COLLECTIVE VIOLENCE

Effective Strategies for Assessing and Interviewing in Fatal Group and Institutional Aggression

COLLECTIVE VIOLENCE

Effective Strategies for Assessing and Interviewing in Fatal Group and Institutional Aggression

Edited by

Harold V. Hall
Leighton C. Whitaker

CRC Press
Boca Raton London New York Washington, D.C.

Library of Congress Cataloging-in-Publication Data

Collective violence : effective strategies for assessing and interviewing in fatal group and institutional aggression / edited by Harold Hall, Leighton C. Whitaker

p. cm.

Includes bibliographical references and index.

ISBN 0-8493-7002-7

1. Violence—Psychological aspects. 2. Violence—Prevention. 3. Violent crimes. 4. Political violence. 5. Aggressiveness (Psychology) 6. Genocide. 7. Collective behavior. I. Hall, Harold V. II. Whitaker, Leighton C.

HM281.C552 1998

303.6--dc21 98-37387

CIP

International Standard Book Number 0-8493-7002-7
Library of Congress Card Number 98-37387
Printed in the United States of America 1 2 3 4 5 6 7 8 9 0
Printed on acid-free paper

Acknowledgments

Collective Violence: Effective Strategies for Assessing and Intervening in Fatal Group and Institutional Aggression was prepared with the generous assistance of many individuals. The contributors of the chapters and appendices alone represent over 500 years of combined professional experience. Special thanks are due to the Consulting Editors who reviewed every manuscript from an interdisciplinary perspective.

I wish to thank the Institute on the Holocaust and Genocide, which allowed reprinting of Director Israel Charny's classic article "Toward a Genocide Early Warning System," which is presented in Appendix C The system is a comprehensive method of calculating genocidal potential for any country or region, based on the Holocaust in World War II and other genocidal atrocities at other times in various parts of the world. The U.S. Secret Service provided information on serial bombing in general and the Unabomber in particular. The Federal Bureau of Investigation made available valuable information on domestic and international terrorism which was cited in this book.

The Pacific Institute is indebted to the late Carl Sagan, Ph.D., of Cornell University in New York, who clarified his predictions on the probability of wars of increasing magnitude. Dr. Sagan made clear that the point where the acceptability of the magnitude of global war equals the rising population of the Earth (i.e., Armageddon) is within the lifetime of most of the readership but partially within our control. The late Professor Saburo Ienaga of the Japanese History Department at Tokyo University provided many deep insights into the motivation of the Japanese to fight wars of atrocities. He achieved a remarkable victory for the freedom of writing and publishing unbiased school textbooks, which were finally endorsed by the Japanese Supreme Court in an unprecedented recognition of this principle.

U.S. Senator Daniel K. Inouye, one of the greatest statesmen of this century, consistently provided encouragement and support for the Pacific Institute's program of intervention with violently traumatized victims.

The National Defense University, through its symposia, provided state-of-the-art training on economic and security issues of vital concern to the United States and other countries. The governments of Great Britain, through the Queens University in Belfast; Poland, through the Marie-Sklovensky University in Lublin, and the Special Schools for Higher Education in Warsaw; and the People's Republic of China, through Fudan University in Shanghai and Peking University in Beijing, are thanked for their interest in understanding the principles of violence and the nonviolent solutions which flow from them. Special recognition and immeasurable thanks are due to Jerilynn Ono Hall, my wife, who, as the Managing Editor, gave voluminous amounts of her time and expertise in the preparation of this book.

Harold V. Hall
Kamuela, Hawaii

Preface

Someday, when seen from another planet, perhaps by our own species of Earth humans at a later time after who knows how much, if not all, of this planet of ours has been destroyed by our own folly, or perhaps seen by another creature which has evolved with no less wisdom than that which is already in our grasp as humans, it will be very easy to understand that the human species on Earth stupidly remained addicted to violence, which ultimately destroyed its existence.

Even for those of us who genuinely love knowledge and the delivery of same in wonderful new books, it is easy to look at still another book in intellectual, professional, and aesthetic anticipation without realizing the enormity of the subject being addressed and therefore without mobilizing our own deepest spiritual and energetic commitments to furthering the work that is so seriously needed in that area. Granted, cool scientific heads and diligent academicians do contribute to our developing knowledge, yet there are times when it is only the passion of the scientist-practitioner to find a cure for an illness or to apply new public health measures to society that will move us forward to an extent that is sufficient to make a difference in respect to the enormity of the problem.

This is a book of overriding importance.

Lethal violence is a terrifying, disgusting, widespread, urgent problem for all of us who care about human life. Our planet is polluted with acts of incredible torture, maiming, and full-blown destruction of human creatures.

Clearly, at its base, lethal aggression derives from a necessary mechanism in the evolution of self-defense. Clearly too, the need for power and violence in self-defense remains an existential given at every level of human experience — from an individual's ability to stand off a would-be attacker, to an ethnic group's ability to defend itself against ethnic cleansing and genocide, to a nation being able to stand up against invasion by an aggressor. However, the first and major problem with the concept of self-defense is that virtually *all* human beings experience themselves as victims in conflict with others and also demonize others, and then justify attacking the other violently in many instances where there would have been no violence from the other or the violence could have been contained through peaceful conflict resolution. In addition, it is natural and apparently inevitable that even in the process of legitimate self-defense, there is a grave tendency to escalate the means and extent of violence.

Indeed, violence seems to be addictive and intoxicating, and like the underlying principle that power corrupts, the exercise of violence even in self-defense corrupts and leads to savagery and overkill and the deaths of innocent people, as we actually know to be true of totalitarian beasts, but also far more than we have wanted to know in the romantic histories we have written of democracies going to justified wars or of victimized peoples defending themselves or revolting against tyranny as they must. There is no doubt that our planet is fighting a battle against time to evolve means within the international system that will enable responding in proper self-defense to aggression, and also to contain the violence of responses in self-defense, as well as to prevent wars as much as possible. The issue is urgent more than ever because the means for mass destruction are growing from moment to moment and, much as science fiction writers and our imaginations have told us, can lead to the destruction of everyone and everything.

Moreover, the story of human destruction is not limited to major events we have known as wars. Increasingly, new forms of major destruction of huge numbers of people are appearing, such as in terrorism and genocide. We are accustomed to thinking of both of these as the actions of nation-states, but increasingly, it appears that the machinery of destruction is moving to a variety of groups and even individuals who take upon themselves missions of extermination of other human beings.

Thus, where genocide has been a function of nation-states as in the Ottoman government's genocide of the Armenian people from 1915 on, or the Nazi Holocaust especially of the Jews but also of a variety of other peoples from 1940 on, any number of recent cases of genocide are more functions of ethnic identities spilling death on one another — thus, the Hutu and Tutsi in Rwanda, or the Serbs and the Croats in the former Yugoslavia, or even the work of self-defined political power groups, in effect along the lines of magnified gangs, turning against their own people — thus the madness of the Khmer Rouge in Cambodia killing their own people with very little of the "reasons" we are accustomed to "understand," simply because at that moment the victims were perceived as not of the Khmer gang.

Indeed, the possibility of genocide being executed even by smaller and smaller units, cults or gangs, or even a handful of people, and for all we know even by a single individual, becomes more probable as the possibilities of exercising enormous mass destruction spread in an age where mega-scientific weapons are and will be increasingly within the reach of an unlimited number of groups and people. Harbingers have already appeared, such as by a cult in Japan spreading deadly gas in a public transportation area, and in the blowing up of the Murrah Federal Building in Oklahoma City by a small number of self-styled domestic terrorists. If the 20th century has been characterized as the century of genocide,[1] then it is highly possible that the 21st century will prove to be one of runaway demonic violence and genocides.[2]

The pollution of violence is evident at every level of human life. In the marvelous drama of democracy and freedom that has developed in the world's greatest superpower — the U.S. — the fact is that in most parts of the country, one dare not walk the streets without expecting the danger of being attacked, the rates of everyday murders are obscene, and the basic cultural climate is one of educating for violence as the preferred and expected way of being in this world. It will indeed be a joke when the anthropologists of the other planets look down on this period of history on Earth through the television and cinematic records that we have left revealing how we taught our children to disqualify sentiment, integrity, and respect for the imperative, *Thou shalt not kill.*

Harold Hall's book is clearly the urgent call of a decent man who, using the tools of his profession as a psychologist and social scientist is trying with deep feeling to contribute something to the prevention of a lethal outcome for humanity. He asks, correctly, whether there is time in which we can reframe our

[1] Totten, S., Parsons, W.S., and Charny, I., Eds. (1997) *Century of Genocide: Eyewitness Accounts and Critical Views*. New York: Garland Publishing.

[2] Private conversation between Yves Ternon, M.D., author of *L'etat Criminel: Les Genocides au Xxe Siecle*. Paris: Editions du Senil, 1998, and Israel Charny on the occasion of the International Symposium on the "Genocide of the Armedians" at the Sorbonne University in April 1998.

priorities. To do so, he leads us, with the collaboration of a wonderful group of colleagues, through a fascinating but disturbing maze of the phenomena of violences in groups, institutions, and the media.

There are a variety of institutions which are explicitly committed to doing destructive aggression. And there are a variety of others which implicitly do so while ostensibly being devoted to justice and self-defense. There are population groups which take off into their own specialized forms of violence against others. There is violence by actual criminals, but also hate groups and terrorists. And there is a variety of deadly culture-infecting and polluting themes which desensitize the citizens and societal institutions to deadly force, even by officers of the law, and desensitize us to preparations for catastrophic violence, even by the military of democratic countries that are committed to using force for the defense of life. Culture-wide themes justify, legalize, and reify violence, including at times by the finest of our scientific establishment and ugly pollution has become synonymous with the performing arts that are rendered by the media.

The voices of Harold Hall and his colleagues call us to study, learn, and create newly effective strategies for intervening in fatal group and institutional aggression. These voices, among which I am proud to participate, are the loveliest sounds of our humanity. May their anthem of prayer for decency and life prevail.

Israel W. Charny
Executive Director
Institute on the Holocaust and Genocide
Jerusalem

CONTRIBUTORS

Chief Editors
Harold V. Hall
Leighton C. Whitaker

Associate Editors
Sally H. Barlow
Claudia J. Clayton

Consulting Editors
Lucien A. Buck
Israel Charny
Patrick E. Cook
Robert F. Eme
Gary Jackson
Rosalie G. Matzkin
Sandra B. McPherson
David M. Paltin
Joseph G. Poirier
Lita L. Schwartz

Managing Editor
Jerilynn Ono Hall

Contributors
Bonnie Ballif-Spanvill
Dennis R. Baltzley
Sally H. Barlow
Randy Borum
Lucien A. Buck
Israel Charney
Claudia J. Clayton
Patrick E. Cook
James F. Craine
Thomas A. Crum
Joseph Davies
John Doe
Robert F. Eme
Theodore B. Feldmann
Charles J. Golden
Harold V. Hall
Reed Hayes
Dayle L. Hinman
Kimon Ianetta
Michele L. Jackson
Rosalie G. Matzkin
Dennis G. McLaughlin
Sandra B. McPherson
David M. Paltin
Joseph G. Poirier
Chanan Rapaport
Frank C. Sacco
Lita L. Schwartz
Harley Stock
William H. Tucker
Stuart W. Twemlow
Leighton C. Whitaker

About the Editors

Harold V. Hall, Ph.D., a forensic neuropsychologist, is the Director of the Pacific Institute for the Study of Conflict and Aggression. He has served as a consultant for a wide variety of criminal and civil justice system agencies, including the Federal Bureau of Investigation, the National Bureau of Prisons, the U.S. Secret Service, and district, family, and circuit courts at state and federal levels. He has written or edited six books and over 40 peer-reviewed articles, primarily on the subjects of violence and aggression. Dr. Hall is a Diplomate in both Forensic Psychology and Clinical Psychology from the American Board of Professional Psychology and is a Fellow of the American Psychological Association. He is board certified in Forensic Neuropsychology from the American Board of Psychological Specialties. Most recently, he was inducted into the National Academy of Practice in Psychology, which limits its membership to 100 living professionals from that discipline in the United States and Canada. He has investigated and trained others in individual and collective violence since the late 1960s in the Pacific Basin, on the continental United States, and in Europe.

Leighton C. Whitaker, Ph.D., is in private practice, and is Adjunct Clinical Professor at Widener University's Institute for Graduate Clinical Psychology, and editor of the *Journal of College Student Psychotherapy*. His 70 professional publications address a wide variety of clinical and social subjects and include the *Whitaker Index of Schizophrenic Thinking* (Western Psychological Services, 1980) and *Schizophrenic Disorders* (Plenum Press, 1992). His previous positions include Associate Professor and Director of Adult Psychology for the University of Colorado Health Sciences Center, Professor and Director of the University of Massachusetts Mental Health Services, and Director of Swarthmore College Psychological Services. He has done forensic work for many years and has been consultant to the U.S. Department of Labor's Job Corps. His work with youth has been featured on television and in newspapers.

Contents

APPENDICES

Introduction

COLLECTIVE VIOLENCE: CAN WE REFRAME OUR PRIORITIES IN TIME?

Harold V. Hall

"America feels like its unraveling. ... Unraveling eras reflect a social mood that has become newly personal, pragmatic, and insecure. These are times of buccaneers and barnstormers, of courtly intrigue and treacherous alliances, of civil unrest and boom-and-bust markets. Contrasts abound — between the rich and the poor, the garish and the sober, the sacred and the profane. People act out, welcoming conflict while disdaining consensus. All relationships seem in flux, all loyalties in doubt, all outcomes chancy. Society fragments into centrifugal parts, with small-scale loyalties rising amid the sinking tangle of civilization. The pace of life quickens, and time horizons shorten. Mounting secular problems are either deferred or deemed insoluble." (William Strauss and Neil Howe, *The Fourth Turning: An American Prophecy,* 1997)

Collective violence evokes the full panoply of my emotions and thoughts when I reflect upon my clinical-forensic experience over the last 30 years: I recall 17-year-old Mark, who, as an "old" member of a Hispanic gang, killed a member of a competing gang in a drive-by shooting because the rival was encroaching on Mark's crystal methamphetamine trade. And Darci, a 30-year-old, middle-class, black female with no record of criminality who, exploding after experiencing a lifetime of prejudice from whites, became caught up in a race riot and burned down a grocery store, incinerating the owner and his family within. And 38-year-old George, a black male awaiting death by electrocution for murdering three white men in a bar after robbing them along with two others, who had spent his entire life in a violent display of reverse discrimination. And Silas, who belonged to the Jonestown cult whose members, including children, had been ordered to commit suicide by drinking Kool-Aid laced with cyanide; luckily, Silas was in the U.S. on a supply and recruitment mission at the time. And 35-year-old Vinnie "the Knife", an enforcer for a syndicated crime family, who viewed prison as an interlude between "hits". And 26-year-old Eric, whose primary job in his white supremacist group was to restrain victims while they were knifed or clubbed by other skinheads. And 45-year-old James, a major in a militia group in California, who trained the men and women in his cell in guerilla tactics in preparation for armed combat with the federal government, and awaited the word of the organizational leader to mobilize in concert with other cells. And 42-year-old Dick, a paranoid schizophrenic with revenge fantasies arising out of his service in Vietnam, who plotted the assassination of a U.S. Senator. And the Unabomber, who, as the most prolific serial bomber, over the course of 17 years, killed three people and maimed two dozen others with his homemade bombs. I recall 31-year-old Ted, a veteran police officer who shot an unarmed motorist who had cursed at him and refused to stop for a traffic ticket. And 51-year-old Paul, a Special Forces officer in the U.S. Army who was recruited by the Central Intelligence Agency (CIA) for its infamous Phoenix Program in Indochina involving the roundup, interrogation, and killing of tens of thousands of Vietnamese civilians. And 63-year-old Howard, bilingual in Russian and English, who had pronounced misgivings about his role as a nuclear policy planner for the U.S. for World War II scenarios, but only after he had retired.

At this point in history, we hear stories more frequently than at any time in the past of war, terrorism, genocide, organized crime murders, deadly drug wars, involuntary human experimentation by governments, and other violent enterprises. Nuclear destruction of this planet is, and will continue to be, a distinct possibility. Lethal violence by groups and institutions, also known as collective violence and defined in this book as acts by representatives of those organizations which lead to the death of others, is certainly the most distinct challenge of our times.

Certainly, collective lethal violence has always been with us. The 5600 years of recorded history have produced more than 14,600 wars or about 2.6 wars every year (Baron, 1977). Only 10 of the 185 generations in recorded history have been free of war. The 20th century has certainly been the bloodiest in all of human history. Counting only casualties from war, the 18th century produced a rate of 50 deaths per 1 million population per year compared to 60 deaths per 1 million during the 19th century and 460 deaths per 1 million so far in the 20th century, during which there has been 250 wars (Tehranian, 1997). Over 50 wars have been raging around the world in the 1990s (Gurr, 1993; Turpin and Kurtz, 1997). Half of the world's governments spend more on developing and maintaining military forces and weapons than on health and education (Barnaby, 1997). Would you be surprised to know that war is only the *second* most frequent cause of this downward historical trend of lethal violence by groups and institutions?

On a worldwide basis, being killed by one's own government is more probable than dying in war. R.J. Rummel (1990, 1992, 1994), a political scientist at the University of Hawaii who was nominated for the Nobel Peace Prize for his work on genocide, documented that for every person killed in war as a combatant, four to five are killed by their own government. Most of these murders are planned and rehearsed, which then increases their lethality. As examples, group murder by quota, a particularly sinister method of killing, was perpetrated by Stalin in the Great Terror from 1936 to 1938 (Rummel, 1990, 1994), by Nazis in concentration camps during World War II (Levi, 1958), by Ho Chi Minh in North Vietnam during the 1950s (Rummel, 1994), and by ex-CIA Director William Colby in the CIA-sponsored Phoenix Program during the Vietnam War (Branfman, 1978; Chomsky and Herman, 1977).

The U.S., as the focus of this book, is experiencing an explosion of violent activities. The following show that no place in this country is safe from violence:

- Since the two-ton bomb destroyed the Alfred P. Murrah Federal Building in Oklahoma City on April 5, 1995, killing 168 people and representing the most deadly terrorist attack in U.S. history, militias have largely retreated underground but have reported a sevenfold increase in membership (*Law Enforcement News,* 1996).
- In many American cities, gunfire is heard on a nightly basis. Despite admonitions that inner city violence is exaggerated by the media, only a foolish person would walk unescorted or unguarded in most of our inner cities, which are in an advanced state of decay after decades of neglect. Large sections of our cities are not even patrolled by police officers, because they become targets of opportunity if they venture into these areas.

- Explicit instructions on building an atomic bomb (the technology for which has been available on the open market for over 20 years), in addition to manuals on everything from construction to procurement of poison weapons, homemade explosives, and night scopes and silencers for firearms, are available on the open market (e.g., see Delta Press catalog, 1996).
- In this century, the U.S. warred more than most other nations. Our country was the first to wreak thermonuclear holocaust against our enemy and has never renounced a first strike (preemptive) option (Kull, 1988).
- Murder, ostensibly to punish deviance and to enforce rules as well as to serve greed and anger, is part and parcel of the "business" activities of the 24 Cosa Nostra crime families in the U.S., consisting of Sicilians and other Italians, as well as numerous other organized crime syndicates who, broken down by ethnic group, include blacks, Chinese, Mexicans, Vietnamese, Japanese, Cubans, Colombians, Irish, Russians, Canadians, and various combinations (Beirne and Messerschmidt, 1995). Arrests for these murders are reported as individual violence when they are truly collective violence in planning, substance, and execution.
- According to the Final Report of the Advisory Committee on Human Radiation Experiments (Faden, 1996), over 4000 radiation experiments were performed by the Atomic Energy Commission and other government agencies on thousands of unwitting U.S. citizens from 1944 to 1974, and may still be conducted today. With no intended medical benefit, comatose patients were injected with radioactive isotopes, the testicles of prison inmates were irradiated, hospital patients were injected with plutonium, and radiation was intentionally released into the environment. In one study at Vanderbilt University, newborn babies were transfused with blood laced with chromium-50 in order to determine the onset of hemorrhaging.
- Representing over 20 *million* Americans, if the results can be generalized, an ABC-*Washington Post* survey in May 1995 found that 9% of more than 1000 adults answered "yes" to the question, "Is it ever justified to take violent action against the government?" Thirty two percent indicated that they did not trust the government, and 36% responded "yes" to the question, "Does the U.S. threaten personal rights?"

In *Collective Violence: Effective Strategies for Assessing and Intervening in Fatal Group and Institutional Aggression*, we attempt to understand the changing nature of deadly aggression by groups and institutions in and by the U.S. — their similar and unique characteristics, how they evolve through the violence cycle, why they are increasingly in conflict with one another, what we can do about these organizations — and make predictions about future scenarios, given the transitional nature of our society. This is a tall order for a book, especially because it is very likely to ruffle some feathers and meet stiff opposition, given that individual readers may have allegiance to one or more of the groups and institutions scrutinized.

The information in this book comes from publicly available sources and can be checked for accuracy. We assume that effective change requires accurate knowledge of groups and institutions. The task has been made feasible by the host of quality contributors to this volume, all of whom were charged with presenting an effective blueprint for action in the areas of their expertise. The contributors to this book call for definitive societal action to construct a more humane and peaceful world.

This is not a book focusing on people of the U.S. or people engaged in constructive efforts to build a greater community or the many opportunities for quality living afforded by this great nation. Nor is it about the success of our nation in meeting the challenges of the times over a 200-year history. Instead, this book focuses on the violent side of some of our most cherished groups and institutions. The authors try to help counter the trend of increasing collective violence through understanding and suggestions for correction.

Our starting point as contributors and for the book as a whole is a certain moral stance in favor of peace and against violence. It is an orientation that demands sober evaluation, patience, kindness, tenacity, ingenuity, and respect for all people, including those we wish to change. As individual authors and editors, we realize that none of us can save the world from gratuitous violence and destruction, but we believe that by adhering to the spirit of a psychology of peace and helping to foster a like-mindedness in others, we can contribute to reversing the downward trend. Thus, our attempts to live up to our moral stance are based on faith that group and institutional reform can be cultivated effectively.

First and foremost, this book seeks a generalization of this attitude to our daily routine. As Vaclav Havel (1997, p. 113), the writer who emerged victorious as President of his nation over no less an adversary than Czechoslovakia's Communist system, stated in *The Art of the Impossible*:

"It is possible to imagine thousands of tiny, inconspicuous, everyday decisions whose common denominator is precisely the spirit and ethos of a politics that is aware of the global threat to the human race and does not support general consumer resignation but, rather, seeks to awaken a deeper interest in the state of the world and rally the will to confront the threats hanging over it. Above all, however, it is possible to imagine that, through the agency of thousands of properly chosen, carefully combined, and well-timed public actions, the positive local climate in a country — that is, a climate of solidarity, creativity, cooperation, tolerance, and deepening civil responsibility — can slowly, inconspicuously, but steadily be strengthened."

Two types of collective violence are examined in this book — nongovernment and government. While the two often overlap, as when the CIA hired La Cosa Nostra figures to assassinate Fidel Castro (Hersh, 1997), they can be differentiated for valid purposes.

Organized crime, hate and supremacist groups, the emerging militia groups (e.g., Patriots), cults, violent juvenile gangs, and other private collectivities all share a disenfranchisement from the government. Each group is characterized by rigid rules for membership, a code of conduct, and leader domination, as opposed to a democratic process. As we shall see, the psychopathology that individuals bring into the group and that develops in the course of membership contributes synergistically to destructive outcomes. The formation and continuation of collectivities are encouraged by significant portions of the community which derive rewards and satisfactions from their existence. As a general trend, these groups and institutions are becoming more systematic, organized, group-focused, and dangerous. The chief danger of these private organizations is in their combining strengths to overthrow the government through violent means and thereby accelerating the loss of human rights. Thus, such groups represent no improvement over our present way of life.

Government groups are a second focus of this book. On the whole, in this country, lethal violence committed by legally ruling elites and institutions, including the government, is viewed as more acceptable than lethal violence committed by those not in power. Unfortunately, legal violence tends to be standard behavior in our country, justified as necessary to maintain order and security, protect U.S. interests, and prevent further violence.

Congruent with several principles discussed later (e.g., violence begets violence), violent social problems are often reacted to by committing more "legitimate" violence in an attempt to solve the problems. The government typically defines as acceptable certain violent actions perpetrated by corporations, the medical profession, and the government itself against disenfranchised or weak groups, for example, foreigners/immigrants, homosexuals, and activists (Elias, 1997). The government finds unacceptable violence by the disenfranchised groups toward the same powerful, legally constituted groups.

As Elias (1997, p. 128) maintained, our system routinely suppresses various groups and communities as diverse as the Native Americans, civil rights groups, and Earth First!. As he stated, "We have an intellectual culture that is so committed to the rule of force that it never ceases to be baffled when that violence routinely fails (e.g., in winning over the Vietnamese, in stopping crime, and so forth)."

Elias (1997) opined that it would be scandalous for Americans to know that our programs designed to combat violence may do more to create than reduce crime, and that ostensibly antidrug policies do more to promote the drug trade, including its violent offshoots, than to stop it. Likewise, it would be ironic to discover that government departments and agencies charged with providing intelligence and security do more to destabilize our country than to insure our safety.

We seek solutions in this book. To help our society get back on track, a time-honored and unalterable two-step process must be followed. First, based on concern and respect for others, we must be honest with ourselves, even if it hurts. In the analysis of lethal violence, we search for "ground truth" — the interactions and contributions of perpetrator, victim, and context variables at a given point in time when killing occurs. Ground truth is the reality of the violent act, stripped of deception and camouflage. As such, it is often ugly. The human radiation experiments, genocide perpetrated by our government, the willingness to destroy the world through nuclear holocaust to prevent the enemy from "winning", and the butchery of organized crime groups are all ugly truths that must first be understood in order to be changed.

We must discover and learn from ground truth in order to make effective change possible. Thus, we must ruthlessly probe the reality of various collective organizations — such as hate groups, terrorist groups, and violent agencies of the federal government — all of which appear to distort truth in the direction of their vested interests. Because people have a natural inclination to avoid horror and death, we are also reluctant to ask whether and how we are denying, condoning, or even supporting violence and death within our culture of violent solutions.

Foundational chapters covering issues common to all group and institutional violence are presented first in this book, followed by chapters on violent private collectivities, then violent government entities. In Chapter 1, this author examines a variety of violent entities and the principles which flow from such an analysis, preparing the way for predictions and recommendations for constructive action. One exciting finding concerns the application of many of the same principles to both individual and collective violence. Inhibitions to violence, a vital topic in understanding why violent individuals and collectivities do not aggress continually or indefinitely, are addressed by Leighton Whitaker in Chapter 2. Importantly, he shows how those inhibitions can be identified and reframed into meaningful intervention strategies.

The all-important link between the media, in all of its forms, to violence and aggression is presented by Lita Schwartz and Rosalie Matzkin in Chapter 3. They offer a rare opportunity to explore the now firmly established contribution of the media to collective violence and to polarization, especially among our youth. They discuss and elaborate upon solutions, ranging from strategies for rating television programs to limitations of violence-enhancing messages in music.

Developmental aspects of violence and aggression are addressed by Robert Eme in Chapter 4. Eme articulates clearly the biopsychosocial mechanisms, starting with our genetic endowment, that may place us at higher risk for developing violent patterns of behavior. He shows convincingly that developmental windows of opportunity can be exploited to reduce needless aggression.

In Chapter 5, Joseph Poirier discusses the problem of juvenile delinquency, its pervasiveness, and a variety of methods to reduce this type of violence. In Chapter 6, Sally Barlow and Claudia Clayton examine the subject of violence against women by individuals and institutions, with micro-violence increasing macro-violence and vice versa. They propose interventions which, consistent with proposals by other commentators (e.g., Brock-Utne, 1997; Turpin and Kurtz, 1997), take into account micro-violence (e.g., spouse battering, rape-murder), structural violence (e.g., economic inequality), and macro-violence (e.g., war, genocide). In addition to reducing overt violence, for real change there must also be improvement of the life span, freedom of choice, and economic opportunity for women.

Chapter 7, in which Lita Schwartz discusses cults, begins the section of the book on lethal violence perpetrated by private groups and institutions with an analysis of cults. Between 2000 and 5000 cults exist in the U.S., with almost half espousing apocalyptic beliefs that the world will soon come to an end (Hoffman and Burke, 1997). Schwartz's principal position is that societal conditions may be a factor in joining a cult, but individual psychosocial factors (and psychopathology) are more important in maintaining membership in certain groups.

Crimes have increased against members of religious groups, racial and ethnic groups, women, lesbians, gays, and bisexuals. In Chapter 8, Charles Golden, Michele Jackson, and Thomas Crum focus on hate groups. Interestingly, they found few articles that documented therapeutic success with perpetrators of hate crimes.

In Chapter 9, Claudia Clayton, Sally Barlow, and Bonnie Ballif-Spanvill probe the topic of group violence, with an emphasis on terrorism and enunciate a series of violence-related observations from their analysis. They discuss in-group/out-group dynamics which have direct relevance for intervention in group violence.

Dayle Hinman and Patrick Cook, in Chapter 10, discuss profiling multiple perpetrators. Hinman and Cook apply profiling methods to FBI cases involving serial rape-murder, as well as other lethal violence.

Chapter 11 deals with large-scale hostage and barricade incidents, with implications for negotiating strategies and training. Theodore Feldmann presents the various means by which law enforcement personnel and the mental health community can work together to effect nonviolent resolutions to such incidents.

Deaths resulting from violence perpetrated by institutions, primarily the government, are discussed by this author in Chapter 12. The chapter notes that war, genocide, and other group actions account for far more deaths than are caused by individual violence.

In Chapter 13, Harley Stock, Randy Borum, and Dennis Baltzley discuss the use of deadly force by police. They classify violent police officers into several types and offer specific policies geared toward intervention with these individuals.

David Paltin discusses biological and chemical warfare, used largely by governments but also by private groups, in Chapter 14. The shift to biological weapons — constituting the poor man's nuclear bombs — by terrorist groups constitutes an increasing danger. Paltin offers interventions at individual, group, and societal levels.

In Chapter 15, Leighton Whitaker probes the CIA's 50-year history of violence and reform since it was founded in 1947, revealing misery and death inflicted by that agency in its most violent eras. For example, while involved in Vietnam in the 1960s, in Afghanistan in the 1970s, and in Nicaragua in the 1980s, the CIA has been associated with gross increases in drug use in this country through its direct or indirect support of drug lords.

Sandra McPherson discusses death penalty legislation and events over the decades, including forensic considerations, in Chapter 16. Capital punishment is shown to have *no* rehabilitative value (as shown by independent studies over the last few decades) and, worse, possibly to contribute to the very outcome that is feared. McPherson outlines alternatives to the death penalty as we know it, including abandoning this type of government intervention.

In Chapter 17, William Tucker discusses ways in which science has been used to justify collective violence. He analyzes the many rationalizations used by intellectuals to justify violence and notes that some of the most credentialed and learned of our contemporaries have a long history of supporting policies that could yield collective violence on a massive scale.

Lucien Buck, in Chapter 18, addresses conflict, competition, and violence in terms of how they can be prevented or rendered less destructive by judicious use of Gandhian concepts of love, humanism, and life affirmation. He explains and illustrates critical aspects of the nonviolent approach (e.g., the civil rights movement led by Dr. Martin Luther King, Jr.).

In Chapter 19, Stuart Twemlow and Frank Sacco address methods for intervening in violent communities. They describe ways in which entire communities can be changed by working with the police departments, schools, and members of the greater community.

The last chapter, by this author and Leighton Whitaker, sounds the clarion call for a fundamental restructuring of our scientific-military-business community to avoid the consequences of current pathological trends. This chapter includes predictions for the next several decades if current trends continue, with suggestions for dealing with the fundamental changes to come.

In Appendix A, Sandra McPherson discusses two generations of CIA interrogation manuals, both of which, although heavily redacted prior to their release under the Freedom of Information Act in January 1997, contain abundant evidence of gross violations of human rights through sensory deprivation, hypnosis, brainwashing, and a host of psychological threats and ploys. A former military officer in Vietnam, John Doe, in Appendix B, shares his experience in the first phase of the Phoenix Program, an interrogation, torture, and murder program of the CIA implicated in the deaths of literally tens of thousands of innocent Vietnamese. Early warning signs of genocide are presented in Appendix C by Israel Charny and Chanan Rapaport of the Holocaust Center in Jerusalem. Their classic contribution articulates stepwise criteria to forecast genocide. In Appendix D, techniques for facilitating the assessment of dangerousness using handwriting characteristics are presented by Kimon Iannetta. These techniques appear to yield valid measurements of perpetrators of collective as well as individual violence. Joseph Davis, in Appendix E, describes his experience after the bombing of the Federal Building in Oklahoma City in 1995 and discusses the importance of critical incident stress debriefing to communities in crisis.

References

Barnaby. F. (1997) Can we redefine national security in time? *Peace and Conflict: Journal of Peace Psychology, 3*, 217–219.

Baron, R.A. (1977) *Human Aggression*. New York: Plenum Press.

Beirne, P. and Messerschmidt, J. (1995) *Criminology*, 2nd ed. Fort Worth, TX: Harcourt Brace College Publishers.

Branfman, F. (1978) South Vietnam's police and prison system: the U.S. connection. In H. Frazier (Ed.), *Uncloaking the CIA*, pp. 110–127. New York: Free Press.

Brock-Utne, B. (1997) Linking the micro and macro in peace and development studies. In J. Turpin and L. Kurtz (Eds.), *The Web of Violence: From Interpersonal to Global*, pp. 149–160. Urbana: University of Illinois Press.

Chomsky, N. and Herman, E.S. (1977) The U.S. versus human rights in the Third World. *Monthly Review, 29* (July-Aug.), 22–24.

Elias, R. (1997) A culture of violent solutions. In J. Turpin and L. Kurtz (Eds.), *The Web of Violence: From Interpersonal to Global*, pp. 117–148. Urbana: University of Illinois Press.

Faden, R. (1996) *Final Report to the President on the Human Radiation Experiments*. New York: Oxford University Press.

Gurr, T. (1993) *Minorities at Risk: A Global View of Ethnopolitical Conflicts*. Washington, D.C.: U.S. Institute of Peace.

Havel, V. (1997) *The Art of the Impossible*. New York: Alfred A. Knopf.

Hersh, S. (1997) *The Dark Side of Camelot*. Boston: Little, Brown & Company.

Hoffman, B. and Burke, C. (1997) *Heaven's Gate: Cult Suicide in San Diego*. New York: Harper Collins.

Kull, S. (1988) *Minds at War: Nuclear Reality and the Inner Conflicts of Defense Policymakers*. New York: Basic Books.

Levi, P. (1958) *Survival in Auschwitz*. New York: A Touchstone Book.

"Policing keeps an eye on the radical right" (1996) *Law Enforcement News*, Dec. 31, p. 24.

Rummel, R.J. (1990) *Lethal Politics: Soviet Genocide and Mass Murder Since 1917*. New Brunswick, NJ: Transaction Publishers.

Rummel, R.J. (1992) *Democide: Nazi Genocide and Mass Murder*. New Brunswick, NJ: Transaction Publishers.

Rummel, R.J. (1994) *Death by Government, Genocide and Mass Murder Since 1900*. New Brunswick, NJ: Transaction Publishers.

Strauss, W. and Howe, N. (1997) *The Fourth Turning: An American Prophecy*. New York: Broadway Books.

Tehranian, M. (1997) Death by design. *Honolulu Advertiser*, May 18, p. A3.

Turpin, J. and Kurtz, L. (1997) *The Web of Violence: From Interpersonal to Global*. Urbana: University of Illinois Press.

Part I

FOUNDATIONAL ISSUES

Chapter 1

VIOLENT GROUPS AND INSTITUTIONS IN THE UNITED STATES

Harold V. Hall

"Whoever fights monsters should see to it that in the process he does not become a monster. And when you look into an abyss, the abyss also looks into you." —Friedrich Nietzsche (in *Thus Spake Zarathustra*)

"Violence is an American as cherry pie." —H. Rapp Brown

Some years ago, this author attended a seminar presented by two prominent Federal Bureau of Investigation (FBI) agents on organized crime and gang-related atrocities. Toward the end of the training, the lead presenter showed a slide of a dead female lying on her stomach, a long staff impaling her to the ground through her rectum, the staff jutting into the air at a 45-degree angle. Suddenly, he burst into prolonged, uncontrollable laughter and commented that the victim looked foolish and comical in that position. The participants did not share his humor, instead reacting with silence and immobility. The positive impact of his presentation had evaporated.

At that time, this author thought of the quote from Nietzsche cited above and was reminded that too frequent or intense involvement with violence does indeed affect one in deleterious ways. The presenter obviously had some form of post-traumatic stress disorder (PTSD) from prolonged contact with the dark side of life. Yet, some emotion, some feeling for the tragedy of violence is necessary to empathize with the victim. Nothing is more vapid than a detached, academic view of killing and murder. Perhaps patterns run through individual and collective violence which, if understood, could eventually affect the very phenomenon that we are studying. For example, if we knew that perpetrators, victims, and others present at the scene of the violence were all prone to suffer from PTSD to varying degrees, we then should not be surprised to discover that the accuracy of their reporting is suspect and that their later symptoms will be almost universal. Perhaps intervention methods exist which make constructive change in violent individuals and groups more probable.

This chapter first presents a sampling of common forms of group and institutional violence in and by the U.S., expanding on those which are not addressed separately in the remainder of the book. Indeed, patterns do emerge which then lead to a preliminary set of violence-related principles. The ultimate goal in articulating these principles is eventually to develop an applied theory of human violence which can then be utilized for interventions designed to help the affected individuals and the community at large.

Mob Violence

Mob violence, such as race riots (as the least organized type of collective violence), has common characteristics which include (1) like-mindedness, (2) emotionality, and (3) irrationality (Greenberg, 1996). Contagion, the spreading of affect and convergence tendencies — such as the act of like-minded individuals joining a mob — explains the apparent mental homogeneity in such a group.

Recall Darci, the 30-year-old black female mentioned in the Introduction, was a manager at a laundry chain. She had no history of criminality but became involved in a race riot in Watts. Darci helped start the fire at the grocery store which resulted in the death of the Korean owner, his wife, and their two children. She looted goods from that store and others. After several days, sickened by her own behavior and learning that she had contributed to ending the lives of innocent people, she discontinued her involvement in the collective violence. In keeping with most riots of protracted duration, the leaders who then emerged were sociopaths with long histories of predatory violence. The riot ended with the deaths of several dozen people and the gutting of several square miles of inner city. Darci, who was never arrested in connection with her role in the riot, resumed her previously law-abiding lifestyle, but will always be scarred by her experience.

From a review of data-based studies, the American Psychological Association (APA, 1993, p. 31) stated the following regarding mobs:

- Mob violence, like gang participation, can serve many psycho-social needs.
- Data on participants in mob violence are inadequate, but the available information suggests that male adolescents and young adults are the most frequent participants.
- Typically, those who participate in the initial phases of mob violence are not criminals or delinquents.
- A loss of individual self plays an important facilitative role for those who participate.
- In the course of mob violence, the members enter into a process of change along a "continuum of destruction". Violence can escalate quickly through a "process of contagion".
- Bystanders have the ability to influence the mob by their action or passivity; the earlier that bystanders act as the mob is forming, the greater their potential influence.

Certainly, all participants should be held morally and legally responsible for their misdeeds, especially when mob behavior is associated with looting and other indicators of secondary gain. In our emerging typology of collective violence, however, mob behavior is typically the most impulsive and poorly executed. In many ways, a learned helplessness model is aptly descriptive when self-destructive behavior occurs after the perpetrators have gone through repeated frustration and denial created by their poverty, loss of identity, and second-class status. Mob behavior is rarely seen in the upper income portions of U.S. cities and suburbs. As a type of collective violence, mob behavior is the least dependent on prior learning experiences of violence. Senseless violence becomes homogeneous in mob involvement through contagion, convergence, loss of perceived responsibility through anonymity, and the impression that everyone is approving of collective violence at the time.

Early intervention through direct contact with involved parties stands the best chance of diluting mob power by depriving it of its most psychologically normal members. Once this is accomplished, the remaining mob members (i.e., predatory sociopaths) can be targeted for coercive methods of control if the violence continues.

Gang Violence

The American Psychological Association (APA, 1993) and others (Cheatwood, 1996; Huesmann et al., 1984; Patterson et al., 1972) noted that gangs in this country are overwhelmingly comprised of young males from minority ethnic groups who joined because of needs for belonging and self-definition and a sense of connection. Although only a small percentage of youths joins gangs, homicide and aggravated assault are three times more likely to be committed by gang members than by non-gang members. The APA (1993, p. 29) stated:

"Gang violence appears to have increased in levels and lethality during the 1980s. Studies in the early 1970s reviewed few or no homicides in the United States attributable to gang violence. By 1980, however, there were 351 gang-related homicides in Los Angeles alone and more than 1500 gang-related homicides in Los Angeles between 1985 and 1989.

"Gang demographics changed in the beginning of the 1980s. Delinquent gangs no longer are confined to certain states and to the inner city, and their membership encompasses a wide age range, with members as young as 9 and as old as 30."

American gang-related violence and activities have spread to the Pacific Basin. There are huge increases in drug-related activities and associated violence from mainland gangs in Pacific Basin countries and in Hawaii, Guam, and American trust territories.

American gangs have spread to Europe, as well. The California-based Hell's Angels, for example, established a chapter in Copenhagen, Denmark, in the early 1980s, followed shortly thereafter by the Bandidos and other gangs (Carl, 1996). An escalating series of violence emerged as a result of competition for the international drug trade. Car bombs, machine guns, sawed-off shotguns, and high-tech weaponry have become part and parcel of the Danish street scene. Carl (1996, p. 45) reported the following about a gang war, which had been escalating for over 3 years:

"The war peaked in October, when members of a rival group (police suspect the Houston-based Bandidos) fired an antitank missile at a Hell's Angels' clubhouse in Copenhagen. The missile passed over the heads of the police posted outside, bored through the brick wall of the fortress-like building, and exploded inside, killing two and wounding 19. This was just a few weeks before the start of the trial of six Angels for their involvement in the March 10 murder of one of their rivals at Copenhagen's airport."

In recent years, juvenile gangs within major cities may kill more over business than character disputes. In an intensive study of 102 homicide cases in Baltimore, MD, from 1987 to 1989, Cheatwood (1996) noted that, nationally, multiple-offender killings of both loosely organized and complex gangs with established membership and leadership roles account for 11% of all homicides (and in some years up to 30% in some urban areas). He observed that single-offender homicides follow a lethal violence sequence of (1) two intimates or acquaintances interacting in an informal setting, with a history of affectively based interchanges (baseline); (2) challenges and argumentation by both participants, with one eventually defining the threat as so severe that violence is appropriate, either to "save face" or as a preemptive strike (acceleration phase); (3) perpetration of the violence; and (4) an absence of even weak remorse after the killing (post-violence phase).

Cheatwood (1996) found that the stages in multiple-offender homicides where no concurrent felony was committed (63% of multiple offender homicides) differed significantly from single-offender homicides. According to Cheatwood (1996):

1. During baseline activities, the offenders had multiple contacts with future homicide victims but the contacts were less likely than single-offender homicide contacts to involve character disputes. Instead, these confrontations dealt with territory, sale of drugs, and other collective activities.
2. In those multiple-offender cases where a confrontation took place hours or days before the killing, during the acceleration stage, confrontation became the prelude for the homicide, suggesting anticipation of the killing. In most multiple-offender homicides, planning and rehearsal were common and the acceleration period more spread out than in single-offender homicides where impulsive, short-term violence was often shown. A decision was made to

kill and operational plans were made based on the demands of a business or commercial reputation, or maintaining a good name. Usually, one primary actor within the gang sought to enlist the support of other members to confront the victim. These members were generally aware that a killing was probable (the primary actor often obtained the actual "shooter" from these ranks). Final statements to victims indicated a clear awareness of the impending killing (e.g., "Remember me?" or "Die, motherfucker.").

3. The violence was perpetrated with efficiency. Often, the others present operated as a cheering section by urging the violence on (e.g., "Finish him off." or "Do a head shot.").
4. During the recovery period, the multiple offenders escaped the scene to avoid detection and apprehension. No guilt or remorse was expressed. Instead, they often openly told others of the killing in an attempt to gain prestige or to impress and to bring meaning to the event. The perpetrators' affect was positive. For male perpetrators, the first person they told was usually a girlfriend, especially because she was often needed to provide an alibi or a place to stay, or to conceal evidence or weapons.
5. During the return to baseline period, many multiple offenders reveled in retelling the events of the killing, suggesting self-reinforcement of the violence-related act, feelings, and thoughts.

The total disregard for the victim, combined with the often overt knowledge of the identity of the perpetrators, of course, set the stage for revenge and ensure that the killing cycle will continue.

Given the above, it should come as no surprise that violent gangs, some of which more resemble crime syndicates than disorganized groups of street toughs, are spreading from urban to rural areas of the U.S. (Skorneck, 1997). Ironically, the proliferation of gangs often stems from families' geographic moves in an attempt to provide a better life and a safer place to raise their children. The FBI noted that, once in the community, local names for the new gangs are often adopted and that, ultimately, the new gangs are often more violent than the nationally known gangs they seek to emulate.

The Federal Gang Violence Act of 1997 seeks federal prosecution of gang members by establishing the members' association with the gangs and obtaining the forfeiture of gang-related assets such as drug money. The Act increases penalties for a variety of activities and includes a 4-year mandatory minimum sentence for recruiting a minor.

Research over the last quarter century suggests that, to be effective, intervention must start well before the teen years. Early violence eventually begets violence and persists into later life, suggesting that the aggressive personality is essentially formed by late childhood or adolescence. Investigations have shown that, once ingrained, aggression tends to persist. Aggression at age 8 is a good predictor of violence toward one's offspring 22 years later (Huesmann et al., 1984). In Europe, as well, aggression at age 8 has been found to be predictive of self-reported violence at age 30 (Farrington, 1994).

In this country, especially in urban areas, children are often raised in a subculture of violence in which the perpetrator is rewarded. In a classic study, Patterson, Cobb, and Ray (1972) reported that 80% of young normal children's assaultive behaviors across common situations produced rewarding consequences, which accounted for their persistence. In a study involving over 1600 children, Dodge and his colleagues (1997) found that young children who are proactively aggressive — bullying, calculating, and less emotional — are more likely than reactive aggressors to both expect and receive rewards for their violence. Evidence supporting this finding is so strong that Dodge proposed a classification system based on the two types of aggressive behavior.

So what can be done about youth aggression? Relevant to primary prevention, during child development, non-violent parents inhibit violent tendencies in their children by modeling non-violence (Bandura, 1973; Hoffman, 1960). The child learns to think in terms of non-violent options. In general, the most powerful predictor of non-violence is a history of non-violence. As Robert Eme discusses in Chapter

4, secondary prevention efforts involve identifying high-risk youth before they have internalized a predatory attitude toward significant others and society.

Tertiary efforts have not been remarkably successful. The failure of tertiary approaches in reform schools and prisons was shown by the fact that approximately 5000 out of 9000 youths incarcerated in California Youth Authority facilities were gang members in 1989 and by findings that gang cohesiveness *increased* rather than decreased as a function of incarceration (Goldstein, 1994). The APA (1993) has proposed a variety of tertiary prevention efforts based on the finding that intervention of this type is difficult, but not hopeless. Common characteristics of successful programs, as discussed by the APA and by Joseph Poirier in Chapter 5, include interventions that are multi-modal, sustained, and coordinated.

Syndicated Crime

According to the President's Commission on Organized Crime (1986), the annual gross income of crime syndicates is $66 billion. This figure increases to $226 billion if legal ventures funded by illegally earned money are included, making crime networks one of the top U.S. industries (Albini, 1971; Chambliss, 1988). Generally, in most major cities in this nation, a loose affiliation of business people, police officers, politicians, and union leaders covertly supports illegal services and materials based on informal relationships with organized crime groups. Some evidence, revealed by investigative journalism and declassified documents, shows that the U.S. federal government used organized crime figures and resources during World War II, in France during the 1950s, in Indochina, against Castro, and at other times (Beire and Messerschmidt, 1995; Bellis, 1981; Myers, 1997; Pearce, 1976; Stanton, 1976).

Besides traditional gambling, prostitution, loan sharking, garnering political favors, and racketeering, syndicated crime activities in the last few decades have included pervasive distribution and sale of hard drugs in remote and otherwise relatively inaccessible places (e.g., prisons, rural areas, the military), hazardous waste disposal in at least one third of the states, and direct investment (read criminally lucrative or "sweetheart contracts") in the construction, clothing, and trucking industries (Beirne and Messerschmidt, 1995). In the 1980s, for example, several crime groups imposed a 2% "tax" on New York City contractors on the pouring of cement for structures exceeding $2 million (President's Commission on Organized Crime, 1986). The groups made over $71 million from just 10 jobs, including the Trump Plaza in Manhattan.

Salvador "Sammy the Bull" Gravano, who was the underboss in the Gambino organized crime family until he became a government witness against Gambino Boss John Gotti, made the point that killing is both necessary and desirable (Maas, 1997, p. 46):

> *"Committing a murder — making your bones — was not a prerequisite for induction into Cosa Nostra. But, more often then not, it would happen. Murder was the linchpin of Cosa Nostra — for control, for discipline, to achieve and maintain power. For made members and associates, it was an everyday, accepted fact of life. The code that could trigger a hit was very clear. If someone broke the rules, he would be whacked. Murder was the means to bring some semblance of order to what otherwise would be chaos."*

No statistics can be presented on murders perpetrated by the Cosa Nostra or by the other ethnic-based crime syndicates in this country. If the perpetrator is known, homicides are reported for that individual, not for perpetrator groups or institutions.

Various Chinese, Black, Mexican, Vietnamese, Japanese, Cuban, Columbian, Irish, and Russian syndicates require that members be of that particular ethnic group. In the 24 Cosa Nostra "families" nationwide (each participant thinks of himself as a member of a specific crime family whether or not the members are related by blood), members are all male Sicilians or of other Italian descent (Beirne and

Messerschmidt, 1995). In the last decade or two, it has become permissible to have merely one parent, usually the father, of Sicilian or other Italian descent (Maas, 1997).

Ressler et al. (1993), in their FBI-based *Crime Classification Manual*, emphasized that syndicate murders are almost always planned and rehearsed and result from territorial and business disputes. These criminal competition homicides are often preceded by both intra-group (e.g., within a family) and inter-group (e.g., between families) conflict.

The crime scene usually evidences a well-planned murder that reflects awareness of incriminating behaviors by the killer. The offender almost always has a history of violence. The killing itself is done quickly and expeditiously, usually with a firearm brought to the scene, with pre-designated escape routes and decoys, if necessary. Staging of the scene — deliberate modification of the context of the killing to make it appear that it was not murder (e.g., suicide, accident) — usually does not occur. Vital body parts of the victim are targeted in terms of two scenarios. If the perpetrator group intends the murder to make a statement or announcement, a bombing, public killing, or open execution-style shooting will be seen. If the intent is to simply eliminate the victim, he is likely to be shot in the head with a small-caliber, untraceable handgun.

The agency most responsible for arrests of organized crime figures has been the FBI, especially since the death of J. Edgar Hoover (Beirne and Messerschmidt, 1995; Kessler, 1993). Hoover, notably, did not substantially target organized crime.

In light of the above, we can surmise that (1) organized crime in the U.S. is a business supported, or at the very least tolerated, by the greater community and to a lesser degree by the government; otherwise, it simply could not exist, and (2) murder is an acceptable business practice with few real long-term aversive consequences to the organized crime group itself. Under these conditions, even with the best law enforcement, organized crime can never be eradicated. Ironically, in this country and abroad, it appears that we indirectly create or at least tolerate some of the murder we fear is the result of collective lethal violence. The U.S. government's practice of hiring organized crime figures to kill or otherwise inflict violence on others should be considered illegal, because, among other untoward consequences, it legitimizes and condones such behavior.

Hate Crimes

Hate-motivated crimes are increasing across the nation (Craig and Waldo, 1997; see also Wisconsin v. Mitchell, 1993) and often involve violence directed at members of religious, racial, ethnic minority and majority groups, women, lesbians, gays, and bisexuals (Comstock, 1989; Herek and Berrill, 1992; Levin and McDevitt, 1993). An increase in racist, sexist, anti-Semitic, and homosexually targeted crimes, including murder, arson, bombings, looting, verbal harassment, and assault, has been confirmed by statistics gathered by various groups such as the National Gay and Lesbian Task Force (1994), the Center for Democratic Renewal (1987), and the Anti-Defamation League (1994).

For 1995, in order of frequency, reported hate crimes were most often perpetrated against (1) male homosexuals (1031 as opposed to 131 against lesbians), (2) individuals of a different ethnicity/national origin (958; as separate categories, Hispanic and Jewish victims numbered 685 and 350, respectively); and (3) those of a different religion, other than those, such as Jewish victims, reported in the previous category (U.S. Dept. of Justice, 1997).

Hate crimes are less likely to be reported than other crimes. Only one third of hate-crime victims reported the violence to the police, compared to 57% of victims of non-hate crimes (Mjoseth, 1998). Whether reported or not, victims of hate crimes are likely to have higher levels of psychic distress and PTSD than victims of other crimes (Mjoseth, 1998).

Pursuant to the Hate Crime Statistics Act of 1990, enacted to document the rate of hate crimes more accurately, the FBI reported that 4558 bias-motivated offenses were committed in 1991 (as cited in Wisconsin v. Mitchell, 1993) and that 7947 were committed in 1995 (U.S. Department of Justice, 1997). Blacks are the most frequent targets of reported racially motivated violence, with individuals of Asian, Latino, and Native American descent also being targeted (Center for Democratic Renewal, 1987; Finn and McNeil, 1987; U.S. Department of Justice, 1997). The highest rate of crime toward blacks occurs when blacks move into all-white neighborhoods, suggesting that violence will increase in the suburbs in the next few years as more minorities move into those areas (Mjoseth, 1998).

A new federal bill (51529), introduced by Senators Edward Kennedy (Democrat from Massachusetts) and Arlen Specter (Republican from Pennsylvania), builds on the 1994 Hate Crimes Sentencing Act and calls for stiffer sentences for hate-crime offenders. As of 1998, 38 states have enacted laws that increase sentences for those convicted of perpetrating violence toward others on the basis of race, religion, national origin, gender, or sexual orientation (Mjoseth, 1998).

Although the most common hate group perpetrator is a young white male, many minority perpetrators are every bit as racially prejudiced as their white counterparts. Some black-on-white violence, for example, carries a racial component (U.S. Dept. of Justice, 1997). Statistics support this interpretation of minority reverse prejudice. Although black victims of hate crimes are the most frequent (3945 in 1995) compared to white victims (1554 in 1995), black perpetrators of hate crimes (2253; about 27% of the total), who represent about 12% of the total population, are over-represented compared to whites (4991) who comprise 59% of the perpetrator group. The Justice Department presented, but downplayed, these figures in the spirit of the current Zeitgeist; such statistics are neither politically correct nor likely to yield research funds for investigators to probe these racial disparities.

Case Illustration 1

The author evaluated 26-year-old Eric, a member of a white supremacist group, for criminal responsibility relevant to insanity on charges of aggravated assault, negligent homicide, driving under the influence of alcohol, grand theft auto, and felon in possession of firearms. Like many "skinheads", he had a history of substance abuse, predatory violence, and violence-related incarceration. Because of his large size but slow reactions, his role in a number of violent incidents was to restrain victims while they were assaulted by other members of his group. He estimated that he was a "holder" in between 20 and 30 assaults over his 5 years in a white supremacist group in California, with several of the victims dying of their wounds. He expressed pride in the efficacy of his behavior. The instant offenses involved his ingesting "ice" (the smokable form of methamphetamine) with several gang members, assaulting a black homosexual drag queen so badly that he was later hospitalized in a coma, stealing the victim's late-model car, and crashing into two other vehicles while being chased by police officers, killing a lone driver in another car in the process. Eric was addicted to ice and experienced auditory hallucinations, such as hearing voices telling him that he was the Devil and that he should "kill, kill, kill" and other severe symptoms. His defense attorney hoped a sanity evaluation would yield exculpatory information, as there was no chance of misidentification by the police for the crime. He was found competent to stand trial and criminally responsible. A subsequent dangerousness evaluation was cited by the presiding judge as a basis for sentencing him to an extended term of imprisonment of 20 years to life, with a 15-year minimum.

Hate crimes are discussed more thoroughly by Golden, Jackson, and Crum in Chapter 8. Within a general finding that no known effective therapies exist for hate-crime offenders, the authors cogently argue that efforts at change must start at a young age and present a variety of preventive interventions for school-age children.

Domestic Terrorism

In a most ominous trend, militia leaders claim that membership in "patriot" groups has increased sevenfold since the Oklahoma City bombing of the Alfred

P. Murrah Federal Building in 1995 to a high of 250,000 members nationwide (*Law Enforcement News*, 1996). The Anti-Defamation League found that, as of 1994, 40 states had active militias, with a total of approximately 15,000 hardcore members.

In May 1996, the Southern Poverty Law Center, which has studied the domestic terrorism movement more closely than any other organization except the U.S. government, identified 441 militias, twice as many as in 1994 (Roy, 1996). Terrorists do not welcome the negative publicity. The staff and physical facilities of the Southern Poverty Law Center have been the target of attacks by militias. On November 9, 1995, several members of the Oklahoma Constitutional Militia were arrested as they were preparing explosives intended for use against the Southern Poverty Law Center and four other organizations.

According to the Southern Poverty Law Center, the weapons and equipment found in the possession of antigovernment extremists in 1994 and 1995 alone included (1) AK-47, M-16, AR-15, Uzi, and SKS assault rifles; (2) 9-mm machine guns; (3) .50-caliber rifles; (4) fully automatic Mac-10 pistols; (5) freeze-dried bubonic plague bacteria; (6) Ricin, a biological poison — in March 1995, for example, four members of the Minnesota Patriots Council who possessed sufficient Ricin to kill 1400 people and had learned to manufacture the poison from a mail-order manual were convicted of conspiracy to use Ricin to kill federal agents and law enforcement officers; (7) M-203 grenade launchers; (8) homemade C-4 explosives; (9) silencers; (10) machine guns and component parts; (11) automatic weapon conversion kits; (12) armor-piercing ammunition; (13) night-vision binoculars; and (14) body armor and gas masks. These resources represent opportunity factors associated with violence. Mere possession of some of these weapons is a crime in itself.

The incidents described below occurred between 1994 and 1996 and encompass most of the violence inflicted on others by alleged militia members during this 2-year period (Roy, 1996). In September 1994, a police officer in Missouri was wounded at his home by a sniper shot from a high-powered rifle. The shooting was believed, but not proven, to be in retaliation for a raid on a Patriot Order of the Citizens of the Kingdom of Christ. In 1995, bombs went off at a U.S. Forest Service Office in Nevada; no one was killed. In April 1995, 168 people were killed by a homemade bomb (made from fertilizer) at the Murrah Federal Building in Oklahoma City. Also in April 1995, as a result of a gun battle, three deputies were wounded by militia members in Indiana. In September 1995, in Utah, a member of the Army of Israel militia was charged with assault. He was also arrested for attempting to steal explosives. On October 9, 1995, an Amtrak train derailed in Arizona. An antigovernment message was found at the scene. No one was killed. In January 1996, a Patriot member attacked a state highway patrol trooper in Ohio. The Patriot, who was allegedly a member of the Unorganized Militia of Ohio, was charged with felonious assault. In April 1996, three members of the Phineas Priesthood were charged with bank robbery and conspiracy to commit two other bank robberies during which they planted pipe bombs to divert attention.

Would the perpetrators have committed the crimes if they had not belonged to a militia group? Probably not, unless those individuals had a background of violence. History is the best predictor of dangerousness, and most militia members do not have a substantial background of violence. Clearly, it is the potential of the movement, rather than the absolute number of violent acts, that concerns authorities.

Militia books and pamphlets, to the extent that they reinforce the attitude that violent overthrow of the government is an acceptable solution to current problems, should be studied in order to understand the psychology of the movement. Additionally, they may provide knowledge of the suggested methodology of violence. Excerpts from the *Turner Diaries* (Pierce, writing under the pseudonym of Andrew MacDonald, 1978, 1980) illustrate the ideological framework for a modern American revolution as the hero tells the story of his resistance against the government. A dispassionate reading of this book, for which its printing history claims sales of almost 200,000 copies as of February 1995, implies that the hero, an American white male, has been repeatedly victimized by the federal government. The increasing restrictions on firearm ownership, the contemplated internal passport program (where Americans would have credit card-like objects with a built-in computer chip for positive identification of the owner), the favoring of minorities over the majority, are all cited as grievances and proof of victimhood to which a violence response is necessary. A spiritual connection is emphasized (MacDonald, 1978, 1980, pp. 34, 35):

"But one thing which is quite clear is that much more than our freedom is at stake. If the Organization fails in its task now, everything will be lost — our history, our heritage, all the blood and sacrifices and upward striving of countless thousands of years. The Enemy we are fighting fully intends to destroy the racial basis of our existence. ...If we fail, God's great Experiment will come to an end, and this planet will once again, as it did millions of years ago, move through the ether devoid of higher man."

In the *Turner Diaries*, the Jewish people are reported to have concocted the Holocaust in order to involve the U.S. in World War II against Germany. Hitler is exalted as the "Great One". Jews are described as archetypically evil, shrewd, and controlling, unleashing the power of the media on the white majority. But Jews are not the only targets. The book states that the goal is to kill all Jews and non-Caucasians toward the end of creating an all-white, non-Jewish society. A striking passage springs from the *Turner Diaries* (MacDonald, 1978, 1980, p. 171):

"My most profound impression comes from the fact that every face I saw in the fields was White: no Chicanos, no Orientals, no Blacks, no mongrels. The air seems cleaner, the sun brighter, life more joyous. What a wonderful difference this single accomplishment of our revolution had made!"

After describing taking control in the U.S. through a revolution and nuclear blackmail, the book ends with a fantasized genocidal extermination of a large section of the Earth involving about 2 billion people (MacDonald, 1978, 1980, p. 210):

"Therefore, the Organization resorted to a combination of chemical, biological, and radiological means, on an enormous scale, to deal with the problem [of non-white control]. Over a period of four years some 16 million square miles of the Earth's surface, from the Ural Mountains to the Pacific and from the Arctic Ocean to the Indian Ocean, were effectively sterilized. Thus was the Great Eastern Waste created."

Importantly, the book provides lessons on how to carry out revolutionary activities. The hero blows up the FBI building in Washington, D.C., after a long explanation about how to accomplish this with certain types of explosives and a particular *modus operandus* (which Timothy McVeigh is alleged to have used in the Oklahoma City bombing).

Patriot literature provides members and potential members with the knowledge and means to overthrow the U.S. government. The *Militia Battle Manual* (Koch, 1996, pp. 15–16), for example, starts off with these lethal thoughts:

"Don't kill just any politician you see on the street. Kill the ones who are opposed to the cause and trying to get the most extreme measures against it passed. Don't just blow up any building. Blow up the people and buildings that are most against the cause or will give you a strategic advantage in the field."

The six cardinal rules of the militia organization in preparation for armed conflict are then provided (Koch, 1996):

1. Use cells consisting of one or more people who know and trust one another. (The cell system, borrowed from the Communists, is highly frustrating to law enforcement agencies because, if organized correctly, it minimizes their ability to uncover members' identities.)

2. Let cells and the organization grow naturally. Don't transfer members between cells. Joining a cell is always voluntary. (Joiners may be subject to lengthy deception-detecting interrogations in an effort to identify informers.)
3. Be realistic; set reasonable goals for cells. Don't have a cell with one sniper hold down a police station, for example, while other cells blow a bridge.
4. Keep the organization as simple as possible and still do the job. Simplicity leads to flexibility and effectiveness of combat operations.
5. Keep paperwork to a minimum. The output should never be traced back to you. Do not make copies and never put a name or title on anything written.
6. Establish a clear chain of command. If the leader is killed or wounded, all members know who will assume command. A cell leader is a captain, a major has two cells under command, and a colonel has five or more cells.

A fully articulated cell organization is depicted in Figure 1.1.

In sum, domestic terrorist groups are growing and appear motivated to remain on the American scene. They are almost impossible to eliminate because of their cell system. Anti-minority, and particularly anti-Jewish, in nature, they are projected to become increasingly lethal in the coming decades. As Bob Fletcher, a member of a militia in Montana, predicted (Roy, 1996), "Expect more bombs."

Intervention against terrorist groups has been largely punitive and tertiary, the least effective methods for changing others (Bandura, 1973; Elias, 1997; Turpin and Kurtz, 1997). The Southern Poverty Law Center noted that anti-militia laws are on the books in 24 states, and its first recommendation was that such laws be enacted in the remainder of the states and that

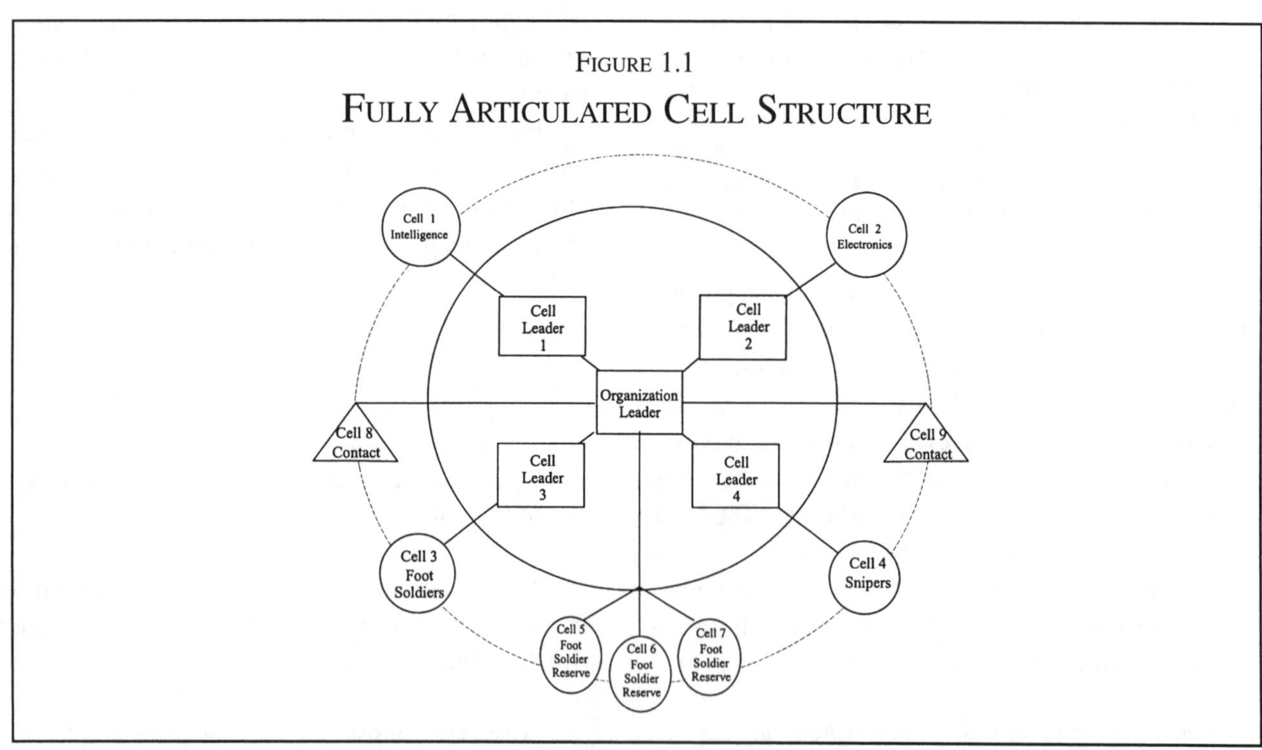

Cell structure in Phase 2 (operations) after Phase 1 (creation) is completed. In inner circles, Organization Leader knows identities of cell leaders but not cell members, except for contacts with access to important information. Cell members do not know identities of individuals in other cells (broken line). Phase 3 would be an all-out war. (Adapted from Koch, T. (1996) *The Militia Battle Manual*. El Dorado, AR: Desert Publications.)

current violations be prosecuted (Roy, 1996, p. 42). The Center's second and third recommendations broaden to include federal jurisdictions. Existing and proposed anti-militia laws would ban *all* nongovernment military and paramilitary organizations. Anti-paramilitary training laws would prohibit training with weapons (including explosives) that is carried out with the knowledge or intent to use such training to foment civil disorder. The Center has won multiple civil awards against Patriot and white supremacist groups in litigation since about 1980 — for example, enjoining the white Patriot Party from training or even existing as a para-military organization (Person v. Miller, 1988). Observations and interventions regarding terrorism are offered in Chapter 9 by Clayton, Barlow, and Ballif-Spanvill.

Lethal Violence by the Government

Unfortunately, "legitimate" killing by the government in the form of police deadly force, wars, and violent actions by government agencies and departments is common (Stanton, 1976; Tehranian, 1997; Turpin and Kurtz, 1997; Woodward, 1988). As we already know, lethal violence by individuals acting on their own behalf has become more frequent with the aid of improved technology, the breakdown of the family, changing moral values, violent lifestyles, desensitization to violence through the media, racism, and other destabilizing factors (Herrnstein and Murray, 1994; Ropp, 1962; Sagan, 1980, 1995, personal communication; Toplin, 1975). When police officers or government agents kill a civilian, however, the resulting public backlash and eventual civil unrest can be profound.

The public outcry is based on the underlying assumption that the government has abused its monopoly on the legitimate use of violence, which it is accorded only to protect civil society from violence both within and outside the country. Thomas Hobbes (1928), an Enlightenment theorist, presented the essentials of this "social contract" we have with the state: Recognizing that the use of violence must be regulated by any social system, we (as citizens) relinquish the right to use force in exchange for liberty and security.

Increased crime, civil unrest, riots, rebellions, and revolution occur when the government fails in its part of the social contract. As stated eloquently in 1928 by U.S. Supreme Court Justice Louis Brandeis (cited in Archer and Gartner, 1984, p. 95):

> *"Our government is the potent, the omnipresent teacher. For good or ill, it teaches the whole people by its example. Crime is contagious. If the government becomes a lawbreaker, it breeds contempt for the law."*

Over the last two centuries in this country, illegitimate violence by individuals acting alone or under the umbrella of collective entities has come to be legally considered murder. The *Law of Homicide,* by Frank Bowlby (1907), covered legal thought in America from the last half of the 19th century to the early part of the 20th century and defined justified killing in detail. The theoretical underpinnings of the *Law of Homicide* remain current in the interpretation of state and federal statutes (Kopel and Blackman, 1997; U.S. Congress Senate Subcommittee on Terrorism, Narcotics, and International Operations, 1989; U.S. Department of Justice, 1983).

How do you apply the rules of law in practical situations? As the *Law of Homicide* explained, police officers engage in deadly force under restricted conditions where the rules of engagement are known to all parties beforehand. The restricted conditions may change according to jurisdiction, but the basic rules are known to all players. For example, in some jurisdictions, police are trained not to shoot unless necessary to defend themselves or others in the vicinity.

What about war? According to the *Law of Homicide* (Bowlby, 1908, p. 14), "... Killing even an alien enemy, unless such killing occurred in the actual exercise of war, would be murder." Any lethal action, whether individually or collectively motivated, constitutes murder when a person kills at the instigation of another. Bowlby stated metaphorically that a person who deliberately let loose a dangerous beast, which then killed an individual, should be held responsible for murder.

Today, depending on how laws differ among jurisdictions, one could be charged with being an accomplice to murder for providing firearms to a person who uses them in a felony murder. Applying Bowlby's metaphor, letting loose a wild beast is like equipping and training others to kill, as several agencies and departments of our government have done. Whether this type of killing is perpetrated by an individual, a gang, a militia, or the CIA, it is murder.

Inserting federal agencies into civilian affairs by using the military can constitute criminal behavior. The Posse Comitatus Act of 1878 was passed to forbid the use of federal troops in response to allegedly civilian criminal behavior except where expressly permitted by the Constitution or by an act of Congress. In part, the amended act provided as follows (as cited in Kopel and Blackman, 1997, p.85):

> *"Whoever, except in cases and under circumstances expressly authorized by the Constitution or Act of Congress, willfully uses any part of the Army or the Air Force as a* posse comitatus *or otherwise to execute the laws shall be fined no more than $10,000 or imprisoned not more than two years, or both."*

The basic idea is that anything that makes law enforcement appear military-like is onerous and repugnant to the American people and has been so since the framing of the Constitution. With regard to the Posse Comitatus Act, Chief Justice Warren Burger observed "a traditional and strong resistance of Americans to any military intrusion into civilian affairs" (Laird v. Tatum, 1972, pp. 15–16).

Nevertheless, the federal government has persistently violated the spirit of *posse comitatus* in disregard of the law of the land. As documented by Kopel and Blackman (1997), the Army broke up a miner's strike in Cour d'Alene, ID, in 1899, and imprisoned some strikers for months without charges. The Army was used to spy on union organizers, pacifists, and black demonstrators during World War I. President Truman's seizure of the steel mills may have been unconstitutional. During Vietnam, military intelligence was applied against war demonstrators and resistors. Both Ruby Ridge and Waco were run like military operations, with the Department of Defense providing advice and FBI personnel being trained to drive tanks and operate other military equipment.

Kopel and Blackman (1997) pointed out the "drug law" loophole in the Posse Comitatus Act, meaning that military assistance may be provided if a drug connection to a civilian act is shown. This explains why the Bureau of Alcohol, Tobacco and Firearms (BATF) classified Waco as a drug investigation, despite evidence that Koresh had notified law enforcement officials when, upon assuming leadership, he discovered a methamphetamine laboratory in the Branch Davidian compound.

Our definition of collective lethal violence focuses on individuals acting in their group or institutional roles, causing or allowing the death of others. As we will discuss, this definition includes the human radiation and biological/chemical experiments in which individuals on the U.S. government payroll acted within their roles in lethal ways without the consent, knowledge, or approval of the subjects. If a physician administers a drug that has no intended medical benefit, stating that it is another drug and knowing full well the potential harmful side-effects of the administered drug, the physician may be considered to have committed murder if the patient dies as a result.

The Police

The use of deadly force by police, including retrospectively determined unauthorized killing, is addressed by Stock, Borum, and Baltzley in Chapter 13. These authors found that the use of deadly force by police officers is rare (less than .05% of all encounters with citizens). Individuals at high risk for killing others do so as a joint function of their organization's belief system and their own individual violence histories and personal problems.

Two groups of killers emerge: (1) those whose institutional roles involve high risks of violence (e.g., SWAT team members), and (2) those who kill by overreacting to a provocative situation. Poor training, psychological problems, and a history of impulsive behavior may all contribute to the latter category.

Stock et al. point out that within these two groups are five types of high risk police officers:

1. Chronic risk group of individuals who have a lifelong history of conflict with others and may be described as being hypersensitive to threat, manipulative, lacking in insight, projecting of blame, and frequently substance abusing. There is almost always a history of severe relationship problems. An Antisocial Personality Disorder diagnosis would fit these individuals even if they had not joined a destructive collective entity.
2. Job-related (traumatic) experience group including police officers who have direct experience with killing and have difficulty re-integrating into routine work after a violent event. They almost always suffer from PTSD and are more vulnerable to further violent acting out unless treated with immediate debriefing after action and follow-up PTSD intervention if any of the cardinal signs are shown (e.g., flashbacks, nightmares, dissociative episodes, survivor guilt, symptoms of depression and anxiety).
3. Early career problems group characterized by "gung ho" police officers who enjoy the power and authority that come with their role in the group or institution. They lack the judgment and impulse control that come with time and experience. These individuals need proper models and leaders to monitor and provide feedback for them.
4. Personal problem group consisting of police officers, exclusive of the violence trauma group, who experience a breakdown in coping mechanisms and impulse control when faced with personal losses such as a divorce or demotion. PTSD may or may not occur, but should be considered. An early warning system can detect these often bitter and disillusioned officers who were already vulnerable before the stresses were applied.
5. Inappropriate problem-solving style group of police officers who ignore mediation and compromise in dealing with the public. They do not respond to intervention by their organizations because their interpersonal style is acquired over time rather than resulting from ingrained personality traits first manifested during their early development.

The inappropriate problem-solving style group of police officers may have traits in common with all violent collective entities. The primal belief of individuals in this group is that force is necessary to bring situations under control. Psychologically, they are "normal" but tend to be cynical and unwilling to relinquish control. This style has worked for them in the past, so they ignore negotiation-based approaches. Some individuals in this group rise to the leadership of a collective enterprise as their personality style is acquired over time. Subordinates within an organization typically respond better to intervention for inappropriate behavior because of the relatively recent nature of their acquisition of their coping style. Leaders of police organizations, on the other hand, often only begrudgingly respond to outside pressure, such as from the media and higher authority. Internal dissent may be seen as disloyalty.

The following are among the standard suggestions for "successful" police interrogation (Hall and Pritchard, 1996; Royal and Schutt, 1976):

- Isolate suspect from all intrusions and resources.
- Keep suspect immobile as much as possible.
- Establish dependence on the part of the suspect.
- Use one examiner who is friendly, concerned, and firm.
- Ask open-ended questions for new information.
- Proceed from the general to the specific.
- Ask precise questions for concrete data.

- Occasionally ask questions randomly to upset faking patterns.
- Summarize statements in sequence of events.
- Have the suspect verify each part of summarized sequence material.
- Suggest excuses for the crime to the suspect before the suspect spontaneously mentions them.
- Project indifference to the suspect's criminal behavior ("everybody does it").
- Induce stress when appropriate.
- Provide relief after an admission, then induce stress again; repeat the cycle
- Continue until a confession is obtained

In an attempt to extract a confession, due process is often violated, and the interrogation methods themselves may be more unethical than the suspected offense. Yet, deception by interviewers is pervasive — personalizing the suspect, minimizing wrongdoing, and using the "good cop-bad cop" technique and other gimmicks and ploys. Even well-prepared suspects tend to wear down and be caught off guard under these circumstances. Having reviewed hundreds of transcripts of interrogations and interviewed dozens of police detectives, this author is amazed that anyone suspected of any crime would talk to the police about anything. In this country, individuals (rightly or wrongly) suspected of crimes need not incriminate themselves or even verbally interact with the police. It is best to say nothing except (repetitiously, if necessary) to ask for one's attorney.

National police agencies as well as local police departments commonly use the same methods, which are taught by several large firms specializing in "honesty" testing and interrogation techniques (e.g., Reid and Associates, 1986, 1988). Even the context is manipulated in fine detail. Note the following recommendations for setting up an interrogation room in order to obtain a confession (Reid and Associates, 1988, p. 7):

"Shorten the front legs of a straight chair 3/8 of an inch and keep the seat waxed. The person who comes in showing indifference is not going to talk to you. He wants to show you how cool he is by stretching out and taking up a lot of space. Normally when you sit in a chair, it leans slightly backward to support body weight. By changing the tilt, [the suspect will] lean slightly forward. It's really hard to stretch out and be indifferent when you're falling off the chair.

"People have an intimate zone of 6 to 18 inches from the body and a personal zone of 1-1/2 to 4 feet. By stepping in close to the individual to produce anxiety and backing off when you get what you want, you mentally program that person to be cooperative.

"Paint the room a neutral color, such as pale yellow."

In consultation and training with police officers, this author has often found them reluctant to relinquish power and control, including coercive and otherwise inappropriate interrogation techniques. Some confessions, for example, are extracted before or after a polygraph test is administered (i.e., independent of the results), with the "lie detector" itself adding an aura of invincibility and being described by the operator as a machine that cannot be beaten. Police investment of time, money, and energy in these methods is considerable. The techniques themselves are based on power-adversarial reasoning, congruent with the attitudes of many police officers. The long-term loss to individuals and the community in exchange for short-term gain for the police is especially unfortunate given the availability of newer, effective, non-coercive methodologies to uncover deception and distortion (Hall, 1986, 1990, 1996; Hall and Pritchard, 1996; Roberts, 1988; Shooter and Hall, 1990).

The Federal Bureau of Investigation

In Chapter 10, by Hinman and Cook, on profiling methods for multiple perpetrators, and in Chapter 11, by Feldmann, on the FBI's role in hostage negotiations, the authors probe the exceptional efficiency of the FBI in various interventions. This author has worked with the FBI on serial rape murder cases and on a serial bombing case. In all of these interactions, the FBI possessed and applied state-of-the-art methodology; however, the FBI is not without problems. A dangerous side of the FBI, focusing on domestic terrorism, is discussed below.

In the face of a potentially catastrophic problem represented by domestic militia groups, such as the violent overthrow of our government, the governmental reaction has been disappointing. The authorities' counter-responses have been persistently violent and have caused human rights abuses. Worse yet, these responses may actually strengthen the militia movement, as certain historical facts suggest.

A wave of ostensible terrorism occurred in this country in the 1960s and early 1970s, including on college campuses. The FBI and other government agencies were involved in numerous illegal activities, such as implementing strategies to disrupt and "neutralize" domestic organizations felt by federal authorities to threaten the social order (Beirne and Messerschmidt, 1995; Kessler, 1993). Then, as now, FBI informers infiltrated opposition groups and encouraged, albeit indirectly, the very acts for which opposition members were eventually arrested. After concluding that the domestic terrorists, almost all of whom were white, were psychologically normal, simply spoiled, labile, over-privileged kids prone to paranoia, an FBI paper (1976, pp. 2–3) pronounced:

"Yet many of the American terrorists have never experienced the deprivation which American sociologists describe so vividly. They are from the group where the least crime is spawned. They have been, since birth, immersed in the American middle class milieu, the segment of the society that more than any other has traditionally fostered and taught those stolid virtues expressed in the Protestant work ethic including respect for authority. There is no obvious reason why a young American should choose the terrorist role especially if that role is not forced upon him or her by circumstances of deprivation, poverty and family disorganization, which are the factors traditionally thought to effect such choices of deviant life style." [emphasis added]

Several decades ago, domestic "terrorists" were thus viewed as paranoid and unstable in their intense antigovernment feeling, with no acknowledgment by the government for creating the very phenomenon that was being investigated. No learning appears to have taken place since the above was written in 1976. The Associated Press (1997), for example, reported that the government's initial portrayals of terrorists as paranoid, violent individuals who are well equipped with lethal weaponry were grossly exaggerated in several instances. In four major raids on militias in 1996 — Georgia, Washington, West Virginia, and Arizona — no evidence of real violent intent was discovered.

In the 1990s, the FBI itself may have been responsible for some of the alleged crimes. The 12th Georgia Militia claimed that an informant had boasted of his bomb-making skills which were to be used against federal targets, the subject of a later indictment of militia members. An FBI undercover agent gave a West Virginia Mountain Militia $50,000 for photographed blueprints of the FBI fingerprint center in Clarksburg, VA. Transcripts of tapes of militia team meetings in Arizona (i.e., the Viper group) describe an informant repeatedly steering members in discussions toward plans for violence that eventually would be the evidentiary bases for conspiracy charges against them.

We can anticipate an increase in this type of investigations. According to the Associated Press (1997), after the Oklahoma City bombing, Louis Freeh, the current FBI director, told a congressional committee that his agency would "broadly and proactively" act against domestic terrorism. Freeh's policy may be based on a fundamental misreading of the character of domestic terrorists and dooms all but the relatively ineffective tertiary strategies to failure. The view of domestic terrorists as psychologically flawed (not to mention disloyal and paranoid) places all blame on militia activists and relieves federal agencies of acknowledgment of their contribution to the movement. It smacks of the "rush to the dispositional" (Zimbardo, 1997), meaning that negative outcomes are attributed to negative traits or dispositions of the perpetrator rather than to the interaction of perpetrator and victim. The rush to the dispositional has little predictive value. The prophecy is self-fulfilling, as illustrated below.

The public is well aware of the 1992 killing of Randy Weaver's wife and 10-month old daughter by an FBI sniper, Lon T. Horiuchi, at Ruby Ridge. The fact that Marshal William F. Degan was killed by Kevin Harris, a companion of Weaver, does not change the story told by *both* sides that the government fired first in the interchange. In the thoroughly documented *No More Wacos* (1997), David B. Kopel, an attorney, and Paul H. Blackman, a criminologist, brought to light that a BATF informant had repeatedly pressured Weaver into shortening two shotgun barrels and stocks to below their legal limit, and that Weaver had initially declined several times, but later acquiesced. The BATF then threatened Weaver with the loss of his house and with imprisonment if he did not serve as an informer on the activities of the Aryan Nations, a Patriot group.

The BATF targeted Weaver as a violent conspirator when his wife told Aryan Nations members of the BATF plan. An unsuccessful effort by the BATF to hold Weaver in jail after a bogus arrest (false allegations of drug distribution), failing to inform Weaver of a change in the court calendar so additional charges could be filed and a bench warrant issued for his arrest, and a 16-month surveillance of the Weaver cabin all preceded the attack. The 1995 Congressional Hearings established that FBI supervisor Larry Potts approved license-to-kill language and that FBI agent Richard Rogers, the "Hostage Rescue Team" leader, had proposed a plan that included *no* possibility of a peaceful, negotiated end to the conflict.

On September 25, 1997, the Ninth Circuit Court of Appeals in San Francisco held that the "shoot to kill" policy was "a gross violation of constitutional principles and a wholly unwarranted return to lawless and arbitrary wild-west school of law enforcement" (Weinstein, 1997). In a unanimous decision, the Ninth Circuit Court stated that the FBI's acts "violated clearly established law and any reasonable law enforcement officer should have been aware of that fact." The panel rejected the arguments of 13 FBI agents (including Special Agent Horiuchi) and U.S. Marshals that they were entitled to immunity from prosecution for their acts at Ruby Ridge (Weinstein, 1997).

On April 19, 1993, an FBI tank assault on the Branch Davidian complex in Waco, TX, involved ramming the buildings of the compound in order to inject chlorobenzalmalonitrile (CS), a chemical warfare agent which was barred by the Chemical Weapons Convention, signed by the U.S. in Paris in January 1993. This was followed by the fiery deaths of dozens of adults and 27 children. As amply shown by Kopel and Blackman (1997), the deaths were unnecessary and followed a grim comedy of errors including (1) BATF agents deliberately avoiding several opportunities to arrest David Koresh, the cult leader, when he left the compound previously; (2) the total lack of justification for a military assault to serve a search warrant after the BATF notified the media of the upcoming event as a publicity stunt to garner more congressional support for the agency; (3) the BATF attacking *after* losing the element of surprise, when it knew the Branch Davidians were aware of the attack (several of the four BATF agents killed and others wounded may have been struck by "friendly fire"); (4) a foolish FBI strategy of psychological warfare, including broadcasting loud noises, the sounds of rabbits being slaughtered, and other unpleasant noises which, from a psychological perspective, would naturally lead to angry, noncompliant responses; (5) the miscalculation that Koresh and his followers were not willing to commit (mass) suicide; and (6) the FBI misinforming Attorney General Janet Reno and others on the particulars of the assault plan and the supposedly non-harmful effects of the CS agents (some Branch Davidians may have died from inhalation of hydrogen cyanide, a CS agent byproduct).

Kopel and Blackman (1997) pointed out that not since the Wounded Knee massacre in 1890 had so many Americans been killed by the federal government. The number of deaths at Waco represented over 50% of the total number of Americans killed in the Gulf War. It involved the largest number of civilian and law enforcement deaths in a single operation ever in this nation. Kopel and Blackman strongly recommended that a special prosecutor be appointed for the purpose of revealing the truth about Waco based on the assumption that law enforcement officers should obey the law. In its official versions of descriptions of terrorist activities, the FBI, through the U.S. Department of Justice (1997), continued to minimize and deny its role in the deaths of many innocent Americans at Waco.

Nevertheless, the hyperaggressive responses of the FBI and other federal agencies are viewed as contributing to the emergence of domestic terrorist groups. Richard Baudouin of Klanwatch, which tracks such groups, bluntly stated that the behavior of federal law enforcement personnel at Ruby Ridge and Waco "created the militia movement as we know it today" (Republic of Texas, 1997).

The federal agencies involved have developed a tarnished image which may take years to repair (compare this to the hero status FBI agents enjoyed in earlier decades). At the very least, federal law enforcement agencies need to cease and desist in their onerous practice of paying informants on a contingency basis. As Kopel and Blackman noted, contingency payments increase the already huge incentives for informants to lie and deceive in order to obtain a conviction, oftentimes of innocent persons.

There may be some evidence of change over time on the part of the FBI and other federal institutions. In Chapter 11, Theodore Feldmann writes of the Montana Freeman situation which ended in a negotiated surrender. In 1997, the FBI remained on the periphery of the armed confrontation between the anti-government group Republic of Texas. ("Republic of Texas ...", 1997). Three hundred state troopers managed to end a week-long siege peacefully, without assistance from the FBI. Indeed, history shows that, short of total extermination of dissident groups, an adversarial stance by the government worsens stability in a country, extends the duration of conflict, and eventually intensifies violence by both sides. Repression breeds resistance, which in turn yields more repression, which then crystallizes revolutionary activities. Clearly, what is needed is a shift from a model of control and domination to one of win-win outcomes, especially as these groups become increasingly disenfranchised with the government that is supposed to protect them. An arbitration paradigm (amplified on later) is suggested for both entities to experience positive outcomes.

The first rule of medicine and psychology is to do no harm to the patient or client whom one is serving. Similarly, the government should exercise caution in its actions toward the citizens it is supposed to serve. Federal agencies would better contain domestic terrorism by eliminating their own behaviors that help give rise to collective violence before attempting to eradicate these groups. Using infiltrators to create the very crimes for which American citizens are later prosecuted and attacking groups of men, women, and children with blunt-force trauma, together with avoidance of responsibility for wrongdoing on the part of the government, are ingredients for a recipe for certain disaster.

The U.S. Military

For over two centuries since the founding of our Republic, the withdrawal from Vietnam in 1975 notwithstanding, the U.S. military has never been defeated in direct conflict with the enemy. As the only remaining superpower since the collapse of the U.S.S.R. in 1991, the U.S. military continues to enjoy multi-dimensional power projections to all points of the globe. It is likely that American military power will extend into planetary orbit and space travel and exploration in the coming decades.

Activities ensuring the continuation of this unrivaled power base include but are not limited to the following (National Defense University, 1997):

1. The Revolution in Military Affairs (RMA) represents the current rapid development of electronic instruments through advances such as cyberspace-enhanced command and control centers. Higher-impact, flexible, and environment-specific weaponry (e.g., fiberoptic guided missiles; brilliant submunitions and mines delivered by mortars, artillery, and aircraft; silicon-based battle platforms for over-the-hill targeting) and weapon systems (e.g., 21st century infantry personnel are likely to have full night vision capability and sufficient firepower to eliminate large numbers of the enemy) can be anticipated. Within the next several years, a synthesized "mother of existing systems" will give the U.S. military dominant battlefield knowledge (DBK) in any future war or conflict. DBK translates into instant death for the enemy once their location is known.
2. Increased competency of military personnel (e.g., only 1/16 of Navy personnel on active duty in 1975 would be promoted today) along with decreasing overall numbers of military personnel as RMA progresses.
3. Continued nuclear, biological, and chemical superiority, despite reductions in accord with treaties and current policy. The U.S. already has the world's largest and best-equipped conventional force.
4. The perception by most countries, with an expanding NATO in Europe and a host of multi-lateral agreements in the Pacific Region, that the U.S. represents a stabilizing influence.

For these and other reasons, not the least of which is other nations attempting to build up their economy while keeping a modest or even token military force (as the U.S. provides the lion's share of security costs), no country or even combination of countries will be in a position to challenge the U.S. militarily in the next decade or two.

From a security standpoint, at least in the short term, most of this sounds good. From a geopsychological point of view, however, the overall picture shows that the U.S. is actually vulnerable to a variety of factors and events. Extant threats come from (1) the erosion of ethics caused by the acceptance of atrocities in the conduct of U.S. warfare, (2) the huge economical and environmental costs of maintaining superior power, (3) the inability of our military to deal with nonconventional and domestic adversaries, and (4) the creation of violent agencies and departments after the cessation of hostilities, which then operate on a war mentality and see themselves as beyond the law. Let's take these in order.

While few question the necessity of waging war in defense of family and country, armed conflict tends to activate extremes of human destructiveness. When a war is won, history books are written by the winners, and those extreme destructive behaviors (at least on the part of the victor) are commonly minimized. They are not forgotten, however.

Since its inception, the U.S. military's history of atrocities includes (1) the near extermination of American Indians based on a belief system of superiority of values and lifestyle over the original inhabitants of this hemisphere that persists to this day; (2) systematic starvation and lethally harsh treatment of prisoners of war on both sides of the Civil War; (3) unnecessary killing of Filipinos who resisted the takeover of their country by the U.S. after the Spanish-American War. Though little known, even at the time, Filipino men, women, and children above the age of 10, both as prisoners of war and detainees for questioning — active rebels, and suspected rebels — were slaughtered by the U.S. Army with the idea that "goo-goos" (referring to Filipinos) were no better than dogs (Bilton and Sim, 1992). Subsequently, for decades, Filipinos were allowed to serve in the U.S. Navy but only as stewards (read servants); (4) use of poison gas along with its allies and the Germans in World War I (Barnaby, 1984); (5) firebombing urban civilian areas in Germany and Japan in World War II, followed by nuclear attacks on Hiroshima and

Nagasaki in 1945 (although one argument for the nuclear attacks on Japanese cities was the saving of American lives, setting an awesome precedent that the U.S. military would not stop at employing weapons of mass destruction to defeat the enemy); and (6) systematic starvation of German prisoners at the hands of the French and Americans after World War II. Based on Bacque's (1989) painstaking research involving interviews of hundreds of individuals and examination of thousands of documents regarding American prisoner of war (POW) camps, at least 750,000 Germans, including scores of thousands of women, children, and old men may have died of starvation or related causes. Bacque convincingly showed how the POWs were crowded together and fed insufficiently despite the U.S. military possessing adequate food and how the Red Cross was not allowed to deliver packages from home. His book provoked controversy as well as additional eye-witness accounts from German-Americans who were at the camps (D. Schilling, personal communication, 1997).

U.S. atrocities since the end of World War II, the temporal focus of this book, have also been minimized, thus ensuring that each generation of Americans is shocked, traumatized, and hardened and eventually represses or denies the implications of killing in the service of control and domination. Vietnam is a case in point. The downplaying of the slaughter, torture, and rape of hundreds of noncombatants in several hamlets of Song My Village in Quang Ngai Province, from March 16 to 19, 1968, by U.S. troops of the Americal Division was only one of many atrocities committed by the U.S. military in a concerted effort to exterminate the enemy (Bilton and Sim, 1992).

The primary effect of the atrocities on most thinking individuals was expressed by Jonathan Schell in 1969, when most Americans believed that the massacre was an example of excesses which are bound to happen in war (as cited in Bilton and Sim, 1992, p. 37):

> *"When we look at the photographs published in* Life *and see the bodies of children and women in piles, and look into the faces of an old woman and a young girl who [we are told] are about to be shot, we feel a kind of violence is being done to our feelings, and that the massacre threatens to overpower us. To block it out, we may freeze. If we face the massacre for what it is, we are torn by almost unbearable grief, but if we turn away and let the rationalizations crowd into our minds to protect us, we are degraded. We want to go on with our daily lives, and we may wonder, Why should my life be interrupted by this? Why should I take on this suffering on behalf of these victims? However much we may resist it, the choice has been made for us, irrevocably. Whether we manage to bear the grief or whether we freeze, the massacre enters into us and becomes a part of us. The massacre calls for self-examination and for action, but if we deny the call and try to go on as before, as though nothing had happened, our knowledge, which can never leave us once we have acquired it, will bring about an unnoticed but crucial alteration in us, numbing our most precious faculties and withering our souls. For if we learn to accept this, there is nothing we will not accept."* [emphasis added]

Bilton and Sim (1992) amply demonstrated in their well-researched book that My Lai was not an isolated atrocity. They made clear that, during the same time period, other villages were attacked by U.S. forces who raped, tortured, and killed noncombatants. Yet, most U.S. military participants were not punished. Military courts found Lieutenant William Calley guilty of mass murder, but freed him after only several years of imprisonment and house arrest. Ex-Lieutenant Calley married and has worked in his father-in-law's jewelry store in Columbus, GA, in the 1990s. Captain Ernest Medina, who, according to several witnesses gave the order for the massacre, was found not guilty of all charges and eventually left the Army to work for a helicopter manufacturing company owned by his defense attorney, F. Lee Bailey.

My Lai was sandwiched within a series of sinister events that bespoke loathing for those in opposition to U.S. interests and our ready willingness to commit murder and other atrocities. Robert

McNamara (1995), among others, opined that the U.S. entered Vietnam under false pretenses because of the Tonkin Gulf Resolution in 1964 that was itself blown out of proportion by President Johnson. The sum of the enemy assault was a North Vietnamese PT boat attack on a U.S. destroyer (deliberately sent in to provoke a response) which produced no casualties and very little damage. Potential catastrophes emerged. Then-Defense Secretary McNamara was appalled at the willingness of the Joint Chiefs of Staff to expand the war in 1966 to include "nuking" China, thus risking World War III.

After My Lai, tens of thousands of Vietnamese civilians, at this point called "gooks" by the U.S. military, were killed in the infamous CIA-sponsored Operation Phoenix (Branfman, 1978; Chomsky and Herman, 1977). Quotas for the number of Vietnamese to be "neutralized" each month were set by William Colby of the CIA (Branfman, 1978). From 1968 to 1971, at least 40,000 civilians were murdered, and thousands more were tortured. Current estimates by actual CIA operatives at the time suggest that *at least 10 times these numbers* were actually killed and tortured. (A true account of experiences in the Operation Phoenix is provided by "John Doe", an ex-Special Forces officer in Vietnam, in Appendix B.)

The overall effect of war and related atrocities, aside from warping the souls of the perpetrators and inducing PTSD in victims and witnesses, is eventual retaliatory aggression and strengthening of the enemy's will to seek revenge. Like many federal agencies, the military creates its own business by generating violence interlocks and death.

The economic and health costs of preparing for war, with concomitant destruction of the Earth, are enormous. Ruff (1992) noted that at least one third of all scientific research and development is for military purposes. U.S. military expenditures have increased many times more than the world population. The cost of one Trident submarine ($1.4 billion) would fund a 5-year child immunization program for six virulent diseases, and the price of one Stealth Bomber ($68 billion) would fund two thirds of the cost of clean water goals in the U.S. by the year 2000 (Winter, 1994). The approximately 510 atmospheric tests out of the 2034 tests of nuclear bombs have led so far to only 15% of the predicted cancers of the 1.2 million cases of cancers predicted for the next several decades from those tests (Beardsley, 1995). To prevent the destruction of the oceans once radioactive material seeps through the containers in which they were disposed, we must bear the huge economic cost of cleaning up the 48 nuclear warheads and seven nuclear-power reactors on the ocean floor, should it become possible to locate them. The cost of repairing the holes in the ozone layer of the atmosphere (the military causes 76% of the halon-1211 emissions and one half of the emissions of CFC-133, a chlorofluorocarbon) is incalculable and, at this point, we do not have the necessary technology.

No one person, group, or government has set an upper limit on the extent to which we are willing to damage the Earth, squander its resources, and kill its inhabitants, all in the name of winning and control. Consider nuclear war. Because our government's principal goal is to preserve its political power, avoiding the destruction of the Earth and its inhabitants is only its second priority. Indeed, the entire philosophy behind our nuclear arms policy, as expressed by Mutually Assured Destruction (MAD) and nuclear policy planners, is the absolute willingness to launch a mass nuclear attack if ordered (Kull, 1988). To ensure credibility, that absolute willingness to attack assumes that the enemy sees our resoluteness and believes that we are not bluffing. Thus, we will be forced into a nuclear winter if the enemy violates our arbitrary criteria. Such was the willingness of President Kennedy in October 1962 to risk Armageddon when the U.S.S.R. placed missiles in Cuba. The Cuban missile crisis was recently found to be more dangerous than previously believed, largely because the U.S. and U.S.S.R. ignored or disregarded the crisis as viewed by the Cubans, who wanted the Soviets to preemptively launch a nuclear strike on the U.S.

(Blight and Lang, 1995). Without the CIA-inspired Bay of Pigs, the crisis would never have occurred (Blight and Lang, 1995), and Khrushchev would never have deployed the missiles to Cuba in the first place.

The danger of nuclear war is probably greater today than at the time of the Cuban missile crisis. Blair, Feinseson, and Hippel (1997), who have studied nuclear arms policies intensively, showed that the outdated "launch on warning" policy means that an unexplained "blip" on a radar screen in the U.S. *or* Russia could trigger nuclear war. The risk of a nuclear attack, accidental or unauthorized, is extremely high given the outmoded and deteriorated status of the Russian military. Blair et al. provided a prescription for change, calling for the U.S. to disable, store, or place on low alert many of its nuclear warheads, followed by reciprocal action by the Russian president. Unfortunately, the success of the plan calls for bilateral action, the very ingredient lacking in previous attempts to reduce risks of nuclear war. Currently, some nuclear warheads are being deactivated via bilateral agreement, but the remaining warheads are sufficient to destroy the world many times over.

The Central Intelligence Agency (CIA)

Theoretically, the only function of the CIA is to gather foreign intelligence for the President, National Security Council, and those who make and execute U.S. national security policy. According to its mission statement, the CIA's counterintelligence, "special activities", and "other functions" are directed by the President.

Recent disclosures suggest that the CIA has overreached its mandated role. The CIA organized training and published manuals on how to interrogate, psychologically break, and torture those unfortunate enough to fall under its direct control. In January 1997, the CIA declassified its manuals entitled *Counterintelligence Interrogation* (1963) and *Human Resources Exploitation* (1983). See Appendix A, in which Sandra McPherson discusses these manuals in detail and notes a reference to a March 1992 memorandum regarding proper oversight of these programs. Director John Deutsch announced that the CIA would continue to work with immoral people and actually expand covert actions (Morrison, 1995). Thus, we should expect the continuation of human rights abuses by the CIA. In this volume, Whitaker explores the CIA further and uncovers an apparent chronically recurring pattern of human rights violations that, if true, is deadly, multidimensional, and a threat to U.S. citizens.

The CIA's practice by which individuals provided with intelligence are sworn to secrecy obviates challenges to the agency. For example, operatives in the super-secret FRAM units during Vietnam entered China to conduct operations (Smith, 1996), and members of the infamous Operation Phoenix were asked to sign the standard 25-year agreement of silence (Diamond, 1997; see Appendix B). A congressperson serving on the Senate Intelligence Committee is in a similar bind. If a senator is not among the few who are given secret information about the CIA's illegal activities, any complaints he or she may make are limited by the incomplete information base. And, if the senator is informed more completely by any government agency, the senator is sworn to secrecy, thus muzzling that individual on that issue and all connecting issues for the next 25 years.

Based on publicly available information, a table showing the history of CIA aggression, presented by Whitaker in Chapter 15, suggests that routine human rights violations and abuses have occurred frequently since the early 1950s. As recently as 1995, the FBI investigated CIA officials on charges that they had attempted to assassinate Saddam Hussein of Iraq ("Report of plot...", 1998). (Since the 1991 Gulf War, a "Presidential Finding" by ex-President George Bush authorized covert action against Iraq which, because the finding was labeled "lethal", meant that the CIA could circumvent with impunity the U.S. laws which forbid killing a foreign leader.) The FBI dropped the case in 1996, and the U.S. Justice Department decided not to prosecute. George Stephanopoulos (1996), who worked in President Clinton's campaign and administration, openly advocated assassination of Hussein.

Despite the mandate forbidding the CIA to engage in domestic spy activities, some CIA activities have caused the deaths of U.S. citizens. These activities include chemical experiments involving LSD and human radiation experiments which the CIA is still authorized to perform. The Final Report of the President's Advisory Committee on Human Radiation Experiments (Faden, 1996) revealed that, in 1972, CIA Director Helms ordered the destruction of all files labeled MKULTRA that pertained to human radiation and mind control experiments with CIA involvement. Also included is the opening up of the Golden Triangle in the 1960s and the Golden Crescent in the 1970s by working with foreign drug lords and organized crime figures, thus allowing the distribution of heroin to American soldiers in Vietnam and to citizens in the U.S. A conservative estimate is that in excess of 20,000 heroin cases, resulting in deaths by overdose and criminal activity to support the habits of many U.S. citizens, were caused by the various CIA-involved operations over those two decades (Beirne and Messerschmidt, 1995). In addition, the CIA worked with Cosa Nostra figures, thus helping, albeit indirectly, their violent and deadly activities in the U.S., and they also attempted to assassinate Fidel Castro at least eight times and orchestrated and trained terrorists for the ill-fated Bay of Pigs invasion of Cuba which, as noted earlier, led directly to the Cuban Missile Crisis, thus bringing the risk of nuclear war to all people on earth (Blight and Lang, 1995). A recently released 150-page report blamed the debacle on the CIA and impelled the Associated Press to state, "The CIA's ignorance, incompetence, and arrogance toward the 1400 Cuban exiles trained and equipped to mount the invasion was responsible for the fiasco. …" (Nelson, 1998). In October 1961, the report so outraged CIA officials that they destroyed all but one copy. CIA officials feared that release of the report would provoke criticism of the agency. The CIA also failed to inform U.S. field commanders of biological/chemical weapon sites in Iraq and lied about it once it was fairly well-established that U.S. troops had been contaminated and that the CIA had known of the sites for years.

Intelligence gathering is vital to our national security, and many successful operations cannot be discussed, but many of the more negative outcomes were the result of Presidential-inspired encouragement and even directives (Nelson, 1998; Woodward, 1988). Traditionally, the CIA will take the heat for an operation rather than imperil the office of the President, no matter how wrong or foolish that President had been.

Although the CIA is a government-sanctioned agency, its members (similar to persons in the military) are obligated to refuse unlawful directives. Why should we support an organization that drains our resources, creates massive social and drug problems, brings us to the brink of nuclear destruction, mispredicts the major events in the last half of the 20th century it is supposed to know about, and shows little incentive to abolish itself or change fundamentally?

Legal remedies have had only a minor impact on the CIA. It paid death benefits in a wrongful death suit after the CIA and the Army were discovered in 1975 to have conducted LSD experiments on unwitting subjects, and one such subject, Frank Olson, a government scientist, committed suicide a short time later (see Barrett v. United States, 1987). The Army secretly paid half of an $18,000 settlement to Olson's family. Both the CIA and the Army paid the benefits, fearing that adverse publicity might undermine their ability to continue their secret projects.

On October 5, 1988, the CIA announced a settlement in what amounted to the largest amount of money ever awarded to foreign citizens by this country (Weinstein, 1990). Eight Canadians were awarded $750,000 (American) for having been involuntarily placed in mind-control experiments from 1957 to 1961 under Ewen Cameron, M.D., at the Allan Memorial Institute at McGill University in Montreal. As explained by Whitaker in Chapter 15, they had been subjected to experimental drugs, intensive shock treatments, sensory deprivation, and forced sleep for weeks on end, all toward the goal of providing the CIA with data about interrogation methods. The CIA never acknowledged its acts or issued an apology.

Atomic Energy Commission/ Department of Energy

Government agencies may engage in human rights abuses and unethical conduct for years, decades, or indefinitely if their actions are not revealed. In an unheralded study initiated by President Clinton, which outraged the federal agencies under scrutiny, a well-documented book was produced entitled "Final Report of the Advisory Committee on Human Radiation Experiments" (Faden, 1996). One intentional release of radioactive gases in southeast Washington state — termed the "Green Run" because of the color of the fuel elements containing iodine 131 that flowed from tall smokestacks at Hanford's T Plant — took place on December 3, 1949, but remained classified (secret) until 1986 (see Faden, 1996). Airborne devices detected radioactive gases at a distance over 100 miles from the release site. Measurements showed radioactivity on vegetation as high as 400 times the then-permissible concentration. Animal thyroid specimens showed contamination levels up to 80 times the maximum permissible limit. People downwind of the gases were never warned before the experiment and were not informed after it had taken place.

Through a diligent search of existing records, almost a half century after the experiments, the Final Report team also determined that from 1944 to 1947, Hanford released 685,000 curies of radioiodine into the environment (about 80 times the amount released during Green Run) in an effort to determine how iodine could contaminate the food supply in the event of nuclear war or nuclear accident. During the study, Hanford researchers used deception to collect data by having staff pretend to be agricultural inspectors while surreptitiously measuring iodine levels in animal thyroids. One biologist who worked on contract for the project wrote the following (Faden, 1996, p. 324):

> *"I was introduced to two security agents of the Manhattan Engineer District ... who were to be my escorts and contact men during the day. They proved to be the best straight-faced 'liars' I had ever known. I was no longer 'Karl Herde of DuPont' but through the day would be known and introduced as Dr. George Herd of the Department of Agriculture. I was to simulate an animal husbandry specialist who had the responsibility of testing a new portable instrument based on an unproven theory that by external readings on the surface of the farm, the 'health and vigor' of animals could be evaluated. I was advised not to be alarmed if at times during the conversation with farmers that they appeared critical or skeptical. I was to be very reserved and answer questions as briefly and vaguely as seemed acceptable. They agreed to carry a clipboard. ...I was to concentrate on the high readings (thyroids, of course) and furnish those for recording when not being observed.*
>
> *"That day we visited several diversified farms under irrigation from the Yakima River between Topenish and Benton City. ...Smooth talk and flattery enabled us to gain one hundred percent cooperation. ...*
>
> *"I was successful in placing the probe of the instrument over the thyroid at times when the owner's attention was focused on the next animal or some concocted distraction."*

The effects of the intentional releases were significant. One farmer in the affected area, while testifying in Spokane in 1994, pointed to an area on a map called "death mile", where *100%* of the families who drank the water and ate the locally grown food had members who developed thyroid problems and cancer and gave birth to disfigured and handicapped children.

As the Final Report (Faden, 1996) clearly documented, some physicians participated in the human radiation experiments in order to receive grant funds.

Government personnel, on the other hand, appeared motivated by power. In either case, the decision to harm and the possibility of killing people stemmed from a cold, hard, unbending logic which held human life as an object of manipulation. This thinking was expressed by a military participant in a 1950 Department of Defense Committee on Medical Sciences (Faden, 1996, p. 301):

"Now we are very much interested in long-term effects ... but when you start thinking militarily of this, if men are going out on these missions anyway, a high percentage is not coming back, and the fact that you may get cancer 20 years later is just of no significance to us." [emphasis added]

The radiation experiments continued for 30 years, from 1944 to 1974, by which time they were ostensibly stopped by stringent federal research rules. Selected studies are presented in Table 1.1 to show the pervasive and diverse nature of this lethal phenomenon. Table 1.2 lists and describes biological and chemical experiments discussed in the Final Report (Faden, 1996). The media exposed the studies in the 1960s and 1970s, with government spokespersons initially denying the report, then fabricating cover stories as knowledge of the experiments emerged. In 1996, in the opening remarks to the Final Report (Faden, 1996), President Clinton stated that deception was employed to cover the embarrassment and impropriety of the studies, and that the perpetrators knew they were wrong, but chose to proceed anyway.

Rules of ethical conduct in research known since the Nuremberg tribunals, reformulated in the now-famous Nuremberg code (see Table 1.3, presented in its original words from the Final Report, Faden, 1996) and made more explicit in the Wilson memorandum (espousing the same ideas and limitations), were typically ignored. One excuse used by our government was that we were in a Cold War with the U.S.S.R. Yet, the federal agencies which conducted the radiation experiments started them *before* the Cold War (1944) when the Soviets were our allies and ended *before* the collapse of the U.S.S.R. in 1992, thus lending little credence that Cold War tension motivated the studies. The Final Report (Faden, 1996) showed that investigative journalism and an increasing number of lawsuits, the two powers of a free society which leaders in the federal government fear the most, applied pressure for the end of the experiments.

The Final Report (Faden, 1996) showed that the 4000 or more radiation studies overall did not improve our national security, even though, in yet another fabrication, national security was presented both as the motivation for the studies and as the excuse not to reveal their existence. The experiments were much more consistent with the desire of the power elite to maintain the U.S. as the dominant nuclear power on this globe, regardless of who our ostensible enemy was or whether we were in a hot or cold war or at peace. More about the phenomenon of the sterility of "scientism" or pseudoscience is presented in Chapter 20.

Currently, according to the Final Report (Faden, 1996), several federal agencies are still authorized to conduct these experiments (including the Department of Defense and CIA) and are budgeted funds for that purpose. The Final Report ended with a statement of a key committee member, Jay Katz, that the safeguards provided by research rules are not sufficient to prevent the reoccurrence of these experiments. His conclusions on the Committee's review of contemporary radiological research suggested that 50% raised serious ethical issues, mostly related to consent and risk, with 24% raising ethical issues that should not be taken lightly. He proposed that a National Human Investigation Board promulgate research policies as well as administer and review the studies themselves. Indeed, if the Final Report is correct, the experiments have never stopped.

This author attempted to determine whether relevant professional associations and institutions acknowledged that, during the period from 1944 to

TABLE 1.1

HUMAN RADIATION EXPERIMENTS BY THE U.S. (SELECTED STUDIES, 1944–1974)

Date	Experiment	Related Behavior/Remarks	Agency/Site/Location
1940s	Radioactive iron was administered to 820 poor, pregnant whites.	A proffered drink, called a "cocktail", was given to subjects with no explanation of its contents; in 1963–1964, offspring were found to have higher rate of malignancies.	Vanderbilt University with Tennessee Department of Health
1944–1961	244 intentional releases of lanthanum-14-emitting gamma rays.	"Shots were fired [intentionally] when the wind was blowing to the northeast" over several Pueblo Indian and Spanish-speaking communities.	Atomic Energy Commission (AEC) at Los Alamos, NM; termed "Rala Tests"
1946–1953	Radioactive iron and calcium were placed in breakfast food of 74 training school retardates during two separate studies.	Ostensible purpose was to determine how the body absorbed various minerals. The Quaker Oats Company continued to deny the wrongness of their role in these experiments up to 1997.	Massachusetts Institute of Technology (MIT) staff at Fernald School in Massachusetts; funded by National Institute of Health (NIH), AEC, and Quaker Oats Company
1949–1952	65 field tests intentionally released 13,000 curies of tantalum.	Radioactive tantalum was dropped in the form of small particles to see how much would render a territory uninhabitable.	U.S. Army Chemical Corps at Dugway, UT
1950s–1960s	Blood of 10 prisoners was removed, irradiated, returned to their bodies.	One prisoner stated, "They told us nothing about the tests. They just said it wouldn't bother us."	AEC in Utah prisons
1950s–1960s	4100 male uranium miners worked in unventilated mines.	Researchers agreed not to "alarm" miners by warning them of hazardous conditions. As of 1960, 4-1/2 times more lung cancer was found than expected. By 1990, 10% of work force had died of lung cancer while remainder suffered from health problems.	Public Health Service and State of Colorado; mines located in plateau area of Colorado
1951	Atomic bomb was dropped on Nevada test site, with several thousand soldiers 7 miles from ground zero to test radiation effects.	Troops were told that "no danger of immediate radiation remains 90 seconds after air burst;" they were also told it was safe to move into the spot directly below the burst right after the explosion wearing regular field clothing.	U.S. Army at southern Nevada test site (Desert Rock), termed the "HumRRO" experiments

Table 1.1 (continued)

Human Radiation Experiments by the U.S. (selected studies, 1944–1974)

Date	Experiment	Related Behavior/Remarks	Agency/Site/Location
1951	Four children with nephrosis were injected with sulfur-35, along with two other children with other conditions.	Study was done to determine if children had impaired protein production or excessive renal losses.	University of Minnesota
1952	12 subjects watched burst in darkened trailer about 6 km from detonation site.	Six subjects wore protective goggles, while remaining six did not; study was terminated when two subjects incurred retinal burns.	AEC in Nevada; termed the "Flashblindness Experiments"
1953	34 children with hypothyroidism, 2–15 years old, were given iodine-131.	Conducted to study cause of hypothyroidism; this was a nontherapeutic research study with no known medical benefits.	Johns Hopkins in Baltimore, MD
1954	Solders were called on to eat foods exposed to cobalt radiation.	Religious organizations called on Army to halt this practice.	U.S. Army, Fitzsimmons Hospital, CO
1954	Bikini "bravo" shot atomic test.	Device was exploded despite adverse weather forecast, causing fallout to affect hundreds of Micronesians with a concomitant increase in thyroid abnormalities and deaths as late as 1987. Follow-up "treatment" for monitoring only. Extracted teeth analyzed for radioactive content.	AEC and U.S. military services in the Marshall Islands area of the Pacific Ocean
1955	Ground crews were asked to a rub radioactive fuselage with either gloved or bare hands.	Test conducted to determine if plane needed to be washed down after it flew through radioactive cloud.	AEC and Air Force in Nevada during Operation Teapot
1955, 1956	Several dozen pilots were asked to fly through atomic clouds.	Studies were done to learn exactly "how much radiation penetrates into the human system." Findings made no contribution to science as data had already been collected by flying drone aircraft into clouds.	Termed "Operation Teapot" (1955) and "Redwing" (1956); location assumed to be in Nevada
1956–1957	200 administrations of iodine-131 to 120 subjects, including 84 Eskimos and 17 Indians.	Experiment to determine role of thyroid gland in extreme cold. Some subjects were pregnant or lactating. Eskimos were overly trusting (there is not word for "radioactivity" in the language).	Air Force Aeromedical Laboratory in Alaska

Table 1.1 (continued)

Human Radiation Experiments by the U.S. (selected studies, 1944–1974)

Date	Experiment	Related Behavior/Remarks	Agency/Site/Location
1957	3224 participants of one atomic test showed cluster of 9 leukemias.	Participants were told that no damage would result; it was later discovered that, contrary to study design, some subjects had witnessed other atomic test shots, thus raising their risk. About 220,000 soldiers participated in at least one nuclear test.	AEC in Nevada during test shot "Smoky" as reported by the Centers for Disease Control in 1980
1958	Researchers contaminated a creek with radioactive soil from Nevada.	Researchers later claimed that they removed the soil and burned it in above-ground mounds; in 1993, mounds of soil were shipped to Nevada test site for disposal.	U.S. Geological Survey near Cape Thompson in Alaska; termed "Project Chariot"
1958, 1963	90 soldiers were asked to perform "typical army maneuvers" on soil contaminated with radioactive lanthanum.	In the first study, soldiers were asked to crawl over contaminated ground after a shallow underground shot; in the second study, soldiers were asked to maneuver on ground contaminated with artificial fallout.	Camp Stoneman, CA, and Camp McCoy, WI; termed "Operation Jangle"
1960s	Five prisoners were transfused with radioactive iron or radioactive phosphorus.	Study was designed to determine the survival time of red blood cells during periods of severe iron deficiency or rapid cell formation.	AEC at Colorado State Penitentiary
1961	Radioactive iodine was administered to 70 retardates.	Ostensibly designed to test countermeasure to nuclear fallout.	Harvard Medical School, Massachusetts General, and Boston University School of Medicine, staff at Wrentham State School
1963–1968	30 tests were conducted to study trace quantities of radioisotopes in environment.	In one study, seven subjects drank milk from cows that grazed in a contaminated pasture; in others, about 20 subjects stood downwind of intentional releases.	Idaho National Engineering Laboratory in Idaho and Washington

Table 1.1 (continued)

Human Radiation Experiments by the U.S. (selected studies, 1944–1974)

Date	Experiment	Related Behavior/Remarks	Agency/Site/Location
1963–1973	181 healthy "volunteer" adult male prisoners were submitted to testicular irradiation.	Associated with painful biopsies to testicles and vasectomy at the end of the study.	AEC in prisons in Oregon and Washington State

1947, their members and staff were likely involved in the experiments; to ascertain what, if anything, had been accomplished in the way of investigation; and to obtain a copy of each association's or institution's ethics code. The author contacted 16 professional associations that were in existence during that period and several grant-awarding corporations, including the major associations that focused on nuclear and radiological medicine, and chemical and biological societies, such as the Oak Ridge Associated University. These associations could have easily verified whether or not their members were involved (names of all known researchers in the human radiation experiments are listed in the index of the Final Report).

Despite repeated mailings of the letter of inquiry, the only professional associations to respond were the American Medical Association (AMA) and the American Psychological Association (APA). In December 1997, the AMA claimed that it had no "jurisdiction to investigate individual physician behavior" (contrary to its Code of Medical Ethics) and suggested that the state medical societies in which each physician practiced be contacted. In January 1998, the APA acknowledged that it actively investigates mistreatment of human subjects, but stated that the length of time since the alleged misconduct had occurred was too great. The APA has a limitation of 10 years; therefore, the Ethics Office opined that it could not investigate members' involvement in the human radiation experiments.

The only grant-awarding institution to respond was the Quaker Oats Company. Resulting from an uncoordinated effort, two response letters were received in January 1998 — the first from its Corporate Communications Department and a second from its Consumer Response Unit. The letter from the Corporate Communications Department claimed that the Quaker Oats Company's role was limited to awarding a small research grant to the Massachusetts Institute of Technology, whereas the letter from the Consumer Response Unit indicated that Harvard University may have received a grant as well. Both letters failed to mention that the National Institutes of Health and the Atomic Energy Commission were co-funders of the project. The first response stated, "Then, *as today*, Quaker relies on the procedures and policies that exist in university and research institutes to ensure that research is done in a safe, ethical, and legal manner" [emphasis added]. It stated that a 1994 task force of the Massachusetts Department of Mental Retardation investigating the original studies found

Table 1.2

Human Biological/Chemical Experiments by the U.S. (selected studies, 1944–1974)

Date	Experiment	Related Behavior/Remarks	Agency/Site/Location
1932–1973	Despite availability of penicillin by the mid-1940s, 200 blacks were denied treatment for syphilis.	Subjects were enticed to participate in experiments with offers of free medical examinations and "special free treatments" such as lumbar punctures which were purely diagnostic. Over the 40-year span of the program, 28 subjects died and 100 more suffered blindness and severe mental disease.	Public Health Service in Tuskegee, AL; exposed by an investigative journalist
1950s	Studies using drugs (such as LSD and mescaline) and other chemical, biological, and psychological means for mind control; 150 CIA studies were conducted under the MKULTRA code name alone.	Frank Olsen, an Army scientist, committed suicide a week after being given LSD without his awareness; Harold Bauer, a professional tennis player and unwitting subject in an Army study, died after being given mescaline. MKULTRA records were deliberately destroyed by then-CIA Director Richard Helms. There is some evidence that human radiation was part of the MKULTRA program but that CIA worked through second parties to obtain information.	CIA and Department of Defense (DOD); despite the ban on such studies by several presidents, CIA and DOD are still authorized to proceed
1956–1972	Profoundly retarded children and adolescents were systematically injected with hepatitis.	Consent form implied that the subjects were to receive a vaccine against a virus. Only route for admission to the school was through the hepatitis unit.	Willowbrook State School for the Retarded on Staten Island and New York University
1963	Live cancer cells were injected into indigent elderly patients.	Research was approved over the objections of physicians who were consulted; physicians who were responsible for experiment were placed on probation for 1 year.	Brooklyn Jewish Chronic Disease Hospital and Sloan-Kettering Cancer Research Center

that the small amount of isotopes had no discernible effects on the health of the subjects.

The above responses failed to reveal that neither the 74 training school retardates nor their guardians were informed of the risks involved. The Final Report (1996) showed that the parents of the retardates, who were sent letters, were not even informed that a radioisotope would be used (Final Report, 1996, pp. 211–213). No medical benefit to the subjects was ever intended. In a blazing indictment of the Fernald School, the Final Report noted that parents were bribed to participate by promises of rewards above what their children ordinarily received in their frugal and impoverished environment. The original letter

Table 1.3

The Nuremberg Code

1. The voluntary consent of the human subject is absolutely essential. This means that the person involved should have legal capacity to give consent, should be so situated as to be able to exercise free power of choice, without the intervention of any element of force, fraud, deceit, duress, overreaching, or other ulterior form of constraint or coercion; and should have sufficient knowledge and comprehension of the elements of the subject matter involved as to enable him to make an understanding and enlightened decision. The latter element requires that before the acceptance of an affirmative decision by the experimental subject there should be made known to him the nature, duration, and purpose of the experiment; the method and means by which it is to be conducted; all inconveniences and hazards reasonably to be expected; and the effects upon his health or person which may possibly come from his participation in the experiment. The duty and responsibility for ascertaining the quality of the consent rest upon each individual who initiates, directs or engages in the experiment. It is a personal duty and responsibility which may not be delegated to another with impunity.

2. The experiment should be such as to yield fruitful results for the good of society, unprocurable by other methods or means of study, and not random and unnecessary in nature.

3. The experiment should be so designed and based on the results of animal experimentation and a knowledge of the natural history of the disease or other problem under study that the anticipated results will justify the performance of the experiment.

4. The experiment should be so conducted as to avoid all unnecessary physical and mental suffering and injury.

5. No experiment should be conducted where there is an *a priori* reason to believe that death or disabling injury will occur; except, perhaps, in those experiments where the experimental physicians also serve as subjects.

6. The degree of risk to be taken should never exceed that determined by the humanitarian importance of the problem to be solved by the experiment.

7. Proper preparation should be made and adequate facilities provided to protect the experimental subject against even remote possibilities of injury, disability, or death.

8. The experiment should be conducted only by scientifically qualified persons. The highest degree of skill and care should be required through all stages of the experiment of those who conduct or engage in the experiment.

9. During the course of the experiment, the human subject should be at liberty to bring the experiment to an end if he has reached the physical or mental state where continuation of the experiment seems to him to be impossible.

10. During the course of the experiment, the scientist in charge must be prepared to terminate the experiment at any stage, if he has probable cause to believe, in the exercise of good faith, superior skill, and careful judgment required of him, that a continuation of the experiment is likely to result in injury, disability, or death to the experimental subject.

from the Fernald School to the parents read, in part (Faden, 1996, p. 211):

"... We have asked for volunteers to give a sample of blood once a month for three months, and your son has agreed to volunteer because the boys who belong to the Science Club have many additional privileges. They get a quart of milk daily during that time and are taken to a baseball game, to the beach, and to some outside dinners and they enjoy it greatly."

The second response from the Quaker Oats Company falsely claimed that the company had "no information about the process and forms that were used to gain consent from parents or guardians of the children." The process and letter used to gain parental consent had already been published in the Final Report (1996) two years earlier.

Thus, the passage of time and even disclosure of wrongdoing by a Presidential Committee are no guarantees that denial and minimization of wrongdoing will not continue. Most culpable organizations chose simply not to respond to this author's inquiries. The three that did respond tried to claim that they were not responsible or minimized the harm.

Genocide

Genocide is the deliberate and systematic destruction of a racial, religious, political, or ethnic group. The United Nations Genocide Convention specifically declared that the following actions, which, when carried out against a national, ethnic, racial, or religious group in order to destroy that group, in full or in part, fall under the rubric of genocide: (1) killing persons belonging to the group, (2) causing grievous bodily or spiritual harm to members of the group, (3) deliberately enforcing upon the group living conditions which could lead to its complete or partial extermination, (4) enforcing measures designed to prevent births among the group, and (5) forcibly removing children from the group and transferring them to another group (H. Silverman, personal communication, April 1997). According to this definition, genocide can occur before the actual killing of target victims. Silverman (personal communication, April 1997) noted that laws passed between 1933 and 1935 by the German government aimed to reduce the future number of genetic "inferiors" through involuntary sterilization programs. Approximately 500 children of mixed (black/German) racial backgrounds and between 320,000 and 350,000 individuals judged to be physically or mentally handicapped were subjected to surgical or radiation sterilization procedures. Supporters of sterilization argued that the handicapped burdened the community with the costs of their care. Many of Germany's 30,000 gypsies were also eventually sterilized and prohibited, along with blacks, from intermarrying with Germans. New laws combined traditional prejudices with the new racism of the Nazis which defined gypsies, by race, as "criminal and asocial".

Most, but not all, genocide is perpetrated by government entities which kill four to five citizens of their own to every one who dies in war. Table 1.4 displays the distribution of government murders in this century throughout the world.

R.J. Rummel, a professor of political science at the University of Hawaii who was nominated for the Nobel Peace Prize for his works on genocide, has accumulated the most comprehensive and accurate statistics on this phenomenon (1990, 1991, 1994). Genocide by the government, which Rummel terms "democide", has always been part of human history. Over a million victims were massacred and stacked into pyramids by the Mongols in some captured cities. Burying groups of people alive seemed to be a favorite method of the Chinese emperors. During the Black Death of 1347 to 1352, thousands of Jews were killed after they were blamed for poisoning the water. In Germany and in the low countries, few Jews were left at the end of the plague. Rummel cited data for the period after 1900 that show that well over 100 million people were murdered by their own governments.

TABLE 1.4

SOME MAJOR DEMOCIDE EPISODES AND CASES

Episodes/Cases	Democide (000)[a]	Years	Victims	Regime(s)
Concentration/ labor camps	39,464	1917–1987	Anyone	U.S.S.R.
Jewish Holocaust	5291	1942–1945	European Jews	Hitler
Intentional famine in Ukraine	5000	1932–1933	Peasants	Stalin
China land reform	4500	1949–1953	Rich/landlords	Mao Tse-Tung
Collectivization	3133	1928–1935	Peasants/landlords	Stalin
Cambodian Hell	2000	1975–1979	Cambodian people	Pol Pot
Cultural revolution	1613	1964–1975	Communists/officials/ intellectuals	Mao Tse-Tung
German expulsion	1583	1945–1948	German ethnics	Poland
Bengal/Hindu genocide	1500	1971	Hindus/Bengali leaders/	Pakistan
Armenian genocide	1404	1915–1918	Turkey's Armenians	Young Turks
Great Terror	1000	1936–1938	Communists	Stalin
Serbian genocide	655	1941–1945	Serbs/Jews/gypsies	Croatian Ustashi
Indonesian massacre	509	1965–1966	Communists/sympathizers	Indonesian army
Ugandan massacres	300	1971–1979	Critics/opponents/tribesmen	Idi Amin
Boat people	250	1975–1987	Vietnamese/Chinese	Vietnam
Spanish Civil War	200	1936–1939	Republicans/Nationalists	Spanish Republican government/ Nationalist army
Rape of Nanking	200	1937–1938	Chinese	Japanese army
"La Violencia" massacres	180	1948–1958	Liberals/conservatives	Colombia liberal/ conservative governments
East Timor massacres	150	1975–1987	Timorese	Indonesian army
Colonial massacres	132	1900–1918	Hereros/Hottentots/others	German kaiser

[a] Most probable estimates from a low to high average. Estimates are from or based on Rummel (1990, 1991, 1992) and various tables of sources and estimates published in *Statistics of Democide.*

Source: Rummel, R.J. (1994) *Death by Government, Genocide and Mass Murder Since 1900*, Table 1.5. New Brunswick: Transaction Publishers. With permission.

Rummel showed a convincing link between this type of killing and form of government. The more democratic and less totalitarian a government, the less democide (or war) occurs. The primary cause of democide (and war) is unchecked power in the hands of dictators who justify the killing in the name of national unity, racial purity, glory, doctrine, or utopia. Absolute power does corrupt absolutely, which Rummel restates for democide as the "power principle" — power kills, and absolute power kills absolutely. Of course, this does not mean that elements of democratic governments cannot engage in mass killing (see previous sections on war and the CIA). The risk for democide is much lower as a function of increased freedom within a country, including the freedom to challenge the power elite, and to effect grass-root changes.

The first step in eliminating genocide, given that most readers are not in a position to effect national political change readily, is to understand the conditions under which it occurs. Perhaps then genocide can be predicted just like other violent phenomena. Israel Charny, the Director of the Institute on the Holocaust and Genocide in Jerusalem, has done just that in his *Toward a Genocide Early Warning System* (1982, 1997). This system, presented in Appendix C in its entirety, has been proven valid in many contexts since its original publication, to include sanctioned massacres and other genocidal acts in Africa and the Former Yugoslavia (Charny, personal communication, 1997). All serious students of group and institutional violence should read and analyze this classic piece. Charny cogently stated that if only a few lives are saved by those who read about this predictive system, correctly anticipate a genocidal outcome, and take measures to protect themselves, it will be worth the effort devoted to this cause.

Bozydar Kaczmarek, of the Institute of Psychology at the University of Maria Curie-Sklodowska in Lublin, Poland, addressed the support of genocide by the greater community (personal communication, June 1997). He pointed out that not only did S.S. officers at the extermination camps do their best to fulfill their duties, but that a great number of German businessmen also competed to procure orders for death equipment and to furnish Zyklon-B crystals. He provided a letter from one of the firms (cited in Shirer, 1967, p. 1265):

"Following our verbal discussion regarding the delivery of simple constructions for the burning of bodies, we are submitting plans for our perfected cremation ovens which operate with coal and which have hitherto given full satisfaction.

"We suggest two crematoria [furnaces] for the building planned, but we advise you to make further inquiries to make sure that the two ovens will be sufficient for [your] requirements.

"We guarantee the effectiveness of the cremation ovens as well as their durability, the use of the best material and our faultless workmanship.

"Awaiting your future word, we will be at your services.

"Heil Hitler!

"C.H. Kori, GM. B.H."

Silverman (personal communication, April 1997) observed that the evolution of the Nazi assault — isolating Jews in ghettos and camps, abusing and dehumanizing them, literally abducting them from their homes and deporting them to destinations beyond anything they could imagine, destroying lives, families, and entire communities — depended on the collaboration, indifference, or silence of local inhabitants. The assault could not have acquired momentum without the tacit consent of influential third-party observers, religious authorities, and the "free world".

Kaczmarek (personal communication, June 1997) also shared information recently obtained from archives maintained by the Soviets showing that genocide victims were fully exploited by the Nazis. As an example, Erich Muhsfeld, Chief of the crematorium at Majdanek, located just outside Lublin where Dr. Kaczmarek teaches, testified as follows (Kaczmarek, personal communication, June 1997):

"At the bottom of the ditch I placed a sort of wooden grate on which the prisoners would place the bodies further away in the ditch. When the pyre was ready I poured methane over and set fire to it. ... When, the pyre having burned down, the ashes were [cooled], the prisoners from my kommando brought them onto the surface, and there the ashes were crushed in a special grinder."

Kaczmarek learned that the ashes and bones were prepared in the above-described way to constitute a component of the compost which was later used as a fertilizer in the camp kitchen gardens. As a further example, Kaczmarek (personal communication, June 1997) noted:

"Not only were personal belongings of the prisoners grabbed, but the practically minded Nazi also utilized their hair, as well as silver and gold teeth. The hair was spun and used for knitting warm socks for submarine crews."

At Majdanek, before cremation of gassed or shot victims, the teeth were pulled out on a table installed in the building of the large crematorium. The operation was performed by a German prisoner Bruno Horn, who was also a camp dentist. The gold and silver were later melted and sent to the banks in Switzerland where, as we have recently learned, Nazi deposits are still held.

There is also one shocking fact that reflects the way of thought of S.S. officers (Kaczmarek, personal communication, 1997). The chief of the crematorium had his house heated with the warmth gained during the cremation. To be able to do so, the house was built in close vicinity to the crematorium. Moreover, his wife and children used to visit him during holidays and stayed at the house!

On the basis of his analysis of the genocide in Rwanda in April to July 1994, in which 500,000 to 800,000 were killed and over 2 million displaced, Wessells (1996) recommended the following interventions: (1) political restructuring for inclusiveness; (2) constructing a civil society with norms of civility, room for peaceful dissent, reduction of extremism, and decreased centralization of control; (3) addressing the traumas and other psychological wounds of the genocide; (4) establishing an effective system of justice, ending the culture of impunity that has persisted over the decades; (5) protecting human rights; (6) integrating refugees economically and socially; (7) reconciling and resolving conflict by nonviolent means through methods such as community dialogues, interactive problems-solving sessions, and cooperative efforts across lines of conflict; and (8) paying careful attention to the needs of young people.

A key question involves whether or not Charny's early warning system can be applied to contemporary U.S. In particular, are we moving toward genocide of blacks and other vulnerable minorities (e.g., Hispanics, Asian-Americans, an increasing white underclass)? Based on the study of genocide throughout history, Charny and his colleagues proposed the following seven stages (see Appendix C):

1. Societal forces supporting human life are weaker than societal forces moving toward destruction of human life.
2. Key historical, economic, political, legal, and social events act as triggers to a cognitive set and ideology conducive to genocide.
3. Genocidal fantasy and ideology are formed.
4. Precipitating factors and context are set into motion.
5. Means to genocide are mobilized.
6. Genocide is legitimized and institutionalized.
7. Genocide and experience-denying mechanisms are executed.

Stage 1, involving societal forces, suggests that a baseline or starting point for any given country or people should be obtained. Assuming that forces within individuals, groups, and nations are involved in experiences of creating life and destroying life, so long as a balance occurs, no danger of genocide exists. Indeed, an integrated balance of the constructive and destructive processes equates with aliveness and the cyclic nature of social history, according to Charny and his colleagues.

Although in the U.S. freedom of expression, initiative, and risk are generally encouraged, this society's prevailing atmosphere, a critical index of its value system, is changing. The country is swinging toward the right. Factors suggesting destructiveness in this country include the strong pursuit of power over others; a loss of national purpose, confidence, and pride; the easy availability of weapons together with a cultural glorification of the use of weapons; and our government's dedication to arms development combined with an effort to minimize its arms limitations within the existing terms of international conventions unless it is to our power advantage (e.g., witness the recent treaty regarding landmines, which the U.S. refused to sign).

Key historical events (Stage 2) in this country, as factors which force a momentum toward genocide of blacks, include the race riots of the last third of the 20th century, the dissatisfaction of the white majority with the outcome of the O.J. Simpson murder trial, and the disproportionate number of rapes and murders and other crimes of violence committed by black Americans.

Many black Americans have fallen into a self-appraised genocidal victim role. They perceive AIDS, the alleged spread of cocaine in urban areas by the CIA, and the disproportionate number of blacks executed in capital punishment cases as deliberate attempts to destroy the black race. The fact that one third of adult black males are in the criminal justice system suggests that a sizable percentage of blacks feel disenfranchised from and perceive themselves as victims of the establishment (Hall, 1996). A critical mass toward eventual black-white conflict may have already been reached.

Genocidal fantasies and ideology (Stage 3) have already been articulated and promoted by the leaders of many collective entities labeled "hate", "white supremacist", "militia", or "Patriot" groups. (Although still primarily the expression of extremist individuals or fringe groups, there appears to be growing support for the notion that blacks are responsible for society's ills.) Increasingly, mainstream "white America" holds that black crime, blacks procreating with whites, black ghettos, and the welfare system are all conspiring to destroy the "American way of life". Therefore, the emerging reasoning goes, we must contain or control these inferior subhumans before they fatally degrade the white race or further contaminate our government.

To illustrate how this reasoning has permeated mainstream thinking, Herrnstein and Murray (1994), in their controversial book, *The Bell Curve,* predicted an increasing isolation in this country within the "cognitive elite" comprised of those individuals in the upper 1% of the intelligence spectrum, as suggested by scores on a variety of scholastic aptitude measures and education at the "best" schools in the U.S. (e.g., Ivy League universities). According to those authors (and probably true), the cognitive elite wield an inordinate amount of influence on the direction of American society. These high-IQ individuals usually socialize with each other and not outside their group, tending to form coalitions with the affluent and the successful. Interestingly, in recent decades, Jews and Asian-Americans are increasingly entering the ranks of the cognitive elite. On the other end of the intelligence spectrum are the disadvantaged minority groups and a growing white underclass. In regard to blacks and poor whites, Herrnstein and Murray noted that three fourths of all illegitimate births are to women of below-average IQ.

Based on hundreds of studies of intelligence, Herrnstein and Murray (1994) went on to suggest that the black inner city has a population with a mean IQ in the low 80s at best. This statement explains why their book has provoked outrage — they posited that high or low intelligence is the driving force behind success and failure in our society, and that blacks in particular are significantly less intelligent than other races when rated by standardized measures of intelligence. They predicted that the collective white reaction to continued high rates of crime and violence by blacks will be increased suppression by the government, making an already bad situation explosive. They forecast that blacks may be placed in ghettos from which they cannot escape, possibly resulting in genocide. Herrnstein and Murray (1994, p. 526) stated:

"In short, by custodial state, we have in mind a high-tech and more lavish version of the Indian reservation for some substantial minority of the nation's population, while the rest of America tries to go about its business. In its less benign forms, the solutions will become more and more totalitarian. Benign or otherwise, "going about its business" in the old sense will not be possible. It is difficult to imagine the United States preserving its heritage of individualism, equal rights before the law, free people running their own lives, once it is accepted that a significant part of the population must be made permanent wards of the state.

"Extrapolating from current trends, we project that the policies of custodialism will be not only tolerated but actively supported by a consensus of the cognitive elite. To some extent, we are not even really projecting but reporting. The main difference between the position of the cognitive elite that we portray here and the one that exists today is to some extent nothing more than the distinction between tacit and explicit."

Precipitants to genocide (Stage 4), including symbolically charged events such as full-scale war or famine under which cover genocide is likely to take place, have not yet occurred. Neither has the mobilization of means to genocide (Stage 5), much less the institutionalization and execution of genocide itself (Stages 6 and 7), but the reader is reminded that such events can transpire in a few months to a few years (Charny, 1982, 1997; Rummel, 1990, 1991, 1994).

Given the temporal stages of genocide, it appears that the U.S. is somewhere in the third stage in its progression toward genocide of blacks and other vulnerable minorities. Almost always, the remaining steps will be within the context of some other catastrophic event. The time required for completion of the remainder of the stages is relatively short and is characterized by intense changes and a shift to authoritarian systems of control.

Assassins and Bombers: Lone Perpetrators Against the System

Individual violence against groups and institutions should be contrasted with violence perpetration by collective entities. Persons acting as group representatives are easier to apprehend because law enforcement agencies can play one member off against another and because of the greater chance that increased numbers will result in mistakes. Individuals acting alone, on the other hand, who threaten or consummate violence toward collective entities, represent a difficult challenge, particularly if the anticipated or actual violence is organized and the perpetrator does not wish to be caught.

When the identity and aim of the possible perpetrator are known (a plan to kill a U.S. official, for example), the key question is one of dangerousness. If the identity is unknown, say that of a cautious, methodical serial bomber, the priority becomes one of identification through profiling and other means. In Appendix D, the analysis of handwriting characteristics in evaluating dangerousness is presented by Kimon Ianetta (1993), who demonstrates and illustrates the unique handwriting characteristics of assassins, mass killers (including Timothy McVeigh), and other violent types. Ianetta (1993, p. 3) found that "whether the writing instrument is held in the hand, the mouth, the crook of the arm, or between the toes, the person's writing retains his or her individualized characteristics and can be analyzed accurately."

Two examples of lone perpetrators — one disorganized and the other organized — are provided. The first example is an outpatient at a Veterans Administration (VA) clinic who, in 1973, revealed plans to kill then-President Nixon; the second is the individual known as the Unabomber, whom this author profiled in 1990.

Case Illustration 2

Ex-staff sergeant James Marker verbally vented his rage against the U.S. government to anyone who would listen, and especially to the VA outpatient staff in St. Petersburg, FL, where he was diagnosed as chronic paranoid schizophrenic. He was drawing a 100% service-connected disability from the VA following a psychiatric hospitalization toward the end of a third tour in Vietnam as a Special Forces staff sergeant. His plan was simple and reminiscent of President Kennedy's assassination. He planned to intercept the President on a tour of a city and shoot him with a sniper rifle from a tall building. He had already followed the President on a previous visit, although he had not carried any weapon. He claimed to have an arsenal, and, while in the Army, he had qualified on the 1000-meter range to hit human-size targets. As he related his thought that it did not matter if he died in the process, his intended effect was believable. Wearing a vest covered with Vietnam medals and patches and no shirt, bearing tattoos of predatory creatures on his thin arms, balding, and staring from his two piercing brown eyes set in an angular, darkly tanned face, this 35-year-old Caucasian struck the floor with a long staff, as he emphasized his points. Because this author is a Vietnam veteran, he would understand, ex-Staff Sergeant Marker explained. "We were sold out, betrayed in Vietnam by gutless politicians and an officer corps whose members were only punching their tickets." During his tours in Vietnam, he worked both phases of Operation Phoenix—first, the outright assassination of suspected enemy civilians and, second, the roundup and execution of civilians suspected of collaborating with the Vietcong. Yes, he explained, he had developed some unusual reactions to the constant killing, such as having an orgasm when he shot females in the chest with his .45. Yes, after being discharged, he almost killed his Vietnamese wife several times at night by strangulation, as he would awake from nightmares of bodies marching toward him, holding their heads in their hands until they reached him, and he awoke in a fit of panic and suffocation. Yes, he heard voices calling him an "asshole" and a "Judas" for being the sole survivor in an ambush in which his men were killed. He provoked fights with others on the street for "infractions" as simple as staring at him, hitting them with his staff, which he used in an expert fashion. The last this author saw of Staff Sergeant Marker was when he asked if the author had informed any federal agency of his threats, as two Secret Service agents had questioned him. The author answered in the affirmative, stating that he had no other choice, as Staff Sergeant Marker's medication had not restrained his violent impulses, psychotherapy was not working, and the author did not want to see him hurt himself or another person. He responded that he did not feel as if he was a real threat as he never initiated aggression and was only "three fourths serious" about shooting Nixon. Yet, when asked if he would have acted on his impulses if he had not been confronted by the federal agents, he claimed he did not know but stated that, if he had acted, he would have certainly killed the President. Four months later, Staff Sergeant Marker was killed in a bar in retaliation for using a broken beer bottle to cut the throat of a patron who had allegedly insulted his wife.

Several methods for assessing dangerousness were suggested by Staff Sergeant Marker's case, although all were conceived retrospectively; the methods were not typically used in the 1970s. How does the potential presidential assassin compare to actual presidential assassins? Table 1.5 presents the U.S. Secret Services' (1988) description of the etiological factors associated with incidents from 1835 to 1986. Table 1.6 presents the commonalities among the 18 presidential assassins (successful and attempted) from 1835 to 1986 (U.S. Secret Service, 1988).

Most assassination attempts are not successful. Yet, in Staff Sergeant Marker's case, the similarities between him and presidential assassins were strong. At 35 years of age, he was close to the median age of 38. He was of less than average height (about 5'8-1/2" tall), white, male, only a high-school graduate, living on disability, and probably psychotic, and he had told several authorities of his feelings and intentions.

Other similarities between Staff Sergeant Marker and actual presidential assassins (successful and attempted) were suggested by the clinical and forensic literature. Harris (1978), in a classic paper, examined presidential assassins since 1835 in an attempt to identify a core psychology and to differentiate them from other types of violent perpetrators. The main features of assassins are related to rebellious/rivalrous personalities who are mentally disturbed social loners. Like Staff Sergeant Marker, they tend to be "low man" in the dominance hierarchy in their development and, perhaps not surprisingly, are almost always later-born sons. During development, because

Table 1.5

American Presidential Assassination Incidents: Etiology and Associated Features

Year	Target	Perpetrator	Motive	Associated Feature
1835	Jackson	Lawrence	Mental	Believed victim was the King of England
1865	Lincoln	Booth	Political	Confederate
1881	Garfield	Guiteau	Mental	Perpetrator believed he was "Stalwart of the Stalwarts"
1901	McKinley	Czolgosz	Political	Anarchist
1912	T. Roosevelt	Schrank	Mental	Dreamed of visit by McKinley
1933	F.D. Roosevelt	Zangara	Personal	Nihilist
1950	Truman	Collazo Torresola	Political	Puerto Rican nationalists
1958	Nixon	Mob	Political	Anti-American demonstration
1960	J.F. Kennedy	Pavlick	Mental	Psychotic commands
1963	J.F. Kennedy	Oswald	Political	Marxist
1968	R.F. Kennedy	Sirhan	Political	Palestinian
1972	Nixon	Bremer	Personal	Attention seeking
1972	Wallace	Bremer	Personal	Attention seeking
1974	Nixon	Byck	Personal	Alienation from family
1975	Ford	Fromme	Political	Manson family agenda
1975	Ford	Moore	Personal	Seeking refuge
1979	T. Kennedy	Osgood	Mental	Psychotic
1980	Carter	Hinckley	Personal	Attention seeking
1981	Reagan	Hinckley	Personal	Attention seeking
1981	Reagan	Nassar	Political	Lybia/PLO revenge
1986	Reagan	Chukaku-Ha	Political	Left-wing element

Source: Prepared by U.S. Secret Service (1988). Includes acts toward presidential candidates and those not resulting in death, including stalking.

their generally smaller size puts them at a disadvantage at overcoming their arrogant, older brothers, they learn deception and surprise. They compensate for low self-worth with grandiosity.

As adults, the lethal violence sequence starts with typical baseline behavior consisting of the above traits and characteristics. During a prolonged acceleration period, depression and despair over a traumatic event or loss emerge. In Staff Sergeant Marker's case, he was 2 years removed from his relatively high status in the Green Berets. During this stage, the assassin seeks a new identity that commands respect. Staff Sergeant Marker attempted to create a self that spoke of the horror and betrayal in Vietnam. His challenge to the system flowed from the dynamics of his personality, superimposed on his wartime ordeal. In this sense, his assassination plan was based on a need for revenge.

The literature shows that American presidents are stalked frequently (Cain, 1982; Harris, 1979). The violence is preceded by anticipatory excitement, and the assassin's self-image becomes that of a self-styled hero who has done a public good. After the killing, the perpetrator maintains this delusion to further bolster and protect self-esteem, but knowledge of assassins' precise mental dynamics after the

Table 1.6

Commonalities Among American Presidential Assassins (1935–1986)[a]

Age	Range 21-73; median 38
Immigrant	8 themselves, or parents
Height	Male, 5'–5'11"; female, 5' – 5'3"
Race	White
Sex	15 males; 3 females
Aliases	5 used
Education	No college graduates
Economic status	14 unemployed, retired, living off savings
Veterans	4 (1 U.S. Marine Corps; 2 U.S. Army; 1 Italian Army)
Political or fringe group	11 belonged or adhered to beliefs
Mental illness	6 psychotic; 5 personally motivated
Tidiness	5 dapper; 1 sloppy
Situational variables	8 running out of money
Threats	8 orally threatened to authorities or acquaintances; 9 wrote about their intentions prior to their acts
Stalking	9 passed up potential opportunities

[a] Data collected by U.S. Secret Service (1988). Total incidents = 18 and refer to attempted and successful presidential assassinations.

recovery periods is lacking due to their small numbers and because many are killed in the act or executed before they can be studied.

In his review of the literature on document examiners' findings regarding presidential assassins, Cain (1982) found many of the same traits as Harris (1978), especially the grandiosity in their mental disturbances. Assassins typically make oral statements or write letters, or both, that justify and "require" the death of the President. Their motivation to kill is repressed initially but can be inferred from stresses such as loss of a job or loved ones. The President, as the principal representative of "the System", is then held responsible. Sexual inhibition, poor frustration tolerance, undue concern with the morals of others, hostility, and persistent focus on killing are common. (Sirhan Sirhan wrote "RFK must die!!" more than 20 times in the last page of his notebook.) These psychological characteristics were not yet formulated in the behavioral literature in the 1960s. Staff Sergeant Marker met later, empirically derived criteria for dangerousness in that he had a history of multiple acts of violence, some recent and life-threatening; skill in using firearms and the opportunity to use them; and triggers to aggress, including command hallucinations to kill as part of his severe psychosis (Hall, 1987, 1993, 1996).

The U.S. Secret Service (1988) has also articulated dangerousness criteria. It looks for a history of violence behavior or threats and tries to determine whether or not weapons and mobility are available to potential assassins. It views mental illness and interest in political assassins and assassinations as contributing factors. Altogether, four categories of questions pertaining to critical areas of inquiry are covered in the Secret Service evaluation, as shown in Table 1.7.

Observe that many of the violence-related questions in Table 1.7 do not deal with actual history,

Table 1.7

U.S. Secret Service Questions to Determine Dangerousness

Category 1 History of Violence/Threats	Category 2 Weapons and Mobility	Category 3 Mental Illness as a Contributing Factor	Category 4 Interest in Political Assassination
1. Does the subject have a history of violent behavior? 2. Has the subject threatened (directly or indirectly) a person protected by this Service? 3. Are there known factors have access to weapons or in the subject's life and environment that might increase or decrease the likelihood that the subject might attempt to injure a protectee? 4. Does the subject possess a violent attitude toward an administrative or legislative decision, policy, or action of federal, state, or local government? 5. Does the subject have a history of hostility toward authority figures — school/employment/parents/military/law enforcement/politicians? 6. Does the subject have a history of personal visits to offices, government agencies, and/or public officials to voice or exhibit strong feelings of animosity or hatred?	1. Does the subject have a history of weapon use, and is there data to suggest that the subject might be inclined to use weapons to harm a a protectee? 2. Does the subject currently other means of injuring a protectee? Might the subject be likely to gain access through such means? 3. Does the subject have the means and/or capacity to travel to an area where he/she might come in proximity with a protectee?	1. Does the subject have a history of mental illness with any of the following symptoms? a. Command hallucinations b. Command delusions c. Beliefs that he/she is being persecuted, threatened, attacked, mutilated, injured d. Severe depression with belief that world is coming to an end e. Serious suicide attempts f. Beliefs that someone whom the subject cares about is being injured or hurt by a protectee 2. Has the subject had any recent experiences that might lead to feelings of desperation? 3. Does the subject have a history of being a social isolate? Does he/she have a support system (family, friends, etc.)? 4. Has the subject ever been diagnosed by mental health professionals as being dangerous to himself/herself or others? 5. Does the subject's mental history (records) use such terms as explosive, impulsive, hostile, unpreditable, aggressive, poor control, grudge against society, angry, homicidal, suicidal, agitated, belligerent to describe subject's personality or behavior?	1. Does the subject adhere to hate beliefs or philosophies that advocate the overthrow of the government by force or subversion? 2. Does any evidence exist to suggest that the subject may be interested in political assassination (e.g., newspaper clippings, books, personal scrapbooks, diaries, poems, photographs of protectee (etc.)? 3. Does evidence exist to suggest that the subject may admire or be attempting to emulate past assassins or notorious figures? Is the subject attempting to model himself/herself after Oswald, Sirhan, Bremer, Moore, Fromme, Hinckley, etc.?

opportunity, or triggers, but rather address more subtle suggestive signs such as indirect threats to kill and a violent attitude. Less than 1% of severely mentally disturbed persons who threaten to kill ever do so (Hall, 1996; MacDonald, 1978), and almost no homicide threats, by any category of perpetrators, uttered during the escalation stage culminate in the death of a victim. The connection between a violent attitude by itself and actual violence is almost non-existent (Baron, 1977, 1984; Baron and Richardson, 1994; Blumenthal, 1976; Hall, 1996).

A word on ethics before closing this section on dangerousness prediction — one effect of labeling all persons who threaten to kill or have violent attitudes as potential assassins is to create false positives (individuals wrongfully identified as potentially violent who later do not aggress). Considering the high stakes in presidential assassin cases, evaluators are usually willing to pay the price for being wrong, setting aside the moral and societal costs of falsely labeling someone as dangerous, on the remote chance that the given individual will indeed be an assassin. Setting a high threshold for correctly predicting that a potential violent perpetrator will be violent (e.g., trying to include 99.9% of all true positives) means — because the state of the art in dangerousness prediction is rudimentary — that a great many individuals who are evaluated will erroneously be labeled dangerous, thereby negatively affecting any interrogated individuals who are innocent but falsely accused. Such false positive errors alienate these individuals from the government.

The following is an illustration of how possible excessive false positives are generated. The MOSAIC-2 program is one of a series of computer programs that draws on more than 250,000 communications and 18,000 cases and generates a narrative report on an individual (de Becker, 1997a). A case is compared to thousands of others in which the outcomes are known. Clients include the CIA, U.S. Supreme Court police, U.S. capitol police for threats against Congress members, and others. MOSAIC-3 is used by the U.S. Marshal's Office to predict violence against officials in the federal judiciary. Neither MOSAIC-2 nor MOSAIC-3 is available outside of government agencies.

MOSAIC reports may be based on piecemeal, fragmentary data in individual cases and thus generate many false positives. Even a discrete, limited threat or a history of violence in the suspect is not necessary for inclusion. The method is based on the beliefs that there is "no downside to false positives" and that, if 500 people are assessed in order to identify just one genuine threat, then the procedure and cost are worthwhile (de Becker, 1997a, 1997b).

Case Illustration 3

The Unabomber, previously known by federal enforcement agencies as the "Junkyard Bomber" for his construction of bombs from material available at a junkyard or hardware store, killed three people and wounded two dozen others over a span of 17 years. The bombings stopped with the arrest of Theodore J. Kaczynski, a Harvard-educated mathematics professor who taught at the University of California at Berkeley prior to becoming a recluse at his Lincoln, MT, cabin (Douglas and Olshaker, 1996). The Unabomber is reputed to have produced the Unabomber Manifesto *(1996), in which he identified himself as the author, "FC". The Justice Department sought the death penalty in this case (Knight-Ridder Service, 1997), but Kaczynski later pled guilty and was sentenced to life imprisonment without the possibility of parole.*

In 1989, a team of clinical-forensic professionals, including this author, offered to profile this case pro bono *for the U.S. Secret Service. At that time, the Unabomber had set off 12 devices and killed one person (see Table 1.8). He had been sighted once in Salt Lake City, UT, on February 20, 1987. A composite drawing was produced from that sole sighting. Based on material provided by the Secret Service, this author generated a profile delineating the lethal violence sequence for the Unabomber (see Figure 1.2). In 1990, the U.S. Secret Service sent the profile to the FBI at Quantico, VA, where it was considered together with several other profiles (and was subsequently rejected because it suggested that the Unabomber was college educated, as opposed to the FBI's belief that he was a blue-collar worker, probably a machinist, due to the precise construction of his bombs). In 1996, after the Unabomber wrote*

Table 1.8

The Unabomber Series

No.	Date of Bombing	Location	Device	Injuries
1	May 26, 1978	Northwestern University, Evanston, IL	Pipe bomb filled with match heads	Slightly injured campus police officers
2	May 9, 1979	Northwestern University, Evanston, IL	Bomb with match heads	Graduate student treated for minor cuts/burns
3	November 15, 1979	American Airlines plane, between Chicago, IL, and Washington, D.C.	Bomb with altimeter	12 passengers treated for smoke inhalation
4	June 10, 1980	Lake Forest, IL	Package bomb	President of United Airlines injured on hands, face, and thighs
5	August 8, 1981	University of Utah, Salt Lake City, UT	Package bomb	No injuries as bomb placed in unoccupied business classroom
6	May 5, 1982	Vanderbilt University, Nashville, TN	Pipe bomb with match heads and gun powder	Injuries to secretary when opening package
7	July 2, 1982	University of California, Berkeley, CA	Small metal pipe bomb	Serious injury to victim
8	May 15, 1985	University of California, Berkeley, CA	Bomb with ammonium nitrate and aluminum powder	Victim lost partial vision in one eye and two arteries were severed
9	June 13, 1985	Boeing Company, Auburn, WA	Mail bomb	Bomb did not detonate
10	November 15, 1985	Ann Arbor, MI	Package bomb	Assistant to psychology professor suffered powder burns and shrapnel wounds
11	December 11, 1985	Sacramento, CA	Bomb filled with nails and left in parking	Killed computer store owner with shrapnel to heart
12	February 20, 1987	Salt Lake City, UT	Bomb disguised to look like boards	Computer store owner injured; perpetrator sighted
13	June 22, 1993	Tiburon, CA	Package bomb	Geneticist seriously injured
14	June 24, 1994	Yale University, New Haven, CT	Package bomb	Computer scientist seriously injured
15	December 10, 1994	North Caldwell, NJ	Package bomb	Advertising executive killed instantly when opened package
16	April 24, 1995	Headquarters of California Forestry Association (CFA) Sacramento, CA	Pipe bomb	President of CFA killed when opened package

FIGURE 1.2

UNABOMBER'S LETHAL VIOLENCE SEQUENCE

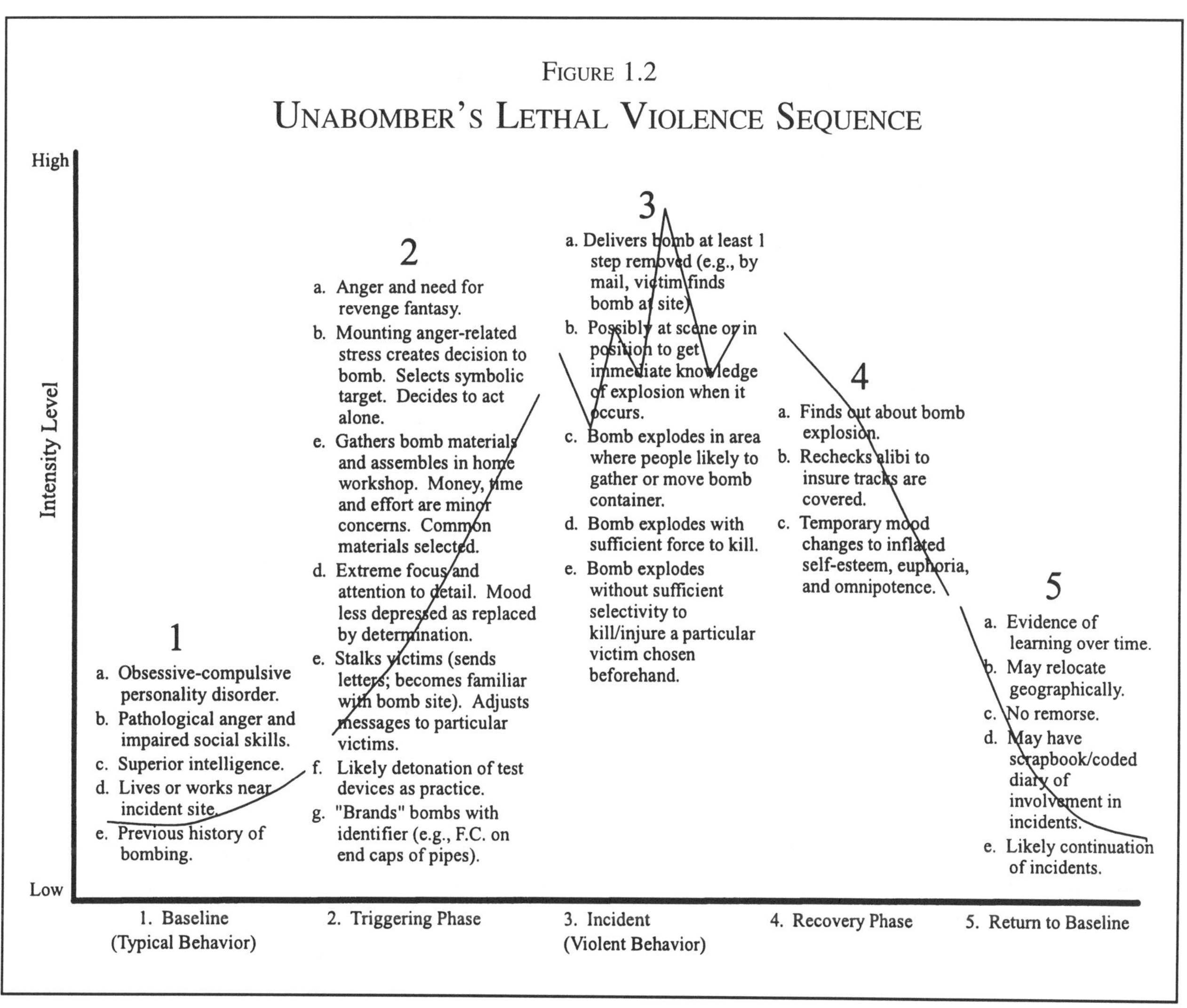

the Unabomber Manifesto, *the profile was updated with further information obtained by the Secret Service.*

Profilers are advised to place their findings in a lethal violence sequence to give a sense of temporal flow to the violence. In this case, data suggested that the Unabomber was right-handed, U.S. born, and obsessive-compulsive, with pathological anger that he kept bottled up in an overcontrolled fashion. He was seen to have superior intelligence and a college education. He was not psychotic nor were there any indications of a thought disorder. It was likely that he lived near the bomb sites at the times of the first few bombings but then geographically relocated for the bombings in the latter part of the series. He loved the outdoors and the wilderness. He was not comfortable around others and could be described as a social loner. The probability was exceptionally high, absent death or apprehension or lack of opportunity, that he would continue his bombings.

The profile provided a vast number of inferences based on epidemiological data, the circumstances of the bombings, and other factors. Almost all bombers are male. The suspect was seen as right-handed because photographs of the wiring of the bombs showed that it was assembled with right-handed twists. Bomb makers are exceptionally careful individuals and rarely switch hand dominance when they are constructing bombs. He was seen as U.S. born because he wrote fluently and used colloquialisms in his letters to several victims, including Percy Wood, who was president of United Airlines at the time of receiving the bomb. The explosion caused Mr. Wood to lose part of his hand and finger when he opened the bomb (June 10, 1980). The Unabomber wrote like a native when he sent a letter together with a bomb to University of Michigan psychology professor, James V. McConnell. A research assistant was injured when he opened the letter. Obsessive compulsiveness was seen in the rigorous, methodical way he constructed his bombs, painstakingly assembling the devices, as well as making some of the components himself. His obsessive-compulsiveness was so strong that the associated features of this disorder from the *Diagnostic and Statistical Manual*, fourth edition (DSM-IV), were inferred as part of the profile. Pathological anger was suggested by the bombings themselves, killing and wounding strangers, as well as the indirect, deceptive nature of the bombings as a means of violent expression.

Later, extreme anger and a tendency to intellectualize, as part of his obsessive-compulsive style, were also seen in the *Unabomber Manifesto*. His superior intelligence was revealed by his letters, which used concepts, words, and structure suggesting excellent abstract intelligence. The conclusion that he was college educated was inferred from the fact that colleges were targeted, that the suspect was of high intelligence, given his use of words common to college graduates, and that the letters discussed college requirements for graduate study. The suggestion that he lived near the bombing sites initially came from base rate data, relocation being part and parcel of this type of organized violence sequence for bombers after they commit a few acts of violence. The love of the outdoors was deduced from the fishing wire and gunpowder used for the bombs. A single black hair from a dog or cat suggested possible ownership of pets. He was seen as a loner based on evidence that he acted alone (despite his claim in the *Unabomber Manifesto* that he was part of a group) and because bombers who act alone also tend to be uncomfortable around others socially.

Despite the hiatus in bombings, barring death or apprehension, for several reasons he was seen as likely to continue bombing. He first killed on December 11, 1985, and then bombed again on February 20, 1987. This suggested that the fact that one of his bombs had resulted in death did not serve as an inhibition to continued violence. Second, age data show that serial bombers, like serial rape-murderers and assassins, rarely "burn out" because their central motives— anger and narcissism — can never be satisfied. Third, his increasing sophistication and learning over time, as well as his written productions, suggested that he was enjoying the process. In almost all violence of this organized type, the perpetrators avidly read accounts of their exploits in the newspapers, thus self-rewarding the violence and ensuring its continuation.

Overall, criminal profiles draw from a confluence of base rate data, crime scene information, the projected psychology of the perpetrator, and other information. John Douglas, now retired from the FBI, also profiled the Unabomber (Douglas and Olshaker, 1996). Douglas stated that to be successful, a profiler must put himself or herself in the mind of the perpetrator, a degree of empathy shown by few investigators. Importantly, Douglas noted that criminals reveal more clues when they attempt to deceive investigators or to justify their action because they then project their minds into the deception. A pattern emerges which suggests more leads and clues, which then point the way to investigatory strategies (such as the FBI encouraging the Unabomber to publish his work, based on his assumed grandiosity, which ultimately led to Kaczynski's arrest).

Yet, in all of the thousands of bits of data provided to this author and the millions of bits of data the federal agencies had in their possession (including a computer database of tens of thousands of students and faculty at major universities around the country), not one fact or combination of facts could have led or did lead to the likely perpetrator or even his general location. Reliance on informers, as always, was critical. The Unabomber's brother, David Kaczynski, recognized the style of writing and expressions in the *Unabomber Manifesto* on the Internet, which led the FBI to his brother's cabin in Lincoln, MT.

Principles of Violence and Implied Interventions

Humankind's innumerable experiences with violence and the vast literature on empirical and clinical investigations of aggressive and harmful behavior in the last half of the 20th century suggest patterns and outcomes which point to helpful preventive interventions for both individuals and communities. Because all types of human violence — domestic, acquaintance, stranger, and institutional — have commonalities, certain "violence principles" may be inferred. The types themselves overlap when individual persons, representing a community, kill others.

Killing is but one form of violence to others, often serving the same basic functions and having the same characteristics as nonlethal violence, depending on circumstances (Archer, 1988; Archer and Gartner, 1984; Hall, 1987, 1996; Richardson, 1960). Thus, we need not confine ourselves to knowledge about fatal aggression in the derivation of violence principles. Whether we speak of a husband shooting his wife out of a need for domination, a police officer using deadly force because no other response was possible, two perpetrators beating a homosexual to death in a hate crime, gangs fighting a deadly turf war to control a drug trade, or the CIA killing an enemy through an intermediary out of a misguided sense of mission, the same dynamics and functional characteristics may apply. Needs for control and retribution and to accomplish some objective run through these violent acts in various degrees. Thus, violence can be analyzed in terms of the principles which, depending on the type and circumstances of the violence, form the bases for individual treatment or large-scale prosocial intervention.

Robust models and theories of human aggression of a general sort, each having strong proponents, have been presented (Hall, 1996), with foci ranging from the ethological (e.g., Archer, 1995; Lorenz, 1966), aggressive-cue (e.g., Berkowitz, 1965, 1969), excitation-transfer (e.g., Zillman et al., 1972), cognitive neo-association (e.g., Berkowitz, 1969, 1988), and social learning (e.g., Bandura, 1973, 1977, 1983, 1986; Tedeschi and Felson, 1994). Unfortunately, none of the theories accounts for the diversity of human violence.

In contrast, the principles in this chapter do not stem from any single model or theory but are supported by evidence from many approaches and disciplines. No violence can be understood in isolation. The principles, in the author's view, lend themselves to application for evaluation, intervention, and organizational change. These principles are presented here primarily to reframe the violent event in terms of systematic patterns and to refocus our limited resources and maximize effective intervention. They represent the crystallization of key points for evaluating and changing violence-related phenomena. The interventions which may be implied from the principles are all nonviolent actions that rest on the assumption that both the perpetrator and victim are worthwhile and deserving of respect.

To change American society for the better by reducing violence, a time-honored and unalterable two-step process must be followed. First, we must be honest even if it hurts. In analyzing lethal violence, we call this "ground truth" — the interaction of the contributions of perpetrator, victim, and context variables at a given point in time when killing takes place. Ground truth is the reality of the violent act, stripped of deception and camouflage. As such, it is often ugly. Its realization conflicts with our natural inclination to avoid horror and death. Because groups and institutions, like individuals, try to survive and avoid censure, through their representatives, they often avoid, deny, or minimize ground truth. Nevertheless, ground truth must be known in order for effective change to take place. Thus, we must ruthlessly probe the ground truth of different collective organizations — from hate groups to terrorists to the U.S. federal government — all of which typically distort information in the direction of their vested interests. The Johari Window, presented in Figure 1.3, can be applied to collective entities in our effort to frame distortion and deception committed by institutions. In essence, any group or organization has information that is known to themselves or to outsiders to varying degrees *and* information that is hidden or unknown. Uncovering blind, hidden, and unknown information as much as possible renders that organization more responsive to the needs of the greater community.

FIGURE 1.3
THE JOHARI WINDOW

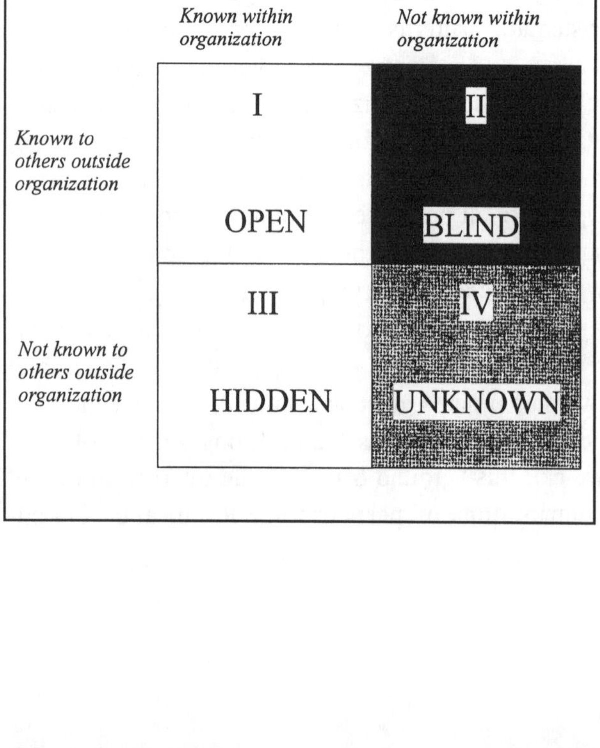

	Known within organization	*Not known within organization*
Known to others outside organization	I OPEN	II BLIND
Not known to others outside organization	III HIDDEN	IV UNKNOWN

Second, with the ground truth in our grasp, interventions must be congruent with the principles of violence in order to reduce the negative and strengthen the positive. As a conceptual foundation based on a century of data in various disciplines, human behavior has repeatedly been demonstrated to be lawful, and individual and collective violence has been determined to unfold in orderly and predictable ways (Bandura, 1973, 1977, 1983, 1986; Baron, 1977; Baron and Richardson, 1994; Buss, 1961; Dollard et al., 1939; Geen, 1991; Kutash et al., 1978; Monahan, 1981; Richardson, 1960). The following ten applied principles and their implications for intervention are presented in Table 1.9. In the author's opinion, ignoring these principles dooms intervention to failure.

Principle 1: Violence and the Threat of Violence Preempt Other Events for Attention and Action

Implied interventions: Knowledge of nondeliberate distortion about violent events should be factored into our observations.

This principle holds true for both animals (Archer, 1988, 1995) and humans (Buss, 1961; Hall, 1996; Hall and Sbordone, 1993; Kull, 1988; Tedeschi and Felson, 1994; Toplin, 1975). Cognitively, perceptually, and emotionally, the focus of the perpetrator, victim, and others present is on the killing event. If someone shoots at us with a sidearm, we don't pay attention to the holster. If a terrorist group plans to use a weapon of mass destruction, the terrorists are not interested in the proportion of well-dressed to poorly dressed members of the target group. As an adaptive mechanism, this focus is natural because it maximizes the chances of victim survival or perpetrator success.

As a starting point for intervention, our first principle implies that although violence may not be a

Table 1.9

Ten Applied Principles of Violence

Principles	Implied Interventions
1. Violence and the threat of violence preempt other events for attention and action.	Knowledge of nondeliberate distortion about violent events should be factored into our observations.
2. The perpetrator group, victim group, and context in interaction constitute the violent event for collectivities.	Because violence is often the result of mutual contributions, the designation of perpetrator group or victim group should be based on careful interactional analysis.
3. Perpetrator violence involves a temporal series of discrete stages.	Interventions can be targeted to any stage in the violence sequence.
4. Deliberate deception by the perpetrator typically occurs at every stage of the lethal violence sequence.	Deception should be accounted for in order to plan appropriate intervention effectively.
5. History, opportunity, and triggers to violence, operating in concert against inhibitions, are the principle contributions to violence.	Inhibitions acting to reduce the incentive to behave violently should be developed and implemented.
6. Violence is always a choice after costs are weighed and nonviolent options are excluded.	The decision path of organizations that lead to violence should be articulated before intervening.
7. Successful violence is frequently followed by self-reinforcing thoughts, feelings, and behaviors.	Care should be taken to ensure that violence is neither successful nor reinforced socially.
8. Interventions that respond violently to violent events lead to self-generating violent interlocks.	Violence interlocks are initially broken by unilateral, non-violent actions, not by bilateral actions.
9. Micro-violence and macro-violence are functionally similar and tend to potentiate each other.	Expect and plan for micro and macro changes affecting each other.
10. Reframing and redirecting our violent mindsets require transcending violent interlocks to cycles of affection and gratitude.	Training in altruism and the advocacy of others, even of our perceived adversaries, should start in childhood and proceed throughout the lifetime of each individual.

total surprise to the identified victim (who may have been exposed to cues associated with the upcoming aggression), a strong, limiting cognitive focus by all parties should be expected. For perpetrators, the focus allows them to complete the task with a greater probability of success by avoiding distraction and attention to non-essential details. For victims, the focus permits them a chance to escape harm by keeping them alert for avenues of defense or avoidance. For bystanders or others who are aware of the violence, the focus enables them to learn by vicarious experience.

Learning is demonstrated by the degree to which the violent event is accurately reported and later measured. That dataset of observations is the basis for identification of the perpetrator(s) and for later intervention. The identification of the perpetrator(s) often rests on the collection of facts considered nonessential at the time of the violent event (e.g., weather, social events).

To increase accuracy of reporting, nondeliberate distortion should be kept to a minimum while not compromising the safety of the victim or onlookers. Hall and Pritchard (1996), in a compendium of methods for detecting distortion and deception, noted that onlookers and others reporting the violent event are almost always affected by the stress of the event and the threat to them personally. Factors other than stress that may limit focus include limited general intelligence, impoverished attentional and memory skills, and psychosis. Normal persons focus intently on any threatening behavior or weapon shown by the perpetrator; thus, non-threatening stimuli are usually ignored. For example, reports of clothing color and estimates of time are typically deficient due to being poorly reported by witnesses to violence.

The violent act itself may be subject to distortion (Buckhout, 1980). Hall and Pritchard (1996) found that nondeliberate distortion increased if the violence was brief or seen as weak in relation to the harm done to the victim. The reported event is poorly focused upon if physical barriers are present, distractions are operative, or no stimulus-ground uniqueness emerges (e.g., violence committed at night by perpetrators wearing dark clothing). Table 1.10 presents a list of nondeliberate distortions associated with impaired focus as evidenced by later measurements of recall for the violent event.

Even individuals who are well trained in violent confrontations are subject to problems in focus and later reporting of the event. The following presents the experiences of a veteran police officer who was shot with his own sidearm while struggling with a suspected burglar:

Table 1.10

Nondeliberate Distortion Factors

1. Reporting person
   a. Stress
   b. Physical disability
   c. Limited intelligence
   d. Poor attention skills
   e. Recall problems
   f. Psychosis
2. Reported event
   a. Memory focus
   b. Brief duration
   c. Physical barriers
   d. Weak intensity
   e. Distractions
   f. Figure-ground merging
   g. No stimulus uniqueness
3. Evaluation errors
   a. Unreliable measures
   b. Invalid measures
   c. Inadequate training
   d. Leading questions/procedures
   e. Emotional context of evaluation

Case Illustration 4

After the shooting, Officer Jones reported that his alleged assailant was between 5'7" and 5'10" tall and weighed "far more" than 200 pounds (actually, the perpetrator stood 5'4" tall and weighed 180 pounds). Temporal events were seen as stretched out in duration (the victim estimated 10 minutes for the entire time span of the violence; actually, independent sources agreed that it was closer to 2 or 3 minutes, at most). He did not recall several relevant details (e.g., the license plate number of the vehicle allegedly belonging to the defendant, the behavior of the nearby witness during the time of the shooting). The officer subsequently developed severe post-traumatic stress disorder (PTSD), which further distorted his memories of the event.

Research has shown that as people switch from normal states into general adaptational syndrome (GAS) behaviors which may be associated with threats to their lives or well-being, they become less attuned to details because they are more concerned with immediate safety needs. Generally, memory for some details and sequences can be demonstrated, but recall is less clear overall than normal. Time estimates are especially vulnerable to exaggeration — in some studies by a factor of 2.5 to one (e.g., see Buckhout, 1980). Size and weight of the defendant are usually overestimated, with poor recall of the perpetrator's clothing, as in the case of the above-described officer-victim (Hall and Pritchard, 1996, p. 27).

Organizations tend to focus on violent events that compromise their security or otherwise threaten their safety. Nonintentional distortion in regard to actual or threatened attacks can influence how the group or institution typically reacts, making them prone to error and misreporting. Research shows that distorted memory of the violence is accepted as real and becomes resistant to extinction (see Hall and Pritchard, 1996). Violent gangs, for example, almost always report that the opposing gang started the gang war. Prior to the conflict, the number of weapons and opposing gang members are almost always exaggerated.

In short, limiting nondeliberate distortion translates into keeping the stress of the threatened or actual violence to the level necessary to show effectual responses. High perceived stress tends to disorganize behavior and compromise accurate recall of the event.

Principle 2: The Perpetrator Group, Victim Group, and Context in interaction Constitute the Violent Event for Collectivities

Implied interventions: Because violence is often the result of mutual contributions, the designation of perpetrator group or victim group status should be based on careful interactional analysis.

Although the emphasis of this book is on perpetrator groups, the victim group and the context must also be considered, as all of these elements are necessary for the violence to occur (see Figure 1.4). The relative contributions to violence by each of these three factors should be assessed. Answers to the following questions are often unclear: Who started the violence? Who is the "real" perpetrator group? Who is the "real" victim group?

FIGURE 1.4
VIOLENT EVENTS FOR COLLECTIVITIES

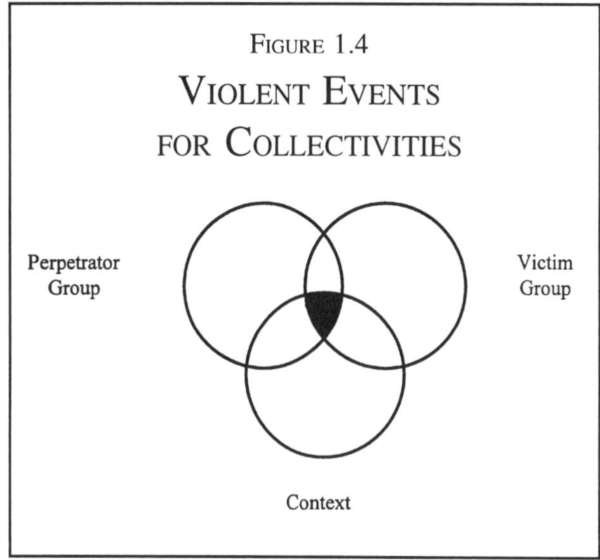

Most studies are based on the study of violent individual or group perpetrators (Cornell, 1993; Daly and Wilson, 1988; Daniel and Robins, 1985; Goetting, 1989; Lester, 1977; Mann, 1992; O'Brien, 1987; Poussaint, 1983), the factors that are assumed to underlie violence (Brooks and Harford, 1992; Hesieh and Pugh, 1993; Smith et al., 1992; Ullah, 1988), or epidemiological data (Kelly, 1966; U.S. Department of Justice, 1997). These investigations and reports imply that perpetrators always decide upon and institute violence and, more basically, that we know with certainty who the victim and the aggressor are. Yet, the roles of the perpetrators and victims are often confused.

The literature on victim-precipitated homicide (VPH), in which the victim sets the stage for his or her own death, is instructive on this point. The VPH literature has been given scant attention despite its frequent relevance (Curtis, 1974; Foote, 1996; Goetting, 1989). Wolfgang (1958) found that 26% of 588 cases of homicide in Philadelphia were victim precipitated. Voss and Hepburn (1968) replicated Wolfgang's classic research and found that 28% of the 420 homicides in their study were precipitated by the victim. Curtis (1974) found that 39% of the homicide cases across the U.S. are victim precipitated. Goetting (1989) determined that 60% of the marital homicide cases he studied were victim precipitated, while Mann (1989) presented a phenomenal 83% victim-precipitated homicide figure for homicides by women in six large cities across the U.S.

What does this mean? At least one fourth of the homicide cases in this nation may be victim precipitated. We should know when victims initiate or contribute to the violence sequence which leads to the death of the perpetrator. The traditional focus on the identified perpetrator may be too limiting for identification and intervention efforts. A weak group of adolescents that preemptively attacks an organized crime group out of fear for the safety of its members should be treated differently than a predatory group with purely commercial motives. Police officers who apply deadly force to uphold a "macho" image or who react primarily out of fear are motivationally dissimilar to officers who kill only when all other possible options are excluded. Suicidal attacks by kamikaze warriors in World War II or Chinese mass assaults during the Korean War have peculiar characteristics (such as disinterest in body armor) which qualify as victim-precipitated killing. In sum, the evaluator of violence-related events should carefully consider the interactional effects of perpetrator, victim, and context. To do otherwise, by immediately labeling who is the injurer and who is the injured party, often creates inaccurate predictions of future aggressor behavior as well as inappropriate interventions.

Principle 3: Perpetrator Violence Involves a Temporal Series of Discrete Stages

Implied intervention: Interventions can be targeted to any stage in the violence sequence.

For all classes and types of fatal aggression, perpetrator violence involves a temporal sequence of events consisting of baseline, acceleration, the actual violence, post-violence adjustment, and return to baseline. As Figure 1.5 shows, every act of violence is part of a process which can be further analyzed as follows: (1) a baseline period of typical behavior, (2) an acceleration or triggering stage wherein the perpetrator prepares to inflict violence, (3) the violent act, (4) an adjustment stage in which recovery from the violence takes place, and (5) a return to typical ways of behaving, if such is possible. Interventions can be geared to any part of the lethal violence sequence, but the earlier the intervention, the more successful it is likely to be.

The Baseline Period. Stage 1 of the lethal violence sequence — the baseline period — covers the entire history of the individual or group entity, including early development, typical characteristics, and organization. Social and cultural factors are part and parcel of this baseline endowment. The history of a group's violence should be scrutinized because, almost always, the most recent killing bears some resemblance to past violence, if not in lethality then in function and form. Ignoring a group's violent history condemns us to the common error of focusing too exclusively on recent events and provides an inadequate view of the background of the collective entity, thereby resulting in inaccurate prediction and ineffective intervention. Baseline traits involving distinction and judgments leading to violence or peacefulness are important to consider and are discussed below.

As discussed by this author in *Lethal Violence 2000: A Sourcebook on Fatal Domestic, Acquaintance, and Stranger Aggression* (1996), the avoidance of exaggerating distinctions and appreciation of differences among groups and individuals are associated with *less* violence; distinction-exaggerating tendencies are associated with *increased* violence. Distinction-creating tendencies are fostered by having time-limited objectives with pressure to achieve, establishing dominance hierarchies, contingent affection, orderliness, precision, power and control strategies, and perceiving members of one's group as superior to others. Military and quasi-military groups tend to exaggerate distinctions between themselves and others, often to the disadvantage of members who do not actually conform or of avowed victim group targets. Predatory and proactively aggressive, these groups, as they achieve power and are rewarded for violence, tend to perpetuate themselves. Outliving their usefulness and hostile to outside influences but having dominant status within their society in their efforts to maintain power, control, and status, they tend to become dangerous to the very nation which gave rise to them. Thus, powerful military groups should be greatly reduced after a war.

Distinction-dissolving traits include tolerance of differences, holism, intuition, complexity, ambiguity, non-contingent affection, and reciprocal power relationships. The main factor in nonviolent societies associated with less development of violent tendencies is lavish physical affection toward infants and children (Prescott, 1975). A similar effect results from the nonsuppression of premarital sexual activity during

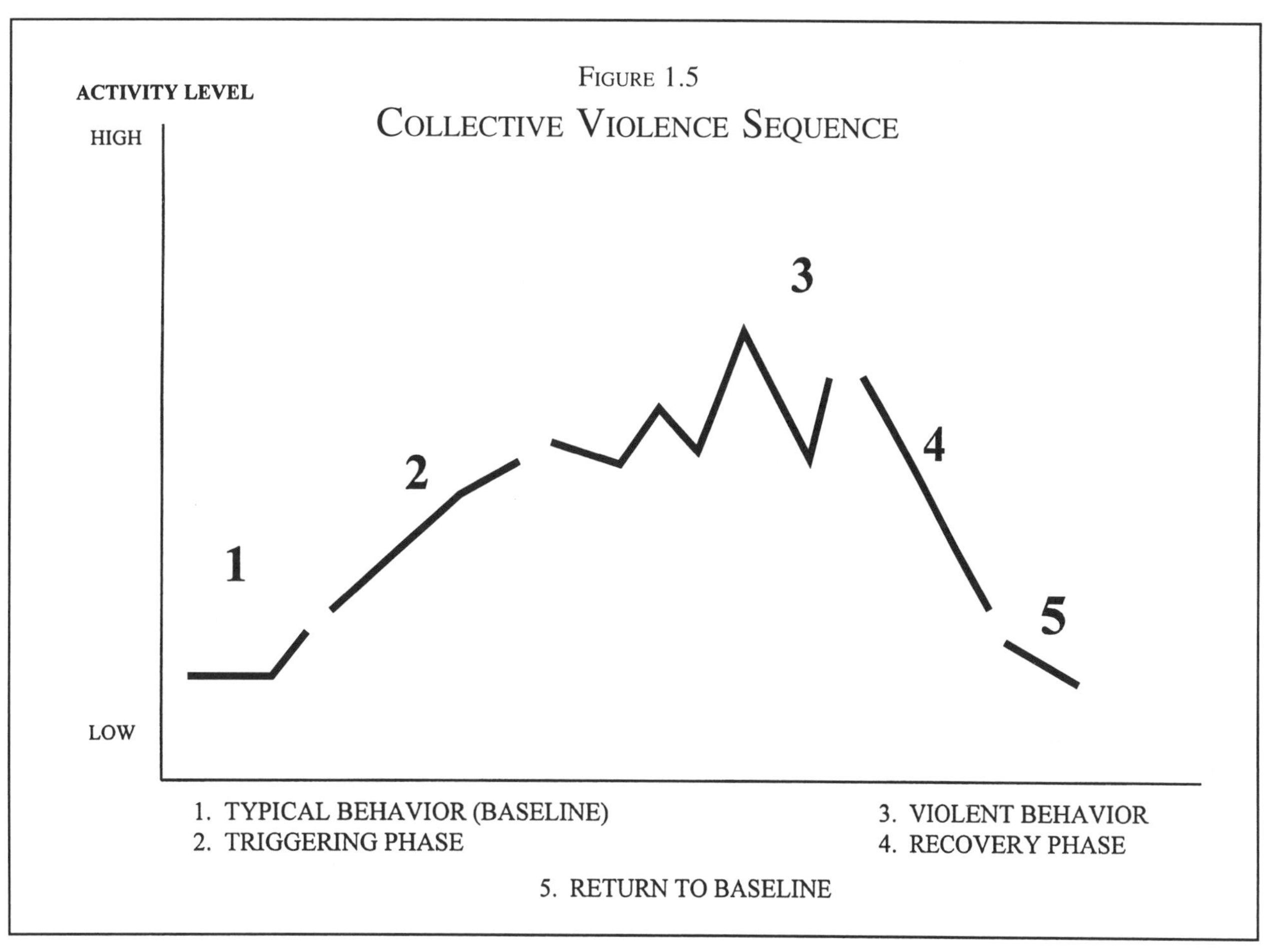

FIGURE 1.5
COLLECTIVE VIOLENCE SEQUENCE

adolescence. Based on a study of 400 pre-industrial societies, Prescott found that there was only a 2% chance of a society becoming violent if both factors (i.e., lavish physical affection and unsuppressed premarital sexual activity in adolescence) were present ($p < .0001$).

Distinction-dissolving groups tend to use nature as a model and aggress only when forced into defending their homeland or their way of life. If such groups continue to aggress after sustaining heavy losses, they may prevail; otherwise, they lose and generally are not absorbed easily into the dominant society.

Baseline information can be used to identify the perpetrator group or institution. A youth gang with a collective history of violence will, during the relatively quiescent periods in its existence, have members who advertise the group by wearing their colors and displaying the gang's authority and activities. The military, a federal agency, or a terrorist group may train for war during peacetime. The numbers of soldiers, the nature of the training, the state of preparedness, attitudes, and the aggression policy can be revealed thereby.

Intervention strategies during this stage, when there is little expressed aggression, carry the best prognosis for violence reduction ultimately. As examples:

1. To prevent the development of violent gangs, implement FASTract (Family and School Together) programs to eliminate violence by children in preschools and schools and at home (Dodge, 1997).
2. Decrease media violence and support non-violent models in the media.
3. Provide "peacekeeper" training in schools. Switch hero status from sports skills to "peacekeeper" status with training in resolving and mediating disputes.
4. Provide programs to reduce sexism, racism, and reverse racism.
5. Substantially increase government support for efforts to resolve conflict at local levels using local resources.
6. Develop programs for full educational and employment opportunities.
7. Provide psychological training to produce abilities and mental states that help to eliminate motivation to induce chemically altered states of consciousness.

Acceleration Stage. Events suggestive of violence make for tense times for all parties who may be involved. Triggers to violence start the acceleration stage. Primary triggers for groups and institutions include (1) disruption in their ability to control others, (2) threat of violence from another entity, (3) conflict within the organization, (4) misinterpreted instructions to aggress (e.g., as in nuclear attack accidents), and (5) orders from higher authorities to aggress. During this stage, the perpetrator group tends to project hostility and blame onto the victim group for various misdeeds and anticipated actions. Perpetrator group members are expected to buy into the labeling of victim group members as inferior, unethical, and dangerous. Cohesiveness increases within the aggressor group based on their assumptions that violence is necessary and that everyone should "pull together" to achieve victory.

The characteristics and capabilities of the victim group are important. The perpetrator almost always targets a weaker entity (e.g., Germany attacked Poland and other weaker countries; the U.S. invaded Panama and Grenada; terrorist groups select unsuspecting individuals for assassination; hate groups often victimize single victims). Some types of collective violence, such as bombing or use of advanced weapons, are almost impossible to defend against. Genocide by a well-prepared state, execution of mob members within an organized crime family, and other types of collective violence are likewise difficult to avoid unless members of the victim group remove the opportunity for aggression by leaving the area or adopting special defensive measures.

Violence escalates toward a flash point in synergistic fashion during the acceleration stage. The first act by the perpetrator-to-be (e.g., an argument between leaders, violation of neighborhood or national boundaries) makes violence more probable. The response of victim group members (e.g., arguing back, counter-violations) increases the chances of collective violence even more. The perpetrator group responds in an escalating series of events. Inhibitions to violence as a function of increasing emotion may erode in their ability to prevent aggressive responses. The idea of violence, never far from the thinking of some groups, is formulated. Logistical planning and weapons are selected and prepared. The victim group is made available in a particular context or the perpetrator group moves to an advantageous predatory site. Perpetrator anger and other emotions increase; perception becomes selectively biased during the acceleration stage. The focus is on upcoming violence, and blame is increasingly projected onto the victim group. The perpetrator group will do almost anything to place the chosen victim group at a disadvantage before striking, including massive use of denial of intent and mobilization of resources. Violence is initiated after choosing to exclude non-violent options.

During the acceleration period, high-risk groups may be targeted for preventive intervention. Secondary prevention strategies include the following:

1. Short-term dispute resolution and mediation between violent parties
2. Informing collective entities that their plans are known and that the cost of aggression is prohibitive; the perpetrator groups must believe that they will be punished if they aggress
3. Individual crisis intervention with members of certain groups (e.g., hate groups, participants in mob violence, stressed police officers)
4. Peer-group counseling (e.g., for members of youth gangs)
5. Anger management and cognitive reframing methods with perpetrator group members
6. Procedures to eliminate opportunity factors (e.g., having high-risk groups surrender firearms)

While not as effective generally as primary prevention, secondary prevention during the acceleration stage may represent the only window of opportunity for intervention. As with all interventions, secondary prevention must be orchestrated within an interdisciplinary, multilevel approach to any particular set of violence-related problems. Most groups and institutions with violence potentials, from the police to the Cosa Nostra to the military, resent and resist secondary prevention interventions from outside their organization. In these cases, meaningful change may occur only as a result of action by higher authority or external circumstances (e.g., presidential directives banning CIA assassinations, the dissolution of the KGB caused by the collapse of the Soviet Union, godfathers in crime families avoiding all drug transactions). History shows that even these changes are typically thwarted by violent organizations as they deflect attempts at control and displace aggression onto safer targets.

Violence Stage. Violence is usually task oriented, fully focused, and goal directed but may be modulated by a pre-determined plan to limit violence. In general, whoever "wins" a conflict is the one who can outlast the other, not the one who can inflict the most damage at any given point unless that damage eliminates the enemy. The turning point in many conflicts is marked by massive efforts to defeat the enemy while in the throes of an apparently losing campaign. In the American Revolution, the continental army was repeatedly on the brink of extinction before the victory at Yorktown. The 1968 Tet offensive by the North Vietnamese and the Vietcong is another example. Although defeated by the U.S. in nearly every battle and having sustained huge losses, the Vietcong and soldiers of the North Vietnamese Army managed to surprise attack most South Vietnamese cities and to turn American opinion against the war, causing our eventual abandonment of the Vietnamese people in 1975. The U.S. public asked how an enemy we supposedly had all but defeated, according to the body counts and other data in reports by General Westmoreland and other leaders, could launch successful countrywide surprise attacks. After Tet, the U.S. shifted from an offensive to a defensive war that was widely and rightly seen as highly politicized and unjust.

Most people, especially victims and bystanders, are disgusted by violence. Yet, violence is often rewarding to perpetrators. A Vietnam veteran stated the following (Tanaka, 1996, p. 77):

"As anyone who has fired a bazooka or an M60 machine gun knows, there is something to that power in your finger, the soft seductive touch of the trigger. It's like the magic sword, a grunt's Excaliber: all you do is move that finger so imperceptibly, just a wish flashing across your mind like a shadow, not even a full brain synapse, and poof! in a blast of sound and energy and light a truck or a house or even people disappear, everything flying and settling back into dust."

Violence as a turn-on is not limited to war. For the several thousands of violent offenders evaluated by this author, many of whom belonged to predatory gangs, hate groups, organized crime syndicates, and other such organizations, the infliction of violence on others became a rewarding stimulus as the violence unfolded. The violence becomes highly addicting.

Sonny "the Bull" Gravano, who over the years as a Gambino crime underboss was reputed to have murdered over 20 people, spoke of his first kill after he blew off the back of the head of a fellow member of the crime family in a car with the help of accomplices (Maas, 1997, p. 51):

"The car was a mess. Back in the neighborhood, we washed down the inside real good. We were all scared, not like afraid, but excited. I can't really describe it. But then I felt a surge of power. I realized that I had taken a human life, that I had the power over life and death. I was a predator. I was an animal. I was Cosa Nostra."

The above are not isolated examples. The power, excitement, and stimulation value of violence are primal to some perpetrators. Once ingrained as an addiction, these primal conditioning experiences appear irreversible. The combination of the "two potencies" (to give life and to give death) is irresistible in these cases. Consider a serial rape murder. Some men find that killing women is sexually exciting. The serial murderer's ultimate fantasy is to have the victim die at the point of the murderer's orgasm, with many perpetrators stopping the strangulation or torture and then starting it again in non-lethal proportions, in order to achieve this aim. No mental health treatment has ever been shown to be effective in changing the desire for lust killing. In fact, serial murderers, like some killers who operate within a collective context, do not "burn out" or lose interest in killing even as they enter their 40s or 50s (Cook and Hinman, 1996; Schlesinger, 1996).

This author has concluded that violent perpetrators rarely believe they have done wrong. The victim deserved it, the perpetrators were only following orders (and therefore someone higher up was responsible), the perpetrators themselves were abused as children, or events created a violent situation where no other response was possible. These rationalizations, of course, stand squarely in the way of effective intervention.

Interventions at the point of violence are the most limited and consist of self-defense by members of the victim group or rescue efforts by third parties. In the author's view, this is the only stage wherein counter-violence may be necessary because the alternative may be death. Almost always, though, the perpetrator group decides the extent to which violence will be exhibited (e.g., achieving conquest of a nation, a "favorable" body count, control of drug trade in a section of a city). Which group maintains its control depends primarily on preparation and training, the will to win, effective leadership, and other factors already set into place in the acceleration period.

Post-Violence Adjustment. By concealing or altering the results of their aggression, perpetrators routinely pretend that they were not involved or that they were forced to commit the violence. When successful, these attempts allow the perpetrator group to escape the aversive consequences of the recent violent actions. Some perpetrators recover after their stressful experience. They begin, almost immediately, to evaluate their violent behavior as "good" or "bad", and this judgment, once entrenched, is highly resistant to change. Others' evaluations (e.g., peers, supervisor) assist this process by communicating to the perpetrator that the violence was both necessary and successful. A negative reaction by significant or knowledgeable others (e.g., one's spouse, the public) may dilute the positive effects of the violence somewhat, but some support from one's perpetrator group almost certainly takes place. At this point, interventions should be directed at the cognitive framing of the violence by the perpetrator as well as immediately applying negatively sanctions against the perpetrator group or institution; however, that is sometimes impossible.

History provides many examples of after-the-fact psychological assimilation of violence in perpetrators' minds. Lifton (1997) wrote of Nazi doctors' tendency to double, or divide the self into two functioning wholes (e.g., the protector of the Aryan race who experiments on inferiors vs. the healing physician who does not harm his patients). In order to adjust to a death environment such as a concentration camp, a part-self (i.e., the master Aryan) acts as the entire self during times of violence.

Doubling may be seen as adaptive, holistic, and unconscious. It functions to avoid guilt. It also involves a dialectic between the two selves in terms of freedom to choose and a connection to a set of stimulus demands, suggesting that Nazi doctors needed a death environment to provide and give meaning to the violent part-self. The self that violates one's original self and standards uses the original self and skills to amplify power and abilities. In this sense, according to Lifton (1997), although unconscious in motivation, one is responsible for the perpetrated violence. In such a death-dominated environment, one had to double after only a short time in order to survive. Auschwitz, as an atrocity-producing setting, could not have existed without the doubling phenomenon. Lifton maintained that doubling became the group norm. He argued that, in less violent settings, doubling is a more gradual process, down a slippery slope of moral compromises.

Clearly, doubling is a universal phenomenon, not only in German culture, but throughout the world. Note the doubling that occurs when an execution takes place in a Cosa Nostra family — "it is only business, nothing personal" — or in the CIA's insistence that any violent acts by the agency or its henchmen are in the interest of national security. The same phenomenon occurs in most violent groups and institutions. Some form of doubling is necessary for psychological adjustment to and assimilation of the killing events.

Return to Baseline. The final step in the violence sequence is a return to typical behavior after the killing has taken place. In the author's experience, deadly perpetrator groups put a great amount of effort into holding themselves blameless for the killing. Typically, they first deny and then, if discovered, project the blame for the killing onto the victim group or others. Their inhibitions to kill in the future may be reduced by doing so, because they have not accepted responsibility for their lethal conduct. In general, any violence makes future violence more probable, given the opportunity to aggress and the availability of the correct triggers. In this stage, perpetrator groups often refine methods for future lethal violence.

In general, interventions can be geared to any part of the lethal violence sequence but are typically less successful in the last two stages. Prevention is always better than cure, and the earlier the intervention, the more likely it is to be preventive. To focus on the early baseline events of a race riot means to examine the poverty and frustration that tend to give rise to the mob behavior in the first place. To focus only on the conduct of a war that is economically motivated rather than on the underlying economic motivational dynamics means that we are doomed to repeat such wars should a similar situation occur.

The entire sequence must be taken into account in any effective intervention programming. Program evaluators are strongly encouraged to construct a lethal violence sequence to better understand the relative contributions of key factors to the killing event.

Principle 4: Deliberate Deception by the Perpetrator Typically Occurs at Every Stage of the Lethal Violence Sequence

Implied interventions: Deception should be accounted for in order to effectively plan appropriate intervention.

Deception by collective entities is almost universal in regard to planning, executing, and distancing themselves from lethal violence. When deception is uncovered prior to a lethal act, the violence may not occur for fear of adverse consequences to the perpetrator group. After a violent act occurs, however, coverup, denial, faking, and just plain lying are typical and to be expected. Deception, commonly overlooked in the analysis of aggression, functions to maintain control and protect the collective enterprise from censure and attack both from without and within. From the Trojan Horse to Goebel's Nazi propaganda to denial by the White House of wrongdoing, deception has been seen as necessary for the entity to survive and prosper. And, it usually works, at least in the short run. Eventually, most deception related to lethal violence is uncovered because of the primacy of the killing event in the minds of the perpetrators and the ambivalence that it engenders.

One reason for the usual immediate efficacy of deception is that we believe that we have taken falsehood into account. Most professional evaluators believe that they already possess the ground truth about the violent groups and institutions being scrutinized. Actually, databases on groups and institutions almost always lack or contaminate information. When the information about a perpetrator group is congruent with the evaluator's own prior beliefs, vested interests, and biases, the evaluator often believes the source and ignores conflicting data.

Members of most collective entities use two main types of deliberate deception: *faking good* by concealing or minimizing their own negative traits and exaggerating positive characteristics, and *faking bad* by exaggerating or fabricating the enemy's negative traits (e.g., potential for harm) and minimizing the enemy's positive traits (Table 1.11 illustrates these two basic deceptive styles.). In most violent collective enterprises, as in war, truth is certainly the first casualty.

Handel (1982, p. 145) observed the following:

> *"Since no effective measures to counter or identify deception have yet been developed, the inevitable conclusion is that deception — even if it does not achieve its original goals — almost never fails and will therefore always favor the deceiver, the initiating party. ...Perceptual and cognitive biases strongly favor the deceiver as long as the goal of deception is to reinforce a target's preconceptions or simply create ambiguity and doubt about the deceiver's intention. ...Rationality dictates that a move which involves little cost and little risk of failure should always be included in one's repertoire."*

As discussed in the earlier section on methods of interrogation, police are adept at deception. The Associated Press (1997) reported that police sent letters to 3800 individuals wanted on charges ranging from theft to drug dealing, inviting them to become "extras" at more than $200 per day for a movie entitled *The Rocky Marciano Story*. The 54 suspects who showed up were promptly arrested.

Sammy Gravano made definitive statements connecting faking and lethal violence (Maas, 1997, p. 123): "Now deception is at the core of a clean mob hit. It's absolutely essential. It knows no bounds." Maas (1997, p. 46) stated:

> *"In theory, a Cosa Nostra hit required a precise procedure. A case had to be made. It had to be sanctioned by the family boss. A murder that had not been authorized invited immediate retribution. Yet time after time, transgressions occurred out of fear, jealousy, desperation, greed."*

Table 1.11

Deception by Collective Entities: Fake Good and Fake Bad Styles

	Positive Presented	Negative Presented
	Fake Good	*Fake Bad*
Exaggerate/ Fabricate	1. Human radiation experiment portrayed as medical benefit for patient. 2. A meal before a Mafia "hit" is characterized to victim as a happy social event.	1. Terrorist group falsely claims responsibility for bombings. 2. Gang member exaggerates role in murder of informer for prestige.
	Fake Good	*Fake Bad*
Minimize/ Deny	1. CIA claims it had no role in assassination of a state leader. 2. Terrorist cell goes underground, with members taking conventional jobs.	1. To terrify enemy, battle leader says that no prisoners of war will be taken. 2. Police interrogators create compliance by downplaying need for counsel.

The military provides excellent examples of deception throughout the lethal violence sequence. (Handel, 1977, 1982; Reit, 1978; Whaley, 1969, 1982). Vast sums of money have been spent by the federal government in the systematic study of operational deception from which principles have been applied in modern American wars. Hall and Pritchard (1996) discussed the application of tactical deception in military operations. In general, deception is viewed favorably by the military because it serves as a force multiplier by magnifying the ostensible strength of friendly forces or by misdirecting the enemy in some other advantageous manner. Cunning and faking may be the only hopeful strategies when friendly forces are actually understrength. An inverse relationship is usually found between the amount of deception employed and the strength of one's forces because less faking is needed when a group is strong. Overall, deception is cheap in terms of labor and capital.

Mao Tse-Tung, probably the worst mass murderer in human history, accounted for at least 38 million deaths from 1923 to 1976 (Rummel, 1991, 1994). Mao provided a model of deception fused with the acceptability of killing for taking control of a nation. Statements attributed to Mao (in Griffith, 1961) include: "Uproar in the East, strike in the West" and "Political power comes out of the barrel of a gun." Griffith, a retired U.S. Marine Corps Brigadier General, explained why Mao's ideas on deception and killing have become standard tactical doctrine for most nonconventional fighting forces in the world (Griffith, 1961, p. 26):

"Here we find expressed the all-important principles of distraction on the one hand and concentration on the other; to fix the enemy's attention and to strike where and when he least anticipates the blow. Guerrillas are masters of the arts of simulation and dissimulation; they create pretenses and simultaneously disguise or conceal their true

semblance. Their tactical concepts, dynamic and flexible, are not cut to any particular pattern. But Mao's first law of war, to preserve oneself and destroy the enemy, is always governing."

The mass media may distort by using narratives to interpret violence and thus help set norms about legitimate vs. illegitimate violence. As such, the media deserve special comment because we tend to believe what it tells us. Classically, the media are seen as attempting to link macro-violence and social structure to the micro-level of individual interpretation, conscience, and judgment (Durkheim, 1950). Master narratives define certain media-portrayed historical sequences of violence as tragic, heroic, exhausting, or simply mundane (Frye, 1957). These narratives change valence over time and history. For example, the infanticide of the Greeks and the genocidal homicide of Native Americans by the U.S. military are now held to be morally corrupt, whereas they were at one time regarded positively.

Currently, the master narrative ranges along a continuum of self-interest vs. altruism. At one end, lethal violence is perpetrated in self-defense or for selfish reasons; at the other, it is perpetrated for the good of the other, the racial or ethnic group, or even the world. Smith (1997) noted that, at all points of the continuum, violence is viewed as legitimate when it is deemed necessary and as a resort for those with global motivations, such as the protection of society. The current master narrative holds that fighting against an "evil other" justifies the legitimate use of violence. "Good" violence requires "bad" violence as a stimulus toward which to react.

Smith (1997) noted two events in which master narratives were formed by the public and then changed by the media and, along with it, public opinion. The first is the case of Bernhard Goetz who, on December 22, 1984, in a Manhattan subway, shot four black youths with his .38-caliber handgun. During the first few weeks following the incident, Goetz's behavior was viewed as highly legitimate because the state had failed to uphold its obligation to protect its citizens from violent group predators in the subways. At that time, national surveys indicated that the majority of Americans approved of Goetz's actions. Numerous callers encouraged him to run for mayor. On January 25, 1985, a grand jury decided not to indict him. Later, when it was revealed that Goetz had shot some of his alleged assailants in the back with "dum-dum" bullets (and, by his own account, bent over one wounded man and shot him again, saying, "You seem to be doing all right; here's another one"), no longer did his behavior seem coerced. Hence, the master narrative changed. Six weeks after the first grand jury's decision, a second grand jury indicted Goetz on several charges, including attempted murder.

Smith's (1997) second example was President Bush and the Gulf War. The initial prevailing narrative portrayed by the media (to which many hold) was that the war was a titanic struggle between good and evil. It was revealed that Saddam Hussein, as a youth of 22, had assassinated President Adul-Karem Kassim. When Hussein took power, he had almost two dozen of his rivals executed. He invaded innocent, nonbelligerent Kuwait in August 1990, then proceeded to rape and plunder the country. All the while, according to the master narrative, Hussein, who had developed a chemical arsenal and other doomsday machines, was prepared for total war.

The master narrative began to suffer when it was revealed that the U.S.'s true interest was economic — protection of our oil supply — and that the U.S. had ignored (or started) dozens of other wars around the globe involving equivalent or worse suffering and death. Meanwhile, then-President Bush proclaimed a vision of a "New World Order" which frightened many Americans in its ramifications for even more control by the U.S. government, while at the same time having a domestic policy that made him appear weak and foolish. It was revealed that prior to the invasion of Kuwait, April Glaspie, U.S. Ambassador to Iraq, had conveyed a message to Saddam Hussein (eventually determined to stem from

State Department superiors), that the U.S. had "no opinion on Arab-Arab conflicts." Once we knew that Hussein's invasion was imminent, but before it was launched, Bush issued no warning to enable the potential aggressors to retreat. The U.S. bombing of an Iraqi bomb shelter, which killed many civilians, was initially denied and then distorted by the U.S. military. This action failed to observe the distinction between using weapons for purely military objectives and those likely to involve civilian casualties. In the end, however, the master narrative survived, even after the U.S. failed to help the Kurds in Northern Iraq, who had supported our position and then were left vulnerable. The media were strongly instrumental in favorably contrasting President Bush with Hussein in order to legitimize the violence.

A decision rule has been proposed by several commentators from the current dialectics of state and civil society as portrayed by the media (Smith, 1997; Turpin and Kurtz, 1997). In order to legitimize violence, three criteria must be met; otherwise, the violence is not legitimate:

1. The violence must be the least harmful possible, and be expressed only when no other options are available.
2. The violence must be expressed by a "good", "heroic", "patriotic", or otherwise positive person or group against an "evil" other.
3. The violence must be motivated by selfless and universal reasons.

Virtually every organization engaging in violence or exploitation of others uses deception because it takes so little effort, increases the chance of success, and lowers the risk of discovery. Deception was used by government workers and physicians in the human radiation and biological/chemical experiments and is used by the media, through its overreliance on master narratives; by the police and other investigative agencies; and by organized crime, violent cults, and youth gangs and hate groups. Deception is truly a universal phenomenon.

The dangers of deception greatly offset its advantages. One danger is self-deception — believing and acting on one's own distortions. Typically, members of violent organizations display unjustified arrogance after a few initial successes, although deception never lasts indefinitely. Human experience reveals innumerable examples of the deceived party recovering and eventually gaining the upper hand. The deceived party tends to improve its deception-detecting skills and reacts to the perceived enemy with more determination. After being duped and wronged, revenge is sought as well as victory.

Other dangers regarding deception are abundant. As evaluators, the more skeptical we are of information, the more we tend to rely on preconceptions which may or may not be accurate in particular cases. Most members of a violent organization are very reluctant to change their values because those group values have been rewarded and because, as dissidents, they would be seen as traitors. Thus, they may be poor sources of information for the purpose of obtaining ground truth about an event. Police often believe that an interrogated suspect perpetrated a crime — for example, because the cost of wrongly thinking that a suspect is innocent runs counter to the primary purpose of law enforcement. Conversely, once a source is seen as credible, it is more difficult for evaluators to disregard the data, even though the person may deceive and distort, as happens with double agents and informers.

In sum, deception occurs during every stage of a violent sequence and should be accounted for in order for effective intervention to take place (Hall, 1996; Hall and Pritchard, 1996). We have to know what to treat. We may never uncover all the deception operative within a violent group, but we should be aware of the group's style of faking. As discussed and illustrated, deception consists of variations of faking good and faking bad styles. It is generally viewed favorably by those who employ it as it tends to set the victim up for the violent event and results in the avoidance of negative sanctions, at least in the short run. In general, ground truth may be established and, when stripped of deception or at least knowledge of faking styles, often leads to intervention and eventual reduction of violence. Uncovering ground truth will be resisted by perpetrators and by those with a vested interest in concealing the truth to maintain power and control and may even be hazardous for the deception detector. Whistle-blowers, investigative journalists, attorneys, and others who uncover falsehoods are often subject to censure or worse by the exposed collective entity in its effort to protect itself.

The decision process to determine where the faking has occurred is the first strategy for uncovering deception. Figure 1.6 presents a decision process for deception that involves distinguishing non-deliberate from deliberate distortion. The goal is to delineate which faking style is being used by the deceiver at any particular time. Mixed and fluctuating styles, as well as attempts to invalidate the evaluation process (e.g., walking out of a nuclear disarmament meeting, refusing to respond when interrogated), emerge as the most common variations of faking good and faking bad. Critically, the evaluator must understand that deception can and does occur both during the lethal violence sequence and later at the point of evaluation. Detecting deception needs to cover both temporal periods.

Principle 5: History, Opportunity, and Triggers to Violence, Operating in Concert Against Inhibitions, Are the Principle Contributors to Violence

Implied Interventions: Inhibitions acting to reduce the incentive to behave violently should be developed and implemented.

Consider the following formula for expressing violence (V) as a function of history (H), opportunity (O), and triggers (T) minus the influence of inhibitions (I) (Hall, 1987):

$$V = f(H + O + T - I)$$

Except in most unusual circumstances, the classic literature and clinical/forensic experience clearly show that violence does not occur without historical precedent. The most influential historical factors associated with violence include multiple acts of serious violence by the individual or group (Petersilia et al., 1977; Wolfgang, 1977, 1978), lethal or potentially lethal violence (Steadman and Cocozza, 1974), recent violence (Michigan Corrections Dept., 1978), and a belief that violence is necessary to solve the problem at hand (Blumenthal, 1976). A potent historical factor is violence followed by social reward rather than punishment (Webster et al., 1979). Lack of accountability for violence by itself tends to increase its frequency because no aversive consequences have been experienced (Monahan, 1981). In Chapter 4, Eme convincingly shows that these historical precedents extend to the temperament traits of the neonate and young child and may serve as possible genetic contributions to later violence.

In violent groups and institutions, and in virtually all the collective entities discussed in this book, the individual member with no history of violence gradually incorporates the violent history of that entity as part of the member's personality, self-esteem, and identity. Because history is the best predictor of violent behavior, investigators should inquire about a group's or institution's history of violence over time. Unless fundamentally changed, violent organizations tend to repeat their histories, given the availability of weapons and victims.

Opportunity factors such as victim availability, victim proximity, and possession of weapons make violence possible and can increase its effects (Bandura, 1973; Berkowitz and LePage, 1967; Monahan, 1981). Richardson (1960), for example, found that wars are more likely to be waged against contiguous neighbors. Almost always, organized crime hits involving firearms are against victims in the geographical proximity of the perpetrators.

Sociopathic individuals, solo perpetrators against the government, and members of violent groups and

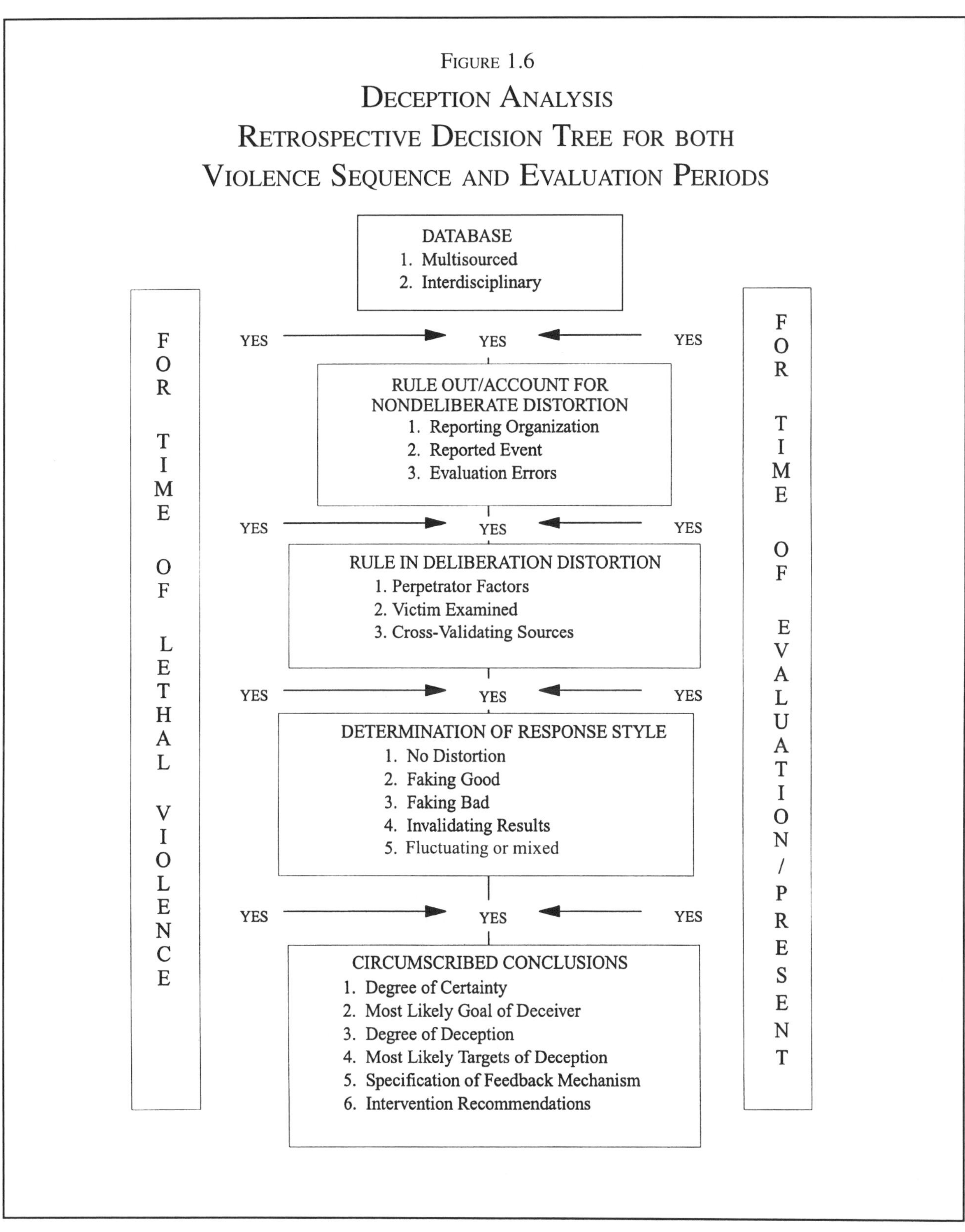
FIGURE 1.6
DECEPTION ANALYSIS
RETROSPECTIVE DECISION TREE FOR BOTH
VIOLENCE SEQUENCE AND EVALUATION PERIODS
DATABASE
1. Multisourced
2. Interdisciplinary
FOR TIME OF LETHAL VIOLENCE
FOR TIME OF EVALUATION/PRESENT
YES
YES
YES
RULE OUT/ACCOUNT FOR NONDELIBERATE DISTORTION
1. Reporting Organization
2. Reported Event
3. Evaluation Errors
YES
YES
YES
RULE IN DELIBERATION DISTORTION
1. Perpetrator Factors
2. Victim Examined
3. Cross-Validating Sources
YES
YES
YES
DETERMINATION OF RESPONSE STYLE
1. No Distortion
2. Faking Good
3. Faking Bad
4. Invalidating Results
5. Fluctuating or mixed
YES
YES
YES
CIRCUMSCRIBED CONCLUSIONS
1. Degree of Certainty
2. Most Likely Goal of Deceiver
3. Degree of Deception
4. Most Likely Targets of Deception
5. Specification of Feedback Mechanism
6. Intervention Recommendations

institutions generally set violence into motion by themselves. The triggering stimuli are internal decisions to aggress should the opportunity arise and the costs are not seen as prohibitive. Entitles such as organized crime, the CIA, hate groups, and gangs do not need external triggers to aggress; they are motivated by policy or internal values governing how violence is to be executed, their own violent history, expected rewards following the violence, and the availability of victims.

Inhibitory stimuli include all conditions associated with reduced probability of violence. For both individual and collective violence, the best inhibitor is an absence of historical violence. Momentary inhibitors, such as the presence of a police officer at the elbow of an individual contemplating robbing a bank or the fear of nuclear retaliation should a preemptive strike be launched, are poor inhibitors over the long run because the motivating force behind the violence is held in check only by a temporary set of environmental circumstances that does not change the perpetrator's underlying belief in the acceptability, if not desirability, of the violent response in order to achieve control and power. Even the ultimate aversive consequence of violence — death — inhibits a wide range of aggressive behaviors only so long as punishment is perceived as quick and certain.

The violence prediction decision tree can be applied to data collected on collective entities in order to frame critical questions for projections of aggression (see Figure 1.7). Once it is determined that adequate knowledge is available on a violent group or institution, that information should be scrutinized for non-deliberate and deliberate distortion and deception in order to complete a deception analysis. An adequate database and analysis are basic to the retrospective decision process.

All collective entities should be examined to estimate the extent and type of previous violence perpetrated on other organizations or individuals. If a history of violence is absent, it is extremely likely that the organization will be nonviolent. Never predict violence in the absence of past violence unless individuals in the perpetrator organization have, outside their organizational roles, acted violently. All of the collective entities discussed in this book have a history of violence.

Next, opportunity variables that make possible or expand the nature of violence should be examined, such as superior weaponry or technological breakthrough. The American Indians were defeated by superior weapons and by new diseases to which they had no resistance (in some cases, deliberately unleashed diseases; Hall, 1996). The Germans in World War II were logistically inferior to the allies and fought on two fronts and thereby lost their final push for victory. The Japanese finally surrendered after the second atomic bomb was dropped on Hiroshima.

The next step in the decision process is to determine triggering stimuli — typically short-term in duration and intense in import — which set violence into motion. The killing of a gang member may trigger revenge by the victim group. As stated earlier, some individuals or groups do not require an external trigger in order to aggress, especially in cases of carefully thought out violence, as opposed to impulsive reactions to another group's aggression.

The last step in the retrospective decision process is to present replicable conclusions and outcome measures of the prediction such as body counts or severity of wounds inflicted. The evaluator of collective violence is strongly advised to specify the temporal boundaries of the prediction, as failure to do so implies an indeterminate prediction for which the predictor may be held accountable.

Principle 6: Violence Is Always a Choice After Costs Are Weighted and Nonviolent Options Are Rejected

Implied interventions: The decision path of organizations that lead to violence should be articulated before intervening.

FIGURE 1.7
DANGEROUSNESS PREDICTION DECISION TREE FOR COLLECTIVITIES

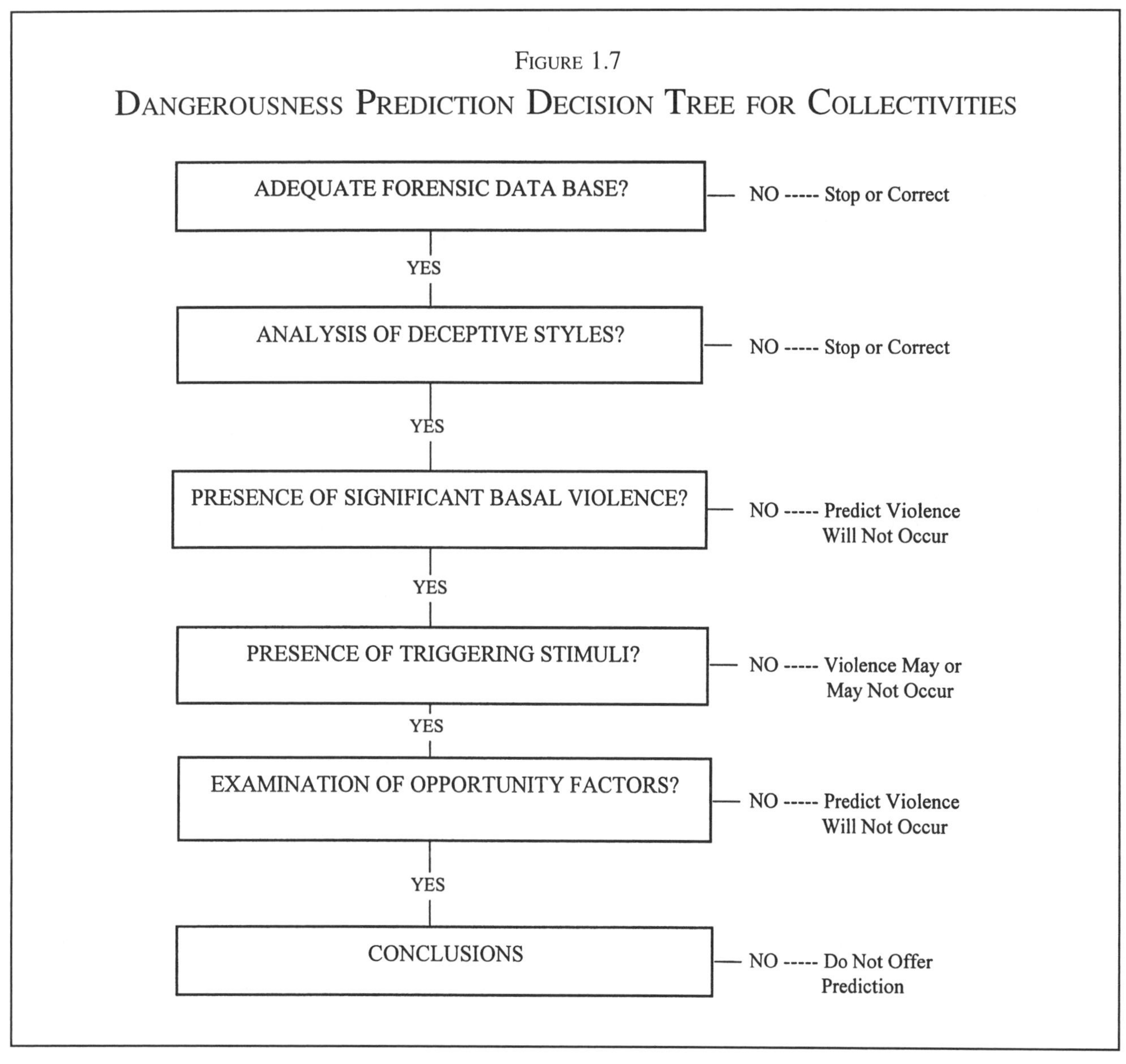

This principle focuses on key cognitive events during the violence sequence. Violence never occurs by accident. Whether "impulsive" or meticulously planned, the decision to aggress is based on a belief of success or pay off after other alternatives are considered and rejected. Even the degree of violence shown is optional, thus showing that a further choice is made. In hate crimes, members of youth groups and mobs often state that they are willing to inflict only a certain amount of harm (e.g., wounding but not killing opponents). In war, aggressors may elect to kill combatants but not non-combatants. Syndicated crime families kill some but not all of their opposition. All violence is modulated to some degree, with an eventual decision to stop. Even global wars are limited, with an eventual decision to stop.

Seven stages leading to genocide were posited earlier from knowledge of this type of mass killing for the last millennium (Charny and Rapaport, 1981). In the first and second stages, conditions conducive to genocide occur, including the formation of genocidal fantasy and precipitating crises that set the process into motion in Stages 3 and 4. A clear intent to kill members of a target group is expressed by the mobilization of means to genocide in Stage 5. A choice is made at this time, prior to the institutionalization and execution of genocide in Stages 6 and 7.

As a choice, violence is subject to behavioral control. Typically, only a few members of any organization decide to initiate the violence sequence (Baron, 1977; Hall, 1996: Kull, 1988). Usually, the leader or a small group within the organization decides whether or not to commence violence, how to modulate it as it is expressed, and when to stop.

Taking personal responsibility for violence is possible only after perpetrators acknowledge making a deliberate choice to inflict violence. One must acknowledge the choice to kill in order to move on to the next step, namely changing attitudes, beliefs, and behavior.

Principle 7: Successful Violence Is Frequently Followed by Self-Reinforcing Thoughts, Feelings, and Behaviors

Implied interventions: Care should be taken to ensure that violence is neither successful nor reinforced socially.

Repeatedly violent individuals are small in number but account for the vast majority of violent acts (e.g., school bullies, robbers, infantry commanders; Bandura, 1973; Monahan, 1981, 1988, 1992; Wolfgang, 1958, 1977). After many experiences of assimilation and recovery, one's violent behavior becomes ego syntonic, positively regarded, and self-reinforced. Such repeatedly violent individuals see a wide range of victim behaviors as justifying violence. Violent acts are habit forming and addicting as they satisfy both expected and unexpected needs.

Although reported as individual crimes, most deadly violence by groups and institutions does not result in arrest, conviction, or other negative sanctions by the criminal justice system. Murder has a clearance ("get away with") rate of between 70 and 80% in this country; the likely perpetrator is not even identified or brought into custody in 20 to 30% of homicides. A typical murderer has less than an even chance of being apprehended (Hall, 1996). In the author's experience, it is the careless, non-organized killers who are convicted and imprisoned. Group perpetrators who are acting under direction from their leaders are typically less careless and better organized.

Members of organizations who kill are rarely convicted of murder, whether they are police officers who unjustly use deadly force (see Chapter 13), organized crime hit men (Maas, 1997), CIA operatives (see Appendix B), FBI snipers or assault team members (Kopel and Blackman, 1997), or combat infantry leaders (Richardson, 1980). The reality is that most perpetrators of institutional violence may kill with impunity over extended periods of time. Most genocide occurs under the umbrella of war (Levi, 1958; Rummel, 1990, 1991, 1994), with only a small fraction of the perpetrators brought to justice.

To be maximally effective, traditional beliefs hold that punishments applied for violence should be immediate and intense and allow no means of escape. Otherwise, the perpetrators internalize the self-reward associated with violence; witnesses die, forget, or otherwise become unavailable; and the wrongdoers suffer no adverse consequences. According to these traditional beliefs, the bully in the schoolyard who attacks should be beaten senseless at the first opportunity; group perpetrators should be identified quickly, arrested, and convicted for maximum effect; even better, we should execute them.

Traditional interventions for members of perpetrator groups during this tertiary intervention stage include the following, alone or in combination:

1. Executing leaders and key followers
2. Dissolving the perpetrator group by coercive methods
3. Using invasive physical procedures (e.g., chemical approaches, psychosurgery) and noxious psychological interventions such as aversive stimulation
4. Instituting work rehabilitation and forced labor
5. Using structured intervention (hospitalization, imprisonment)
6. Imposing other punishments and sanctions on members of violent groups and families

The next principle shows why these traditional strategies are exactly the wrong reactions.

Principle 8: Interventions that Respond Violently to Violent Events Lead to Self-Generating Violent Interlocks

Implied interventions: Violence interlocks are initially broken by unilateral, rather than bilateral, nonviolent actions.

Violence begets violence whether the revenge is immediate or delayed for decades (as has occurred in the former Yugoslavia by the Serbs against the Croatians and Muslims). Both the Occidental and Oriental worlds appear to believe in the Biblical "eye for an eye and a tooth for a tooth." In order to right the violence balance, the thinking goes, the perpetrator must be punished for misdeeds. Given this attitude, we should expect retaliation from victim groups and institutions when they are attacked. Then the perpetrator group, now victimized itself, plots its revenge and attacks when given the opportunity. This is why the traditional interventions implied by Principle 7 are risky. Even if a victim group is killed off completely, relatives, friends, or members of similar groups may perpetuate the cycle when the power shifts in their favor. Violent interlocks tend to persist for extended periods, even over generations. The Irish-British tit-for-tat in Northern Ireland has persisted for many decades. Victims may turn into perpetrators of violence, perpetrators may turn into victims of PTSD, and perpetrators may become worse, immediately or years later. Ultimately, the whole world suffers.

The Cuban missile crisis of October 1962, which brought us to the edge of oblivion, is an example of a violence interlock. The U.S. built and used nuclear bombs, the secret formula for which was stolen by the U.S.S.R. in the 1950s. The Communists then infiltrated and conducted covert operations in Latin and South America, and the U.S. responded in kind to counter the threat. The Bay of Pigs incident, a bungled CIA operation, then motivated Castro to request assistance and protection from the U.S.S.R. The U.S. responded with a threat of military action once it discovered that missiles had been placed in Cuba. Then-President Kennedy made a covert deal with the Soviets for the U.S. to remove NATO missiles from Turkey if the U.S.S.R. would remove its missiles in Cuba. For the next three decades, the U.S.S.R. and Cuba continued the interlock by continuing threatening and violent actions (see Figure 1.8).

Timothy McVeigh sought revenge on the federal government for its actions in Waco, TX, with the 1995 bombing of the Murrah Federal Building in Oklahoma City close to 2 years after the Waco incident. This author predicts that his execution will generate revenge by domestic terrorist groups, which will thereby provide a rationale for more violent suppression by the government (see Figure 1.9). On and on the cycle goes.

History has shown that interlocks are broken by one party — the current perpetrator group or, more usually, the victim group — withdrawing from the conflict and addressing the violence in a nonviolent manner. Leaving the country, for example, as Jews escaped Germany before World War II, may be the only way to survive. But assuming that one's ethnic, religious, or other identity is not immediate grounds for execution, victim groups may remain in the country and assertively attempt to change the aversive conditions, as when Gandhi changed Africa forever

FIGURE 1.8

VIOLENCE INTERLOCKS: CUBAN MISSILE CRISIS

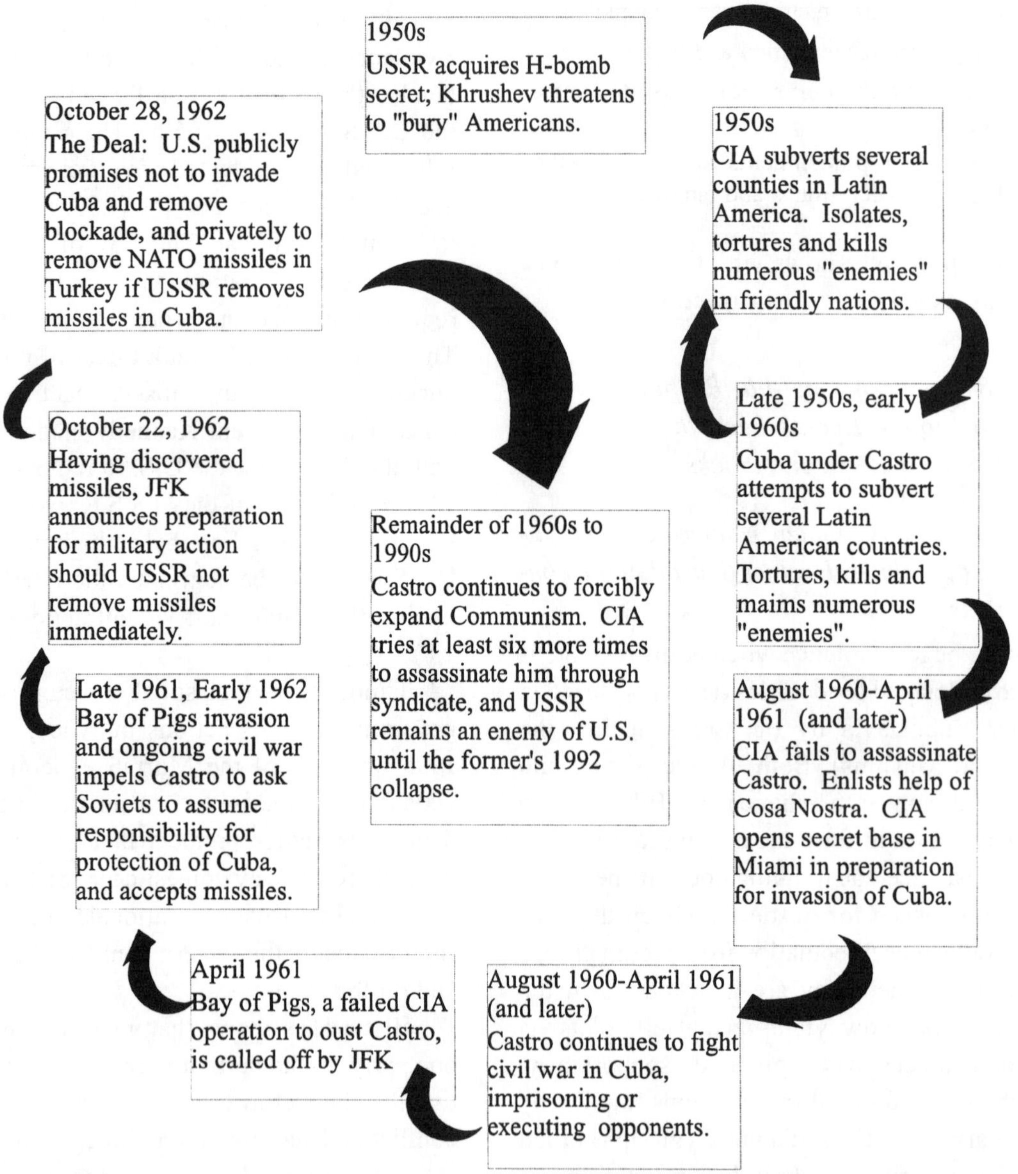

1950s
USSR acquires H-bomb secret; Khrushev threatens to "bury" Americans.

1950s
CIA subverts several counties in Latin America. Isolates, tortures and kills numerous "enemies" in friendly nations.

Late 1950s, early 1960s
Cuba under Castro attempts to subvert several Latin American countries. Tortures, kills and maims numerous "enemies".

August 1960-April 1961 (and later)
CIA fails to assassinate Castro. Enlists help of Cosa Nostra. CIA opens secret base in Miami in preparation for invasion of Cuba.

August 1960-April 1961 (and later)
Castro continues to fight civil war in Cuba, imprisoning or executing opponents.

April 1961
Bay of Pigs, a failed CIA operation to oust Castro, is called off by JFK

Late 1961, Early 1962
Bay of Pigs invasion and ongoing civil war impels Castro to ask Soviets to assume responsibility for protection of Cuba, and accepts missiles.

October 22, 1962
Having discovered missiles, JFK announces preparation for military action should USSR not remove missiles immediately.

October 28, 1962
The Deal: U.S. publicly promises not to invade Cuba and remove blockade, and privately to remove NATO missiles in Turkey if USSR removes missiles in Cuba.

Remainder of 1960s to 1990s
Castro continues to forcibly expand Communism. CIA tries at least six more times to assassinate him through syndicate, and USSR remains an enemy of U.S. until the former's 1992 collapse.

and freed India from British control with his non-violent movement. Martin Luther King, Jr., used may of the same methods in the successful civil rights movement in this country. Throughout the world, non-violent movements have broken violent interlocks and changed the course of history.

In sum, persistent, organized, and respectful non-violent interventions may break violence interlocks

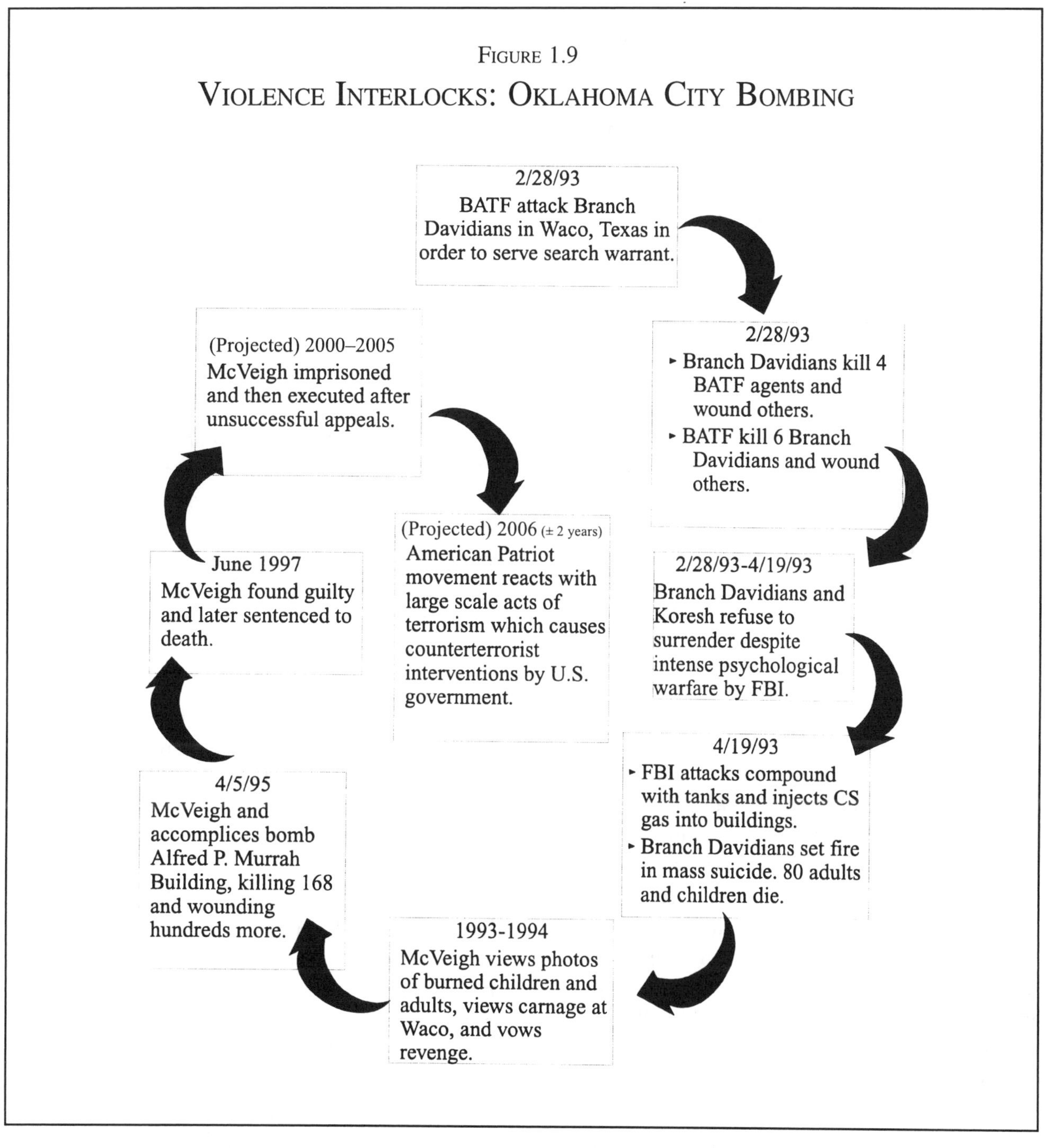

and lead to self-generating win-win cycles. In Chapter 19, Twemlow and Sacco discuss ways to change violent communities by teaching individuals to assume and apply the peacekeeper role in positive, concrete ways. True reduction of violence and redirection of our energies into peaceful pursuits require that intervention be directed at several cycles of violence for a particular entity, perhaps for as long as several years to several generations. In Chapter 18, Buck provides a Gandhian model of non-violence which embraces differences and respect for the adversary, even to the point of informing that party of all intended actions. This model goes beyond the conflict-competition-violence cycle so prevalent in Western society. Based on a wealth of previous positive outcomes, Buck concludes that cooperation yields success as long as one continues to maintain a cooperative stance.

Principle 9: Micro-Violence and Macro-Violence Are Functionally Similar and Tend To Potentiate Each Other

Implied Interventions: Expect and plan for micro- and macro-changes affecting each other.

This principle suggests that we are all in this violent arena together. We are all affected when war occurs in a foreign country or when a drunkard beats his wife in our neighborhood. All violence serves to wrest or maintain control and serves to demean us. This principle suggests that micro-violence on an individual level (e.g., felony-murder, solo assassination) and macro-violence on a collective level (e.g., wars, organized crime hits) are not functionally different. Both flow through the violence sequence which eventually involves the death of a person: a decision to kill emerges (the motivation stemming from one of the "big four" since the dawn of civilization — greed, lust, revenge, or fear), plans are formulated, victim availability is ensured, and the killing is accomplished. Perpetrators then typically try to escape the aversive consequences of killing by covering their tracks, staging, or some other form of deception which further complicates the violence sequence. Eventually, everyone is affected because this is a mutually dependent, highly interactive world.

Similar behavioral and functional patterns emerge across micro- and macro-levels of violence. War is murder writ large (Richardson, 1960; Rummel, 1994; Sagan, 1980), and homicide rates within countries are influenced in a positive direction by war (Archer and Gardner, 1984). Even though individuals within collective entities may not have a history of violence before their first kill, they soon incorporate the values and history of the violent group or institution as their own. Through a variety of means and incentives, from military boot camp to cash payments, collective entities ensure a rapid and pervasive incorporation of the acceptability of killing.

Richardson's 1960 mathematical treatment of 300 wars and conflicts from 1835 to 1949, presented in his classic *Statistics of Deadly Quarrels*, demonstrated a trend toward killing ever-increasing numbers of people over the decades. He presented a compelling but little cited data-based argument that group influences tend to foster individual violence and vice versa. He first studied banditry in Manchuria in 1835, analyzing the 4784 raids carried out that year by hundreds of bandit groups. He then analyzed a study of 1313 gangs in Chicago in the 1920s, involving the killing of from one to three people at a time. A between- and within-groups comparison showed that, aside from a general tendency toward aggregation for aggression (i.e., violence tended to be a group phenomenon in the gangs he studied), the smaller incidents were much more frequent. Killings by groups resembled a battle and showed other similarities to war. The mean slopes, plotted over time as a function of frequency, showed a remarkable similarity with larger, fatal quarrels such as war. This implies that the two types of fatal quarrels (by large and small collective enterprises) represent two ends of the same continuum having as a common denominator an acceptability for killing. Richardson concluded that there is no scientific reason for terminating a list of fatal quarrels at any magnitude above zero.

In another data analysis of the killing and acceptability continuum, Richardson found that insurrection, revolts, and riots are perpetrated by small groups of individuals. Large groups consisting of government individuals engaging in collective violence, such as war or genocide, are unlikely to be punished and, in fact, are often praised by the system in which they operate. Richardson observed that, ironically, it is considered evil to kill one person but glorious to kill 10,000. "Does mere multiplicity excuse?" he asked in observing that, across many cultures, murders by individuals often result in execution while group murderers, whether in a mob or infantry platoon, almost always escape the death penalty for killing.

Archer and Gartner (1984) found that war tends to legitimize the general use of lethal violence in domestic society. In their rigorous and often cited cross-national study of homicide, they determined that wars increase the rate of violence in both combatant and non-combatant groups. Archer and Gartner (1984) noted that arrests for homicide in the U.S. increased dramatically during the 10-year period of the Vietnam War, including homicide arrests for those over the age of 45 (who were not likely to be Vietnam veterans). They argued convincingly that war both models and legitimizes lethal violence whether or not the eventual perpetrator even participated in that collective aggression.

What are the implications of this principle for intervention? First, we must repeatedly intervene at both micro- and macro-levels of lethal violence. If war, genocide, and gang violence increase individual violence, with the opposite being true as well, then we must treat both the individual and collective aspects of violence. We must recognize that tolerating unbridled aggression by gangs, the CIA, or hate groups increases the chance of both war and domestic violence by creating a mindset that accepts and legitimizes violence, and by creating grievances that motivate retaliation. The solution, of course, involves individual as well as systems interventions on many levels across the entire temporal span of violence.

Principle 10: Reframing and Redirecting Our Violent Mindsets Require Transcending Violent Interlocks to Cycles of Affection and Gratitude

Implied interventions: Training in altruism and the advocacy of others, even of our perceived adversaries, should start in childhood and proceed through the lifetime of each individual.

Considering all the preceding principles and implied interventions, it is not sufficient to describe, measure, apply, and change violence intervention methods and to eliminate violence in various collectivities. Violent events are not isolated or static. Violence interlocks connect to other violence interlocks in a pervasive pattern of progressively negative outcomes. In a general sense, we must reframe and redirect our violent energies in ways that will not only prevent violence but that will ensure a positive, enduring reciprocity of outcomes. In other words, we need to attend to the process of nonviolent behaviors leading to win-win outcomes, rather than focus exclusively on the content of violence and the need for revenge and control.

In abusive marital relationships, the clinician's job is only half done when the battering stops. Long-lasting and loving relationships require learning new problem-solving methods to earn respect and to enhance the other person. War, like marriage, does not end violence unless the vanquished are supported and then encouraged to act nonviolently toward the rest of the world. To achieve these outcomes, we must try to transcend our own self-gain or national interests to achieve the long-term positive reciprocal benefit for all parties.

Kohlberg's (1963, 1967) moral development theory has generated hundreds of empirical studies in the last three decades (Corsini and Auerbach, 1996). His highest form of morality considers not only the actual laws and rules of society and various organizations, including those reflecting self-gain and self-interest, but also self-chosen standards of justice and respect for human dignity. Moral individuals dedicate themselves to redirecting the negativity in violent group and individual behavior so as to avoid condemnation by their own consciences.

According to Kohlberg's (1963, 1967) analysis, there are six stages of moral development. Most of the violent groups and institutions discussed in this chapter operate from Stage 1 (deferring to the power of authority figures to avoid trouble and punishment) or Stage 2 (seeking to satisfy their own needs by behaving in ways that yield rewards and the return of favors). Some collectivities apparently make decisions based on ensuring approval from others (Stage 3) or out of a sense of duty (Stage 4). None of the violent entities — private or government — think in terms of the rights of others or even conform to the laws and standards established by the majority (Stage 5). They do not behave in ways that would be respected by an impartial observer (Stage 6), opting instead for violent acts covered by deception and distortion.

Kohlberg found entities separated by two or more stages to be unable to communicate using the same assumptions. It is thus no wonder that Stage 6 thinking and values would threaten most violent entities.

The stage-by-stage development is universal. Kohlberg (1963, 1967) determined that moral development takes place in similar fashion in Mexico and Taiwan, and other studies have generalized this finding to dozens of other countries (Corsini and Auerbach, 1996), thus arguing compellingly for training children early in morality, as discussed in detail by several contributors to this book.

Conclusions

This chapter presents and analyzes a sampling of collective violence and ten applied principles with implied interventions. Most, if not all, forms of group and institutional violence in this country, and indeed the world, are supported by a significant portion of the populace and by leaders and power groups within the government. All perpetrators have a base of power, an ideology, targeted victims, self-reinforcement for violence, and particular characteristics that differentiate them from other virulent perpetrators of group violence.

Whether private or governmental, without exception, all violent groups and institutions are trapped in violent interlocks with victims or other collective entities. This is an unavoidable aspect of violence. Responses to a real or imagined grievance and a counter-response for revenge or to gain power result in further violence from the now-wronged original perpetrator entity.

To break violent interlocks, this chapter and all those which follow hold to the fundamental proposition that durable change equals nonviolent change. This nonviolent stance does not preclude self-defense during the course of violence, legal remedies seeking compensation for the damage resulting from the violence, exposure of the perpetrator groups, or other attempts to obtain compensation or redress legitimately. Eventual forgiveness, respect for the adversary, persistence, and an unwillingness to compromise the underlying equalitarian position of the non-violent movement characterize those interventions which succeed and endure over time.

Annotated Bibliography

1. Archer, D. and Garner, R. (1984) *Violence and Crime in Cross-National Perspective*. New Haven, CT: Yale University Press. This book provides a cross-national, quantitative comparison of violence and relates the findings to such critical questions as (a) Does the level of domestic violence in a society increase after that nation has participated in a war? (For most nations, the answer is a strong "yes".) (b) Does the death penalty deter violence and crime? (Almost universally, the answer is "no"; in fact, the death

penalty may even indirectly increase violence.) (c) Do large cities have unusually high homicide rates? (The answer depends on the size of the city relative to the overall homicide rate of the country.)

2. Bandura, A. (1973) *Aggression: A Social Learning Analysis.* Englewood Cliffs, NJ: Prentice Hall. This classic, and still very relevant, textbook probes the origins of aggression, instigators of aggression, and maintaining conditions from a social learning perspective. Modification and control of violence are discussed in terms of modeling principles, differential reinforcement, institutional remedial systems, and changes in social systems. A major theory of aggression and violence is presented.

3. Graham H.D. and Gurr, T.R., Eds. (1969) *The History of Violence in America. Historical and Comparative Perspectives.* New York: Frederick A. Praeger. This edited work stemmed from a report submitted to the National Commission on the Causes and Prevention of Violence. Presented at a time when this country was in the midst of both Vietnam and domestic turmoil, this book outlines the history of violence in America in splendid detail. Findings suggest that the conflict in the 1960s was not unique, but represented a shift in attitude on the part of Americans toward each other and their society. The value of the book lies is the historical treatment of both individual and collective violence.

4. Rummel, R.J. (1994) *Death by Government.* New Brunswick: Transaction Publishers. In his fourth book on genocide and government mass murder (what the author calls "democide"), Rummel presents a historical overview on genocide and offers detailed tables for offender nations in this century. The primary conclusion that emerged was that the less freedom and control exercised at a grass roots level by the citizens, the more likely it is that genocide would occur. Rummel found that democratic societies tend to be nonviolent, a finding that also applies to previously totalitarian governments which turned democratic. War and genocide were found to be part of the same social process where power and control reign supreme.

5. Tedeschi, J. and Felson, R. (1994) *Violence, Aggression and Coercive Actions.* Washington, D.C.: American Psychological Association. In this well-documented book, a theory of coercive action (the preferred term for violence and aggression), focuses on social identity, power, influence, retributive justice, and other social psychological concepts. A social interactionist approach emerges that explores face-to-face confrontations and the intent of the violent perpetrator.

References

Albini, J. (1971) *The American Mafia: Genesis of a Legend.* New York: Appleton-Crofts.

American Psychological Association (1993) *Violence and Youth: Psychology's Response. Vol. I: Summary Report of the American Psychology Association Commission of Violence and Youth.* Washington, D.C.: American Psychological Association.

Anti-Defamation League (1994) *Hate Crime Laws: A Comprehensive Guide.* New York.

Archer, D. and Gartner, R. (1984) *Violence and Crime in Cross-National Perspective.* New Haven: Yale University Press.

Archer, J. (1988) *The Behavioral Biology of Aggression.* Cambridge, England: Press Syndicate of the University of Cambridge.

Archer, J. (1995) What can ethology offer the psychological study of human aggression? *Aggressive Behavior, 21*, 243–255.

Associated Press (1997) Black victims to get apology, *The Honolulu Advertiser*, May 2, p. A6.

Bacque, J. (1989) *Other Losses*. Toronto, Canada: Stoddart Publishing.

Bandura, A. (1973) *Aggression: A Social Learning Analysis*. Englewood Cliffs, NJ: Prentice Hall.

Bandura, A. (1977) *Social Learning Theory*. Englewood Cliffs, NJ: Prentice-Hall.

Bandura, A. (1983) Psychological mechanisms of aggression. In R.G. Geen and E.I. Donnerstein (Eds.), *Aggression: Theoretical and Empirical Reviews*, Vol. 1. pp. 1–40. San Diego, CA: Academic Press.

Bandura, A. (1986) *Social Foundations of Thought and Action: A Social Cognitive Theory*. Englewood Cliffs, NJ: Prentice Hall.

Barnaby, F. (1984) *Future Wars: Armed Conflict in the Next Decade*. United Kingdom: Multimedia Publications.

Baron, R.A. (1977) *Human Aggression*. New York: Plenum Press.

Baron, R.A. (1984) Reducing organizational conflict: an incompatible response approach. *Journal of Applied Psychology, 69*, 272–279.

Baron, R.A. and Richardson, D.R. (1994) *Human Aggression*, 2nd ed. New York: Plenum Press.

Barrett v. United States, 660 F.Supp. 1291 (E.D.N.Y. 1987).

Beardsley, T. (1995) Testing's toll. *Scientific American, 273*, 28.

Beirne, P. and Messerschmidt, J. (1995) *Criminology*, 2nd ed. Fort Worth, TX: Harcourt Brace College Publishers.

Bellis, D.J. (1981) *Heroin and Politicians: The Failure of Public Policy To Control Addiction in America*. Westport, CT: Greenwood.

Berkowitz, L. (1965) The concept of aggressive drive: some additional considerations. In L. Berkowitz (Ed.), *Advances in Experimental Psychology*, Vol. 2, pp. 301–329. New York: Academic Press.

Berkowitz, L. (1969) The frustration-aggression hypothesis revisited. In L. Berkowitz (Ed.), *Roots of Aggression*, pp. 1–28. New York: Atherton Press.

Berkowitz, L. (1984) Some effects of thoughts on anti- and prosocial influences of media events: a cognitive-neoassociation analysis. *Psychological Bulletin, 95*, 410–427.

Berkowitz, L. (1988) Frustrations, appraisals, and aversively stimulated aggression. *Aggressive Behavior, 14*, 3–11.

Berkowitz, L. and LePage, A. (1967) Weapons as aggression-eliciting stimuli. *Journal of Personality and Social Psychology, 7*, 202–207.

Bilton, M. and Sim, K. (1992) *Four Hours in My Lai*. New York: Penguin Books.

Blair, B., Feiveson, H., and Non Hippei, F. (1997) Taking nuclear weapons off hair-trigger alert. *Scientific American, 277*(5), 74–81.

Blight, J. and Lang, J. (1995) Burden of nuclear responsibility: reflections on the critical oral history of the Cuban missile crisis. *Peace and Conflict, 1*, 225–264.

Blumenthal, M. (1976) Violence in America: still viewed by many as a necessary tool for social order, social change. *Institute for Social Research, 4*, 2–23.

Bowlby, F. (1907) *TheLaw of Homicide*, 3rd ed. Rochester, NY: The Lawyer's Cooperative Publishing Company.

Branfman, F. (1978) South Vietnam's police and prison system: the U.S. connection. In H. Frazier (Ed.), *Uncloaking the CIA*, pp. 110–127. New York: Free Press.

Brooks, S. and Harford, T. (1992) Occupation and alcohol-related causes of death. *Drug and Alcohol Dependence, 29*, 245–251.

Buck, L.A. (1996) Beyond conflict and competition: diversity, cooperation, and life affirmation as alternatives to violence. In H.V. Hall (Ed.), *Lethal Violence 2000: A Sourcebook on Fatal Domestic, Acquaintance and Stranger Aggression,* pp. 589–611. Kamuela, HI: Pacific Institute for the Study of Conflict and Aggression.

Buckhout, R. (1980) Eyewitness identification and psychology in the courtroom. In G. Cooke (Ed.), *The Role of the Forensic Psychologist*, pp. 175–185. Springfield, IL: Charles C Thomas.

Buss, A.H. (1961) *The Psychology of Aggression*. New York: Wiley.

Cain, S. (1982) The psychodynamics of the presidential assassin and an examination of the theme/graphic variables of his threatening correspondence. *Forensic Science, 19*, 39–50.

Carl, C. (1996) Hell's Angels in Denmark, *U.S. News and World Report,* Dec. 23, *112*, 58.

Castro, J. (1988) The cash cleaners. *Time*, Oct. 24, 65–66.

Center for Democratic Renewal (1987) *They Don't All Wear White Sheets: A Chronology of Racist and Far-Right Violence — 1980–1986.* Atlanta, GA: Center for Democratic Renewal.

Chamblis, W. (1988) *On the Take: From Petty Crooks to Presidents*. Bloomington, IN: Indiana University Press.

Charny, I. (1982) Toward a genocide early warning system. In *How Can We Commit the Unthinkable? Genocide, the Human Cancer,* Boulder, CO: Westview Press, pp. 283–331.

Cheatwood, D. (1996) Interactional patterns in multiple-offender homicides. *Justice Quarterly, 13*, 108–127.

Chomsky, N. and Herman, E.S. (1977) The United States versus human rights in the Third World. *Monthly Review,* July-Aug., *29*, 22–45.

Comstock, D.G. (1989) *Violence Against Lesbians and Gay Men*. New York: Columbia University Press.

Cornell, D.G. (1993) Juvenile homicide: a growing national problem. *Behavioral Sciences and the Law, 11*, 389–396.

Craig, K.M. and Waldo, C.R. (1997) "So, what's a hate crime anyway?" Young adults' perceptions of hate crimes, victims, and perpetrators. *Law and Human Behavior, 20*(2), 113–123.

Curtis, L.A. (1974) Victim precipitation and violent crime. *Social Problems, 21*, 594–605.

Daly, M. and Wilson, M. (1988) *Homicide*. New York: Aldine de Gruyter.

Daniel, A.E. and Robins, A.J. (1985) Violent women. *Psychiatry in Family Practice*, September 1, 96–108.

de Becker, G. (1997a) *The Gift of Fear: Survival Signals that Protect Us From Violence*. New York: Little, Brown and Company.

de Becker, G. (1997b) *An Introduction to Threat Assessment and Management*. Studio City, CA: Gavin de Becker.

Diamond, J. (1997) Spies, critics, look back on CIA's 50 years. *West Hawaii Today*, September 14, p. 8A.

Dodge, K. (1997) Untitled. *Journal of Abnormal Psychology, 106*, 1–15.

Dollard, J., Doob, L., Miller, N., Mowrer, O.H., and Sears, R.R. (1939) *Frustration and Aggression*. New Haven, CT: Yale University Press.

Douglas, J. and Olshaker, M. (1996) *Unabomber: On the Trail of America's Most-Wanted Serial Killer*. New York: Pocket Books.

Elias, R. (1997) A culture of violent solutions. In J. Turpin and L. Kurtz (Eds.), *The Web of Violence: From Interpersonal to Global,* pp. 117–148, Chicago: University of Illinois Press.

Faden, R. (1996) *Final Report of the Advisory Committee on Human Radiation Experiments*. New York: Oxford University Press.

FC (1995) *The Unabomber Manifesto: Industrial Society and Its Future*. Berkeley, CA: Jolly Roger Press.

Farrington, D.P. (1994) Childhood, adolescent, and adult features of violent males. In L.R. Huesman (Ed.), *Aggressive Behavior: Current Perspectives*, pp. 215–240, New York: Plenum Press.

Federal Bureau of Investigation (1976) *Terror: The Crime of the Privileged: An Examination and Prognosis*. Quantico, VA: Special Operations and Research Unit, FBI Academy.

Finn, P. and McNeil, T. (1987) *The Response of the Criminal Justice System to Bias Crime: An Exploratory Review*. Contract report submitted to the National Institute of Justice, U.S. Department of Justice. Also available from ABT Associates, 55 Wheeler St., Cambridge, MA 02138-1168.

Foote, W.E. (1996) Victim-precipitated homicide. In H.V. Hall (Ed.), *Lethal Violence 2000: A Sourcebook on Fatal Domestic, Acquaintance and Stranger Aggression*, pp. 175–202, Kamuela, HI: Pacific Institute for the Study of Conflict and Aggression.

Geen, R.G. (1991) *Human Aggression*. Pacific Grove, CA: Brooks/Cole.

Goetting, A. (1989) Men who kill their mates: a profile. *Journal of Family Violence, 4,* 285–296.

Goldstein, R. (1974) Brain research and violent behavior. *Archives of Neurology, 30*, 1–18.

Greenberg, M. (1996) Mob psychology. In R. Corsini and A. Auerbach (Eds.), *Concise Encyclopedia of Psychology*, p. 573, New York: John Wiley & Sons.

Griffith, S. (1961) *Mao-Tse-Tung on Guerrilla Warfare*. New York: Praeger Publishers.

Hall, H.V. (1986) The forensic distortion analysis: a proposed decision tree and report format. *American Journal of Forensic Psychology, 4*, 31–59.

Hall, H.V. (1987) *Violence Prediction: Guidelines for the Forensic Practitioner*. Springfield, IL: Charles C Thomas.

Hall, H.V. (1990) Extreme emotion. *University of Hawaii Law Review, 12*, 39-82.

Hall, H.V., Ed. (1996) *Lethal Violence 2000: A Sourcebook of Fatal Domestic, Acquaintance, and Stranger Aggression*. Kamuela, HI: Pacific Institute for the Study of Conflict and Aggression.

Hall, H.V. and Sbordone, R.J. (1993) *Disorders of Executive Function: Civil and Criminal Law Applications*. Winter Park, FL: Paul M. Deutsch.

Hall, H.V. and Pritchard, D. (1996) *Detecting Malingering and Deception: The Forensic Distortion Analysis*. Winter Park, FL: GR Press.

Handel, M. (1977) The Yom Kippur War and the inevitability of surprise. *International Studies Quarterly, 21*, 461–502.

Handel, M. (1982) Intelligence and deception. *Journal of Strategic Studies, 5*, 133–154.

Harris, B. (1978) Assassins. In I.L. Kutash, S.B. Kutash, L.B. Schlesinger et al. (Eds.), *Violence: Perspective on Murder and Aggression*. San Francisco, CA: Jossey-Bass.

Herek, G.M. and Berrill, K.T., Eds. (1992) *Hate Crimes: Confronting Violence Against Lesbians and Gay Men*. Newbury Park: Sage.

Herrnstein, R.J. and Murray, C. (1994) *The Bell Curve: Intelligence and Class Structure in American Life*. New York: Simon & Schuster.

Hobbes, T. (1928) *Leviathan*. London: Dent.

Hoffman, M. (1960) Power assertion by the parent and its impact on the child. *Child Development, 31*, 129–143.

Hsieh, C. and Pugh, M. (1993) Poverty, income inequality, and violent crime: a meta-analysis of recent aggregate data studies. *Criminal Justice Review*, Autumn, 182–202.

Huesmann, L.R., Eron, L.D., Lefkowitz, M.M., and Walder, L.O. (1984) Stability of aggression over time and generations. *Developmental Psychology, 20*, 1120–1134.

Kessler, R. (1993) *The FBI*. New York: Simon & Schuster.

Knight-Rider Service (1997) Timothy McVeigh, May 6, p. A7.

Koch, T. (1996) *The Militia Battle Manual*. El Dorado, AR: Desert Publications.

Kohlberg, L. (1963) The development of children's orientation toward a moral order. 1. Sequence in the development of moral thought. *Vita Humana, 6*, 11–33.

Kohlberg, L. (1967) Moral and religious education and the public schools. In T. Sizer (Ed.), *Religion and Public Education*. Boston: Houghton Mifflin.

Kopel, D. and Blackman, P. (1997) *No More Wacos*. Amherst, NY: Prometheus Books.

Kull, S. (1988) *Minds at War: Nuclear Reality and the Inner Conflicts of Defense Policymakers*. New York: Basic Books.

Kutash, I.L., Kutash, S.B., Schlesinger, L.B. et al. (1978) *Violence: Perspective on Murder and Aggression*. San Francisco, CA: Jossey-Bass.

Laird v. Tatum, 408 U.S. 1 (1972)

Lester, D. (1977) The prediction of suicide and homicide rates cross-nationally by means of stepwise multiple regression. *Behavior Science Research, 1*, 61–69.

Levi, P. (1958) *Survival in Auschwitz*. New York: A Touchstone Book.

Levin, J. and McDevitt, J. (1993) *Hate Crimes: The Rising Tide of Bigotry and Bloodshed*. New York: Plenum Press.

Lifton, R. (1997) Doubling the Faustian bargain. In J. Turpin and L. Kurtz (Eds.), *The Web of Violence: From Interpersonal to Globa*, pp. 29–44, Chicago: University of Illinois Press.

Lorenz, K. (1966) *On Aggression*. New York: Harcourt, Brace and World.

Maas, P. (1997) *Underboss: Sammy the Bull Gravano's Life in the Mafia*. New York: Harper Collins.

MacDonald, A. (1978, 1980; written as W. Pierce) *The Turner Diaries*. Hillsboro, WV: National Vanguard Books.

MacDonald, J. (1968) *Homicidal Threats*. Springfield, IL: Charles C Thomas.

Mann, C.R. (1989) Getting even? Women who kill in domestic encounters. In S.L. Johann and F. Osanka (Eds.), *Representing Battered Women Who Kill*, pp. 8–26, Springfield, IL: Charles C Thomas.

Mann, C.R. (1992) Female murders and their motivees: a tale of two cities. In E.C. Viano (Ed.), *Intimate Violence. Interdisciplinary Perspective*. Washington, D.C.: Hemisphere Publishing.

McNamara, R.S. with VanDeMark, B. (1995) *In Retrospect: The Tragedy and Lessons of Vietnam*. New York: Random House.

Michigan Corrections Department (1978) Reported in Monahan, J., *The Clinical Prediction of Violent Behavior*. National Institute of Mental Health, DHHS Publication Number (ADM) 81–92. Washington, D.C.: U.S. Government Printing Office.

Mjoseth, J. (1998) Hate groups demand unique legall, psychological and policy responses. *American Psychological Association Monitor*, January, p. 25.

Monahan, J. (1981) *The Clinical Prediction of Violent Behavior*. National Institute of Mental Health, DHHS Publication Number (ADM) 81–92. Washington, D.C.: U.S. Government Printing Office.

Monahan, J. (1988) Risk assessment of violence among the mentally disordered: generating useful knowledge. *International Journal of Law and Psychiatry, 11*, 249–257.

Monahan, J. (1992) Risk assessment: commentary on Poythress and Otto. *Forensic Reports, 5*, 151–154.

Myers, L. (1997) After CIA offered $150,000, mob said it would kill Castro for free. *West Hawaii Today*, July 2, p. A5.

National Defense University (1997) Military forces in the Asia-Pacific region: cooperation and conflict. 1997 Pacific Symposium, April 28–29, Honolulu, HI.

National Gay and Lesbian Task Force (1994) *Anti-Gay/ Lesbian Violence, Victimization and Defamation in 1993*. Washington, D.C.: National Gay and Lesbian Task Force Policy Institute.

Nelson, C. (1998) Top secret CIA report blames spy agency for Bay of Pigs fiasco. *West Hawaii Today*, Feb. 23, p. 7A.

O'Brien, R.M. (1987) The interracial nature of violent crimes: a reexamination. *American Journal of Sociology, 4*, 817–835.

Patterson, G., Cobb, J., and Ray, R. (1972) A social engineering technology for retraining the families of aggressive boys. In H. Adams and I. Unikel (Eds.), *Issues in Transient Behavior Therapy*. Springfield, IL: Charles C Thomas.

Pearce, F. (1976) *Crimes of the Powerful*. London: Pluto Press.

Person v. Miller, 854 F.2d 656 (4th Cir. 1988)

Petersilia, J., Greenwood, P., and Lavin, M. (1977) *Criminal Careers of Habitual Felons*. Santa Monica, CA: Rand.

"Policing keeps an eye on the radical right" (1996) *Law Enforcement News*, Dec. 31, 24.

Poussaint, A.F. (1983) Black-on-black homicide: a psychological-political perspective. *Victimology, 8*(3-4), 161–169.

Prescott, J.W. (1975) Body pleasure and the origins of violence. *Bulletin of the Atomic Scientist*, November, p. 10.

President's Commission on Organized Crime (1986) *The Impact: Organized Crime Today*. Washington, D.C.: U.S. Government Printing Office.

Reid and Associates (1986) 1986 seminar schedule. *The Reid Techniques of Interviewing and Interrogation Based on over 200,000 Successful Interviews and Interrogations*. Chicago: Reid and Associates.

Reid and Associates (1988) *The Investigator,* Spring, *4*(2), 21–40.

Reit, S. (1978) *Masquerade: The Amazing Camouflage Deceptions of World War II*. New York: Hawthorn.

"Report of plot against Saddam led FBI to investigate CIA" (1998) *The Honolulu Advertiser/Los Angeles Times*, February 16, p. A2.

"Republic of Texas: less menace than legal menace" (1997) *Law Enforcement News,* Dec. 1, *23*(480), 11.

Ressler, R., Douglass, J., Burgess, A.W., and Burgess, A.G. (1993) *Crime Classification Manual*. London: Simon & Schuster.

Richardson, L. (1960) *Statistics of Deadly Quarrels*. Pacific Grove, CA: Boxwood Press.

Rogers, R., Ed. (1988) *Clinical Assessment of Malingering and Deception*. New York: Guilford Press.

Ropp, T. (1962) *War in the Modern World*. New York: Collier Books.

Roy, J., Ed. (1996) *False Patriots: The Threat of Antigovernment Extremists*. Montgomery, AL: Southern Poverty Law Center.

Royal, R.E. and Schutt, S.R. (1976) *The Gentle Art of Interviewing and Interrogation: A Professional Manual and Guide*. Englewood Cliffs, NJ: Prentice-Hall.

Ruff, T. (1992) The environmental effects of military activities. *Global Society*, 9–12.

Rummel, R.J. (1990) *Lethal Politics: Soviet Genocide and Mass Murder Since 1917*. New Brunswick: Transaction Publishers.

Rummel, R.J. (1991) *China's Bloody Century: Genocide and Mass Murder Since 1900*. New Brunswick: Transaction Publishers.

Rummel, R.J. (1994) *Death by Government, Genocide and Mass Murder Since 1900*. New Brunswick: Transaction Publishers.

Sagan, C. (1980) *Cosmos*. New York: Random House.

Schell, J. (1969) An account of destruction in Quang Ngai and Quang Tin, *New Yorker*. Dec. 20, pp. 37–44.

Shooter, E. and Hall, H.V. (1990) Explicit alternative testing for deliberate distortion: toward an abbreviated format. *Forensic Reports, 3*, 115–119.

Skorneck, C. (1997) Gangs spread through U.S. *The Honolulu Advertiser*, April 24, p. A8.

Smith, W. (1996) *Covert Warriors: Fighting the CIA's Secret War in Southeast Asia and China 1965–1967*. San Francisco, CA: Presidio.

Smith, M.D., Devine, J.A., and Sheley, J.F. (1992) Crime and unemployment: effects across age and race categories. *Sociological Perspectives,35*(4), 551–572.

Stanton, D. (1976) Drugs, Vietnam and the Vietnam veteran: an overview. *American Journal of Drugs and Alcohol Abuse, 3*, 557–570.

Steadman, H. and Cocozza, J. (1974) *Careers of the Criminally Insane*. Lexington, MA: Lexington Books.

Stephanopoulos, G. (1997) Why we should kill Saddam. *Newsweek*, Dec. 1, 34.

Tanaka, Y. (1996) *Hidden Horrors: Japanese War Crimes in World War II*. Boulder, CO: Westview Press.

Tedeschi, J. and Felson, R. (1994) *Violence, Aggression and Coercive Actions*. Washington, D.C.: American Psychological Association.

Tehranian, M. (1997) Death by design. *The Honolulu Advertiser*, May 18, p. A3.

Toplin, R.B. (1975) *Unchallenged Violence: An American Ordeal*. Westport, CT: Greenwood Press.

Turpin, J. and Kurtz, L. (1997) *The Web of Violence: From Interpersonal to Global*. Chicago: University of Illinois Press.

Ullah, P. (1988) Unemployment and psychological well-being. In J.G. Howells (Ed.), *Modern Perspectives in Psychosocial Pathology*, pp. 247–267, New York: Brunner/Mazel.

U.S. Congress Senate Subcommittee on Terrorism, Narcotics, and International Operations (1989) *Drugs, Law Enforcement, and Foreign Policy*. Washington, D.C.: U.S. Government Printing Office.

U.S. Department of Justice (1983) *Report to the Nation on Crime and Justice* (NCJ-87068). Washington, D.C.: U.S. Government Printing Office.

U. S. Department of Justice (1997) *Hate Crime — 1995*. Federal Bureau of Investigation, Criminal Justice Information Services (CJIS) Division, Uniform Crime Reports, at www.FBI.gov.

U.S. Secret Service (1988) *American Presidential Assassination: Etiology and Prediction*. Washington, D.C.: United States Secret Service Office of Training.

Voss, H.L. and Hepburn, J.R. (1968) Patterns of criminal homicide in Chicago. *Journal of Criminal Law, Criminology and Police Science, 59*, 499–508.

Webster, C., Slomen, D., Sepejak, D., Butler, B., Jensen, F., and Turral, G. (1979) *Dangerous Behavior Rating Scheme (DBRS): Construction and Inter-Rater Reliability*. Unpublished manuscript, Toronto, Ontario.

Weinstein, H. (1990) *Psychiatry and the CIA: Victims of Mind Control*. Washington, D.C.: American Psychiatric Press.

Weinstein, H. (1997) Ruby Ridge ruling assails FBI. *The Honolulu Advertiser*, Sept. 26, p. A11.

Wessels, M.G. (1996) Genocide in Rwanda: origins and psychological tasks of reconstruction. Paper presented at the 104th Annual Convention of the American Psychological Association, August 11, Toronto, Canada.

Whaley, B. (1969) *Strategem: Deception and Surprise in War*. Cambridge, MA: Center for International Studies, MIT.

Whaley, B. (1982) Toward a general theory of deception. *Journal of Strategic Studies, 5*, 178–192.

Winter, D. (1994) Peace from an ecofeminist perspective: boys will be boys unless… . *Peace Psychology Bulletin, 3*, 6–14.

Wisconsin v. Mitchell, 113 S. Ct. 2194 (1993)

Wolfgang, M. (1958) *Patterns in Criminal Homicide*. London: University of Oxford Press.

Wolfgang, M. (1977) From boy to man — from delinquency to crime. National Symposium on the Serious Juvenile Offender, Minneapolis, MN.

Wolfgang, M. (1978) An overview of research into violent behavior. Testimony before the U.S. House of Representatives Committee on Science and Technology.

Woodward, B. (1988) *Veil: The Secret Wars of the CIA 1981–1987*. New York: Simon & Schuster.

Zillman, D., Katcher, A.H., and Milavsky, B. (1972) Excitation transfer from physical exercise to subsequent aggressive behavior. *Journal of Experimental Social Psychology, 8*, 247–259.

Zimbardo, P. (May 1997) What messages are behind today's cults? *APA Monitor, 5*, 14.

About the Author

Harold V. Hall, a forensic neuropsychologist, is the Director of the Pacific Institute for the Study of Conflict and Aggression. He has served as a consultant for a wide variety of criminal and civil justice system agencies, including the Federal Bureau of Investigation, the National Bureau of Prisons, the U.S. Secret Service, and district, family, and circuit courts at state and federal levels. Dr. Hall is a Diplomate in both Forensic Psychology and Clinical Psychology from the American Board of Professional Psychology and is a Fellow of the American Psychological Association. He is board certified in Forensic Neuropsychology from the American Board of Psychological Specialties. Most recently, he was inducted into the National Academy of Practice in Psychology, which, as with other National Academy disciplines such as medicine and dentistry, limits its membership to 100 living professionals from that discipline in the U.S. and Canada. He has investigated and trained others in individual and collective violence since the late 1960s in the Pacific Basin, on the continental U.S., and in Europe.

CHAPTER 2

INHIBITING FATAL GROUP AND INSTITUTIONAL AGGRESSION

Leighton C. Whitaker

This chapter addresses group and institutional lethal aggression in terms of its dynamics and ways to inhibit it. Factors instrumental in facilitating or inhibiting this type of violence are elucidated from examples of both legal and illegal institutions, including professions, sports organizations, military institutions, deadly cults, and the militia movement.

The inhibition of violence is a grave topic emotionally laden with ethical, political, social, psychological, and spiritual issues, especially when it means inhibiting not just violent individuals but whole groups and institutions. It is at the heart of the fundamental question of social as well as personal rights and responsibilities. Often, this topic is addressed with considerable feeling but little light, as possibilities for understanding are short-circuited by the heat of impassioned reactions or are reacted to with a sense of helplessness. We will do well, therefore, to strive for a thorough understanding rather than a rush to judgment or a facile giving up. Thus, we will have to guard against a blind righteousness on the one hand and an unseeing apathy on the other.

The term "institution" is defined broadly here as any organization of group effort to benefit the group, others, or both. The very term evokes the notion of inhibitions on the expression of individuals in favor of conformity to the group ethos. Membership in an institution, however, does not necessarily mean inhibitions against violence toward others outside of the group or even members within the group. In their pursuit of group conformity, institutions variously lure and pressure individual members to renounce certain personal behaviors and values for the sake of the group ethos. The members are thereby trained in the institution's particular ethnocentrism, a habitual disposition to judge foreign individuals or groups by the standards and practices of one's own culture or ethnic group. The tendency to become ingrown and intolerant of other people is, therefore, endemic to institutions as well as individuals.

The term "inhibition" is also defined broadly here. The most satisfactory definition this author has found is from *Webster's Third New International Dictionary* (Gove, 1966) wherein the primary meaning of the term is "an act or an instance of formally forbidding or barring something from being done," while an important extension of the term is "a desirable restraint or check upon the free or spontaneous instincts or impulses of an individual effected through the operation of the human will guided or directed by the social and cultural forces of the environment." The primary meaning relates to an agent or force external to the individual that represses the individual. The further meaning, which is not even mentioned in some dictionaries, includes restraining forces that are internal to or within the individual.

External restraints are usually obvious, whereas internal restraints tend to be subtle, though certainly no less important. The latter include the conscience, in both its prohibiting and idealistic forms; we may choose not to be violent in order to avoid consequent feelings of guilt, because we are empathic with and love the potential victims of our violent tendencies, or both. We may also be inhibited because we fear retaliation and loss. Often, there are admixtures of external and internal inhibitions in any given instance and, over time, what was an external inhibition can be transformed into an internal inhibition and vice versa.

The purpose of this chapter is to understand better the ways in which the violence potentials of institutions may be inhibited, including from the inside of institutions and from inside the individual members. A series of realizations must be arrived at to achieve this purpose. First, all institutions, by their inherent nature, may tend to commit violence toward both outsiders and their own members. Second, this tendency to commit institutional violence toward both insiders and outsiders is greatest when "group centricity" is maximized so that there is little accountability to outsiders. Third, in order to be constructive toward insiders as well as outsiders, an institution must deliberately build in safeguards and inhibitions against its own institutionally inherent destructive tendency. Fourth, effective inhibitions against institutional violence can be incorporated in the design of new institutions, applied to the process of monitoring existing institutions, and used for intervention when egregious institutional violence is imminent or actual. Fifth and finally, the basis for any truly constructive society or group ethos must value nurturant partnerships more than violent dominator relationships.

Before suggesting specific ways to inhibit institutional violence, this chapter will emphasize developing a clear understanding of the context and workings of institutions in terms of their violence proclivities. Their structures and dynamics can be understood by explicating examples and deriving certain principles that, in combination, show us how institutional violence proclivities are facilitated or inhibited. We may learn thereby to inhibit institutional violence effectively in a variety of ways.

The Inherently Violent Tendency of Institutions

Most institutions have the potential for violence. In striving for group conformity, institutions require that their members make certain sacrifices "for the common good", ostensibly for the good of the membership as a whole. So, the members are at some risk according to the kinds of sacrifices they must make. Outsiders are at risk, too, because the goals of any given institution may be against outsiders' interests. It is not always true that "what is good for General Motors is good for the country" or the rest of the world. Thus, any institution may engender harm to both members and outsiders.

Because of their size and the synergy of interindividual relationships, institutions have greater violence potentials than an individual acting alone. As will be illustrated and explained, individuals may, as members of a group or institution, commit atrocities which they would never commit as an individual acting alone. Often, therefore, inhibitions against institutional violence, to be effective, must be greater.

On close examination, no institution is totally free of harmful tendencies. Though most do not perpetrate lethal violence directly, it is evident that even the most respected institutions, when they pursue unenlightened group interests, may wittingly or unwittingly contribute to violence against outsiders. More subtly, the pursuit of "groupish self-interest" can readily damage the membership as well by requiring harmful self-sacrifices, as will be illustrated. Furthermore, externally directed violence begets internally directed violence by modeling uncaring, violent relationships or through unconscious guilt which seeks relief by means of denial and projection or by punishing oneself.

If an institution increasingly proceeds to demand conformity and to disdain nonconformists, the "progressive group centrism" exerts more and more pressure on its members to deny individual and group responsibility except as it may serve what is perceived, expediently, as the group interest. But, even this "benefit of group allegiance" lessens as the group becomes more centric and authoritarian until it is only the leader who is deemed important. When the group ethos becomes really only the ethos of an authoritarian figure, no behavior is considered acceptable except slavish devotion to the wishes of the leader. Yet, even such devotion carries no assurance of safety or even survival, as when the leader demands the deaths of loved ones or even the members themselves.

Most clearly, it is extremely authoritarian-led groups which fit this model of progressive group centrism leading to a kind of "black hole" destruction of its members. Vivid examples readily come to mind: the Nazi progression from dominating and destroying outsiders to attempts on Hitler's life by insiders to his eventual suicide, and the so-called Jonestown massacre in Guyana where the leader and his followers, abhorring outside influences, committed suicide together.

Deikman (1990, p. 104) delineated the deadly course as follows:

"The more authoritarian the human social system, the more likely a separatist world view will arise because any anger or resentment stimulated in the follower by his or her submission to the leader requires displacement onto other persons — the outsider, the infidel, the non-believer. Feelings of rebellion toward the leader, which are defined by the group as evil, make the cult member anxious, even ready to believe in Satanic possession, an apt metaphor to describe the sensation of being invaded by unwanted feelings and images."

Most groups do not become so authoritarian as to engage in progressive centrism or "black holeism" actively and continually to the point of lethal violence. This fact holds out hope for efforts to check or ameliorate institutional violence. What happens within as well as outside of institutions to inhibit the blinding, destroying extremity of group centrism? Why do some institutions "hold the line" or even become more constructive toward their members and nonmembers? Some answers can be found in how many of our common, everyday institutions both engage in violence and check their own violence proclivities. While these organized group cultures do exact some destructiveness, they also manage to retain a modicum of general social approval as society actively evaluates whether they are beneficial overall or, at least, not harmful to an unacceptable degree.

Inhibitions against institutional violence include external surveillance and controls, the rules and ethos of the institution itself, and the personal, internal inhibitions of the individual members. The risk of institutional violence is directly related to the presence or absence of three sources of inhibition — external, intra-institutional, and intra-individual — which dynamically affect one another. With this framework in mind, let us consider as examples some familiar institutions.

Examples of Mandated, Legally Limited, Institutional Aggression

The institutions to be reviewed illustrate the fact that *many, if not most, institutions require that their members be willing and able to materially damage — physically or psychologically — persons construed to be opponents*. An individual's failure to conform to this requirement will result in certain negative consequences for the individual's standing in the institution, such as low ratings, exclusion, or death.

The Legal Profession

As traditionally conceived, the law serves the causes of fairness and justice. Like democratic government, which makes and enforces law, the law as a profession is designed to be an implementer of the principle of checks and balances, a principle intended to maximize fairness and justice. But, the lawful pursuit of justice is based on the adversary system which inherently guarantees deceit, and often more conflict and violence, adding to the conflict and violence which occurred originally to bring the matter to a court of justice. Attorney and ethicist Walt Bachman observed in *Law v. Life: What Lawyers Are Afraid To Say About the Legal Profession* (1995, p. 35):

> *"And behind it all, the cross-examining lawyer is motivated — indeed, ethically driven — not by a sense of justice, not by a desire for truth, not by fairness or decency, but always by the interests of the client. Flowing from the overriding imperative of zealous advocacy is the duty to attack and, if possible, destroy a harmful witness by any means permitted by law. A trial lawyer, as the executioner of this obligation, wields a fearsome power."*

Not limiting himself to trial lawyers, Bachman (1995) asserted, "Law is the only learned profession in which one is ethically obligated to hurt people" (p. 36). "The lawyer's professional life is filled with aggressive, manipulative, half-truthful and other destructive behaviors" (p. 107). For example, "When the principle of free religious expression is challenged, a lawyer will come forth not only in its defense, but also to profess the freedom of religious cults to brainwash converts" (p. 89). Bachman emphasized that the harrowing pursuit of the ethical ideals of one's profession results not only in perpetrating violence on others but violence on attorneys themselves as the conflict between professional ethics and society-wide ethics takes its toll emotionally.

Like other socially accepted or at least tolerated institutions, the legal profession is systematically restricted externally by the extant body of law and other socially constructed inhibitions and within the institution by its own ethical standards. But, intra-individual inhibitions are complicated by pressures on the lawyer to abide by the ethic of advocacy for his or her client, even at the expense of abusing others. This admixture of inhibitions means that no lawyer is permitted to commit murder as such, though a lawyer might substantially cause loss of life. For instance, a defendant or witness becomes so distressed by a trial lawyer's harrowing tactics in court as to commit suicide, but the suicide is not considered to be a murder. Thus, what observers might view as a "murderous attack" is, legally, not a murder and, like other legally accepted institutions, the law profession is not allowed to commit murder *per se*. And neither would the law profession itself, given its own institutional ethics, condone murder *per se*.

While Bachman (1995) made a compelling case for the destructiveness of the lawyering institution, other authors have made a case for including their own professional institutions as inherently destructive. They would not agree, apparently, that the law is the only learned profession in which one is ethically obligated to hurt people.

The Profession of Journalism

Janet Malcolm, in speaking of her own profession in *The Journalist and the Murderer* (1990), likened the journalist's profession to that of the malevolent trial lawyer. She noted the "... ironic parallel between the methods of trial lawyers and of journalists" (p. 45). "Evidently, to be a good trial lawyer you have to be a good hater. A lawsuit is to ordinary life what war is to peacetime. In a lawsuit, everybody on the other side is bad. A trial transcript is a discourse in malevolence" (p. 63). But, she observed that, unlike the trial lawyer, whose adversary role is clear, the journalist must pose from the very outset as a kind of friend, even a psychotherapist, leaving the question of how to justify the "murderous" act. Malcolm (1990, p. 3) stated:

"Every journalist who is not too stupid or too full of himself to notice what is going on knows that what he does is morally indefensible. He is a kind of confidence man, preying on people's vanity, ignorance, or loneliness, gaining their trust and betraying them without remorse. Journalists justify their treachery in various ways according to their temperaments. The more pompous talk about freedom of speech and 'the public's right to know'; the least talented talk about Art; the seemliest talk about earning a living."

We are all familiar with a myriad of other institutions which even more clearly not only permit, but have as their essential reason for existence, the purposeful commission of violence, albeit violence shy of outright legally defined murder. Among such institutions, sports offer clear examples.

Sports

Sports may be defined generally as entertaining exercises in sublimated warfare that are characterized by competition and striving for dominance short of deliberate lethality. Deliberately lethal acts in sports are illegal.

Boxers are physically and mentally trained to hurt an opponent to the point that the opponent cannot continue. The preferred method is to induce a state of unconsciousness in the opponent, what is called a "knockout", a condition dependent on inducing insult to the brain, typically in amounts resulting in permanent brain damage. In the long and much-revered tradition of the pugilistic arts, a boxer is rated not merely according to wins and losses but also by the number and proportion of knockouts, or brain damaging results, he has achieved. To become a boxer-hero, one has to have done considerable damage to one's opponents and, almost always, have tolerated considerable damage to one's own body and brain. None of the many boxing deaths in the history of boxing (an average of five per year in recent years) has ever resulted in a murder conviction though thousands of fans have knowingly and exultantly shouted "murder".

"Ultimate fighting", one of the names for a "new sport", continues to draw strenuous objections but is now legal in many states including New York (Barry, 1997), where the state legislature was strongly supportive. Its supporters claim that it not as dangerous as boxing because there have been no reported deaths so far, and that it is better to legalize it in order to establish some control. *Esquire, The Magazine for Men,* devoted eight pages to an article on "ultimate fighting" (Kriegel, 1996), second only to a 10-page article entitled "In Praise of Dangerous Women," referring to women who ruin men's lives.

The object of ultimate fighting is to cause pain and submission. A fighter does whatever he can to cause his opponent so much pain and injury that the opponent is rendered unconscious or gives up but, it is hoped, not before the typically vast audience has thoroughly enjoyed the brutality. Thus, according to Kriegel (1996, p. 94), a leading hero is "[a] purveyor of pain, he plays perfectly: His skill is nothing less than an American preoccupation. People just love to see the bad guy kick ass." The hero is avidly followed by "the best-looking chicks". Except for eye-gouging, biting, and throat kicking, no moves are off limits. A fighter can kick his opponent in the groin, knock his teeth out, or rip his lips off. This ostensibly new sport, which is at least as old as Roman gladiators, is appealing to both the fighters and audiences because of its extreme sado-masochism. Like all sado-masochism, which ostensibly is highly sexual, it shows a preference for violence over sexuality, as made clear by a statement by its biggest "ultimate fighter" hero: "I'd rather fight than fuck" (Kriegel, 1996, p. 98).

Football is a North American game that is inherently violent. While not explicitly designed to injure opponents seriously or to kill them, many of its heroes are the really "hard hitters" who down their opponents with a vengeance that has often resulted in crippling injury or even death, though not murder charges. Football players' much-valued toughness is associated with a willing personal acceptance of punishment and injury. Special recognition is given for "playing injured" provided the player does not handicap his team thereby. Fans as well as players zealously endorse not only "beating" the opposing team but may be especially pleased at their team members hitting opponents hard enough to force them out of the game.

A "Special NFL Classic Edition" of *Sports Illustrated* (1995) featured on the cover "The Toughest Quarterback Ever," and a section called "Tough as Nails" glorified the most violent players. For example, a noted Hall of Famer, albeit not the very toughest or meanest, was quoted as saying (p. 20):

"'... when we played, there was no such thing as dirty play. It was dirty if you got caught. I was looking to head butt someone on every play. I'd set guys up by throwing a few cross-body blocks, then throw a leg whip. And, at 6'9", I could leg whip the crap out of you.' This was a scary dude, on and off the field."

All sports feature planned competition within the rules, but the rules may not be enforced. Just as football players can get away with "dirty play" when the rules are not rigorously enforced, so too do other kinds of athletes exceed the official limitations on violence. Often, it is the beyond-the-rules activity that is most attractive to the fans.

Professional ice hockey players engage in a great many extracurricular battles on the ice which have nothing to do with the game of ice hockey. Their brawls, resembling a cross between wrestling and boxing, often persist for a minute or more as the referees stand by and fans are stirred to greater enthusiasm. A young superfan told me that he and his friends enjoy their season tickets primarily because they can see so many of these brutal battles.

Baseball, the quintessential American game, involves a great many potentially injurious events over the course of a single game even when played within the rules. Players may bend the rules and "accidentally" injure one another — for example, by running for a base "with flying spikes". And, though intimidation is part of the game, players are not killed. Players who are so skillful as to come *close* to harming opponents without actually harming them may get special recognition. For example, baseball pitchers make reputations on their abilities to intimidate but not physically harm opposing batters. "Sal the Barber" Maglie, pitcher for what was then known as the New York Giants, was less known for tonsorial skills as such than for his skill at "shaving" the faces of batters with his very close pitches. In *The Ultimate Baseball Book* (Okrent and Lewine, 1991, p. 281), a famous Dodger pitcher defined his occupation, thereby explaining how he had opposing batters dodging his pitches and striking out instead of hitting:

"Sandy Koufax — 'Pitching,' he said, 'the art of instilling fear by making a man flinch.' Yet his control was such that in 1966, Koufax set a National League record by pitching 323 innings without hitting a single batter."

Examples of Illegal Violence in Legal Institutions

Thus far we have examined only examples of institutions bound simultaneously by law, ethically defined limits, and careful supervision by a governing body. What happens when otherwise high-minded, legally constituted institutions are effectively exempt from the law and even their own institutional rules? This situation illustrates the principle that *exemption from the law, due to lack of enforcement or secrecy, serves to enhance violence proclivities.*

Colleges and Universities

Institutions of higher education have long failed, in relation to their students, to enforce laws, policies, and rules applicable to people outside of their campuses. They have been especially lax with regard to students' use of alcohol and other drugs and in relation to activities of fraternities. For example, state laws against underage drinking tend to be merely communicated to students rather than enforced. Because these "theoretical inhibitions" are not really enforced, they are not "real" rules. Much of campus violence, including virtually all instances of date rape, occurs under the influence of alcohol (Rivinus and Larimer, 1993). In the absence of enforcement of the existing laws, policies, and rules by colleges and universities or by local police, there is institutional sanction for, rather than against, this and other forms of campus violence.

John Silber, the president of Boston University, observed in a *New York Times* op-ed piece entitled "Students Should Not Be Above the Law" (1996): "But today colleges and universities tend to circumvent the courts and bury serious criminal cases in their own judicial systems." What happens when effective exemption from the law is compounded by secrecy rather than openness? College fraternities, which by their nature are secretive, provide an example.

Matthews (Crothers and Matthews, 1996, p. 50) reported that, "The fraternity initiation remains the most secret of campus rituals — and the most debauched." She and photographer C. Taylor Crothers documented many hazing rituals at a conservative, selective, well-endowed East Coast university where students were joining one of the ten largest North American fraternities. The fraternity's national headquarters said that the organization's purpose was to develop social responsibility and that hazing is officially condemned. Nevertheless, "new members of an all-fraternity drinking club entertain hundreds of students and alumni by drinking up to a case of beer apiece, chased by a fifth of vodka, tequila, or 40-proof 'Mad Dog' wine, followed by raw trout or Vienna sausage." Of course, such practices result in serious injury and even death. Matthews quoted a fraternity rush chairman: "Hazing is very educational about human nature. ...[T]he nicest, politest, most churchgoing people turn out to be so mean and angry. And cruel, if you give them a little power."

By maintaining that its practices must be secret, an institution has free rein to engage in violent behavior. Then, even an institution supposedly governed by a superordinate entity, such as when a fraternity is governed both by its national organization and its college or university, can commit violence. The example of college fraternities illustrates that non-enforcement of the rules and secrecy allow and thereby foster institutional violence.

The Military

Military institutions in the U.S. clearly prepare for and engage in lethal aggression. Whereas sports may be thought of as sublimated warfare, the military is explicitly and usually legally devoted to actual warfare. Yet, most military institutions are mandated only to defend their countries and are restricted to "gentlemanly conduct", the rules of the Geneva Convention, and the like. They are not supposed to engage in exploitation and cruelty. Ostensibly, the military does not encourage cruelty, though some militaries, such as the Nazis, are trained to be cruel in order to reduce resistance and to break the will of the enemy. In any case, the dangerous business of training people to be violent can readily lend itself to even blatant forms of cruelty, particularly if rules against cruelty are not enforced and practices are carried out secretly.

Critics complain about episodes of cruelty in the U.S. military, as though it is not integral to the legally and socially mandated mission of military institutions to train their members to injure and kill. Public outrage ensues when it is discovered that a particular military training facility is a culture of abuse and is even violent toward the students it is designed to teach and protect. Thus, a *New York Times* editorial

("The Citadel's Culture of Abuse", 1997) said: "It is a sad commentary on campus morality that it took the presence of women to expose deviant conduct that victimizes male students as well. The Citadel's hazing tradition teaches young men that brutalizing others and denigrating women is what it takes to be a military officer." But, this tradition is inherent to all institutions pledged to train its members in violence. "Hazing" is, of course, a euphemism; the practice is more accurately termed "training in cruelty".

Institutional inculcation of cruelty requires systematically training members to abide their own suffering as well as that of others. Eisler (1996, p. 96) noted: "It is instructive in this connection that the training of the Nazi S.S. officers who manned the mass extermination camps is said to have included the raising of puppies, which they were then ordered to feed, play with, and care for in every way — and then kill with no signs of emotion." Whether called hazing or training in cruelty or simply obedience training, all institutions that have as at least one of their purposes the infliction of pain engage systematically, officially or non-officially, in fostering callousness to their own and others' pain. As Eisler put it, "... once empathy and love are in any context habitually suppressed, this tends to result in what psychologists call blunted affect — a reduced and highly compartmentalized capacity to respond to feelings (affect) other than anger, contempt, and similar 'hard' emotions."

On Thursday, January 30, 1997, the television program "Headline News" showed an amateur videotape of 1991 and 1993 U.S. Marine Corps hazings marking the completion of paratrooper training. Officially, upon completion of that training, Marines are awarded their "wings" in the form of a medal that is supposed to be pinned onto the Marine's uniform. In the videotape, however, each of the many medal recipients wore only a t-shirt and stood still while another Marine pinned the medal into his chest, making sure to maximize the pain by punching the medal in and rubbing the already inserted medal back and forth to further increase the wound and the pain. The recipients were shown grimacing and screaming in pain.

The Marine Corps officially proscribed this hazing practice of "blood winging" or "gold winging", which means smashing the medal into the chest, but recognized that the hazing was going on in previous years and is continuing now. A quite similar hazing of a Navy submariner eventuated in a sailor's suicide after he was pressured to reveal the names of his tormentors or be court-martialed, as reported on the 6:30 p.m. news on February 12, 1997 (National Broadcasting Company, NBC). Clearly, the official training in the military lends itself to such behavior which, therefore, must be vigilantly guarded against. In his comments on the hazing, Army General John Shalikashvili, chairman of the Joint Chiefs of Staff, said (Ruane, 1997): "People get very charged up in this business. We demand people who are tough and who can stand up to adversity." But, of course, the legally authorized training itself is readily conducive to cruel behavior.

Anti-Government Extremists, Terrorists, and Deadly Cults

"There is no cruelty like the cruelty of the righteous."
(Arthur Deikman, *The Wrong Way Home,* 1990, p.106)

Having illustrated the propensities for and limitations against institutional violence in legally constituted and thus socially allowable institutions, let us examine institutions that simultaneously exempt themselves from the law, have no accountability whatsoever to anyone but themselves, are highly secretive, have as their purpose the commission of violence, demand that members commit even lethal violence to gain rank, and provide members with a sense of great righteousness for doing so. Anti-government extremists, terrorist groups, and deadly cults are three overlapping kinds of institutions that fit these criteria. It is important to understand their range of attributes, the differences among them, and their essential similarities.

This chapter will focus on two at least superficially quite dissimilar examples — the Patriot or militia movement in the U.S. and the Aum Doomsday Cult in Japan. The Patriots consist largely of economically and educationally poor white individuals, while Aum draws considerable wealth and its members tend to be especially well educated in the formal academic sense.

In light of the principles previously articulated and the institutional characteristics of the Patriot and Aum groups, we will be able to grasp why they commit even lethal violence. But, we will also ask why these groups are not more deadly than they are. What inhibits them in the absence of outside governance? Because they require violent behavior, act as though exempt from the law, are secretive, and are motivated by "righteousness", what is to stop them? To answer this question, we must examine their natures closely, asking along the way what causes such violent institutions to form, how they maintain themselves, how they can resist the inhibitions that society promotes, and how their members can avoid becoming conscious-stricken. What already considered or new extra-group, intra-group, and intra-individual inhibitions are or can be effective?

The Anti-Government Extremist Patriots

This seemingly loosely organized collection of anti-government extremists functions in an institutional manner that strongly encourages violence, albeit sometimes in the name of "protection" for themselves and perhaps others outside the group. The U.S. groups commonly label themselves "Patriots" (Southern Poverty Law Center, 1996, p. 6). They are overwhelmingly white and Christian, are predominantly male, and are "... a potpourri of the American right, from members of the Christian Coalition to the Ku Klux Klan — people united by their hatred of the federal government."

Floyd Cochran (1996) is a former youth recruiter and national spokesman for the white supremacist movement Aryan Nations. Since leaving the movement, he has been making presentations as "acts of atonement" designed to unseat the movement. He characterized Aryan Nations members as poor in education and literacy and stated that they spread their hate messages through the Internet, radio, and comic books. He gave talks and showed a videotape on November 6, 1996, at Delaware County Community College in Pennsylvania, during which he noted that 14- to 25-year-olds have been joining the movement in great numbers and stated that, as a young man, "I joined a hate group because it made me someone." He and other recruiters used public relations techniques, such as friendly socialization, and they focused on rural, all-white areas where people are quite isolated. Cochran was able to use the media to propagandize: "My bigotry became palatable to the media who would just repeat what I said." He estimated that there are 3500 "skinheads" (young neo-Nazis) and 51 hate groups in Pennsylvania alone but said that the groups "do not mass in numbers because of their paranoia."

The movement's deadly aims are obfuscated by their methods for developing a following. Members approach potential recruits with friendliness and recourse to the Bible. They proclaim that their racist orientation is called for in the Bible and that what they do is in the name of God and Christianity. These messages provide justification for hating and make the movement acceptable. The videotape shown by Cochran featured young male neo-Nazi members exulting in their strident messages such as: "God is hate." ... "I love my race to the point I kill." ... "Whatever is destroying our race must be eliminated." ... "The Bible says the Jews are descendants of Satan."

Having had ample time now for considerable thinking, the former evangelist for the Aryan Nations has said that ignoring the groups will not work and neither will combating them with violence, because they truly are like the hydra that grows two heads when one is cut off. He strongly recommended countering them with a vigorous, multi-faceted educational approach. Cochran has felt that such groups exist because of what is not taught in society, and that people are not sufficiently challenged to think. He urged that the clergy should emphasize correct quoting and interpretation of the Bible to counter the false versions and that stereotypes should be countered with the reality of human diversity. Cochran also suggested that other states should emulate Georgia's anti-masking law. In summary, he said that economic difficulties, poor education, and lack of information play key roles in recruitment susceptibility.

The Patriot movement followers may number as many as 5 million nationwide, according to Dees (1996). This figure may include anyone who is supportive of the Patriots. The hard-core Patriots, however, who may number anywhere from 15,000 to 250,000, could be enough, given sufficient secrecy and the right equipment, to overthrow a nation violently, even the U.S.

The hard-core Patriots appear to have a kind of group paranoia which stirs them to prepare to do what they fear the government is going to do to them. Helped by radical white supremacists, this anti-government alliance proposes that extreme action is necessary and, because the government is armed, they, too, must be armed. Accusing the government itself of unlawful activity that is destructive to its citizens and their rights, they react with unlawful activity themselves, including terrorist forms of violence. Though most citizens disapprove of their tactics, in part, they are able to gather sympathizers because not only they, but many other people, perceive the government as too restrictive of individual rights. The very notion of the government inhibiting them inspires more fear, hatred, and preparation because they are united by hatred of the government.

Dees (1996), the chief trial counsel for the Southern Poverty Law Center and its Militia Task Force, has emphasized the relentlessness of the Patriots' loathing of the federal government. Inhibiting anti-government extremists is especially difficult, as the Patriots' image of the "hydra" suggests that each act of inhibition or suppression may inspire a counter-reaction more severe than anything that preceded it.

The Southern Poverty Law Center (1996, p. 45) made 14 recommendations for limiting the power and dangerousness of the Patriots. The first nine suggest legal and regulatory procedures. The next four suggest preventive actions by government employees, journalists, clergy, and schools. The last recommendation, which states that, "Charges of government misconduct must be investigated promptly and thoroughly," raised the issue of how government can and does inspire aggression against it and the citizens it represents.

Government Facilitation of Anti-Government Extremists

No government can afford to be merely an inhibitor or repressor of its citizens. Its citizens must feel that they are nurtured and served in return for the self-sacrifices required in any organizational endeavor. Thus, highly repressive governments tend to be overthrown, albeit often in favor of equally or more repressive governments. For instance, the Russian revolution of 1917 seems inevitable in retrospect because czarist rule was blatantly out of touch with and negligent of its starving citizens, who felt they had to revolt or die. Of course, czarist tyranny was immediately replaced by communist tyranny.

A wise government will ensure that its nurturance of and sensitivity to its citizens' needs take precedence over its inhibitory and regulatory actions, just as parents should make sure that their love of their children is paramount, with discipline guiding, rather than stifling, them. The identifying characteristic of a totalitarian government is its intolerance of individual freedom. Even a democratic government, however, can begin to behave in such an inhibitory manner as to cause a loss of freedom that is indistinguishable from a clearly authoritarian or totalitarian government.

Such is the text of Howard's book, *The Death of Common Sense* (1994), in which he showed how the U.S., by wrapping itself in ever more laws and regulations, has tended to strangle not only the actions of its citizens but their ability to develop judgment and common sense. He noted that the number of federal agencies doubled from 1960 to 1980; that federal statutes and formal rules now total about 1 million words; that our tax law now has 36,000 pages; that the greater the number of regulations, the more loopholes can be found by lawyers to subvert their intent; and that, therefore, "[a] culture of resistance sets in" (p. 49). Citizens react negatively to the enmeshment of their bread-and-butter institutions — schools, hospitals, and workplaces — in regulatory law. For example, "Hospitals now spend on the order of 25 percent of their budget on administration, mainly to comply with these procedural requirements. ...Forty percent of all doctors say they would not choose the profession again, the main reason being the hassle factor — the growing levels of paperwork" (Howard, 1994, pp. 93, 94). Of course, people with less income and less education than doctors or lawyers are injured far more because they have fewer resources with which to cope.

The growing gap in income between richest and poorest (Holmes, 1996) increases the aggravation. As of 1996, the U.S. had more children in poverty than any other industrialized nation. A large portion of the most violence-ready followers of the Patriot movement, such as the Aryan Nation, tend to be low income and, therefore, are especially affected. They tend to blame their troubles on cheap laborers from other countries and are against the United Nations as a symbol of a potential one-world government. Another possible source of their employment problems is that, by and large, they have been left behind in our rapidly escalating high technology society.

As Howard (1994, p. 154) observed, "The injuries are mounting, and Americans are building up a reservoir of hatred. Just listen to the radio talk shows." Government is increasingly seen as the enemy, especially when its protective functions are perceived as being simultaneously restrictive of freedom and wasteful of taxpayers' money — for example, in 1994, when it was discovered that the Defense Department was spending more on procedures for travel reimbursement ($2.2 billion) than on travel ($2 billion) (Howard, 1994). Quite significantly, as Dees (1996, p. 69) explained, the militia movement, which crystallized in 1992, was formed by people who "felt frustrated by too many regulations, threatened by a one-world economy, and frightened by a government that had gotten too big and too powerful."

Similarly, in 1995, NBC began a series of programs called "The Fleecing of America" which showed one government project after another that produced nothing or close to it, all at taxpayer expense. On June 4, 1996, NBC anchorman and narrator Tom Brokaw announced that, so far, their investigators calculated that these projects had cost $58.2 billion. As of this writing, the "Fleecing of America" series about wasteful government spending has continued.

In light of these developments, such anti-government institutions as the Patriots may be seen as representing merely an extreme version of disenchantment with the U.S. government, albeit a version that may readily lapse into paranoia and violence rather than non-violent protest and reform. As in all cases of possible paranoid ideation and behavior, it is important to ferret out any basis in objective reality. Paranoid phenomena, which will be discussed more fully later in this chapter, often have some basis in reality, although not nearly enough to explain the phenomena fully.

Like many other citizens, the Patriots resent being regulated minutely, taxed deeply, and subjected to wasteful spending of their hard-earned money. The author makes these observations not as excuses for the Patriots' violence but as a basis for understanding and helping to re-direct their efforts. Ironically, the paranoia of the bigoted Patriots is remarkably similar to the "paranoia" of which blacks were accused in the 1960s (Whitaker, 1970, 1972a) when racial tensions erupted into violence as this disenfranchised population grew so frustrated with a government they saw, often correctly, as far more restrictive and unjust than nurturing (Higginbotham, 1996). Like the current Patriots, blacks did not trust the government, were prepared to be violent, and were determined to own rather than serve in others' institutions (Whitaker, 1972b).

Part of the solution is to improve our government through democratic means, making it more sensitive and empathic, thereby lessening the motivation to act violently and showing the viability of peaceful reform. Having less to rebel against in our society might lessen the rebellion, at least by reducing the reality basis for group paranoia. In order for people to trust institutions, the institutions must provide meaningful, empowered belonging (Deikman and Whitaker, 1979).

Dees is widely known for his stand against the militia movement, whose members have often made threats on his life. But, like all those who realize they have to understand "the enemy" to defeat or at least change that enemy, he is also empathic. Having studied events at Ruby Ridge (near Naples, ID), the Waco (TX) Branch Davidian tragedy, and the Oklahoma City bombing, he has shown an understanding of where its members are coming from. He presented the following hypothetical defense of Timothy McVeigh, who was convicted of the Oklahoma City bombing, as McVeigh's best chance to avoid the death penalty (Dees, 1996, p. 167):

"The jury would learn about McVeigh's obsession with his hero in The Turner Diaries *who blew up a federal building; his valiant service in the Desert Storm campaign; his anguish at seeing American soldiers serving under United Nations command in Somalia; his fears that his country's values will be lost to a godless one-world government; his outrage that FBI agents would murder innocent women and children; his anger at corrupt, overpaid politicians."*

While empathy for murderous people might appear odious indeed, it provides both a realistic understanding of motivation and practical ways of inhibiting them. For one thing, it leads to a clear realization that military training, i.e., training to harm and destroy as well as to protect, can readily be transferred to causes unintended by the trainers. Historically, civil wars and overthrows of governments have usually involved people using government training and tactics that were designed originally to defend the government to war against the government. The old adage seems to hold: Those who live by the sword die by the sword. Our government should emphasize nurturance and negotiation more than training in destruction.

Institutional training in paralethal and lethal violence is dangerous for all concerned, including the government or other institutions that conduct such training. All that need happen is that the trainees become disenchanted with their trainers, such as the government, and ache, like Hitler did, to use that training against the trainers. Currently, as Dees (1996, p. 213) has noted, a clandestine group called the Special Forces Underground, formed in 1992, has as its goal forcing the federal government "back into its constitutional prison." This group relies mostly on active duty military personnel and ex-service members who have had covert operations training. Furthermore, there are periodic reports of active duty soldiers linked to white supremacist groups killing black citizens; for example, a white paratrooper was charged with shooting and killing a black couple in Fayetteville, NC, in December 1996 ("Soldier tells of...", 1997).

The Aum Doomsday Cult

Aum, a cult originating in Japan, is in many ways the exact opposite of the Patriot movement. Whereas the

Patriots are loosely configured to the point of being without an apparent leader, Aum is tightly organized and clearly headed by an absolute leader. The Patriots are virtually all white, Aum virtually all Asian. The Patriots are poor in formal education and financial resources, while Aum members tend to be very highly educated in the natural sciences and have immense financial resources. Aum's five "commandos" who led the massive nerve gas (sarin) strike in the Tokyo subway system on March 20, 1995, were a cardiovascular surgeon, a graduate student in particle physics, an applied physics graduate, an applied physicist who graduated at the top of his class, and an electronics engineer. Aum "... is the story of the ultimate cult: a wired, high-tech, designer-drug, billion-dollar army of New Age zealots, under the leadership of a blind and bearded madman, armed with weapons of mass destruction" (Kaplan and Marshall, 1996, pp. 2, 3).

These apparently gross differences between the Patriots and Aum, however, are rather superficial compared to the similarities in their core identities and ideologies. Though the Patriots claim to be leaderless and state that they realize that fostering antigovernment sentiments is more acceptable in public than preaching racism and Aryan superiority, some of the most violently inclined, including Timothy McVeigh, have been known admirers of Hitler (Cochran, 1996; Dees, 1996). Thus, it is highly probable that the Patriot movement, particularly the Aryan Nation, is more identified ideologically with Hitler than would appear from what they offer for public consumption. Some members who resemble Hitler in stridency, righteousness, and bigotry have been ideologic leaders of the movement. But, knowing that blatant bigotry turns most people off and not wishing to lose potential recruits, even these leaders often downplay their bigotry in public in favor of culling animosity toward the government. Both the Patriots and Aum are authoritarian to the core.

Furthermore, both institutions preach impending doom. Aum's leader, Shoko Asahara, links his authority to Lord Shiva, the Destroyer who reigns over the Hindu pantheon of gods. Thus, members of Aum, like the Patriots, predict a doom they themselves appear to be implementing. Aum, too, engages avidly in actions that would wreak havoc even on nonmembers, all in the name of what Aum calls the supreme authority or the supreme truth.

Both institutions maintain that they are serving a spiritual good, a cleansing action that would make a holy re-creation possible. The idea is that first we must destroy, and that the process will require supreme sacrifices. The holy figures in these cases are Hitler and Asahara, who himself has venerated Hitler. This observation leads to yet another similarity.

Both institutions carry out recruitment, training, and the mandating of sacrifices by engaging in bold lies. According to Kaplan (1992, p. 676), Hitler claimed that "the great masses of the people ... will more easily fall victims to a big lie than a small one." Asahara has engaged in big lies, also. He has pretended to be able to levitate, read minds, see the future, hear the voice of God, and more. Asahara even repackaged his dirty bath water as "miracle pond" and sold it for nearly $800 per quart (Kaplan and Marshall, 1996, pp. 18, 19): "Believers who donated over $2000 to the Shambalization Plan Fund received the best prize, two gallons of Asahara's dirty bath water."

Aum's recruitment tactics involve Aum members pretending to have no affiliation with the group, but then leading on potential recruits (Whitaker, 1996). Like most duplicitous cults, Aum also convinces members to give up large amounts of money to the cult as protection from doom. The message common to the Patriots and Aum, and myriad other deadly cults, is that only devout members would survive the certain advent of doomsday. Both of these institutions are totally devoid of humor about themselves; they are deadly serious. People who are severely paranoid are strikingly devoid of a sense of humor. We might say that they take themselves far too seriously.

The natural progression of such a cult follows the same general pattern regardless of its initial constitution. The differences in the initial characteristics of cult members and the society in which they emerge — for example, the differences between the Patriots and Aum — recede in significance. Their progressively greater secrecy, lying, unaccountability, repression of dissent, and urging of violent behavior in the name of religion result in their having to exert more and more control against (1) the threat that members will begin to question and think for themselves, and (2) attempts by those external to the cult to redress its wrongs. Such a cult, therefore, engages more and more in paralethal and lethal practices against both members and outsiders. As the practices of high pressure indoctrinations become inadequate in the face of growing skepticism both inside and outside of the cult, outright punishments must be introduced, and when even harsh punishments are not enough to suppress dissent, then atrocities, including murders, must be committed.

In the case of Aum, initial appeals to alienated youth have to be girded by stripping them of their possessions, isolating them from their families and outside society, and separating them as much as possible from their identities as individuals. Members were made to endure extreme hardships in hypnosis-inducing circumstances featuring extreme isolation, sleep and food deprivation, and ceaselessly strident propagandizing. Later, members were made to submit to what was acknowledged as "brainwashing" by means of drugs and cranial electrical shocking devices. Members were told that their paths to higher spiritual enlightenment would be facilitated by these devices which would reduce brain activity, as measured by electroencephalography, to the almost nonexistent level of their supreme master himself. Asahara falsely claimed to have achieved that low level himself. If a member was still questioning and wanting to leave the cult, that member had to be murdered without a trace of the body left for would-be investigators to discover. At the insistence of their leader, Aum members also murdered an attorney who was investigating them, together with the attorney's wife and children (Whitaker, 1996).

The Art and Science of Inculcating Violent Behavior

Violent behavior can be induced quickly and fairly readily in most people who are subjected to strong authoritarian pressure that suggests they would be right in submitting. Social psychologist Solomon Asch (1952) demonstrated in a classic series of experiments that even the pressure of a group of six students (who were Asch's confederates) could induce a given individual to override his or her own visual perception of lengths of lines in favor of conforming to the group's clearly incorrect judgment. As Eisler (1996, p. 388) has pointed out, "What has not received even a fraction of the attention paid to that finding is what Asch's experiments demonstrated about dissent: that when just *one* of Asch's six confederates disagreed with the answers of the majority, the rate of conformity declined to a mere 5 percent!" Clearly, an individual would-be dissenter can be greatly encouraged to dissent if supported by even one other individual in an otherwise unified group pressure situation. But, when there is no one supporting the would-be dissenter in such a situation, even quite "normal" people may perform egregious forms of aggression.

Studies by Stanley Milgram (1974) strongly suggested that most apparently normal people could be induced to administer what they believed to be severe shock to an apparently hapless experimental "subject" as instructed by a white-coated experimenter and his assistant. Of the real subjects, who thought they were teaching memory tasks to the "subject", 90% actually pressed the switches that indicated the most extreme pain, despite hearing the subject screaming in apparent pain, if they were at a physical distance from the subject. As one of Milgram's subjects said, "You really begin to forget that there's a guy out there, even though you can hear him. For a long time I just concentrated on pressing the switches and reading the words" (p. 38). Thus, the combination of an authoritarian leader and distance from the victim, which serves to dehumanize the victim, can induce ordinary people to inflict pain and suffering on innocent persons.

Like all deadly cults, the Aryan Nation and Aum rely on these two techniques — authoritarian leadership and distance from the victims — and on certain additional conditions and techniques because highly reliable training in violent behavior must not rely merely on inducements of a temporary sort, but on thorough inculcation which is effected by frequent repetitions and admonitions which can be optimally effective with especially vulnerable subjects. Thus, among the conditions necessary are voids in the nurturance and education of young potential recruits and the ability to structure the environment in ways favorable to hypnotic forms of transformation.

The Aryan Nation or, more broadly, the Patriots have tended to recruit especially poorly educated youths whose ignorance greatly facilitates bigotry and suggestibility. Though Aum has recruited many youths who were exceptionally well educated in the physical sciences, like others in Japan's school systems they lacked much schooling in anything else. Other conditions were also important. Kaplan and Marshall (1996, p. 289) put the matter succinctly: "It would be easy to dismiss Aum as a peculiarly Japanese case, and indeed there are conditions in Japan that shaped the cult's unique character. The straitjacket schools and workplaces, the absentee fathers and alienated youth no doubt helped fuel Shoko Asahara's rise to power. But … ineffective and bungling police, fanatic sects, and disaffected scientists are hardly limited to the Japanese."

Like other youths lured into cults, Aum inculcates them in a "religion" that promises to fill their spiritual voids with supreme truth while requiring that they submit to an absolutely authoritarian leader who is to be their god. Their old straitjackets are replaced by even more constricting garments. Asahara declared himself to be the divine leader of a completely non-violent religion. As stated by Kaplan and Marshall (1996, p. 23):

"Inside the growing communes, though, Asahara or his disciples would beat followers for the smallest act of disobedience. This was termed 'karma disposal', the dumping of spiritual baggage that holds one back in this life or the next. 'I often pick on my disciples,' Asahara freely admitted. 'It's not because I am a sadist. It is because I have to rid them of negative karma.' Asahara's theory of karma was simple: pleasure bad, pain good."

A similar progression characterized the Nazi movement as it was largely freed from societal inhibitions thanks to enabling by economic distress together with widespread bigotry not only in Germany but in other countries where there were ample sympathizers. Currently, the Patriots are aware that their bigotry is relatively unpopular in the larger society so they must be careful to emphasize only the government as the enemy of the people. But, with fewer inhibitions emanating from society, the Patriot movement could quickly become even more openly bigoted and destructive.

Reality vs. Paranoia

Frequently, various cults, hate groups, terrorists, and the like are dismissed as being simply "paranoid" or, in less restrained terminology, they are called "crazies", but we have seen that the matter is far more complex. A considerable foundation of pervasive social and personal conditions underlies and supports lethal group and institutional aggression. We must take into account the supportive structure for lethal institutional aggression, which is schematized in Table 2.1, if we are to understand and effectively inhibit it. The apparent paranoia of these groups is largely shared and supported in various forms by a vast number of other persons and groups.

TABLE 2.1

SUPPORTIVE STRUCTURE FOR LETHAL INSTITUTIONAL AGGRESSION

Terrorists
Hate groups
Authoritarian institutions
Excessively regulating government
Societally pervasive dominator mentality
Failure to educate for partnership relationships

Was Asahara's claim that Aum's development of weaponry is only for purposes of self-defense or the Patriots claim that they must arm for self-defense merely the propaganda of con artists, or are such claims believed by the "liars" themselves? The answer depends on understanding all of the contributions to these claims. As we have seen, sometimes there is a partial reality base to claims of persecution. And sometimes, leaders knowingly lie while members are inculcated to believe. Typically, however, both the leaders and members of deadly cults share at least some genuinely paranoid proclivities, albeit proclivities shared, to a lesser degree, by a vast supportive structure in the larger society. To survive, massive myths must have massive support.

While the paranoia of the militia, terrorist groups, and deadly cult institutions has some grounding in truly oppressive conditions — such as difficult economic straits in Hitler's pre-Nazi Germany and in a large segment of today's U.S. or the alienation of Japanese youth — the paranoia also has a genuinely morbid or irrational aspect. When such institutions portray certain outsiders as the sole cause of their difficulties, their claims are at most grounded in only partial truths. Their slogans falsely suggest that they would be fine "if only we could get rid of the Xs or the Ys or the Zs!" (fill in Jews, blacks, Catholics, homosexuals, the mentally ill, any non-believers, people with genetic defects, or the federal government). Ultimately, this kind of failure to admit or to discover factual truth leads to the extermination of anyone who is different. Inevitably, its success would result in a biological genetic disaster as well as a psychogenetic disaster, because extreme inbreeding weakens and eventually destroys the hereditary line, both physically and psychologically. In reality, it is not the destruction of variety among or within species but the natural diversity of humankind as well as all animal and plant life which gives the greatest promise of survival. If disobeyed, this natural law, which favors diversity, also destroys the "in-group".

The following are among the bases upon which an individual personality may develop a paranoid condition (Whitaker, 1992, p. 7):

"Common to schizophrenic, bigoted, and paranoid conditions are extreme problems with self-esteem or self-worth. Paranoid and bigoted orientations are ways to raise oneself, no matter how irrationally, from a condition of devastatingly low self-esteem. Schizophrenic persons differ from groups of bigoted people in that they have not established a consensus or communion with others with whom they can share their beliefs; they are unable to convince others of the correctness of their beliefs. Schizophrenic persons are exceedingly individual, or idiosyncratic."

The paranoid form of morbidity manifest in scapegoating would be called a paranoid psychosis were it not so fully shared in common with other scapegoaters. Clinical psychology and psychiatry have no adequate clinical terms for group paranoid disorders, with the small exception of *folie a deux* (literally, "madness of two"), which means that two people may share the same delusional beliefs. But, as Erich Fromm noted in *The Sane Society* (1955, 1990, p. 15), "Just as there is a 'folie a deux' there is a folie a millions."

How can we further distinguish, for the practical purpose of knowing whether or what kind of intervention is advisable, genuinely morbid paranoid group phenomena from other group movements that are more rationally grounded? What is the difference, if any, between the current Patriot movement and the American Revolution, for example? A key difference is that between autonomy and domination strivings.

The revolutionaries who created the U.S. aimed to be free of English domination but had no evident aim to conquer England or to cleanse the world, as it were, of English citizens. They were content to gain their freedom from what they perceived as English oppression. In sharp contrast, the Nazi movement aimed not simply to establish or fortify German independence or autonomy but to conquer the world and to "cleanse" the world of its seemingly innumerable "inferior" peoples. Insofar as the members of the Patriot, Aum, or other aggressive group movements strive not merely to establish their own independence but to dominate and destroy others to assert their superiority and to eradicate the "inferiors", they are acting out a form of paranoid ideology — "If it were not for the inferiors, whom we must dominate and destroy, we would be recognized as the superiors," for example, as racially superior.

Even people who would individually be perceived as quite normal may become very destructive if they are subjected sufficiently to the conditions and training that make for blind obedience. Because there is a vast number of individuals who have the rather common tendency to engage in unwarranted blaming of others for their problems, it is not difficult to understand the making of deadly cults. While paranoid proclivities make vulnerable recruits, however, being schizophrenic does not.

Paranoid schizophrenic persons show a greater idiosyncrasy than can be tolerated in group paranoia. Persons who are schizophrenic are so idiosyncratic or distinctively different from others, including other schizophrenic persons, that idiosyncrasy is a hallmark of schizophrenic disorders (Whitaker, 1992). Thus, if a schizophrenic patient is confronted with another person who has the same delusion, something gives. For example, in the case of two women who thought they were the Virgin Mary, one concluded that she was not the Virgin Mary but must be Mary Magdalene, thus preserving each woman's claim to individual distinction. Group identity and cohesion are not staples with persons who are schizophrenic, but individuals who are paranoid, though not paranoid schizophrenic, are more likely to band together, provided they can agree on a common enemy.

The extreme cohesiveness of Aum, whose members shared patently absurd beliefs inculcated by their leader, surely suggests a highly consensual "folie a group" to use Fromm's concept. Members of the militia and Patriot groups appear to be a strongly united force only in terms of having the government as their common enemy, but many are united also in their belief that minorities, homosexuals, whites who enjoy and support black culture, etc. are also common enemies. Similarly, but in their more advanced phase, Aum members believe that they have to rid the world of all outsiders in order to cleanse it, to make a clean start in preparation for a new world order. Given this kind of thinking, but not a pervasive kind of thought disorder, these extremists would not be called schizophrenic, but they might meet the criteria for a paranoid disorder if we had such a designation for a group.

The structure of the militia movement allows and even promotes extreme individuation within the bounds of the single-faceted scapegoating group identity. *Leaderless Resistance* (Beam, 1992) is the title of the most popular militia operations manual other than *The Turner Diaries* (Pierce, writing under the pseudonym of Andrew MacDonald, 1978, 1980). Leaderlessness serves the strategic purpose of making it difficult, if not impossible, for the government to focus its detection, surveillance, and anti-terrorist work on any overall organization. Instead, there is a movement consisting mostly of "cells" as small as a few members each. Members of a cell can claim, with some evidence, that they are basically unrelated to any other group or cell that the government challenges. This strategy happens also to lend itself to a kind of "paranoid" freedom of ideation and expression that suits highly idiosyncratic individuals who detest authority of any kind, whether it be irrational (authoritarian) or rational and democratically determined, but this apparent "leaderlessness" could quickly give way to clearer centralization of authority.

Given the strategic and psychological characteristics of "leaderless" cells, what would it take to unite such groups into an even more destructive, massively united movement? One decisive condition would be many, if not most or all, cells perceiving a new "clear" and massive injustice on the part of the government. Ruby Ridge and Waco have provided considerable grist for the milling of a united movement, because many people besides militia members could question the need for the "harsh" government tactics that were employed. In the case of the Oklahoma City bombing, clearly the worst terroristic attack in the history of our country, the bombing has been touted by extreme members as a government plot.

A second decisive condition is that militia members' insistence on individualism or resistance to becoming more massively united is lessened if they find other scapegoats in common. Dees (1996, p. 200) noted that "of the 441 militia and 368 Patriot groups that existed between 1994 and 1996, 137 had ties to the racist right — to groups like the Aryan Nations and the Ku Klux Klan. Of all the militias, these groups and the types of members they attract are the most dangerous."

Both the Aryan Nation and Aum fit the paranoid pattern which comprises two synergistically interacting dynamics which can be captured in the assertions "I would be very great if I were not so very persecuted" and "I am persecuted because of my great qualities." Grandiose and persecutory delusions go hand in hand to form an explanation which simultaneously serves to boost self-esteem and to vent hostility. As exemplified by *The Turner Diaries*, the paranoid process engenders a grand pseudocommunity in which everything that exists fits into the underlying delusional system.

Youths who become alienated through lack of nurturance and social success must somehow raise their self-esteem and avoid feeling inferior. It is then but an easy step to feeling oppressed and seeking redress in a "family" that elevates their self-esteem by identifying them with supremacist groups like the Aryan Nation and Aum.

Having become members, they are then strongly bonded with supposedly only superior people. The group's unifying mission — to cleanse the country and eventually dominate the world — satisfies their powerful need to turn the tables on the innumerable "inferior" beings who have contaminated or would contaminate them. If fully adopted, this mindset fits the paranoid pattern: the now-denied sense of inferiority, unworthiness, and vengeance is projected onto other people. When acted out, this mindset means behaving in the oppressive, hostile manner they attribute to their "persecutors". If the available supply of persecutors dwindles and resentment toward the leader and other members increases, intra-group violence will increase as members doubt one another. To paraphrase an old saying, "Sometimes I think only me and thee are acceptable and sometimes I doubt thee." Ultimately, paranoid group movements tend to evolve into a "black hole" mentality wherein the members find each other unacceptable and may even commit lethal violence within the group.

A Blueprint for Inhibiting Institutional Violence

Many methods can be effective for inhibiting group and institutional lethal aggression. No one method is likely to be very effective by itself but certain combinations may be very effective. As noted previously, we can categorize inhibitions as coming from three sources — extra-institutional, intra-institutional, and intra-individual. Table 2.2 shows examples of

TABLE 2.2

SOURCES AND EXAMPLES OF INHIBITIONS AGAINST INSTITUTIONAL VIOLENCE

Extra-institutional

Enacting laws against the forming of militias whose intent is the violent overthrow of the U.S., wearing masks in public, or using telephones, the mails, or Internet for hate messages. (Banning masks or clothing used for disguise may be unconstitutional.)

Conducting surveillance, such as by electronic devices to monitor telephone calls, meetings, and other communications initiated by or among suspects.

Conducting searches, in conformity with search-and-seizure laws; for example, having police look for materials and resources that could be used to commit violent acts.

Educating for democratic living, such as teaching empathy, tolerance, compassion, and personal responsibility at home, in schools, and in society generally.

Intra-institutional

Developing democratic processes, such as free and open elections, allowing dissent, and actively reviewing complaints and suggestions.

Encouraging extra-institutional relationships; for example, involvement with family, friends, and other groups in the broader community.

Actively cultivating diversity to enrich the institution ethnically, by encouraging a broad variety of personal viewpoints and opinions.

Taking stands against bigotry, both within and outside of the institution, through education, formal protests, and reaching out to help oppressed people.

Intra-individual

Examining one's own tendencies to project and displace hostility vs. accepting personal responsibility and contributing to democracy.

Checking with others outside to see what they would think of the workings of one's institution or group and what changes they suggest.

Taking periodic leaves of absence from the institution in order to look more objectively at it and to belong elsewhere for awhile as a broadening experience.

Participating actively in democratic processes by becoming well-informed, voting, and reaching out to educate and help others to exercise their rights and responsibilities as citizens.

inhibitions that can be effected within each of these categories.

The following blueprint suggests both potentially effective inhibitions and their limitations, beginning with the most simply reactive and, therefore, probably the least effective, and progressing to the level of potentially more effective solutions. The less-effective solutions are included here because they may be partially effective in some circumstances where harm is imminent and are sure to be included in any politically acceptable program of intervention and thus are important to take into account.

Repression

The most common governmental reactions to unlawful violent behavior are repressive. Essentially, repression means trying to identify and deactivate those suspected of wrongdoing. In the case of anti-government militants, the federal government and the state governments (albeit under federal control) would be authorized to undertake surveillance methods that may be useful to identify and convict the wrongdoers. At the extreme, we would allow the government unlimited development and use of intelligence equipment, including covert auditory and visual recording devices, weapons and other intimidation methods, prosecutions, incarcerations, and punishments. In short, we would declare all-out war on the "outlaws". We would become as thoroughly militarized "as necessary" to eradicate the "bad elements" in our society. In this extreme version, certain costs and dangers of repressive tactics become quite clear.

Such all-out repression would destroy the democracy we seek to protect. Our society would then become that which its anti-government militants say we now are. Effectively, we would give truth to the lie.

The U.S. Constitution, which is at the heart of our democracy, would be only a relic. We would have destroyed ourselves, thereby saving anti-government militants the effort and assuring them of victory.

The common-sense reaction to this danger of self-destruction is to lessen the repression and to practice it in a more moderate fashion. Recognition that some repression is probably necessary, especially in the short run, should be coupled with the realization that it is a dangerous tool. Any repressive effort tends to inspire more militant rhetoric and action as well as to inhibit unlawful forms of protest. Many people who are already militant would increase their efforts, and many presently non-militant citizens, seeing their government practice harsh repression, would conclude that the government is indeed becoming like the militants suggested it is, and thereby become more militant themselves. The net effect could easily be more, rather than less, unlawful militancy. Historically, we have instructive examples from our government's attempts in the 1960s to repress black militant dissidents and from our conduct of the Vietnam war.

Inevitably, the use of repressive measures is a tricky business. Paradoxically, the use of repression in a democratic society must be coupled with strong inhibitions against its use. Any increases in our repressive tactics against anti-government militants would have to be matched by increases in surveillance and prosecution of government agents exceeding limits on their powers. The checks and balances characteristic of a democratic government would have to be further mobilized. As a consequence, the "repressive solution" means expense not only in terms of direct expenditures for the repressive measures themselves but also expenditures to fund vigilant and inhibitory actions against these measures. By analogy, it is as if we were to drive faster while applying the brakes harder at the same time, thereby surely generating more friction and compromising our forward progress.

In conclusion, while repression may be necessary, especially in the short run, to save lives, it is hardly a first-rate solution. Rather, it is a dangerous, costly, and potentially quite divisive solution which, if carried to the extreme, would guarantee destruction of our democracy. Those who would regard repressive medicine as a cure in itself should be advised: "This medicine must be used sparingly, as excessive use may cause more harm than the disease it is intended to cure." And in further service of truth in packaging, the warning should say, "Our only guarantee is that symptoms will persist or worsen if nothing is done except to use this medicine."

Negotiation

Though unappealing to "macho" mentalities, negotiation has a long and successful history of resolving disputes if used early enough in the conflict process.

Its success depends considerably on ascertaining early signs of conflict as well as bringing an open mind, empathy, and goodwill to the negotiating table. Respect for opponents has a way of easing discussion and engaging them unless it is clear that an aggressor is already absolutely determined to dominate, as occurred when Hitler was not inclined at all toward sincere, peaceful negotiation and British Prime Minister Chamberlain misread him. Typically, negotiation does not work when matters have already gone very far, but when adversaries can be brought to the negotiating table early in the hostilities, it is possible to generate feelings of empathy and respect for one another.

Negotiators would do well to regard their "adversaries" as at least potentially constructive people with whom talking could be helpful. Carl Rogers, the psychologist whose principles of counseling extended far into other areas of discourse, posited an especially important principle for viewing interpersonal conflicts in need of peaceful resolution. As stated by Kirshenbaum (1995, p. 39):

> *"[Rogers] ... acknowledged the powerful destructive forces within people but saw no evidence to suggest that they were* primary. *He saw negative* and *positive impulses existing side by side within the individual. ...[H]e saw that when the therapist could provide the conditions of congruence, empathy, and unconditional positive regard, this helped the individual to accept both the positive and negative feelings within himself. Once the individual could understand and accept all parts of himself and his inner experience more fully, that person tended to choose more constructive courses of action."*

The use of empathy in negotiation is a method for facilitating intra-group and intra-individual inhibitions against violence. It is much more difficult to behave violently toward people if you get to know them as fellow human beings and are in a position to become able to "feel for them". And, when one shows empathy, it tends to beget empathy in others, too. Ultimately the sense of empathy may carry the day. The reverse is also true. Perceived lack of empathy readily facilitates "negative" behavior including violence and rebellion.

Intra-Individual Inhibitions Against Violence

Leaders attract followers in many ways. On balance, the leader must be perceived as benefiting the followers in order for the followers not to leave. Even extreme forms of coercion and total lack of support for dissent cannot guarantee that a leader will keep followers if the followers are made thoroughly miserable by the leader. Two examples are offered here.

An older student, returning to study at the university he had left several years before, told his story about joining and then leaving a very large religious cult that demanded major personal sacrifices. He had achieved a high position of financial responsibility in the cult and attained a close personal relationship with the leader, but his years of hard work and devotion to the cause, which delayed his education and greatly restricted his freedom, were not enough for the leader. The leader demanded that he submit to an arranged marriage to be formally performed together with many others. Even this further sacrifice of his personal freedom was not enough for him to leave the cult. His own family of origin had been fraught with conflict and turmoil, and he greatly valued his place in his "new family", especially because he had such a close relationship with the "father". So he went through with the marriage, hoping that with time and his own dutiful efforts the marriage would become tolerable and thus confirm the far-seeing wisdom of the cult's leader. A couple of years passed during which he was thoroughly miserable with his arranged marriage and could not find grounds for compatibility. Finally, he left the marriage and the cult, albeit not without severe regrets for his relatively wasted years and the loss of his "father".

Cochran, the aforementioned national spokesman for the Aryan Nation, said he left the movement after a sacrifice they demanded got him thinking. As a prominent member of the Aryan Nation, he had avidly pursued his role as propaganda minister, recruiting many youths to the movement by giving them "just cause" for attacking minorities and others who were "racially inferior". As in Hitler's Nazi movement, the Aryan Nation was also dedicated to rooting out any "genetically inferior" members of their own "race" so as to make it "pure".

This theoretically satisfactory approach to racial purity foundered badly when Cochran was told that his own son, who had a cleft palate (and therefore was imperfect) would have to be "sacrificed" (killed) for the cause. Cochran not only then left the Aryan Nation but began to see that his former dedication had supported and furthered atrocities by that organization. He went from a sense of righteousness to a sense of having committed the most egregious sins. Whatever previous sense of guilt and inhibition that was kept at bay while he was a member was unleashed and became a tremendous, continual dedication to what he called "atonement". Everywhere he could, he made presentations to unmask the propaganda he had previously so fervently preached. The experience of having the cult's violence turned on his own flesh and blood served as a wake- up call. The movement had gone too far; it had threatened to kill someone precious to him.

These case examples illustrate that the "black hole-ism" tendency of deadly cults inevitably begins to destroy or lose their members through death or desertion. This phenomenon of progressive pressure to conform partially explains why authoritarian groups and institutions do not commit lethal aggression more often than they do.

Typically, when people are willing to become violent in a war against the government, there is, as previously emphasized, at least some reality basis for their inclinations. They feel, and often are, disenfranchised. Seldom are they the happy owners of highly successful and legal enterprises, nor are the majority well educated. Cochran, the former propaganda minister of the Aryan Nation, who possessed only a GED himself, claimed that he was appointed to his major spokesman role only because he was so rare in his ability to speak a simple sentence "without having to consult a dictionary." He emphasized that the vast majority of his fellow members were not only poorly educated in the academic sense but lived in very isolated places where there were few voices of any kind, let alone dissenting voices. And because people who are very ready to join a paranoid cult have paranoid tendencies themselves, one can imagine the difficulty of getting through to these people any message that would cause them to stop echoing the party line and reflect on other possibilities. Receiving strong group emotional support for blaming "inferiors" is highly attractive. These considerations lead to recommending certain steps designed to make possible peaceful resolution.

Suggested ways to relate to potentially violent anti-government activists include the following:

1. *Take their complaints very seriously.* Draw them out by listening with a ready ear. Empathize as much as possible with their own subjective feelings as well as any facts that they present which may support their claims. A sympathetic ear will engender some constructive relatedness that can help the militant person(s) get out of the black hole of their paranoid community. This approach does not mean humoring people, i.e., speaking or acting as though the listener is convinced that the complaints are valid in the sense of proven facts. It does mean, however, listening with an open mind and being attentive to what may well be at least some substance to the complaints.
2. *Encourage and cooperate with factual investigations.* Ralph Nader-like studies will tend to make legitimate complaints clear and believable instead of quickly judged "paranoid delusions". During the Denver Model Cities hearings in the 1960s with citizens from poor areas of the city (Whitaker, 1970), some citizens complained that a supermarket chain charged higher prices in the ghetto than in a wealthy neighborhood. A city councilman scoffed, saying, "How could the chain charge more in a poor area

where people can't afford to pay as much?" As an advisor, the author suggested that the offended citizens conduct an objective study, which they carried out meticulously. They were then able to show that, indeed, their claim was entirely justified. The "paranoid" complaints of the black, Chicano, and poor white citizens then received more serious and sympathetic attention.

3. *Where interest is shown, provide factual information related to the complaints.* When people experience a ready ear, they often respond with a ready ear. For instance, in the case of the Denver Model Cities citizen participation project, the Denver Black Panthers took on progressively more constructive and well-informed roles. And though some might have carried a gun and seemed ready for violent confrontation, they did vastly more studying and proposing peaceful projects than they espoused violence. The very governments, city and federal alike, that have been labeled enemies became far more welcome as the processes outlined above were sensitively and sincerely implemented. Although a massive change in the presidency and executive branch of the U.S. dashed most of the funding prospects (Whitaker, 1972a), the spirit of constructive involvement persevered. Several former black militants became important members of city government, and an education strategy begun by a former failed college student became the vehicle for many successful Chicano college graduates.
4. *Educate.* If we would inhibit evil, we must educate people to be good, and not simply try to repress evil. As Eisler (1996, p. 382) has suggested, "... on the human level a far more useful way of looking at evil is as the absence of those qualities that make us uniquely human: our enormous capacity for consciousness, choice, and most important, empathy and love." Traditionally, education has been defined as a formal academic process in which values as such are not taught. The mere mention of teaching values in the public school system is objected to on the grounds that it violates separation of church from state, but there is no need to select or use any religion to teach the values of a democratic society interested in survival.

The core values necessary for a democratic society to survive and to be constructive in the world are respect for and empathy with other living beings and our natural heritage. Yet, our schools in the U.S., let alone educational institutions in more authoritarian countries, do too little to prepare us for peaceful means of resolving conflicts. We should be especially careful not to emphasize the physical sciences at the expense of a liberal education. A broad education can teach respect for oneself and others through a wide array of subjects including the arts, humanities, and social sciences. Narrowly restricted education facilitates narrow mindedness, a crucial component of bigotry-motivated human violence.

A truthful education will also inhibit violence. What is most wrong with our gigantic violence entertainment industry is that it does not portray violence honestly. As Eisler (1996) emphasized, it eroticizes violence, even though, inherently, real violence is exactly the opposite of sexual pleasure. Furthermore, as McWilliams noted (1993), the violence entertainment industry sanitizes violence though real violence is the opposite of sanitary. Consider here, for example, that favorite hate cult oxymoron "ethnic cleansing". McWilliams proposed a solution (1993, p. 590):

"All of this sanitized violence only makes real violence a more acceptable solution to problems. It's not that violence is shown, and that causes violence; it's that violence is shown as the solution *to problems;* that *causes violence. 'A single death is a tragedy; a million deaths is a statistic,' said Joseph Stalin (who should know). If, however, the way in which each of these million died and the suffering they went through had to be viewed one at a time in great detail, perhaps it would no longer be a statistic, and perhaps such tragedies would happen less often."*

Harold Pagliaro (1996) provided an excellent illustration of front-line combat in war, a group and institutional endeavor that otherwise is almost always shown as eroticized and sanitized entertainment in movies, television, and children's games. His book *Naked Heart* is as freeing as only the truth can be.

Truthful, realistic education in human relations is what is most needed in school curricula and in society at large. In its absence, we will continue to have a predominantly dominator mentality that adversely affects not only male-female relationships but all relationships involving positions of power; otherwise, most of our institutions will continue to stress domination of others.

If we continue in serious pursuit of stereotypic masculine ideals of domination, inevitably we will promote, rather than inhibit, fatal group and institutional aggression. But, if we trade in the male stereotype model of domination which masquerades as the ultimate power, we can have a far more powerful model, the power to nurture and safeguard not only our lives and rights but those of others. Eisler's (1996) partnership model emphasizes nurturance, nonviolent conflict resolution, a more egalitarian social structure, mutual respect and freedom of choice in sexuality, empathy and unconditional love, pleasure bonding, and the enhancement of giving, nurturing, and illuminating life as the highest power. If we select the partnership model over the presently preeminent dominator model, we can certainly inhibit personal, group, and institutional lethal aggression.

Summary

This chapter proposes principles and methods useful for inhibiting group and institutional lethal aggression. It documents that all institutions have the potential for violence, as illustrated by various legally and societally approved professions such as law and journalism, by sports, by colleges and universities, and by the military. In the process, the relative effectiveness of their particular extra-institutional, intra-institutional, and intra-individual inhibitions is noted. This review and commentary is then used to contrast those institutions with anti-government extremists, terrorists, and deadly cults, using the anti-government Patriots in the United States and Aum in Japan as examples of the latter.

The Patriots and Aum appear to be very different in many ways but have certain characteristics which in combination define a cult — dependence on a leader, compliance with the group, avoidance of dissent, and devaluation of the outsider. The more authoritarian the leadership and the more coercive the conformity, the more likely it is that hostilities will be projected onto and acted out against outsiders, but members suffer losses themselves, including training in cruelty that requires becoming insensitive to their own emotions and desires. Ultimately, as such groups become more ingrown and intolerant, members tend to turn on one another.

The readiness of such groups to attack the government arises in part from justified concerns such as feeling uncared for and not listened to while being stringently regulated and taxed by a government seen as wasteful and negligent of their needs, but the members tend also to share paranoid proclivities as well as the all too human susceptibility to authoritarian leadership that promises to save them from some kind of doomsday. A cult's own vengeful brand of religion is used to compensate for feelings of persecution and low self-esteem while freeing members from inhibitions against committing violence. The people most likely to be recruited are alienated youths who find a "family" in the cult.

The author's blueprint for inhibiting institutional violence includes, but notes the considerable dangers of, repressive methods. Negotiation, if conducted early enough, can be very useful. Intra-individual inhibitions against violence, which are usually held in check by group pressures to conform, can be unleashed by even one dissenter, or by an individual's increasing sense of oppression, as illustrated by case examples. What is most fundamentally needed is early education in human relations and democratic living, with greater emphasis on partnership than dominator models.

Annotated Bibliography

1. Dees, Morris (1996) *Gathering Storm: America's Militia Threat*. New York: Harper Collins. As chief trial counsel for the Southern Poverty Law Center and its Militia Task Force and an award-winning author, Dees knows what militias are about and conveys his knowledge well. His years of investigative research enable him in this book to give richly detailed accounts of the militia movement both from the outside and the inside. The resultant picture is persuasive. The reader comes to understand that what we read in the newspapers or see on television is merely the tip of the iceberg. The movement's motivational impetus becomes clear in terms of its scapegoating nature and strong resemblance to the Nazi movement which has largely been reborn as a purer than thou "patriotism".

2. Deikman, Arthur J. (1990) *The Wrong Way Home: Uncovering the Patterns of Cult Behavior in American Society*. Boston: Beacon Press. The author, a psychiatrist especially well known for his research on states of consciousness, shows clearly that cult behavior — dependence on a leader, compliance with the group, avoiding dissent, and devaluing the outsider — pervades the "normal" institutions on which we are dependent. He makes understandable the deadly extremes of authori-tarianism that militia and terrorist cults fanatically pursue. Deikman's outstanding ability to illuminate the vicissitudes of dependency dynamics that underlie cult behavior is reminiscent of Erich Fromm's brilliant book, *Escape from Freedom,* that related the tragic lure of Hitler's Nazi ideology to its facilitation by social institutions in the pre-World War II era. Like Fromm, Deikman found that "[t]he structure of cults is basically authoritarian; obedience and hierarchical power tend to take precedence over truth and conscience when they conflict, which they often do" (see p. 73).

3. Eisler, Riane (1996) *Sacred Pleasure: Sex, Myth, and the Politics of the Body*. New York: Harper Collins Publishers. This 405-page book is at once a powerful condemnation of violence in all its ubiquity and iniquity and a correspondingly powerful appreciation of love and nurture. It is astonishingly sane. For that reason, the reader is made acutely aware that much of what we blithely accept as normal turns out to be the insanity of everyday life, all the more destructive for its banality. Eisler's highly readable text brims with sophisticated scholarly analyses that have immediate practical applications in every sphere of life. She shows that "... if we are to construct a society where sex will be linked not with violence and domination but with the truly erotic — with the life-and-pleasure-giving powers within us and around us in the world — we need to fully extricate ourselves from all that has for so long unconsciously bound us to painful and unhealthy myths and realities" (see p. 200).

4. Pagliaro, Harold (1996) *Naked Heart: A Soldier's Journey to the Front*. Kirksville, MO: Thomas Jefferson University Press. A distinguished professor of English literature gives an eloquent but literally and figuratively down-to-earth personal account of his actual World War II front-line experiences as an 18-year-old infantryman. Presented in the humane context of his family experiences and values, the contrast is powerfully instructive. On the one hand, he is brought up to love and to revere life, and on the other he is forcibly trained to kill under the dictum of "kill or be killed!" A premonitory dream at age 14 depicted "exploding artillery shells that broke across the skies, lighting them in deep shadowed blazes of fire and shaking them with thunder. I remember the dream, as intense as hallucination, the live painting of a world gone mad" (see p. 3). The dream and reality become isomorphic, leaving no doubt that war is indeed a hellish nightmare utterly different from its vapid idealization.

References

Asch, S.E. (1952) *Social Psychology*. Englewood Cliffs, NJ: Prentice-Hall.

Bachman, W. (1995) *Law v. Life: What Lawyers Are Afraid To Say About the Legal Profession*. Rhinebeck, NY: Four Directions Press.

Barry, D. (1997) Outcast gladiators find a home: New York. *The New York Times,* January 15, pp. A1, B6.

Beam, L. (1992) Leaderless resistance. *The Seditionist.* February, pp. 22–27.

"The Citadel's culture of abuse" (1997) *The New York Times,* January 14, p. A14.

Cochran, F. (1996) Presentation on the Aryan Nations. November 6, Delaware County Community College, PA.

Crothers, C.T. and Matthews, A. (1996) Hazing days. *The New York Times Magazine*, November 3, pp. 50, 51.

Dees, M., with Corcoran, J. (1996) *Gathering Storm: America's Militia Threat.* New York: HarperCollins.

Deikman, A.J. and Whitaker, L.C. (1979) Humanizing a psychiatric ward: changing from drugs to psychotherapy. *Psychotherapy: Theory, Research and Practice, 16*(2), 204–214.

Deikman, A.J. (1990) *The Wrong Way Home: Uncovering the Patterns of Cult Behavior in American Society.* Boston: Beacon Press.

Eisler, R. (1996) *Sacred Pleasure: Sex, Myth, and the Politics of the Body*. New York: Harper Collins Publishers (originally published in 1995).

Fromm, E. (1990) *The Sane Society.* New York: Henry Holt & Co. (originally published in 1955).

Gove, P. (1966) *Webster's Third New International Dictionary of the English Language, Unabridged*. Springfield, MA: Merriam.

Higginbotham, A.L., Jr. (1996) *Shades of Freedom: Racial Politics and Presumptions of the American Legal Process*. New York: Oxford University Press.

Holmes, S.A. (1996) Income disparity between richest and poorest rises. *The New York Times*, June 20, pp. A1, A18.

Howard, P.K. (1994) *The Death of Common Sense*. New York: Warner Books.

Kaplan, J., Gen. Ed. (1992) Adolf Hitler. In *Bartlett's Familiar Quotations,* 16th ed., p. 676. Boston: Little, Brown and Company.

Kaplan, D. E. and Marshall, A. (1996) *The Cult at the End of the World*. New York: Crown Publishers.

Kirshenbaum, H. (1995) Carl Rogers. In M.M. Suhd (Ed.), *Positive Regard: Carl Rogers and Other Notables He Influenced,* pp. 1–90. Palo Alto, CA: Science and Behavior Books.

Kriegel, M. (1996) Gentlemen, start your bleeding. *Esquire*, March, pp. 94–101.

MacDonald, A. (1978, 1980, written as W. Pierce) *The Turner Diaries*. Hillsboro, WV: National Vanguard Books.

Malcolm, J. (1990) *The Journalist and the Murderer*. New York: Knopf.

McWilliams, P. (1993) *Ain't Nobody's Business If You Do: The Absurdity of Consensual Crimes in a Free Society.* Los Angeles: Prelude Press.

Milgram, S. (1974) *Obedience to Authority*. New York: Harper and Row.

National Broadcasting Company (1997), broadcast February 12.

Okrent, D. and Lewine, H., Eds. (1991) *The Ultimate Baseball Book.* Boston: Houghton Mifflin.

Pagliaro, H. (1996) *Naked Heart*. Kirksville, MO: Thomas Jefferson University Press.

Rivinus, T.M. and Larimer, M.E. (1993) Violence, alcohol, other drugs, and the college student. In L.C. Whitaker and J.W. Pollard (Eds.), *Campus Violence: Kinds, Causes, and Cures,* pp. 71–119. New York: The Haworth Press. Published simultaneously in *Journal of College Student Psychotherapy, 8*(1/2,3).

Ruane, M.E. (1997) Cohen assails hazing by Marines. *Philadelphia Inquirer,* February 1, p. A1.

Silber, J. (1996) Students should not be above the law [op-ed]. *The New York Times,* May 9, p. A 27.

"Soldier tells of admission in double murder" (1997) *The New York Times,* February 16, p. A 19.

Southern Poverty Law Center (1996) *False Patriots: The Threat of Anti-Government Extremists.* Montgomery, AL: Southern Poverty Law Center.

Sports Illustrated (1995) Special NFL classic edition, Fall.

Whitaker, L.C. (1970) Social reform and the comprehensive community mental health center: the Model Cities experiment, Part I. *American Journal of Public Health, 60*(10), 2003–2010.

Whitaker, L.C. (1972a) Social reform and the comprehensive community mental health center: the Model Cities experiment, Part II. *American Journal of Public Health, 62*(2), 216–222.

Whitaker, L.C. (1972b) Community mental health wars and black ownership. *Professional Psychology,* Fall, pp. 307–310, 321–323.

Whitaker, L.C. (1992) *Schizophrenic Disorders: Sense and Nonsense in Conceptualization, Assessment and Treatment.* New York: Plenum Press.

Whitaker, L.C. (1996) Social inducements to paralethal and lethal violence. In H.V. Hall (Ed.), *Lethal Violence 2000: A Sourcebook on Fatal Stranger, Domestic, and Acquaintance Aggression,* pp. 143–174. Kamuela, HI: Pacific Institute for the Study of Conflict and Aggression.

About the Author

Leighton C. Whitaker, Ph.D., ABPP, is in private practice, is Adjunct Clinical Professor at Widener University's Institute for Graduate Clinical Psychology, and is the editor of the *Journal of College Student Psychotherapy.* His 70 professional publications address a wide variety of clinical and social subjects and include the *Whitaker Index of Schizophrenic Thinking* (Western Psychological Services, 1980) and *Schizophrenic Disorders* (Plenum Press, 1992). His previous positions include Associate Professor and Director of Adult Psychology for the University of Colorado Health Sciences Center, Professor and Director of the University of Massachusetts Mental Health Services, and Director of Swarthmore College Psychological Services. He has done forensic work for many years and has been a consultant to the U.S. Department of Labor's Job Corps. His work with youth has been featured on television and in newspapers.

Acknowledgments

The author thanks Arthur Deikman, M.D., for reading an early version of this manuscript, making suggestions, and providing useful readings. Thanks go also to Benjamin Whitaker for helping prepare the final manuscript.

CHAPTER 3

VIOLENCE, VIEWING, AND POLARIZATION: THE CONTRIBUTION OF VIOLENCE IN THE MEDIA AND SOME SOLUTIONS

Lita Linzer Schwartz and Rosalie G. Matzkin

Across all regions of the nation, Americans are becoming preoccupied with identifying and reinforcing their personal and group identities, while being less concerned with what is in the public interest. Amidst the riches of our natural resources, ongoing advances in technology, and international movements to eliminate weapons of mass destruction, our people seem increasingly polarized and confounded by unresolved tensions and conflicts. Many of these tensions and conflicts erupt into hate crimes and violence, especially among our youth. The purpose of this chapter is first to scrutinize some of the most pervasive kinds of polarization, as well as to examine problems within some major institutions which the authors believe contribute to the spread of messages of conflict, hatred, and violence. There is also a second, perhaps even more important purpose: to provide data about current, mostly new, efforts being introduced across the country to combat our national fears and discontents.

Media reports of the use of lethal violence to end disagreements, whether personal or public, bombard us daily. Violence against children, and increasingly *by* children, has become a national crisis. According to a report released by the Centers for Disease Control and Prevention in February 1997 (Havemann, 1997, p. A2), "Nearly three quarters of all the murders of children in the industrialized world occur in the United States." The report also found that "the United States had the highest rates of childhood homicide, suicide, and firearms-related deaths of any of the world's 26 richest nations."

That study strongly supported the results of previous investigations which also tracked the problems of violence and children. In fact, in the 1997 *National Television Violence Study* (NTV Study, 1997), researchers felt compelled to quote statistics from the American Psychological Association's 1993 study because they believed the data were still valid. Stressing the fact that we live in a violent society, the authors noted that "we rank first among all developed countries in the world in homicides per capita" (p. 8). The NTV Study listed some of the staggering statistics:

- Every five minutes a child is arrested for a violent crime.
- Gun-related violence takes the life of an American child every 3 hours.
- Every day, 100,000 children carry guns to school.

- In a recent survey of fifth graders in New Orleans, more than 50% reported being a victim of violence, and 70% have seen weapons used.
- Adolescents account for 24% of all violent crimes leading to arrest. The rate has increased over time for the age group 12 to 19 and is down for the age group 35 and older.
- Among individuals ages 15 to 24, homicide is the second leading cause of death, and for black youth, it is the leading cause.
- A child growing up in Chicago is 15 times more likely to be murdered than a child growing up in Northern Ireland.

Although violence in America takes many forms, during the 1990s a less familiar form — domestic terrorism — has literally exploded in many of our communities. In fact, in 1995 alone, there were nearly 8000 reported hate crimes committed across the country. Many others go unreported (Uniform Crime Reports Program, Division of Federal Bureau of Investigation, West Virginia, personal communication, June 10, 1997). The fear and anxiety produced by bombings of churches, government buildings, abortion clinics, offices, and even homes, often involving fatalities, are now adding even more pressure to the already troubled American psyche. Places such as Waco, TX; Oklahoma City, OK; and the summer Olympics park in Atlanta, GA, now evoke graphic images in our collective unconscious, underscoring our conflicts over how to assess, deal with, and prevent future repetition of such tragedies.

America's preoccupation with issues of violence is not, of course, limited to the real world. Our popular culture eerily reflects and sometimes distorts the images of aggression, pain, physical abuse, rapid car chases, explosions, and gunfire. Actual, or make-believe, those scenes are available on a regular schedule, prime time, after school, on the 5:30 p.m., 6 p.m., and 6:30 p.m. or late evening news broadcasts. The circumstances of these events are taking their toll on our sensibilities and those of our over-exposed children. The almost addictive consumption of mass media entertainment and the blurring of the lines between entertainment and reality-based programming add to the problem.

Clearly, we in contemporary society are increasingly dependent on the media. The news media and free speech *are* essential to democracy and are integral components of any democracy. Moreover, most of us enjoy the media's many attributes and riches. The intrinsic tensions existing between audience needs and wants and those of its marketplace foundations will undoubtedly continue to be revised and reviewed, as they have been historically, since the first meaningful Federal Communications Commission (FCC) was initiated in 1912. But, our more intense contemporary dependency, particularly on electronic media, has inherent flaws, not the least of which is the danger that some who engage in lethal violence may use (and may be used by) mass media for purposes of conveying their own messages of hate or fear. It is the interaction of violence, the media, and the climate of polarization that the media help to engender with which this chapter is primarily concerned. To provide a context for this interaction, a needed discussion of relevant political and economic factors of the mass media is also included.

A Historically Fractious Nation

"Lethal violence in America provides many models in the industry of death. History has shown that Americans as a whole, although resourceful and very willing to help others, are an incorrigibly violent people. Ours was a society that repeatedly used lethal violence to attain such lofty goals as national independence... " (Hall, 1996, p. 669)

In fact, as early as the arrival of the Puritans in what became the New England Colony, those who did not accept the established religion were ousted from the Colony. In addition, by 1634, Pilgrims and Puritans were killing each other for control of the beaver trade. In one particularly violent episode involving the fatal aggression by members of one group against the other, the outcome impelled a general court in Boston to disavow the action and to state, "... besides [the governor] had brought us all and the gospel under a common reproach of cutting one another's throats for beaver" (Dofstadter and Wallace, 1972, p. 48; taken from James Kendall, *Original Narratives of Early American History,* Vol. VII, 1908).

Those already here in the 19th century, and again especially after the First World War, resented newer immigrants, harassed them, and succeeded in having immigration laws modified in the 1920s to prevent Eastern and Southern Europeans, as well as Asians, from coming to this country. The ideal view early in the 20th century, exemplified by Israel Zangwill's (1908) *The Melting Pot*, was that the U.S. was a "melting pot" into which all newcomers were poured and stirred and from which they emerged as assimilated "Americans". (This did not include the former slaves whose race could not "melt", obviously, especially in the South.)

Virtually all of the early immigrants had grave economic problems. Many came from countries where little education was available to them, so they were illiterate. Stereotypes of newcomers included the view that they were political radicals.

The practice of enforcing "Americanization", so prevalent in many American institutions, and the contempt and disdain expressed so openly by many Americans toward the immigrant and his culture, had long-term ramifications (Isser and Schwartz, 1985, p. 19): "... [D]emands for conformity tended to lead to the destruction, or at least the weakening, of marital relationships, as well as creating social anomie. Delinquency, materialism, and alcoholism were frequently the fruits of the policy of destroying traditional family and community relationships." As we know from a wide variety of sources, these negative outcomes contribute to violent behavior.

The concept of cultural pluralism introduced by Kallen (1915), on the other hand, supported the idea of maintaining cultural and ethnic traditions within a larger society that had a common language (English), rules, and social goals. Whether we use nation of origin as the source of tradition, or the practice of various religions under the protection of the First Amendment, cultural pluralism allows for people of different backgrounds to live, function, and worship under the same flag, enriching the national image as they do so. The ideals of cultural pluralism, however, in recent years, have been perverted into ethnic, religious, and political polarizations that have sometimes erupted into lethal violence. Some of these incidents have involved fatalities to adults and children. They have been reported repeatedly in the media, both print and electronic, with unintended impact on children's incidental learning about people unlike themselves as well as about how to interact with them.

Mass Media and Juvenile Homicide

In a previous work entitled "Violence, Viewing, and Development" (Schwartz and Matzkin, 1996), the authors found widespread condemnation of the mass media by many public and professional groups. The media's portrayals of violence were perceived as being responsible for the high rate of juvenile homicides. Other groups blamed variously heredity, parents, teachers, poverty, drugs, and peer groups. The authors concluded, however, that it is the interaction of these many factors that creates vulnerable youth — youth who are less resistant to situations that may lead them to acts of violence such as shooting or knifing someone. As a result of this interaction of factors, children in the same family may vary in their degree of vulnerability to external factors such as violence in the mass media, with the result that one may become a killer and another a solid citizen. The media's role *is* important here, though not exclusive, because like family, school, and government, the media has taken on a life of its own that, for better or worse, contributes to people's attitudes, behaviors, values, and lifestyles.

FIGURE 3.1

THE PERSON *VIS-A-VIS* VIOLENCE

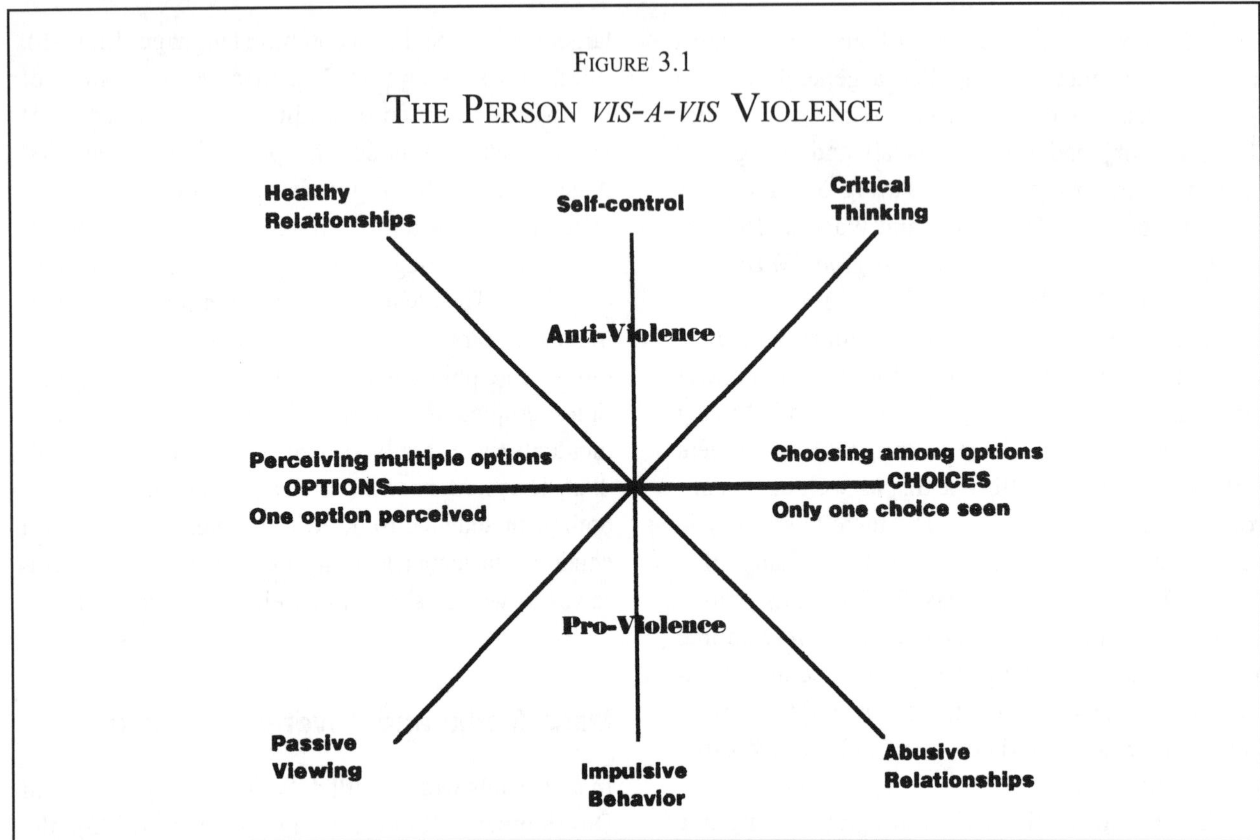

The authors also found that too many children and youth exist with little hope that they will live past age 20, with the perception that they have no choices in life (and have little, if any, experience in how to make them), and with a propensity for impulsive behavior (Schwartz and Matzkin, 1996). Many of these young people lack the necessary social and psychological mechanisms (learned or innate) necessary to enable them to exercise self-control. Those who have lived in families where abusive and violent behaviors are common tend to perceive such behavior as the norm. They then are more likely to engage in violence themselves. Their personal experiences and personal qualities either contribute to, or detract from, their ability to avoid violence through perceiving options and making informed choices. The interaction of these factors can be seen in Figure 3.1.

Those lacking the qualities and experience that would enable them to avoid violent behavior are also more easily drawn into the polarized groups that too often promote violence. They may display what Farley (1991) called Type-T (or Big-T) behavior. Such individuals are arousal seekers, preferring high risk, novelty, unpredictability, high intensity, low structure, and high conflict rather than the simpler and quieter lifestyle of "small-t" individuals. Type-T personalities may seek stimulation through positive or negative pathways and in mental or physical activities. Type-T personalities who engage in negative activities via socially disapproved sources of stimulation harbor "a dangerous side, which is the destructive aspect of taking risks and seeking thrills" (Farley, 1991, p. 375). And it is this type of youth who is apt to seek out more violent entertainment programming and become aroused to violence.

A Climate of Polarization

One of the complex and confounding characteristics of our contemporary society is its apparent inability to find common ground among those who actually acknowledge the existence of our problems. While not all serious disagreements lead to violence, we appear to be living in a time when issues become intensely sensationalized, resulting in ideological disparity. Hotly contested issues range from the political arena to the world of sports. It is these disparities which capture the headlines and most of the attention, to the belittlement of the equally important reality of the beliefs and attitudes that also bind us. One way of perceiving the discordance and polarization or extremism is to glance at the 1996 elections as a sign of how wide the gulf is between political parties and voters. American voters continued to reinforce a national split by electing two branches of government from two different parties that have found it difficult to work together. According to Wolman and Fuller (1997), "Regardless of public calls for cooperation, voters in the last two elections have made bipartisanship less likely."

Another way to see how hostile we become over our disagreements is to look at the frequency of conflict that exists in and around the world of sports. When owners and players were unable to agree on a new contract, the 1995 World Series had to be canceled. Violence has become common in many of our national games and sports, both on the field/court and off, with verbal and physical aggression occurring not only among players, but against fans, referees, and umpires as well.

Of course, the causes and provocations for the violence are neither new nor unrelated. In an address to the 104th Annual Meeting of the American Psychological Association (August 1996), Atlanta Mayor Andrew Young observed:

"In spite of all our progress in human relations, largely in relation to race, [Americans] find ourselves becoming more polarized than ever before. And understanding that polarization, and understanding the effects of the rapid social change that we've been involved in, I think, is critical to our survival, particularly as we approach this 21st century."

The Economic and Social Contexts of Polarization

Tumultuous socio-economic changes and disparities have been occurring over the last two decades. Ironically, this has all been taking place as the Cold War with the (former) Soviet Union has ended and as the perception of a global economy has been influencing not only how we conduct business, but also the kinds of business we conduct.

We cannot expound on the problems that divide us without looking at the serious underlying issues festering below the surface and episodically exploding into open view, including:

- Joblessness
- Crime
- Racism
- Reverse racism
- Drugs
- Easy access to guns
- Child abuse
- Homelessness
- Breakdown of the family
- Domestic violence
- Public cynicism
- Lack of adequate health care
- Fetally addicted babies
- Distrust of government or of government programs
- Terrorist acts

Economic disparities, brought about by the loss of manufacturing jobs for millions of Americans, as well as the loss of the small family farm or shop, have encouraged the development of a virtually permanent underclass. Lack of options for entry-level jobs, with the kind of potential growth offered the unskilled, has helped to increase family instability. The cycle of family instability often then leads to increases in racism, intolerance, extremism, and chemical dependency, as well as cynicism toward a government that appears to many to be too bloated, bureaucratic, or simply too expensive to support.

Some controversies over privacy and personal rights, abortion, adoption, and gun control have led to acts of violence and murder. Most alarming, perhaps, has been the rise of the militia movement in America. As stated by Stern (1996, pp. 44–45):

"Many of the people who join militias see themselves as Klan members did in the 1960s. They do not define themselves as belonging to hate groups, but as citizens trying to reclaim and preserve a way of life under attack. They count on their neighbors' shared concerns about gun control or the environment or abortion; about outside forces such as government and hidden power groups trying to change the way they live. And, like the Klan of the 1960s, they want to intimidate their perceived opponents in order to gain a feeling of political strength and perhaps real political power as well. But as much of their political tactics resemble Klan thuggery, the history of hate and conspiracy from which today's militia have grown, is much broader.

"Go to a militia meeting and pick up the literature. There are charts depicting the 'Conspiracy To Rule the World', ... literature from the Christian Patriots, the Posse Comitatus, Christian Identity groups, Bo Gritz, the John Birch Society, and the Ku Klux Klan. This rich compost of conspiracy theory and hate has fermented on the fringes of America for decades. The ideas found in all these right-wing groups have not faded away. They have been reborn as part of the militia movement. This time around, the ideas are more dangerous, for their proponents are heavily armed."

As we noted earlier, many political campaigns have become increasingly, intensely, and bitterly partisan with the aid of electronic media coverage. This factionalism seems to explain, at least in part, why only 48% of eligible voters went to the polls in 1996. This may indicate that the majority has gone from being polarized to paralyzed, staying at home rather than even bothering to register their complaints by voting.

As an advertising-driven society, we are encouraged to become constant consumers. As consumers, we are encouraged to demand or purchase what we do not need and may not even really want. One of the most cynical ploys of business has been the recognition, growing and expanding since the 1950s, of the youth market. Separating out youthful consumers from their parents with youth-oriented products has been a boon to the recording, entertainment, and fashion industries which have created the products. Creating avid consumers out of very young children is an even more recent phenomenon. As Hillary Rodham Clinton (1996, p. 289) stated, "Those of us who believe in the free market system should worry about what we are in danger of becoming: a throw-away society in which people — especially children — define self-worth in terms of what they have today and can buy tomorrow."

Persistently, the advertising messages of our media-saturated world remind viewers how important it is to have this or that product, reminding them, too, that without this or that product they are somehow less adequate. Such messages over time can provoke crime, as young people seek to possess the currently popular jacket, sneakers, or other object or to acquire the money to buy them. Ewing (1990a, p. 161) noted, "Impoverished youngsters are more likely to become involved in juvenile gangs, commit economically motivated crimes such as robbery, and be exposed to the temptations of the drug trade often flourishing in their disadvantaged and decaying urban neighborhoods."

In a nation of such diversity, conflicts and differences are, of course, natural and sometimes healthy. However, our present problems of violence, particularly among the young in America, and the nation's overall mood of disengagement, cynicism, or polarization are complex and difficult to mend. No single facet of American life can be held liable as the source or basis for the discontent that confronts us. In fact, the problems are connected so tightly that as one aspect worsens, the other problems also escalate (Schwartz and Matzkin, 1996).

The Community and Polarization

While much research focuses on the individual and violence, Twemlow and Sacco (1996) have been studying cultural factors that influence violence. In addressing in depth the notion that lethal violence does not occur in a vacuum, these researchers emphasized the importance of social context and the mores of the larger group beyond the immediate family. Twemlow and Sacco (1996, pp. 619–623) identified a group of psychological attributes within a violent community. They include:

1. Anti-intellectualism (lack of emphasis on reflection or abstract thinking processes)
2. Desire for personal power and a belief that altruism is weakness
3. Need for immediate gratification
4. Lack of stable political or family systems

Today, whether we are looking at the dysfunctional or violent community or at a reasonably healthy or stable one, contemporary lifestyle changes have precipitated other dramatic alterations in familial and community relations. Far more than in earlier times, peer pressure plays a part in the modern technocratic community. Peer pressure is far more influential than it was several decades ago. According to Prothrow-Stith and Weissman (1991, p. 59):

"In the age-segregated society in which we live, many adolescents have little contact with adults, including their parents. I was interested to read some research documenting this. Sociologists interviewed hundreds of students attending an economically and socially diverse midwestern high school. The young people kept detailed logs of what they did and with whom during a two-week period. The researchers found that their teenage subjects, busy with school, after school jobs that stretch into the dinner hour, and peers often spent as little as one hour a week with their parents. Many families did not eat dinner together. Nor, in general, did the students have other adult friends or advisors."

In earlier eras, traditional family roles were sharply defined, and fewer households required two full-time working parents. Then, single parents raising families had a support network more often than they do today. As a result, the availability of positive role models or mentors within the extended family has decreased for many youths today.

In weak or dysfunctional communities, there is also a tendency to adopt attitudes of being a victim of, rather than to accept responsibility for, the miseries being experienced. This is often accompanied by an unwillingness to engage in basic, constructive survival activities, especially when those in ailing communities do not know how to organize and work together, and when they do not understand the collaborative process.

However, it is not merely within poorer or less structured communities and regions that a sense of cooperation is lacking. As observed by Hall (1996, p. 674), Americans maintain "the continued belief that competition, with its violent offshoots, as opposed to cooperation, is necessary (and even healthy) to sustain our quality of life." Our emphasis on individualism (an historically perceived virtue) and on "doing one's own thing" (a contemporary American belief) now often take precedence in many areas over a desire to participate in what is understood to be in the common interest.

Public Schools

Schools, particularly public schools, once the true inspiration for notions of hope and possibility, are beleaguered by complex problems, targeted for attack by groups who seek to undermine their validity and usefulness and who wish more tax dollars would be made available to private education. Since the end of World War II, as black southerners moved north and gradually as new immigrant groups from Asia and Latin America arrived in larger numbers, our cities have become more crowded with these populations. This has led to the abandonment of the cities by large numbers of middle and upper middle class populations. This has also led to businesses and corporations quitting the city, leaving the cities minus their once healthier tax bases.

In major cities, the polarization surrounding cultural differences and problems of how to cope with drugs, violence, and guns in the schools have resulted in constant administrative staff changes and provoked deep suspicion that power is more important than learning to many local political and educational leaders. As stated by Applebom (1997): "Whether couched in the rhetorical excesses of liberals or conservatives, when the subject is society and its ills, the solution is invariably education."

Now that faith is being tested, as never before. A changing work force has put an increased premium on education as the single most important key to success. A fractured populace has different views of what schools must provide. And a near-mania for improvement on standardized test scores has coincided with the public's expectations that schools are out to deal with the ills of poverty and violence in poor neighborhoods.

"As a society, we have a long history of continually looking at schools as a sort of first line of defense against whatever is defined as the problem du jour," said Mike Rose, a professor at the University of California at Los Angeles, who wrote *Possible Lives: The Promise of Education in America.* "We're at a time when we are particularly conflicted as a culture. So you can imagine how contradictory and confusing the messages can be at the school level" (Rose, 1996, p. E4).

Educators at all levels, however, from nursery school to graduate school, face more challenges today due in part to the media's omnipresence. Because children spend so much time in front of the television set, learners are demanding that education be entertaining. Teachers are expected to "perform" for their students, whether in kindergarten or in college. Educators feel a pressure to keep up with the newest fads in popular culture and a need to endorse the latest trends in video and film, or else face the possibility of finding themselves considered "out of it" or irrelevant to their students. This is a kind of emotional blackmail, and it speaks volumes about the issue of who is influencing whom.

Contemporary popular culture, in its various forms, genres, formats, and media arrangements offers us a sweeping but useful reflection of our growing societal fragmentation. Our differences are continually underscored through media news reports as well as entertainment programming. Ideological differences aired in hateful speech, marches, inflammatory rhetoric heard and printed across the electronic media and on the Internet are abetting the disequilibrium.

Polarization and the Mass Media

Media and Audiences: The Relationship

In a previous work (Schwartz and Matzkin, 1996), the authors touched briefly on how research has helped to illuminate the relationship between media and audiences, particularly children and youth. Findings from several areas of research which looked at media content and its relationship to attitudes and behavior were summarized. Virtually all of the research, from several differing approaches and disciplines, concluded that media currently impact significantly on society, on the individual, and particularly on the child. Among the studies were those based on modeling theory, social learning theory, cognitive dissonance, arousal theory, and cultivation analysis.

The many and complex ways in which people are affected by mass media encounters have been the subject of study in a variety of often interrelated disciplines within the social sciences for more than 50 years. During this period, as social science research techniques have changed and become increasingly sophisticated, findings have been modified, new issues have been discovered and received new attention, and new areas of exploration continue even now to unfold.

Mass media studies, in particular, focus on media content, media channels (or technologies through which messages are sent and received), and the very nature and meaning of the communication act. "Uses and gratification" research seeks to understand why people use a special medium, with what expectations, and whether or not these expectations are fulfilled. Media studies also explore related issues including polling, advertising, and the media's role in political campaigns. Cultural studies examine forms, genres, and types of entertainment arts (including mass mediated formats), often from a historical perspective.

While during the 1930s many researchers accepted the hypodermic (or "magic bullet") concept of human behavior, by the 1940s and 1950s, research had largely modified that view of a mass and homogeneous audience and had come to acknowledge individual differences and the notions of selective attention, perception, and retention (Blumler and Katz, 1974; Davison and Yu, 1974; DeFleur and Ball-Rokeach, 1975). During the 1950s, studies by Katz and Lazarsfeld (1955), for example, observed the minimal effects theory of mass media, because "personal influences" were perceived as more important than mass media in shaping opinions, attitudes, and beliefs. Since the 1960s and 1970s, most research has reverted to considering the cumulative effects of mass media exposure depending on how heavy the viewing habits and what type of content is being viewed, as well as personal characteristics and contexts of the audience.

In repudiating the "magic bullet" phenomenon, which implied that media could immediately target an audience member and modify his or her pre-existing beliefs or behaviors, research was characterizing audiences as active and individualistic, rather than merely passive. The rationale has become that the audiences who watch television, listen to the radio, read newspapers, or go out to the movies, are active, in the sense that they have turned on their sets or left their homes and freely chosen to engage in their encounters. They are mass audiences, therefore, from only the most vague and ambiguous perspectives. As noted by Baughman (1992, p. xv):

"[T]he numbers of consumers and the ease with which they can be manipulated by the mass media should not be overstated. On command, TV cannot drive millions to extreme antisocial behavior, nor can advertising hypnotize legions of consumers and voters. The great majority carry in their heads different individual filters — fashioned by class, race or ethnicity, family upbringing, formal education — that limit the effectiveness of mass communication."

Furthermore, outside of the media, family, and school, there are other important socializing agents, such as adolescent peers or opinion leaders in the community, who also impact on our lives and those of our children. In the case of adolescent peers, according to Croteau and Hoynes (1997, p. 15), "These unofficial socializing agents can promote messages that contradict the ones being espoused by the 'powers that be'." When parents chastise their teenage children for hanging around with "the wrong crowd", they are implicitly aware that the potential socializing influence of peers can work to counter parental influence.

On the other hand, the use of media, particularly television, video, and satellite, has come to dominate the lives of millions of consumers of all ages during the past two decades. Although the television is turned on in the average American home for at least 6 hours a day, the perceived viewing requires about the same brain activity as eating, according to major studies by Kubey and Csikszentmihalyi (1990, p. 81).

As television viewing habits have changed, television's content and how and who it reaches have also changed. During earlier decades, television provided a world of popular entertainment and news shared by so many millions, regardless of demographics, that it was deemed a unifying element in America's melting pot society. The advent of cable, satellite, and other technologies has dramatically altered all that. Today's audiences are actually smaller and more sharply defined. They are carefully sought and bought.

Still, because television uses certain common denominators, most people can understand its content in a similar manner. Kubey and Csikszentmihalyi (1990, p. 81) concluded that even if viewers of television, for example, "choose ... what they are exposed to and are able to interpret messages in line with their needs and background, ... the mass media bring about rather uniform and immediate responses in substantial portions of their audience."

The prevailing view in mass media research of the 1980s and 1990s is that media influences are far more potent and long-lasting than had previously been believed. In other words, the effects of media messages must be examined in terms of both individual differences and shared experiences. Croteau and Hoynes (1997, p. 212) stated:

"We can speculate that the influence of the media may have increased since the 1950s and 1960s as children and adolescents have spent more and more time with the mass media. Exposure to the mass media is now a central means by which young people learn and internalize the values, beliefs, and norms of our political system, a socialization that lays the foundation for much of later political life. ...[T]he lessons of such socialization sometimes emanate from entertainment television as well as news and public affairs media."

Some researchers argue that we "learn" about crime even while we are watching entertainment (Croteau and Hoynes, 1997, p. 15).

Underlying the pervasiveness of mass media in our daily lives and our growing dependency on it is another important factor: the mass media's continued consolidation of its own power. Media conglomerates have been bought up by other giant corporations, thus reducing the number of organizations of ownership. Consolidation of power in cultural production and distribution has put virtual control over what is shown on television, in the movie theaters, and heard on the radio, if not in magazines and other print outlets, into the hands of a comparatively small group of business people. While we take this for granted and rarely give much consideration to the ways in which the mass media are structured, it is that very set of underpinnings, with its emphasis on the "bottom line" in a marketplace economy and the prominent role of advertisers, that must be adequately understood in order to deal fully with the effects of mass media on audiences. In sum, it is not so much the direct effects of mass media exposure, but rather the long-term indirect effects, which shape public opinion, engender desensitization, and promote disharmony. It is also important to acknowledge that in a free enterprise system, there may very well be conflict between what is profitable and what is in the best interest of the public, a notion that the media corporations make a special public relations effort never to admit (Auletta, 1991; Croteau and Hoynes, 1997).

In a previous work (Schwartz and Matzkin, 1996), the authors also noted that it is not the direct consequences of media exposure that produce the most noticeable effects on most audiences. Rather, the indirect effects, which occur cumulatively over time, impact on individuals and help to shape our national character.

As electronic media, especially, fight for market share, they also fight to distinguish their shows and films from others. In promoting a sense of urgency to their potentially competing audiences, producers help to "hype" dissonance, aggression, and luridness.

The Hollywood Motion Picture Industry

Popular culture tells us a great deal not only about our entertainments but also about our attitudes, values, beliefs, heroes, and even our enemies. Its forms play not only to our hopes, dreams, and fantasies, but also to our unconscious fears, anxieties, and insecurities. It is probably interesting to speculate what values are espoused when *Braveheart* — produced, directed, scripted by, and starring the popular Mel Gibson — won the 1995 Academy Award as "Best Picture of the Year". The film, a historical war epic, is based on events that occurred during the 13th century involving Scottish patriots seeking political separation from the villainous British. The last third of the film portrays countless acts of terrorism planned and carried out by the Scottish patriot, William Wallace (Mel Gibson), and his rebels against their enemies. The film's many war sequences are its most outstanding, magnificently choreographed, and artistically shot.

Braveheart's theme of revenge is unequivocally graphic. While many moviegoers, as well as politicians of all persuasions, are critical of Hollywood's seeming emphasis on violence and sex in their entertainments, how viewers interpreted *Braveheart* (along with the good guy/bad guy action adventures starring Arnold Schwartzenegger) often have a political flavor. Many who are angry about Hollywood excesses favor movies like *Braveheart*, seeing in its war themes positive examples of physical heroism, nationalism, and patriotism. Supporters of *Braveheart* found virtue in the clear line the story draws between its good and bad guys. The acts of violence and terrorism, which included shockingly graphic, ruthless, and murderous intrusions into the towns and homes of Wallace's enemies were shown as justifiable acts of revenge, punishment, and patriotism. For those who see less merit in *Braveheart*, the screenplay lacked believable character development, dialogue, and plot and depicted excessive killing and brutality.

In 1929, 110 million people went to the movies each week. Sixty years later, attendance had declined to about 22 million a week, with teenagers accounting for 25% of all ticket sales. In addition, surveys show that many Americans — 44% — do not go to the movies at all (Merrill et al., 1990). Even with such low audience populations, Hollywood influences the worlds of film and popular culture in terms of the direction its movies take, if not in terms of who directs them.

After trailing the art and industries of England and France in the first years of commercial filmmaking, the American film asserted its dominance in the years just preceding World War I and, with the help of that war (and the films of Griffith, Sennett, and Chaplin; the star system; and the beginnings of the studio system) established a commercial supremacy that has never been challenged (Mast and Kawin, 1994, p. 104).

There is much to suggest that the Hollywood film industry helps define the direction of all electronic entertainment. This is in part because television, catering to much larger and today more heterogeneous audiences, has not wanted to offend its advertising-targeted consumers (Baughman, 1992, p. 203):

"The demographics of the movie audience also partly explain Hollywood's new sexuality. The percentage of films rated R (usually denoting nudity) by the MPAA rose from 23% in 1968–69 to 56% in 1985. The [1980s'] most popular films shared certain characteristics. Almost all appealed primarily to younger consumers or adults who shared their children's fascination with the comic strip characters Superman *(1978),* Batman, *and* Dick Tracy *(1990). Although most did not carry an R rating, many contained violent scenes that would offend some older adults. A TV director could not show a horse's head in a character's bed as Francis Ford Coppola did in* The Godfather.*"*

Demographics, especially by age groups, play a major role in movie production and advertising costs, although that does not guarantee that a film will be profitable. Still, it is not surprising, considering who movies are made and targeted for, that *Variety* ("Top 100...", 1997) listed four action adventure films as the top grossing films of 1996. They were *Independence Day*, *Twister*, *Mission Impossible*, and *The Rock*. Their ticket sales outdistanced other respected films for the period including *Babe*, *101 Dalmatians*, *The Birdcage*, *Courage Under Fire*, and *Dangerous Minds*. More substantive comedies and dramas, such as *Sense and Sensibility*, *Dead Man Walking*, *The Postman*, *The American President*, *Emma*, and *Secrets and Lies* were rated far below in terms of ticket sales.

A list of videos most often rented in 1996 from Blockbuster (a chain of video rental and sales stores) included most of the same films, but was topped by *Seven*, an extremely bleak and gory serial murder film which starred Brad Pitt. Other action adventure films which feature graphic violence that were Blockbuster rental hits included: *Get Shorty*, *Die Hard with a Vengeance*, *Twister*, *Heat*, *Braveheart*, and *Golden Eye*. Such movies cater to an ever-increasing demand for heightened stimulation by an ever-increasingly desensitized, mostly young, viewing public.

That non-violent Hollywood movie genres can generate audiences and influence other media is most clearly shown in the example of the film *Clueless*. A clever and successful contemporary comedy about a high school teenager and her family and friends, *Clueless* (an updated version of Jane Austen's *Emma*) was transposed into a television series the following year.

The National Television Violence Study

In contrast to films, television, with its hundreds of millions of simultaneous viewers, has more far-reaching influence, and far more extensive mass media research has been done on its audiences. Studies of violent content shown on television and its effects continue to provoke more research, the most notable of which is the *National Television Violence Study* (NTV Study).

As reported by Mediascope (1996, p. i), who conducted the NTV Study in conjunction with four universities, it "sought a three-part assessment of television, including an independent analysis of the amount, nature, and context of violence in entertainment programming, a study of the effectiveness of content advisories and ratings, and a review of televised anti-violence educational initiatives." In the research segment developed by the University of California, Santa Barbara, the sample included 2693 programs shown over a 20-week period between October 8, 1994, and June 9, 1995, on commercial, independent, public, basic cable, and premium cable television stations, with two daily half-hour time slots randomly selected for each channel each week during the sample period. Overall, some of the findings were that 57% of programs contained violence, 33% had nine or more violent interactions, 73% had unpunished violence, 58% showed no pain on the part of the victims, and 57% showed repeated behavioral violence (Mediascope, 1996, p. 11). Almost one third of all programs (32%) showed no negative consequences of violence. Slightly more than half of the programs depicted short-term negative consequences of violence (52%). Only 16% of all violent programs depicted the long-term negative repercussions associated with violence (Mediascope, 1996, p. 16).

In the research segment carried out at the University of Texas at Austin, the focus was on reality programming (talk shows, public affairs programs, documentaries, news, entertainment news, non-news shows, etc.). The sample included 384 reality programs shown on 23 channels. Of these shows, 38% had some visual violence, and an additional 18% talked about violence. In each group (visual and talk), only 13% presented long-term negative consequences of violence. In the daytime hours, 6 a.m. to 6 p.m., 41 to 60% of the programs showed visual violence, while discussions of such acts varied from 21 to 40% in the 6 to 9 a.m. period to 61 to 80% in the 9 a.m. to 3 p.m. and 6 to 8 p.m. periods, and 41 to 60% in the 3 to 6 p.m. and 8 to 11 p.m. periods (Mediascope, 1996, p. 33).

Violent acts in visual sequences on televised programs (N = 384) were present in 41 to 60% of shows on between 6 a.m. and 6 p.m., with an increase to 61

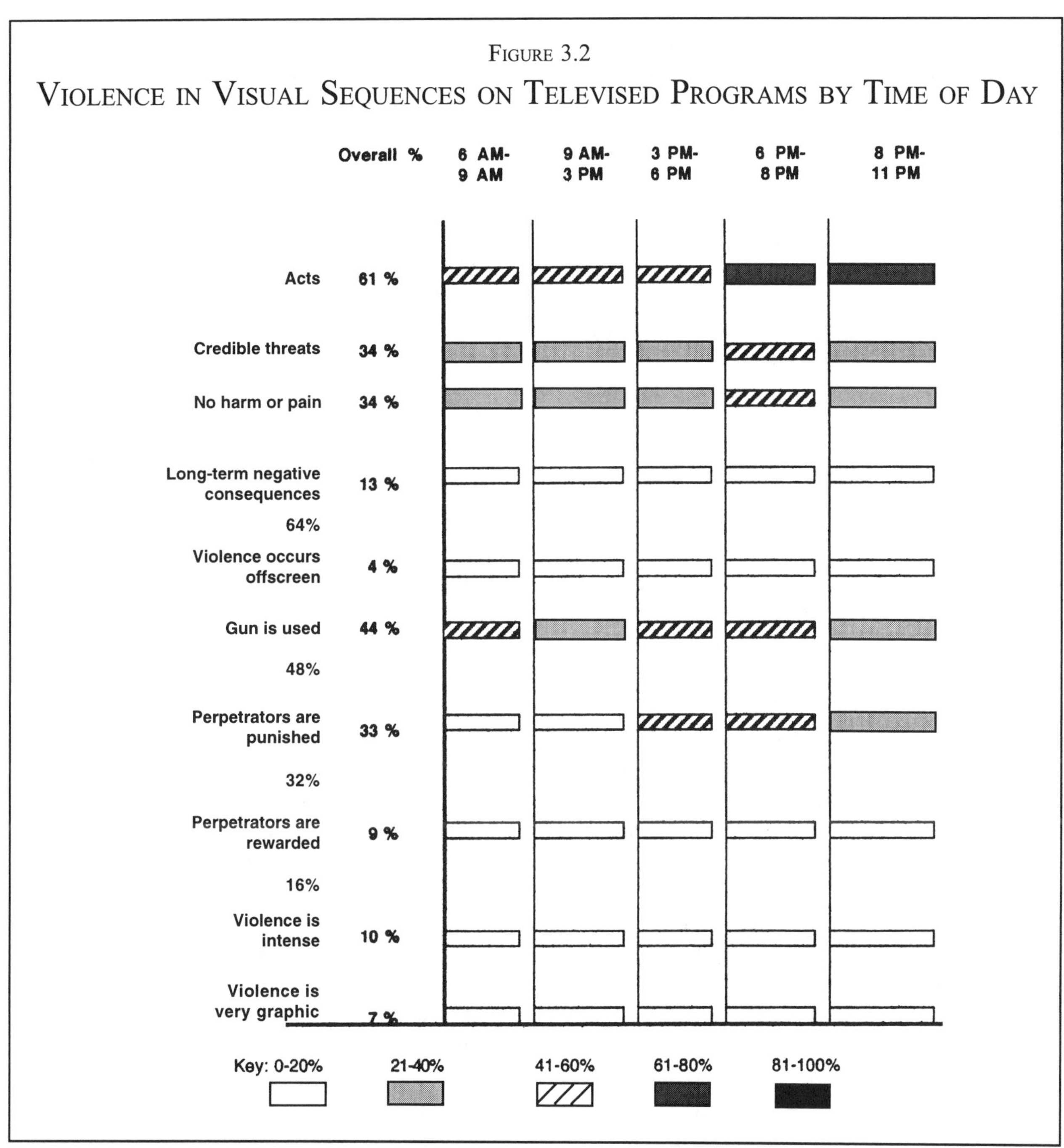

Adapted from *National Television Violence Study: Executive Summary, 1994–1995.* Studio City, CA: Mediascope, Inc., 1996.

to 80% from 6 p.m. to 11 p.m, as shown in Figure 3.2. In addition, violence occurring offscreen and long-term negative consequences were shown in 20% or fewer shows between 6 a.m. and 11 p.m., as was also true for perpetrators being punished in programs shown between 6 a.m. and 3 p.m. More punishment was shown in the after-school and early evening hours, but this was true in only about half of the programs (Mediascope, 1996). The studies clearly emphasized that such programming presented at least three anti-social effects (Mediascope, 1996, p. 143):

1. Viewers may learn aggressive attitudes and behaviors from these exposures.
2. Continued exposure to violence in the mass media will undermine feelings of concern, empathy, or sympathy (i.e., desensitization effects).
3. The viewing of media violence increases general feelings of fear of crime or victimization in viewers.

In the second year of the NTV Study, there were some small percentage changes in the overall industry averages from those presented in Figure 3.2. For example, the percent of programs with violence increased by 3%; violent scenes with "no remorse, criticism, or penalty for violence" increased by 2%; violent interactions that depicted harm unrealistically increased by 5%; and the violent programs that showed long-term negative consequences decreased by 3% (Federman, 1997, p. 26).

Examining programs by genre or type, the NTV Study found that the average percentage for "programs with violence" was 57% for all categories of programs (drama, comedy series, children's series, movies, reality based, and music/videos), while the average percentage for programs with an anti-violence theme was 4% (Mediascope, 1996). An average of 73% of the programs had unpunished violence. (A more detailed breakdown of factors in the profile of violence is shown in Figure 3.3.) It is interesting to note that, in the second year of the study, it was found (Federman, 1997, p. 28) that "... in a typical week of television, there are over 800 violent portrayals that qualify as high risk for children under 7. ...[O]f all genres, children's programs contain the greatest number of these high-risk violent portrayals."

The fact that too many daytime programs and children's series, particularly, show violence, frequently without punishment for the perpetrator or any indication of long-term negative consequences, is deplorable. Among the recommendations made by the Texas researchers was that the television industry "consider airing violent reality programs, especially police programs, in late-evening time periods when children are less likely to be watching" (Mediascope, 1996, p. 40). Making such adjustments in program content and time of presentation is a joint responsibility of the television stations or networks, the advertisers, and those who create programs.

It is important to underscore the notion that television is not simply "a toaster with pictures" as President Reagan's appointment to chair the Federal Communications Commission, Clay Fowler, had observed. Television is, instead, a total environment which pervades the atmosphere and mood of any given location. In the next several pages, the authors discuss each of several types of programs with respect to violence and their contribution to the polarizing of the population. While many of the programs discussed are of virtually no interest to younger audiences, indirect effects can make their way into a family's everyday domestic life, influencing the overall mood of the home. Children pick up on subtle changes. While someone in the vicinity of the television may not appear to be focused on the conversation in which the televised personalities are engaged and may seem unmindful of the utterances being expressed, the overall dynamics, mere emphasis and changes in volume, the sounds of shouting, screaming, sirens, musical sequences, and underscoring can have an impact on these seemingly unfocused and unsuspecting non-listeners. In addition, the signals that actual listeners project during and after particularly disturbing media engagements, such as action/adventure, graphic news reports, or dramatizations in which reporters and guests verbally attack each other, can influence familial interactions, projecting feelings of unease, restlessness, fear, or displeasure.

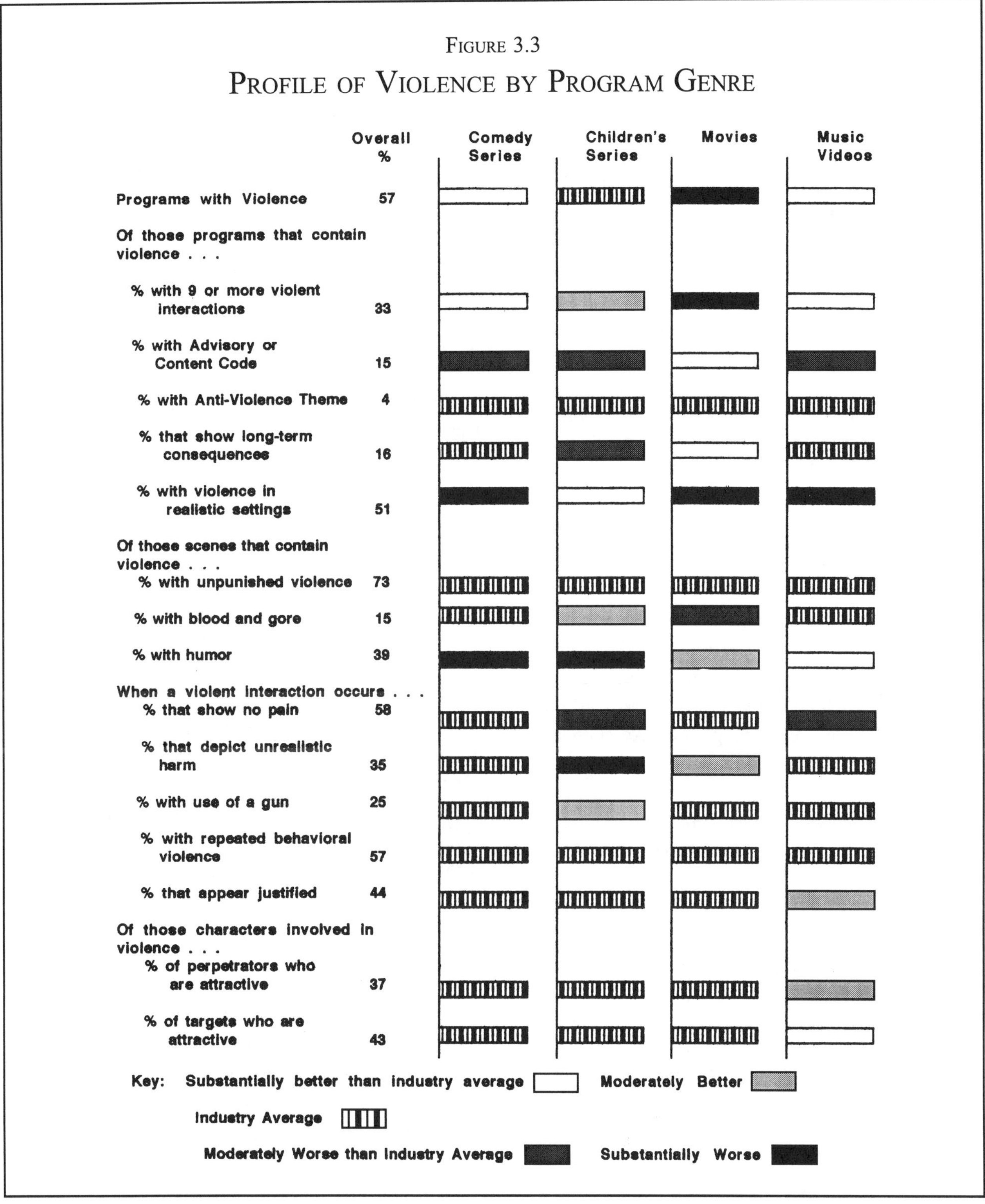

FIGURE 3.3
PROFILE OF VIOLENCE BY PROGRAM GENRE

Adapted from *National Television Violence Study: Executive Summary, 1994–1995.* Studio City, CA: Mediascope, Inc., 1996.

Types of Programming

Television Sitcoms/Dramatic Series

Television sitcoms are among the most popular prime time television series. Generally speaking, they are less subject to instances of graphic violence than some other genres. Reruns of sitcoms are shown on local cable stations and frequently rate higher than current programming against which they are running. Most of us would agree that one of the primary entertainment values of the television sitcom is its capacity to evoke laughter. Laughter, humor, and comedy provide the public with a necessary and healthy outlet from life's stresses; however, who is laughing at what indicates another area of division.

Most sitcoms follow a set of rather familiar conventions, the most common of which is their focus on family life. While in the early days of television, most sitcoms depicted more or less stereotypical or traditional family units, today's scripts involve the trials and tribulations, usually humorous in tone, of some less-conventional variations on the family. Members of this family become embroiled in a tragicomic dilemma which must be neatly resolved during the 22 minutes of playing time. As stated by Kenevy (1994, p. G1):

"A quick remote-control journey through network prime time sitcom-land reveals a lineup of programs divided by race. Most shows feature white characters; a growing number have black performers as stars. But few offer both races in major roles.

"Our viewing habits mirror those divisions. A recent breakdown of Nielsen Media Research ratings showed a wide disparity between black and nonblack households in viewing preferences. And the preferences gap is widening. In a similar survey 8 years ago, the Top 20 lists for black and nonblack audiences featured 15 programs that were on both."

It is also significant that, considering the makeup of our country today, there are literally no sitcoms featuring Asian, Hispanic, or Native Americans individuals or families. Minority ethnic groups are considerably underrepresented, as are religious groups such as Jews or Muslims. In the case of Jewish characters, as in *Seinfeld* or *The Nanny*, they are either stereotyped or their ethnicity or religious affiliation is made so incidental that the characters seem totally assimilated. Although exaggeration and caricature can be inventive and funny, they can also lead to stereotyping. When no other sorts of portrayals of the same group are shown, this is problematic because vast reaches of the audience may have no other exposure except those stereotypical portraits.

While sitcoms seem to be generally less multicultural in their regular episodes, dramatic series, including action adventure programs, have introduced many more interracial casts. Even during the 1970s, such programs as *Hawaii Five-O*, *The Rockford Files*, and *Quincy* portrayed central characters of different races who worked together without rancor. When they did present racial issues, as in *In the Heat of the Night*, somewhat later, the issue itself was race. Many of the current dramatic television series, including a series premiering during the 1996–1997 season called *Touched by an Angel*, introduced interracial casts. For the most part, however, their situations also involve violence and trauma (i.e., *ER*, *NYPD Blue*, *Homicide*), occurrences often arising from polarized thinking on the part of one or more characters. In other words, there are few, if any, new or original dramatic series or full-hour shows whose themes are not either violence or health/crisis related.

Children's Programming

As observed by Signorielli (1991, pp. 63, 64, 89), children's television programming is increasingly geared to boys rather than girls and is "male-dominated; women in children's programs are under-represented by a factor of four." Signorielli further commented that the "basic dimensions of programming for children ... have been remarkably stable for more than 20 years. ...The most important (theme) is violence, appearing in 94% of these programs at average rates of about 6 acts of violence per program and 22 acts of violence per hour of programming." Further, she wrote that "[p]ain, suffering or medical help rarely follow this mayhem, whose function is not preventative or therapeutic but dramatic and social."

According to research findings, children's programming contains many more actual acts of violence than does adult programming, or even prime-time or public television (Signorielli, 1991). Further, most children's shows broadcast on networks, other than the Public Broadcasting System (PBS), are advertising driven and initiated and packaged by sponsors, thus helping to create consumers among the very young.

Children watching "children's shows" and then being exposed further to adult tabloids and the like are getting double doses of negative programming. Research cited by Prothrow-Stith and Weissman (1991) and others indicate that young children who are heavy viewers of violent children's programs such as *Power Rangers, Mortal Kombat,* and *Mutant Ninja Turtles* often turn more aggressive in their interactions immediately following viewings. Their aggressive behavior can lead, and has led, to lethal violence (Schwartz and Matzkin, 1996).

We must note, however, that there are non-violent television shows that provide positive images of sharing and of peaceful resolutions to differences. These include *Barney & Friends*, *Sesame Street*, and *Mister Roger's Neighborhood*, geared to children in the pre-school and early elementary school years and all shown on public broadcasting. *Where in the World Is Carmen San Diego?*, also shown by PBS, introduces some action and adventure for the elementary school-age child. (We should note that action and adventure do not necessarily equal violence.) In the Roper Youth Report, a study of 6- to 12-year-olds conducted for the Corporation for Public Broadcasting in 1996, it was found (Lemon, 1997, p. 7) that children who watched PBS programs became "more motivated to engage in activities such as reading a book, making something, researching a subject further or doing an experiment. ...And they are more likely to report that their parents have rules about what and how much they can watch on TV."

Arcade Games

In an earlier study, the authors addressed the negative effects on some youths of violent arcade and computer games (Schwartz and Matzkin, 1996). Although their contribution to dissonance and separatism is unknown, they can contribute to the exacerbation of acting-out behavior in connection with children's and young people's experiences of anger, hatreds, jealousies, and similar negative feelings. Some youths become virtually addicted to fantasy games, such as *Dungeons and Dragons*, which, according to Ewing (1990b, p. 74) "involve themes of satanic sacrifice, witchcraft, demonology, monsters, and killing." In cases where those who are vulnerable to such stimuli have become homicidal, they appear to have been significantly influenced by such games. Two examples suffice to make the point.

In one case, five teenagers who were part of a self-styled "Vampire Cult" murdered the parents of one of their group ("Florida girl...", 1996). In a second case, two teenaged boys had been planning to kill a female acquaintance "for more than a year — for no apparent reason. They had even shown friends a hit list with her name on it" (Goldberg, 1997). Once they killed her, early in January 1997, they murdered her family in case family members might reveal that the girl had gone to meet them. Both boys had been "kicked out" of their family homes and were school dropouts. "But what has particularly gripped and baffled the town ... is the two teen-agers' involvement with fantasy games like *Dungeons and Dragons*, their apparent attraction to a small macabre subculture known as Goth, and their enthusiasm for the popular *Highlander* television show." They were also said to have played fantasy games so zealously that they had been kicked out of an informal group of players by other participants for overdoing it (Goldberg, 1997).

Clearly, these games are moneymaking enterprises for their developers, manufacturers, and the arcades where they are offered. As is true for a number of other media enterprises, however, there appears to be no overarching sense of responsibility for possible negative consequences for the players.

MTV/Rap/Rock/Country and Western Music

It has become a common practice to suggest that MTV and its competitors offer music and talk which are coarse, demeaning to females, emphasize machismo and salacious thoughts and behavior, promote violence, and avoid tenderness and other more positive values. On the other hand, while MTV appears to pit the lifestyle of youth against older generations, it must be given some credit for introducing programming encouraging young people to vote, interviewing political leaders, having special anti-drug messages, and often being very innovative. MTV, with much competition from other music television stations, is a continually evolving network, which is using many new programming formats in addition to videos. In addition, adolescent males are more often the viewing audiences and appear to have a physiological need for a place to hang their own newly developing energies and emotional fantasies. While MTV's music does not place a healthy emphasis on romantic love and seems to serve up too many images of intensely abusive or vulgar sexuality, in comparison to other programming it appears to be the least damaging, although it, too, has the capacity, if viewed over extended periods of time, to desensitize viewers.

In some kinds of rock music, but particularly *some* rap music, there are messages that reflect a sense of marginalization and isolation experienced by many adolescents and especially by many inner-city youth. The rap song can be a healthy and creative outlet for frustration, bewilderment, and anger. With that said, however, in a special report on "hip, hop, and rap" (1992), the Anti-Defamation League's specialists on popular music (ADL, 1992, p. 1) wrote that:

> *"Rock and roll music, like other forms of cultural and artistic expression, has often been associated with the freeing of the individual from musical convention. Recently, however, there have been notable and disturbing instances in which certain performers have exhibited the most stifling and unimaginative mindsets of all by conforming to notions and forces of bigotry, violence and hate. Guns 'n' Roses, Public Enemy, Ice Cube, Sister Souljah, and other groups featured here have immense followings, enjoy lucrative record contracts, and receive generous coverage on radio and television. Whether their popularity has grown because of or in spite of their forays into prejudice, they have been allowed — and perhaps even encouraged — to expose millions of young people to this destructive message. It is their constitutional right to express themselves no matter how offensive their beliefs are. But it is also their right — indeed a moral obligation — for those who abhor and unequivocally reject hatred to expose and denounce such poisonous messages in whatever form they are spread.*
>
> *"... Words, images, and ideas conveying anti-Semitism, as well as hostility toward minorities and women, formerly the domain of the gutter or the extreme right, have begun to seep into mainstream culture to find surprising acceptance and legitimacy — with unfortunate consequences for their targets and for the social atmosphere of our nation."*

In 1990, Madonna issued a remix of a single called "The Beast Within" in which she sang, "I know your tribulations and your poverty and the slander of those who say they are Jews. They are not. They are a synagogue of Satan." According to the ADL (1992, p. 1) report, it may have been more than coincidental that the release of Madonna's record was followed by the vandalizing of "three synagogues and a high school in Ventura County, California."

Lyrics by other popular rap groups, including Public Enemy and Ice Cube, have also been associated with anti-Semitic, homophobic, and racist lyrics. For example, in "Black Korea" Ice Cube warns Koreans in his neighborhood not to follow him, "Or your little chop suey ass will be a target/So pay your respect to the Black fist..." (ADL, 1992, p. 3). In 1997, new songs and new interpretations of old songs continue to use dark and violent images. One example is an interpretation of "Still Killing Us Softly" that offers up literal examples of killing and mayhem.

Country and western music, a genre that once crossed over regional, racial, and even ethnic lines, appears presently to be returning to mostly segregated musical genre (Feiler, 1996, p. H38):

"And yet as critical as black music was to the formation of traditional country music, 30 years after these legends were at the height of their popularity, country music seems more removed from black America than at any time in its history. Despite three decades of record increases in sales and listenership, there are no black artists with major record deals in Nashville, no black label executives, only one or two black songwriters and only a handful of black backup musicians. With Nashville commanding as much as one third of the radio market, country music may be the largest segregated corner of American music today."

Sports Television

The 1996 Summer Olympics offered viewers a respite from political campaigns during the summer, and from other tragic events including the TWA air tragedy. Although violence in sports is generally not lethal, fans observing the fights between players during the Olympics or during regularly scheduled games are being shown that violence is the response to differences of opinion. This is a poor model for our youth. During the first day of Olympic competition, on at least two occasions involving two different sets of competitions (one in men's swimming, the other in women's bicycle racing), sports anchors described competitors who were said to "hate" each other. The bombing that took place at the stadium park in Atlanta may have contributed to improving the mood, because following that tragedy, reporters and all involved in the Olympics became more circumspect in their reporting.

A study by Jackson (1993) used sports to examine issues of social class, gender, and race. He found that women's sports events are still underrepresented in the mass media and that athletes of color are described with too much attention given to their "natural athletic prowess" and not enough attention given to their other individual strengths. Again, the media reinforces stereotypes that contribute to increasing racial polarization.

Television Talk Shows

Tabloid talk shows put much emphasis on bizarre and dysfunctional stories. Studio audiences, as well as home viewers attracted to tabloid programming, can choose from a variety of daily shows with topics that include:

1. I lost my girlfriend as a result of learning something about her on your show — she was a porn movie actress (Jerry Springer, January 14, 1997)
2. Sisters competing for and living with the same man (Jenny Jones, January 15, 1997)
3. Women who love/have loved murderers and ex-convicts (Montel Williams, January 15, 1997)

Despite questions regarding the legitimacy of some guests who appear on tabloid talk shows, producers who are constantly faced with deadlines often advertise on their own shows, seeking other controversial guests of a particular type for another program. It is encouraging to note, however, that one award-winning news anchor at the Chicago station that hired Springer in early 1997 resigned in protest, and that Springer himself left his new post after only two broadcasts (Carter, 1997c).

If such confessional programs were helping to sensitize the public and create more compassion, more acknowledgment of the legitimacy of the need for psychological counseling, and more overall understanding of the complexities of human experience, then perhaps we would find some reasonable way to defend tabloid talk shows. However, the public's disinterest in the dramatic changes prior to and following passage in 1996 of a new Welfare Reform Bill indicates that human understanding is not what these programs breed.

The fact that a number of tabloid talk shows have engaged members of fanatical hate groups to appear and freely express their extremist views to their audiences, while certainly legally acceptable, does seem to be a curious phenomenon, considering how few programs give voice to groups that preach more positive, non-extremist messages of tolerance and community. That bigots and zealots are invited on many morning shows following network morning broadcasts seems to legitimize their inflammatory and inaccurate notions and enables others who are vulnerable to or leaning toward such thoughts to have them legitimized and reinforced (ADL, 1992). The resulting extremist perceptions can lead to lethal violence. The point here is not that talk shows should be censored, but rather that there should be opportunities for those representing other views to be heard in order that inaccurate and distorted statements and opinions be corrected.

Why have these shows proliferated, one may ask. The answer is quite simple. Money. Talk shows are the cheapest kinds of programming to produce. Guests are not paid except for transportation and board. There are no sets required and no complicated script writing and rehearsals.

Movies Made for Television

While critics often refer to made-for-television movies as "crisis of the week" dramas, there are television movies which critics admire and which are considered highly entertaining. One trouble spot, however, is the docudrama or movie based on real-life events which is frequently either fictionalized in part or has its more lurid scenes exaggerated. In one winter sweeps period, for example, all three major networks produced and broadcast movies about Amy Fisher, a Long Island teenager who was arrested, tried, and incarcerated for shooting her much older boyfriend's wife.

More recently, two military academy first-year cadets allegedly murdered a high school classmate while they were all in their senior year of high school. The NBC network and the film's producers rushed to produce and telecast the story before the case went to trial. According to Carter (1997a, p. C11), the network was apparently concerned with filling a "valuable two-hour spot in the network's schedule for February, one of the three most important ratings periods in the season, known as sweep months." Because neither cadet had yet been tried, there was not even the opportunity to show the long-term negative consequences of the murder they admitted committing.

The general manager of the Dallas-Fort Worth NBC affiliate apparently watched a tape of the film and was guided by his conscience to refuse to show the film as scheduled (Carter, 1997b). The network, however, was reportedly frustrated by his decision because of the potential negative effects this would have on the national ratings. Adding a further sense of irresponsibility to this "bottom-line" attitude, as Carter (1997b, p. 17) observed, was NBC's prompt move "... to turn the KXAS decision to its advantage. By Thursday night (February 6, 1997), it had begun broadcasting promotions for the movie ending with the line: 'The movie some people don't want you to see!'" Again, lethal violence was being used to arouse viewer interest without conveying an anti-violence message.

Public Affairs, News, and Political Discussion

"The media's impact on the political world is real and undeniable. ...This influence reaches not only presidents and political elites, but also ordinary citizens." (Crotreau and Hoynes, 1997, p. 199)

Today, the media may not tell us what to think, but they can tell us what to think about. It is the media decision-makers (editors, publishers, producers, department heads) who select the stories they want covered in their news broadcasts or on their news pages. It is the media which omit stories they do not wish to present to the public, for whatever reasons. And it is they who select, as well, how prominently each story should be featured and where in the television news lineup or on which page it should appear. While editorial commentary (which selects, dissects, and analyzes events of interest to the public) goes as far back as the early days of the newspaper, radio, and television, television editorial commentary with its emphasis on oppositional news perspectives is more recent and more intrusive.

Whether it is *Crossfire*, *The McLaughlin Group*, *Firing Line*, *The David Brinkley Show*, Chris Matthews on *Hardball*, or even the PBS *Jim Lehrer Show*, when it comes to political discussion, the trend is clearly adversarial. Television news analysis generally introduces a liberal vs. a conservative, a Democrat vs. a Republican, a "pro" vs. an "anti". In many cases, the emphasis is on hyping controversy and choosing sides. We are expected to believe that by putting two combatants such as Jerry Falwell and Larry Flynt on the same *Larry King Live* telecast (January 10, 1997), for example, we will be hearing a meaningful and reasoned discussion of two sides of First Amendment issues.

Viewers who tune in to most of the televised political analysis shows meet mainly white, middle-aged men confronting or disagreeing with each other, often talking simultaneously. While these programs have become as familiar as other kinds of entertainment or news series, what many viewers may not realize is that these political analysis shows have carefully prepared dialogue. According to journalist James Fallows (1996), news discussion programs are scripted to follow a format similar to that of the sitcom. Fallows stated (1996, pp. 116–117):

"So it was with Leave it to Beaver, *and so it is with* This Week with David Brinkley. *It is because we know that George Will is starchy and Sam Donaldson gets his goat that we want to see how they'll handle whatever they disagree about in this week's news. It is because we know that John McLaughlin is a blowhard that we enjoy his posturing, exactly as we did with blowhards like Fred Flintstone and Ted Baxter. Debate shows like* Crossfire *are set up in an even more rigidly predictable way, with one host structurally forced to take the liberal side of any issue and the other host the conservative. Such typecasting is down to a science when it comes to producing tv shows — but it is exactly contrary to the way a reporter should think. ...In addition to predictability, the talk show world cultivates an ethic of polarization and overstatement."*

Equally important, the content of news analysis and interview broadcasts dwells mainly on political strategy and tactics rather than tackling in-depth exploration of hard-core issues such as the budget, campaign reform, the environment, foreign policy, health care, and the like. News reporters and their research staffs sift through miles of faxes, satellite memos, and reprints seeking the day's best sound bites. Sound bites may not truly inform, but they can provoke. A new sound bite or tidbit, unsubstantiated or not well researched, may become an item and then a series of hard hitting news stories and sidebars. Such stories come and go after a few days of tantalizing allegations, often unresolved. Kurtz (1996, p. 14) stated:

"At the very least, like violence-soaked movies, sex-saturated sitcoms, and the more virulent strains of rap music, trash talk helps degrade a culture that is slowly sinking into the gutter.

"While radio talk shows excel at turning up the volume, it is the television pundits who have the loudest megaphone of all. A political charge — say that Clinton is a foreign policy bumbler — is leveled by Pat Buchanan on Crossfire *Friday night, seconded by Robert Novak on* Capital Gang *on Saturday night, and kicked around by Tim Russert and Bob Schieffer on Sunday morning. By the time* Newsweek *and* Time *and* U.S. News & World Report *hit the street Monday, they are carrying headlines like 'Clinton's Foreign Policy Mess' and 'Can He Recover?'. This in turn provides fodder for Al Hunt on* Today *and Chris Matthews on* Good Morning America *and Fred Barnes on* CBS This Morning.

"In short, the most dedicated consumers of political talk shows are other journalists, who fertilize and spread the latest fodder down through the media food chain. No good idea goes uncopied."

Presidential campaigns, which go on in the U.S. far longer than in most other Western democracies, have grown more partisan over the past decade and a half. Political ads pollute the airwaves with messages designed to incur fear and wrath in the minds and hearts of potential voters. While campaigns may be too long, the role and prestige of the politician, including that of the presidency, seem to be diminishing, while that of the nightly news anchor and political commentator seem to be on the rise. In some ways, this appears to illustrate a diminution of the significance of the politician. Presidential press conferences, for example, are actually no longer carried live on any of the three original television or radio networks. (NBC, CBS, and ABC carried presidential press conferences live until the end of the Bush presidency.) CNN continues to carry more live press briefings than the other networks. (Neither PBS nor its radio affiliates, APR or NPR, forces its affiliates to carry press conferences or briefings.) Instead of hearing the actual words of a president or some other politician, it is more likely that viewers will hear anchors, commentators, or both offering interpretations of that speech or briefing. As observed by Hallin (1997, pp. 61, 65):

"... [M]odern TV news is much more mediated than the TV news of the 1960s and 1970s. During the earlier period the journalist's role as a communicator was relatively passive. Most television journalism ... was dominated more by the words of candidates and officials than by those of journalists. One should notice that Cronkite ... spent much of his time quoting the candidates. ...

"Today's television journalist displays a sharply different attitude toward the words of candidates and other newsmakers. Today those words, rather than simply being reproduced and transmitted to the audience, are treated as the raw material to be taken apart, combined with other sounds and images, and integrated into a new narrative. ...It puts image making at the center of politics and pushes real political debate to the margins."

Despite the fact that viewers have selective processes which help filter out what they do not want to think or believe, over enough time, the news media make a powerful contribution to the shaping of public opinion, as well as the shading of the point of view of an individual. Volatile issues, reinforced by persistent, repetitive, and aggressive media coverage, can arouse particularly those who are unable to absorb intemperate comments, think them through, and work out their personal frustrations in positive ways. Certainly, the extremist fringe in this country has many more opportunities to have their views reinforced and their emotions heightened to the boiling point by media coverage that encourages the "feeding frenzy".

On the other hand, television news broadcasts highlight crimes, the bloodier the better, as their lead stories, with repetition between news shows as well as on them. Claude Lewis (1997), an African-American columnist, deplored what he perceived as journalism's slide on "the slippery slope into sleaze." Lewis (1997, p. A13) stated:

"For years, TV fed the public hunger for violence and sensation with nightly reports of bloody shootings and burning buildings. But now, this no longer has the same shock effect, and newscasts increasingly traffic in the salacious and even the bizarre. ...Being first with the most sensational stories is often more valued than being the most accurate or the most informative."

One wonders how much television provokes violence when reality mimics that medium. A case in point: On May 13, 1997, the *TV Guide* for the Philadelphia area listed for the theme of the *NYPD Blue* show that evening that a hijacker took over a city bus. At about 4 p.m. that afternoon, a man who had just attempted to rob a store in Camden, NJ, across the river from Philadelphia, hijacked a Camden bus. He held the driver and a passenger hostage for 4 hours until a police negotiator talked him into disembarking and surrendering. Had he seen that program summary in the paper? Or was this just a coincidence that could have escalated into lethal violence?

Tabloid Television News Programming

Tabloid news programming offers the re-enactment of a violent news event or a replay of some aspect of a violent or sexual news event, usually with heightened sound, special effects, a voice-over reporter, and dramatic music. Many tabloid news shows such as *Hard Copy*, *Inside Edition*, and *American Journal* are broadcast during late afternoon or early evening hours when children are home from school. Their trailers and promos, provided at increased volume, are sometimes misleading. Research suggests that these shows promise more "sex and violence" than they actually deliver. Nonetheless, tabloids usually focus on the bizarre, the dark, the underside of life. Since the murder of JonBenet Ramsey on December 26, 1996, these programs have pursued the story. On the very day that Ennis Cosby was found murdered, a promo promised that listeners could "hear the inside story of the murder of Ennis Cosby tonight on *Entertainment Tonight*!" (Jan. 16, 1997). In these promos and programs, lethal violence is being used as entertainment, a diversion from routine. In both the Ramsey and the Cosby cases, as well as others more local in focus, the tantalizing emphasis is on blood and gore rather than on the straight facts. In effect, lethal violence is being "glamorized". Moreover, many of these tabloids are being broadcast during the late afternoon hours when children may be within hearing distance.

Talk Radio

More extreme and far more blatantly vituperative than most of television's discussion and polemics is what is conducted over talk radio. Here, insults fly, rumors are uttered aloud, innuendoes are acceptable, demonizing is commonplace, and millions of listeners may be misinformed and misled.

There is general agreement that talk radio offers large, long doses of right-wing commentators assaulting middle-of-the-road and liberal viewpoints. Here, the effects of polarization are most obviously political. Here, too, there is no room for a meaningful discussion of complex public policy or for a continuum or crossover of perspectives. Thus, those who are regular listeners and others who perhaps tune in occasionally to radio talk, have little opportunity on radio of accessing more moderate perspectives about a politician or issue. By offering up bitter invectives, with no ameliorating conditions, those who listen can find their views reinforced and hardened and their cynicism intensified.

A number of troubling and even tragic acts of violence have been traced to talk radio shows, including the shooting death, several years ago, of Alan Berg, a liberal talk show host in Denver. More recently, late in 1996, in New York City, conservative host Bob Grant touched off a hot racial controversy. Because of his bitter attacks on blacks, culminating with some extremely demeaning remarks about then newly deceased U.S. cabinet secretary Ron Brown, Grant was fired from WABC but was immediately picked up by radio station WOR. This created much dissension at the station and among listeners. At WOR, travel columnist and host Arthur Frommer resigned because he did not wish to be associated with Grant's beliefs. In the same spirit, shortly afterward, the Dime Savings Bank withdrew its advertising (Barron, 1996; Egan, 1996; Lu, 1996).

During President Clinton's first term, talk show hosts hostile to his presidency offered dangerous fantasies, including suggestions that he might be right for assassination. In a show anchored by G. Gordon Liddy (April 24, 1995), while delivering a commentary attacking some government agencies, Liddy "shocked even some of his most loyal listeners by advising them to shoot agents of the Bureau of Alcohol,

Tobacco, and Firearms (BATF) if they came to their homes" (Relin, 1995, p. 27). Asked if he was sorry about the controversy his comments created, he answered, "I take back what I said about shooting agents in the head. ...You should aim for the chest and the groin."

Some print journalists express concern about balancing the needs and rights in a democracy of a free press with the complications that an irresponsible press may provoke through its inclination to excess. Kurtz (1996, p. 19) stated that:

"It would surely be unfair to blame the talk shows for the decline of American civilization and other assorted sociological ills. This is, after all, a country in which politicians run vicious attack ads accusing each other of being liars, weasels, tax cheats, hypocrites, and soft on murderers and rapists. It is a media-saturated world in which the leader of the free world feels compelled to announce on MTV that he wears briefs, not boxers. It is a culture in which people prattle on before the cameras about their experiences with adultery, incest, impotence, and child abuse. Talk shows simply mirror the best and the worst of society.

"They have also become a powerful vehicle, however, that trumpets the most extreme and polarizing views, that panders to sensationalism, that spreads innuendo and misinformation with stunning efficiency. Talk shows have altered the nature of journalism, shifting the center of gravity from those who ask questions to those who seem to have all the answers."

Advertising

In a market-based economy, the laws of supply and demand are considered preeminent. And in a market-based economy made up of products and consumers, advertising plays a major role in communicating to consumers what is available to buy and sell. Newspapers, despite decreased readerships, still service advertisers, and actually depend on advertising for their survival.

The language and visuals of print advertising in magazines, newspapers, billboards, and mailings is a complex and important subject of study which has been researched extensively. In both electronic media and print, motivational research is touted. Psychographics, for example, is a marketing strategy that goes beyond simpler demographics to understand and target consumer differences in lifestyle, values, motivation, goals, and tastes. It is used to sell many kinds of products from automobiles and detergents to food and beverages (Black and Whitney, 1988, p. 433).

Electronic advertising, however, has been forced to become ever more innovative as audiences have become accustomed to using remote control channel changers. Advertisers' efforts in the last decade have been aimed at defeating the powerful channel changer or zapper in order to prevent viewers from switching channels during commercial breaks. With the aid of high-tech editing techniques and other sophisticated tools, advertisers have produced some dramatic and entertaining commercials. The uses of various attention-getting devices designed to block out viewers' opportunities for critical thought are often over-stimulating, especially for children. The same focus on the sponsor's "bottom line" is evident in many of the programs that advertisers sponsor. Programming itself is often designed to appeal to one group to the exclusion of others. Commercials are blatantly pitched to that desired group or product (within the world of advertising, the "product" is the consumer audience or market share.)

It is not surprising that the cost of airing commercials may exceed that of the productions the commercials are sponsoring. For the 1996 Superbowl Game broadcast on the Fox Network, such advertisers as Anheuser-Busch, AT&T, Coca-Cola, IBM, Oscar Mayer, Pizza Hut, and Honda paid as much as $1.3 million for a 30-second commercial, a 19% increase over the previous year's $1.1 million for the same spot on NBC's 1995 broadcast of the Superbowl (Johnson, 1997, p. 12). Why does this matter? It matters because if sponsors are willing to invest millions and even billions of dollars to research, test market, and create commercials in order to persuade audiences to buy products, they must believe in their efforts. If ads can make an impact in just a few seconds, it makes sense that media's capacity to impact, cumulatively, can apply to all content, whether it be of ads, entertainment, or news.

What Is Wrong With Media Sensationalism?

Our previous section provides an overview of some of the damaging aspects of various formats of mass media programming. Clearly, the media contribute much that is positive and worthwhile to modern life, and there are many talented, creative, and dedicated artists and business people committed to quality work. However, the authors found a strong tilt toward callousness, brutality, incivility, and sensationalism which are believed to have an impact on audiences, the vulnerable and the young, in particular (Schwartz and Matzkin, 1996). The indirect effects of such images on viewers, but especially on heavy viewers, are by no means insignificant. Desensitization, increasing cynicism, and fear about the world are all effects which the authors have previously discussed (Schwartz and Matzkin, 1996).

In media storytelling, the insatiable taste for violence has taken us far afield from the great myths of the past (biblical, classical, psychological), which for centuries we have continued to inherit and transmit. Protagonists and central characters in today's big commercial entertainments hardly resemble those men and women of transcendent characteristics and abilities, who struggled with enormous moral problems or issues, who learned difficult lessons, who offered us moral insights. Our contemporary protagonists seem but shadows of those past cultural icons. Too often cardboard-like, flat, and devoid of truly heroic qualities, vision, moral centeredness, or wisdom, they are often merely performers of feats behind whom we can read the winks of stars playing their latest screen roles.

Even in other formats, such as television news, the influence of ratings and, since the 1980s, profits, has forced important changes. As news has had to compete with other programming, the lines between it and entertainment have become increasingly blurred.

As Boorstin (1961) prophesied, we have come to confuse heroes and celebrities and have become a nation obsessed with celebrityhood and consumption. Our performers are more real to us than the people they are portraying or their ideas. In public affairs, those who do the analysis are given more prominence and respect than those they are analyzing, and discussions of public affairs, like most other entertainments, demand sensational talk, quick fixes, and 6-second soundbites. We are less frequently exposed to characters, programs, or newspersons who are actually seen contemplating or pondering a serious thought or issue. Pauses and deliberation are expensive and in the media, time, even just 15 seconds, can be measured in dollars. In addition, sponsors, fearing rejection and competition by zapper-bearing viewers, insist on action programming. Thus, there is little emphasis on in-depth investigative journalism. During the 1950s, 1960s, and early 1970s, aside from light-hearted entertainment and dramas, CBS, NBC, and ABC regularly featured one- and two-hour documentary broadcasts, often dealing in-depth with a single issue. According to the late Richard Salant, former president of CBS (personal communication, September 1992), the introduction of the TV series *Sixty Minutes*, which features roughly three major pieces per show, changed the course of in-depth news analysis permanently. Today's documentary lasts about 10 minutes. In short, sensationalism sells. As Postman (1985, p. 28) observed:

"We are now a culture whose information, ideas and epistemology are given form by television, not by the printed word ... to be sure, there are still readers and there are many books published, but the uses of print and reading are not the same as they once were, not even in schools, the last institutions where print was thought to be invincible. There is no parity here. Print is now merely a residual epistemology, and it will

remain so, aided to some extent by the computer and newspapers and magazines that are made to look like television screens. ...Our public discourse [our political, religious, informational, and commercial forms of conversation]—a television-based epistemology—pollutes public communication and its surrounding landscape."

Our discussion of genres also attempted to illustrate how virtually every media format seems to encourage oppositional and confrontational behaviors and attitudes, rather than rational discourse or thoughtful analysis. What has resulted is an ever-deeper emphasis on individualism and the search for personal goals, and diminishing concern for the community and what is in the public interest. This, in turn, has led to fractionalization and polarization as people separate along personal and special interest concerns. Thinking less deeply or introspectively, we have become more impatient and intolerant. We have even become suspicious of those who may not yet have surrendered themselves up to the new pragmatism. Lacking a sense of community, the overly media-exposed come to perceive the world as a darker and more menacing place. In a menacing world, it becomes reasonable to support the idea of every man or woman for himself or herself. The notion of what is in "my" best interest has come to pervade our society and was addressed by Mitroff and Bennis (1989, pp. 178–179)

"Crowding, if not crashing, up against the Complexity From Without [the complexities and economic dislocations being fostered here by the new global economy] is the Rot From Within. This part of America's morality play has to do with the general effects of the larger TV and show business culture, of which increasingly every facet of our society from education to politics is affected, on our growing inability to handle complex issues. ...

"The argument has been essentially this: By the very nature of the medium, TV works by breaking everything down into 15- to 30-second segments or blips. Since the primary purpose of each blip is to grab and hold the attention of the viewer, the content of any blip is nowhere as important as how it delivers it and how the presenter looks. The primary purpose of TV is not to inform, or to educate, and strangely enough not to entertain, but to keep the viewer from switching dials by holding his or her attention. ...[T]he inevitable result not only is a society that is uninformed about anything, but one that has lost the even more fundamental ability to know it is uninformed. ...Worse yet, it may have lost the ability and the very soul to care. ...

"In psychoanalytic terms, the counter protagonist as represented by TV and show business to that of the mature ego and superego demanded by the new global economy, is an incredibly primitive intellect—in other words, Freud's Id."

Today, the worlds of media entertainment and news are tightly connected within the larger corporate structures of tobacco, liquor, gambling casinos, and other special interests. Time Warner, for example, which until the mid-1980s was actually two wholly separate and hugely profitable corporations, is now TimesWarnerCNN. Disney now owns several film production companies and, perhaps even more relevant, recently acquired the ABC network. Loews, which owns theaters, hotels, and Republic Pictures, also owns the Lorillard Tobacco Company. And the buying and selling is not over yet.

It is fruitless to argue that the ways in which the media are structured and operated are irrelevant or only indirectly related to the subject of violence in the media or society. If we do not understand how the media work, we cannot realistically even begin to bring about meaningful change, change which we do not think should have anything to do with censorship of any kind. The cumulative effects of the many kinds of polarizing messages that the media all too predictably employ and encourage in their efforts to deliver audiences to sponsors is involved and deeply embedded in our economic and political system, but the media are not impervious to consistent calls for change (Schwartz and Matzkin, 1996).

In 1986, a low-budget film called *River's Edge* (directed by Tim Hunter), a story of youthful alienation, murder, and callousness, opened around the country. Based on a true story, the film depicted a group of high school teens who discovered that one of their classmates had murdered his girlfriend. The youngsters set about making arrangements to help the friend cover up his inexplicable homicidal act. Dark and somber, the film depicted these unemotional teenagers as lacking any kind of moral compass; they are completely matter of fact about the murder. The film's underlying tone suggests a cautionary tale designed to warn a contemporary society of the numbing of a nation, and especially the numbing of the young.

When little children can hear the sounds of car crashes, screams, sirens, gunfire, and the like in their homes, even if they are not in the viewing room there are effects. When they can hear angry media voices arguing about issues they may be too young to understand, there can also be effects. When children sense that their parents are made anxious, tense, angry, or cynical through violent or polemical and outrageous media exposures, children can be affected. We cannot protect children from all of these and other harmful ramifications of incidental learning — learning that actually may be starting as early as birth or before, but we can try to raise the consciousness of audiences, media owners, and producers, for the sake of the children.

When children and teens plead with parents and educators that they are not going to be affected by watching a particularly gory film, broadcast, video, or game because they have seen others and such encounters have not bothered them, they are delivering the most convincing argument against constant and repeated exposure to violent entertainment and media programming. They already bear the legacy of what they have seen, what it has done, and what it continues to do to an entire generation.

Positive Currents in the Sea of Problems

Amidst the cacophony being waged on radio and television, computer networks, and in the newspapers, there are, nonetheless, new movements being initiated and implemented by persistent, determined, and often inspired individuals, groups, organizations, and agencies who are taking responsibility and who want to make a difference. They believe in change and wish to engender more emphasis on our communal nature. They stress critical thinking skills with respect to the media. They teach alternative dispute resolution techniques to avert violence, especially among our youth.

Several dramatic initiatives have been undertaken recently to deal with the linked issues of media, violence, and polarization. The government's hearings on the media, the television industry's introduction of ratings, and Congress' adoption of the V-chip have received virtually all of the national attention. These other long-term programs, however, may turn out to be more beneficial by getting the public involved.

Two Radically New Media Movements

The Cultural Environment Movement. In March 1994, the Cultural Environment Movement (CEM) was founded by a coalition of individuals and organizations under the leadership of Dr. George Gerbner, Dean Emeritus of the Annenberg School for Communication, University of Pennsylvania. A major goal of CEM is to improve the nation's cultural environment through greater involvement of parents and the public in the creation of media stories that are transmitted to children. The coalition, a nonprofit umbrella organization, has members from over 150 independent media, labor, environmental, and minority groups.

In a telephone interview (January 8, 1997), Gerbner said, "In order to create richer, more diverse stories and a more varied cultural environment, society has to play a more active role in the formation of cultural politics, something we do not do presently." He added that "the role of television in our lives is very different from that of earlier technologies and different from that of earlier technologies." In that same conversation, Gerbner explained:

"Years ago, people went out to a movie. Perhaps they went once a week. Even twice. It was something one did for a few hours. Television is something quite different and quite unique in the world. With television we create an environment. It is on, and you may not be watching, but there is some kind of communication going on. Whether you are attending to it consciously or not, whether it is white noise, it is there as a kind of permanent and pervasive presence. And the public, which actually owns the airwaves from which network television operates, has no say in how programming is selected, implemented, or funded or in other issues of public policy. In fact, the public does not have a voice in much of the cultural policy decisions made in this country, which is different from the situation in most other democratic countries. And even though we have no representation, we are nonetheless being taxed. We are actually financing television network programming. I say we are being taxed, because advertising is a tax-deductible business expense which all the media corporations and sponsors are able to take. The money that media do not have to put into the federal budget is what we — the public — have to make up for."

With 30 years of research in cultivation analysis, Gerbner has examined, documented, and evaluated the effects of television violence on audiences. His findings convinced him that the public needs to understand the structures and operations of the handful of global media conglomerates whose decisions control most entertainment, news, and other programming and thus control so much that is routine in people's daily lives. "They need to understand how media operate or they will never be able to implement changes," he emphasized (personal communication, June 3, 1997).

Ultimately, what Gerbner is seeking is an organized effort on the part of the public to wrest control away from the handful of media conglomerates and to place more control into the hands of the public. One high-profile project being considered by CEM's board of directors is the formation of an international judicial tribunal which would investigate and put on trial media executives involved in "egregious violations of human communications rights" — rights which are laid out in the CEM program. Defense and prosecution jurists could be hired to participate in the trials which might be held at The Hague (Gerbner, personal communication, June 3, 1997). Gerbner suggested that there may also be awards given to media executives who make contributions to improving operations and programming in the interest of the public.

The Center for Media Literacy. While the CEM seeks to enter the offices of board chairpersons of corporations and media organizations in order to promote structural, employment, and programming modifications, the second radical new movement, the Center for Media Literacy, seeks to encourage and promote critical thinking skills. It offers a broad range of programs, strategies, and curricula designed to foster activism in order to help the public learn how to use the media, rather than be used by it. The Center is located in Los Angeles, under the direction of its founder, Elizabeth Thoman, a leading expert on media violence. Thoman explains the goals of the Center (personal communication, January 7, 1997):

"The nation has tried analyzing the public health issues related to media uses, the psychology of media uses (why we use the media and whether we do or do not get what we want). ...All of the attempts at turning the problems of media attention around have been basically interpersonal — trying to get families to work together, trying to work on issues of conflict. There are new programs out there for peer counseling and mediation resolution. What we are about is promoting notions that what we are watching on television is providing us with troubling images that have become the norms — and that there is something wrong with these norms. Media literacy is something different because it is an effort to help people to cope with media. Instead of castigating people and instead of studying how media influence the culture of violence, we are teaching families, schools, teachers, administrators and communities how to take charge of children."

The Center's programs are concerned with three stages of media literacy. The first stage helps parents and families learn to balance their media "diets" by making choices about how much time is to be spent with media, and by developing good viewing habits. The second stage involves developing the tools of critical analysis. The third and most advanced stage encourages analysis of the ownership, structures, and operations of the media and asks questions such as "who produces, who profits, who loses and who decides?"

Some of the Center's teaching materials are geared to home use; others are for schools and community centers. Titles of media subject units include: "Media Literacy: Keys to Interpreting Media Messages", "The Smart Parent's Guide to Kids' TV", "Sold Separately: Parents and Children in Consumer Culture", "Dancing in the Dark: Youth, Popular Culture and the Electronic Media", "Selling Addiction", and "Enlightened Racism: The Cosby Show, Audiences, and the Myth of the American Dream".

In *Beyond Blame*, the Center takes on the issue of violence with a five-unit curriculum that teaches media skills to all age groups, starting with fourth and fifth graders, and including programs for middle schools, teens, and parents as caregivers. The fifth unit in the series provides a 90-minute introduction and overview for a Town Hall meeting where citizens, teachers, religious leaders, and other interested members of the community can come together to assert their common concerns about media violence. The *Beyond Blame* package includes unit outlines, lesson plans, worksheets, and video segments, as well as background resources and bibliographic materials for leader preparation.

One goal of the *Beyond Blame* program is to motivate activism in learners. For example, elementary school children are asked to count the number of acts of violence (as they have learned to define violence) in a particular television show. Older children have to create peaceful endings to media stories that are currently resolved through violence.

Other Efforts

Other organizations are also strongly endorsing media education. The National Council of Teachers of English, for example, which has been encouraging the use of media instruction since 1970, strongly endorsed media literacy in a 1996 summary of position reports (Suhor, 1996):

"The Commission on Media sees both encouraging and discouraging indicators about media literacy becoming a central focus of the K–12 English language arts curriculum. On the one hand, growing societal concern across the ideological spectrum about the negative impacts of various media on youth has generated calls from national officials, community leaders, teachers, parents, and the general public to do something. Often, unfortunately, such concerns lead to efforts to censor media and to condemn media producers. On the other hand, means of making media literacy an integral part of the school curriculum languish for lack of funds for materials and equipment, a dearth of effective pre-service training for teachers, and confusion about where media literacy instruction should occur in the curriculum."

Beginning in 1993, meetings were held at the University of Virginia Graduate Center that brought together parents, human services professionals, and representatives from the community, including youth service agencies, law enforcement, school systems, public administration, and local business because of their common perception of and common concern about an increase in youth violence (Sheras et al., 1996, p. 401). The project, presented in a variety of formats so as to reach people of diverse levels of experience, was multi-disciplinary and action oriented. Four instructional objectives were developed (Sheras et al., 1996, p. 402):

1. Help participants become informed consumers of media information.
2. Adopt a risk factor perspective on the causes of violence. A risk factor model allows participants to recognize the role of multiple factors in the etiology of violence which range from innate differences in temperament to family learning experiences and to incorporate concepts of cognitive and affective development as well as societal influences.
3. Teach participants to avoid stereotypes, to be sensitive to context, and to pay attention to multicultural issues.

4. Focus on positive actions, emphasizing prevention and education.

Training programs for the project, involving more than 40 hours of direct instruction, were provided through week-long summer institutes, weekend programs spread throughout the school year, and satellite links. It was found that video interviews with juveniles involved in disputes, potential victims, police officers, teachers, and others are very effective training tools. They also provide "an indirect means to build a shared sense of purpose and community across the state and to inspire greater commitment to using outside resources" (Sheras et al., 1996, p. 404). The local and national media covered aspects of the project, which made more people in Virginia and elsewhere aware of the effort being made. Apart from the strongly significant gains made in knowledge by participants, at least 10 poster or essay projects involving students were developed in the first 2 years of the project, ranging from contests on safety or violence-related topics to discussion groups, plays, and puppet shows, to the development of mediation and conflict resolution programs (see Table 3.1).

Yet another approach that may contribute to the reduction of violence and polarization is represented in a newly introduced curriculum called *A Study of Heroes*. This pilot program is being used in New York City in public and private schools, in a locked correctional facility for juvenile offenders, and in both High Point, NC, and Houston, TX. According to its designer, Dr. Kathy Morin, a curriculum specialist, the program includes a flexible set of student activities, worksheets, and learning units that integrate skill areas such as history, reading, creative writing, political/social topics, and debate and conflict resolution (Morin, personal communication, October 8, 1996). One of the program's goals is to help end the confusion that exists among today's youth over the concepts of "hero" and "celebrity". The program attempts to accomplish this goal through its use of the theme of heroes to teach basic skills. *A Study of Heroes* provides study materials ranging from kindergarten through high school. For young children just learning to read, there is a unit called "Real Heroes from A to Z" which is used to teach vocabulary. There are intergenerational homework units, a unit on heroes and holidays, and a study of great educators as heroes. Among the subject units for which materials have already been provided are Eleanor Roosevelt, Jacobo Timerman, Anwar Sadat, Martin Luther King, Jr., Harriet Tubman, Mother Teresa, Albert Schweitzer, and Mahatma Gandhi.

The Southern Poverty Law Center in Montgomery, AL, publishes *Teaching Tolerance*, a magazine which it sends without charge to 200,000 school teachers nationwide. Published twice a year, the magazine provides teaching suggestions on a variety of topics to encourage interracial and multi-cultural understanding in the classroom. The materials, resources, and ideas it offers can be adapted for teaching at all levels and grades within the school system.

The Impetus of Conflict Resolution

Earlier generations, especially those influenced by the Depression, were taught to save for a rainy day, to delay gratification, to control impulses, to seek alternatives. That is not the situation today. As Zimbardo (1970, p. 240) asserted almost 30 years ago:

> *"All about us — from the mass media, from our everyday observations, from reliable anecdotes — the evidence overwhelmingly points to a very different conception of the human organism. Reason, premeditation, the acceptance of personal responsibility, the feeling of obligation, the rational defense of commitments appear to be losing ground to an impulse-dominated hedonism bent on anarchy."*

If we can persuade people to slow down enough in their reactions to situations, then the picture painted by Zimbardo might be eradicated. That is, people, especially our youth, would think about alternative responses or long-term consequences of their actions. Violence would not be the initial response.

Table 3.1

Organizations and Sources of Information Related to Conflict Resolution

ACT (Action for Children's Television)
Attn: Peggy Charren
20 University Road
Cambridge, MA 02138
Telephone: (617) 876-6620

ADL (Anti-Defamation League)
823 United Nations Plaza
New York, NY 10017

American Federation of Teachers
555 New Jersey Ave., NW
Washington, D.C. 20001

American Academy of Pediatrics
141 Northwest Point Blvd.
P.O. Box 927
Elk Grove Village, IL 60007
Telephone: (312) 228-5005

A Study of Heroes
Attn: Kathleen D. Morin, Director of Curriculum
575 Lexington Avenue
New York, NY 10002
Telephone: (212) 628-8596

CEED (Center for Early Education and Development)
University of Minnesota
51 East River Rd.
Minneapolis, MN 55455
Telephone: (612) 624-3567

CEM (Cultural Environment Movement)
Attn: Dr. George Gerbner
University Science Center
3624 Market Street
Philadelphia, PA 19104

CML (Center for Media Literacy)
Attn: Elizabeth Thoman
4727 Wiltshire Blvd., Suite #403
Los Angeles, CA 90010
Telephone: (213) 931-4177

ERIC Clearinghouse on Elementary and Early Childhood Education
University of Illinois, College of Education
805 W. Pennsylvania Ave.
Urbana, IL 61801-4897
Telephone: (217) 333-1386

ESR (Educators for Social Responsibility)
National office
Attn: Larry Dieringer, Executive Dir.
23 Garden St.
Cambridge, MA 02138
Telephone: (617) 492-1764
New York City chapter
475 Riverside Drive, Rm. 450

National Congress of Parents and Teachers
Attn: June Dykstra
330 N. Wabash Ave., Suite 2100
Chicago, IL 60611-3690
Telephone: (312) 670-6782

NCTE (National Council of Teachers of English)
Attn: Millie Davis, Director of Affiliate and Member Services
Urbana, IL

Pennsylvania Department of Education
Attn: James Buckheit, Acting Director
333 Market St., Harrisburg, PA 17126
Telephone: (717) 783-3755

People for the American Way
2000 M Street
Washington, D.C. 20036

RCCP (Resolving Conflict Creatively Program)
Attn: Linda Lantieri, Director
163 Third Ave., Suite 103
New York, NY 10003
Telephone: (212) 387-0225

SAVE
Attn: Julie Good
633 W. Rittenhouse St.
Philadelphia, PA 19144
Telephone: (215) 438-9070

Teaching Tolerance, Southern Poverty Law Center
Attn: Morris Dees
400 Washington Ave.
Montgomery, AL 35104
Telephone: (334) 264-0286

The Media Center for Children
Attn: Dr. Alvin Pouissant, Director
Judge Baker Children's Center
2 Blackfan Circle
Boston, MA 02115-5794
Telephone: (617) 232-8390, ext. 2303

The Raoul Wallenberg Committee of the U.S.
Attn: Rachel Oestricher Berheim, President
575 Lexington Avenue
New York, NY 10002
Telephone: (212) 350-4875

The American Psychological Association (APA, 1997), in a briefing paper stated that we could reduce the chance of violence in our youth by giving them the ability to arrive at nonviolent solutions to problems by teaching them such skills as:

- Problem-solving
- Stress management
- Assertiveness
- Anger control
- Impulse control

Further, the APA asserted that, to be effective, youth intervention programs must start as early as possible, must educate parents in prevention strategies including nonviolent coping skills, and must include numerous components of the child's environment. Some of these programs must include critical thinking skills and media literacy in addition to attempting to reduce aggression and anti-social behavior through the development of conflict resolution techniques.

If the Cultural Environment Movement and the Center for Media Literacy are broad associations whose efforts are aimed at confronting dissonance and violence, there are other new initiatives emerging, some of which are centered in the schools. A growing trend since the mid-1980s is the use of conflict resolution and peer counseling in public schools. The Resolving Conflict Creatively Program (RCCP) is one such school-based program focused on conflict resolution and intergroup relations that provides a model for preventing violence and creating caring, learning communities. According to Gurewitz (personal communication, July 31, 1996), the RCCP attempts to show…

"… young people that they have many choices besides passivity or aggression for dealing with conflict; gives them skills to make those choices real in their own lives; increases their understanding and appreciation of their own and other cultures, and shows them that they can play a powerful role in creating a more peaceful world."

The Resolving Conflict Creatively Program serves 5000 teachers and 150,000 children in 325 schools nationwide, including New York City. Linda Lantieri, one of the organizers of RCCP, wrote a new curriculum and a book that details issues of peace in the schools (Lantieri and Patti, 1996).

Another program, *Second Step: A Violence Prevention Curriculum*, in use in more than 10,000 schools in the U.S. and Canada, involves a series of 30 lessons offered in 35-minute weekly or twice-weekly sessions designed to teach empathy, problem-solving, and anger management to children from preschool through ninth grade, with curricula geared to grade level (Grossman et al., 1997). As reported by Tanner (1997), comparisons of children in experimental and control groups (all second- and third-graders) in the Seattle schools, evaluated prior to the program and again 2 weeks and 6 months after the conclusion of the program, showed that the experimental subjects "exhibited about 30 fewer acts of aggressive behavior every day than children who did not take the course. The subjects also exhibited 800 more neutral or positive acts per class every day than children who did not take the course." Aggressive behaviors included hitting, kicking, and shoving. As Rosenberg (1997, p. 1642) and his associates at the National Center for Injury Prevention and Control, Centers for Disease Control and Prevention, have cautioned, however, use of this curriculum or any other requires the support of school administrators as well as the commitment of time and resources for effective implementation. They concluded their editorial comment with the statement: "As far as our children are concerned, leaving violence at its current level is something we cannot afford to do."

An overview of catalogues of college and graduate school offerings indicates that higher education is finally putting new effort forth to provide mediation counseling programs for teachers and programs to prepare children for peer counseling. Lesley University in Boston is the first university in the U.S. to offer a Master's degree in Mediation Counseling, but, clearly, schools of education and graduate schools are realizing the importance of trying to help children begin very early to deal with negative feelings — theirs and others — and to develop skills that may help protect them from threatening experiences. According to Gerbner (1997), by the time a child in the U.S. is 6 years old, the child's exposure to violence and brutality, whether in his or her real life home world or via the media, has had a permanent influence.

The recent focus on introducing and implementing school programs in mediation and peer counseling is indeed being taken seriously by cities, states, and the federal government. At the Springfield (Delaware County) School District in southeastern Pennsylvania, for example, which has a quite homogeneous population, teachers and administrators spent nearly 2 years putting together a proposal dealing with cultural diversity and peer counseling to compete for a state grant. The program was funded and coordinating efforts between various areas of instruction in junior and senior high schools are being worked out to permit the highest levels of consistency for success (on-site visit, October 8, 1996). Of course, budgeting money for school programs is always problematic. When federal revenue sharing was virtually eliminated during the 1980s under federal efforts at deregulation, many state and local educational organizations became underfunded, making it necessary to get communities to raise local taxes — never a popular move. In addition, the climate of the nation has become so anti-bureaucracy and anti-federal government that local authorities insist that only they can decide what money can be used for education, and how it should be used.

A major new focus in Pennsylvania is on funding for instructional technologies, according to Jim Buckheit of the state's Department of Education, where he is head of the media literacy program (personal communication, January 13, 1997). Buckheit believes that as long as the nation maintains emphasis on local control, funding for media programs will remain local as well, a situation which he observes has both strengths and weaknesses. Knowing how to use the technologies is not the same as having an understanding of their implications and consequences or having the best critical skills to use them to their best advantage. Most educators involved with either conflict resolution or media literacy expressed concern about how unprepared schools, administrators, and teachers in particular are to implement such new programs. A spot check of some 15 colleges and universities indicated that while there were scattered courses available, there does not seem to be a department of media literacy or a requirement for it at most schools of education.

In the law enforcement area, there are increasing efforts to teach criminals and drug abusers to use cognitive thinking skills rather than to act or react in a "knee-jerk reflex" manner. These programs are in widespread use in Canadian prisons and halfway houses as well as in many facilities in the U.S. and appear to have positive effects (Cass, 1997). If children and adults can be taught that there are numerous techniques for resolving disputes and that they need to consider the potential consequences of their acts, we can have hope that the knee-jerk reflex reaction of whipping out a knife or gun will be reduced. If the use of weapons is reduced, lethal violence should be reduced. It ought to be obvious that such alternative techniques need to be taught and modeled at home, in the schools, and on television.

Communities Take Action

While schools, colleges, and umbrella organizations formulate and expand programs on how to help youngsters become better communicators, more peaceable friends, and more critical users of the media, community action groups are forming as well. One such organization — SAVE — has just celebrated its tenth year of activity in the Philadelphia area. This small but growing organization is trying to find ways of helping to defuse polarization through modeling. SAVE brings college graduates into the public schools to engage with troubled populations and to act as role models. Each young male tutor is committed to spending a full year at a particular high school where he works with young people and teaches the basics of conflict resolution, mediation, and anger management and helps pupils understand the impact of media violence. Funded by the private sector, SAVE was begun by three sets of parents in the Philadelphia area who had experienced the death of one of their children through a violent act (Good, personal communication, September 20, 1996).

In Boston, several community programs are apparently proving effective in reducing killings of and by juveniles. As reported by Clinton (1996, p. 191), the annual *Team Harmony* event in Boston "brings middle and high school students and teachers together with local sports figures and business leaders to take a stand against prejudice and bigotry. Local television and radio stations, newspapers, churches, and synagogues get involved." The *Violence Prevention Curriculum for Adolescents* developed by the Educational Development Center is teaching conflict-resolution skills to youngsters (Prothrow-Stith and Weissman, 1991), and the probation department has accelerated its activity in cooperation with the police department so that nightly house calls are made to youths on probation (Operation Night Light) by a probation officer and a police officer (Goldman, 1997, p. A1). The result has been that Boston "has seen none of its teenagers under 17 killed by gunfire since July 1995. And the homicide rate for those under 24 dropped more than 70% in the last year. Arrests for assault with a gun by a juvenile declined 81% since 1993." These data provide a wonderful positive contrast to the statement cited earlier by the authors to the effect that the homicide rate in Boston had increased 45% in 1990 over the previous year (Schwartz and Matzkin, 1996).

The Child Study Center at Yale University School of Medicine is another community-based program which focuses on underserved inner-city children, families, and other members of the community. Years of research by a collaborative effort of the Center's faculty, the New Haven Department of Police Services, the Child Development and Policing Program, and the New Haven schools have led to the creation of model programs on conflict resolution, research and treatment of troubled children and their families, and evaluation activities (Cohen, 1996).

Dealing With Racism

As the authors have noted earlier (Schwartz and Matzkin, 1996), acceptance by peers is important to children, with such acceptance playing an ever-greater role as they move into adolescence. The youth who is troubled at home or at school and who cannot find acceptance among his or her "socially acceptable" peers will take acceptance where he or she finds it and adopt the group's attitudes A particularly graphic and very unusual example is Tom Leyden. According to Helfand (1996, p. A22):

> *"[Leyden's] life began to unravel around age 15, when [his] parents divorced. Leyden dropped out of school and began hanging out with punk rockers. On weekends, he'd escape the shouting at home by running off to concerts where he could vent his rage by slam-dancing and fighting. Leyden's penchant for violence won him friends among skinheads at the shows, and he began hanging out with them, adopting their violent attitudes. Soon he helped start a skinhead group with about 20 teenagers."*

Fifteen years later, Leyden had become sufficiently disillusioned and distressed by the beliefs and practices of skinheads that he went to the Simon Wiesenthal Center in Los Angeles to offer his knowledge to the Center to fight hate groups. Apparently, a major part of his change of perspective was related to the "angst of watching his sons — ages 4 and 2 — grow up as hatemongers saluting the Nazi and Confederate flags" (Helfand, 1996, p. A22). The older boy even turned off a television program that featured black actors, saying that he and his brother were not allowed to watch shows with black actors. The skinheads and "new world order" call for eliminating members of minority groups, the handicapped, and the police. This affected Leyden personally, for his mother was handicapped and his brother was a police officer. Leyden's new perspective led him to divorce his wife, a member of the skinhead group, and to seek custody of his sons, in addition to turning his knowledge of the skinhead and similar movements to more constructive uses. Thus, his effort, an individual one, can reach youths because of his "inside" experience.

Acknowledging that in the U.S. the issue of racism and its role in violence that is often lethal are serious problems, a number of national organizations are focusing their efforts on solutions. One of these is the American Psychological Association which announced, in a banner headline in its monthly *APA Monitor*, a major two-pronged effort to educate the public on racial issues ("Proposed TV rating...", 1997, p. 40). One prong was a "National Conversation on Racism", a year-long event that sought to stimulate dialogue on the causes of racism. It was made up of a series of conferences, workshops, professional meetings, lectures, and other forums on racism. The second prong was a mini-convention within APA's 1997 annual meeting in Chicago.

Newsweek's November 25, 1996, issue took a big step toward encouraging its nearly 3 million readers to help end racism with a four-page article by Ellis Cose entitled "Twelve Steps Toward Racial Harmony" (Cose, 1996, pp. 54–55). Among the 12 steps Cose suggested were the notion that "ending hate is the beginning, not the end, of our mission ... we must do a better job at leveling the playing field ... [and] we must become serious about fighting discrimination."

Lowering the level of the rhetoric is a goal of *Common Quest*, a new magazine dealing with race relations, which has two co-editors, one black and the other Jewish. Reporting on the new publication, Eisner (1996, p. E7) said, "Providing a safe space for discussion doesn't mean offering up pablum. ...It means acknowledging that the wounds and suspicions between these two fascinating subsets of American society are real and deep and well founded, but the ties are still special and important enough to warrant the hard work of honest talk."

Another publication, *At-Risk Resources*, published by the Bureau for At-Risk Youth in Plainview, NY, displayed a full-page advertisement on its back cover for a new 10-part video series on violence prevention, called *Peace Talks*. The series features conversations between students and Michael Pritchard, a well-known youth counselor.

Each of these efforts is based on the premise that reducing racial and other polarizations can play a role in reducing hate crimes and lethal violence, especially among our youth. Further, learning to think (and view) critically and to develop alternative means of resolving conflicts, can similarly contribute to a reduction in lethal violence. All of these efforts and concerns are intertwined, for each of them affects the individual to some degree and, over time, reshapes the individual's thinking and behavior.

The Media Reflects on Itself

Amid the conflicts and polemics over the roles, responsibilities, and impact of the media, there are ripples within the media institutions themselves that indicate some degree of responsiveness to criticism leveled at them. ABC's *Nightly News with Peter Jennings* has begun a regular feature called "Solutions" which focuses on national issues and the hopeful or positive efforts to resolve them. *CBS Morning* spent a week sending its staff back to their hometowns, followed by a round-table summary. Tom Brokaw suggested that America is basically healthy and that the climate of the country is far more stable and cohesive than we may sometimes be led to believe.

While Brokaw's optimistic tone might not play well in places such as Oakland, Boston, Philadelphia, New York City, or Washington, D.C., it may have comforted some who cannot deal with ambiguity.

National Network Ratings

The introduction of a national television ratings system has finally been implemented after much public and publicized discussion and warnings from Attorney General Reno and other national leaders. Following Congressional hearings on the effects of the media on children, members of the media industries agreed to create a system that would help families select programming appropriate for children. The new guidelines are supposed to guide parents in choosing which television programs are considered by the networks appropriate for children of varying ages, but even in the days just prior to and following the implementation, controversy continued concerning their potential purposes and efficacy. While Jack Valenti, president of the Motion Picture Association of America (MPAA), has said that the new television ratings system offered American families is the best that can be achieved here, Canadian families will be using a more sophisticated system that is said to give parents far greater control over what their families will be watching on television (DePalma, 1996).

Responding to the network ratings effort, Gerbner has called the ratings "the rating game shame". He disputed the MPAA's claim that this was the most workable plan. Addressing Valenti, Gerbner said that all organizations urged Valenti "to design a rating system that provides reasons for the ratings such as sex, violence, foul language, so that parents can make informed decisions." According to Gerbner (1997, p. A17), the system that has been "rammed down the public's throats" has four fatal flaws:

- It ignores what public interest groups have demanded: information about the reasons for the ratings rather than only age classifications.
- It confuses the choices made in movie-going with the very different decisions of television viewing.
- Producers rating their own programs results in inconsistencies.
- Ratings designed by the industry and programmed into the V-chip are like "letting the fox guard the chicken coop".

Gerbner continued by saying, "Violence needs no translation. It is image driven. It speaks 'action' in any language; therefore, what global program syndicators may lose domestically, they more than make up by selling cheaply to many countries. When you can dump a Power Rangers on 300 million children in 80 countries every night, shutting out domestic artists and cultural products, you don't have to care who wants it and who gets hurt in the process."

It is not only communications specialists such as Gerbner who question the outcome of the new ratings system. In a study of ratings systems by the University of Wisconsin at Madison, part of the NTV Study, younger children (ages 5 to 9) and older children (ages 10 to 15) were given eight programs and descriptions with varying rating designations (Federman, 1997, p. 35). They were then asked "how much they wanted to see each one. ...The MPAA ratings increased children's interest in restricted programs, but none of the content-based systems had this effect." Psychologists joined lawmakers, parents, and children's advocates early in 1997 in calling on the television industry to develop a rating system that specifies the content of a program, not the age group that should see it. Apparently, some major broadcasters have heeded the call as, early in June 1997, the Fox and ABC networks, as well as cable network owner Ted Turner, announced that they would introduce S (sex), V (violence), and L (language) symbols to the age ratings previously introduced (Farhi, 1997).

On the other hand, what good are television rating systems if offensive commercials are shown during programs intended for watching by all ages? A case in point occurred on December 1, 1996, on the

Fox Network which was showing a figure-skating competition from 4:30 p.m. to 6:00 p.m. (EST). An inappropriate commercial for a pornographic videotape — titled "Cops Too Hot 2" and available by telephone or mail — was shown not once, but twice, during commercial breaks. This is not an uncommon occurrence. While it is clearly not illegal to air such a commercial, common sense alone would dictate that the hour and the program were not the appropriate venues for this commercial and that it should be aired during a later programming time slot.

Norman Lear Talks to His Media Colleagues

Writer/producer Norman Lear, whose controversial hit comedy series *All in the Family* attempted to shoot holes in the aura of bigotry, is also the founder of the People for the American Way, a not-for-profit organization dedicated to bringing people together. In a keynote address entitled "Our Lost Passion for Something Better" and given before the Humanitas organization, Lear (1996) spoke candidly to his television colleagues concerning the media's need to examine itself more critically:

"Today, it seems to me, our industry is being born yet again with the conglomerizing that sees Disney's purchase of Cap Cities/ABC, TimeWarner's planned buyout of Turner Broadcasting, Westinghouse's acquisition of CBS, and many other electronic media. ...My concern is the very plausible scenario that we may soon have only three or four humongous, homogeneous funnels through which all news, information, and entertainment will pass — with little support for localism, diversity of programming, or robust free speech. ...

"I suspect it is up to the independent companies, and to we writers, producers, directors — those of us who happen not to be caught up in the conglomerizing of the moment — to begin the discussion. The electronic media is, after all, fast becoming — if it has not become already — the nervous system for human consciousness. ...

"But given the bottom-line, short-term ethos that dominates our business culture, can the media develop the kind of socially [sic], visionary leadership that was present at the first *birth of television? ...If television is indeed failing its promise to America, as our critics charge, it is because we in television are not living up to* our *full potential. ...The fact is that* America *— which happens to include business, government, and nonprofits as well as television — is failing its promise. ....*

"I believe that we in television got here when, starting many years ago and escalating over time, we began to subjugate our potential for creative leadership to the relentless reckoning of perceived public tasters whose fluctuations are measured minute by minute seven days a week. ...Living and making decisions by the numbers has infected most other industries as well — and politics. ...

"A culture that becomes a stranger to its own inner human needs — which are, for better or worse, unquantifiable, intuitive and mysterious — is a culture that has lost touch *with the best of its humanity."*

Positively Focused Commercials

Print ads and television commercials from some of the major corporations of the world, and occasionally from a network, are cropping up which take a stand for cooperation, tolerance, responsibility, choices, and consequences. International Paper Corporation, for example, has sponsored several positive television ads. In one, a father urges his son to play in a ball game to enjoy himself, not just to win. This is a novel idea for many youths and for their parents. The company has also produced similar positive messages on its Web site. Microsoft Corporation had a two-page ad in *Time* (November 18, 1996, pp. 26–27) against racism. In it, a child asks her mother, "… if the laws don't keep us apart anymore, what does?"

The USA Network has itself sponsored daily 15- or 20-second commercials promoting the messages "Heal the Hate" and "Erase the Hate" and has used Dennis Franz and Jimmie Smits of *NYPD Blue* and Rick Rossovich of *Pacific Blue*, as well as President Clinton, to convey the messages. Similarly, a brief public service spot with Dennis Franz was seen on the ABC Network on November 2, 1996, urging adults to be a mentor.

What We Can Do Now

The attitudes that underlie polarization and the resulting behaviors, especially among our youth, cannot be wished away or expected to vanish overnight. There are, however, a number of ways in which we can help the "positive currents" to flow more effectively to make the media a more positive influence and ultimately to reduce juvenile homicide.

Recommendations of the NTV Study, Year 2

Researchers at the University of California, Santa Barbara; the University of Texas, Austin; the University of Wisconsin, Madison; and the University of North Carolina, Chapel Hill, who participated in the second-year NTV Study effort concluded their report with a number of recommendations to the television industry, policy makers, and parents. They pleaded for a de-escalation of graphic violence in all forms of programming and for greater effort on the part of programmers to portray both short-term and long-term negative consequences of violence. Some other recommendations included (Federmann, 1997, pp. 45–49):

For the television industry:

- Be creative in showing more alternatives to the use of violence for solving problems and less justification for violent actions.
- Be sensitive to the time of day that programs containing violence are aired.
- When reality programs present violent themes, include expert information or helplines that suggest alternative means of conflict resolution or other ways viewers can appropriately respond to violence.
- Consider changing the television industry rating system, because similar age-based ratings have been found to attract children to restricted content.
- Design anti-violence public service announcements (PSAs) better to maximize their impact. Parents may be an overlooked and important target audience for anti- violence messages intended to reduce youth violence.

For policy makers:

- Recognize that context is an essential aspect of television violence and rely on scientific evidence to identify the context features that pose the most risk.
- Continue to monitor the nature and extent of violence on television.

For parents:

- Take an active interest in your children's television viewing and watch and discuss programs with them.
- Consider the context of violent depictions in making viewing decisions for children.
- Consider a child's developmental level when making viewing decisions.
- Recognize that certain types of violent cartoons pose particularly high risk for young children's learning of aggression.

One of the most significant observations of the study was its conclusion that (NTV Study, 1997, p. 526), "Because of the heavy competition from messages that glamorize violence, the volume of anti-violence messages will probably have to be significantly higher to cause changes in interest and attitudes about violence." Whether observations such as this or the above recommendations will have genuine effect will depend to a large extent on whether they are publicized. They need to be available in full-page print ads in newspapers and magazines, on handbills distributed by social agencies, and perhaps even on billboards. The authors do not expect that they will receive the consistent and needed publicity on television, except, perhaps, for public broadcasting stations. Even so, it will take the persistence of a fully aroused public and a conscious and prolonged set of public forums for meaningful change to occur.

Parenting Education

There are those who assume that knowing how to parent comes as naturally as knowing how to create babies. This may be an instinctive ability among animals; it is not a human instinct. It must be learned, either by example or by instruction. Perhaps education for parenting should be required in every state as a condition for a marriage license for all those under age 75 years. After all, we require special learning to be acquired to attain a driver's license. Perhaps every child should have a Tamagotchi "cyber pet" which clamors for attention and "dies" without it, much like a human infant (Boccella, 1996). More realistically, perhaps practical parenting education should be made a curriculum requirement for all students to take and pass before graduating from high school.

Whether the parents are teenagers themselves or chronologically adults, they are their children's initial models for behavior and, one hopes, their initial and continuing sources of psychological and caring support. As DiIulio (1996, p. A15) put it:

> *"Even impoverished kids living in crime-ravaged neighborhoods tend to make it if they have an adult — parent, teacher, coach or clergy — to protect and guide them. Those who commit the worst crimes, however, "have almost always been raised without adult care and supervision. Indeed, they usually have suffered a lifetime of abuse and neglect."*

In a pilot study, Curtner-Smith (1994, p. 466) found that an "authoritarian parenting style was the single best predictor of adolescents' susceptibility to antisocial peer pressure, followed by fathers' negative discipline." This suggests that extreme parenting styles may be as harmful to children, in some ways, as abuse and neglect.

On the other hand, there is the opposite problem of parental "intimidation" which again the media help to foster. Parents, particularly in the youth-oriented culture in which we are living, feel frightened and intimidated when their children tell them they are old fashioned, not with it, or not cool. These accusations are not unique to the current generation. Today, however, they may be followed by the use of physical force or acting-out behavior in a way far different than was true 30 or more years ago. In part because they want to respond supportively and in part because there is psychological fear being supplied to parents by their children in general (a form of emotional blackmail), the notion that they must appreciate whatever their child likes becomes a motivating factor. The notion that parents must be "forever young" is also supported by movies, advertising, and popular culture in general. Parents may be doing their children the disservice of offering them only reinforcement of what is ultimately not in their best interests, thus contributing more to the problem.

If all the parents who secretly disapproved of certain programming and movies would organize in their school districts or communities or among friends to discourage children from viewing such performances, many fewer of these entertainments would be made, because the industry, with all of its hype and seductive persuasions, might be more disposed to get the message. They could also use the NTV Study, Year 2 recommendations, as a topic for parent-teacher association meetings and newsletters.

Summary

While this chapter began with a description of the climate of polarization that has been emerging in this country and the dangers it presents for the future of our democratic society, the authors have also introduced a number of new and positive currents. These currents indicate that there is much support for change that is constructive, nonpartisan, humanistic, and new. In many communities across the country, activists are struggling to heighten the consciousness of those who feel paralyzed, overwhelmed, indifferent, left out, or even cynical. Activists do not usually find themselves in the majority. Through their sense of optimism, good will, and commitment, however, they often can lead, inspire, and invoke hope in others. To build the bridge to the 21st century in which Americans of all persuasions have a place will take time, effort, and a lot of shared ideas. We need to find the right keys to unlock the sense of isolation and polarization so many seem to be experiencing. We need to find the right combination to unlock the sense of unity out of diversity that has always been America's most intangible and most miraculous essence.

It is the authors' position that the problems of violence to and by children are complex and cannot be resolved by a single action or piece of legislation. Many are indeed the victims of community polarization fostered by adults. The factors involved in juvenile homicide are so interwoven that violence and children is truly a major problem. Many different, but coordinated, actions must be taken to reduce and eliminate it eventually. The authors have endeavored to suggest some appropriate starting points for community groups, for industry, and for the media to engage in a positive fight — the one against polarization and other factors that contribute to juvenile homicide.

One can find in the concept of an orchestra a metaphor useful to describe both our polarization and its antithesis. Orchestras are composed of various groups of instruments — e.g., reeds, strings, tympani, wind — with each group itself being composed of various instruments. If each musician played his or her own line of music without regard to the role of others, the result would be discordance and disharmony. On the other hand, given a musical composition to play, if each musician contributes the unique sound of his or her instrument to the common effort, what is heard can sound harmonious, beautiful, and satisfying to the listener, who greets it with delighted applause. At times, the composition may call for a solo performance, but it is supported by everyone as essential to the piece being played. Although different compositions call for different soloists, as do different life situations, the purpose is never to negate the common supportive effort that is achieved by the whole.

Polarization within the community reflects, in the context of the orchestral analogy, each group performing a solo voice without hearing or attending to other voices. The result is a din of sounds, making it difficult to make sense out of any of them. As each voice struggles to be heard, it frequently becomes harsher, more strident — what, in behavioral terms, might be perceived as more violent. In the polarized situation, there is "black" or "white" but no "gray". Hatreds of particular class, ethnic/racial, and gender groups fester and are rationalized.

What we do now will affect everyone's lives from today on into the unknown future. Those who are children now are our future. Their care and development are not political matters, but rather a matter of national survival. As an anonymous *New York Times* editorial writer (June 1, 1996, p. 18) put it, "If a true measure of a society is how well it treats its children, then America is in trouble."

We close with the thought expressed by President Clinton as he ended his 1997 State of the Union speech:

" ...we must never believe that diversity is a weakness — it is our greatest strength. ...People on every continent can look to us and see the reflection of their own greatness, as long as we give all our citizens, whatever their background, an opportunity to achieve greatness. We are not there yet. We still see evidence of abiding bigotry and intolerance. ...We must fight against this, in our country and in our hearts."

Annotated Bibliography

1. Federman, J., Ed. (1997) *National Television Violence Study,* Vol. 2: *Executive Summary.* Santa Barbara, CA: The Center for Communication and Social Policy, University of California, Santa Barbara.

2. Mediascope, Inc. (1996) *National Television Violence Study: Executive Summary, 1994–1995.* Studio City, CA: (author).

3. Mediascope, Inc. (1997) *National Television Violence Study,* Vol. 1. Thousand Oaks, CA: Sage. These three works represent the accumulated

efforts of four universities to study violence on television, especially with regard to its effects on children. In the Federman summary, specific recommendations are made to the television industry, policy makers, and parents with regard to the quantity and nature of violence shown, as well as the fact that relatively few negative consequences for crime were shown and few anti-violence messages were conveyed. These are large-scale, comprehensive studies whose findings are relevant to all groups in society.

4. Auletta, K. (1991) *Three Blind Mice: How the TV Networks Lost Their Way.* New York: Random House. Ken Auletta, a writer for *The New Yorker*, has been working both inside and outside of the television media for over 20 years. He has been a television correspondent for WNBC-TV, WCBS-TV, and New York's public television station. *Three Blind Mice* details the stories of the actual sales transactions of the three original owners of the ABC, NBC, and CBS networks by three global corporations. Having tracked the events leading up to and through these media buys, Auletta carefully documents the kinds of formatting, advertising, and programming changes that have since transpired. How those changes have influenced public awareness, attitudes, values, and beliefs is a dramatic and powerful story. Auletta insists it is crucial to understand the complex network of interrelationships between corporate America and the media because so much of public, cultural, and political policy is centered around the web of relationships. Implicit in the telling is the real underbelly of the story — how media operations and profit concerns turn on notions as simplistic as the notion that violence is not only big business, but good business.

5. Blumler, J. and Katz, E., Eds. (1974) *The Uses of Mass Communications: Current Perspectives on Gratifications Research.* Beverly Hills, CA: Sage. During the 1970s, mass media studies entered a new era of re-evaluation and change of emphasis. New questions were being raised which were far broader and less academic. Uses and gratifications studies, a central set of theories and approaches to audience studies, began to go beyond social science questions that focused on statistical data, and empirical analysis and the uses of numbers to substantiate evidence (sizes of audiences, who experiences what under what conditions, and with what effects) Studies and questions about studies became increasingly refined, on the one hand, to include cultural studies issues and, on the other hand, became more economically oriented as research began to explore more deeply the issues of the media and hegemony. In some ways, research out of the 1970s resembled the classic more qualitative and humanistic studies of the 1940s as to who reads a newspaper or who watches soap operas and why. Questions of content and the qualitative cultural experiences in which individuals were freely choosing to engage became more pertinent.

6. Davison, W.P. and Yu, F.T.C., Eds. (1974) *Mass Communication Research: Major Issues and Future Directions.* New York: Praegar. Davison and Yu's book is an excellent sourcebook which provides an overview of the history of mass media research and the differing directions that have been taken over the decades. Although published some 20 years ago, this work lays out a framework for much of the future work that has been ongoing in the field. *Mass Communication Research* examines methodological and theoretical approaches and studies of the individual and the media and the collective audience. It looks at differing perspectives on the functions of the mass media, how we study mass media in the nation state and in the political system, changing technologies, and how research has been and continues to evolve.

7. Fallows, J. (1996) *Breaking the News: How the Media Undermine American Democracy.* New York: Pantheon Books. Fallows, an editor for *The Atlantic Monthly*, questions with concern the functions of the news media today and whether they may actually be getting in the way of the public's ability to hear, digest, and understand independently what is happening in government. *Breaking the News* is a careful scrutiny of the contemporary news media, full of colorful and authentic anecdotes from both print and electronic journalism.

8. Ivengar, S. and Reeves, R., Eds. (1997) *Do the Media Govern? Politicians, Voters, and Reporters in America.* Thousand Oaks, CA: Sage. A very current study of the interrelated roles of media, government, and the public, with excellent chapters by leading journalists, editors, media critics, mass media researchers, and students of public policy. Issues explored in thoughtful multi-dimensional discussions include: reporters, reporting, and the business of news; reporters and public officials — who uses whom; media-based political campaigns; the effects of news on the audience — minimal or maximal effects; and the use of the media in the policy process.

9. Kubey, R. and Csikszentmihalyi, M. (1990) *Television and the Quality of Life: How Viewing Shapes Everyday Experience.* Hillsdale, NJ: Lawrence Erlbaum Associates. The authors' research is based on findings from nearly a dozen different studies conducted over 15 years. Thousands of self-reported observations concerning the role and meaning of television in daily life were collected and analyzed. The 1200 participants included Americans, Canadians, Europeans, and some Africans, ranging in age from 18 to 63. This research develops a series of very human profiles of certain kinds of television viewers. While its central concern is to place audience viewing into some kind of routine or daily life context, and to look closely at how different kinds of people use and encounter television differently, it also looks at the physiological and mental activity involved in viewing and distinguishes between the uses and effects of heavy and light viewing.

10. Lantieri, L. and Patti, J. (1996) *Waging Peace in our Schools.* Boston, MA: Beacon Press. This book is an encouraging personal report as well as a plea for more emphasis in the schools on teaching and learning skills associated with critical thinking and conflict resolution. The writers give detailed accounts of urban public school life, the problems of violence, and the underlying causes, documenting the importance of helping children learn early in life to manage their emotions. *Waging Peace* is very readable, full of touching insights and personal anecdotes that underscore the usefulness of programs that help teach children to get in touch with their feelings and to learn tolerance and self control.

References

American Psychological Association (1993) *Violence and Youth: Psychology's Response*, Vol. I. Washington, D.C.: (author).

American Psychological Association Task Force on Violence and the Family (1996) Annual Convention of the APA, August 19, Toronto, Canada.

American Psychological Association (undated) *Clarifying the Debate: Psychology Examines the Issues. Is Youth Violence Just Another Fact of Life?* (a briefing paper of the American Psychological Association posted on the World Wide Web) Washington, D.C.: (author). Retrieved May 4, 1997, from the World Wide Web: http://www.apa.org./ppo/violence.html.

Anti-Defamation League (1992) *Hip to Hate: Hateful Lyrics in Rap and Rock* [pamphlet]. New York: (author).

Applebome, P. (1997) Schools as America's cure-all. *The New York Times*, Jan. 12, p. E4.

Auletta, K. (1991) *Three Blind Mice: How the TV Networks Lost Their Way.* New York: Random House.

Barron, J. (1996) Bob Grant is back on the air picking up where he left off. *The New York Times*, April 30, p. B3.

Baughman, J.L. (1992) *The Republic of Mass Culture: Journalism, Filmmaking and Broadcasting In America Since 1941.* Baltimore: Johns Hopkins University Press.

Black, J. and Whitney, F. (1988) *Introduction to Mass Communication*, 2nd ed. Dubuque, IA: Wm. C. Brown.

Blumler, J. and Katz, E., Eds. (1974) *The uses of Mass Communications: Current Perspectives on Gratifications Research.* Beverly Hills, CA: Sage.

Boccella, K. (1997) In mere days, the cyber pet from Japan is latest craze. *The Philadelphia Inquirer*, May 16, pp. A1, A22.

Boorstin, D. (1961) *The Image.* New York: Atheneum.

Carter, B. (1997a) TV film about teen-ager's murder draws protest on network's timing. *The New York Times*, Feb. 3, pp. C11, C16.

Carter, B. (1997b) Texas station rejects movie about local murder case. *The New York Times*, Feb. 8, pp. 11, 17.

Carter, B. (1997c) Springer quits news show, citing attacks. *The New York Times*, May 9, p. A22.

Cass, J. (1997) Thinking things through heads off return to prison. *The Philadelphia Inquirer*, Feb. 17, pp. A1, A6.

Clinton, H.R. (1996) *It Takes a Village and Other Lessons Children Teach Us.* New York: Simon & Schuster.

Clinton, W.J. (1997) State of the Union address, February 4, Washington, D.C.

Cohen, D.J. (1996) *Child Study Center: Yale University School of Medicine Annual Report.* New Haven: Yale University Press.

Cose, E. (1996) Twelve steps toward racial harmony. *Newsweek*, Nov. 25, pp. 54–55.

Croteau, D. and Hoynes, W. (1997) *Media/Society: Industries, Images, and Audiences.* Thousand Oaks, CA: Pine Forge Press.

Cultural Environment Movement (1996) *The Cultural Environment Monitor, 1*(1), 1.

Curtner-Smith, M.E. (1994) Family process effects on adolescent males' susceptibility to antisocial peer pressure. *Family Relations, 43*, 462–468.

Davison, W.P. and Yu, F.T.C, Eds. (1974) *Mass Communication Research: Major Issues and Future Directions.* New York: Praegar.

DeFleur, M. and Ball-Rokeach, S. (1975) *Theories of Mass Communication*, 3rd ed. New York: David McKay.

DePalma, K. (1996) Canadian parents test limits on TV access. *The New York Times*, Dec. 30, pp. C9, C14.

DiIulio, J.J., Jr. (1996) Stop crime where it starts. *The New York Times*, July 31, p. A15.

Dofstadter, R. and Wallace, M., Eds. (1972) *American Violence: A Documentary History.* New York: Alfred A. Knopf.

Egan, T. (1996) Talk radio or hate radio? Critics assail some hosts. *The New York Times*, Jan. 1, p. 22.

Eisner, J.R. (1996) A needed new forum for racial dialogue. *The Philadelphia Inquirer*, Dec. 1, p. E7.

Ewing, C.P. (1990a) *Kids Who Kill.* Lexington, MA: Lexington Books.

Ewing, C.P. (1990b) *When Children Kill: The Dynamics of Juvenile Homicide.* Lexington, MA: Lexington Books.

Fallows, J. (1996) *Breaking the News: How the Media Undermine American Democracy*. New York: Pantheon Books.

Farhi, P. (1997) Some TV networks to use additional rating symbols. *The Philadelphia Inquirer*, June 3, p. A4.

Farley, F. (1991) The T-Type personality. In L. Lipsett and L.L. Mitnick (Eds.), *Self-Regulatory Behavior and Risk Taking: Causes and Consequences*, pp. 371–382, Norwood, NJ: Ablex.

Federman, J., Ed. (1997) *National Television Violence Study, Vol. 2: Executive Summary*. Santa Barbara, CA: The Center for Communication and Social Policy, University of California, Santa Barbara.

Feiler, B. (1996) Has country music become a soundtrack for white flight? *The New York Times*, Oct. 20, p. H38.

"Florida girl and 4 other teems are accused of killing her parents" (1996) *The Philadelphia Inquirer*, Nov. 29, p. A13.

Gerbner, G. (1997) Global market wins out on TV. *The Philadelphia Inquirer*, Jan. 30, p. A17.

Goldberg, C. (1997) Family killings jolt a tranquil town. *The New York Times*, Feb. 3, p. A10.

Goldman, H. (1997) Death takes a holiday among Boston teens. *The Philadelphia Inquirer*, Jan. 26, pp. A1, A10.

Grossman, D.C., Neckerman, H.J., Koepsell, T.D., Liu, P., Asher, K.N., Bland, K., Frey, K., and Rivara, F.P. (1997) Effectiveness of a violence prevention curriculum among children in elementary school: a randomized controlled trial. *Journal of the American Medical Association, 277*, 1605–1611.

Hall, H.V. (1996) Death by institutional violence. In H.V. Hall (Ed.), *Lethal Violence 2000: A Sourcebook on Fatal Domestic, Acquaintance and Stranger Aggression,* pp. 663–690, Kamuela, HI: Pacific Institute for the Study of Conflict and Aggression.

Hallin, D.C. (1997) Sound bite news. In S. Ivengar and R. Reeves (Eds.), *Do the Media Govern? Politicians, Voters, and Reporters in America*, pp. 60–64, Thousand Oaks, CA: Sage.

Havemann, J. (1997) U.S. tops survey on homicides of children. *The Philadelphia Inquirer*, Feb. 7, p. A2.

Helfand, D. (1996) Former skinhead lends his expertise to those he once hated. *The Philadelphia Inquirer*, Nov. 29, p. A22.

Isser, N. and Schwartz, L.L. (1985) *The American School and the Melting Pot: Minority Self-Esteem and Public Education*. Bristol, IN: Wyndham Hall Press.

Jackson, S.J. (1993) The end of innocence: learning to critique violence through the media analysis of sport. *Journal of Experiential Education, 16*(3), 40–46.

Johnson, B. (1997) Super Bowl advertisers, *Advertising Age*, January 20, p. 12.

Kallen, H.M. (1915) Democracy versus the melting pot. *The Nation, 100*, 219–220.

Katz, E. and Lazarsfeld, P.F. (1955) *Personal Influence*. New York: Free Press.

Kenevy, B. (1994) TV in black and white. *The Philadelphia Inquirer*, June 5, pp. G1, G9.

Kubey, R. and Csiksentmihalyi, M. (1990) *Television and the Quality of Life*. Hillsdale, NJ: Lawrence Erlbaum Associates.

Kurtz, H. (1996) *Hot Air: All Talk All the Time*. New York: Random House.

Lantieri, L. and Patti, J. (1996) *Waging Peace in the Schools*. Boston: Beacon Press.

Larry King Show (1997) Discussion with Larry Flynt and Jerry Falwell. January 10, Philadelphia: KYW-TV.

Lear, N. (1996) Our Lost Passion for Something Better. Humanitas Prize speech, July 11, Universal City, CA.

Lemon, S.M. (1997) Ready to learn update: some good news about watching PBS. *Philadelphia: Applause*, May, p. 7.

Lewis, C. (1997) The slippery slope into sleaze is changing the news and tastes. *The Philadelphia Inquirer*, May 12, p. A13.

Lu, S. (1996) After I misspoke, more and more radio affiliates started listening. *The New York Times,* April 22, p. D9.

Mast, G. and Kawin, B.F. (1994) *A Short History of Movies*, 6th ed. Needham Heights, MA: Simon & Schuster.

Mediascope, Inc. (1996) *National Television Violence Study: Executive Summary, 1994–1995.* Studio City, CA: (author).

Merrill, J.C., Lee, J., and Friedlander, A.J. (1990) *Modern Mass Media*, 2nd ed. New York: Harper Collins.

Mitroff, L.I. and Bennis, W. (1989) *The Unreality Industry: The Deliberate Manufacturing of Falsehood and What it Is Doing to Our Lives.* New York: Carol Publishing Group.

Morin, K. (1996) *A Study of Heroes: A Program That Inspires and Educates Through the Example of Heroes.* Longmont, CO: Sopris West.

National Center for Health Statistics (1997) Births, marriages, divorces, and deaths for November 1996. *Monthly Vital Statistics Report, 45*(11), Hyattsville, MD: National Center for Health Statistics.

National Television Violence Study, Vol. I (1997) Thousand Oaks, CA: Sage.

Postman, N. (1985) *Amusing Ourselves to Death.* New York: Viking/Penguin.

"Proposed TV rating system is criticized" (1997) *APA Monitor*, January, pp. 8, 10.

Prothrow-Stith, D. and Weissman, M. (1991) *Deadly Consequences.* New York: Harper Collins.

Relin, D.O. (1995) Anger on the airwaves. *Media Monitor*, Sept. 1, p. 27.

Rosenberg, M.L., Powell, K.E. and Hammond, R. (1997) Applying science to violence prevention. *Journal of the American Medical Association, 277*, 1641–1642.

Schwartz, L.L. and Matzkin, R.G. (1996) Violence, viewing, and development. In H.V. Hall (Ed.), *Lethal Violence 2000: A Sourcebook on Fatal Domestic, Acquaintance and Stranger Aggression,* pp. 113–142. Kamuela. HI: Pacific Institute for the Study of Conflict and Aggression.

Sheras, P.L., Cornell, D.G., and Bostain, D.S. (1996) The Virginia youth violence project: transmitting psychological knowledge on youth violence to schools and communities. *Professional Psychology, 27*, 401–406.

Signorielli, N. (1991) *A Sourcebook on Children and Television.* Westport, CT: Greenwich Press.

Stern, K.S. (1996) *A Force Upon the Plain: The American Militia Movement and the Politics of Hate.* New York: Simon & Schuster.

Suhor, C. (1996) Summaries of informal annual discussions of the commissions of the NCTE. In *NCTE Trends and Issues in English Instruction: Six Summaries.* Urbana, IL: National Council of Teachers of English.

Tanner, L. (1997) Study says children can learn to be less violent. *The Philadelphia Inquirer*, May 28, p. A3.

"Top 100 world-wide box office champs" (1997) *Variety,* January 10–26, p. 14.

Twemlow, S.W. and Sacco, F.C. (1996) The violent community: a view from an evolving nation. In H.V. Hall, Ed., *Lethal Violence 2000: A Sourcebook on Fatal Domestic, Acquaintance and Stranger Aggression*, pp. 613–634. Kamuela, HI: The Pacific Institute for the Study of Conflict and Aggression.

Wolman, N. and Fuller, A.A. (1997) As for bipartisanship, the future looks dim. *The New York Times*, Feb. 14, p. A36.

Young, A. (1996) *Urban Problems and Opportunities* [tape]. Annual meeting of the American Psychological Association, Toronto, Canada.

Zangwill, I. (1908) *The Melting Pot* (stage presentation).

Zimbardo, P.G. (1970) The human choice: individuation, reason, and order versus deindividuation, impulse, and chaos. In W.J. Arnold and D. Levine (Eds.), *Nebraska Symposium on Motivation: 1969,* pp. 237–307. Lincoln: University of Nebraska Press.

About the Authors

Lita Linzer Schwartz, Ph.D., is Distinguished Professor Emerita of Educational Psychology and Professor Emerita of Women's Studies at The Pennsylvania State University and is a Diplomate in Forensic Psychology of the American Board of Professional Psychology. She is a graduate of Vassar College (A.B.), Temple University (Ed.M.), and Bryn Mawr College (Ph.D.). **Rosalie Greenfield Matzkin, Ed.D.,** is a Lecturer in Films, Communication, and Popular Culture at The Pennsylvania State University. She is a graduate of Syracuse University (B.A.), and Teachers College, Columbia University (M.A., M.Ed., and Ed.D.). Prior to studying for her doctorate, she worked as a reporter/editor for a New York City-based trade newspaper and in local news research for WNBC-TV. Both authors can be reached at The Pennsylvania State University, Abington College, Abington, PA 19001.

Chapter 4

MODES OF JUVENILE VIOLENCE

Robert F. Eme

"Every day, crime shatters the peace in our Nation's neighborhoods. Violent crime and the fear it engenders cripple our society, threaten personal freedom, and fray the ties that are essential for healthy communities. No corner of America is safe from increasing levels of criminal violence, including violence committed by and against juveniles." (Reno, 1996, in Loeber and Hay, 1997, p. 1)

This statement by Attorney General Janet Reno starkly and crisply summarizes the current situation in the U.S., which has the highest level of violence of any industrialized country (Loeber and Hay, 1997). More precisely, the violent crime that is shattering, threatening, and fraying our society is primarily perpetrated by male juvenile offenders. Archer (1994, p. 1) noted in his excellent book entitled *Male Violence*: "Male violence may even outrank disease and famine as the major source of human suffering." See Eme (1996) for a discussion of reasons for the greater male prevalence and Rowe et al. (1995) for research supporting a common etiology for male and females. The majority of criminal offenders are teenagers, with official rates of crime peaking sharply at about age 17 and dropping precipitously in young adulthood. By the early 20s, the number of active offenders decreases by over 50%, and by age 28 almost 85% of former delinquents desist from offending (Caspi and Moffitt, 1995). This prevalence and incidence of male adolescent crime applies to most types of crime during recent historical periods and in numerous Western nations (Caspi and Moffitt, 1995).

The occurrence of adolescent male violence takes on an even more ominous cast with the grim forecasts of a coming "storm" of juvenile violence. In the most comprehensive report ever assembled on crimes committed by young people, the Justice Department predicted that if current trends continue, the number of arrests for violent crimes will double by the year 2010 (DiIulio, 1996). Hence, in a few years, we can expect to encounter the "youngest, biggest, and baddest generation any society has every known" (Bennett et al., 1996). Furthermore, Fox (1996), in his March 1996 report to Attorney General Reno, cautioned that we should not be deceived by recent reports of a declining rate of violent crime. The overall drop in crime obscures the fact that there are actually two crime trends in America — one for the young and one for the mature — and that these are moving in opposite directions. For example, from 1990 to 1994, the overall rate of murder declined slightly (4%), while the rate of murder committed by teenagers ages 14 to 17 jumped 22%. Also, while the overall rate of juvenile crime declined 2.9% in 1995 and declined again in 1996 (Butterfield, 1997), this good news is tempered by the fact that the number of teenagers is expected to increase by about 1% per year through 2010. Thus, even if the crime rate held steady, this substantial increase in the number of juveniles would markedly increase the total number of violent crimes committed (Bennett et al., 1996; Butterfield, 1996). Hence, President Clinton, being well aware of the import of these predictions, stated in a February 19, 1997, speech on youth crime to an audience at Boston University (Mitchell, 1997, p. A1):

"So we know that we've got about six years to turn this juvenile crime thing around or our country is going to be living in chaos. And my successors will not be giving speeches about the wonderful opportunities of the global economy; they'll be trying to keep body and soul together for people on the streets of these cities."

We now know that the storm clouds begin gathering in very early childhood (Caspi and Moffitt, 1995; Moffitt, 1993a,b; Moffitt et al., 1996) and that these "early starters" account for a substantial number of adolescents who become chronic violent offenders (Patterson et al., 1991). For example, Moffitt et al. (1996) reported that boys who became "life-course-persistent" offenders were distinguished by difficult behavior as early as age 3 years, and Stattin and Magnusson (1996) reported a significant relationship between externalizing problems at 4 and 5 years and registered delinquency up to the age of 30 years. Similarly, Patterson's (1993) research on the stability of the antisocial trait concluded that the antisocial acts of the 5-year-old are the prototypic acts of the delinquent adolescent. Eron et al. (1991) reported that by the time children are 6, patterns of aggressive behavior seem so well established that they persist into adulthood, despite a wide variety of environmental contingencies and events. Finally, Masse and Tremblay (1997) reported that the behavior of boys in kindergarten predicted the onset of substance abuse in adolescence. Thus, this very early manifestation of antisocial behavior takes place before the deviant peer process begins and provides the circumstances that lead to violent gang involvement (Patterson et al., 1991). Furthermore, it is precisely this relatively small number of chronic juvenile offenders (5 to 7%) who account for a vastly disproportionate number of crimes (50%) and who are also disproportionately likely to commit violent offenses (Caspi and Moffitt, 1995).

Hence, if effective intervention is to take place to reduce significantly and decisively the gang violence endemic to many of our cities and which is forecast to become much worse, it must start taking place in very early childhood when the antisocial traits of the chronic offenders, which underlie the various subsequent forms of antisocial behavior (Martin, 1997; Patterson, 1993), are being formed. Moreover, for intervention to be effective, it must be guided by a clear understanding of the developmental roots of aggression and violence in their various modalities (Kazdin, 1993). The purpose of this chapter is to provide such an understanding which will furnish the basis for a discussion of "promising" interventions that will be presented in the final section of the chapter.

With regard to the terms "violence" and "aggression", we will adopt Archer's (1994, p. 2) definition of violence as "physically aggressive behaviors that do, or potentially could, cause injury or death." He indicated that the emphasis on damage caused is the crucial distinction between physical aggression and violence. The first focuses on the act and the second on the consequences. Furthermore, there is virtually unanimous agreement that human aggression is not a unitary phenomenon, but that there are different categories of aggression with different functions and antecedents (Feshbach, 1997). This chapter will explore the developmental manifestation of the different modalities of the physically aggressive behaviors that eventually come to have violent consequences. In addition, it will identify the most significant biologically based and learning/environmentally based factors that contribute to the development of the various modalities. It acknowledges the current emphasis on the dynamic, interactive processes between individuals and their environments which require models that incorporate multiple biological and environmental processes to explain developmental changes and differences among individuals (Rutter, 1997; Zahn-Waxler, 1996).

The model that the author finds most useful for this chapter has been put forth by Archer (1996, p. 19) and is termed "gendered socialization as a coevolutionary process." This model proposes that biological factors provide predispositions which gendered socialization processes can accentuate, attenuate, modify, etc. Hence, according to this analysis, gendered socialization represents not the imposition of roles that arise by historical accident but cultural learning that interacts with biological predispositions to produce individuals who are able to pursue strategies appropriate for their own sex that have been adaptive in our evolutionary past. Note that it is the "dispositions" (the likelihood of acting in a certain way under specific circumstances) that are hypothesized to have been adaptive, not the actual behavior (Archer, 1995). Last, it should be noted that although this model has been constructed primarily to demonstrate the compatibility of evolutionary and social role explanations of sex differences in social behavior, it can be easily generalized to include predispositions that are not rooted in evolution (e.g., diathesis-stress models of psychopathology; see Fowles, 1992).

Modes of Aggression

Although there is no formal classification of modes or kinds of aggression that is universally accepted, there is very widespread acceptance for certain kinds of aggression that are clearly distinct from one another (Coie and Dodge, 1997; Hinshaw and Anderson, 1996; Vittiello and Stoff, 1997). This chapter will draw upon this acceptance and will sketch when a particular form of aggression appears to emerge or become salient developmentally. In addition, it will examine the major biologically based and learning-based factors that influence the various modalities. The four modes of aggression that will be considered in developmental sequence are (1) emotional aggression, (2) instrumental aggression, (3) dominance aggression, and (4) proactive aggression. The definition of the various modes and the rationale for the sequencing will be provided in the following discussion.

Emotional Aggression (Ages 0 to 1)

Definition. Perhaps the most famous longstanding explanation of aggression is that of frustration-aggression in which emotional arousal is theorized to give rise to aggression (Fabes and Eisenberg, 1992). This hypothesis has its most current, comprehensive statement in the work of Leonard Berkowitz (1989, 1992, 1996), who posited two systems of aggression. The first system is what he calls emotional aggression.

Development. Berkowitz (1989, 1992, 1996) maintained that there is an innate, biological predisposition of the organism to respond with negative affect to aversive stimuli which then instigates the classic fight-or-flight tendencies. Parenthetically, it should be noted that the central command neurons of the sympathetic nervous system that provide the basis of the fight-or-flight response have recently been identified (Jansen et al., 1995). The relative strengths of these opposing tendencies are determined by biological, learning, and situational factors. The rudimentary anger experience stems from the negative affect-produced internal physiological reactions and involuntary emotional expressions produced by the unpleasant occurrence. It is this emotional experience that provides the instigation to hostile aggression — behavior that deliberately attempts to achieve the goal of hurting another person. In less technical terms, Berkowitz (1992, p. 79) stated that this simply means "we're nasty when we feel bad." His theorizing receives strong support from the child developmental literature in which there is a consensus that states of discomfort in young infants can be observed that are indicative of either an innate emotional repertoire or innately aversive events (Coie and Dodge, 1997; Kopp, 1989). For example, newborns whose rhythmic sucking was interrupted responded with angry cries and thrashing (Cole and Cole, 1993). Thus, Loeber and Hay (1997), in their superb literature review of the key issues in the development of aggression and violence from childhood to early adulthood, correctly reported that the earliest manifestations of aggression occur in the infant's earliest encounters with the social world, with most infants showing signs of frustration and rage. Furthermore, the emergence of this emotion is thought to be crucial to survival because of its self-regulatory and social communication functions in that it prepares the body to initiate self-protective and instrumental activity (Coie and Dodge, 1997).

In summary, the earliest mode of aggression is an automatic, involuntary reaction to aversive stimuli that produces a state of discomfort/distress in the infant and a tendency to fight, given appropriate biological, learning, and situational factors. This negative affect becomes more richly differentiated as anger, aggression, and eventually hostility, which is defined as an unfavorable judgment of another that arises from negative affect and the aggressive instigation that stems from negative affect (Berkowitz, 1992).

Biological Factors: Difficult Temperament. Caspi and Moffitt (1995) reported that the earliest roots of antisocial behavior probably begin with some factor capable of producing individual differences/deficits in the neuropsychological functions of the infant nervous system. When children with such deficits are raised in an unstable family environment, they are 2.3 times more likely than control group children to develop violent criminal offending in young adulthood (Raine et al., 1996). Such differences may be heritable in origin or may result from pre- or postnatal exposure to toxic agents or from delivery complications. In addition, the brain may also be altered by neonatal deprivation of nutrition and stimulation and by maltreatment. For example, Kotulak (1996) summarized various research on the effects of violence and stress on the development of children's brains. This research indicated that the stresses caused by maltreatment can actually affect genes, switching them on or off at the wrong time, forcing them to build abnormal networks of brain-cell connections. Thus, a highly stressful environment can cause genes important for survival to become overexpressed, making the child more likely to become aggressive and violent.

There are many routes by which compromised neuropsychological functioning might lead to aggressive behavior. In infancy, the most relevant route is the development of a difficult temperament, which greatly increases the likelihood that the infant will manifest negative emotionality, i.e., the degree to which negative emotions are elicited and the intensity with which these emotions are experienced and expressed (Fabes and Eisenberg, 1992). This proneness to negative emotional reactivity is clearly associated with a greater likelihood of aggressive behavior (Caspi et al., 1995; Fabes and Eisenberg, 1992; Henry et al., 1996; Loeber and Hay, 1997; Prior, 1992; Prior et al., 1993).

Learning-Situational Factors: Disorganized-Disoriented Attachment. The most relevant learning and situational factors that transform negative emotionality (more commonly seen in a child with a negative temperament) into aggression are those that promote an attachment that is known as disorganized-disoriented. In their masterful review of the application of attachment theory to psychopathology, Cicchetti and Toth (1995) traced the discovery of a disorganized-disoriented attachment. In 1981, researchers first reported on a number of infants who could not be classified according to the conventional criteria. These infants did not seem to possess a coherent strategy to deal with the stress of separation/reunion. Rather, upon reunion, these infants either blended contradictory features of several strategies (e.g., strong proximity seeking followed by strong avoidance) or appeared dazed and disoriented. Cicchetti and Toth theorized that it was the injection of fear into the caregiving experience (in addition to behaviors that are unresponsive or override clear infant communication and goals; Lyons-Ruth, 1996) that was essential for the development of a disorganized-disoriented attachment. Carlson et al. (1989, p. 529) indicated that:

"... the concurrent activation of the fear/wariness and attachment behavioral systems produces strong conflicting emotions to approach the caregiver for comfort and to retreat from him or her for safety. Proximity seeking mixed with avoidance results as infants attempt to balance their conflicting approach and avoidance tendencies. Freezing, dazing, and stilling are thought to result from a mutual inhibition that results when the two opposing desires of approach and avoidance are activated simultaneously and in equal strength."

The most important cause of the disorganized-disoriented attachment pattern is child maltreatment (Lyons-Ruth, 1996). Studies indicate that as many as 82% of maltreated infants develop this pattern (Cicchetti and Toth, 1995). Furthermore, research now clearly documents a relation between disorganized-disoriented attachments and childhood disruptive behavior (Shaw et al., 1996), aggression (Lyons-Ruth, 1996), and serious forms of delinquency (Smith and Thornberry, 1995). As disorganized infants make the transition into toddlers and preschoolers, they are much more likely to exhibit deviant levels of hostile aggression and to develop various forms of controlling and coercive behaviors toward their caregivers, along with strong avoidance tendencies (Lyons-Ruth, 1996). Cicchetti and Toth (1995, pp. 41–42) indicated that these hostile, controlling, and coercive behaviors emerge from insecure attachments in three ways:

1. The crystallization of working models in which relationships are viewed as characterized by anger, mistrust, chaos, and insecurity
2. Child behavior that serves as a strategy to gain the attention of and proximity to the caregiver when other strategies have failed
3. Insecure attachments that provide a motivational basis for developing a non-prosocial/resistant orientation to relationships

Furthermore, as Berkowitz (1992) noted, insofar as these children continue to be mistreated as they develop, their disposition to be highly aggressive becomes more crystallized and they become more violence prone. These children become emotionally reactive aggressors who are often quick to anger and inclined to lash out at others who bother them.

Instrumental Aggression (Ages 1 to 2)

Definition. Although aggression always involves an intention to do harm (Archer, 1994; Berkowitz, 1992), injury is not always the main objective. Berkowitz indicated that aggression can have other goals (e.g., hitting another child to obtain a toy). When this kind of action is carried out for some extrinsic purpose, rather than for the pleasure of doing it, it is termed instrumental aggression. Hence, instrumental aggression is a means to obtain some other objective that is more important than inflicting injury.

Beginning in the second year of life, behavioral signs of temper tantrums and aggression toward adults and peers can be observed (Loeber and Hay, 1997). "Habit training" becomes the most common elicitor of aggressive behavior, and the majority of conflicts between 21-month-old children are concerned with object or possession struggles (Park and Slaby, 1983). Indeed, up to half of all peer exchanges among children 12 to 18 months old can be characterized as involving conflict (Coie and Dodge, 1997). Personal/hostile aggression is infrequent and rarely shown at the very beginning of a conflict as opposed to the later stages of a dispute (Loeber and Hay, 1997). At this young age, children learn that instrumental behaviors (e.g., tugging a toy, displaying active resistance) are more likely than communicative actions (e.g., gesturing, verbally requesting) to lead to yielding. Thus, the modality of instrumental aggression emerges and becomes salient. The most elegant and comprehensive exposition of the development of this modality is found in the coercion model of Patterson and his colleagues (1991, 1993).

Development: Coercion Model. The coercion model has been detailed in many publications (e.g., Patterson, 1993; Patterson et al., 1989), with its most current statement being that of Dishion et al. (1995). This model is based on the learning principals of positive and negative reinforcement in which the parents directly train the child to perform aggressive behavior. In some instances, the demandingness and possessiveness so characteristic of toddlers (Ames and Ilg, 1976) are positively reinforced by allowing the child's coercive behavior to succeed and hence be instrumental in achieving a goal. An example would be allowing a toddler to hit a sibling in order to get a toy. The most important form of reinforcement, however, is negative reinforcement. For example, as parents engage in "habit training" to socialize their child's autonomy (Erikson, 1950) or as peers attempt to influence the child, the child experiences these interactions as aversive and attempts to terminate them by actions such as hitting, arguing, whining, throwing a temper tantrum, and so forth. To the extent that these aggressive behaviors are instrumental in terminating the aversive/negative stimuli of parental socialization demands or peer intrusions, they become negatively reinforced. As Dishion et al. (1995, p. 439) indicated:

"The child learns to avoid parent demands through a process of negative reinforcement. Repeated over thousands of trials, the child learns to use coercive behaviors to gain control over a disrupted, chaotic, or unpleasant family environment. These patterns become overlearned and automatic and operate without conscious, cognitive control. In the absence of contravailing forces, the child may progress from displaying these trivial aversive behaviors in the family to exhibiting similar patterns with other people in other settings, to engaging in other antisocial behaviors, including physical aggression, lying, or stealing. At the hub of the coercion process is the parents' inconsistent, harsh, or erratic efforts to set limits on their young child."

Based on this model, Patterson and his colleagues have demonstrated a progression from noncompliance to temper tantrums to physical attack for toddlers 18 months of age (Dishion et al., 1995). Others have also demonstrated strong support for this model as the pathway from preschool coercive behavior to increasingly high levels of aggression in childhood for males (McFadyeen et al., 1996). Hence, it is clear that in toddlerhood, a very powerful developmental precursor of subsequent juvenile violence, emerges with the onset of the modality of instrumental aggression.

Biological Factors: Attention Deficit/Hyperactivity Disorder. There is a consensus that childhood attention deficit hyperactivity disorder (ADHD) is a biologically based disorder (Barkley, 1996) that poses a major risk factor for the subsequent development of conduct disorder (Loeber, 1990; Loeber and Keenan, 1994; Lynam, 1996; Robins, 1991), especially when it is properly conceptualized as a disorder of impulsivity/behavioral disinhibition/self-control rather than motor overactivity or inattention (Barkley, 1995–1997).

Lynam (1996) conducted the most extensive review to date on the two models that have been developed to account for this relationship. The first, the stepping-stone model, proposes that ADHD would maximize interpersonal conflict, behavioral dyscontrol, etc., which in turn would lead directly to the development of an oppositional defiant disorder (ODD), which in turn could escalate to various conduct problems (CP), aggression, violence, and so forth. For example, ADHD, when combined with the normal oppositionality in the toddler which has previously been described, may tax the skills of the parent "and lead to the adoption of coercive childrearing techniques" (Lyman, 1996, p. 222).

The second model, risk-factor, is very similar to the stepping-stone model, except that it assumes that an ODD is already present. Hence, it proposes that problems and consequences that ADHD behavior creates on top of ODD behaviors may escalate into CP.

In addition to these two models which have appeared frequently in the literature, Lynam (1996, p. 224) proposed a third model which suggests that children with symptoms of both ADHD and CP are afflicted with a virulent strain of conduct disorder best described as fledgling psychopathy. This psychopathy develops out of what he terms a "psychopathic deficit" — a "failure to inhibit a dominant response, or more specifically goal-directed behavior, in the face of changing environmental contingencies." Parenthetically, it should be noted that, although Lynam was inexplicably unfamiliar with Barkley's (1995–1997) recent theorizing on ADHD, his conceptualization of a failure in inhibition was virtually identical to Barkley's theory. Lynam then proposed that the child with this deficit will have grave difficulty in incorporating feedback from the environment and using this information to modulate responses while pursuing rewards. For example, the child will not respond to admonitions from his or her parents while pursuing rewards or will respond impulsively in the face of rewards.

In summary, the foregoing theories clearly indicate how the neurobiological disorder of ADHD can strongly predispose a child to the development of a coercive style in the preschool years and future conduct problems. They also help explain the growing body of evidence that disruptive behavior problems in the preschool years often persist and that children identified as showing relatively severe behavior problems in early adolescence often have a history of problems that began in the preschool years (Campbell, 1995).

Learning-Situational Factors. Dishion et al. (1995) listed a number of "contextual variables" that increase the likelihood that a coercive process will develop. The variables that are most relevant for this period of development when instrumental aggression first emerges are single parenting and extensive child-care.

During the toddler stage, parenting becomes much more challenging, as a major qualitative change takes place — the onset of socialization pressure (Maccoby and Martin, 1983). In addition to needing to continue the sensitive, responsive, involved caretaking required to establish the secure attachment and basic trust of infancy, parents begin the process of socializing the child's drive for autonomy and individuation. Children at this stage must learn to inhibit disruptive behavior and engage in socially required or approved behavior. This is no small task, as children in these terrible twos "... may be, above all else, imperious, bossy, and demanding" (Ames and Ilg, 1976, p. 14). Hence, it comes as no surprise that the most common elicitor of anger outbursts at this age is habit training (Ross and Slaby, 1983). If these outbursts are not to eventuate in a lifestyle of chronic power struggles (Dreikurs, 1964) and coercive interactions, highly skilled and consistent parenting is needed. This is a formidable task for two parents working together; for a single parent with one or more children, it is all the more so.

Unfortunately for children, single parenting is becoming more and more common. The percentage of families with children headed by a single parent (usually a woman because of divorce or being born to an unmarried mother), which has doubled since 1970 (U.S. Census Bureau, 1997), is currently approximately 30% ("Single families...", 1995). Furthermore, half of all children in the U.S. spend some time as part of a single-parent family before reaching age 18 (National Advisory Mental Health Council [NAMHC], 1996). The voluminous research on the effects of single parenting was recently reviewed by the NAMHC's Basic Behavioral Science Task Force, which falls under the National Institute of Mental Health (NIMH). This task force consisted of 52 eminent behavioral and social scientists in the Division of Neuroscience and Behavioral Science of NIMH.

They concluded that single parenting often has long-term negative effects on children and that children who grow up with two parents do better in many ways than children who grow up with only one parent (National Advisory Mental Health Council, 1996). One of the major negative effects on boys of being raised by a single parent is that they are more likely to engage in antisocial behavior.

The impact of the increased stress of single parenting with its eventual long-term negative effect of elevated risk of antisocial behavior in boys becomes manifest in toddlerhood in the following way. Elevated levels of day-to-day stress increase the likelihood of a coercive interaction that results in antisocial behavior. This, in turn, results in a toddler progressing from noncompliance to temper tantrums to physical attack (Dishion et al., 1995) and to problem behavior by age 6 to 7 (Fagot, 1990).

The debate on the effects of child care may be the most contentious of any of the 20th century's conflicts on the proper way to raise children (Karen, 1994). The importance of this discussion is illustrated by the fact that as of 1991, 58% of all preschoolers in the U.S. with employed mothers were in some form of nonrelative care, with the largest group (28%) receiving center-based care (Chira, 1995; Scarr and Eisenberg, 1993). Recently, several clear and consistent findings have emerged which have significant implications for the development of instrumental aggression.

First, Scarr and Eisenberg (1993, p. 633), in their comprehensive review of child care research, concluded that:

"No one denies that an examination of children with extensive child care experience may reveal elevated levels of some negative behaviors. Regardless of methodology, increased aggression in children using center care has been found to be a fairly robust finding and is no longer targeted for sole investigation."

Lamb (1997), in the most extensive review to date on this topic, reached a similar conclusion. These conclusions should come as no surprise, as it has long been known that the interactions of preschool children are marked by high levels of social conflict. Parke and Slaby (1983) reported that approximately half of interchanges among children in nursery school could be viewed as conflictual, with the majority of conflicts being struggles over possessions. Furthermore, these conflicts provide very rich schedules of positive reinforcement for coercive behavior, with 80% of coercive behavior producing successful outcomes (Dishion et al., 1995). In sum, as Park and Slaby (1983, p. 569) observed, these early social conflicts serve as a "... training ground for learning effective strategies for initiating and terminating conflicting aggressive interactions." Hence, if a high frequency of instrumental aggression which is richly reinforced is normative for preschool children, it is small wonder that child-care centers that are overcrowded, understaffed, or staffed with unskilled workers can provide super-enriched reinforcement schedules for instrumental aggression.

Second, and most disturbing, is the finding that care at most child-care centers is so poor, according to the most extensive study of the quality of center-based child care to date, that it threatens children's intellectual and emotional development (Carnegie Task Force, 1996). Researchers at the University of Colorado at Denver, the University of California at Los Angeles, the University of North Carolina, and Yale University examined 400 care centers in California, Colorado, Connecticut, and North Carolina. They concluded that the level of care at most of the centers, especially in infant/toddler rooms, did not meet children's needs for health, safety, warm relationships, and learning. Most care was deemed to be sufficiently poor to interfere with children's intellectual and emotional development (Carnegie Task Force, 1996).

Thus, if poor-quality center care increases aggression and most centers provide poor care, it follows with syllogistic inexorability that a very significant proportion of our most vulnerable children are in essence being tutored in the aggressive arts in settings that Oliver Twist and the Artful Dodger might find familiar.

This foregoing conclusion receives support from the preliminary findings of the most extensive and definitive study of daycare in the U.S. to date. In 1989, the National Institute on Child Health and Human Development (NICHD) began a 10-site longitudinal study of the effects of day care and continues to follow 1300 children from birth to age 7 (Azar, 1996). Before considering the relevant findings, two observations are in order. First, there is a major difference between this study and previous ones in that the quality of child care provided at the sites is judged by the study's coordinator, Dr. Sarah Friedman, to be much better than what is commonly found, although inferior to care provided by fathers or relatives or care in the home by a caregiver (Chira, 1996). Thus, whatever final conclusions emerge from this study, they will not change the dismal findings on aggression if most center-based care continues to be as poor as it has been in the past. Second, the variable of aggression has yet to be examined (Azar, 1996; Chira, 1996).

Keeping these observations in mind, the relevant findings at 15 months of age are as follows (Azar, 1996). First, on a positive note, the study found that child care did not directly threaten the mother-child bond; however, child care did have an adverse effect on attachment if mothers were insensitive and unresponsive or showed more signs of depression or anxiety. Moreover, this increased risk of having an insecurely attached child was compounded by poor-quality child care, being in child care for 10 hours or more a week, and switching or starting additional care arrangements.

The study found that boys who were in child care for 30 hours or more a week were slightly more likely to have insecure relationships with their mothers (Azar, 1996). This result is fully congruent with previous findings of a disproportionately high preponderance of insecure attachments among boys (Carlson et al., 1989) as well as the greater prevalence of negative effects of nonmaternal care on males (Baydar and Brooks-Gunn, 1991; Belsky, 1988; Scarr and Eisenberg, 1993), although this area of research is not without controversy (Belsky, 1990; Belsky and Braungart, 1991; Clarke-Stewart, 1989; Silverstein, 1991). It is also consistent with the finding that when maternal employment in the preschool years does have a negative effect, it tends to have a stronger effect on males (Hoffman, 1989).

A very interesting example of this negative effect was seen in a study by Coon et al. (1993), who found that high maternal IQ had a negative effect on boys' but not girls' achievement scores. They attributed this surprising finding to the facts that mothers with higher intelligence tend to have more prestigious jobs and that maternal employment has been found to exert a negative effect on the achievement scores of young males.

Finally, it should be noted that the validity of these foregoing findings is buttressed by research of Rutter and his colleagues (1985, 1997). Beginning in 1970, they detected sex differences in children's responses to a number of specific family contexts — for example, parental mental illness, discord, short-term residential care of children, and daycare participation. Rutter found then and reaffirmed in 1985 the hypothesis that, analogous to greater male susceptibility to biological stress, males have a greater susceptibility to psychological stress as well. More recently, Zaslow and Hayes (1986) and Earls (1987) reviewed the literature in this regard and concluded that Rutter was correct: psychosocial stress appears to have more serious effects on boys than on girls. Additional support came from a recent study of neonates by Davis and Emory (1995), who found greater behavioral and physiological stress reactions for males to a mildly stressful behavioral assessment procedure. They also noted that their findings parallel similar sex differences in stress reactivity in infant rhesus monkeys and human adults.

Finally, it should be noted that a more recent analysis of the findings of the NICHD study extended the negative effects of extensive day care to include both boys and girls (NICHD, 1997). The researchers reported that the amount of nonmaternal care (30 hours per week or more) was weakly associated with less sensitive and less engaged mother-child interactions: The more time infants and toddlers spend in nonmaternal childcare arrangements, the less sensitive and positively involved mothers were with their children at 6 months of age, the more negative they were with them at 15 months of age, the less positively affectionate the children were toward their mothers at 24 and 36 months of age, and the less sensitive mothers were to their toddlers at the 36-month point.

In summary, the most common form of extensive non-parental child care — center-based care — is poor and thus increases the likelihood of male aggression. Moreover, even in quality center-based care, preliminary conclusions indicate adverse effects for vulnerable children or children with extensive child care.

Dominance Aggression (Ages 3 to 6)

Definition. Dominance aggression refers to aggression that allows the individual to gain the prerogatives that accompany attaining high rank in certain species (Weisfeld, 1994). The concept is primarily rooted in ethological theory which indicates that dominance hierarchies are frequently seen in group-living species in which resources are strongly contested. However, dominance aggression goes beyond the simple tendency to fight for resources (instrumental aggression) and is a distinct motive in and of itself. For example, fighting frequently occurs in the absence of any contestable resources (Weisfeld, 1994) and thus is motivated by relations in the dominance hierarchy.

Development. Dominance aggression seems to emerge at around 3 years of age (Weisfeld, 1994) and it is at this age that the gender difference in levels of aggression becomes marked (Loeber and Hay, 1997). Thus, in contrast to earlier instrumental aggression in which the objective seemed not to be focused on hurting another child, but simply attaining a goal (e.g., securing a toy), many researchers have reported marked increases in competitiveness at this age. This takes such forms as running races, play-fighting, seeking approval, and comparing heights; tangible resources do not seem to motivate these comparisons (Weisfeld, 1994).

One of the clearest sex differences in preschool children is that of rough-and-tumble play which involves fighting and chasing action patterns that are playfully motivated and delivered (Boulton, 1994). Human and nonhuman males predominate in this play pattern (Bouton, 1994; Maccoby, 1991). These rough-and-tumble play episodes that characterize preschool males are one of the ways in which boys compete to work out dominance relations (Weisfeld, 1994). A close connection between the formation of dominance hierarchies and aggression has been demonstrated by Strayer's (1992) observations of 3- and 4-year-olds in nursery school. He identified a specific pattern of aggressive interaction among children: when one child aggresses, the other child almost always submits by crying, running away, flinching, or seeking help from an adult. These dominance hierarchies formed an orderly pattern of social relationships within the group and influenced who fought with whom and under what circumstances.

In summary, dominance aggression is not primarily a function of negative emotionality or reinforcement but is driven by a predisposition to compete and dominate.

Biological Factors. Psychology has recently rediscovered Darwin and hence there has been a growing interest in evolutionary psychology, which is the science that studies the psyche in the light of current knowledge and theory about the evolutionary processes that created it (Daly and Wilson, 1994). Evolutionary psychology predicts that the sexes will be the same or similar in all those domains in which males and females have faced the same or similar adaptive problems and will differ in those domains in which they have faced different sorts of adaptive problems. Thus, to an evolutionary psychologist (Buss, 1995, p. 164): "The likelihood that the sexes are psychologically identical in domains in which they have recurrently confronted different adaptive history is essentially zero."

As applied to child development, an evolutionary functional explanation has been offered for rough-and-tumble play as being necessary for "the practice and perfection of extremely complex and fast-paced species-typical motor skills useful in predator avoidance and in intraspecific fighting" (Symonds, 1979, p. 36). More specifically, this rough-and-tumble play is viewed as "practice fighting" providing preparation for the intrasexual competition for increased access to more numerous or desirable female mates (Boulton, 1994; Buss, 1995). In our evolutionary past, those males who were most adept at this intraspecific fighting would have had a distinct advantage in terms of their fitness, and hence this selection pressure would have made it more likely that they and their offspring would have survived (see Wrangham and Peterson, 1996, in their book *Demonic Males: Apes and the Origins of Human Violence* for a cogent argument in establishing an evolutionary continuity of male violence from apes to humans). Although rough-and-tumble play is no longer adaptive in this respect in present circumstances, evolutionary theory argues that our inherited design is the same regardless of our present circumstances and hence males retain this predisposition.

In summary, in terms of evolutionary selective pressures, males have needed to fight more than females for mates and to avoid predators; therefore, males have needed more practice and engaged in more rough-and-tumble play (Boulton, 1994). As the preschool male child matures, this rough-and-tumble play pattern evolves into a propensity for high-risk competition which predisposes him to escalated physical aggression in the face of a challenge to social status or reputation (Archer, 1995; Buss, 1996).

Robust support for this theory is found in the exhaustive review of the literature on the influence of prenatal and neonatal gonadal hormones on human sex differences by Collaer and Hines (1995). They concluded that the evidence is very strong that sex differences in levels of these hormones predispose males to rough-and-tumble play. Criticism that this conclusion is rendered equivocal because of other factors was effectively countered by Eme (1996).

Learning-Situational Factors. Strayer's (1992) research on the development of agonistic and affiliative structures in preschool play groups indicated that social dominance is developmentally the earliest stable dimension of peer group social organization. Furthermore, it is quite clear from the work of Maccoby (1991), as well as many others (Ruble and Martin, 1997), that beginning in preschool the cluster of play behaviors in boys (rough-and-tumble, along with an assertive-dominant interaction style), which was previously discussed, is a central element in the spontaneous segregation of children into same-sex play groups. Maccoby's research indicated that this segregation into same-sex play groups is indeed spontaneous and not primarily a function of adult pressure, nor is it closely linked to involvement in sex-typed activities. This sex segregation then results in a divergence of interactive styles for the sexes (Maccoby, 1990). Boys in their groups are more likely than girls in all-girl groups to interrupt one another; use commands, threats, or boasts of authority; refuse to comply with another's demand; heckle a speaker; or call another child names. This differential peer socialization for a rough-and-tumble, assertive-dominant interaction style would clearly seem to predispose males to becoming more oppositional, aggressive, and violent.

Similarly, Hoynega (1993) indicated that the sexes differentially emphasize nurturance vs. competition, or what she calls prosocial dominance vs. egoistic dominance. Prosocial dominance includes acts that tend to maintain social structures and relationships. Acts of egoistic dominance serve the purpose of maintaining or increasing one's own status in the social group and include overt aggression as well as competition. She concluded that, cross-culturally, there is no doubt that girls engage in more nurturant behaviors and that boys engage in more egoistic dominance and challenge.

In summary, it is clear that beginning in preschool, the sexes begin to have markedly different peer group socialization experiences that are primarily driven by spontaneous sex segregation. Indeed, this type of socialization is so important that Harris (1995) made a credible case for the theory that it is the peer group rather than the family that is primarily responsible for the transmission of culture and for the environmental modification of children's personality characteristics. The peer group socialization experience for males is a major factor in their developing dominance aggression.

Preschool males who develop high levels of dominance aggression (as well as other forms) tend to have this aggression consolidated through two different processes as they mature: (1) initial rejection by nonaggressive peers, and (2) subsequent selection of deviant peers (Loeber and Hay, 1994). Thus, Patterson's coercion model (Patterson, 1993; Patterson et al., 1989, 1991), as well as the social cognition and social network model of Cairns and Cairns (1991), suggest that training for antisocial behavior in the home results in aggressivity that is rejected by the normal peer group, which then provides the basis for peer groupings based upon deviance. This theory finds strong support in the literature (Parker et al., 1995), which clearly shows that the aggressive child is at high risk not only for rejection by the normal peer group, but also for an intensification of aggressive behavior through the retaliations and provocations the aggressive behavior elicits. Peers are thought to supply the child with attitudes, motivations, and rationalizations to support antisocial behavior as well as to provide opportunities to engage in specific delinquent acts. Criminological theories developed by sociologists and criminologists which implicate delinquent subculture as a major criminologic factor support the validity of this theorizing (Tedeschi and Felson, 1994). This deviant peer group membership thus becomes a major training ground for delinquent acts. For example, national survey data in the U.S. indicated that the percentage of students reporting gangs operating in the schools increased from 19% in the sixth grade to about 40% from the ninth grade on (Loeber and Hay, 1997), and the first-ever nationwide survey of youth gang problems found that 49% of reporting agencies described gang activity as "getting worse" (Burch and Chemers, 1997).

Thus, as previously discussed, Maccoby's research (1988, 1990, 1991) has shown how same-sex peer groups provide males with powerful socialization experiences in competition, dominance, and assertiveness. The implications of this differential peer group socialization for antisocial behavior are twofold (Maccoby, 1986, p. 275). First, "groups of a given sex vary in how much they encourage the display or inhibition of borderline antisocial behaviors." For example, in male groups, the factors which are more likely to promote antisocial behavior include a greater likelihood of male retaliatory fighting, a greater probability of competitive and risk-taking behavior, and a greater likelihood of male play in large groups on streets and playgrounds where they will not be supervised and monitored by adults. Second, Maccoby indicated that "individual temperament may lead certain boys who like rough play to seek out other like-minded boys." Hence, given the greater male prevalence in ADHD and the attendant impulsivity and low frustration tolerance this disorder implies, it can easily be seen how males with this disorder might have these characteristics amplified by the culture of male groups (analogous to the type of magnification of male rough-and-tumble play seen in same-sex groups in non-human species; Breedlove, 1994). This amplification would bring males closer to the borderline between social and antisocial behavior.

Evidence for the efficacy of this kind of socialization in male groups comes from a fascinating study of female delinquency. Caspi et al. (1993) found that early puberty in females is associated with behavior problems only for girls enrolled in mixed-sex educational settings. Their interpretation was that the presence of boys in mixed-sex educational settings served to dilute school norms for tolerable conduct, with the resultant adverse impact on females. Thus, males from preschool on are more exposed to such norm dilution which then becomes maximized in deviant peer groups, gangs, etc. Gangs, in turn, make a considerable contribution to violent behavior. For example, homicide and aggravated assault are three times more likely to be committed by gang members (who are as young as 9 years of age and overwhelmingly male) than by nongang delinquents (American Psychological Association [APA], 1993). Also, it should be noted that almost 90% of gang members are ethnic minorities (American Psychological Association, 1993). Gang membership also helps explain the remarkably consistent inverse relationship between socioeconomic status and antisocial behaviors in males such that lower socioeconomic status is correlated with a greater prevalence of male antisocial behavior and severe delinquency (Dohrenwend et al., 1992).

Proactive Aggression (Ages 7+)

Definition. It is taken to be a truism that different individuals exposed to the same environment experience it, interpret it, and react to it differently. Various theories emphasizing scripts, working models, or personal theories suggest that early experiences can set up anticipatory attitudes that lead a child to project particular interpretations onto new social relationships and ambiguous situations (Caspi and Moffitt, 1995; Loeber and Hay, 1997). Once a schema becomes well-organized, it filters experience and makes individuals selectively responsive to information that matches their expectations and views of themselves. This type of organization first takes place developmentally in the Piagetian concrete operational stage which normatively begins about age 7. It is at this stage that the internal representations of the preoperational stage gradually form integrated systems (Flavell, 1963).

Hence, a distinct type of aggression, known as proactive aggression, results from the maturing information processing abilities of children at this stage (Hinshaw and Anderson, 1996). Proactive aggression is defined as unprovoked, aggressive/violent behavior intended to harm, dominate, or coerce another person, i.e., bullies (Brown et al., 1996). In contrast to emotional aggression, which is characterized by an intense pattern of autonomic arousal, this type of aggression is characterized by little autonomic arousal but involves highly patterned appetitive behavior oriented toward a reward (Coie and Dodge, 1997). The most thorough theoretical exposition of this mode of aggression was presented by Tedeschi and Felson (1994), who view aggression as a decision to use coercion to influence others, express grievances, or assert social identity. In the clinical/anecdotal literature, this type of aggression was extensively described by Yochelson and Samenow (1976) and in a more abbreviated form by Samenow (1984). They contended, in contrast to the trauma or deprivation theories of crime which were in vogue, that criminals essentially had a different world view. This enables them to maintain high self-esteem and to view themselves as "decent people".

These foregoing clinical observations have received very impressive empirical support. A comprehensive review of the relationship between violence/aggression and self-esteem by Baumeister et al. (1996, p. 26) concluded that:

"The traditional view that low self-esteem is a cause of violence and aggression is not tenable in light of the present

evidence. Most studies failed to find any support for it, and many provided clear and contradictory findings. Aggressors seem to believe that they are superior, capable beings. Signs of low self-esteem ... seem to be rare among violent criminals and other aggressors. Violent and criminal individuals have been repeatedly characterized as arrogant, confident, narcissistic, egotistical, assertive, proud, and the like."

In summary, what proactive aggression adds to the preceding modalities is the cognitive component in which aggression is seen as a value and becomes a salient characteristic of what Patterson (1993, p. 918) termed the "antisocial trait" — i.e., a style that seeks "to maximize short-term gains but adds to long term increases in misery." This trait, in turn, provides the foundation for a particularly ominous development — psychopathy. The personality core of psychopathy is regarded by many as the shallow, callous exploitation of others (Kosson and Newman, 1995; Mealey, 1995a). Consequently, psychopaths are much more willing to engage in violent behavior that is proactive, i.e., purposeful, decisive, remorseless exploitation of others to satisfy their own needs.

Development: Social Information Processing. In the area of aggression research, the most influential model emphasizing the role of organized cognitive factors is that of Dodge (1986, 1993) and his colleagues (Dishion et al., 1995). Dodge outlined a social information processing model which suggested that biases or deficits at any step in the model (encoding, mental representation, response access, response decision, enactment) can lead to aggressive behavioral responses. There is now considerable empirical evidence to support this claim (Crick and Dodge, 1994; Dodge, 1993; Waldman, 1996). In terms of the stage most relevant to this discussion — the response decision stage — children are hypothesized to evaluate the previously accessed responses and select the most positively evaluated response for enactment. Research has shown that aggressive children have been found to evaluate aggression more positively, to expect that aggression will come easily for them, and to feel that inhibiting aggression will be especially difficult (Crick and Dodge, 1994; Dodge, 1993; Guerra et al., 1995).

Biological Factors. Mealey (1995a,b) conducted the most current, comprehensive exploration of the possible biological basis for psychopathy, as a result of which she proposed that individuals with primary psychopathy (those with a greater genetic predisposition in contrast to those with a more learned/environmentally based secondary psychopathy) often adopt a cognitive (vs. affective) style of processing information. That is to say, primary psychopaths are genetically predisposed to experience little of the social emotions such as anxiety, guilt, shame, empathy, etc. Consequently, being impaired in the empathic understanding that most of us rely on much of the time, they will process the social encounters of everyday life primarily in a "... pure cost-benefit approach based upon immediate personal outcomes with no 'accounting' for the emotional reactions of others with whom they are dealing." This sociobiological evolutionary theory provoked a lively commentary by 42 experts in various relevant areas, as well as Mealey's own response. Interesting support for her theory was provided by Bjorklund and Kipp (1996) in their review of the empirical and theoretical literature on gender differences in the evolution of inhibition mechanisms. They hypothesized that cognitive inhibition mechanisms evolved from the necessity to control social and emotional responses in small groups of hominids for the purposes of cooperation and group cohesion. Furthermore, their review found that females consistently exhibited greater control in inhibiting certain prepotent responses, potentially inappropriate responses, or both. They hypothesized that this difference was consistent with differential evolutionary pressure on females for greater parental investment in offspring. For example, for eons of evolution, in contrast to male humans, female humans have had pregnancies which involve 9 months of carrying the fetus, followed by several years when they provide nourishment for their children. It is small wonder, then, that various theorists have consistently emphasized the more communal, empathic personality of girls and women (e.g., Block, 1973; Eagly, 1993, 1995; Zahn-Waxler et al., 1991) or that Feingold (1994), in his meta-analysis of gender differences in personality, concluded that women were especially higher than men in tender-mindedness (e.g., nurturance). Furthermore, the work of Zahn-Waxler and her colleagues (Zahn-Waxler et al., 1991, 1996; Zahn-Waxler and Robinson, 1995) has clearly demonstrated that among aggressive girls, the "moral emotions" of guilt and empathy are much more likely to be present than they are among aggressive boys. In the most extensive review of the literature to date on sex differences in personality traits and social behavior in children and adolescents, Ruble and Martin (1997, p. 960) concluded:

> *"Are females more socially oriented and sensitive as gender stereotypes suggest? The results of meta-analyses suggest that they are ... women appear to be better than men at decoding others' emotions and to have a greater tendency to take the perspective of another when the opportunity arises. ...Females also appear to be more socially expressive and responsive."*

Finally, it should be noted that the very exciting research of Skuse et al. (1997) has provided preliminary evidence of a possible genetic basis on the X chromosome for the greater female social orientation. In a study of children with Turner's syndrome (i.e., females who are missing one X chromosome), Skuse et al. determined that if a Turner's girl inherited her lone X chromosome from her mother, she was much more likely to display greater social skill deficits than if her one X chromosome came from her father. For example, she was more likely to be characterized as engaging in socially offensive or disruptive behavior, lacking an awareness of other people's feelings, and less likely to respond to commands. Skuse et al. accounted for this finding by proposing that "imprinting" (chemical modification of a gene that causes it to be silent) caused a gene to be silent on the maternal chromosome, while the same gene remained active on the paternal chromosome. They theorized that this gene somehow influences the formation of the brain's prefrontal cortex, which in turn enhances social intelligence. The relevance of these findings, beyond Turner's syndrome, are that because males invariably inherit only the maternal X chromosome, their copy of the putative social enhancement gene is always silent. In contrast, girls invariably inherit one of their X chromosomes from their father and thus always have an active social enhancement gene. Hence, it may be that a genetically based female superiority in social cognition is a major factor strengthening their inhibitory mechanisms, thereby increasing the likelihood of their experiencing empathic rather than narcissistic emotions.

In summary, the extensive reviews of two bodies of different, yet related, literature by Mealey (1995b) and Bjorklund and Kipp (1996) (as well as the supportive research of Skuse et al., 1997) nicely complement one another in establishing a biological basis for experiencing empathic, as opposed to purely narcissistic, emotions. To the extent that a child is less disposed to experience more empathic emotions, the child is more likely to evaluate an aggressive/violent action as an appropriate, self-serving response.

Learning-Situational Factors. We know that there is a high degree of intergenerational similarity for antisocial behavior (Patterson et al., 1989) such that having an antisocial parent places a child at risk for antisocial behavior, and it is clear that many aggressive children come from homes in which at least one parent is exceptionally violent (Perry et al., 1990). Additionally, Robins (1991) reported that children of criminal and alcoholic parents have a greatly increased risk of conduct disorder. Eron and Huesmann (1990) and Frick (1994) also provided evidence for an intergenerational transmission of aggression. These clear findings, which may also have biological influences (Lytton, 1990a,b) and which may not be exclusively due to modeling (Tedeschi and Felson, 1994), establish the importance of cultural context and values to which the child is exposed.

Social and cultural influences in early childhood may have a life- long impact on a child's attitudes toward violence (American Psychological Association, 1993; Staub, 1996a). There are subcultures of violence, which is a concept used to describe groups in society in which violence has become acceptable, and even valued or required (Staub, 1996b). In such subcultures, there exists, in addition to economic poverty, a moral poverty — the poverty of being without loving, capable, responsible adults who teach the young right from wrong (Bennett et al., 1996). If children are raised in such an environment, the likelihood of involvement with violence is greatly increased. On the positive side, early exposure to cultural influences can help a child build a positive identity and a sense of belonging to a group with shared values and traditions that may help buffer the child against social risk factors for involvement in violence (American Psychological Association, 1993).

One of the most remarkable illustrations of the relevance of subculture to violence is the study of one neighborhood during the 1960s in San Francisco (Wilson and Herrnstein, 1985). This neighborhood had the lowest income, the highest unemployment rate, the highest proportion of families with incomes under $4000 per year, the least educational attainment, the highest tuberculosis rate, and the highest proportion of substandard housing of any area of the city. This neighborhood was called Chinatown. Yet, in 1965, there were only five persons of Chinese ancestry committed to prison in the entire state of California.

An equally compelling demonstration of the importance of values and subculture comes from a study of Indochinese refugee families and academic achievement (Caplan et al., 1992). During the late 1970s and early 1980s, devastating circumstances forced many Indochinese families to seek a new life in the U.S. Their children had lost months, even years, of formal education while living in refugee relocation camps. They suffered disruption and trauma as they escaped Southeast Asia and arrived in the U.S. knowing virtually no English and often with little more than the clothes they wore. With regard to prior educational and social status, these refugees were ordinary people, not the elites who had fled earlier.

All the children attended schools in low-income, metropolitan areas which were not renown for outstanding academic achievement. They were fairly evenly distributed throughout the school levels in grades 1 through 11. After being in the U.S. for an average of 3-1/2 years, their academic performance was examined and the results were astounding. Their overall grade point average was a B, and their mean overall score on the California Achievement Test was at the 54th percentile.

If these children had remained low achievers for years or developed serious behavior problems (e.g., aggression/violence), there would have been no dearth of sage explanations focusing on environmental disadvantage, prior trauma, poor English skills, etc., that would argue for the relative hopelessness of their situation amid a host of powerful, adverse geographic and demographic factors. Yet, they triumphed against all odds. The secret of their astounding success was that their parents (illiterate though they were in English) valued education. Hence, with two loving parents, loving siblings, and lots of homework, they achieved admirably in inner-city schools. In summary, subcultures that either promote or discourage violence as a response to adversity are an extremely powerful factor influencing proactive aggression. Thus, violence in this context becomes more and more a rational choice (Tedeschi and Felson, 1994) to achieve the individual's goals.

Nearly four decades of research on television viewing and other media have documented the almost universal exposure of American children to high levels of media violence (American Psychological Association, 1993, p. 33; Donnerstein et al., 1994).

In reviewing this vast literature, the American Psychological Commission on Violence and Youth concluded as follows:

"There is absolutely no doubt that higher levels of viewing violence on television are correlated with increased acceptance of aggressive attitudes and increased aggressive behavior. Three major national studies ... reviewed hundreds of studies to arrive at the irrefutable conclusion that viewing violence increases violence. In addition, prolonged viewing of media violence can lead to emotional desensitization toward violence."

This conclusion was echoed by Huston and Wright (1997) in the most comprehensive literature review to date on the effects of mass media on children's development. Thus, it would seem that mountainous "irrefutable evidence" has clearly closed the discussion regarding whether or not there is a causal relationship between the effects of media to which all children are exposed and the increased likelihood of violence. Yet, Tedeschi and Felson (1994, p. 122), in their review of much the same literature, concluded that "it is difficult to draw firm conclusions about the effect of exposure to media violence, given the inconsistent findings." What, then, is a reader to make of this contradictory interpretation?

It appears that Tedeschi and Felson's major quarrel with the orthodox interpretation of this literature is the lack of clarity regarding "to what extent that message repeats lessons learned from other sources of influence" (Tedeschi and Felson, 1994, p. 122). Their critique seemed to revolve around the extent of the redundancy provided by the media to some children. Thus, to the extent that they were correct in their interpretation, it may be that violent mass media has its most deleterious effect on children who are already being raised in a subculture of violence, for whom there are few, if any, messages to contradict the legitimacy of violent behavior as a rational choice. Its very redundancy with the violent subculture helps ensure the consistency and pervasiveness of the violent message. Schwartz and Matzkin (1996) came to a similar understanding in their review when they concluded that it was the interaction of many factors which created youth who would be more vulnerable to violence in the mass media. (See Chapter 3 for a discussion of violence in the media.)

In summary, it would appear to be safe to conclude, along with the APA, Huston and Wright, and many others, that a causal connection of significant magnitude between violent television viewing and aggression has been established. In addition, it would also appear safe to conclude along with Tedeschi and Felson, Schwartz and Matzkin, and perhaps others, that this causal connection would seem to be all the more significant for the more vulnerable youth.

Conclusion and Promising Interventions

Weisfeld (1994) correctly noted that despite the fact that real-life examples of aggression obviously often involve more than one type of aggression, it is useful to try to specify the type of aggression involved. By identifying the various modes involved, the aggressive behavior can be more adequately understood and treated. This is especially important because little in the way of effective treatment for juvenile violence has been generated (Kazdin, 1997). There are, however, several promising approaches (DeV. Peters and McMahon, 1996; Edwards, 1995; Kazdin, 1995, 1997; Tate et al., 1995; Yoshikawa, 1994), but even these have serious limitations with regard to the magnitude and maintenance of therapeutic change (Kazdin, 1997). In short, the overall picture is far from optimistic, and the gloom is deepened by the results of the most comprehensive study ever of crime-prevention programs which showed that some of the most popular programs, including boot camps, midnight basketball, neighborhood watches, and drug education classes in schools, have little impact (Butterfield, 1997).

It is hoped that this foundational chapter has added to the recommendations for prevention/treatment that have been well explored in the aforementioned citations (as well as others unknown to the author) clear documentation that perhaps the single most important, underemphasized, or overlooked fact with regard to the treatment of violent youth is that, as indicated in the introduction to this chapter, it must begin very early. This position has been strongly put forth by the Human Capital Initiative — a consortium of dozens of organizations (including the APA) that informs policy makers about the contributions social scientists can make in solving the nation's most pressing problems (Martin, 1997). This chapter fully supports that position, as it concluded that at least by age 7 children have acquired all the major modalities of aggression. Hence, it is small wonder that Patterson (1993) reported that the antisocial acts of the 5-year-old are the prototypic acts of the delinquent adolescent, and that Eron et al. (1991) reported that, by the time children are 6, patterns of aggressive behavior seem so well established that they persist into adulthood despite a wide variety of environmental contingencies and events. Thus, for those readers who are most concerned with the vulnerability of juveniles to the social and collective factors associated with violence (e.g., gangs), it is imperative that their work begin much earlier than is typically the case and that it be guided by a clear understanding of the developmental roots of aggression and violence in its various modalities (Kazdin, 1993).

What form should these interventions take? As there already exist several excellent discussions of "promising" interventions for juvenile violence (e.g., DeV. Peters and McMahon, 1996; Edwards, 1995; Kazdin, 1995, 1997; Tate et al., 1995; Yoshikawa, 1994) which the interested reader can consult, it is beyond the limits of this chapter to replow this field; however, what this chapter can perhaps add to this literature is an identification of a "promising" interventions that would be most relevant to a particular mode of aggression.

A Promising Intervention With Emotional Aggression (Ages 0 to 1)

The discussion of emotional aggression proposed that the major environmental factor in the development of a disorganized-disoriented attachment, which so often places a child in the developmental trajectory that leads to early onset of emotional aggressive behavior disorders, involves deficient parenting skills and hostile and rejecting parental behavior. In her masterful review of the recent attachment-related studies of early aggression, Lyons-Ruth (1996) concluded that early attachment relationships can be positively influenced by well-targeted family and parenting support groups (Jacobson and Frye, 1991; Lieberman et al., 1991; Lyons-Ruth et al., 1990). The interventions cited in these studies involved frequent home visits by either master's level professionals or "volunteer coaches" and would seem to be readily adaptable to diverse situations. Parenthetically, a note of caution needs to be attached to these "promising" interventions. Because maintenance of change was not evaluated, one cannot say with confidence that these changes lasted, especially in light of the failure to maintain change in the largest, most comprehensive, and intensive early intervention program to date (Baumeister and Bacharach, 1996).

A Promising Intervention With Instrumental Aggression (Ages 1 to 2)

The discussion of instrumental aggression proposed that the most elegant and comprehensive exposition of the development of this mode of aggression was the coercion model (Dishion et al., 1995; Patterson, 1993; Patterson et al., 1989). Fortunately, this model has also generated one of the most promising and well-researched treatments for this type of aggression — Parent Management Training (Kazdin, 1997).

In this method, parents meet with a trainer who teaches them to use specific procedures to alter interactions with their child, to promote prosocial behavior, and to decrease deviant behavior. The achievement of these goals requires the development of several different parenting behaviors, such as establishing rules for the child to follow, providing positive reinforcement for appropriate behavior, delivering mild forms of punishment to suppress behavior, negotiating compromises, and other procedures. These parenting behaviors are systematically and progressively developed within treatment clinic sessions and eventually implemented in the home.

Treatment effects have been evident in marked improvements in child behavior on a wide range of measures, and the effects of treatment have also been shown to bring problematic behaviors within normative levels for peers who are functioning adequately within the community. Follow-up assessment has shown that the gains are often maintained 1 to 3 years after treatment, with one study reporting maintenance gains 10 to 14 years later (Kazdin, 1997).

In summary, no other technique for treating instrumental aggression has been studied as often or as well (Kazdin, 1997). Furthermore, the availability of treatment manuals for parents and therapists (e.g., Sanders and Dadds, 1993) makes this treatment intervention one that can be readily applied in a variety of settings.

A Promising Intervention With Dominance Aggression (Ages 3 to 6)

The discussion of dominance aggression proposed that beginning in the preschool period, a form of aggression emerges which is not primarily a function of negative emotionality or reinforcement but is driven by a predisposition to compete and dominate. This predisposition in the context of aggressive peer socialization experiences was hypothesized to provide the breeding ground for subsequent gang involvement.

A promising intervention to address this type of aggression, which can be implemented beginning in the first grade, is a violence prevention curriculum entitled *Second Step: A Violence Prevention Curriculum* (Grossman et al., 1997). This program is designed to prevent aggressive behavior by increasing prosocial behavior and interpersonal conflict resolution skills. A recent well-designed evaluation of this intervention with 790 second- and third-grade students concluded that 6 months after the intervention had ceased, it had modestly positive effects in reducing observed physically aggressive behavior and in increasing neutral and prosocial behavior in the school setting (Grossman et al., 1997). It should be noted that these modest effects were not evident in the home setting or teacher report, but only in the reports of blind observers who viewed the children in multiple school settings.

A Promising Intervention With Proactive Aggression (Ages 7+)

The discussion of proactive aggression proposed that the most influential model emphasizing the role of organized cognitive factors in aggression was that of Dodge and his colleagues (Crick and Dodge, 1994; Dishion et al., 1995; Dodge 1986, 1993). As with the case of instrumental aggression, it is fortunate that the developers of this model have generated one of the most promising approaches for treating proactive aggression — Cognitive Problem-Solving Skills Training (Kazdin, 1997). The basic aspects of this approach have been succinctly summarized by Kazdin (1997, p. 164) as follows:

"Problem-solving skills training (PSST) consists of developing interpersonal cognitive problem-solving skills. Although many variations of PSST have been applied to the conduct of problem children, several characteristics are usually shared. First, the emphasis is on how children approach situations, i.e., the thought processes in which the child engages to guide responses to interpersonal situations. The children are taught to engage in a step-by-step approach to solve interpersonal problems. They make statements to

themselves that direct attention to certain aspects of the problem or tasks that lead to effective solutions. Second, behaviors that are selected (solutions) to the interpersonal situations are important as well. Prosocial behaviors are fostered (through modeling and direct reinforcement) as part of the problem-solving process. Third, treatment utilizes structured tasks involving games, academic activities and stories. Over the course of treatment, the cognitive problem-solving skills are increasingly applied to real-life situations. Fourth, the therapists usually play an active role in treatment. They model the cognitive processes by making verbal self-statements, apply the sequence of statements to particular problems, provide cues to prompt use of the skills, and deliver feedback and praise to develop correct use of the skills. Finally, treatment usually combines several different procedures including modeling and practice, role-playing, and reinforcement and mild punishment. These are deployed in systematic ways to develop increasingly complex response repertoires for the child."

With regard to an overall evaluation of its efficacy, Kazdin (1997) concluded that although several central questions have yet to be answered, Cognitive Problem Solving Skills Training remains highly promising because its treatment effects have been replicated in several controlled studies.

Summary

In his address to the 1996 Circumpolar Health Conference (cited in Rosenberg et al., 1997, p. 1641), William Foege, the senior public health statesman whose containment strategy played a central role in the eradication of small pox, observed that:

"The most devastating plague of the 20th century is not AIDS, not Ebola *virus, not drug abuse, and not violence. It is the plague of fatalism: the paralytic frame of mind which says that we cannot change the way things are, so why even try."*

The foregoing identification of some "promising interventions" is meant to inoculate the reader against such fatalism with regard to interventions for reducing juvenile violence. On the other hand, those who tend toward starry-eyed optimism in this regard would do well to bear in mind the sobering judgment of Alan Kazdin (who is perhaps the premier authority on treatment for juvenile violence) that, "little in the way of effective treatment has been generated for conduct disorder" (Kazdin, 1997, p. 161). For these optimists, a health dose of cynicism (as defined by Andrew Bierce, 1993, in his *Devil's Dictionary*), might provide an appropriate antidote. For Bierce, a cynic is a "blackguard whose faulty vision sees things as they are, not as they ought to be."

Annotated Bibliography

1. Archer, J. (1996) Sex differences in social behavior: are the social role and evolutionary explanations compatible? *American Psychologist, 51*, 909–917. This article clearly and cogently provides a model for integrating social role and evolutionary explanations for aggressive behavior.

2. Barkley, R. (1997) Behavioral inhibitions, sustained attention, and executive functions: constructing a unifying theory of ADHD. *Psychological Bulletin, 121*, 65–94. This article is essential reading for understanding the nature of the impulsive-hyperactive type of ADHD that is such a important factor in contributing to aggression.

3. Berkowitz, L. (1992) *Aggression: Its Causes, Consequences, and Control*. New York: McGraw Hill. This book is essential reading for those who want a sophisticated exposition of emotional aggression.

4. Collaer, M. and Hines M. (1995) Human behavioral sex differences: a role for gonadal hormones during early development? *Psychological Bulletin, 118*, 55–107. This article is essential reading for establishing the important role of prenatal hormonal influences on the development of aggression.

5. Harris, J. (1995) Where is the child's environment? A group socialization theory of development. *Psychological Review, 102*, 452–489. This article is essential reading for those who are interested in a sophisticated model of the role of peer relations in the development of aggression.
6. Kazdin, A. (1997) Practitioner review: psychosocial treatments for conduct disorder in children. *Journal of Child Psychology and Psychiatry, 38*, 161–178. This article by arguably the leading authority on the treatment of conduct disorder is essential reading for those interested in being educated on the most current psychosocial approaches to treating aggressive behavior.

References

American Psychological Association (1993) *Violence and Youth.* Washington, D.C.: (author).

Ames, L.B. and Ilg, F. (1976) *Your Two-Year-Old: Terrible or Tender.* New York: Delacorte.

Archer, J. (1994) *Male Violence.* New York: Rutledge.

Archer, J. (1995) What can ethology offer the psychological study of human aggression? *Aggressive Behavior, 21,* 243–255.

Archer, J. (1996) Sex differences in social behavior: are the social role and evolutionary explanations compatible? *American Psychologist, 51,* 909–917.

Azar, B. (1996) Psychologists cautious about day-care results. *APA Monitor,* June, p. 18.

Barkley, R. (1995) *Taking Charge of ADHD.* New York: Guilford Press.

Barkley, R. (1996) Attention-deficit/hyperactivity disorder. In E.J. Mash and R.A. Barkley (Eds.), *Child Psychopathology* (pp. 63–112) New York: Guilford.

Barkley, R. (1997) Behavioral inhibition, sustained attention, and executive functions: constructing a unifying theory of ADHD. *Psychological Bulletin, 121,* 65–94.

Baumeister, A. and Bacharach, V. (1996) A critical analysis of the infant health and development program. *Intelligence, 23,* 79–104.

Baumeister, R., Boden, J., and Smart, L. (1996) Relation of threatened egotism to violence and aggression: the dark side of high self-esteem. *Psychological Review, 103,* 5–33.

Belsky, J. (1988) The "effects" of infant day care reconsidered. *Early Childhood Research Quarterly, 3,* 235–272.

Belsky, J. (1990) Parental and nonparental child care and children's socioemotional development: a decade in review. *Journal of Marriage and the Family, 52,* 885–903.

Belsky, J. and Braungart, J. (1991) Are insecure-avoidant infants with extensive day-care experience less stressed by and more independent in the strange situation? *Child Development, 62*, 567–571.

Bennett, W., DiIulio, J., and Walters, J. (1996) *Moral Poverty and How To Win America's War Against Crime and Drugs.* New York: Simon & Schuster.

Berkowitz, L. (1989) Frustration-aggression hypothesis: examination and reformulation. *Psychological Bulletin, 106*(1), 59–73.

Berkowitz, L. (1992) *Aggression: Its Causes, Consequences and Control.* New York: McGraw-Hill.

Berkowitz, L. (1996) On the determinants and regulation of impulsive aggression. In S. Feshbach and J. Zagrodzka (Eds.), *Aggression: Biological, Developmental, and Social Perspectives,* pp. 187–211. New York: Plenum Press.

Bierce, A. (1993) *The Devil's Dictionary.* New York: Dover.

Bjorklund, D. and Kipp, K. (1996) Parental investment theory and gender differences in the evolution mechanisms. *Psychological Bulletin, 120,* 163–188.

Block, J. (1973) Conceptions of sex role: some cross-cultural and longitudinal perspectives. *American Psychologist, 28*, 512–526.

Boulton, M. (1994) The relationship between playful and aggressive fighting in children, adolescents and adults. In J. Archer (Ed.), *Male Violence*, pp. 23–41. London: Routledge.

Breedlove, S. (1994) Sexual differentiation of the human nervous system. In L. Porter and M. Rosenzweig (Eds.), *Annual Review of Psychology*, pp. 389–418. Palo Alto, CA: Annual Reviews, Inc.

Brown, K., Atkins, M., Osborne, M., and Milnamow, M. (1996) A revised teacher rating scale for reactive and proactive aggression. *Journal of Abnormal Child Psychology, 24,* 473–480.

Burch, J. and Chemers, B. (1997) *A Comprehensive Response to America's Youth Gang Problem.* Office of Juvenile Justice and Delinquency Prevention, Fact Sheet #40, March 1997. Washington, D.C.: U.S. Government Printing Office.

Buss, D. (1995) Psychological sex differences. *American Psychologist, 50,* 164–168.

Buss, D. (1996) Sexual conflict: evolutionary insights into feminism and the "battle of the sexes". In D. Buss and N. Malamuth (Eds.), *Sex, Power and Conflict*, pp. 296–319. New York: Oxford University Press.

Butterfield, F. (1996) Crimes of violence among juveniles decline slightly. *The New York Times,* Aug. 9, p. A1, A9.

Butterfield, F. (1997) Most efforts to stop crime fall far short study says. *New York Times,* April 4, p. A16.

Butterfield, F. (1997) F.B.I. report finds that crime is down for 5th straight year. *New York Times,* Oct. 5, p. A16.

Campbell, S. (1995) Behavior problems in preschool children: a review of recent research. *Journal of Child Psychology and Psychiatry, 36,* 113–149.

Caplan, N., Choy, M., and Whitmore, J. (1992) Indochinese refugee families and academic achievement. *Scientific American,* February, 36–43.

Carlson, V., Cicchetti, D., Barnett, D., and Braunwald, K. (1989) Disorganized/disoriented attachment relationships in maltreated infants. *Developmental Psychology, 27*(1), 108–118.

Carnegie Task Force (1996) *Years of Promise: A Comprehensive Leaning Strategy for America's Children. The Report of the Carnegie Task Force on Learning in the Primary Grades.* New York: (author).

Caspi, A., and Moffitt, T. (1995) The continuity of maladaptive behavior: from description to understanding in the study of antisocial behavior. In D. Cichetti and D. Cohen (Eds.), *Developmental Psychopathology,* Vol. 2, pp. 472–511. New York: John Wiley & Sons.

Caspi, A., Lynam, D., Moffitt, T., and Silva, P. (1993) Unraveling girls' delinquency: biological, dispositional, and contextual contributions to adolescent misbehavior. *Developmental Psychology, 29*(1), 19–30.

Caspi, A., Henry, B., McGee, R.O., Moffitt, T.E., and Silva, P.A. (1995) Temperamental origins of child and adolescent behavior problems: from age three to age fifteen. *Child Development, 66*, 55–68.

Chira, S. (1995) Care at child day centers is rated poor. *The New York Times.* April 3, p. A1.

Chira, S. (1996) Study says babies in child care keep secure bonds to mothers. *The New York Times.* Sept. 15, pp. A1, A11.

Clarke-Stewart, A. (1989) Infant day care. *American Psychologist, 44*, 266–273.

Cicchetti, D. and Toth, S. (1995) *Attachment Theory: Social, Developmental, and Clinical Perspectives.* Hillsdale, NJ: Analytic Press.

Coie, J. and Dodge, K. (1997) Aggression and antisocial behavior. In W. Damon and N. Eisenberg (Eds.), *Handbook of Child Psychology: Social, Emotional, and Personality Development*, 5th ed., Vol. 3, pp. 779–862. New York: John Wiley & Sons.

Cole, M. and Cole, S. (1993) *The Development of Children*. New York: W.H. Freeman.

Collaer, M. and Hines, M. (1995) Human behavioral sex differences: a role for gonadal hormones during early development? *Psychological Bulletin, 118,* 55–107.

Crick, N. and Dodge, K. (1994) A review and reformulation of social information-processing mechanisms in children's social adjustment. *Psychological Bulletin, 115,* 74–101.

Daly, M. and Wilson, M. (1994) Evolutionary psychology of male violence. In J. Archer (Ed.), *Male Violence,* pp. 253–288. London: Routledge.

Davis, M. and Emory, E. (1995) Sex differences in neonatal stress reactivity. *Child Development, 66*, 14–27.

DeV. Peters, R. and McMahon, R. (1996) *Preventing Childhood Disorders, Substance Abuse, and Delinquency.* London: Sage.

DiIulio, J. (1996) Stop crime where it starts. *The New York Times,* July 31, p. A10.

Dishion, T., French, D., and Patterson, G. (1995) The development and ecology of antisocial behavior. In D. Cicchetti and D. Cohen (Eds.), *Developmental Psychopathology,* Vol. 2, pp. 421–471. New York: John Wiley & Sons.

Dodge, K.A. (1986) A social information processing model of social competence in children. In M. Perlmutter (Ed.), *Eighteenth Annual Minnesota Symposium on Child Psychology,* pp. 77–125. Hillsdale, NJ: Lawrence Erlbaum Associates.

Dodge, K.A. (1993) Social-cognitive mechanisms in the development of conduct disorder and depression. In L.W. Porter and M.R. Rosenzweig (Eds.), *Annual Review of Psychology*, Vol. 44, pp. 559–580. Palo Alto, CA: Annual Reviews, Inc.

Donnerstein, E., Slaby, R., and Eron, L. (1994) The mass media and youth aggression. In L. Eron, J. Gentry, and P. Schlegel (Eds.), *Reason To Hope: A Psychosocial Perspective on Violence and Youth*, pp. 232–234. Washington, D.C.: American Psychological Association.

Dohrenwend, B., Levav, I., Shrout, P., Schwartz, S., Naveh, G., Link, B., Skodol, A., and Stueve, A. (1992) Socioeconomic status and psychiatric disorders: the causation-selection issue. *Science, 255*, 946–951.

Dreikurs, R. (1964) *Children: The Challenge.* New York: Hawthorn/Dutton.

Eagly, A. (1995) The science and politics of comparing men and women. *American Psychologist, 50,* 145–158.

Earls, F. (1987) Sex differences in psychiatric disorders: origins and developmental influences. *Psychiatric Developments, 1,* 1–23.

Edwards, R. (1995) The search for a proper punishment. *APA Monitor,* December, p. 30.

Eme, R. (1996) Sex differences in juvenile violence. In H.V. Hall (Ed.), *Lethal Violence 2000: A Sourcebook on Fatal Domestic, Acquaintance and Stranger Aggression*, pp. 79–112. Kamuela, HI: Pacific Institute for the Study of Conflict and Aggression.

Erikson, E. (1950) *Childhood and Society*, 2nd ed. New York: W.W. Norton.

Eron, L., Huesmann, L., and Zelli, A. (1991) The role of parental variables in the learning of aggression. In D. Pepler and K. Rubin (Eds.), *The Development and Treatment of Childhood Aggression*, pp. 169–188. Hillsdale, NJ: Lawrence Erlbaum Associates.

Fabes, R. and Eisenberg, N. (1992) Young children's emotional arousal and anger/aggressive behaviors. In A. Fraczek and H. Sumkley (Eds.), *Socialization and Aggression*, pp. 85–100. Berlin: Springer-Verlag.

Fagot, B. (1990) Sex differences in responses to the stranger in the strange situation. *Sex Roles, 23,* 123–132.

Feingold, A. (1994) Gender differences in personality: a meta-analysis. *Psychological Bulletin, 116*, 429–456.

Feshbach, S. (1997) The psychology of aggression: insights and issues. In S. Feshbach and J. Zagrodzka (Eds.), *Aggression: Biological, Developmental, and Social Perspectives*, pp. 213–235. New York: Plenum Press.

Flavell, J. (1963) *The Developmental Psychology of Jean Piaget.* New York: D. Van Nostrand.

Fowles, D. (1992) Schizophrenia: diathesis-stress revisited. *Annual Review of Psychology, 43,* 303–336.

Fox, J. (1996) *Trends in Juvenile Justice.* Washington, D.C.: Bureau of Justice Statistics.

Frick, P. (1994) Family dysfunction and the disruptive behavior disorders. In T. Ollendick and R. Prinz (Eds.), *Advances in Clinical Child Psychology*, Vol. 16, pp. 203–226. New York: Plenum Press.

Grossman, D., Neckerman, H., Koepsell, T., Liu, P., Asher, K., Beland, K., Frey, K., and Rivara, F. (1997) Effectiveness of a violence prevention curriculum among children in elementary school. *Journal of the American Medical Association, 277,* 1605–1611.

Guerra, N., Huesmann, L., Tolan, P., Van Acker, R., and Eron, L. (1995) Stressful events and individual beliefs as correlates of economic disadvantage and aggression among urban children. *Journal of Consulting and Clinical Psychology, 63,* 518–528.

Harris, J. (1995) Where is the child's environment? A group socialization theory of development. *Psychological Review, 102*, 452–489.

Henry, B., Silva, P., Caspi, A., and Moffitt, T. (1996) Temperamental and familial predictors of violent and nonviolent criminal conviction: age 3 to age 18. *Developmental Psychology, 32,* 614–623.

Hinshaw, S. and Anderson, C. (1996) Conduct and oppositional defiant disorders. In E. Mash and R. Barkley (Eds.), *Child Psychopathology*, pp. 113–149. New York: Guilford.

Hoffman, L. (1989) Effects of maternal employment in the two-parent family. *American Psychologist, 44*(2), 283–292.

Hoynega, K. (1993) Sex differences in human stratification: a biosocial approach. In L. Ellis (Ed.), *Social Stratification and Socioeconomic Inequality,* Vol. 1, pp. 139–157. Westport, CT: Praeger.

Huston, A. and Wright, J. (1997) Mass media and children's development. In W. Damon and N. Eisenberg (Eds.), *Handbook of Child Psychology. Child Psychology in Practice*, 5th ed., Vol. 4, pp. 999–1058. New York: John Wiley & Sons.

Jansen, A. , Zay, V., Karpitskiy, V., Mettenleiter, T., and Loewy, A. (1995) Central command neurons of the sympathetic nervous system: basis of the fight-or-flight response. *Science, 270,* 644–646.

Jacobson, S. and Frye, K. (1991) Effect of maternal social-support on attachment: experimental evidence. *Child Development, 62,* 572–582.

Karen, R. (1994) *Becoming Attached: Unfolding the Mystery of the Infant-Mother Bond and Its Impact on Later Life.* New York: Warner Books.

Kazdin, A. (1993) Treatment of conduct disorder: progress and directions in psychotherapy research. *Development and Psychopathology, 5,* 277–310.

Kazdin, A. (1995) *Conduct Disorders in Childhood and Adolescence,* 2nd ed. London: Sage.

Kazdin, A. (1997) Practitioner review: psychosocial treatments for conduct disorder in children. *Journal of Child Psychology and Psychiatry, 38,* 161–178.

Kopp, C. (1989) Regulation of distress and negative emotions: a developmental view. *Developmental Psychology, 25,* 343–354.

Kosson, D. and Newman, J. (1995) An evaluation of Mealey's hypotheses based on the psychopathy checklist: identified groups. *Behavioral and Brain Sciences, 18,* 562.

Kotulak, R. (1996) *Inside the Brain.* Kansas City: Andrews and McMeel.

Lamb, M. (1997) Nonparental child care: context, quality, correlates, and consequences. In W. Damon and N. Eisenberg (Eds.), *Handbook of Child Psychology: Child Psychology in Practice*, 5th ed., Vol. 4, pp. 73–134. New York: John Wiley & Sons.

Lieberman, A., Weston, D., and Pawl, J. (1991) Preventive intervention and outcome with anxiously attached dyads. *Child Development, 62*, 199–209.

Loeber, R. (1990) Development and risk factors in juvenile antisocial behavior and delinquency. *Clinical Psychology Review, 10*, 1–41.

Loeber, R. and Hay, D. (1994) Developmental approaches to aggression and conduct problems. In M. Rutter and D. Hay (Eds.), *Development Through Life: A Handbook for Clinicians*, pp. 488–516. Oxford: Blackwell Scientific.

Loeber, R. and Hay, D. (1997) Key issues in the development of aggression and violence from childhood to early adulthood. In L. Porter and M. Rosenzweig (Eds.), *Annual Review of Psychology*, Vol. 48, pp. 371–410. Palo, Alto, CA: Annual Reviews, Inc.

Loeber, R. and Keenan, K. (1994) Interaction between conduct disorder and its comorbid conditions: effects of age and gender. *Clinical Psychology Review, 14*(6), 497–523.

Lynam, D. (1996) Early identification of chronic offenders: who is the fledgling psychopath? *Psychological Bulletin, 120*, 209–234.

Lyons-Ruth, K. (1996) Attachment relationships among children with aggressive behavior problems: the role of disorganized early attachment patterns. *Journal of Consulting and Clinical Psychology, 6*, 64–73.

Lyons-Ruth, K., Connell, D., and Grunebaum, H. (1990) Infants at social risk: maternal depression and family support services as mediators of infant development and security of attachment. *Child Development, 61*, 85–98.

Lytton, H. (1990a) Child and parent effects in boys' conduct disorder: a reinterpretation. *Developmental Psychology, 26*(5), 683–697.

Lytton, H. (1990b) Child effects — still unwelcome? Response to Dodge and Wahler. *Developmental Psychology, 26*(5), 705–709.

Maccoby, E. (1991) Gender and relationships: a reprise. *American Psychologist, 46*, 538–539.

Maccoby, E. and Martin, J. (1983) Socialization in the context of the family: parent-child interaction. In E.M. Hetherington (Ed.), *Handbook of Child Psychology*, Vol. IV, pp. 1–87. New York: John Wiley & Sons.

Martin, S. (1997) APA among those calling for more violence research. *APA Monitor,* April, p. 8.

Masse, L. and Tremblay, R. (1997) Behavior of boys in kindergarten and the onset of substance abuse during adolescence. *Archives of General Psychiatry, 54,* 62–68.

McFadyeen, S., Bates, J., Dodge, K., and Pettit, G. (1996) Patterns of change in early childhood aggressive-disruptive behavior: gender differences in predictions from early coercive and affectionate mother-child interactions. *Child Development, 67,* 2417–2433.

Mealey, L. (1995a) Primary sociopathy (psychopathy) is a type, secondary is not. *Behavioral and Brain Sciences, 18,* 579–587.

Mealey, L. (1995b) The sociobiology of sociopathy: an integrated evolutionary model. *Behavioral and Brain Sciences, 18,* 523–599.

Mitchell, A. (1997) Clinton urges campaign against youth crime. *The New York Times*, Feb. 20, p. A15.

Moffitt, T. (1993a) Adolescent-limited and life-course-persistent antisocial behavior: a developmental taxonomy. *Psychological Review, 100,* 674–701.

Moffitt, T. (1993b) The neuropsychology of conduct disorder. *Development and Psychopathology, 5,* 135–151.

Moffitt, T., Caspi, A., Dickson, N., Silva, P., and Stanton, W. (1996) Childhood-onset versus adolescent-onset antisocial conduct problems in males: natural history from ages 3 to 18 years. *Development and Psychopathology, 8,* 399–424.

National Advisory Mental Health Council (1996) Basic behavioral science research for mental health: social influence and social cognition. *American Psychologist, 51,* 478–484.

National Institute of Child Health and Human Development (1997) Results of NICHD Study of Early Child Care. Presented at Society for Research Child Development Meeting. Retrieved April 3, 1997, from the World Wide Web: http://www.nih.gov/nichd/news/rel4top.htm.

Park, R. and Slaby, R. (1983) The development of aggression. In P. Mussen (Ed.), *Handbook of Child Psychology,* Vol. 4, pp. 548–610. New York: John Wiley & Sons.

Parker, J., Rubin, K., Price, J., and DeRosier, M. (1995) Peer relationships, child development, and adjustment: a developmental psychopathology perspective. In D. Cicchetti and D. Cohen (Eds.), *Developmental Psychopathology*, Vol. 2, pp. 72–95. New York: John Wiley & Sons.

Patterson, G. (1993) Orderly change in a stable world: the antisocial trait as a chimera. *Journal of Consulting and Clinical Psychology, 61*, 911–919.

Patterson, G., Capaldi, D., and Bank, L. (1991) An early starter model for predicting delinquency. In D. Pepler and K. Rubin (Eds.), *The Development and Treatment of Childhood Aggression*, pp. 390–410. Hillsdale, NJ: Lawrence Erlbaum Associates.

Patterson, G., DeBaryshe, B., and Ramsey, E. (1989) A developmental perspective on antisocial behavior. *American Psychologist, 44*(2), 329–335.

Perry, D., Perry, L., and Boldizar, J. (1990) Learning of aggression. In M. Lewis and S.M. Miller (Eds.), *Handbook of Developmental Psychopathology*, pp. 135–142. New York: Plenum Press.

Prior, M. (1992) Childhood temperament. *The Journal of Child Psychology and Psychiatry and Allied Disciplines, 33*(1), 249–279.

Prior, M., Smart, D., Sanson, A., and Oberklaid, F. (1993) Sex differences in psychological adjustment from infancy to 8 years. *Journal of the American Academy of Child and Adolescent Psychiatry, 32*(2), 291–304.

Raine, A., Brennan, P., Mednick, B., and Mednick, S. (1996) High rates of violence, crime, academic problems, and behavioral problems in males with both early neuromotor deficits and unstable family environments. *Archives of General Psychiatry, 53,* 544–549.

Robins, L. (1991) Conduct disorder. *The Journal of Child Psychology and Psychiatry and Allied Disciplines, 32,* 193–209.

Rosenberg, M., Powell, K., and Hammond, R. (1997) Applying science to violence prevention. *Journal of the American Medical Association, 277,* 1641.

Ross, P. and Slaby, R. (1983) Development of aggression. In E. Hetherington (Ed.), *Handbook of Child Psychology*, Vol. IV, pp. 1–87) New York: John Wiley & Sons.

Rowe, D., Vazsonyi, A., and Flannery, D. (1995) Sex differences in crime: do means and within-sex variation have similar causes? *Journal of Research in Crime and Delinquency, 32*, 84–100.

Ruble, D. and Martin, C. (1997) Gender development. In W. Damon and N. Eisenberg (Eds.), *Handbook of Child Psychology: Social, Emotional, and Personality Development*, 5th ed., Vol. 3, pp. 933–1016. New York: John Wiley & Sons.

Rutter, M. (1985) Resilience in the face of adversity. *British Journal of Psychiatry, 147*, 598–611.

Rutter, M. (1997) Nature-nurture integration: the example of antisocial behavior. *American Psychologist, 52*, 390–396.

Samenow, S. (1984) *Inside the Criminal Mind.* New York: Times Books.

Sanders, M. and Dadds, M. (1993) *Behavioral Family Intervention.* Needham Heights, MA: Allyn & Bacon.

Scarr, S. and Eisenberg, M. (1993) Childcare research: issues, perspectives, and results. In L. Porter and M. Rosenzweig (Eds.), *Annual Review of Psychology*, Vol. 44, pp. 613–644. Palo Alto, CA: Annual Reviews, Inc.

Schwartz, L. and Matzkin, R. (1996) Violence, viewing, and development. In H.V. Hall (Ed.), *Lethal Violence 2000: A Sourcebook on Fatal Domestic, Acquaintance and Stranger Aggression*, pp. 113–142. Kamuela, HI: Pacific Institute for the Study of Conflict and Aggression.

Shaw, D., Owens, E., Vondra, J., Keenan, K., and Winslow, E. (1996) Early risk factors and pathways in the development of early disruptive behavior problems. *Development and Psychopathology, 8,* 679–699.

Silverstein, L. (1991) Transforming the debate about child care and maternal employment. *American Psychologist, 46*(10), 1025–1032.

"Single families total 30% of homes" (1995) *Chicago Tribune,* Jan. 10, p. 8.

Skuse, D., James, R., Bishop, D., Coppin, B., Dalton, P., Aamodt-Leeper, G., Bacarese-Hamilton, M., Creswell, C., McGurk, R., and Jacobs, P. (1997) Evidence from Turner's syndrome of an imprinted X-linked locus affecting cognitive function. *Nature, 387,* 705–708.

Smith, C. and Thornberry, T. (1995) The relationship between childhood maltreatment and adolescent involvement in delinquency. *Criminology, 33,* 451–477.

Staub, E. (1996a) Altruism and aggression in children and youth. In R. Feldman (Ed.), *The Psychology of Adversity*, pp. 116–143. Amherst: University of Massachusetts Press.

Staub, E. (1996b) Cultural-societal roots of violence: the examples of genocidal violence and of contemporary youth violence in the United States. *American Psychologist, 51,* 117–132.

Stattin, H. and Magnusson, D. (1996) Antisocial development: a holistic approach. *Development and Psychopathology, 8,* 617–645.

Strayer, F. (1992) The development of agonistic and affiliative structures in preschool play groups. In J. Silverberg and J. Gray (Eds.), *Aggression and Peacefulness in Humans and Other Primates*, pp. 150–171. New York: Oxford University Press.

Symonds, D. (1979) *The Evolution of Human Sexuality.* New York: Oxford University Press.

Tate, D., Reppucci, N., and Mulvey, E. (1995) Violent juvenile delinquents: treatment effectiveness and implications for future action. *American Psychologist, 50,* 777–781.

Tedeschi, J. and Felson, R. (1994) *Violence, Aggression, and Coercive Actions.* Washington, D.C.: American Psychological Association.

U.S. Census Bureau (1997) Census Bureau Report on the State of the Nation, March 26, posted on the World Wide Web. Retrieved September 18, 1997, from http://www.census.gov/Press-Release/cb97-48.html.

Vittiello, B. and Stoff, D. (1997) Subtypes of aggression and their relevance to child psychiatry. *Journal of the American Academy of Child and Adolescent Psychiatry, 36*, 303–315.

Waldman, I. (1996) Aggressive boys' hostile perceptual and response biases: the role of attention and impulsivity. *Child Development, 67*, 1015–1033.

Weisfeld, G. (1994) Aggression and dominance in the social world of boys. In J. Archer (Ed.), *Male Violence*, pp. 42–69. London: Routledge.

Wilson, J. and Herrnstein, R. (1985) Race and crime. In J. Wilson and R. Herrnstein (Eds.), *Crime and Human Nature*, pp. 459–474. New York: Simon & Schuster.

Wrangham, R. and Peterson, D. (1996) *Apes and the Origins of Human Violence.* Boston: Houghton Mifflin.

Yochelson, S. and Samenow, S. (1976) *The Criminal Personality,* Vol. 1, *A Profile for Change.* New York: Aronson.

Yoshikawa, H. (1994) Prevention as cumulative protection: effects of early family support and education on chronic delinquency and its risks. *Psychological Bulletin, 115,* 28–54.

Zahn-Waxler, C. (1996) Environmental, biology, and culture: implications for adolescent development. *Developmental Psychology, 32.* 571–573.

Zahn-Waxler, C., Cole, P., and Barrett, K. (1991) Guilt and empathy: sex differences and implications for the development of aggression. In K. Dodge and J. Garber (Eds.), *Emotional Regulation and Dysregulation*, pp. 243–272. New York: Cambridge University Press.

Zahn-Waxler, C. Cole, P., Welsh, J., and Fox, N. (1996) Psychophysiological correlates of empathy and prosocial behaviors in preschool children with behavior problems. *Development and Psychopathology, 7,* 27–48.

Zahn-Waxler, C. and Robinson, J. (1995) Empathy and guilt: early origins of feelings of responsibility. In K. Fischer and J. Tangney (Eds.), *Self-Conscious Emotions: Shame, Guilt, Embarrassment and Pride.* New York: Guilford Press.

Zaslow, M. and Hayes, C. (1986) Sex differences in children's response to psychosocial stress: toward a cross-context analysis. In M.E. Lamb, A.L. Brown, and B. Rogoff (Eds.), *Advances in Developmental Psychology,* Vol. 4, pp. 285–333. London: Lawrence Erlbaum Associates.

Zahn-Waxler, C. Cole, P., Welch, J., and Fox, N. (1996) Psychophysiological correlates of empathy and prosocial behaviors in preschool children with behavior problems. *Development and Psychopathology, 7,* 27–48.

About the Author

Robert Eme, Ph.D., received his doctorate in Clinical Psychology from Loyola University of Chicago, IL. He currently is a Professor of Clinical Psychology at the Illinois School of Professional Psychology located in Rolling Meadows, IL. His prime area of interest and publication in the academic sphere is sex differences in juvenile psychopathology. In the more applied/clinical sphere, his area of interest and practice is the diagnosis and treatment of attention deficit disorders in children, adolescents, and adults.

Chapter 5

JUVENILE DELINQUENCY AND VIOLENT CRIME

Joseph G. Poirier

Violent juvenile crime is the extreme expression of juvenile delinquency. Violent juvenile crime was once an isolated problem, restricted to large inner city areas. Today, the problem of violent juvenile crime is a concern of every community, regardless of size or location. The extent of the problem has been labeled a "national crisis" by the Coordinating Council on Juvenile Justice and Delinquency Prevention (CCJJDP) (1996a, p. v). Graphic evidence demonstrates that violent juvenile crime has progressively escalated over the past 20 years. The available data are not entirely clear, but it appears that youth gangs are responsible for close to half of all violent youth crime. The problems of violent juvenile crime and youth gangs exist worldwide, but the author has confined the current study to the domestic problem.

Data for the last 5 years show that juveniles are responsible for 1 out of 5 violent crimes. Of those violent juvenile crimes, juveniles in groups perpetrated 1 out of 7 violent crimes (Snyder and Sickmund, 1995). Substance abuse, weapon possession, and especially gang involvements were primary factors associated with violent juvenile crime. Less obvious, but of profound influence, are changes in the traditional role of the family (Loeber and Dishion, 1984; Lewis et al., 1988). Also important are a variety of other sociocultural changes that have served to change the identity of today's youth, particularly adolescents.

This chapter explores the problem of group violent juvenile crime with a focus on juvenile gangs. The chapter will review pertinent statistical data from a historical perspective, describe conditions associated with violent juvenile crime, and discuss factors that contribute to violent crime by youth gangs. Finally, the chapter explores action plan proposals designed to address prevention, diversion, and treatment strategies with violent juvenile offenders.

Literature and Lore

An initial problem with the topic of juvenile delinquency is arriving at a definition of the term. Juvenile delinquency can be defined either as a legal concept or in behavioral terms (Mulvey et al., 1993). According to statutory definitions in most states, a juvenile is a person 18 years of age or younger. Minor variations exist across states in the criteria of defining a juvenile. Illinois and Texas, for example, limit statutory delinquency to age 17 and under. Statistics reflect that the modal age range of juveniles who commit violent crime is between 9 and 18. Recent data reflect that younger persons are increasingly becoming involved in violent offenses, often because of association with gangs.

There is also no standardized definition of what constitutes a gang or gang activity (Curry et al., 1994). This has hampered efforts to document statistically violent crimes committed by gangs. Several criteria, however, have evolved as essential to definitions of gang behavior: (1) formally organized structure, (2) identifiable leadership, (3) identified with a territory, (4) recurrent interaction, and (5) engaging in serious or violent behavior (Howell, 1994).

The law recognizes the malleability of delinquent youth, as compared to adult criminals. The legal system has historically recognized that children cannot be held responsible for their behavior in the same way as adults. In the early 1900s, this thinking led to the establishment of the nation's juvenile courts. In this regard, the law recognizes juvenile status offenses. Status offenders are juveniles who commit acts that are illegal because of the juvenile's age. Examples of juvenile status offenses are truancy, the purchase or ingestion of tobacco products, and the purchase or ingestion of alcohol. Many violent juvenile offenders have prior histories as status offenders. Further, status offenders often offend initially as members of a group. The focus in the juvenile court is more rehabilitative than punitive, compared to adult criminal court.

The Juvenile Court System

The juvenile courts have primary responsibility for determining dispositions of youth involved in delinquent behavior. The juvenile court process is central to understanding the judicial management of delinquency. The Office of Juvenile Justice and Delinquency Prevention (OJJDP) devised a generic model of the juvenile judicial process (Butts et al., 1996, p. 1). The model described six processing functions of the juvenile justice system as follows:

1. *Intake.* An intake unit screens all initially referred cases. The main function of the intake unit is to decide if a case referred by the police will be forwarded to the court. The intake unit may decide on informal disposition such as non-judicial probation with referral to a community-based support agency, restitution, or similar diversion efforts.
2. *Transfer.* This is the process of a juvenile offender matter being transferred from the juvenile court to the adult court. In some jurisdictions, statutes stipulate that certain serious offenses by a juvenile (e.g., murder, rape, and armed robbery) automatically "waive" a juvenile into adult court. In other jurisdictions, a petition is filed asking the juvenile bench to consider waiving a case into the adult court because of the seriousness of an offense.
3. *Petitioning.* The intake unit decides whether or not a case should be formally handled in the juvenile court. A decision for formal handling results in the filing of a petition. The petition will result in the case being placed on the juvenile court docket for an adjudication hearing.
4. *Adjudication.* At the adjudication hearing, the juvenile bench judges a delinquent as involved or not involved. If the juvenile is deemed involved, then the case is scheduled for a disposition hearing. Juvenile court adjudication is comparable to a trial in the adult court, which results in a determination of guilt or non-guilt.
5. *Disposition.* At the disposition hearing, the juvenile judge decides what sanctions are appropriate for the offending juvenile. Disposition is comparable to sentencing in the adult court.
6. *Detention.* For reasons of safety, of either the community or the juvenile, an offender may be placed in a juvenile detention facility at virtually any point of the adjudication process.

TABLE 5.1

1988 TO 1992 JUVENILE AND ADULT ARREST RATE INCREASES IN EACH COMPONENT OF THE VIOLENT CRIME INDEX

	% Increase	
Crime Category	**Juvenile**	**Adult**
Murder	51	9
Forcible rape	17	3
Robbery	50	13
Aggravated assault	49	23

Statistical and Clinical Associations to Violent Juvenile Crime

Several federal agencies, particularly the Federal Bureau of Investigation (FBI), monitor the incidence and prevalence of violent crime. OJJDP, a federal agency within the Bureau of Justice, tracks juvenile offense data based on arrest data from the FBI and on disposition reports from juvenile courts.

The FBI and OJJDP use police and juvenile court data to generate national trend reports. The FBI developed the Uniform Crime Reporting System. Reports are published annually (e.g., FBI, 1992–1996a[1]). The FBI also developed the Violent Crime Index, which is derived from arrest data for four types of offenses: murder, forcible rape, robbery, and aggravated assault.

According to the Violent Crime Index, for the 27-year period from 1965 to 1992, the incidence of all violent crime increased 43%. The 10-year period from 1983 to 1992 reflected a 54% increase in reported crime (Snyder, 1994c). Both adult and juvenile offenses were included in these data.

The FBI arrest data for the period from 1988 to 1992 indicated an 11% increase in juvenile arrests contrasted with a 6% increase in the total arrest rate for adults. According to the Violent Crime Index, juvenile arrests for violent crimes increased by an alarming 47% compared to a 19% increase for adults (Snyder, 1994b). The data in Table 5.1 compare the adult to juvenile arrest rate increases for each component of the Violent Crime Index from 1988 to 1992. These data reflected greater juvenile increases in violent crime categories as compared to adults.

The most recent OJJDP *Juvenile Court Statistics* report (Butts et al., 1996) was the 67th in the series and updated juvenile court data through 1993. The 1993 data were based on records from approximately 1800 juvenile courts and nearly 690,000 case records. The dispositions of more than 67% of all youngsters appearing in juvenile court matters were represented in the data. The 1993 data reflected a 2% increase in juvenile court cases from 1992 and a 23% increase compared to 1989 (Butts et al., 1996).

There was a total of 122,000 Violent Crime Index offenses in 1993. These included 38% of all person offenses committed by juveniles, and 8% of all crimes committed by juveniles in 1993 (FBI, 1993). According to these FBI arrest data, juvenile arrests for homicide increased 45% between 1989 and 1993

---

[1] The Uniform Crime Reporting System provides a Crime Index that is a combination of the Violent Crime Index and the Property Crime Index. The Property Crime Index combines the offenses of burlary, larceny-theft, motor vehicle theft, and arson.

Table 5.2

1985 to 1994 Juvenile to Adult Violent Crime Index Arrest Rate Increases

	Percent Change in Arrests			
	1990–1994		1985–1990	
	Juvenile (%)	Adult (%)	Juvenile (%)	Adult (%)
Crime index total	9	–8	18	17
Violent crime index	26	0	75	48
Murder	15	–9	150	11
Forcible rape	0	–12	6	–5
Robbery	32	–14	57	12
Aggravated assault	25	6	97	71

and 14% between 1992 and 1993. These data were comparable to similar increases in juvenile court processing of homicide charges (Butts et al., 1996). Between 1989 and 1993, there was a greater increase in person crimes by juveniles in comparison to an overall decrease in property crimes by juveniles (Butts et al., 1996). During 1994, there were 2.7 million juvenile arrests nationwide (Snyder et al., 1996). This represented a 28% increase in juvenile arrests since 1984, compared to a 19% increase in adult arrests for the same period. Of all arrested juveniles in 1994, 35% were 15 years of age or younger. The proportion of juvenile arrests involving youth younger than 15 increased slightly between 1985 and 1994. Snyder et al. (1996) showed that this increase occurred in most offense categories.

Of particular note in the 1994 data was a 71% increase in juvenile arrests for murder involving 16- and 17-year-old youths. Coinciding with this increase in juvenile homicide crimes was a significant increase in juvenile weapon use. Also of significance was a dramatic increase in violent crime by females between 1985 and 1994. Female juvenile arrest rates were higher than for male juveniles for violent crimes of robbery and aggravated assault.

Table 5.2 presents a comparison of juvenile and adult arrest rate increases in the Violent Crime Index from 1985 to 1990 and from 1990 to 1994. The proportionate increases in juvenile arrest rates are apparent. According to Snyder et al. (1996), juveniles accounted for 19% of all arrests for violent crime in 1994. The authors pointed out that, because juveniles tend to commit crime in groups, the 19% juvenile arrest figure may inflate the actual extent of juvenile involvement in violent crime. That is, the 19% figure represents the number of juveniles charged for violent crime offenses and who entered the juvenile court system. A more accurate estimate of actual juvenile involvement in violent crime may be the FBI estimate of 14% of juveniles cleared by law enforcement in 1994. A cleared case is an incident closed with the adjudication of a juvenile being found involved and a disposition being rendered. Thus, cleared cases were based on reported crimes that underwent investigation and legal scrutiny beyond what is represented in unscreened initial arrest data. Based on

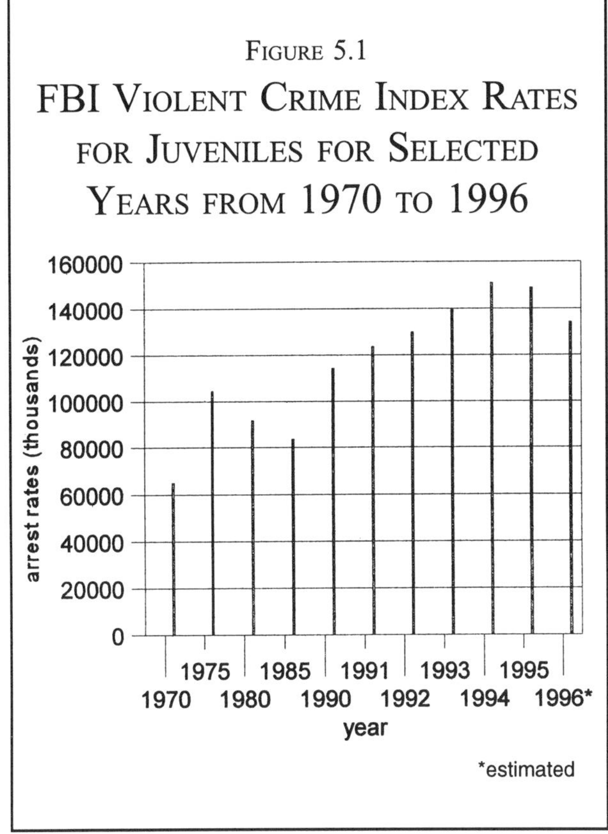

FIGURE 5.1
FBI VIOLENT CRIME INDEX RATES FOR JUVENILES FOR SELECTED YEARS FROM 1970 TO 1996

the 1994 data for cleared cases, the Violent Crime Index rates for juvenile involvement were as follows: 10% for murder, 13% for aggravated assaults, 14% for forcible rapes, and 20% for robbery (Snyder et al., 1996).

According to the 1994 FBI Violent Crime Index data, 94% of juvenile arrests were for robbery and aggravated assault; by comparison, the categories of murder and rape accounted for only 6% of the arrests (Snyder, 1994a; Snyder et al., 1996). In the totality of the arrest and cleared case data, therefore, juvenile offenses represented a comparatively small percentage when compared to adults.

The juvenile arrest rates from the Violent Crime Index (FBI, 1997a) for selected years from 1970 to 1996 are depicted in Figure 5.1. The 1996 annual figure was an estimate based on the most currently reported FBI data for all violent crime for 1996 (FBI, 1997b; Thomas, 1997). The data specifically for juvenile crime were not yet available. The violent crime arrest data for juveniles indicated that, from 1975 through 1988, the number of juvenile arrests for violent crimes essentially varied with the size of the juvenile population. Beginning in 1989, however, the juvenile violent crime arrest rate escalated beyond the historic range (Snyder et al., 1996). The data in Figure 5.1 reflect the alarming upward spiral of juvenile arrests for violent crimes from 1989 through 1994. In 1994, the data began to reflect a significant rate decrease that has continued through the preliminary 1996 data.

FBI Uniform Crime Report data[2] for 1995 (FBI, 1996b,c; Suro, 1996) showed that the drop in the upward trend of violent juvenile crime for that year was particularly evident for juvenile offenders under the age of 15. It is important to emphasize that although the recent drop in violent crime was encouraging, the 1995 rate of violent crime still remained 64% higher than it was in 1987. The rate decreases that continued through 1996 nonetheless constituted a substantial juvenile violent crime problem. The 1995 data indicated a 2.1% increase in juvenile female arrests and a 3.4% decrease in juvenile male arrests. There was a 1.7% decrease in the overall arrest rate for juveniles ages 15 to 17, and a 4.6% decrease in the overall arrest rate for juveniles ages 10 to 14.

At the present time, it is difficult to interpret what the recent decreases in violent crime rates really mean. Did the decreases reflect an isolated, temporary fluke in a nearly two-decade trend of increases in violent juvenile crime? Another explanation may be that the national effort to address the problem of violent juvenile crime has begun to have a meaningful impact. Almost $17 million in federal grants are now available to states for delinquency prevention and intervention programs. Was the recent drop in

[2] As noted earlier, the volume of data that constitute the Uniform Crime Report and the Violent Crime Index is so extensive that there is typically a 1- to 2-year delay in data reporting.

the violent juvenile crime rate a reflection of this effort? In any event, the data, now consistent for more than a 3-year period, have represented a modest, but significant, reversal in the progression in violent juvenile crime from 1980 through 1996.

The gathering of statistical data on a comprehensive basis regarding gang activity has been a relatively new endeavor and a less than sophisticated effort until very recently. Early studies from 1975 through 1983 were summarized by Curry et al. (1994). Those data were drawn from very small national samples and the findings were so diverse that it was not possible to draw any meaningful conclusions except that the magnitude of gang activity was significant and apparently growing. In 1995, OJJDP entered into a cooperative arrangement with the Institute for Intergovernmental Research to establish the National Youth Gang Center (NYGC). One of the primary functions of NYGC is to conduct periodic national surveys in an effort to develop a comprehensive data base regarding the problem of youth gangs (Moore, 1997). The first NYGC survey captured data for 1995. These data reflected that 2007 of 3400 reporting jurisdictions acknowledged gang activity. The study estimated 23,338 gangs and 664,906 gang members in the reporting jurisdictions (Moore, 1997).

The NYGC survey defined a gang as "a group of youths in the [respondent's] jurisdiction, aged approximately 10 to 22, that [the respondent] or other responsible persons in [the respondent's] agency or community are willing to identify or classify as a 'gang'" (Moore, 1997, p. 1). The age range encompassing juveniles and adults was justified by existing data (Howell, 1994), which reflected the age range of gang members to be from about 12 to 25 years. There is agreement among researchers of gang behavior that the most appropriate statistic for assessing the magnitude of gang behavior is the number of crimes committed by gangs as opposed to estimates of the number of gang members (Curry et al., 1994).

Based on a 1992 national study (Curry et al., 1994), it was made clear that gang-related crime involved primarily violent acts. The authors reported that homicide and other violent crimes accounted for about half of all gang-related crime incidents. The same authors reported that in terms of gang membership characteristics, the proportion of female to male gang members was relatively small; females represented only 3 to 4% of reported gang membership. The 1992 data also indicated that black and Hispanic youth were the overwhelming majority of gang members, but that white youth were increasingly becoming involved.

The results of the NYGC 1995 study were based on surveys mailed to 4120 jurisdictions. There were responses from 3440 jurisdictions, with 58% (2007) acknowledging youth gang activity. Half of the reporting jurisdictions had populations fewer than 25,000 residents. According to Moore (1997), all 50 states reported youth gang activity, and 90% of the reporting agencies stated that the gang problem was remaining stable or getting worse. The 1995 NYGC study indicated that all states and most large cities reported a youth gang problem. The study also reflected that gangs were appearing in new localities to include smaller cities and even rural counties. The 1995 data were the most recent and probably the most accurate estimates of gang activity and gang crime yet available. The study was an initial effort based on a random sampling of jurisdictions. Because all law enforcement agencies were not queried, it is likely that the estimates are less than what actually exists. A 1996 effort, still underway, solicited data from all law enforcement agencies as well as other sources. These data should provide an even more accurate picture of gang activity (Moore, 1997).

One other recent study of gang activity examined prosecutors' perceptions of gang-related crime (Johnson et al., 1995). In this study, 80% of the prosecutors from 36 states acknowledged gangs to be a significant problem in their jurisdiction. The prosecutors reported that gangs formed on the basis of racial or ethnic origin were the most prevalent types in both large and small jurisdictions. The most frequently reported type of gang crime was drug trafficking, but the prosecutors agreed that extreme violence was an integral element of the gang subculture. The prosecutors noted that existing state statutory codes were not designed for the serious violence that characterizes street gang crime, nor did the wording of existing statutes regarding gang activity apply specifically to juvenile offenders. The provisions of existing statutes also did not cover the peculiarities of gang crime, e.g., drive-by shootings, street turf fights, and multiple offenders brandishing weapons. The prosecutors were in agreement that early intervention and services designed to improve family functioning were the most important prevention measures to address gang violence and crime.

Etiological Factors of Violent Juvenile Crime

Historically, a wide array of etiological factors has been associated with violent juvenile crime, gang involvement, and the interrelationship of the two (Offord et al., 1975; Busch et al., 1990; Spergal et al., 1993; Curry et al., 1994; Henggeler, 1996; Moore, 1997). These factors are summarized in Table 5.3. These data reflect that the earlier focus on neurological associations has been supplanted in more recent studies by emphasis on behavioral and social factors. The data in Table 5.3 also indicate the wide range of factors that researchers have associated with serious youth crime.

The Juvenile Violence Event

As with many forms of violence, there is no single, predictable course of juvenile violence. Some forms of violence (for example, certain types of domestic violence) have identifiable cycles (Poirier, 1996). Hall (1996) summarized child and adolescent developmental conditions that are potential markers for later violence. Violent juvenile crime is perhaps distinguished from adult violent crime by being more random and precipitous. Factors associated with juvenile violence can coexist in an unstable condition without violence actually occurring. Then, with unpredictability and suddenness, violent juvenile behavior can take place. Violent crime emanating from the gang context may be portended when gangs are involved in conflicts (e.g., over street-territory claims or drug trafficking disagreements), but this assumes insiders' knowledge of gang activity.

Gang Violence

Youth gangs existed long before the problem of violent juvenile crime. The classic version of the youth gangs of young America was perhaps best portrayed in the imagery of the old "Our Gang" silent and sound movies. The recreational pursuits of youth gangs of just 20 years ago, however, have been transformed into contemporary gang involvement in violent behavior (Miller, 1982; Ryan et al., 1993; Hutson et al., 1994a,b). According to Skolnick (1995), youth gangs are often rooted in neighborhood identities, frequently with cultural or ethnic origins. Gang identities can thereby persist through generations. Other parameters leading to gang activities include social isolation coupled with poverty and community disorganization (Spergal et al., 1993; DuRant et al., 1995; Myers et al., 1995). Ethnic conflicts within communities can also lead to the formation of gangs as youths seek consolation and safety by bonding together.

Gang violence is often prompted by perceived threat to the integrity of the gang (Oliver, 1995). The organization of gangs can range from casual to highly structured. Some gangs have vague membership requirements, while other gangs have strict eligibility codes. In some gangs, there are penalties for dissidents. Once a youth is initiated into a gang, there is opportunity for becoming involved in activities of increasing import. Codes of loyalty and secrecy serve

TABLE 5.3

ETIOLOGICAL FACTORS ASSOCIATED WITH VIOLENT JUVENILE CRIME

Factor		Sample Study
I.	*Neurological deficits*	
	a. Perinatal trauma, head and face trauma	Lewis, Shanok, & Balla (1979)
	b. Epilepsy	Taylor (1969)
	c. Temporal lobe epilepsy	Ounsted (1969)
	d. General neurological deficits	Pontius (1982)
	e. Attention deficit disorder	Satterfield et al. (1982)
II.	*Learning disability*	
	a. History of educational difficulties	Hurwitz et al. (1972) Broder et al. (1981) Karniski et al. (1982)
	b. School dropout, poor academic performance, low commitment to school, school environment offers weak structure	Busch et al. (1990)
	c. Early academic failure	Hawkins et al. (1987) American Psychological Association (1993)
III.	*Psychological control/impulse problems*	Stearns (1975) Yeudall et al. (1982) Brickman et al. (1984) Lewis et al. (1985)
IV.	*Psychopathology*	
	a. Depression	Deykin et al. (1987) Cooley-Quille et al. (1995) DuRant et al. (1995)
	b. Low social conformity, favorable attitude toward antisocial behavior, cognitive bias to attribute hostile intentions to others	Henggeler (1996) Lewis et al. (1979)
V.	*History of family dysfunction*	
	a. Murder in family	Duncan and Duncan (1971)
	b. Family violence	Easson and Steenhilber (1961)
	c. Parental psychiatric history	Offord et al. (1975)
	d. Family lower socioeconomic status	Lewis et al. (1985)
	e. History of family member criminal violence	Busch et al. (1990)
	f. Lack of parental monitoring, inept discipline, parental substance abuse, family member psychiatric illness, low warmth and cohesion	Peterson et al. (1994) Thornberry (1994) Henggeler (1996)
	g. Family history of substance abuse	Bohman (1978) Goodwin (1985)
	h. Teenage mothers, parents who are high school dropouts	Slavin (1990)
	i. Lax parental attitude toward crime and substance abuse	Brook et al. (1990)

TABLE 5.3 (CONTINUED)

ETIOLOGICAL FACTORS ASSOCIATED WITH VIOLENT JUVENILE CRIME

Factor		Sample Study
VI.	*Neighborhood and community deficits*	
	a. Criminal subculture supporting activities such as drug dealing and prostitution, resident mobility and transition, low social support from community organization	Rivara et al. (1995) Sigler (1995) Henggeler (1996)
VII.	*Juvenile offender substance abuse*	Deykin et al. (1987) Busch et al. (1990) Osgood (1995)
	a. Alcohol and nicotine	Snyder and Sickmund (1995)
	b. Illicit substances	Snyder and Sickmund (1995) Maxson et al. (1996) Snyder et al. (1996)
VIII.	*Juvenile offender weapon possession*	
	a. Firearm use	Snyder and Sickmund (1995) Maxson et al. (1996) Snyder et al. (1996)
IX.	Peer group/gang association	Busch et al. (1990) American Psychological Association (1993) Spergal et al. (1993) Curry et al. (1994) Snyder and Sickmund (1995) Maxson and Woods (1996) Snyder et al. (1996) Moore (1996)
	a. Association with troubled peers	Elliott et al. (1989) Henggeler (1996)
X.	Juvenile offender ethnic differences in violent crime rate	American Psychological Association (1993)
XI.	Time of day of violent juvenile crime	
	a. Most serious juvenile crime committed between 2 p.m. and 6 p.m. on school days	Snyder et al. (1996)

to perpetuate a gang's longevity. The same codes result in gangs being resistant to law enforcement detection. The extent of gang violence can range from mischievous acts of theft or vandalism to serious crimes such as armed robbery, rape, arson, and homicide. In comparison to non-gang offenders, gang members commit a disproportionate percentage of serious and violent offenses and are more likely to engage in substance abuse (Hutson et al., 1995; Spergal et al., 1993).

According to the Bureau of Justice Statistics (Butts, 1994), for the 5-year period from 1987 to

1992, the use of firearms in violent crimes by teenagers (16 to 19 years old) reflected per capita rates of handgun victimization ranging from 2 to 17 times that for adults. Firearm homicides generally increased from 1979 to 1991 across all ages. Young black males (15 to 24 years of age) were overrepresented as perpetrators and victims; as victims, they accounted for nearly 60% of all firearm homicides. Snyder et al. (1996) cited a study by the National Institute of Justice in which 4000 arrestees were interviewed. Gang membership and involvement in drug sales were associated with gun ownership among the arrestees. The study also found that juveniles who had been violently victimized (i.e., threatened or actually fired upon) were more likely to admit owning a gun.

Gang migration is a recently described aspect of gang violence. Maxson et al. (1996) described relatively few cities (13%) reporting gang migration occurring before 1986. Most cities (54%) indicated that local gang problems preceded indications of gang migratory behavior. The same researchers noted that the reasons for gang migration were complex and varied from one region to the next. Most reporting jurisdictions indicated that the number of gang migrants was small.

According to currently available data, more than half of all violent juvenile crime is committed by individual perpetrators. Gang activity alone, therefore, is not responsible for the problem of juvenile violence, but demographics clearly indicate that gang activity is becoming an increasingly pervasive factor in violent juvenile crime (Curry et al., 1994).

Violent Juvenile Offender Characteristics

Eighty percent of all juvenile violence is committed by males. More specifically, 78% of offenses against persons, 80% of property offenses, and 88% of drug law violations by juveniles were committed by males (Butts et al., 1996). Between 1989 and 1993, the volume of delinquency crimes by males increased 21%, compared to a 31% increase for females. For the same period, offenses against persons committed by juveniles increased by 49% for males and by 68% for females (Butts et al., 1996).

The FBI juvenile offense data for the period from 1988 to 1993 indicated an 18% increase in delinquency offenses for white (including Hispanic) youth, compared to a 34% increase for black youth and a 32% increase for youths of all other races (Butts et al., 1996). One significant statistic was that black youth (61%) were more likely to have their delinquency cases handled by formal disposition than were white (49%) or other race youth (48%).

Between 1980 and 1994, 26,000 juveniles committed homicides. The number of juvenile perpetrators who committed homicides decreased from 1980 to 1984 and then rose progressively through 1994. There were more than 2300 victims of juvenile homicide in 1994; this was nearly three times the number of juvenile homicide victims in 1984 (Snyder et al., 1996). A comparison of male and female juvenile homicide perpetrators in these data indicated that females were more likely to kill family members and that males were more likely to kill strangers. The female perpetrators were also more likely (35%) to kill other juveniles in comparison to the male homicide perpetrators (25%). The data of Snyder et al. (1996) showed that 88% of the juvenile homicide offenders were older teens between the ages of 15 and 17, 11% were juveniles between the ages of 12 and 14, and 1% were juveniles under the age of 12. Older juvenile homicide offenders were more likely to kill acquaintances and strangers. Younger juvenile offenders were more likely to murder family members, and their victims tended to be younger in age.

Between 1980 and 1994, juvenile homicide offenders were most likely to kill a victim from their own race (Garrett, 1995; Snyder et al., 1996). Snyder et al. extracted descriptive data indicating that white offenders killed white victims 90% of the time and that black offenders killed black victims 76% of the time. Black offenders were more likely to kill strangers

(33%) compared to white offenders (27%) and black offenders were less likely to kill family members (7%) in comparison to white offenders (15%).

For the 14-year period from 1980 to 1994, the majority (7 out of 10) of juvenile offender homicides involved firearms; knives or other blunt objects were the weapons in 2 out of 10 homicides; and personal weapons, defined as hands, fists, or feet, were the lethal weapons in 5% or less of the homicides (Snyder et al., 1996). The 14-year FBI data reviewed by Snyder et al. (1996) reflected that approximately half of the juvenile violence offenders acted alone and that the other half had at least one other person involved with them. Of the latter group, half acted with one other person and the other half acted in a group of three or more.

Juvenile female offenders (65%) were more likely than male offenders (49%) to act alone. Younger offenders were more likely to kill in groups. A comparison of black and white juveniles indicated that both were equally likely to have killed alone (50%), in pairs (23%), or in groups of three or more (27%). When juveniles committed homicides in groups, there was an adult accomplice 60% of the time (Snyder et al., 1996). The latter data reflected violent juvenile crimes committed by more than one juvenile perpetrator.

Triggering Phase of the Violent Juvenile Crime Incident

Contemporary society continues in an ongoing struggle to cope with the challenges posed by adolescence. Conversely, adolescents struggle with the challenge of how they are perceived by society. The contemporary adolescent is prone to perceiving many circumstances as menacing (Stearns, 1975). Virtually any stimulus viewed as threatening can be sufficient cause for a violent act. The naiveté, impulsivity, and immature cognitive restraint of adolescence combined with adult physical strength meld together in a potent crucible for violent juvenile behavior.

There are a multitude of preconditions that can help trigger juvenile violence, but an important distinction in understanding the triggering phase of violent juvenile crime is whether the crime involves a solo perpetrator or a gang. Both solo and gang juvenile crime can be premeditated, but gang crime is more likely to involve impulsive, wanton, and indiscriminate violent behavior (Henggeler et al., 1993). These factors contribute to the highly lethal nature of gang crime. Other contributing factors are the high incidences of substance abuse and possession and use of weapons among gangs (Oliver, 1995). All of these characteristics of adolescence and youth gang sociology serve as triggering phenomena of violent youth crime. The more preconditions that are present, the greater the likelihood that violent behavior will occur, but no single precondition, or combination thereof, will necessarily cause an incident of violent juvenile behavior.

Recovery and Return to Baseline Phases of Violent Juvenile Crime

The aftermath of juvenile violence incidents when victims and offenders are involved in pre-incident relationships should be considered. Such relationships can include situations with family members (Duncan and Duncan, 1971; Poirier, 1996) or with peers (Brook et al., 1990). In these situations, the violence is often precipitated by some dynamic of the relationship going awry. Following violence in relationships, both perpetrators and victims struggle with feelings of the relationship having been violated. Thus, feelings of shared remorse and shame can be characteristic of both offenders and victims in nonstranger juvenile violence. In relationship-based juvenile violence, the reality of the prior relationship can either temper or exacerbate post-violence feelings of needs for revenge and vindication. Intervention with relationship-based juvenile violence should always address post-trauma needs of both victims and perpetrators. In some cases, this may include conjoint sessions with an offender and the victim(s). Obviously, these interventions must be undertaken with discretion and careful timing.

Stranger-to-stranger violent juvenile crime involves different offender and victim dynamics. Intervention strategies involve different considerations than those involved in relationship violence. The aftermath of gang violence involves the gang's approval or disapproval of the offender's performance. Some forms of stranger-to-stranger crime involve premeditation and careful planning; this type of violence clearly implicates more involved antisocial personality dynamics. The long-term psychological sequela on the violent juvenile offender is not well established (Singer et al., 1995). We know that juvenile offenders who have perpetrated violence are at higher risk for continued violent behavior unless the cycle is interrupted (Snyder and Sickmund, 1995). In recent years, the media, especially television and movies, have portrayed graphic and electrifying youth gang activity. These portrayals often depict youth gangs as functioning in a manner similar to that of adult terrorist groups. While such youth gang activity may exist, the more typical scenario for clinicians who actually work with violent juvenile offenders is far more subdued and less sophisticated. The following two case examples describe actual situations. While perhaps less sensational in circumstances than media portrayals, the very real tragedies that occurred in the following case examples were, nonetheless, equally compelling.

Case Illustration 1: Johnny, Alvin, and the Plowheads

This case situation occurred in a rural, agricultural area that adjoined a large metropolitan community. The victim in this sad and unusually vicious act of juvenile violence was 8-year-old Johnny. The circumstances of Johnny's death were not typical of gang violence, but gang involvement was a contributing factor.

Johnny's nude body was found in a large, sealed, transparent plastic bag in a snowy field. Johnny had been missing for 2 days; he was found by a search party organized by family members, neighbors, and friends. The crime scene was a wretched experience for the search party members, many of whom had known Johnny personally. Johnny's body was badly mutilated. His tongue had been hacked off with a crude cutting implement, his nipples were pierced with large safety pins, and his penis was horribly lacerated in an apparent attempt to sever it. His oral and anal cavities were stuffed with dirty, coarse cloth. The plastic bag contained the body, the severed tongue, and a partially rusted, medium-sized kitchen knife. An autopsy determined that the immediate cause of death was asphyxiation; Johnny was mutilated and unconscious when he was placed inside the plastic bag, where he subsequently died.

Friends and family members agonized over the horrific circumstances of Johnny's death. He was described as mischievous, but also as caring and affable. Subsequent police investigation led to telling evidence that Johnny had been murdered by a single perpetrator. The perpetrator was eventually identified as Johnny's best friend, 11-year-old Alvin. Alvin and Johnny had been constant playmates. The two youths went to the same school, rode together on the same school bus, and spent virtually all after-school hours together. Approximately 6 months prior to Johnny's death, Alvin befriended a small youth gang that frequently gathered at the nearby home of an adolescent neighbor. Spring had arrived, and Alvin was spending more time outside, especially in the evening hours. This would occur after the younger Johnny had returned home at the end of the day. The adolescent gang was called the "Plowheads" in reference to the agricultural nature of the community. The somewhat derogatory designation only served as a bonding element for the gang members against the ridicule of other peers. Alvin was the youngest participant in the ill-formed gang.

The gang regarded Alvin as a humorous nuisance; the gang members teased Alvin unmercifully about his well-known family circumstances, his youth, his lack of sexual prowess, and any other issue perceived to be sensitive. Alvin was the youngest of seven siblings. The next oldest sibling was 8 years Alvin's senior. At the time of the incident, Alvins's alcoholic father was approaching his 70th birthday. Alvin's father had a well-established arrest record for theft, public intoxication, and domestic violence. The father had been incarcerated on numerous occasions for minor offenses, but was known as a "good provider" when not drinking. Over the years, Alvin's mother and all the older siblings had periodically incurred the father's inebriated wrath. Alvin had witnessed much of this history of domestic violence. He had escaped being physically victimized by his father but had been psychologically tormented. Alvin was also physically and emotionally abused by two of his older brothers. Some of this taunting by the older brothers involved sexual references. In one instance of physical abuse by an older brother, Alvin suffered a compound elbow fracture. The older brother was convicted of child abuse and incarcerated for 18 months, at which point he returned home. Alvin's involvement with the gang began several months thereafter. Subsequently, the older brother moved out of the home to live with friends.

Following the initial police investigation, Alvin was charged as an adult, as statutorily required because of the nature of the offense (i.e., first degree murder). Subsequent adjudication, however, resulted in Alvin's case being maintained in the juvenile court. During the juvenile court adjudication and later disposition hearings, the author met with Alvin, his family members, and also several of the gang members who were facing various other juvenile offenses. At the point of the court-ordered assessment process Alvin would only speak in negative terms about his association with the gang. It was apparent, however, that although he was treated miserably by the gang, Alvin had enjoyed the camaraderie the gang members had offered him. The gang members were heavily into alcohol and cannabis abuse, and there was overt sexual activity between the older male and female gang members. Alvin was exposed to these activities, albeit in a teasing and taunting manner. As a child, Alvin had been exposed to substance abuse and sexual innuendo through his older siblings. With the gang, Alvin appeared to enjoy perceiving himself as one step closer to being a participant in adult activities than he had been in his family situation.

For a variety of reasons, including the steadfast denials of Alvin's family, the maneuvering of the attorneys, and Alvin's poor recollection, the exact circumstances of Johnny's death were never fully determined. We did establish that Alvin and Johnny were playing, and that they became involved in a dispute over wearing each other's jackets. The conflict escalated to throwing rocks and at one point, Johnny was struck on the head by a rock thrown by Alvin. Johnny was seriously injured by the blow and apparently disoriented. Alvin became frightened, confused, and then angry. Alvin apparently thought that Johnny was pretending to be hurt and became more antagonistic.

As is often the case with tragic dynamics involving youthful victims and offenders who are acquaintances, it was difficult to determine who was the greater victim, Johnny or Alvin. The latter statement is in no way intended to dismiss the tragedy of Johnny's death and the reality of Alvin's treachery. From the objectivity of the clinical perspective, however, the impact of the overall situation was pathetic for both Johnny and Alvin. Johnny was dead, and Alvin faced spending the remainder of his youth under the scrutiny of the juvenile system. Alvin would also carry the psychological and social repercussions of the experience for life. The challenge posed to professionals working with Alvin to undo and correct the realities of his prior history was indeed formidable.

Case Illustration 2: Maria G. and the Diablos

Clinicians who work with troubled adolescents quickly recognize the common denominator of disturbed family situations. The lack of consistent caring and support from the family leads the adolescent to try to meet those needs in peer relationships. All too often, adolescents who share disturbed family backgrounds find each other and merge into groups.

Maria was native to El Salvador. When she was 4, the rural village where she lived with her parents and an older brother was pillaged by a rebel military band. The men of the village were herded together and mass murdered. The elderly, women, and children were gathered together in a confined area and held hostage for several weeks. Many of the women, including Maria's mother, were sexually harassed, raped, or both by the captors. As an adolescent, Maria had only vague recollections of the experience; her primary memory was of the rebels offering her candy. Maria had confused memories of hearing her mother crying out and apparently attempting to fend off her multiple attackers. She had vivid and very unpleasant memories of the aftermath of the situation. Maria, her mother, and an older brother grieved the death of the father and shared the village's remorse over the many community members who had died.

Maria's most intense memory was of her mother's outrage over being sexually victimized. Maria recalled with considerable difficulty that at the time she had interpreted her mother's cries as grief over the death of Maria's father. For years afterward, Maria's mother shared with Maria her bitter, angry memories of the sexual attacks, memories that were only intensified by her husband's death.

When Maria was 9 years of age, she and her mother immigrated to the United States. Her brother remained in

El Salvador with relatives. Maria and her mother settled into a large Hispanic community in a prosperous suburb. They struggled for a year or so, subsisting with the assistance of community and religious resources. Maria's mother found work at a small Hispanic restaurant and eventually married the restaurant owner. The new husband was a divorcee and had two small children from a prior marriage in his care. With time, it became apparent that Maria's stepfather abused alcohol and was often abusive to Maria's mother. There also were episodes of the stepfather consuming alcohol and being inappropriately sexually suggestive with Maria.

Frustrated, and feeling abandoned by her mother, Maria found solace in staying out with friends. Maria was physically precocious and was soon introduced to experimental use of tobacco, alcohol, cannabis, and phencyclidine, as well as to sexual activity with male peers. Maria was 13 years of age when she and several of her older female friends were invited to join a youth gang known as the "Diablos". The youth gang was made up predominantly of Hispanic adolescents. At first, Maria understood the gang to be primarily social in its purpose. The gang members were encouraged to shun contact with youngsters who were not gang members. The gang code expected fierce loyalty. There were ill-defined expectations of secrecy, open sharing of requested sexual favors, and shared substance abuse. Hispanic, young, street-sophisticated, and attractive, Maria found herself quickly percolating to the top of the gang hierarchy. Shortly before her 14th birthday, she became the girlfriend of the gang leader.

The gang leader was a 20-year-old Hispanic male named Marcos. Marcos was known for being ruthless and cunning, but also charming. Maria soon became aware of the gang's involvement in trafficking illicit substances. After several months of enjoying her new status and having become very enamored with Marcos, Maria got involved in aspects of the illicit drug activities. Remarkably, throughout this time, Maria maintained herself in good standing both at home and at school.

The situation came to a critical point when Marcos advised Maria that one of her friends, a girl named Felicia, was jeopardizing the welfare of the gang. Felicia was one of Maria's older friends; ironically, Maria and Felicia had been initiated together into the Diablos. Marcos indicated that Felicia was romantically involved with a rival gang member. Additionally, Felicia's boyfriend was delinquent in satisfying an outstanding illicit substance loan of $110 to the Diablos. Marcos charged Maria with confronting Felicia and satisfying the wrongs to the Diablos. Marcos gave Maria a small-caliber pistol and instructed her to "frighten" Felicia; Marcos suggested, "Felicia may need to be hurt a little."

Maria was accompanied by two of Marcos' favored male accomplices, both of whom smoked phencyclidine immediately prior to the confrontation. Maria declined the phencyclidine but consented to smoke marijuana to "calm" herself. The time and circumstances of the confrontation were well-planned. Unexpected by Maria was Felicia's revelation that she was Marcos' ex-girlfriend. Felicia suggested to Maria that Marcos' real intention was to intimidate her into re-establishing a relationship. Maria was stunned and confused. She was also egged on by her male accomplices. Felicia responded to Maria's threats with the handgun by drawing a concealed knife. The males encouraged Maria to "shoot the bitch." One of the males threw a small packing crate at Felicia. Felicia was injured and became outraged. She thrust the knife at Maria, causing a chest wound. Maria fired the pistol multiple times in indiscriminate, angry retaliation.

Felicia died of gunshot-induced abdominal and head injuries. Maria was charged with manslaughter; she was adjudicated in the adult court and eventually received a sentence of 10 years in a female adult correctional center. The two male accomplices, Marcos, and other gang members were also charged with various offenses. The public court hearings were well attended by family members and outraged members of the community. The citizen demands for justice were no doubt part of the judicial deliberations. In such matters, the views of the community are often tainted by personal relationships, individual allegiances, and jaded perceptions. Maria's family members were present during her trial, but they were a very small voice compared to that of the families of the victim and the other gang members involved.

Unfortunately, no degree of judicial temperament or wisdom can ever really address the fundamental issues in such a situation. The fundamental purpose of the judicial system is to pursue justice and to impose consequences. The courts cannot begin to address the problem of family backgrounds, nor the conditions of the community that serve to foster and maintain youth gang activity. Other resources must address these prevention and treatment issues. When those resources do not exist, or are not effective, then tragedies such as those reflected in these case illustrations occur.

Maintaining Conditions and Difficulties in Intervention

The dynamics of violent juvenile crime are maintained by the presence or persistence of the etiological factors previously summarized in Table 5.3. Intervention difficulties are created by inadequate responsiveness by the juvenile justice system, insufficient intervention resources, or both. The most serious and most violent juvenile crimes are committed by a small proportion of offenders (e.g., see Wolfgang, 1958, 1978; Krisberg and Onek, 1995). Howell (1995, p. 5) summed up the situation by saying, "If we want to reduce the overall level of violence in society, we must successfully intervene in the lives of high-risk offenders, who commit about 75% of all violent juvenile offenses."

There is unanimity among experts that a basic problem in the effort to address adolescent violence is insufficient coordination of existing services and resources. Beyond that point of agreement, there is great diversity in thought about how to approach the problem. Some criminal justice experts call for radical initiatives within the justice system, while others cite the need for reform of the legal and penal systems. Melton and Pagliocca (1992) described research indicating that mere exposure to the adjudication process is not a very effective "socializing" experience for youngsters. Unless youngsters are actively involved in ongoing education about the judicial system, they do not learn from simple exposure to the juvenile court.

From a research vantage point, it is difficult to ascertain the impact of judicial sanctions vs. the impact of treatment interventions on delinquency. Particularly with violent offenders, there are usually multiple sanctions and interventions linked together over a period of time. There are often multiple service providers. Other empirical problems with assessing intervention efficacy occur because of differences across jurisdictions in policies and in available services. An inner-city juvenile court, for example, will have a different posture toward gang-involved, substance-abusing, violent juvenile offenders than will a judge in a small rural town.

Clinical Assessment of the Violent Juvenile Offender

Violent juvenile offenders are initially identified by the Juvenile Justice System and most often by police officers conducting initial investigations. As these youngsters traverse the juvenile system, many are referred to mental health resources for clinical assessment. A juvenile offender may have a history of offenses, none of which involve florid violence, but clinically, the circumstances implicate a troubled, angry youth. Substance abuse, for example, would significantly increase the clinical risk for such a juvenile offender (Deykin et al., 1987; Dembo et al., 1995). In a similar vein, youth gangs can maintain a socially acceptable "cover" while at the same time engaging in illegal activities. For example, the author was involved in the assessment of several youthful offenders who were members of the same gang. A police undercover operation found a component of the gang to be involved extensively in the sale of small firearms. Several months earlier, the same gang had been publicly recognized as a community group because its female membership sold the largest volume of Girl Scout cookies in the community. Staff working with juvenile offenders need to be trained properly and receive ongoing supervision; otherwise, they will be no match for the cunning, streetwise manipulations typical of this population.

Clinicians are occasionally asked by the juvenile bench to evaluate violent juvenile offenders on a pre-adjudication basis with regard to specific concerns. Such pre-adjudication concerns could include competency to stand trial (i.e., competency of the juvenile to participate in the adjudication process) and recommendations for interim placement (e.g., need for inpatient psychiatric care or need for detention in a juvenile center). The more typical requests for clinical assessment follow adjudication and a finding by a judge that a juvenile offender was "involved" in an offense. At this juncture, clinicians are asked to conduct clinical assessments to generate dispositional recommendations. Ideally, clinicians are provided with some direction as to the assessment issues. For example, there may be a need for a better understanding of an offender's aggressive behavior. Or, there could be a request for a family-based assessment to understand better the offender's background and to determine whether or not there is a reasonable expectation that the family can offer necessary structure and support to the offender.

Another frequent assessment question posed to clinicians is that of "dangerousness", a forensic concept. "Risk assessment" is a more appropriate clinical phrasing of the assessment issue. Assessing dangerousness and potential responsiveness to treatment is part of the treatment process with violent juvenile offenders (Henggeler et al., 1993; Litwack et al., 1993; Wiebush et al., 1995).

Compared to adult offenders, tracking juvenile offenders, particularly repeat juvenile offenders, is perhaps a more accurate process. This is attributable to several factors, such as the narrower age range of youthful offenders and a more sophisticated monitoring system for young offenders as compared to adult offenders, at least in most jurisdictions. It would seem that such data could be utilized to assess the potential for violent behavior with known offenders. Two measures frequently used by researchers to assess juvenile dangerousness are prior arrests for violent crimes and self-reports of violent behavior. Henggeler et al. (1993) conducted research to see if these two variables accurately indexed violent criminal behavior by juveniles. The findings failed to support predictive validity of the two measures utilized either individually or together. Clearly, we are in need of continued research to develop more meaningful assessment techniques and more valid assessment variables and combinations of variables (Monahan and Steadman, 1994).

In the meantime, clinicians must continue to respond to an unending flow of risk assessment requests from the juvenile courts. Risk assessment of the juvenile offender is an attempt to identify behavioral risk factors whereby the juvenile poses a serious or emergent threat to himself or herself or to others. Implicit in the request are the issues of whether or not the juvenile may become a threat in the future and what can be done to minimize any future threat. Also implicit in risk assessment of the juvenile offender is what level of restrictive placement is necessary to minimize risk. If there is a significant risk, then the juvenile bench seeks clinical recommendations both as to appropriate dispositional placement and long-term treatment goals.

The assessment of serious juvenile violence matters must follow the same stringent guidelines for conducting any meaningful forensic evaluation. The forensic clinician must be well grounded in the usual clinical skills. In addition, he or she must be well trained in the foundations of the judicial process, be familiar with pertinent case law precedents, understand principles of the admissibility of evidence, and be knowledgeable of the adversarial process. There must be a thorough and comprehensive effort to access pertinent records, including any relevant legal, medical, educational, mental health, and other documents. The clinical evaluation will ideally include a review of police investigation reports and witness and victim statements. The latter materials are useful because they are usually the records made closest in time to the occurrence of the offense. Needless to say, all evidentiary materials must be reviewed with a keen awareness that observer and witness accounts are subject to distortion and bias. Psychological testing may be an integral aspect of clinical/forensic evaluation. The usual ethical constraints of appropriate use of tests apply. Tests should be appropriately validated for the clinical issue at hand, and interpretations based on test findings should not extend beyond the limits of the particular instrument being utilized.

In most evaluations of violent juvenile offenders, an evaluation will not be complete without a conjoint family evaluation. The exceptions would be when family members are unwilling to participate or are otherwise unavailable, or when the bench requests assessment of a very specific issue (e.g., need for hospitalization, suicidality concerns, or substance-abuse history). In each of these excepted situations, the clinical report must qualify the limited nature of the assessment. In some circumstances, it may be possible to collaterally interview other gang members. In most instances, however, such an effort will be met with objections from defense attorneys that their client's rights will be placed in jeopardy by such conjoint assessment efforts. Clinical findings and recommendations should always stop short of going beyond the purpose and scope of the assessment. Recommendations must always acknowledge the competency limits of the clinical-forensic assessment process.

Intervention Guidelines With Violent Juvenile Offenders

From 1991 through 1993, the American Psychological Association (APA) convened a Commission on Youth and Violence. In a summary report of its findings and recommendations, the Commission concluded that youth violence was not random, uncontrollable, or inevitable. The Commission stressed that many interpersonal contacts to which a child was exposed have the potential for instilling aggressive proclivities. The Commission concluded that early and systematic intervention programs were essential to meaningfully address the problem of juvenile violence.

In a comprehensive review article addressing prevention and treatment issues with juvenile delinquency, Mulvey et al. (1993) concluded that interventions directed at juvenile delinquency must be broadly based and extend over long periods of time. The reviewers emphasized that there were significant methodological problems involved in the attempt to determine which interventions were truly effective with delinquency. Many studies have assessed the efficacy of different interventions with delinquency. Many more of these studies have professed to identify effective interventions. Still other researchers have suggested that no interventions are effective with delinquency or at least that effectiveness cannot be clearly demonstrated because of flaws in study design (e.g., Van Voorhis, 1987; Basta and Davidson, 1988).

The basic methodological predicament with delinquency studies is inconsistency in defining or establishing operational connections between delinquency and identified parameters. Our level of empirical sophistication is simply not such that we have clearly established any causal relationships (Mulvey et al., 1993; Justice, 1994; Brewer et al., 1995; Hawkins et al., 1995). It is not always clear if a given factor has a causal relationship with delinquency. Therefore, it is not clear whether controlling or manipulating that factor has any impact on delinquency. For example, does dropping out of school, substance abuse, or gang involvement really increase the risk for delinquency? Alternatively, is the risk for delinquency related to a combination of all three factors, or is it related to an entirely different set of factors. These concerns, of course, are not unique to delinquency studies.

The literature contains many proposed systems for classifying juvenile delinquency interventions. For the sake of simplicity, we have adopted a four-category arrangement of types of interventions. These four categories are as follows: (1) prevention, (2) diversion strategies, (3) treatment and correctional interventions, and (4) monitoring and follow-up strategies. These categories offer a simple, albeit somewhat artificial, means of grouping the spectrum of initiatives.

Prevention Models

The basic notion of primary prevention comes from public health models of disease control and prevention. The goal of primary prevention is to identify individual and environmental risk factors before a problem occurs. Formal prevention programs designed to address the needs of at-risk children have been operational since the turn of the century. The CCJJDP (1996a,b) estimated that it now costs between $34,000 and $65,000 per year to incarcerate one juvenile defendant. The estimated cost to taxpayers for the rehabilitation of a single young adult's criminal career is $1.1 million (CCJJDP). These numbers do not even begin to account for indirect costs to victims and consumers. In comparison, it now costs $4300 per year for a single at-risk youngster to attend a Head Start school readiness program. To the extent prevention measures are effective, the benefits of redirecting the lives of at-risk youngsters are inestimable.

The most basic forms of delinquency prevention initiatives are an array of prenatal, natal, and perinatal education programs for disadvantaged and at-risk parents, designed to address a multitude of problems. Prevention programs designed to reduce infant malnutrition, teenage pregnancy, parental substance abuse, and domestic abuse probably all contribute to a reduction in later violent behavior by children and adolescents (Hawkins and Weis, 1985).

Delinquency-prevention models employing parent education and parent training approaches are widely available. Different models use various combinations of didactic and experiential approaches, but a common strategy is to meet with small groups of parents with shared interests. The group bonding that takes place among the participants is believed to enhance the willingness of individual parents to adopt new parenting styles.

Early intervention programs target youngsters at risk for delinquency. The intervention is offered long before delinquency may occur. Thus, in terms of measuring outcome, the strength of these programs is at the same time their major research weakness. For this reason, Mulvey et al. (1993, p. 138) suggested that "these programs should probably be thought of as an effort to increase family resiliency to a variety of possible negative outcomes in their children (e.g., mental health problems) rather than a preventive effort focused solely on delinquency prevention."

The nuclear family must be a vital focus of prevention initiatives with juvenile delinquency and juvenile violence. Prevention efforts at the family level, however, are a sensitive endeavor. Such work will often be viewed as intrusive and also as prematurely labeling family situations as high risk. Additionally, cultural, ethnic, and religious prejudices can become confounded by one's intent to be helpful.

One effective prevention approach with juvenile crime has been the establishment of community-wide curfew hours for juveniles. Snyder et al. (1996) reported that curfew restrictions did reduce the incidence of juvenile crime but that the impact was not dramatic. The authors also noted that curfew efforts paradoxically appeared to increase some types of serious juvenile crime. For example, when a curfew resulted in youngsters being confined in troubled family circumstances, there was evidence of an increase in family member victimization. According to Snyder et al., juvenile crime peaked daily between 2 p.m. and 4 p.m. and then steadily declined throughout the evening hours. One of five incidents of all violent juvenile crime occurred between 2 p.m. and 6 p.m. on school days.

Another relatively new prevention model involves providing critically troubled families with short-term but intensive services. The Intensive Family Preservation Services (IFPS) model was designed as a prevention strategy, but IFPS is most appropriately regarded as a hybrid of prevention and treatment (Brewer et al., 1995). This designation is appropriate because the intended consumers of IFPS are families which are already experiencing problems. IFPS intervenes swiftly and intensively to prevent an at-risk child or adolescent family member from being removed from the family. Removal of a youngster from his or her home usually entails placement in a special-needs residential program. Such programs are very expensive and often are not available locally. As a result, these youngsters require out-of-local jurisdiction placement. In addition to the expense, such non-local placement hampers the family's involvement in treatment.

The academic setting provides a second level for much-heralded prevention programming for at-risk youth. School programs offer specialized classroom formats (e.g., Head Start; see Haskins, 1989, and Rosen, 1993), preschool (Schweinhart, 1987), and also various behavior management interventions. Studies have reviewed the impact of these specialized programs on school attendance, academic performance, and school vandalism; the findings have reflected varying degrees of success.

Engaging students in school governance is another delinquency prevention strategy. The intent is to instill leadership and mature social values in youngsters. Recent derivations of this model are designed to teach anger management and conflict resolution skills (Eggert, 1994). These approaches include violence prevention curricula, peer-based mediation, and peer-counseling models. These programs attempt to engage students directly in problem-solving and mediation skills through a variety of cognitive-behavioral techniques.

Teen Court programs are another recent approach designed to teach the application of principles of justice to youth by direct involvement in the judicial process (Godwin, 1996). Brewer et al. (1995, p. 73) reported that, "Relative to comparison students, experimental students improved significantly in their empathy, interpersonal problem solving, anger management, and behavioral social skills as measured by hypothetical social conflict situations." These approaches may be utilized as prevention efforts but are also useful with offenders. Unique to these approaches is that their design is rooted in the theoretical dynamics of antisocial behavior (Mulvey et al., 1993).

Many community youth programs are designed to provide prevention programming for at-risk youth. These programs are sponsored by many national youth organizations, local government entities, and independent agencies. Examples are programs offered by the National 4-H Club, Scouts of America, local recreation departments, and Young Men's Christian Associations (YMCAs). Other examples of community delinquency prevention programs include neighborhood watch programs and youth citizen patrols, such as the Guardian Angels.

Spergel and his associates (1993) conducted nationwide assessments of prevention approaches directed at street gang violence. They reported that respondents from large cities with significant gang activity felt that providing youth opportunities (e.g., job finding, remedial education, and structured recreational programs) was the most effective prevention strategy. The next most effective strategies were community organization approaches designed to address the problem of gang crime. In jurisdictions where the gang problem was perceived as "emerging", community organization alternatives were deemed the most effective strategy. Suppression strategies involving increased law-enforcement activity were judged as less effective, except when used in conjunction with other approaches.

Diversion Strategies

Diversion is a legal/correctional term that refers to procedures that attempt to divert a juvenile offender into a structured program that will avoid placement in a juvenile detention or correctional facility. According to the public health prevention model, diversion is secondary prevention. Secondary prevention is the identification of an early-stage disease (i.e., delinquency) and intervention at an opportune time to prevent the problem from escalating.

Diversion programs for delinquents offer community-based intervention and treatment. Diversion is more effective than residential placement. Juvenile court disposition data reflect a current trend to attempt to place violent juvenile offenders in highly structured, well-supervised, community-based programs as opposed to juvenile correctional settings (Krisberg et al., 1995). Maintaining a juvenile offender with his or her family of origin offers greater likelihood of a positive response to treatment. In turn, there is also a greater likelihood of long-term benefit from treatment. Diversion of a delinquent youth into a community-based program can avoid weeks or months of resistance because the delinquent, his or her family members, or a combination, are angry at the "system" for removing the offender from the community. A significant motivation with diversion is the desire of the delinquent to avoid detention. Such coercive motivation may not be as humanistic as self-motivation but can be just as effective. Diversion is not always a viable strategy with juvenile offenders who have committed serious offenses. Juveniles with serious/chronic offense histories always present with risk for reoffending. Although our ability to predict reoffending is less than empirically based, the concern for public safety is always an overriding consideration with violent juvenile crime.

Depending on jurisdictional procedures, juvenile offenders are diverted into specialized programs. In some jurisdictions, diversion occurs before offenders are referred to the juvenile court. Examples of diversion efforts include outpatient substance abuse education and treatment programs, specialized programs for juvenile arsonists or juvenile sexual offenders, and programs whereby delinquents visit adult correctional facilities and meet face-to-face with adult inmates. Diversion is a vital strategy in helping to channel early delinquent youth to appropriate resources. Diversion serves to disrupt the cycle of offenders evolving into a pattern of seriously aggressive behavior. Diversion is most useful with younger delinquents and with those who do not already have an entrenched pattern of antisocial behavior.

The adjudication and disposition of juvenile gang members who are responsible for crimes are addressed on an individual basis in the juvenile court. Disposition, therefore, never results in a gang as a unit being referred into stipulated treatment. This may be an area for future exploration. Perhaps mechanisms could be developed to refer gangs, or at least components of gangs, to specialized programs. Youth gang crime is complex social behavior which, in most instances, will not be responsive to crisis or short-term intervention. Rehabilitation efforts with gang-involved youth and their families will require long-term treatment with skilled, well-trained clinicians.

Beginning in the early 1970s and continuing to the present, there have been numerous diversion initiatives specifically designed for serious and chronic juvenile offenders (Krisberg et al., 1995). In 1993, OJJDP awarded a competitive grant to the National Council on Crime and Delinquency (NCCD), which conducted an extensive search of prevention and intervention programs designed for juvenile offenders with serious, violent, or chronic histories. One initial observation by NCCD was the lack of consistent intervention with juvenile offenders following their immediate contact with police. This is a critical juncture in the juvenile justice system process; NCCD recommended a national effort to develop consistent procedures following initial police intervention with violent juvenile offenders.

The violent offender intervention programs deemed promising by NCCD all employed some form of graduated sanctions. A basic assumption with the graduated sanctions model is that community-based intervention models are more effective than placement in traditional correctional centers. Krisberg et al. (1995) concluded that although research on the graduated sanctions approach was limited, it was possible to draw some meaningful conclusions. Graduated sanctions programs in the community appear to be at least as successful as traditional incarceration in reducing recidivism. More intensive and better-structured graduated sanctions programs appear to be more effective than placement in correctional facilities. Another important consideration is that community-based graduated sanctions programs are usually significantly less costly than their traditional counterparts.

Acknowledging that no single schema would be satisfactory to everyone, OJJDP (Wilson and Howell, 1993) adopted a four-tiered level of graduated sanctions as follows:

1. Intermediate sanctions within the community for first-time, nonviolent offenders
2. Intermediate sanctions within the community for more serious offenders
3. Secure care programs for the most violent offenders
4. Aftercare programs that provide high levels of social control and treatment services

The purpose of a continuum of care approach is to permit movement of violent juvenile offenders through the sanction levels in a manner that optimizes exposure to needed services, while affording protection for the community. The primary drawback of the proposed model is that many jurisdictions have gaps in available services, such that a graduated continuum is not feasible.

The intervention programs deemed promising by NCCD varied in points of emphasis. One model, for example, offered an initial intensive, month-long assessment process. This intensive assessment allowed sufficient time for caseworkers to sift through the background circumstances of each offender and then coordinate a plan of appropriate interventions. Another approach, called Project Care, utilized citizen volunteers who had been screened by juvenile probation officers. The citizen volunteers worked in committee settings as well as in one-on-one settings with juvenile defendants and their parents. The goals of Project Care were to develop intervention plans, make recommendations to the juvenile bench, and assess services for juveniles on probation. Other models have featured interventions completely outside the juvenile justice system. Still other models have provided intensive case management and, for example, required daily contact between the offender and the supervising juvenile services case worker. The latter approach was used primarily with early offenders judged at-risk for becoming serious or chronic offenders (Krisberg et al., 1995).

Residential Treatment and Correctional Facility Interventions

Residential treatment and correctional facility interventions are particularly relevant with violent juvenile perpetrators. Although not primary or secondary prevention, correctional and treatment interventions offer tertiary prevention impact (DeFazio and Warford, 1993). That is, it is hoped that placement of youngsters in residential or correctional programs will benefit some of them so that recidivism is reduced. According to 1992 Juvenile Court data, detention occurred in 24% of person offense cases, 17% of property offense cases, and 35% of drug offense cases (Butts, 1994).

Between 1988 and 1994, there was a 68% increase in the number of requests for juvenile offenders to be transferred to adult court systems (Butts, 1994). Transfer to the adult court is prompted by the seriousness of the offense (e.g., murder, armed robbery, and rape) and consideration of the delinquent's amenability to juvenile system resources.

Juveniles were adjudicated in more than half (57%) of the 743,700 cases in 1992. Adjudication resulted in the majority of the juveniles being placed on formal probation. Twenty eight percent of the juveniles were placed out of the home in residential facilities, and 11% received other dispositions (Butts, 1994). Cases not adjudicated by the juvenile court (43% in 1992) are usually dismissed because of a lack of sufficient evidence.

An incident of violent crime requires decisive intervention to protect public safety. In some instances, there is a need to intervene to provide protection for an out-of-control, offending juvenile. The delinquent may be out of control because of anger, substance abuse, a psychiatric condition, or some combination thereof. The long-term goal is to offer the juvenile perpetrator the opportunity for rehabilitation (Cellini, 1994). The APA Commission on Youth and Violence (1993, p. 59) observed: "By the time youth with antisocial behavior are referred clinically, their dysfunction often is pervasive and severe, and multiple counter influences need to be brought to bear to achieve significant impact."

Professionals working with violent juvenile offenders must learn to contend with their characteristic capacity to be charming and, at the same time, deceitful. Many violent juvenile offenders present with a street-honed ability to be cunning and conniving. These qualities are encouraged and maintained by gang involvement. Such youngsters can be impressively creative in their efforts to manipulate caretakers and treatment providers.

Programs for serious and chronic juvenile offenders are not popular initiatives when it comes to funding. It is largely because of inadequate funding that programming for violent juvenile offenders in correctional settings is primarily homogenous in nature. Historically, correctional facilities have provided little more than "warehousing" of violent juvenile offenders (Mulvey et al., 1993). There is also the inevitable problem of bonding among juvenile offenders in correctional facilities, which can only serve to exacerbate any proclivity for violent behavior. Krisberg et al. (1995) reported that the most effective secure corrections programs capped the number of detainees and allowed only a small number of participants. These programs also provided individualized services. The authors stated that "large training school" facilities have not proven to be effective in rehabilitating juvenile offenders (Krisberg et al., 1995).

The NCCD study also found that one singularly effective approach utilized by secure correctional settings was a behavior modification system of rewards and sanctions. The behavior modification strategies were most effective when the avenues for achievement were visible and realistic. Effective programs also offered cognitive-behavioral models that addressed management of hostility and aggression; a key aspect of these programs was well-trained staff (Krisberg et al., 1995).

Monitoring and Follow-Up Strategies

Monitoring the status of adjudicated delinquents usually occurs throughout the course of the stipulated probation. Appropriate long-term monitoring of violent juvenile offenders is a vital aspect of the treatment process, although such monitoring significantly increases intervention costs. Juvenile courts vary in their willingness to establish periods of probation that will coincide with recommended lengths of treatment. Although some clinicians, usually those with a humanistic orientation, resist the coercive element of court sanctions as part of the treatment process, stipulated involvement in treatment is essential with violent offenders. Civil rights activists also complain of infringement on the rights of juveniles. Depending on the provisions of local statutes, the jurisdiction of the Juvenile Court typically expires when the juvenile reaches the age of majority. Some jurisdictions allow for continued jurisdiction of the Juvenile Court until the juvenile is 21 years old, if deemed necessary.

The Reader and the Problem of Violent Juvenile Crime

If there is a single theme that permeates the juvenile delinquency literature, it is that any meaningful effort to address the problem must be multi-dimensional

(Rosenfeld and Decker, 1993; National Council of Juvenile and Family Court Judges, 1994; Borduin et al., 1995; Henggeler, 1996). Studies have also consistently indicated that prevention and intervention initiatives must occur at the community level (Schwab-Stone et al., 1995). These two recommended approaches are invitations for lay-person involvement in addressing the problems.

The Coordinating Council on Juvenile Justice and Delinquency Prevention (1996a) surveyed a large volume of studies addressing the problem of delinquency. Based on these data, CCJJDP proposed an Action Plan. The Action Plan framed the fight against juvenile violence with eight objectives that can be organized at the federal and state levels. These initiatives can then be implemented at the local community level. The Action Plan recommendations were based on research and program evaluations that have been demonstrated to be effective with juvenile crime. The Action Plan emphasized the need for multi-disciplinary assessment teams and centers. These facilities are envisioned as bringing together in a single place a broad range of juvenile service workers that would include intake, probation, and parole workers from youth service agencies, as well as workers from education, social services, and mental health. These teams or centers would accurately identify the sentencing, treatment, and rehabilitative needs of each juvenile defendant. The Action Plan's eight objectives incorporate many of the points made thus far in this chapter. As a whole, the objectives provide a focus for mobilizing prevention and intervention strategies. The eight objectives are as follows (CCJJDP, 1996a, p. 3):

1. Provide immediate intervention and appropriate sanctions and treatment for delinquent juveniles.
2. Prosecute certain serious, violent, and chronic juvenile offenders in criminal court.
3. Reduce youth involvement with guns, drugs, and gangs.
4. Provide opportunities for children and youth.
5. Break the cycle of violence by addressing youth victimization, abuse, and neglect.
6. Strengthen and mobilize communities.
7. Support the development of innovative approaches to research and evaluation.
8. Implement an aggressive public outreach campaign on effective strategies to combat juvenile violence.

Summary

Approximately half of all violent juvenile crime is committed by individual perpetrators. Nonetheless, the phenomenon of violent juvenile crime cannot be divorced from the broad web of juvenile gang involvement. Violent crimes committed by individual youths and by juvenile gangs are the result of a complex pattern of aggressive behavior, the seeds of which begin in early development. Juvenile violence usually flows from an explicit progression of aggressive behavior. Therefore, early identifications of aggressive behavior and involvement in gang activity are critical steps in effective prevention of violent juvenile crime. If early identification is followed by well-planned, comprehensive intervention, data are encouraging that the cycle of aggressive behavior by youths and youth gangs can be interrupted.

Studies have identified key areas of etiological and sustaining factors of violent juvenile crime. These include a wide array of family and community problems, substance abuse, weapon possession, and, of utmost importance, gang involvement. These risk factors have evolved from societal changes that have occurred in the last 20 to 30 years. The factors have had a profound impact on the identity and role of our nation's youth.

The scope and impact of violent juvenile crime are almost overwhelming, but there are multiple initiatives underway to address the problem. FBI arrest statistics show that beginning in late 1994 and continuing through early 1996, the rate of all violent crime was on a downward trend for the first time since the early 1980s. This downward trend has included violent crimes perpetrated by juveniles.

The ultimate response to juvenile gang violence will probably require reconfiguring of the family's role in contemporary life. It is perhaps unrealistic to expect that the role of the family of 30 to 60 years ago is still relevant today. However, families remain the developmental nurseries of the minds and personalities of today's youth. We cannot afford to underestimate the vital role of the family in the genesis of troubled youth and youth vulnerability to gang activity. The response to violent juvenile gang behavior must be a multi-dimensional effort that focuses on the roles of the family and the community as etiological factors. The process must involve partnerships at many levels beginning with the family and the community and extending to the police and the juvenile courts. From there, the entire juvenile justice system must work effectively with an extensive network of community resources and professionals from varied disciplines. There is an impressive existing database that documents the magnitude of the violent juvenile crime problem. We understand many of the etiological and sustaining factors of violent juvenile crime. While there is an unending need to explore and develop new intervention approaches, there are effective resources at hand. Now there must be a committed and sustained effort to employ those resources to prevent and combat the problem of violent juvenile crime.

Annotated Bibliography

1. Howell, J.C., Ed. (1995) *Guide for Implementing the Comprehensive Strategy for Serious, Violent and Chronic Juvenile Offenders.* Washington, D.C.: Office of Juvenile Justice and Delinquency Prevention. This readily available document contains very contemporary "best practice" information regarding the problem of serious juvenile crime. A comprehensive technical report, the document is an invaluable resource for researchers. The intervention approach is based on risk assessment combined with a model of graduated sanctions.

2. Mulvey, E.P., Arthur, M.W., and Reppucci, N.D., (1993) The prevention and treatment of juvenile delinquency: a review of the research. *Clinical Psychology Review, 13*, 133–167. This recent and comprehensive review article addresses juvenile delinquency prevention and research. The topic of juvenile delinquency has generated a large research base, but that research has not always adhered to rigorous empirical standards. The authors are very attuned to this problem and attempt to focus on empirically based research findings. This is a thorough, well-referenced article. The critical review of the research is balanced and thoughtfully presented.

3. Snyder, H.N. and Sickmund, M. (1995) *Juvenile Offenders and Victims: A National Report.* Washington, D.C.: Office of Juvenile Justice and Delinquency Prevention. This technical report underwent a second printing in 1996. The authors designed the report as a series of briefing papers. Several sections provide statistics and demographics in a variety of key areas regarding delinquency. This is a comprehensive report wherein the reader can pick and choose from selected areas of interest. The report represents one of the best single resources regarding delinquency that was currently available. If the interested reader were to be directed to any single resource regarding the topic of delinquency, this would be it.

References

American Psychological Association (1993) *Violence and Youth: Psychology's Response*. Washington, D.C.: (author).

Basta, J.M. and Davidson, W.S. (1988) Treatment of juvenile offenders: study outcomes since 1980. *Behavioral Sciences and the Law, 6*, 355–384.

Bohman, M. (1978) Some genetic aspects of alcoholism and criminality. *Archives of General Psychiatry, 35*, 269–276.

Borduin, C.M., Mann, B.J., Cone, L.T., Henggeler, S.W., Fucci, B.R., Blaske, D.M., and Williams, R.A. (1995) Multisystemic treatment of serious juvenile offenders: long-term prevention of criminality and violence. *Journal of Consulting Psychology, 63*(4), 569–578.

Brewer, D.D., Hawkins, J.D., Catalano, R.F., and Neckerman, H.C. (1995) Preventing serious, violent, and chronic delinquency and crime. Childhood, adolescence and the community. In J.C. Howell (Ed.), *Guide for Implementing the Comprehensive Strategy for Serious, Violent, and Chronic Juvenile Offenders*, pp. 61–131. Washington, D.C.: Office of Juvenile Justice and Delinquency Prevention.

Brickman, A., McManus, M., Grapentine, W.J., and Alessi, N. (1984) Neuropsychological assessment of seriously delinquent adolescents. *Journal of the American Academy of Child and Adolescent Psychiatry, 23*, 453–467.

Broder, B.K., Dunivant, N., and Smith, E.C. (1981) Further observation on the link between disability and juvenile delinquency. *Journal of Education Psychology, 43*, 838–850.

Brook, J.S., Brook, D.W., Gordon, A.S., Whiteman, M., and Cohen, P. (1990) The psycho social etiology of adolescent drug use: a functional interactional approach. *Genetic, Social and General Psychology Monographs, 116*(2), 20.

Busch, K.G., Zager, R., Hughes, J.R., Arbit, J., and Russell, R. (1990) Adolescents who kill. *Journal of Clinical Psychology, 46*(4), 473–485.

Butts, J.A. (1994) *Delinquency Cases in Juvenile Court*, Fact Sheet # 18. Washington, D.C.: Office of Juvenile Justice and Delinquency Prevention.

Butts, J., Snyder, H.S., Finnegan, T.A., Aughenbaugh, A.L., and Poole, R.S. (1996) *Juvenile Court Statistics 1993*, Statistics Report. Washington, D.C.: Office of Juvenile Justice and Delinquency Prevention.

Cellini, H.R. (1994) Management and treatment of institutionalized violent juveniles. *Corrections Today, 56*(4), 100–102.

Cooley-Quille, M.R., Turner, S.M., and Beidel, D.C. (1995) Emotional impact of children's exposure to community violence. *Journal of the American Academy of Child and Adolescent Psychiatry, 34*(10), 1362–1368.

Coordinating Council on Juvenile Justice and Delinquency Prevention (1996a) *Combating Violence and Delinquency: The National Juvenile Justice Action Plan.* Washington, D.C.: Office of Juvenile Justice and Delinquency Prevention.

Coordinating Council on Juvenile Justice and Delinquency Prevention (1996b) *Combating Violence and Delinquency: The National Juvenile Justice Action Plan Summary.* Washington, D.C.: Office of Juvenile Justice and Delinquency Prevention.

Curry, D.G., Ball, R.A., and Fox, R.J. (1994) *Gang Crime and Law Enforcement Record Keeping,* Research in Brief Series, NCJ 148345. Washington, D.C.: National Institute of Justice.

DeFazio, T.M. and Warford, R.G. (1993) Violence prevention programming within juvenile detention. Part 2. Violence experience survey. *Journal for Juvenile Justice and Detention Services, 8*(1), 9–18.

Dembo, R., Turner, G., Sue, C.C., Schmeidler, J., Borden, P., and Manning, D. (1995) Predictors of recidivism to a juvenile assessment center. *International Journal of Addiction, 30*(11), 1425–1452.

Deykin, E.Y., Levy, J.C., and Wells, V. (1987) Adolescent depression, alcohol and drug abuse. *American Journal of Public Health, 77*, 178–181.

Duncan, J.W. and Duncan, G.M. (1971) Murder in the family: a study of some homicidal adolescents. *Journal of Psychiatry, 127*, 1498–1502.

DuRant, R.H., Getts, A., Cadenhead, C., Emans, S.J., and Woods, E.R. (1995) Exposure to violence and victimization and depression, hopelessness, and purpose in life among adolescents living in and around public housing. *Journal of Developmental Behavior in Pediatrics, 16*(4), 233–237.

Easson, W.M. and Steenhilber, R.M. (1961) Murderous aggression by children and adolescents. *Archives of General Psychiatry, 4*, 27–35.

Eggert, L.L. (1994) *Anger Management for Youth: Stemming Aggression and Violence*. Bloomington, IN: National Education Service.

Elliot, D.S., Huizinga, D., and Menard, S. (1989) *Multiple Problem Youth: Delinquency, Substance Abuse and Mental Health Problems*. New York: Springer-Verlag.

Federal Bureau of Investigation (1992) *Crime in the United States 1991*. Washington, D.C.: U.S. Government Printing Office.

Federal Bureau of Investigation (1993) *Crime in the United States 1992*. Washington, D.C.: U.S. Government Printing Office.

Federal Bureau of Investigation (1994) *Crime in the United States 1993*. Washington, D.C.: U.S. Government Printing Office.

Federal Bureau of Investigation (1995) *Crime in the United States 1994*. Washington, D.C.: U.S. Government Printing Office.

Federal Bureau of Investigation (1996a) *Crime in the United States, 1995*. Washington, D.C.: (author).

Federal Bureau of Investigation (1996b, May) *Uniform Crime Reports, 1995 Preliminary Annual Release*. Washington, D.C.: (author).

Federal Bureau of Investigation (1996c) Uniform Crime Reporting Program Press Release, October 13. Washington, D.C.: (author).

Federal Bureau of Investigation (1997a, February) *Violent Offense Arrests by Age, 1970–95*. Washington, D.C.: (author).

Federal Bureau of Investigation (1997b) *Preliminary Uniform Crime Report*. Washington, D.C.: (author).

Garrett, D. (1995) Violent behaviors among African-American adolescents. *Adolescence, 30*(117), 209–216.

Godwin, T.M. (1996) *A Guide for Implementing Teen Court Programs*, Fact Sheet # 45. Washington, D.C.: Office of Juvenile Justice and Delinquency Prevention.

Goodwin, D.W. (1985) Alcoholism and genetics: the sins of our fathers. *Archives of General Psychiatry, 42*, 171–174.

Hall, H.V. (1996) Overview of lethal violence. In H.V. Hall (Ed.), *Lethal Violence 2000: A Sourcebook on Fatal Domestic, Acquaintance and Stranger Aggression*, pp. 1–51. Kamuela, HI: Pacific Institute for the Study of Conflict and Aggression.

Haskins, R. (1989) Beyond metaphor: the efficacy of early childhood education. *American Psychologist, 44*, 274–282.

Hawkins, J.D., Catalano, R.F., and Brewer, D.D. (1995) Preventing serious, violent, and chronic juvenile offending: effective strategies from conception to age 6. In J.C. Howell (Ed.), *Guide for Implementing the Comprehensive Strategy for Serious, Violent, and Chronic Juvenile Offenders*, pp. 57–60. Washington, D.C.: Office of Juvenile Justice and Delinquency Prevention.

Hawkins, J.D., Lishner, D.M., Jenson, J.M., and Catalano, R.F. (1987) Delinquents and drugs: what the evidence suggests about treatment and prevention. In B.S. Brown and A.R. Mills (Eds.), *Youth at High Risk for Substance Abuse*, DHHS Publication No. ADM. 97-1537.

Hawkins, J.D. and Weis, J.G. (1985) The social development model: an integrated approach to delinquency prevention. *Journal of Primary Prevention*, (6), 20.

Henggeler, S. (1996) Treatment of violent juvenile offenders — we have the knowledge: comment on Gorman-Smith et al. (1996) *Journal of Family Psychology, 10*(2), 137–141.

Henggeler, S., Melton, G.B., Smith, L., Foster, S., Hanley, J., and Hutchinson, C.M. (1993) Assessing violent offending in serious juvenile offenders. *Journal of Abnormal Child Psychology, 21*(3), 233–243.

Howell, J.C. (1994) *Gangs*, Fact Sheet #12. Washington, D.C.: U.S. Department of Justice, National Institute of Justice.

Howell, J.C., Ed. (1995) *Guide for Implementing the Comprehensive Strategy for Serious, Violent, and Chronic Juvenile Offenders*. Washington, D.C.: Office of Juvenile Justice and Delinquency Prevention.

Hurwitz, I., Bibace, R.M., Wolff, P.H., and Rowbotham, B.M. (1972) Neuropsychological function in normal boys, delinquent boys, and boys with learning problems. *Perceptual and Motor Skills, 356*, 387–394.

Hutson, H.R., Anglin, D., Kyriacou, D., Hart, J., and Spears, K. (1994a) The epidemic of gang-related homicides in Los Angeles County from 1979 through 1994. *Journal of the American Medical Association, 274*(3), 1031–1036.

Hutson, H.R., Anglin, D., Mallon, W., and Pratts, M.J. (1994b) Caught in the crossfire of gang violence: small children. *Journal of Emergency Medicine, 12*(3), 385–388.

Hutson, H., Anglin, D., and Spears, K. (1995) The perspectives of violent street gang injuries. *Neurosurgery Clinics of North America, 6*(4), 621–628.

Johnson, C., Webster, B., and Connors, E. (1995) *Prosecuting Gangs: A National Sssessment*, NIJ Research in Brief Series, NCJ 151785. Washington, D.C.: U.S. Department of Justice, National Institute of Justice.

Justice, B. (1994) Making behavioral change the outcome measure in research on violence. *Psychology Reports, 75*(3, pt. 1), 1202.

Karniski, W., Levine, M.D., Clarke, S., Palfrey, J.S., and Meltzer, L.J. (1982) A study of neurodevelopmental findings in early adolescent delinquents. *Journal of Adolescent Health Care, 3*, 151–159.

Krisberg, B., Currie, E., and Onek, D. (1995) Graduated sanctions for serious, violent, and chronic juvenile offenders. In J.C. Howell (Ed.), *Guide for Implementing the Comprehensive Strategy for Serious, Violent, and Chronic Juvenile Offenders*, pp. 133–187. Washington, D.C.: Office of Juvenile Justice and Delinquency Prevention.

Krisberg, B. and Onek, D. (1995) A blueprint for implementing the comprehensive strategy for serious, violent, and chronic juvenile offenders. In J.C. Howell (Ed.), *Guide for Implementing the Comprehensive Strategy for Serious, Violent, and Chronic Juvenile Offenders*, pp. 17–55. Washington, D.C.: Office of Juvenile Justice and Delinquency Prevention.

Lewis, D.O., Moy, E., Jackson, L.D., Aaronson, R., Ritvo, U., Settu, S., and Simons, A. (1985) Biopsychosocial characteristics of children who later murder: a prospective study. *American Journal of Psychiatry, 142*, 1161–1166.

Lewis, D.O., Pincus, J.H., Bard, B., Richardson, E., Prichep, L.S., Feldman, M., and Yeager, C. (1988) Neuropsychiatric, psycho educational, and family characteristics of 14 juveniles condemned to death in the United States. *American Journal of Psychiatry, 145*, 584–589.

Lewis, D., Shanok, S.S., and Balla, D.C. (1979) Perinatal difficulties, head and face trauma and child abuse in the medical histories of serious delinquent children. *American Journal of Psychiatry, 146*, 419–423.

Litwack, T.R., Kirschner, S., and Wack, R. (1993) The assessment of dangerousness and predictions of violence: recent research and future prospects. *Psychiatric Quarterly, 64*(3), 245–273.

Loeber, R. and Dishion, T.J. (1984) Boys who fight at home and school: family condition influencing cross-setting consistency. *Journal of Consulting and Clinical Psychology, 52*(5), 759–768.

Maxson, C.L., Woods, K.J., and Klein, M.W. (1996) Street gang migration: how big a threat? *National Institute of Justice Journal,* February, 26-31.

Melton, E.P. and Pagliocca, P.M. (1992) Treatment in the juvenile justice system: directions for policy and practice. In J.J. Cocozza (Ed.), *Responding to the Mental Health Needs of Youth in the Juvenile Justice System*, pp. 107–139. Miami, FL: The National Coalition for the Mentally Ill in the Criminal Justice System.

Miller, W.B. (1982) *Crime by Youth Gangs and Groups in the United States*. Washington, D.C.: National Institute of Juvenile Justice and Delinquency Prevention

Monahan, J. and Steadman, H., Eds. (1994) *Violence and Mental Disorder: Developments in Risk Assessment.* Chicago: University of Chicago Press.

Moore, J.P. (1997) *Highlights of the 1995 National Youth Gang Survey,* Fact Sheet #63. Washington, D.C.: Office of Juvenile Justice and Delinquency Prevention.

Mulvey, E.P., Arthur, M.W., and Reppucci, N.D. (1993) The prevention and treatment of juvenile delinquency: a review of the research. *Clinical Psychology Review, 13*, 133–167.

Myers, W., Scott, K., Burgess, A.W., and Burgess, A.G. (1995) Psychopathology, biopsychosocial factors, crime characteristics, and classification of 25 homicidal youths. *Journal of the American Academy of Child and Adolescent Psychiatry, 34*(11), 1483–1489.

National Council of Juvenile and Family Court Judges (1994) *Where We Stand: An Action Plan for Dealing with Violent Juvenile Crime*. Reno, NV: (author).

Offord, D.R., Allen, N., and Abrams, N. (1975) Parental psychiatric illness, broken homes and delinquency. *Journal of American Academy of Child and Adolescent Psychiatry, 17*, 224–238.

Oliver, M. (1995) *Gangs: Trouble in the Streets*. Springfield, NJ: Enslow.

Osgood, D.W. (1995) *Drugs, Alcohol and Adolescent Violence*, Paper No. 2, F-1077. Boulder, CO: University of Chicago Institute of Behavioral Science Center for the Study and Prevention of Violence.

Ounsted, C. (1969) Aggression and epilepsy, rage in children with temporal lobe epilepsy. *Psychosomatic Research, 13*, 2237–2242.

Peterson, P., Hawkins J.D., Abbott, R.D., and Catalano, R.F. (1994) Disentangling the effects of parental drinking, family management, and parental alcohol norms on current drinking by black and white adolescents. *Journal of Research on Adolescents, 4*(2), 203–227.

Pontius, A. (1982) Neurological aspects of some types of delinquency, especially in juveniles. *Adolescence, 7*, 289–308.

Rivara, F.P., Shepard, J.P., Farrington, D.P., Richmond, P.W., and Cannon, P. (1995) Victim as offender in youth violence. *Annals of Emergency Medicine, 26*(5), 609–614.

Rosen, T. (1993) Violence prevention: the newest challenge, *School Safety, 3,* 9–12.

Rosenfeld, R. and Decker, S. (1993) Where public health and law enforcement meet: monitoring and preventing youth violence. *American Journal of Police, 12*(3), 11–57.

Ryan, M., Leighton, T., Pianim, N., Klein, S., and Bongard, F. (1993) Medical and economic consequences of gang-related shootings. *American Surgery, 59*(12), 831–833.

Satterfield, J.H., Hoppe, C.M., and Schell, A.M. (1982) A prospective study of delinquency in 110 adolescent boys with attention deficit disorder and 88 normal boys. *American Journal of Psychiatry, 139*, 795–427.

Scalia, J. (1997) *Juvenile Delinquents in the Federal Criminal Justice System*, Special Report NCJ-163066, Bureau of Justice Statistics. Washington, D.C.: U.S. Department of Justice, Office of Justice Programs.

Schwab-Stone, M., Ayers, T., Kasprow, W., and Voyce, C. (1995) No safe haven: a study of violence exposure in the urban community. *Journal of the American Academy of Child and Adolescent Psychiatry, 34*(10), 1343–1352.

Schweinhart, I.J. (1987) Can preschool programs help prevent delinquency? In J.Q. Wilson and G.C. Loury (Eds.), *From Children to Citizens. Vol. III. Families, Schools and Delinquency Prevention*, pp. 135–153. New York: Springer-Verlag.

Sigler, R.T. (1995) Gang violence. *Journal of Health Care for the Poor and the Underserved, 6*(2), 198–203.

Singer, M.I., Anglin, T.M., Song, L.Y., and Lunghofer, L. (1995) Adolescents' exposure to violence and associated symptoms of psychological trauma. *Journal of the American Medical Association, 273*(6), 477–482.

Skolnick, J.H. (1995) Drugs and violence: police departments under siege. Issue III. Gangs and crime old as time but drugs change gang culture. *Drugs and Violence, 4*(4), 81–91.

Slavin, R.E. (1990) Achievement effects of ability grouping in secondary schools: a best-evidence synthesis. *Review of Educational Research, 60*, 471–499.

Snyder, H.N. (1994a) *Juveniles Account for 1 in 8 Violent Crimes Cleared by Arrest*, Fact Sheet #15. Washington, D.C.: Office of Juvenile Justice and Delinquency Prevention.

Snyder, H. N. (1994b) *Law Enforcement Agencies' Arrests of Persons Below the Age of 18 in 1992,* Fact Sheet #13. Washington, D.C.: Office of Juvenile Justice and Delinquency Prevention.

Snyder, H.N. (1994c) *Violent Crime Index Offenses Reported in the U.S.,* Fact Sheet #16. Washington, D.C.: Office of Juvenile Justice and Delinquency Prevention.

Snyder, H.N. and Sickmund, M. (1995) *Juvenile Offenders and Victims: A National Report.* Washington, D.C.: Office of Juvenile Justice and Delinquency Prevention.

Snyder, H.N., Sickmund, M., and Poe-Yamagata, E. (1996) *Juvenile Offenders and Victims: 1996 Update on Violence*, Statistics Summary. Washington, D.C.: Office of Juvenile Justice and Delinquency Prevention, U.S. Department of Justice.

Spergal, I., Curry, G.D., Chance, R., Kane, C., Ross, R.E., Alexander, A., Rodriguez, P., Seed, D., Simmons, E., and Oh, S. (1993) *Gang Suppression and Intervention: An Assessment.* Washington, D.C.: Office of Juvenile Justice and Delinquency Programs.

Stearns, A.W. (1975) Murder by adolescents with obscure motivation. *American Journal of Psychiatry, 114*, 303–305.

Suro, R. (1996) Violent crime drops among teens. *The Washington Post*, Dec. 13, pp. A1, A19.

Taylor, D.C. (1969) Aggression and epilepsy. *Journal of Psychosomatic Research, 13*, 229–236.

Thomas, P. (1997) Violent crime rate drops 7 percent nationwide. *The Washington Post*, June 2, pp A1, A8.

Thornberry, T.P. (1994) *Violent Families and Youth Violence*, Fact Sheet #21. Washington, D.C.: Office of Juvenile Justice and Delinquency Prevention.

van Voorhis, P. (1987) Correctional effectiveness: the high cost of ignoring success. *Federal Probation, 51*, 56–62.

Wiebush, R., Baird, C., Krisberg, B., and Onek, D. (1995) Risk assessment and classification for serious, violent, and chronic juvenile offenders. In J.C. Howell (Ed.), *Guide for Implementing the Comprehensive Strategy for Serious, Violent, and Chronic Juvenile Offenders*, pp 189–230. Washington, D.C.: Office of Juvenile Justice and Delinquency Prevention.

Wilson, J.J., and Howell, J.C. (1993) *A Comprehensive Strategy for Serious, Violent, and Chronic Juvenile Offenders: Program Summary*. Washington, D.C.: U.S. Department of Justice, Office of Juvenile Justice and Delinquency Prevention.

Wolfgang, M.E. (1958) *Patterns in Criminal Homicide*. Philadelphia: University of Pennsylvania Press.

Wolfgang, M.E. (1978) An Overview of Research into Violent Behavior. Testimony before the U.S. House of Representatives Committee on Science and Technology.

Yeudall, L.T., Fromm-Auch, D., and Davies, P. (1982) Neuropsychological impairment of persistent delinquency. *Journal of Nervous Mental Disease, 170*, 257–265.

About the Author

Joseph G. Poirier, Ph.D., ABPP, is a clinical psychologist with a specialty in forensic psychology. He is the Clinical Director of the Child and Adolescent Evaluation Service (CAFES) in Montgomery County, MD. CAFES is a multi-disciplinary team that conducts evaluations on Juvenile Court referred juveniles and their families. CAFES is also responsible for the county's Juvenile Sexual Offender Program. Dr. Poirier is also the Co-Director of the Prince George County, MD, Circuit Court Mental Hygiene Service. This service conducts forensic assessments of criminal, juvenile, civil, and domestic matters. Dr. Poirier is board certified in the specialty areas of forensic, clinical, and family psychology by the American Board of Professional Psychology (ABPP). His mailing address is 10620 Georgia Avenue, Suite 209, Silver Spring, MD, 20902. Dr. Poirier can also be contacted by e-mail: jgpoirier@erols.com.

Chapter 6

WOMEN AND AGGRESSION

Sally H. Barlow and Claudia J. Clayton

Violence against women is multi-faceted, as demonstrated by the following examples. On one of the airport billboards staring out at passengers as they hurry to their next destination is the face of a woman and the sobering text beneath, "A woman is seven times as likely to be assaulted in her own home. Stop domestic violence." In a recent story aired on National Public Radio's (NPR) *All Things Considered*, Carol Bellamy reported that according to a UNICEF study, 60 million women in South America, Africa, and several other countries "vanished simply because they were female" (NPR, 1997). The notion that violent rape of women is one of the spoils of war was reaffirmed in the most recent outbreak between Bangladesh and Pakistan, the Bosnian-Serb conflict, and the latest revelations about Japanese World War II mass rapes at Nanking (Chang, 1997). In peacetime in America, a woman has a one in four chance of being raped during her lifetime, as well as being subjected to the ever-increasing violence of other forms of aggression. At home and abroad, while at war or during peacetime, each woman confronts an enormous legacy of interpersonal violence, both criminal and intimate, individual and group. "Every three minutes a woman is beaten/every five minutes a women is raped/every ten minutes a lil girl is molested/yet I rode the subway today," begins the poem by Ntozake Shange (1978, p. 114). Most researchers believe violence against women is the most immediate result of the inequality between the sexes, and that it has reached epidemic proportions in the U.S. Thus, women are subjected to individual violence, but they may also become victims of aggressive groups, including armies, gangs, and terrorists. Women are often subjected to aggression that can result from inequality, as well, instigated by gender, racial, ethnic, and religious factions. Regardless of the great variation in lethal group aggression,[1] there are some essential aspects held in common by the perpetrators of violence that include the goal to remain in control and the use of tactics to intimidate through the use of violent strategies which are bolstered by the cohesive small group process that encourages certain kinds of behavior from its members.

Given the enormity of this problem, a solution requires that we explore the empirical and theoretical literature in the fields of biology, ethology, psychodynamics, and postmodernism, as well as the current climate that allows and fosters violence toward women. Certainly, men and children of both genders are subjected to violence, but those topics are dealt

[1] There is a vast body of literature that deals with the differences as well as similarities between the terms "aggression" and "violence" (see Chapter 9).

with in other chapters. The current exploration of women and violence considers the processes of the physiological body, the study of patterns found in animal behavior in their natural environments — in particular, non-human primates who share an estimated 98.5% DNA with humans (Eibl-Eibesfeldt, 1989) — and the motivational forces, both conscious and unconscious, that determine human behavior and attitudes.

Biological Differences That Act as Moderator Variables in Aggression Toward Women

Possible differences between the genders that may have a relationship to aggression and violence are size and physiological factors such as neurohormones and chromosomes. There was a time in history when other differences between the genders were highlighted, often as a result of the gendered science perspective written about by Keller (1985). For instance, it was routinely assumed that women were less intelligent then men until sound empirical data gathered in the 20th century disproved these earlier beliefs. However, it has always been clear that men are, on average, larger than women.

Size

During a recent archeological dig, evidence was uncovered of a race of Amazon warriors, women of unusual strength and fighting prowess ("Ancient ruins...", 1997). The Roman soldiers found them to be so fierce in battle that they deliberately avoided that region; until now there was little proof of such a society, and these female warrior races are clearly an exception. This biological difference between women and men may help cement the androcentric view wherein larger size is equated with superiority.

There are instances where the reverse is true (smaller men or women aggress against larger men and women). Nevertheless, these are exceptions to the rule and are likely not verified by the Federal Bureau of Investigation (FBI) Uniform Crime Reports (see Table 6.1). Certainly, other variables may be operating in concert with size. There is anecdotal evidence of smaller women assaulting larger men and smaller men assaulting larger men, illustrated by the biblical story of David and Goliath. Given what we know about incidence rates of various crime categories, however, males are much more likely to commit violent crimes against women than the reverse. Even in the area of filicide, where parents batter their children to death, males (fathers, stepfathers, boyfriends) are far more likely to commit the deed. Only in one crime category — infanticide — are women as likely as men to kill their recently born children (Barlow and Clayton, 1996).

To be "mightier than" appears to be one of the factors in determining who aggresses against whom. Is this the deciding factor in rape? The vast majority of rape cases involve men raping women. There are cases of men raping men and men raping children, fewer cases of boys raping younger children, and rare cases of women raping women or men; in one study, 3 to 4% of men reported being physically forced by women to copulate (Hall and Flannery, 1984). If women were on average larger than men, would they be the gender that rapes? Do contributions from chromosomal and neurohormonal studies add explanatory power to the notion of size?

Neurohormonal and Chromosomal Possibilities

Though factors such as lowered IQ or cortical damage have been related to violent behavior, no single brain behavioral process has been clearly correlated to group violence. Many studies of violence and aggression have highlighted neurophysiological components such as the influence of testosterone (Constantino et al., 1993), as well as hypothalamo-

TABLE 6.1

ARRESTS BY GENDER FOR SELECTED CRIMES, 1993

Crime	Number of Persons Arrested		Percent (%)	Percent (%)
	Male	Female	Male	Female
Aggravated assault	372,557	69,518	84.3	15.7
Burglary	304,702	33,536	90.1	9.9
Drug abuse violations	811,493	157,113	83.8	16.2
Forcible Rape	32,107	416	8.7	1.3
Forgery	58,425	31,062	65.3	34.7
Fraud	335,580	199,297	59.4	40.6
Larceny-theft	842,658	408,619	67.3	32.7
Motor vehicle theft	148,932	19,863	88.2	11.8
Murder	18,375	1900	90.6	9.4
Prostitution	31,712	57,138	35.7	64.3
Robbery	140,128	13,405	91.3	8.7
Runaways	65,051	87,081	42.8	57.2
Weapons violations	206,990	17,405	92.2	7.8

Source: Uniform Crime Reports for the United States 1993, Federal Bureau of Investigation, U.S. Department of Justice, U.S. Government Printing Office, Washington, D.C.

pituitary-adrenal (HPA) functioning where dysregulated HPA function could have a causative effect on severe forms of violence, in some cases revealed by exposure to excessive amounts of alcohol (Buydens-Branchey and Branchey, 1992). While studies by Dabbs and colleagues (1987, 1988) have revealed strong relationships between testosterone and criminal activity in males and females, others (Constantino et al., 1993, p. 1217) have suggested that these inferences are spurious:

"All published studies on testosterone in aggressive humans have been performed on pubertal or post-pubertal males. It is widely recognized, however, that the origins of aggressive behavior, particularly in delinquent and criminal populations, very often can be traced back to early childhood at a time in an individual's life when testosterone levels are two orders of magnitude lower and, in fact, equivalent in boys and girls."

Their research seriously questioned the causative role of androgens. Nevertheless, Ellis (1991) made a compelling argument for the causative role of androgens in male sexual aggression, labeling it an unlearned drive that is the result of organizational and activational stages of masculinizing the brain that leads to a higher sex drive in males. He also noted an interesting combination: neuroandrogenic factors result in an increased sex drive and a decreased sensitivity to noxious stimuli (punishment, as well as other environmental cues) that might explain, for instance, a rapist's apparent lack of concern for the suffering of others. Ellis (1991, p. 635) cited a number of studies that implicate not only a causative but also a maintenance role of testosterone; that is, males exposed to sexual stimuli (e.g., pornography) increase their levels of circulating testosterone that subsequently influence their drive for sex.

Researchers (Halpern et al., 1994; Sarne et al., 1995) have also examined the role of serotonergic (serotonin, 5-HT) functions in aggressive and nonaggressive males. Sarne and colleagues (1995) presented a method to detect a biological difference between aggressive and nonaggressive individuals, though they conceded that everyday behavior is probably affected more by cultural factors. Netter and Neuhäuser-Metternich (1991, p. 418) studied catecholamine responses to defined stressors indicating sympathetic arousability, noting that all aggressive subjects exhibited lower levels and delayed stress responses of norepinephrine. They concluded that, "There is definitely a relationship between catecholamine levels and the trait of aggression."

The idea of the extra-aggressive male (XYY chromosomes) has also been studied in an effort to explain hyperaggression; however, controversy exists regarding these findings. Some researchers have suggested that the extra Y chromosome results in lower intelligence and a higher rate of crime (as evidenced by the higher representation of XYY men in prisons). Nevertheless, a problem with methodology may have obscured the variables, such as IQ and crime potential, associated with this chromosomal abnormality (Rollins, 1996, p. 41).

Raine et al. (1995, 1996) have accumulated impressive data examining, among other responses, electrodermal, cardiovascular, and cortical activity and their relationship to later crime rates. These researchers concluded that underarousal of both the central nervous system (CNS) and the autonomic nervous system (ANS) is related to criminal behavior, and that such underarousal is evidence of early neuromotor deficits. This bolsters the view that genetic predisposition to criminality may find its expression through ANS and CNS underarousal.

These studies suggested findings that physiological processes may predispose males to violence which then may find expression in sexual aggression, specifically, and aggression generally via a number of mechanisms including biology and experiential learning. The majority of sociocultural research has added the important component of cultural influences that are interpreted by the individual person as a "go" or a "no-go" on those felt impulses. What New York City gangs reportedly called "wilding" in referring to their brutal gang rape of a young female professional jogging through Central Park in 1989 was clearly influenced by their specific culture of gang violence (they felt entitled to vent their need for wild adventure on whatever object passed within their territory), as well as by the influence of the wider culture that assumes that violence is an unfortunate but present and apparently immutable quality of industrialized society (see Table 6.2). This particular instance also illustrated the racial differences in the perpetration, as well as our awareness, of crime. The victim was a white woman who was attacked by members of a black gang. The story was in the national headlines for days. At the same time and in the same city, however, black women were being raped and beaten as well, yet their stories were not as conspicuously present in the media (Rollins, 1996, p. 199). Other contributions might be implicated in the above act of violence: extremely inadequate parenting (data which emerged in subsequent interviews of the young men) or early training and less access to direct power or majority/minority group issues, including unequal access to education and occupation (see Table 6.3). These precipitants may have combined to make this activity look like the "lethal male raiding" found in non-human primate societies described below.

Evidence from the Ethological Literature

The data from the ethological literature, specifically non-human primate studies, suggest that aggression parallels, in part, the data from humans. Manson and Wrangham (1991) examined intergroup aggression in chimpanzees and found that small groups of adult males deliberately raided neighboring social groups in order to injure or kill others. They labeled this

Table 6.2

Assault Cycle of Societal Violence Against Women, Gang Aggression

Step 1a	A violent-prone culture, born of a number of contributing sources, rewards aggressive behavior through media, sports heroes and the like — a child is born.
Step 1b	The government routinely engages in aggressive activities beyond its borders in order to "keep the peace" in "unstable" countries — the child becomes a toddler.
Step 2	Women reinforce the prevalence of violence by not confronting it in their own personal relationships and by enculturating their male children to accept the messages from the media, coupled with training from school systems that do not examine and eliminate their part in the transmission of a violent-prone culture — the child goes to school.
Step 3	Violence occurs as a function of impulsive, aggressive personality characteristics being played out against a background of male-dominated subcultural norms that reinforce the prevailing ethic of hypermaleness — the child acts out in school, is rewarded, and routinely chooses action over insight, attenuating verbal development.
Step 4	The inner city continues to erode, the family structure of single-parent homes becomes beleaguered by financial and social demands — the child joins a gang.
Step 5	American's obsession with violence as sport is reinforced by top-rated television shows, newspapers and movies, and the public becomes immune — one of the gang's violent activities makes the local news, and the child, as newly enculturated gang member, becomes an anti-hero.

"lethal male raiding" (p. 370). Enquist and Leimar (1990) noted that fatal aggression can occur as a consequence of dangerous actions initiated originally to win a valuable resource (receptive females, food sources, territory). Are these lethal attacks between social groups a result of an imbalance of power? Is group aggression simply an adaptive mechanism for obtaining resources? Manson and Wrangham (1991) cited different instances that support this notion; for instance, subgroups of at least three males usually made up the raiding parties who then attacked solitary males or females or male/female pairs, demonstrating clear superiority. The victim groups that feared these attacks often traveled in large numbers in order to ward off such aggression. (Interestingly, human's access to superior weaponry can often overcome an imbalance of numbers.) Manson and Wrangham (1991, p. 376) stated, "The combination of hostile intergroup relationships and sufficient imbalance of power create sufficient conditions for fatal attacks to be favored."

Many of the accounts of intergroup aggression speak to the issue of control over reproductive resources. Hamai et al. (1992) suggested that within-group infanticide, a specific form of lethal aggression in chimpanzees, serves to coerce females into copulating less promiscuously and with higher ranking adult males, which Barlow and Clayton (1996, p. 206) described as being "an evolutionary strategy of male-male competition." Goodall's observations at the Gombe Reserve suggested that the attacks of stranger males upon mothers was for the purpose of recruiting the adolescent daughters, who often traveled with their mothers, into the group. Goodall documented

Table 6.3

Assault Cycle of Societal Violence Against Women, Individual Aggression

Step 1	A baby boy is born. He is deprived of warmth, comfort, consistency.[a] He is unable to master completely Mahler's subphases of separation individuation (Mahler et al., 1975). His ability to soothe himself, and achieve object constancy are seriously attenuated.
Step 2	The boy seeks stimulation in a desperate attempt to feel something. A father figure moves in and out of the home as the mother's inconsistency spreads to choices in mates. Her faulty parenting continues in undulations of neglect and overstimulation that leave the boy confused. He is a bed wetter and a poor student throughout elementary school.
Step 3	Previous acting out (fire-starting and animal killing) blossoms into the juvenile offenses of car theft and petty burglary. Drug offenses accumulate. He regularly beats up his girlfriend, who is pregnant by him. He drops out of high-school.
Step 4	After two moderate stints in the local juvenile jail, he attempts to clean up his act by getting a full-time job and working on his GED. However, his mother overdoses. He is ambivalent about her death and begins drinking again. On one of these benders, he rapes a clerk when he surprises her while robbing a convenience store. This opportunity rape is reinforced by such experiential learning that then leads to future rapes.

[a] While it is dangerous to draw parallels from the work of Harry and Margaret Harlow (Restak, 1979, 1984), it is compelling to consider the human version of the wire/cloth mother-child relationship.

17 attacks on stranger females with infants, usually by adult males. The objects of the attacks were the adult females, but the infants often were injured or killed and sometimes eaten, by the males. These behaviors are considered to promote the survival of the group and hence are evolutionary explanations for aggression. The majority of ethological researchers suggest that when females are present, they are usually in a supportive, rather than directly aggressive, role. The exception to this is a rare account of a pathological relationship between a chimpanzee mother and daughter pair which was suspected in the deaths of at least seven infant gorillas over the span of several years (Goodall, 1986).

In an intriguing series of studies (Azar, 1997), low serotonin was associated with monkeys who were inappropriately aggressive, antisocial, and willing to drink alcohol until intoxicated (unusual for monkeys) while in the lab. In the wild, these monkeys sought danger, often making very risky leaps. As described by Azar (1997, p. 29), "These traits have dire consequences. Male rhesus monkeys typically leave their home troupe at puberty and find their way into another troupe. But troupes oust impulsive males well before adolescence. They tend to become loners ... are unsuccessful at mating, and often die within a year."

Several non-evolutionary explanations for aggression have been suggested, such as crowding or other stressful conditions that likely increase irritability (Burke, 1984), although primates have relatively sophisticated behaviors for conciliation and avoidance of conflict in crowded situations (de Waal, 1989), and social stability is a more important determinant of primate aggression than is population density. Goodall (1986) suggested chimpanzee xenophobia as an explanation for attacks on mothers by stranger males. Eibl-Eibesfeldt (1989) wrote of chimpanzee "temper tantrums" — their tendency to lose control when they are in a state of strong emotional arousal. Such situations may occur during feeding and competitive male displays, and the aggression may be displaced toward females or infants.

In summary, the aggressive behavior of non-human primates appears to have several outcomes: establishment of territory, dominance, sexual advantage, discipline, protection from predators, and, in a sense, morality — that is, survival of the group (see Chapter 9). Wilson (1975) suggested that all of these categories have their parallel in human behavior, though a direct grafting of behaviors from non-human primates to humans would be inappropriate given the complex way in which humans construct their past histories as well as their ability to project themselves into the future. Still, the gender differences are compelling and suggest that while allowing for a certain symbolization of status, human males fight for territory, compete for females, discipline children sometimes to the point of death (filicide), collectively aggress under the aegis of moralistic wars, and sometimes engage in lethal male raiding.

When female non-human primates engage in aggression, it is either in a supportive role or as a result of pathological, not adaptive, behavior, a role currently employed by human females as well. Perhaps if human females actually engage in more and more aggressive acts, we may see a shift from the belief that aggression in women is pathological to the sad realization that it has become normative. This stems from a controversial notion suggested by some that the numbers of women in traditionally male crime categories are increasing. However, Rollins (1996, p. 233) offered an alternative view, suggesting that the numbers have not increased at all for women. Noting changes in the Uniform Crime reports per gender category over the years may be one indicator that proves or disproves this notion of increasing crime for women.

Psychodynamics of Male Aggression

The effects of human physiology (perhaps embedded in evolutionary adaptation) cannot be presented as causative given the lack of conclusive evidence. They might more reasonably be labeled physiological moderator variables. Several other moderator variables include those psychological and group dynamic variables invoked by, among others, social role construction theories of aggression that warrant further scrutiny. These variables covary with the expression of violence. Taking a psychosocial point of view, author Roger Horrocks (1994, pp. 134, 135) stated:

> *"Why are men violent to women? I want to counterpose the question, 'Why are men violent to men?' In other words, why are men violent at all? What must be tackled is the amount of violence that men commit — football hooliganism, war, terrorism, mugging, murder. My answer is straightforward, men are conditioned and trained to carry out the violence of the whole culture. In this sense, women who are fascinated/obsessed with male violence are actually projecting their own violence onto such men. And we all project our violence onto violent men. As Jung stated in a discussion about the Second World War, 'We love the criminal and take a burning interest in him because the devil makes us forget the beam in our own eye when observing the mote in our brother's, and in that way, outwits us.'"*

This intriguing quote suggests several other sources of violence: interpersonal issues that include role expectations such as the projection of violence by some onto males who then bear the entire burden of "carrying it" for the culture, invoking the biblical scripture as well as theme and title of Flannery O'Connor's novel, *The Violent Bear It Away*.

Eagly and Steffen (1986) conducted a meta-analytic review of male-female differences, confirmed the societal expectation notion, and agreed essentially that aggressiveness was more attributable to males based on perceived roles. While men may be trained more to express aggressive impulses, women may certainly be a part of their hyperaggressiveness by not "owning" their own aggressive impulses, relying on males to act out such aggression vicariously.

Macro- and Micro-Violence: Blurred Boundaries, Mutual Influence

Culturally reinforcing, highly contextualized exchanges have their origins in a number of issues (control, power, attachment) that surface in forms of group aggression as well as stranger, acquaintance, and intimate rapes; domestic abuse; pornography; and prostitution. These examples of micro-violence can theoretically be contrasted to macro-violence which has been defined as aggression by groups and institutions. This latter form of collective violence is defined as aggressive acts of representatives of those organizations. Because organizations, institutions, and governments operate according to certain belief structures that implicitly and explicitly influence an individual member's behavior, it is possible to consider prejudice (racial, ethnic, gender, religious) as a guiding value that links micro-violence to macro-violence. For instance, during the Bosnian conflict, Muslim women were the subject of attack by soldiers, perhaps as a result of religious, ethnic, and gender prejudice. Another way that macro-violence (e.g., war) influences micro-violence has to do with the perception of power. The phrase "might makes right" refers to the tolerance of violence from the ruling elites or ruling institutions (governments) that directly or indirectly influences the behavior of groups who are not in power. The individual violent behavior of a gang member is clearly influenced by a societal norm that one should aggressively pursue one's goals. Gang members often refer to other ostensibly legal organizations' identical ethic — hostile takeovers by corporate big business and government violence in the form of CIA-instigated insurrections in third-world countries — when justifying their own behavior. In the same way, male batterers refer to the larger norm group — "males should be in control" (Dutton, 1987) — when justifying their assaultive behaviors toward their victims. There is continuing controversy about where individual and group responsibility overlap. That is, how much responsibility can one attribute to the influences of the group (e.g., emotional contagion, group coerciveness) vs. the influences within the individual (e.g., genetic predisposition)? Perhaps it is exactly here in the blurred boundaries between an individual and a group that micro- and macro-violence represent a process of mutual influence. Empirical data (Brock-Utne, 1997) convincingly portray this relationship between micro-level violence (spouse abuse, rape) and structural violence at the macro-level (economics, inequality, war). For this reason, those specific aggressions defined as micro-violence are considered below. Each area — pornography, marital violence, rape, and prostitution — is a possible exemplar of those influences found within and across biological, ethological, and psychodynamic domains.

Micro-Violence: Exemplars of Macro-Violence

Pornography

Pornography has often been portrayed as a "victimless crime" and has been distinguished from "erotica" in that the latter involves print and film media produced for males and females where neither gender is being subjected to denigration. Research about pornography has a controversial past that intersects American's strong beliefs about First Amendment rights as well as a negotiation of these rights as interpreted within individual communities. Beliefs about pornography range from the idea that it is harmless to the claim that it is potentially lethal.

Pornography is included in this chapter on women and violence because a content analysis of most pornographic material reveals that a majority is based on domination of women by men (Cowan et al., 1988), a theme which explicitly reinforces the idea that force is acceptable in sexual relations. In addition, despite the early belief that pornography was harmless, enough current data suggest that it has resulted in sexual aggression toward women (U.S. Attorney General's Commission on Pornography, 1986). Erotica also takes its toll on relationships by developing a taste for certain kinds of sexual relations that are neither realistic nor healthy (Weaver et al., 1984).

As pornographic films gained wider audience appeal in the 1980s (some say as a backlash against the women's movement; see Faludi, 1992), Hollywood saw a ready market and began producing an increasing number of such films. The victims are seen as willing, or if unwilling, deserving of their fate as a result of their "bitchiness" or overt sexuality. Linda Lovelace, the star of the popular film *Deep Throat* recounted behind-the-scenes events in her exposé of the pornographic film industry under her real name, Marchiano, in her books, *Ordeal* (1980) and *Out of Bondage* (1986). Film critic Gene Siskel (1980, p. E3) believes that the most damaging consequence of pornographic movies is that they "shape the public's attitude toward attacks on women as some kind of sport" and cater to the young adult male who is still developing ideas about what is normal and abnormal sexuality. Many movies of this type present their material as representing the status quo, thus reinforcing the notion that this type of sexuality is normal. A number of studies have attempted to demonstrate that normal college-aged males can be conditioned to respond to sexuality with violence (Check and Malamuth, 1985; Malamuth, 1981, 1988). From this data, it becomes clear how an increasing appetite for sex and violence begins to drive the taste of the American viewing and reading public (Zillmann and Bryant, 1986).

Violence in Marriage

Spouse abuse (including battering, rape, and some forms of emotional abuse) occurs between married and unmarried, heterosexual and homosexual pairs, although it is most prominently inflicted by men against women. Domestic violence is the leading cause of injury to women in the U.S. (Rollins, 1996). It has been estimated that one third of all women will be battered at some time in their lives (Straus et al., 1980), and most researchers agree that spouse abuse is seriously under-reported. It is an example of the cross-over between micro- and macro-violence, as batterings accumulate not only over time for an individual spouse and may lead to death, but also across women, as a category, in the case of the total number of assaults registered nationwide in one day.

The historical definition of marital contracts according to legal sanctions worldwide (some still extant in a number of countries) gave men enormous power and essentially characterized women and children as chattel (property) to do with as men pleased. Numerous accounts of beatings and killings are found throughout history. As late as the 19th century, a law allowing a man to act as he saw fit toward his wife was still on the books in England (Lips, 1997, p. 340). Even in the present day, it is not unusual to hear of a woman being killed in India because her dowry was not extensive enough (death is apparently easier to deal with than divorce). In the 20th century, there are many accounts of judges unwilling to interfere with a man's "castle", a term not coined until post-industrial revolution to denote the demarcation between the harshness of the work place and the sanctuary of the home. The likelihood that a battered women will be rescued by the courts is small, given this notion that a man's home should be inviolate. Dutton (1987a) stated that a husband who assaults his wife has a 6.5% probability of being detected and an even smaller probability of being arrested. As Dutton (1987b, 1995) has also suggested, these assaulting males blame their wives for their violent behavior.

Others (Rosenbaum and O'Leary, 1981) have suggested that batterers have fewer verbal or assertive skills and resort to violence as a way of "speaking" their distress.

One of the reasons marriages are "places" where violence can occur is that intimate relationships include a complex interaction of power, control, and attachment. In addition, marriages take place against a backdrop of societal expectations about what is considered normal and aberrant behavior. The majority of men eschew violence; however, according to Dutton (1986), even men who believe violence is wrong, may engage in it.

In an intriguing social psychology experiment conducted by Harris et al. (1986), participants viewing videotapes of couples fighting indicated that two male friends engaged in an argument needed outside intervention to stop an escalating disagreement. This was not their belief regarding heterosexual couples who were arguing; however, both kinds of couples were viewed as engaging in escalating disputes in which physical force seemed to be the "next logical step". A follow-up on this type of research needs to be conducted to determine if these social/psychological findings hold up in actual marriages; for instance, do homosexual pairings escalate more quickly to angry expression than do heterosexual pairings?

Holtzworth-Munroe and Stuart (1994) suggested that there are three kinds of batterers: (1) the type suggested by Dutton who manifest underlying conflicts about attachment, strike out at their wives when they fear abandonment, and may also be violent outside the family; (2) the type whose violent behavior occurs within the family only and who may have a passive-dependent personality; and (3) the type whose behavior is generally violent and anti-social, within and outside the family, and who may also be dependent on alcohol and drugs. While men are generally the initiators of violence in marriage, women often fight back, dangerously escalating the attacks so that medical attention is eventually necessary for one third of the victims (MacLeod, 1980). The naive notion that women remain in such relationships because of their own masochistic personalities (Goldstein, 1983) has been largely debunked (Unger and Crawford, 1996). The notion of masochism has been replaced with the alternative hypothesis that the long-term pattern of isolation, coupled with economic dependence, seems insurmountable to many of these women. In addition, once a woman does separate from her spouse, she becomes a target for lethal violence by him (Pagelow, 1993).

Dutton (1987b) suggested that the act of battering is often the consequence of borderline personality organization (BPO). Less severe than borderline personality disorder (*Diagnostic and Statistical Manual, DSM,* 4th ed., 1994), BPO operates within the male as a sequence of internal beliefs that climaxes in angry outbursts as an attempt to re-establish a sense of control. Dutton's work, the culmination of several decades of research, is one of the most comprehensive explanations of assaults of husbands against wives. It includes compelling intrapersonal and interpersonal or relationship dynamics that help explain the assaultive cycle. These dynamics could be corroborated by some of the more sophisticated analysis systems such as the Structural Analysis of Social Behavior (SASB; Benjamin, 1996), in which hostile enmeshment (lack of autonomy, angry attachments between the couple) can be interpersonally tracked to its unfortunate conclusions—battering (attack). The remorse that follows starts the cycle all over again. As Dutton (1987b) has pointed out, this cycle is well in place and, verbal attestations aside ("I'm so sorry, it will never happen again!"), will, in fact, continue until the husband has a new way of supporting his unstable sense of self that does not require instantaneous affirmations from his wife. The wife usually does not realize what the husband is seeking because the expectation is embedded in an intricate but often elusive set of maneuvers not explicitly known to either. In a review of "risk markers" of batterers, Hotaling and Sugarman (1986) identified a number of markers for male-to-female abuse which included witnessing violence as children (the only marker which was also true for the wife), having lower occupational and income status, and being non-assertive and somewhat psychologically deviant.

In one of his experiments, Dutton (1987b) showed that assaultive males become angrier and more aroused than other men when watching videotaped scenes of male-female arguments in which there is a strong perceived threat of the female leaving the male. He viewed this finding as further corroboration of his theory that assaultive men are terrified of their dependence on women and use violence to "face down the specter of abandonment" (Lips, 1997, p. 341). This conclusion is supported by additional empirical research that shows jealousy as the main trigger for assaultive behavior (Bowker, 1983). Dutton's work consisted essentially of summaries of actual clinical cases. The work of Harris et al. (1986) was based on university students observing actors on videotapes. Extrapolations from both of these databases to "normals" must be done with caution. Gottman (1979) has conducted a number of studies on normal couples communicating, including during conflicts. These studies were executed ingeniously to determine a fairly reliable rate of dispute, some of which led to physical abuse, but the majority of which did not.

For domestic violence to occur, a number of variables in combination must be present: (1) a type of modeling (witnessing violence as a child), (2) a context that supports and expects violence as the normal course of events, (3) a temporary relief that is powerfully reinforcing, and (4) an eventual build-up of tension. Sometimes, these factors are exacerbated by environmental pressures (job, money, children); however, these variables are usually additive, not causative. It is clear from the combined empirical data that domestic violence is different from stranger violence in that the relationships are current and historical. Stranger violence may include some of these elements when the object of the aggression may be a substitute for the spouse, an illustration of displacement. A number of intervention strategies have been attempted, including the establishment of women's shelters, resocialization (many judges will defer sentences if the batterer receives anger management therapy), and proposals for early education for young males (Ballif-Spanvill et al., 1997).

Dutton's work helps conceptualize the conflictual position to which males are enculturated regarding dependence. Enculturation essentially means the transmission of cultural expectations about how to carry out one's gender assignment successfully. Men are encouraged to be independent/self-reliant, not dependent/other-reliant. When they realize that they are dependent upon their wives, they act out (fight back) against this "awful" realization, based on what they have been instructed to be, feel, and think. They have been taught that the best jobs go to the fastest, biggest, smartest, not the most tender and dependent. Society must find a new interactional, interpersonal language focused on interdependence — that individuals who constitute a couple can and must be legitimately interdependent upon each another without risk to an autonomous self-representation.

Rape

There are numerous perspectives regarding the origins of rape, including: (1) evolutionary — rape is an adaptation that has species survivor benefits; (b) social-biological — rape is a result of two unlearned drives, the sex drive and the drive to possess and control; (3) psychological — rape is a behavior congruent with perceived role; (4) feminist — rape is a means of social control; and, finally, (5) macro-sociological — rape is a spillover from other endorsements of violence and social disorganization (Valentich, 1994). Each theory promotes a different treatment strategy (Marshall et al., 1990).

The evolutionary theorists form two main camps: those who believe that rape is selected, in the evolutionary sense, to promote the species, and those who believe that rape is a byproduct of evolutionary forces, not an adaptation. While this is a fascinating body of literature, in the main the evolutionary perspective has not held up in the empirical data; however, the work of the Thornhills (1992), who stated that rape is a side-effect of a more general adaptation, is important because it suggested that brain mechanisms perceive cues which result in sexual coercion, and that contexts that discourage rape can be identified from these cues. The sociobiologists (Ellis, 1991; Wilson and Daly 1985) who believe that rape is the product of inherited, unlearned drives have had slightly better empirical success in correlating rape with these biological drives. This is especially true when explaining the more gruesome forms of rape by serial killers whose need to possess the victims fits this biological drive for ownership. Evolutionary and sociobiological theories have not been received well by the general public, however, because they both appear to convey the message that "men can't help themselves".

The psychological approaches to understanding rape are concerned with offenders' roles and motivations. (Barbaree and Marshal, 1991, warned that the data were derived from two very different populations: criminals and college undergraduates). A number of researchers (Hall et al., 1991; Malamuth et al., 1991; Yourell and McCabe, 1989) have suggested that a multidimensional model is needed to understand rape including physiological arousal, dysfunctional attitudes that promote violence, affective dyscontrol, abusive home environments, and misogyny (see Table 6.4). As Hall and Barongan (1997, p. 13) stated:

"Mainstream cultural experiences in the United States may place men at risk for becoming sexually aggressive. Risk factors include the conditioning of sexual arousal to deviant stimuli, the development of cognitive distortions that reduce the perceived impact of sexual aggression, condoning anger toward women, and developmentally related personality problems that may lead to sexual aggression and other problems."

Acquaintance/date rape is one of the potent examples of such mainstream enculturation. One of the results of the women's movement has been an increase in the reporting of rape, which revealed a number of startling findings: first, that rape occurs far more frequently than we imagined and, second, that domination or humiliation, not mere sexual satiation, is the goal. Benderly (1982, p. 40) stated, "Sexual violence is not innate; it depends on the status of women, the relationships between the sexes, and the attitudes taught to children." She echoed the beliefs of feminists who maintain that rapists are not sexually deprived; rather, they are hostile, aggressive men who enjoy engaging in violence against women. Continuing research efforts are likely to offer a more multi-dimensional etiology, suggesting that rape is not a unidimensional act and that all rapists are not alike. For instance, Ellis (1991) pointed out that for some men, the goal is sex, with aggression being the means to achieve that goal. Others have suggested that for another type of rapist, the goal is aggression, and sex is a byproduct (Yourell and McCabe, 1989).

Sanday (1981), who found cultures in which rape is practically nonexistent, corroborated Benderly's claim. Sanday compared rates of rape among 156 tribal societies as well as the function and meaning of rape in these societies. She suggested that a high incidence of rape is embedded in a distinguishably different cultural configuration in which tribes are faced with depletion of resources, migration, and other factors contributing to a dependence on male destructive capacities in contrast to relying on female fertility. In times of adequate food resources, male and female attributes are valued equally, but, in times of distress, males are equated with greater status which also "forces men to prove their status" (Sanday, 1981, p. 25). Benderly (1982) cited Sanday's research to counter the popular beliefs promoted by some feminist writers (Brownmiller, 1975) that rape is inherent to male and female relationships and went on to cite her own anthropological research corroborating the notion that rape-prone societies have histories of unstable food supplies, warfare, and migration.

TABLE 6.4

ETIOLOGICAL COMPONENTS OF AGGRESSION AND POSSIBLE INTERVENTION STRATEGIES FOR GANG RAPE

Source	Biological	Sociological	Psychological
	Neurohormonal (sexual drive, control drive)	Cultural entrainment for violence from macro societal level to micro family level	Dysfunctional attitudes (women as objects etc), personality problems
Action	Sexual arousal Aggression	Spillover from other areas into female relationships	Affective dyscontrol: sex, aggression, or both
Normal	Initiate sex Appropriately express anger, etc.	Culture promotes that needs can be negotiated Aggression is tolerated in acceptable contexts	Individual has skills to express sexual intimacy, or… Irritation and anger
Abnormal	Rape, molestation Assault	Subculture rewards both sexually aggressive and aggressive behaviors	Personality problems that promote anti-social or intermittent explosive disorders, etc.
Treatment	Neurohormonal Interventions	Strengthening anti-crime legislation, education	Step programs that promote individual responsibility
Hopes	Drives regulated Less aggression Heritability	Cultural ethic that promotes well-being via peaceful strategies	Affect regulation, sense of self, reality testing that promote health

One might counter that American males are not generally suffering from unstable food supplies. However, because the U.S. has the highest crime statistics for rape in the industrialized world, and rape is the fastest growing crime of violence in the country, a suitable explanation must be sought. We must remember that, according to Wilson (1975), a translation from the concrete to the symbolic occurs from primitive to industrialized societies that renders resources necessary for survival (food, water, shelter) into potent symbols of status (income, possessions), including demonstrations of dominance. These demonstrations are most readily apparent in times of war.

Ehrenreich (1997) suggested that engaging in the "passions of war" is one of the ways we band together in groups to overcome our fears of annihilation. According to her treatise, these blood rites of killing occur equally in males and females; however, the occurrence of rape during times of war is perpetrated mostly by males against females. For example, Valentich (1994) noted that between 20,000 and 50,000 women have been raped in the former Yugoslavia since the civil war began there. Men and boys were also raped, but nowhere near the numbers of adult males raping females. These female victims were mostly Muslims in Bosnia-Herzegovina, supporting the notion that rape is a violent act of denigration and domination, which in this case, focused on "ethnic cleansing" or genocide. "Public, brutal rape was the *coup de grace* to ensure that the remaining women would never want to return to their homelands" (Valentich, 1994, p. 54). Valentich noted from survivor accounts that pornography was involved. She stated that "there [is] a relationship between pornography consumed [by the soldiers who filmed many of the rapes], the sexualization of the environment of torture and predation, and the sexual acts performed" (Valentich, 1994, p. 57). Historians have noted that such rapes are not often punished when they serve to forward a political agenda that is part of a plan to terrorize and conquer a racial group. In fact, one of the reasons the rapes perpetrated during this war (and other current conflicts such as in Pakistan and Bangladesh) have come to light is the outcry of women worldwide and the subsequent organization of the Ad Hoc Women's Coalition (1993) to declare rape during war a war crime. Valentich suggested that a combination of theories explains the high incidence of rape during war time, including social disorganization, traditional roles that reinforce hyper-masculinity, and the reduction of the mitigating effects of religion (Stack and Kanavy, 1983). She concluded that the evolutionary perspective of rape is not sufficiently explanatory, and that we must develop an encompassing theory so that intervention can occur.

A number of authors have promoted the notion that rapes that occur during wartime as well as peace time are essentially acts of terrorism. Sheffield (1997, pp. 111, 112) suggested that many women feel controlled by an invisible force and that most women are angry about being …

"… unfree: a hostage of a culture that, for the most part, encourages violence against women, instructs men in the methodology of sexual violence, and provides them with a ready justification for their violence. …Sexual terrorism includes nonviolent sexual intimidation and the threat of violence as well overt sexual violence. For example, although an act of rape, an unnecessary hysterectomy, and the publishing of Playboy *magazine appear to be quite different, they are in fact more similar than dissimilar."*

What these behaviors have in common is that they all appear to be predicated on the wish to dominate women through the engendering of fear and hostility.

Prostitution

One reason prostitution might warrant inclusion in a chapter on violence and women is that, although it is ostensibly voluntary, the backgrounds of most women who are prostitutes would suggest that "conscription" into this "army" is based on powerful "pretraining" that includes significant rates of molestation as children (Barry, 1979; Silbert and Pines, 1983). Prostitutes also continue to be abused by their "johns" as well as the police who believe that prostitutes are fair game for abuse (Carmen and Moody, 1985). Barry (1979) went so far as to say that a number of women and girls who are not prostitutes experience "sexual slavery" without ever having to leave their homes, as they are the victims of husbands and fathers instead of pimps.

Postmodernism: A Deconstruction of Extant Theories of Violence Against Women

The descriptions of biological, ethological, and psychodynamic explanations of violence do not include the recent contributions of postmodern thinkers, taking their lead from Derrida (Evans, 1991), who seriously assess the very paradigms of reality we take for granted. Several authors, Bem (1993), Heilbrun, (1990), Irigaray (1993), and Keller (1985), representing a number of disciplines, have contributed to our understanding of violence against women. They have suggested that the trilogy of explanatory theories — biology, ethology, psychodynamics — require such deconstruction given that they rest upon basic tenets of humanism, which they assert is only one way to view reality. These authors question the validity of the scientific method and the objective "truths" that result from utilizing such empirical methods. While it is not within the scope of this chapter to explore these in depth, a cursory view may assist us, given that the extant theories of violence against women, while they may have served to orient us in the past, might, because of that very orientation, continue to obscure the truth.

The psychologist, Bem (1993), stated that our culture constructs gender differences by invoking biological essentialism, androcentrism, and gender polarization as a way to maintain different valuing systems for males and females. She cited decades of gender-difference research based on questionable methods. The literary critic, Heilbrun (1990), highlighted a social deconstruction by analyzing accounts in literature of women's stories (e.g., Penelope's strategy to ward off suitors by unweaving Odysseus' death shroud at night) that illustrate an entirely different view of reality. Irigaray's (1993) particular brand of psychoanalytic feminism explored the roots of gender differences, essentially promoting a stance of "alterity" which eschewed all forms of power over others. The scientist, Keller, suggested the compelling thesis that science itself has contributed to the inequality between the genders by promulgating a male-dominated world based on the seemingly irrefutable evidence of scientific experiments which proved, among other things, that women are inferior. She speculated that perhaps one motivation for this might be male fear of the emotional aspect of life represented by the feminine, and hence his attempt to denigrate emotion as well as intellect in women. As evidence of this, the renowned psychologist G. Stanley Hall once wrote, "The woman who uses her brain loses her mammary function first and has little hope to be other than a moral and medical freak" (cited in Rollins, 1996, p. 59). Simone de Beauvoir wrote, "Representation of the world, like the world itself, is the work of men; they describe it from their own point of view, which they confuse with the absolute truth" (cited in Keller, 1985, p. 3). These authors represent a growing body of literature which asserts that gender politics is a morass of unconscious and conscious, political-psychological-social-historical factors which, although difficult, might be understood if we do not hang onto useless constructions of reality rooted in humanism. Deconstructionist writers have been accused of sitting on the limb that they are eagerly sawing off, but this task of dismantling the world in which they themselves reside is exactly what they view as important, even if it means crashing down with it. Because we have not, as a society, eradicated the roots of violence, the postmodern position has some allure in its willingness to go to any lengths to discover the truth of the human experience. Still, we must not throw out the baby with the bath water by discarding all that research has learned about violent behavior.

Conclusions

Group aggression toward women (gang rape, terrorism, war) represents documented acts of macro-violence. Pornography, violence in marriage, rape, and prostitution represent micro-violence, those individual acts that may be linked to levels of macro-violence because of the total numbers of aggressive incidences that become life-threatening to women as a group. A satisfactory theory that explains and eradicates these acts does not, as yet, exist. Examinations of ethology, biology, and psychodynamics are helpful, in part, but do not, taken as a whole, explain the sheer amount of aggression and violence promulgated toward women. And while early efforts of postmodernist thinkers may aid us in the construction of just such an all-encompassing theory, their efforts are only on the horizon of our understanding.

The Seeds of Violence

Inside the Individual, Family, Culture, Society. Phillip Zimbardo (1970) warned us about the "rush to the dispositional" — when violence occurs we often look for the simplest solution by finding defects inside the person (positioning the cause squarely on the side of nature). Indeed, some of the compelling evidence from non-human primates and humans suggests that we carry the seeds of aggression within us, perhaps as an adaptational tool, but locating the source of violence so narrowly is specious at best and, at worst, dangerous to our survival as a species. If the sources of violence are not necessarily located only within the individual, are they to be found in society? Such questions face us with the age-old debate — nature vs. nurture. Is a gang member part of the group, for instance, because of psychological factors (childhood influences) or physiological factors (heredity)? Bronfenbrenner and Ceci (1994) suggested a non-additive, synergistic effects model that would account for the heredity-environment interaction, focusing on proximal processes which transform genotypes into phenotypes. Of the current models that attempt an explication of the nature-vs.-nurture debate, this is perhaps the most reasonable.

In order to consider the relative contribution from both sides of the nature-vs.-nurture debate in this non-additive synergistic effects model, one must examine the data from biological, ethological, and environmental influence studies. Our brains appear to be designed with mechanisms for obtaining resources in order to survive and for determining the risk/benefit of actions designed to obtain those resources. In addition, our society is not equitable, thus presenting the context of an imbalance of power — one of the precursors to lethal attacks — where resources can, in fact, be seized by one group over another. Although there is controversy about what has created such an imbalance of power, issues of territoriality (nationalism, gang drug turf, or control over sexual objects) continue to foster the climate for violence. But, as Zimbardo (1997) suggested, solutions to violence involve a much more complex picture. For instance, it is more reasonable to assume that gang members are not simply an aggregate of individual "bad boys and girls" with bad childhoods, but rather part of a gang culture that performs a critical function which society at large apparently has not fulfilled.

In addition to avoiding the rush to the dispositional, we must face the clearly implicated dynamics of social role. Zimbardo also demonstrated early in his career the enormous influence of social role expectation in the now classic prisoner studies in which college students took on the roles of prisoner or guard to such an extent that the experiment had to be stopped. We are apparently willing to be either harsh or submissive, depending upon the role we have been assigned (Haney et al., 1970; Milgram, 1974).

Simple vs. Complex Solutions. Simplistic solutions include increased crime legislation, the elimination of the military, etc., but an issue as complicated as violence requires a multi-disciplinary approach that utilizes history, psychological knowledge, social contexts, legal issues (both criminal and civil), and an appeal to a higher law of conduct toward one another whether we label this religion, philosophy, or spirituality (see Table 6.5).

Hall and Barongan (1997, p. 13) suggested that an appreciation of diversity may be the key to eliminating some kinds of aggression in our society. They stated, "Both feminine socialization and certain aspects of socialization in ethnic minority cultures may serve as protective factors against sexually aggressive behavior because they encourage empathy and sexuality in the context of committed relationships." Perhaps this offers an antidote to the moral disengagement that encourages a lack of empathy for victims during aggressive acts. Nevertheless, in order for these sources to be valued, we will have to turn the world upside down, and that, in itself, is perhaps a violent, if not revolutionary, act.

As Hall noted in the opening chapter of this volume, we must not shrink from acknowledging "ground truth" about violence, including what violence we

Table 6.5

Violence Prevention Wish List or "Global Cooling"

1. Make millions of dollars available for researchers from National Institutes of Health and Mental Health and other funding organizations to develop strategies to prevent violence. Funding would only be renewed if pilot programs proved useful. After several years of collecting data, the funding agencies would tabulate information from all levels (biological, psychological, sociological, ethological) to develop a meta theory about violence instigation, maintenance, and prevention.
2. Appoint a new Cabinet position for Domestic Peacemaking. Subsumed under this Cabinet Minister would be liaisons to other branches of government such as the Attorney General (to examine civil rights violation, case law), Congress (to strike useless legislation and create laws), and Education (to promote learning at elementary levels on up) to create an unprecedented but necessary combination of all branches of government.
3. Financially reward states with reduced crime rates, especially gang-related. Grant sanctioning power to governors and mayors to tie local and federal funding (roads, schools) to maintenance of standards.
4. Begin a series of exchanges between the leading authorities of all nations regarding the possible interaction between aggression and imbalance of power. Their eventual goal would be to propose a plan for an equitable world based on an exchange of goods, services, land, and resources, as well as to curtail covert aggression against nations and other collective entities without prior knowledge and approval of Congress.
5. Make marriage a two-step licensing process, in which a preliminary period determines compatibility and an additional period determines right to reproduce.

condone and why, and the contributions of both the victims and the perpetrators, as well as the reality about the principles of violence and the laws of human behavior that we do know. Because micro-level violence can lead to macro-level violence and because each level is involved in an overlap of mutual influence, the intervention strategies we devise must include indirect as well as direct tactics.

Ultimately, the gender disparity shown by violence toward women will result in the destruction of society if we do not intervene. Efforts to reduce violence toward women must include restoration of the principles upon which the U.S. Constitution was built — a government of the people, by the people, for the people. This means that the illegal activities at elite institutional levels (CIA, FBI, and other governmental agencies) must cease if we are ever to hope for a non-violent society. When the highest levels of government exercise absolute power, they indirectly sanction the illegal activities of others, from people in organized crime to inner-city gangs.

Also included should be legislation that lengthens sentences for career criminals and funds prevention programs aimed at children before the age of 8, as research continues to show that only this type of intervention is viable (Venables, 1989); recommitment to civil rights legislation in order to reduce inequality; and gun control legislation to keep firearms from violent criminals. While the debate regarding the arming of America has fierce critics on both sides, we quote the noted art critic, Sister Wendy, who represents our viewpoint as she described several of Goya's paintings of men beating each other to death, "Human stupidity, especially human stupidity armed … is a threat, darkness, hell is there" (British Broadcasting Company, *The Story of Painting*). In addition, there should be a further crackdown on alcohol- and drug-related lethal violence.

These possible intervention strategies only scratch the surface and run the risk of constituting exactly those simplistic solutions we wish to avoid. In addition, the above strategies involve national concerns only. Yet, violence is a worldwide phenomenon. A much longer list is needed that crosses intervention levels (micro and macro), international boundaries, genders, races, ethnicities, cultures, religions, individual psychologies, and the human heart if we are to hope for a better world. As Solzhenitsyn (1974, p. 168) stated,

"If only there were people somewhere insidiously committing evil deeds, and it were necessary only to separate them from the rest of us and destroy them. But the line dividing good and evil cuts through the heart of every human being. And who is willing to destroy a piece of his heart?"

In Gergen's relational theory (Roberts, 1997), we are considered to be co-creators of action, and as such must become ethical advocates, regardless of biological presses, evolutionary endowments, psychological interpretations, or social constructions. We must change the existing paradigm of "power over", which has resulted in domination and violence by both men and women, to "power to"in order to create and maintain a world of peace.

Summary

In order to understand the legacy of violence that faces women today, a number of perspectives are needed: biological, ethological, psychodynamic, sociological, and postmodern theories. Group aggression is expressed toward women in many forms, including gang rape and other physical assaults that occur during war and peacetime. While there is great variation in lethal group violence, there are some essential aspects held in common by the perpetrators of violence. These include, but are not limited to, the goals of gaining control (whether initiated by impulsive rage or careful planning) and maintaining control through the use of tactics to intimidate by employing violent strategies. These may be bolstered by the cohesive small group process that encourages certain kinds of behavior from its members. Some authors have suggested that the social construction of power maintains the imbalance of power and directly contributes to group violence against women. If this is true, it could be construed that group aggression includes any violent behavior, wherein a more powerful gender dominates a less powerful gender. Given this interpretation, individual acts such as rape and spouse abuse become exemplars of group aggression because they collectively harm women; that is, they are instances in which micro-violence may be cumulatively lethal which inextricably links micro- to macro-level violence.

Annotated Bibliography

1. Wilson, M. and Daly, M. (1985) Competitiveness, risk-taking, and violence: the young male syndrome. *Ethology and Sociobiology, 6*, 59–73. The Wilson and Daly research team constitutes what many consider to be the leading experts in the U.S. on the topics of murder and violence. This articles explores the relationship between the variables of competition, risk, and violence and suggests future areas of needed research.

2. Bem, S. (1993) *The Lenses of Gender: Transforming the Debate on Sexual Inequality*. New Haven: Yale University. Dr. Bem's career has been spent observing and understanding the relationships of women and men, culminating in this thoughtful book that promotes a new way of looking at gender, as if through a set of lenses. After decades of significant research on the differences as well as similarities of men and women, and the development of the most widely used Bem Sex Role Inventory (BSRI), she provides us

with three notions that make up these lenses, so implicitly embedded in our society that we are not consciously aware of them: biological essentialism, androcentrism, and gender polarization.

References

"Ancient ruins of Amazons" (1997) *The New York Times*, Feb. 25, p. A12.

Ad Hoc Women's Coalition Against War Crimes in the Former Yugoslavia (1993) *Call for Action*. New Brunswick, NJ: Center for Women's Global Leadership at Rutgers University.

American Psychiatric Association (1994) *Diagnostic and Statistical Manual of Mental Disorders,* 4th ed. Washington, D.C.: (author).

Azar, B. (1997) Environment is key to serotonin levels. *APA Monitor*, April, pp. 26, 29.

Ballif-Spanvill, B., Clayton, C., and Barlow, S. (1997) *Grant Proposal To Develop Training Tapes on Conflict Resolution for Elementary Age Children*. College of Family, Home, and Social Sciences, Brigham Young University.

Barbaree, H. and Marshall, W. (1991) The role of male sexual arousal in rape: six models. *Journal of Consulting and Clinical Psychology, 59*(5), 621–630.

Barlow, S. and Clayton, C. (1996) When mothers murder: understanding infanticide by females. In H.V. Hall (Ed.), *Lethal Violence 2000: A Source Book on Fatal Domestic, Acquaintance and Stranger Aggression*, pp. 203–230. Kamuela, HI: Pacific Institute for the Study of Conflict and Aggression.

Barry, K. (1979) *Female Sexual Slavery*. Englewood Cliffs, NJ: Prentice-Hall.

Bem, S. (1993) *The Lenses of Gender: Transforming the Debate on Sexual Inequality*. New Haven: Yale University.

Benderly, B. (1982) Rape free or rape prone? *Science*, October, pp. 40–43.

Benjamin, L. (1996) *Interpersonal Diagnosis of Personality Disorder,* 2nd ed. New York: Guilford Press.

Bowker, L. (1983) *Beating Wife Beating*. Lexington MA: Heath Publishers.

British Broadcasting Company (1997) *The Story of Painting with Sister Wendy*. London: BBC.

Brock-Utne, B. (1997) Linking the micro and macro in peace and development studies. In J. Turpin and L. Kurtz (Eds.), *The Web of Violence: From the Interpersonal to Global*, pp. 149–160) Chicago: University of Illinois Press.

Bronfenbrenner, U. and Ceci, S. (1994) Nature-nurture reconceptualized in developmental perspective: a bioecological model. *Psychological Review, 101*, 568–586.

Brownmiller, S. (1975) *Against Our Will: Men, Women, and Rape*. New York: Simon & Schuster.

Burke, B. (1984) Infanticide: why does it happen in monkeys, mice, and men? *Science, 84*(5), 26–31.

Buydens-Branchey, L. and Branchey, M.H. (1992) Cortisol in alcoholics with a disordered aggression control. *Psychoneuroendocrinology, 17*(1), 45–54.

Carmen, A. and Moody, H. (1985) *Working Women: The Subterranean World of Street Prostitution*. New York: Harper & Row.

Chang, L. (1997) *The Rape of Nanking: The Forgotten Holocaust of World War II*. New York: Basic Books.

Check, J. and Malamuth, N. (1985) An empirical assessment of some feminist hypotheses about rape. *International Journal of Women's Studies, 8*, 414–423.

Constantino, J., Grosz, D., Saenger, P., Chandler, D.W., Nandi, R., and Earls, F.J. (1993) Testosterone and aggression in children. *Journal of American Academy of Child and Adolescent Psychiatry, 32*(6), 1217–1222.

Cowan, G., Lee, C., Levy, D., and Snyder, D. (1988) Dominance and inequality in X-rated videocasettes. *Psychology of Women Quarterly, 12*, 299–311.

Dabbs, J., Frady, R., Carr, T., and Besch, N. (1987) Saliva testosterone and criminal violence in young adult prison inmates. *Psychosomatic Medicine, 49*, 174–182.

Dabbs, J., Ruback, R., Frady, R., Hooper, C., and Sgoutas, D. (1988) Saliva testosterone and criminal violence among women. *Personality and Individual Differences, 1*, 103–110.

deWaal, F. (1989) *Peacemaking Among Primates*. Cambridge: Harvard University Press.

Dutton, D. (1986) Wife-assaulters' explanations for assault: the neutralization of self-punishment. *Canadian Journal of Behavioral Science, 18*(4), 381–390.

Dutton, D. (1987a) The criminal justice response to wife assault. *Law and Human Behavior, 11*, (3), 189–206.

Dutton, D. (1987b) Wife assault: social-psychological contributions to criminal justice policy. *Applied Social Psychology Annual, 7*, 238–261.

Dutton, D. (1995) Intimate abusiveness. *Clinical Psychology: Science and Practice*, *2*(3), 207–224.

Eagly, A.H. and Steffen, V.J. (1986) Gender and aggressive behavior: a meta-analytic review of the social psychological literature. *Psychological Bulletin, 100*, 309–330.

Ehrenreich, B. (1997) *Blood Rites: The Origins and Nature of the Passions of War*. New York: Henry Holt.

Eibl-Eibesfeldt, I. (1989) *Human Ethology*. Hawthorne, NY: Aldine de Gruyter.

Ellis, L. (1991) A synthesized (biosocial) theory of rape. *Journal of Consulting and Clinical Psychology, 59*(5), 631–642.

Enquist, M. and Leimar, O. (1990) Evolution of fatal fighting. *Animal Behavior, 39*, 1–9.

Evans, J. (1991) *Strategies of Deconstruction: Derrida and the Myth of Voice*. Minneapolis, MN: University of Minnesota Press.

Faludi, S. (1992) *Backlash: The Undeclared War Against Women*. London: Chatto & Windus Press.

Goldstein, D. (1983) Spouse abuse. In A. Goldstein (Ed.), *Prevention and Control of Aggression* (pp. 37–65) New York: Pergamon Press.

Goodall, J. (1986) *The Chimpanzee of Gombe: Patterns of Behavior*. Cambridge, MA: Belknap Press.

Gottman, J. (1979) *Marital Interaction: Experimental Investigations*. New York: Academic Press.

Hall, E. and Flannery, P. (1984) Prevalence and correlates of sexual assault experiences in adolescence. *Victimotology, 9*, 398–406.

Hall, G., Hirschman, R., and Beutler, L. (1991) Introduction to special section on theories of sexual aggression. *Journal of Consulting and Clinical Psychology, 59*(5), 619–620.

Hall, G. and Barongan, C. (1997) Prevention of sexual aggression: sociocultural risk and protective factors. *American Psychologist, 52*(1), 5–14.

Halpern, J.M., Sharma, V., Siever, L.J., Schwartz, S.T., Matier, K., Wornell, G., and Newcorn, J.H. (1994) Serotonergic function in aggressive and nonaggressive boys with attention deficit hyperactivity disorder. *American Journal of Psychiatry, 151*(2), 243–248.

Hamai, M., Nishida, T., Takasaki, H., and Turner, L. (1992) New records of within-group infanticide and cannibalism in wild chimpanzees. *Primates, 33*, 151–162.

Harris, L.M., Gergen, K.J., and Lannaman, J.W. (1986) Aggression rituals. *Communications Monographs, 53*, 252–265.

Heilbrun, C. (1990) *Hamlet's Mother and Other Women*. New York: Columbia University Press.

Holtzworth-Munroe, A. and Stuart, G. (1994) Typologies of male batterers: three subtypes and the differences among them. *Psychological Bulletin, 116*(3), 476–497.

Horrocks, R. (1994) *Masculinity in Crisis: Myths, Fantasies and Realities*. New York: St. Martin's Press.

Hotaling, G. and Sugarman, D. (1986) An analysis of risk markers in husband to wife violence: the current state of knowledge. *Violence and Victims, 1*, 101–124.

Irigaray, L. (1993) *Sexes and Genealogies*. New York: Columbia University Press.

Keller, E. (1985) *Reflections on Gender and Science*. New Haven: Yale University Press.

Lips, H. (1997) *Sex and Gender: An Introduction*, 3rd ed. Mountain View, CA: Mayfield Publishing.

MacLeod, L. (1980) *Wife-Battering in Canada: The Vicious Circle*. Hull, Quebec: Canadian Government Publishing Centre.

Mahler, M., Pine, F., and Bergman, A. (1975) *The Psychological Birth of the Human Infant: Symbiosis and Individuation*. New York: Basic Books.

Malamuth, N. (1981) Rape proclivity among males. *Journal of Social Issues, 37*, 138–157.

Malamuth, N. (1988) Predicting laboratory aggression against male and female targets: implications for sexual aggression. *Journal of Research in Personality, 22*, 474–495.

Malamuth, N., Sockloskie, R., Koss, M., and Tanaka, J. (1991) Characteristics of aggressors against women: testing a model using a national sample of college students. *Journal of Consulting and Clinical Psychology, 59*(5), 670–681.

Manson, J. and Wrangham, R. (1991) Intergroup aggression in chimpanzees and humans. *Current Anthropology, 32*, 369–390.

Marshall, D., Laws, L., and Barbaree, H. (1990) *Handbook of Sexual Assault: Issues, Theories and Treatment of the Offender*. New York: Plenum Press.

Milgram, S. (1974) *Obedience to Authority*. New York: Harper & Row.

National Public Radio (1997) *All Things Considered*, July 22.

Netter, P. and Neuhäuser-Metternich, S. (1991) Types of aggressiveness and catecholamine response in essential hypertensives and healthy controls. *Journal of Psychosomatic Research, 35*(4/5) 409–419.

Pagelow, M. (1993) Justice for victims of spouse abuse in divorce and child-custody cases. *Violence and Victims, 8*(1), 69–83.

Raine, A., Venables, P., and Williams, M. (1990) Relationship between central and autonomic measures of arousal at age 15 and criminality at age 24 years. *Archives of General Psychiatry, 47*(11), 1003–1007.

Raine, A., Venables, P., and Williams, M. (1996) Better autonomic conditioning and faster electrodermal half-recovery time at age 15 years as possible protective factors against crime at age 29 years. *Developmental Psychology, 32*(4), 624–630.

Restak, R. (1979) *The Brain: The Last Frontier*. New York: Doubleday Books.

Restak, R. (1984) *The Brain*. Toronto: Bantam Books.

Roberts, T. (1997) *The Lanahan Readings in the Psychology of Women*. Baltimore, MD: Lanahan Publishers.

Rollins, J. (1996) *Women's Minds, Women's Bodies: The Psychology of Women in a Biosocial Context*. Cambridge, NJ: Prentice-Hall.

Rosenbaum, A. and O'Leary, D. (1981) Marital violence: characteristics of abusive couples. *Journal of Consulting and Clinical Psychology, 49*, 63–71.

Sanday, P. (1981) The socio-cultural context of rape: a cross-cultural study. *Journal of Social Issues, 37*(4), 5–27.

Sarne, Y., Mandel, J., Goncalves, M.H., Brook, S., Gafni, M., and Elizur, A. (1995) Imipramine binding to blood platelets and aggressive behavior in offenders, schizophrenics and normal volunteers. *Neuropsychobiology, 31*, 120–124.

Shange, N. (1978) With no immediate cause. In N. Shange (Ed.), *Nappy Edges*, pp. 114–117. New York: St. Martin's Press.

Sheffield, C. (1997) Sexual terrorism. In L. O'Toole and J. Schiffman (Eds.), *Gender Violence: Interdisciplinary Perspectives*, pp. 110–128. New York: New York University Press.

Silbert, M. and Pines, A. (1983) Early sexual exploitation as an influence in prostitution. *Social Work, 28*, 285–289.

Siskel, G. (1980) Nauseating film trend puts plague upon the land. *Salt Lake Tribune*, Sept. 26, p. 3E.

Solzhenitsyn, A. (1974) *The Gulag Archipelago: 1918–1965. An Experiment in Literary Investigation*. London: Book Club Associates.

Stack, S. and Kanavy, M. (1983) The effect of religion on forcible rape: a structural analysis. *Journal of the Scientific Study of Religion, 22*(1), 67–74.

Straus, M., Gelles, R., and Steinmetz, S. (1980) *Behind Closed Doors: Violence in the American Family*. New York: Anchor Press.

Thornhill, R. and Thornhill, N. (1992) The evolutionary psychology of men's coercive sexuality. *Behavioral and Brain Sciences, 15*(2), 363–375.

Unger, R. and Crawford, M. (1996) *Women and Gender: A Feminist Psychology*, 2nd ed. New York: McGraw-Hill.

U.S. Attorney General's Commission on Pornography (1986) *Final Report*. Washington, D.C.: U.S. Government Printing Office.

Valentich, M. (1994) Rape revisited: sexual violence against women in the former Yugoslavia. *The Canadian Journal of Human Sexuality, 3*(1), 53–64.

Venables, P. (1989) The Emanuel Miller Memorial Lecture 1987: childhood markers for adult disorders. *Journal of Child Psychology and Psychiatry and Allied Disciplines, 30*(3), 347–364.

Weaver, J., Masland, J., and Zillmann, D. (1984) Effect of erotica on young men's aesthetic perception of their female sexual partners. *Perception and Motor Skills, 58*, 929–930.

Wilson, E. (1975) *Sociobiology*. Cambridge: Harvard Press.

Wilson, M. and Daly, M. (1985) Competitiveness, risk-taking, and violence: the young male syndrome. *Ethology and Sociobiology, 6*, 59–73.

Yourell, A. and McCabe, M. (1989) The motivations underlying male rape of women. *Australian Journal of Sex, Marriage, and Family, 9*(4), 215–224.

Zillmann, D. and Bryant, J. (1986) Shifting preferences in pornography consumption. *Communications Research, 13*, 560–578.

Zimbardo, P. (1970) The human choice: individuation, reason and order vs. deindividuation, impulse and chaos. In W. Arnold and D. Levine (Eds.), *Nebraska Symposium on Motivation*, pp. 237–307. Lincoln, NE: University of Nebraska Press.

Zimbardo, P. (1997) What messages are behind today's cults? *APA Monitor, 5*, 14.

About the Authors

Sally H. Barlow, ABPP, teaches in the areas of diversity, the social psychology of groups, psychodynamic treatment, and advanced objective assessment at Brigham Young University in the Psychology Department where she has been the recipient of the Excellence in Teaching Award. She earned her ABPP Diplomate in Clinical Psychology in 1991 and has published in the area of diversity, process, and outcome research in time-limited group psychotherapy and personality disorders. She has received numerous research grants, and has presented papers at both national and international conferences. **Claudia J. Clayton, Ph.D.,** is an assistant professor of psychology at Brigham Young University. She holds a Ph.D. in anatomy, with emphases in neuroscience and pharmacology, from the University of Utah School of Medicine, and a Ph.D. in clinical psychology from Brigham Young University. She received postdoctoral training at the University of Rochester School of Medicine and Dentistry and the University of North Carolina at Chapel Hill. Her interests include developmental psychology, biological psychology, personality disorders, and family dynamics.

Part II

COLLECTIVE VIOLENCE BY PRIVATE GROUPS AND INSTITUTIONS

Chapter 7

CULTS: PREDISPOSED TO COMMUNAL VIOLENCE?

Lita Linzer Schwartz

When we hear the word "cult" we might have any one of several mental images. Some might recall saffron-robed Hare Krishnas with shaved heads singing on street corners or soliciting contributions in airports; others may think of the Moonies and their mass marriages; still others might visualize the tragedies of Jonestown or Waco or Heaven's Gate. In some settings, these groups are perceived as religions and therefore non-profit bodies; in other locations, they are taxed as a business. As activist groups in recruiting, fundraising, and proselytizing, they may be regarded as highly assertive bodies; as groups that cause death to others or themselves, they would have to be labeled lethally violent. On an individual level, a cult member might regard the group as a source of salvation; the member's family may perceive the cult as having stolen their child.

What *is* a cult? Is it a religion? A threat? A source of violence? Or a source of salvation?

What Is a Cult?

According to the general dictionary definition, a cult is a group of people who share beliefs, principles, or a leader, or all of these; it may or may not be religious. From a mental health point of view and as defined by Levine (1980, pp. 123–124), a cult is...

"... a group which follows a dominant leader, often living, who may make absolute claims that he is divine, God incarnate, the messiah, or God's emissary, and that he is omniscient and infallible. Membership is contingent on complete and literal acceptance of the leader's claims and acceptance of his doctrines and dogma. Complete, unquestioning loyalty and allegiance are demanded together with a total willingness to obey the cult leader's commands without question — which may include a unique way of viewing the world, of acting, of dressing, or of thinking."

This total acceptance and obedience has been observed in many of the groups that are regarded as cults. One example has been the willingness of Moonies to sell flowers for 15 hours or more each day to meet their fund-raising quotas for the Unification Church or to allow Reverend Moon to select their spouses. Similarly, the fanaticism of the followers of the Shree Bhagwan Rajneesh, when he resided in Oregon, extended to large financial contributions that were converted into Rolls Royces as well as attempts to establish a political base in the state. On the violent side, there have been the People's Temple suicides in Jonestown in 1978, the Branch Davidians' tragedy at Waco in 1993, the Solar Temple suicides in Canada and Europe in 1994, and, later, the nerve gas attack by the Aum Shinrikyo cult in Tokyo in 1995 and the Heaven's Gate suicides in 1997, all in response to the leaders' desires.

There are those who deny that the groups just mentioned are cults, and others who regard any extremely fundamentalist or highly orthodox religious groups as cults. Although these latter groups may use some of the same techniques as cults, they must be evaluated on an individual basis in terms of the perception of the leader, whether the recruit is informed before joining of the nature of the group and its beliefs, and similar criteria (Isser and Schwartz, 1988). There are several groups that have "unconventional" beliefs and lifestyles, including the Latter Day Saints (Mormons), the "Father Divine" movement, the Amish, and Jehovah's Witnesses. They are generally regarded today as non-traditional sects or subdivisions of Christianity. Commentators such as Kephart and Zellner (1991) provided descriptions of several of these groups. The Committee on Psychiatry and Religion of the Group for the Advancement of Psychiatry (GAP; 1992, p. 3) distinguishes between sects and cults in this way: "Groups that define themselves as dissidents within particular religions [are] sects, and those that define themselves by creating or pursuing alien forms of worship [are] cults."

Another way to differentiate cults from sects and other subdivisions of major religions is to compare the ways in which they do or do not exhibit the characteristics identified as typical of cults. Schwartz and Kaslow (1981) developed an 8 × 10 factor grid, where a check could be noted for each group on each characteristic, that summarizes these traits. The grid included the following groups and criteria:

Groups (vertical axis)	*Criteria* (horizontal axis)
Lubavitcher Chassidim	Charismatic leader
Amish	Submission to authority
Roman Catholic	Communal life-style
Mormons	Rigid ideology
Unification Church	Restricted communications
Church of Scientology	Isolation from family
Alamo Federation	Active recruiting
Children of God	Physiologic deprivation
	Hate/fear of outsiders
	Assets turned over to group

The only characteristics shared by all eight groups were "submission to authority" and "rigid ideology"; otherwise, the first four groups can be distinguished from the last four in a number of ways:

	First Four	*Last Four*
Assets:	Tithing and contributions	All financial assets
Recruiting:	Identify the group	Rarely identify group
Isolation:	Rare	Fairly common
Hate/fear:	Rare	Preached
Life-style:	Individual family residences	Frequently communal in close-knit neighborhoods
Charisma:	High respect for but no worship of leader as God	Virtual deification of leader

Even in non-religious groups that function in a cult-like manner, the individual is accepted only if he or she becomes a committed believer in the wisdom of the omniscient leader, an obedient follower of that leader, and an active financial contributor to the leader's "cause." Examples of these groups include *est* and its sequels founded by Werner Erhard, Lifespring, the Sullivanians, Charles Manson's followers, and the Symbionese Liberation Army. A number of "skinhead" groups also share some of the characteristics of cults, particularly in-group loyalty vs. hate and fear of outsiders, rigid ideology, and submission to authority.

Robert Lifton, whose work on "thought reform" in China during the 1950s and later studies of brainwashing in other settings are classics, has provided a briefer definition of a cult (Lifton, 1991, p. 2):

"Cults can be identified by three characteristics: (1) a charismatic leader who increasingly becomes an object of worship as the general principles that may have originally sustained the group lose their power; (2) a process I call coercive persuasion or thought reform; (3) economic, sexual, and other exploitation of group members by the leader and the ruling coterie."

In both religious and secular cult groups, according to Lamberg (1997), the leader, or guru, "forms the cult and directs its activities. While he or she has enormous power, this power comes only from disciples. Without disciples, there is no guru."

The cult leader may manifest one or more of the following roles: Hero, Outsider (i.e., persecuted by society), Narcissist, Charismatic Figure, or Entrepreneur (GAP, 1992). Charisma is such a necessity that it is almost a given, with one or more of the other roles also part of the leader's *persona*. It is the leader's revelation and rebirth that typically are the bases for the beliefs and behaviors of the disciples, no matter how silly that narrative might seem to a non-believer. For example, Marshall Herff Applewhite and Bonnie Lu Trusdale Nettles, otherwise known as "Guinea and Pig" and "Bo and Peep" and "Do and Ti" (Bearak, 1997), were both divorced, middle-aged, and reasonably observant in a traditional religious sense. They wrote soul-searching letters to each other, sharing their thoughts, for several years. Bearak (1997, p. B8) observed that these letters represented "a journey from sincere religious zeal to delusional beliefs in a divine calling and finally to what most psychiatrists would call outright psychosis." As early as the 1970s, as reported by Dolbee (1997, p. A1), the pair claimed to be from outer space and to be seeking "to recruit a crew for a spaceship that would come and take them to a higher plane." The psychosis, with its doctrine rooted in scriptures and mysticism, led ultimately to the group suicide that we know as "Heaven's Gate" in response to the appearance of the Hale-Bopp comet.

There are relatively few female gurus. The widow of Father Divine kept his Peace Mission alive long after his death; Susan Alamo was co-leader with her husband Tony of the Alamo Foundation until her death; and Elizabeth Prophet headed the Church Universal and Triumphant until the mid-1990s, when she stepped down from her position. Each of these women had the leadership characteristics and magnetic quality that kept her disciples under control.

In all of the cult groups, emphasis on being part of the "in" group is accompanied by hostility toward, and perhaps fear of, non-believers. Outsiders include family members, who may be contacted or seen only with permission of the leader and usually for the purpose of obtaining funds for the group. Once in the group, the other cult members become each other's family. Adding to the separation from the larger society is the use of a special vocabulary or the assignment of special meanings to common expressions, all known only to members of the group (Landa, 1991). If the cult is a religious one, the official message is typically that only members of the in-group will be "saved" when the apocalypse occurs.

Margaret Singer, a premier researcher on the cults, described these groups very well (Singer, 1995, pp. xxii–xxiii):

"Myriads of false messiahs, quacks, and leaders of cults and thought-reform groups have emerged who use Orwellian mind-manipulation techniques. They recruit the curious, the unaffiliated, the trusting, and the altruistic. They promise intellectual, spiritual, political, social, and self-actualization utopias. These modern-day pied pipers offer, among other things, pathways to God, salvation, revolution, personal development, enlightenment, perfect health, psychological growth, egalitarianism, channels to speak with 35,000-year-old 'entities', life in ecospheres, and contact with extraterrestrial beings."

There are people who disagree with Singer's view and that of others who perceive many of these groups as cults. They believe that the critics of the groups are anti-religion, or are psychotherapists who reinterpret "innocent spiritual involvements" as "induced psycho-pathologies", thereby enlarging their psychotherapeutic practices (Schwartz, 1985, pp. 152–153; also see Anthony and Robbins, 1992). That is, some who support cults as religions allege that mental health therapists are of the opinion that anyone who joins a cult is mentally ill and really needs therapy and that all ex-cult members need therapy. There is little or no evidence to support this accusation against psychotherapists or any other opponents of cults. In fact, however, former members may need help to deal with their feelings about having been in a cult or with experiences they may have had there, and their parents may need help in dealing with, first, their child's disappearance and, second, the child's preference for the cult over the family. These realities are hardly an attempt to expand therapists' private practices; they meet a real need.

Recruiting and Retention

There are, as already noted, many religious sects and groups that proselytize actively and solicit funds openly. If their members knock at your door, they immediately identify themselves as Jehovah's Witnesses, Mormons, or Christian Scientists, to cite just a few. Cult members generally do not. They befriend the loner, the altruist, the seeker, and the alienated without identifying the group to which they belong. Their implication or assertion (known as "heavenly deception"), however, is usually that they are working for the betterment of mankind, or to help the aged, or to enhance the individual's self-esteem, knowledge, chance of salvation, personality, or some other aspect of the person's life. They then invite the prospective recruit to a dinner or a lecture or to visit "our farm" to learn more about the group's work.

As Zimbardo (1997) has described the recruiting process, who among the emotionally needy could resist becoming part of a group …

"... in which you will find instant friendship, a caring family, respect for your contributions, an identity, safety, security, simplicity, and an organized daily agenda. You will learn new skills, have a respected position, gain personal insight, improve your personality and intelligence. ... Your leader may promise not only to heal any sickness and foretell the future, but to give you the gift of immortality, if you are a true believer."

Those who are vulnerable to the recruiter's appeal may be emotionally confused or distraught at the moment because of personal traumas, such as the breakup of a relationship, loss of a job, being away from home for the first time, confronting a major change in status, or feeling a void in their life (Fennell, 1993; Lamberg, 1997; Sheffield, 1997; Sullivan, 1997). In addition, they tend to have strong dependency needs, a distaste for making choices, and self-doubt. They often come from families where the parents are overly permissive or are highly authoritarian and where there is a weak or non-existent relationship between child and father (Schwartz and Kaslow, 1979; GAP, 1992). Other factors may include parents who expect too much of their child, an overwhelming desire or need for peer (or other) acceptance, low self-esteem, a kind of naive idealism, angst in a new situation, and the breakdown of family ties (Schwartz and Kaslow, 1981; GAP, 1992).

The recruits are usually bright, from middle-class homes, lonely, and without the "street smarts" that youths from less well-endowed neighborhoods usually learn. They are poorly prepared to resist cult recruiters, who are very convincing.

One member of the Aum Supreme Truth (Aum Shinrikyo) group in Japan, who joined *after* the subway gas attack, is quoted as saying that she joined because, according to Sullivan (1997), she "was feeling spiritually unfulfilled and unsatisfied with life. 'I felt like I really wanted to serve something and to be of help.'" While most laypersons would think that this woman (and others like her) was clearly mentally ill, most psychologists and psychiatrists agree that relatively few recruits suffer from psychopathology, averring, as reported by GAP (1992. p. 31), "that seriously disturbed people are a minority in cult populations. Truly psychotic individuals do not make good converts or group members."

Once on site for a discussion or a lecture, the naive recruit may be subject to intensive mind manipulation without even being aware of it. What might have taken weeks or months of patient instruction many decades ago has been refined and accelerated in more recent years to a matter of days or hours (Isser and Schwartz, 1988). Zimbardo's "prison" experiment with his students (1973) provided a vivid example of the speed with which an individual's mind-set and self-perception could be changed.

For those unfamiliar with this experiment, Zimbardo divided his class randomly into "prisoners" and "jailers", prepared "cells" in the basement of a campus building in which the "prisoners" were housed, and discovered that within 2 or 3 days, the prisoners were cowering from their jailers' verbal abuse. The jailers, for their part, had become abusive, punitive, and dictatorial. Even Zimbardo had not been prepared for this rapid change in mental state, and he quickly drew his experiment to a close.

Brown (1991) argued that, while proselytization is a corollary of the First Amendment right to freedom of religion for religious groups, when cults (religious or otherwise) use mind manipulation techniques, often called brainwashing, to destroy an individual's right to choose not to join, this constitutes the tort of false imprisonment rather than religious freedom.

If the group can get the recruit to accept one or two premises or activities, it becomes easier to ensnare him or her more quickly. This is similar to the good salesperson's "foot in the door" technique. The group's dogma is communicated through clichés and slogans, delivered in chants, mantras, familiar melodies sung with special group-oriented lyrics, and repetition of religious-type greeting phrases. Through abundant use of behavior modification techniques, especially positive reinforcement, the recruit is drawn deeper into the group. This technique is usually referred to as "love-bombing".

If the recruit rejects the friendship and reinforcement offered, feelings of guilt are engendered over the prospective abandonment. On the other hand, successful recruiting leads to close bonding among the members against the outside world, although within the group, they are encouraged to watch their peers for any deviation from the "true path". Individual autonomy is surrendered in exchange for acceptance by the leader and the group and the promise of extraordinary bliss. Langone (1994, p. 10) described the process: "Cultic groups foster unhealthy forms of dependency by focusing on submission and obedience to those in authority. Such groups operate under a dynamic of deception, dependency, and dread (the 'DDD syndrome') in order to maintain control over members."

Part of the instruction is a kind of depersonalization, i.e., breaking down the individual's persona in order to create a new one that conforms to the image of the group and its leader (Schwartz, 1991b). To a degree, this is similar to what was done to novices when they entered a convent or seminary. The difference, however, is that in the latter case, the novice entered the order voluntarily, knew what to expect in terms of lifestyle, and had the option to withdraw if he or she could not adapt to the new life. Withdrawal from a cult is not as easy.

While in the cult, members relinquish independent thought and judgment. They typically withdraw from college or the work-force in order to meet the expectations or demands of the group and work devotedly at their assigned tasks within the group for virtually no pay (other than the approval of the group), little rest, and a less than balanced diet.

Cults of Abuse and Violence

In the rare instances when a member attempts to avoid a group requirement or task, or refuses to obey the leader, punishment can be extremely harsh. Corporal punishment may even be practiced on infants

(Langone and Eisenberg, 1993). The disobedient one may be beaten, put on a strict minimal diet, shunned, isolated, or even killed. The murder of 40 to 50 defectors by the Aum Shinrikyo group is an example of this last extreme measure (Lamberg, 1997). Lifton (1991) alluded to this as the "dispensing of existence" in which those who have not embraced the truth as pronounced by the cult are labeled "evil" and deemed to lack the right to exist. In other words, conformity is everything; defection brings the threat of extinction.

Child Abuse

Some groups, such as Jim Jones' People's Temple and the Branch Davidians, initially welcome entire families into their midst. In other cults, where the new members are late adolescents and young adults, a natural result of lengthy affiliation is the birth of children to cult members. In both settings, the children are as subject to the rules of the group as are adults, with shame and humiliation or corporal punishment inflicted for any transgressions. According to Landa (1991, p. 609):

> *"A cult's abusive practices generally apply to everyone in varying degrees of severity, depending on each member's status within the group. It is not uncommon that preferential treatment be given first to the leader's offspring, second to those born into the cult, and last to those brought into the cult by their parents."*

Landa (1991, p. 615) went on to say, "A parent's willingness to participate in or allow the abuse of his or her children at the leader's request is one indicator the leader uses to test the parent's devotion to the cult." If, on the other hand, the parents protest harsh treatment of their little ones, they, too, may be whipped or otherwise punished, usually in front of the entire group as an example and warning to others. In a variation of this, in Jonestown, children were punished for their parents' activities, such as speaking privately to each other (Wooden, 1981). In a sense, the children were held hostage for their parents' behavior. Punishments of children have ranged from forced sex to isolation and starvation in a box, from beatings to psychological abuse (Landa, 1991). At the extreme, especially in Satanic-type and fundamentalist cults, children may be horribly sexually abused or killed ritualistically (Clifford, 1994; deMause, 1994; Langone and Eisenberg, 1993).

Children in cults and some religious groups are often subject to so much physical and psychological abuse and medical neglect that their conditions may result in death as the parents rely on prayer or a leader's "spiritual healing" instead of appropriate medical treatment. One example of medical neglect is the case of a 22-month-old boy who died from loss of blood because his parents not only would not seek medical help because of their religious beliefs, but they said they would have resisted attempts to provide such help by others. They did have their pastor pray over the child after the child cut his foot. This did not help (Gibbons, 1997). An autopsy showed that the toddler had hemophilia. The parents were subsequently charged with involuntary manslaughter.

In another case, a couple who belonged to the Faith Tabernacle Church lost one child because of lack of medical treatment in 1991 and pleaded guilty to manslaughter. Six years later, they lost a second child because their pastor's anointing the child with oil could not relieve a diabetic coma ("Second faith healing...", 1997).

Faith Assembly, founded in 1963 by Hobart Freeman and primarily based in Indiana, is another church that condemns medications and the field of medicine. Hughes (1990, p. 108) reported that, "Freeman contends that Satan controls the visible, sensory realm of nature, and that he works through the occult forces of medicine, science, and education. Medical treatment is regarded as unbelief, bringing on sickness and death from Satan. The power of Satan increases in direct proportion to one's disobedience or doubt of

God." Freeman asserted that demons reside in hospitals and live within medical drugs. Clearly, anyone who disagreed with him was possessed by demons and under the influence of Satan. Members of Faith Assembly followed his teachings, even when it was their children who were ill.

Hughes (1990, p. 112) suggested that the parents' submission to Freeman in these situations was characterized by ego-splitting, limited affective attachment, ethical confusion, and counterphobic defenses: "When faced with childhood illness, these parents could not assess the situation realistically. From fear of disobeying God or Freeman-the-father, they practiced faith healing techniques consistent with a paranoid conception of illness." As a result, several cases of little children with treatable illnesses that went untreated medically resulted in infanticide.

Rudin (1984) cited a number of deaths from faith-healing religious groups, which continue to be reported in newspapers in the late 1990s. These bring to the fore questions about religious freedom and parental rights to raise their children according to their beliefs versus the state's duty to protect the welfare of children. The U.S. Supreme Court, in its 1944 ruling in Prince v. Commonwealth of Massachusetts (Prince v. Commonwealth of Massachusetts, 1944), attempted to resolve this conflict. The decision included these statements: "Parents may be free to become [religious] martyrs themselves. But it does not follow that they are free to make martyrs of their children." Unfortunately, this ruling has not been as effective a protector of children as most people might wish. Even laws in all 50 states which mandate the reporting of suspected child abuse have not effectively protected children in cults from abuse. As stated by Malcarne and Burchard (1992, p. 84):

"The state's primary interest lies in the protection of the children, not the parents' right to parent freely. However, religious cults can present novel problems, in that the parental behaviors defined by the state as abusive or neglectful may not be perceived as such by cult members, and further may be both intentional and well-meaning."

Children of cult members are abused in another way. They rarely receive traditional formal schooling opportunities, although they may be sent to cult-run boarding schools or to ashrams for children only. According to Langone and Eisenberg (1993, p. 337), they have "little knowledge about the world, especially if their group was isolated ... their capacity to think critically and act independently may be deficient, not merely 'blocked' as may be the case with ex-cultists who joined as adults." The few who may attend public schools are a puzzle to their peers because of their narrow range of life experience (Holmes, 1995).

It is the cruelty to children that may drive one or both parents to try to leave the group; however, if only one of the parents seeks to leave, he or she may have great difficulty in taking the children out, too, and may seek aid from the courts. Rudin (1984, p. 13) found that, "Many parents and grandparents claim the groups do not let them see the children, do not honor their legal visitation rights, or do not turn the children over when they gain custody". One grandmother in Britain successfully sought to have her grandson made a ward of the court when he was 8 days old because his mother was raising him in The Family, a/k/a The Children of God. According to *The Times* of London (as cited in American Family Foundation, 1996), when the case was heard again 3 years later, the Lord Justice said that the boy could remain with his mother in the cult, but "insisted that the mother and The Family's leaders must renounce the preachings of their late leader, David Berg, who promoted incest, prostitution, and sex with children."

Practices in the Sullivan Institute for Research in Psychoanalysis, a non-religious cult, have led a number of nonmember parents to try to gain custody of their children. As reported by Kandel (1988, p. 123), "The core of the Sullivanian theory is that the nuclear family and all strong dyadic relationships are psychologically destructive, and that parent-child bonds in particular are the root of all evil and the mainspring of maladjustment." All members of the group must be in perpetual therapy with therapists of the group, and the therapist's consent is necessary to bear or raise a child. There is no therapeutic confidentiality about this or any other aspect of therapy, as the therapists report everything to the group's leaders. The biological parents are displaced by "foster parents" from within the group, on a rotating basis, in order to prevent the development of parent-child bonding.

When one parent leaves the group, he or she may have to prove to the court how dangerous the Sullivanians are in order to demonstrate the potential psychological and physical injury the child may suffer within the group. The limits on the time that a parent could spend with his or her own child, especially private quality time, are seen as a strong argument against allowing the child to remain with the Sullivanian parent. The state will examine all aspects of the child's life within the cult to determine whether they pose a danger to the child's health, safety, and general welfare. Kandel (1988, p. 125) further observed that:

"Former Sullivanian parents testified that they had been forced to surrender their children or required to send them to boarding school at ages as young as three years. Testimony was given by young adults who had been raised within the Sullivanians on the suffering they had experienced. (One Sullivanian-raised young adult had become a teenage alcoholic. Another had committed suicide.)"

It is not only the Sullivanians who deride the traditional family unit. Father Divine was referred to as "Father" and his wife as "Mother" from the time he founded his Peace Mission in the early 1930s (Cantril and Sherif, 1938). There was no sex, no marriage, and no (other) family for those who belonged to the Mission. However, despite the way it was portrayed in its heyday, the Mission was nowhere near as evil as the other cults mentioned here (GAP, 1992, p. 11):

"Father Divine's Peace Mission was a syncretistic blend of Pentecostal faith, positive thinking, and secular pragmatism. It became an emotional support system for hundreds of American blacks who were struggling in the process of urbanization. In return for submission to the group, which regarded Divine as the personification of God, members received food, clothing, and housing at minimal cost. In addition, the Mission supported civil rights and welfare for the poor."

In the Unification Church, Reverend Sun Myung Moon and his wife are regarded as the "True Parents". Jim Jones and his wife functioned in the same way in the People's Temple. A child who has been well indoctrinated may refuse to cooperate with his or her parents if they leave the group or may divulge their plans to defect to the "True Parent" (Landa, 1991). Even if children leave a cult, it may be difficult for them to become attached to or to respect their biological parents because of lessons learned in the group.

Adult Abuse

Ostracism, whippings, and other physical and psychological abuses await erring adults in cults as well as the children. Their diet, already restricted, may be reduced even more. They may be shamed in front of other members. Some cases have been reported where the member who had not met a day's quota had to continue selling the roses, books, or other commodities until the quota *was* met, no matter how many hours it took or how tired the individual might be.

Adult abuse may be physical, as described above, or psychological. If a member is punished by being shunned by peers in the group, this could make him or her suicidal at the rejection. The leader may ignore the individual or place him or her at the foot of the group's dinner table rather than in the person's accustomed place. The individual may not be allowed to participate in certain activities within the group or, where there had been contact with the original family, may not be permitted to make phone calls or have visits even for important family occasions.

Any downgrading of the member's status in the cult can be devastating even as it forces the member back to conformity.

If a cult member is ill or injured, the leaders rarely permit the member to see a physician or to be hospitalized. Their fear, of course, is that someone from outside the cult will attempt to contact and deprogram the member. In addition to rejecting medical treatment for group members, most cults reject any form of psychological or psychiatric treatment for those who may need it. A case in point involved the death of a 36-year-old Scientologist who was in a minor traffic accident in Clearwater, FL, but had not been hurt. For no apparent reason, she stripped off her clothes and began to walk in her naked state down the street. She was taken to a hospital for a psychiatric examination, but several Scientologists arrived to remove her from the hospital, saying that their religion did not believe in psychiatry. According to Frantz (1997, p. A1):

> *"Seventeen days later, after being kept under 24-hour watch at a Scientology-own[ed] hotel in downtown Clearwater, Ms. McPherson was dead. By church accounts, she had spit out food, banged violently on the walls of her room, and hallucinated. The county medical examiner said Ms. McPherson was deprived of water for at least her last 5 to 10 days and died of a blood clot brought on by severe dehydration."*

McPherson had received some limited medical care, but obviously not of a quality to prevent her death. Had she received appropriate psychiatric as well as medical care, she might still be alive.

Suicide and Homicide

Although the Mormons (Church of Jesus Christ of Latter Day Saints, LDS) are now considered members of a sect, having 10 million members worldwide as of 1997, there have been breakaway groups from that Church that are more cult-like and also more homicidal. In 1977, it was estimated that 25 deaths could be associated with one such group in Texas. A second occurrence in a breakaway group took place in Kirtland, OH, in 1989 when a family of five was killed. (It should be noted that the Kirtland group had broken away from the main LDS church more than a century ago.) In each case, the victims were regarded as apostates (Langone and Eisenberg, 1993).

In 1978, the mass homicide-suicide of People's Temple members and others took place in Jonestown, leaving a total of 913 dead, including 276 children. Conway and Siegelman (1995) estimated that from the Manson Family murders in 1969 through the Oklahoma City bombing in 1995, there were a total of 1078 adults and 340 children killed. Not all of these deaths were cult related, although they did stem from the actions of alienated individuals, if not groups.

In some groups of adolescent Satanists who perceive Satanism as a religion, heavy metal music is considered to be religious music. The titles of songs speak to the religious aspect — "Sabbath Bloody Sabbath", for instance; to suicide, which, according to Tucker (1993, p. 362), "is promoted as an answer to life's problems, as a kind of religious act of courage and devotion," with song titles such as "Killing Yourself to Live" and "Mandatory Suicide"; and to ritual killing and mutilation, which are encouraged with songs such as "Bodily Dismemberment" and "Killing Is My Business ... and Business is Good!" The emotionally needy youths who belong to these groups are likely to be the most vulnerable to such messages. Although Tucker (1993, p. 362) did not include any of the lyrics, which could be heard at any record store, he asserted that, "This music may be just a commercial scam, but its content speaks directly to Satanism, and its thrust is much more than just entertainment."

Two decades after the Jonestown tragedy, we have been confronted with several additional instances of mass suicides or homicides just within a 4-year period, from 1993 to 1997. It is one thing to adore a guru, to follow his or her dicta, and to believe what that person believes. To most of us, it seems quite another thing to allow oneself to be led to suicide rather than return to the outside world. It must be understood that cult members, especially those who have been in the group for an extended period, sincerely believe that people outside the group will do them harm and that death with the group leader is more desirable than remaining in any part of the non-cult world. There is also the reality that the guru has "enforcers" just as any mob leader does. Those at Jonestown who did not take their portion of poisoned Kool-Aid were shot by Jim Jones' aides. Branch Davidians who did not wish to die with David Koresh at Waco were killed by Koresh's aides (or placed in a position to be killed by the FBI) or in the fires set within the compound.

The Branch Davidians and the Church Universal and Triumphant (CUT) both amassed large stashes of weapons at their respective headquarters sites. These were allegedly for their protection against outside forces, i.e., all of those who were non-believers and who intended harm to the "enlightened". The weapons were apparently used at Waco, although they have not as yet been used by CUT members.

On the other hand, the 39 members of Heaven's Gate who peacefully committed suicide in California in 1997 believed that they were enroute to a better place aboard an extraterrestrial spaceship hidden in the tail of the Hale-Bopp comet (Gleick, 1997). These were all bright, highly capable, computer-savvy, celibate individuals who were convinced that they were going to a place better than Planet Earth. Unlike some of the other cults described here, they were not violent toward outsiders; they simply rejected life as most people live it and felt that there was nothing on earth for them. After hearing one follower say on the farewell videotape that "... I've been on the planet for 31 years and there's nothing here for me," one columnist (Jenkins, 1997, p. A1) added, "Nothing. No human embrace. No sunsets. No dreams. Nothing." This alienation is not unique to the Heaven's Gate member who said it. Levine and Slater (1976, p. 413), in a study of 106 cultists in nine cults found that 40% of their subjects had joined a cult because "life had no meaning, they were drifting."

Some members of Heaven's Gate had castrated themselves like their leader, Marshall Applewhite. They made videotapes in which they discussed their imminent departure, the shedding of their body shells or "containers" which they would no longer need, and their eager anticipation of becoming part of the Kingdom Level Above Human. Zimbardo (1997) and others have expressed concern that this type of behavior, though perhaps not as neatly organized, may become more common as the millennium approaches.

The Order of the Solar Temple suicides and homicides in 1994 and later (December 1995 and March 1997) also represented a willingness or readiness to die rather than have to deal with the outside world. Like the members of Heaven's Gate, they expected their suicides to transport them to a new planet — Sirius (Branswell, 1997; "Yet more Solar Temple...", 1997). In the original incident, some bodies were discovered in the Province of Quebec and some in Switzerland. Apparently, adult members killed the children and some of the adults and then committed suicide after arranging for mass immolation. The adults who had been shot were ceremonially lying together, much as the Heaven's Gate suicides were found later. Haught (1995) reported that, "Farewell letters said the believers were leaving this earth to escape 'hypocrisies and oppression in this world.'"

The Solar Temple group had been unknown until the first group of bodies was found in 1994, and a full understanding of both their belief system and their rationale for death is still lacking. Allegedly, its founder, Luc Jouret, a Belgian homeopath, traced the group's ideas back to the Knights Templar of the Crusades (Walsh, 1996). These were combined into a New Age philosophy that also included astrology and health prescriptions and were packaged as personal development seminars for business people (Branswell, 1997). Unlike the members of most cults, those in the Solar Temple were largely middle-class, financially successful business people and professionals rather than young adults or late adolescents ("Trying to understand...", 1994). In this first group were a former mayor, a journalist, and a large company executive. Those killed in the 1995 suicide/homicide/immolation episode included a psychotherapist, an architect, and two policemen, one of whom shot his own two daughters, ages 2 and 4 years (Walsh, 1996).

A different picture is painted by the activities of the Aum Shinrikyo cult in Japan. Shoko Asahara, the guru of the group, appears to have been a psychopath from his childhood when, as a half-blind student at a school for the blind, he attacked those weaker than himself. He was not a particularly bright student academically, but was gifted in the social skills of a "con man". Before becoming a cult leader, for example, he aggressively sold bogus health tonics. Then, according to the religious mythology he propounded as a guru, he had a religious awakening that brought him special powers that he could teach to his followers. (Other religious cult leaders typically have had the same sort of experience and similarly suffer from megalomania.) Asahara's message was a mixture of Hindu and Buddhist beliefs with scientific experimentation (sold to the followers for thousands of dollars each) and science fiction elements added (Chisolm, 1995). He appealed to others who were depressed and restless (Matraux, 1997).

As he developed his political ideas, Asahara emphasized meditation to achieve enlightenment and praised Adolf Hitler. Sullivan (1997) wrote that Asahara "preached that Armageddon is imminent, that the Japanese and U.S. governments were planning to attack Aum, and that mass murders were necessary not simply to thwart the government but to save the souls of those killed." The release of toxic fumes in the Tokyo subway finally brought a government crackdown on the cult and on Asahara that had been forestalled earlier by the group's alleged status as a religious corporation. Although the police had been aware of some of the crimes previously committed by the group's members, including murders both within and outside of the group, and of the storage of poison gases, the group had been protected by a government afraid to use its power to close down a subversive group. According to Sullivan (1997, p. A21):

"That 1952 law has never been used, and a government panel last January unanimously decided that using it against Aum would set a dangerous precedent. The Japanese have painful memories of life earlier this century under a government with virtually unchecked power. The notion of the government banning a religious group, even one as universally despised as Aum, had too many ominous overtones, even for many of Aum's staunchest critics."

The death of more than 20 adults and injury of over 5000 people in the Tokyo subway, however, dissolved any restraints on government action following the subway gas attack. The group itself continues to exist.

Reducing the Impact of Cults

The heyday of the cults was rooted in the counterculture of the 1960s and 1970s. A major difference between the cults of 25 to 30 years ago and those functioning today, even those that have continued throughout this period, is that today's groups tend to be more organized, more focused, and far more violent both within the group and toward outsiders. The earlier emphasis was on recruiting large numbers of young people, principally to obtain the money that they could earn and raise and sometimes to protest some public policy, such as the Vietnam war. The emphasis today is much more on acting out every grievance the group's leadership has against society in general and some other groups in particular.

Some of the groups may have seemed more exotic and possibly harmless years ago, and even mental health and other professionals were unaware of the psychological damage they could do to those who joined them. The damage occurred even when the membership was relatively brief. One young man, for example, had difficulty reconciling his pre-cult and post-cult self-perceptions. "How could I — a bright, well-liked guy — swallow the line those people were feeding me? There must be something more wrong with me than I thought!" Others were upset by the pain they had caused family and friends. Many ex-cultists found that cultic slogans kept surfacing in their minds and interfered with memory, that they distrusted all organized groups, and that they felt that no one who had not had their experience could understand what they were feeling (Giambalvo, 1993).

Some parents were initially unaware of what their children's involvement with a particular group (usually described in glowing terms by the recruit) meant; others had some sense of the danger this involvement posed for their children. The latter group sought out ex-cult members and others who might know ways to extricate their children from the cult. These methods were known collectively as de-programming.

Deprogramming

Several years ago, parents would hire someone virtually to kidnap their children from cults, isolate them for several days (or as long as it took), and, in a sense, "re-brainwash" them to re-enter conventional society. That is not the pattern today, in part because deprogrammers were then seen as kidnappers and sometimes were imprisoned for that crime and in part because ex-cult members are more often the "exit counselors" today, able to draw on *their* experiences to help current cult members (Garvey, 1993; Giambalvo, 1993). They are also able to provide emotional support for the anguished parents of cult members.

Those who leave the cults, either on their own initiative or with the "help" of exit counselors, have a number of problems, some of which may persist over long periods of time. When they first come out of the cult, according to Schwartz (1991a, pp. 160–161), they ...

"... often experience guilt, both for the grief they caused their families and for the friends they left in the group; thought diffusion, where they are unable to focus their thinking on the task at hand; awkwardness in explaining the time period of cult membership when completing employment applications; physical ill-health from the poor diet and lack of sleep, although this is generally remediable; and some experience visual or auditory hallucinations that are both upsetting to them and that interfere with their daily functioning."

The difficulty with employment applications is that prospective employers may look at an unaccounted-for time period as possibly prison time or as an indication of the instability of the applicant. They may not realize what an effort it took for the job applicant to withdraw from and overcome the rigors of cult membership, and the applicant may find it awkward to explain the situation. In addition, women who have been in cults where they were used sexually by the leader for his pleasure or to recruit new members live in fear that employers will discover this aspect of their history and somehow use it against them (Rosedale, 1995).

Working with both the ex-cultists and their parents requires that the professional be familiar with the patterns associated with cults in terms of recruiting, thought processes, and interpersonal relationships, as well as the difficulties of separation from the cult. The therapist needs to know not only the general format used by cults, but also the specific history, techniques, and beliefs of as many cults as possible. The groups *do* differ in many ways, from their living arrangements to their views on sexuality, and it is important in dealing with the ex-cultist to know from which group the individual is coming.

One of the first things that has to be communicated to the parents, certainly, is not to greet their returning child with anger, blame, and accusations. They may seek supportive counseling while their child is in the cult and be invited by their child's therapist to an occasional session as appropriate once the child is out of the cult. It is rare that all parties are at every session, for the needs of the parents and of the youth differ in terms of both reintegrating the youth into society and dealing with any family relationships that may have contributed to the youth's earlier vulnerability.

Second, both the therapist and the ex-cult member need to be knowledgeable about why individuals are vulnerable to cult recruitment as well as the techniques used by cults to recruit and control their members. They can move from the general pattern to the specific aspects of vulnerability and how to reduce them as part of therapy. Third, Goldberg (1993, p. 240) noted that, "It is important that the therapist 'normalize' post-cult symptoms and emotions. Ex-cultists need to know that their reactions usually are related to cultic suggestions, practices, and manipulations, and to their actual separation from the cult." Somatic symptoms, for example, may stem from the cult's suggestion that anyone leaving the cult will develop a serious illness, maybe even a fatal one. Forced celibacy or sexual abuse within the cult can create awkwardness in new social relationships.

Children who were raised in a cult or similar group may be more of a challenge for exit counselors and psychotherapists. They need to learn about the larger society, including its vocabulary and its mores; to acquire what are regarded as common social skills and to have socialization experiences; to become educated in the cognitive sense; and to have long-term psychotherapeutic support (Langone and Eisenberg, 1993).

Current Factors

In the 1970s, and even into the 1980s, many parents were reluctant to impose their values on their children. Society was in flux, with a strong emphasis on moral "relativism". These factors continue today along with a multitude of diverse entertainment and sports "models" who are paid huge sums of money for talents that are sometimes socially questionable, but who become "celebrities" with large numbers of followers. The element of peer acceptance, particularly for adolescents, also continues to play a role in who young people follow and how they behave. There are choices involved in choosing *who* you want to accept you, and the outcomes of those choices must be dealt with, as well as (where the outcome is unlawful or injurious) the effects of unwise choices. Too many youths have not been taught how to choose among options and how to anticipate the effects of their choices. The need to make decisions can be overwhelming for those who have not been prepared by their parents to learn the techniques of and to take responsibility for decision-making (GAP, 1978). How can they be helped?

Invulnerability to Cults

There are many people who are attracted to cults for a variety of reasons, as we have seen. There are also, however, many individuals who have been approached with equal fervor and with the same techniques and have been invulnerable to the recruiters. Why?

In one study of 40 ex-cult members, 70% of the respondents indicated that the cult gave them a sense of purpose that had been absent in their family life (Schwartz, 1983). By contrast, in a study of those who were invulnerable to the recruiters, subjects reported that they had a strong relationship with their fathers, either positive or negative (Schwartz, 1979). They also viewed themselves as self-directed. Their internal locus of control meant that they would not turn over control of their lives to someone else. Even if they were "loners" and perhaps opposed to their parents' values, disenchanted with their peers' behaviors, or maybe even a bit low in self-esteem — all characteristics of those vulnerable to cult recruiters — the invulnerable were different. They had developed enough coping strategies and resilience to have inner direction, that internal locus of control, and to have the sense to listen to what they called their "inner ear". They did not want or need the rigid guidelines of the cults to direct their lives.

Coping *can* be learned. The caretaking adult can suggest to the child, "Let's pretend that [some problem has arisen]" and ask the child to work out a solution while under supervision. Given a variety of such opportunities, the child will be better prepared to think, rather than act impulsively when confronted with a problem (or a cult recruiter).

Coping Skills

Everyone faces a difficult situation at some time that calls for an atypical response. That is, the usual responses do not apply, so alternate solutions must be sought. Can young children be taught to do this, to cope?

What is being asked of children in coping is the ability to look for and perceive alternatives, to weigh them for possible consequences, and then to select the response that has a high probability of resolving the problem with minimal negative effects. In Piagetian theory, pre-adolescents are not supposed to be capable of such abstract, even creative, thinking (Piaget, 1952). Yet, observing toddlers and preschoolers, they can be seen pausing in their play to consider which "tool" can be used to construct a sand castle, or where they can best hide in a game of hide and seek. Some children are more adept than others at this kind of thinking and at an earlier age, but almost all young children can be given opportunities to learn how to reason out possible answers to problems and then to choose one. Indeed, some children suggest alternative solutions that are creative, although simple in design. The combination of creativity with the ability to seek alternatives markedly increases a child's coping skills. There is also a need for children to develop in early childhood a sense of autonomy that is preparation for the later stages of initiative, industry, and identity integration in Erikson's model (1950). All of these abilities contribute to reduced vulnerability to cult recruiters in later years.

Resilience

Similarly, when the child is confronted with disappointment because something expected has gone awry, adults can help build resiliency by encouraging the youngster to shift gears rather than be swamped by tears or anger. Resilience is the ability to bounce back, to recover from disappointment with poise and possibly with a better alternative. Garmezy (1980), a pioneer in studies of invulnerability, drew upon a quote attributed to Robert Louis Stevenson in discussing this trait: "Life is not a matter of holding good cards but of playing a poor hand well." Thus, if an activity has been rained out, the child might substitute a related indoor activity. If a grade is less than expected, the parent might help the child seek an alternative means of mastering the academic task. If the child knows that he or she is really capable most of the time, loved, perceived as good, and supported in efforts even when falling short of perfection, the child can develop the positive sense of self-esteem that contributes to resiliency.

According to Flach (1988), the resilient personality has a strong yet supple sense of self-esteem, perceives and develops his or her abilities, is independent in thought and action, is open-minded, is willing to dream, and has a high tolerance for disappointment and distress. This gives the resilient individual a sense of focus, a commitment to life, and a framework for experience that encompasses both meaning and hope — all qualities that cult members have indicated they do not have.

Locus of Control

Some people, even adults, see themselves only in terms of how they think others perceive them; other people have a self-image derived from looking inward. The first group, which tends to seek direction as well as approval from others, is said to have an *external* locus of control. Those in the second group, who are more self-directed, have an *internal* locus of control. Coping skills and resiliency are more often associated with the internal locus of control.

One element of an internal locus of control is decision-making. Parents can begin to teach toddlers how to make and live with their own decisions by asking them to choose which of two T-shirts they prefer to wear each morning. It is not a calamity if the child chooses a striped shirt that clashes with plaid pants today; tomorrow he may choose a solid shirt to wear with plaid pants. Even in childhood, there are thousands of choices to make over the years, and the more experience children have with making decisions (within reasonable limits), the more secure they will be operating from an internal locus of control when confronted with truly critical choices. If the family is supportive of the child developing a variety of experiences, the child will be more likely to respond effectively to life events, and less likely to exhibit disruptive and dysfunctional behavior patterns.

If an adolescent or young adult has been reared in a family that shared warmth, acceptance, and consistency, and has authoritative (not authoritarian) parents, that young person has most likely had his or her psycho-social as well as survival needs met. If the young person has been prepared from early childhood to develop coping skills, resiliency, and an internal locus of control, it is likely that a cult recruiter's invitation will be effectively refused. It thus becomes critical to help children develop strategies that support these characteristics. If this is done, cult leaders will have fewer followers. If they have fewer followers, as was indicated earlier, they have less power and less control over others' lives.

Concluding Comments

Attempts to define a cult or to understand why people join them evoke varied responses, sometimes depending on one's professional or religious orientation. When a cult erupts with violent behavior toward its own members or against the larger society, the responses are even more diffuse. The suggested remedies for their recruiting techniques, their alleged abuses, and their very existence range from the ineffective to the potentially preventive.

It is apparent that cults share certain characteristics that may be beneficial to their leaders but may not be as healthy for their followers. Many cults have exhibited violence within the group in the form of child and adult abuse; a few have gone beyond abuse to commit homicide or mass suicide. Those groups that claim to be religious in focus are protected by the freedom of religion provisions of the First Amendment. Even their abuse of children is often permitted when they point to biblical injunctions on child-rearing. It is often difficult to restrain assertive or aggressive cultic activities under our laws, but Brown (1991) believes that tort liability for false imprisonment created by mind manipulation techniques would pass constitutional scrutiny whether for religious or secular cults.

Other alternatives to functioning cults must be found. One possibility lies in prevention. We may not be able to prevent individuals from trying to develop a cultic following or from being violent, but it is possible to reduce the number of potential gurus who succeed. This can be done, as has been shown, by making more of the potential followers invulnerable to the seductive appeals of cult recruiters. As with many other efforts, this preventive effort has to be started early in life so that fewer individuals fall prey to cults as they approach adulthood. A second possibility is education, i.e., publicity about the practices of cults and the ways in which they control people's lives. Such an effort would have to be carefully designed so as not to make the cults more attractive to the more vulnerable. A third endeavor would be to reduce access to both guns and chemicals that might be used to make bombs, thus decreasing the violence that cult groups can commit with such materials. Stiff penalties for child abuse, and for adult abuse as well, when the victims are willing to testify, might have some negative effects on those practices.

Obviously, cults cannot be swept away by a single law, government action, or court decision. Those cults that disappear tend to do that to themselves. For the others, we shall have to nibble away at their recruiting and their abusive practices, lessening their impact and their aggression wherever possible.

Annotated Bibliography

1. Kephart, W.M. and Zellner, W.W. (1991) *Extraordinary Groups: An Examination of Unconventional Life-Styles*, 4th ed. New York: St. Martin's Press. This is very useful as a text for a course on non-traditional religious groups because the groups discussed include the Shakers as well as Father Divine's Mission, Jehovah's Witnesses, the Hasidim, the Amish, and other groups that are now regarded as sects. Their behaviors and beliefs can be useful in demonstrating how such groups differ from those we regard as cults.

2. Langone, M.D., Ed. (1993) *Recovery from Cults: Help for Victims of Psychological and Spiritual Abuse*. New York: W.W. Norton. Langone, a psychologist, is Executive Director of the American Family Foundation and editor of the *Cultic Studies Journal*. In this volume, he has collected 20 chapters that are focused on mind control, leaving the cults, facilitating recovery, and special issues (such as teen Satanism). The chapters are clearly written and provide abundant additional sources for the reader in their reference lists.

3. Singer, M.T., with J. Lalich (1995) *Cults in Our Midst*. San Francisco: Jossey-Bass. Singer is one of the most experienced therapists in the country when it comes to working with ex-cult members and their families. She has helped thousands find their way back to the world of their families. In a combination of theory and example, she and Lalich present the mental health, and sometimes physical health, hazards posed by the cults, how they recruit and entice new members, and how they operate in the community.

There are a few older books that are not cited here, but which underlie many of the more current references, and which the reader may find of great interest. They were among the sources Isser and Schwartz (1988) used in moving from a study of the forced conversion of a few 19th-century French girls to a study of the highly successful recruiting of the 1960s, 1970s, and later by a variety of cults and cult-like groups. Among the key books in what was a 25-page list of references are:

4. Downton, J.J., Jr. (1979) *Sacred Journeys: The Conversion of Young Americans to Divine Light Mission*. New York: Columbia University Press.

5. Levine, S.V. (1984) *Radical Departures: Desperate Detours to Growing Up*. Chicago: University of Chicago Press.

6. Lifton, R.J. (1961) *Thought Reform and the Psychology of Totalism: A Study of "Brainwashing" in China*. New York: W.W. Norton.

7. Meerloo, J.A.M. (1956) *The Rape of the Mind*. New York: World Publishing.

Lifton and Meerloo's volumes are particularly valuable aids in understanding how the recruit can become an active advocate and committed cultist in a very short time.

References

American Family Foundation (1996) Judge says "The Family" is reforming. *The Cult Observer, 13*(1), 8.

Anthony, D. and Robbins, T. (1992) Law, social science and the "brainwashing" exception to the First Amendment. *Behavioral Sciences and the Law, 10*, 5–29.

Bearak, B. (1997) Odyssey to suicide. *The New York Times*, April 28, pp. A1, B8–B10.

Branswell, B. (1997) Deadly voyages. *Maclean's, 110*(14), 46–47.

Brown, L.B. (1991) He who controls the mind controls the body: false imprisonment, religious cults, and the destruction of volitional capacity. *Valparaiso University Law Review, 25*, 407–454.

Cantril, H. and Sherif, M. (1938) The kingdom of Father Divine. *Journal of Abnormal Psychology, 33*, 147–167.

Chisolm, P. (1995) Japan's nightmare. *Maclean's, 108*(22), 38–39.

Clifford, M.W. (1994) Social work treatment with children, adolescents, and families exposed to religious and Satanic cults. *Social Work in Health Care, 20*(2), 35–59.

Conway, F. and Siegelman, J. (1995) *Snapping: America's Epidemic of Sudden Personality Change,* 2nd ed. New York: Stillpoint Press.

de Mause, L. (1994) Why cults terrorize and kill children. *Journal of Psychohistory, 21*, 505–518.

Dolbee, S. (1997) Origins of the cult: "Bo and Peep" began doomsday odyssey in '70s. *The San Diego Union-Tribune*, March 28, pp. A1, A7.

Erikson, E.H. (1950) *Childhood and Society.* New York: W.W. Norton.

Fennell, T. (1993) Nightmare tales. *Maclean's, 106*(6), 26–27.

Flach, F. (1988) *Resilience: Discovering a New Strength at Times of Stress*. New York: Fawcett Columbine.

Frantz, D. (1997) Death of a Scientologist heightens suspicions in a Florida town. *The New York Times*, Dec. 1, pp. A1, A16.

Garmezy, N. (1980) Children under stress: perspectives or antecedents and correlates of vulnerability and resistance to psychopathology. In A. Robin, J. Arnoff, A. Barclay, and R. Zucker (Eds.), *Further Explorations in Personality,* pp. 196–269. New York: John Wiley.

Garvey, J. (1993) The importance of information in preparing for exit counseling: a case study. In M.D. Langone (Ed.), *Recovery from Cults: Help for Victims of Psychological and Spiritual Abuse*, pp. 181–200. New York: W.W. Norton.

Giambalvo, C. (1993) Post-cult problems: an exit counselor's perspective. In M.D. Langone (Ed.), *Recovery from Cults: Help for Victims of Psychological and Spiritual Abuse*, pp. 148–154. New York: W.W. Norton.

Gibbons, T.J., Jr. (1997) Parents charged in death of tot. *The Philadelphia Inquirer*, Aug. 19, p. R1.

Gleick, E. (1997) The marker we've been ... waiting for. *Time*, April 7, pp. 28–36.

Goldberg, L. (1993) Guidelines for therapists. In M.D. Langone (Ed.), *Recovery from Cults: Help for Victims of Psychological and Spiritual Abuse*, pp. 232–250. New York: W.W. Norton.

Group for the Advancement of Psychiatry (1978) *Power and Authority in Adolescence: The Origins and Resolution of Intergenerational Conflict*, Report No. 101. New York: (author).

Group for the Advancement of Psychiatry (1992) *Leaders and Followers: A Psychiatric Perspective on Religious Cults,* Report No. 132. Washington, D.C.: American Psychiatric Press.

Haught, J.A. (1995) And now, the Solar Temple. *Free Inquiry, 15*(1), 31.

Holmes, K. (1995) Hare Krishna movement faces loss of the young faithful. *The Philadelphia Inquirer*, Jan. 16, pp. B1, B5.

Hughes, R.A. (1990) Psychological perspectives on infanticide in a faith healing sect. *Psychotherapy, 27*(1), 107–115.

Isser, N. and Schwartz, L.L. (1988) *The History of Conversion and Contemporary Cults*. New York: Peter Lang.

Jenkins, L. (1997) Closing Heaven's Gate. *The San Diego Union-Tribune*, March 30, pp. A1, A15.

Kandel, R.F. (1988) Litigating the cult-related child custody case. *Cultic Studies Journal, 5*(1), 122–131.

Kephart, W.M. and Zellner, W.W. (1991) *Extraordinary Groups: An Examination of Unconventional Life-Styles*, 4th ed. New York: St. Martin's Press.

Lamberg, L. (1997) Apocalyptic violence in Heaven's Gate and Aum Shinrikyo cults. *Journal of the American Medical Association, 277*, 191–193.

Landa, S. (1991) Children and cults: a practical guide. *Journal of Family Law, 29*(3), 591–634.

Langone, M.D. (1994) Reflections on child custody and cults. *The Cult Observer, 11*(8), 9–10.

Langone, M.D. and Eisenberg, G. (1993) Children and cults. In M.D. Langone (Ed.), *Recovery from Cults: Help for Victims of Psychological and Spiritual Abuse*, pp. 327–342. New York: W.W. Norton.

Levine, S.V. (1980) The role of psychiatry in the phenomenon of cults. In S.C. Feinstein, P.L. Giovacchini, J.G. Looney, A.Z. Schwartzberg, and A.D. Sorosky (Eds.), *Adolescent Psychiatry,* Vol. 8, pp. 123–137. Chicago: University of Chicago Press.

Levine, S.V. and Slater, N.E. (1976) Youth and contemporary religious movements: psychosocial findings. *Canadian Psychiatric Association Journal, 21*, 411–420.

Lifton, R.J. (1991) Cult formation. *Cultic Studies Journal, 8*(1), 1–6.

Malcarne, V.L. and Burchard, J.D. (1992) Investigations of child abuse/neglect allegations in religious cults: a case study in Vermont. *Behavioral Sciences and the Law, 10*, 75–88.

Matraux, D.A. (1997) Aum sweet home: the appeal of Aum Shinrikyo to Japan's restless and depressed youth. *American Asian Review, 15*(3), 191.

Piaget, J. (1952) *The Origins of Intelligence in Children* (M. Cook, trans.) New York: International Universities Press.

Prince v. Commonwealth of Massachusetts, 321 U.S. 158 (1944).

Rosedale, H.L. (1995) Women and cults: a lawyer's perspective. *Cultic Studies Journal, 12*(2), 187–194.

Rudin, M. (1984) Women, elderly, and children in religious cults. *Cultic Studies Journal, 1*(1), 8–26.

Schwartz, L.L. (1979) Cults: the vulnerability of sheep. *USA Today, 108*, 22–24.

Schwartz, L.L. (1983) Family therapy and families of cult members. *International Journal of Family Therapy, 5*(3), 168–178.

Schwartz, L.L. (1985) Viewing the cults: differences of opinion. In B.K. Kilbourne (Ed.), *Scientific Research and New Religions: Divergent Perspectives*, pp. 149–159. San Francisco: American Association for the Advancement of Science, Pacific Division.

Schwartz, L.L. (1991a) Resisting the powers of religious cults. In W.A. Rhodes and W.K. Brown (Eds.), *Why Some Children Succeed Despite the Odds*, pp. 159–170. New York: Praegar.

Schwartz, L.L. (1991b) The historical dimension of cultic techniques of persuasion and control. *Cultic Studies Journal, 8*(1), 37–45.

Schwartz, L.L. and Kaslow, F.W. (1979) Religious cults, the individual, and the family. *Journal of Marital and Family Therapy, 5*, 15–26.

Schwartz, L.L. and Kaslow, F.W. (1981) The cult phenomenon: historical, sociological, and familial factors contributing to their development and appeal. *Marriage and Family Review, 4*(3/4), 3–30.

"Second faith healing death in family" (1997) *Daily News* (Naples, FL), April 22. [Reprinted in *The Cult Observer, 14*(3), 8, 1997.]

Sheffield, E. (1997) Cults target vulnerable students. *The Guardian* (London), Oct. 1, p. 10.

Singer, M.T., with J. Lalich (1995) *Cults in Our Midst.* San Francisco: Jossey-Bass.

Sullivan, K. (1997) Japan cult survives while guru is jailed: group worships leader on trial in gas attack. *The Washington Post,* Sept. 28, p. A21.

"Trying to understand Solar Temple debacle" (1994) *The Cult Observer, 11*(9, 10), 19–21.

Tucker, R. (1993) Teen Satanism. In M.D. Langone (Ed.), *Recovery from Cults: Help for Victims of Psychological and Spiritual Abuse*, pp. 356–381. New York: W.W. Norton.

Walsh, J. (1996) The sunburst sacrifices. *Time, 147*(2), 45.

Wooden, K. (1981) *The Children of Jonestown.* New York: McGraw-Hill.

"Yet more Solar Temple suicides" (1997) *The Cult Observer, 14*(3), 9.

Zimbardo, P.G. (1973) The psychological power and pathology of improvement. In E. Aaronson and R. Helmreich (Eds.), *Social Psychology in the World Today*, pp. 162–165. New York: Van Nostrand.

Zimbardo, P.G. (1997) What messages are behind today's cults? *APA Monitor, 28*, 14.

About the Author

Lita Linzer Schwartz, Ph.D., ABPP, is a Distinguished Professor Emerita of The Pennsylvania State University. She is a Fellow of Divisions 41, 43, and 46 of the American Psychological Association and holds a Diplomate in Forensic Psychology. She has been studying cults and conversion techniques for more than two decades, has written on them extensively, and presently serves on the Editorial Advisory Board of the *Cultic Studies Journal.*

CHAPTER 8

HATE CRIMES: ETIOLOGY AND INTERVENTION

Charles J. Golden, Michele L. Jackson, and Thomas A. Crum

Two gay men walking across a park were attacked by a gang of youths and left dead. ...A black man training in a white neighborhood for a marathon was attacked and shot in the chest. He died in an ambulance on the way to a hospital. ...In an attack that lasted several hours, neo-Nazis beat a skinhead to death after discovering that he was Jewish. ...A white driver was pulled out of his car and beaten to death after he had a flat tire in South-Central.

Hate crimes are reportedly on the rise throughout the U.S. (Craig and Waldo, 1996). While many hate crimes are not violent and involve destruction of property and verbal assaults, a significant minority of these crimes involves physical violence and personal injury, with a smaller group resulting in lethal violence. Levin and McDevitt (1993) described, in chilling detail, the excesses of many hate crimes when they reach violent proportions. Such crimes are often much more vicious and violent when they do occur because they are motivated by hate rather than by the simple desire to eliminate someone who may be standing between the perpetrator and a specific goal. Hate crimes are intimately interwoven with other types of lethal violence (e.g., juvenile crimes) and the differentiation of a crime as a hate crime must be determined on the basis of the motivation and rationale of the perpetrator.

Herek (1989) defined hate crimes as those which are intended to harm or scare an individual simply because of his or her membership in a specific group. This group can be defined on the basis of religion, skin color, country of origin, culture, sexual preference, or any of a number of other factors. The individual who is attacked is usually personally unknown to the attacker, and the assumptions about the victim are based on prejudices and stereotypes unrelated to the victim's actual behavior. Hate crimes can involve murder, violent assaults, property crimes, bombings, arson, looting, harassment, threats, or intimidating acts (Herek and Berrill, 1990). Berk (1990) noted that members of non-minority groups (e.g., whites) as well as minority groups may be, and in fact often are, the victims of hate crimes.

A thief's attack on a victim would not be considered a hate crime, regardless of the group to which the victim belonged; however, an attack on the victim simply because he or she was Jewish, black, or gay would be a hate crime. The motivation of the perpetrator must be considered. Hate crimes which result in lethal violence are distinguished from terrorism by their lack of a specific political agenda or the desire to inspire fear in a large group to gain political ends.

Berk (1990) noted that hate crimes are generally considered to be very different from other crimes. For example, most cases of murder and violence involve people who know each other, while hate crimes typically occur between strangers. Hate crimes which involve property result in the destruction of property, while most property crimes involve taking rather than destroying. Lethal violence is generally perpetrated by one person, whereas hate-motivated lethal violence is most often seen from larger groups. Berk (1990) expressed concern, however, that the lack of good empirical evidence regarding hate crimes may bias our current perception of such crimes.

Classification of a crime as a hate crime requires an understanding of the motivation of the perpetrator, something which is not easily inferred unless voluntarily provided by the perpetrator to the police or some other reliable source. In cases where the perpetrator is not caught, we can only guess as to whether a crime was motivated by hate. In other cases, the intent of the perpetrator is ambiguous. We cannot assume, because the victim is a member of a minority group, that the crime was motivated by hate. For example, if a Latino gang member kills a black gang member, is the crime gang related or hate motivated (Berk, 1990)? The ways in which particular jurisdictions handle these and similar issues of classification can result in a large variance in statistically reported hate crimes.

Berk (1990) attempted to draw a line between symbolic victims and actuarial victims. Symbolic victims are individuals who are attacked because they represent something hateful to the attacker, whether that be religion, skin color, or sexual orientation. Actuarial victims are attacked because of expectations of what can be derived from the attack. If a well-dressed gay man is attacked, it may be because of his symbolic value (he represents all gays) or his actuarial value (well-dressed people may carry more money). A hate crime exists only when the attack is for symbolic rather than actuarial reasons.

Until recently, the counting of hate crimes has been unsystematic. In response to the demands of many victim's groups, Congress enacted the Hate Crimes Statistics Act (1990) which mandates reporting and recording of hate crimes; however, reports of hate crimes still remain a problem. Unlike crimes reported and cataloged by such obvious factors as geographical region of the crime, gender and age of the victim, gender and age of the perpetrator, family relationships between the perpetrator and victim, and other easily identified characteristics, hate crimes are not as easily classified or recognized.

Another difficulty is that not all hate crimes are reported. This may be for a variety of reasons. Berrill and Herek (1990) suggested that gay victims may not report crimes because of a fear of secondary victimization. This may be because they view the police as anti-gay or because they fear being publicly disclosed as gay, making them the focus of violence from other perpetrators. Blacks may feel that white police officers condone and participate in hate crimes against them. Victims may not report crimes because they fear they will be blamed, as is often the case with rape victims. It may be suggested that the victim caused the attack because of his or her behavior (Berrill, 1986). In cases of a more minor nature, the victim may be unsure whether he or she was the victim of a hate crime or simply excessive behavior for another reason.

Most observers agree that blacks are the most frequent victims of racially motivated hate crimes (Finn and McNeil, 1987). However Latino, Asian-Pacific, and Native Americans are also often victims (Chen and True, 1994; Craig and Waldo, 1996). The Anti-Defamation League of B'nai B'rith (1986) has suggested that there has been an increase in anti-Semitic crimes, while crimes against Moslems have increased with the rise of terroristic acts such as the World Trade Center bombing. A significant increase has been seen in hate crimes against gays and lesbians as well (Herek et al., 1997).

The earliest examples of hate crimes in the U.S. were those directed toward Native Americans in the 16th, 17th, and 18th centuries (which later became the genocidal attack on Native Americans in the 19th century). These attacks were often justified by classifying Native Americans as "savages".

The best known hate crimes were those organized by the Ku Klux Klan (KKK or the Klan) following the Civil War. By 1867, the KKK had adopted a white supremacist platform as its organizing principle (Goldberg, 1981). The object of the KKK's hate is anyone who is not of Anglo-Saxon descent and Protestant religion. The target victims of the KKK have typically been blacks and Jews, but gay men and lesbians have increasingly come under attack (Lutz, 1987). The KKK's tactics for furthering its cause have included hanging, castration, mutilation, shooting, tar and feathering, and fire and acid branding. The Klan membership decreased rapidly through the 1970s but has recently experienced a resurgence, along with other supremacist and separatist groups (George and Wilcox, 1996).

The Klan's new approach not only has appealed to traditional stereotypes and bigotry, but has also painted the U.S. government as a conspirator against the U.S. itself. For example, the Klan has appealed to farmers and others in the rural south and midwest by declaring that the U.S. government is conspiring with minority groups against the white race using such issues as affirmative action as a rallying point. According to the Anti-Defamation League of B'nai B'rith (1986), farmers have been encouraged to engage in violent confrontations with authorities to avoid foreclosure. Other groups have sold hate under the guise of religion and a return to morality using violent means as a way of protection and demonstration (Reed, 1989; Young, 1990). These groups have expanded their net from traditional scapegoat groups to include police officers, sheriffs, and federal agents who are now seen as part of a plot to deprive innocent and good people of their liberties.

Despite the increasing incidence of hate crimes in the U.S., actuarial data on its prevalence are scarce. Each target group tends to have a national organization which keeps track of these crimes, but little is done on a national level to document their occurrence. The Federal Bureau of Investigation reported 9895 hate crime offenses in 1995, but it is estimated that the actual number may be as much as 10 times that amount.

Other studies have attempted to use survey methods to estimate the number of hate crimes (although such methodology is obviously inappropriate with victims of lethal violence). The National Gay and Lesbian Task Force (NGLTF; 1984) has attempted to compile information regarding the victimization of gay men and lesbians. This study retrospectively asked more than 2000 gay men and lesbians in eight U.S. cities about their experiences as victims of hate crimes. Among those surveyed, 19% reported being physically assaulted, i.e., punched, kicked, or beaten, at least once because of their perceived sexual orientation. Forty-four percent of participants indicated that they had been threatened with physical assault. An astounding 94% reported some other type of victimization, ranging from being verbally abused to being pelted with objects. Gender differences were also found, with gay men being victimized more often than lesbians.

Comstock (1989) examined the relationship between race/ethnicity and hate crimes committed against gay men and lesbians. In a sample of 291 respondents, which was approximately two thirds whites, blacks, and Hispanics, gay men and lesbians were more likely to have been victims of violence or threats of violence. Race was unrelated to the hate crimes of vandalism, arson, or being spat upon. Gay men and lesbians of minority racial groups were also more likely than their white counterparts to be victimized in areas identified as gay/lesbian, i.e., outside gay establishments. This finding is not unexpected, given the increased risk of violent crime for racial minorities (Bureau of Justice Statistics, 1994). These results suggest that gay men and lesbians of minority racial groups face "double jeopardy" in a society plagued by racial and anti-gay hatred (Berrill and Herek, 1990).

Factors in Hate Crimes

Not surprisingly, there is little hard data on the characteristics of people who commit hate crimes. Many of these crimes are committed anonymously, and others are performed only when in groups. Frequently, we are dealing not only with the psychological characteristics of the individual but also with the characteristics of the societies in which they live. Thus, we must include both sociological and psychological factors in understanding these processes. We must also understand that the motivation which leads to this type of lethal violence in one individual will not be identical to that of another individual. Thus, we cannot discuss one clear set of etiological factors but rather must consider a complex set of interacting forces which has a greater or lesser impact in any given instance.

Hamner (1992) attempted to use social identity theory to explain these phenomena. He argued that individuals need self-esteem, and that self-esteem is tied directly to the way their group (the "in-group") is evaluated, defining the individual's place in society. It is especially important that the in-group be clearly valued well above perceived "out-groups". Out-groups are defined by a number of factors (discussed below), and one group deals with the individuals in the other group as being representative of the whole group rather than as individuals. Attacking the out-group results in an increased value for the in-group and a decreased value for the out-group, enlarging the perceived distance between the two groups.

Many factors play a role in determining which group constitutes an out-group and allowing the attacker to justify the attacks on such a group. One of the most common factors among all of these crimes is the ability to dehumanize the individual who is attacked. Bar-Tal (1990), writing about genocide, identified the devaluation of an out-group as "delegitimization". He defined delegitimization as the categorization of a group into negative social categories that are outside acceptable norms and values (Bar-Tal, 1988, 1989). Individuals may be dehumanized by labeling them as inhuman or immoral or by giving them negative political labels.

Delegitimization makes the suspect group a non-human entity, laden with negative characteristics and threatening to the greater society. The in-group perceives the threatening goals of the out-group as far-reaching, unjustified, and in opposition to the goals of the in-group (LeVine and Campbell, 1972). The more the individual sees the person being attacked as inhuman, the more likely that lethal violence can be employed. As a result, attacks are almost always on strangers rather than people known to the attacker. For example, Herek (1992) pointed out that laws which stigmatize homosexual behavior can help lead to anti-gay violence. Condemnation by religious institutions can have similar effects, as can stories of conspiracies often attributed to Jews and blacks.

A strong respect for authority may also predispose an individual to turn against an out-group (Staub, 1996). Individuals may be swayed by gang leaders or political voices which target specific groups. In some cases, the perpetrator subverts his or her own identity to the leader. Pluralistic societies, or those that have many subcultural variations, may be prone to group violence or individual crimes of hate. Pluralism creates richness and diversity for a society, but it may also create destructive undercurrents when the characteristics of a subgroup differ significantly from the majority. In the U.S., there is an influx of newcomers whom many believe do not share the views and culture of the majority. Some members of society may view such an influx as a threat to the dominant culture as well as a threat to their way of life. When this is combined with economic and political challenges, it can lead to situations ripe for the development of hate crimes.

Another related factor is the question of visibility (Gamson, 1995). The degree to which a group is easily differentiated increases the ability of others to target members of that group for hate crimes. Thus, individuals whose skin color is different, whose dress is different, or who possess other visible signs of being "different" are more likely to become the object of both hate rhetoric and hate crime. As a group becomes more aggressive and more visible, there may be an increase in hate crimes, as has been seen in the increased attacks on gay men and lesbians as they have become more open about their sexual orientation (Berk, 1990).

The extent of the differences between the out-group and perpetrators increases the likelihood of hate crimes. Physical attributes are a particularly salient way to discriminate against a group because identification of the out-group members is easy. At times, the exclusion criteria may be hidden, such as religious or political values. The Native Americans in North America were easy targets to eliminate because the differences between them and the Europeans encompassed many domains and were extreme in nature. Similarly, blacks, Pacific Islanders, and other groups are readily identified and may have many other cultural differences.

The concepts of authorization and routinization are additional factors in individual and group hate crimes (Gamson, 1995). Authorization (by the in-group) defines and sanctions the violent behavior while removing the individual's moral responsibility. Authorization may also be caused by the failure of the government or police to take the crimes seriously and to prosecute them in a vigorous manner (Berrill and Herek, 1990). Routinization occurs as acts of violence become routine and organized, leaving little time to ask moral and philosophical questions. As the acts become more routine, the degree of violence escalates to lethal levels.

Several reports (National Asian Pacific Legal Consortium, 1994; U.S. Commission on Civil Rights, 1992) have attempted to identify the specific factors within the U.S. which have led to increases in hate crimes and violence against Asians and Pacific Islanders. These reports identified several factors, including (1) a long history of prejudice and discrimination; (2) increased visibility due to immigration; (3) conflicts between cultural and religious practices of immigrants with the dominant culture; (4) resentment toward the success of Japan following World War II, resulting in a misplaced jealousy of the success of Asians and Pacific Islanders; (5) perception that these groups receive unfair subsidies and assistance from the government; (6) a decrease in social services which is blamed on immigrants; (7) abrupt racial integration of neighborhoods which were previously of the majority race; (8) insensitive media coverage of the groups which strengthens stereotypes; and (9) poor police response to hate crimes. It is clear that the full intensity of hate crimes is highly dependent on the presence of many of these factors, not just a single cause.

The Violent Event

The first example below is adapted from a conversation with a convicted felon who had committed a hate-related murder. It has been altered to protect confidentiality. Language content has been edited but grammar and syntax have not.

Case Illustration 1

I always knew that the blacks were out to get us. When I was a small child, I saw a group of blacks attack my older brother and beat him severely. My father said they did it because they were trying to take over the town. We moved away from there after that, but I never forgot the need to watch out for people like that. We moved to a new town where there were no blacks and things were fine until I was a teenager. That's when they passed the g—d— affirmative action rules. My father lost out on a big promotion on the "line" because they gave it to a black who had no skills whatsoever. The blacks started to move into our town and our neighborhood, acting like they owned the place.

I got involved with a gang which was trying to protect the neighborhood from them. We would send them warnings, like bricks through the windows, and paint words on their houses. The first ones moved out after they got the message but they all just kept coming back. They didn't know their place. My father got passed over for another promotion, and he started to drink because he was so unhappy. He blamed it all on the blacks. One day, when he was drunk, he ran his car into a tree and died. It was all the blacks' fault If they had stayed away, we would have been fine. My mother lost the will to live after that and she wouldn't leave the house. She died a year later, when I was 17. They said she died of pneumonia but I knew what she died of.

I got more involved with the gang. We would go out and look for blacks who were alone. When we found one, we'd beat them up. The more they fought, the harder we hit. After we were done, we'd go and smoke some joints and get some girls and celebrate. We didn't kill no one. We just wanted them to leave us alone.

The night the killing happened we had been drinking and we were driving around. We were driving down the street when we saw this n—— walking down the street all secretly like he was up to no good. We jumped out of the car and rushed him. He screamed as we hit him. I told him he was a "g—d— n——" and that he was a crook. He wouldn't shut up, so we hit him harder. He drew out a knife and told us to back off. I told him that no n—— was going to try and slice me up. We surrounded him and we wrestled him down and got the knife, though Rory got sliced up on his left arm while we were doing it. We decided we had to teach the n—— a lesson, so we stuck a rag into his mouth and we took turns holding him down and cutting him up. He finally passed out so it was no fun hitting him anymore. Someone kicked him a few times and then we left. We went and partied because we had shown the n—— that you can't fool around with us.

Case Illustration 2

On the night of March 3, 1991, a lone black man was driving his car, reportedly speeding, when he saw blue and red lights in his rear view mirror. It took him a couple of minutes to decide what to do. Should he pull over and find out what the police wanted, or should he attempt to outrun them so that he did not have to put up with the hassle that would surely follow? The cocaine and alcohol that were in his blood stream made the choice a little harder to make. He finally decided to pull over but he apparently made the decision too late because when the first police officer came to his car door, the officer's gun was drawn and pointed at his face. Just then, a few more police cars arrived at the scene. He did not know it yet, but there were 15 white police officers either at the scene or on their way. The police ordered him to the ground. When he attempted to ask them questions about why he was being treated in this way, he was struck on his back by a baton. He attempted to stand, to get away from the beating, but the four officers standing over him continued to hit him with their batons, kicked him, stomped on him, and even used an electric stun gun in order to "restrain" him. Racial epithets filled his ears right before the blood. He could feel the bones in his ankle, face, and skull crack. His eye started to fall out of its socket but there was nothing he could do to prevent the blows. You could see him attempt to cover his face but the blows found their mark elsewhere until his hands moved from his face. This incident was videotaped by a resident of a nearby apartment complex, who watched in horror as this civilian was savagely beaten by those who were responsible for serving and protecting his community. This 2-minute videotape showing 56 blows to the body and face of Rodney King captured the attention of the nation and proved, with graphic detail, that hate-motivated police brutality occurs.

Personality and Characteristics of the Perpetrator

Personality studies on hate group members or terrorists are rare. The limited studies have found that imprisoned terrorists have low self-esteem and externalize blame for their failures to the society-at-large (Post, 1987). Levin and McDevitt (1993) found that perpetrators were primarily young white males seeking excitement (often accompanied by drinking), juveniles who see themselves as defending their turf, or members of hate groups. It is this latter group which is most likely to commit violent and lethal acts of hate. Hate groups attract individuals, typically men in early adulthood (mean age of 22.5 years; Falk, 1988), who tend to have paranoid personality features (Post, 1987), and who are intelligent (Kampf, 1990), industrious, and committed to their cause (Falk, 1988).

Low self-esteem and a tendency to externalize make these individuals prone to blame others for their problems and focus on whatever out-group is dictated by their own affiliations and culture. Berk, Boyd, and Hamner (1992) suggested that those who commit hate crimes are generally males in their teens to mid-20s, and that they outnumber their victims by two to one, have had little contact with the victim, attack the person outside of a personal residence, usually on evenings or weekends, and do not commit the hate crime in the course of another crime.

Of hate crimes committed by whites, 60% are motivated by racial bias, with up to 20% related to sexual orientation (Witkin and Thornton, 1997). Fifty-six percent of incidents of lethal violence related to hate are committed by offenders under 21 years of age (Witkin and Thornton, 1997).

Olmstead-Rose (1990) found that the perpetrators of crimes against gay men were generally young men believed to be age 21 or younger. More than half of the perpetrators committed their crimes while they were in groups. It is unfortunate, but not surprising, to learn that members of minority groups that have historically been victimized have taken to perpetrating hate crimes. Perpetrators were inordinately members of minority groups themselves: 42% were identified as white, 32% as black, 22% as Hispanic, and 3% as Asian. However, perpetrators who were members of minority groups were typically not members of organized hate groups.

Some perpetrators may feel that they are protecting themselves rather than initiating an attack. They are likely to have few family ties and may have poor social relationships. In many cases, commission of a hate crime is accompanied by a sense of thrill at attacking the feared group as well as a related boost in self esteem. In some cases, the perpetrators join hate groups more for the thrill and the danger than for the hate. Rarely are the perpetrators readily identified as "psychotic" or having a major psychiatric disease. Their cognitive processes are generally within normal limits and may even be superior. Individuals with low self-esteem may also be more threatened by the success or simple visibility of groups against whom they are prejudiced. This may be exploited by leaders within the community who intensify their fears of and feelings of threat from the minority group.

As seen in Case Illustration 2, there is evidence of hate crimes perpetrated by the police and other official groups. The 1991 police beating of Rodney King is but one example provided by the National Association for the Advancement of Colored People (NAACP; 1995). Although it is said that verbal abuse and harassment are the most common forms of hate-motivated police activity, the Rodney King incident and the thousands of reported and unreported police beatings of minority group members appear to provide evidence of a nonlocalized, systemic pattern of hate-motivated crimes perpetrated by police.

Many police departments are attempting to retrain their officers in less harmful ways of detaining and arresting while others are regrouping their departments in order to provide community-based programs that will enable the community members and police to discuss and act upon problems together instead of in an adversarial manner (National Association for the Advancement of Colored People, 1995).

Our understanding of the roots of hate-motivated violence can also be extended by examining the psychology of "heroic helpers" who resist external pressures to be involved in violent hate crimes. Staub (1993) summarized this work as suggesting that such individuals do not identify themselves as part of the in-group. They are able to maintain an independent perspective and see value across groups. They are raised with strong moral values toward helping and valuing others. They are inclusive, rather than exclusive, in defining people as human. They focus on the welfare of other people, believe that we are personally responsible to help others, and have an ability to show empathy. They are close to their families and associate with groups which preach protection and help rather than violence. They are not swayed by the actions of others and have faith in their own competence, a willingness to disregard personal consequences, and a high tolerance for risk. They relate to others as humans rather than as Jews, blacks, or Arabs. In many respects, these individuals appear very much the opposite of the individuals who commit violent hate crimes.

Demographics of the Victim

The demographics for the victims of hate crimes vary considerably depending on the specific situation and circumstance. Victims may be of any age, racial group, gender, or sexual orientation. Thus, while a young black man may be the victim of a hate crime, he, in turn, can be the perpetrator of a hate crime against a Korean druggist or a white middle-class man. Victims are typically judged to be in a situation where they are relatively helpless and outnumbered. The choosing of a person as a victim lies primarily in his or her symbolic value as a group member, not in the person's own individual characteristics or identity.

Triggering the Lethal Hate Crime

A lethal hate crime is usually the end-product of a slow process involving escalating crimes. The initial crimes may involve property rather than violence against persons. As these are tolerated, or even applauded, there may be increasingly violent confrontations (Staub, 1996). In these cases, early harm to a group or individual may be minimal; for example, throwing eggs at houses, disrupting gravestones, or causing minor physical harm. Only a very small minority of perpetrators move from property crimes and less violent acts to lethal violence. However, a lethal hate crime is rarely the first hate crime committed by the perpetrator.

Laboratory studies involving the administration of electric shock have demonstrated the principle of escalating violence (Buss, 1966; Goldstein et al., 1975). In these studies, teachers shocked learners who failed on a task. Teachers who were able to determine the shock level were found to increase the intensity of the shock over trials. This occurred despite controls for the learner's error rate (Goldstein et al., 1975).

As the level of violence increases, the chances for lethal violence also increase. The actual lethal act is rarely planned, but rather is somewhat accidental as a result of the increasing violence of the attacks (and may even be accidental in the sense that murder was not intended). The likelihood of violence is increased by the ingestion of alcohol or drugs which lowers inhibitions, as well as by the presence of others who encourage the attack. While the victim is usually a random individual who typically is not known to the attacker, in some cases the victim may be an individual who is seen as being too aggressive or to have committed some insult.

The violent event itself typically involves weapons which happen to be present. It is rarely preplanned but is more spontaneous. In some cases, the intention is simply to beat up and "scare" the individual, but the violence goes too far. In many cases, the degree of violence employed is well out of proportion to subduing or even killing the individual. The attacks may resemble a frenzy of hatred and violence rather than simply the desire to kill.

After the event, the attack may be celebrated and the violent individuals seen as heroes by the group. Interviews with attackers reveal that they feel a type of euphoria during the attack, followed by a feeling of kinship with the group involved in the attack, allowing the perpetrators a sense of increased self-esteem (Hamner, 1992). The violence is most likely to be condoned and rewarded by groups with which they associate. The act may be adequate for a period of time, temporarily increasing the perpetrators' self-esteem and standing within the group, but eventually another cycle of attacks begins which can lead to further violence.

Case Illustration 3

I never knew any blacks or Jews when I was young, but I knew how bad they were. My father would tell me stories of how they attacked white women and how we had to protect ourselves. He also kept a gun in the house and in the car because we never really knew when one of them might come after us. We lived in a very rural county, and we needed to be able to protect ourselves. My father ran a farm and I helped, but times got tough and many of the farms went up for sale. We lost our farm to the Jew bankers who stole it from us. They sold it and we had to move into town where everyone was living off government checks and anything they could scrounge up. This was all the fault of the Jews and the blacks. They worked together to take everything away from good Christian Americans. The Jews gave lots of things to the blacks so they would be their muscle and help them bring down the whole country. They controlled a lot of the government, and they started to hassle us about guns and everything.

I found a group that was out to save the country. They lived on one of the farms, and they were storing up an arsenal for the day when the Jews would send the blacks against us. I moved out there and helped all I could. Raleigh was our leader, and he had things figured out real well. He could tell when they were lying, and he told us the real truth. Things were getting real bad. They had taken over the sheriff's office and they had hired a n—— deputy sheriff. He was out hassling all the white folks, especially the women. He was forcing girls to sleep with him by threatening or encouraging them to betray their race, but it was all hushed up because they controlled the government. Raleigh said we had to get him and all the other n——— before they got us and corrupted the white race completely. Raleigh started sending us on n—— hunts. We'd go out and look for n——— who we'd beat up and kick out of the county. I really liked that. We were helping the country and showing what real white men could do. We were sending them a message. We'd go back to the farm and celebrate, but Raleigh wouldn't let it go too far because he said that it was only one and there were many more. The sheriff kept trying to get us but they couldn't prove who did it and we would have massacred them anyway if they had come out to the farm.

Things got more and more tense. The n—— sheriff said we were the Ku Klux Klan and trying to scare all the white people into thinking we were some kind of nuts. The big problem started when we went out on patrol one afternoon. We went down by the river and we saw a n—— on the beach with a white woman. She was probably Jewish. They were tangled together and didn't even see us. We snuck up on them and caught them nearly naked, wearing swimsuits. The n—— kept screaming at us to let them go and threatening to go to the police. He told us he would kill us if we touched his little Jew. We tortured the bitch and her n—— playmate by playing with her. You should have seen the foam coming out of the n——'s mouth. We had him hog tied and he would scream and thrash and try to bite while we had a good time with the Jewish bitch. She cried and begged and moaned, but she deserved everything she got. She was a traitor to the white race. After we were finished with her we beat both of them to a pulp. You could hardly tell who was white and who was black.

We only got caught because there was some kind of a spy in our group who alerted the sheriff. He showed up and cornered us, but not before we had taken care of the n—— and his bitch. We had a shoot-out. I got one deputy before they shot me in the stomach. I was in the hospital for about ten days. We're going to get out of here before the trial, though — Raleigh will come for us. It doesn't matter, no God-fearing Christian jury would ever find us guilty for stopping that sh—. You can bet any n—— 'round here is going to think twice before going off with a white woman, and any white woman traitor is going to think twice too. I think we got our message out that they can't mess with us anymore.

Difficulties In Intervention

Intervention with individuals committing hate crimes is difficult for several reasons. First, hate crimes are as much a product of society as they are of the individual. Stereotypes and prejudices held within a society are transmitted from generation to generation and are difficult to eradicate. Hate crimes also tend to increase when times are bad and individuals feel threatened economically or personally. Thus, intervention requires changes on a society-wide basis, not just in the individual guilty of the crime.

A second problem is that hate crimes are often applauded by a small section of society which sees the victims as getting what they deserve. In criminal cases, the victim is often blamed for the behavior of the attacker. In such cases, the attacker sees his or her behavior as proper and justified, if not actually heroic.

In such cases, there is no motivation to change and, indeed, the motivation is to maintain the behavior and to urge others to behave the same way. Such attitudes are transmitted through generations, creating new attackers, and are often based on old prejudices or stereotypes. The process of dehumanization removes any stigma of guilt. The thrill of the act, which may come from simply doing something asocial (violence) along with external support again increases the likelihood of such behaviors repeating themselves.

Herek (1989) pointed out that problems in dealing with hate crimes include simply admitting to their frequency and gathering significant data on their nature and occurrence. This has not occurred in any organized manner, with many crimes being underreported. Berrill and Herek (1990) viewed secondary victimization as another major impediment to the reporting of hate crimes. Because many are afraid to report crimes due to an anticipated negative reaction from the police, the problem of hate crimes can easily be swept under the rug or classified as some other type of crime. When the gay or black communities distrust the police, they will not cooperate with attempts to report or help stop violence and the less serious crimes which lead to violence.

Evaluating the Perpetrator

Psychological evaluation of the perpetrator has been a largely neglected area in the literature. This is partly due to a greater focus on the evaluation of the victim, who is more easily identified, and the failure to identify the attacker in many of these cases. Lethal violence stemming from hate crimes is generally committed by a stranger with no connection to the victim and in out-of-the-way places where the only witnesses are the attackers. In such cases, typical police methods are not effective in tracking down the perpetrators. Only in cases where there is a witness or clear evidence is someone actually apprehended. Many of these cases are thus classified as unsolved.

When such individuals are caught, there is no standard profile for their evaluation. In the authors' own experience, administration of personality tests such as the Minnesota Multiphasic Personality Inventory-2, Rorschach, Sentence Completion, and Thematic Apperception Test can be useful in eliciting dimensions of personality (assuming that the perpetrator is cooperative). These individuals are rarely psychotic, but they may show signs of personality disorders and social problems on these tests which give insight into their way of thinking.

Often, the best way to get information from these individuals is through an interview. But, while these individuals are rarely ashamed of their behavior, they are highly suspicious of government organizations and people interviewing them, whom they may see as part of the system which encourages whatever deviance they believe they are fighting. However, if their confidence can be gained, it may be found that they are often proud of what they have done and will discuss their actions and justifications in extensive detail. The key to such trust is showing a strong interest in taking their beliefs seriously. Questions which imply disapproval of their behavior or beliefs will quickly lead to an end of the useful conversation. By appearing sympathetic and serious (and not challenging their racial epithets and similar language), insight into their motivations and the assessment of the likelihood of such events happening again can be achieved. It is routine to find that the crime of which they are accused is just one of many.

Cognitive and intellectual testing is rarely indicated in these cases, but occasionally can be useful with individuals who appear to be of low intelligence. In most cases, a cognitive screening examination is adequate.

Intervention

Intervention for hate crimes is most often aimed at society rather than at the individual attacker.

Individuals are regarded as the tip of the iceberg and a reflection of a much more pervasive societal problem. Treatment of the hate crime offender is not well documented in the literature, other than suggestions for incarceration in order to emphasize the seriousness of the crimes. Berrill and Herek (1990) suggested that attackers be required to receive education and training which focus on understanding, tolerance, and respect for those they attacked. Innovative sentencing involving restitution which increases contact with the persecuted group and their "humanness" may also be useful. However, these suggestions focus on individuals who have committed less serious hate crimes which did not involve death or serious impairment. In the latter cases, the consensus appears to be to incarcerate the individual for an extended period of time as punishment and as a sign to others that these are activities which will not be tolerated.

Sandhu and Brown (1996) emphasized that a more comprehensive theory of prejudice needs to be developed in order for interventions to be enacted and studied more effectively. They suggested that multi-modal individual therapy can be effective if the therapist is able to focus on the specific aspect of prejudice that the perpetrator exhibits. For example, if the perpetrator has erroneous beliefs about the hated group, the therapist can provide education and information to the client and can facilitate the exploration of the reasons why these beliefs are important to the client. If the client is expressing prejudice because of low self-esteem and fear of the hated group, the therapist can assist the client in believing in himself or herself and discussing the reasons why the group is feared. The therapist can also provide a nonjudgmental environment where the client can explore his or her beliefs and can experiment with newly developed beliefs. It appears as though Sandhu and Brown (1996) were developing a strategy of intervention with which most therapists already have experience. Although Sandhu and Brown (1996) were not specifically discussing the perpetrators of hate crimes, their philosophy on treating prejudice may have implications for the treatment of the perpetrators of hate crimes.

While intervention at a societal level is difficult, there are many things which can be done to lessen the incidence of these crimes. There is, unfortunately, a paucity of any research on which of these techniques work; rather, there are simply opinions on the causes of hate crimes and reasonable suggestions as to how they might be ameliorated.

A major issue for intervention is the more obvious one of documentation. Herek and Berrill (1990), while writing about anti-gay and anti-lesbian hate crimes, emphasized the need for full and proper documentation of hate crimes including how and where they occur. They suggested studying demographic issues, the type of crime, the situation of the crime, and other relevant factors to better understand the underlying factors and the potential risk factors of hate crimes. Berk (1990) outlined eight factors which should be evaluated for each crime: (1) the number of perpetrators, (2) the ages of the perpetrators, (3) the ratio of perpetrators to victims, (4) the relationship of the perpetrators to the victims, (5) the location of the crime, (6) when the crime occurred, (7) the gender of the perpetrators and victims, and (8) other associated crimes committed at the same time. There is also a need to determine risk factors which may influence the choice of victims. For example, are more hate crimes aimed at Jews who dress in traditional Orthodox garb or who wear Jewish stars?

Levin and McDevitt (1993) suggested that government reactions to hate crimes are a major issue. They argued that as long as the government ignores or downplays these issues, hate crimes will increase because of perceived tacit government support. Berrill and Herek (1990) argued for increased sensitivity training for police and criminal justice personnel so that they learn to understand that hate crimes are real crimes, even if they are relatively minor or directed at a group toward which the "system" itself may feel prejudice. Because lethal violence based on prejudice is almost always an outgrowth of smaller acts, proper early reaction can help eliminate the more violent crimes. In addition, the system must react strongly to cases where the police or the justice system itself is the perpetrator of the hate crime.

Levin and McDevitt (1993) argued for a need to modify affirmative action programs to include all disadvantaged people (e.g., all poor Americans not just poor member of a particular group) so that such programs are more even-handed. They suggested that programs which seem to give more to one disadvantaged group than another can engender a sense of unfairness which may translate into hate crimes.

Government is also implicated in hate crimes, as noted earlier, by placing certain practices and peoples outside the law. Herek (1992) argued that laws and moral codes taught by religions which label homosexuality as deviant and evil contribute to anti-gay violence. He suggested that there is a tendency to alternately try to hide and to condemn homosexuality which leads to increased chances of violence. He suggested the need for institutional changes which accept homosexuals (or any other group) as an important prerequisite to long-term changes. Berrill and Herek (1990) called for enacting statutes that facilitate the arrest and prosecution of those who commit hate crimes, imposing more severe penalties for hate crimes, and making it easier for victims of hate crimes to file for damages and compensation against their attackers.

Herek (1989) cited the importance of greater trust and cooperation between minority communities and the police as a key to intervention. Agencies need to make efforts to show that they are fair and will not further victimize those minority members, as well as make a commitment to investigate and solve hate crimes at all levels. Allowing less severe crimes to go unpunished (or even seeing them as simply juvenile pranks) provides for the escalation of violence leading to lethal violence at its endpoint.

Herek (1989) also identified community education as a major intervention factor. He strongly suggested that federal funds are needed to develop and implement programs aimed at lessening prejudices against all minority groups. He stated that these programs should be heavily aimed at children and juveniles, because juveniles are overrepresented as the perpetrators of hate crimes. Sensitivity training for teachers and students are necessary. Simple programs are advocated for university settings as well.

The role of the school as a place of education as well as socialization with other children with different characteristics and beliefs cannot be overemphasized. Because day care or preschool may begin as young as several weeks old in many families, the role of the school is even more important than it was 50 years ago. Schools must teach children the general values of getting along with each other and of valuing each other despite our differences.

Schools need to encourage independent thinking and questioning. They must teach children to think for themselves and to problem solve. Schools themselves must react to cases of prejudice by child against child with rational discussion and problem solving so that the children can understand their errors. We must remember that most school misbehavior does not represent prejudice or hate, but that those cases which do must be clearly identified and handled in a manner which addresses the prejudice, not the child. There must be sufficient adult supervision so that cases of prejudicial behavior are readily identified and addressed rather than overlooked or ignored. Children and adults armed with strong values are likely to be better able to resist the misinformation and invitations to violence found in the community.

Staub (1996) emphasized the importance of how we define "us". By extending the boundaries of what we consider "us", we see more people as part of our in-group and tend to see others less as outsiders. To the extent that we can teach people not to view an individual as an outsider, our ability to stop crimes of hate becomes greater. To do this, we must emphasize our similarities rather than our differences. Staub suggested the importance of recognizing the historical roots of differences among people — why people developed in different ways — to emphasize how we all might react in similar ways to similar circumstances. Thus, although we are different, we are the same underneath, possessing the same goals, feelings, intelligence, and humanity. These again are basic attitudes which need to be taught early and reinforced through the mass media.

Staub (1996) indicated the importance of training parents in methods of positive socialization and promoting a positive attitude toward others. Such training can involve individual or group training and can include churches and other community organizations, the support of schools at all levels, and the involvement of the social services system. Such training is needed at all levels of society, not just for poor parents or minority parents, as prejudicial behavior has its roots in the values of parents from all classes and of all colors and ethnic groups.

Community organizations must also attempt to instill strong values in parents, and parents must be willing to support those values even when their own children are the violators of appropriate values and behaviors. Because childhood learning comes from other sources (babysitters, daycare, and preschool personnel), training must extend to anyone working in such settings. It is important to emphasize that many of the tolerant values and views we wish to teach develop at very young ages. By the time a child is an adolescent, these views are generally strongly formed and require much more effort to change. Thus, early parent training of the child as well as school involvement are essential if we wish to cause major changes within society.

It is important to create cross-cutting relationships that involve deep, rather than superficial, contact between different groups (Staub, 1996). Unfortunately, at present, we encourage integration, but integration without deep contact. It is not unusual in an "integrated" school to find whites, blacks, and Hispanics at their own tables, creating a segregation which is voluntary but which prevents any real interaction. By using learning techniques which emphasize cooperation (rather than individual learning alone) and by forming cooperative learning groups of members from different "factions", we can allow individuals to gain a better sense of one another and come to respect each others' strengths and weaknesses as humans. Such techniques may be employed in work and social settings as well with the same goals.

There have been successful attempts at increasing positive intercultural relationships in children in preschools (Harper and Dawkins, 1985), sports (Slavin and Madden, 1979), and extracurricular activities (Crain et al., 1982; Patchen, 1982). These programs were designed to increase cooperative, rather than competitive, activities among children of different cultural backgrounds. Slavin (1996) supported programs that divided classrooms into smaller teams consisting of culturally diverse groups of children. Grades were assigned based on group achievement rather than individual achievement. Because the children were acting in a cooperative manner and striving for a community goal, they were able to view their group members as the in-group and to learn about the similarities that they shared.

The mass media has a strong impact on the views and beliefs of American society and is therefore a powerful tool in combating prejudice in America. The way that the media presents minority members on television, in movies, in music, and in the news fosters negative attitudes and stereotypes in prospective perpetrators (Chen and True, 1994). However, the mass media can show how people can work together, despite their differences, against a common enemy (such as natural catastrophes). This does not require the use of dehumanizing concepts. Musical lyrics can emphasize discord or can incorporate love and cooperation. The media can show us how people have similar wants, needs, fears, and goals despite our differences and make differences commonplace and acceptable rather than frightening. We must encourage the media to promote our positive rather than negative values.

Summary and Conclusions

Hate crimes offer a major challenge for our society. While the exact incidence of hate crimes is unknown, they clearly occur far more frequently than they are reported. It is equally uncertain what percentage of lethal violence can be attributed to hate crimes because of the difficulty of classifying a crime as a hate crime without knowing the inner motivations of the perpetrator.

Hate crimes are manifestations of individuals regarding others as symbols of a given group or idea rather than as people. In most cases, the attacker is trying to build his or her own self-esteem by lowering the value of a group whose beliefs or behavior he or she sees as contradictory or threatening to the attacker's beliefs or way of life. Such factors as dehumanization, stereotyping, routinization, historical conflicts, authorization, imagined threats, visibility, and cultural differences provide an atmosphere consistent with, and conducive to, hate crimes.

The perpetrator of a hate crime is generally a young male with poor self-esteem and poor family ties, who typically does not act out alone. His level of self-esteem is very dependent on the importance of his group rather than his own behavior. He is usually of normal intelligence and is unlikely to be psychotic. He looks up to and respects leaders who may be bigoted and who may encourage violence openly or on a more subtle level. He usually commits less serious hate crimes such as property crimes first and slowly escalates the seriousness of the crimes as he is encouraged and rewarded by the response of his peer group and the lack of punishment from society.

A lethal outcome is often unplanned. The perpetrator rarely knows the victim and selects the victim because the perpetrator has the opportunity to attack with impunity. Attackers generally outnumber victims by a 2-to-1 margin. The intent initially may not be to kill but rather to injure as a warning to others. After the attack, the attacker may feel euphoric and show an increase in self-esteem. Rewards may come from the peer group, increasing the likelihood of further similar behavior. In many cases, the attacker is never identified.

Intervention is difficult because these crimes may not reflect individual pathology on the part of an attacker but rather reflect symptoms of more serious symptoms within society. As a result, intervention suggestions have focused more on the community than on the individual, aiming at changes in laws, police procedures, sensitivity training, training of school personnel, school procedures, parent training, and in how the media portrays minority groups.

It is suggested that future study in the area of hate crimes and prejudicial violence will be necessary because of our lack of hard knowledge regarding the etiology, intervention, and societal effects of these incidences. Such focus should be on the comprehensive psychological evaluations of the perpetrators and the personal and societal factors which lead to violence. More work is needed to identify when crimes are hate related and to deal with those crimes in an effective manner by studying the outcome of varying approaches. Research should also focus on identifying the effectiveness of societal interventions in changing both prejudices and stereotypes as well as on addressing hate crimes through both prospective and retrospective studies.

Annotated Bibliography

1. Able, D. (1995) *Hate Groups.* New York: Enslow Press. This book provides a useful description of hate groups and hate crimes in the U.S., examining the issues of the influence of such issues as freedom of speech in inciting hate crimes.

2. Ezekiel, R.S. (1995) *The Racist Mind.* New York: Viking Penguin. This book follows a Jewish researcher as he attends white supremacist rallies and interviews the white supremacist group members and leaders. He finds hope in the relationships he is able to build with people who "hate" him.

3. Garoogian, R. and Garoogian, A. (1995) *Crimes in America's Top Rated Cities: A Statistical Profile.* New York: Universal Reference Publishers. A statistical look at the incidence of hate crimes (as well as other crimes) throughout the U.S.

4. Hawley, W.D. and Jackson, A.W. (1995) *Toward a Common Destiny: Improving Race and Ethnic Relations in America.* San Francisco: Jossey-Bass. An excellent compilation of research describing ethnic identity and the improvement of race relations.

5. Levin, J. and McDevitt, J. (1993) *Hate Crimes: The Rising Tide of Bigotry and Bloodshed.* An excellent introduction to hate crimes intended for a wide audience of professionals and lay people. The book describes hate crimes, the possible motives of predators, and possible interventions on the part of the community.

6. McLaughlin, K.A. (1997) *Healing the Hate: National Hate Crime Prevention Curriculum for Middle Schools.* Newton, NJ: Education Development Center. A proposed curriculum for dealing with the problem of hate crimes aimed at juveniles who are most likely to be later perpetrators. An excellent start for considering intervention programs.

References

Anti-Defamation League of B'nai B'rith (1986) *The American Farmer and the Extremists.* New York: ADL.

Bar-Tal, D. (1988) Delegitimizing relations between Israeli Jews and Palestinians: A social psychological analysis. In J. Hofman (Ed.), *Arab-Jewish Relations in Israel: A Quest in Human Understanding*, pp. 217–248. Bristol, IN: Wyndham Hall.

Bar-Tal, D. (1989) Delegitimization: the extreme case of stereotyping and prejudice. In D. Bar-Tal, C. Graumann, A. W. Kruglanski, and W. Stroebe (Eds.), *Stereotyping and Prejudice: Changing Conceptions*, pp. 169–188. New York: Springer-Verlag.

Bar-Tal, D. (1990) Causes and consequences of delegitimization: models of conflict and ethnocentrism. *Journal of Social Issues, 46*(1), 65–81.

Berk, R.A. (1990) Thinking about hate-motivated crimes. *Journal of Interpersonal Violence, 5*(3), 334–349.

Berk, R.A., Boyd, E.A., and Hamner, K.M. (1992) Thinking more clearly about hate-motivated crimes. In G.M. Herek and K.T. Berrill (Eds.), *Hate Crimes: Confronting Violence Against Lesbians and Gay Men*, pp. 123–143. Newbury Park, CA: Sage.

Berrill, K.T. (1986) *Anti-Gay Violence: Causes, Consequences, Responses.* Washington, D.C.: National Gay and Lesbian Task Force. (Available from the National Gay and Lesbian Task Force, 1517 U St., NW, Washington, D.C. 20009.)

Berrill, K.T. and Herek, G.M. (1990) Violence against lesbians and gay men. *Journal of Interpersonal Violence, 5*(3), 269–273.

Bureau of Justice Statistics (1994) *Criminal Victimization in the U.S.: 1993,* Ref. No. NCJ-145125. Washington, D.C.: U.S. Department of Justice.

Buss, A.H. (1966) The effect of harm on subsequent aggression. *Journal of Experimental Research in Personality, 1,* 249–255.

Chen, S.A. and True, R.H. (1994) Asian/Pacific Island Americans. In L.D. Eron, J.H. Gentry, and P. Schlegel (Eds.), *Reason to Hope: A Psychological Perspective on Violence and Youth*, pp. 145–154. Washington D.C.: American Psychological Association.

Comstock, G.D. (1989) Victims of anti-gay/lesbian violence. *Journal of Interpersonal Violence, 4,* 101–106.

Craig, K.M. and Waldo, C.R. (1996) "So, what's a hate crime anyway?" Young adults' perceptions of hate crimes, victims, and perpetrators. *Law and Human Behavior, 20*(2), 113–129.

Crain, R., Mahard, R., and Narot, R. (1982) *Making Desegregation Work.* Cambridge, MA: Ballinger.

Falk, R. (1988) *Revolutionaries and Functionaries.* New York: Dutton.

Federal Bureau of Investigation (1996) *Uniform Crime Reports: Hate Crime 1995.* Available online: http://www.fbi.gov/uct/hatecm.htm.

Finn, P. and McNeil, T. (1987) *The Response of the Criminal Justice System to Bias Crime: An Exploratory Review,* contract report submitted to the National Institute of Justice, U.S. Department of Justice. (Available from ABT Associates, Inc., 55 Wheeler St., Cambridge, MA 02138-1168.)

Gamson, W.A. (1995) Hiroshima, the Holocaust, and the politics of exclusion. *American Sociological Review, 60,* 1–20.

George, J. and Wilcox, L. (1996) *American Extremists: Militias, Supremists, Klansmen, Communists, and Others.* Amherst, NY: Prometheus Press.

Goldberg, R.A. (1981) *Hooded Empire: The Ku Klux Klan in Colorado.* Chicago, IL: University of Illinois Press.

Goldstein, J.H., Davis, R.W., and Herman, D. (1975) Escalation of aggression: experimental studies. *Journal of Personality and Social Psychology, 31,* 162–170.

Hamner, K.M. (1992) Gay-bashing: a social identity analysis of violence against lesbians and gay men. In G.M. Herek and K.T. Berrill (Eds.), *Hate Crimes: Confronting Violence Against Lesbians and Gay Men*, pp. 179–190. Newbury Park, CA: Sage.

Harper, F.D. and Dawkins, M.P. (1985) The Syphax child care center. *Journal of Negro Education, 154,* 438–450.

Hate Crimes Statistics Act (1990) Public Law 101-275, 28, U.S.C. 534.

Herek, G.M. (1989) Hate crimes against lesbians and gay men: issues for research and policy. *American Psychologist, 44* (6), 948–955.

Herek, G.M. (1992) The social context of hate crimes: notes on cultural heterosexism. In G.M. Herek and K.T. Berrill (Eds.), *Hate Crimes: Confronting Violence Against Lesbians and Gay Men*, pp. 89–104. Newbury Park, CA: Sage.

Herek, G.M. and Berrill, K.T. (1990) Documenting the victimization of lesbians and gay men: methodological issues. *Journal of Interpersonal Violence, 5*(3), 301–315.

Herek, G.M., Gillis, J.R., Cogan, J.C., and Glunt, E.K. (1997) Hate crimes victimization among lesbian, gay, and bisexual adults: prevalence, psychological correlates, and methodological issues. *Journal of Interpersonal Violence, 12*(2), 195–215.

Kampf, H.A. (1990) Terrorism, the left wing, and the intellectuals. *Terrorism, 13*(1), 23–51.

Levin, J. and McDevitt, J. (1993) *Hate Crimes: The Rising Tide of Bigotry and Bloodshed.* New York: Plenum Press.

LeVine, R.A. and Campbell, D.T. (1972) *Ethnocentrism: Theories of Conflict, Ethnic Attitudes and Group Behavior.* New York: Wiley.

Lutz, C. (1987) *They Don't All Wear Sheets.* New York: National Council of Churches.

National Asian Pacific American Legal Consortium (1994) *Audit of Violence Against Asian Pacific Americans, 1993: Anti-Asian Violence, A National Problem.* Washington, D.C.: (author).

National Association for the Advancement of Colored People (1995) *Beyond the Rodney King Story: An Investigation of Police Conduct in Minority Communities.* Boston, MA: Northeastern University Press.

National Gay and Lesbian Task Force (1984) *Anti-Gay/ Lesbian Victimization: A Study by the National Gay Task Force in Cooperation with Gay and Lesbian Organizations in Eight U.S. Cities.* Washington, D.C.: Gay and Lesbian Task Force.

Olmstead-Rose, L. (1990) *1989 Statistical Analysis, Community United Against Violence.* Unpublished manuscript.

Patchen, R.E. (1982) *Black-White Contact in Schools: Its Social and Academic Effects.* West Lafayette, IN: Purdue University Press.

Post, J.M. (1987) Rewarding fire with fire: effects of retaliation on terrorist group dynamics. *Terrorism, 10,* 23–35.

Reed, B. (1989) Nazi retreat. *The New Republic,* July 3, pp. 10–11.

Sandhu, D.S. and Brown, S.P. (1996) Empowering ethnicity and racially diverse clients through prejudice reduction: suggestions and strategies for counselors. *Journal of Multicultural Counseling and Development, 24,* 203–217.

Slavin, R.E. (1996) Enhancing intergroup relations in schools: cooperative earning and other strategies. In W.D. Hawley and A.W. Jackson (Eds.), *Toward a Common Destiny*, pp. 291–314. San Francisco, CA: Jossey-Bass.

Slavin, R.E. and Madden, N.A. (1979) School practices that improve race relations. *American Educational Research Journal, 16*(2), 169–180.

Staub, E. (1993) The psychology of bystanders, perpetrators, and heroic helpers. *International Journal of Intercultural Relations, 17*, 315–341.

Staub, E. (1996) Cultural-societal roots of violence: the examples of genocidal violence and of contemporary youth violence in the United States. *American Psychologist, 51*(2), 117–132.

U.S. Commission on Civil Rights (1992) *Civil Rights Issues Facing Asian Americans in the 1990s.* Washington, D.C.: U.S. Commission on Civil Rights.

Witkin, G. and Thornton, J. (1997) Pride and prejudice. *U.S. News Online*, July 7–22. Available online: http://www.usnews.com/usnews/issue/RACE.HTM.

Young, T.J. (1990) Violent hate groups in rural America. *International Journal of Offender Therapy and Comparative Criminology, 34*(1),15–21.

About the Authors

Charles Golden, Ph.D., is a Professor of Psychology at Nova Southeastern University, FL, working in the Psy.D. and Ph.D. programs in clinical psychology. He has published over 200 books, chapters, and articles in psychology over a wide variety of topics to include violence related evaluation. **Michele L. Jackson** is a fifth-year student at Nova Southeastern, currently completing her internship as the last requirement for her doctoral degree. She has worked as a social worker with the Public Defender's office (Capital Crimes Unit) in Dade County, Miami, FL. **Thomas Crum** is currently beginning his third year in the Nova Southeastern doctoral program in Clinical Psychology.

Chapter 9

PRINCIPLES OF GROUP VIOLENCE WITH A FOCUS ON TERRORISM

Claudia J. Clayton, Sally H. Barlow, and Bonnie Ballif-Spanvill

Violence, or the threat of violence, is having an impact on the lives of individuals in virtually all parts of the globe. Given the pressing need to understand and curb violent and aggressive behavior, why has so little progress been made? Pepitone (1984) suggested that our attempts have been blocked by a lack of interdisciplinary cooperation. A comprehensive theory of violence requires an understanding of individual reality, collective reality, sociopsychological processes, and habitual emotional and behavioral tendencies (e.g., Markus and Kitayama, 1994). This requires information about the interplay of many factors, including biological, psychological, familial, peer group, cultural, religious, historical, economic, and political influences on human behavior. This book presents views from many areas in order to help remedy this problem.

Group violence has many sources and takes many forms. It is perpetrated by gangs; terrorists; spectators at sporting events; organized crime; opposing religious, ethnic, racial, and political factions; countries at war; and even by governments against their own citizens. These categories are not mutually exclusive (e.g., narcoterrorism, ecoterrorism, ethnic/political conflict in central Africa, ethnic/religious/political conflict in Bosnia, street gang conflict over drug turf). In spite of the many varieties of group violence, the authors believe they have some fundamental aspects in common.

In this chapter, the authors present a compendium of psychological principles that contribute to understanding group violence, followed by a discussion of terrorism as an example of group violence. The authors then propose a general model of motivation for participating in group violence and summarize the processes that contribute to the development of such motivation. Finally, some suggested ways for dealing with terrorism in light of the model are offered.

Psychological Principles that Contribute to the Understanding of Group Violence

Violence as an Instinctive Mechanism for Obtaining Resources

Studies across species indicate that violence, including group violence, may be instinctive. According to Manson and Wrangham (1991, p. 369), an evolutionary approach can provide some insights into lethal group violence as a "biologically adaptive mechanism for obtaining material, and/or reproductive resources." Pepitone (1984, p. 331) stated that, "A comprehensive theory of aggression will not only require identification of biological sources but [will need] to link them systematically to sources at other levels at which individuals and groups function."

Wilson (1975) suggested that animals, which are genetically programmed and the product of natural selection, display aggressive behavior to establish and defend feeding and living areas, compete for females for mating, secure unreceptive females, prevent young from straying, attack predators, and cooperate to promote certain normative, collective policies that ensure survival of the group. Thus, their aggressive behavior appears to have several results: establishment of territory, dominance, sexual advantage, discipline, protection from predators, and, in a sense, morality (i.e., survival of the group). Wilson (1975) further suggested that parallels can be drawn to human behaviors. Although there is a certain symbolization of status that occurs, humans still fight for territory, including access to food; compete for females and aggress sexually against them; discipline children, sometimes to the point of great harm, as in the case of battering that leads to filicide; and collectively aggress with a strong moralistic component in wars, "police actions", and the like. He also implied that human mob violence has parallels in other species.

A form of lethal group violence known only in one species of non-human primate — chimpanzees (although similar behavior may occur in some non-primate species) — is termed "lethal male raiding" (Manson and Wrangham, 1991). It has been observed at both major sites of chimpanzee observation in the wild: Gombe National Park, Tanzania (Goodall et al., 1979; Goodall 1986) and Mahale Mountains National Park, Tanzania (Nishida et al., 1985). The behavior consists of unprovoked forays of adult males into the territory of a neighboring group during which they hunt, attack, and often kill members of the other group. This behavior is similar to raiding by adult males in some human societies (Otterbein, 1970), wherein small groups of men hunt for victims in neighboring territories, trying to take them by surprise and to inflict violent injury or death.

The Choice of Violence in Light of Risk/Benefit Analysis Regarding Group Survival

Sociobiological theories of behavior usually are based on risk/benefit or cost/benefit analyses, the benefit having to do with the adaptive value of the behavior in terms of species survival. Species survival depends on the ability of individuals to survive and reproduce. The adaptive value of intergroup aggression in non-human primates may be that the winners achieve access to resources such as territory, food, or reproductive females (Manson and Wrangham, 1991). These authors have analyzed the costs and benefits of lethal male raiding in chimpanzee societies, using information provided by the original observers of the behavior (Goodall, 1986; Nishida et al., 1985). The costs appear to be low. Groups of males, along with a female or two at times, stealthily move along the border of their territory. If they do not find any members of the other group, they either return to their own territory or make a foray into the neighboring territory. If they come upon a lone male, a female who is not sexually receptive, a mother and infant, or a male-female pair, they may attack in a most aggressive fashion. Goodall (1986) observed five attacks that resulted in deaths of the victims and many other attacks during which the intended victims were wounded but escaped. Some of the aggressors held the victim(s) down and dragged them along the ground while they and the other aggressors bit, stomped, and beat them. Manson and Wrangham (1991) concluded that the element of surprise, the degree of aggression, the immobilization of victims (not seen in aggression in other non-human primate species), and the superiority in numbers of the aggressors make this a low risk activity.

Interestingly, Manson and Wrangham (1991) found no evidence that lethal male raiding provides benefits greater than those occurring through other mechanisms in species in which the females relocate to other groups before they reproduce. They suggested that this form of aggression occurs because of its low risk. That is, they hypothesized that imbalance of power promotes lethal attacks and suggested that, "Long-term social bonds facilitate the formation of cooperatively attacking subgroups, and variation in subgroup size reduces the cost of damaging aggression to attackers with sufficient numerical superiority." According to this hypothesis, they predicted that, "The cost to the aggressors will be low, attacks will be restricted to occasions of overwhelming superiority, potential victims will attempt to travel in large subgroups, and attacks will occur whenever the opportunity arises" (Manson and Wrangham, 1991, p. 371).

Do these predictions hold true in humans? Manson and Wrangham (1991) suggested that humans carry out their activities in subgroups of various sizes and that small subgroups may invite aggression by larger subgroups in adversarial situations, even though variation in subgroup size in humans is less important than in chimps, as humans have such a wide variety of tactics and so many sources of power imbalance. Still, the preferred military approach to conflict in humans is to use maximum force against the enemy, including numerical force, even with modern weapons (Keegan, 1976). Although it is difficult to evaluate the cost of human group aggression, Manson and Wrangham cited Bueno de Mesquita, who stated that over 85% of the initiators of international wars benefit from the war. Also, an analysis by Ember (1978) revealed that ambushes appear to be the tactic of preference in human foraging societies, although some use open group warfare or a combination of ambush and open group tactics.

The Choice of Objects of Aggression as Related to the Extent to Which Resources Can Be Seized

Another interpretation of the basis for choosing objects of aggression involves judging whether resources important to survival and reproduction can be seized (resource alienability). Manson and Wrangham (1991, p. 374) hypothesized that, "If material resources of sufficient value (i.e., importance to reproduction) are alienable, competition over females should give way to competition over material resources." To test this hypothesis, they analyzed group aggression in 42 foraging societies. They found that in societies that had access to alienable (obtainable) resources, those resources tended to be the objects of aggression, whereas when there were not such accessible resources, the conflict tended to be over women.

Additional support for the alienable resource hypothesis was provided by Sanday (1981), although she interpreted her findings differently. She studied 156 tribal societies regarding the incidence, function, and meaning of rape in tribal societies and found the incidence of rape to be greater in times of distress than in times of adequate food resources. This is congruent with the resource alienability hypothesis. Sanday's suggestion was that a high incidence of rape is embedded in a distinguishably different cultural configuration in which tribes are faced with depletion of resources, migration, and other factors contributing to a dependence on male destructive capacities, as opposed to relying on female fertility. Her interpretation was that male and female attributes are valued equally during times of adequate resources, but in times of distress, males are equated with greater status which "forces men to prove their status" (Sanday, 1981, p. 25), and the incidence of rape increases. While this last interpretation does not necessarily follow from Sanday's research, it is somewhat similar to that proposed by DeMause (1990) based on his examination of infanticide-prone cultures. He suggested that if infanticide were a result of depleted resources (not enough food to go around), the rates would be equal for male and female infants. But, if it occurred to fill some other function (as a method of appeasing the harvest gods, for example) the ratio of male deaths to female deaths would decrease, reflecting the valuing of males over females. Barlow and Clayton (1996) presented similar results, comparing rates of infanticide related to economic hardship or religious ritual in several ancient and modern cultures.

In-Group/Out-Group Dynamics and the Choice of Violence

Boone (1991, p. 377) posited another objective of lethal male raiding in chimps and primitive human societies: "... direct elimination of competitors for critical resources that are so thinly or irregularly distributed as to make it inefficient or impossible to defend or seize the area containing them." He regarded imbalance of power as a contributing factor, but not as immediately causal. Patterson (1991) entertained the hypothesis that chimps have the ability to label in-group and out-group populations as friends and enemies and may even share the capacity to extend that categorization to "us/non-food" and "them/food/prey". He cited Eibl-Eibesfeldt's model implying that the ability of humans to categorize others of their species as non-human underlies their ability to kill each other without suffering inordinate guilt.

Alexander (1989) suggested that intergroup aggression in humans and chimps has its roots in three characteristics: territoriality, cooperation between males, and the movement of females from their group of origin to other groups while the males are philopatric (that is, they remain with the groups in which they were raised). Interestingly, aggression in chimps and humans is largely carried out by the males, with females playing a supporting role, an unusual phenomenon among primates.

The Framework Beyond Biology for Understanding Human Violence

Bauermeister (1977, p. 245) stated, "Activity in which mankind has engaged so widely since time immemorial must be nurtured by psychological forces which are a part of the normal biological and social makeup." The non-human primate research may provide important clues about motivations for lethal group aggression in humans, but it is not clear to what extent that framework extends to complex human societies. Wilson (1975) noted that the "moralistic" behavior of many animals shows little variation, whereas human behavior is enormously variable because it is biologically constituted to be influenced by culture and the ability to learn from experience.

Explanations of human aggression in terms of mechanisms within the individual have been proposed widely throughout the scientific literature, sometimes subjected to empirical scrutiny and sometimes not. Early experience, exposure to others' behavior (modeling), and individual personality and psychological structure, including susceptibility to emotion, appear to contribute to a person's propensity for violence. Other mechanisms are related to group as well as individual phenomena. These include emotional contagion, identification with the group, ritual processes, and disengagement of self-sanctions.

The Influence of Social Learning on Violent Behavior

Early experience and exposure to violence are correlated with behavior problems. The role of early experience has been studied by Botsis et al. (1995), who assessed 79 psychiatric patients to determine the impact of early parental loss and exposure to family violence on behavioral problems. The patients were boys who had experienced parental loss. Their first-degree relatives also were assessed. It was found that exposure to family violence, as perceived by the patient, was significantly correlated with behavior problems in themselves and their first-degree relatives. Also, maternal loss at an early age was significantly correlated with suicide and violence. The authors suggested that these variables differentially predict the possibility of aggression directed inwardly (risk for suicide) or directed towards others (risk for violence).

Prino and Peyrot (1994) studied the interaction of early experience and modeling (i.e., the demonstration of behavior by another person). They compared aggressive, prosocial, and withdrawn children who had come from three settings: abused, non-abused but neglected, and non-abused, non-neglected as a controlled comparison. Their findings suggested that both forms of maltreatment resulted in a particular form of maladjustment compared to the control group. The physically abused children displayed much more aggression than the other groups, while the neglected children were more withdrawn. The children who were neither abused nor neglected exhibited more prosocial behavior than the others.

Personality Traits and the Reaction to Violent Models

Boyatzis et al. (1995) examined the effect of watching violent cartoons on elementary school children's behavior during play. Children who were assigned to watch Mighty Morphin Power Rangers cartoons exhibited seven times as much aggression during play than the control group. The boys in the cartoon group were more aggressive than the girls in that group, and it was noted that they imitated precisely the kicks and other aggressive moves of the Power Rangers. Dunand et al. (1984) examined the effects of modeling (watching aggressive films) plus the presence of an active or passive confederate. Subsequent aggression was increased for those who watched in the presence of an active confederate, suggesting the principle of social facilitation. Celozzi et al. (1981) studied the interaction of modeling and personality traits on the aggressive behavior of 81 high school boys. They found that viewing aggression had an effect, but it was not consistent across the subjects. The boys who had low scores on measures of aggressive personality traits were less affected than those with high trait aggression scores.

Aggression and the Psychoanalytic View of Individual Psychology

Aggression may be seen an instinctive reaction to the thwarting of drives. According to Sigmund Freud (1930, 1961), aggression or destructiveness is a basic instinct, though he considered it a secondary instinct, one operating in reaction to the thwarting of the pleasure-seeking drives. Freud reformulated his theories of aggression at the outbreak of World War I and added the idea of the death instinct at the beginning of World War II. While there are some notable exceptions to the dearth of empirical research on Freudian concepts (Eagle, 1984; Henry et al., 1994), generally Freud's complex ideas about the workings of the aggressive drives within the human psyche have not been validated empirically. Nevertheless, modern reworkings of Freud's ideas retain their vitality in the views of many because of their explanatory power, as evident in the following discussion.

Otto Kernberg's (1992) recent contribution of expanded theoretical notions based upon his clinical work represents the single best example of Freud's conceptualizations in the present day. Kernberg's work on personality disorders, narcissism in particular, led him to postulate the character type of the malignant narcissistic personality-disordered individual who gains political power over people who can be easily led into violent acts that mirror the individual leader's psychopathology (Kernberg, 1995). It takes a leader like Hitler or Stalin *and* a followership willing to worship such a leader. Malignant narcissists see others as idols, enemies, or fools, all in an exaggerated way. They see themselves as the embodiment of good and are able to rationalize their own antisocial behavior as appropriate to dealing with such enemies.

Aggression can center around hatred, which derives from rage. Kernberg (1992) made connections between aggression and rage, and rage and hatred. He explored the consequences of chronic hatred and secondary defenses against this hatred. He viewed hatred (p. 21) as being "the core affect of severe psychopathological conditions. ...Hatred derives from rage, the primary affect around which the drive of aggression clusters." He viewed the early appearance of rage as the infant's attempt to eliminate frustration, coming and going relatively quickly. Hatred is a complex aggressive affect, and, in contrast to the acuteness of rage reactions, it is chronic and stable. Kernberg (1992, p. 23) stated, "The primary aim of one consumed by hatred is to destroy its object." Hatred is not necessarily pathological. It can serve a much-needed survival function against a real threat. In pathological hatred, the object of the hatred is a person both needed and desired, as well as hated and envied, but the need and desire typically are not within conscious awareness. Pathological hatred can be expressed in murder and suicide, as well as other violent actions and obsessive thoughts. Kernberg (1992, p. 28) hypothesized that such hatred is more likely in individuals whose mothers' behavior combined "abandonment, violence, chaos, and a teasing overstimulating together with chronic frustration."

Other Viewpoints Supporting the Emotional Basis of Violence

People who are violent often appear to be cold and distant, unmoved by the tragedies they have brought about. Because they rarely display remorse, violence may mistakenly be considered emotionless behavior. Yet, an individual's decision to engage in violence is primarily based on that person's stage of emotional development, accumulated affective learning, and present emotional state. Perpetrators choose to be aggressive, in part, because of their emotions, not because they have no feelings. However, the specific emotions that influence their decisions to be violent differ markedly from those emotions experienced in similar situations by most other people. This may be due, in part, to the impact of difficulties they have experienced in their lives and the emotional reactions they have observed in close associates. Nonetheless, it is their emotions, albeit distorted, that are almost always involved with aggressive behavior. Chronically violent individuals act in ways consistent with their feelings and in anticipation of more positive affect and a rewarding emotional payoff (Atkinson, 1964; Ballif, 1977).

Violence is viewed as instrumental in bringing about success and its concomitant positive feelings. While the capacities to experience affect are biologically based, emotions seem to be largely acquired and can be "taught" in the sense that they can be socially engineered. Tedeschi and Felson (1994) argued that among those individuals who participate in group violence, learned behavioral scripts are firmly in place in which aggression is the means of acquiring various rewards and incentives. They acknowledged the sociological views that values which are related to harm-doing vary, and that nonviolent ways to achieve are often blocked. However, they emphasized that learned patterns of aggressive behavior that have been successful time and again are a major factor in encouraging groups to engage in violence.

Emotions and the Decision-Making Process Regarding the Use of Violence. The effects of emotion on the cognitive decision to carry out violence cannot be underestimated. Negative emotions have been found to greatly reduce the ability to think clearly about different alternatives (Hettena and Ballif, 1981). In fact, certain emotions have been shown to limit perception, discrimination, learning, memory, decision-making, and judgment (Izard, 1977; Zajonc, 1980; Bower, 1981; Ballif, 1989).

Anger usually accompanies violent acts. Averill (1983) concluded that the most important fact about anger is that it is a reaction to some perceived misdeed. Several researchers have cast light on how anger clouds judgment (White, 1968; Masters et al., 1981; Tarvis, 1982; Meichenbaum and Gilmore, 1984; Tedeschi and Felson, 1994). They have found that anger limits what will be attended to and the ability to think flexibly in terms of cognitively organizing events, understanding situations, and making appropriate decisions. It disrupts complex thinking and intensifies behavioral responses to the object of aggression. Angry people tend to fixate on the unjust episode and focus on punishing the perpetrators, disregarding the future and the possible aftermath of their actions. It is because the arousal of anger disrupts and disorganizes cognitive processes that it is difficult for angry people to consider ultimate long-range consequences of their acts. Angry people simplify information processing and tend to make single-minded judgments.

Assaults on identities, sometimes resulting in "losing face", can provoke intense anger. Coercion may then be used as a means of protecting the desired identity. People are socialized to believe that blameworthy actions should be punished and are motivated by this belief to try to maintain justice between themselves and others (Tedeschi and Felson, 1994). For example, when one gang attempts to intimidate another gang that has worked hard to establish a reputation as being tough, this "tough" gang may interpret that action as an attack on who they are. This same "tough" gang may then attempt to save face by lowering the status of the provoking gang through insults or counterattacks. When targets believe that the antagonist has belittled and demeaned them, they are likely to feel humiliated. By retaliating, the target can nullify that negative identity and reduce humiliation (Vogel and Lazare, 1990).

Personal identity and status combine with normative systems when group members are deeply committed to their group identities. In this case, people emote and act according to the norms of their group in order to experience affirmation of self through the reflected appraisals of others (Burke and Reitzes, 1991).

Contagion of Emotions. Emotions seem to spread from one person to another and can be "caught" (Hare, 1976; Burt, 1982; Knoke and Kuklinski, 1982; Bradley, 1997). Luschen (1980) suggested that we study sport as a way to further understand aggression, as it is a regulated system in which conflict is displayed. According to him, sport represents a general structural reality in all societies from primitive to industrialized. Certainly, there are numerous newspaper accounts of violence erupting at sporting events throughout the world. The notion of contagion is used to explain some of these instances; for example, when a foul is committed on the field of a sports event or a limited violent act occurs in the stands, other violent episodes are triggered. Convergence factors — the fact that like-minded people may be attracted to aggressive sports and thus might be more likely to behave similarly — may also be operating.

Interestingly, McPhail (1994) noted that extensive observational studies of crowds showed that neither participants nor non-participants in civil rights and anti-war demonstrations were transformed by the crowd into irrational pawns of suggestion and contagion. He suggested that emotional contagion may occur mainly in collective situations where conditions encourage altered states of consciousness. This seems consonant with sporting events where adrenalin is high and there is a significant amount of drinking or other substance use.

Scheidlinger (1994) proposed that three processes combine to contribute to teenage violence. The first comes from the group's temporary emotionalized state where reason, control, and judgment give way to unbridled emotionality, often found in crowd-like conditions. The second is the process in which a person is prevented or hindered by situational group factors from becoming aware of himself or herself as a separate individual. The third process is that of emotional contagion, in which emotional behavior is spread from one person to another. Similarly, Hatfield et al. (1993) believed that emotional contagion may help us understand crowds and group behavior, including those associated with Adolf Hitler.

Further studies are refining our understanding of this process. For example, Sullins (1991) found that the moods of people become more alike when the people in a dyad were about to experience the same circumstances. Hatfield et al. (1993) found that in conversation people automatically mimic and synchronize their movements with the facial expressions, voices, postures, and movements of others. Also, subjective emotional experience is affected by the activation of and feedback from facial, vocal, postural, and movement mimicry (Adelmann and Zajonc, 1989; Hatfield et al., 1993; Laird and Bresler, 1992).

The Contribution of Group Processes to Violence

Part of what appeals to individuals about joining groups is that group membership increases individual anonymity, personal safety and protection, and some power. At the same time, it decreases personal responsibility. Long ago, Gustave LeBon (1896) argued that crowds of people may act as entities unto themselves, as if the whole were controlled by one irrational mind with primitive motivations, with members of the crowd losing their individual sense of responsibility.

Festinger, Pepitone, and Newcomb (as reported in Forsyth, 1994, p. 442) coined the term "deindividuation" to describe how individuals become "so submerged in the group that they no longer stand out as individuals." Zimbardo (1969) continued the research and developed a process model that noted that the lowered threshold of normally restrained behavior is brought about by a sense of anonymity and diffusion of responsibility. Other studies have extended Zimbardo's research by expanding the understanding around loss of self-awareness and altered experience. The critical ways in which deindividuation leads to violence appear to include feelings of anonymity and reduced responsibility, as well as internal changes that include reduced self-awareness and perceptual disturbances. The outputs are extreme behaviors that are uncharacteristic of the individual under normal circumstances (Diener, 1977).

The other concept that should be included in this discussion is the process of groupthink (Janis, 1982, p. 552) — "a mode of thinking that people engage in when they are deeply involved in a cohesive in-group, when the members' striving for unanimity overrides their motivation to realistically appraise alternative courses of action." Groupthink reinforces and is in turn reinforced by the shared beliefs of the group members. It may lead to the perception that the risks to the participants in terrorist activities, for example, are relatively small.

Stronger group identity appears to be associated with increased violence. In an archival study, Mullen (1986) analyzed newspaper accounts of lynch mobs in the U.S. in the late 1800s to early 1900s. He noted that as lynchers became more numerous relative to the victims, the lynchers became less "self-attentive" and more deindividuated. Their deindividuation led to a breakdown of the normal self-regulation processes which, in turn, led to an increase in "transgressive behavior represented by the composite index of atrocity" (burnings, hangings, dismemberment, etc.; see Mullen, 1986, p. 194). These finding echo the conclusions of Scott's (1975) article detailing the mind of the murderer in which there is a qualitative shift in mental functioning. Watson (1973) presented anthropological evidence that the more brutal a group's customs, the more likely members are to paint their faces or wear uniforms, thus diminishing their personal identities. Uniforms that signify group membership help members merge into the group and distinguish between actions of the group as a whole and actions of individual members. This method of fostering the individual's sense of anonymity is most useful in training groups, such as armies, that may have to engage in violent activities that would normally be extremely repugnant to individual members.

Individuals still weigh risks against costs, however. McPhail (1994) concluded that no rational individual will participate in collective action unless the prospects of private benefits exceed the risk of private cost. He further argued that perpetrators of violent behaviors are not the victims of psychological deindividuation; rather, they are purposive actors adjusting their behaviors to make their perceptions match their objectives. In this case, the advantages reaped from group membership would be taken into consideration in a cost/benefit analysis of possible participation in group violence.

Emotions and Group Bonding

Collins (1981) proposed that emotions felt in common by group members are generated in rituals. These charismatic emotional energies create social solidarity and preserve and disseminate normative group patterns. Desecrating a symbol usually elicits anger and conflict between groups or between group factions, but reaffirming symbols generates positive emotion and synchronization within a group. Collins held that the inherent emotionality of even commonplace interaction rituals is the glue that holds society together and the driving force that mobilizes social change (Heise and O'Brien, 1993).

Violence can become ritualized in groups. For traditional behaviorists, aggression is a determined outcome of antecedent events, genetic or environmental; that is, aggression is predictable. But Harris and colleagues suggested that their research indicated a more voluntary quality. Harris et al. (1986), as well as Gottman (1979, 1994), found that repetitive patterns between couples suggest a perceived obligation to defend their position against verbal attacks that seemed to propel them into increasingly forceful efforts to "save face", suggesting the notion of ritual. Harris et al. observed conflicts in cross-cultural contexts corroborating this notion of ritualized escalating antagonism. They predicted that aggression would be reciprocated at every level of intensity, supporting the notion that once people have embarked on a given ritual, it becomes increasingly difficult to select alternative options. Physical violence is an almost welcome, often inevitable, termination of the ritual.

Harris et al. (1986) also studied aggressive rituals and asked subjects to predict, advise, and evaluate videotaped encounters of heterosexual couples fighting, and then two males fighting. The majority of subjects expected or condoned the physical expression of aggression for both couples and friends. The possibility for voluntary termination of aggression in couples was noted in contrast to the view that male friends needed outside intervention to stop. The authors noted that rituals account for much interaction and are based on the shared meanings of participants. For example, what appears as violent or disorderly public behavior may prove under informed observation to be based on unspoken but well-established rules of the group (Marsh, 1978; Marsh et al., cited in Harris et al., 1986).

This view moves an explanation of aggression beyond simple modeling to a meta-psychology that must include context to be fully understood. This notion of aggression as a ritual implies that human aggression cannot be studied apart from other human activity, but rather should be studied as part of a sequence or extended pattern amid other human behaviors.

Disengagement of Moral Reactions to Justify Violence

Bandura (1986, 1990) posited three categories of psychosocial mechanisms that can operate to distance people from morally based self-control: (1) moral justification; (2) minimizing, ignoring, or misconstruing consequences; and (3) dehumanizing the objects of aggression.

Moral Justification. Several forms of moral justification deserve mention. Bandura (1990, p. 10) suggested that it is much more difficult for aggressors to justify to themselves the killing of innocent people than that of political figures and, therefore, that it requires "intensive psychological training in moral disengagement ... to create the capacity to kill innocent human beings as a way of toppling rulers or regimes or of accomplishing other political goals."

Violence is seen as defensible when nonviolence has been ineffective against a highly destructive adversary. However, according to Bandura (1990, p. 166), violence also may be used against enemies who have not inflicted great suffering "on the grounds that, if left unchecked, they will escalate in severity to the point at which they will eventually exact a high toll in loss of liberties and in suffering."

Cognitive reframing can change one's conception of what originally was believed to be abhorrent behavior. A well-known example is that of Sergeant York, who sought conscientious objector status based on his Christian beliefs until his commanding officer used the Bible to convince him that fighting and killing were acceptable to God under certain circumstances (Skeyhill, 1928). The majority of Americans probably would agree that American involvement in World War I was morally justified and perhaps even imperative.

More problematic is the unthinkable suffering inflicted throughout history by people who, on the basis of their religious beliefs, were intent on ridding the world of evil (see Rapoport and Alexander, 1982). Ryan (1997) suggested that the concept of "chosenness", particularly in the Judeo-Christian tradition, has been a driving force in the self-righteous justification of destroying or subjugating groups seen as "not chosen". This sensitive issue is extremely difficult to deal with, as reflected in the 1990s by the protracted debates about the appropriateness of and responsibility for outside intervention in such areas as Somalia and Bosnia.

Minimizing, Ignoring, or Misconstruing the Consequences. This category includes euphemistic labeling, advantageous comparisons, displacement or diffusion of responsibility, and distancing of consequences. Euphemistic labeling can cause behaviors to be understood in a relatively benevolent light. For example, the sense of personal responsibility can be diminished in gang members who "off", "waste", or "take care of" someone rather than "murdering" or "killing" the perceived enemy. Likewise, they "initiate" new members rather than "beat them up".

Advantageous comparisons also contribute to cognitive restructuring of violent behavior. As Bandura (1990, p. 171) stated, "Self-deplored acts can be made to appear righteous by contrasting them with flagrant inhumanities. The more outrageous the comparison practices, the more likely it is that one's own destructive conduct will appear trifling or even benevolent."

People are more likely to behave in ways that harm others if someone in authority takes on the responsibility (Diener et al., 1975), allowing participants to minimize their own actions. Such displacement of responsibility was demonstrated in a famous experiment on the extent to which people would obey authority (Milgram, 1974). Subjects were told their task was to shock other subjects ("learners") who were not performing properly on a learning task. In actuality, the "learner" was not being shocked, but an audio recording was used to produce verbal responses to the task and sounds appropriate to someone receiving electric shocks, and the subjects believed this was the case. Psychiatrists and scientists who were polled prior to the study estimated that only about 1/3 of 1% of the subjects would go all the way to the strongest shock, 450 volts, and that the rest would refuse to continue far before reaching that point. To everyone's astonishment, nearly 70% of the subjects actually progressed to maximum shock, depending on the conditions. One of the factors that contributed to the subjects' willingness to continue administering painful shocks to the "learner" even though they were clearly uncomfortable doing so was that the experimenter told each subject that it was the experimenter's, not the subject's, responsibility for what was happening (e.g., balking subjects were told that "the experiment requires that you continue"). Bandura (1990 p. 173) stated that "people [who] view their actions as springing from the dictates of authorities rather than from their own volition ... are spared self-prohibiting reactions."

Diffusion of responsibility occurs when people in a group feel less responsible for acting or making decisions than they would if they were alone (Schwartz and Gottlieb, 1980). There are several ways this can happen. Division of labor may allow attention to shift from the implications of the task as a whole to the details of the individual's fractional contribution; group decision-making makes it easy for no single individual to feel responsible for the consequences; and collective action facilitates the ability of individuals to place the majority of the responsibility on the behavior of all the other members of the group (Bandura, 1990).

Milgram's (1974) obedience experiments illustrated some effects of the distancing of consequences. For example, it was found that commanded obedience decreased when the subject was in the same room as the "learner", who pretended to receive the electric shocks. Thirty percent of the subjects still proceeded to maximum shock even when they were told to hold the "learner's" arm on the shock plate during shock administration! Nevertheless, this supports the supposition that it is easier to minimize or ignore harmful consequences of one's actions if one is not able to actually see those consequences.

Much of modern weapons technology acts at such a distance that it enables its users to remain impersonal. Viewing mass destruction on a radar or television screen, or even from the height of an airplane, can be more analogous to playing at target practice or a computer game than to causing injury or death to hundreds or thousands of people. Kilham and Mann (1974) suggested that in a hierarchical system, those at an intermediate level find it easier to disengage personal control than those lower in the system who must actually perpetrate the violence. The middle-level people neither make the major decisions nor have to carry them out and thus tend to be more obedient to commands involving destruction.

Dehumanizing the Objects of Aggression. Dehumanization of the opponent enhances people's willingness to use violence. Lack of empathy is a common mechanism for seeing another as less than human. Bandura (1990) made the point that empathic responses to others' experiences depend in large part on whether or not we view them as similar to ourselves and that empathic responses strengthen self-sanctions against harming the object of our empathy. This can be seen anecdotally with people who are not strictly vegetarian but who will not eat "anything that has a face". Also, prosecutors say that one of the most challenging aspects of winning jury trials of accused abusers or murderers of infants is getting the jury to regard the infant as fully human. They spend a great deal of time helping juries understand such issues as the potential of the baby and his or her value to family and society (R. Parrish, personal communication, 1995).

The perception of social roles can foster dehumanization. The influence of the social environment generally is more powerful than that of individual characteristics in promoting a dehumanizing attitude. Authoritarian institutional influences are particularly powerful. In a landmark experiment, Zimbardo and his colleagues at Stanford (Haney et al., 1973) turned the basement of one of the older buildings on campus into a simulated prison. They then randomly selected student volunteers to serve as guards or prisoners. The experiment had to be terminated early because the students were turning their roles into an unexpected reality. The prisoners became depressed and submissive, while the guards became abusive and tyrannical. Thus, the powerful quickly differentiated themselves from the powerless and took full advantage of their positions. This finding is congruent with that of Larsen et al. (1971) who, on the basis of shock-administration studies, concluded that subjects' personalities did not predict their willingness to administer shocks to another person nearly as well as did social influences imposed in the experimental situation. The Milgram (1974) studies showed similar findings.

Dehumanizing attitudes and techniques are not difficult to find in society. For example, during Gulf War press briefings, military leaders often used the term kill "it" (referring to the Iraqi army) rather than kill "them" (referring to the Iraqi soldiers). Police and criminals sometimes use pejorative terms when referring to each other, and corporate leaders have been in the news for using demeaning codewords for minorities and women. Such efforts designed to reduce the status of victims of harmful behavior do not necessarily lead to violence, but they can help groups and individuals justify inappropriate actions toward those they see as being less human than themselves.

The various psychological concepts and empirical findings discussed in this section have been selected because of their probable roles in motivating individuals to engage in group violence, including terrorism. It is, after all, individuals who actually perpetrate the violence and are ultimately responsible for their own actions.

The authors now proceed to a discussion of terrorism, addressing incidence, types of events, and definitions and dealing with some common characteristics and motivations of terrorist organizations in light of many of the principles discussed above.

Terrorism

In 1987, federal charges were brought against 14 Christian white supremacists for conspiring to poison the water supplies of two major U.S. cities. According to the indictment, members of the Aryan Nation from throughout Canada and the U.S. met at the group's Idaho headquarters in 1983 to plan the overthrow of the U.S. government and the establishment of an independent Aryan nation. Their proposed tactics included assassinating Jews, politicians, and government officials and bombing and polluting municipal water supplies. The seriousness of the threat was confirmed in April 1984, when law enforcement officers raided a white supremacist enclave in Arkansas and found 30 gallons of cyanide (Hoffman, 1995).

Hoffman (1995) described the Christian Identity movement as the unifying thread of the Christian white supremacists in the U.S. The movement is hostile to any government entity beyond the county level, views non-whites and Jews as children of Satan, is obsessed with purifying the U.S. in terms of race and religion, believes that Jewish interests have conspired to control the government of the U.S., and advocates overthrowing the federal government, which it calls the "Zionist Occupation Government". This sobering example of a terrorist group within the U.S. describes only one of about 50 known terrorist groups active throughout the world.

The Impact of Terrorism

Terrorism is of particular interest to governments, law enforcement organizations, and social scientists because of its impact on enormous numbers of people around the globe. Peace negotiations between bitterly opposing political factions are time and again disrupted by terrorist operations. Business and government executives, and even people in "everyday" jobs such as teachers at foreign universities, take special security precautions. Only a tiny percentage

TABLE 9.1

INTERNATIONAL TERRORIST INCIDENTS, 1977–1996

Year	Incidents	Year	Incidents
1977	419	1987	665
1978	530	1988	605
1979	434	1989	375
1980	499	1990	437
1981	489	1991	565
1982	487	1992	363
1983	497	1993	431
1984	565	1994	322
1985	635	1995	440
1986	612	1996	296

Data are from U.S. Department of State (1996).

of the world's population has been directly victimized by terrorist acts, but the very fear of such acts has caused great numbers of people to modify their behavior. This affects economies as well as lives. For example, thousands of travelers have avoided certain airlines, airports, buses, department stores, or other locations during particular terrorist threats.

According the U.S. Department of State (1996), the incidence of international terrorism has tended to decrease since 1987 (see Table 9.1), but its impact remains serious. There were 440 incidents in 1995, with a death toll of at least 168 from the Oklahoma bombing alone, and 296 incidents in 1996, with a death toll of 311. The increased deaths were due to the use of more powerful weapons and the targeting of civilians. For example, bombing and firebombing were involved in 187 of the 296 international terrorist incidents in 1996. The U.S. was the target of 73 attacks on foreign soil during that year. Table 9.2 lists the total number of international terrorist events and those directed against U.S. targets, according to type of attack. The U.S. has remained relatively immune to international terrorism within its borders, with two attacks each in 1991 and 1992, one in 1993, and none from 1994 through 1996 (U.S. Department of State, 1996). However, the U.S. government continues to take the possibility of such attacks very seriously (Terrorism Research Center, 1997).

Meanwhile, domestic terrorism in countries such as Algeria, India, Sri Lanka, and Pakistan is becoming at least as serious as international terrorism (U.S. Department of State, 1996), and domestic terrorism is a serious issue in the U.S. The Federal Bureau of Investigation (1997) published the number of terrorist incidents in the U.S. from 1980 to 1995, as well as the number of suspected terrorist incidents and terrorism preventions from 1982 to 1995 (see Table 9.3). These numbers include the few incidents originating internationally, as described above, but the majority are of domestic origin. For example, according to the Centre for National Security Studies (1995), 11 of the 12 terrorist incidents in 1993 involved domestic perpetrators. Nine of those occurred

TABLE 9.2

INTERNATIONAL TERRORIST INCIDENTS BY TYPE OF EVENT, 1996

Type of Event	Incidents Against All Targets	Incidents Against U.S. Targets
Armed attack	39	3
Arson	31	7
Assault	1	—
Bombing	116	55
Firebombing	71	1
Hijacking	2	—
Kidnapping/hostage	28	6
Other	9	—

Data are from U.S. Department of State (1996).

in Chicago on a single night when animal rights activists placed incendiary devices in stores selling furs. Most domestic terrorist groups in the U.S. in recent years have involved special interest extremists, such as animal rights activists, anti-abortion activists, and right-wing extremists such as militia groups often having a religious agenda, with racist or anti-government ideologies (Centre for National Security Studies, 1995; Federal Bureau of Investigation, 1995; Hoffman, 1995; Ranstorp, 1996).

Definitions

Terrorism is a subjective term for which numerous definitions have been posited. For example, Schmid (1984) listed over 100 definitions formulated between 1936 and 1981. Statistics on the incidence of terrorism from various sources do not always agree due to the use of differing definitions of terrorism (U.S. Department of State, 1996), and the debate over the nature of terrorism has impeded its systematic study.

The authors have formulated the following definition of terrorism, incorporating elements from those of several authors: Terrorism is a strategy involving the premeditated threat or use of unlawful violence aimed at persons (usually noncombatants) or property. It is intended to instill fear in a wider group than its immediate victims, and the public is especially terrorized when civilians are targeted in unpredictable ways, leading to widespread feelings of personal vulnerability. Terrorism is considered domestic or international depending on the group's origin, base of operations, or activities. Its purpose may be political, religious, or ideological, and its goal is to coerce a government, an organization, or a segment of society into acting in accordance with the terrorists' objectives (Cooper, 1974; Adams, 1986; Bassiouni, 1987; Pomerantz, 1987; Bandura, 1990; Title 22, United States Code, Section 2656f(d); U.S. Department of State, 1988, 1996).

Table 9.3

Domestic Terrorist Incidents, Suspected Incidents, and Preventions in the U.S., 1980–1995

Year	Incidents	Suspected Incidents	Preventions
1980	29	n/a	n/a
1981	42	n/a	n/a
1982	51	0	3
1983	31	2	6
1984	13	3	9
1985	7	6	23
1986	25	2	9
1987	9	8	5
1988	9	5	3
1989	4	16	7
1990	7	1	5
1991	5	1	4
1992	4	0	0
1993	12	2	7
1994	0	1	0
1995	1	1	2

Data are from Federal Bureau of Investigation (1996).

Common Characteristics of Terrorist Groups

Some definitions of terrorism are so broad as to include virtually any kind of political violence. Long (1990) suggested it might be more useful to try to identify "the most common characteristics of terrorism, regardless of whether any particular one or combination of them is present in any given case" (p. 4). He listed four categories: goals, strategies, operations, and organization.

Goals. Terrorists' goals are usually political, which distinguishes them from ordinary criminals. Their grievances may involve social, economic, or other issues (e.g., ecoterrorism is becoming more common), and they believe that terrorism is their last resort (Knutson, 1981). Their goals may include demonstrating that the existing government cannot protect its citizens, thus creating the potential for political unrest and an eventual revolution. According to Feierabend and Feierabend (1970, p. 214), terrorist activities also may facilitate extended periods of social frustration among the populace during which "levels of social expectations, aspirations, and needs are raised for many people for significant periods of time, and yet remain unmatched by equivalent levels of satisfactions." Long (1990) noted that terrorist groups are fanatic seekers of vindication and that they perform terrorist acts knowing that the probability is very low that they will actually achieve their political aims. They often justify their actions by appealing to religion or some other "higher truth" even though the doctrines of major religions do not support terrorism. (For example, Shiite Moslems have committed many suicide bombings in Lebanon, but Islam clearly forbids suicide.)

Strategies and Tactics. The strategy of terrorism is to create terror. Prior to each act, planning and operating in complete secrecy are of great importance. After an act is committed, however, maximum exposure is essential in order to produce fear in the population, which will in turn coerce governments to alter their policies in line with terrorist goals. The desire for exposure dictates the choice of victims as well as the timing and location of the acts. As a consequence, the availability of publicity through the news media has profoundly influenced terrorist tactics.

Along with instant worldwide communication, technology has advanced the ability of terrorists to strike at global targets in a matter of hours. Probably the most influential technological influence was the introduction, in the 1960s, of large-scale, international jet transportation (Anderson and Sloan, 1995). An even more terrifying turn of events is the black market dealing of nuclear, biological, and chemical warfare technology that has occurred partly as a result of the collapse of the eastern bloc.

Operations. Terrorism involves the use or threat of violence. The threat of violence, alone, is not enough; the threat must be based on a willingness to actually commit violent acts in order to be credible (Anderson and Sloan, 1995). Terrorist operations include murder or infliction of injury by various means, kidnapping or hostage taking (e.g., hijacking), sabotage, arson, or other destruction of property.

There is an old platitude that says, "One man's terrorist is another man's freedom fighter." Long (1990, p. 7) believed that the criminal nature of terrorist acts distinguishes them from the military nature of guerillas or other insurgents, which, "while not fully sanctioned as conventional warfare, are still considered appropriate military behavior. Terrorist acts cannot be so justified." The nature of terrorist acts is to inflict violence while usually trying to avoid direct combat. There is no distinction made between military and nonmilitary targets and, in fact, the victims often are noncombatants. The acts are not part of a purely military mission, and their objects are chosen to propagate fear and unrest.

Terrorist operations are inexpensive relative to the arming and training of conventional forces, which makes this option open to organizations with limited funds. The involvement of secrecy and deception helps keep costs low and serves as a "force multiplier" (Hall and Pritchard, 1996) that increases the chance of success. For example, even sophisticated operations such as the bombing of Pan Am Flight 103 over Lockerbee, Scotland, in 1988, usually cost less than $250,000 (Long, 1990).

Organization. Terrorists almost always operate in groups. These usually are small, as large groups present greater discipline and security problems, and some members tend to become paranoid after being in the group for a time. If the group is large, it usually is divided into subsections (i.e., cells), and people in each subsection are not privy to the membership or operations of the others. The groups exert powerful influences on individual members. For example, membership can become a powerful source of self-esteem, and group membership itself can be a stronger motivation for committing terrorist acts than the political goals of the group (Long, 1990).

Explanations of Terrorism

The most prominent explanations of terrorism fall into three categories: structural, rational choice, and psychological (Ross, 1993). Structural theories utilize the view that terrorism is caused by environmental, political, cultural, economic, and social factors in societies; rational choice theories explain terrorism in terms of cost/benefit analysis by the participants; and psychological theories address individual and group dynamics in relationship to the formation of terrorist groups and the commission of terrorist acts. The central aspects of these three explanations are summarized below.

Structural Explanations. Ross (1993) constructed a causal model based on structure. He posited three "permissive" causes: geographical location, type of political system, and level of modernization, and seven "precipitant" causes (listed in order from least to most important): social, cultural, and historical facilitation; organizational split and development; presence of other forms of unrest; support; counterterrorist organization failure; availability of weapons and explosives; and grievances. The permissive causes act as facilitators of the precipitant causes. One example of location is the greater likelihood that terrorism will occur in cities than in rural areas because of logistical advantages (i.e., more resources such as banks to be robbed, larger pools of recruits, more targets, easier media access). The importance of the type of political system is illustrated by the fact that oppositional terrorism is most common in democracies, less common in underdeveloped nations, and rare in countries with totalitarian governments, either left- or right-wing. Democratic societies provide civil liberties such as freedom of movement and media access, and they tend to encourage diverse political values and narrow constituencies around issues such as race, class, or ethnicity. Many democracies still face unresolved issues of colonialism (e.g., Northern Ireland) or other difficult ethnic or separatist conflicts (e.g., the Basque separatist movement in Spain, or the Bosnian conflict and others in eastern Europe, which emerged upon the removal of authoritarian government). Also, most democracies provide easy accessibility for foreign terrorists (e.g., Al Fatah attacks in France).

Ross (1993, p. 322) suggested that the level of modernization is the most important of the permissive factors. He listed six factors of modern societies that encourage terrorism: "better, more sophisticated, vulnerable targets; destructive weapons and technology; mass media; populations with increased literacy; conflicts with traditional ways of life; and networks of transportation." He also stated that modern societies tend to press for democratic governments. Thus, the more modern the society, the greater the number of grievances and the ability to express or act on them.

The seven precipitant causes have a more immediate impact on the development of terrorism. Social, cultural, and historical facilitation are based on shared values, beliefs, and traditions that foster the development of subgroups within the population. These deeply held, shared views and attitudes foster group identity and cohesion. If the ideology of the group supports violence (or is interpreted as supporting violence, Long, 1990), then the motivation toward violent activity becomes particularly high.

In his discussion of organizational development or split, Ross (1993, p. 323) agreed with Laquer (1977, p. 103) that "most terrorist groups come into existence as the 'result of a split between the moderate and the more extreme wings of an already-existing organization' (e.g., political party)." Ross postulated that the more splitting that occurs within terrorist organizations, the greater the likelihood that at least one of the splinter groups will advocate or use terrorism. Crenshaw (1990) mentioned the Red Brigades and Prima Linea — two Italian left-wing groups that became divided over the issue of whether to work clandestinely or to use propaganda and other organizational strategies to work with a larger protest movement. The Red Brigades chose the former and Prima Linea the latter. Ross also postulated that other forms of political unrest (e.g., strikes, riots, revolution, demonstrations, etc.) within the population will increase the probability that subgroups will identify and act upon grievances.

Terrorism is facilitated by outside support. Support may be in the form of "finances, training, intelligence, false documents, donations or sales of weapons and explosives, provisions of sanctuary or safe housing, propaganda campaigns, ideological justification, public opinion, legal services, and a constant supply of recruits" (Ross, 1993, p. 324; see Long, 1990). Ross hypothesized that the greater the amount of support, the greater the failure of counterterrorist efforts, and, conversely, the greater the failure of counterterrorist efforts, the greater the amount of support for terrorists.

Ross suggested that the greater the availability of weapons and explosives, the greater the incidence of terrorism. According to Avrich (1984, p. 166), 19th century anarchists believed the invention of dynamite provided a "great equalizing force, enabling ordinary workmen to stand up against armies, militias, and police, to say nothing of the hired gunmen of the employers." Weapons can be obtained by purchase, theft, gift, or construction. Many weapons and materials for bombs are legally available in the U.S. Timothy McVeigh, for example, was able to buy materials to make the deadly truck bomb that took 168 lives and wounded hundreds of others in Oklahoma City in 1995 (FBI, 1996). The presence of weapons and weapons materials is particularly high in countries that have recently undergone civil strife.

The last and most important precipitant cause is grievances. Ross (1993, p. 326) parceled them into seven categories: economic, ethnic, racial, legal, political, religious, and social. These grievances can be directed against "individuals, groups, organizations, classes, races, and ethnicities, both public and private (e.g., the government, businesses, unions, military, police, religious organizations, political parties)." Left unaddressed, serious grievances can result in the formation of social movements or interest groups that can, under the influence of the factors mentioned above, evolve or split into terrorist organizations.

Rational Choice Explanations. Crenshaw (1990) discussed terrorism as a logical political strategy, a choice made among alternatives, that results from the collective rationality of the group. She cited several advantages of analyzing terrorist behavior by trying to understand the quality of their choices.

The rational choice approach allows groups to be compared to some standard of rationality. For example, questions may be asked about a group's grasp of reality, its ability to judge the consequences of its actions, and factors that may diminish or enhance rational action. This approach also suggests questions about the real motives of a group. For example, is hostage-taking intended as a bargaining strategy, or are there other motives?

At the theoretical level, the development of terrorism through history can be outlined in terms of rational choice, revealing "similarities in calculation of ends and means. The strategy has changed over time to adapt to new circumstances that offer different possibilities for dissident action — for example, hostage taking. Yet, terrorist activity considered in its entirety shows a fundamental unity of purpose and conception" (Crenshaw, 1990, p. 10; see Crenshaw, 1985).

Another advantage of this approach is that it discourages us from dismissing terrorism as an irrational or inexplicable aberration. Indeed, the belief that terrorism is the only viable option is one way by which group members may overcome their moral compunctions (Bandura, 1990).

The rational choice approach highlights the specific advantages and costs of terrorism. It can help us understand several circumstances under which extremist groups find terrorism useful. For example, terrorism often has been used when other strategies have failed, and its development can be the result of a learning process. Terrorists learn from others' examples as well as from their own experience. This process is particularly important because of the intense media coverage and instant worldwide communication now available.

Terrorism can be useful in setting public agendas and can even serve as a preliminary step to revolution. Also, the fact that it may foster further government repression may actually be an advantage insofar as it heightens public discontent. Crenshaw (1990) cited the failure of nonviolent movements in 19th century Russia, the failure of Parnell's constitutionalist efforts in Ireland, and the Arab's failure at conventional warfare against Israel. Castro's terrorist acts against the Baptista government actually invited further repression, which eventually fomented revolution as innocents were killed by the government.

Among the costs of terrorism are that it invites a punitive reaction that could harm the group and it can result in increased government repression of activities of the general public, which can result in diminished popular support. Loss of public support also may result from what citizens interpret as excessive or indiscriminate harm of innocent victims. The latter is less likely in an ethnically divided society in which victims (or the government, for that matter) can be identified as enemies. Lastly, some revolutionaries may not support terrorism because they find it elitist and believe that the people should take responsibility for their fate.

Rational choice explanations also address the reasons that terrorist groups generally remain weak in the sense that they are unable to attract large numbers of constituents or garner sufficient military power to effect political or societal changes by other means. Such groups may be unable to attract a significant following because they are so extreme that their appeal is limited, and they resort to terrorism to even the odds. Also, groups may not have the resources, or perhaps the temperament, to do the difficult and time-consuming work required to mobilize large-scale support. Contrast, for example, the IRA, a terrorist organization, and its legal counterpart, Sinn Fein (Crenshaw, 1990).

Another reason terrorist groups may remain weak is that people living under repressive governments may refrain from joining because they are particularly afraid of government retaliation or because they do not learn of the opportunity due to censorship of the news media. Such situations eventually may foster the formation of terrorist groups because, according to Crenshaw (1990, p. 13), "the likelihood of popular dissatisfaction grows as the likelihood of its active expression is diminished." However, such groups may remain disadvantaged because they are unable to test their popularity in any straightforward way, so they tend to develop fantasies about positive responses of the general population. According to Crenshaw, such unrealistic expectations are not unusual in radical underground organizations in Western democracies.

According to the rational choice approach, terrorism may be a defensive response to threat or to a downturn in a group's fortunes, as well as a response to an opportunity. For example, the IRA Provisionals (PIRA) utilized terrorism to counter its appearance of weakness, even though this alienated public opinion (McGuire, 1973).

Terrorist leaders may use poor judgment because they tend to want action. However, impatience also can result from an analysis of the situation that indicates an immediate window of opportunity for success, such as an increase in the vulnerability of the regime in power or a significant increase in the power or resources of the terrorist group (e.g., money, weapons, training, information, strategic innovation, etc.). For example, religious terrorists schedule their attacks according to their theological beliefs or to cause maximum disruption of their enemies' religious holidays or other sacred times. Timothy McVeigh apparently patterned his attack on the Alfred P. Murrah Federal Building in Oklahoma after *The Turner Diaries* and based the timing on the second anniversary of the demise of the Branch Davidians in Waco, TX, which he blamed on the FBI (Ranstorp, 1996).

Psychological Explanations. According to Reich (1990, p. 263), psychological. explanations of terrorism have not dealt with the enormous variety and complexity of the issue. He observed, "Even the briefest review of the history of terrorism reveals how varied and complex a phenomenon it is, and therefore how futile it is to attribute simple, global, and general psychological characteristics to all terrorists and all terrorisms." As with group violence in general, single-factor explanations do not suffice to explain the phenomenon. The propensities of individuals interact with group dynamics and external factors.

The study of terrorist psychology is still in its infancy. Much of the present information on the subject has been gleaned from interviews and assessments of captured terrorists, terrorist leaders willing to be interviewed in secure and secret locations, and even autobiographies of terrorists (e.g., Begin, 1977; Savinkov, 1931; Yacef, 1962). It is often difficult, if not impossible, to distinguish the person's rationalization of his or her behavior from genuine motivations. Nevertheless, there are several hypotheses and conclusions that run through the literature.

Some types of background are over-represented in terrorists. Post (1990) cited evidence from several extensive studies of terrorists' backgrounds that indicate that many of them came from the margins of society or were unsuccessful in their personal lives, jobs, and educations, or both. For example, an examination of the life course of 250 West German terrorists (Jager et al., cited by Post, 1990, p. 28) revealed a high incidence of severe problems in the families of origin. About 25% of the leftist terrorists "had lost one or both parents by the age of fourteen; loss of the father was found to be especially disruptive. Seventy-nine percent reported severe conflict, especially with the parents (33%), and they described the father, when present, in hostile terms. One in three had been convicted in juvenile court. [They were] advancement oriented and failure prone, [and their careers in terrorism] were the terminal point of a series of abortive adaptation attempts." These findings generally have been confirmed in studies of members of other terrorist groups, although Miller (cited by Long, 1990) described the typical terrorist as being a single male from a middle- or upper-class background, relatively well educated, although often a university drop-out, who was likely to have joined the group while attending the university. This description seems to apply more to the "terrorists" of the 1960s and early 1970s who engaged in campus riots and demonstrations against the establishment.

Tedeschi and Felson (1994) emphasized that learning from the repeated success of aggressive behavior is a major factor in encouraging groups to engage in violence. Terrorists capitalize on this fact among themselves by continually associating violence with the achievement of success through brainwashing, modeling, and reinforcement. There can be little doubt that they understand that building certain emotional expectations for success is a critical factor in maintaining organized aggressive behavior. Such learning takes place within terrorist groups as new recruits are gradually indoctrinated in terrorist ideology and behavior (Bandura, 1990).

The literature indicates that, contrary to common belief, terrorists usually are not mentally disturbed (Crenshaw, 1981; Heskin, 1980; Long, 1990; Post, 1984). Although there is no striking psychopathology or particular personality type that is strongly associated with terrorists, some traits and tendencies do appear to be overrepresented in this population.

Low self-esteem and lack of success in their personal lives seem to be common among members of terrorist groups (Long, 1990; Post, 1990). Long (1990, p. 18) stated that people with low self-esteem "tend to place unrealistically high demands on themselves and, when confronted with failure, to raise rather than lower their aspirations. Bitter at failure, they tend to be drawn to groups espousing equally unrealistic aspirations. They commonly feel out of control of their own lives and are convinced that their lives are controlled by external sources," perhaps accounting for the hatred of outside forces which they express by terrorist ideation and acts. According to psychoanalytic theory, they may defend themselves against their own self-hatred by projecting that hatred onto outside "objects" such as governments or other established authority. When they join a tight group of others who also blame outside causes for their (or the world's) problems and who are willing to express their shared hatred violently may be the first time they feel accepted by others, the first time they truly belong (see Post, 1990). These views are congruent with that of Lawler (1992), who concluded that people become emotionally attached to groups that strengthen their general sense of control. Choices that bring about a high sense of control produce positive emotion, which in turn strengthens attachments to groups responsible for the opportunity to make the choices.

Long (1990) noted that many terrorists have ambivalent feelings about the use of violence that causes human suffering. (Most of his information was gleaned from interviews with captured terrorists, and it is important to note that some of them did appear to have no guilt or moral qualms about their violent acts.) It is likely that hostage taking is a popular tactic in part because the perpetrators can displace responsibility for any violence that occurs, blaming the authorities for refusing to comply with the terrorists' demands (Bandura, 1990; Long, 1990). Bandura noted that this process also occurs in battered spouse syndrome, in which the batterer blames the victim for whatever trouble ensues after the batterer enters the justice system.

Terrorists often rationalize and minimize their actions by comparing them with historical events (Bandura, 1990). Such comparisons help eliminate self-sanctions against violence and become a vehicle for self-approval serving destructive actions. For example, the present democracies of France, Great Britain, and the U.S. originated in violent rebellion against oppressive governments. This comparison is commonly made during news interviews by members of right-wing separatist groups in the U.S.

Russell and Miller (1983) evaluated information about captured or known terrorists from a wide variety of sources and concluded that terrorist leaders tend to be more hostile and narcissistic than the average follower. Leaders' images of themselves as the good ideal and of the outside object as completely bad, observed Long (1990, p. 18), provides "a grandiose self-image that projects confidence and purpose and attracts others to its glow."

Terrorists generally are not impulsive, either individually or in groups. On the contrary, successful operations of this nature demand the ability to plan carefully and withhold action until everything is in place (see Crenshaw, 1981). On the other hand, they do exhibit the propensity to take risks. Crenshaw distinguished between two types of risk-takers among terrorists: those who take risks individually, as exemplified in leaders who, as a manifestation of their narcissism, risk danger as a means of self-affirmation; and collective risk-takers, who derive an identity from being group members *per se*, rather than from the group's activities.

A high proportion of terrorists appear to be stimulus seekers. They are attracted to stressful situations and are quickly bored when inactive (Long, 1990). In fact, Zawodny (1978) concluded that the most important factor in the decision-making process of groups that have been forced underground is the psychological climate in the group, rather than the external situation. Inaction is extremely stressful for these stimulus seekers and results in considerable tension if it goes on for very long. Zawodny went so far as to say that terrorist groups must actually commit terrorist acts to justify their existence. Leaders sense the buildup of tension and plan terrorist activity in order to release the group's aggressions, rather than risking the possibility that they will turn on themselves (or their leader). Post (1990) asserted that this climate fosters groupthink, leading to riskier choices than an individual alone would make.

Terrorists may see terrorism as an end in itself. Post (1990, p. 35) argued that, although the ostensible cause for terrorist acts is the group's political goal, the terrorism is actually the end itself. That is, "*The cause is not the cause*. The cause, as codified in the group's ideology, according to this line or reasoning, becomes the rationale for acts the terrorists are driven to commit. Indeed, the central argument of this position is that *individuals become terrorists in order to join terrorist groups and commit acts of terrorism.*" According to Post, an important corollary of this is that if terrorists actually achieved their stated goals or demands, there would be no further need for their existence! Thus, their demands in hostage situations, for example, sometimes are set so high as to be unobtainable.

Post's (1990) stance is partially tenable from a psychological viewpoint, and the authors believe it should be tempered by additional views. It is important to remember that emotions are influenced by experience and are thus largely developed and acquired. For example, advertisers often pair warm, exciting, and other positive emotions with products they are trying to sell, as does the military in its efforts to recruit soldiers. Through contiguous association, some of the positive affect attaches to the product name and makes it more desirable. Similarly, terrorists use calculated procedures to actively and continually socially "engineer" the emotions of fellow terrorists, as discussed above.

Heise and O'Brien (1993) presented another finding important to the understanding of emotion management in terrorist groups. Emotions that erupt during social interaction in terrorist groups are judged for suitability according to the cultural and ideological standards of the group. These emotions are managed in order to produce culturally acceptable displays that yield social accord in the sense that individuals' constellations of emotional meaning resonate with or suppress each other during social interaction. Thus, norms emerge that reflect the composition of the group.

Terrorists use coercion as a form of social influence (Tedeschi and Felson, 1994). Tedeschi and Felson have identified three primary social motives for using coercion: (1) to influence others to obtain some benefit, (2) to express grievances and establish justice, and (3) to assert or defend social identities. Although one of these motives may be salient in any given coercive episode, it is not unusual for all three to be implicated in a single episode. According to this model, individuals engage in a limited form of rationality based on their perceptions of benefits and costs and probabilities of success, but decisions are often made quickly, under the influence of emotion or alcohol or drugs, resulting in a failure to consider costs of alternative choices.

Bandura (1990, p. 186) presented the congruent view that terrorist behavior evolves through a process of gradual moral disengagement. He cited evidence that…

> *"... terrorist behavior evolves through extensive training in moral disengagement and terrorist prowess, rather than emerging full blown. The path to terrorism can be shaped by fortuitous factors as well as by the conjoint influence of personal predilections and social inducements. ...The disinhibitory training is usually conducted within a communal milieu of intense interpersonal influences insulated from mainstream social life. ...Initially [recruits] are prompted to perform unpleasant acts that they can tolerate without much self-censure. Gradually, through repeated performance and repeated exposure to aggressive modeling by more experienced associates, their discomfort and self-reproof are weakened to ever higher levels of ruthlessness. ...Eventually, acts originally regarded as abhorrent can be performed callously."*

Moral disengagement becomes difficult when aggressors develop empathy for their victims. Examples abound of hostages and hostage-takers who develop sympathy and compassion for each other as they become personally acquainted. It appears that the better acquainted the captors become with their captives, the more difficult it is for them to harm the hostages. The extent to which the captors themselves elicit sympathy seems to depend on several factors, including the extent to which they interact with their captives in a personal way, revealing their personalities and problems; the amount of compassion with which they treat the captives; and their explanation of their (or their people's) plight that led them to take captives in the first place. It is possible for terrorist captors to be so cold or cruel to their hostages that little or no empathy develops on either side (Bandura, 1990). It is not unusual that the total dependency of the hostages on the captors, especially in prolonged situations, engenders hostage identification with the captors (Long, 1990). Strentz (1982) wrote about this phenomenon, popularly known as the "Stockholm Syndrome" after a 1973 bank robbery in Sweden in which bank employees were held hostage. He suggested that captives may regress to an infantile identification with the captors in a way similar to that in which abused children sometimes come to identify with their abusers.

Characteristics of Terrorists Consistent with a General Understanding of Group Violence

Although the study of terrorism is difficult and far from complete, the evidence suggests the following general characteristics of these groups, reflecting many of the principles that apply to group violence in general:

- Individuals and groups are influenced by their environment, including political, cultural, historical, economic, and social factors.
- When deciding on a course of action, they weigh risks/costs vs. benefits in service of obtaining desired goals or resources.
- They use strategies, tactics, and operations to create an imbalance of power in the terrorists' favor.
- They work to create a strong group identity, with an "us vs. them" (in-group vs. out-group) mentality. This fosters groupthink.
- Members typically are not deranged.
- Although there is no personality profile that could be characterized as typical of terrorists, certain traits appear to be over-represented among groups members, including risk-taking (although they are not impulsive), low self-esteem, feeling out of control of their lives, and ascribing their failures to outside sources. Many of them come from the margins of society, and it is not uncommon for them to have experienced significant disruption of life during childhood.
- Terrorist leaders are, on the average, more hostile and narcissistic than their followers.
- Leaders manipulate followers' emotions, and utilize coercion and disengagement of moral responses to help enable the perpetration of violence, especially on innocent people.

An Explanatory Model of Participation in Group Violence

Taken together, the findings in psychology suggest that in order for any person to join others in carrying out violent actions, that person must have certain ideas, feelings, and expectations related to doing harm. These specific thoughts and emotions are critical in the sense that without them, an individual would not be motivated to join with others in aggressive behavior. These patterns of thinking and feeling fall into three basic clusters, which are listed in Table 9.4.

The first cluster concerns perpetrators' individual and collective expectations of the beneficial outcomes of violence. The most sought-after outcomes are those which bring positive emotional payout. Usually, the results are related to providing basic survival and to

Table 9.4

Three Patterns of Thinking Critical to Motivation for Participating in Group Violence

Individuals anticipate beneficial outcomes as a result of the violence.
Individuals view themselves as capable of bringing about a desired result and as personally responsible for doing so.
Violence is viewed as the most effective way to accomplish the desired result.

enhancing a sense of belonging and social position. Some examples of positive outcomes individuals typically expect from engaging in terrorist violence are

- An object of hate is destroyed.
- A blameworthy act is punished.
- A misdeed is put right.
- Justice is maintained.
- Power is balanced.
- A reputation is established.
- A desired identity is protected.
- Negative identities are nullified.
- Humiliation is reduced.
- Group position is affirmed.
- Negative consequences are minimized.
- Position of power is obtained.
- The world is freed from less desirables.
- The greater good is brought forth.

Individuals who carry out acts of violence in groups do so expecting that they will be able to reap benefits such as those listed above. They believe that their actions will, in fact, bring about justice, power, the greater good, or whatever reward they are seeking. These accomplishments, however, are always defined from the group members' own perspectives, which usually are not shared by the larger community.

The second pattern of thinking focuses on the individual's view of himself or herself as not only capable of bringing about the desired result but personally responsible for doing so. No one attempts to accomplish a goal without believing that there is a chance of success (Atkinson, 1964). People who engage in violence are no exception. They will not participate in violent acts unless they believe that they will be able to bring about the benefits they pursue. In some cases, self-confidence is amplified by messianic delusions. Such individuals not only believe that they can be successful, but that they must be. They feel it is their personal responsibility. They often feel that they are the only ones who can restore justice or right whatever wrongs they perceive. Listed below are some of the thought patterns that cluster around the sense violent people have of themselves, individually and collectively:

- They see others as idols, enemies, or fools, all in exaggerated ways.
- They dehumanize their targets of aggression.
- They see themselves as the embodiment of good having to deal with enemies.
- They think they are chosen, selected by God to carry out their missions.
- Their personal identities merge with the group's identity.
- As the group's identity increases, so does the anonymity of the individual.
- They believe that responsibility for what they do is not theirs but that of the group.
- Self-regulation procedures give way to group regulation processes.
- They believe that they will be safe and protected by the group.

When any individual truly believes that it is possible to bring about personal adulation from those in the group as well as make the world a better place by participating in violent acts, it is a little easier to understand why he or she would be willing to do so. When those thought patterns are coupled with the beliefs that he or she has been chosen to bring these great benefits about and that the group will be responsible for any problems, it seems amazing that there are not more who would take part in violent acts!

The third pattern of thinking concerns violence being viewed as the most effective way to accomplish sought-after results. Wanting certain results and believing that one can obtain them are insufficient to cause an individual to join others in violent acts. Potential participants must also believe that violence is the most effective way, if not the only way, of obtaining success. This kind of thinking is simple and straightforward: violence is seen as the best and possibly only way to obtain benefits successfully. From the point of view of the individual, all other ways are judged to be less fruitful or blocked altogether.

It is important to remember that these three patterns of thinking must all be present in some degree in order for the violent behavior to occur. Should any one of them weaken or change into something else, the individual would withdraw from participation.

The processes by which aggressors acquire these patterns of thought are complex. These processes, addressed throughout the opening discussion of the psychology of group violence, may be grouped into four categories: biological, environmental, developmental, and social. They have been summarized in Table 9.5. Although it has been demonstrated that these processes can weave together to increase the probability that violence will occur, they do not completely predict its presence or absence. It is important to understand that individuals with very similar innate and environmental inputs can differ to some degree in their choice of behavior. This suggests that each individual still has the potential to decide how to respond to whatever inputs they encounter. It is possible that their sense of purpose, meaning, or self is the basis for their unique responses to similar situations. This may account for the fact that some individuals who have biological propensities for violence, difficult environmental influences, or both, and who find themselves in groups with enormous sophistication in exerting pressure on them to engage in violence are able to resist becoming involved in violent acts. For the most part, however, the authors believe that these are the processes that create the thought patterns that are critical in motivating individuals to participate in group violence. This synthesis of the findings into a working model provides the basis for suggesting solutions to the problem of terrorism.

Solutions to Terrorism

Solutions to terrorism are desperately needed and overwhelmingly difficult. Long (1990) noted that the threat of terrorism is almost certain to continue because the political, economic, and social conditions that give rise to it are not likely to be solved any time soon. Nevertheless, counterterrorist efforts are essential, and the decline in state-sponsored terrorism has been attributed to increased zero-tolerance policies among governments (U. S. Department of State, 1996).

Solutions should address the motivations to violence or the processes that lead to those motivations. The U.S. government sees neutralizing terrorist groups as the general objective of counterterrorism, thus addressing the thinking patterns listed in Table 9.4. The specifics of this objective include identifying and monitoring terrorist groups, weakening the organizations, preventing attacks, minimizing the effects of attacks, and reducing the vulnerability of potential targets (Terrorism Research Center, 1997). Three general rules are stressed (U. S. Department of State, 1996): (1) the government does not make deals with terrorists and does not submit to blackmail; (2) terrorists are pursued aggressively, treated as criminals,

TABLE 9.5

PROCESSES INVOLVED IN ACQUIRING PATTERNS OF THOUGHT THAT LEAD TO GROUP VIOLENCE

Process	Elements
Biological	Humans have biologically based constitutions capable of violence. Innate tendencies for aggressive behavior vary in strength. The biologically based capacity for aggression can be modified by societal influences and other forms of learning.
Environmental	People learn how to behave by watching the behavior of others. Environmental influences to become violent have more effect on those who already have an innate propensity toward violence. Individuals tend to respond to the things they see in ways that are similar to the responses of those they are with.
Developmental	Early experiences may lack certain ingredients or contain too much of others, altering normal emotional development. These abnormal emotions form reference points upon which decisions to engage in violence are made.
Social	People can catch the emotions of others. Through identification with a group, individuals disengage personal responsibility and self-sanctions. Stronger group identity is created through such experiences as rituals and initiations. Internal states such as emotions also impact the decision to become violent. Cognitive restructuring increases the value of violence and decreases the perceived extent of suffering it is expected to cause. Repetitive violence can become ritualized and rhythmically continued in that context. Social roles and authoritarian influences are particularly powerful ways for participants to justify aggressive behavior.

and subjected to the rule of law; and (3) economic, diplomatic, and political sanctions are used to apply pressure on countries that support terrorists, and other countries are urged to follow suit.

Several overarching policy objectives are important (Long, 1990; Terrorism Research Center, 1997):

- The policy must be global, emphasizing international cooperation. This may necessitate focusing on the criminality of terrorist acts, rather than on the terrorist groups *per se*, thus avoiding value judgments as to the legitimacy of the terrorists' political goals.
- Interagency cooperation is paramount. Both the components (the operating principles and specific counterterrorist measures) and the process (means of administration) of the policy must be addressed. This involves patient negotiation and consensus-building.
- The policy must be long term.
- The policy must be adaptable to the wide variety of terrorist situations.
- Governments should talk directly to terrorists, as a rule, because dialogue generally is necessary to peaceful resolution of conflict.

- Patience, perseverance, and willingness to forego recognition are necessary in those responsible for tracking down and thwarting terrorists. (Such a low-key approach can run counter to American culture!)
- Restraint is necessary to avoid premature action that may foreclose the obtaining of further intelligence and to prevent overreaction such as inappropriate repression of the populace, which can undermine the legitimacy of the government.

In determining how to eliminate the benefits of terrorist acts, it is important to consider what, if any, concessions to terrorists governments should be prepared to make. There is general agreement that government or law enforcement entities should negotiate to resolve specific situations or political issues only if this provides no reward for terroristic actions. Levitt (1988) suggested viewing the response in terms of four principles:

- Governments should strive for consistency in their categorization and condemnation of terrorist acts.
- Clarity of policy is important, notwithstanding the fact that it may evolve over the years.
- Antiterrorism policy must be credible. That is, it must attempt to make the costs of terrorist activity prohibitively high in ways that are reasonably possible to accomplish. It should avoid extravagant claims about eradicating terrorism.
- Striving for international consensus is paramount. Even unilateral responses should be made within the framework of collective policy.

Levitt (1988) also discussed three types of political measures for dealing with terrorists:

- Long-term political measures should be designed to resolve the broad political problems that encourage terrorism. In reality, this is impossible to accomplish fully. Even so, it should be recognized that changing laws, altering geographic boundaries, providing education to change destructive traditions, refraining from inflammatory acts, and so forth, can have a long-term effect in reducing the motivation for terrorist acts.
- Vigorous and persistent diplomacy should be used to "encourage, maintain, and increase international cooperation against terrorism and isolate terrorist groups and states supporting them until they are induced to cease [and to] provide and share technical assistance for antiterrorism" (Levitt, 1988, p. 148). Extradition treaties should be expanded and informal working relationships among various professionals fostered. (The latter is often difficult, as "turf" is so important to governmental, military, and police agencies.)
- Public affairs measures include formulating and publicizing a clear, consistent, credible public policy; dealing with the news media by providing "the conceptual simplicity that the reporter requires without resorting to simplistic polemics that ill-serve the decision-makers, the media, and the public alike" (Levitt, 1988, p. 150); maintaining close communication with airlines, businesses, and other private sector entities that may be targets; supplying adequate travel warnings and other advisories; maintaining a sympathetic relationship with victims and their families; and depoliticizing terrorist acts by focusing on the criminal aspects.

It is important to facilitate aggressors seeing themselves as more peaceful and their victims as more human. The news media may contribute to how terrorists see themselves and their victims. Bassiouni (1987) described problems of media coverage of terrorist incidents:

- The very reporting of violence may encourage others to commit violent acts.
- "Excesses or deficiencies in media coverage may enhance the climate of intimidation which the terrorist seeks to generate; this would not only further unnecessarily the perpetrators' objectives, but it would also engender pressures for counterproductive governmental repression and cause undesirable social consequences" (Bassiouni, 1987, p. 183).
- Intense or repeated media coverage may deaden the public's outrage at terrorist acts and increase its tolerance of violence, thus necessitating increased violence to achieve the effect desired by the terrorists. Also, such coverage can render impersonal or abstract

> the violence and its consequences, thus diminishing the humanity of the victims and terrorists.
>
> Media reports may endanger the lives of hostages and otherwise interfere with law enforcement. This is most likely during coverage of events as they are occurring. On the other hand, Bassiouni (1987) noted that media coverage also can serve as a "safety valve" by publicizing terrorist viewpoints that otherwise would be brought to public attention by violent actions. Also, the media may have access to intelligence unavailable to official organizations, and they sometimes can serve to secure the release of hostages, such as by agreeing to publish the terrorists' rhetoric.

Patient negotiation with captors may help them come to see their hostages as more human as they come to know them and as they come to see the hostages' human value to the negotiators, thus increasing the chances of hostage survival. Also, a patient approach on the part of police or military may help the terrorists see their way to accomplishing at least some of their objectives using alternatives to violence. Unfortunately, highly ideological terrorists are likely to degrade and torment their hostages, who in turn are less likely to develop any sympathy with their captors; thus, personalization often does not develop on either side (Bandura, 1990).

Prevention of Thought Patterns that Lead to Violence

In addition to specific responses to terrorism, intervention in the processes that lead to participation in group violence (see Table 9.5) can help prevention in the long run. Such approaches must involve diverse social entities including families, neighborhoods, schools, communities, governments, and churches if they are to have the necessary widespread and ongoing effect. Such cooperation and singleness of purpose seem impossible, but there has been a ground swell of awareness in the U.S. in recent years in response to the many forms of violence prevalent in our society. Diverse responses to violence are proliferating. These include neighborhood watches, church-sponsored marital and premarital counseling, establishment of peace curricula in the schools, public service messages about parenting skills, and anti-domestic violence initiatives by government and private organizations.

Although innate biological propensities for aggressive behavior will continue to exist, they can be softened through early experiences in kind and loving families and through more peaceful socialization. Let us first briefly consider the enormously influential role of early experience in the family.

Families Need To Bond Deeply and Develop Strong Feelings of Belonging

It is in the family where a young child first develops a sense of individuality and belonging to a group. Parents and siblings also provide the child with guidelines delineating effective and appropriate behavior. Healthy families assist the child to grow and develop normal cognitive and affective patterns of thinking and feeling. Although a discussion of the family's role in providing for children's basic needs including love and belonging cannot be included here, it must be emphasized that the family plays a critical role in producing emotionally healthy family members who have learned by precept and example how to relate to other human beings.

The growing disintegration of the family unit is leaving more and more young children hungry for normal attention and affection and desperate for a sense of belonging. Consider the children whose fathers and mothers spend most of their time and energy outside the home, as well as the rising number of young children born to unwed women living in poverty and often working long hours to earn a living. The opportunities these children have for developing self-worth and a sense of family unity may be diminished, as it is sometimes all these parents can do to manage necessary household tasks, let alone spend the enormous amount of time and effort it takes to teach their children the nuances of managing their lives and relationships in peaceful, productive ways. Failed by inadequate early experiences, sometimes in fragmented families, those youngsters may learn little about kindness to others and may be vulnerable to groups who offer a chance to belong. As children from all socio-economic backgrounds are wounded by a lack of family security and guidance, they turn to other sources of influence around them. Unfortunately, they often find sources that only accelerate their aggressive tendencies.

Widespread Violence Must Be Replaced with More Peaceable Behavior

Constant exposure to violence in early years teaches children that violence is acceptable and effective. The severity of children's exposure to violence is due to the fact that it is almost epidemic in the U.S. Violence is the second leading cause of death for Americans between the ages of 15 and 24 years and the leading cause of death for black Americans in this age group (Rosenberg, Powell, and Hammond, 1997). Many young children have witnessed muggings or shootings, and even seen dead bodies. In addition, large numbers of assaults and robberies among teenagers happen within schools, where 3 million crimes occur per year. Furthermore, millions of children who have been abused in their homes or who have witnessed parental violence, experience first hand violent role models, leaving them not only physically and emotionally injured, but with nothing but violent behavior to imitate.

These direct personal experiences with violence also are impressed on young children's minds through the socializing influence of television. As early as 1981, television violence occurred 25 times an hour during weekend daytime children's programming (Gerbner, 1981). Recently, it has been found that 6 out of 10 programs feature violence and that more than half of all major characters are involved in violence (Gerbner, 1994). With preschoolers watching more than 27 hours of television per week (Centerwall, 1993) and high school graduates spending more time in front of a television than in the classroom, is it any wonder that violent behavior is turned to as an effective way of accomplishing personal and group goals? As long as young minds are inundated with violence, directly and indirectly, their aggressive tendencies will be exaggerated and they will become more and more violent themselves. Without a serious shift away from violence in all parts of society, violence will continue to grow as a viable option for individual and group behavior.

The tragedy is that if violence could be replaced with cooperation and consideration, children would grow up with totally different behavioral repertoires. These broad, sweeping changes in society seem impossible to bring about, but failing to do so will only escalate the use of violence as the primary means to an end, the view many have of violence today. Both strengthening families and teaching more peaceful behavior patterns improve the probability that individuals will not develop the three thought patterns related to becoming violent. It is clear that such an effort requires the coordinated efforts of governments, religions, the media, and other institutions with widespread influence.

Concluding Comments

The authors have addressed many psychological aspects of group violence, viewed it through the lens of terrorism, and formulated a general model that takes into account its specific characteristics. The model encompasses other types of group violence as well. One of the most salient conclusions to be drawn from this work is that the difficulty of achieving a peaceful world is enormous, even overwhelming, but the necessity is compelling. Clearly, it is idealistic to believe that peaceful means can be substituted for violence everywhere and in every situation. Nevertheless, individuals and societies must not lose sight of this objective.

Ultimately, our best hope may be that each of us keep as a reference point the desire to see others as human, to learn the many skills involved in maintaining peaceful interactions, to make the effort to achieve our objectives peacefully, to teach peacemaking to our families and others whose lives we touch, and to participate as fully as possible in the development and maintenance of social systems that support humane and compassionate behavior.

Annotated Bibliography

1. Long, D.E. (1990) *The Anatomy of Terrorism.* New York: The Free Press. David E. Long served as director of regional policy formulation and coordination in the Office of Counter Terrorism, U.S. State Department, from 1985 through 1987. In this book he essentially constructs a terrorism theory by dealing with six basic issues: the nature of terrorism, understanding terrorist behavior, profiles of leading terrorist groups, sources of support for terrorists, planning and execution of terrorist acts, and counterterrorism. The work culminates in a highly informed discussion of antiterrorism policy.

2. Pepitone, A. (1984) Violent aggression from the multiple perspectives of psychology. *Journal of Social and Economic Studies, 1*(4), 321–355. Albert Pepitone, a professor at the University of Pennsylvania, explores the varied approaches to understanding and preventing violence in this groundbreaking article that offers reasonable explanations for why we have failed to confront and eradicate violence thus far. He categorizes conceptual types of aggression, details theoretical contributions from the psychological and sociological literature, and explores the notion of normative aggression. In his section on intergroup aggression, he points out the need for a multi-disciplinary approach in which psychological processes are integrated with the dynamics of social and political systems. He uses the exemplars of conflicts between organized groups, cultural conflicts, and mass violence to further illustrate these mechanisms of psychological and sociological motivations that combine to create the myriad of violent activities that take place worldwide.

3. Tedeschi, J.T. and Felson, R.B. (1994) *Violence, Aggression, and Coercive Actions.* Washington, D.C.: American Psychological Association. After presenting and synthesizing traditional theories of aggression and bringing together literature on power and influence, conflict and competition, retributive and redistributive justice, self-presentation, cognitive attribution, and criminal violence, the authors present their own social interactionist theory. From a social psychological perspective, they abandon the concept of aggression and substitute coercive actions. The resulting social interactionist theory of coercive actions is a theory of rational choice, with decisions made to obtain three goals: to gain compliance, to restore justice, and to assert and defend identities. This position provides a particularly strong foundation for practical analysis and intervention. The authors themselves relate their framework to real social problems including sexual coercion and parenting styles.

References

Adams, J. (1986) *The Financing of Terror: How the Groups that Are Terrorizing the World Get the Money To Do It.* New York: Simon & Schuster.

Adelmann, P.K. and Zajonc, R. (1989) Facial efference and the experience of emotion. *Annual Review of Psychology, 40,* 249–280.

Alexander, R.D. (1989) Evolution and the human psyche. In P. Mellars and C. Stringer (Eds.), *The Human Revolution*, pp. 455–513. Edinburgh: Edinburgh University Press.

Anderson, S. and Sloan, S. (1995) *Historical Dictionary of Terrorism.* New Jersey: The Scarecrow Press.

Atkinson, J.W. (1964) *An Introduction to Motivation.* Princeton, NJ: C. van Nostrand.

Averill, J.R. (1983) Studies on anger and aggression: implications for theories of emotion. *American Psychologist, 38,* 1145–1160.

Avrich, P. (1984) *The Haymarket Tragedy.* Princeton: Princeton University Press.

Ballif, B.L. (1977) *A Multidimensional Model of Motivation for Learning.* Paper presented at the meeting of the American Educational Research Association, New York, NY.

Ballif, B.L. (1989) *The Delicate Dance Between Emotions and Cognitions.* Paper presented at the meeting of the American Educational Research Association, San Francisco, CA.

Bandura, A. (1986) *Social Foundations of Thought and Actions: A Social Cognitive Theory.* Englewood Cliffs, NJ: Prentice-Hall.

Bandura, A. (1990) Mechanisms of moral disengagement. In W. Reich (Ed.), *Origins of Terrorism: Psychologies, Ideologies, Theologies, States of Mind*, pp. 161–191. Cambridge and New York: Woodrow Wilson International Center for Scholars and Cambridge University Press.

Barlow, S.H. and Clayton, C.J. (1996) When mothers murder: understanding infanticide by females. In H.V. Hall (Ed.), *Lethal Violence 2000: A Sourcebook on Fatal Domestic, Acquaintance and Stranger Aggression*, pp. 203–229. Kamuela, HI: Pacific Institute for the Study of Conflict and Aggression.

Bassiouni, M.C. (1987) Terrorism, law enforcement, and the mass media: perspectives, problems, proposals. *Journal of Criminal Enforcement Bulletin, 56,* 14–17.

Bauermeister, M. (1977) Women victims and their assailants: rapists, victims and society. *International Journal of Offender Therapy and Comparative Criminology, 21*(3), 238–248.

Begin, M. (1977) *The Revolt* (S. Katz, trans.). Los Angeles: Nash.

Boone, J.L. (1991) Comment on J.H. Manson and R.W. Wrangham, intergroup aggression in chimpanzees and humans. *Current Anthropology, 32*(4), 377.

Botsis, J.A., Plutchick, R., Kotler, M., and van Praag, H.M. (1995) Parental loss and family violence as correlates of suicide and violence risk. *Suicide and Life-Threatening Behavior, 25*(2), 253–260.

Bower, G.H. (1981) Mood and memory. *American Psychologist, 36,* 129-148.

Boyatzis, C.J., Matil, G.M., and Nesbit, K.M. (1995) Effects of the Mighty Morphin Power Rangers on children's aggression with peers. *Child Study Journal, 25*(3), 45–55.

Bradley, R.T. (1997) *Charisma and Social Structure.* New York: Paragon.

Burke, P.J. and Reitzes, D.C. (1991) An identity theory approach to commitment. *Social Psychology Quarterly, 54,* 239–251.

Burt, R.S. (1982) *Toward a Structural Theory of Action: Network Models of Social Structure, Perception, and Action.* New York: Academic Press.

Celozzi, M.J., II, Kazelskis, R., and Gutsch, K.U. (1981) The relationship between viewing televised violence in ice hockey and subsequent levels of personal aggression. *Journal of Sport Behavior, 4*(4), 157–162.

Centerwall, B.S. (1993) Television and violent crime. *The Public Interest, 111* (Spring), 56–71.

Centre for National Security Studies. (1995) *Recent Trends in Domestic and International terrorism.* Available online: http://nsi.org/library/terrorism/tertrend/html.

Collins, R. (1981) On the micro foundations of macro sociology. *American Journal of Sociology, 86,* 984–1014.

Cooper, H.H.A. (1974) *Evaluating the Terrorist Threat: Principles and Applied Risk Assessment*, p. 4. Gaithersburg, MD: International Association of Police Chiefs.

Crenshaw, M. (1981) The causes of terrorism. *Comparative Politics, 13,* 379–399.

Crenshaw, M. (1985) *The Strategic Development of Terrorism.* Paper presented at the meeting of the American Political Science Association, New Orleans, LA.

Crenshaw, M. (1990) The logic of terrorism: terrorist behavior as a product of strategic choice. In W. Reich (Ed.), *Origins of Terrorism: Psychologies, Ideologies, Theologies, States of Mind*, pp. 7–24. New York: Woodrow Wilson International Center for Scholars and Cambridge University Press.

DeMause, L. (1990) The history of child assault. *The Journal of Psychohistory, 18*(1), 1–28.

Diener, E. (1977) Deindividuation: causes and consequences. *Social Behavior and Personality, 5,* 143–156.

Diener, E., Dineen, J., Endresen, K., Beaman, A.L., and Fraser, S.C. (1975) Effects of altered responsibility, cognitive set, and modeling on physical aggression and deindividuation. *Journal of Personality and Social Psychology, 31,* 143–156.

Dunand, M., Berkowitz, L., and Leyens, J.P. (1984) Audience effects when viewing aggressive movies. *British Journal of Social Psychology, 21,* 69–76.

Eagle, M. (1984) *Recent Developments in Psychoanalysis.* New York: McGraw-Hill.

Ember, C. (1978) Myths about hunter-gatherers. *Ethnology, 17,* 439–448.

Federal Bureau of Investigation (1997) *Terrorism: The Year in Review.* Available online: http://www.fbi.gov/publish/terror/terrorin.htm.

Feierabend, I.K. and Feierabend, R.L. (1970) Aggressive behaviors within polities, 1984–1962: a cross-national study. In E.I. Megargee and J.E. Hokanson (Eds.), *The Dynamics of Aggression*, pp. 213–226. New York: Harper & Row.

Forsyth, D.R. (1994) *Group Dynamics*, 2nd ed. Pacific Grove, CA: Brooks/Cole.

Freud, S. (1930, 1961) *Civilization and Its Discontents.* New York: W.W. Norton.

Gerbner, G. (1981) Statement on Violence on Television Before the U.S. House Subcommittee on Telecommunications, Consumer Protection, and Finance, 97th Conference. *Congressional Record* (serial no. 97-84), p. 155.

Gerbner, G. (1994) In S. Jhally (producer/director) *The Killing Screens: Media and the Culture of Violence* [video]. Northampton, MA: The Foundation.

Goodall, J. (1986) *The Chimpanzees of Gombe: Patterns of Behavior.* Cambridge: Belknap/Harvard University Press.

Goodall, J., Bandora, A., Bermann, E., Busse, C., Matama, H., Mpongo, E., Pierce, A., and Riss, D. (1979) Intercommunity interactions in the chimpanzee population of the Gombe National Park. In D.A. Hamburg and E.R. McCown (Eds.), *The Great Apes*, pp. 13–53. Menlo Park, CA: Cummings.

Gottman, J. (1979) *Marital Interaction: Experimental Investigations.* New York: Academic Press.

Gottman, J. (1994) *Why Marriages Succeed or Fail.* New York: Simon & Schuster.

Hall, H.V. and Pritchard, D.A. (1996) *Detecting Malingering and Deception.* Boca Raton, FL: CRC Press.

Haney, C., Banks, C., and Zimbardo, P. (1973) Interpersonal dynamics in a simulated prison. *International Journal of Criminology and Penology, 1,* 69–97.

Hare, A.P. (1976) *Handbook of Small Group Research,* 2nd ed. New York: Free Press.

Harris, L.M., Gergen, K.J., and Lannaman, J.W. (1986) Aggression rituals. *Communications Monographs, 53,* 252–265.

Hatfield, E., Cacioppo, J.T., and Rapson, R.L. (1993) Emotional contagion. *Current Directions in Psychological Science, 2*(3), 96–99.

Heise, D.R. and O'Brien, J. (1993) Emotion expression in groups. In J.M. Haviland and M. Lewis (Eds.), *Handbook of Emotions,* pp. 489–497. New York: The Guilford Press.

Henry, W., Strupp, H., Schacht, T., and Gaston, L. (1994) Psychodynamic approaches. In S. Garfield and A. Bergin (Eds.) *The Handbook of Psychotherapy and Behavior Change,* pp. 467–503. New York: Guilford Press.

Heskin, K. (1980) *Northern Ireland: A Psychological Analysis.* New York: Columbia University Press.

Hettena, C.M. and Ballif, B.L. (1981) Effects of moods on learning. *Journal of Educational Psychology, 73,* 505–508.

Hoffman, B. (1995) Holy terror: the implications of terrorism motivated by a religious imperative. *Studies in Conflict and Terrorism, 18,* 271–284.

Izard, C.E. (1977) *Human Emotions.* New York: Plenum Press.

Janis, I. (1982) *Groupthink: Psychological Studies of Policy Decisions and Fiascoes,* 2nd ed. Boston: Houghton Mifflin.

Keegan, J. (1976) *The Face of Battle.* Middlesex: Penguin.

Kernberg, O. (1992) *Aggression in Personality Disorders and Perversions.* New Haven: Yale University Press.

Kernberg, O. (1995) *The Effects of the Narcissistic Leader on the Group.* Paper presented at the American Group Psychotherapy Association Annual Meeting, Atlanta, GA.

Kilham, W. and Mann, L. (1974) Level of destructive obedience as a function of transmitter and executant roles in the Milgram obedience paradigm. *Journal of Personality and Social Psychology, 29,* 696–702.

Knoke, D. and Kuklinski, J.H. (1982) *Network Analysis.* Beverly Hills, CA: Sage.

Knutson, J.N. (1981) Social and psychodynamic pressures toward a negative identity: the case of an American revolutionary terrorist. In Y. Alexander and J.M. Gleason (Eds.) *Behavioral and Quantitative Perspectives on Terrorism,* pp. 143–144. New York: Pergamon Press.

Laird, J.D. and Bresler, C. (1992) The process of emotional feeling: a self-perception theory. In M. Clark (Ed.), *Review of Personality and Social Psychology.* Vol. 13. *Emotion.* Newbury Park, CA: Sage.

Laqueur, W. (1977) *Terrorism.* Boston, MA: Little, Brown.

Larsen, K.S., Coleman, D., Forges, J., and Johnson, R. (1971) Is the subject's personality or the experimental situation a better predictor of a subject's willingness to administer shock to a victim? *Journal of Personality and Social Psychology, 22,* 287–295.

Lawler, E.J. (1992) Affective attachments to nested groups: a choice process theory. *American Sociological Review, 57,* 327–339.

LeBon, G. (1896) *The Crowd*. London: Ernest Benn.

Levitt, G.M. (1988) *Democracies Against Terror: The Western Response to State-Supported Terrorism,* pp. 93–105. Washington Papers No. 134, Center for Strategic and International Studies, Washington, D.C., New York: Praeger.

Long, D.E. (1990) *The Anatomy of Terrorism,* New York: The Free Press.

Luschen, G. (1980) Sociology of sport: development, present state, and prospects. *Annual Review of Sociology, 6,* 315–347.

Manson, J.H. and Wrangham, R.W. (1991) Intergroup aggression in chimpanzees and humans. *Current Anthropology, 32,* 369–390.

Markus, H.R. and Kitayama, S. (1994) The cultural shaping of emotion: a conceptual framework. In S. Kitayama and H.R. Markus (Eds.), *Emotion and Culture: Empirical Studies of Mutual Influence*, pp. 339–351. Washington, D.C.: American Psychological Association.

Marsh, P. (1978) *Aggro, The Illusion of Violence.* London: J.M. Dent.

Masters, J.C., Felleman, E.S., and Barden, R.C. (1981) Experimental studies of affective states in children. In B. Lahey and A.E. Kazdin (Eds.), *Advances in Clinical Child Psychology*, Vol. 4, pp. 91–114. New York: Plenum Press.

McGuire, M. (1973) *To Take Arms: My Year With the IRA Provisionals.* New York: Viking.

McPhail, C. (1994) The dark side of purpose: individual and collective violence in riots. *The Sociological Quarterly, 35*(1), 1–32.

Meichenbaum, D. and Gilmore, J.B. (1984) The nature of unconscious processes: a cognitive-behavioral perspective. In K. Bowers and D. Meichenbaum (Eds.), *The Unconscious Reconsidered*, pp. 273–298. New York: Wiley.

Milgram, S. (1974) *Obedience to Authority: An Experimental View.* New York: Harper & Row.

Mullen, B. (1986) Atrocity as a function of lynch mob composition: a self-attention perspective. *Personality and Social Psychology Bulletin, 12*(2), 187–197.

Nishida, T., Hiraiwa-Hasegawa, M., Hasegawa, T., and Takahata, Y. (1985) Group extinction and female transfer in wild chimpanzees in the Mahale National Park, Tanzania. *Zeitschrift fur Tierpsychologie, 67,* 284–301.

Otterbein, K.F. (1970) *The Evolution of War.* New Haven: HRAF Press.

Patterson, J.D. (1991) Comment on J.H. Manson and R.W. Wrangham, Intergroup aggression in chimpanzees and humans. *Current Anthropology, 32*(4), 382.

Pepitone, A. (1984) Violent aggression from the multiple perspectives of psychology. *Journal of Social and Economic Studies (n.s.), 1*(4), 321–355.

Pomerantz, S.L. (1987) The FBI and terrorism. *FBI Law and Criminology, 72,* 1–51.

Post, J. (1984) Notes on a psychodynamic theory of terrorist behavior. *Terrorism, 7,* 241–256.

Post, J.M. (1990) Terrorist psycho-logic: terrorist behavior as a product of psychological forces. In W. Reich (Ed.), *Origins of Terrorism: Psychologies, Ideologies, Theologies, States of Mind*, pp. 25–40. Cambridge: Woodrow Wilson International Center for Scholars and Cambridge University Press.

Prino, C.T. and Peyrot, M. (1994) The effect of child physical abuse and neglect on aggressive, withdrawn, and prosocial behavior. *Child Abuse and Neglect, 18*(10), 871–884.

Ranstorp, M. (1996) Terrorism in the name of religion. *Journal of International Affairs, 50,* 41–62.

Rapoport, D.C. and Alexander, Y., Eds. (1982) *The Morality of Terrorism: Religious and Secular Justification.* Elmsford, NY: Pergamon Press.

Reich, W. (1990) Understanding terrorist behavior: the limits and opportunities of psychological inquiry. In W. Reich (Ed.), *Origins of Terrorism: Psychologies, Ideologies, Theologies, States of Mind*, pp. 261–279. Cambridge: Woodrow Wilson International Center for Scholars and Cambridge University Press.

Rosenberg, M.L., Powell, K.E., and Hammond, R. (1997) Applying science to violence prevention. *Journal of the American Medical Association, 277*(20) ,1641–1642.

Ross, J.I. (1993) Structural causes of oppositional political terrorism: towards a causal model. *Journal of Peace Research, 30,* 317–329.

Russell, C.A. and Miller, B.H. (1983) Portrait of a terrorist. In L. Freedman and Y. Alexander (Eds.), *Perspectives on Terrorism*, pp. 45–60. Wilmington, DE: Scholarly Resources.

Ryan, E.S. (1997) *The Criminal Belief Rationality: The Theology of Crime*. Paper presented at the concurrent conferences of the Peace Studies Association and the Consortium on Peace Research, Education, and Development, Georgetown, MD.

Sanday, P.R. (1981) The socio-cultural context of rape: a cross-cultural study. *Journal of Social Issues, 37*(4), 5–27.

Savinkov, B. (1931) *Memoirs of a Terrorist* (J. Shaplen, trans.). New York: A. and C. Boni.

Scheidlinger, S. (1994) A commentary on adolescent group violence. *Child Psychiatry and Human Development, 25,* 3–11.

Schmid, A. (1984) *Political Terrorism: A Research Guide*. New Brunswick, NJ: TransAction Books.

Schwartz, S.H. and Gottlieb, A. (1980) Bystander anonymity and reactions to emergencies. *Journal of Personality and Social Psychology, 39,* 418–430.

Scott, E.M. (1975) The act of murder. *International Journal of Offender Therapy and Comparative Criminology, 19*(2), 154–163.

Skeyhill, T., Ed. (1928) *Sergeant York: His Own Life Story and War Diary*. Garden City, NY: Doubleday, Doran.

Strentz, T. (1982) The Stockholm syndrome. In F.M. Ochberg and D.A. Soskis (Eds.), *Victims of Terrorism*, p. 152. Boulder, CO: Westview Press.

Sullins, E.S. (1991) Emotional contagion revisited: effects of social comparison and expressive style on mood convergence. *Personality and Social Psychology Bulletin, 17*(2), 166–174.

Tarvis, C. (1982) *Anger: The Misunderstood Emotion.* New York: Simon & Schuster.

Tedeschi, J.T. and Felson, R.B. (1994) *Violence, Aggression, and Coercive Actions*. Washington, D.C.: American Psychological Association.

Terrorism Research Center (1997) *The Basics of Terrorism*. Available online: http://www.terrorism.com/terrorism/bpart1.html.

Title 22, United States Code, Section 2656f(d).

U.S. Department of State (1988) *Patterns in Global Terrorism.* Washington, D.C.: U.S. Government Printing Office.

U.S. Department of State (1996) *Patterns in Global Terrorism*. Washington, D.C.: U.S. Government Printing Office.

Vogel, W. and Lazare, A. (1990) The unforgivable humiliation: a dilemma in couples' treatment. *Contemporary Family Therapy, 12,* 139–151.

Watson, R.I. (1973) Investigation into deindividuation using a cross-cultural survey technique. *Journal of Personality and Social Psychology, 25,* 342–345.

White, R.K. (1968) *Nobody Wanted War: Misperception in Vietnam and Other Wars.* Garden City, NY: Doubleday.

Wilson, E. (1975) *Sociobiology*. Cambridge: Harvard Press.

Yacef, S. (1962) *Souvenirs de la Bataille d'Alger*. Paris: Julliard.

Zajonc, R.B. (1980) Feeling and thinking: preferences need no inferences. *American Psychologist, 35,* 151–175.

Zawodny, J.K. (1978) Internal organizational problems and the sources of tensions of terrorist movements as catalysts of violence. *Terrorism, 1,* 277–285.

Zimbardo, P.G. (1969) The human choice: individuation, reason, and order versus deindividuation, impulse, and chaos. In W.J. Arnold and D. Levine (Eds.), *Nebraska Symposium on Motivation*, pp. 237–309. Lincoln: University of Nebraska Press.

About the Authors

Claudia J. Clayton, Ph.D., is an assistant professor of psychology at Brigham Young University, where she teaches introductory psychology, research design and analysis, and developmental psychology. She received the Excellence in Teaching Award in 1994. She holds a Ph.D. in anatomy, with emphases in neuroscience and pharmacology, from the University of Utah School of Medicine, and a Ph.D. in clinical psychology from Brigham Young University. She received postdoctoral training and was on the faculty at the University of Rochester School of Medicine and Dentistry and the University of North Carolina at Chapel Hill. Her research interests include human development, violence and peacemaking, and the biology of behavior. **Sally H. Barlow, ABPP,** a graduate of the University of Utah in 1978, earned her ABPP Diplomate in Clinical Psychology in 1991. She has published in the areas of individual and group psychotherapy research, has received numerous grants, among them an NIMH grant to study common and specific factors in short-term group psychotherapy, and has presented papers at national and international conferences. As an associate professor, she teaches graduate courses in assessment, psychodynamic treatment, group theory and intervention, and diversity at Brigham Young University, where she received the Excellence in Teaching Award. Her recent interests include the regulation of psychology as a profession, as well as the education of future psychologists. **Bonnie Ballif-Spanvill, Ph.D.,** is a professor of psychology and director the Women's Research Institute at Brigham Young University, where she received her Ph.D. in 1966. She returned to her alma mater in 1994 after 25 years as a professor in the graduate school of Fordham University at Lincoln Center in New York City. Her research, papers, and publications in human emotion and motivation earned her Fellow status in the American Psychological Association in 1984 and the American Psychological Society in 1987. She is currently involved in studying peace and violence in women and men across ages and cultures worldwide.

Chapter 10

PROFILING AND CRIMINAL INVESTIGATIVE ANALYSIS OF VIOLENT CRIMES WITH MULTIPLE OFFENDERS

Dayle L. Hinman and Patrick E. Cook

Overview and Epidemiology

In this chapter, the authors examine profiling and crime scene analysis and discuss their uses in investigating crimes of violence committed by two or more individuals (see Cook and Hinman, 1996, for a discussion of profiling as an important investigative tool).

There is a superabundance of contemporary examples of violent crimes committed by multiple perpetrators. For example:

- In Eustis, Florida, four teenagers, alleged to be obsessed with vampires, have been accused of beating a friend's parents to death.
- Two teenagers from Texas have been charged with murdering a 16-year-old girl. The accused were first-year cadets at U.S. military academies.
- The number of juvenile gang killings (in which there are often multiple perpetrators) reported each year in the U.S. more than doubled (542 to 1157) between 1989 and 1995 (Federal Bureau of Investigation, 1994, 1996).
- On February 26, 1993, an explosion rocked the World Trade Center in New York City. In the largest incident of international terrorism conducted within the borders of the U.S., six people were killed, more than 1000 were injured, and the harsh reality of international terrorism was brought home to the citizens of the U.S.
- Two years later, the bombing of the Murrah Federal Building in Oklahoma City in April 1995 brought a new awareness of another growing threat of violence — domestic terrorism.

Until recently, Americans were less likely to be murdered by strangers than by family members, friends, or acquaintances acting alone. That is no longer true (Federal Bureau of Investigation, 1994). For some kinds of homicides, such as "drive-by" shootings and major terrorist acts, there is a high likelihood that there are multiple perpetrators; in others, there may or may not be more than one perpetrator. When there are no witnesses, and when the suspects are unknown, it may be difficult to determine whether there is one or more than one perpetrator.

TABLE 10.1

NUMBER OF HOMICIDES REPORTED IN THE UNITED STATES AND PERCENTAGES INVOLVING SINGLE, MULTIPLE, AND UNKNOWN VICTIMS AND OFFENDERS FOR THE YEARS 1991-1995

	1991	1992	1993	1994	1995
Homicides	20,863	21,701	22,175	21,093	19,143
Incident type (%):					
Single victim/ single offender	52.8	52.3	52.7	53.0	53.0
Single victim/ multiple offender	11.6	10.4	11.2	11.5	11.1
Single victim/ unknown offender(s)	32.4	33.4	32.5	31.5	31.9
Multiple victims/ single offender	1.6	2.0	1.9	1.9	1.9
Multiple victims/ multiple offenders	0.6	0.7	0.6	0.8	0.8
Multiple victims/ unknown offender(s)	1.0	1.2	1.1	1.3	1.4

Data compiled from the Uniform Crime Report data base and provided to the authors by the FBI.

Obviously, knowing whether there is one suspect or there are multiple suspects is essential in the identification and apprehension of all the parties responsible for a crime. For the purposes of this chapter, the authors consider only those individuals whose criminal responsibility derived from active participation in the violence.

According to the *Uniform Crime Report*, published each year by the FBI, 19,143 murders were reported to have been committed in the U.S. in 1995 (FBI, 1996). Not all agencies cooperate in reporting murders in their jurisdictions. Not all murders are recognized as such by the authorities, and not all bodies of homicide victims are found. Most murders involved only one offender and one victim. Table 10.1 presents a summary of the number of reported homicides in the U.S. for the years 1991 to 1995 and the percentages involving single, multiple, and an unknown number of victims and offenders.

How can investigators discern which crimes were committed by single offenders and which involved multiple offenders? In any crime of lethal violence, more than one active participant (primary perpetrator) can be involved. The types of lethal violent crimes that may involve multiple perpetrators include:

- Homicide
- Felony murder
- Sex crimes
- Bombing and arson
- Terrorism
- Hijacking
- Hostage taking
- Physician-assisted suicide

Multiple perpetrators are common in single homicides. In both classic and spree types of serial murder, multiple perpetrators are rare, but not unknown (Cook and Hinman, 1996). Henry Lee Lucas and Otis Elwood Toole are serial killers who killed individually and as a team. Lawrence Bittaker and Roy Norris met in prison. They used a van to abduct five teenaged girls whom they tortured and killed.

Felony murder refers to deaths that occur during the commission of a felony such as aggravated battery or armed robbery. It is common to find multiple perpetrators in these types of crimes.

Research has shown that sexual sadists, many of whom kill their victims, may have compliant victims (Hazelwood et al., 1993), some of whom act as accomplices. A study of 30 sexual sadists found that 11 (36.7%) had accomplices (totaling 11 males and 7 females) (Dietz et al., 1990).

Some bombers work in teams, especially when large bombs are involved. Arsonists usually act alone.

As defined by the Terrorism Research and Analytical Center (TRAC; 1993, p. 28), terrorism is "the unlawful use of force or violence to intimidate or coerce a government, the civilian population, or any segment thereof, in furtherance of political or social objectives." Terrorists may operate alone or in teams.

Between 1961 and 1989, 306 American airplanes were hijacked. In 22.5% of the incidents, multiple hijackers were involved. Multiple hijackers were more successful than lone hijackers (75% vs. 46%) (Feldmann and Johnson, 1996).

Call (1996) identified six types of hostage-takers — emotionally disturbed, political extremists, religious fanatics, criminals, prison inmates, and others — and 12 subtypes. Deliberate political extremist hostage-takers who planned to take hostages are more likely to be willing to execute their hostages than are those who did not plan to take hostages.

Whether assisted suicide should be considered a crime is the subject of much debate. Physician-assisted suicide involves two or more people participating in a lethal act on one of the individuals — the "victim" is also an accessory.

For many specific crime areas, there are professionals (e.g., Bureau of Alcohol, Tobacco, and Firearms agents; fire marshal investigators; hostage negotiators; suicidologists) who collect data regarding the methodology and characteristics of typical types of crimes and typical types of offenders. Drug Enforcement Administration agents have used research to develop drug courier profiles to spot individuals who are likely to transport narcotics. Store detectives are trained to identify the movements of and typical clothing worn by shoplifters to conceal merchandise. Profilers use this type of information to focus investigations, perfect new investigative tools, and continue to add to the knowledge base necessary for effective criminal investigations.

Can profiling be used to determine the number of offenders who have *actively* participated in a particular crime? If profiling can suggest the kind of suspect to look for, can it suggest when investigators should look for one perpetrator, when they should look for two, and when they should look for a large group, gang, or terrorist organization? From early in the Unabomber investigation, the mail bomber was believed to be a single person, acting alone. The Oklahoma City and World Trade Center bombers were, from the outset of the investigations, believed to be multiple perpetrators, with some type of organizational support. Why?

Louis J. Freeh, Director of the FBI, has said that agents must use behavioral psychology to be able to deal with the many types of criminals and terrorists they face today (Franks, 1996). In this chapter, the authors discuss the use of profiling in the investigation of violent crimes committed by multiple offenders.

In the following section, the authors discuss profiling and criminal investigative analysis, indicate the types of crimes most likely to be profilable, and suggest the indicators of single and multiple perpetrators for a given violent crime. In subsequent sections, the authors briefly address the effects of multiple perpetrators on the violent event cycle, discuss the difficulties in profiling crimes with more than one perpetrator, and suggest guidelines for evaluating violent crimes so that indicators of multiple perpetrators will not be overlooked. The authors use cases to illustrate important points and conclude with brief comments about profiling bombing and other acts of terrorism.

Profiling, Criminal Investigative Analysis, and Detection of Multiple Offenders

Profiling

There is often confusion about what is meant by "profiling" of violent crimes (Cook and Hinman, 1996). The profiling of serial killers has been the most widely publicized application (in news and true crime literature), and the most glamorized (in novels, movies, and television series). Profilers are not clairvoyant, nor do they have other forms of extrasensory perception as is often attributed to them in works of fiction. More factual accounts, such as the recent books by former FBI Behavioral Science Unit agents who developed profiling, gloss over many of the details of their procedures. One reason for oversimplifying the profiling process for the public is to deprive criminals of specific knowledge of profiling techniques (Ressler and Shachtman, 1997).

The FBI defines profiling as an investigative technique by which to identify the major personality and behavioral characteristics of the offender based on an analysis of the crimes committed (Douglas and Burgess, 1986). It should be understood that people are not profiled. The focus of the analysis or profile is the behavior of the perpetrator or perpetrators within the crime scene. Profiling is an investigative tool. It is not separate from the investigation. It is an integral part of it. The profile can suggest directions for the investigation. New evidence must always be analyzed and the profile modified when appropriate.

Investigators regularly use profiling techniques without calling what they do "profiling". When a crime occurs, investigators use their training and experience to try to determine: What happened? Why did it happen? And, who did it?

Profilers analyze the criminal activity in order to describe the person or persons responsible. Essentially, this amounts to making an educated guess based on logic, common sense, crime-scene experience, years of shared investigative experience, and intuition — what police call a "gut feeling".

A case on which the authors consulted provides a good example. An unknown person shot and killed two girls who were spending the afternoon sunning at the beach. Each girl was shot twice in the head at close range with a .38-caliber revolver. The nature of the victims' wounds ("double tapped" and "head shots") and the weapon used (until recently, police duty weapons were most commonly used .38 caliber revolvers) suggested an increased probability that the killer was a current or former law enforcement officer, as opposed to someone such as a jilted boyfriend or a drug dealer. The killer was ultimately determined to be a former police officer.

Why Profiling May Be Helpful

Profiling may be helpful in increasing the efficiency and effectiveness of police investigations for a variety of reasons, including:

- Focusing the investigation
- Suggesting proactive strategies

- Suggesting interview strategies
- Suggesting trial strategies
- Directing interventions in ongoing crimes
- Preventing violent crimes

Profiling can aid in the apprehension of an unknown perpetrator by focusing the investigation on more likely types of offenders (e.g., "The suspect is likely to be a single 20- to 25-year-old white male who is unemployed and lives within a one-mile radius of the crime scene") and eliminating others.

Profiling can often suggest proactive investigative strategies. Proactive techniques are designed to predict or manipulate the perpetrator's behavior (e.g., likely to return to the body dump site) and cause the perpetrator to do something that helps in his or her own apprehension. With knowledge of individual profiles and group dynamics, investigators can try to turn multiple perpetrators against each other. For example, investigators may surmise that one of the perpetrators may be a weak link. They could then use the media to publicize their (true) belief that one of the partners in crime could be in danger of being killed by his or her partner. This could cause the weak link to come forward for protection.

Profiling can also suggest interview strategies that will be effective with particular suspects. For example, props can be helpful when some suspects are interrogated. They can help convince the suspect that the police know more than they actually do, or that they have unlimited technical resources. The psychological defenses of some types of suspects may be overwhelmed by a display of maps, files, computer printouts, or high-tech gear.

A profiler may provide helpful advice to the prosecutor for courtroom tactics that could elicit incriminating behavior from a defendant. FBI profiler John Douglas provided this kind of advice to the prosecutor in the trial of Wayne Williams, the Atlanta Child Killer. The prosecutor followed Douglas' advice and got the defendant to lose his composure and show his rage to the jury by waiting until the appropriate moment, putting his hand on Williams' arm, and asking him what it was like to strangle the victims (Douglas and Olshaker, 1995).

Profiling may give direction to interventions in a series of crimes or a crime in progress. In hostage and armed standoff situations, the behavior and communications of the hostage-taker and intelligence information that is developed may enable the negotiator to profile the suspect and tailor the negotiation strategy or tactical response to the situation.

One example of using profiling to prevent violent crimes would be preparing to interdict terrorist threats by profiling individuals or groups most likely to target Olympic teams from specific countries. This was one approach used in protecting visiting Olympic teams during the 1996 Olympics in Atlanta.

Crimes that Lend Themselves to Profiling

The types of crimes that lend themselves to profiling include:

- Series of similar crimes
- Unusual crimes
- Crimes accompanied by communications
- Crimes suggesting mental illness

One reason that profiling may be helpful with series of similar crimes such as serial murders, rapes, bombings, and arsons is that these are the crimes about which the most profiling information has been developed. A second reason is that serial crimes may provide multiple samples of the perpetrator's work. When serial crimes are determined to be linked, the accumulated evidence may help to produce a more accurate and helpful profile. Changes in crime behavior over time also can provide helpful information. Many investigations are impeded when investigators and agencies fail to share information and fail to recognize serial crimes as such, due to what Egger (1990) called "linkage blindness".

Unusual crimes with repeated *modus operandi* (MO) activity, signature characteristics, behavior prints, and signs of staging are often more easily profilable than garden-variety violent crime. The MO refers to the actions taken by the offender to accomplish the crime and avoid apprehension (e.g., entering through an open window, wearing latex gloves, stabbing with a screwdriver, etc.). The *signature* is ritualistic behavior at the crime scene that reflects the offender's fantasy and motivation that is not necessary for the perpetration of the crime (e.g., posing the body in a specific manner, postmortem mutilation, and exploration). The signature can be so individual and specific that its repetition, like fingerprints, can be recognized as a behavior print. In its broadest sense, a *behavior print* is a sign of activity left at the crime scene by the perpetrator or perpetrators. *Staging* is purposefully altering the crime scene to misdirect the investigation (Douglas and Munn, 1992). Profilers look for data regarding the offender's activities with the victim, crime scene evidence, and evidence of the offender's preparation and technical attention to details. The Unabomber's meticulously crafted bombs were examples of his signature. On occasion, multiple signatures or behavior prints at a crime scene indicate the presence of multiple perpetrators.

Crimes accompanied by communications such as terrorist communiques, kidnappers' ransom notes, or graffiti taunting the police may be more easily profiled because of the psychological information contained in the communications.

Some crimes may suggest that the perpetrator suffers from a major mental illness such as schizophrenia, bipolar disorder, or drug-induced delirium. Bizarre aspects of the crime may help the profiler identify related characteristics of the offender (e.g., obviously confused and disoriented).

As Geberth (1996) and others have observed, it is not the offense *per se* that determines a crime's profilability, it is the behavior that is exhibited by the perpetrator at the crime scene. Profilers are taught to know the enemy and look at the scene. In an earlier work on serial murder (Cook and Hinman, 1996), the authors suggested that profiling is a skill that is not easily acquired. People who attempt to do "psychological profiling" based only on psychological theory or research literature do not have the requisite investigative training and experience. They often do more harm than good.

Criminal Investigative Analysis

FBI Director Freeh observed that good investigators have always used behavioral psychology, but that they now have a discipline to enable them to do it better (Franks, 1996). This is due in large measure to the databases and profiling techniques developed by the FBI. Now referred to as criminal investigative analysis, this highly specialized form of profiling is used when investigators of serial murders and similar crimes of violence focus on the forensic and behavioral crime scene evidence. The purpose of this investigative technique is to identify the major personality and behavioral characteristics of the offenders in order to understand, identify, and apprehend them. It is based on a detailed analysis of the crime or crimes committed (Douglas et al., 1986).

Criminal investigative analysis requires extensive training and familiarity with the research findings of the FBI's National Center for the Analysis of Violent Crime (Douglas and Olshaker, 1995; Douglas et al., 1986).

The FBI Police Fellowship

In 1982, FBI administrators queried several large police agencies to determine if there was interest in participating in a behavioral science fellowship program. The first fellow began his training in 1984. By 1991, a total of 33 experienced investigators from the U.S. and other countries were trained in profiling.

The training consisted of an academic phase and an application phase. The first 3 months involved intensive training in topics that provide the basis for the profile and assessment process. The officers attended courses in homicide and rape investigation, abnormal psychology, equivocal death evaluation, blood spatter interpretation, forensics, and a myriad of other topics. The remainder of the time was dedicated to developing the analytical and profiling skills of the officers. The officers participated in group consultations and were assigned cases to work on under the guidance and supervision of experienced profilers. The officers had the opportunity to study hundreds of cases and benefit from all of the experiences and special expertise of the group. Each FBI Fellowship lasted a year, which was not an unrealistic amount of time for an individual to become proficient in the art of profiling (Hazelwood, 1986).

After the FBI discontinued the program, the Fellowship graduates formed an association to select, train, and certify understudy candidates. At the conclusion of all phases of the training, the candidates are tested by representatives of the FBI and the Fellowship Association. Successfully passing the test allows them admission to this small group of certified profilers. Sadly, there are individuals who conduct courses or workshops that last only a few days and certify the attendees as profilers. In such a short time, trainees cannot possibly develop the expertise they need to be competent profilers.

The Profiling Process

The authors have found that working in a small group is the best way to facilitate the profiling process. At various times, the group may include investigators and crime-scene technicians from several law enforcement agencies, a medical examiner, a forensic psychologist, and a blood spatter expert. Case conferencing brings everyone up to speed on the status of the case and all potentially related cases in a series. Reviewing case information with each other and brainstorming often leads to a suggestion or new idea that yields positive investigative results.

In their seminal article on profiling, Douglas et al. (1986) identified six stages in the criminal profile generating process:

- Profiling inputs
- Decision process model
- Crime assessment
- Profile
- Investigation
- Apprehension

The process begins with profiling inputs. The first stage includes the gathering of all the case information and available facts. It should be emphasized that the profile will only be as accurate as the information on which it is based. Erroneous, inaccurate, or incomplete information will undermine the entire process. Comprehensive case information is gathered regarding the crime scene, forensics, case background, photographs, and victimology. Victimology is the study of victim characteristics in order to better understand the crime. These data should include all of the information that can be obtained regarding the victim's lifestyle, habits, personality, employment, physical condition, reputation, and family relationships. An outline of the data used in constructing a profile, as contained in the submission requirements for homicide case consultation for one agency's criminal assessment profile program, is presented in Table 10.2.

Once all of the pertinent information has been gathered and reviewed, the profilers can move on to the second stage, which is the decision process stage. During this stage, the case is organized and reviewed for patterns that may prove meaningful. The basic information is expanded to consider seven decision points: (1) homicide style, (2) primary intent of the homicide, (3) victim risk, (4) offender risk, (5) escalation, (6) window of opportunity for the crime, and

Table 10.2

Data Used in Constructing a Profile: Submission Requirements for Homicide Case Consultation

1. Case background
   a. Synopsis of crime
   b. Initial complaint reports and follow-up investigative reports
   c. Detailed interviews of witnesses and any other pertinent information
   d. Investigative officer's reconstruction of the sequence of events
   e. Copies of (or synopsis of) local media attention to the crime
2. Photographs (color, if possible)
   a. Complete photographs of the crime scene
   b. Photograph of the victim before the incident
   c. Autopsy photographs detailing the depth and extent of the wounds
   d. If inside a building, photographs of the other rooms
   e. If available and appropriate, submit aerial photographs
3. Crime scene sketch (to include distances and directions)
4. Map (with plottings and key) representing:
   a. Scale
   b. Time/location where the victim was found
   c. Location of the victim's residence
   d. Location of the victim's vehicle (if pertinent)
   e. Location of the crime scene (if it is different from where the victim was found; also, any other related crime scenes
   f. Location of any other pertinent areas, i.e. evidence found, attempts on other victims, etc. (note: state the distances between the points)
5. Medical examiner's report (autopsy protocol)
   a. Toxicological/serological results, including drugs, alcohol, presence of sperm, etc.
   b. Findings/impressions of the medical examiner regarding estimated time of death, type of weapon, suspected sequence of the delivery of the wounds and any other appropriate data available
6. Neighborhood and complex (Racial, ethnic, social data and economic breakdown
7. Describe the victim's activity prior to death (where victim was last seen and by whom)
8. Background of the victim
   a. Age
   b. Sex
   c. Race
   d. Physical description including dress at time of incident
   e. Marital status/adjustment
   f. Intelligence, scholastic achievement/adjustment
   g. Lifestyle, recent changes
   h. Personality style/characteristics
   i. Demeanor
   j. Residency, former and present, in relation to crime scene
   k. Sexual adjustment
   l. Occupation, former and present
   m. Reputation at home and work
   n. Medical history, physical and mental
   o. Fears
   p. Personal habits
   q. Use of alcohol or drugs/social habits
   r. Hobbies
   s. Friends and enemies
   t. Recent court action and prior record
   u. Relatives in area
   v. List names of all persons known to have seen victim during the 24 hours before incident
9. Complete list of evidence recovered

The reader will note the emphasis on victimology. Ebert (1987) suggested a similar list to be used in conducting a psychological autopsy in cases of equivocal death.

(7) crime location. All of these points serve to focus or expand the direction of the investigation.

In the crime assessment stage, the profilers use the information obtained and organized in the first two stages to reconstruct the sequence of events and the actions of the offender and the victim. The profilers interpret the dynamics of the crime and the actions based upon their own experience with similar crimes. Broad aspects such as the degree of planning that was exhibited, victim selection, method of control, and sequence of events are considered. Then, more specific aspects of the dynamics are reviewed such as location of the crime scene, cause of death, method of killing, location of wounds, excessive trauma, position of the body, items taken, etc. (Ressler et al., 1988). At this stage, the number of offenders is addressed.

The first three stages deal with what happened, how it happened, and why it happened. The fourth stage deals with the type of persons who committed the crime and their behavioral organization with relation to the crime. All of these factors interact to lead the profilers to link the crime-scene dynamics to specific criminal personality traits or patterns. Once the type of person has been described, the profilers can suggest an investigative strategy. The strategy should include how a suspect would respond to a variety of investigative efforts.

No two offenders are exactly alike. There is a wide range of individual differences among offenders who commit similar offenses. They also may share common traits. For this reason, novice profilers are cautioned not to think in terms of "always" or "never". Profilers focus on the common denominators that have been discovered between the psychological make-up of the criminal and the psychological "clues" that are found in the crime scene. The individuals who developed the FBI research did not intend for the information to be used as a "cookbook" to define or limit the description of potential suspects. Rather, this information has been provided to help the investigator read and interpret the scene. It is based on the combined experience of other investigators working on similar cases that have been solved. The common elements that link crime-scene dynamics to specific personality patterns can then be suggested. The what, why, and who can be translated into: If this happened, for this reason, the perpetrator is likely to be this type of person.

Detailed profiling of a crime can often suggest such potential identification factors as sex, race, education, type of employment, and various lifestyle factors (e.g., proximity of residence to the crime scene, transportation, hobbies, and sexual and social development). The offenders' selection of the victim, preparation for the crime, and the elements of the actual offense can suggest the approximate social/emotional ages of the offenders. The social/emotional age may differ from their chronological age. Offenders who have been incarcerated for significant periods of time (when normal sexual and social development would be expected to occur) may be difficult to profile with regard to age because of "arrested development" (Cook and Hinman, 1996).

In the fifth stage, the profile is provided to the investigating agency. Suspects matching the profile are evaluated. If a suspect is identified, apprehended, and confesses, the goals have been met. If other similar cases subsequently occur, the profile should be evaluated and revised to include the new information.

Finally, information regarding the subject is obtained and compared with the profile in the apprehension stage for validity and accuracy. It is important to evaluate continually the accuracy of the offender characteristics that were suggested. Knowing how and why different aspects of the crime occurred helps profilers interpret or make investigative sense out of similar cases they see in the future.

Indicators of Lone vs. Multiple Perpetrators

Some crimes are typically committed by an individual acting alone. A person who spends hours carefully constructing a letter bomb is not generally a sociable individual. It would be rare for him or her to have an accomplice. Some crimes are more likely to involve more than one perpetrator. Examples include gang-related violence and felony murders. Terrorists who target a major government or commercial building with a car bomb loaded with hundreds of pounds of explosives generally have assistance. They need it physically to accomplish the crime. Acts of international terrorism may involve strike teams of terrorists.

Given the nature of the violent crime which has occurred, the profiler first should consider what is statistically typical for that type of crime. Is this a typical homicide? Is it an act of group terrorism or gang violence? As another example, product tampering is rarely done by multiple perpetrators (although when they elect to communicate, they often claim to be acting as part of a group).

Next, the crime must be evaluated to determine the minimum number of participants necessary to commit the crime in the way it was carried out. The profiler tries to estimate accurately how many perpetrators would be required to control the victims, move the body, ransack the house, load the fuel oil/fertilizer explosive into the truck, etc. The defense in the criminal and civil O.J. Simpson trials tried to raise doubts about their client's guilt by suggesting that two people may have murdered Nicole Brown Simpson and Ron Goldman. There was no forensic evidence of a second killer. There were no behavior prints of a second killer. Some people, including some defense experts, seemed ready to accept the premise that it would have taken two assailants to accomplish the grisly murders, or that one murderer acting alone could not have committed the crimes in a short period of time. In real life, violent crime does not happen in slow motion. It also does not take as long in real time as in the typical dramatization. Many people are surprised to learn that most real gunfights are usually over in seconds. Anyone who has seen law enforcement training exercises or training videos on edged weapons understands how quickly a man with a knife could kill two people in a small, enclosed area.

Seeing the available space in which the crime occurred is one of the reasons that, when possible, profilers try to visit the crime scene. Actually viewing the scene, seeing the dimensions, determining what can be seen from the location, and what surrounding areas offer as a view of the scene — "getting a feel for" the scene — can be very helpful. Often, clues can be found in visiting the scene and "walking through" the interaction that took place between the victim and the attacker. One of the questions asked is, "What is the smallest number of offenders that would be necessary to carry out this crime, at this place, in this particular fashion?" Crime-scene videotapes and photographs are also helpful in this regard, but visiting the scene of the crime in person can provide information and a feel for the context of the crime that the profiler cannot get from videos and photographs (Geberth, 1996). Viewing crime scenes from the air can reveal patterns of body placement that suggest that more than one murderer could be involved in a series (Ressler and Shachtman, 1997). Maps, aerial photographs, crime scene photos, videos, and crime-scene visits each provide a unique perspective and are not interchangeable.

A visit to the scene was quite valuable in a homicide case involving a middle-aged couple. The female victim was found just inside the door of her residence. She was dressed in the clothing she would have worn to work at her night job. Her purse was over her arm and her keys were beside her. She had been stabbed multiple times and her throat had been slashed repeatedly. Her boyfriend had been struck once on the head with a heavy ashtray. He had fallen over the railing on the deck and his nude body was discovered in the back yard. His clothing had been dropped on the deck, apparently while he was attempting to flee. The two types of weapons and the vast difference in the severity of the wounds suggested that two perpetrators had been involved in the murders of the two victims. The killers were soon determined to be the male victim's juvenile son and one of his pals.

In a series of three geographically close robberies, the number of weapons used was also an indication of the number of perpetrators present in each case. In the first robbery, a convenience store clerk was shot in the left eye at close range with a .22-caliber magnum. He was then shot in the back of the head with a .357 revolver. There was evidence of a struggle. No money was taken. In the second robbery, a motel clerk was shot with a .357 and his wallet was taken. In the third robbery, a lone gunman robbed a restaurant that had only one visible employee. He shot the dishwasher as he exited the kitchen, then made off with the money. When the men were arrested, it was learned that they split up after the first botched robbery. One of the criminals had learned it was more profitable to go it alone.

The perpetrator's ability to control or intimidate the victim(s) is an issue for consideration, as is the age and size of the victim(s) and the use of weapons and restraints. Two of the three apartments that serial killer Danny Rolling entered in Gainesville, FL, were occupied by two persons. Rolling quickly found and executed the "extra" persons. He then bound and gagged the targeted victim. The investigators' conclusion that he had acted alone was reinforced by his use of bindings to incapacitate his victims. A singular individual can control the actions of multiple victims if they are stunned by a blitz attack, if they are sufficiently intimidated and believe that one or all will be harmed if they do not comply, or if the perpetrator is armed with a dangerous weapon. Victims will agree to tie up other victims if they believe that complying with the demands of the offender will increase their chances for survival.

The total extent, order, and types of crime activity must always be considered when attempting to determine how many individuals were involved. Crimes that specifically indicate more than one person are sometimes evident from forensic evidence. Examples include autopsy evidence; fingerprints of more than one perpetrator; more than one type of semen in a sexually motivated crime; crime-scene/clothing/blood patterns, when a body has been moved, indicating that the victim was carried by the hands *and* feet or a heavy body has been lifted over the top of a high-walled dumpster; or void (non-bloodstained) areas in blood spatter showing where perpetrators were standing when the bloodshed occurred. Voids on surfaces within bloodstained patterns are due to intervening objects or persons (James and Edel, in press).

In a recent case that involved the murders of a woman and her infant, bloodstain patterns and voids helped to guide the crime scene analyst in her assessment. At the time of the double homicide, the adult victim was seated in the driver's seat of her vehicle wearing a safety belt. The baby was strapped into her car seat in the back seat of the car. The mother had been stabbed multiple times. The angles of the wounds and blood spatter indicated that the victim was stabbed both from the right and from behind. Her baby had been stabbed three times. The evidence strongly suggested that the offender did not inflict wounds from the passenger seat, then run around and get into the back seat to continue the attack. The investigators cleared this case with the arrest of the baby's father and his cousin.

It is important to remember that the foundation of the profile is the processing of the information obtained from the crime scene and the investigation. Additionally, the value of an extensive and thorough investigation of the victim's background (victimology) cannot be overstated. This must be undertaken for the profilers to assess the type of person or persons who would target a particular victim.

A case that demonstrates this point is one the authors were asked to review after all of the leads had grown cold. The crime scene photographs showed that the victim was completely covered by a sofa cover. When the cover was removed, it was obvious that the elderly, crippled, black woman had been struck in the face and head with a fireplace tool. Her dress had been pulled up to expose her genital area and was open at the neck to expose her breasts. No semen was present, so the investigators surmised that she was fondled by a sexual pervert. For weeks the investigation had centered around white sexual offenders who had been released from prison into the area and had long blond hair that matched hairs found on the victim.

When the investigators were asked to provide a victimology to the profilers, they re-interviewed the victim's sister. It was during this interview that they discovered that *she* had covered the body! It is not unusual for family members to cover the gruesome sight of their murdered loved ones, but it is critical for the investigators to know this.

The scene photos told the investigators that the victim's dress could have been pulled up as she fell backwards. The victimology revealed that she frequently kept money in her bra. With this new information, the profilers could develop a scenario for how the crime may have unfolded. It was suggested that the primary offender was likely to be a young black male who lived in the neighborhood and had taken money from the victim in the past. Perhaps the anger and aggressive behavior were related to a need for drug money and were triggered on this occasion when she refused to give him any money. With this new focus, the homicide investigators teamed up with the narcotics unit. A quick resolution to this case occurred with the arrest of a female drug dealer who had long blond hair. When a hair standard was requested for comparison to a homicide case, she instantly provided the name of the young man to whom she had sold drugs on that fateful night. Her hair was shed at the scene when she attempted to stop the buyer from striking the victim when she refused to give him money. As this case demonstrates, it is easier to find something if you know what you are looking for.

Effects of Multiple Perpetrators on the Violent Event Cycle

Some of the earliest treatises on social philosophy and social psychology addressed the relationship between crowds and mob violence. Profilers must have a basic understanding of the effects of the presence of more than one participant in a crime, the interactions of the participants with each other and with the victim or victims, and the behavioral input of each participant. These factors determine whether or not a violent act occurs. If a violent act does occur, these factors influence what takes place.

Adding a second perpetrator changes the variables in what Megargee (1982, 1993) termed the "algebra of aggression" — the equation conceptualizing the psychological process that determines whether an individual will make a particular aggressive response. According to Megargee's stimulus-response analysis, whether or not an individual engages in aggressive or violent behavior is a result of the interaction of five factors: (1) instigation to aggression refers to the internal factors that motivate an individual to behave violently; (2) the habit strength of a particular violent act depends upon its reinforcement history — whether the individual has been rewarded or punished for the act in the past; (3) inhibitions against aggression are the internal factors, based on past experience, which oppose the instigation and habit strength for aggression against a particular target; (4) situational factors are the external factors that may increase or decrease aggressive behavior as the individual interacts with the environment, including the presence of a weapon, the presence of witnesses, and the behavior of victims, bystanders, and associates; and (5) reaction potential, which refers to the strength of the aggressive response that occurs after the opposing and favoring factors are weighed against each other.

In discussing the behavior of associates, Megargee mentioned that social psychological experiments have shown that a group will take a more extreme position than the individual members and that a group member may accept aggressive behavior by the group that violates his or her personal values. Additional participants can influence the equation (and thus the behavioral outcome) in a variety of ways. For example:

Person 1 says to Person 2: "Are you going to put up with that? We ought to teach that mother-f—— a lesson!" This situational factor increases intrinsic or angry instigation and decreases inhibition by suggesting that violence is appropriate.

Person 1 says to Person 2: "Let's not leave any witnesses." This increases extrinsic or instrumental instigation by pointing out that murder facilitates escape. It also decreases inhibitions by suggesting violence.

Person 1 says to Person 2: "Don't do it! It isn't right," which increases "moral" inhibition, or "Don't do it! You'll never get away with it," which increases "practical" inhibition.

These are oversimplified examples. They are not intended to do justice to the complex interactions of partners in crime who plan a murder, or to groups of individuals unexpectedly thrown into situations (criminal and non-criminal) in which lethal violence occurs seemingly spontaneously. Depending on the combinations of personalities and circumstances, lethal violence may be more likely to be committed by some dyads, and less likely by others. According to Gavin de Becker (1997), murder by juveniles is most likely to occur during the commission of a crime (felony murder) when two or more juveniles are involved. Peer pressure is a factor, according to de Becker. Adding a third person alters the dynamics again. Adding a group alters the dynamics even more. A body of social psychological knowledge supports this view regarding dyadic and group interactions. Base rate information about crime dynamics and how the social matrix of violence is affected by the number of perpetrators is more limited, and primarily anecdotal.

Criminals commit crimes, so it is no surprise that groups of criminals commit crimes. What happens when two psychopaths team up? Hare (1993, p. 65), one of the foremost experts on psychopaths, says that psychopaths don't usually get along, but when they do become partners, there is a "grim symbiosis" with unfortunate outcomes for others. The dynamics are different when two perpetrators participate in the same crime. According to Douglas and Olshaker (1995), there generally is a more dominant and a more compliant partner. Usually, one is more organized and one is less organized. Douglas and Olshaker (1995) observed that serial killers are inadequate, and that the most inadequate are the ones who need partners to help them commit their crimes.

Cults and hate groups spawn violent behaviors by their members. Often, it is a disturbed member who acts out the message of hate after having been incited by the group's rhetoric (e.g., some abortion clinic violence) or who has been intentionally programmed by the group's leadership (e.g., Charles Manson and followers). Pathological cognition and attitudes of the leader often become the norm, many times in the absence of intentional programming. In some instances, malignant group influences include shared paranoid delusions of persecution or grandiosity.

Often, it is instructive to analyze a violent crime by tracking the perpetrator *and* victim through the phases of the lethal violence sequence. Hall (1987, 1996) identified the five stages of the lethal violence sequence as:

1. Baseline, including history of personality characteristics and events and typical behavior
2. Escalation or triggering phase
3. Killing time/violent event
4. Recovery phase
5. Return to baseline

For profilers, the task is to start with all the available information about the violent event (crime scene and victimology) and work both backward and forward in the sequence. They work backward to attempt to determine why this happened to this victim, at this location, at this particular time. What did the killer(s) do to prepare for the violent event? Knowing the killer's level of preparation helps profilers understand the perpetrator's motivation and fantasy.

Probably very few murders occur without the offender having a prior fantasy. An organized serial killer usually has a very well-developed fantasy (Cook and Hinman, 1996). A "gang-banger" who shoots another adolescent for his athletic shoes probably entertained a fantasy about shooting someone at some time before he went on the prowl with a loaded semi-automatic pistol in the waistband of his shorts. Law enforcement officers who engage in lawful self-defense shootings must have fantasized shooting bad guys. They may not want to do it or enjoy the prospect of doing it. but they *have* imagined doing it, and they have accepted that they could do it if they have to defend themselves or others. They trained to do it — they shot at silhouettes and cartoon bad guy targets in training. An abused spouse fantasizes a violent act of self-defense before enacting it, even if only long enough to pick up a weapon and use it. This does not imply, however, that for all lethal violent crimes involving more than one perpetrator, the participants communicate their fantasies to each other, share the same fantasies, or are even aware that the others may have a homicidal fantasy of any kind.

Working forward in the cycle, the profiler asks: How did the perpetrators attempt to avoid detection? How did he, she, or they leave? What did they do next? What was their post-offense behavior? How might their behavior have stood out or exposed them to detection? What might set off another cycle of violence?

In considering each phase in the lethal violence sequence, the profiler must always consider whether there might be any indications of more than one perpetrator. If there are, then it may be possible for some of their characteristics to be deduced from the available information. The behavioral characteristics may then be compiled into meaningful descriptions of each offender. For example, a crime scene may show evidence of both organized and disorganized behavior. This could indicate that there is a single offender with mixed characteristics, a staged crime scene, or two offenders, one who is organized and one who is disorganized. The following case illustrates some of the points covered thus far.

Case Illustration 1

A double homicide in a rural area in Florida was initially believed to have been committed by multiple offenders, perhaps during a robbery. A male restaurant owner/cook and a waitress were discovered in the early morning hours. Their throats had been cut multiple times. Their hands and feet were bound with lengths of rope. The knots on the rope that bound the male victim were considerably different from the knots on the rope that secured the woman. Two extra lengths of rope were found on the floor. Flour was found on the back of the woman's chair. There was no evidence of sexual activity. There were no signs of forced entry into the restaurant. No money or property was known to be missing from the restaurant, and the victims' vehicles were undisturbed.

The location of the crime and time of crime were considered to be important. It would have been more profitable for the offender to commit a robbery at the close of business. In the morning, only a small amount of start-up money was available.

An important consideration was that two people had been killed together. The killer could have arrived early to kill the male. He could have waited in the parking lot to kill the female. Also, the presence of the extra set of binding ropes was cause for suspicion that more than one victim and possibly more than two victims were targeted.

The locations, number, and severity of the injuries were considered. The male victim was stabbed numerous times in the neck. The attractive female victim had been slashed repeatedly in the throat. This type of vicious, perseverative attack is best described as overkill. *It is often seen in crimes of passion.*

While reviewing this case and attempting to establish the motive for this crime, the profiler considered what the minimum number of offenders necessary to commit this crime might be. The two different types of knots could mean that two different people tied the ropes. This could suggest that there were at least two perpetrators. However, both of the victims could have been sufficiently intimidated and controlled by a single person while the female victim tied the male victim's hands and feet. With the stronger victim secure, the killer could put down his weapon and tie up the weaker victim. The question then arises, why tie them up at all? Some of the most common reasons for restraining victims are to control the victims so the perpetrator can search for valuables without interference or distraction, to secure extra time for an escape, or to dominate/intimidate them and, often, say something to them.

Several individuals who were familiar with the restaurant were interviewed by investigators. They reported that the owner was the only person who cooked in the kitchen. The discovery of flour on the back of the chair in which the waitress was seated was significant. The profilers offered the opinion that the waitress transferred flour to her hands when she tied the cook's hands. She then sat down and transferred the flour from her hands to the back of her chair. The suspect tied her hands and feet with a different type of knot.

In this case, the significance of the third set of bindings and a thorough review of the victims' lives preceding the violent event helped to focus the investigation. The investigators were able to identify a third person who was supposed to begin work on the morning of the homicides. The question then became, who would specifically desire to kill these three people, at this location, at this particular time? A man was soon charged with these two murders. He had gone to the restaurant to kill his former wife on the first day of her job at the restaurant. He imagined that her roommate (the waitress) was involved in an affair with her and that the cook was also her lover. He bound the victims so that he could await the arrival of his former wife. When she arrived, the three individuals he despised could be killed together. His plans went awry when his ex-wife's vehicle failed to start that morning. The killer simply ran out of time, and he forgot to take the bindings he had brought for his wife (the extra set) when he left.

Could this crime have been committed by more than one offender? Certainly. However, only one perpetrator was required to complete all of the criminal activity at the scene. There was no forensic evidence (fingerprints, etc.) suggesting that a second perpetrator had been present. There were no behavior prints of a second killer. It would be unlikely (but not unheard of) for another person to risk being charged with murder in order to stand by and watch as another person carried out a crime of revenge.

Difficulties in Profiling Multiple Perpetrators

For many crimes, the investigators and profilers may fail to accurately determine the number of perpetrators. Often, there is just not enough evidence. Sometimes, the criminal behavior is at variance with what normally occurs in similar crimes. The investigator's ultimate success depends on his or her ability to recognize and interpret the available evidence. When there is a lack of forensic and behavioral evidence, it may be impossible to let the crime scene tell the true story. In some situations with multiple perpetrators, one partner may be dominant and active, while the other is submissive and passive. The inactive participant is less likely to leave forensic evidence. He or she is also less likely to interact with the victim in a way that leaves behind a signature or other behavior print. When that occurs, only the signature of the dominant/active perpetrator may be apparent. As an illustration, consider the following homicide case.

Case Illustration 2

The body of a 71-year-old woman was discovered in a vacant field approximately three miles from her home. She was lying on her back with her feet together. Her wrists were bound (but not tied together) with telephone cord. She was dressed in a knee-length sleep shirt and panties that had been cut across the crotch. She had been sexually battered vaginally and anally, but no semen was identified. She had been shot twice in the head.

Profilers took note of the location of the victim's body in relation to her residence (the point of initial confrontation) and the time of the crime. It appeared that the victim had walked from a vehicle to the location where she laid down and was shot.

Inspection of her residence revealed that the telephone cable had been pulled from the box and the screen on the back porch had been cut to facilitate opening the door. The kitchen window had been pried from the frame, and pieces of glass were neatly placed on a nearby table. The victim's 10-year-old poodle was missing. The cords from both telephones had been removed. In the victim's bedroom, the sheets and a comforter had been removed from the mattress and placed under the bed. There was evidence of blood and fecal material on the sheets.

The victim was the widow of a police chief. His service revolver was missing from a strong box under her bed. Currency from the victim's purse, jewelry, and a VCR had been taken from the house. A towel and latex glove were found on the bathroom counter. Small amounts of blood were found on a bedroom wall and in the garage.

A patrol officer discovered the victim's sedan parked in a wooded area to the north of the victim's residence. Small sticks had been wedged into the door and trunk locks. An oven mitt and a latex glove were recovered near the vehicle.

In order to assess this case and focus on the most likely offender, the investigators looked into the victimology of the deceased woman. She had been a widow for 8 years. Her two grown children and friends described her as an independent and feisty person. She had lived in her home for 15 years. She was described as security conscious and not the kind of person to allow a stranger into her home, especially at night. The victim was last seen in the company of close friends celebrating her birthday at a local restaurant. Neighbors heard the victim's dog bark at approximately 1:30 a.m.

With regard to the scene and time of day (or the "what"), it appeared that the perpetrator came to the residence sometime during the night after the victim returned home and changed into her nightgown. He brought latex gloves, a screwdriver, and a knife, suggesting that he was prepared to force entry into the house and confront the victim. He did not expect to be admitted voluntarily. He disabled the telephone from the outside, cut the screen, broke the window, and climbed inside. Wearing latex gloves, he removed the cords from both telephones. It would be logical to assume that the victim was targeted for a confrontation. If the perpetrator had surveilled her even briefly, he would have known that she led a very active life and was frequently away from her home. If he had wanted only her property, he could have chosen a time when she was absent to commit a burglary.

The location, amount, and severity of the victim's injuries were considered. It seemed reasonable to assume that the victim had been tied to her bed to facilitate a sexual battery and allow the offender to move about the house to search for valuables. The evidence of a confrontation was confined to the victim's bedroom. The offender killed the dog. At the second crime scene (the murder scene), the victim's head had been placed on a pillow. She had been shot in the head twice through the pillowcase. Because nothing in her victimology suggested a different reason for someone to kill her, it seemed most likely that she was killed because she recognized her attacker.

To estimate the age of the offender, the profilers considered several facts. Because the victim's vehicle was taken, it was possible that the offender did not have one. The removal of the VCR, the disposal of the car nearby, and the sticks in the car locks led profilers to suspect some local youth who would be known to or recognized by the victim. This proved to be correct.

What was not surmised in the analysis of the crime and crime scene was the presence of a second teenager. His activity at the scenes was confined to killing the dog to silence its barking. The primary offender could have carried out this homicide alone.

An individual who simply stands and watches while a crime is perpetrated and does not act or interact is virtually invisible even to the best investigator. A second participant can serve as a resource, helping to stage the crime scene or removing evidence from the scene.

The authors recently consulted on a case in which a woman was found bound and strangled. Many aspects of the crime suggested that this was a revenge killing done by a single perpetrator. There was no forensic evidence of a second participant. A troubling aspect of the case was that the victim had been posed in a sexual position; otherwise, the crime did not appear to have been sexually motivated. The sexual posing could have been the signature of a second perpetrator, or it could have been staging. The investigation proved that it was both. There had been an accomplice present in the victim's house. He reportedly did not participate in the actual murder. He confessed to helping to stage the crime to look like a sexual murder. In doing so, he left his own behavior print — he had previously served time for sexual battery.

Guidelines for Evaluating Crimes for Indicators of Multiple Perpetrators

Simplicity can be a key element in the investigation of violent crime that is often overlooked or

Table 10.3

Checklist of Indicators of Single and Multiple Perpetrators of a Violent Crime

Data Type	Data	Single Perpetrator	Multiple Perpetrators
Statistical	Crime statistics — what is typical for type of crime?	Most often single perpetrator (e.g., letter bomb, rape-murder, work-place murder)	Most often involves more than one perpetrator (e.g., drive-by shooting, lynching, large bombing)
Logistical	Location, physical requirements (e.g., weight of victim), number of victims, time frame, etc.	Crime can be carried out by one person, or can *only* be carried out by one person	Crime requires more than one perpetrator
Forensic	Forensic evidence includes fingerprints, shoe prints, serology, blood spatter, hair and fiber, number of weapons, autopsy evidence	No evidence of more than one perpetrator	Evidence suggests more than one perpetrator (e.g., obvious forensics, multiple weapons, wounds inflicted by left- and right-handed person)
Behavioral	Behaviors in committing the crime include *modus operandi*, signature, staging, behavior prints	No evidence of more than one perpetrator	Evidence of more than one type (e.g., "organized" and "disorganized" behavior, different activities with victim)

misunderstood. Investigators sometimes attempt to attach creative scenarios and highly involved motives to essentially simple crimes. For many reasons, they may hypothesize extravagant motivations and complicated mechanics in the commission of murder. According to crime reconstruction expert Rod Englert (personal communication, November 1995), essentially, all murders are committed for fear, revenge, sex, or theft.

The authors caution investigators against developing elaborate hypothetical scenarios with casts of multiple perpetrators unless the crime and crime scene data warrant it. Determining the number of subjects at a crime scene is important in effectively concluding a case and bringing the responsible individuals to justice. It is just as important to be able to rule out the presence of additional suspects. In *Unnatural Death: Confessions of a Medical Examiner* (Baden and Hennessee, 1989), former New York City Medical Examiner Dr. Michael Baden described how forensic pathology (including autopsy findings) provides crucial evidence in murder investigations. At times, forensic pathologists can determine the presence of more than one perpetrator. They may also be able to debunk popular conspiracy theories about multiple assassins of a young President.

Table 10.3 presents a checklist of indicators of single and multiple perpetrators for a given violent crime. Unless the particular crime is one generally associated with groups of offenders *and* the crime and crime scene factors outlined in the checklist point to more than one perpetrator, the authors suggest that the best investigative approach is to look for the minimum number of participants necessary to commit the crime in the way it was carried out. However, keep in mind that additional perpetrators may have been "invisible" with regard to evidence of their presence at the crime scene. FBI profiler Special Agent Joe Navarro (personal communication, 1996) said it very well: "Absence of evidence is not evidence of absence."

Profiling Bombers and Terrorists

The current state of knowledge that allows us to profile violent crimes was developed by law enforcement professionals who studied convicted serial killers and other violent criminals. Their atheoretical, empirical research was augmented by many years of investigative experience and practical information. The core knowledge was accumulated by identifying typologies (e.g., organized and disorganized offenders), identifying commonalities, and understanding the linkages between crime scene behaviors (e.g., MOs and signatures) and offender characteristics (Douglas et al., 1986). It is important that this kind of research be continued and extended to additional types of group and institutional violence, including terrorism and gang violence. Detailed examinations of the various types of group and institutional violence are found elsewhere in this handbook. In what follows, the authors briefly consider typologies that have been developed for bombers and terrorists. As more becomes known about them, better profiles may be developed which will lead to more effective investigative strategies and techniques.

Types of Bombers

Douglas and Olshaker (1996) identified three types of bombers: personal cause, group, and mixed. Personal cause bombers seek revenge or criminal profit. They usually act alone and are often antisocial or paranoid. Group bombers act in conjunction with others. They may belong to an informal group of like-minded individuals, a formal militia group, or a terrorist organization. Recent examples include the terrorist bombing of the TWA plane over Lockerbee, Scotland; international terrorists' bombing of the World Trade Center; and the domestic terrorists' bombing of the Murrah Federal Building in Oklahoma. Some abortion clinic bombings in which an unbalanced person is encouraged by a group to act violently could be categorized as mixed. Groups may also mix. For example, there have been some reports of right-wing terrorist groups supporting anti-abortion groups (Burghart, 1995).

Investigations of arson and bombing always necessitate careful forensic analysis. Physical evidence is often the key to determining whether the event was an intentional crime or accidental. Bombers often can be profiled by their preferred explosives and detonators, and arsonists by their preferred accelerants. Unfortunately, some organizations have opposed legislation mandating the addition of identifying markers in explosives, propellants, and chemicals used to make explosives, thus making it much more difficult to track down the purchasers of materials used in deadly explosions.

Types of Terrorists

There are two general types of terrorism in the U.S. (TRAC, 1993). In domestic terrorism, individuals or groups without foreign direction target the government or citizens. International terrorism refers to terrorist acts committed by individuals or groups based in foreign countries, directed by individuals, groups, or countries outside the U.S., or whose terrorist activities cross national borders.

In 1993, 12 incidents of terrorism were reported in the U.S. Only one terrorist act was committed by international radical fundamentalists — the car bombing of the World Trade Center on February 26. American Front Skinheads were responsible for two bombings in the state of Washington in July. Members of the Animal Liberation Front were responsible for nine bombing incidents in Chicago during a 2-day period in November (TRAC, 1993).

Domestic terrorist groups include left-wing groups, right-wing groups, and special interest groups. The goal of left-wing groups is to bring about socialist revolution. The United Freedom Front and Puerto Rican Armed Forces of National Liberation (FALN) are examples of left-wing groups. Right-wing groups may be racist, anti-Semitic, or both. Right-wing groups include "hate" groups such as the Ku Klux Klan and Skinheads; neo-Nazi groups such as the Aryan Nation; Christian identity groups such as the Aryan Nation, The Order, and the Posse Comitatus; numerous militia groups; and compound dwellers. At a recent presentation to the annual meeting of Hostage Negotiators of America, Dr. Waymon Mullins reported that the favorite weapons of far-right terrorist groups now include explosives, heavy military ordnance, and chemical and biological warfare agents (Leak, 1996). Special interest groups include the Animal Liberation Front and some anti-abortion groups.

Bolz et al. (1996) discussed the purposes and characteristics of terrorism, which include the use of violence to persuade; selection of targets and victims (including women and children) for maximum propaganda value; the use of unprovoked attacks; the use of surprise to circumvent countermeasures; the use of threats, harassment, and violence to create an atmosphere of fear; loyalty only to themselves or kindred groups; and equal employment opportunity for females.

With the emergence of international radical fundamentalism, it is likely that there will be more terrorism directed toward Americans at home and throughout the world. According to the Terrorist Research and Analytical Center (1993, p. 12), "...the international terrorist threat in the United States has both changed and increased, as the aura of invincibility against terrorist attacks on U.S. soil has now been challenged."

The FBI believes that there has been an increase in right-wing terrorist activities in recent years. Whether we have more to fear from acts of terrorism committed by our disaffected fellow citizens or by foreign terrorists remains to be seen. In the final analysis, acts of violence committed by terrorists are subject to the same kinds of investigations as other crimes of violence. With the use of all the investigative techniques available, including forensic laboratory analysis, crime-scene evidence, and profiling, crimes of terror will (it is hoped) be solved, and those responsible brought to justice.

Summary

All evidence indicates that crimes of violence will continue to plague society in the 21st century. Violent crimes committed by multiple perpetrators, such as gang violence and terrorism, are expected to increase. In this chapter, the authors discussed profiling and criminal investigative analysis and a variety of ways to determine whether more than one perpetrator was involved in a violent crime. Profiling is an investigative process with six stages: profiling inputs, decision process model, crime assessment, profile, investigation, and apprehension. Indicators of the number of active participants in a violent crime can be classified as statistical (is this a crime that is typically committed by multiple offenders?), logistical (is this a crime that could not be carried out by an individual acting alone?), forensic (is there forensic evidence such as prints, serology, blood spatter, fibers, autopsy findings, etc. that indicates multiple offenders?), and behavioral (is there behavioral evidence of multiple perpetrators, such as signatures and behavior prints?). The authors used case examples to illustrate key points, discussed the difficulties in profiling multiple offenders, and suggested guidelines for evaluating crimes in which there may have been multiple perpetrators.

Given the predicted increase in violent crimes with multiple perpetrators, it is essential that investigative and profiling knowledge and techniques be developed, extended, and refined to meet these threats to the public safety.

Annotated Bibliography

1. Douglas, J., Ressler, R.K., Burgess, A.W., and Hartman, C.R. (1986) Criminal profiling from crime scene analysis. *Behavioral Sciences and the Law*, *4*(4), 401–421. This article is considered by many to be the "classic" publication on profiling.
2. Geberth, V.G. (1996) *Practical Homicide Investigation: Tactics, Procedures, and Forensic Techniques*, 3rd ed. Boca Raton, FL: CRC Press. A good introduction for law enforcement and for mental health professionals interested in learning the basic "nuts and bolts".

References

Baden, M.M. and Hennessee, J.A. (1989) *Unnatural Death: Confessions of a Medical Examiner*. New York: Random House.

Bolz, F., Dudonis, K.J., and Schultz, D.P. (1996) *The Counter Terrorism Handbook: Tactics, Procedures and Techniques.* Boca Raton, FL: CRC Press.

Burghardt, T. (1995) Neo-Nazis salute the anti-abortion zealots. *Covert Action*, Spring (52), pp. 26–31, 33.

Call, J.A. (1996) The hostage triad: takers, victims, and negotiators. In H.V. Hall (Ed.), *Lethal Violence 2000: A Sourcebook on Fatal Domestic, Acquaintance, and Stranger Aggression*, pp. 561–587. Kamuela, HI: Pacific Institute for the Study of Conflict and Aggression.

Cook, P.E. and Hinman, D.L. (1996) Serial murder. In H.V. Hall (Ed.), *Lethal Violence 2000: A Sourcebook on Fatal Domestic, Acquaintance, and Stranger Aggression*, pp. 363–382. Kamuela, HI: Pacific Institute for the Study of Conflict and Aggression.

De Becker, G. (1997) *The Gift of Fear: Survival Signals that Protect Us From Violence*. Boston: Little, Brown, & Company.

Dietz, P.E., Hazelwood, R.R., and Warren, J. (1990) The sexually sadistic criminal and his offenses. *Bulletin of the American Academy of Psychiatry and Law*, *18*(2), 163–178.

Douglas, J. and Burgess, A.W. (1986) Criminal profiling: a viable investigative tool against violent crime. *FBI Law Enforcement Bulletin*, *55*, 9–13.

Douglas, J. and Munn, C. (1992) Violent crime scene analysis: modus operandi, signature, and staging. *FBI Law Enforcement Bulletin*, February, 2–10.

Douglas, J. and Olshaker, M. (1995) *Mind Hunter: Inside the FBI's Elite Serial Crime Unit*. New York: Scribner.

Douglas, J. and Olshaker, M. (1996) *Unabomber: On the Trail of America's Most-Wanted Serial Killer.* New York: Pocket Books.

Douglas, J., Ressler, R.K., Burgess, A.W., and Hartman, C.R. (1986) Criminal profiling from crime scene analysis. *Behavioral Sciences and the Law*, *4*(4), 401–421.

Egger, S.A. (1990) Linkage blindness: a systematic myopia. In S.A. Egger (Ed.), *Serial Murder: An Elusive Phenomenon*. New York: Praeger.

Federal Bureau of Investigation (1994) *Crime in America: Uniform Crime Reports 1993*. Washington, D.C.: U.S. Government Printing Office.

Federal Bureau of Investigation (1996) *Crime in America: Uniform Crime Reports 1995*. Washington, D.C.: U.S. Government Printing Office.

Feldman, T.B., and Johnson, P.W. (1996) Aircraft hijacking in the United States. In H.V. Hall (Ed.), *Lethal Violence 2000: A Sourcebook on Fatal Domestic, Acquaintance, and Stranger Aggression*, pp. 403–439. Kamuela, HI: Pacific Institute for the Study of Conflict and Aggression.

Franks, L. (1996) Don't shoot: in the new F.B.I., patience comes first. *The New Yorker*, July 22, pp. 26–31.

Geberth, V.G. (1996) *Practical Homicide Investigation: Tactics, Procedures, and Forensic Techniques*, 3rd ed. Boca Raton, FL: CRC Press.

Hall, H.V. (1987) *Violence Prediction: Guidelines for the Forensic Practitioner*. Springfield, IL: Charles C Thomas.

Hall, H.V. (1996) Overview of lethal violence. In H.V. Hall (Ed.), *Lethal Violence 2000: A Sourcebook on Fatal Domestic, Acquaintance, and Stranger Aggression*, pp. 1–51. Kamuela, HI: Pacific Institute for the Study of Conflict and Aggression.

Hare, R.D. (1993) *Without Conscience: The Disturbing World of the Psychopaths Among Us*. New York: Pocket Books.

Hazelwood, R. (1986) The NCAVC training program: a commitment to law enforcement. *FBI Law Enforcement Bulletin*, December, pp. 23–26.

Hazelwood, R., Warren, J., and Dietz, P. (1993) Compliant victims of the sexual sadist. *Australian Family Physician, 22*(4), 474–479.

James, S.H. and Edel, C.F. (in press) *Forensic Applications of Bloodstain Pattern Interpretation*. Boca Raton, FL: CRC Press.

Leak, G. (1996) The right wing. *The U.S. Negotiator*, Spring, pp. 1, 3.

Megargee, E.I. (1982) Psychological correlates and determinants of criminal violence. In M. Wolfgang and N. Weiner (Eds.), *Criminal Violence*, pp. 81–170. Beverly Hills, CA: Sage.

Megargee, E.I. (1993) Aggression and violence. In H.E. Adams and P.B. Sutker (Eds.), *Comprehensive Handbook of Psychopathology*, 2nd ed., pp. 617–644. New York: Plenum Press.

Ressler, R.K., Burgess, A.W., and Douglas, J.E. (1988) *Sexual Homicide: Patterns and Motives*. Lexington, MA: Lexington Books.

Ressler, R.K. and Shachtman, T. (1997) *I Have Lived in the Monster: A Report from the Abyss*. New York: St. Martin's Press.

Terrorism Research and Analytical Center, National Security Division, Federal Bureau of Investigation (1993) *Terrorism in the United States: 1993*. Washington, D.C.: U.S. Department of Justice.

About the Authors

Dayle L. Hinman is a Special Agent for the Florida Department of Law Enforcement and is the Statewide Coordinator of the Criminal Assessment Profile Program. She consults with law enforcement investigators and offers assistance in the analysis of homicide crime scenes. With over 21 years of law enforcement experience, she instructs at numerous police academies in the areas of serial murder investigation and profiling through crime-scene analysis and reconstruction. Special Agent Hinman received a B.S. degree from Florida State University and is currently working on a Master's degree. She was the recipient of a year-long fellowship in the Behavioral Science Unit at the FBI Academy and is one of only 33 graduates of the program. **Patrick E. Cook, Ph.D.,** (University of Texas at Austin), is a Diplomate in Clinical Psychology of the American Board of Professional Psychology. Before entering the private practice of clinical, forensic, and police psychology in Tallahassee, FL, he was an Associate Professor in the Psychology Department at Florida State University. He consults with a number of public safety agencies, including four police departments and a fire department. He is the psychologist on the Tactical Apprehension and Control Team of the Tallahassee Police Department. Dr. Cook is a consultant to the Florida Department of Law Enforcement and a member of the department's Criminal Assessment Profile Program team.

Acknowledgments

The authors wish to thank the following people for their helpful comments on this chapter: John S. Farrell, Chief of the Prince George's County (MD) Police Department and former Chief of Investigations, Metro-Dade Police, Miami, FL; FBI Special Agent, profile coordinator, and counterintelligence expert, Joe Navarro; and Dr. Carolyn Stimel, forensic psychologist.

Chapter 11

DEALING WITH LARGE-SCALE HOSTAGE AND BARRICADE INCIDENTS: IMPLICATIONS FOR NEGOTIATION STRATEGIES AND TRAINING

Theodore B. Feldmann

Hostage and barricade situations represent a serious form of lethal violence; many incidents are on record in which loss of life has occurred. The risk to victims in these incidents can vary considerably depending upon the presence or absence of high risk factors (Fuselier et al., 1991). Factors associated with an increased risk of violence include multiple psychosocial stressors, interpersonal problems with victims, lack of family or social support, and the verbalization of suicidal intent.

The risk factors identified above have come primarily from incidents involving a single subject who is either barricaded alone or who holds a small numbers of hostages. Indeed, it is this type of hostage or barricade situation that is most commonly encountered by police. An on-going study of these events, conducted at the University of Louisville, revealed that nearly 90% of hostage and barricade incidents involved a perpetrator acting alone (Feldmann, 1997).

Although single-perpetrator situations are most common, another type of hostage/barricade event poses an even greater risk of violence for police negotiators. Protracted, large-scale incidents, characterized by organized groups of hostage-takers with many hostages, present a much different management problem. Negotiation strategies employed successfully with a single subject may be ineffective or inadequate when multiple subjects are involved. The potential for lethality also increases markedly under these circumstances. In order to better understand the complexity of large-scale incidents, this chapter: (1) reviews the literature on hostage/barricade situations, (2) examines the dynamics of hostage negotiations, (3) examines four highly publicized incidents along with the negotiation techniques used to address them, (4) discusses the unique aspects of these incidents and their implications for negotiation strategies, and (5) discusses the importance of mental health consultation in these situations.

Historical Overview of Hostage-Taking

The phenomenon of hostage-taking has existed throughout history but has become commonplace during the past 25 years (Call, 1996). A *hostage situation* is defined as one in which a person or persons are held against their will, with release contingent upon certain demands being met (Feldmann and Johnson, 1993). Essential to the hostage situation is the presence of a specific demand. The nature of the demand may vary, including, but not limited to, money, weapons, transportation, food, and alcohol or drugs. Regardless of the type of demand made, the hostage-taker clearly communicates that the hostages will not be released unless certain conditions are met. Thus, without demands, a hostage situation does not exist. This is in contrast to a *barricade situation* in which an individual isolates himself or herself, and perhaps others, but makes no demands other than "go away" or "leave me alone". In such an instance, there is no leverage or bargaining point around which release of those held can be obtained.

The motivations for hostage-taking are many, but traditionally have been summarized as follows: (1) to effect an escape from an interrupted criminal act, (2) to elicit sympathy for radical causes, and (3) to embarrass governments and force a change in domestic or foreign policy (Federal Bureau of Investigation, [FBI], Special Operations and Research Unit, 1981; Fuselier, 1981). More recently, a trend has emerged in which hostages are taken in an attempt to gain retribution for a real or perceived wrongful act, as in domestic violence or workplace violence (Feldmann and Johnson, 1993).

Jenkins et al. (1977) have defined two basic types of hostage situations. The first is the traditional kidnaping in which a hostage is taken to an unspecified location and held for ransom. The second type is the hostage-barricade situation in which one or more persons are seized but no attempt is made to reach a hideout. Rather, the hostage-takers allow themselves to be surrounded in a public place where negotiations are conducted.

A review of case studies by law enforcement officers reveals four categories of persons who take hostages (Fuselier, 1981; Gray, 1981): (1) persons with mental disorders, (2) criminals without mental disorders who planned to take hostages in the commission of a crime or who took hostages because they were interrupted during the crime, (3) prisoners in penal institutions who take hostages in order to escape or effect some change in the penal system, and (4) terrorists who take hostages in order to secure retribution or alleviation of disturbing social conditions.

The mentally ill group comprised over 50% of all hostage-takers (Fuselier, 1981). These persons represent four traditional diagnostic groups: (1) schizophrenia, (2) depression, (3) antisocial personality disorder, and (4) inadequate personality disorder. This latter group corresponds to an outdated *Diagnostic and Statistical Manual*, 2nd ed., diagnostic category which is characterized by low self-esteem and inept responses to stress (American Psychiatric Association, 1968; Strentz, 1983). The inadequate personality may be viewed as related to several of the *Diagnostic and Statistical Manual,* 4th ed. (American Psychiatric Association, 1994) personality disorders which are marked by a high degree of impulsivity and low self-esteem (e.g., the borderline personality disorder).

It has traditionally been thought that the taking of hostages represents an "irrational, mindless, ineffective, or necessarily perilous" activity (Jenkins et al., 1977). In a study conducted by the Rand Corporation, however, Jenkins et al. found that these acts actually have a very high rate of success. In virtually all cases, the hostage-takers receive extensive publicity, and this is often a major objective for the perpetrators. Furthermore, the hostage-takers have nearly an 80% chance of escaping apprehension, punishment, or death. Thus, hostage-taking is an extremely effective and successful type of criminal activity.

History of Hostage Negotiations

In response to the problem of hostage-taking, law enforcement agencies have developed strategies for hostage negotiation. The main impetus for these protocols was the terrorist action against Israeli athletes during the 1972 Munich Olympics (Fuselier, 1981; Schrieber, 1972). As a result, law enforcement agencies around the world have been forced to address the problem of hostage-taking; this has been accomplished through the formation of negotiation teams as well as special weapons and tactics (SWAT) teams (Vandiver, 1981).

The emergence of hostage negotiation teams in the U.S. was pioneered by the New York City Police Department (Schlossberg, 1980). This program was based upon two basic premises: (1) the hostage has no value to the hostage-taker other than serving as a tool or device to attract an audience and gain attention, and (2) the prevention of violence is in the interest of both police and the hostage-taker. The act of hostage taking was viewed as an outcome of frustration and a maladaptive attempt at problem solving. This, in turn, led to hostage negotiation being conceptualized as a specialized form of crisis intervention.

When hostage situations occur, law enforcement personnel must establish meaningful contact with hostile, desperate, or mentally ill individuals. In weighing the demands of hostage-takers vs. the welfare of hostages, negotiators must attempt to engage the subjects through active and empathic listening while, at the same time, leaving open the option of tactical assault (Fuselier, 1986; Noesner and Webster, 1997). Due to the potential for a tragic outcome, a thorough understanding of the dynamics of hostage situations is essential.

The basic goals of hostage negotiation may be summarized as follows: (a) to establish contact with the hostage-takers; (b) to elicit specific information about the event including the number of hostages and hostage-takers, demands, illness or injury to the hostages, and motivations for the incident; and (c) to conduct a meaningful dialogue with the hostage-takers which will result in surrender of the subjects and safe release of the hostages. This dialogue may involve a mutual give-and-take in which some demands are met in exchange for the safe release of the hostages (e.g., trading food for the release of hostages). Other demands, such as for weapons or for a getaway car, are not met under any circumstances. The overall objective of the negotiations is to obtain release of the hostages without any injuries to them, law enforcement officers, or hostage-takers, and without the use of tactical personnel (e.g., SWAT). These strategies have been described extensively by Fuselier (1981).

The Dynamics of Hostage Situations and Negotiations

Hostage situations are fluid events which are influenced by many variables. As a result of these variables, the negotiation of hostage incidents takes on a dynamic quality. A variety of factors, both internal and external to the hostage situation, influences the progress of the negotiations. In order to arrive at a successful outcome, the hostage negotiator must fully understand the dynamics of the situation and be prepared to alter negotiation strategies as needed (Feldmann and Johnson, 1995).

A process with distinct stages may be observed to develop in hostage negotiations. These stages include: (1) exploration of the problem — for example, how many hostages are being held and what are the demands of the hostage-taker; (2) development of a working alliance between the negotiator and the hostage-taker, which is essentially an agreement to work together to resolve the situation; (3) working to achieve a goal — the successful release of the hostages; and (4) termination, which would include the surrender-ritual and the release of the hostages.

As mentioned previously, the interaction of the negotiator with the hostage-taker is complex. The negotiator must possess the ability to develop a working relationship with the hostage-taker. This is often a difficult undertaking because the two parties frequently have conflicting goals. The hostage-taker most often views escape as the optimal outcome of the situation, whereas police negotiators seek surrender or apprehension of the subject. Another difficulty stems from the fact that the hostage-taker may readily resort to violence to obtain his goals, while the negotiator strives to prevent injury or loss of life. When the negotiator is successful in developing a relationship with the hostage-taker, he or she may become a significant and influential figure for the hostage-taker. An appreciation of this may be very helpful in guiding the negotiator.

The emergence of transference-like reactions between the hostage-taker and the negotiator may also occur (Feldmann and Johnson, 1995). During negotiations, for example, the hostage-taker may experience a desire to become one with the negotiator, thus acquiring strength and stability from the relationship. The hostage-taker may manifest a need for accepting and confirming responses from the negotiator. In other instances, there is an idealization of the negotiator as an all-powerful, benevolent figure. When this occurs, the hostage-taker develops an intense trust for the negotiator and desires to gain his or her acceptance. At other times, the hostage-taker comes to view the negotiator as someone very much like himself or herself, essentially an alter-ego. These transferences closely parallel the transferences described in the literature on self psychology (Wolf, 1988).

The stress of the hostage situation may likewise lead to some degree of fragmentation in the hostage-taker. The extent of the fragmentation will be determined in part by the degree of psychopathology present in the hostage-taker. The nature of the hostage situation will also influence the degree of fragmentation. If psychopathology is already present (e.g., the borderline or "inadequate personality" hostage taker), this will be more pronounced. In response to the fragmentation, certain behaviors may be utilized to restore partial cohesion. This may increase the risk of harm to the hostages, particularly if substance abuse or violence is the primary manifestation.

Empathic responses by the negotiator can decrease the degree of fragmentation and stabilize both the fragmenting personality and the negotiation process. In essence, the negotiator must be able to establish a meaningful relationship with the hostage-taker and utilize that relationship to bring about a successful resolution. In addition, during the course of the negotiation process, the negotiator must also use the relationship to stabilize a potentially explosive situation and to convince the hostage-taker that it is in the hostage-taker's best interest to surrender. Many variables complicate this process, including the criminal or violent tendencies of the hostage-taker, the nature of the events which led to the hostage-taking in the first place, the degree of ego integrity possessed by the hostage-taker, and the skill of the negotiator. Other external variables over which the negotiator may have little control, such as media intrusions or unpredictable behavior by the hostages, will also influence the outcome. Thus, the negotiation process is an exceedingly complex one.

Hostage Negotiation Training for Law Enforcement Officers

Hammer et al. (1994) studied the characteristics of police hostage negotiation teams. Their results indicated that over 80% of negotiators were white males. For the majority of officers, hostage negotiation team duty was a part-time activity; most were assigned to patrol or detective operations. Only 45% of teams surveyed had written selection procedures for negotiators.

Training of negotiators was relatively brief; 74% received less than 10 days of initial training, and 44% received less than 5 days of training. Eighty-two percent of teams received less than 10 days of additional training per year, and 61% less than 5 days per year. Joint hostage negotiation team/SWAT training occurred in 44% of teams. In most instances, training was provided by the FBI or by senior team members who had participated in hostage negotiation courses offered at the FBI Academy.

In addition to the formal training of hostage negotiation teams, Noesner and Dolan (1992) have advocated training for uniformed officers who are first responders to the scene of a hostage or barricade situation. Essential components of first responder training include intelligence-gathering functions, attempting to calm the subjects, ensuring the safety of those in the immediate area, and establishing firm perimeters around the scene. Another fundamental component of first-responder training consists of guidelines to help officers avoid entering into premature negotiations with the subjects. The goal of this strategy is to prevent making promises or agreements with the hostage-takers that might complicate or limit the work of the hostage negotiation team. In short, first-responder training should be geared toward control and containment rather than actual negotiation.

Hammer et al. (1994) reviewed the type and frequency of hostage negotiation team call-outs. They found that most hostage negotiation teams (72%) responded to 10 or fewer incidents per year. The most common types of situations to which they responded were barricades, domestic violence, and suicide threats. Mental health professionals were utilized as consultants by 56% of the teams surveyed. In most instances, the sole function of the consultants was to provide post-incident counseling for negotiators.

All of the respondents surveyed cited the need for additional training and information. Specific areas identified included the recognition of psychopathology, assessment of the hostage-taker's emotional stability, resolution strategies, communication skills, and suicide intervention.

The Stockholm Syndrome

The Stockholm Syndrome is defined as an emotional response on the part of persons held hostage in which they develop strong positive feelings toward the captors and simultaneous negative feelings toward the police (Strentz, 1980). This syndrome was first identified in 1973 following a bank robbery in Stockholm, Sweden, in which four female bank employees were held hostage for 131 hours by a pair of armed robbers. Over the course of this incident, the hostages came to believe that their captors were actually protecting them from the police. Two of the hostages went on to develop romantic attachments to the robbers, with one of them eventually marrying one of the subjects.

This phenomenon can be understood as an unconscious reaction to stress in which the victim identifies with the captor as a way of dealing with the trauma of the event. It may be considered a function of the defense mechanisms of identification with the aggressor and regression. One factor that appears to influence the development of the Stockholm Syndrome is time; the longer the hostages are held, the more likely this phenomenon will be observed. The behavior of the hostage-takers will also influence its development. Hostage-takers who are viewed as relatively benign, or even considerate, will more likely be identified with in a positive manner. The Stockholm Syndrome has been observed in a number of hostage incidents and may interfere with negotiations because the hostages view police, not the hostage-takers, as the real threat.

The Protracted Large-Scale Incident

Hostage negotiation teams are most often confronted with a single subject who is either barricaded alone or holds only a small number of hostages (Feldmann, 1997). The offenders are most often motivated by an interpersonal dispute or grievance complicated by an underlying psychiatric disorder. In fact, 91% of 155 subjects studied in Kentucky had a psychiatric diagnosis. The majority of these incidents was associated with some expression of suicidal intent. The success of negotiation in these cases, therefore, depended greatly on the crisis intervention skills of the negotiator.

A much different situation exists in those cases involving multiple hostage-takers or barricaded subjects who have complex demands and goals. The presence of significant numbers of hostages also complicates management strategy. By virtue of their complexity, these situations often are of protracted durations. This section of the chapter examines four such incidents. The case illustrations presented here are not intended to serve as critiques of negotiation plans or tactical options, but rather are discussed to illustrate the unique aspects of large-scale hostage/barricade situations.

The Atlanta and Oakdale Prison Riots

In November 1987, the two longest simultaneous sieges of U.S. prisons occurred in Oakdale, LA, and Atlanta, GA (Fuselier et al., 1989). These incidents originated with the "Marielito" boatlift which occurred between April and October 1980, when approximately 125,000 Cuban refugees arrived in the U.S. from the Cuban port of Mariel. Among this group were 2750 men imprisoned in Cuba for various crimes or psychiatric conditions, all of whom were deemed by the U.S. Immigration and Naturalization Service (INS) as unfit for admission into the U.S. As a result of the INS ruling, these men were detained at federal correctional facilities in Atlanta and Oakdale.

On November 20, 1987, the U.S. State Department informed the Department of Justice that an agreement had been reached with the Cuban government that would result in many of the Cuban detainees being returned to their homeland. In spite of efforts to increase prison security, 987 detainees at Oakdale rioted on November 21, 1987, taking 36 hostages and setting fire to prison buildings. On Monday, November 23, 1987, 1370 Cuban detainees in Atlanta rioted, setting fire to three buildings and taking 102 hostages. The Oakdale siege lasted until November 29, 1987, while the Atlanta standoff ended on December 4, 1987.

These incidents were managed jointly by the FBI and the Bureau of Prisons (BOP). Negotiators from both agencies were sent to Oakdale and Atlanta. Negotiators from the Atlanta Police Department also responded to the Georgia incident.

The primary demand by inmates at both sites was that none of them be returned to Cuba. The far-reaching nature of this demand led to a complex command structure in which the on-scene commanders at Atlanta and Oakdale reported to senior officials at the FBI and BOP, who in turn consulted with other government officials through the office of the Attorney General.

Negotiation strategies were governed by concern for the potential large-scale loss of life. The development of an effective negotiation plan was complicated by a number of factors (Bell et al, 1991). A major difficulty, particularly at Atlanta, was the physical configuration of the prisons. Buildings had been added to both facilities over time as needed, making it impossible to visually observe all areas of the prisons. Thus, the gathering of intelligence was greatly limited. Hostages were held at multiple locations at both Oakdale and Atlanta, and many of the prison buildings were separated by substantial distances. As a result, two significant difficulties were encountered. First, it was impossible to accurately ascertain the number of hostages being held. Second, uncertainty about where the hostages were being held precluded the development of assault strategies, a fact that the inmates fully recognized.

Another complicating factor for negotiation involved communication problems. This issue emerged in response to the sheer number of individuals involved in the incident, competition between various inmate groups for control and influence, and the large number of law enforcement and emergency personnel responding to the incident. For example, face-to-face negotiation generally involved five or six federal negotiators and a like number of inmates.

Proposals outlined during these sessions were then taken by hostage negotiators to the on-scene command post and then relayed to senior officials in Washington, D.C. In a similar manner, the inmate negotiators required prolonged periods of time to discuss negotiation points with the larger inmate population. It was not uncommon for relatively minor issues to require up to 10 hours to notify all parties.

Closely related to the problem of communication was the difficulty authorities had in identifying inmate leaders. Multiple factions emerged from the inmate population and claimed to represent the entire group. Many incidents occurred in which agreements reached with self-proclaimed leaders were rejected by other inmate groups. Although no clearly defined leader ever emerged, negotiators did identify a loose coalition of inmates with the greatest influence over the entire group. Ultimately, it was more important to identify the inmates' decision-making process than individual decision makers.

Language was a major problem for negotiators from the outset. Spanish was the primary language for all the Cuban detainees; only a few of the inmates spoke English well enough to negotiate in that language. The first FBI negotiator on the scene was fluent in Spanish, but difficulty was encountered in finding enough Spanish-speaking negotiators for the duration of the incident. At one point during the incident, a decision was made by the on-scene commanders to conduct negotiations in English only. The rationale for this decision was twofold. First, it ensured that the government's position was clearly articulated. Second, it forced the Cuban detainees to think through their responses carefully. This activity also added to the stress and fatigue experienced by the inmates. Eventually, the detainees requested to speak to bilingual negotiators and released hostages as a gesture of good faith when the government agreed. This led to an increased use of Spanish-speaking negotiators during the final days of the siege.

An issue closely related to language concerned the cultural differences between the Cuban detainees and the negotiators. Dramatic speeches about their plight and emotional outbursts, such as threats to kill all of the hostages, were frequently observed early in the negotiation process. As the incident progressed, negotiators realized that these statements were more cultural expressions of bravado than actual statements of intent. The threats could, therefore, be interpreted in another context. Concessions on both sides were also viewed differently because of cultural issues. The Cuban detainees were less interested in bilateral exchanges and, instead, placed great value on one side making a unilateral concession as a gesture of good faith. According to their view of the negotiation process, the other side was then obligated to reciprocate. When this was recognized by government negotiators, the negotiation process accelerated rapidly.

Obviously, the duration of the incident placed great stress on both sides. The government utilized two different negotiation teams, each working 12-hour shifts. Although this plan helped the negotiators deal with fatigue, it also disrupted continuity. Lengthy orientation and "catch up" periods were required at the beginning of each new shift.

Mental health professionals were utilized throughout the incident. One member of the mental health team sat in on face-to-face negotiations in order to observe the inmate negotiators and monitor the dynamics of the event. Others were assigned the tasks of developing psychological profiles of the inmate leaders, assessing stress and fatigue, and reviewing prison medical records for the presence of psychiatric illness among the inmates.

The successful resolution of the Atlanta and Oakdale sieges resulted from careful attention to each of the factors described above. The circumstances surrounding these two incidents necessitated that usual negotiation strategies be modified to fit the unique characteristics of these events. Negotiations were constantly modified and reassessed according to the changing nature of the incidents.

Ruby Ridge, Idaho

In 1983, Randy and Vicki Weaver moved to northern Idaho from Cedar Falls, IA. The Weavers were Christian fundamentalists whose religious views led them to reject modern society (Morganthau et al., 1995). They were survivalists who believed in the imminence of a biblical Apocalypse and were also sympathetic to many beliefs espoused by the Aryan Nation group.

In 1986, Randy Weaver sold two sawed-off shotguns to Kenneth Fadeley, an informer for the Bureau of Alcohol, Tobacco, and Firearms (BATF). The BATF later tried to use the threat of prosecution to force Weaver to spy on the neo-Nazi underground in Idaho and Montana. Weaver refused to cooperate, and in early 1991 was arrested and charged with a weapons violation. Weaver and his family then fled to a cabin on Ruby Ridge, where they stayed for 18 months. The U.S. Marshals Service tried in vain to negotiate with Weaver and finally decided to force him out despite the fact that Weaver was known to have a large number of weapons and an ample supply of ammunition in the cabin.

On August 21, 1992, a team of marshals on a reconnaissance mission ran into Weaver's 14-year-old son, Sammy, and 24-year-old Kevin Harris, near the family cabin. Sammy Weaver and a Deputy U.S. Marshal, William Degan, were killed in an ensuing shootout. The next day, the FBI's Hostage Rescue Team (HRT) was deployed around the cabin.

According to FBI Director Louis J. Freeh (1995), the FBI responded to Ruby Ridge subsequent to the BATF investigation of Randy Weaver. The FBI response came after the U.S. Marshals Service had conducted an 18-month investigation and surveillance of Weaver. The actual FBI deployment occurred on August 21, 1992, after Degan's death. The FBI acted upon information provided by other law enforcement agencies; this information led the FBI to believe that it was facing a grave threat that required a prompt response.

The rules of engagement adopted by the HRT at Ruby Ridge stated that, under certain circumstances, certain persons "can and should" be the subject of deadly force. Although such rules were contrary to FBI policy, some SWAT personnel on the scene interpreted the rules as a "shoot-on-sight" policy.

On August 22, 1992, an FBI sniper fired two shots, one of which killed Vickie Weaver. The sniper took his first shot when he observed Randy Weaver raise a rifle toward the sky; the sniper believed that Weaver was attempting to fire at a police helicopter. The second shot, which struck Mrs. Weaver, was intended for an armed subject the FBI agent saw running toward the cabin. The sniper testified before a congressional hearing that he did not see Mrs. Weaver standing in the vicinity.

In 1993, Randy Weaver and Kevin Harris went on trial for Degan's death. An Idaho jury acquitted both men of murder and conspiracy; Weaver ultimately served 4 months in prison for missing his court date on the original weapons charge. The Weaver family sued the government for $200 million for the wrongful death of Vicki Weaver. Following months of negotiation, the Department of Justice agreed to pay $3.1 million to Randy Weaver and his three surviving children for the shooting death of his wife and their mother. The eventual settlement agreement admitted no wrongdoing or legal liability by the Department of Justice (Morganthau et al., 1995).

The Branch Davidian Siege

Perhaps the most widely known and most controversial large-scale hostage/barricade incident is the Branch Davidian standoff in Waco, TX, which lasted from February 28, 1993, until April 19, 1993. The culmination of this siege was an FBI raid on the compound in which David Koresh, leader of the Branch Davidians, and 85 of his followers died in a fire that was thought to have been set by the group. The following summary of events in Waco was compiled from documents prepared for the government's investigation of the incident (Dennis, 1993; Department of Justice, 1993).

The initial raid on the compound was conducted by the BATF on Sunday morning, February 28, 1993. Government agents were attempting to execute arrest and search warrants against Koresh and his followers. The precipitant for the assault was evidence that the group had amassed large quantities of illegal weapons and ammunition. The Branch Davidians, who apparently had advance knowledge of the government raid, opened fire on the federal agents, killing four BATF officers and wounding 16 others. An undisclosed number of Branch Davidians, including Koresh, were wounded.

By Sunday afternoon, units of the FBI's HRT arrived on the scene, and the FBI assumed overall command of the incident. Telephone negotiations with Koresh began almost immediately. Among the first major developments in the negotiation process was a decision to allow Koresh to broadcast his religious beliefs on a Dallas radio station and to give an interview to the Cable News Network (CNN).

The initial set of negotiations produced promising results, as indicated by the release of 10 children from the complex on Monday, March 1. Later that day, however, Koresh became agitated when FBI agents in armored vehicles were deployed around the perimeter of the compound. Negotiators also cut the telephone lines for all outgoing calls except to the negotiating command post. In spite of his displeasure with these developments, however, Koresh repeatedly assured negotiators that a mass suicide was not being contemplated.

The primary demands verbalized by David Koresh early in the standoff were for a forum in which he could articulate his religious beliefs. On March 2nd, he prepared a 1-hour audio tape of his religious teachings and agreed to surrender if the tape was broadcast nationally. In spite of the government's agreement to allow the Christian Broadcasting Network to play the tape, Koresh later refused to leave the compound.

Over the next few days, several children and adults left the compound. One of the released children carried a note stating that the adults in the compound were prepared to die. In spite of vague threats and references to the end of the world, Koresh continued to deny plans for a mass suicide. On March 4th, two FBI profilers warned that increased tactical presence by authorities could result in violence by the Branch Davidians. Other experts, however, provided what the FBI called "inconsistent information" regarding the risk of violence.

By Saturday, March 6, FBI negotiators were frustrated by the lack of progress and expressed concern that negotiations were at an impasse. During that weekend, the FBI refused to allow delivery of milk to the compound unless more children were released. Koresh rejected this position by saying that the children were his biological descendants. At this point, the debate within the FBI over tactical options began to increase.

Electrical power to the compound was cut on March 9. Koresh responded to this by breaking off negotiations until the power was restored. In an effort to maintain the negotiation process, the government agreed to turn the power back on. At the same time, HRT members reported seeing weapons in the windows of the compound, further increasing concerns that a negotiated settlement was not possible.

The on-scene commanders expressed considerable concern that Koresh was exerting too much control over the situation and not negotiating in good faith. In response to that issue, electrical power was again cut off on Friday, March 12. It was also hoped that this decision would increase the level of stress and discomfort within the compound and persuade additional Branch Davidians to surrender.

On Sunday night, March 14, the FBI began to illuminate the compound with the intention of disrupting the Davidians' sleep and placing more pressure upon them; an additional reason cited by federal authorities was to increase the safety of HRT personnel deployed around the compound. Another change in strategy was the FBI's decision to refuse to listen or respond to Koresh's extended religious statements.

Subsequent FBI negotiation strategies included an increasingly confrontational stance with the Branch Davidian leader. Negotiators challenged Koresh about his truthfulness and sincerity in the negotiation process. Simultaneously, the FBI made a decision to increase the tactical pressure on the compound. This began on March 18, when a message was broadcast over loudspeakers to the Branch Davidians saying that all those who surrendered would be treated fairly by the government.

In spite of these efforts, little progress was made. On March 19, in response to concerns expressed by the group, legal documents from Koresh's attorneys were delivered to the compound. The response from Koresh was that he was ready to surrender. At the same time, two people left the compound and were taken into custody. The next day, another woman left the compound. Early on Sunday morning, March 21, two other Davidians came out; Koresh, however, still refused to leave. That evening, in response to the latest perceived impasse, the FBI decided to begin playing Tibetan chants over loudspeakers surrounding the compound. The response from Koresh was that no other people would leave the compound.

On Monday, March 22, the FBI held a meeting to discuss negotiation and tactical strategy. One option considered was the introduction of teargas as a nonlethal alternative to clear the compound. FBI negotiators, however, continued to press for a peaceful resolution to the incident. The next morning, another Branch Davidian left the compound; this person would be the last of the group to surrender. During the nights of March 23 and 24, the FBI resumed its pressure tactics of shining bright lights into the compound and playing both Tibetan chants and Christmas music. Audiotapes of messages from Branch Davidians who had left the compound and of previous negotiation sessions, as well as sounds of rabbits being slaughtered, which sounded like the cries of infant humans, were also played. The goal, again, was to raise the level of psychological pressure on the people within the compound, forcing either surrender or a resumption of meaningful negotiations. When these efforts were unsuccessful, FBI negotiators became more confrontational with Koresh by calling him a liar and a coward.

After several days of inactivity, the FBI decided to allow a face-to-face meeting between Koresh and his attorney on Monday, March 29. Two more meetings took place the following day. As a result of these meetings, Koresh issued a vague statement indicating that the group would surrender in early April following their observance of Passover. This pledge was reiterated on April 4. During this time frame, the FBI continued to broadcast loud music throughout the night. In spite of Koresh's assurances, however, the group did not surrender after Passover. This latest setback in the negotiation process once again triggered a debate about tactical options, including the use of teargas.

On Friday, April 9, Koresh sent a letter to the FBI saying, "the heavens are calling you to judgment." Behavioral science experts examined the letters and concluded that Koresh was possibly psychotic and unlikely to voluntarily leave the compound. This belief, in part, led the FBI to finalize an assault plan using teargas; this option was then presented to U.S. Attorney General Janet Reno for approval. In the interim, HRT members began installing concertina wire around the compound.

On April 13, Koresh stated that he would not leave the compound until God instructed him to do so. Negotiations were complicated by his insistence on citing and interpreting biblical passages. The next day, Koresh sent a message to the authorities indicating that he would not consider surrender until he had completed writing a manuscript explaining the Seven Seals from the Book of Revelations.

During this time, the FBI continued to examine its tactical options, particularly with respect to the effects of teargas on children. Those in favor of a tactical resolution not only cited the impasse in negotiations but also the fact that the Davidians were thought to have enough provisions to last 1 year. The FBI had come to believe that time was no longer on their side; fatigue had started to plague HRT snipers, along with fears that their positions were within range of the Branch Davidians' .50-caliber rifles. Officials also believed that Koresh was becoming more paranoid; psychological profiles developed of Koresh portrayed him as someone who believed himself to be invincible. Finally, authorities were also concerned about reports that Koresh was sexually abusing children within the compound. Against this backdrop, assault appeared to be the only viable option left.

By Friday, April 16, Koresh announced that he had finished his manuscript on the First Seal. That same day, Attorney General Reno rejected the teargas assault plan. On Saturday, however, a meeting was held in Washington, D.C., to reconsider a tactical resolution and to outline the rules of engagement. The plan was then approved and presented to President Clinton on Sunday.

At 5:59 a.m. on Monday, April 19, the Branch Davidians were notified that an assault was imminent and were ordered to surrender. Koresh was told exactly where the teargas was coming from so that he could move the children away; in response to this gesture, Koresh threw the telephone out the front door. Shortly after 6:00 a.m., two combat engineering vehicles began inserting teargas into the compound. The Branch Davidians responded with gunfire, and Koresh instructed his followers to don gas masks. The compound was gassed throughout the morning, but by 9:30 a.m., high winds began dispersing the teargas. Assault vehicles then began breaching the walls of the main building to provide the Davidians an exit route; this activity continued until 11:45 a.m. At 12:07 p.m., the Davidians began setting fires throughout the compound. Koresh was called again at 12:12 p.m. and was told to lead the group out of the compound. Nine people left at that point and were taken into federal custody. By 12:25 p.m., gunfire was heard from within the compound, leading to fears that the Davidians were killing themselves or each other. Firefighting efforts began at 12:41 p.m., but were largely unsuccessful. By the time the fires were extinguished, 86 Branch Davidians, including Koresh, were dead.

The Freemen Standoff

The Freemen standoff, which occurred near Jordan, MT, lasted 81 days, from March 25 until June 13, 1996. The origin of this incident can be traced to March 8, 1994, when the group announced a $1 million bounty for the arrest and conviction of public officials involved in a foreclosure action against Ralph Clark's farm. The group itself was loosely organized around opposition to all forms of organized government (Piernick, 1997). Scattered cells of the group, located primarily in the western U.S., attempted to disrupt local and state governments by placing property liens against elected officials.

In September 1995, the Freemen moved their headquarters to Clark's property (Annin and Hosenball, 1996). On October 3, 1995, U.S. Marshals sold the farm at an auction, but the group refused to vacate the area. During the ensuing months, the FBI investigated LeRoy Schweitzer, the group's leader, and his second in command, Daniel Petersen, on charges of fraud, conspiracy, armed robbery, and threats against federal officials. On March 25, 1996, FBI agents captured the men on the edge of the Clark property. Agents then surrounded the ranch, marking the beginning of the standoff.

When the incident began, 26 people were in the complex referred to by the Freeman as "Justus Township". The group initially ate barbecue meals together and watched satellite television (Beals and Peyser, 1996). One member of the organization, who later surrendered, described the atmosphere as "like camping". Over time, however, the group became bored and riddled with competing factions which were unable to agree on demands or a negotiation strategy.

Throughout the incident, various members of the Freemen left the ranch and surrendered to authorities. By the time the standoff was resolved on May 16, 1996, only 16 people remained in the compound.

Negotiations were conducted continuously throughout the duration of the incident (Romano, 1997). Certain demands, such as for cigarettes, were met by the FBI, but these were delivered only one pack at a time. The FBI negotiation strategy was described as accommodation coupled with slowly increasing levels of pressure.

During the course of the incident, the FBI allowed 45 outside mediators to negotiate with the Freemen. On April 17, 1996, five Freemen met with Montana State Representative Karl Ohs. On April 27, 1996, the FBI allowed James "Bo" Gritz, a right-wing activist, to enter the compound; by May 1, however, Gritz gave up negotiation attempts, saying that the Freemen had taken an "oath to God" not to leave the compound until their demands were met. On May 15, 1996, Colorado State Senator Charles Duke arrived in Jordan and arranged the first face-to-face meeting between the Freemen and two FBI negotiators. These talks, however, broke down on May 21 following a confrontation between Duke and one of the Freemen.

Negotiations were complicated by the absence of clear-cut demands. At various times, the Freemen attempted to argue their constitutional right to self rule as well as their belief that the federal government had no jurisdiction over them. On other occasions, the group demanded the release of Schweitzer and Petersen as well as guarantees that all charges related to the case would be dropped. When the Montana attorney general agreed to drop all state charges against the group, however, the Freemen refused to surrender. FBI negotiators reported that the Freemen would stamp negotiation documents with the phrase "refused for cause" at the end of each session. In the end, the Freemen settled for a promise to allow a Montana state legislator to safeguard a truck full of documents that they believed substantiated their complaint against the government.

One problem for negotiators was the presence of children in the compound. Members of the group used the children as shields. One participant, who sought refuge at the ranch rather than lose custody of her two children, was quoted as saying, "They absolutely knew that the FBI would not come in as long as the children were there." In fact, the 16 remaining Freemen gave up 1 day after the last child departed.

On May 31, 1996, the FBI moved three armored cars and a helicopter to its staging area in an attempt to increase the pressure on the group. Electricity to the compound was shut off on June 3, and the helicopter began making aerial patrols over the ranch. This may have been the turning point in the incident. The Freemen had already run out of certain items, such as toothpaste and toilet paper. Without electricity, the water pump that supplied the compound went dry. Although the Freemen had generators, they barely supplied enough power to keep essential appliances working. Food supplies in the compound were dangerously low.

The Clark property was comprised of eight buildings occupying an area of 960 acres. As a result, there was no viable assault option (Romano, 1997). In spite of this fact, which was not fully appreciated by the Freemen, the FBI decided to gradually increase the threat of force. This was done by moving the news media farther away from the compound and by positioning armored vehicles within visual range of the compound. These actions, coupled with the helicopter overflights and the loss of electricity, served to heighten the Freemen's sense of vulnerability.

On June 6, 1996, four subjects, including two children, left the compound. Three outside negotiators from a right-wing legal foundation met twice with Freemen inside the ranch on June 10. The next day, Edwin Clark, who had assumed leadership of the group, was flown to Billings, where he presented a proposed surrender agreement to Schweitzer, who reportedly gave his approval. When the last child left the compound on June 12, the FBI began dismantling the negotiating tent and relocating the vans parked nearby in apparent preparation for the surrender. This act further reinforced for the Freemen that their position was untenable. On June 13, 1996, the 16 remaining Freemen surrendered to authorities.

Implications for Hostage Negotiation Strategies

The case illustrations presented in this chapter indicate that significant differences exist between hostage/barricade situations involving multiple subjects as compared to those involving perpetrators acting alone. Clearly, each of the incidents described above was associated with unique characteristics which complicated negotiation and overall management. This implies that negotiation strategies must take these characteristics into consideration in order to maximize the success of negotiations.

Factors Influencing the Outcome of Negotiations

In crisis situations, such as hostage or barricade incidents, certain key factors can be identified. These factors include the passage of time, the amount of intelligence available on the situation, media intrusions, public opinion and other political considerations, decision-making processes, psychopathology and the related issues of suicide and substance abuse, and unexpected developments. The successful crisis manager exerts maximal control over these factors to reach a successful outcome (Bracey, 1980).

Passage of Time. In general, the passage of time is viewed as an ally in hostage/barricade situations. This occurs for several reasons. First, time is required for negotiators to establish a working relationship and rapport with the subjects. As that relationship evolves, negotiators are able to obtain more information about the nature of the situation. Time also allows the on-scene commander to consult with both negotiators and tactical personnel to better formulate management strategy. Finally, if hostages are present, the passage of time generally leads to some degree of personalization of the relationship between the hostage-takers and hostages. In most instances, the greater degree of personalization that occurs, the lower the risk of harm to the hostages. The effect of a personal relationship between the hostages and hostage-takers may be summarized as follows: When the hostage-takers view hostages as unique individuals, as opposed to nameless/faceless objects, they will be much less inclined to do anything that will cause harm or injury.

During protracted incidents, however, the passage of time may both help and hinder negotiations. In all four of the situations described in this chapter, law enforcement personnel had adequate time to establish command and control procedures. Likewise, deadlines or demands issued by the perpetrators were never an issue. During the Atlanta/Oakdale standoffs and the Freemen incident, time was used effectively to build a negotiation process which ultimately led to the surrender of all barricaded subjects and the safe release of all hostages. At Ruby Ridge and Waco, however, a point arrived when authorities came to view the passage of time in a negative way.

The common denominator in the Ruby Ridge and Waco sieges was the perception that failure to negotiate a settlement within a time frame deemed reasonable by command personnel represented an impasse that could only be resolved by increased pressure. At Ruby Ridge, this pressure was manifested by rules of engagement permitting snipers to open fire on the cabin. Increased pressure at Waco was accomplished at first by a change in negotiation strategy followed by emphasis on a tactical resolution.

Stone (1993) described the marked transformation of negotiation styles that occurred at Waco. He referred to the initial phase of the engagement as one of "conciliatory negotiation". This strategy resulted in the establishment of an on-going dialogue with Koresh and the surrender of 37 people, including 21 children. In spite of that progress, Koresh had broken one agreement after another with the negotiators. This led to increased frustration among both negotiators and on-scene commanders, and created increasing pressure from tactical leaders for an assault option. The result of this process was a shift to what Stone called a "mixed-message" strategy in which negotiators became more confrontational, mocking, and harassing. During the final phase of the standoff, the process of negotiation was abandoned except as a means of maintaining communication with the compound. Additionally, various tactics were used to disorient and stress the barricaded subjects. These included the use of bright lights and noises at night to disrupt sleep, and the deployment of armored vehicles in proximity to the compound to intimidate the Branch Davidians. In the end, the on-scene commanders and officials in Washington, D.C. equated the passage of time with failure. Thus, the only option left was the insertion of teargas into the compound followed by an assault.

How can differences in the view of time between Atlanta/Oakdale and the Freemen standoff, on the one hand, and Ruby Ridge and Waco, on the other, be explained? Although many complex factors came into play, the most obvious difference in the latter two situations was that federal officers were killed and wounded. That tragic fact generated an intense, and understandable, pressure to act, resulting in what Stone (1993) described as an "action imperative" and "military mentality". Organizational, command, and budgetary issues also influenced decision-making processes as both incidents progressed. These factors may well have overridden the traditional view that time is on the side of law enforcement during protracted standoffs.

Intelligence. The gathering of accurate and reliable intelligence about a hostage or barricade situation is essential to effective crisis management and, ultimately, a peaceful resolution. Essential information includes data collected from direct communication with or observation of the perpetrators including identity, motivation for the event, goals that the subjects hope to achieve, demands, weapons present, observable symptoms of mental illness, suicidal ideation, and drug or alcohol use. Information regarding the hostages must also be obtained. This includes the number of people held, their condition, and relationship (if any) to the hostage-takers. External sources of intelligence are also extremely important; prior criminal history, mental health records, and collateral interviews with witnesses, family members, and friends should be conducted by members of the negotiation team.

In the large-scale incidents discussed in this chapter, intelligence gathering was hampered by several factors. The most obvious was the size of each incident. The prison layouts in Atlanta and Oakdale prevented direct visual observation of both inmates and hostages. The same situation applied at Waco. In both instances, information about what was happening within the prisons and compounds was limited to what negotiators were told by the subjects. There was no way for this information to be validated. This, in turn, increased the pressure on negotiators to establish open and trusting relationships with the perpetrators.

A somewhat different situation existed during the Ruby Ridge and Freemen situations. The respective compounds were more open to direct observation but the nature of the surrounding landscape made it impossible for the deployment of forward observation posts without placing officers in dangerously exposed positions. This necessitated gathering visual intelligence from great distances.

Difficulty was also encountered in determining the number and identity of both the subjects and the hostages. This, in turn, made it difficult to identify the group leaders, particularly at Atlanta and Waco. Even more disturbing to law enforcement officers on the scene was the lack of information about weapons possessed by the barricaded subjects. Intelligence at Waco and Atlanta tended to underestimate the weaponry in possession of the subjects, while at the Freemen standoff, armament was overestimated. The combination of inadequate information regarding the number and identity of subjects and their weapons created an unstable and insecure environment for police that led to frequent disagreements between negotiators and tactical personnel.

Media. Dealing with the media is often problematic during hostage/barricade situations. These are high-profile events from a media standpoint and are guaranteed to attract intense coverage. The major areas of concern regarding media relationships are the following: (1) intrusion of reporters or camera crews inside the outer perimeter, (2) direct contact via telephone or other modality between the hostage-takers and the media, (3) live television coverage of the incident which allows the perpetrators to observe tactical planning and maneuvering, and (4) media criticism of or commentary about incident management that unduly influences command decisions. Close cooperation between the on-scene commander and the agency's public affairs officer can minimize many of these disruptions. Likewise, secure telephone lines and control over electricity into the crime scene is essential.

In all four of the cases presented in this chapter, media coverage was extensive. Due to its isolated location, Ruby Ridge received the least amount of live coverage. Nevertheless, media reports about the duration of the standoff led to public perception of an impasse which may have hastened a change in the rules of engagement. Media response to the Atlanta incident was so extensive that logistical problems were encountered in moving personnel and supplies into the prison. A similar situation existed at Waco, where media vehicles clogged the county roads leading into the compound, resulting in delays in moving essential traffic in the staging areas. The relatively flat, wide-open geography around the Freemen in Montana led to problems maintaining a secure outer perimeter; media units, particularly during the early stages of the standoff, frequently ventured too close to the buildings on the farm.

The most significant impact of media coverage, however, concerned public perception of how the incidents were managed. Marked contrasts existed between the Ruby Ridge and Waco incidents as compared to the Atlanta/Oakdale and the Freemen incidents. The former were widely criticized by the media, leading to a general view that the government was not in adequate control of the situations. The latter incidents, however, were seen as models of effective negotiation and restraint. These perceptions engendered by the media, whether positive or negative, invariably influenced management decisions at the scene and also at higher administrative levels in Washington, D.C.

Public Relations. Effective management of the news media interfaces closely with image and public relations issues. Other considerations include external political considerations that may force a premature tactical intervention. For example, consider the political ramifications of an extended barricade situation occurring on a busy downtown street during rush hour. Although extended negotiation may result in surrender of the subject, disruption of traffic patterns as well as inconvenience to businesses and the public may force department administrators or city officials to pressure the on-scene commander into an early assault. Tactical intervention, in turn, increases the risk of injury to the perpetrators, hostages, law enforcement officers, and the public. Unfortunately, on-scene commanders often find themselves in a difficult position *vis-a-vis* these external pressures.

This was clearly the case at Waco. Stone (1993), in his review of the Branch Davidian incident, described a flawed decision-making process which was influenced, at least in part, by political and budgetary considerations. As that situation progressed, the negotiating team had less input into the management process while advocates of a tactical solution gained increasing influence. On the other hand, the lessons learned from Waco allowed the government to adopt a much different stance during the Freemen standoff. The FBI took a more proactive position in managing public relations in Montana, allowing the on-scene commanders to focus on a negotiated settlement. Public relations issues must never be underestimated during protracted group hostage or barricade incidents.

Decision-Making. Decision-making processes clearly influence the management of these situations. The successful resolution of hostage and barricade incidents requires a clearly defined chain of command, as well as open communication between the parties involved. In most police departments and federal law enforcement agencies, the tactical and negotiation commanders report directly to the on-scene commander. Inevitably, some disagreement occurs between negotiation and SWAT personnel regarding management of the incident. The on-scene commander must fully appreciate the roles and capabilities of both teams in order to make effective decisions. It is often difficult to determine the point at which negotiation is no longer a viable option; negotiators tend to push for open-ended time frames, while tactical officers often rush to an assault. The on-scene commander must carefully evaluate and weigh these competing interests.

The Atlanta/Oakdale prison riots can be viewed as models for interagency coordination and cooperation. The FBI and BOP established a clear chain of command both on the scene and in Washington, D.C. A similar situation existed during the Freemen incident. It is interesting to note that no viable assault option existed in any of these situations. As a result, conflicts between negotiators and tactical leaders were minimal. The on-scene commanders in all three cases were able to report to their supervisors that extended negotiations represented the only hope for a peaceful resolution.

The Ruby Ridge and Waco situations, in contrast, were marked by poorly defined chains of command and a lack of coordination between agencies (Freeh, 1995; Stone, 1993). At Ruby Ridge, the initial management was handled by the BATF and the U.S. Marshals Service. During Waco, the BATF initiated the assault and managed the early stages of negotiation. In both cases, the FBI entered the management process after the incidents were underway. The need for a coordinated management policy during large-scale crisis events was articulated by Stone (1993) and Dennis (1993) in their reports to the Attorney General.

Psychopathology Among Perpetrators. A major concern in any hostage or barricade situation is the presence of psychopathology among the perpetrators. Issues such as personality style, unconventional belief systems, overt psychosis, suicide risk, and alcohol or drug intoxication will influence negotiation strategy. Failure to recognize the signs and symptoms of psychiatric disorders will not only jeopardize the effectiveness of negotiations but will also increase the likelihood of violence.

During the Atlanta and Oakdale riots, the mental and emotional stability of the inmates was of significant concern. It was known from prison medical records as well as immigration files that a large number of the Cuban detainees had psychiatric histories. The diagnostic entities encountered covered a spectrum of categories within the *Diagnostic and Statistical Manual,* 4th ed.

Schizophrenia, major affective disorders, substance abuse, and personality disorders were all identified in the inmate population. As a result, negotiators were confronted with two major tasks. First, it was important to identify and facilitate communication with those inmate leaders who displayed the greatest degree of mental stability. Second, negotiators faced the dilemma of dealing with unpredictable outbursts and behavior from the more unstable members of the inmate population. Fortunately for the negotiating team, the Cubans themselves acted quickly to segregate the more unruly individuals within the prison. Both sides recognized that the fragile nature of the negotiations could be undermined by those persons with obvious psychopathology.

The situation at Ruby Ridge with respect to psychopathology was more subtle but, in many ways, more complicated to manage. The Weaver family and their followers displayed little in the way of overt pathology, but possessed a deep-seated distrust and suspicion of government authority. These personality traits created barriers to the establishment of any meaningful dialogue. As a result, negotiations never reached the point of mutual trust necessary for a successful resolution.

The Branch Davidian standoff in Waco was complicated by both the personality style of Koresh and the strength of the unconventional belief system embraced by the group. Stone (1993) described the paranoid, grandiose, and narcissistic character traits displayed by Koresh. These reached such a level of intensity at various times during the incident that behavioral science experts monitoring the siege questioned whether or not Koresh was psychotic. Much of the frustration experienced by FBI negotiators was the result of Koresh's insistence that he control all aspects of the negotiation process. These behavioral tendencies, in retrospect, could be understood as directly related to his personality structure. The group psychology of the Branch Davidians was also largely unrecognized during the course of the incident.

Unlike Waco, where authorities dealt primarily with one individual, the Freemen standoff in Montana was characterized by a loosely organized group of subjects with different personality styles and varying agendas. No common belief system united the Freemen, except for a general distrust of government authority. Some of the barricaded subjects adhered strongly to the Freemen philosophy while others were motivated by personal issues unrelated to political or ideological views. Within the group, paranoid, narcissistic, antisocial, and dependent personality traits were seen. Power struggles within the compound forced negotiators to deal with multiple "spokesmen" at different times during the 81-day siege. While negotiators were able to exploit this dynamic to split the group, it also placed the negotiating team in the difficult position of recognizing and reacting to many different personality styles.

Alcohol and Drugs. Alcohol and drugs are frequently implicated in hostage situations. In Atlanta, many inmates raided the prison infirmary and confiscated large quantities of minor tranquilizers, such as Valium, and other controlled substances. The Freemen had substantial quantities of alcohol in their compound. This resulted in negotiators being forced to deal with intoxicated subjects whose behavior and judgment were unpredictable.

When present, alcohol and drugs complicate the negotiation process and significantly increase the risk of a tragic outcome. One reason that alcohol and drugs pose a significant danger during a hostage incident is that they cause a general increase in the level of impulsivity in the hostage-takers. This impulsivity may cause the captors to take unnecessary chances which could jeopardize the safety of the hostages. When these substances are added to the otherwise volatile nature of a hostage situation, the potential for injury becomes much greater.

Alcohol and drugs also cause impairment in judgment. When under the influence of alcohol or drugs, for example, hostage-takers may have difficulty in realistically evaluating the nature of their actions and the possible consequences. A false sense of confidence or bravado may ensue, which influences the hostage-takers to behave in ways they might ordinarily resist. This further increases the risk of injury or death to the hostages, law enforcement officers, and perpetrators.

In a related area, the use of alcohol, drugs, or both, may increase the risk of aggression. The disinhibiting nature of these agents is well known. Rage reactions have been clearly documented for alcohol and for many drugs. When an armed, and potentially dangerous, captor is under the influence of these substances, the threshold for violence is significantly reduced.

Police officers recognize the dangers inherent in responding to incidents associated with substance abuse. These situations are often complicated by some personal dispute where affect levels are already extremely high. This creates an extremely volatile situation. Negotiations must then be conducted with an angry, and possibly irrational, person whose judgment is significantly clouded by the effect of alcohol or drugs. Of all hostage situations, these are usually the most explosive and have the greatest potential for tragic outcome.

Finally, it is extremely difficult to negotiate with an individual who is intoxicated. Clinicians have long recognized that interviews with intoxicated persons yield only limited information; about the only thing that can be assessed is the level of intoxication. That person may appear quite different when he or she is sober. The same phenomenon occurs in hostage negotiations. Alcohol or drug intoxication clearly adds a significant degree of difficulty to the negotiation process.

The Suicidal Hostage-Taker. In many hostage incidents, depression and suicidal ideation complicate the situation. This was most evident in Waco in the willingness of Koresh and his followers to commit mass suicide rather than surrender. Another example of this phenomenon was the Heaven's Gate suicide in San Diego, in which 39 people took their own lives. Persons who subscribe to unconventional religious beliefs or who are deeply committed to a social or political cause may view death as a viable alternative to prosecution, or perceived persecution, by the government.

The taking of hostages may also result from feelings of hopelessness or desperation associated with depression or an overwhelming psychosocial stressor. This is encountered more commonly in individual rather than group incidents, although it was clearly present in Atlanta and Oakdale, where some inmates were willing to die rather than return to Cuba. The suicidal hostage-taker may hope that police will eventually kill him or her and may even attempt to provoke police into shooting (a phenomenon known to police as "suicide by cop"). It is essential that the negotiators be aware of this possibility and look for indicators of depression and suicide. Negotiators must also be comfortable with discussing these impressions with the hostage-takers and utilizing crisis intervention techniques to defuse the situation. It is essential in any hostage or barricade situation that law enforcement officers ask the question, "Are you going to kill yourself?"

One of the most pressing considerations in dealing with a barricaded subject, whether with hostages or alone, is the possibility that the subject might commit suicide (DiVasto et al., 1992). In many jurisdictions, law enforcement agencies utilize hostage negotiation teams to deal with these incidents. As a result of this practice, negotiators must possess the skills to assess and defuse suicide potential.

In assessing the relative suicide risk of a barricaded person, several factors must be taken into consideration. These include the subject's level of hostility, recent events in the individual's life, the social support system available to the person, and the use of alcohol or drugs.

For example, hostile statements directed at another, such as, "she'll see" or "they'll know now how they made me feel" not only reflect the possible origin of suicidal ideation but can also be used by the negotiator to direct further dialogue. Expressed hostility also signals an increased danger for hostages or law enforcement officers on the scene.

Recent psychosocial stressors, including loss of job, divorce or separation, or criminal indictment, may serve as triggers for the hostage or barricade incident. In these instances, the negotiator should facilitate a discussion of the problem, attempting to assist the subject in arriving at a nonviolent resolution. During these situations, collateral information is of great value in guiding the negotiator, particularly if the subject is reluctant to talk about the problem.

Assessment of the person's social support system is also of value in dealing with the suicidal hostage-taker. In general, the absence of a support system increases the risk of suicide. When dealing with this type of individual, the negotiator must offer alternative sources of support such as hospitalization or referral to mental health professionals. The relationship that develops between negotiator and subject may also be utilized as a source of temporary support.

When family members or friends are present at the scene, the negotiator may be confronted with difficult decisions. Clearly, the information provided by these individuals may be invaluable in assessing the severity of the situation. At the same time, however, these persons may offer suggestions that are counterproductive. A common example is when family members volunteer to talk directly to the subject. While this ultimately may be successful in convincing the hostage-taker to surrender, it is, nevertheless, fraught with peril. The high affect levels associated with family conflicts may inflame the situation further, often precipitating suicide. As a rule, family, friends, or other civilians should not be allowed to speak directly to the subject. Rather, an audiotape or videotape can be prepared and then played. This strategy allows negotiators to screen the tape in advance for potentially inflammatory material.

Finally, negotiators must recognize that suicide is not always preventable. This is a common fact known to mental health professionals, but is something with which negotiators invariably struggle.

Unexpected Developments. Finally, unexpected developments often disrupt management of hostage and barricade situations. These events, such as loss of electrical power or equipment failure, may be beyond the control of everyone involved. Other complications include impulsive or irrational behavior on the part of the hostage-takers, the effects of stress and anxiety on both hostage-takers and negotiators, unpredictable behavior on the part of the hostages, and either inadvertent or deliberate intrusion of outside parties onto the scene. Although the unexpected can never be fully prevented, anticipation of and planning for complications will help minimize their disruptive effect. Maintenance of secure inner and outer perimeters decreases the likelihood of civilian intrusions. Frequent testing of equipment, coupled with the presence of backup systems, is also essential. Liaison with public utility companies also decreases the risk of unexpected disruptions of service.

The utilization of third-party negotiators is another example of a potentially disruptive and unpredictable occurrence. The FBI, in its hostage negotiation training course, discourages the use of outside persons as negotiators. Under certain circumstances, however, authorities may find themselves with no other alternative.

The Waco incident serves as a useful example. Koresh made many demands to broadcast his religious beliefs through various media outlets. Some of these requests were granted, while others were rejected. As direct negotiations with Koresh became less productive, the FBI decided to allow him to meet with his attorney. It had been hoped that these meetings would facilitate an acceptable surrender agreement. In the end, however, this approach was unsuccessful.

Third-party negotiators were also used at Ruby Ridge, the Freemen standoff, and Atlanta, with mixed results. Some of the outside intermediaries involved with the Freemen clearly helped make surrender more attractive to the group. Likewise, the Catholic Archbishop of Miami was successful in establishing trust with the Cuban inmates in Atlanta. The opposite effect occurred at Ruby Ridge, where the Weaver family became more intransigent.

Clearly, the utilization of external persons in negotiation introduces a variable over which police have limited control. The advantages and disadvantages must be weighed carefully before any decision is made. Evaluation must take place on a case-by-case basis.

Mental Health Consultation to Police Hostage Negotiation Teams

Given the high levels of psychopathology among hostage-takers, the complex dynamics of the negotiation process, and the levels of stress inherent in such situations, mental health professionals have been utilized as consultants by police hostage negotiation teams. Consultants can provide valuable assistance to negotiators in a number of areas: (1) diagnosing and assessing subjects, (2) evaluating negotiation and management strategies, (3) monitoring stress during the incident, (4) training negotiators on basic mental health issues, (5) developing training scenarios for both negotiators and tactical units, and (6) researching the characteristics of hostage/barricade incidents and the success of various negotiation strategies. This section outlines the roles for mental health professionals with hostage negotiation teams.

Before addressing the functions of the consultant, a fundamental question must be addressed: What qualifications are necessary for working with a hostage negotiation team? First, the consultant must possess adequate clinical training and experience and the ability to convey that information to law enforcement officers who may not be familiar with mental health issues. A familiarity with basic forensic issues is also desirable in order to appreciate fully the perspective of police officers and the legal ramifications of hostage and barricade situations. Obviously, an interest and willingness to work with law enforcement is extremely important. In a related area, an understanding of the unique function and organization of law enforcement agencies and a willingness to work within that system are crucial. Related components include flexibility, availability, and recognition that the consultant must ultimately defer in decision-making to the on-scene commander. Finally, familiarity with basic hostage negotiation concepts must be present. Ideally, the consultant should go through the same training that negotiators receive.

One important caveat must be emphasized regarding consultation with hostage negotiation teams. The consultant, regardless of his or her credentials or experience, should not attempt to assume the role of a hostage negotiator. This is a function that should be reserved only for trained law enforcement officers. The successful management of hostage or barricade situations requires a complex interaction between negotiation, tactical, and command personnel. No mental health professional, for example, is trained to make the decision to terminate negotiations and initiate a tactical assault. A host of ethical and liability issues make it imperative that the mental health professional restrict his or her activities solely to consultation.

Diagnosis and Assessment

A primary example of the mental health professional's function is the assessment of mentally ill hostage takers. Crucial diagnostic information may be obtained by monitoring the content of the negotiations. This diagnostic information is useful in assisting negotiators and on-scene commanders in the formulation of effective negotiation strategies. Examples include depressed and suicidal persons who attempt to provoke the police into a fatal assault, psychotic individuals, those intoxicated with alcohol or drugs, and persons with unconventional belief systems (e.g., the Branch Davidians). Assisting officers in understanding complex group dynamics is also important. The consultant, regardless of professional discipline, must also possess a thorough understanding of the physiological and behavioral effects of psychotropic medications and other psychoactive substances (Feldmann, 1992).

Consultants can also be of use in gathering intelligence and evaluating information obtained about hostage-takers. For example, reviewing hospital records for subjects with psychiatric histories will be of benefit in determining the degree to which the individual may be influenced by a mental illness. Other sources of information readily available to police, such as prison or probation records, may yield valuable clinical data. The mental health consultant can also facilitate liaison with other therapists who have treated the subjects. Finally, the consultant may be utilized to conduct on-scene interviews with family members, friends, and witnesses. This function is of particular importance in understanding the motivations and belief systems of members of religious sects or fringe groups.

Negotiation and Management Strategies

The mental health consultant can also provide insights into the dynamics of the incident, which assists the negotiators in maintaining objectivity and neutrality during the incident. In this role, it is useful for the consultant to listen directly to the negotiations; this practice was successfully employed at the Atlanta prison. Evidence of subtle shifts in mood, stress levels, signs of intoxication, or symptoms of thought disorder may then be shared immediately with the primary negotiator. The emphasis in this function is on active listening and facilitating communication between the negotiator and the subject.

At the same time, the consultant is also monitoring the dynamics and progress of the situation. Of particular importance is the nature of the relationship between the negotiator and the subject. Indicators of positive or negative feelings on the part of the subject may be easily missed by the primary negotiator, who is often attending to several different sources of information at once. The affective reaction of the subject toward the negotiator is extremely important and can often be utilized to direct the negotiations toward a successful outcome.

Finally, there are three levels of consultation that can be addressed by the mental health consultant: negotiators, command personnel, and SWAT team members. In this role, the consultant provides information regarding mental health issues to all parties involved in management of the situation and also facilitates communication among the three groups.

Dealing With Stress

Another important function of the mental health consultant is monitoring stress levels during the incident. Stress can be defined as the physiological and psychological responses to a painful or threatening stimulus (Horowitz, 1986). On a physiological level, stress leads to a variety of changes, generally referred to as the fight-or-flight reaction. This reaction consists of the activation of the sympathetic nervous system, suppression of the parasympathetic nervous system, activation of the pituitary-adrenal-cortical axis leading to catecholamine production, and mobilization of the reticular activating system. The physiological manifestations of these changes lead to: (1) increased energy mobilization (glucose metabolism), (2) increased heart rate and cardiac output, and (3) increased capacity for physical activity through increased blood flow to the skeletal muscles. A variety of physical manifestations occur in response to this process. First, the individual experiences a rapid heart rate and increased blood pressure. Another clinical manifestation is hyperventilation. Other associated physical findings include dry mouth, sweating, decreased appetite, nausea, and tremor.

While acute stress leads to the fight-or-flight reaction, exposure to chronic stress leads to the conservation-withdrawal reaction. The pattern of adaptation associated with this response is characterized by: (1) a predominance of parasympathetic activity, (2) withdrawal from the environment, (3) decreased heart rate and blood pressure, (4) decreased level of activity and muscle tone, and (5) decreased body temperature. The conservation-withdrawal reaction may be seen in hostages who have been held captive for extended periods of time.

On a psychological level, stress is associated with a myriad of responses. These include (1) fear, (2) anxiety or panic, (3) irritability, (4) anger, (5) helplessness, (6) decreased sleep, (7) hypervigilance, (8) startle reactions, (9) obsessive thoughts, (10) forgetfulness and decreased concentration, (11) somatic complaints, and (12) depression.

It can easily be seen that physical and psychological effects of stress are likely to destabilize a hostage or barricade situation. A major function of the mental health consultant, therefore, is to assist negotiators in the management of stress reactions. Three levels of evaluation must be maintained: (1) stress on the negotiators, (2) stress levels among the hostage-takers or barricaded subjects, and (3) reactions of the hostages.

In all instances, stress may exert both positive and negative responses. On a positive level, stress may influence the hostage-taker to bring the incident to an early conclusion. The task of the negotiator then becomes ensuring that the resolution is a peaceful one. Negative effects of stress, on the other hand, are to be avoided. These include impulsivity and aggression, impaired judgment, alcohol or drug use to cope with stress, and suicide. In the majority of hostage and barricade situations, the cumulative effects of stress are likely to be negative. The consultant, therefore, must constantly be aware of the impact stress is having on all the parties involved.

Bohl (1992) identified both external and internal sources of negotiator stress. External sources of stress include conflicts with on-scene commanders over negotiation strategies and pressure from SWAT team members for a tactical assault. Internal sources of stress consist primarily of fears that the incident will not be resolved peacefully. Most negotiators believe that a tactical assault equates with negotiation failure. Thus, a real or perceived breakdown in the negotiation process impacts the negotiator's sense of competence. Feelings of guilt may also ensue if hostages or fellow officers are killed or injured. Identification with the hostage-taker may also occur; this appears most common with depressed subjects who are threatening suicide. A completed suicide may leave the negotiator with feelings of inadequacy; this is often manifested by the negotiator literally saying, "If only I had done more, I could have prevented the suicide."

In dealing with negotiator stress, Bohl (1992) emphasized the importance of the triad of education, peer support, and crisis debriefing. Education consists of clearly defining the negotiator's role and responsibilities, having realistic expectations regarding what constitutes success and failure in a hostage/barricade incident, training in basic mental health issues (with particular emphasis on suicide and crisis intervention), and recognizing the signs and symptoms of stress. Education must also address negative coping skills, such as the excessive use of denial, intellectualization, or alcohol to deal with stress. Peer support includes letting the negotiator know that he or she is not alone; every negotiator has successes and failures. It is imperative that this fact be reinforced. Crisis debriefing allows the primary negotiator and other team members to review the management of the incident objectively. The emphasis should be on a critical evaluation of negotiation strategies with the goal being to educate and improve handling of future situations. The debriefing process must also allow for the examination and working through of all emotional reactions to the incident.

Finally, stress may influence hostages to act in unpredictable ways that complicate management of the situation. Fear, anxiety or panic, and helplessness can trigger impulsive, and sometimes irrational, acts on the part of hostages. This is clearly one dynamic involved in the Stockholm Syndrome, discussed earlier in the chapter. Exposure to violence or the experience of being held captive may also result in stress-induced psychopathology (North et al., 1989;

Ochberg, 1988; Simon and Blum, 1987). Again, careful assessment of stress levels by the consultant will assist negotiators in calming and stabilizing the situation.

Basic Mental Health Training for Negotiators

Most training for hostage negotiators includes some discussion of basic mental health issues. The quality and quantity of this training, however, is often spotty and superficial. An essential role for the mental health consultant is the provision of adequate information regarding such areas as interviewing skills, suicide assessment, recognition of mental illness, the signs of alcohol and drug intoxication, and crisis intervention techniques.

Negotiator training in these areas must be provided at two levels. First, all negotiators should receive exposure to these issues during their initial training. In addition, regular updates and in-depth sessions on particular topics should be included as part on the on-going training that team members receive. Table 11.1 outlines a basic mental health curriculum that has been used to train hostage negotiation teams in Kentucky.

Development of Training Scenarios

In addition to training sessions dealing with mental health issues, the mental health consultant can also be utilized in the development of training exercises and scenarios. The consultant, for example, can develop training scenarios involving mentally ill subjects in which the negotiators must deal with suicidal, intoxicated, or psychotic persons. Role playing is utilized in these exercises and the "hostage-taker" utilizes a script reflecting the type of behavior and verbal responses characteristic of the illness being portrayed. These training sessions should be as realistic as possible and should be carried out in conjunction with the SWAT team.

Table 11.1

Sample Curriculum: Mental Health Training for Hostage Negotiators

1. Basic interviewing and listening skills
2. Psychopathology for hostage negotiators
    a. Psychotic disorders
    b. Affective disorders
    c. Neuroses
    d. Personality disorders
    e. Organic mental disorders
3. Suicide assessment
4. Drug and alcohol abuse
5. Overview of psychotropic medications
6. Crisis intervention techniques
7. The dynamics of hostage situations
    a. Course of the event and stages of a hostage situation
        1. Establishing contact with the hostage-taker
        2. Information and intelligence gathering
        3. Developing a relationship with the hostage-taker
        4. Dealing with demands
        5. Negotiation stages
        6. Resolution and the surrender ritual
    b. Monitoring change and progress
        1. Indicators of progress
        2. Stalemates and lack of progress
        3. Danger signals
    c. The relationship between the negotiator and the hostage-taker
    d. Dealing with the hostages (includes Stockholm Syndrome)
    e. Dealing with unexpected or outside events (media, families, etc.)
    f. Sociocultural factors influencing negotiations
8. Negotiator stress and stress reactions associated with the incident
9. Crisis debriefing

Another useful training tool consists of visits to psychiatric units. Volunteer patients are selected to be interviewed by members of the negotiation team. In this manner, the negotiators acquire first hand knowledge and experience of the symptoms of psychiatric illnesses. This type of experience helps to familiarize negotiators with the kinds of psychopathology they are likely to encounter during real hostage or barricade incidents.

Finally, evaluation of training effectiveness is an important function for the consultant. Pre- and post-training evaluation instruments should be utilized, as well as self-evaluation by the negotiators. The goal of such activities is to increase negotiator sensitivity to mental health issues and to improve recognition of pathology. This, in turn, allows the negotiator to be better equipped to deal with actual situations.

Research

Although much has been learned about the management of hostage and barricade situations, negotiation remains an intuitive rather than an empirical activity. Mental health consultants, working in conjunction with police officers and forensic behavioral scientists, can foster research into the effectiveness of various negotiation and management strategies as well as training programs. The establishment of research databases, such as the one currently underway at the University of Louisville, will be of great assistance in determining what factors influence success and failure in negotiation.

For example, an on-line database of hostage/barricade incidents can be utilized via a notebook computer housed in the hostage negotiation team command post. As intelligence is gathered on a given situation and offender, incidents with similar characteristics can be retrieved from the database. Negotiators, consultants, and commanders may then review what worked and what did not work in similar situations. While no database can replace the experience of trained negotiators, the database is of value in evaluating various management strategies and in anticipating unexpected complications.

Summary

Hostage and barricade incidents are not rare or unusual occurrences. A search of the news media for any given week or month yields literally hundreds of these events. Whenever an armed subject, who may be intoxicated or mentally ill, holds others against their will, the risk of lethal violence becomes obvious.

This risk increases significantly in those situations involving multiple, heavily armed subjects who are operating in an organized and coordinated manner. Demands in these cases are often complicated and may involve political, religious, social, or delusional overtones.

In the past, law enforcement agencies have tended to treat all of these incidents as if they were identical. The illustrations presented in this chapter suggest otherwise. Effective management of hostage and barricade situations requires an understanding of many different factors. First and foremost, the motivation for the incident must be understood. Negotiators cannot defuse a potentially explosive event unless they fully appreciate why it is occurring. Likewise, it is insufficient merely to know that a given perpetrator has a history of mental illness; the nature of the illness and its effects on behavior must also be recognized. Finally, negotiators must possess a thorough grasp of the dynamics of the negotiation process.

Utilization of mental health consultants and continued study of the characteristics of hostage and barricade incidents will improve management strategies. Continued emphasis on training will also help police negotiators be better prepared when incidents occur. Although it is impossible to prevent hostage and barricade situations, effective crisis management techniques will greatly reduce their lethality.

Suggested Readings

1. Call, J.A. (1996) The hostage triad: takers, victims, and negotiators. In H.V. Hall (Ed.), *Lethal Violence 2000: A Sourcebook on Fatal Domestic, Acquaintance, and Stranger Aggression.* Kamuela, HI: Pacific Institute for the Study of Conflict and Aggression.
2. Feldmann, T.B. and Johnson, P.W. (1993) Hostage situations and the mental health professional. In P. Blumenreich and S. Lewis (Eds.), *Management of the Violent Patient: A Clinician's Guide.* New York: Brunner/Mazel.
3. Fuselier, G.D. (1981) A practical overview of hostage negotiations. *FBI Law Enforcement Bulletin, 50* (6), 2–11.
4. Knutson, J.N. (1980) The dynamics of the hostage taker: some major variants. In F. Wright, C. Bahn, and R.W. Rieber (Eds.), *Forensic Psychiatry and Psychology.* New York: New York Academy of Sciences.
5. Meyer, R.G. (1992) *Abnormal Behavior and the Criminal Justice System.* Lexington, MA: Lexington Books.

References

American Psychiatric Association (1968) *Diagnostic and Statistical Manual of Mental Disorders*, 2nd ed. Washington, D.C.: American Psychiatric Association.

American Psychiatric Association (1994) *Diagnostic and Statistical Manual of Mental Disorders*, 4th ed. Washington, D.C.: American Psychiatric Association.

Annin, P. and Hosenball, M. (1996) Why the Feds are closing in on a band of radicals. *Newsweek,* April 8. Available online via www.aol.com.

Beals, G. and Peyser, M. (1996) How the Feds avoided a Waco-style bloodbath. *Newsweek,* June 24. Available online via www.aol.com.

Bell, R.A., Lanceley, F.J., Feldmann, T.B., Worley, T.H., Fuselier, D., and van Zandt, C. (1991) Hostage negotiations and mental health: experiences from the Atlanta prison riot. *American Journal of Preventive Psychiatry and Neurology, 3*(2), 8–11.

Bohl, N.K. (1992) Hostage negotiator stress. *FBI Law Enforcement Bulletin, 61* (8), 23–26.

Bracey, D.H. (1980) Forensic psychology and hostage negotiation: introductory remarks. In F. Wright, C. Bahn, and R.W. Rieber (Eds.), *Forensic Psychology and Psychiatry*, pp. 220–249. New York: New York Academy of Sciences.

Call, J.A. (1996) The hostage triad: takers, victims, and negotiators. In H.V. Hall (Ed.), *Lethal Violence 2000: A Sourcebook on Fatal Domestic, Acquaintance, and Stranger Aggression*, pp. 561–588. Kamuela, HI: Pacific Institute for the Study of Conflict and Aggression.

Dennis, E.S.G. (1993) *Evaluation of the Handling of the Branch Davidian Stand-Off in Waco, Texas, February 28 to April 19, 1993.* Washington, D.C.: U.S. Government Printing Office.

Department of Justice (1993) *Report to the Deputy Attorney General on the events at Waco, Texas, February 28, 1993 to April 19, 1993.* Washington, D.C.: U.S. Government Printing Office.

DiVasto, P., Lanceley, F.J., and Gruys, A. (1992) Critical issues in suicide intervention. *FBI Law Enforcement Bulletin, 61*(8), 13–16.

Federal Bureau of Investigation (1993) *Response and Management of Critical Incidents.* Special Operations and Research Unit. Quantico, VA: FBI Academy.

Federal Bureau of Investigation Special Operations and Research Unit. (1981) A terrorist organizational profile: a psychological role model. In Y. Alexander and J. Gleason (Eds.), *Behavioral and Quantitative Perspectives on Terrorism*, pp. 35–50. New York: Pergamon Press.

Feldmann, T.B. (1992) Psychopharmacology in criminal justice. In R.G. Meyer (Ed.), *Abnormal Behavior and the Criminal Justice System*, pp. 265–283. Lexington, MA: Lexington Books.

Feldmann, T.B. (1997) *Psychiatric Consultation to Police Hostage Negotiation Teams.* Paper presented at the meeting of the American College of Forensic Psychiatry, Vancouver, B.C., Canada.

Feldmann, T.B. and Johnson, P.W. (1993) Hostage situations and the mental health professional. In P. Blumenreich and S. Lewis (Eds.), *Management of the Violent Patient: A Clinician's Guide,* pp. 111–130. New York: Brunner/Mazel.

Feldmann, T.B. and Johnson, P.W. (1995) The application of psychotherapeutic and self psychology principles to hostage negotiations. *Journal of the American Academy of Psychoanalysis, 23*(2), 207–221.

Freeh, L.J. (1995, October) Opening Statement, Ruby Ridge Hearing, Committee on the Judiciary, U.S. Senate, Washington, D.C. Available online: www.fbi.gov.

Fuselier, G.D. (1981) A practical overview of hostage negotiations. *FBI Law Enforcement Bulletin, 50*(6), 2–11.

Fuselier, G.D. (1986) What every negotiator would like his chief to know. *FBI Law Enforcement Bulletin, 55*(3), 12–15.

Fuselier, G.D., Van Zandt, C.R., and Lanceley, F.J. (1989) Negotiating the protracted incident: the Oakdale and Atlanta prison sieges. *FBI Law Enforcement Bulletin, 58*(7), 1–7.

Fuselier, G.D., Van Zandt, C., and Lanceley, F.J. (1991) Hostage/barricade incidents. *FBI Law Enforcement Bulletin, 60*(1), 6–12.

Gray, O. M. (1981) Hostage negotiations. *Texas Police Journal, 29*(11), 14–18.

Hammer, M.R., Van Zandt, C.R., and Rogan, R.G. (1994) Crisis/hostage negotiation team profile. *FBI Law Enforcement Bulletin, 63*(3), 8–11.

Horowitz, M. (1986) *Stress Response Syndromes*, 2nd ed. Northvale, NJ: Jason Aronson.

Jenkins, B., Johnson, J., and Renfeldt, D. (1977) *Numbered Lives: Some Statistical Observations from 77 International Hostage Episodes.* Santa Monica, CA: The Rand Corporation.

Morganthau, T., Isikoff, M., and Cohn, B. (1995) The government quietly capitulates in a lawsuit over the bloody '92 standoff with the separatist Weaver Family. *Newsweek,* August 28. Available online via www.aol.com.

Noesner, G.W. and Dolan, J.T. (1992) First responder negotiation training. *FBI Law Enforcement Bulletin, 61*(8), 1–5.

Noesner, G.W. and Webster, M. (1997) Crisis intervention: using active listening skills in negotiations. *FBI Law Enforcement Bulletin, 66*(8), 13–19.

North, C.S., Smith , E.M., and McCool, R.E. (1989) Short-term psychopathology in eyewitnesses to mass murder. *Hospital and Community Psychiatry, 40,* 1293–1295.

Ochberg, F.M. (1988) Post-traumatic therapy and victims of violence. In F.M. Ochberg (Ed.), *Post-Traumatic Therapy and Victims of Violence*, pp. 83–88. New York: Brunner-Mazel.

Piernick, K. (1997) *Militia Groups.* Paper presented at the FBI/Baltimore County Police Hostage Negotiation Seminar, Baltimore, MD.

Romano, S. (1997) *Incident Critique of Jordan, Montana.* Paper presented at the FBI/Baltimore County Police Hostage Negotiation Seminar, Baltimore, MD.

Schlossberg, H. (1980) Values and organization in hostage and crisis negotiation teams. In F. Wright, C. Bahn, and R.W. Rieber (Eds.), *Forensic Psychiatry and Psychology*, pp. 113–116. New York: New York Academy of Sciences.

Schrieber, M. (1972) *After-Action Report of Terrorist Activities: 20th Olympic Games, Munich, West Germany.* Quantico, VA: FBI Academy.

Simon, R.I. and Blum, R.A. (1987) After the terrorist incident: psychotherapeutic treatment of former hostages. *American Journal of Psychotherapy, 41,* 194–200.

Stone, A.A. (1993) *Report and Recommendations Concerning the Handling of Incidents Such as the Branch Davidian Standoff in Waco, Texas.* Washington, D.C.: U.S. Government Printing Office.

Strentz, T. (1980) The Stockholm syndrome: law enforcement policy and ego defenses of the hostage. In F. Wright, C. Bahn, and R.W. Rieber (Eds.), *Forensic Psychiatry and Psychology*, pp. 137–150. New York: New York Academy of Sciences.

Strentz, T. (1983) The inadequate personality as hostage-taker. *Journal of Police Science and Administration, 11*(3), 363–368.

Vandiver, J.V. (1981) Hostage situations require preparedness. *Law and Order, 9,* 66–69.

Wolf, E.S. (1988) *Treating the Self: Elements of Clinical Self Psychology.* New York: Guilford Press.

About the Author

Theodore Feldmann, M.D., is Associate Professor in the Department of Psychiatry and Behavioral Sciences, University of Louisville School of Medicine. He is board certified in general psychiatry and forensic psychiatry. Dr. Feldmann's research activities have included the study of aircraft hijacking, workplace violence, hostage and barricade incidents, and juror stress. He has served as an expert witness in over 100 civil and criminal cases in state and federal courts. Dr. Feldmann has also served as a consultant to the Federal Bureau of Investigation, the Kentucky State Police, the Louisville Police Department, and the Jefferson County (KY) Police Department. In those capacities, he has provided on-scene consultation at hostage situations, development of training exercises, and psychological profiling of offenders. He received training in hostage negotiation at the FBI Academy in Quantico, VA, and has also served as an instructor at both the FBI Academy and the Kentucky State Police Academy.

PART III

COLLECTIVE VIOLENCE BY GOVERNMENT INSTITUTIONS

Chapter 12

DEATH BY INSTITUTIONAL VIOLENCE

Harold V. Hall

Even though social scientists have in the past amassed impressive experimental evidence that violence can be produced through imitation or modeling, they have in general neglected the possibility that government — with its vast authority and resources — might turn out to be the most potent model of all. This powerful influence of governments on private behavior seems to be what Justice Louis Brandeis had in mind when he wrote in 1928: "Our government is the potent, the omnipresent teacher. For good or ill, it teaches the whole people by its example. Crime is contagious. If the government becomes a lawbreaker, it breeds contempt for the law." (Archer and Gartner, 1984, p. 94)

In this chapter, the historical lethal influences of institutional entities, particularly the government, on both individuals and other groups will first be discussed. Next, variables critical to fatal group violence, particularly power and control by government, will be described. Finally, the attitudes and behaviors that are required for the prevention and control of collective lethal violence will be examined. A key belief is that war and other mass killings are not inevitable. Collective violence truly begins and ends in the minds of men and women.

A Brief History of Institutional Violence

Embedded within a belief that society is deteriorating, it is easy to conclude that the human ability to self-control lethal behaviors is particularly weak and poorly controlled at this point in history. As an analysis makes clear, however, the foundation for violence seen today was laid centuries ago. The current increase in lethal violence may be but one reflection of this long-term trend.

Modern brain development in humans occurred several hundred millennia ago as an adaptation to the demands of the stimulus environment. Humans were hunter-gatherers and, as mounting archeological data suggests, quite capable of communicating, making fire, expressing spirituality, designing tools and weapons, stalking and hunting animals, and, when necessary, killing their own kind. The best evidence indicates that humans not only lived in synchrony with nature, but also in balanced kinship within relatively small groups of relatives and accepted others (Fromm, 1973; Sagan, 1980).

Killing, when it did occur, evoked different behaviors by the initiator and target. Data on mammals and most early human groups suggest that initiators of lethal violence showed four primary patterns (Archer, 1988, 1995; Sherman, 1981):

1. Interspecies predatory behavior in order to obtain food. The target reacted with fight-or-flight behavior or, in some cases, deception, such as feigning death.
2. Intraspecies competition, associated with attempted dominance and control in order to win access to resources or remove threats to status or position. Fight-or-flight behavior on the part of the aggressor or the target was the usual response to escalating violence.
3. Defensive aggression in order to prevent harm to self, offspring, others, or territory.
4. Infanticide, so that defective or weak individuals would not compromise the species' ability to survive.

Several investigators have differentiated between affective and predatory behavior in animals (Chi and Flynn, 1971; Eichelman, 1990; Reis, 1974) and in clinical-forensic settings with humans (Meloy, 1988). Affective modes are those characterized by intense emotion to internally or externally perceived threat (i.e., competitive and defensive violence and infanticide). There is a heightened and diffuse awareness and an impulsive, brief attack aimed at reduction of the threat stimulus. Predatory modes of violence are characterized by preparation for attack, minimal fear during the attack sequence, and a heightened and focused awareness, with all factors operating toward a prey that is the target of consumption. Self-controlled or organized violence, such as robbery, serial murder, and the use of deadly force by police, is the modern equivalent of predatory aggression.

The use of predatory aggression among early humans is instructive. No more game was killed than was necessary to sustain life. Cannibalism was rare and was held as an early taboo. Early "wars" with other tribes were territorial and self-limiting. The basic function of predatory aggression was attack for the purpose of consumption or exploitation. Stalking and deception were the essence of this type of aggression in an orchestrated, organized attempt to seize the prey. The sequence for predatory aggression may be summarized as follows:

goal setting → planning → execution →
seizing prey → consumption

Killing associated with competition for resources with other humans was a type of affective aggression which followed animal patterns of aggression. It was aimed, not at consumption, but at removing a threat to resources or status. Communication between the initiator and responder was an associated feature of this type of aggression for both animals and humans. Here, attack was usually preceded by an aggressive display or by a communication of superior status (i.e., dominance), by sight, by sound, or even by scent. This was followed by providing the target a chance to withdraw. If the opponent ignored the signal, aggression followed ritualized patterns in order to reduce harm (e.g., only head butting is displayed in fighting between horned ungulates; fangs or poison are not used in confrontations between rattlesnakes; weapons of war are forbidden in intrafamilial conflicts).

As one or the other party started to lose, flight by the losing party signaled defeat. If flight was impossible, appeasement signals were rendered by the loser in order to inhibit the attacker from further attack. A defeated wolf bares the vulnerable underside of its neck to the victorious wolf as a functional equivalent of defeat. Subordinate baboons crouch in a sexual presentation to the dominant baboon. Humans may cry or show other disorganized, infantile behavior, or both, which clearly communicates defeat to the winner (and may elicit parental feelings).

At this point, the aggressive sequence is over and the social transaction complete. Occasionally, the contestants bond as a result of the mutual competition and as they settle into an implicit dominance hierarchy. The sequence is

threat → display →
attack or flight → conflict resolution

Although nonlethal outcomes far outweigh instances in which the loser dies, it is possible to be killed in competitive violence. Many herbivorous animals show intense aggression during the mating season, but very few opponents actually die as a result of their wounds. Humans have killed others in disputes throughout the ages, secondary to attempts to dominate opponents. In short, there is, in this type of aggression, an overwhelming evolutionary tendency to achieve control by winning, but to avoid lethal outcomes if at all possible.

Defensive violence involves intense affect due to a preemptory attack by an intruder. Occasionally, a brief threat display by the defender to ward off the new threat is presented. If approach behaviors continue, however, the intruder is attacked with all weapons at the disposal of the defender. No rules of conduct are followed. Anything goes. Bears protecting their cubs can inflict lethal harm very quickly with teeth and claws. Humans defending their kind will persistently attack intruders, even to the point of sacrificing their own life. At the termination of the violence, the defender (if alive) returns to the defended territory or protected others. Following an unsuccessful attempt, the intruder (if alive), retreats to a familiar and safer area. Setting aside technology for a moment, humans engaging in defensive violence, as with all other animals, have an evolutionary edge over intruders and usually experience favorable outcomes.

Infanticide is another type of affectively driven violence. The killing of offspring by their parents or allowing its occurrence (e.g., by mates) bestows a variety of benefits in the animal world (Archer, 1988; Ridley, 1978; Sherman, 1981). With humans, infanticide is usually accompanied by rituals to overcome maternal bonding and the intense affect experienced in killing one's offspring. There appears to have been a cultural factor in the bias toward sons, with female infants being killed in disproportionately greater numbers. Barlow and Clayton (1996) comprehensively reviewed the literature on infanticide in lower primates and humans. In their analysis, they found that males perpetrate the vast majority of infanticide in lower primates, such as apes and chimpanzees. With humans, females commit the majority of infanticide.

Gender differences emerge among the four types of lethal violence discussed above. Males predominate in predatory and competition-based violence. In the past, men hunted, fought battles with other tribes, and engaged in contests to gain leadership of the tribe. Throughout the ages, men engaged in these two types of lethal violence far more than women. This holds true today in *every* society that has maintained crime records (Meyers, 1993). For example, in the U.S., men are arrested eight times more frequently than women for violent crimes. Eme (1996) presented a compelling case that sex differences in violence among juveniles are due to a confluence of genetic, congenital, neonatal, and psychosocial experiences, culminating in males being at high risk for violence and acting out. In Chapter 6, Barlow and Clayton discuss the ubiquity of male on female aggression and violence. Defensive violence has been exhibited by both genders, depending on circumstances, and throughout human history.

These four primary kinds of lethal violence in humans can be collapsed into two types — predatory violence and that characterized by intense affect. Archer (1988) suggested that predatory violence is fundamentally different from affective violence in terms of both neurobiology and basic function (to consume rather than remove a threat or aversive stimulus). He noted from the animal literature that there are no real neurological differences between competitive and defensive violence. Indeed, no neurological differences between competitive and defensive aggression in humans have ever been demonstrated in humans (Archer, 1988, 1995; Reis, 1974; Ridley, 1978).

The best evidence suggests that fatal aggression in early humans occurred within and between balanced kinship groups in their quest for survival (Barash, 1977; Fromm, 1991; Sagan, 1980). Successful adaptation implied two sets of culturally idiosyncratic traits operating within a balanced kinship — distinction-making and distinction-dissolving. It is hypothesized that these two tendencies stimulate a cognitive-behavioral-psychosocial process which makes the killing of another person more or less probable. An individual or a tribe has both distinction-making and distinction-dissolving tendencies. An imbalance occurs when one set of traits dominates the other.

Distinction-making traits refer to activities such as creating dominance hierarchies, having a narrow focus of attention, paying close attention to detail as opposed to the whole, valuing precision and orderliness, such as weapon-making or planning for battle, and training subordinates to kill efficiently. These traits are necessary for survival. The knife must cut deep, the arrow must fly true, and control must be established to deal effectively with violent crises. When an individual or group values these traits over distinction-dissolving traits, however, a breakdown in empathy occurs. We then see ourselves as not only different, but superior and self-entitled, especially if previous outcomes involving attempted dominance on our part have been favorable.

Distinction-dissolving traits value richness of experience, intuition, complexity, ambiguity, and holism. Examples include ritualistic dancing as animals to celebrate a successful hunt and attempted communication with the spirits to ask for a vision to meet a major life task. These traits are necessary as well for survival. They ensure creativity, flexibility, intuition, and diversity within an appreciation of the whole. New ways to solve old problems may thus be found to successfully adapt to the environment. When these traits are valued over distinction-making, the individual or group has no clear focus or organization and will most likely be seen as ineffectual.

History shows that distinction-dissolving traits are more fragile than their distinction-creating counterparts, perhaps because the former requires an integration with nature and the animal world for its nurturance and maintenance. When both are imbalanced, distinction-dissolving tendencies generally lose out. This appears to have started on a gradual basis on this planet about 10 to 15 millennia ago, secondary to the erosion of the hunter-gatherer lifestyle in favor of farms, ranches, and villages. In the course of events, spiritual power associated with nature was relinquished by the individual to organized religion and government, which then wielded an extraordinary degree of external control in everyday life.

Church and State became inseparable. Cities and countries formed, and the old distinction-dissolving ways gradually faded in favor of technological, economic, and bureaucratic accomplishments. Metal weapons and shielding had no early competitors. The concept of the standing army was introduced. The city-state and then the nation were in positions to enforce their will over weaker neighbors. Alcohol from fermented plant products was available for the first time, thus providing a powerful disinhibition to all types of violence (alcohol and other intoxicating substances were routinely allowed prior to battle up to the 20th century). Infanticide expanded to child abuse and neglect, as the value of offspring decreased. During this great changeover from hunter-gatherers to food producers, self-mutilation and genocide occurred for the first time in human history, setting the stage for more lethal violence to come.

Predatory and affective aggression appeared to merge in both function and form. Perpetrators began to show victim-like behaviors, as in suicide and self-mutilation, and victims showed characteristics of perpetrators. As war was introduced on a massive scale, family, criminal, and institutional violence began to have common qualities. Imbalanced kinships became imbalanced societies and cultures in their aggressive pursuit of dominance, material possessions, and self-aggrandizement. A few historical examples illustrate the general breakdown of distinction-dissolving traits in favor of killing those who are different:

- The Old Testament contains numerous references to (righteous and unrighteous) killing at group and institutional levels.
- When Troy was captured by the Greeks in 1184 B.C., all postpubescent males were slaughtered and the surviving children and women were sold into slavery.
- Genocide was perpetrated systematically against many weaker groups, including the Mongols against other Asians and Europeans, the Arabs against the Africans, and the Chinese against Tibetans and Indochinese. As early as the 14th century, the plague was deliberately introduced to enemies by warring European factions (Barnaby, 1984). Most national boundaries were established by blood.
- Tens of thousands of individuals lost their lives in the Crusades and various other religious wars, inspired first by the Catholic Church and later, by Protestant sects. During the Spanish Inquisition (1420 to 1498), thousands of individuals were tortured to death or burned alive at the stake in the name of Church and State. Millions of American Indians were systematically killed off by European powers through war, disease, starvation, and slavery.

The introduction of gunpowder-driven projectiles in the 15th century accelerated the decline of distinction-dissolving tendencies and psychologically changed lethal violence forever. First, firearms were superior and afforded even more control over others to the bearer of arms. Although cumbersome and slow in operation, these weapons represented a quantum leap in the technology of death. The two-man musket, introduced by the Spaniards around the time of Columbus, for example, could destroy any existing body armor at close range with its two-ounce ball or disable a horse at 300 yards (Ropp, 1962). Cannons rendered the mounted warrior and fixed defenses, such as castles, obsolete. For many countries, lethal violence, particularly war, was viewed as a legitimate and even honorable means of national advancement (a trend that has continued throughout the 20th century).

To overcome the human tendency to be non-violent except to obtain food or remove imminent threats, governments and military strategists found ways to create psychological distance between perpetrators and victims. One method was to remove the contact and communication between perpetrators and victims that are inherent in most killing acts. This was remarkably successful. Very few highly motivated warriors who killed at long distance (e.g., with artillery and later with modern bomb crews) would be willing to maim, strangle, stab, burn, or otherwise mutilate children and adults with their own hands. Instead, there is a tendency to stop short of killing once distress and appeasement signals are wrenched from their victims (Kemp, 1987).

Encouraged by those in power, the common citizen-soldier was trained to become more predator-like, with an emphasis on deception, precision, strategy, quick kills, and a clear focus on eliminating the enemy. Pejorative labels were used to prevent soldiers from seeing the enemy as fellow human beings. Personal communication with the opponent was blocked. Except for dominance displays, communication with the enemy was frowned upon and was highly ritualized when it occurred. Individual weapons which killed quickly at close range were introduced. Warriors, through the use of weapons, particularly firearms, were taught *not* to recognize distress cues from opponents and were taught to see their own flight as an act of cowardice (Kemp, 1987). Violent attitudes were reinforced and equated with loyalty to unit, corps, God, and country (interestingly, U.S. Marine recruits are taught this four-factor sequence of loyalty in boot camps). The vanquished were treated as predators treat their prey, for consumption and exploitation, with the spoils bequeathed to the victors. In this manner, those in control through the use of religion, government, military, and technology have aided and abetted in the usurpation of our non-violent tendencies.

The brutalizing effect on those who came to the Western hemisphere was manifested and reinforced by the genocidal treatment of Indians by the first European intruders, particularly the Spanish, French, and English. The horror stories began not long after Christopher Columbus landed in the Caribbean. In their thoroughly researched *Chronicle of America*, Daniel et al. (1995) described how Columbus, desperate to pay the financers of his expeditions, imposed a gold tax on the Indians in Hispaniola in 1508. The few Indians who could pay the tax had a copper necklace placed on them; those found without a necklace often had both of their hands chopped off. Daniel et al. noted that a ship traveling from Lucayos (Bahamas) to Hispaniola could "without compass or chart, guide itself solely by the trail of dead Indians who had been thrown from the ships" (original quote in Pietro Martire d'Anghiera's *De Orbe Novo*, 1525). Other Indians worked as slaves under the Spanish system known as "encomienda". After a few years, of 250,000 Indians in Hispaniola, only 60,000 remained. Today, "pure" Indians in the Caribbean are a rarity and have all but died out.

The Conquistadors in Central America and South America destroyed extant Indian cultures by war and conquest, often pitting tribes against one another. After direct conquest, the bulk of the native population was killed off by disease, the encomienda system, and the unjust political/religious system. Daniel et al. (1995) documented that, in 1576, one epidemic alone in New Spain killed off nearly 40% of the Indians, and that tens of thousands of Indians became slaves to Spanish landowners each year (with most perishing within a year of enslavement). Indians were executed, often by being burned at the stake, for refusing to convert to Catholicism.

Certainly, the norms for conflict in North America were more barbaric than those of Western Europe. Killing by opportunity (i.e., without provocation) was common, with the intruders usually winning because of superior weaponry. The newcomers were suspected to be responsible for the deliberate spread of diseases to the Indians. A smallpox epidemic in New England in 1618 killed Indians from the Penobscot River (in Maine) to Rhode Island, wiping out as much as 90% of the population of the tribes (Daniel et al., 1995). The epidemic was believed to have started originally with African slaves, themselves victims of genocide, whose owners allowed them to mix with the Indians. In the 1760s, the British routinely deceived Indians into taking smallpox-infested blankets for trade or as gifts (Barnaby, 1984). Daniel et al. (1995) noted that, in 1763, General Jeffrey Amherst, British Commander in the Great Lakes region, wrote to a vice commander, Colonel Henry Bouquet, advising him to inoculate rebellious Indians with smallpox by means of infected blankets. While some were alarmed, the proposal received generally wide support and was implemented with deadly effect.

Murder, massacre, and torture of prisoners prior to hanging were practiced by both sides in the American Revolutionary War. Richard Maxwell Brown (1969a, p. 64), an eminent historian, discussed a key dynamic of the American character as shown by the events of that war:

"Two things stand out about the Revolution. The first, of course, is that it was successful and immediately became enshrined in our tradition and history. The second is that the meanest and most squalid sort of violence was from the very beginning to the very last put to the service of Revolutionary ideals and objectives. The operational philosophy that the end justifies the means became the key-note of Revolutionary violence. Thus given sanctification by the Revolution, Americans have never been loathe to employ the most unremitting violence of any cause deemed to be a good one."

Frantz (1969, p. 148), a historian, shared with us the following account, which clearly illustrates the deadly trend of collective violence into the 19th century:

"Nowhere has the lust for blood been more deeply etched than in the infamous Sand Creek massacre. Shortly after sundown on November 28, 1864, Col. J.M. Chivington and his men left Fort Lyon, Colo., to surround the followers of

Chief Black Kettle. At dawn Chivington's militia charged through the camp of 500 peaceful Indians, despite Black Kettle's raising an American and then a white flag. Not just warriors were killed. Women and children were dragged out, shot, knifed, scalped, clubbed, mutilated, their brains knocked out, bosoms ripped open. Four hundred and fifty Indians in varying stages of insensate slaughter lay about the campground. There is no defense whatsoever for the action. It was bloodier than Chicago or Detroit or Harlem ever thought of being. Chivington and his cohorts were widely hailed as heroes by many of their fellow Americans."

In fairness, Indians, both as individuals and as tribes, were also lethally violent toward the intruders. Entire groups of settlers were wiped out by Iroquois, Sioux, Apache, and other tribes. Torture, rape, and slavery by the vanquished Indians were common practices; yet, as hunter-gatherers with highly developed distinction-dissolving tendencies, the Indians accepted the intruders' presence until their land and food supply was threatened. The acquisitiveness of the intruders left no room for compromise, and, equipped with firearms, they rendered the Indians nearly extinct.

These events were not isolated, but occurred systematically within the context of opening the North American continent for people of European extraction. The genocide perpetrated against the Indians in North America began in Virginia in the early 1600s and continued for nearly three centuries until Wounded Knee in South Dakota in 1890. With the Americans' firearms and superior numbers, the Indians never really had a chance to win or even maintain their holdings. Ironically, there was plenty of room for expansion in North America, a vast area rich with resources, without resorting to the tactics of extermination. Racial prejudice and greed, monetary and social payoff, all encouraged and supported by those in power, were the chief motivators.

In summary, lethal violence in America provides many models in the industry of death. History has shown that Americans as a whole, although resourceful and very willing to help others, are an incorrigibly violent people. Ours was a society that repeatedly used lethal violence to attain such lofty goals as national independence (Revolutionary War), continental domain (Indian Wars), a thriving economy (slavery), preservation of the Union (Civil War), containment of outlaws (vigilantism), and protection of international security (foreign wars and support of dictators who commonly abuse human rights). Such a society would be reluctant to unequivocally condemn its own use of lethal violence. An unacknowledged value system emerged in this country which depended on lethal violence to attain our most cherished dreams and hopes, but frowned on its individual expression in non-governmental (i.e., "non-approved") contexts.

Worldwide, the 20th century has been the bloodiest in all of human history. There have been approximately 250 wars since 1900 (Tehranian, 1997), resulting in about 40 million deaths (Rummel, 1994). During this same time period, an incredible 170 million have been murdered by their own governments (Rummel, 1994). According to Rummel's (1994) well-researched *Death by Government*, political unrest in Mexico during the time of revolutions (1890 to 1920) resulted in the murder by the government of about 2 million people. In Poland after World War II (1945 to 1949), almost a million Germans were killed. About 1.5 million Bengali Hindus were killed in Pakistan in 1971. From 1945 to 1987, about 4 million Vietnamese people deemed opponents of the regime in power were murdered.

Rummel (1994) identified the top killers of this century. Casualties from war were not included in his tally. Joseph Stalin was the most prolific murderer, killing about 42 million of his own people from 1929 to 1935. Mao Tse-Tung accounted for about 38 million deaths from 1923 to 1976. Adolf Hitler was third, with about 21 million deaths from 1933 to 1945. Surprisingly, Chiang Kai-Shek, a longtime ally of the U.S., was the fourth leading megamurderer in this century, with about 10 million deaths from 1921 to 1948. Vladmir Lenin killed about 4 million people from 1917 to 1924. Hideki

Tojo was responsible for about 4 million deaths from 1935 to 1945, primarily civilians in China and Korea before and during WWII. From 1968 to 1987, Pol Pot of Cambodia killed off about 2.5 million people in his country, representing a higher rate of genocide than all other countries in this century. Yayaha Khan of Pakistan in one year, 1971, was responsible for the murders of over 1.5 million individuals, mostly Hindus. Joseph Tito of Yugoslavia, finishing up the list of the worst 10 killers in this century, from 1941 to 1987, was responsible for the deaths of over 1 million men, women, and children.

Overall, Rummel (1994) noted that most of the victims came from Russia and China. Since the inception of World War II, about 1 out of 20 Chinese was killed by Japanese or by his or her own government. In Indochina, in less than 4 years, 31% of Cambodians died at the hand of Dictator Pol Pot and his Khmer Rouge.

The most prolific murderers in this century were all dictators and account for an estimated 170 to 360 million deaths, according to Rummel (1994). No other century has seen murder of this magnitude. In his important work, Rummel noted that the dynamic that makes all this killing possible is a belief in absolute truth combined with absolute power. He came to the startling conclusion that death by one's own government is a more probable event than death in war (about 38 million people were killed in wars in the 20th century). For every one person killed in war as a combatant, four or five people have been murdered by their own government.

Nuclear, biological, and chemical warfare, particularly disgusting and dishonorable ways to fight, represent the epitome of noncommunication between perpetrators and victims and further eroded the evolutionary tendency toward nonviolence. Philip Morrison (1995, p. 45), a professor emeritus at Massachusetts Institute of Technology who worked on the Manhattan Project and also inspected Hiroshima soon after the blast, shared his excitement about his work:

> *"The Trinity Test, the first test of a nuclear bomb, went off as planned on July 16, 1945, leaving lifelong indelible memories. None is as vivid for me as that brief flash of heat on my face, sharp as noonday for a watcher 10 miles away in the cold desert predawn, while our own false sun rose on the Earth and set again. For most of the 2000 technical people at Los Alamos — civilians, military and student-soldiers — that test was the climax of our actions. The terrifying deployment less than a month later appeared as anticlimax, out of our hands, far away."* [emphasis added]

Professor Frank Barnaby (1984), a nuclear physicist and former Director of the Stockholm International Peace Institute (SIPI), estimated that, in the early 1980s, the U.S. alone had about 38,000 tons of killer chemical warfare agents (particularly nerve agents, such as VX and SARIN, and lethal dermal agent mustard gas). Only a portion of these lethal chemicals have been destroyed in the last few years. During World War I, 100 million kilograms of chlorine, phosgene, and mustard gas were used by *both* sides to kill 100,000 solders and to injure another million or more (Barnaby, 1984). Chemical agents were used by the Italians in Ethiopia from 1935 to 1936, an act which pales in comparison to the Nazis, in World War II, who gassed millions of victims, primarily Jews, and also gypsies, handicapped individuals, homosexuals, Jehovah's Witnesses, Socialists, Communists, and Democrats. Almost 6 million Jews alone may have been exterminated (about two thirds of the European-Jewish population). In Chapter 14, David Paltin discusses modern-day applications and strategies of chemical and biological warfare. With the increase in terrorism, the chances of chemical attacks, biological attacks, or both are mounting.

Japan has a proud and ancient history. In the 1930s and 1940s, however, Japan's military, apparently reasoning that an enemy people are to be destroyed at any cost, used biological agents in their war against the Chinese, including parachuting plague-infested rats into cities in Northern China (Barnaby, 1984). Japanese prisoners of war testified that Japan's military disseminated a plague into China by using fleas that were attracted to humans (*Pulex irritans*) as the carrier. These incidents took place in central China, where no plague epidemics had been recorded previously. It has long been suspected that the Japanese operated a death camp in China before and during World War II.

In August 1991, the Associated Press reported that dozens of fragmented skulls and thigh bones that had been discovered in Tokyo were disposed of by the Japanese government. It was highly likely, according to Kanagawa University history professors who were interviewed at the time of the discovery, that the bones were remains of prisoners who died in germ warfare experiments conducted by Unit 731 in Northern China. There, prisoners were injected with typhus, cholera, and other diseases, in addition to having gangrene induced, within a variety of other medical experiments. Some of these historians believe that the staff and others responsible for Unit 731 activities were not prosecuted or even identified by the U.S. in exchange for information helpful to our own biological warfare efforts. Yuki Tanaka (1996), previously a Research Fellow at the Australian National University, documented the biological warfare experiments conducted by Unit 731 and other atrocities committed by the Japanese during World War II.

Japan's denial of atrocities has extended to the schools. Denying the past (or not discussing aspects of it) does not allow for learning of true history to take place and thus raises the risk of repetition. Professor Saburo Ienaga (1970; personal communication, 1992), a former distinguished history professor at Tokyo University, successfully pursued court action to have the Ministry of Education's system of certifying textbooks declared unconstitutional. The Stone Age, as well as the atrocities of World War II, were left out of the typical history textbook. Instead, Japanese history usually started with tales of the "age of the gods" (i.e., myths about the origin of the imperial family as recorded in the *Kojiki* and *Nihon Shoki*). According to Ienaga (1970), this mythology leads to the notions that the willing sacrifice of one's life in war is the supreme morality, that war in general is to be idolized as a struggle against inferiors (i.e., non-genetically pure Japanese), and that the denial of these misdeeds once the war is over is an indication of loyalty.

Biological and chemical warfare continued after World War II. Mycotoxins, which are poisons produced naturally by fungi and create massive bleeding from the stomach and death within an hour, were used by the U.S.S.R. against the Afghans, by Laos and Vietnam against the Hmong people, and by Vietnam against the indigenous people of Kampuchea (Barnaby, 1984). In August 1995, Iraq, long known to use biological weapons on its own people for political control, admitted, for the first time, that it had started producing *Clostridium botulinum* and *Bacillus anthraces* in 1989 for offensive purposes.

On March 20, 1995, a nerve gas attack in Tokyo's subway system shattered the illusion that Japan is insulated from the lethal violence it has perpetrated on other countries (this incident is discussed by Leighton Whitaker in Chapter 2 and by David Paltin in Chapter 14). Major news carriers reported that Sarin was used by a radical cult, killing 12 people and sickening 5500. Even though those thought to be responsible were arrested, including the cult leader, Shoko Asahara, the fear in Japan is that this could easily occur again with greater lethality. Japan's self-image of safety and order was shaken by the event, which marked a psychological milestone for the country. The shattering of the sense of security was intensified by authorities realizing that the event may have been the tip of an iceberg. The cult was also allegedly planning an airborne Sarin attack on the capital and was forming a guerilla army with a chemical, biological, and conventional arsenal. As noted above, the U.S. and other countries possess Sarin for possible use on the enemy. Without diminishing the heinous nature of the attack in Japan, we have another example of how the same weapon is viewed differently depending on who is perceived as the "legitimate" aggressor.

According to Barnaby (1984), the U.S. (the Pentagon, in particular) has an interest in the possible military applications of research in recombinant DNA, opening up the prospect of artificially created life forms and viruses as weapons of mass destruction. The current status of this research is unknown. In a well-documented and haunting book entitled *Emerging Viruses: AIDS and Ebola: Nature, Accident, or Intentional*, Leonard Horowitz (1997) discussed how the U.S. government in the 1960s and 1970s developed countless immune-system-ravaging viruses. He detailed how, during that time and later, numerous viral vaccine experiments were conducted simultaneously in New York City and Central Africa in the populations most plagued by AIDS. The CIA in particular, among other agencies, has been implicated in the use of the AIDS virus for military purposes.

In this country, experimentation with the effects of nuclear radiation continued long after Hiroshima and Nagasaki. As elaborated on by this author in Chapter 1, the U.S. Energy Department admitted that about 9000 Americans, including children and newborns, were used in 154 human radiation tests during the Cold War (Burns, 1995). The Final Report to the President on the Human Radiation Experiments (Faden, 1996) revealed that over 4000 radiation experiments, involving tens of thousands of unwitting U.S. citizens, were performed. One of the reported experiments took place at Vanderbilt University in Nashville, TN, in 1969, where 86 newborn babies were given blood laced with chromium-50, a radioactive substance, to measure red blood cell counts and determine the timing of hemorrhaging.

Nuclear weapons are probably the single, greatest threat to the survival of the human species. This threat is based on the following:

1. The history of prior use by the U.S., with history representing the best predictor of future violence — This country has never renounced first-strike options (Kull, 1990), meaning that there are strategic scenarios that call for initiating thermonuclear war in other than a retaliatory capacity.
2. Proliferation — At least seven countries possess "the bomb" (U.S., Russia, United Kingdom, France, China, India, and Pakistan), and others are concealing their nuclear capabilities (e.g., Israel and, until they abandoned their programs, South Africa, Argentina, and Brazil). Heirs to Soviet nuclear weapons include the Ukraine, Belarus, and Kazakhstan, which may not have surrendered all their weapons as promised. In theory, any nation that has nuclear breeders accumulates plutonium, which can be fashioned into nuclear weaponry. To date, nations capable of building nuclear weapons include Canada, Germany, Italy, Japan, South Korea, Sweden, Taiwan, Switzerland, Belgium, the Netherlands, and Finland. Those with suspected nuclear plans include North Korea, Iraq, and Iran, the last two of which were signatories of the renewed Non-Proliferation Treaty in May 1995. Although the treaty has been extended indefinitely, a criticism is the nonbinding nature of the goals as well as the impossibility of airtight guarantees that non-weapon states will never be the target of nuclear attack by the major powers. The possession of nuclear weapons implies a willingness to engage in thermonuclear war, as all strategies of nuclear deterrence are based on the assumption that nuclear weapons will be used if necessary in either a first strike or retaliatory capacity. Kull (1990), in a remarkable psychological analysis of the inner conflicts of nuclear policy makers, noted that most U.S. nuclear planners assume that nuclear war is inevitable.
3. Huge stockpiles of nuclear weapons, enough to kill every living person and animal on the planet many times over — Even after a planned reduction in thermonuclear weaponry as announced over the last few years, whether hydrogen bombs or ICBMs, the remainder is sufficient to end all life on Earth. Of the 2034 tests of nuclear bombs that have been conducted worldwide since 1945, 511 have been atmospheric tests (Beardsley, 1995). Beardsley showed that, when combined with standard risk factors, as shown by assessments by the United Nations, such testing could easily lead to 1.2 million fatal cancers. Only 15% of the predicted cancers resulting from the atmospheric tests have been diagnosed; the remainder will be contracted over the coming centuries.
4. Power, prestige, and money associated with nuclear weapons outweighing the perceived disadvantages

— All the permanent members of the United Nations Security Council are nuclear weapon states, a fact not lost on the rest of the world. A huge nuclear industry has been created worldwide. Winter (1994) noted that one Trident submarine (costing about $1.4 billion) would fund a 5-year child immunization program for six virulent diseases and that one Stealth bomber ($68 billion) would fund two thirds of the estimated costs to meet clean-water goals in the U.S. by the year 2000.

5. Increased military expenditures — In regard to the environmental effects and costs of military activities, Ruff (1992) documented that since the 1930s, military expenditures have increased 2.6 times more than the world population. Eighty-six percent of all U.S. government energy use is military. At least one third of all scientific research and development is for military purposes. According to Ruff, the U.S. Defense Department accounts for 76% of halon-1211 emissions and about one half of the emissions of CFC-133, a chlorofluorocarbon. Ruff noted that 48 nuclear warheads and seven nuclear-power reactors (e.g., in submarines) remain on the ocean floor as a result of military accidents or sabotage.
6. The many ways in which a nuclear war could break out — This includes a small group of scientists/ technologists or a terrorist group making a bomb from information readily available to the public. Barnaby (1984) conjectured that a bomb could easily be made and exploded by a team of four, including one physicist (he noted that a young American physics graduate student had designed a thermonuclear device using only publicly available information). Each submarine with nuclear missiles is, by itself, capable of starting World War III. Accidental nuclear war is a possibility that cannot be dismissed. From 1977 through 1984, for example, the U.S.' early warning system generated over 20,000 false indications of missile attacks on the country, although only 5% were serious enough to require a second look (Kreger, 1989). Only one believable "attack" is necessary to ignite a nuclear conflagration.
7. On an individual level, the belief that one has little impact on whether we continue to support nuclear warfare — Most people do not try to change the *status quo*, thus guaranteeing its continuation.
8. The continued belief that competition, with its violent offshoots, as opposed to cooperation, is necessary (and even healthy) to sustain our quality of life — Related beliefs that maintain our high-risk status are that dominance over and control of others are necessary for survival, and that war, including nuclear war, is inevitable.
9. The misperception that the odds for favorable outcomes are on our side — The main flaw in the deterrence policy is that it is not possible to repeatedly risk nuclear war (or any catastrophic event) without the event becoming more probable.

Carl Sagan (1980, p. 329), in *Cosmos*, stated the following:

"How do we explain the global arms race to a dispassionate extraterrestrial observer? How would we justify the most recent destabilizing developments of killer-satellites, particle beam weapons, lasers, neutron bombs, cruise missiles, and the proposed conversion of areas the size of modest countries to the enterprise of hiding each intercontinental ballistic missile among hundreds of decoys? Would we argue that ten thousand targeted nuclear warheads are likely to enhance the prospects for our survival? What account would we give of our stewardship of the planet Earth? We have heard the rationales offered by the nuclear superpowers. We know who speaks for the nations. But who speaks for the human species? Who speaks for Earth?"

The links between war, genocide, and state-sanctioned killings, on the one hand, and family, acquaintance, and stranger violence, on the other, are pervasive and fundamental. First, institutional violence tends to legitimize the general use of violence in domestic situations. Nonverbally, it models that it is acceptable to kill, given sufficient power and moral righteousness. Killing others outside an institutional context is bound to increase under these circumstances, as individuals tend to incorporate the values of the superordinate power.

Archer and Gartner (1984) studied homicide from a cross-national perspective of 154 nations. They found that the level of lethal violence in 50 nations increased after the country participated in a war. The increase applied to both veterans and nonveterans of both sexes. Further, they determined that, after World War II, homicides increased for both men and women in an 11-nation European group for which data were available.

Archer and Gartner (1984) noted that arrests for homicide in this country increased dramatically for both males and females (101 and 59%, respectively) during the 10-year period of the Vietnam War — from 1962 until our military forces were withdrawn in 1973. Homicide arrests increased for all age groups, including those over the age of 45 (who likely were not Vietnam veterans).

In their cross-national study, these authors showed that an increase in homicides occurred consistently after both large and small wars, whether a country was defeated or victorious or had a good or poor economy, for both men and women and for several age groups. They speculated that war lowers the threshold for homicide as a means of settling conflict in everyday life because war provides concrete evidence that killing others under some conditions is acceptable and because of the powerful influence of government as a model of legitimacy. Finally, war provides instruction in the technology of death to its citizen soldiers.

Inhibitions to Violence

Given all of the above, one may wonder why there is not more war, genocide, and mass murder. Why do people or governments not simply kill those who displease them? Some do, as we have seen, with governments generally exercising less restraint than most individuals. Generally, however, all except predatory violence is avoided if possible by both individuals and groups. Why? The answer lies in inhibitory factors, those characteristics of the perpetrator, victim, and context of violence that may lower the probability that violence will occur.

Analysis of inhibitions must figure into all descriptions and prognostications of violence and thus bears close scrutiny. Our hope for a non-violent world lies in inhibitions to aggress. In Chapter 2, Leighton Whitaker discusses this concept in detail and with an eye toward applying the few inhibitions of which we are aware.

As a weak inhibitor of violence, some countries tend to avoid war as a generalized extension of the propensity of the people and leaders in power at the time to avoid confrontation and violence whenever possible. For example, Richardson (1960) found that the Confucian-Taoist-Buddhist orientation of China yielded very few wars and exercised a general role as a pacifier in regional disputes until the 1911 revolution. A bloody history has been revealed, as discussed, in subsequent decades. Richardson found that during the period from 1820 to 1939, only Sweden, Switzerland, and Persia had no wars of a significant magnitude. Yet, each of these countries has a bloody past and in one case (the Middle East area in old Persia), the present is filled with lethal violence.

Running cross-grain to popular opinion, the worst overall offender from 1480 to 1941, in terms of the number of wars and conflicts with other nations, was Great Britain. Great Britain has been involved in lethal violence continually since 1941 — in the Korean War, Ireland, the Falkland Islands, and a host of other areas. Since our country was formed, the U.S. may run a close second, especially if undeclared wars and other lethal acts of aggression toward other nations and peoples are counted.

Once control is established, usually by violent means, many political and religious institutions discourage lethal violence among its members. Despite the actual history of Western religious leaders and sects, as we have seen, most teach that killing by individuals is unacceptable. In another domain, youth movements across the world attempt to instill values of cooperation and altruism. On an individual basis, these values become internalized and weigh against pressures or desires to inflict lethal harm on others. They assume inhibitory status when they contribute to a decision not to aggress.

Social pressure to inhibit violence can be considerable. Smaller, more vulnerable groups (i.e., the Pueblo Indians of New Mexico, the Amish, the Hutterites, and the Mormons), preserve their cultural identity by nonviolent defensive adaptations (Siegal, 1969). All of these groups have rigorous codes of conduct for their members, as defined by an authoritative elite. Innovations are screened carefully by the leadership. From a developmental standpoint, Siegal (1969) noted that training in self-control starts at an early age, with the subordination of the individual to the welfare of the group. Communication with the outside world in these groups is conventional but deceptive in the use of denial on sensitive issues such as sex and aggression.

The Death Penalty

As another form of institutional violence, there is a recent trend toward acceptance of capital punishment as shown by data for the period from 1930 to 1993 (Stephen and Brien, 1994). In the U.S., executions rose to about 200 a year in the 1930s, followed by an overall decline, until they stopped altogether in 1972, when the Supreme Court ruled the death penalty unconstitutional as then administered.

Stephen and Brien (1994) documented that ten states executed 38 prisoners during 1993, the largest annual number since the U.S. Supreme Court upheld the constitutionality of revised state capital punishment laws in 1976. At the end of 1993, 2716 prisoners were being held under sentences of death by 34 states and the federal prison system.

In terms of the age at which the death penalty is allowed, 11 states and the federal prison system required a minimum age of 18; 16 states require an age of eligibility between 14 and 17. Lethal injection and electrocution are the usual means of inflicting death, but it is still possible to be executed by hanging (Montana, New Hampshire, and Washington) or by firing squad (Idaho and Utah). The majority of those executed are white, as opposed to black or Hispanic. Only a handful of women have been executed, with no executions of women in 1993.

Except for the executed individual, capital punishment does not act as an inhibitor to lethal violence and does not save lives. When all is said and done, its primary function appears to be revenge by the state for wrongful behavior. Indeed, the murder risk in some geographical areas of this country *increased* when executions were resumed in the 1980s. Barnett and Schwartz (1989), for example, in comparing the murder risk for the period from 1976 to 1977 (when there was no capital punishment) with the period from 1984 to 1986 (when capital punishment was reinstituted) found that the murder risk for Southern cities increased 13%. They noted that, in the mid-1930s, executions averaged two per month, with a total death row population of about 2000 inmates, a high rate for the population at that time, showing that capital punishment had insignificant deterrent value.

Despite all of the arguments in favor of the death penalty, including the total removal of threat from an executed offender, the critical argument against the death penalty is that it again models the acceptability of killing others as a solution to a problem. Despite this opinion, there is considerable popular support for the death penalty. When Ted Bundy was executed in Florida, people outside the prison cheered and clapped. On November 28, 1994, the Associated Press reported that Jeffery Dahmer, a serial killer who had strangled and dismembered 17 males (and ate some of them), was beaten to death, his face battered beyond recognition, by a fellow inmate (himself convicted of murder) at the Columbia Correctional Center. Not only members of the victims' families but others expressed the opinion that the perpetrator was a "hero" and should be honored and not punished. In Chapter 16, Sandra McPherson further probes the psychopathology behind the death penalty.

Outlaws, Gangs, and Organized Crime

In the worst terrorist attack in U.S. history, the bombing of the Murrah Federal Building in Oklahoma is seared in the minds of Americans as a brutal, cowardly act that indiscriminately killed 168 children and adults. Yet, we learn of increasing numbers of Americans who express disenchantment with the government and federal enforcement agencies. The quasi-hero status that these institutions once enjoyed is fading rapidly. Concurrently, anti-establishment figures in gangs, terrorist groups, and organized crime have gained considerable support and even admiration from large segments of the public. Unlawful group activity has affected every facet of our lives, from the increased time and expense of airport security to the perception that the police simply cannot protect the citizenry from violence.

In truth, Americans have always had mixed feelings about outlaws and their gangs. In the American West, gangs plied their trade with relative impunity. In 1877, for example, Texas alone had a phenomenal 5000 men on its wanted list (Rister, 1933). The greatest gunfighters — Wild Bill Hickok, Doc Holliday, Ben Thompson — often played both sides of the law. Vigilante gangs formed in response to outlaws — those outside the law — often had the strongest support. As President, Andrew Jackson once advised Iowa settlers to punish a murderer by vigilante action (Brown, 1969b). In his younger days, Theodore Roosevelt attempted unsuccessfully to join a vigilante movement. Folk hero status has been accorded to some, such as Jesse James, Billy the Kid, John Wesley Hardin, and, in the 20th century, Al Capone, Pretty Boy Floyd, Dillinger, and Ma Barker. We keep the hero status alive through our literature and movies. The great majority of these "heroes" attained their power through small groups of like-minded individuals who would stop at nothing to achieve their ends.

Gangs provide much of the infrastructure of American society. They could not survive without support from individuals whose needs are satisfied by the groups' stock and trade. Based on several decades of experience, this author speculates that for every gang of several dozen core individuals, several hundred non-gang members — families and extended families, customers, bribed parties, individuals and groups who receive no material benefits but support the gangs out of common ideology or beliefs — actively work to keep gangs in existence, or at least reinforce their behavior. Taking into account their pervasive activities, organized crime affects virtually every facet of life and constitutes a second form of government in this country. When murder occurs between the gangs, public fear and anxiety turn to apathy when the public realizes that gang members are killing one another. A temporary public outcry for vigorous enforcement of the laws more likely occurs when a non-gang member is murdered.

Most modern-day gangs received their impetus from society's need to experience altered states of consciousness, as in alcohol during Prohibition or drugs in the last few decades. The Sicilian Mafia — "La Cosa Nostra" — has expanded greatly since the 1930s to include a wide range of illegal activities in all parts of the country — gambling, prostitution, fencing, labor racketeering, loan sharking, smuggling, money laundering, and murder for hire. Networking was effected with other groups. Jewish organized crime, for example, has been allied with Italian families (Abadinsky, 1990). Eventually, legitimate businesses were entered into in order to launder money and provide increased capital for mob ventures. Lethal violence was, and is, routinely engaged in to enforce business rules or as murder for hire.

A proliferation of gangs has taken place in the country in the last several decades. The enduring gangs tend to have strong economic ties to the drug trade. As with all institutions, crimes which result in arrests are documented for individuals, rather than the groups to which they belong. In juvenile gangs, many members remain involved long into their adult years (e.g., Crips, Bloods). Their *modus operandi* is to hide behind an intricate organization of high rollers, who are successful drug traffickers, and "baby" gangsters, ages 12 to 15, who work the streets for sales. Motorcycle gangs include the five largest — Hell's Angels, Pagans, Outlaws, Bandidos, and the Sons of Silence (Richardson, 1991). Richardson predicted that these and other gangs will make methamphetamine the drug of choice in future years. Richardson also predicted an increase in international networking, as well as forays into legitimate business, in order to launder money. Lethal violence is projected to increase as gangs expand their operations and as police try to disrupt their operations. It is important to know the mindset of these groups concerning murder. Killing others is not perceived as inappropriate behavior but, rather, as a legitimate tool for revenge, enforcement, or additional revenue.

Throughout the 1970s and 1980s, gang members have shown an increased willingness to assault and murder law enforcement officers (NIJ, 1990). Chinese gangs and "tongs", which are involved in heroin trafficking, are becoming increasingly violent toward the police and the general public (Joe, 1992).

Jamaican posses are known for their drug trafficking and posse-related murders in their attempts to terrorize and control (Gay and Marquart, 1993). The shift from the sale of marijuana to cocaine in the 1980s was associated with an increase in lethal violence. Although these posses generally trace their origins to Jamaica, they now have working relationships with West Coast street gangs and the Columbian narcotics cartel.

Some enduring gangs in America have international agreements with other groups, much like peace treaties, to divide the spoils of war. According to the U.S. Congress Senate Committees (1991, 1992a,b), the four major Asian organized crime groups which operate in many U.S. urban areas include: (1) the Chinese groups, including triads (which originally evolved as a resistance group to the Manchu Dynasty), tongs (business/fraternal organizations which stem from triads), and increasingly violent street gangs; (2) the Japanese criminal society known as the Boryokudan or Yakuza, which alone has over 3000 groups and 86,000 members (Mosquera, 1993); (3) Vietnamese groups, often associated with the Chinese groups or Viet Ching; and (4) Korean gangs, some of which are associated with the Japanese Boryokudan. Other international gangs are from South America and Europe.

When trends are considered, an expansion of international gang activities into the U.S. is taking place at an accelerated rate. These activities include computer chip theft, the black market for transplant organs, illegal arms trading, and illicit disposal of toxic wastes. All of these activities have involved murder as part and parcel of the need for deception and to avoid apprehension.

The groups themselves may be supported strongly by the societies in which they are embedded. Japanese police, as an example, allow the Boryokudan to function in certain areas as long as no cultural taboos are violated (Huang and Vaughn, 1992). The pachinko parlors, illegal drugs, gambling houses, and prostitution are perceived by the Japanese as serving to alleviate stress from their daily lives and society's rigid social structure. When an individual is murdered, or innocent bystanders are hurt in a gang-related incident, the police experience increased public pressure to investigate. Much like in the U.S., no real change takes place in the structure or activities of organized crime. As mentioned above, the statistics on arrests and convictions reflect sanctions for individuals rather than for the groups that perpetrated the violence.

The burgeoning literature on terrorism indicates clear trends, as the following sections document. At this time, terrorist groups are trained specifically for operations in the U.S. by Libya, Syria, and other Middle East countries. Other terrorist groups consisting of disillusioned Americans have been formed within this country.

A Rand report suggested that for 1988, at least one person was killed in about 20% of all international terrorist acts. Bombings were the most common tactic (Gardela and Hoffman, 1992). Most acts were symbolic and designed to call attention to terrorist interests. Many of the terrorist attacks were by Islamic groups, with Libya, Syria, and other Middle East countries often providing the training for hijackings, bombings, extortion, and assassinations. Although Europe has a long history of dealing with Islamic extremists, some commentators, such as Builta (1993), and certainly many federal authorities, suggest that the U.S. may be the real target. As part of his analysis, Builta explored the many links between Sheik Omar Abel-Rahman and his accomplices in the World Trade Center bombing. Recent court outcomes regarding this bombing suggest these links are not coincidences.

Terrorist groups formed within the U.S. are increasing as a conjoint function of accelerating distrust of the federal government, and the opportunity provided for self-aggrandizement and exploitation. Mullins (1990) correctly predicted that terrorist activity would increase in virulence and frequency in the 1990s. He speculated that terrorists would engage in large scale operations and use state-of-the-art weaponry, if available. Narcoterrorism would become a reality, with the bond between terrorism and drugs more commonplace and formalized. He correctly predicted an increase in violent forms of expression for anti-abortionists.

A reasonable prediction is that collective violence of institutions and the lethal behavior of its members will persist well into the 21st century as the influences of the family, school, government, and other institutions continue to erode. The influence of the police simply will not be sufficient to quell the expected widespread disorder. Should our government cease to exist due to any combination of causes, these groups will most likely compete for the control and direction of everyday life.

Racial and Ethnic Violence

Lethal violence in this country cannot be understood outside the context of race and ethnicity. Blacks, in particular, show differential responses to family, criminal, and institutional violence as a result of their history and common experiences of prejudice.

From the onset, slavery — especially the sale of humans once they had arrived at their destinations — implied a willingness to become involved as accessory to murder. Coupland (1939) determined from archival research that four or five lives were lost for every slave delivered at Zanzibar, the point of debarkation for many slave ships. He estimated that around the time of the American Civil War, East Africa alone lost 80,000 to 100,000 lives annually to the slave trade. A minority of Africans survived the kidnaping, slave ships, or initial years at sites in the Western hemisphere (Graham and Gurr, 1969). Once they arrived, the right of the masters to kill their slaves was absolute. After the Civil War, as an expression of white supremacy during the post-Reconstruction period, almost 2000 blacks were killed by Southern males (Brown, 1969a). Overall, 5000 blacks were killed, primarily by lynching, between 1865 and 1955 (Comer, 1969).

Open murder of blacks, associated with competition and prejudice, occurred quite regularly in the South, traditionally the most violent region of our country. In a classic study covering 49 years in 14 southern states, Hoveland and Sears (1940) found that the number of lynchings of blacks varied as a function of the farm and acre value of cotton. Although correlational in nature, the results suggested that negative economic conditions increased this type of murder. Importantly, the findings were confirmed in a re-analysis of the original data using more sophisticated statistical techniques and a more accurate measure of economic conditions (Hepworth and West, 1988).

As violence begets violence, blacks responded with lethal aggression of their own. The first slave uprising in this country — in New York City in 1712 — was put down with great ruthlessness because the slaves were not armed sufficiently (Brown, 1969a). The majority of race riots — 76 between 1913 and

1963 — occurred after emancipation in the 20th century (Janowitz, 1969). Generally, far more blacks than whites were killed during these confrontations, again because blacks had limited resources and weapons.

The riots in Harlem/Rochester in 1964 and Watts in 1965 reversed a pattern that has continued up to the present (including the massive 1992 riot in Los Angeles). During those riots, for the first time, blacks inflicted more lethal violence on majority race individuals than they sustained (Brown, 1969; Janowitz, 1969). A shift from reactive to proactive aggression of all types was seen, with assaults and robbery predominating.

Violence rates for blacks, as both perpetrators and victims, are higher than for other racial groups. Foote (1996) and Bixenstine (1996) presented convincing data that the violence rates, including murder, have been consistently higher for blacks compared to other ethnic groups. A multitude of statistics from the NIJ and the FBI suggest that blacks perpetrate rape, robbery, murder, and assault far out of proportion to their numbers.

Despite some gains, polarization between the races may be increasing in this country. As blacks react with increased violence to their own victimhood, an increased backlash from the victims of blacks can be expected, resulting in a vicious cycle. Backlash movements are likely to come in the form of vigilante-type responses or by the police. Indeed, we have seen significant examples in the last few years. It is hoped that a counterbalancing trend will emerge from the increasingly large black middle class, supported by equal access into the military, training institutions, and affirmative action.

The net effect of the continued victimization of and perpetration of violence by blacks is "anomie" (Durkheim, 1951). Anomie represents a social condition in which there is a deterioration in existing rules of society or when desired goals are not accessible through legitimate means. Associated features include feelings of isolation, powerlessness, and estrangement from others, even from one's own race. Anomie is associated intimately with violence in that the normal inhibitions and societal rules regarding harming others are weakened. The plight of blacks, as well as other disenfranchised groups in this country, reflects a substantial degree of anomie Unfortunately, anomie increases as a function of expressed violence and sets the stage for an entrenched cycle of aggression.

Summary

On a global level, the story of humankind over the millennia describes the spread of unbalanced civilization by lethally violent means. The vast majority of significant events — wars, assassinations, executions, rebellions, and crucifixions — have something to do, directly or indirectly, with lethal institutional violence. The 5600 years of recorded history have produced more than 14,600 wars, or a rate of about 2.6 wars every year (Baron, 1977). Only 10 of the 185 generations of humans in recorded history have been free of war. The fragile cognitive processes leading to distinction-dissolving and altruistic behavior have been largely driven underground by the technology of death and the need of institutions to maintain order and control. In concordance with the influences of these institutions, we have individually become more accepting of lethal violence toward others. From this legacy, lethal violence in modern times has taken on unique and dangerous characteristics.

Primitive modes of adaptive violence — particularly predator-prey and defensive aggression, which kept us alive, and competitive aggression, which shaped a necessary dominance hierarchy for survival under harsh conditions — were subverted in the last few millennia into a virulent combination, characterized by a need for dominating, hurting, or destroying the opponent, and deception to cover the tracks of the perpetrators. Lethal violence continues to be used by individuals, groups, and countries to achieve their own ends, at an enormous cost to humans and the environment. In a deep psychological sense, our history of support for institutions and individuals associated with lethal violence and winning at any cost has affected our attitudes, behavior, fantasies, hopes, and certainly our ability to survive as a species. With few exceptions, we have become a nation of competitive, impulsive, self-aggrandizing, distinction-creating people who care little for self-sacrifice and altruism. Toward what have we evolved?

Several critical differences emerge between contemporary collective violence and that before the development of nuclear weapons. These differences make current times especially challenging for those who strive to make the world less violent. First, in the past, killing, for all its brutality, did not threaten the existence of the entire human species. Today, several nations are capable of destroying all life on Earth many times over. Due to the realities of conducting nuclear war (e.g., from submarines, bombers, missile silos) and in spite of fail-safe mechanisms (which have not prevented dozens of nuclear accidents), many people are aware of how to initiate a nuclear war and may therefore have it within their power to start a thermonuclear war and thus end existence as we know it on Earth. The reader should never forget that, in order to represent a credible influence, the mindset required of those who possess nuclear, biological, and chemical weapons involves the absolute willingness to use those devices when target groups violate arbitrary criteria (Kull, 1990).

In the last few decades, lethal violence has been the focus of vigorous scientific inquiry. New methods of perpetrator identification have emerged (e.g., DNA printing, forensic engineering, P-300 wave analysis). Just as capital punishment will not reduce the overall murder rate because it has no deterrent value, so too can sure-fire methods of perpetrator identification not be expected to reduce lethal violence. Technology, for all its glamour and promise, will never reduce the rate of murder. To do that, we must change the values by which people live and die. We need to teach ways to self-control violent responses and, additionally, to bond with others who are different from us in a meaningful, positive, win-win fashion. In short, we need to become more distinction-dissolving in our attitudes toward others.

Can institutional violence be stopped? Should we even try? Some say "no" and point to the violence and war that have raged since the beginning of human history. Theoretical support for the notion comes from evolutionary approaches. Over the eons, the reasoning is that we have aggressed against our own kind for food, sex, territory, and other reinforcers. Genes associated with violence have endured because they were adaptable (Barash, 1977). Thus, why fight against our "natural" state?

The Seville Statement, which scrutinized biological findings in order to challenge the deterministic idea that violence and war are inevitable, stands as a counter to the above. The Seville Statement is an optimistic declaration that points to the possibility of a nonviolent future. Table 12.1 presents the Statement in its entirety. The American Psychological Association (APA), which endorsed the statement in 1987, saw it is a social statement designed to counter unfounded assumptions on the inevitability of violence and war. The APA asserted that the Seville Statement constitutes a socially and scientifically responsible action that was congruent with the empirical literature.

A criticism of the Seville Statement is that it was motivated by fear and politics (Beroldi, 1994). Yet, we are living with the reality of the Doomsday Clock, black market thermonuclear devices, rising criminal violence, and the disintegration of the American family. No sane person could fail to see the ominous signs and fear for the future. It should come as no surprise that the signatories of the Seville Statement were also driven by fear and that they wished to address lethal violence on a large scale within a legislative arena. The key question is whether their endorsement of the statement will lead to action culminating in a less destructive world. To make the world more violence free and to transform our society into a more gentle, altruistic place, the contributors to this volume believe that an attitude of optimism and cognitive flexibility, such as is found in the statement, will be required.

Annotated Bibliography

1. Archer, D. and Gartner, R. (1984) *Violence and Crime in Cross-National Perspective*. New Haven: Yale University Press. This book provides a cross-national, quantitative comparison of violence and relates the findings to critical questions such as: (1) does the level of domestic violence in a society increase after that nation has participated in a war? (for most nations, the answer is a strong "yes"); (2) does the death penalty deter violence and crime? (for almost everywhere, the answer is "no"; in fact, the death penalty may even indirectly increase violence); (3) do large cities have unusually high homicide rates? (the answer depends on the size of the city relative to the overall homicide rate of the country)

2. Graham, H.D. and Gurr, T.R., Eds. (1969) *The History of Violence in America. Historical and Comparative Perspectives*. New York: Frederick A. Praeger. This edited work stems from a report submitted to the National Commission on the Causes and Prevention of Violence. Presented at a time when this country was in the midst of both Vietnam and domestic turmoil, this book in splendid detail outlines the history of violence in America. Findings suggest that the conflict in the 1960s was not unique, but represented a shift in attitude on the part of Americans towards each other and their society. The value of the book lies in the historical treatment of both individual and collective violence.

3. Kull, S. (1982) *Minds at War. Nuclear Reality and the Inner Conflicts of Defense Policymakers*. New York: Basic Books. In what should be mandatory reading for all serious students of institutional violence, this work provides a glimpse of how those in power process information about nuclear war. When interviewing high-ranking statesmen, military leaders and policymakers about nuclear war with the former U.S.S.R., Kull deliberately withheld the fact that he had been a practicing psychotherapist for years before he undertook the project as a Fellow in political science at Stanford University. His results are startling. Among other findings, he determined that those in power believed nuclear war to be inevitable. Until that war occurs, most of what is done in terms of nuclear strategy is motivated by political perceptions in order to satisfy the citizens and influence other countries. His results appear relevant today, in spite of recent moves toward disarmament.

4. Richardson, L. (1960) *Statistics of Deadly Quarrels*. Pacific Grove, CA: The Boxwood Press. Richardson's contribution to our understanding of lethal violence is enormous. First, he presents a list of 300 wars, from 1820 to 1949, with precise statements of the causes, the conditions, and the approximate number of war dead. Second, Richardson applies statistical methods to extract highly probable conclusions from the data. Last, and most important, are the conclusions he offers. The Richardson Curve is well known today. Basically, it states that wars of increasing magnitude are occurring with greater frequency. At some point, the willingness to kill will equal or exceed the population of the Earth.

5. Rummel, R.J. (1994) *Death by Government*. New Brunswick: Transaction Publishers. In his fourth book on genocide and government mass murder (what the author calls "democide"), Rummel presents a historical overview on genocide and offers detailed tables for offender nations in this century. The primary conclusion that emerged was that the less freedom and control exercised

Table 12.1

The Seville Statement on Violence

Believing that it is our responsibility to address from our particular disciplines the most dangerous and destructive activities of our species, violence and war; recognizing that science is a human cultural product which cannot be definitive or all-encompassing; and gratefully acknowledging the support of the authorities of Seville and representatives of Spanish UNESCO; we, the undersigned scholars from around the world and from relevant sciences, have met and arrived at the following Statement on Violence. In it, we challenge a number of alleged biological findings that have been used, even by some in our disciplines, to justify violence and war. Because the alleged findings have contributed to an atmosphere of pessimism in our time, we submit that the open, considered rejection of these misstatements can contribute significantly to the International Year of Peace.

Misuse of scientific theories and data to justify violence and war is not new but has been made since advent of modern science. For example, the theory of evolution has been used to justify not only war, but also genocide, colonialism, and suppression of the weak.

We state our position in the form of five propositions. We are aware that there are many other issues about violence and war that could be fruitfully addressed from the standpoint of our disciplines, but we restrict ourselves here to what we consider a most important first step.

It is scientifically incorrect to say that we have inherited a tendency to make war from our animal ancestors. Although fighting occurs widely throughout animal species, only a few cases of destructive intra-species fighting between organized groups have ever been reported among naturally living species, and none of these involve the use of tools designed to be weapons. Normal predatory feeding upon other species cannot be equated with intra-species violence. Warfare is a peculiarly human phenomenon and does not occur in other animals.

The fact that warfare has changed so radically over time indicates that it is a product of culture. Its biological connection is primarily through language which makes possible the coordination of groups, the transmission of technology, and the use of tools. War is biologically possible, but it is not inevitable, as evidenced by its variation in occurrence and nature over time and space. There are cultures which have not engaged in war for centuries, and there are cultures which have engaged in war frequently at some times and not at others.

It is scientifically incorrect to say that war or any other violent behavior is genetically programmed into our human nature. While genes are involved at all levels of nervous system function, they provide a developmental potential that can be actualized only in conjunction with the ecological and social environment. While individuals vary in their predispositions to be affected

at a grass roots level by the citizens, the more likely it is that genocide would occur. Rummel found that democratic societies tended to be nonviolent, a finding that also applied to previously totalitarian governments which turned democratic. War and genocide were found to be part of the same social process where power and control reign supreme.

Table 12.1 (continued)

The Seville Statement on Violence

by their experience, it is the interaction between their genetic endowment and conditions of nurturance that determines their personalities. Except for rare pathologies, the genes do not produce individuals necessarily predisposed to violence. Neither do they determine the opposite. While genes are co-involved in establishing our behavioral capacities, they do not by themselves specify the outcome.

It is scientifically incorrect to say that in the course of human evolution there has been a selection for aggressive behavior more than for other kinds of behavior. In all well-studied species, status within the group is achieved by the ability to cooperate and to fulfill social functions relevant to the structure of that group. "Dominance" involves social bonding and affiliations; it is not simply a matter of the possession and use of superior physical power, although it does involve aggressive behaviors. Where genetic selection for aggressive behavior has been artificially instituted in animals, it has rapidly succeeded in producing hyper-aggressive individuals; this indicates that aggression was not maximally selected under natural conditions. When such experimentally created hyper-aggressive animals are present in a social group, they either disrupt its social structure or are driven out. Violence is neither in our evolutionary legacy nor in our genes.

It is scientifically incorrect to say that humans have a "violent brain". While we do have the neural apparatus to act violently, it is not automatically activated by internal or external stimuli. Like higher primates and unlike other animals, our higher neural processes filter such stimuli before they can be acted upon. How we act is shaped by how we have been conditioned and socialized. There is nothing in our neurophysiology that compels us to react violently.

It is scientifically incorrect to say that war is caused by "instinct" or any single motivation. The emergence of modern warfare has been a journey from the primacy of emotional and motivational factors, sometimes called "instincts", to the primacy of cognitive factors. Modern war involves institutional use of personal characteristics such as obedience, suggestibility, and idealism; social skills such as language; and rational consideration such as cost-calculation, planning, and information processing. The technology of modern war has exaggerated traits associated with violence both in the training of actual combatants and in the preparation of support for war in the general population. As a result of this exaggeration, such traits are often mistaken to be the causes rather than the consequences of the process.

We conclude that biology does not condemn humanity to war, and that humanity can be freed from the bondage of biological pessimism and empowered with confidence to undertake the transformative tasks needed in this International Year of Peace and in the years to come. Although these tasks are mainly institutional and collective, they also rest upon the consciousness of individual participants for whom pessimism and optimism are crucial factors. Just as "wars begin in the minds of men", peace also begins in our minds. The same species who invented war is capable of inventing peace. The responsibility lies with each of us.

Seville, May 16, 1986

References

Abadinsky, H. (1990) *Organized Crime*, 3rd ed. Chicago, IL: Nelson-Hall Publishers

Archer, D. and Gartner, R. (1984) *Violence and Crime in Cross-National Perspective*. New Haven: Yale University Press.

Archer, J. (1988) *The Behavioral Biology of Aggression*. Cambridge: Press Syndicate of the University of Cambridge.

Archer, J. (1995) What can ethology offer the psychological study of human aggression? *Aggressive Behavior, 21*, 243–255.

Barash, D.P. (1977) *Sociobiology and Behavior*. New York: Elsevier.

Barlow, S.H. and Clayton, C.J. (1996) When mothers murder: understanding infanticide by females. In H.V. Hall (Ed.), *Lethal Violence 2000: A Sourcebook on Fatal Domestic, Acquaintance and Stranger Aggression*, pp. 203–229. Kamuela, HI: Pacific Institute for the Study of Conflict and Aggression.

Barnaby, F. (1984) *Future Wars: Armed Conflict in the Next Decade*. London: Multimedia Publications.

Barnett, A. and Schwartz, E. (1989) Urban homicide: still the same. *Journal of Quantitative Criminology, 5*, 83–100.

Baron, R.A. (1977) *Human Aggression*. New York: Plenum Press.

Beardsley, T. (1995) Testing's Toll. *Scientific American, 273*, 28.

Beroldi, G. (1994) Critique of Seville Statement on violence. *American Psychologist, 49*, 847–48.

Bixenstine, V.E. (1996) Spousal homicide. In H.V. Hall (Ed.), *Lethal Violence 2000: A Sourcebook on Fatal Domestic, Acquaintance and Stranger Aggression*, pp. 231–257. Kamuela, HI: Pacific Institute for the Study of Conflict and Aggression.

Brown, R. (1969a) Historical patterns of violence in America. In H. Graham and T. Gurr (Eds.), *The History of Violence in America*, pp. 45–84. New York: Frederick A. Praeger.

Brown, R. (1969b) The American vigilante tradition. In H. Graham, and T. Gurr (Eds.), *The History of Violence in America*, pp. 154–217. New York: Frederick A. Praeger.

Builta, J. (1993) Origins and future of terrorist acts. *CJ Europe, 3*, 4–6.

Burns, R. (1995) About 9000 involved in human radiation tests. *West Hawaii Today*, Feb. 10, p. A.

Chi, C. and Flynn, J. (1971) Neural pathways associated with hypothalamically elicited attack behavior in cats. *Science, 171*, 703–706.

Comer, J. (1969) The dynamics of black and white violence. In H. Graham and T. Gurr (Eds.), *The History of Violence in America*, pp. 444–463. New York: Frederick A. Praeger.

Coupland, R. (1939) *The Exploitation of East Africa 1856–1890*. London: Faber & Faker.

Daniel, C., Kirshon, J.W., and Berens, R., Eds. (1995) *Chronicle of America*. New York: Dorling Kindersley Publishing.

Durkheim, E. (1951) *Suicide: A Study in Sociology*. Translated by J.A. Spalding and G. Simpson (Eds.) New York: Free Press, 1951 (originally published 1897).

Eichelman, B. (1990) Aggressive behavior: from laboratory to clinic. *Archives of General Psychiatry, 49*, 448–492.

Eme, R.F. (1996) Sex differences in juvenile violence. In H.V. Hall (Ed.), *Lethal Violence 2000: A Sourcebook on Fatal Domestic, Acquaintance and Stranger Aggression*, pp. 79–112. Kamuela, HI: Pacific Institute for the Study of Conflict and Aggression.

Faden, R. (1996) *Final Report of the Advisory Committee on Human Radiation Experiments,* New York: Oxford University Press.

Foote, W. (1996) Victim-precipitated homicide. In H.V. Hall (Ed.), *Lethal Violence 2000: A Sourcebook on Fatal Domestic, Acquaintance and Stranger Aggression*, pp. 175–202. Kamuela, HI: Pacific Institute for the Study of Conflict and Aggression.

Frantz, J. (1969) The frontier tradition: an invitation to violence. In H. Graham and T. Gurr (Eds.), *The History of Violence in America*, pp. 127–154. New York: Frederick A. Praeger.

Fromm, E. (1973) *The Anatomy of Human Destructiveness*. New York: Holt, Rinehart, & Winston.

Gardela, K. and Hoffman, B. (1992) *Rand Chronology of International Terrorism for 1988*. Santa Monica, CA: Rand Corporation.

Gay, B.W. and Marquart, J.W. (1993) Jamaican posses: a new form of organized crime. *Journal of Crime and Justice, 16(2)*, 139–170.

Graham, H. and Gurr, T. (1969) *The History of Violence in America*. New York: Frederick A. Praeger.

Hall, H.V. (1987) *Violence Prediction: Guidelines for the Forensic Practitioner*. Springfield, IL: Charles C Thomas.

Hepworth, J.T. and West, S.O. (1988) Lynchings and the economy: a time-series reanalysis of Hoveland and Sears (1940), *Journal of Personality and Social Psychology, 55*, 239–247.

Horowitz, L. (1997) *Emerging Viruses: AIDS and Ebola: Nature, Accident or Intentional?* Rockport, MA: Tetrahedron.

Hoveland, C.I. and Sears, R.R. (1940) Minor studies in aggression. Vol. 1. Correlation of lynchings with economic indices. *Journal of Psychology, 9*, 301–310.

Huang, F.F.Y. and Vaughn, M.S. (1992) Descriptive analysis of Japanese organized crime: the boryokudan from 1945 to 1988. *International Criminal Justice Review, 2*, 19–57.

Ienaga, S. (1970) The historical significance of the Japanese textbook lawsuit. *Bulletin of Concerned Asian Scholars, 2*, 1–12.

Janowitz, M. (1969) Patterns of collective racial violence. In H. Graham and T. Gurr (Eds.), *The History of Violence in America*, pp. 412–443. New York: Frederick A. Praeger.

Joe, K. (1992) *Chinese Gangs and Tongs: An Exploratory Look at the Connection on the West Coast.* Paper prepared for presentation at the 44th Annual Meeting of the American Society of Criminology, November 4-7, New Orleans, LA.

Kelly, C. (1976) *Crime in the United States: Uniform Crime Reports*. Washington D.C.: Superintendent of Documents, U.S. Government Printing Office.

Kemp, G. (1987) The biology of nonviolence. *Medicine and War, 3*, 181–190.

Kreger, D.E. (1989) *Accidental Nuclear War*. MA: Physicians for Social Responsibility, Central Massachusetts Chapter.

Kull, S. (1988) *Minds at War: Nuclear Reality and the Inner Conflicts of Defense Policymakers*. New York: Basic Books.

McNamara, R.S. with van de Mark, B. (1995) *In Retrospect: The Tragedy and Lessons of Vietnam*. New York: Random House.

Meloy, R. (1988) *The Psychopathic Mind: Origins, Dynamics, and Treatment.* Northvale, NJ: Jason Aronson.

Meyers, D.G. (1993) *Social Psychology*, 4th ed. New York: McGraw-Hill.

Morrison, P. (1995) Recollections of a nuclear war. *Scientific American, 273*, 42–46.

Mosquera, R. (1993) Asian organized crime. *Police Chief, 60*(10), 65–66.

Mullins, W. C. (1990) Terrorism in the '90s: prediction for the United States. *Police Chief, 57*, 44–46.

Reis, D. (1974) Central neurotransmitters in aggression. *Research Publication of the Association for Research of Nervous Mental Disease, 52*, 119–148.

Richardson, A. (1991) *Outlaw Motorcycle Gangs: USA Overview*. Rockville, MD: National Institute of Justice.

Richardson, L. (1960) *Statistics of Deadly Quarrels*. Pacific Grove, CA: The Boxwood Press.

Ridley, M. (1978) Paternal care. *Animal Behavior, 26*, 904–932.

Rister, C. (1933) Outlaws and vigilantes of the southern plains, 1865–1885. *Mississippi Valley Historical Review, XIX*, 544–545.

Ropp, T. (1962) *War in the Modern World*. New York: Collier Books.

Ruff, T. (1992) The environmental effects of military activities. *Global Society*, 9–12.

Rummel, R.J. (1994) *Death by Government, Genocide and Mass Murder Since 1900*. New Brunswick: Transaction Publishers.

Sagan, C. (1980) *Cosmos*. New York: Random House.

Sherman, P.A. (1981) Reproduction competition and infanticide in Belding's ground squirrels and other animals. In R.D. Alexander and D.W. Tickle (Eds.), *Natural Selection and Social Behavior: Recent Research and Theory*, pp. 311–331, New York: Chiron.

Short, J.F., Ed. (1968) *Gang Delinquency and Delinquent Subcultures*. New York: Harper & Row.

Siegal, B. (1969) Defensive cultural adaptation. In H. Graham and T. Gurr (Eds.), *The History of Violence in America*, pp. 764–787. New York: Frederick A. Praeger.

Tanaka, Y. (1996) *Hidden Horrors: Japanese War Crimes in World War II*. Boulder, CO: Westview Press.

Tehranian, M. (1997) Death by design. *Honolulu Advertiser*, May 18, p. 3A.

U.S. Congress Senate Committee on Governmental Affairs (1991) Asian Organized Crime: Hearings Before the Senate Permanent Subcommittee on Investigations of the Committee on Governmental Affairs, 102nd Congress, 1st Session, October 3, November 5–6, 1991.

U.S. Congress Senate Committee on Governmental Affairs (1992a) Hearing on Asian Organized Crime: The New International Criminal. Permanent Subcommittee on Investigations, National Institute of Justice.

U.S. Congress Senate Committee on Governmental Affairs (1992b) Hearing on Asian Organized Crime, Part 4. Permanent Subcommittee on Investigations, National Institute of Justice.

Wilson, L. and Rogers, R.W. (1975) The fire this time: effects of race of target insult, and potential retaliation on black aggression. *Journal of Personality and Social Psychology, 32*, 857–864.

Winter, D. (1994) Peace from an ecofeminist perspective: boys will be boys unless… . *Peace Psychology Bulletin, 3*, 6–14.

About the Author

Harold V. Hall, Ph.D., a forensic neuropsychologist, is the Director of the Pacific Institute for the Study of Conflict and Aggression. He has served as a consultant for a wide variety of criminal and civil justice system agencies, including the Federal Bureau of Investigation, the National Bureau of Prisons, the U.S. Secret Service, and district, family, and circuit courts at state and federal levels. Dr. Hall is a Diplomate in both Forensic Psychology and Clinical Psychology from the American Board of Professional Psychology and is a Fellow of the American Psychological Association. He is board certified in Forensic Neuropsychology from the American Board of Psychological Specialties. Most recently, he was inducted into the National Academy of Practice in Psychology, which, as with other National Academy disciplines such as medicine and dentistry, limits its membership to 100 living professionals from that discipline in the U.S. and Canada. He has investigated and trained others in individual and collective violence since 1969 in the Pacific Basin, on the continental U.S., and in Europe.

Chapter 13

POLICE USE OF DEADLY FORCE

Harley V. Stock, Randy Borum, and Dennis Baltzley

When one civilian uses deadly force against another civilian, the results are obviously tragic. However, such an act is unlikely to have a significant impact on those who did not know the victim or the perpetrator. Certainly, it can be argued that anyone's death by violent means diminishes us as individuals and as a society, but reality reflects that these individual acts occur multiple times on a daily basis across the world with hardly a blip on the collective consciousness of the population. For better or worse, such behavior has become, if not acceptable as a way of life, at least acknowledged as a tragic consequence of a changing society with fluctuating moral values. However, when a police officer uses deadly force against a civilian, the societal ramifications can be significant. Like a stone thrown in a pond, the ripple effect can cause civil unrest that results in the loss of substantial life and property.

Legal Justification for Use of Deadly Force

Old English law established that unless the sovereign (King or Queen) granted permission for a lawsuit to be filed against the kingdom, no such action could be forthcoming. The concept of "sovereign immunity" was extended to governmental agencies until the 1960s, when several limitations were identified. Specifically, for example, under California law, the governmental entity was determined to be generally liable for negligent or wrongful acts occurring during employment (1) if the employee is personally liable for such an act or omission, (2) when the governmental body failed to exercise reasonable diligence to ensure appropriate compliance with statutory standards for safety and performance, and (3) when negligent selection, retention, or training can be shown to have been the proximate cause of the injury. In addition, there is no immunity for false imprisonment or arrest (California Tort Claims Act).

Until 1985, it was difficult for citizens to claim a constitutional violation of their rights when police allegedly used excessive force against them. In Tennessee v. Garner (1985), the U.S. Supreme Court reframed such actions by police to fall under the Fourth Amendment. The Court commented that, "Whenever an officer restrains the freedom of a person to walk away, he has seized that person … there can be no question that application of deadly force is a seizure subject to the reasonableness requirement of the Fourth Amendment." This case essentially abolished the over-broad use of the "fleeing felon" doctrine by striking down the use of "all necessary means" to apprehend fleeing suspects. For example, deadly force may not be used against a fleeing felon unless the officer has probable cause to believe that the suspect poses a significant threat of death or serious physical injury to the officer or others. Thus, a purse snatcher, who appears unarmed and jumps over a fence, should not be shot in the back. Additionally, when feasible, the subject must first be warned before deadly force is used. The Garner case was extended in 1989 (Graham v. Connor, 1989) with the concept of "reasonableness". That is, was the officer's use of force reasonable, given all the current and past circumstances known to the law enforcement agent when he took action? This standard is determined from the perspective of a reasonable officer on the scene of the crime. For example, suppose an officer confronts a man with a weapon in the middle of a robbery. The officer commands him to drop the weapon. The man turns toward the officer and points the gun in the officer's direction. The officer shoots and kills the man. It is then discovered that the weapon was really a well-constructed toy model of a gun. If this event is not placed in the proper contextual framework of a reasonable perception standard, this officer theoretically would be guilty of shooting an unarmed man. The only "solution" to this problem is to let the perpetrator shoot first so the officer can verify that he or she is being challenged with a "real" gun. Obviously, such an alternative is unrealistic.

Prior to the use of such force, there has to be a governmental termination of freedom of movement by the officer through intentionally applied means (Reed v. Hoy, 1991). The Court had previously recognized the problem of "second guessing" a police action by stating (Graham v. Connor, 1989): "Not every push or shove, even if it may later seem unnecessary in the peace of a judge's chambers, violates the Fourth Amendment".

While these cases have addressed the proper behavior expected of a law enforcement officer under specific situations, it should also be recognized that when approached by a duly qualified police officer who gives a lawful command, the person being arrested or questioned has a duty not to resist such detainment or arrest. If the person chooses not to comply, the officer may lawfully use that amount of force needed to overcome this resistance.

Other than those in the military, police officers are the only organized group given the authority to commit institutional homicide. That is, based solely on the premise of being a sworn law enforcement agent, an officer can use his or her discretion to take another life, within legal and departmental guidelines. This was not always the case. Police officers did not routinely carry firearms until the 1850s (Miller, 1975). Since then, virtually all police departments have regulated those special circumstances under which deadly force can be utilized. Such requirements closely emulate the legal definition for justifiable use of force.

Historically, courts have recognized that killing someone is not always first degree murder. For example, a person can use deadly force when that person, or members of the immediate household, reasonably believe such force is necessary to prevent imminent death or great bodily harm to himself or herself or another or to prevent the imminent commission of a forcible felony. Police officers are given additional special statutory entitlement. While citizens generally have a duty to retreat, when possible, from a deadly encounter, police have no such restrictions. Indeed, while the average citizen usually tries to escape from a deadly situation, police officers have the responsibility to proactively move toward the problem.

However, restrictions on the use of deadly force do exist. Police are not given *carte blanche*. A police officer is justified in using deadly force when (1) the officer reasonably needs to defend himself or herself or others from bodily harm when making an arrest,

(2) preventing an arrested subject in custody from escaping, (3) capturing an escaped felon, or (4) arresting a felon who is fleeing from justice and the felon has committed a crime involving the infliction or threatened infliction of serious physical harm to another person. When feasible, some warning is given; however, police cannot use deadly force to make an unlawful arrest (Gould and Gould, 1992).

Deadly force has been defined statutorily (Gould and Gould, 1992) as that force "… which is likely to cause death or great bodily harm and includes, but is not limited to: (1) the firing of a firearm in the direction of the person to be arrested, even though no intent exists to kill or inflict bodily harm, and (2) the firing of a firearm at a vehicle in which the person to be arrested is riding."

Thus, a public policy problem emerges: How does a police officer maintain civil order by enforcing a public policy as mandated by law, while using the precisely correct amount of force, in a constantly changing environment, to control a subject, protect the victim, decrease the risk of harm to bystanders, and safeguard the officer's own life? This set of behaviors operates in an environment that encourages second guessing of such action by laymen with little knowledge of the actual job requirements of a police officer. What starts out as a tactical decision by a well-trained professional operating in a paramilitary organization can become a lightning rod for dissident groups espousing obvious, and hidden, agendas. Some civilian groups believe that the police have too much discretion in the use of deadly force and need to be carefully monitored through civilian review processes. It should be noted that, according to the American Civil Liberties Union (1992), "[b]y the end of 1991, more than 60% of the nation's largest cities had civilian review systems, half of which were established between 1986 and 1991." Other militant groups are afraid that the eroding of police powers in favor of the "bad guy" will accelerate the decline of society. The U.S. is not the only country facing this dilemma. Studies in China (Fairbairn and Sykes, 1987), Australia (Elliot, 1979), and Canada (Chappell and Graham, 1985) reflect the increasing use of deadly force by police around the world.

Frequency of Use of Deadly Force by Police

How often is deadly force, which results in a justifiable homicide, used by our nation's police agencies? Nobody knows for sure. Multiple hurdles currently exist that impede the interpretation of meaningful data. These include: (1) reporting mechanisms within individual police departments, (2) definitions of what constitutes a critical incident, (3) policies defining the use of deadly force, (4) officer training in a "use of force" continuum, (5) reported crime levels within a community, (6) local victimization rates, (7) contextual factors, and (8) low reporting rates of use of force by police agencies. In addition, some police agencies do not report an incident by a police officer who shoots at a perpetrator and misses as a "shooting by a police officer". Even though this officer clearly intended to use deadly force, but because of some factor was unsuccessful, this action does not seem to "count".

When the International Association of Chiefs of Police, the major "membership" group for police administrators, launched its first attempt to quantify data on justifiable homicide rates by police, only 42% of those agencies surveyed responded (Matulia, 1982). However, other research has evidenced higher return rates. A Police Foundation study had a 93% response rate (Sherman and Cohn, 1986). Even so, the actual number of police-involved homicides fluctuates greatly, depending on the reporting source. The National Center for Health Statistics of the U.S. Health Service initiated a reporting mechanism for medical examiners to describe "Death by Legal Intervention of Police" (National Center for Health Statistics, 1967). Significant criticism of this system (Blumberg, 1989) suggests that the reported rate of

200 to 300 citizens killed by police each year underreports the actual occurrence rate by 50 to 75%. In a New York study, public health records accurately captured only 38% of homicides already reported by police (New York State Commission on Criminal Justice, 1987).

Further, although the Federal Bureau of Investigation (FBI), through its Uniform Crime Reporting System, has maintained information on justifiable homicides by police since 1940, problems of data interpretation exist. Submission of information by police agencies is largely voluntary. While there are over 15,000 police departments and sheriff offices across the U.S., an average of only 9000 agencies report data to the FBI. This presents an interesting dilemma in terms of defining the true scope of the problem. The FBI has captured detailed data on the number of police officers killed in the line of duty. Generally, between 1986 and 1996, between 140 and 160 officers were killed yearly in the line of duty, with about half killed feloniously; however, because only about 60% of all law enforcement agencies report fatal actions taken by the police, a significant flaw is evident.

Some research (Sherman and Cohn, 1986) suggests a "ratio" of one police officer slain on duty for every 12 citizens (1 to 12) justifiably killed by the police in large cities. Analysis of FBI data suggests an actual ratio of 1 to 4.4 nationwide (Federal Bureau of Investigation, 1979, 1980, 1988, 1991). Thus, annual estimates of justifiable fatal shootings by police range from 250 to 300 (Sherman and Langworthy, 1979) to over 1000 (Fyfe, 1988). If only 60% of all police agencies report such data to the FBI, and if the reporting mechanism is flawed, an extrapolated ratio of approximately one officer feloniously killed for every eight police-initiated justifiable killings of citizens (1 to 8) can be derived, suggesting approximately 500 to 600 fatal police shootings annually.

Geller (1986) estimated that police attempt to shoot fatally about 3600 people per year. Of these, 600 perpetrators are fatally wounded, 1200 are wounded but not killed, and 1800 are shot at but missed. In general, justifiable fatal shootings by police have been decreasing (Sherman and Cohn, 1986). However, it should be noted that each time a police officer shoots at a suspect, the intent is to stop the person's aggressive actions. This may or may not result in death. The idea of "shooting to wound" is the stuff of television fantasy and certain civilian groups' naiveté. Police officers are trained to shoot at the "center mass" of a subject, that is, the middle of the chest. Any other wounding of an individual is generally the outcome of unintended circumstances. An attempt to quantify this slippery issue statistically really misses the point. The vast majority of police contacts with citizens do not result in the use of deadly force.

The probability of any one police officer becoming involved in a fatal shooting is less than the proverbial being struck by lightning. For example, given that the average officer retires after 25 to 30 years of service, a police officer employed in Jacksonville, FL, theoretically would have to be on duty 139 years before being involved in a fatal shooting (Sherman and Cohn, 1986). In Portland, OR, an officer would have to work 193 years (Snell and Long, 1992). Even in New York City, the use of firearms by police against civilians is rare. Of 1762 events in which physical force was used to subdue a subject, officers resorted to the use of a firearm on only five occasions (New York State Commission of Criminal Justice, 1987). In the entire state of New Jersey in 1990, police responded to approximately 8.5 million calls. Officers fired their weapons on 167 occasions (Sullivan, 1992). The FBI estimated that during 1990, almost 1.8 million individuals were arrested for what could collectively be viewed as violent crimes (assaults, robbery, murder, and rape). Yet, as described previously, less than 1/20 of 1% of all encounters with citizens resulted in a fatal shooting committed by a police officer (FBI, 1991).

The authors believe that police officers, in general, tend to underreact with regard to the use of deadly force in situations where such force is legally justified. While there is scant evidence in the research literature to support this view one way or the other (Dwyer et al., 1990), the authors' clinical experience with thousands of police officers suggests that before an officer uses deadly force, he or she considers a variety of issues. The factor most frequently reported to the authors in informal surveys, and the least discussed in the police literature, is liability. When faced with the prospect of having to defend one's life, or that of someone else, an officer often worries that trouble will result from his or her actions.

While in many ways it may seem encouraging that police are not killing as many citizens as might be "justified", one potential concern is that a tendency for officers to underreact when additional force is necessary (not merely allowed) may actually endanger more officers and civilians. Thus, fear of liability may inhibit an officer from taking justifiable action. These averted deadly force opportunities need to be examined carefully to ensure that police officers are responding appropriately and to identify those tactics which can be employed on a systematic basis to deescalate a potentially deadly encounter. Very few police departments gather any information in this regard (Greenberg, 1990; Jamieson et al., 1990).

Use of Deadly Force Models

Multiple police tactics exist that can be construed as deadly force. For example, a police car ramming a fleeing vehicle can obviously cause it to crash and kill the occupants (or innocent bystanders). One technique for halting a fleeing vehicle is called "precision immobilization" and is used by some law enforcement agencies (Pearson, 1992). While theoretically, such a tactic may be sound, fleeing felons often do not obey the rules of the road.

The U.S. Supreme Court has reviewed a procedure that is known as the "dead man's roadblock". This occurs when a roadblock is intentionally erected by the police on the roadway so that the fleeing person's observation of the impasse is restricted until it is unlikely that he or she can avoid it and the vehicle crashes (Brower v. the County of Inyo, 1989). Other police interventions that can result in deadly force, intentional or not, include: (1) incendiary devices, such as "flash-bang" grenades; (2) high-speed pursuits; (3) inappropriately applied defensive physical techniques, such as choke holds; (4) road spikes that flatten tires; (5) fatal attacks by police dogs; (6) fatal TASER shocks; (7) chemical agents, such as teargas; (8) striking devices, such as batons; and (9) firearms.

There is no general agreement in the police literature on what constitutes "deadly force". The International Association of Chiefs of Police Model Deadly Force Policy (1990), the Commission on Accreditation for Law Enforcement Agencies Standards on Use of Deadly Force (1988), and the National Organization of Black Law Enforcement Executives (1990) each approach the issue from slightly different perspectives and suggest somewhat different rules and regulations.

Police officers always have a range of options from which to choose in a confrontational (tactical) situation. These levels are often described in terms of a "use of force continuum". Desmedt and Marsh (1990) have defined the following levels of officer response in a use of force continuum:

1. Social control — Using positive body language to set appropriate boundaries. Just having a police officer on a scene can quell a potentially violent situation; however, too many officers confronting one subject may induce "panic" and increase aggressive actions of a subject.
2. Verbal control — Verbal directions given in short bits of information that can be readily followed to ensure compliance, i.e., "Drop the gun. Do it now."
3. Weaponless control techniques — (a) Pain compliance holds cause the subject to shift his or her attention from the officer to the site of the pain. As

compliance to commands is forthcoming, the painful stimuli are decreased to reinforce appropriate behavior. Pain compliance holds are based on stimulating nerve pathway transmissions and are not intended to cause permanent physical destruction of tissue. (b) Control (short stick) instruments can also be used. These are non-impact devices. They maximize pain but do not produce permanent physical damage. The ability of a subject to tolerate pain, as well as altered states of consciousness induced by drugs or alcohol, may render pain compliance techniques unreliable for gaining control over a resisting subject.

4. Stunning techniques — Physical blows that cause temporary stunning will inhibit resistance without causing permanent physical damage (although there is some probability of physical injury). A stunning technique overwhelms the sensory input and causes short-term disorientation.
5. Direct mechanical techniques — Significant leverage or impact pressure is used directly against the skeletal structure of the body, as opposed to muscle groups. This can fracture bone or cause damage to tissue.
6. Neck restraint immobilization techniques — Such techniques must be applied appropriately in a specified way to avoid depriving the brain of oxygen for a significant period of time or causing heart arrhythmia. This is to prevent a non-lethal maneuver from becoming a fatal one. These holds include carotid restraint, lateral vascular restraint, and "choke holds". While a vascular restraint may cause pain and confusion, choke holds constrict air to the lungs and may induce severe physical damage that can only be remediated by surgical intervention to the throat cartilage.
7. Electrical shocking devices — Non-lethal electrical field discharge weapons (TASER) are commonly referred to as stun guns. Disadvantages include limited range and immobilization ability.
8. Chemical agents — Often referred to as teargas, this class of control options has a variety of different chemical compositions. Problems with these agents include unpredictable effects, the time required for the chemical to become reactive against the subject, and a lack of guarantee of immediate incapacitation.
9. Impact weapons — These include batons and flashlights and are used to apply increased mechanical pressure at specific points of the body, including nerve pathways and joints. They may also be used to stun the subject. General police instruction is to use such weapons only below shoulder level.
10. Firearms — This refers to the use of a handgun, shotgun, or rifle. Attempts by officers to gain control and compliance of subjects are not unilateral. As Desmedt and Marsh (1990) noted, "... the officer will control with the subject's consent, if possible, but force the subject to comply, if necessary." In a police encounter with a civilian, three types of subject responses have been identified: (a) the cooperative subject, (b) the resister, and (c) the assailant. The cooperative subject is essentially compliant with police commands. The resister is not being responsive to verbal or social control but is not proactively aggressive towards the officer. The passive resister does not attempt to flee but also does not follow the officer's directions. Such an individual may grasp a fixed object, such as a telephone pole, to immobilize himself or herself. The active resister continually tries to maintain a physical space between the resister and the officer. Such maneuvers may include swinging the arms to avoid being detained or running away. Three levels of the assailant have been identified. In the first, the subject moves toward the officer and attempts to make physical contact. The action is not likely to cause significant physical damage to the officer but may limit the officer's responses. At the second level, the actions of the subject will probably cause physical injury. This is considered an "attack", although it usually occurs without a weapon. The likely injury outcome to the officer is not "serious". It may include sprains, minor broken bones, cuts, or damage to the officer's teeth. At the third level, the subject's actions will probably cause death or serious physical injury. Imminent threat of serious physical injury or death to the officer or innocent civilians is clear. The mode of infliction of damage can be varied, i.e., gun, car, or tire iron. This is considered to be the use of "lethal force" by the subject (Desmedt and Marsh, 1990).

As a way to help officers apply use of force guidelines in practice, a number of agencies have adopted a "use of force continuum" (as noted above), which suggests the range of appropriate officer responses based on the level of subject resistance

(Kazoroski, 1987; Desmedt and Marsh, 1990; Graves and Connor, 1992). The potential value of this visual and conceptual aid is that it provides a heuristic or model that the officer can use to evaluate and plan his or her response. However, the utility of a continuum depends on two key variables — defensibility and applicability. That is, the continuum must be consistent with a defensible departmental policy that has adequately considered appropriate legal standards, and it must be easily understood and applied by officers in field situations.

There are several models which have sought, in different ways, to address these two important issues. An empirical approach was taken by Samuel Faulkner (1991) at the Ohio Peace Officer Training Academy. Faulkner developed an Action-Response Continuum, which is based on research with over 5000 law enforcement officers and trainers. He also collected data on responses by members of the community and civil rights protection groups. This enhanced the defensibility of his approach. In addition, he took this research and placed it in the context of a continuum where areas of subject resistance and officer responses are conducive to images which are easily remembered. Therefore, this type of continuum can be more easily recalled and applied in actual confrontations.

Another comprehensive and well-integrated use of force continuum has been developed by Desmedt and Marsh (1990), as illustrated in Figure 13.1. This model shows how an assailant's action leads to the choice of "force options" available to the officer and how an "officer reaction" occurs based on which force option was chosen. For example, a person may be cooperative but may be standing physically too close to an officer so that the officer's safety is compromised. The use of verbal direction is appropriate at this level ("please back up"), but certainly not pain compliance techniques. However, if the subject cannot be controlled by verbal directions, such as persuasion or warning, and continues to be "resistant", pain compliance maneuvers are indicated. Yet, it would be inappropriate to put a "choke hold" on this subject. As the subject's behavior escalates by becoming more aggressive, the officer has more counter-aggressive responses to choose from. While such a continuum may suggest a smooth fluidity, this is often not the case. A perpetrator may be relatively calm in response to the officer's verbal commands and then produce a gun. The officer clearly will not have the luxury of going through pain compliance techniques, then "stunning" maneuvers, and then the use of chemical agents. An officer may "jump" the continuum to the use of lethal force. This is referred to as "One Plus One" response. The officer uses one level of force higher than the level of resistance offered by the suspect.

The officer must have the "ability to disengage or escalate" during such an ongoing event (Americans for Effective Law Enforcement, 1988). This implies that, in addition to a purely physical response to a situation, appropriate judgment is also needed to sort through the multi-level, multi-task, situation-specific response the officer is going to make. The authors recommend that psychological training in decision-making under stress be incorporated into tactical training (Borum, 1993).

Meyer (1991) evaluated eight nonlethal force strategies. The TASER (stun gun) and chemical irritant sprays are potent agents to stop physical aggression and produce little physical injury. Other acceptable alternatives (baton, flashlight, physical attack) cause significant injury. Newer methods of restraint (capture nets, for example) could decrease injury to officers and civilians, increase positive public perception of police tactics, and reduce liability claims. Kornblum and Reddy (1991) noted that upon investigating 16 deaths thought to be caused by TASER use, 11 actually resulted from drug overdoses, three from gunshot wounds, one from a combination of heart disease and TASER shock; the cause was undetermined in the remaining case.

Advances in technology suggest that sophisticated alternatives to lethal force are on the horizon (American Society of Law Enforcement Trainers,

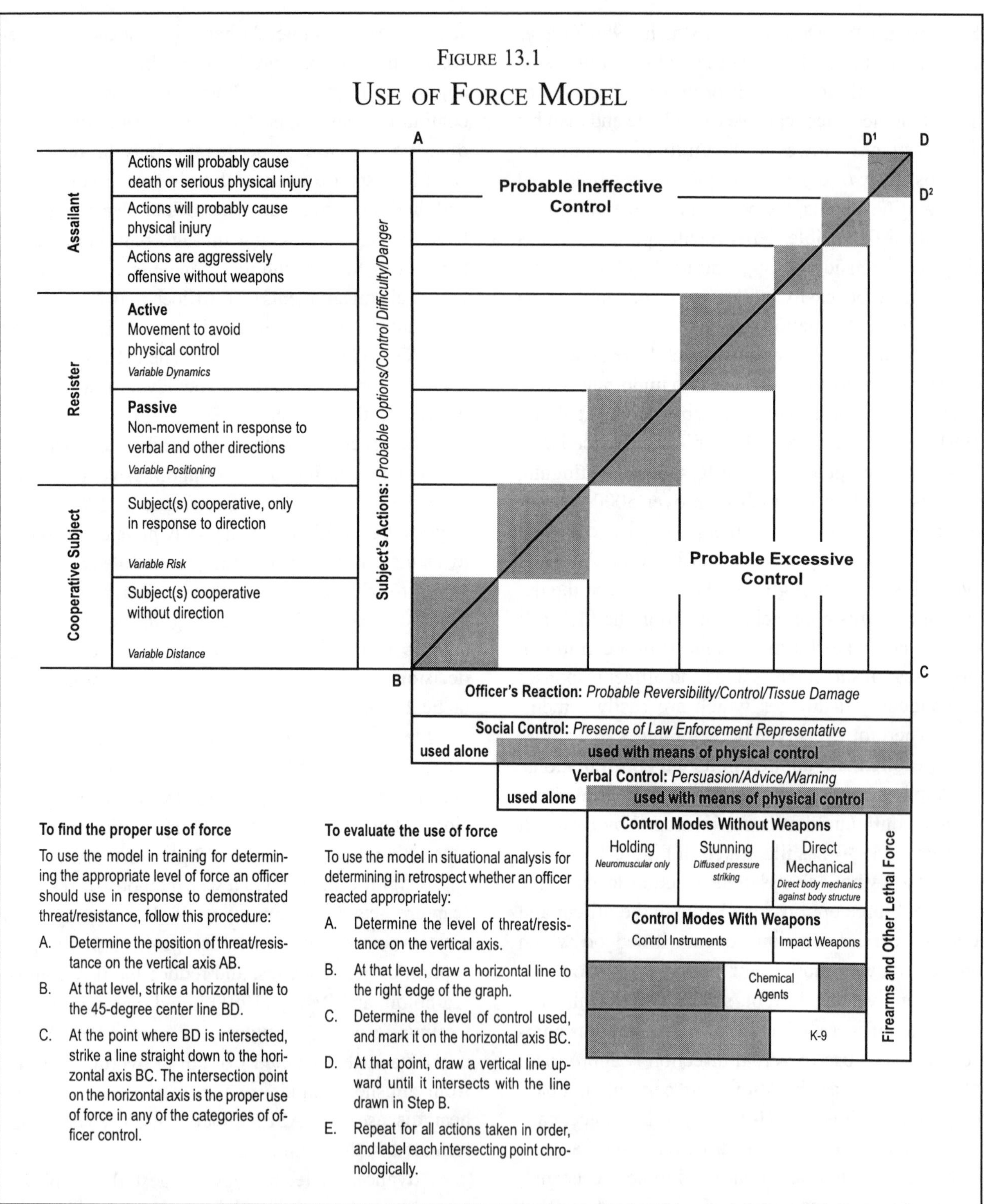

FIGURE 13.1
USE OF FORCE MODEL

Copyright 1990 John C. Desmedt. Used with permission.

1995). Aqueous foam will immerse the individual in a solution that causes disorientation. This has application to riots and prison uprisings. Sticky foam creates a "synthetic spider web" that entangles the individual. Unfortunately, if a sufficient amount is applied to the subject's head, suffocation may occur. A "smart gun" is being developed that will only operate once it "recognizes" the operator of the weapon. These options are being evaluated by cooperation between governmental agencies and private industry.

After reviewing the multiple possible agents of lethal force, the authors suggest the adoption of a definition of deadly force by police as any tactically approved technique which reasonably can be expected, when appropriately applied, to have as an intentional outcome the death of a person. For example, one person in 10,000 may have an allergic reaction to the application of CS (tear) gas. Such a death cannot be reasonably anticipated, nor was the application of this controlling agent intended to kill. Thus, this would not be an intentional application of deadly force.

What Kind of Police Officer Uses Excessive Force

As noted previously, the use of excessive force by a police officer is a complex, interactional event and cannot be explained solely by the officer's personality dynamics. Scrivner (1994), however, described the following five profile types of violence-prone officers, listed in ascending order of frequency.

Chronic Risk Group

These individuals appear to have a lifelong, ingrained pattern of problematic behaviors that bring them in conflict with others. They are threat-sensitive and manipulative and may abuse psychoactive substances. They tend to project blame onto others for their problems and, because they do not seem to learn from past experiences, are likely to get into trouble repeatedly.

Job-Related (Traumatic) Experience Group

Officers involved in critical incidents, such as fatal shootings, often have difficulty re-integrating into routine police work. Such incidents may leave officers more vulnerable to "acting out" if proper psychological debriefing and follow-up treatment are not initiated.

Early Career Stage Problems Group

Some police agencies only require a high school education for employment. Thus, individuals as young as 20 years old are hired. In one department with which the senior author consulted, they hired such an individual and issued him a gun, but not the ammunition. He had to have his father go to the local sporting goods store to buy bullets for him because he was under 21. Young officers are often "gung ho". They like the power and authority given to them. Unfortunately, they often do not have extensive life experiences to help them modulate their impulses. A strong field training officer (FTO) program, in which a specially trained senior officer monitors behavior and gives corrective feedback, will often guide the youthful officer through a maturational process.

Inappropriate Patrol Style Group

As some officers progress in their career, they become more cynical. They believe that using force will generally bring most situations under control. Because this style often "works", they ignore a more problem-solving orientation; however, these officers will often respond to interventions by the agency, because their interpersonal style is acquired over time, rather than resulting from fixed personality traits, as seen in the chronic risk group.

Table 13.1

Officers Referred for Counseling Due to Excessive Force

Officer Profile Type	Percent Referred (%)
Personal problems	28
Patrol style	21
Early career problems	18
Job-related experience	17
Chronic risk	16

Source: Adapted from Scrivner, E.M. (1994) *The Role of Police Psychology in Controlling Excessive Force.* Washington, D.C.: National Institute of Justice Research (NCJ 146206).

Personal Problems Group

For these officers, their "emotional glass" may have already been almost full. When faced with a personal loss, such as divorce or perceived change in job functioning, their behavior may deteriorate. Such officers may exhibit pre-incident behavioral characteristics that can be detected by an early-warning system. As shown in Table 13.1, the five categories are not equally distributed.

Who Gets Shot and Why

Retired Officer Mark Fuhrman, of the Los Angeles Police Department, who will forever be marked as a racist and a liar for his testimony in the O.J. Simpson double murder trial, represents what most Americans identify as a "rogue cop". In a transcript obtained by *The New York Times* (Reibstein et al., 1995, p. 24), Fuhrman stated, "Most real good policemen understand that they would just love to take certain people and just take them to the alley and just blow their brains out. All gang members for one. All dope dealers for two. Pimps, three." Even if such statements were made for "self-aggrandizement", people view them as representative of police behavior.

The 81-second beating of Rodney King that was captured on videotape on March 3, 1991, showed him to be shot with a TASER, kicked, punched, and also hit with a baton 56 times. This beating was administered by three officers, with one sergeant assisting. Approximately 20 police officers stood by and watched. That King did not die is more likely attributable to luck than skillfully administered tactical blows by the police. The jurors saw the tape differently. One of the jurors noted after the verdict that King appeared to be proactively resisting arrest and "was in full control" of his behavior (Daniels, 1992). Yet, approximately 86% of white Americans and 100% of black Americans polled felt the verdict was unjust (Marshall, 1992). Such demonstrations by police officers fuel the perception of the public that they need to be afraid of those who have sworn to protect them. Two separate reports following the King beating suggested that significant attention needs to be paid to the selection process of police officers (Independent Commission on the Los Angeles Police Department, 1991; Kolts, 1992).

The rate of fatal police shootings is not evenly distributed across the country, or even within a given jurisdiction (Geller and Karales, 1981; Horvath, 1987). Indeed, some of the most seemingly tranquil parts of the country (San Diego, California) report amongst the highest rates of fatal shootings per 1000 police officers (4.1). The New York Police Department reports among the lowest (0.7) (Geller and Scott, 1992).

Many of the fatal shootings by police take place in black communities. Black perpetrators were 7.7 times more likely to be shot at than whites in St. Louis, Missouri (St. Louis Metro Police Department, 1992), six times more likely than whites in New York (Fyfe, 1981a,b), and four times more likely than whites in Chicago (Geller and Karales, 1981). Between 1970 and 1984, the number of black civilians killed by police dropped significantly (Sherman and Cohn, 1986). In general, fatal shootings by police have decreased over the past decade. Data on Hispanic Americans is more difficult to recover because of problems in ethnic classification.

Data on who kills police officers are enlightening. From 1981 to 1990, of 1030 persons who killed police officers, 42% were blacks, 55% were white, and 3% were of "other" classified races (Federal Bureau of Investigation, 1991). Eighty-seven percent of officers killed were white, 12% were black, and 1% were of "other races" (Federal Bureau of Investigation, 1989). There appears to be a fairly strong correlation between arrest pattern and shooting victims. For example, Horvath and Donahue (1982) reported that in an urban population center of Michigan, 75% of those arrested were black, as were 82% of those at whom shots were fired. In a non-urban area, Horvath (1987) reported a black arrest rate of 36%, with blacks comprising 35% of those at whom shots were fired. Similar findings were suggested by Binder et al. (1982) and Meyer (1980). Interpretation of these data is difficult in that multiple possible explanations arise:

1. It has been reported that blacks proportionally commit more crime (Matulia, 1985).
2. Blacks have a higher unemployment rate than whites and thus come into contact with police more often (Milton et al., 1977).
3. Police racism — As observed by Sherman (1980), "The evidence of racial discrimination in arrests undermines any use of arrest rates to show an absence of discrimination in police homicide. ...Neither suspects' attitudes nor a complainant's preferences constitute proper grounds for enforcement decisions." Interestingly, black officers shoot civilians (Geller and Karales, 1981) and are shot by civilians (Konstantin, 1984) at a much higher rate than expected.
4. Several factors, other than race, seem to dictate when lethal force is used by police. These include whether the suspect engages in threatening behavior or has a weapon, and the type of crime being committed (Alpert and Fridell, 1992). Almost all the suspects shot by police are male. Donahue and Horvath (1991) indicated that those who were fatally shot by police in Detroit were usually armed, threatened use of a weapon, and had a higher number of prior misdemeanor and felony charges and convictions.

Obviously, many more possible explanations exist; however, a general review of existing research on the interaction of police shootings and the race of subjects evidences significant methodological problems (Alpert and Fridell, 1992). "Easy" explanations should be avoided. Most likely, all lethal outcomes involving police use of deadly force occur from multiple causes.

The following case study is based on an actual police incident involving use of lethal force. Names, dates, and locations have been changed. Variables associated with key events are in parentheses.

Case Illustration 1

On the evening of July 14, 1993, the rain was falling heavily and impaired visibility (attribute of setting). John Collins, a 33-year-old, Caucasian male, heard his neighbor's burglar alarm go off at 1:30 a.m. (mobilizing event). His neighbor was away, and John had the key to the house. He went to investigate. Finding nothing unusual, he turned the alarm off with the code his neighbor had left with him.

Shelly Green, who lived behind John, also heard the alarm sound. She called the police (mode of mobilization — police dispatch); however, she thought the alarm was coming from John's house and provided his address.

When Officer Pete Mattheson, a 23-year-old black officer, arrived at the scene, he was dressed in a departmentally issued black rain coat. He was wearing a baseball-type hat that had the name of the police agency stenciled in one-inch high white letters. He was not required by departmental regulations to remove his badge from his uniform and place it on the outside of his rain gear. His partner, Sam Leonard, a white 29-year-old, was similarly dressed.

When Mr. Collins returned to his house, he inadvertently did not pull the outside living room door completely shut. The driving rain and wind subsequently blew it open. He returned to bed. Thus, when Officers Mattheson and Leonard arrived at the scene of the supposed dispatched burglar alarm, they found Mr. Collins' door ajar.

Officer Leonard, with a shotgun, decided to maintain a perimeter (i.e., a boundary or line of force) on the step leading up to the door. Officer Mattheson went in and announced "police". Mr. Collins was aroused from his sleep by a noise, got up, and peered around the corner into his living room. He turned on a light. There, he saw a black male, in a black rain coat and baseball-type hat, with a gun (attribute of participants). He jumped Officer Mattheson. The two struggled for control of Officer Mattheson's weapon (actions, intentions, and resources of suspect). In the struggle, they fell through the open door and out onto the step where Officer Leonard was standing. Now, faced with two perceived assailants, Mr. Collins went for Officer Leonard's shotgun. Officer Mattheson shot and killed Mr. Collins.

Officer Mattheson was subsequently fired from the department and charged and tried for manslaughter. He was eventually acquitted. He received extensive psychological counseling for post-traumatic stress disorder. He was unable to get another job as a police officer and now works as a security guard. Mr. Collins' family successfully sued the police department for wrongful death.

Multiple coincidental events, unfolding in cascading fashion, shaped this particular use of lethal force:

1. The neighbor gave police the wrong address of the burglary alarm.
2. The door to Mr. Collins' house was blown ajar due to the weather conditions.
3. Officers Mattheson and Leonard, while in departmentally issued rain attire, were not easily identified as police officers.
4. Officer Mattheson thought he was at the correct address of a possible burglary, found a door open, and got no response when he announced "police", thus his "vulnerability awareness" was high.
5. Mr. Collins had already answered an alarm next door and was hypervigilant.
6. Officer Mattheson decided he "had to do something" so he moved forward into the house.
7. Mr. Collins, awakened from his sleep, saw a black male with a gun in his living room. He went into a "survival" mode, and responded.
8. Some tactical problems, as related to training, existed at this juncture. Officer Mattheson should have continually yelled, "Police. Get down on the floor!" and used furniture or his free hand to keep a distance between himself and Mr. Collins. However, "real life" action does not always allow for theoretical training.
9. As the struggle continued, Officer Leonard became involved. Neither he nor Officer Mattheson shouted "police". Instead, they were fighting for their lives. Officer Mattheson committed to a "here goes" strategy and shot Mr. Collins.

This case illustrates how a situation that started with a dispatch call to the wrong address, complicated by inappropriate regulations concerning officer uniform display and perhaps a lack of sufficient tactical training, caused misperceptions in both the police officer and the victim that led to a fatal shooting.

Various sociological theories have emerged to explain who becomes the "victim" of a police shooting. Terms such as institutional racism, social deprivation, lack of appropriate opportunity for employment, or an oppressive environment suggest that perpetrators of violence may not always be fully accountable for their actions (Cloward and Ohlin, 1960). A competing theory holds that there is a "subculture of violence" within certain segregated sections of a community. This subculture is defined by Wolfgang and Zahn (1983, p. 849) as "… a cluster of values that support and encourage the overt use of force in interpersonal relations and group interactions." However, this viewpoint appears to paint with too broad a brush. Certainly, the large percentage of people who emerge from such an environment are not violent. The authors believe that a police-involved shooting is a much more complex, interactional event. It encompasses a specific officer with unique attributes, under certain situational variables, in a broader contextual environment. Thus, while one officer may elect to use fatal force, under the same circumstances, another may not.

There do appear to be situationally mobilizing events that are frequently associated with a police shooting. The "pre-intervention situation" (Sherman, 1983) is the type of call that compels an officer to respond. A mobilizing aggressive event on the part of the subject then causes the officer to engage in a tactical response. Consistently, robbery calls and domestic and non-domestic disturbances account for between 53% and 66% of police shootings (Fyfe, 1978; Geller and Karales, 1985; Milton et al., 1977).

A police-civilian shooting episode is always interactional. While an officer may start a "confrontation" just by arriving at a crime scene in progress, it is the perpetrator who determines how the interaction will proceed by his or her level of compliance with lawful police directions. The events leading up to the shooting may take place over a long time, as during a stand-off. Or, such events may transpire in "split-seconds" as when an officer comes upon a crime scene and the suspect reacts with overtly aggressive behavior that could be construed as life-threatening to the safety of the officer or others. The International Association of Chiefs of Police (1989) claims that about 90% of police shootings take place within a 3-second time frame; however, it is unclear when the clock starts to toll. The authors' interpretation is that the time starts from the first aggressive movement by the subject which the officer determines is life-threatening to the officer or others. Fyfe (1989), an opponent of the concept of "split-second syndrome", believes that examining and modifying officers' approaches to potentially violent encounters is more likely to reduce violence in police-citizen encounters than are changes in officers' actions during the encounter.

Psychological Factors in the Use of Deadly Force

Solomon (1990) described five stages in the "dynamics of fear" that an officer goes through in a potentially violent encounter. These stages are fluid and an officer can "jump" from Stage I to Stage IV, for example, instantaneously.

> *Stage I.* "Here comes trouble" — The officer has reason to believe that a situation has the potential to become problematic.
>
> *Stage II.* "Vulnerability awareness" — The officer may believe that he or she is becoming vulnerable to the threat or may lack immediate control to contain the situation.
>
> *Stage III.* "I've got to do something" — There is a cognitive shift in this stage from internal focus on perceived vulnerability to the adoption of an action plan.
>
> *Stage IV.* "Survival" — If life-threatening behavior on the part of the perpetrator continues, perceptual narrowing may occur to focus on the immediate threat and survival strategies are illuminated.
>
> *Stage V.* "Here goes" — The officer commits to engage in the survival strategies as the only viable option to the perceived threat.

Scharf and Binder (1983) have taken another approach to deconstructing these high-risk encounters into identifiable stages:

1. *Anticipation* — This stage covers the period from when the officer becomes aware of a need for intervention (e.g., radio call) up to the officer's arrival on the scene.
2. *Entry and initial confrontation* — This is the stage at which the officer physically enters the scene or makes initial citizen contact. Tactical decisions here include observations about possible use of cover and concealment to protect the officer.
3. *Dialogue and information exchange* — This is referred to as the "definitional phase" when the officer makes an assessment, issues orders if necessary, or attempts to negotiate with the subject/citizen about the nature of the problem, possible solutions, or both.

4. *Less-than-lethal control tactics* — This stage, added by Geller and Scott (1992), suggests that the officer should consider whether non-lethal control tactics could be effectively utilized. These might include weaponless defensive tactics or weapon-assisted leverage and compliance techniques, or even chemical, electrical, or impact weapons.
5. *Final frame decision* — At this critical point, an officer must make a decision about whether or not to shoot.
6. *Aftermath* — This is the post-event stage encompassing any departmental and administrative response, procedure, or review related to the encounter.

The authors believe a similar "model" is also working in the mind of the perpetrator. Fear is contagious. If the officer is afraid because of the situation, the perpetrator is also likely to be afraid. As discussed by Hockey (1979), the ability of a person to respond to a stressful situation involves a complex relationship among arousal, perception of the task, and capacity to respond efficiently and effectively as first described by Yerkes and Dodson (1908): "(1) For any task there is an optimal level of arousal such that performance is related to arousal in the form of an inverted U. (2) The optimum level of arousal is a decreasing monotonic functioning of the difficulty of the task." Stress or anxiety can increase performance until it reaches a point where it becomes overwhelming, and then performance rapidly decreases.

The authors interpret this to address the issue of lack of requisite behavioral variety under stress. That is, when faced with an unfamiliar or stress-arousing situation, the perpetrator engages in Option A, which does not work to solve the problem. The perpetrator then tries Option B. That does not work. Neither does Option C. The perpetrator then reverts to Option A. It still will not work, but, because of high arousal levels, the capacity to choose from other alternatives is diminished. For example, the subject during a home-invasion robbery points a gun (Option A) at the responding officer and is commanded to "drop it". The perpetrator turns and looks for an avenue of escape (Option B), which may be blocked, then runs into a bedroom (Option C) and is cornered. The perpetrator cannot think of any other options, again points the gun (Option A) at the officer and is fatally shot. The interactional nature of a police/perpetrator situation is described in Table 13.2.

Based on what the authors have learned from the research on deadly force encounters and the psychological factors that operate therein, several prescriptive strategies can be recommended.

Suggested Strategies To Lessen the Use of Deadly Force by Police

Tracking System

A nationwide, systematic tracking system should be developed that can accurately collect data on the fatal and nonfatal use of force by police officers. The National Highway Traffic Safety Administration maintains the Fatal Accident Reporting System (FARS) related to vehicular accidents. Data are uniformly collected in 90 different categories (Teret et al., 1992). A similar system should be constructed for incidents involving police use of force. This data can be utilized to enhance training programs.

This proposed reporting system should be mandatory. All law enforcement agencies would be required to comply, either by law or to maintain accreditation. While the following is not intended to be all inclusive, the information might describe the reported event as follows: (1) weather conditions, (2) lighting, (3) patrol assignment, (4) perpetrator biography, (5) type of crime, (6) gun and ammunition used by officer, (7) number of shots fired by officer, (8) tactical decisions (reason for discharge of weapon), (9) number of perpetrators, (10) number of victims, (11) relationship of victim and offender, (12) officer on or off duty, (13) level of threat by perpetrator prior to shooting, (14) shots fired or weapon used by perpetrator, (15) other options used by officer (mace,

Table 13.2

Dynamics of a Lethal Intervention

Police Officer	Perpetrator
Activating event	
1. Probable cause to believe that a crime is being commited and response to the crime scene.	1. Engaging in behavior that solicits police attention.
Selective attention to the perceived dangerous stimuli	
1. Something is wrong. Environmental cues suggest dangerous situation is evolving. Officer assesses alternatives.	1. Police presence signals that previous acts now have law enforcement scrutiny and avenues of escape are narrowing.
Cognitive changes or distortions	
1. Perceptual narrowing occurs (weapon focus) effect).	1. A perceptual shift from original target of the encounter to the police officer occurs.
2. There is a heightened sense of danger and physiological arousal.	2. Choices narrow — fight, flee, give up.
3. Internally focused response to threat causes changes in thinking patterns.	3. Physiological arousal leads to changes in thinking.
Selected action plan	
1. Based on subject's level of perceived compliance to commands, tactical option selected from internalized use of force continuum.	1. Based on officer's behavior, and avenues of escape available, decision to be compliant or not.
Action plan enactment	
1. The officer enacts an action plan and modifies it continually based on compliance by subject.	1. The suspect can comply with officer demands, or...
2. Avert plan — retreat and reformulate new strategy.	2. Face consequences of non-complying.
3. Develop a new plan and implement it.	

baton, etc.), (16) type of officer injuries, (17) was protective cover used by officer, (18) was officer wearing ballistic vest, (19) prior knowledge of subject or situation, (20) stray shots fired by the officer and by the perpetrator (21) unintentional wounding, (22) demographics of officer, and (23) use of force continuum sequence.

Fyfe (1981a,b) also suggested a shooting typology that might be incorporated to describe these events uniformly. He indicated that some shootings are "elective" by the officer because other options of gaining control of the situation could have been implemented. "Non-elective" shootings are those in which the officer's discharge of a weapon is the only viable choice. Fyfe's typology includes: (1) assaults with guns against police, (2) assaults with knives or other weapons, (3) physical assaults on police, and (4) unarmed or no assault.

Establish Clear Policy

Every agency should develop a written policy directive on the use of deadly and non-deadly force. This policy should contain clear definitions of levels of force, a description of the standard used to judge the appropriateness of an officer's actions, and the conditions under which force or restraint may be used.

The directives should be consistent with constitutional principles and current case law in the jurisdiction. This is imperative because this policy outlines the agency's expectations about officer conduct in use of force situations and provides a consistent standard by which to judge an officer's action in any given situation. However, in developing these policies, it is also important to seek input from line personnel so that feedback from field experience can enhance the "real world" applicability of the directives as they are described.

A number of departments were forced to change their use of force policies following the U.S. Supreme Court's decision in Tennessee v. Garner (1985), which ruled that any policy directives authorizing use of deadly force to apprehend unarmed and nonviolent criminal suspects were unconstitutional. As noted above, this decision did not erase all ambiguity concerning proper standards for deadly force; however, it did establish a national minimum standard. Many of the agencies modified their policies by adopting language more consistent with a defense-of-life standard (which is now required by the Commission on Accreditation of Law Enforcement Agencies, COALEA, for any department seeking to be accredited) (Geller and Scott, 1992). Thus, their policies tended to become more restrictive.

Despite initial concerns that such restrictions might place officers at increased risk, experience with these more restrictive policies suggests that they did reduce the number of shootings by police without producing any negative impact on officer safety. As stated by Geller and Scott (1992):

"The empirical research suggests with remarkable unanimity, but, admittedly, with less data and weaker research techniques than are desirable, that restrictive policies seem to have worked well where they have been tried. ...Adoption of restrictive policies usually has been followed by marked decreases in shootings by police, increases in the proportion of the shootings that are responses to serious criminal activity, greater or unchanged officer safety, and no adverse impact on crime levels or arrest aggressiveness."

Enforcement of Policy

For a policy to have effective force, it must have administrative support and follow-through enforcement. Particularly when an agency moves to a more restrictive deadly force policy, it is important for the written directives to be buttressed by a clear message from the highest levels of the administration that supports the principles of the policy and encourages officers to use restraint in shootings (Sherman, 1983).

Many agencies have some type of internal shooting review system to investigate possible policy violations, and sometimes to aid in enforcement. William Geller of the Police Executive Research Forum has identified several features of Review Boards that appear to be quite promising (Geller and Karales, 1981; Geller and Scott, 1992): (1) conduct reviews of all incidents in which shots were fired, not just those in which an individual was shot; (2) include reviews of "averted shootings" — that is, incidents in which an officer would have been justified to shoot, but was able to resolve the incident by other means; (3) able to provide dispositions or recommendation that are not limited to judgments about the appropriateness of the individual officer's actions, but may also include administrative deficiencies, if relevant; (4) able to go beyond the adjudication of officer liability in the case and to identify and recommend preventive strategies at a systemic level (e.g., training needs, weapon and equipment modification, supervisory changes, etc.).

Pre-Employment Screening

While there is no clear demographic "profile" of the officer with a propensity to use deadly force, and the empirical relationships between individual officer characteristics and the outcomes of high-risk encounters are presently not compelling, law enforcement agencies are still responsible for exercising reasonable care in the selection of employees for public safety positions, and they may be held liable for improper conduct by employees who were not properly screened or evaluated (Bonsignore v. City of New York, 1981).

Many, if not most, major law enforcement agencies currently have comprehensive, multi-stage selection systems that include psychological screenings as one component of the program. Indeed, this component of the screening process has been widely advocated (Milton et al., 1977) and is mandated by COALEA for agencies seeking accreditation. Although pre-employment psychological screening by itself does not guarantee the identification of all applicants who may subsequently use force inappropriately, a careful pre-employment application process consisting of personnel interviews, written tests, and careful background investigation may reveal characteristics, such as a history of impulsive or aggressive behavior or poor emotional control, that could suggest that the applicant would be at higher risk to show an inappropriate response in a stressful use of force encounter. The empirical basis for these assessments is continuing to expand.

Assessment Center

Through the above screening process, departments can reasonably identify minimally qualified candidates who are unlikely to be problems to the department later. This is not sufficient. Using a business model, the customers (the public receiving the services) are demanding highly skilled service providers (police officers). The challenge is to select and promote those individuals who are most likely to be high-level performers. The assessment center concept may be the answer.

The premise of an assessment center is that the closer we can get to having the applicant actually perform the job, the more accurate the test will be and the higher the probability of success on the job. This is the strength of an assessment center. With an assessment center, we identify the critical tasks required to do the job. The applicant is then placed in a scenario where these critical tasks are simulated and has to perform actual job tasks. For example, some of the critical task areas for a new law enforcement officer are to handle interpersonal conflicts (e.g., a domestic violence call) and take reports (e.g., on burglary calls).

An entry level assessment center might place the applicant in a room with arguing spouses, siblings, or roommates. The applicant would have received instructions on what resources are available to him or her prior to going into the simulation. The applicant's task would be to use the appropriate skills to calm the participants down and gather sufficient information to write a simple report or make a determination if one or both of the suspects should be arrested. The applicant might then participate in another simulation involving a recent burglary with witnesses available. This task would measure the applicant's ability to gather sufficient information, through questioning, to complete a basic report. As can be seen, we are measuring many skills, such as leadership, judgment, oral and written communication, and the ability to follow instructions.

The assessment center and job sample methodologies have some negative aspects. This testing is expensive and time consuming to arrange. Some critics note that if care is not taken to provide compelling simulations, realism suffers and applicants are not motivated to perform (Cordner, 1992).

Early Warnings Systems

Some agencies have developed "early warning systems" to monitor officer conduct and identify cases in which further review of an officer's patterns of behavior might be warranted. These systems almost always monitor officers' histories of complaints and disciplinary action, with consideration given to the officers' assignment and the rates and types of complaints that are typically found among similarly situated officers. Specifically, the following factors have been identified in the professional literature as being relevant to include in these warning systems (Geller and Scott, 1992): (1) civilian complaints against the officer; (2) rates of arrest made for resisting arrest or disorderly conduct; (3) involvement in prior shootings or incidents involving injury; (4) record of assignments, including partners and supervisors; (5) record of discipline; and (6) prior commendations and performance evaluations.

Reviews can be conducted by administrators or peer review panels and may also include interviews with the officer involved. If problem areas are identified, the reviewers can make recommendations for remediation where appropriate, which could include re-training in areas of need, specialized new training, psychological counseling, or referral to a psychologist for a fitness for duty evaluation.

Employee Assistance Programs

It is well known that law enforcement is a highly stressful occupation with the potential for family/relationship difficulties (Borum and Philpot, 1993), alcoholism (Pendergrass and Ostrov, 1986), and other stress-related problems that can affect officers' conduct on-duty. Thus, police agencies are well advised to provide access to psychological services for their employees. Many agencies have a psychologist either on staff or retained on a consulting basis to handle referrals for counseling or evaluation. Some departments have moved toward more formal programs for employees' mental health services such as Employee Assistance Programs (EAPs). Police administrators should encourage officers to seek these services when they need them. Officers are unlikely to utilize these services if they believe the administration will view it as a sign of weakness or instability.

Training

Once a clear, defensible use of force policy has been developed and implemented, it becomes necessary to train officers in its interpretation and application so that they can apply it appropriately during encounters in the field. Officers should be able to understand all aspects of the policy and its intent in the context of departmental values and relevant statutory and case law. At least one case from the U.S. Supreme Court (City of Canton v. Harris, 1989) also suggested that agencies are indeed responsible for training officers on constitutional standards regarding the use of deadly force by law enforcement officers.

This level of training should focus on application and implementation. There should be discussions about, and possibly even role playing of, likely field scenarios involving potential use of force and how the policy should guide officers' decision-making. Ideally, this would include participation by command (or management-level) personnel and representation from the city attorney or attorney general's office for legal guidance. Specific types of training are described below.

Dynamic Training. There is a principle of learning called "state-dependent learning" that is important to consider in all aspects of use of force training. This principle suggests that it is easier to recall and apply a skill when the conditions under which it was learned are similar to the conditions in which it is to be applied. This includes not only environmental conditions, but also conditions of physical and mental states. For example, target shooting skills acquired in a distraction-free indoor range and practiced at a relaxed pace may not generalize well to an actual armed encounter because the conditions (internal and external) are dramatically different.

It is sometimes stated that individuals under stress will react according to their training. This is not entirely true. Under conditions of extreme stress, it is not necessarily the "trained" response, but the "dominant" response, that emerges. The goal of training in the appropriate use of force is to make the trained response the dominant one — that is, to train officers in a way that allows the correct response to become reflexive and automatic (Borum, 1993).

This points out the importance of dynamic training or simulation scenario training under "real-life" conditions. Whether training for verbal, physical, or shooting skills, an officer must learn to respond under stressful conditions where the adrenaline is pumping, there are distractions in the environment, and there is a threat to which one must respond. This type of training is called "dynamic" because it changes. The scenario is not set or predictable. The officer must assess and respond to an ongoing situation (Chaney, 1990). Circumstances which are much more similar to actual law enforcement encounters are utilized. The officer can gain a sense of confidence in his or her ability to respond and survive, and, where necessary, can analyze mistakes without having to suffer the actual consequences. Recent advances in the technology of virtual reality show tremendous potential for these types of law enforcement training applications.

Performance Under Stress. Despite advances over the years in use of force training, insufficient attention is still given to the mental and psychological factors involved in stressful confrontations (Borum, 1993; Borum and Stock, 1992). Officers can learn the techniques and physical skills of defensive tactics and shooting, but if they panic, freeze, or overload under pressure, they may not be able to respond appropriately. Stress and anxiety, at extreme levels, can interfere with an individual's thinking and motor skill performance (Nideffer, 1985); therefore, officers must learn about these psychological and physical reactions and be trained to control and minimize their negative effects. It is important for officers to realize that such reactions are normal and that they can learn to control their responses and perform effectively.

Extremely stressful conditions can affect the officer both physically (e.g., tension, rapid breathing, and heart rate) and psychologically (e.g., fear, poor concentration, distracting negative thoughts). Either type of condition can create anxiety at a level that can interfere with judgment and performance. Through training and exercises in relaxation, breathing control, concentration enhancement, positive self-talk, and mental rehearsal, officers can learn to improve and control their physical and psychological responses. These strategies can be used to improve performance generally, and to minimize any negative effects during high-stress situations specifically (Meichenbaum, 1985).

Perceptual Distortion. It is also important to explain to officers and those who investigate shootings about the range of perceptual distortions that can occur during deadly force encounters (Solomon and Horn, 1986). Perhaps the most common of these (up to 83% in one study) is time distortion. Many officers report feeling an expanded sense of time — that the event seemed to be happening in slow motion, where seconds seemed like minutes (67%). Others, however, have reported an opposite effect, where events seemed to happen faster than actual time (15%). Auditory distortion is also quite common (63%) and typically involves either an enhanced (18%) or diminished (51%) intensity of sound during an event. For example, a shot may sound like a cannon or not be heard at all. This "auditory exclusion" phenomenon has obvious implications for reconstruction or investigation of the incident. Another common factor is visual distortion, which was experienced by 56% of the officers in Solomon and Horn's sample. Although some officers may experience a marked increase in perceived detail (18%), the more common distortion is to experience some narrowing of focus, similar to "tunnel vision" (37%). In these cases, the officer becomes completely focused on one specific target area and blocks out all other surrounding objects or events. Some officers even report that objects or persons in focus appeared to be magnified. This narrowing of visual scope may be particularly intensified when a weapon is involved. This phenomenon, known as the weapon focus effect, has been well documented in the social science literature (Kramer et al., 1990; Loftus et al., 1987).

Tactical Training. Clearly, any comprehensive training effort on deadly force use must include extensive tactical and shooting proficiency training. As we have previously noted, firearms training must transcend the firing range and incorporate realistic scenarios and dynamic training. The FBI and a growing number of police departments have created simulated city stages (e.g., Hogan's Alley) where trainers and officers engage in simulated encounters that require officers to make decisions about the proper level of force and to respond under realistic conditions. Officers should also be trained to fire their weapons accurately under a variety of different environmental conditions with variable lighting, after sprinting, and in scenarios with multiple opponents, bystanders, or both (Morgan, 1992). Shooting accurately is an important skill, but the ability to apply (or not apply) that skill appropriately under stressful conditions is equally critical. The goal of tactical training more generally is to teach officers to think critically about *all* stages of a potentially violent encounter.

Human Relations and Cultural Awareness

Many states have begun to include a required training block on "human diversity" in the requirements for basic officer and instructor certification. Training in advanced interpersonal skills and cultural awareness can also have implications for preventing and managing high risk encounters.

Police-suspect encounters are incredibly complex social interactions. Each actor is scanning the other person and the situation for cues of aggression or threat to guide their response. Given that the level of tension in these encounters is often quite high, there is the potential for misinterpreting cues or for inadvertently engaging in behavior that causes the other person to feel a heightened sense of fear or perceived threat. In a survey of Colorado law enforcement agencies, John Nicoletti (1990, p. 39) found that:

"Elevated stress levels, lack of training, lack of control over the situation and lack of self-confidence were the most frequently cited causes for overreaction, while the behaviors mentioned most frequently as being desirable for de-escalation of force were communication and mediation skills, attitude, self-defense and physical condition and anger control."

Thus, the goal of training in human relations and diversity is to help officers to attend appropriately to the interpersonal dynamics of these encounters so that they can better "read" and control the situation.

Conflict Management

A natural extension of human relations training is to broaden skills in conflict management. This goes beyond training in firearms and defensive tactics to helping officers learn about communication, mediation, and negotiation. If an officer lacks appropriate communication and interpersonal skills, the officer may, through his or her own behavior, induce fear in a citizen that could unnecessarily precipitate an aggressive response.

Tactical conflict management or "violence reduction" exercises have been developed in major law enforcement agencies in New York City; Chicago, IL; and Dade County, FL. These programs utilize role playing and scenario exercises to teach officers how to control a potentially violent encounter and to de-escalate, rather than exacerbate, tensions. Offering violence-reduction training also strongly reinforces a departmental philosophy about using the "least injurious control techniques" that would be appropriate in any given encounter. Although there have not been any well-controlled empirical investigations of the effectiveness of these violence-reduction programs, anecdotal accounts from programs such as the one in Metro-Dade (Miami, FL) suggest that there has been some success in reducing shootings by police, enhancing officer safety, and improving relations between police and the community.

Case Illustration 2

Officer John Maynard was dispatched to a "domestic disturbance" at 1410 W. Washington Avenue. Sgt. Stan Norman responded as a "backup" unit. At the scene, Tonya Jackson informed them that her husband, LaMont Jackson, had trapped four relatives in a bedroom and had a knife. He had been drinking heavily and was very angry.

The officers entered the residence, initially drawing their police batons, but not their firearms. The officers encountered Jackson, who was agitated and stabbing the outside of the bedroom door with a knife. Upon seeing the officers, he put the knife down. Officer Maynard directed Jackson to move away from the knife. Instead, Jackson picked it back up and stood still. He was near the kitchen, about 9 to 12 feet from the officers. The four relatives remained in the bedroom, behind Jackson. The officers repeatedly directed Jackson to drop the knife as they drew their firearms. Jackson moved toward the officers, with the knife held in an aggressive posture. When Jackson was about six feet away, Sgt. Norman fired one time, striking Jackson. Jackson continued advancing toward the officers, still holding the knife. Sgt. Norman fired a second round, which caused Jackson to fall to the ground. He subsequently died.

The following considerations are relevant to this example:

1. The officers entered the residence with batons, not firearms, drawn. This demonstrates that they were not predisposed to resort primarily to the use of firearms for physical control or even intimidation.
2. The officers were duty bound to protect occupants behind the bedroom door which they had observed Jackson stab repeatedly; therefore, they could not retreat from Jackson, even for purposes of their own safety.
3. The officers repeatedly and continuously attempted to persuade and direct Jackson to drop the knife.
4. Sgt. Norman waited at his own risk until Jackson was within a distance of about 6 feet from him until he fired at Jackson, thereby placing himself at great risk.
5. To attempt to use a police baton could have been ineffective use of force and could have placed others at danger similar to that in which Sgt. Norman found himself.
6. Sgt. Norman's second shot represented a discreet transaction bought about by Jackson's second attempt to assault with the knife. Each shot was purposeful, and no other alternative existed, given the quickly escalating dynamics of the situation.
7. Forensic findings did not dispute the distance between the subject and Sgt. Norman, as described by Sgt. Norman, at the time he discharged his firearm.

Conclusion

In summary, the available data indicate that the use of lethal force by police is a relatively rare event. In general, police officers appear to be enforcing the law within the constitutional and statutory limitations entrusted to them. Yet, there certainly are some officers who overreact to provocative situations. The authors have attempted to identify the complex interaction between officer and subject that leads to deadly encounters and offer comprehensive strategies to analyze data, select appropriate law enforcement candidates, and train them for the important job they are to undertake.

Annotated Bibliography

1. Geller, W.A. and Scott, M.S. (1992) *Deadly Force: What We Know*. Washington, D.C.: Police Executive Research Forum. This book is

perhaps the most comprehensive, well-researched, and authoritative source on police deadly force currently available. In a series of five chapters, the authors cover the following topics: studying the use of deadly force, the prevalence of shootings, describing and explaining shootings of and by police, and shooting control strategies. A final chapter provides some guidance for law enforcement agencies on setting standards, supporting officers, and managing the public information function and then outlines some directions for future research. The text is full of useful facts, figures, tables, and forms that will be of interest to researchers and practitioners.

2. Fyfe, J.J. (1988) Police use of deadly force: research and reform. *Justice Quarterly, 5*, 165–205. Police use of deadly force first became a major public issue in the 1960s, when many urban riots were precipitated immediately by police killings of citizens. Since that time, scholars have studied deadly force extensively, police practitioners have made significant reforms in their policies and practices regarding deadly force, and the U.S. Supreme Court has voided a centuries-old legal principle that authorized police in about one half of the states to use deadly force to apprehend unarmed, nonviolent, fleeing felony suspects. This essay reviews and interprets these developments.

3. Scrivner, E.M. (1994) *The Role of Police Psychology in Controlling Excessive Force*. Washington, D.C.: National Institute of Justice (NIJ 146206). This report discusses the role of police psychologists in preventing and identifying individual police officers at risk for use of excessive, nonlethal force and the factors that contribute to police use of excessive force in performing their duties. Data are presented from a survey of 65 police psychologists about the type of services they provide to police departments and how those services were used to control force. A typology of five profiles of violence-prone officers is described with some recommendations for intervention at an individual and organizational level.

4. Uniform Crime Reports Section, Federal Bureau of Investigation, U.S. Department of Justice (1992) *Killed in the Line of Duty: A Study of Selected Felonious Killings of Law Enforcement Officers*. Washington, D.C.: Federal Bureau of Investigation, U.S. Department of Justice. This publication reports the results of a largely qualitative study of 51 incidents in which police officers were killed in the line of duty. While the results of the study must be viewed cautiously, they provide some detailed information about the officers, the perpetrators, and the context of the deadly police-citizen encounters. The authors identify what they believe is a "deadly mix" of an easy-going officer who will use force only as a last resort with an offender of aberrant behavior in an uncontrolled, dangerous situation. In the final section, they provide recommendations for interviewing and interrogating these subjects and for enhancing training and procedural review. They also identify for law enforcement managers some "signals" that an officer may be at increased risk to be victimized in a high risk encounter.

References

Alpert, G.P. and Fridell, L.A. (1992) *Police Vehicles and Firearms: Instruments of Deadly Force*. Prospect Heights, IL: Waveland Press.

American Civil Liberties Union (1992) *Fighting Police Abuse: A Community Action Manual*. New York: ACLU.

Americans for Effective Law Enforcement (1988) *Use-of-Force Tactics and Non-Lethal Weaponry*. Chicago, IL: Americans for Effective Law Enforcement.

The ASLET Journal (1995) *The American Society for Law Enforcement Training Journal, 10*(4), 41.

Binder, A., Scharf, P., and Galvin, R. (1982) *Use of Deadly Force by Police Officers: Final Report*. Washington, D.C.: National Institute of Justice (Grant No. 79-NI-AZ-0134)

Blumberg, M. (1989) Controlling police use of deadly force: assessing two decades of progress. In R.G. Dunham and G.P. Alpert (Eds.), *Critical Issues in Policing: Contemporary Readings*. Prospect Heights, IL: Waveland Press.

Bonsignore v. The City of New York, 521 F.Supp. 394 (1981).

Borum, R. (1992) Mental training for high risk encounters in law enforcement. *The American Society for Law Enforcement Training Journal, 1,* pp. 20–26.

Borum, R. (1993) Mental practice in defensive tactics training. *Defensive Tactics Newsletter*, July, p. 67.

Borum, R. and Philpot, C. (1993) Therapy with law enforcement couples: clinical management of the "high-risk lifestyle." *American Journal of Family Therapy, 21*, 122–135.

Borum, R. and Stock H. (1992) Excessive force prevention programs. *Corrections Today*, April, pp. 26–30.

Brower v. County of Inyo, 109 S.Ct. 1378 (1989).

California Tort Claims Act (California Government Code 5.800).

Chaney, R. (1990) Judgment training in the use of deadly force. *Police Chief*, July, pp. 40–44.

Chappell, D. and Graham, L.P. (1985) *Police Use of Deadly Force: Canadian Perspectives*. Toronto: Centre of Criminology, University of Toronto.

City of Canton v. Harris, 109 S.Ct. 1197 (1989).

Cloward, R.A. and Ohlin, L.E. (1960) *Delinquency and Opportunity: A Theory of Delinquent Gangs*. New York: Free Press.

Cordner, G.W. (1992) Human resources issues. In L.T. Hoover (Ed.), *Police Management: Issues and Perspectives*, pp. 227–249. Washington, D.C.: Police Executive Research Forum.

Daniels, L.A. (1992) The jury: some of the jurors speak, giving sharply differing views. *The New York Times*, May 1, p. A10.

Desmedt, J.C. and Marsh, J.F. (1990) *The Use of Force Paradigm for Law Enforcement and Corrections*. Available from The Police S.A.F.E.T.Y. System, LLC; 10108 Baileysburg Lane; Nokesville, VA 22123.

Donahue, M.E. and Horvath, F.S. (1991) Police shooting outcomes: suspect criminal history and incident behaviors. *American Journal of Police, 10*, 17–34.

Dwyer, W.O., Graesser, A.C., Hopkinson, P.L., and Lupfer, M.B. (1990) Application of script theory to police officers' use of deadly force. *Journal of Police Science and Administration, 17*, 295–301.

Elliot, I.D. (1979) Use of deadly force in arrest: proposals for reform in Australia. *Criminal Law Journal, 3*, 50–58.

Fairbairn, W.E. and Sykes, E.A. (1987) *Shooting To Live With the One-Hand Gun*. Boulder, CO: Paladin Press.

Faulkner, S. (1991) *The Action-Response Use of Force Continuum*. London, OH: unpublished manuscript

Federal Bureau of Investigation (1979) *Uniform Crime Reports: Crime in the United States, 1978*. Washington, D.C.: Federal Bureau of Investigation.

Federal Bureau of Investigation (1980) *Uniform Crime Reports: Law Enforcement Officers Killed, 1980*. Washington, D.C.: Federal Bureau of Investigation.

Federal Bureau of Investigation (1988) *Uniform Crime Reports Supplement: Law Enforcement Officers Killed and Assaulted, 1988*. Washington, D.C.: Federal Bureau of Investigation.

Federal Bureau of Investigation (1989) *Uniform Crime Reports Supplement: Law Enforcement Officers Killed and Assaulted, 1989*. Washington, D.C.: Federal Bureau of Investigation.

Federal Bureau of Investigation (1991a) *Crime in the United States, 1990*. Washington, D.C.: Federal Bureau of Investigation.

Federal Bureau of Investigation (1991b) *Uniform Crime Reports Supplement: Law Enforcement Officers Killed and Assaulted, 1990*. Washington, D.C.: Federal Bureau of Investigation.

Fyfe, J.J. (1978) Shots Fired: A Typological Examination of New York City Police Firearms Discharges, 1971–1975. Ph.D. dissertation, School of Criminal Justice, State University of New York-Albany.

Fyfe, J.J. (1981a) Race and extreme police citizen violence. In R.L. McNeeley and C.E. Pope (Eds.), *Race, Crime and Criminal Justice*, pp. 89–108. Beverly Hills, CA: Sage.

Fyfe, J.J. (1981b) Toward a typology of police shootings. In J.J. Fyfe (Ed.), *Contemporary Issues in Law Enforcemen,* pp. 136–151. Beverly Hills, CA: Sage.

Fyfe, J.J. (1988) Police use of deadly force: research and reform. *Justice Quarterly, 5*, 165–205.

Fyfe, J.J. (1989) Police/citizen violence reduction project. *FBI Law Enforcement Bulletin, 58*(5), 18.

Geller, W.A. (1986) *Deadly Force: A Study Guide*. Washington, D.C.: National Institute of Justice. Companion to NIJ videotape entitled *Deadly Force,* a discussion moderated by James Q. Wilson.

Geller, W.A. and Karales, K.J., (1981) *Split-Second decisions: Shootings of and by Chicago Police*. Chicago, IL: Chicago Law Enforcement Study Group.

Geller, W.A. and Karales, K.J. (1985) Chicago Police Department officer-involved shootings (unpublished raw data).

Geller, W.A. and Scott, M.S. (1992) *Deadly Force: What We Know*. Washington, D.C.: Police Executive Research Forum.

Gould, J.B. and Gould, L. (1992) *Florida Criminal and Vehicle Handbook* (776.012-776.08).

Graham v. Connor, 109 S.Ct. 1865 (1989)

Graves, F.R. and Connor, G. (1992) The FLETC use-of-force model. *The Police Chief, 56*, 58.

Greenberg, R. (1990) Personal communication between the chief of the Charleston, SC, police department and William A. Geller, October 8.

Hockey, R. (1979) Stress in police work. In V. Hamilton and D. Warburton (Eds.), *Human Stress and Cognition*. New York: John Wiley & Sons.

Horvath, F. (1987) The police use of deadly force: a description of selected characteristics of intra-state incidents. *Journal of Police Science and Administration, 15*, 226–238.

Horvath, F. and Donahue, M. (1982) Deadly force: an analysis of shootings by police in Michigan, 1976–1981. East Lansing: Michigan State University.

IACP Use of Force: Concepts and Issues Paper (1989) Prepared by the International Association of Chiefs of Police/Bureau of Justice Assistance National Law Enforcement Policy Center. Arlington, VA: International Association of Chiefs of Police.

IACP Model Deadly Force Policy (1990) Available from International Association of Chiefs of Police/Bureau of Justice Assistance National Law Enforcement Policy Center; 1110 N. Glebe Road, Suite 200; Arlington, VA 22201.

Independent Commission on the Los Angeles Police Department ("Christopher Commission") (1991) *Report of the Independent Commission on the Los Angeles Police Department*. Los Angeles: Independent Commission on the Los Angeles Police Department.

Jamieson, J.P., Hull, R., and Battershill, P. (1990) *Recommendations of the [British Columbia Police Commission] Committee on the Use of Less than Lethal Force by Police Officers in British Columbia*. Vancouver: British Columbia Police Commission.

Kazoroski, R. (1987) Use force: a model for the real world of modern policing. *The Florida Police Chief*, August, pp. 32–35.

Kolts, J.G. and staff (1992) *The Los Angeles County Sheriff's Department: A Report by Special Counsel James G. Kolts and Staff*. Los Angeles: Office of the Special Counsel.

Konstantin, D.N. (1984) Homicides of American law enforcement officers, 1978–1980. *Justice Quarterly, 1*, 29–37.

Kramer, T.H., Buckhout, T., and Eugenio, P. (1990) Weapon focus, arousal, and eyewitness memory — attention must be paid. *Law and Human Behavior, 14*(2), 167–184.

Loftus, E.F., Loftus, G.R., and Messo, J. (1987) Some facts about "weapon focus". *Law and Human Behavior, 11*(1), 55–62.

Marshall, S. (1992) Crisis in L.A.: poll — case is evidence of racism. *USA Today*, May 12, pp. 1A, 4A.

Matulia, K.J. (1982) *A Balance of Forces: A Study of Justifiable Homicides by the Police*. Gaithersburg, MD: International Association of Chiefs of Police.

Matulia, K.J. (1985) *A Balance of Forces: Model Deadly Force Policy and Procedure,* 2nd rev. ed. Gaithersburg, MD: International Association of Chiefs of Police.

Meichenbaum, D. (1985) *Stress Inoculation Training*. New York: Pergamon Press.

Meyer, G. (1991) Nonlethal Weapons vs. Conventional Police Tactics: The Los Angeles Police Department Experience. Ph.D. dissertation. Available from University Microfilms; 300 N. Zeeb Road; Ann Arbor, MI 48106.

Meyer, M. (1980) Police shootings at minorities: the case of Los Angeles. *Annals of the American Academy of Political and Social Science, 452*, 98–110.

Miller, W.R. (1975) Police authority in London and New York City, 1830–1870. *Journal of Social History*, Winter, pp. 81–101.

Milton, C.H., Halleck, J.D., Lardner, J., and Albrecht, G.L. (1977) *Police Use of Deadly Force*. Washington, D.C.: Police Foundation.

Morgan, Jr., J., (1992) Police firearms training: the missing link. *FBI Law Enforcement Bulletin*, January, pp. 14–15.

National Advisory Commission on Criminal Justice Standards and Goals: Police (1973) *National Strategy to Reduce Crime*. Washington, D.C.: National Advisory Commission on Criminal Justice Standards.

National Organization of Black Law Enforcement Executives (1990) The FBI's Proposed Revision of Its Deadly Force Policy and the National Organization of Black Law Enforcement Executives' Resolution Opposing the FBI's Plan, July 18.

New York State Commission on Criminal Justice and the Use of Force (1987) *Report to the Governor,* Vol. I. Unpublished report.

Nicoletti, J. (1990) Training for de-escalation of force. *Police Chief*, July, pp. 37–39.

Nideffer, R.M. (1985) *Athlete's Guide to Mental Training*. Champaign, IL: Human Kinetics Publishers.

Pearson, T.L. (1992) Focus on police pursuits: the precision immobilization technique. *FBI Law Enforcement Bulletin*, September, pp. 8–9.

Pendergrass, V. and Ostrov, N. (1986) Correlates of alcohol use by police personnel. In J.T. Reese and H.A. Goldstein (Eds.), *Psychological Services for Law Enforcement*, pp. 489–496. Washington, D.C.: Federal Bureau of Investigation.

Reed v. Hoy, 909 F.2d 324, 329 (9th Cir., 1989), cert. denied, 115 L.Ed.2d 1053 (1991).

Reibstein, L. with Murr, A., Crogan, J., and Foote, D. (1995) Up against the wall. *Newsweek*, September 4, p. 24.

Scharf, P. and Binder, A. (1983) *The Badge and the Bullet: Police Use of Deadly Force*. New York: Praeger.

Scrivner, E.M. (1994) *The Role of Police Psychology in Controlling Excessive Force*. Washington, D.C.: National Institute of Justice Research (NCJ 146206).

Sherman, L.W. (1980) Execution without trial: police homicide and the constitution. *Vanderbilt Law Review, 33*(1), 71–100.

Sherman, L.W. (1983) Reducing police gun use: critical events, administration policy and organizational change. In M. Punch (Ed.), *Control in the Police Organization*. Cambridge, MA: Massachusetts Institute of Technology Press.

Sherman, L.W. and Langworthy, R. (1979) Measuring homicide by police officers. *Journal of Criminal Law and Criminology*, *70*, 546–560.

Snell, J. and Long, J. (1992) Deadly force: police training gets caught in city's budgetary crossfire. *The [Portland] Oregonian*, April 27, pp. A8.

Solomon, R.M. (1990) The dynamics of fear in critical incidents: implications for training and treatment. In *Fear: It Kills! A Collection of Papers for Law Enforcement Survival*. Arlington, VA: International Association of Chiefs of Police/Bureau of Justice Assistance, U.S. Department of Justice.

Solomon, R.M. and Horn, J.M. (1986) Post-shooting traumatic reactions: a pilot study. In J.T. Reese and H.A. Goldstein, (Eds.), *Psychological Services for Law Enforcement*. Washington, D.C.: Federal Bureau of Investigation.

St. Louis, IL, Metropolitan Police Department, Planning and Development Division (1992) Discharge of Firearms by Police Officers. Unpublished internal study.

Sullivan, J.F. (1992) New Jersey panel urges uniform guidelines for police use of deadly force. *The New York Times*, May 11, p. A13.

Tennessee v. Garner, 105 S.Ct. 1694 (1985).

Teret, S.P., Wintemute, G.J., and Beilenson, P.L. (1992) The firearm fatality reporting system: a proposal. *Journal of the American Medical Association, 267*, 3073–3074.

Wolfgang, M.E. and Zahn, M.A. (1983) Homicide: behavioral aspects. In S.H. Kadish (Ed.), *Encyclopedia of Crime and Justice,* Vol. 2, pp. 849–855. New York: Free Press.

Yerkes, R.M. and Dodson, J.D. (1908) The relation of strength of stimulus to rapidity of habit formation. *Journal of Comparative and Neurological Psychology, 18*, 459–482.

About the Authors

Harley V. Stock, Ph.D., ABPP, has consulted with police agencies on the federal, state, and local levels since 1978. He has been an invited instructor at the FBI Academy and the U.S. Secret Service training academy. Dr. Stock has completed a Michigan Law Enforcement Officer Training Council Certified SWAT course and an FBI hostage negotiation course. He has been involved in over 200 hostage situations as part of a hostage negotiation team for various police agencies. Dr. Stock has treated numerous police officers who have been involved in fatal shootings and was chief psychologist at Seafield 911, a treatment facility exclusively for police officers. From 1977 through 1990, he was on the staff at the Center for Forensic Psychiatry in Ann Arbor, MI. There, he was Deputy Director of the Out-Patient Evaluation Unit. He is now a managing partner with The Incident Management Group, a consortium of psychological and security experts which provides consultation to major business organizations. He is a Diplomate of the American Board of Forensic Psychology. **Randy Borum, Psy.D.,** is Assistant Clinical Professor of Medical Psychology in the Department of Psychiatry and Behavioral Sciences at Duke University Medical Center. Prior to this, he served as a sworn officer and Coordinator of Behavioral Science Services in the Palm Bay (FL) Police Department, completed a post-doctoral fellowship in forensic psychology in the Law-Psychiatry program at the University of Massachusetts Medical Center, and served for 2 years as the Chief Psychologist and Forensic Coordinator on the Adult Admission Unit at John Umstead Hospital. He is currently involved in a series of projects on violence, severe mental disorder and the law with the UNC-Duke Violence Research Group and in a study of police and mobile mental health crisis teams. Dr. Borum's work is supported by grants from the National Institute of Mental Health.

Dennis Baltzley, Ph.D., is an Industrial/Organizational Psychologist who received his doctorate from Tulane University. He has over 10 years of applied experience, the past 6 years spent developing complex simulations and testing systems in law enforcement agencies. Prior to that, he worked as a Human Factors Engineer in the evaluation of combat aircraft simulators. He was a principle researcher in reconfiguring the Kennedy Space Center Protective Services Emergency Communication Center. More recently, Dr. Baltzley has served as a personnel director for a large law enforcement agency while restructuring the HR system. Currently, he is employed as a consultant with Personnel Decisions International. He is a team member of PDI's Assessment and Development Center Services which specializes in Strategic Performance Modeling for Fortune 500 companies. Dr. Baltzley currently resides in Minneapolis, MN.

CHAPTER 14

CHEMICAL AND BIOLOGICAL VIOLENCE: PREDICTIVE PATTERNS IN STATE AND TERRORIST BEHAVIOR

David M. Paltin

"The mass of war propaganda against the use of gas and other chemicals has caused the average citizen to have an unholy fear of such agents." (*Chemical Warfare,* 1930)

During the morning rush hour in the Tokyo subway system in late March 1995, ten inconspicuous commuters hurriedly boarded three different cars of the Tokyo line (Kaplan and Marshall, 1996). Their plan had been rehearsed scores of times over the previous weeks, and each move followed a detailed sequence of events. Half of the individuals carried a daily newspaper and a metal-tipped umbrella, while the rest stood close at hand to watch for the police. Each man carrying a newspaper held it under his arm and close to his body to hide the paper's bulky appearance. At the predetermined time, each of the men placed his newspaper on the overhead luggage rack or on the floor and then poked holes in the paper with the umbrella. The men exited the trains as quietly as they had boarded. Minutes after the cars had reached Kasumigaseki Station, screams were heard rising to the street as a frenzied mob of men, women, and children climbed over each other in a rush to escape the underground chamber. Most were able to grope their way out into the sunlight despite blurred vision and overwhelming nausea. There was panic. A number of the injured had blood flowing from their mouths and noses. They laid down on the pavement of the sidewalk and in the street, unable to hold themselves up. The powerful toxic fumes continued to spread underground in the closed chamber, eventually reaching pockets of frightened commuters huddled together in corners and near the gray concrete floor. The Tokyo police scrambled to clear traffic for incoming ambulances. A few of the lucky were able to board the early ambulances to make the trip to the hospital, and the rest waited doubled over and laid on blankets on the sidewalk. Five thousand five hundred people were injured and 12 died in this terrorist attack perpetrated by members of the Aum Shinri Kyo cult. Similar attacks occurred 1 month later in a different city in Japan. When questioned about their motive, cult members admitted that the attack was merely a "contingency plan" designed to redirect the attention of police away from their recent inquiries into cult activity. The Tokyo subway had been chosen for the target as the cult knew it would greatly increase the mortality rate of the attack ("Japan's Frightening Encounter...", 1995).

This chapter describes a rising trend of chemical and biological weapons (CW/BW) use among terrorist and rogue state groups. As observed in the Aum attack, lethal violence against a metropolitan population is quite feasible and meets a variety of terrorist and rogue state goals. Although difficult to manage, chemical and biological materials are easy to acquire and are capable of causing the same casualty rate as nuclear weapons if unleashed in an effective manner. The author notes that, similar to the behavior of the perpetrator and victim in cases of interpersonal violence, predictive patterns begin to emerge when we study the behavior of terrorist groups or rogue leaders accused of using such weaponry. Due to the nature of chemical and biological arms, patterns of behavior occur over months or years prior to actual use.

Citing the lethal violence sequence as a unit of study, we will observe features of group baseline, pre-conflict, lethal event, and recovery behavior that often accompany these attacks. Similar to other acts of genocidal killing, group history with regard to ethnonationalism, mass persecution, and concealment of atrocities becomes a positive predictor of chemical weapons use. Victim and contextual contributions are also described for each phase of the lethal violence sequence. Finally, the chapter describes solutions to the problem of chemical and biological killing. These include becoming personally involved in CW/BW organizations and research, cultivating an active awareness of chemical and biological events that are reported in the media, maintaining congressional and governmental interest in the CW/BW proliferation issue, and supporting methods that identify and address groups which are actively seeking to acquire chemical and biological precursors.

As far back as 1969, the U.S. Department of Defense and other agencies recognized the vulnerability of U.S. cities to chemical and biological terrorism, and a series of exercises were staged to gather data on the defensive options against a biological weapons attack. Remarkably similar to the Tokyo tragedy, one mock drill involved pumping a harmless bacteria into street-level subway vents at various locations in New York City (Simon, 1989). Following the introduction of the material, levels of dispersion, wind carry, and potential death counts were calculated. The results of the study indicated that an actual attack would result in a high casualty rate and that metropolitan police and military officials were incapable of dealing with these types of weapons. Nearly 20 years later, Aum Shinri Kyo proved that this attack scenario was indeed possible to carry out and put the world on notice that the threat of chemical and biological terror is no longer limited to the rural regions of Asia or desert conflict in the Middle East.

The disturbing feature of the Tokyo subway incident was not the cult's ability to synthesize a lethal dose of the nerve agent Sarin, but rather the fact that Aum had been running a chemical weapons research lab with graduate recruits from the Japanese university system for over 5 years (The Henry L. Stimson Center, 1996; Kaplan and Marshall, 1996). During this period, cult chemists not only synthesized a variety of agents, but were also able to buy weapons technology in the international marketplace. Unlike other chemical weapons incidents perpetrated by the Bader Meinhoff Gang in Germany and Hezbollah in Israel, Aum had synthesized most of its chemical weapons technology without a state sponsor, proving that any terrorist cell with adequate chemical training can gain access to the most lethal, non-atomic weapon of mass destruction known to humankind.

Despite ongoing negotiations to reduce the stockpiling of CW/BW materials and technology within the U.S., the United Socialist States, and other large nations, there is a disturbing upward trend in the number of nations that maintain non-conventional weapons programs and in the frequency of lethal CW/BW events and poisonings (*Chemical and Biological: The Urgent Need*, 1989a; Lacey, 1994;

Meselson and Robinson, 1995; Stockholm International Peace Research Institute, SIPRI, 1994). In 1989, William Webster, former Director of the CIA, predicted (*Chemical and Biological*, 1989b) "that as many as 20 countries may be developing chemical weapons, and we expect this trend to continue, despite ongoing multilateral efforts to stop their proliferation." A meta-review of proliferation studies by Spiers in 1994 confirmed Judge Webster's foresight and indicated that 24 nations from the Middle East to Asia had active CW/BW weapons programs. The U.S. and Russian states continue to be the leaders in CW/BW stockpiling, with 40,000 metric tons located across the former Soviet states, and approximately 30,000 metric tons stored in depots in the U.S., primarily in Utah, Johnson Atoll, and Colorado (SIPRI, 1994). Failing to take the lead on the proliferation issue, the U.S. did not ratify the Chemical Weapons Convention treaty until 1996, and as late as the mid-1980s the Reagan administration actively pursued a policy toward increasing U.S. chemical and biological capability, raising spending over a 2-year period from $160 million to $200 million (Bowman, 1994; Worsnop, 1986).

Improving Our Predictions of CW/BW Use

Although weapons control and its associated politics are not the topic of this chapter, proliferation may be linked to a greater risk of lethal incidence (Global Spread of Chemical and Biological Weapons, 1989; McCain, 1989; Meselson and Robinson, 1995). Corresponding with the spread of CW/BW technology, there have also been measured increases in reported and confirmed CW/BW events in various civil, wartime, and terroristic conflicts. Black market trading and theft of biological weapons precursors have become a national security threat, and as the number of nations capable of sustaining a biological and chemical program increases, analysts point out that the frequency of CW/BW incidents will continue to rise (*Chemical and Biological Weapons Threat...*, 1989a; Findlay, 1991; Spring, 1992). In reaching our "coming of age" in the chemical and biological weapons arena, the ability to make accurate, timely predictions of the behavior of groups which possess this capability has become a crucial venture.

This chapter focuses on the prediction of CW/BW use by "rogue" nations during wartime or civil conflict and ethnocentric and ethnonationalist terrorist groups which are most commonly implicated in CW/BW events (Douglass, 1995). Examining data from documented lethal incidents, the author will use the lethal violence sequence as a model for understanding common behavioral patterns that precede and follow these events. In other words, the author will attempt to develop a predictive analog for group or leader behavior in this area. For example, if a police or FBI unit receives intelligence that an identified group was able to acquire biological materials from the American Type Culture Collection (an embarrassing incident which actually occurred in 1985), how could that agency improve its assessment of the risk of an actual attack? In this chapter, the author will describe the central role of (1) group baseline, (2) phase of conflict, and (3) post-event recovery information required for making valid predictions. Finally, solutions and recommendations will be presented that will assist in terrorist intervention and interstate conflict resolution, as well as in future research into violence prevention.

A Short Course in Biological and Chemical Weapons

Historical Accounts of Use

Accounts of the early use of chemical and biological warfare can be found in Hellenic descriptions of battles. As primitive munition delivery was restricted mostly to the catapult or hand-launched weapons, which hardly rendered themselves useful in this type of warfare, ancient reports of biological warfare are confined to water poisonings and other, low-casualty efforts (Russell and Graham, 1996). In the 600 B.C. battle of Solon, an Athenian legislator ordered that hellebores (skunk cabbage) be dumped in the River Pleisthenes in order to incapacitate the defenders of Kirrha. During the Peloponnesian War, the Spartans reportedly soaked wood with pitch and sulfur to create sulfur dioxide torches for use against the Athenians. Eight hundred years later, during Europe's Medieval period, plague-infested cadavers were routinely catapulted over castle walls or placed upstream of enemy troops. In one of the first reports of biological warfare in our era, an account of the Battle of Vicksburg in July 1863 described the poisoning of ponds and lakes with dead livestock by the retreating Confederates.

World War I marked the beginning of the modern chemical era, as industrial technology allowed for the marriage of chemical compounds with shells and cylinders for use on the battlefield (Haber, 1986). Although more than one country experimented with gas bullets and shells during the early weeks of war, it was the Germans who first applied this technology in earnest during a battle with Russian troops at Bolimov. Although this initial attack was ineffective due to weather conditions, a chlorine gas attack against the French at Ypres, perhaps the most well-documented offensive of the entire war, led to 5000 allied casualties and the abandoment of enormous quantities of supplies. The effective use of gas at Ypres reinvigorated the efforts of war departments across the world to develop their own chemical weapons divisions and stockpiles. In the U.S., the Chemical Warfare Service — a group that would last through the Second World War — formed. As technology has improved since those first 5000 deaths, from the discovery of Sarin gas by a German scientist in the 1930s to the most recent development of binary weapons delivery systems, predicted casualty rates for wartime use of chemical and biological weapons have grown exponentially. Any nation or terrorist organization capable of producing and launching chemical or biological weapons is now considered a significant threat to any infantry force or large population center.

Why Are These Weapons So Lethal?

Of the multitude of toxic substances used to kill or incapacitate, the distinction between biological and chemical provides the basic framework for understanding the workings of these classes of weapons. Chemical weapons are defined by the United Nations (1969) as "chemical substances, whether gaseous, liquid, or solid, which might be employed because of their direct toxic effects on man, animals, and plants." In contrast, biologicals are "those that rely on the result of infectious multiplication within the organism" — in other words, toxic organisms that are introduced into their human hosts by air, water, or other transmission (United Nations, 1969). Chemical agents, the less lethal of the two, are further broken down into catagories based on their effects on the intended victim, i.e., burn agents, nerve agents, and tear gas. Perhaps the most familiar of the burn agents (vesicants) is mustard or "dusty mustard". This agent was implicated during the Gulf War as causing the only chemical injury acknowledged by U.S. forces when a marine private entered a grenaded Iraqi storage bunker and exited with severe burns on his skin (Dunn, 1991). Burn agents are designed to cause either blistering and burning of the epidermis or chemical burning and scarring of mucosal tissues and the lungs by being inhaled.

Nerve agents, another class of chemical materials, are clearly the most toxic of the chemical weapons, and include formulations such as Sarin, Soman, Tabun, and VX. These substances, when introduced into the bloodstream, block the synthesis of acetylcholinesterase, thus allowing the toxic buildup of acetylcholine in the nervous system. As acetylcholine regulation is responsible for both involuntary and voluntary muscle functions and a variety of other activities, lethal dosages of nerve agents lead to pupil constriction, headache, breathing difficulty, tremor, convulsions, and finally, death. The effects of even a slight exposure to a toxic nerve agent can last for years, causing peripheral nerve damage and other symptoms (Jamal et al., 1995). Most nerve agents, once synthesized, have a very limited shelf-life, and require careful storage to maintain their strength. For this reason, large-scale, multiple attacks with chemical weapons are often impractical for unorganized states or organizations that are unable to produce new stock. In addition, problems with dispersing the chemical poison at the site of the attack further eliminate other potential chemical users. Following the introduction of nerve agents during World War II, the U.S. quickly overcame both of these obstacles and developed its own nerve agent defense program which included human subjects and ground contamination testing at the Dugway proving grounds in Utah and other locations.

Biological weapons, ranging from disease spores to genetically altered bacteria, are considered the most deadly of all conventional and non-conventional weapons, and easily surpass chemical weapons in lethality (Mullins, 1992). One study estimated that a single aerosol attack of anthrax on the city of New York might cause 600,000 deaths, and only a half ounce of botulinium toxin (if adequately dispersed) could kill every man, woman, and child in the U.S. (Canadian Security Intelligence Service, 1995). The dubious reputation of biologicals stems from the fact that only a minute amount of these substances is required to infect a host organism. Once the respective bacteria or disease takes hold, symptoms of fever, difficulty breathing, chest pain, septicemia (blood poisoning), pneumonia, enlargement of the liver and spleen, anemia, or an influenza-like illness and acute inflammatory skin disease quickly follow (*Arming Iraq...,* 1994a). Although there are innumerable bacteriological toxins listed by the U.S. Bureau of Export Administration as "dual-use" materials (i.e., substances that have both peaceful and military applications), arguably the two most commonly sought are anthrax and botulinium toxin.

Before its introduction as a toxic weapon, anthrax was most familiar to herders and ranchers as a livestock disease. When spores of the anthrax colony are released into the environment and carried via air or contact with contaminated animals, the disease becomes an immediate threat to all forms of life in the area. On April 2, 1979, U.S. satellite reconnaisance identified an explosion at a secret military research lab in Sverdlovsk, Russia (Storella, 1984; Wade, 1980). Soon after the incident, an outbreak of pulmonary anthrax was reported in the neighboring city. Within days, the disease had spread through the human population, causing severe gastrointestinal symptoms among the population and between 500 and 1000 deaths. Like their chemical counterparts, the risk of a major biological weapons attack is tempered by the problem of dispersion. Unless one is armed with a battery of specially equipped warheads and missiles, an attack on a widely dispersed enemy will hardly approach the lethal potential of the weapon. Experts have pointed out, however, that dispersion can be achieved from a helicopter or small aircraft. During the Gulf War, U.S. Defense officials expressed concern when they discovered that, prior to the war, Iraq had purchased 40 industrial aerosol generators capable of spraying tons of bacteriologic material into the prevailing winds (Department of Defense, 1990a).

Descriptive Statistics on Recent Chemical and Biological Incidents

Table 14.1 presents available data on alleged CW/BW incidents that have occurred from 1978 to the present. As predicted by the lethal violence sequence, the data suggest that some perpetrators of CW incidents were also past offenders. The table also presents the

Table 14.1

Descriptive Statistics on Recent Chemical and Biological Incidents

Incident	Perpetrator Classification	Casualties	Source of Data
1975–1980: Vietnamese use of multiple CW agents against Laotian Hmong resistance and Kampuchean army	Rogue nation w/ state sponsors	Fatalities unknown	Eyewitness and physician report; medical data — medical reports of 100–300 affected
1979–1980: Soviet Union use of unknown CW agents against Afghanistan mujahidi	Rogue nation	No accurate data available	Eyewitness and U.S. State Dept.
1980–1985: Iraqi use of phosgene, mustard, and cyanide against Iran	Rogue nation w/ state sponsors	No accurate data available	Eyewitness, soil, and medical data
1985: Rajneesh cult dumping of *Salmonella* in Oregon reservoir to influence local elections	Religious group	50–100 affected	Forensic and medical data
1987: Libyan use of unknown CW agents against Chad	Rogue nation w /state sponsors	No accurate data available	U.S. State Dept.
1991: Iraqi use of mustard against town of Nafaj, Iraq	Rogue nation	Most died shortly thereafter; 300–500 affected	Department of Defense; eyewitness
1991: Gulf War troops report suspicion of CW/BW weapons use and exhibit symptoms of Gulf War illnesses	Rogue nation (in wartime context	49,000–100,000 reporting one or more symptoms; unconfirmed monitoring report of 4400 deaths	Eyewitness; physical/biological evidence
1993: Iraqi dumping CW agents in marshlands, killing Marsh Kurds	Rogue nation	Unconfirmed allegations of "hundreds" of fatalities	Department of Defense
1993: Bosnian Muslims' use of chlorine gas against Serbian forces	Ethno-nationalist group	No accurate data available; three attacks alleged	United Nations; eyewitness
1995: Aum Shinri Kyo use of Sarin in Japan subways	Religious cult	12 fatalities, 5000 affected	Video data; eyewitness

difficulty in gaining accurate casualty data following CW/BW incidents. This difficulty is typically due to regional instability that is the context for many incidents. For example, collection of casualty data on Soviet use of chemicals in Afghanistan was only possible long after the alleged attacks took place due to ongoing battles in the area. Terrorists also appear to be under-represented in the data on successful CW/BW events. This observation does not imply that terrorist groups are less likely candidates to perpetrate an attack. In fact, several "near incidents" have taken place over the past 20 years. However, this information points to the past success of police and government agencies in uncovering plots and hidden caches of dangerous materials prior to an attack taking place.

Who Is Likely To Use These Weapons: Models for Prediction

Having the ability to predict which nationalist group or political leader might use CW/BW technology should be a primary concern of national defense and domestic law enforcement agencies. A number of studies have examined individual factors that contribute to an accurate prediction model (Kellen, 1979; McNitt, 1995; Roberts, 1987; Robinson, 1991), although many of these studies were conducted to analyze specific instances of weapons stockpiling by a particular regime or in preparation of an offensive wartime action. In general, these analyses fall into three basic categories: (1) analyses of characteristics of the weapons themselves and the capability of groups to use them, (2) prediction based on the stages of conflict, and (3) studies of the behavior of "actors" of genocidal violence, including studies of rogue leaders and terrorist groups. Although we will briefly review the first two areas of study, the author suggests that the third category — studies of behavioral "types" and patterns of groups and leaders who have access to CW/BW materials — has greater utility in violence prediction.

Prediction Based on Weapon Characteristics and Capability Analysis

As terrorist incidents increase in frequency, it is crucial for law enforcement and intelligence officials to retain current knowledge on developments in the chemical and biological weapons field. An understanding of current technology can assist in predicting how close a rogue nation or group might be to a successful launch of a chemical or biological attack. Joyner (1990) described attempts by world chemical experts to closely monitor Libya's construction of the Rabta chemical facility near Tripoli in the late 1980s. Even while it participated in CW/BW antiproliferation conferences over the years, Libya had stated on other occasions that the use of chemical weapons against Israel was a justified act of defense. As the plant neared completion, an unexplained, major fire broke out which destroyed most of the facility, which analysts believe may have been set by a nearby country that had also been monitoring Libya's capability. In this instance, defense agencies were able to use their knowledge of weapons technology to predict when the Rabta plant would be considered armed and operational. Technical information about chemical and biological weapons can also be used to evaluate the validity of specific terrorist threats. Studies of weapons development and capability are routinely conducted by national defense departments such as the Defense Intelligence Agency of the U.S. For predictive purposes, it is the study of chemical and biological delivery systems that are the most important in determining potential vulnerable weapons targets.

The question, in other words, is not how deadly a certain chemical could be, but how a group might deliver and spread that chemical over its intended target. For example, recent developments in binary delivery systems have increased the lethal capability of attacks from rogue states. Binary missile systems allow the mixing of chemicals during mid-flight, increasing their toxic lifespan. During the Gulf War,

Iraq threatened numerous times to bomb cities in Israel with chemically loaded scud and Al Hussayn missiles. In the cacophony of Hussein's numerous threats, Coalition officials predicted that this particular one was substantial, as pre-war intelligence reports suggested that Iraq had been able to import binary weapons technology into its own missile program (Department of Defense, 1990c).

Capability analyses combine scientific data on chemical and biological weapons properties with intelligence about the characteristics, size, and organizational level of potential weapons users. Mengel (1979) pointed out that terrorist attacks involving high-technology weapons require a skilled team effort. These attacks not only involve implementation of a plan or threat, but also aquisition of chemical and weapon delivery materials and storage facilities. Hyman (personal communication, September 22, 1995) astutely pointed out that although a determined chemical terrorist can fashion a storage facility out of trash containers in a household bathroom, these chemicals must still be loaded into aerosol generators and specially designed explosive munitions without killing its possessors, then transported undercover to an intended target. While many terrorist groups might be attracted to the potential threat of exotic chemical weapons, fewer are capable of the detailed planning neccessary to work with materials such as mustard, VX, and Tabun. In many instances, sponsorship by a rogue state is a necessary step in acquiring chemical and biological capability and should indicate a higher degree of potential lethal threat to a target community or area.

Prediction of Events Based on Stages of Conflict

The second area of study in CW/BW violence prediction seeks to reveal the stages or levels of intergroup conflict and aggression. Many violent interstate conflicts or wars follow similar patterns of escalation, from declarations of unfairness and historical claims, to phases of pre-hostility and post-hostility engagement (Brockner and Rubin, 1985; Clarke, 1993; Leng and Singer, 1988). An entirely different set of patterns exists for situations involving terrorists and other anti-government groups which may be less reactive to world opinion. Understanding these commonalities during times of conflict can help us predict when non-conventional weapons might be employed, and, likewise, misjudgments in the stages of conflict can lead to a lack of preparation for a chemical or biological attack.

In an interesting review of interstate aggression, Leng (1994) identified the most common types of research study in this field: (1) case studies, (2) "rational choice" and game theory analyses, and (3) quantitative review of event data. Different game rules are present, Leng suggested, at different stages of engagement. For example, in the later stages of conflict, a warring state will often choose a riskier offensive option (e.g., non-conventional weapons) if it perceives that it is time to "turn the tide" of battle. Also important in the field of biological and chemical weapons prediction is an understanding of zero-sum thinking — a phenomenon that occurs when a warring entity uses its "final option" in an already lost battle simply to boost the suffering of the opponent. The U.S. decision to increase its use of napalm and other chemical dessicants in North Vietnam during the final weeks of war might be considered an example of zero-sum thinking, as was Hitler's orders to send troops into the streets of Berlin when it was clear that defeat was at hand.

Clarke's (1993) "rational" model of conflict prediction and termination offered a thorough description of different stages of conflict, as well as dynamic mechanisms that trigger changes from one level of conflict to another. Clarke extended his analysis to include pre-hostility phases, ended with post-dispute and settlement phases, and pointed out that conflict can represent both success-oriented and conflict-oriented objectives. The decision of one side to change the level of hostilities often occurs when that side changes its initial objectives. For example, during the pre-hostility phase of the Gulf War, Hussein's decision to place a group of British citizens under what he euphemistically termed "protective custody" served to increase the probability of hostile conflict with the U.S. Hussein thus changed his initial objective of holding Kuwait to include the collection of human "bargaining chips" that might help prevent active bombing of military targets. Clarke (1993) suggested that the correct strategy in dealing with changes in phases of hostility is to change the objectives of one's opponent and to reduce an opponent's "will to resist".

In dealing with a chemical or biological threat, this means either increasing the negative consequences a group might suffer for using such weapons or distracting an opponent with another objective. When U.S. intelligence officials correctly predicted a phase transition as Hussein moved chemical and biological munitions to the lines of battle, a message was sent to Bagdhad indicating that the U.S. would turn the sands of Iraq into "a glass parking lot" with tactical nuclear weapons if chemicals or biologicals were used. Defense officials later claimed that this threat effectively reduced the Iraqi regime's desire to utilize its chemical weapons (Department of Defense, 1990b). Under this circumstance, familiarity with conflict termination and phases allowed the U.S. to respond to a potentially catastrophic chemical and biological weapons threat.

Predicting the Behavior of the Actor

Whereas capability analyses and technical reviews stand as the "case studies" of chemical and biological violence, the most promising area of inquiry emerges from studies of the actor or perpetrator of lethal CW/BW incidents. By understanding the motivations and behavioral patterns of groups that engage in chemical and biological weapons use, we can identify common behavioral profiles and sequences that might be applied to future threats. Many superpower nations, rogue states, and terrorist organizations possess the capability of developing significant CW/BW weapons programs; however, Simon (1989) argued that some groups are more prone to stage a lethal attack than others who possess the same technology. For example, history suggests that rogue states and terrorist groups are more likely to carry out a chemical weapons attack than superpower nations (Douglass, 1995). Knowing other group characteristics that might predict CW/BW use would also be helpful. For example, recent unconfirmed reports suggesting that Bosnian Muslims may have used chlorine shells in August 1993 were not surprising considering the degree of ethnonationalist conflict in the region, the Muslims' perception that they had been abandoned by the U.S., and their perception of historical victimization (Rummel, 1995). The following qualities and identifying characteristics of groups may be suggestive of a greater likelihood of CW/BW violence:

- *Group solidarity.* Generally, terrorist groups with strong solidarity are more likely to engage in violent behavior than less cohesive groups. As Post (1990, p. 67) suggested, cohesive groups can adeptly magnify the emotional cues underlying their members' behavior, quickly becoming a "psycho-logically unstable group that functions as an emotional hothouse." Research has not yet specified whether solidarity offers a direct link to non-conventional violence, or whether it acts indirectly by discouraging dissenting communication.
- *Group sponsorship by another CW/BW nation.* Alexander (1994) and Spiers (1994) indicated that sponsorship by other countries increases the potential threat of terrorist and rogue groups. Covert transfers of chemical and biological precursors and intelligence through military advisors boost the technological capability of groups while increasing their confidence by the support of a larger state entity. Often, these transfers appear as sales of "agricultural supplies" or "medical products" between legitimate businesses and foreign states which allow sponsor nations to deny their participation if questioned by the world body. In 1989, the CIA described to Congress

a series of transactions that had taken place between German manufacturers and Libyan buyers during construction of the Rabta Chemical Plant. Though state complicity was denied, it was suggested that Bundestag officers may have looked the other way to avoid calling attention to the transactions. Similar accusations were made against the U.S. Department of Commerce after the end of the Gulf War, when it was revealed that Iraq had received between 10 and 20 shipments of biological "dual use" materials originating from the American Type Culture Collection under the guise of agricultural development (*Arming Iraq...,* 1994a).

- *The dangerous leader.* Although often misused as political propaganda, the identification of the dangerous leader may be useful in differentiating chemically armed-and-willing rogue states from their benign counterparts (Aragno, 1991). Mayer (1993, p. 331) described the dangerous leader as having "a low level of connection to other people and high proneness to violence. Other traits are an intolerance of criticism and a grandiose sense of national entitlement. Dangerous leaders murder advisors and citizens, condone torture, are intolerant of the press, feel superior, increase their militaries, and use secret police actions."
- *Religiously inspired and fundamentalist religious groups.* Religious identification offers a complex scheme of motivations and justifications that can be played out in the midst of national or civil conflict. State-sponsored religious beliefs can serve to relieve participants of guilt and victim empathy. In a study of 60 communal genocides that occurred around the world since 1945, Harff and Gurr (1989) found that groups at highest risk for genocide are most heavily concentrated in the Middle East region where there has been an upsurge in both religious fundamentalist acceptance and chemical and biological weapons proliferation (Alexander, 1994; Shultz and Schmauder, 1994).
- *Ethnonationalist groups and regimes.* A number of authors have described the link between mass killing and ethnic-based nationalist movements (Hagopian, 1978; Horowitz, 1985; Kellen, 1979). Ethnonationalism combines ethnic identification with themes of historical dislocation and persecution. Shultz and Schmauder (1994, p. 5) noted that in ethnonationalist conflict, "atrocities are frequent" and "usual conventions of war are ignored."

Motivational Determinants of CW/BW Use

Understanding the psychological or internal motivations of the terrorist group or rogue leader who engages in chemical or biological killing is thoroughly informative. Knowing the emotional and cognitive psychology of the actor can assist in determining the actor's behavioral stability, cycle of violence, and selection of targets.

First, it is important to know something of the history of academic debate which has split the field of terrorist studies into two camps for decades. The initial argument about terrorists, begun by Tilly's (1989) enlightened explanations of seemingly irrational behavior, can be summed up as a debate between the "abnormal patient" vs. the "logical actor". Authors such as Mayer (1993), on the "abnormal" side of the fulcrum, suggested that the behavior of dangerous leaders or terrorists represent irrational acts of madness that should be viewed within the context of mental illness. Khadaffi or members of the Red Army Brigades might be expected to have other symptoms of mental abnormality along the lines of an illness with sociopathic features. The support of lethal violence suggests an abnormal motivation, such as a sadomasochistic striving.

As pointed out by Tilly (1989), however, reliance on theories of frustrated aggression and psychopathology cloud and bias our understanding of these dangerous behaviors. Rather than leading to a descriptive knowledge of genocidal or lethal motivation, the theory of terrorist abnormality promotes the use of ascriptive labels that carry little additional insight. These labels may help the general population reframe its grief and outrage following a lethal terrorist attack, or may provide the political justification for violent military intervention, but they undervalue the motivation of the actor as a point of scientific study.

On the other side of the debate are researchers who believe that the behavior of terrorists and rogue leaders can be understood as "reasoned, instrumental

Figure 14.1
Lifton's Psychohistorical Model of Technological, Genocidal Killing

Psychohistorical dislocation following a period of rapid, traumatic social change	Totalistic ideological response — the search for powerful symbolization	Violent victimization — purging the "germs" of a diseased society

behavior ... which structure the options" and represent rational choice-making in certain, socioenvironmentally determined situations (Crenshaw, 1992, p. 7). This understanding of the motivations of terrorist and rogue leaders is, in this author's observation, the most widely accepted avenue of study and has opened the field in a number of directions.

It is clear that no single genocidal motivation is sufficient to explain all acts of chemical and biological killing. Many researchers have suggested a combination of goals and stimuli that motivate the behavior of the terrorist or state leader. In his study on terrorism and non-conventional technologies, Mengel (1979) suggested a framework of four basic motivators that lead to different varieties of violent public behavior. The motivators are derived from two linear concepts. Violent behavior can be gauged as either *rational* or *emotional* and is elicited by either *internal* or *external stimuli.* The rational/emotional spectrum roughly corresponds to the debate about "rational actors vs. abnormal actors" mentioned at the beginning of this section, while the internal/external dimension refers to the sociopolitical context in which the violence takes place (i.e., the Vietnam war was an external stimulus, while the stimuli for the Salem Witch Trials were internal). Combined, these two linear scales provide the four motivations suggested in Mengel's work: (1) rational/internal stimulus, (2) emotional/external stimulus, (3) emotional/internal stimulus, and (4) rational/external stimulus. According to Mengel (1979), only rational/internal motivations lead to terroristic behavior. The terrorist is a "rational actor" with the goal of effecting political change, but the terrorist's call to violence is prompted by an internal stimulus, for example, believing that his or her personal suffering is actually "purification of the spirit" to commit public violence. By comparison, a group that engages in protest instead of terroristic violence would be placed in the emotional/external stimuli area, as the "gathering cry" of the protest is made up of an emotional momentum that builds after an external political event.

A different approach to genocidal and terroristic motivation was offered by Robert Lifton, a Senior Professor at the Yale Department of Psychiatry. According to Lifton (1976, 1982; Lifton and Falk, 1982; Lifton and Markusen, 1990), genocide, particularly high-technology killing, is the end process of a series of collective psychohistorical experiences that leads certain individuals and groups toward violent victimization of themselves and others. These experiences are enumerated in Figure 14.1. First, psychohistorical dislocation takes place, which refers to "periods in history in which rapid social change, particularly of a traumatic nature, have led to pervasive insecurity, confusion, and anger both on individual and collective levels" (Markusen, 1992, p. 149). During this period, the usual symbolizations and collective ideologies that maintain group cohesion lose their meaning, creating individual and group distress. Next, a totalistic ideological response takes place, in which individuals or group cells within a society try to develop new "meaning structures" that will ease their sense of dislocation. Often, this response carries with it the theme of finding a "cure" which will purge society of its "illness". In the final step, a group identifies certain individuals, organizations, or peoples as the "disease" which caused the group illness. The cure for the disease becomes the genocidal elimination of large groups of people. Lifton further suggested that technological means of killing (i.e., chemical weapons, nuclear weapons) are often preferred by the perpetrators of these events, as they enhance the dehumanization and psychic numbing toward the victims that always precede genocidal murder.

Using Behavioral Analysis To Develop a CW/BW Lethal Violence Sequence

Moving away from the psychodynamics of the terrorist or rogue leader, Margolin (1977) recommended leaving behind the contradictory psychological and motivational theories that have dominated the field of terrorist studies to understand the use of CW/BW. Instead, he suggested a return to the method of careful behavioral observation and data collection. In the behavioral approach, which provides the groundwork for the lethal violence sequence detailed in this chapter, patterns of group behavior, behavioral histories, and other observant data take precedence over group motivational states and group and leader psychology. The emphasis remains focused on details of the actor's past and present behavior. Have past target selections been random or specific, and is the group currently engaged in a practicing phase against a selected target? Have there been attempts to cover up evidence of biological or chemical research? Finally, as pointed out by Hall (1996), a clear understanding of lethal violence, whether genocidal or interpersonal, requires attention to the contributions of the victim and context in the scheme of the event. It is not enough to know only the perpetrator's motivations and behavior. For this reason, sections on context and victim behavior are also included in this review.

As illustrated in the following description of the CW/BW lethal violence sequence, common behavioral patterns emerge when we examine not only the violent event, but also early and late stages of enactment. Readers will note similarities in the sequence of internal/emotional and behavioral events that take place in a chemical weapons incident compared to behaviors we might observe with other violent perpetrators such as participants in genocides and paramilitary operations.

The Lethal Violence Sequence for CW/BW Weapons Use Measuring the Group Baseline

The group baseline provides the starting point for understanding the progression to later stages of the lethal violence sequence. The baseline, more commonly associated with single-subject or single-behavior research, is a frequency measurement of identified behavioral targets (Bootzin et al., 1993). Although it may be helpful to have access to a complete behavioral dossier of a terrorist cell or rogue state leader's past use of violence, only particular aspects of prior behavior are relevant to our purpose of identifying the preliminary stages of CW/BW use. Based on the author's review of actual CW/BW incidents and relevent literature, the following types of behavioral data provide information related to later CW/BW behaviors:

1. Prior acts of violence have been directed toward random (i.e., general population) rather than discriminate targets.
2. Prior attacks have included detailed planning and rehearsal.
3. Group or rogue state has previously used sophisticated weaponry or any type of weapon of mass destruction.

4. Group or state has been accused of actively seeking to purchase CW/BW materials.
5. Prior attacks have resulted in mass casualties.
6. Group or rogue state has engaged in ethnic purges or genocidal programs sanctioned by governing body.
7. Past genocidal killings were followed by official denials or hiding of evidence.

Victim Contributions. Few of us conceive of suddenly becoming the victim of a chemical or biological attack while we are standing in line at a state office building, attending a cultural event, or walking down a city block. We think little about the availability of oxygen from one breath to the next. We are secure in our knowledge that our skin will not likely blister, our eyes burn, and our lungs bleed over the proceeding moments. Chemical and biological violence seems to be the concern of Middle Eastern countries or "traditional" victim groups already being persecuted in Afghanistan, Cambodia, or Basque Spain. Yet, chemical terrorism and biological terrorism within the borders of the U.S. remain a likely part of our future and have already been planned in the past. For example, Bowman (1994, p. 142) cited the 1984 case against a white supremacist group which was planning to dump 200 gallons of cyanide into main reservoirs of Chicago, New York, or Washington D.C.

Why do we distance ourselves from the recognition that we live in a chemically and biologically vulnerable environment? In 1990, the author completed a study of public reaction to the threat of nuclear holocaust, including psychological influences that insulate people who are living under such a threat (Paltin, 1990). One significant finding emerged from this study: People often experience a sense of narcissistic invulnerability (what we might term "selfism") as a common reaction to thinking about and imaging a nuclear event. In other words, participants in the study exhibited a counterphobic psychological defense of self-preservation, an experience of being invincible to annihilation from this type of mass destruction. It is possible that the civilian public, as potential victims, also maintains this defense in reaction to the threat of chemical and biological attack. Rather than taking a proactive, involved stance to influence the future of chemical and biological weapons, the public trusts that its government is doing this activity for them.

During the baseline phase, we might describe the victim's contribution to the approaching event as one of direct or indirect choicemaking regarding chemical and biological security. Issues of CW/BW arms arise almost weekly, with reports appearing both in the popular mass presses and specialized journals (Barry and Watson, 1996; Government Accounting Office, 1991; "War ills...", 1996). Yet, few U.S. communities have well-developed chemical and biological defense plans, and even fewer individual citizens are likely aware of what they should do in a biological emergency. It might be interesting to compare the apathy of U.S. citizens on the topic with the response of citizens of Israel, where preventing and monitoring terrorism is an active part of civic responsibility for each citizen.

Contextual Features. In the case of both terrorist and rogue state violence, context contributes to the situation in our failure to recognize and act upon cues or patterns of violent or threatening behavior. We do not confront what we see. Although the State Department, in cooperation with the Department of Defense, the CIA, and the FBI, maintains current reports on potential "hot spots" across the nation and around the globe, taking preventative action against a rogue state based on baseline data alone does not occur often. The only known instance of a direct proactive strike against a chemical weapons plant is that of the attack on Libya's Rabta Chemical Plant, in which the perpetrators remain unknown. Concerns about political and diplomatic pressure act as inhibitors to taking a proactive stand against countries which have a history of genocidal violence or are known to be developing chemical and biological weapons programs. Political history beginning with the Geneva treaty of 1925, up to the most recent CW/BW anti-proliferation agreement ratified by the U.S. Congress in 1997, shows us that despite the seeming rationality of a program to prohibit and eliminate stockpiling of chemical and biological weapons, debate about the usefulness of and need for such weapons continues. For the past few years, however, some independent and non-profit scientific organizations, such as the Federation of American Scientists, have become vocal advocates of chemical and biological weapons control. Such efforts clearly help to decrease the contextual and diplomatic *laissez-faire* that marks the usual state of affairs during this phase of the violence sequence.

The Pre-Conflict Phase

Weapons Research and Acquisition. The first stage of the pre-conflict phase involves the acquisition of chemical and biological weapons technology and materials. This stage may occur months or years before the group actually decides to use the weapons in an attack or before a target is selected. As noted earlier in this chapter, germ spores such as anthrax or chemical elements such as fertilizers or vesicants are easily obtained from a variety of underground and legitimate sources. During this phase, a group will often aggressively seek an assortment of materials rather than focusing their efforts on a single substance (Timmerman, 1991). Acquisition is also followed by the installation of a "research program" through which the group members increase their familiarity with different areas of weapons use. The goal of the group members in this stage is to increase their capability to utilize what they have aquired and to maintain secrecy about their operations. Schools for training and research for military personnel are established at this stage; for example, larger schools include Russia's Red Banner Academy of Chemical Defense or the Army Chemical School of the U.S.

Bargaining for Demands. Near-entry into the lethal violence phase of the sequence is often characterized by a group's attempts to engage a potential target or government in bargaining for certain political demands or favors. As noted by Mengel (1979, p. 208), vague, universalistic demands such as "overthrow of the oppressors", "peace through anarchy", or "restoration of God's will" are more commonly associated with mass violence rather than specific demands such as "restoration of national elections", "releasing political prisoners", or "exposing presidential corruption". Demands may carry the nuance of a justification for mass violence, as we witness the "internal, psychological motivation" for the attack begin to drive the group's activities. In rare instances where bargaining has been successful, the group will either return to the pre-conflict phase or will submit additional demands.

Selecting the Target. Following the rational objective model of terroristic and rogue state behavior, targets for chemical weapons attacks are often selected based on the goals of the group. For a terrorist organization, induction of mass fear in a population might be the desired goal (Simon, 1989), whereas a rogue state leader might be interested in genocidal elimination of dissenting ethnic or regional groups (Stohl, 1984). Target selection also appears to correspond with baseline data on previous acts of violence. An ethnonationalist group that has a history of conflict with a particular ethnic group might be expected to choose that group as a target for chemical attack.

Victim Contributions. Unfortunately, victims of chemical and biological violence, whether by terrorist or interstate attack, receive little information during the pre-conflict phase that would allow them to maintain some measure of personal protection and defense. Public notification of an impending bomb threat may take place, but suggestions that chemical or biological weapons might be involved are likely to be kept secret, either to control panic or to maintain public trust. Even soldiers entering a known chemical operations theater are often given disinformation about the threats involved or effectiveness of preventive medications (*Is Military Research...,* 1994). Yet, information and defensive equipment are both available and could increase the survivability of a chemical or biological incident if used properly.

Again, Israel provides an example of a government engaging its citizens in personal prevention efforts during an active CW/BW threat. During the Persian Gulf War, Israel negotiated with the U.S. State Department not to actively participate in the offensive against Iraq as long as the U.S. provided adequate defenses against Iraq's chemical and missile operations (Watson et al., 1993). As a result, Israeli citizens were given masks and protective materials, as well as specific and detailed instructions on the use of gas masks and building protective shelters (Wolfe, personal communication, March 6, 1991). Had a chemical-weapon-bearing scud attack on Tel Aviv or Haifa occurred, no doubt such preparations would have decreased the resulting rate of casualty.

Contextual Features. As Leng (1994) noted, the approach toward the active use of force often increases the resolve of the players involved and promotes risk taking. Not coincidentally, the accompanying stress of conflict increases misperceptions of threat on both sides, reduces accurate decision-making, and increases cognitive rigidity (Holsti, 1989). As a result, the context of pre-conflict tension may increase the risk of an organization or country deciding to deploy or ready its available CW/BW arms. This state of posturing and miscommunication also prevents active negotiation that might serve to reduce the risk of CW/BW use during interstate conflict. The situation is even more tense when dealing with terrorist or cult group threats, where negotiation is discouraged to avoid "legitimizing" the cause of the group. Both the U.S. and Israel maintain a "no negotiation" policy with regard to terrorists. As a result, the only remaining strategy for discouraging CW/BW use in this phase is to promote the perception that the use of chemical or biological weapons would result in severe retaliation and would end in the death or life imprisonment of all terrorist or cult members (e.g., a variation of MacNamara's Mutually Assured Destruction policy of the 1960s nuclear era). An alternative strategy that has been used successfully in the past is to employ a recognized state entity or government, a third party, which is able to carry messages and communications to the terrorist leadership regarding potential negotiations. The objective of this type of negotiation is not necessarily to convince the rogue or terrorist to lay down arms, but rather to slow down the escalation of conflict, to promote rational decision-making with all parties involved, and to avoid unnecessary posturing that might trigger an entry into the lethal violence phase of conflict.

Rehearsing the Attack. After a decision to perpetrate violence has been made, the lethal violence phase of a CW/BW attack is preceded by a period of active rehearsal and handling of chemical and biological arms. Practice is necessary due to the complexity of the weaponry. With rogue states, rehearsal may consist of chemical drills and exercises designed to familiarize personnel with weapons use, protective gear, and potential dangers. Care in use of chemical and biological materials is often a key focus in training, as mishandling of these materials is quickly fatal to participants. During the Gulf War, Hussein designated "chemical awareness weeks" during which soldiers received additional practice in working with gas masks, hazardous canisters, and other materials. Identifying rehearsal and drill programs can provide valuable information regarding a group's CW/BW capability.

The Lethal Violence Phase

The Triggering Stimulus. In contrast to the cues that incite violent crime, the identification of a triggering stimulus for a CW/BW event is often quite elusive. However, it is sometimes possible to identify series of events that contributed to the timing of an attack, for example, the failure of bargaining rounds, the anniversary of a prior atrocity, or the death of a political prisoner. Familiarity with a group's historical identifications may be informative. These include past events which are used by the group as a rationale for their existence or which serve to increase the emotional intensity of the group (Crenshaw, 1992).

In many cases, violent collective entities do not need triggers to aggress, as the decision to perpetrate violence may be part of a long-range strategy (Hall, 1996). In these instances, the availability of victims and targets, not triggering stimuli, sets the violence into motion.

The Actual CW/BW Event. Unlike conventional weapons attacks which have the potential to satisfy a terrorist group's hunger with a visual record of an incident in the rubble of a building or an overturned bus, chemical and biological attacks are only successful if they result in human casualty. Mass death, or engaging the opponent's fear of inescapable, noxious death, is the sole emotional payoff of choosing such a complex, hard-to-manage weapon. Due to this fact, potential targets of a chemical or biological weapon are rarely given a warning call or "red letter" prior to the attack in order to prevent human casualty. Once the CW/BW event is underway, it can be assumed that the group has found a sufficient internal justification for the high lethality of the attack and does not feel obligated to warn potential victims.

The CW/BW event phase can be either a discrete, single event or a series of attacks over the active course of an interstate conflict. However, due to the amount of money, time, and preparation involved in the use of these weapons, single-event use appears to be the exception rather than the rule. With regard to prediction, acknowledging that an initial attack may likely be followed by subsequent incidents should allow for increased preparation of potential victims and organization by civil defense or government agencies. We might also expect that a "clustered" attack of simultaneous lethal events would be favored by a terrorist cell with a limited attack time frame, whereas intrastate and wartime use of CW/BW weapons could be extended over months or years, as was the case in the Iran-Iraq war.

Manipulation of the Scene Following the Attack. The end of the lethal violence phase is often signaled by an attempt to reduce the evidence of CW/BW use by its perpetrator. Dismantling and hiding chemical shells, changing locations of research facilities, and mass burials of corpses by military personnel in chemical protective gear, have been reported following past CW/BW incidents. Corresponding to the field of research in genocidal killing, CW/BW perpetrators may engage in this behavior due to fears of violent retribution (Stewart and Zimmerman, 1989) or to avoid angering a state sponsor (Simon, 1989). Due to the brief half-life of compounds such as VX and Soman and biologicals such as anthrax and to delays between the reported date of attack and the arrival of an inspection team, hiding physical evidence of an attack is quite feasible even when inspection involves careful soil and air analyses. This situation may lead to confusion between the compelling, multiple eyewitness reports of attacks and the findings of search teams or observers. Without clear physical markers, the finding "unconfirmed" is often the outcome of post-event site inspections.

Victim Reaction to the Event. The survivors of toxic chemical or biological exposure face the remainder of their lives with a host of debilitating physiological and psychological effects. The physiological damage that occurs from exposure to neurotoxins or biological organisms was described earlier in this chapter, and can include neurological impairment, dermatological complications, major organ involvement, immunological impairment, and neuromuscular impairment. Less known are the psychological effects of survival, the manifestations of acute stress disorder, post-traumatic stress symptoms, and accompanying depression. One Persian Gulf veteran who manifested symptoms of fibromyalgia, asthma, seizures, and chronic pain following his return described his feelings as follows: "I was healthy before the war. Now I'm 33 years old but I feel like I'm 80 years old inside" (B. Jones, personal communication, September 9, 1995). The psychological effects of a successful chemical or biological attack extend outward into the community or population whose members were its target and then expand to the entire human community. Although acts of terrorism, whether chemical or conventional, leave a lasting impression of vulnerability and insecurity in society, the author believes that CW/BW terrorism and genocide are particularly hurtful. For example, there is an abundance of popular hero images that engage our feelings of symbolic immortality. The popular media offer us characters who can survive explosions, automatic weapons fire, and even alien invasion. The author has encountered no parallel psychohistorical images associated with chemical or biological weapons.

Contextual Features Which Influence the Event. The contributions of context during the lethal violence phase are often difficult to discern. Triggering or inhibiting contextual stimuli vary with the type of CW/BW scenario. In terrorist situations, interstate relations between a terrorist surrogate country and a target nation can influence the outcome of a potential lethal event. As Simon (1989) suggested, terrorist groups may be unwilling to go against counter-commands of a sponsoring state if the groups wish to maintain the state's sponsorship. Rogue state use of chemical weapons in ethnic genocide or political cleansing might be vulnerable to threats of embargo outside military intervention, though this level of involvement by outside nations is rare.

Context can also influence the sequence of lethal violence by providing reinforcement for terrorist or rogue leader behavior. For example, if the objective of a terrorist group is to reveal the weakness or vulnerability of a government in protecting its citizens, a successful CW/BW attack becomes the reinforcer for continuation of the lethal violence sequence. If political revenge or economic disruption is the goal, then the threat of mass poisoning can generate the desired result. This was the case with the 1978 Palestinian threat to inject exported Israeli oranges with mercury, as well as the more recent case of poisoning of candy from the Morinaga Candy Factory in Japan. In summary, a successful terrorist event is a self-reinforcing activity.

The Recovery Phase

Denial of the Incident and Expunging of Records. The transition to the recovery phase is often marked by increasing statements of denial of participation in the incident or denials that the incident actually took place. Denials may continue even when evidence to the contrary is readily available. A review of historical CW/BW incidents suggests that this behavior is particularly characteristic of state perpetrators attempting to hide within-state urbanocides on dissenting ethnic groups or political foes. Noting how often multiple eyewitness accounts of CW/BW events are deemed unconfirmed by external investigating agencies and the politics involved in challenging a rogue state with a superpower sponsor, we might conclude that rogue leaders engage in this behavior because it is successful for avoiding sanctions and retribution. From a psychosociological perspective, the manipulation and expunging of acts of violence from the historical record might be considered a form of psychic numbing, or as a final stage of "cleansing" and purification as described by Lifton and Falk (1982).

The Return to Aquisition or Pre-Conflict Bargaining Phase. In the final stage of recovery, the terrorist group or state attempts to re-engage in political dialogue and bargaining to continue its normal political process. If sanctions have been imposed by a regional or world council, reducing or eliminating those sanctions becomes the focus of activity. If concern over CW/BW capability remains intense, bargaining over the scope and protocol of external investigations by the World Health Organization or United Nations investigating teams may be included in post-event bargaining (Federation of American Scientists, 1996). A state or terrorist cell may also renew its process of aquisition of CW/BW technology and arms after external attention toward its behavior has died down. Reports by government investigative agencies may begin to emerge, suggesting that an organization has renewed its imports of CW/BW precursors and materials. An illustrative example of this behavior was the much-publicized case of Iraqi chemical and biological aquisition following world criticism of its use of chemical agents during the Iran-Iraq war ("Ship loaded...", 1990; "U.N. Says Iraq...", 1988). The renewal of aquisition efforts may signal the start of another lethal violence sequence that involves another target.

Case Vignette Illustrating the CW/BW Lethal Violence Sequence. From the time of Assyrian conquest, the history of Iraq has been marked by ethnic tension and conflict. Hammurabi, Sargon, and other ancient rulers of Mesopotamia and Babylon gained the throne through conquest of ethnic foes, although they are equally known for their gifts of legal codification and organization of government (Roux, 1992). During the violent political rise of Saddam Hussein and the Ba'ath (Renaissance) party in Iraq, the tradition of ethnic violence continued, as Kurdish peoples to the north and independent Shi'ites to the south became the target of acts of government terrorism. The West must accept some responsibility for this state of affairs, as Britain left Iraq in 1921 as a hastily arranged conglomeration of territories under a single, autocratic rule. During his first years in power, Hussein recognized the strategic power of acquiring chemical and biological weapons technology. He began acquiring CW/BW technology and chemical precursors from a number of private firms located mostly in West Germany, Holland, and Italy. Military advisors were also engaged to assist Iraq in its development of chemical technology, opening the Samarra plant in the mid-1980s and other plants at other locations. Iraqi chemical weapons officers were well schooled in their craft, many having received advanced degrees at training institutes in the Soviet Union (Department of Defense, 1991b). The ease with which Iraq successfully courted a complete CW/BW development campaign from nations which had committed to chemical arms control is chilling and marked the beginning of a lethal violence sequence that continued for nearly two decades.

Iraq transitioned from its baseline and preconflict phases and entered its first active lethal violence phase during the middle years of the Iran-Iraq war. In the early months of the conflict, Iraq suffered massive casualties at the hands of the new messianic Shi'ite state. The Iranians were surprisingly effective in their offenses and were able to secure territory south of Bagdhad. The situation changed drastically in 1984, when Iraq began its chemical offensive against its enemy. Aircraft loaded with Sarin, Tabun, and mortar rounds of mustard and cyanide were used against strategic Iranian facilities and troops ("U.N. Says Iraq...", 1988). Wisely predicting that Western nations, hypocritical of their prior commitments to chemical treaties, would maintain political silence during Iraqi chemical offenses, Iran brought its chemical weapons victims to hospitals in New York and Western Europe where the news media had a first-hand account of the situation (Hughes, 1988). Iraqi chemical weapons attacks against the Iranians either decreased or ended in 1987, already having doubled the casualty rate endured during the war.

In 1988, Iraq entered a pre-conflict phase of its second lethal violence sequence when it renewed its chemical and germ warfare acquisition efforts. Reports of cyanide shipments and development of a germ warfare plant filtered through to the world media.

Later in 1988, Hussein held a conference in which he invited Iraqi-born physicists and chemists to return from their studies abroad to work on domestic military projects (Department of Defense, 1990a). Despite these indications of a renewal of Iraq's CW/BW capability, the U.S. government maintained official silence on the issue, as the press speculated that Washington wished to avoid embarassment of the Iraqi government ("Iraq said to be...", 1989). Later investigation by Congress revealed that the U.S. had also been exporting shipments of raw chemical and biological materials to Iraq as medical and agricultural development projects ("Arming Iraq...", 1994b). These contextual events preceeded a new lethal violence phase which Iraq entered in 1990, during the months preceeding the Gulf War.

The victims identified in this vignette are the Kurdish tribes of the Iraqi Northern border. Indications during the Gulf War that Iraq had entered the lethal violence phase included active rehearsal and practice of CW/BW operations, and public declarations and threats of chemical capability, such as, "He who threatens us with an atomic bomb will be annihilated by binary chemicals" ("Iraq warns...", 1990).

At the end of the war, Iraqi officials met with their U.S. counterparts under a large canopy set up near Safwan in southern Iraq to discuss the terms of surrender. The U.S. was adamant about keeping Iraqi fixed-wing aircraft grounded. The U.S. believed it had Iraqi aggression fully contained. The Iraqis asked for permission to fly non-fixed-wing aircraft (helicopters) over outlying Iraqi towns in order to drop medical and food supplies to its citizens. This was an odd request, as it was common knowledge that citizens in these areas had been inciting rebellion against Hussein's regime following the war and were considered a threat by Bagdhad. Schwartzkopf and the other Americans at the table unwisely agreed, not recognizing that Hussein was, in effect, requesting permission to fly genocidal missions over Kurdish towns in order to secure his territory ("Interview with Rick Atkinson", 1996).

While developing his autocratic regime, Hussein was never able to gain the allegiance of the Kurdish minority who lived primarily outside of Bagdhad. The Kurds represented a political and personal, but hardly a military, challenge to Hussein. The American agreement provided the contextual trigger that initiated the following chemical lethal violence event. In the proceeding weeks, reports filtered back from the borders that Iraq had launched a number of helicopter-based chemical weapons attacks against the Kurds. In the town of Nafaj, citizens were herded into vacant lots and told to wait for further instructions. Minutes later, helicopters loaded with sprayers showered the crowd with nitric acid, killing hundreds of men, women, and children (Department of Defense, 1991a). Iraq's well-publicized attempts to foil the efforts of the U.N. inspection team identifies the "manipulation of scene" that commonly follows such incidents. Following two cycles of the lethal violence sequence, Iraq re-entered a recovery phase in which it has steadfastly denied that it ever used chemical weapons. Unconfirmed reports suggested that Iraq was again searching for CW/BW materials as early as 1992.

Case Vignette of a Soldier With Gulf War Illness. As of February 1996, 80,000 veterans of the Gulf War had registered with the government regarding symptoms of Gulf War illnesses (GWI). Symptoms of GWI ranged from headaches and dizziness to multiple chemical sensitivity, degenerative joint disease, and skin rashes. One comprehensive study at the University of Texas denoted 51 symptoms associated with the spectrum of illnesses (Haley et al., 1997). Although controversy remains as to whether or not Iraq used chemical or biological weapons during the Gulf War, Hussein's readiness and distribution of these weapons in the field of battle should be considered part of an active phase of lethal violence.

R.M., a Marine veteran with 24 years of service, served as the Ammunition Chief with the 5th Brigade during the Gulf War (R.M., personal communication, March 24, 1997). Prior to the Gulf War, R.M.

considered himself to be in top shape, maintaining his physical condition through marathons and other sports activities. During his deployment, R.M. was exposed to a series of incidents which included scud attacks and exposure to blowback from coalition bombings. He remained in the Gulf during the entire conflict, and returned to the U.S. in May 1991. During the course of his service, R.M. noticed he was having memory problems, difficulty with arithmetic calculation (which was an integral part of his job), and a loss of stamina. These symptoms worsened over the course of the year, and by 1992, he was also experiencing severe rashes, multiple chemical sensitivity, and joint problems. R.M. participated in all three phases of the government's Comprehensive Clinical Evaluation Program in which he was diagnosed with degenerative joint disease and Parkinson's disease. In 1996, 2 years before he was scheduled to end his career with full benefits, R.M. had to retire early. He has not worked following termination of his service with the Marines due to his symptoms.

R.M. has not drawn any conclusions regarding the possibility of toxic exposure to chemical or biological warfare materials during his military service. He has heard explanations from various sources, including the possibility of low-level nerve agent exposure, problems associated with ingestion of pyridostigmine bromide (a preventive inoculation), and infection by a bacteria named *Mycoplasma fermentans*. Although recognized as disabled by the Veterans' Administration (V.A.), R.M. felt that he had received little help from the government in finding appropriate treatments for his condition. He is considering pursuing treatment available from one of the many independent research groups that claim success in working with Gulf War illnesses.

Recommendations for Intervention in the CW/BW Lethal Violence Sequence

Although recent efforts to eliminate stockpiling and proliferation are commendable, singular efforts to reverse the growing threat of chemical and biological weapons use will never be effective without the multidimensional participation of individual citizens, national leaders, multi-national corporations, and world counsels. Solutions must address issues of psychological numbing and ethnonationalist dislocation, as suggested in Lifton's work, and not focus solely on bans and export controls of chemical and biological materials. Prediction efforts by law enforcement and policing agencies must include an understanding of group and leader behavior and, in particular, the characteristics of the CW/BW lethal violence sequence. Utilizing these strategies will increase our ability to practice what Hopple (1993) might term *policy with intelligence,* using baseline knowledge to guide our decisionmaking.

Solutions for Individuals Concerned About the Threat of CW/BW Use

1. Develop an awareness of domestic, as well as international, chemical, and biological arms issues that have an impact on the community. Visualize how these events might endanger personal security and safety. News reports that have bearing on CW/BW issues appear almost weekly. For example, how close do we live to the nearest U.S. chemical weapons stockpile, and is burning used to reduce these stores? Have our communities developed laws and policies for dealing with the use of "pepper spray" as a personal chemical weapon to deter crime? Have we ever spoken with a Gulf War veteran who has opinions on the Gulf War Syndrome?
2. Find out about the activities of professional groups that work toward solutions in the CW/BW arena. Inquire about membership in groups that represent rational views on chemical and biological arms. For example, the Federation of American Scientists and SIPRI actively research and participate in these issues.
3. Find out if local professional societies or national organizations might have an avenue for involvement in the CW/BW arms area. For example, a local psychological association might sponsor a community

lecture by an environmental toxicologist or speaker on terrorism. A law enforcement agency might hold a panel discussion among community leaders on how chemical or terrorist violence might be addressed if it came to their locality.

4. Research in the areas of terrorism and genocide has generally been over-reliant upon individual case studies to make its point. Individuals with a background in social, forensic, and behavioral research might consider addressing this problem by participating in and conducting data-driven research in these areas. For example, too little information exists on effective inhibitors to terrorist behavior.
5. There are presently over 80,000 veterans from the Gulf War reporting one or more symptoms of Gulf War illnesses. Many veterans and members of Congress have been critical of the limited success of the V.A. treatment and research program. In addition, these programs are not accessible by the hundreds of civilian workers who worked in Kuwait and Saudi Arabia during the war. Veterans or civilian workers can find avenues for political involvement and treatment alternatives by contacting one of the many local GWI organizations in their area. A list of these organizations can be found online at http://www.GVWRP.com or by contacting the Desert Storm Justice Foundation at (405) 348-1722.

Solutions for Law Enforcement Officials and Federal Antiterrorist Agencies

1. Learn more about group behavior in terrorist and lethal violence contexts, and disseminate this information within the agency. Learn to identify preparation and baseline phases of a CW/BW lethal violence sequence and their associated behaviors. Develop a file of case examples based on potential scenarios, with suggested interventions that might occur at different phases of the sequence.
2. Form a CW/BW intervention team, similar to a specialist police group, that maintains specialized knowledge and training in this area. Sponsor members of the team to attend conferences on the subject, or to confer across federal and state agencies. Teams might consider forming an E-mail network or contacting the Department of Defense regarding the Chem-Bio Quick Response Force for logistical and informational support.
3. Maintain enough knowledge of CW/BW developments to recognize raw materials and equipment that might be used to construct a chemical or biological device. Learn about chemical, fertilizer, or other related manufacturers in an area, or of potential sources for biological materials such as university agriculture labs or medical research facilities.
4. Learn where to aquire chemical defense equipment that could be used in case of emergencies. Contact local National Guard or equipment suppliers for information on access to masks, protective clothing, or other equipment. Offer information to local hospital and medical center administrators on where to locate medicines or vaccines that might be used in emergency situations.

Manufacturer and Industry Solutions

1. Take the initiative in developing effective chemical taggants that will assist in export monitoring and use, rather than waiting for federal government intervention. Instead of opposing government policies in this area, develop intelligent solutions that will be cost-effective within the industry.
2. Monitor large export sales of heavy equipment, aerosol generators, refrigeration systems, and dual-use chemicals and vaccines to countries suspected of having chemical or biological weapons programs. In particular, consider additional consultation with the Department of Commerce for large exports to Ethiopia, Egypt, Israel, South Korea, China, India, Myanmar, Syria, and Pakistan. Industry executives should be mindful of the lessons learned by companies which were involved in sales with the Iraqi government during the 1980s, and which are now facing civil litigation in Texas.
3. Stimulate new approaches to current issues in global CW/BW proliferation, waste management of chemical stockpiles, and other areas of concern. Encourage original thinking and research in these areas. For example, a large chemical or biomedical research firm might sponsor a conference with a faculty drawn from industry researchers and proliferation monitoring groups such as the Federation of American Scientists.

Government and International Solutions

1. To determine the CW/BW intentions or capability of a terrorist group or rogue state, increase efforts to collect baseline and group behavioral data that will assist in locating that group within its lethal violence sequence. Do not overvalue deployment and logistical intelligence at the expense of information on patterns of past and recent use of chemical or biological arms, rehearsal and training, or information on a country's history of mass killings or other predictors of CW/BW use.
2. Ease confidentiality restrictions on export data maintained by the Bureau of Export Administration of the Department of Commerce. Allow and encourage independent, external monitoring of Department of Commerce decisions. Encourage other governments to develop similar policies for export security. Note the example of the successful interdiction of "supergun" exports from Great Britain to Iraq, which was due to cooperative efforts of both private-sector and government agencies.
3. Encourage ratification of the Chemical Weapons Convention by other countries which have not yet done so. Reinforce these efforts with diplomatic and economic consequences that will guide the success of the treaty. Initiate dialogue with other signatories on their experiences in implementing the Convention and problems encountered in following through with its expectations.
4. Pay heed to researchers who predict an increase in U.S. domestic terrorism and what Nixon once termed "megaterrorism". Be aware that as more incidents occur, terrorists will search for more lethal means of political extortion and newsmaking. Rather than expecting the threats of metropolitan reservoir poisonings that represented the CW/BW capability of terrorists in past decades, plan for attacks as sophisticated as the Tokyo incident — attacks utilizing airborn contaminants in closed facilities with maximized population densities.
5. Psychohistorical dislocation occurs when communities or people undergo rapid change and social upheaval due to civil war, urban migration, and government persecution. This situation leaves fertile ground for reactionary, ultranationalist, and ethnic cleansing movements that may seek chemical or biological capability. Citizens personally identify and align with these movements in order to feel a sense of stability and protection. This author believes it is possible to counter this complex phenomenon by providing "intelligent" foreign affairs and aid support that offer citizens alternative vehicles for personal identification. Specifically, foreign relations and aid programs should work to develop community teams for cooperative building and support projects. For example, U.S. forces in Bosnia could engage in a community building project, developing a combined workgroup of citizens and foreign troops to rebuild local landmarks or a community market. Aid programs should remain micro-sized, stress values of community pride and mutual assistance, and avoid larger national needs such as highway or power plant rebuilding.

Summary

This chapter describes a rising trend of chemical and biological weapons use among terrorist and rogue state groups. As observed in the Sarin attack of the Tokyo subway system perpetrated by the Aum Shinri Kyo cult, lethal violence against a metropolitan population is quite feasible and meets a variety of terrorist and rogue state goals. Although difficult to manage, chemical and biological materials are easy to acquire and are capable of causing the same casualty rate as nuclear weapons if unleashed in an effective manner. The author notes that, similar to the behavior of the perpetrator and victim in cases of interpersonal violence, predictive patterns begin to emerge when we study the behavior of terrorist groups or rogue leaders accused of using such weaponry. Due to the nature of chemical and biological arms, patterns of behavior occur over months or years prior to actual use.

Citing the lethal violence sequence as a unit of study, we have observed features of group baseline, pre-conflict, lethal event, and recovery behavior that often accompany these attacks. Similar to other acts of genocidal killing, group history with regard to ethnonationalism, mass persecution, and hiding of atrocities become positive predictors of chemical weapons use. Victim and contextual contributions are also described for each phase of the lethal violence sequence. Finally, the chapter presents solutions to the problem of chemical and biological killing, including personal involvement, cultivating an awareness of chemical and biological events, maintaining congressional interest in the CW/BW proliferation issue, and identifying and addressing groups which are actively seeking to acquire chemical and biological precursors.

Annotated Bibliography

1. Federation of American Scientists, Working Group on Biological Weapons Verification (April 1996) *Report of the Subgroup on Investigation of Alleged Use or Release of Biological Toxin Weapons Agents*. Washington, D.C.: (author). The Federation of American Scientists, Working Group on Biological Weapons Verification report focuses on the intricacies of biological and chemical weapons detection in field study. Verification of CW/BW use is often hampered by the lack of physical evidence in soil samples or alleged incident sites. This report describes additional sources of evidence of weapons use such as outbreaks of unusual disease strains following an alleged incident.

2. Leng, R.J. (1994) Interstate crisis escalation and war. In M. Potegal and J.F. Knutson (Eds.), *The Dynamics of Aggression*, pp. 307–332. Hillsdale, NJ: Lawrence Erlbaum Associates. This chapter traces the common elements of state and military decision-making that lead to increases in interstate violence. Leng reviews quantitative and qualitative studies in the field of interstate violence. The importance of this chapter lies in the author's description of styles of military thinking that precede a military crisis.

3. Lifton, R.J. (1976) *The Life of the Self.* New York: Simon & Schuster. In this book, Lifton offers a comprehensive framework for understanding the complex relationship between social and military cultures. Based on studies of the nuclear arms race of the 1940s through the 1960s, Lifton proposes that psychohistorical phenomena in groups such as ethnic dislocation and psychic numbing lead to increases in institutionalized violence. Unless society and government become responsive to these issues, Lifton warns, genocidal violence will continue unabated.

4. Simon, J.D. (1989) *Terrorists and the Potential Use of Biological Weapons*, Rand Corp., Report No. R-3771-AFMIC. This Rand report examines two essential areas of study: trends in terrorist activity and inhibitory factors in the use of biological weapons. The report identifies common political motives behind acts of terrorism, then applies a cost-gain analysis to predict the likelihood of biological weapons use among terrorist groups.

References

Alexander, Y. (1994) *Middle East Terrorism: Current Threats and Future Prospects*. Hong Kong: Dartmouth.

Aragno, A. (1991) Master of his universe. *Journal of Psychohistory, 19*, 97–108.

Arming Iraq: The Export of Biological Materials and the Health of Our Gulf War Veterans (1994a) 104th Congress, 1st Session, February 9.

Arming Iraq: The Export of Biological Materials and the Health of Our Gulf War Veterans (1994b) 103rd Congress, 1st Session, testimony of R. Riegle, February 9.

Barry, J. and Watson, R. (1996) Scent of a war. *Newsweek*, September 30, pp. 38–39.

Bootzin, R.R., Acocella, J.R., and Alloy, L.B. (1993) *Abnormal Psychology: Current Perspectives*. New York: McGraw-Hill.

Bowman, S. (1994) *When the Eagle Screams: America's Vulnerability to Terrorism*. New York: Birch Lane Press.

Brockner, J. and Rubin, J. (1985) *The Social Psychology of Conflict Escalation and Entrapment*. New York: Springer-Verlag.

Canadian Security Intelligence Service (1995) *The Threat of Chemical/Biological Terrorism*, Commentary No. 60. Ottawa, Ontario: (author).

Chemical and Biological Weapons Threat: The Urgent Need for Remedies (1989a) 101st Congress, 1st Session, statement of Claiborne Pell.

Chemical and Biological Weapons Threat: The Urgent Need for Remedies (1989b) 101st Congress, 1st Session, testimony of Judge Webster.

Clarke, B.G. (1993) Conflict termination: a rational model. *Terrorism, 16,* 25–50.

Crenshaw, M. (1992) Current research on terrorism: the academic perspective. *Studies in Conflict and Terrorism, 15*, 1–11.

Department of Defense (1990a) Hussein, Filename: 53240051.91r.

Department of Defense (1990b) IZ chemical and biological warhead threat, Filename: 053pgv.oop.

Department of Defense (1990c) Views on Iraqi Chemical Warfare, Filename: 68320747.90.

Department of Defense (1991a) Reprisals against IZ civilians, Filename: 23403244.91r.

Department of Defense (1991b) Iraqi Chemical Warfare, Filename: 23400353.91r.

Douglass, J., Jr. (1995) Chemical and biological warfare unmasked. *The Wall Street Journal*, Nov. 2, p. 2.

Dunn, M.A. (1991) *Information Paper: Chemical Agent Exposure Operation Desert Storm*. Unpublished paper.

Federation of American Scientists, Working Group on Biological Weapons Verification (1996) *Report of the Subgroup on Investigation of Alleged Use or Release of Biological Toxin Weapons Agents*. Washington, D.C.: (author).

Findlay, T., Ed. (1991) *Chemical Weapons and Missile Proliferation: With Implications for the Asia/Pacific Region*. Boulder, CO: Lynne Reinner.

Global Spread of Chemical and Biological Weapons (1989) 101st Congress, 1st Session, Testimony of H.A. Holmes.

Government Accounting Office (1991) *Chemical Warfare: Soldiers Inadequately Trained to Conduct Chemical Operations*, DHHS Publication No. NSIAD 91-197. Washington, D.C.: U.S. Government Printing Office.

Haber, L.F. (1986) *The Poisonous Cloud: Chemical Warfare in the First World War*. London: Clarendon Press.

Hagopian, M. (1978) *Regimes, Movements, and Ideologies*. New York: Longman.

Haley, R.W., Kurt, T.L., and Hom, J. (1997) Is there a Gulf War syndrome? Searching for syndromes by factor analysis. *Journal of the American Medical Association*, January, pp. 217–222.

Hall, H.V. (1996) Overview of lethal violence. In H.V. Hall (Ed.), *Lethal Violence 2000: A Sourcebook on Fatal Domestic, Acquaintance, and Stranger Aggression*, pp. 1–51. Kamuela, HI: Pacific Institute for the Study of Conflict and Aggression.

Harff, B. and Gurr, T.R. (1989) Victims of the state: genocides, politicides and group repression since 1945. *International Review of Victimology, 1*, 23–41.

The Henry L. Stimson Center (1996) *First Anniversary of Tokyo Subway Poison Gas Attack: Is the U.S. Prepared for a Similar Attack?* [news advisory]. Washington, D.C.: (author).

Holsti, O.R. (1989) Crisis decision making. In P.E. Tetlock, J.L. Husbands, R. Jervis, P.C. Stern, and C. Tilly (Eds.), *Behavior, Society, and Nuclear War*, pp. 92–103. New York: Oxford University Press.

Hopple, G.W. (1993) Indications and warning and intelligence lessons. In B.W. Watson, B. George, P. Tsouras, and B.L. Cyr (Eds.), *Military Lessons of the Gulf War*, pp. 146–156. London: Greenhill Books.

Horowitz, D.L. (1985) *Ethnic Groups in Conflict.* Los Angeles: University of California Press.

Hughes, C. (1988) Iran parades survivors of poison gas before the media in New York hospital. Associated Press, April 6.

Interview with Rick Atkinson (1996) *Frontline*, August 5, New York: WGBH Educational Foundation.

"Iraq said to be setting up germ warfare production" (1989) *Los Angeles Times Service,* Jan. 18, p. A8.

"Iraq warns: if attacked, we'll wreck half of Israel" (1990) *Star Bulletin News Services,* May 2, p. A1.

Is Military Research Hazardous to Veterans' Health? Lessons Spanning Half a Century (1994) 103rd Congress, 2nd Session.

Jamal, G.A., Hansen, S., Apartopoulos, F., and Peden, A. (1995) *Is There Neurological Dysfunction in "Gulf War Syndrome"?* Glasgow, Scotland: University of Glasgow, Institute of Neurological Sciences.

"Japan's frightening encounter with chemical terrorism" (1995) *The CWC Chronicle, 1(8)*, 1–2.

Joyner, C.C. (1990) The Rabta chemical factory fire: rethinking the lawfulness of anticipatory self-defense. *Terrorism, 13,* 79–87.

Kaplan, D.E. and Marshall, A. (1996) *The Cult at the End of the World.* New York: Crown Publishers.

Kellen, K. (1979) *Terrorists — What Are They Like?*, Rand Corp., Report No. N-1300- SL.

Lacey, E.J. (1994) Tackling the biological weapons threat: the next proliferation challenge. *Washington Quarterly, 17*(4), 53–64.

Leng, R.J. (1994) Interstate crisis escalation and war. In M. Potegal and J.F. Knutson (Eds.), *The Dynamics of Aggression*, pp. 307–332. Hillsdale, NJ: Lawrence Erlbaum Associates.

Leng, R.J. and Singer, J.D. (1988) Militarized interstate crises: the BCOW typology and its applications. *International Studies Quarterly, 32,* 155–173.

Lifton, R.J. (1976) *The Life of the Self.* New York: Simon & Schuster.

Lifton, R.J. (1982) *Death in Life: Survivors of Hiroshima.* New York: Random House.

Lifton, R.J. and Falk, R. (1982) *Indefensible Weapons: The Political and Psychological Case Against Nuclearism.* New York: Basic Books.

Lifton, R.J. and Markusen, E. (1990) *The Genocidal Mentality: Nazi Holocaust and Nuclear Threat.* New York: Basic Books.

Margolin, J. (1977) Psychological perspectives in terrorism. In Y. Alexander and S.M. Finger (Eds.), *Terrorism: Interdisciplinary Perspectives*, pp. 271–277. New York: John Jay Press.

Markusen, E. (1992) Comprehending the Cambodian genocide: an application of Robert Jay Lifton's model of genocidal killing. *The Psychohistory Review, 20*, 145–170.

Mayer, J.D. (1993) The emotional madness of the dangerous leader. *Journal of Psychohistory, 20*, 331–348.

McCain, J.S. (1989) Proliferation in the 1990s: implications for U.S. policy and force planning. *Strategic Review, xvii*(3), 9–20.

McNitt, A. (1995) Government coercion: an exploratory analysis. *Social Sciences Journal, 32,* 195–205.

Mengel, R.W. (1979) Terrorism and new technologies of destruction: an overview of the potential risk. In A. Norton and M. Greenberg (Eds.), *Studies in Nuclear Terrorism*, pp. 27–52. Boston: GK Hall and Co.

Meselson, M. and Robinson, J.P. (1995) *Strengthening the Biological Weapons Convention.* Paper presented at the 4th Workshop of the Pugwash Study Group on the Implementation of the Chemical and Biological Weapons Conventions, Geneva, Switzerland.

Mullins, W.C. (1992) An overview and analysis of nuclear, biological and chemical terrorism. *American Journal of Criminal Justice, 16*(2), 95–119.

Paltin, D.M. (1990) *The Effects of Nuclear Holocaust Imagery on Self-Concept.* Unpublished doctoral dissertation, United States International University, San Diego.

Post, J.M. (1990) Current understanding of terrorist motivation and psychology: implications for a differentiated antiterrorist policy. *Terrorism, 13,* 65–71.

Roberts, B. (1987) *Chemical Warfare Policy: Beyond the Binary Production Decision*, IX, no. 3. Washington, D.C.: Center for Strategic and International Studies.

Robinson, J.P. (1991) Chemical weapons proliferation: the problem in perspective. In T. Findlay (Ed.), *Chemical Weapons and Missile Proliferation*, pp. 19–35. Boulder, CO: Lynne Rienner.

Roux, G. (1992) *Ancient Iraq*. New York: Penguin Books.

Rummel, R.J. (1995) Democracy, power, genocide and mass murder. *Journal of Conflict Resolution 39,* 3–26.

Russell, R. and Graham, P.V. (1996) *Early History of Chemical, Smoke, Flame, and Biological Weapons.* Unpublished manuscript.

"Ship loaded with cyanide Iraq bound" (1990) Associated Press, Sept. 30.

Shultz, R.H. and Schmauder, J.M. (1994) Emerging regional conflicts and U.S. interests: challenges and responses in the 1990s. *Studies in Conflict and Terrorism (17),* 1–22.

Simon, J.D. (1989) *Terrorists and the Potential Use of Biological Weapons,* Rand Corp., Report No. R-3771-AFMIC.

Spiers, E.M. (1994) *Chemical and Biological Weapons: A Study of Proliferation.* New York: St. Martin's Press.

Spring, B. (1992) *The Chemical Weapons Treaty: An Illusory Search for a Panacea* , Report No.187. Washington, D.C.: (author).

Stewart, J. and Zimmerman, L.J. (1989) To dehumanize and slaughter: a natural history model of massacres. *Great Plains Sociologist, 2,* 1–15.

Stockholm International Peace Research Institute (1994) *Chemical Weapons Destruction in Russia*. Available online: http://www.sipri.se/projects/group-cw/BICC.

Stohl, M. (1984) International dimensions of state terrorism. In M. Stohl and G.A. Lopez (Eds.), *The State as Terrorist: The Dynamics of Governmental Violence and Repression*, pp. 5–12. Westport CT: Greenwood Press.

Storella, M.C. (1984) *Poisoning Arms Control: The Soviet Union and Chemical/Biological Weapons*. Cambridge, MA: Institute for Foreign Policy Analysis, Inc.

Tilly, C. (1989) Collective violence in European perspective. In T.R. Gurr (Ed.), *Protest, Rebellion, Reform,* 2nd ed., pp. 56–70. Beverly Hills: Sage.

Timmerman, K.R. (1991) *The Death Lobby.* Boston: Houghton Mifflin.

"U.N. says Iraq used chemicals" (1988) *The Honolulu Advertiser*, Aug. 2, pp. A1, A4.

United Nations (1969) *Report of the Secretary-General on Chemical and Bacteriological (Biological) Warfare,* Report No. A/7575. Washington, D.C.: United Nations.

Wade, N. (1980) Death at Sverdlovsk: a critical diagnosis. *Science,* September, p. 1501.

"War ills for real, study says" (1996) *The Honolulu Advertiser,* Oct. 13, p. A8.

Watson, B.W., George, B., Tsouras, P., and Cyr, B.L., Eds. (1993) *Military Lessons of the Gulf War.* London: Greenhill Books.

Worsnop, R.L. (1986) Chemical warfare. *The Honolulu Advertiser,* March 10, p. A2.

About the Author

David M. Paltin, Ph.D., is a clinical psychologist in Tustin, CA, and has been recognized as a Diplomate of the American College of Forensic Examiners. He completed his doctoral dissertation on the impact of weapons of mass destruction in society and has studied psychological factors underlying group violence. Since the end of the Persian Gulf War, Dr. Paltin has focused on the development and use of biological and chemical weapons in Iraq and on the use of nonlethal chemical weapons in the United States. Questions and comments may be addressed to the author at 17300 W. 17th St, #J-451, Tustin, CA, 92780.

CHAPTER 15

THE CENTRAL INTELLIGENCE AGENCY AND LETHAL VIOLENCE

Leighton C. Whitaker

"We have seen the best of our time: machinations, hollowness, treachery, and all ruinous disorders, follow us disquietly to our graves." —Shakespeare

How can a covert agency of the U.S. government foster or damage its own democratic spirit, ideals, and well-being as well as that of other nations? Does the "gentlemanly game" of spying, together with sabotage and manipulation intrinsically infuse its players with treacherous impulses and cause corrosive distrust and destruction throughout the world? Or is such clandestine work necessary to minimize evil in the world? What should a democratic government do?

In attempting to answer these and other questions, this chapter addresses (1) the early development and present formation of the Central Intelligence Agency (CIA); (2) the CIA's 50-year history from 1947 to 1997, with emphasis on its cycles of destructiveness and reform; (3) the inevitable ethics questions about covert work; (4) the machinating mentalities necessary to carry out covert operations; (5) CIA mind-control programs; (6) efficacy questions regarding national and world well-being; and (7) prospects and recommendations.

The central question throughout is whether covert actions, including spying, sabotage, and the manipulation of other nations, have a net effect of enhancing or destroying lives in the U.S. and the world. Even if we might sometimes agree that the means justify the ends, do clandestine methods really achieve the ends of peace and well-being? While a conclusion is made difficult because of secrecy and the ubiquitous nature of the consequences of covert actions, at least partial answers are provided.

Early Development and Present Formation

Understanding the CIA requires knowledge of its origins, particularly how world affairs led to its creation and how it came to be an enduring independent executive bureau of the U.S. government. How has it managed to continue beyond the original reasons for its creation?

Early Development

What we know now as the CIA had noble parentage. In 1940, the Axis powers — Germany, Italy, and Japan — were already ominous potential opponents of the U.S. in what was to be called the "good" war. Clearly, so ran popular sentiment, the evil fascists had to be defeated. President Franklin Roosevelt, seeking to develop an intelligence-gathering capacity that could help the U.S. meet an emergent war preparedness need, sent attorney and former general "Wild Bill" J. Donovan on a fact-finding mission to Europe. Donovan proposed that he be designated as the director of a two-part centralized intelligence unit: the Office of Strategic Services (OSS) and the Office of War Information (OWI). The Japanese attack on Pearl Harbor on December 7, 1941, confirmed that the intelligence operations of the U.S. were behind the times. Their covert nature was readily accepted amid the exigencies of such a desperate all-out war.

The OSS was created in 1942 to obtain information about enemy nations and to sabotage their war potential and morale. Its research and analysis section did valuable work but did not get as much after-the-war publicity as the "cloak and dagger" section operatives who bravely infiltrated enemy territory and acted as liaisons with the underground in Nazi-occupied countries. A former OSS officer told this author of his personal experiences of being parachuted behind enemy lines and helping to capture Nazi officials. Like his comrades, he felt entirely that they were performing good in the the "good" war.

At the end of World War II in 1945, the Axis powers having been thoroughly defeated, both the OSS and the OWI were disbanded. But, in 1946, President Harry Truman established the National Intelligence Authority (NIA) within which the CIA was established in 1947. This was the same Truman who said (Kaplan, 1992, p. 655): "Secrecy and a free, democratic government don't mix." Given the seeming conflict with democracy implicit in granting extraordinary powers for clandestine operations, especially in peacetime, how could the President justify the further development of a highly secret, largely independent, and non-accountable agency with what were normally only wartime powers? Truman, together with Prime Ministers Clement Atlee (Britain) and W.L. Mackenzie King (Canada), provided an answer in their Declaration on Atomic Energy on November 15, 1945. As cited in Kaplan (1992, p. 655), they had to guard against "[m]eans of destruction hitherto unknown, against which there can be no adequate military defense, and in the employment of which no single nation can in fact have a monopoly."

Besides his concern about the general availability of atomic weaponry, Truman was personally acquainted with a man who was correctly envisioned as capable of massive lethal violence not only against other aggressor nations but also against his own people. As Josef Stalin was participating in peace negotiations with the Allies and the defeated Axis nations, his "good guy" status was still hostage to his history. According to Goodman (1997), as many as "... 20 million people throughout the Soviet Union were annihilated in the first 30 years of Stalin's reign, not including the losses in war." Would the recent ally become a mortal enemy? The Cold War instantly replaced the hot war. Now the measures taken to protect the nation's security would be, like the Cold War itself, far more covert than overt. The thinking behind this strategizing has been expressed succinctly: "The CIA was founded to prevent another surprise attack such as occurred at Pearl Harbor" (Kessler, 1992, p. 331).

Thus, the National Security Act of 1947 established the CIA as an independent agency within the Executive Office of the President. Of its five allotted functions authorized by Congress, the fifth, especially, left much room for interpretation (Richelson, 1995, p. 13): "To perform other such functions and duties related to intelligence affecting the national security as the National Security Council may from time to time direct." Though this provision was intended only to authorize espionage, the CIA developed according to a maximalist interpretation authorizing covert action. "Because the legislation that set it up gave it little guidance, the agency had to invent itself along the way. There have been many false starts and many mistakes" (Kessler, 1992, p. xxxv). The ambiguity of the legislation allowing maximalist interpretation resulted in the CIA becoming the primary U.S. government agency for intelligence analysis, clandestine human intelligence collection, and covert action; the latter even included attempts to overthrow other governments and to arrange at least indirectly, as the preferred covert method, for assassinations of their leaders.

One of the few stringent legislative limitations was that the CIA must operate internationally, not collect information on U.S. citizens; the Federal Bureau of Investigation (FBI) has the domestic turf. During the long reign of J. Edgar Hoover, the FBI and CIA were often at loggerheads, but the relationship became more complementary when William H. Webster became FBI Director after Hoover's death in 1972. The CIA and FBI even created a joint secret operation in 1980 to recruit Soviet spies in Washington, D.C. Beginning in 1981, when President Reagan signed Executive Order 12333, the CIA was given more latitude to operate within the U.S. Executive Order 12333 stated that "... the CIA may operate domestically in order to collect 'significant' foreign intelligence, so long as the effort does not involve spying on the domestic activities of Americans" (Kessler, 1992, p. 21). This Order, like its ambiguously stated "fifth function", left much room for interpretation; for example, was opening the mail of thousands of U.S. citizens thought to have Soviet connections justifiable?

From its inception after World War II until the collapse of Soviet communism in 1990, the existence of the CIA was justified primarily by the Cold War. During that period of over 40 years, the Cold War went through five phases (Flanders and Flanders, 1993, p. 119): "confrontation from 1945 to 1955; coexistence and competition from 1955 to 1972; a period of détente from 1972 to 1979; renewed confrontation from 1979 to 1985; and a final period of rapidly easing tension from 1985 to 1990." In 1997, the CIA observed its 50th anniversary and continued to try to sell its role in the post Cold War era.

Present Formation: The CIA in the 1990s

By 1992, the CIA had 22,000 full-time employees with a little over half working at its 258-acre compound in McLean, VA. The compound, and sometimes the entire CIA agency, is often referred to as "Langley", the name of a town that used to be there but is no longer on the map. The CIA as a whole is often referred to as "The Agency".

The language used by the CIA is rife with special terms, some of them cryptonyms (e.g., Project MKULTRA) which are secret designations for various individual persons or CIA projects. Other terms are euphemisms, such as "neutralize", which usually means kill, in this context, an extreme version of its ordinary designation of making inoperable or causing to have no effect. Other terms, such as "finding", also go beyond the readily assumed ordinary meaning. A finding in a scientific article or even in a detective's report typically means simply a discovery, but in CIA language it means a written determination by the President of the United States required before covert action may be undertaken, as in "a presidential finding that authorized the covert operation."

CIA language also includes many title designations of the kind that are common in bureaucracies that thereby operate behind a maze of mysterious jargon that defies easy understanding. As the *American Heritage Dictionary* (1992) puts it, together with an illustrative example, "bureaucratese" is a "style of language characterized by jargon and euphemism that is used especially by bureaucrats. 'Soviet bureaucratese, especially the tongue-twisting acronyms and alien-sounding portmanteau words of the state security apparatus.'"

Of the total of 22,000 regular CIA employees, 5000 constitute the Directorate of Operations, the proudest and most secretive, risk-taking, and troublesome CIA component. According to Kessler (1992, p. 4), "By definition, it is the job of this directorate to break the laws of other countries." By 1992, 53 CIA officers had lost their lives in the service of the Agency. The count of officer deaths in the line of duty has risen to 58 according to the CIA headquarters plaque shown on a television special marking the CIA's 50th anniversary (C-Span Washington Journal, 1997). There is no evident record of how many agents — persons recruited to act under control of an intelligence service — have been killed.

As of 1992, to collect foreign intelligence, the CIA maintained stations in 130 countries with a staff of about 3300. Even friendly nations are spied upon, with the exception of Great Britain, Canada, and Australia, and CIA officers may be placed "under cover" in any U.S. government facility abroad except the Peace Corps. The remainder of the staff are located in 22 CIA offices in Washington, D.C., or in the CIA's domestic stations. In addition to regular employees, including CIA officers, the CIA has about 4000 agents.

The size of the annual intelligence budget has not always been clear. It was estimated in 1980 to be about $6 billion, and it was to be increased to more than $20 billion for 1985 during the Reagan administration (Woodward, 1987, p.193). Recently, Gerth (1997, p. A 12) observed that, "Many members of Congress want to reduce the intelligence community's $30 billion budget, or pry open more of its secrets." Weiner (1997d, p. A16) reports that, "The CIA itself spends about $3 billion a year, while the Director of the CIA (DCI) and the Secretary of Defense allocate most of the remainder to military intelligence services like the National Security Agency, which conducts electronic eavesdropping, and the National Reconnaissance Office, which builds spy satellites."

Table 15.1

The United States Intelligence Community: Central Intelligence Agency (CIA)

- State Department's Bureau of Intelligence and Research
- Energy and Treasury Departments' intelligence components
- National Security Agency
- Federal Bureau of Investigation (FBI) counter-intelligence component
- National Reconnaissance Office
- Defense Intelligence Agency
- Army, Air Force, Navy, and Marine Corps intelligence elements
- Other agencies, e.g., Commerce Dept., that have intelligence components but are not full-fledged members of the intelligence community

More recently, on October 15, 1997, the CIA, under pressure from a Federation of American Scientists' lawsuit, stated that the current overall intelligence fiscal year budget is $26.6 billions, but it is still not known exactly how much is spent by each of the 13 agencies, some of which are listed in Table 15.1, that are covered under the spy budget which itself is buried in the Defense Department budget ("Prying open the spy budget", 1997).

The DCI wears three hats: head of the CIA, coordinator of the other intelligence agencies in the government, and primary advisor to the President, through the National Security Council, on foreign intelligence matters. Thus, the DCI has power over the intelligence community as a whole, including the CIA. The Deputy Director of the CIA (DDCI) is the first officer of the CIA itself. Both the DCI and the

DDCI are appointed by the President of the United States with the advice and consent of the Senate.

Besides the President, the CIA is monitored by two Congressional oversight committees (House and Senate), the President's Foreign Intelligence Board, a citizen panel that investigates CIA shortcomings and reports its findings to the president, and the President's Intelligence Oversight Board that is responsible for reporting any intelligence activities which appear to be illegal or improper. Legislation passed in 1990 has placed the CIA's inspector general on the same level of authority on the agency's organization chart as the DCI. But, as former CIA Director Gates (1991 to 1993) has pointed out (C-Span, 1997a) and as CIA Director William Casey clearly demonstrated, the DCI is not responsible to police agencies but is really responsive to the President's own policies. For further information about the structure of the modern CIA, the reader is referred especially to Kessler (1992).

George Tenet, the new DCI, has said that the CIA would focus on 10 or 15 countries and increase its recent emphasis on combating terrorism, drug trafficking, and arms proliferation (Gerth, 1997). One may seriously question whether the CIA's influence has actually *increased* terrorism, drug trafficking, and arms proliferation, as will be discussed later in this chapter.

Deputy Director of Central Intelligence John McLaughlin stated that during the Cold War, 40 to 50% of the Agency's budget was spent in relation to concerns about the Soviet Union but that, since the end of the Cold War, only 20 to 30% is spent on Russia, and that the CIA had been "downsizing" by not replacing retiring or otherwise departing employees until a recent active hiring campaign (C-Span, 1997b). As of this writing, it does not appear that the CIA is substantially smaller. Former DCI Admiral Stansfield Turner said that the mission of the CIA has actually broadened to include about 180 countries whose actions may impact on the welfare of the U.S. (C-Span, 1997b).

The agency's utility as a spy organization has been criticized recently, including by many top former CIA officials. In the 7 years Fred Hitz has been inspector general of the CIA, his caseload has increased fourfold. He has filed classified reports on the CIA's connections with the Bank of Credit and Commerce International, which has a record of operating as a criminal enterprise, and on the CIA's ties to Guatemalan military members who have committed acts of murder, torture, and kidnaping. On October 2, 1997, Hitz, who since October 1990 has served under five different DCIs, announced that he would leave the Agency to teach at Princeton University, where he was recruited to join the CIA 36 years ago (Weiner, 1997f).

As of the end of August 1997, six top CIA positions were unfilled ("Keeping track…", 1997). Tenet's appointment had left the position of DDCI vacant for 8 months. Four new positions, created by Congress on October 11, 1996, to improve management of the CIA and the 12 other U.S. intelligence branches over which the Director of Central Intelligence presides, had yet to be filled (see Table 15.1).

Cycles of Violation and Reform

Since its inception, the CIA has been a kind of legal criminal, authorized to break the laws of other countries, but not its own. The many men and few women who were personally inclined, recruited, trained, and rewarded for breaking laws have not always observed this slippery distinction. Nor were their violations of U.S. law readily detected. Masters of disguise, deception, and cover-up may apply their skills in any direction. Inherently, therefore, the U.S. government and its citizens have dealt with a paradox of our own creation: how to promote criminal behavior without that behavior *excessively* compromising and damaging the democracy it was designed to defend. Table 15.2 shows alleged institutional aggression by the CIA from 1950 to 1995. This table reflects, and the

Table 15.2

CIA Institutional Aggression Over the Decades

Date	Alleged CIA Behavior	Related Behavior/ Remarks	Sample Reference(s)
1950	Recruited syndicate figures in France to form a “criminal terror squad” to force dockers to load arms in ships bound for Vietnam.	Syndicate allowed to refine heroin in Marseilles for shipment to U.S. with knowledge of CIA.	Pearce (1976), McCoy (1997)
1950–on	Opened and photographed mail of over 1 million civilian Americans without their knowledge or consent.	Associated activity included installation of surveillance devices, breaking into homes and offices.	Parenti (1983), Woodward (1987)
1953	Toppled Mohammed Mossadegh of Iran, a democratically elected leader, and installed Shah of Iran, Reza Pahlavi.	In addition to favorable oil concessions to U.S., Iran bought over $18 billion in weapons over next two decades from U.S.	Prados (1986), Moyers (1988)
1954	Overthrew Jacobo Arbenz of Guatemala, who had received 65% of the vote, thus violating rights of a friendly power.	CIA organized terrorists in Honduras who crossed over on June 18,1954, to overthrow the Guatemalan government.	Herman (1982)
1954–on	Trained officers in Guatemala in terrorism and provided weapons, who then tortured, burned, strangled and slaughtered political opponents for several decades.	Termed “Operation Success” by the CIA; all reform measures instituted by Arbenz were terminated, including the right to unionize.	Moyers (1988)
1957	Helped set up Savak, Iranian secret police, who tortured, mutilated, and killed regime’s opponents.	Savak agents trained at USMC base in Quantico and at the CIA complex in Langley, VA.	Chomsky and Herman (1977)
1960	CIA planned assassination of Congolese nationalist leader Patrice Lumumba.	Before CIA plot was effected, Lumumba was murdered by rival faction.	Woodward (1987)
1960s	Recruited syndicate figures to assassinate Fidel Castro. Eventually, at least eight attempted assassinations, two with CIA supplied lethal pills and hypodermic needle, were carried out over several years.	Planners included John Roselli, Sam Giancana, Santo Trafficante, Jr., Rafael “Chi Chi” Quinlero, Feliso Rodriguez, Frank Sturgis, and E. Howard Hunt.	Hinckle and Turner (1981), Myers, (1997), Prados (1986), Woodward (1987)

1960s	Worked with syndicate figures to develop Golden Triangle for opium growing in return for fighting Pathet Lao.	CIA's airline — Air America — transported opium to labs. Heroin was used by GIs in Vietnam and users in U.S.	Bellis (1981), McCoy (1997), Stanton (1976)
1960s	William Colby, ex-CIA Director, appointed bank official for Nugan Hand bank in Thailand.	Much of money from drug trade was laundered through this bank whose branch was close to Golden Triangle.	Sheehan (1988)
1960s	Worked with ITT who, threatened with being nationalized in Chile, toppled Salvadore Allende.	CIA spent $350,000 to bribe members of Congress in Chile and some $13 million to block election.	Simon and Eitzen (1986)
1961	Bay of Pigs, planned and orchestrated by CIA DDO Richard Bissell, failed.	Cuban Missile Crisis of 1962 intimately connected with Bay of Pigs.	Blight and Lang (1995), Woodward, (1987)
1963	KUBARK counterintelligence interrogation manual published and widely distributed.	Presented coercive methods including sensory deprivation, hypnosis, use of threats of violence, and torture.	Declassified and redacted by CIA January, 1997
1965–70	Organized secret MEO Army whose leaders were extensively involved in heroin production. CIA transported opium to clandestine labs through Air America. From 1965 to 1970, active heroin addicts in U.S. grew from 68,000 to 500,000.	Heroin ultimately used by GIs in Vietnam and individuals in U.S. White House surveys showed more than 3000 U.S. troops in Vietnam were addicted to heroin.	Bellis (1981), McCoy (1997), Marshall et al. (1987), Stanton (1976)
1968–1975	Operation Phoenix created by William Colby, first to assassinate suspected Viet Cong (VC) and VC sympathizers and then to assemble, incarcerate and murder Vietnamese civilians.	For the first time in American history, quotas were set for the number of people to be "neutralized". From 1968 to 1971, over 40,000 civilians were murdered and thousands more were tortured.	Branfman (1978), Chomsky and Herman (1977)
1970s	Stockpiling of poison and venom previously banned by Presidential order.	Disregarded executive orders. Lethal pills previously used in assassination attempts.	Woodward (1987)
1970s	Bush was appointed head of CIA in 1976. Provided weapons and money to Angolan rebels, attempted to overthrow Jamaican government, and kept Manuel Noriega of Panama on payroll, who was deeply involved in drug trafficking. Eventually paid $160,000. Disregard of President Ford's (1976) ban on assassination which was reaffirmed by Carter.	In 1976 CIA created "Operation Condor" to monitor and assassinate dissident refugees in member countries (Argentina, Bolivia, Brazil, Chile, Paraguay, and Uruguay).	Corn (1988), Maas (1986), Morrison (1995)

TABLE 15.2 (CONTINUED)

CIA INSTITUTIONAL AGGRESSION OVER THE DECADES

Date	Alleged CIA Behavior	Related Behavior/ Remarks	Sample Reference(s)
1972	Ex-CIA operatives break into Democratic Party's headquarters in Watergate Hotel. James W. McCord retired from CIA's Office of Security two years earlier. CIA supplied operatives with CIA alias identities, a voice-alteration device, and a red wig.	Role of the CIA was downplayed in the most blatant threat to the democratic process in American history.	Kessler (1993), Parenti (1983), Woodward (1987)
1973	Worked with Chilean military to overthrow Allende, resulting in death of 30,000 civilians and President Allende himself.	Augusto Pinochet came to power. Over 20,000 political prisoners were killed between 1973 and 1976. Many more were tortured.	Faden (1996), Simon and Eitzen (1986)
1973	CIA's Technical Services Division destroys secret files on human radiation experiments.	Reported by former CIA official, Scott Breckenridge. Original order from Richard Helms, CIA Director, in 1972.	Ensign and Alcalay (1995), Faden (1996)
1975	Indirectly responsible for 25 to 30 bombings in Dade County, FL, in 1975 by Cubans trained by CIA to fight Castro. This group was also responsible for assassinations in Lisbon, Mexico, New York, and Washington, D.C.	Known as "Cuban Refugee Terrorist Network" whose collective organizations had up to 6000 members. Commentators argued that U.S. drug problem was largely due to CIA training of the terrorists with known drug distribution networks.	Herman (1982), Kruger (1980), Marshall et al. (1987)
1980s	CIA supports Chad Defense Minister Habrè in order to rid Chad of Quadafi's influence.	Habrè turns out, consistent with his past, to brutally suppress human rights in Chad.	Woodward (1987)
1980s	Opens up Golden Crescent to finance Afghan Mujahedin rebels in fight against USSR. Large-scale activities with arrival of CIA on Afghan-Pakistan border.	By 1986, 40% of heroin into U.S. was coming from Golden Crescent and 19% from the Golden Triangle, a switch from the 1960s and 1970s when CIA focused on Indochina.	Bellis (1981), Lifschultz (1988), Sciolino (1988)

1980s	CIA agent Lt. Col. Moses Klanzamation, deputy chief of Doe's personal guard, attempted to assassinate Liberia's leader, Samuel K. Doe.	Klanzamation, after confessing his CIA ties, was executed a week later.	Woodward (1987)
1980–81	Carter White House was stocked with moles, spies and informers who reported to senior Reagan advisors through CIA.	Reagan-Bush campaign officials, with help of CIA, contacted Iran directly, offering more arms than Carter and thus winning Iran's support. Hostages were freed after Reagan was elected.	Hoffman and Silvers (1980)
1982	CIA agents used electric shock device on suspects.	One suspect dies of torture. CIA agent was fired.	Woodward (1987)
1983	In direct opposition to Boland Amendment enacted in 1982, which forbade public money for purpose of destabilizing Nicaraguan government, CIA obtained military equipment and arranged for destruction of oil facilities and storage tanks at Nicaraguan ports, in addition to mining Nicaraguan harbors. One British ship was hit by mine.	Termed "Operation Elephant Herd", CIA also prepared and distributed to contras an assassination manual in violation of Executive Order 12333, which prohibited assassinations. Ignored 1986 World Court ruling that international law was violated and that the U.S. must cease and refrain from such activities.	Emerson (1988), Gutman (1988), Scheffer (1987), Woodward (1987)
1983	CIA hired pollster to conduct surveys and analyze data in upcoming Grenada election after U.S. invasion.	U.S. backed Herbert Blaize won election and, as one of his first acts, asked Reagan to maintain 250 U.S. troops on island.	Woodward (1987)
1983	CIA published and distributed *Human Rights Exploitation Manual.*	Despite a disclaimer that most coercive techniques are improper, the manual details ways to induce aggression through prolonged heat, cold, and exertion.	Declassified and redacted by CIA in January, 1997
1984	Despite a second, stronger Boland Amendment which forbade the support of or involvement in operations in Nicaragua, contras continue to receive money through trafficking in cocaine. Contras continued to receive arms from CIA support activities.	In 1986, at least 25 arms drops were made inside Nicaragua. Contras continued to conduct a campaign of terror. Cocaine use in U.S. increased 38% between 1982 and 1985, and crack cocaine use increased dramatically between 1985 and 1996, the height of the contra arms-for-drugs trade.	Brody (1985), Chomsky (1985), Gutman (1988), Moyers (1988), Scheffer (1987), U.S. Senate (1989)

Table 15.2 (continued)

CIA Institutional Aggression Over the Decades

Date	Alleged CIA Behavior	Related Behavior/ Remarks	Sample Reference(s)
1984	CIA Director Casey testified in Congress on CIA-distributed manual on "Selective Use of Violence" to "neutralize" Nicaraguan officials such as court judges, police and state security officials.	The "Murder Manual" widely used in training and operations in CIA schools and covert operations which were not redacted in all editions read, "If possible, professional criminals will be hired to carry out selective jobs."	Woodward (1987)
1985	CIA proposed selling weapons to Iran despite opposition from Departments of Defense and State.	Iran, at that time, had numerous terrorist operations against U.S.	Woodward (1987)
1990	CIA learned that all but a few of East German recruits were double agents and were feeding false information.	Consistent with previous discovery that, in 1988, all of CIA's agents were actually working for Castro.	Morrison (1995)
1990s	Bank of Credit and Commerce International (BCCI) kept secret CIA accounts to finance contras in Nicaragua and Mujahedin rebels in Afghanistan.	In return, CIA did not interfere with BCCI's involvement in heroin trade in Pakistan and cocaine trade in Central America.	Beaty and Gwynne (1991), Castro (1988), Schmalz (1988), Burns (1997),
1991	Knew of chemical weapons bunker at Khamisiyah in Iraq in mid-1980s which was targeted for destruction by U.S. forces but failed to warn Iraq in March 1991.	Until 1997, CIA maintained it possessed only cursory reports and had uncovered them in 1995. Hundreds of thousands of troops may have been exposed to Sarin and other agents.	Pine (1997)
1992–95	Emmanuel Constant, a Haitian military junta thug, was placed on CIA payroll. Guatemalan colonel implicated in murder of U.S. citizen was retained on covert payroll.	CIA Director John Deutsch stated, "I believe that the US needs to maintain, and perhaps even expand, covert action as a policy tool."	Morrison (1995)
1995	Possible spying on Japanese negotiators during automobile-export negotiations.	Some evidence of CIA as a tool in commercial espionage.	Morrison (1995)

next sections of this chapter document, the cyclical nature of CIA violations and reforms. The years from 1975 to 1980 and from 1985 to 1990 mark periods of reform after major violations were revealed and oversight attempts, including congressional investigations, were instigated.

Into the 1970s

Having been caught off guard by the Pearl Harbor surprise attack, the U.S. quickly developed intelligence services during World War II, but with the Cold War and threats of Soviet takeovers immediately following World War II, the U.S. still found itself trailing both the British and the Soviets in intelligence. Thus, the newly formed CIA was set clearly on a mission to catch up to and, at least contain, the Soviets. What followed, as reported by Flanders and Flanders (1993, p. 733), was authority for almost 30 years "to conduct covert activities including political, psychological, and economic warfare and paramilitary operations." Under President Dwight D. Eisenhower, a 1954 report of the Doolittle Committee reinforced the CIA's authority with a mandate (as quoted in Flanders and Flanders, 1993, p. 733) to "build a covert action service more ruthless and effective than the intelligence agencies of America's adversaries."

Failed missions, such as the U-2 spy plane incident in 1960 over the Soviet Union and the Bay of Pigs Invasion of Cuba in 1961, tarnished the CIA's image but only in regard to questions of CIA competence and control of covert activities, not questions of ethics or human safety or rights. It was not until the mid-1970s, when Congress spearheaded important reforms, that ethics questions came to the fore. Even then, Congress' concern was mostly about infringing on the lives of U.S. citizens and not about violating the rights of people in other countries, with the exception of assassination plots against foreign leaders. Congressional investigative committees, the Senate's Church Committee, and the House's Pike Committee were not formed to look into allegations of ethical and legal violations until there was public outcry precipitated by the press.

May 1973 press reports linked the CIA to a break-in and illegal search of the office of a psychiatrist who had been treating ex-government official Daniel Ellsworth, a pivotal figure in the Pentagon Papers. Investigation of what became known as the Watergate Affair led to disclosure of a secret document called the "Family Jewels" and assembled within the CIA, which listed 700 possible abuses committed by the CIA since the Agency began in 1947. The list revealed acts of CIA participation outside its charter such as illegally opening the mail of U.S. citizens for 20 years, testing mind-altering drugs on unwitting subjects, surveilling domestic individuals and groups (including U.S. citizens opposed to the Vietnam War), and planning assassination attempts or plots against foreign leaders.

Several control measures were instigated as a result of these revelations. In January 1975, President Gerald Ford's administration appointed the Rockefeller Commission to look into CIA activities. Congress formed oversight committees in both the Senate and the House. In February 1976, President Ford issued Executive Order No. 11905 to prevent future intelligence activity violations. Under President Ford, George Bush became DCI for a brief term from 1976 to 1977 with a mandate to restore confidence both within and outside of the Agency. During the next 4 years, President Jimmy Carter and his DCI Stansfield Turner kept the CIA on a tight rein. Concomitant with this period of reform, the United States and the Soviet Union experienced a period of warming or détente in the Cold War from 1972 to 1979.

The 1980s

Pressure to expand covert activity increased in 1979 with the Soviet intervention in the Afghanistan War.

By the early 1980s, U.S.-Soviet hostilities were intensifying under President Ronald Reagan, who called the Soviet Union an "evil empire" and gave support to the CIA for anti-Communist insurgencies worldwide. Thus, the CIA intensified and extended its activities to virtually the world at large. William J. Casey, who served as DCI from 1981 to 1987 under President Reagan, enlarged on the already aggressive mandate. He saw himself as a significant policy maker who was responsible to the President alone. The Congressional Committees and other oversight groups were bypassed as much as possible, resulting step-by-step in major violations of the CIA charter and the rights and responsibilities of legally constituted policy makers in the U.S. government.

While he was running for President, Ronald Reagan and the Republican platform had charged that President Carter had made it virtually impossible for the CIA to conduct effective espionage, and that DCI Turner was overly responsive to the Carter human rights campaign. Turner himself had once referred to President Carter as a "peacenik" (Woodward, 1987, p. 7). President Reagan and Casey "both had contempt for Jimmy Carter and what they thought was his weakness, his indecisiveness and his unhealthy, hand-wringing anxiety" (Woodward, 1987, p. 17).

Casey fit the image of the covert operative. As Woodward (1987) noted, Casey slurred his words with a speech pattern that sounded "like a shortwave broadcast, fading in and out" (p. 14), "showed a hundred different faces to a hundred different worlds" (p. 17), and "let nothing get in his way. He worked nights, weekends. It was a single-mindedness that had to be admired" (p. 19). "He was said to love mystery, the cloak, and a little of the dagger" (p. 30) and saw intelligence operations as "ruthless and cut-throat" (p. 101). "The tough, cold, even hard Irishman was sure he knew right from wrong" (p. 119).

As a member of the OSS in World War II and as a private citizen, Casey was used to living on the edge. His appointment was questioned when it was revealed that, as a 1% partner in a potential pen development company, his $95 investment had yielded him $60,000 in tax deductions, which the IRS had disallowed. As observed in Woodward (1987, p. 182), "Casey had chalk all over his feet from playing close to the foul line most of his life." His political views, including strong endorsement of the "need for covert action", coincided with those of Reagan who was elected President in 1980. Allen Dulles, the DCI during the Eisenhower years, had noted that "presidents always want a hidden way of doing things. That's how the CIA gets its clout with the White House" (Woodward, 1987, p. 42). Thus, Casey appeared to be Reagan's ideal choice as DCI.

After Reagan was elected president, his campaign claims of imminent Soviet domination were unsupported by DCI Turner, who did not estimate that the U.S. was "dangerously" behind the Soviets in weaponry and preparedness for an all-out war. According to Turner, even after a first strike by the Soviets, the U.S. would have enough strategic nuclear weapons to destroy all Soviet cities with a population of over 100,000 (Woodward, 1987, p. 56). But, the new President insisted on more military spending and new weapons systems. The added expense during the Reagan years helped to quadruple the U.S. national debt. The stage for what became known as the Iran Contra Affair had been the 1980 Republican presidential platform which promised an aggressive CIA and stated (as quoted in Woodward, 1987, p. 209), "We deplore the Marxist-Sandinista takeover of Nicaragua … we will support the efforts of the Nicaraguan people to establish a free and independent government."

Casey persistently dominated those around him despite early setbacks in his era and considerable opposition in Congress and within the CIA. His first choice for DDCI, Max Heugel, failed to receive Congressional approval because of income tax violations; the second, Bobby Inman, quit over disagreements with Casey; and the third, John McMahon, became someone Casey wished to avoid, in order to be as autonomous as possible. Though he had to include McMahon in the "paperwork loop", the latter appears to have had little power. According to Woodward (1987, p. 408), "So Casey was not only running the contra operation out of his office, as well as some of the fund-raising effort, he was running his own public-affairs office. He wasn't even telling McMahon what he was up to." Casey's orientation was reinforced by President Reagan's dedication of a new $190 million, seven-story addition to the Langley headquarters, often referred to as the "Casey Memorial Wing" (Woodward, 1987, p. 408).

Feeling responsible only to President Reagan, Casey knew the President's policies but did not know what Reagan would actually do. The President's "wobbly seesawing ... 'Yes' ... 'well' ... 'no'" (Woodward, 1983, p. 380) left room for Casey to operate as he chose, operationalizing what he sensed were the President's policies and ultimately forming policies of his own making, just as he had eagerly wanted to do when he accepted the position of DCI. While Casey was DCI, the CIA engaged in covert action by carrying out the Iran Contra scheme without first obtaining a presidential finding, an absolute legally required prerequisite for such action. Thus, Casey obviated his obligation to the President, as well as his duty to inform Congress, but Casey appeared proud of this complete circumvention of legally constituted authority (Woodward, 1987, p. 539): "To get the Ayatollah to fund the Contras was a strategic coup, a sting of unimagined proportions: having an enemy fund a friend. The DCI labeled this the ultimate covert operation."

The CIA's only direct action was to arrange the details of arms shipments (Kessler, 1992, p.92), but the CIA expedited matters indirectly, as it so often has. In this case, Lieutenant Colonel Oliver North arranged the actual carrying out of the operation through a self-financed arm of the National Security Council and National Security Advisor John Poindexter.

The Iran-Contra scheme had evolved from President Reagan signing a finding on December 1, 1981, providing the initial lethal assistance to the Contras to oppose Nicaragua's Sandanista government (Woodward, 1987, p. 589). It ended with Congressional hearings, the resignation of Poindexter, the firing of North, and Casey's death on May 6, 1987, the day after Congress began its hearings.

In a previous operation, Casey's secret work with the Saudi intelligence service to arrange the assassination of an arch-terrorist by car bombing missed its target but killed at least 80 people, many of whom were innocent (Woodward, 1987, p. 587). Vastly greater destructive actions could be expedited through international arms deals. The CIA was known to place trust in Saudi arms dealer Adnan Khashoggi, the world's richest man, who courted governments and celebrities while he sold huge quantities of deadly weapons. Each of Khashoggi's three commercial-sized planes, outfitted far more lavishly than Air Force One, was fully staffed at all times with U.S. pilots and was ready to fly anywhere in the world with less than an hour's notice (Kessler, 1986, p. 4). Iran-Contra showed that CIA-expedited lethal actions could be carried out on a far greater scale involving circumventing not only the laws of other nations but those of the U.S. itself.

Khashoggi had developed contacts with several U.S. presidents before Reagan, as well as with the CIA, beginning at least as early as 1953 through Kermit Roosevelt when this grandson of Theodore Roosevelt had been head of the CIA's Middle East operations. Later, it was said of Khashoggi (Kessler, 1986, p.64) that, "No one knew for sure where his CIA connections began or ended, magnifying his importance." His contacts with President Reagan included meeting him in person in February 1985 to negotiate the release of $180 million to the Sudan. Having become very well known both for his arms dealings and as a go-between in other massive money matters, he was a "natural" choice to arrange the complicated weapons for money and hostages scheme that eventually became known as Irangate (Kessler, 1986, p. 309):

"What emerged, according to sources, was the Iran arms deal, with plans to involve the Israelis, set up secret Swiss bank accounts, obtain bonds and letters of credit, trade arms for hostages as a way of establishing good faith, and solicit the approval of the U.S. government. It's likely that nobody else in the world could have pulled it off but Khashoggi. ...By doing a favor for the U.S., Khashoggi could win more friends for Saudi Arabia and enhance his own standing in all the countries."

The man the U.S. depended on knew the plan would be revealed eventually and create a scandal, but he thought Reagan's gullibility was not his concern; of course, the President of the United States could not trade guns for hostages with Iran, the country that called the U.S. the "Great Satan". Khashoggi himself was caught up in the intrigue and suffered massive monetary reversals. He lost his status as the world's richest man but still had enough to support himself and lavishly entertain celebrities.

By the end of the Reagan-Casey era, the old CIA violations, first revealed by the press in the 1970s and elaborated upon in the Family Jewels document, had been superseded by more ubiquitously violating activities affecting entire nations and their relationships with one another. It was as if the reforms so belatedly and laboriously constructed in the 1970s had never existed, and, instead of tallying the numbers of individuals killed as direct consequences of CIA activities, the toll of lethalities could only be estimated, at best, through complicated questioning starting with "What if we hadn't done that?"

Has the vast, complicated web of CIA interventions saved more human lives than it has cost? Or has it facilitated greater destruction of human life through its massive system of intrigues designed to limit the "spread of communism"? While we cannot be sure of what would have happened without CIA interventions or exactly how many people died because of them, we do know that many of these interventions eventuated in tremendous numbers of fatalities. For example, as shown in Table 15.2, just within the period from 1968 to 1975, Operation Phoenix resulted in the murder of over 40,000 Vietnamese civilians (see Appendix B), and CIA work with the Chilean military resulted in the murder of over 20,000 political prisoners.

Revelations and Reservations in the 1990s

In 1990, Congress forced the CIA to establish an internal Historical Review Panel which was to propose declassifications of its secret documents. A historian, George Herring, who served on the panel for 6 years called it "a brilliant public relations snow job" (Weiner, 1997a). The Panel did not meet at all between August 1990 and June 1994. In an editorial, *The New York Times* ("Opening up C.I.A. history", 1997) noted, "All records from the agency's directorate of operations are exempt from Freedom of Information requests. Many of the documents the CIA has made public over the years are meaningless because so much information is blocked out."

Furthermore, the CIA has destroyed many of its most important documents. For example, after promising for more than 5 years to make public the files from its covert mission to overthrow the government of Iran in 1953, the CIA said on May 28, 1997, that it had destroyed or lost almost all of them decades ago (Weiner, 1997e).

Inevitably, the CIA's long history of violations, cover-ups, exemptions from disclosure, and failed pledges to make information public have fueled not only tremendously deep and widespread distrust but also many specific conspiracy theories. For example, Representative Maxine Waters, a Democrat from California, and other black leaders have pushed for an investigation into allegations that the CIA knew of or promoted the selling of cocaine by Nicaraguan Contras in the U.S. in the early 1980s to raise money for their cause (Holmes, 1997).

Some revelations have been forthcoming, however. In September 1996, a summary of an investigation into the U.S. Army's School of the Americas

(SOA) together with four pages of translated excerpts from its seven Spanish-language manuals, were released (Priest, 1996). The Defense Department summary noted that, to recruit and control informants, the manuals advised use of "fear, payment of bounties for enemy dead, beatings, false imprisonment, executions and the use of truth serum" (as quoted in Priest, 1996, p. A1). In January 1997, two SOA training manuals in English were declassified and approved for release — *Counterintelligence Interrogation* (U.S. Army, 1963) and *Human Resource Exploitation* (U.S. Army, 1983; see Appendix A).

Established in 1946 in Panama and based in Fort Benning, GA, since 1984, the SOA has trained central and southern hemisphere nationals in the art of war. Among the 57,000 students it has graduated are many significant human rights violators — for example, over 40 Salvadoran officers responsible for major atrocities in Salvador's civil war. Those atrocities included the slaughtering of Archbishop Romero together with four nuns, six priests, and a housekeeper and her daughter.

In the process of revising the English-language manuals over the years and redacting them in readiness for release, some obviously torturous instructions have been lined through and replaced with qualifying remarks or other instructions that would seem to soften the treatment in what may have been a public relations effort. For example, instruction E-27 originally tells the interrogator: "There should be no built-in toilet facilities. The subject should have to ask to relieve himself. Then he should either be given a bucket or be escorted by a guard to the latrine. The guard stays at his side the entire time he is in the latrine." The revised version reads "If there are no built-in toilet facilities, subject he [sic] should …" Often, instructions which are more blatantly torturous have been entirely lined out, or disclaimers have been penciled in. For example, after elaborating on physically and psychologically coercive techniques that may, admittedly, result in permanent damage to the subject, a hand-printed comment appears, such as "This technique is illegal and may not be used." Thus, the predominant residual emphasis is on more subtle psychological methods. These changes in the manuals may not mean changes in the field in active practice.

Nevertheless, even with these "corrections", the 128-page interrogation manual and the somewhat more brief exploitation manual have provided a set of training guidelines that reads like a systematic reversal of how to do beneficial psychotherapy. Some of the SOA methods — for example, sensory isolation, coercion techniques, and mind-altering drugs — are the same as or similar to those used by psychiatrist D. Ewen Cameron in the CIA MKULTRA Project which it cites and which is discussed later in this chapter. As if to underline the anti-therapeutic nature of all of the recommendations, the interrogators and exploiters are forewarned not to develop or permit any personal caring for their human subjects.

The thoroughly insidious nature of the entire SOA orientation is illustrated by how psychological research results are couched. For example (U.S. Army, 1963, p. 90), "The interrogator can benefit from the subject's anxiety. As the interrogator becomes linked in the subject's mind with the reward of lessened anxiety, human contact, and meaningful activity, and thus with providing relief for growing discomfort, the questioner assumes a benevolent role."

Reverend Roy Bourgeois, a Catholic priest of the Maryknoll order, has vigorously protested against the SOA for many years. In 1983, he and two associates secretly gained admission to its base in Fort Benning and were arrested and sentenced to prison. His continuing campaign has been applauded by Representative Joseph Kennedy, Jr., a Democrat from Massachusetts who has attempted, with others in Congress, to close the SOA, but opposition has appeared to be strong (Macklin, 1997, p. D12): "A Pentagon spokesman says there has been no softening in the Defense Department's support for SOA, adding that military budget cuts and staff downsizing have intensified the need for the school, in order to maintain influence in the region."

Ethics Questions

A government that seeks to preserve itself and its people must devote a considerable share of its energies to its neighboring nations. Ideally, at least, some portion of the energy goes into enterprises expressive of, and intended to foster, good will. Other portions are devoted to diplomacy and to arming itself against at least potentially warlike adversaries. Still another portion may be devoted to the covert enterprises of spying, including on one's "friendly" fellow nations, and sabotaging and manipulating other nations in clandestine fashion, such as through propaganda and false information programs.

The actions of a legally constituted institution, when garbed in secrecy and not only authorized, but mandated, to break the laws of other countries, may have far more insidiously destructive consequences than an overtly destructive illegal institution that is readily subject to outside observation and regulation. Its beginnings may be noble in intent, but when its means and even its goals continue to be shrouded in secrecy, it may perpetrate death under the guise of goodness and by means of its covert authority; it may also result in such corrosive distrust as to alienate its own citizens as well as those of other nations. In the case of a democratic nation, heavy reliance on covert actions may seriously undermine or even destroy the very democracy it is supposed to protect. In essence, the clandestine nature of the CIA, together with its mandate to break laws while striving for plausible deniability, virtually guarantees that it will not be fully accountable and that it will violate even its own charter.

The motto of the CIA, borrowed from the Bible, is "Know the truth and the truth will set you free." But this motto, like many of the euphemisms used by the CIA, is unidirectional; the CIA appears truly interested in uncovering the truth about others while maintaining secrecy for itself.

Often, the CIA has aided and abetted murderous actions by recruiting others to do the actual killing, including assassinations. For example, a CIA guerrilla warfare training manual advised the Nicaraguan Contras on "selective use of violence" to "neutralize carefully selected and planned targets such as court judges, police and state security officials, etc." (as cited in Woodward, 1987, p. 444). The manual also stated, "If possible, professional criminals will be hired to carry out selective jobs." As observed in Woodward (1987, pp. 445–446), "This was embarrassingly reminiscent of the CIA's hiring of John Roselli, a member of the Cosa Nostra, to assassinate Castro in the early sixties." The question of "neutralizing" enemies, as well as the CIA's sacrificing or endangering its own officers, agents, and friendly associates, whether directly or, more often, through the enlistment of others, is at the heart of the ethical and governmental issue of whether or not the CIA should exist.

Rationales and Rationalizations

Lethal violence is most likely to be condoned in overt war. Even then, certain rules of decency are supposed to apply, but one extreme answer to the ethics question regarding lethal and paralethal violence is that "all is fair in love and war". As for war, there are both hot and cold wars, the latter intended ostensibly to prevent the former. And as for love, frequently, the spy or saboteur must get close, sometimes in a very friendly way, in order to "recruit" agents, which means getting people to become traitors to their own countries (Thomas, 1995, p. 182): "The most effective tool of recruitment was not cash or thumbscrews or blackmail or ideology — but simple friendship."

Cultivating friendships for this purpose has certain possibly lethal consequences. Although the CIA officer — the recruiter — may be at some risk, the traitor is at much greater risk. Some governments, apparently excepting the U.S., execute traitors who are discovered. For example, the Soviets executed as many as 20 of its traitors after CIA officer Aldrich

Ames, who became a traitor himself, identified them for the Kometét Gosudárstvennoi Bezopásnosti (KGB). And, periodically, cases involving other government retributions come to light, but the clandestine nature of all of this "double-dealing" makes it difficult to ascertain the full measure of the lethal consequences even for the particular traitors, let alone the more insidious, ubiquitous, and often long-term lethal consequences promulgated by the spying business overall. Still, one may hold to the rationale that all is fair in love and war, at least when national security is at stake.

The case of spy and double agent Aldrich Ames, to be discussed in detail later, illustrates fully the deadly results of cultivating close "friendships" in order to recruit agents who thereby become traitors to their own countries. Closeness can be fostered in the doctor-patient relationship wherein patients' institutionalized trust and susceptibility, based on the ostensibly "helping and healing" nature of the relationship, can lead to the destruction of their brains and any semblance of mental well-being, as will be illustrated later in the case of psychiatrist D. Ewen Cameron and CIA Project MKULTRA (Weinstein, 1990). Or, the CIA may be capable of destroying its own, as will be illustrated in the case of a U.S. Army major (Morehouse, 1996). Finally, in addition to damage and death directly attributable to violence against them, CIA leaders, as well as operational officers, may become severely disturbed by their lives in the agency, as will be illustrated in the case of Frank Wisner (Thomas, 1995).

How does the CIA actually rationalize its extraordinarily off-limits behavior? That depends, in large part, on the abilities of its individual members to provide and accept rationales in keeping with the "moral" standards of "gentlemanly" conduct. The early CIA leadership was drawn predominantly from Ivy League universities — Harvard, Yale, and Princeton. During the 1950s, the CIA recruiter at Princeton University was William Lippincott, the dean of students. Another recruiter was Yale crew coach Skip Walz. Frank Wisner, who earned both his undergraduate and law degrees at the University of Virginia when it was likened to the private Ivy League schools, became a high-ranking CIA officer in its formative years. Observers noted (Thomas, 1995, p. 37):

"With his moralistic background, Wisner may have been bothered at some level by the dirty work of spying, but he never showed it. The ability to swallow one's qualms, to do the harder thing for the greater good, was regarded as a sign of moral strength by men like Wisner. At meetings with his staff, he seemed moved less by squishy scruples than by practical necessity. 'We talked about assassinations,' said Jim McCarger, one of Wisner's top aides. 'Wisner's attitude was that the KGB was better at it.'"

Wisner retired in 1962, but swallowing qualms appeared to have played a major role, cumulatively, in his becoming haunted and experiencing cycles of increasing depression (Thomas, 1995, p. 319): "Old ghosts flitted through Wisner's addled mind." In October 1965, he shot himself. "Wisner's death saddened but did not shock his colleagues" (Thomas, 1995, p. 320).

Aldrich Ames (as quoted in Earley, 1997, p. 39) claimed that at "the Farm", a CIA training site, "You were told that you were now part of an elite service, that you were selected because you were one of the best and brightest, and that your job was paramount to the very survival of the United States. Because of these things, you were entitled to lie, cheat, deceive. You did not have to obey laws in any foreign countries."

Whereas Ames took matters a step further by becoming a "mole" in the service of the Soviet Union, CIA officer David Whipple maintained his clandestine but "loyal" adherence to his training. Whipple stated (as quoted in Kessler, 1992, p. 9), "We don't think of it as living a lie. We think of it as a necessary thing. ...You have to protect your identity in order to remain effective. ...It's as if you were a slightly different person."

Duane Claridge, recruited by the CIA in 1954, is the highest ranking American spy directly and personally involved in espionage, war, counter-terrorism, and intrigue to make his life public. For 33 years, he epitomized the CIA's clandestine activities. In his book, *A Spy for All Seasons: My Life in the CIA* (1997, p. 408), he objected to the "serious limitations imposed by the U.S. legal system on the efficacy of a Clandestine Services effort" and the "handwringers" who claim that by collecting information on terrorists and the proliferators of weapons of mass destruction, narcotics, and international crime, the CIA becomes "one of the bad guys." Claridge (p. 409) stated:

"This is absurd. But you do have to deal with undesirables to penetrate the organizations or states involved to obtain information. Mother Teresa, for all her wisdom, unfortunately, doesn't have it. What is disturbing is the hypocrisy on this issue of some in Congress, the executive branch, the media, academia, and, most disgraceful of all, the current CIA leadership. The CIA is lambasted by these worthies for dealing with 'scumbags' to acquire secret intelligence to protect American lives and property, whereas no such condemnation is leveled at the FBI, the DEA, and local law enforcement agencies, which deal routinely with criminals (called paid informants rather than agents) to capture and convict other criminals."

The real issue here is not merely whether the CIA has to "deal with undesirables" but whether killing and other harmful acts are committed with impunity. Actually, dealing with undesirables has often resulted in such acts.

William Casey, DIC, during the increased covert activities era of the Reagan administration, in which Claridge was particularly active, invoked, for the sake of endorsement, the words of General, and later first President of the United States, George Washington (as quoted in Woodward, 1987, pp. 210, 211): "For upon secrecy, success depends in most enterprises of the kind, and for the want of it, they are generally defeated, however well planned and promising." Casey went on with a further rationale: "It is much easier and much less expensive to support an insurgency than it is for us and our friends to resist one. It takes relatively few people and little support to disrupt the internal peace and economic stability of a small country." Thus, ease and economic expediency were offered as suitable rationales. President Reagan's DIC, Casey, also proclaimed his right to be free of substantial oversight by elected officials other than the President. Casey stated: "The business of Congress is to stay out of my business" (as quoted on A and E 20th Century, 1997).

As reported on C-Span (1997c), former CIA Director Gates put the matter bluntly — working for the CIA requires "scams and tricks" and having "strange and unsavory bedfellows," but unsavory behavior by oneself as well as one's close associates raises qualms, whether openly admitted or not.

Qualms and Quibbles

Claims and rationales for the "necessity" of covert actions have been countered by qualms even within the CIA, including among its highest officials. As noted in Woodward (1987, p. 187), Admiral Bobby Ray Inman, who served directly under DCI Casey as DDCI, found it troubling that "covert operations seemed to get started when the White House and the State Department were frustrated with diplomacy … the painstaking steps of negotiation and endless meetings, proposals, and counterproposals. …The secret covert action provided a shortcut, …the comfort of action, the feeling that there was a secret way to get things done." CIA officers in training sometimes quit as they experienced misgivings about the nature of covert operations.

Furthermore, highly placed CIA officers have looked down on the low-life spies beneath them. Ames documented this prejudice by citing former DIC Dulles' attitudes toward the spy (in this case, Benedict Arnold) vs. the spy's superior (British Major John Andre). Ames (as quoted in Earley, 1997, p. 204) said: "Having been both a case officer and a spy, I can tell you clearly ... [t]he agency leadership, as opposed to the rank and file, has consistently denigrated and despised the spy. One of Allen Dulles's favorite lines was Sir Francis Walsingham's line about how he had gone out and hired a low fellow to spy. Meanwhile, Andre is described as the model of professionalism."

Another qualm-raising argument is that the CIA's recruitment of spies to become agents in the service of the U.S. relies on persuading foreigners to become traitors to their own countries. Does persuading someone to become a traitor cultivate a traitorous spirit in oneself, albeit a denied or compartmentalized part?

Yet another criticism of CIA ethics is that the Agency has contracted with people known to be criminals, by the standards of U.S. law, to carry out covert actions on behalf of the U.S. Is there something contradictory about hiring criminals to do the "dirty work" for "a good cause"? Perhaps, once started down the road of covert action, there is no telling where, how, or when, if ever, the repercussions will stop.

In the pursuit of "plausible deniability", the CIA may further cover up the covert actions, but the covers on top of covers may result in far greater distrust and hostility years later. A CIA cover-up of covert aircraft testing in the western U.S. in the 1950s and 1960s led people to believe that their sightings of unidentified objects in the skies were alien spaceships (Wise, 1997). Recent revelations of that cover-up have fed the already widespread suspicion that our federal government is not honest with its citizens. Former DCI Stansfield Turner has said that the CIA is too secretive for its own good; when cover-ups are brought to light, they provoke more investigative interest (C-Span, 1997c).

The media are often asked, in the name of national security, not to reveal CIA activity but to put themselves in a quandary. It is difficult, for example, for respectable newspaper publishers to know where to draw the line. *The Washington Post* considered and reconsidered whether to publish a story about a covert operation involving U.S. submarines picking up messages in Soviet underwater cables. According to Woodward (1987, p. 534), *Post* board chairwoman Katherine Graham reasoned: "If intelligence agencies were trying to overthrow governments, we probably should publish, but how could the United States gather too much intelligence? Listen too much? The Soviets did it to us. Even if we were ahead in the various technologies, should we wait for the Soviets to catch up?"

Machinating Mentalities

"Feelings were the natural enemy of the CIA operative."
(Woodward, 1987, p. 48)

The War Against Feelings

Many people drawn to covert work in its most aggressive and clandestine forms are characterized by machismo, defined by *The American Heritage Dictionary,* (1992) as: "a strong, sometimes exaggerated sense of masculinity stressing attributes such as courage, virility, domination of women, and aggressive manliness." The adjectival form is illustrated by a quote from Arthur M. Schlesinger: "He was a mindless activist, a war lover who found macho relish in danger and felt driven to prove manhood by confrontation."

The macho orientation and morbid behavior are closely associated in terms of "protest masculinity" which presents as bravado and aggressive impulsivity and serves as a cover-up for a lack of deep masculinity (Whitaker, 1987, 1996a). The macho orientation short-circuits careful reflection and demands actions to prove one's manhood. Men who lack a strong, secure sense of masculinity readily become compulsive courters of danger. They are compelled to provide or be provided with "tests of masculinity" but remain insecure about their masculinity even if they "win".

Macho men must try to dominate women in contrast to cultivating equal partnerships with them, and they must deny and forcibly reject all signs of "femininity" in themselves. Thus, women are, at least ostensibly, typically regarded as inferior, and macho men are usually homophobic. The CIA has been extremely male dominated in terms of numbers and authority, and its largely macho orientation shows in its language as well as its actions. Woodward (1987) documented examples. President Reagan repeatedly denigrated Libyan political leader Qaddafi as fay and once remarked (as quoted in Woodward, p. 509): "Qaddafi can look in Nancy's closet any time." Lieutenant Colonel Oliver North, who conducted much of the Iran-Contra affair, remarked that "it was time to kill the cocksucker terrorists" (p. 412). Observing that DDCI John McMahon apparently had an inhibiting effect on his boss, DCI William Casey, the State Department's Tony Motley "wondered whether McMahon maybe had something on Casey." Motley had once said jokingly, "McMahon had somehow caught Casey sucking cock!" (p. 375).

While macho personalities seem drawn to morbid forms of risk taking, even death-defying or death-courting exploits, the fear of involvement in such activity cannot be admitted, sometimes even to oneself. Thus, macho men are also drawn to drugs that help them anaesthetize and deny fear. In the case of CIA operatives, who are not supposed to use illicit drugs but are trained to perform in extremely dangerous situations, alcohol has been the drug of choice. Heavy drinking is said to be so characteristic in the CIA Operations Directorate that nothing short of extremely gross interference with observed work functions is cause for special intervention. For example, Ames habitually imbibed heavily even on duty but was never taken aside for reasons of his problem drinking.

Even problem use of drugs other than alcohol may be observed but discounted. Operatives who became traitors to the U.S. have become so after internal security lights should have been flashing (Kessler, 1992, p. 324): "The CIA knew Edward Lee Howard had a drug problem but prepared to send him anyway to Moscow, where he began working for the Soviets. The agency knew that William P. Kampiles also had a drug problem but allowed him access to the top-secret manual for the KH-11 spy satellite, which he promptly sold to the Soviets."

Disregard for internal security generally has been a major problem within the CIA. Polygraph (lie detector) tests have been omitted or downplayed in major traitor cases including that of CIA officers Ames and David Barnett, as well as Karl Koecher, a Czech Intelligence Service officer who became a CIA employee. Thus, the CIA's expertise in conducting and detecting covert operations is, seemingly paradoxically, not applied within its own organization; professional level self-monitoring is lacking. However, the laxness of its self-monitoring is not paradoxical when viewed in the light of the personalities and ethos involved. The right to break rules, as long as there is "plausible deniability", often seems to permeate the mentality of the CIA. Kessler (1992, p. 331) stated:

"Instead of improving security, the CIA's response over the years to embarrassing spy cases has been to try to cover them up by opposing prosecutions that would make its mistakes public. Thus the CIA's blasé attitude about security is a form of self-protection, a way of insulating CIA officers from accountability. The attitude is fueled by directors of Central Intelligence who consider the subject of security to be both dreary and beneath them."

The macho orientation of spies has a particular characteristic twist. Their clandestine operations are by definition not directly confrontational. Instead, plotting, deception, stealth, and craftiness are needed to accomplish missions. The thrill is in the secrecy as well as the action of derring-do. As Thomas (1995) noted in his book *The Very Best Men,* the CIA preferred to hire college men who gave the appearance of gentlemen; they were certainly not impulsive criminals or the kinds of men who go to bars looking for a fight. They were often good fraternity men or members of gentlemen's secret societies who played by the rules, albeit sometimes rules of their institution's own making. Many were sports teams members who were, accordingly, well disciplined at following the rules of the game. In the CIA, often the rules have been of the Agency's own making, and breaking rules is not only acceptable but needed for effective covert action. To protect themselves and the Agency, officers should strive for what has been termed "feasible deniability". Ideally, of course, officers as well as any agents they have recruited should not be caught, but if they are the Agency may have to deny any connection in an effort to maintain its own deniability in the face of accusations. Thus, the spy may have to be a loner.

Because war and the "blood sport" of hunting require killing and deception, they may very readily lend themselves to other forms of deadly covert action. Other sports, as well as most competitive games, may be regarded as sublimated warfare (Whitaker, 1997) and may involve deception as well as, at least modulated, aggression. After all, chess was invented as a substitute for war. All sports involve tactics that are designed to be deceptive and evasive: end runs in football, curve balls in baseball, fakes in basketball, and so on. These tactics are licit parts of the game, i.e., within the rules. Sportsmen and gentlemen play by the rules, and both sides in a game of sport are required to abide by the same rules.

The CIA also abides by rules, although they are more often secret and allow for lethal consequences. Traditional archenemy, the Russian KGB, and its U.S. counterpart, the CIA, have tacitly observed certain rules to avoid lethal consequences, such as not executing each others' spies, though many double agents (i.e., traitors to their own countries) have been executed by their own governments. Thus far, the U.S. has preferred incarcerating rather than executing its own officers caught spying against the U.S.

So, in the overwhelmingly male world of the CIA, a man can transfer experiences in sports to being a CIA officer and feel somewhat at home, except for two major differences — visibility and independent oversight. In organized sports, spectators are welcome to watch, comment on, debate, and discuss all of the action; umpires or referees and lines people scrutinize every aspect of the game to ensure fair play. In contrast, CIA officers often are not only allowed but required to engage in foul play and to keep secret almost everything they do. Theoretically, the CIA is subject to independent oversight, but it is difficult to ensure.

How do generally intelligent, well-educated, and typically "well-raised gentlemen" come to like this work and to tolerate the inherent emotional conflicts? Part of the answer is drug use, with an emphasis on alcohol.

Covert action with the intent to do harm, including to those one befriends, requires denial and distancing of feelings in the face of very emotionally provocative experiences. Typically, emotions in such situations become too strong to be managed simply by an acute denial reaction, even when blunted by drugs. What is needed is a personality already thoroughly inculcated in the denial of emotion. The covert operative must be already capable of a certain coldness and distance learned in his early years. Fear of emotions and stalwart denial of feelings can be learned early enough to be reliable in later "dangerously emotional" situations so that the operative does not give himself away by being genuinely emotionally expressive. Drugs, including alcohol, can help to suppress any residual proclivity to become emotionally feeling.

Other parts of the answer include automatic, unreflective obedience to authority, and perceiving the enemy as less than human. These characteristics are essentially two sides of the same coin. If an individual is extremely concerned with obeying and satisfying an authoritarian leader, then other people count for very little. Thus, an unreflective, obedient follower can far more easily kill another human being than can a reflective, independent person, because the latter empathizes with and "feels for" the potential victim.

Heroes

The CIA's heroes, as well as its traitors, appear as a group to have been successful generally at warring against their feelings and avoiding genuine emotional intimacy, though sometimes at great cost in terms of personal relationships and their own emotional well-being. In *A Spy for all Seasons,* Claridge (1997, p. 27) disclosed his own subtle but profound early training in denying emotion. "Although not stated, it was made clear that emotional gestures and speech were signs of weakness and to be avoided." This training probably contributed to his social reticence (Claridge, 1997, p. 25): "There was no question that I could do the schoolwork, but I didn't do nearly as well with the social work of growing up. I was a rather shy and withdrawn child — I played with other kids, but never formed the great boyhood friendships that other children did." In his adult years, like so many of his colleagues in the CIA, he became a heavy drinker. Evan Thomas' book, *The Very Best Men* (1995), provided biographic accounts of four CIA operatives who performed feats of derring-do in the relatively free-wheeling era of the 1950s and early 1960s. According to Thomas (1995, p. 12), besides damaging others' lives, "for Wisner, Bissell, Barnes, and Fitzgerald, the personal cost was high as well. The careers of two were ruined; one killed himself; only one lived past the age of sixty-two. They could not see that the mortal enemy was within, that they were being slowly consumed by the moral ambiguities of a life in secrets." Nor were these four men unusual in their eventual disenchantment. Most of some 66 former CIA officials interviewed by Thomas readily acknowledged that there were more CIA failures than successes.

Initially, idealism characterized these and many other leading CIA officers. They were consumed by the moral ambiguities because they were virtuous, highly educated gentlemen reared by their parents and their universities to be idealistic (Thomas, 1995, p. 11): "Patriotic, decent, well-meaning and brave, they were also uniquely unsuited to the grubby, necessarily devious world of intelligence." Confident of the rightness of their actions at the outset but naive about consequences, they headed boldly into tragedies of their own and others' making. Yet, perhaps they had at least some prescience of the fate of adventurous violation. Thomas quoted the old "Whiffenpoof" drinking song sung by Yalemen with their arms linked:

"We're poor little lambs who've lost our way...
Little black sheep who have gone astray...
Gentlemen songsters off on a spree
Damned from here to Eternity."

Romantic, even comradely, idealism was seldom linked to the ability to tolerate deep feelings, unless in the form of an intense yet emotionally distant rather than emotionally vulnerable manner (Thomas, 1995, p. 17): "Frank Gardiner Wisner had grown up in a world that was, like the one the CIA would help create, secretive, insular, elitist, and secure in the rectitude of its purpose. ...In later years, Wisner was regarded, even by intimates, as a remote figure; capable of charm and warmth, yet somehow not quite all there." He showed what was regarded as moral strength: to swallow his qualms and to "do the harder thing for the greater good." He impressed others as a very strong man in command. A manic-depressive, his high energy wore out his men, and by his late 40s he was more floridly manic. For 6 months in 1958 to 1959, he was psychiatrically hospitalized at Sheppard-Pratt where he was given electroconvulsive shock treatments (Thomas, 1995, p. 162). It was his end as head of clandestine services. What others had observed as "a certain fatalism in his character" (Thomas, 1995, p. 70) was consistent with his committing suicide in later life.

Desmond Fitzgerald, the second of the men biographied by Thomas, exemplified, if anything, an even more extreme version than Wisner of the macho, emotionally distant, highly educated, and seemingly fearless gentleman so idealized in that era. He was described by those who knew him as cold and "not one to reveal his feelings" (Thomas, 1995, p. 49). As a well-connected, 31-year-old lawyer, he enlisted in the Army as a private instead of taking a safe rear echelon job and became a combat officer. At 34, he joined the CIA. Wisner placed him in charge of the Office of Policy Coordination's Far East Division and he ran secret armies in Tibet and Laos. Later, he was made director of all clandestine operations for the CIA to which he brought esprit and high standards (Thomas, 1995, p. 127): "[Fitzgerald] wanted his spies to be at once intellectual and macho. His idea of perfection, said one of his case officers, was a Harvard Ph.D. who could handle himself in a bar fight." Although his romantic notion of what could be achieved by an individual was upset by the development of weapons of mass destruction, he persisted with covert projects that would subvert rather than directly confront. Like Wisner before him, Fitzgerald became worn out. In 1967, at age 56, while playing tennis in 97° July weather he collapsed with a fatal heart attack (Thomas, 1995, p. 333).

Tracy Barnes, the third man about whom Thomas wrote, may have been even more extremely macho than Wisner or Fitzgerald. Barnes' relish of risk from an early age may have been related to being "on his own" as a child whose mother favored his older brother. His maternal grandfather had committed suicide. After attending Groton, Barnes matriculated at Yale where he was known to court death by speeding in his car. Looking back on his life, his widow (as cited in Thomas, 1995, p. 75) said, "Tracy invited danger. He couldn't wait for it." She remembered that on the Monday morning after Pearl Harbor, "he enlisted without waiting for breakfast." Others observed that, during his World War II service, he went out of his way to tempt fate. John Bross, the senior prefect in Barnes' class at Groton who got him a position training commandos to drop behind German lines, thereby preventing his almost certain death as a would-be waist gunner in the air force, said (Thomas, 1996, p. 76): "I rather got the impression that he wanted specifically to look death in the eye." Consistent with his clearly macho orientation (Thomas, 1995, pp. 174, 175): "Personal feelings were not to be spoken of at Barnes' dining room table," and, according to his children: "On the tennis court, he could come close to tantrums. He created an atmosphere that was so intense it became unpleasant." Like Richard Bissell, who became his boss in clandestine operations, he was an extremely impatient "doer", rather than a reflective individual.

As a CIA officer, Barnes was surrounded by fanatical devotion to deviousness, for example, in the form of E. Howard Hunt, who became known in later years as one of the Watergate burglars. The 1950s atmosphere even promoted the wildest, most unregulated actions. Accordingly (Thomas, 1995, p. 85): "Barnes was willing to try just about anything. There was little to hold the CIA back. Congress provided almost no operational oversight, while handing out what amounted to a blank check of unrestricted funds. The press was docile, caught up in the thinking that to quibble would be unpatriotic."

Richard Bissell was another Groton and Yale alumnus like Tracy Barnes, and he liked Wisner and Fitzgerald whom he had gotten to know at Georgetown dinner parties. The Georgetown crowd was known for betting, playing games, striving to appear carefree instead of workaholic, and drinking heavily. A member remarked (Thomas, 1995, p. 103): "I never went to a Sunday Night Supper when someone didn't get embarrassingly drunk. ...Just to unwind. It wasn't maudlin. No one threw up. We just drank a hell of a lot. A martini was like a glass of water is now."

As a boy, Bissell, in his own words (cited in Thomas, 1995, p. 89), was "shy and timid, a perfect foil for teasing" who relied on his mother as "my refuge from the cruel world." He was known as the smartest man in Washington, D.C., largely for his work on the Marshall Plan and the U-2 spy plane, when he was appointed head of CIA clandestine services to replace the mentally disabled Wisner.

Bissell took special interest in a top-secret project code-named MKULTRA, dedicated to experiments to turn human beings into robots, which is discussed later in this chapter and, beginning in 1960, to assassinate Cuban leader Fidel Castro. Failed plots involving the Cosa Nostra to kill Castro by poisoning his cigars or his drinks, and later the Bay of Pigs invasion of Cuba, became well-publicized fiascoes which, together with the U-2 spy plane discovery, helped bring down Bissell.

The DCI for most of this free-wheeling period, was Allen Dulles, who served from 1953 to 1961 under Presidents Eisenhower and Kennedy (Thomas, 1995, p. 73): "Dulles does not seem to have been in the least troubled by the ambiguities of intelligence work. He was a man capable of an amiable encounter with the enemy and the Devil; he learned to deal comfortably in perfectly bad faith, without ever violating a personal sense of moral rectitude and decency, wrote his biographer Peter Grose." According to Louis Auchincloss who had worked in the same law firm as Dulles, "Allen was shrewd — but cold as ice."

Traitors

The Aldrich "Rick" Ames case is a thoroughly documented example of the most insidious development of the spying mentality. While "straightforward" spying is itself fraught with dangers to everyone involved, these dangers are multiplied when the "patriotic" spy begins to spy for the enemy. Yet, such a personal transformation is just a further logical step in a sequence already characterized by treacherous behavior.

Ames' father, who had worked for the CIA, told him (as cited in Earley, 1997, p. 31), "You and I know that lying is wrong, son. ...But if it serves a greater good, it is okay to lie. It is okay to mislead people if you are doing it in the service of your country, but it is never okay to lie or mislead people for your own personal benefit." Decades later, the younger Ames would explain that he had sold information to the Soviets for the sake of his wife (whose extravagant tastes he seemed to share). As a CIA officer trained to "recruit" foreigners to betray their own countries, it was both natural and traitorous for him to betray his own country.

Ames' childhood and adolescence had much in common with others in his vocation. As cited in Earley (1997, pp. 26, 28), he recalled a combination of idealism, high standards, and discomfort with feelings: "We did not speak much about feelings. ...The idea was that individual integrity and worth was of paramount importance. ...Stoicism was the virtue." Perhaps he was attempting to fill the emotional void by stuffing himself with food paid for with money stolen from his father, in "solitary greed", before regular family dinners. His later alcoholism may have had the same function of denying and displacing emotional needs. His role model became "The "Saint", a fictional James Bond of the day who rescued damsels, smoked cigarettes, drank highballs, and solved mysteries.

After his father revealed that he worked for the CIA, Ames obtained a summer job with the CIA making counterfeit money. By then, his father's career was floundering, and, just as Ames and two of his three siblings would do later, he became alcoholic. Ames had become, according to those who knew him, a "sincere" liar who "got his kicks from fooling people" (Earley, 1997, p. 33). After flunking out of college in his second year and experiencing blackouts from binge drinking, he continued his interest in acting but began drinking heavily on a regular basis, his living habits deteriorated, and he returned home where his father got him a regular job with the CIA.

At the CIA's training site called "the Farm", Ames' proclivities were furthered by being trained to focus on identifying a person's vulnerability or weakness and to "befriend" the person in order to recruit him or her, the same approach used by deadly cults. His heavy drinking, often with his instructors, fit with the Directorate of Operation's macho image. Ames, as cited in Earley (1997, p. 112), said, "You have to realize that hard drinking had been an accepted part of the CIA culture for many years. James Angleton was famous for getting loaded every day at long lunches. There was still an element of macho pride in being an officer who could go drink-for-drink with other men."

Meanwhile, his heroic idealism continued side-by-side with his machinating mentality. On his honeymoon with his first wife, he saved two boys from drowning, but, according to Ames (as cited in Earley, 1997, p. 43), that idealism did not diminish "...what is at the core of the intelligence officer's world — betraying another person's trust in you." Given the nature of his formative years, his reliance on the anesthetic effects of alcohol to still emotional needs and qualms alike, the "ethical vacuum" of CIA covert operations and the mandate to encourage betrayal, it is not surprising that as Earley (1997) noted through Shakespeare (from *The Merchant of Venice*): "The villainy you teach me I will execute, and it shall go hard but I will better the instruction."

Although not very good himself at recruiting Soviet officials who could be induced to betray their countries, Ames' attainment of a senior position in the CIA Directorate of Operations gave him access in 1983 to files that showed the Agency's penetration of every aspect of the Soviet system. There, he learned of the specific operations and the names of the Soviets recruited to spy within the Soviet intelligence establishment. These "moles" or "double agents" were traitors to their own country and were dependent on the CIA to help protect them from exposure. Now Ames was in a position to "blow the cover" off these traitors. By becoming a mole or traitor himself, Ames could be of great value to the Soviets and be paid handsomely for his betrayal of the Soviet moles and the U.S. If discovered, the Soviet moles would, in all likelihood, be executed while, as a traitor to the U.S., Ames would, at most, be imprisoned for life.

Ames' decision to betray his country and, in effect, give the death sentence to the Soviet moles, appeared to have been based on disillusionment and greed, as well as facilitated by his own machinating mentality. Ironically, his own idealism helped foster the disillusionment. He had become revolted by evidence of CIA abuses as well as the ignoring of accurate information gathered by the CIA in favor of political expediencies that helped to gain and protect presidential offices.

He was especially impressed by the damage done by James Jesus Angleton, the CIA's former chief of counterintelligence. Angleton was a legendary mole hunter who, in the early 1960s, was an increasingly alcoholic and conspiratorial man who would puzzle over counterintelligence cases while having 4-hour lunches at an elite restaurant and downing serial martinis (Thomas, 1995, p. 307). His destructive use of authority included a "hostile interrogation" of double agent Yuri Nosenko, who was still working for the KGB and turned out to be a genuine defector in the service of the CIA and the U.S. The "interrogation" lasted 4 years and 8 months. It included sensory and social isolation, near starvation, disorientation, sleep deprivation, massive shots of Thorazine and other psychotropic drugs, phony lie-detector tests, and telling Nosenko that he was going crazy and that everyone who had known him had abandoned him. Ames was struck by the actual insanity as well as immorality demonstrated by Angleton and his men.

Furthermore, it was apparent that the CIA could not control one of their own who was engaged fanatically in destructive and demoralizing "witch-hunts". By the mid-1960s, Angleton, still the chief of counterintelligence, was hopelessly preoccupied with what he believed was a "monster plot" by the Soviets to plant a mole in the CIA, and he made it difficult for the CIA's Soviet Division to recruit agents. Even the high-ranking Desmond Fitzgerald, noted earlier in this chapter, could not get Angleton to attend important late-afternoon meetings when the chief of counterintelligence may have still been out drinking his lunch. Fitzgerald, himself preoccupied with CIA plans to kill Castro, was aware that Angleton's paranoia was corrosive to the Agency, but was doubtful that DCI Helms would support any effort to curb Angleton in the Spring of 1967. As already noted, the exhausted Fitzgerald died of a heart attack in July of that year. Ironically, having caused much of Fitzgerald's anguish and deadly fatigue, Angleton (as cited in Thomas, 1995, p. 333) wrote the man's widow, "I have just received the breaking of hearts message. To me Des was a man of rare spiritual harmonies."

Disillusioned, heavily in debt, and having learned that the CIA was an organization that could fail to monitor or control even extreme behavior destructive to itself, on April 16, 1985, Ames walked into the Soviet embassy and began a liaison with the KGB that was not discovered until 1995. Meanwhile, he was known to be alcoholic, had compromising lie-detector test results, and had an ostentatious, extravagant life style, since at least the summer of 1986, that contrasted starkly with his modest salary.

Surveillance of his actions was apparently minimal until very near the end. Eight years after he had first become a double agent, he was able, on June 13, 1993, to carry a shopping bag with seven pounds of CIA intelligence reports right past CIA guards as he left work. None of the guards asked to look inside the bag. Even after being placed under intense surveillance by the FBI, Ames had gotten away with making at least two successful "dead drop" deliveries of information to the Soviets. It was not until October 6, 1993, that the FBI began to discover what turned out to be a wealth of definitive evidence against Ames, who was thereby forestalled from collecting another $1.9 million being held for him in Moscow.

Arresting Ames on February 21, 1994, required a very elaborate and expensive set of investigations by the CIA and the FBI. In addition, the CIA's inspector general, Fred Hitz, later required 12 investigators, a review of 45,000 pages of documents, and 300 interviews. His 486-page classified report blistered the CIA for "sleeping on the job and not catching Ames much earlier" (Earley, 1997, p. 333). This report and the Agency's failure to follow its recommendations resulted in Congressional investigations and President Clinton signing a directive that gave the FBI more power in relation to the CIA.

Altogether, Ames identified for the Soviets at least 20 of their officers who had become agents for the CIA. Most of them were subsequently arrested and many were executed. Ames was sentenced to life imprisonment, while his wife, Rosario, who knew the source of their wealth in later years, was sentenced to 5 years in prison. Jeanne Vertefeuille of the CIA, who actually did much to reveal Ames' treachery, summed up her impression (as quoted in Earley, 1997, p. 351): "As I see it, the money was never important to him, until he met Rosario. ...[I]t was a combination of his weakness and Rosario's materialism that caused him to do it."

Other men who were traitors to the U.S. in recent years have been somewhat less troublesome to the CIA's image. Marine Sergeant Clayton Lonetree confessed spontaneously to a CIA officer in 1986 to having been recruited by the KGB as a spy, and two former FBI agents were sentenced to prison recently ("FBI agent who spied...", 1997), but Ames was a CIA insider, one of their own. And the CIA was aware of its own past excesses. As noted in Earley (1997, p. 224), Vertefeuille said, "We *all* agreed that we would not act in any Angletonian fashion."

After Ames was caught, an even higher ranking CIA officer, Harold J. Nicholson, was apprehended in November 1996 and sentenced in June 1997 ("CIA traitor...", 1997). He had been selling secrets to Moscow since 1994. Like Ames, his excuse for endangering lives and even causing loss of lives was financial support his family. Whereas Ames made millions, however, Nicholson reaped only $300,000. In view of his cooperation, Nicholson, age 46, was given a sentence of 23 years and 7 months, calculated to make his release possible before he turned 70 (Weiner, 1997b). Unlike the Ames case, Nicholson's compromising lie detector results were given very careful attention. Prior to the Ames and Nicholson cases, moles had not been caught purely on the basis of detective work. According to Earley (1997, p. 224), "Every spy caught by a U.S. intelligence service in recent history had been nabbed because of a snitch." It had been traitors betraying traitors.

Mind Control Programs

"The prince of darkness is a gentleman." —Shakespeare

In 1953, the CIA Project code-named MKULTRA began a top secret mind and behavior influence program. It was run overall by Sidney Gottlieb of the Chemical Division, who had a Ph.D. from Cal Tech and labeled himself one of the "Dr. Strangeloves" of the technical services staff. Project MKULTRA may be the best single example of complete failure of the adage, "The ends justify the means." In the case of the MKULTRA endeavors, not only were the means illicit, but the ends were seldom, if ever, achieved, just as the Nazi medical experiments on helpless victims contributed little of scientific value, unless one includes the later psychological studies of the perpetrators. It took until 1977 for the general public, through a *New York Times* front-page article in August of that year, to learn anything of the secret 25-year, $25 million project that the CIA operated in the 1950s and 1960s.

According to Thomas (1995, p. 211), Gottlieb was "a pleasant man who lived on a farm with his wife, ...drank only goat's milk, and grew Christmas trees, which he sold at a roadside stand." He and his staff were devoted to harming minds as well as bodies. Their deadly endeavors involved using drugs on totally unknowing citizens, including even CIA-affiliated scientists, one of whom leapt out of a window after unwittingly ingesting LSD. MKULTRA's early emphasis on LSD experiments was inspired by a false intelligence report that the Soviets were trying to buy up the world's stock of LSD. Throughout the 1950s, the CIA covertly tested LSD on unwitting subjects, including in whorehouses they ran in the Greenwich Village section of New York City and in San Francisco, where customers were slipped powerful drugged drinks. CIA case officers watched through one-way mirrors and joked about "operation Midnight Climax" (Thomas, 1995, p. 212). The results contributed no new knowledge of mind control.

As was often the case with CIA projects, MKULTRA also contracted with nongovernmental institutions and individuals. In revelations made possible by the Freedom of Information Act in 1977, the CIA's mind control programs involving 185 nongovernmental researchers in 80 institutions, including 54 colleges and universities, 15 research foundations, 12 hospitals and clinics, and three penal institutions came to light.

D. Ewen Cameron had been part of a team of multinational psychiatrists. He evaluated war criminal Rudolph Hess and considered the impact of the holocaust. In a 1946 paper called "Frontiers of Psychiatry" he used the case of Nazi Germany to exemplify how a society poisoned the minds of its citizens through propagating anxiety. Instead of really rejecting authoritarian methods of influence, however, he chose to perform experiments on unwitting patients in his care with the ostensible aim of countering authoritarian regimes, as exemplified by the fascists and communists, and finding methods to improve society. According to Weinstein (1990, p. 99), "Cameron's solution to the ills of society was simple: Experts should decide who can parent and who should govern. These experts must develop methods of forcefully changing attitudes and beliefs."

Having learned about Dr. Cameron's experiments, the CIA used a front organization to fund his work from 1957 through 1960 in order to gain access to the results of his experimental "treatment" of patients at the Allan Memorial Institute of Psychiatry at McGill

University, Montreal. The Canadian government also helped fund this research.

Cameron was, at various times, president of virtually all of the world's major psychiatric organizations. Shielded by secrecy and his own world renown and never really challenged by colleagues, though they knew something of the aggressive "treatments" he forced on unwitting patients, Cameron was never brought to justice. He died in 1967, 10 years before his "experimental" work came to public attention.

Cameron used frequent, often extremely intense electroconvulsive treatments (ECTs) known as Page-Russells, debilitating psychiatric drugs, sensory isolation, and "psychic driving" consisting of seemingly interminable forcing of verbal messages on the patient, all in the relentless pursuit of what Cameron called "depatterning", which was likened to the "brainwashing" attributed to Communists in Asia. In essence, the purpose of such treatment was to deprive the subject, as thoroughly as possible, of his or her mental faculties.

Psychiatrist Harvey Weinstein's book, *Psychiatry and the CIA: Victims of Mind Control* (1990), provided a detailed account of Cameron's pseudoscientific, thoroughly iatrogenic treatment of nine of his patients, including Dr. Weinstein's father, Lou, who initially presented only an anxiety disorder related to an episode of suffocation in childhood. Cameron repeatedly hospitalized and subjected this previously highly successful man against his will to treatments which so grossly shrunk his faculties as to reduce him to an essentially vegetative condition for the rest of his life. For example, in one 3-month hospital stay, Lou Weinstein was put to drugged sleep continuously for 54 days, given at least 23 ECTs, subjected to psychic driving, and "depatterned" to a state of complete regression. Some temporary success at instituting regression had been achieved but the psychiatric team had to be sure to institute a deeper, longer lasting regression. An excerpt from a psychiatric resident's notes clearly indicates the process and the goal (as quoted in Weinstein, 1990, p. 41):

"Last week he was deeply confused, incontinent, and we plan to keep him on sleep for 10 days prior to driving. He has, however, come out of his confusional state rather rapidly. He is beginning to be oriented, and no longer incontinent. We are then reinstituting Page-Russells twice a day until incontinence is reached, which we hope we will be able to accomplish in 48 hours, and will place him on isolation and on driving immediately."

Like Cameron's other patients, Lou Weinstein was finally discharged, his treatment having broken his brain, his spirit, and his finances. In turn, those who really cared about him were permanently damaged also, in no small part because the damage and its causes would never be acknowledged by the responsible parties.

It took nearly three decades for Cameron's patients to gain a settlement from the CIA. It was only then, October 3, 1988, by which time there were only seven surviving ex-patients *cum* plaintiffs, that they were given, collectively, $750,000 U.S., or about $100,000 Canadian, each. Even then, wrote Weinstein (1990, p. 270), "The response of the CIA through its spokesman, Bill Devine, was quite illustrative. Any settlement, if approved, does not represent a concession of liability on the part of the agency."

While the denial of liability serves as a legal defense against any further lawsuits, it also serves to perpetuate the psychological damage to the patients. People who have been severely traumatized are best helped by defining the trauma and its causes and by being provided with full acknowledgment of responsibility by the actually responsible parties or, at least, their agents. Psychologically, denial serves to continue and even to worsen the hurt.

How can such atrocities be inflicted, be covered over for decades, and be psychologically perpetuated? Is the responsibility merely that of an individual, or is there a collective responsibility? Is it enough to discover and stop the individual perpetrator? These are questions that should be paramount in all cases of grievous wrongs, especially where institutions are directly involved.

Thoroughly understanding the individual perpetrator and his or her actions necessitates knowing the developmental and contemporaneous contexts. Without such thorough understanding, we will only react simplistically and not in ways that will prevent future atrocities. Thus, we need to know both about the individual and the gestalt of formative influences.

Cameron studied and operated within a psychiatric system that was rather authoritarian and gave credence to a wide array of potentially quite harmful but much vaunted physical treatments (Whitaker, 1996a). Egas Moniz, a Portuguese neurologist, was co-winner of the Nobel Prize in 1949 "for his discovery of the therapeutic value of prefrontal lobotomy in certain psychoses" (Valenstein, 1973, p. 54). About 50,000 persons had their brains irreversibly damaged to the point of permanent dementia. The practice was stopped not so much by the sober independent evaluations that made clear that its harmful effects were not compensated by benefits, but by the introduction of powerful major tranquilizers that came to be called antipsychotics.

These neuroleptic drugs, including the phenothiazines, now account for tens of millions of cases of irreversible brain disease, including millions of cases of tardive dyskinesia, but are still considered the treatment of choice for schizophrenic disorders. These and other treatment procedures illustrate the "persistence of shrinking" (Whitaker, 1996b), which is based on a kind of reductionistic fallacy that continues to permeate the field of biological psychiatry. In essence, such treatment is aggressive on the part of the treater and passive on the part of the patient and targets symptoms that appear disruptive, at the expense of long-term results that will really be of benefit. Its motto sometimes seems to be, "If your brain offends you, we will damage it in an effort to banish your offensive symptoms."

Having studied and practiced in this atmosphere, most of Cameron's characteristic treatments were not so much radical departures from, as they were exaggerations of, contemporaneous trends. For example, ECTs were widely used, despite the fact that patients' brains were evidently damaged to the point of causing amnesias, but Cameron increased the frequency of ECT administration, and often he used Page-Russell ECTs, which were up to 75 times the "normal" dosage (Kessler, 1992, p. 308). Cameron combined ECT with both approved and experimental drugs and forced drugged sleep and sensory isolation on his uninformed patients.

At least 100 patients were subjected to brainwashing, according to Cameron's prescriptions. An evaluation of his results on 79 patients hospitalized from 1956 to 1963, who had reached the third stage of depatterning, showed "complications" (such as persisting amnesia and, therefore, brain damage) in 60% of these patients. Altogether, Cameron performed almost 10 years of ever-increasing and intrusive experimentation involving brainwashing procedures on at least 100 patients with no one intervening (Weinstein, 1990, p. 142). The results of Cameron's endeavors yielded no valuable scientific knowledge, and, according to Dr. Sidney Gottlieb, neither did the MKULTRA Project, of which it was only a small part (Weinstein, 1990, p. 143).

In one way, Cameron's actions were unremarkable. Hadn't he done vastly less damage than if he had performed lobotomies? Or if he had been forcing massive, long-term doses of neuroleptics on virtually anyone diagnosed as schizophrenic, as was a common practice? Fifty thousand lobotomies and millions of cases of neuroleptic-induced brain damage dwarfed the damage he did or could do as an individual. Wasn't he, like Moniz, trying to forge a breakthrough treatment for the "mentally ill?"

Cameron had a covert purpose. He was not just trying to help his patients. In fact, in some cases, the patients were individuals who did not present severe psychological or psychiatric disorders. One such patient was a young woman physician who sought to be a psychiatric resident. Cameron said she appeared "nervous" and required a medical examination at Royal Victoria Hospital, affiliated with McGill University and Allan Memorial Institute, where he then subjected her to his depatterning experiments (Weinstein, 1990, p. 166). She, too, became brain damaged.

What lessons, then, can be learned from Cameron's destructive "experiments" and similar medical atrocities? Weinstein (1990, p. 285) offered this sad realization:

"It is the silence and resistance to truth that makes us all vulnerable. I am haunted by the silence of my colleagues who worked at the Allan Memorial Institute in the 1950s and did not speak up; I am appalled by their continued silence in the 1980s when the truth emerged. Medicine has a history of engaging in evil undertakings when the motivation can be reframed so that the outcome is couched under the rubric of 'for the greater good.' The nontreatment of syphilis by the United States Public Health Service, the experimentation of the Nazi doctors for the good of the Fatherland, the irresponsible destruction of psychiatric patients under the guise of 'curing their schizophrenia'—all of these found willing adherents, physicians who would carry out the work for a larger philosophy of good intention. Phillip Zimbardo, a social psychologist at Stanford University, terms this phenomenon the 'structure of evil.' The actors engage in evil for a 'good' reason."

Certainly in the case of Cameron, the road to hell was paved with ostensibly good intentions. Cameron had become very like the Nazi doctors whose "experiments" on hapless victims were supposed to enhance society. The means, and not just the ends, may be crucial. And, very clearly, authoritarian means guaranteed destructive outcomes. These and other endeavors undermined and even permanently ruined the lives of citizens the CIA was supposed to protect. The means had come to severely damage the democratic goal it was supposed to serve.

Psychic Warriors

In the 1970s, it was known that the Soviet Union had been involved in "remote viewing" and related parapsychological studies. Sometime during that era, the Stanford Research Institute in California was conducting a program funded by the U.S. government which became the point of origin for similar studies conducted by the Defense Intelligence Agency, a part of the intelligence community overseen by the CIA. The U.S. research unit, begun in early 1974, was first code-named Sun Streak and later Stargate.

David Morehouse (1996), the distinguished Honor Graduate of many army training programs, was recruited for the unit in early 1988 after he was accidentally shot during an infantry exercise and began experiencing paranormal phenomena. The bullet entered deep into his helmet but did not pierce his skull. Nevertheless, it was this head trauma that opened the door, as it were, to his being trained as a "psychic warrior". His story is remarkable both for its revelations of the content of this top secret research and for what happened to him personally in the process.

The head trauma precipitated an ability or a curse, depending on circumstances, manifested in visions that were revelatory or nightmarish. One theory was that the conduits normally left closed at birth were damaged, that they had been forced open and were not reclosable. Morehouse, then an Army Ranger commander, was seen as someone whose new-found ability could be furthered by training. He was advised by some in the Army not to join the paranormal training program but was invited by others, despite their acknowledgment that such training had been damaging for some trainees. What was he to do about his often frightening experiences? Morehouse's wife wanted him to get professional assistance. In response, "Levy", the head of the paranormal unit, made a cautionary prediction. Ironically, because Morehouse joined the unit instead of seeking professional help, he only temporarily avoided the predicted outcome. Levy said (Morehouse, 1996, p. 98):

"I'll tell you what the doctors will do. They will very carefully document his descriptions of the visions, perhaps even ask him to draw sketches. They will put him through some simple tests. They will classify him as delusional, maybe

even psychotic. And then they will prescribe all sorts of drugs. They will want to control his visions with a chemical straightjacket. They will not be understanding; they will not care; and his career will be over. The best you could hope for would be a medical discharge for psychological disability. Not a very fitting end to an otherwise exceptional career is it?"

Training in "remote viewing" took place in austere, sensorily deprived environments of the kind that make for hypnotic or trance conditions. Having achieved the necessary brain wave frequency, which the viewer did more readily with training, the viewer became removed from his or her earthly body and entered the "ether", an altered state of consciousness whereby the viewer became able to transcend ordinary time and space. Often, the aim was to investigate a specific place or event. Though disembodied, as it were, and therefore never harmed bodily, sometimes the viewer was traumatized by his or her experiences, for example a visionary visit to Nazi concentration camps or to burning Iraqi oil fields in the Gulf War.

Meanwhile, the process was monitored via a variety of physiological measuring devices and, usually, another experienced remote viewer. On returning to ordinary consciousness, the trainee would make notes and sketch what he or she had seen in the space and time travels.

According to then Major Morehouse, the government pumped tens of millions of dollars into paranormal research in half a dozen private and as many state and federal research centers across the U.S., but, due to the secrecy level and the nature of the research, those affiliated with it were feared, ridiculed, scoffed at, mocked, and ostracized and were set apart apparently so as not to be a really accountable part of the intelligence community. His story illustrates the lengths to which the CIA has gone to develop superior intelligence-gathering methods and to which it went, apparently, to stop one of its officers from divulging its secrets, even when the secrets had already been largely disclosed by others. Morehouse (1996, pp.190–191) said:

"I had to define clearly what I was about to do. First I considered whether telling my story would endanger the national security of the United States, the country I loved dearly and had sacrificed for. I concluded that it would not. The Cold War was over. A year ago our Soviet counterparts had told the entire world what they had been doing for the past forty years in the paranormal arena. I wasn't giving away launch codes or the names of top-secret operatives. I was telling a story about psychic spies, whose existence was already an established fact."

What followed initially were threats and phone taps. Cassette tapes of his conversations with various people started showing up in his mail as did little cardboard packages or envelopes with no return address. Next, his home was broken into and his office ransacked. Then, he ascertained that he was being followed as he drove his car, and he had a blowout independently diagnosed as "[t]his here tire's been cut to blow" (Morehouse, 1996, p. 200). After these strategies failed to neutralize him, he was charged by an Army prosecutor with trumped up allegations. Further on, he and his wife and children again had their home invaded. This time, after a generator was moved into the garage, it dispelled a potentially deadly gas into their living quarters. Next, he was psychiatrically hospitalized and, except for a woman psychiatrist who took him seriously (and later lost her position over doing so) and refrained both from diagnosing him as having "biological problems" and drugging him, he was regarded as needing psychiatric drugs.

Brought before the directors of Walter Reed Hospital's psychiatry department, it was decided eventually that Morehouse would be medically retired as no longer fit to do what he had been trained to do and too emotionally unstable to wear a uniform. After the retirement process had begun, he was visited, in the presence of his wife and children, by a major from Sun Streak who asked to speak with him alone, but his wife stayed with him. The visiting major informed soon-to-be-ex-Major Morehouse that he could not let Morehouse destroy the unit with any claims and would do anything necessary to protect it (Morehouse, 1996, p. 224). The visitor ended the conversation ominously with, "Oh, you have no idea who's swinging, my friend. You really don't have any idea at all. And you remember this: in this world, even when you can see who's swinging, you'll never see the one that gets you." The visitor then winked, turned, and walked away.

A few days later, Morehouse relapsed, falling back into the "ether" and experienced being slashed and screeched at. Upon waking from this nightmare, he found his body, face, and bedclothes covered with blood, pages torn from his notebook, and sketches made on the pages in his blood. A single razor blade was found stuck in the table next to his bed. Neither he nor hospital personnel could account for the incident.

Subsequently, he was given Halcion, Prozac, and a number of other psychiatric medications to stop what were regarded by the "biological" psychiatrists as hallucinations and was then transferred to the psychiatric ward at Ft. Bragg's Womack Army Hospital, where the authorities were to proceed with a court martial. Ironically, at Womack, the treatment of Major Morehouse, who had not been a drug abuser, consisted almost entirely of taking prescribed drugs and sitting through classes for drug abusers (Morehouse, 1996, p. 231):

"The drugs I was given were overwhelming — a cupful every day by the time I left the hospital. I was on forty milligrams of Loxitane (a powerful antipsychotic), sixty milligrams of Prozac (an antidepressant), six milligrams of Cogentin (to offset the tremors caused by the Loxitane), and thirty milligrams of Restoril (a tranquilizer). Most mornings these drugs knocked me to the floor. Although I didn't have any dissociative episodes or trips into the ether, I spent every day in a fog."

In this condition and without any actual defense by an attorney, contrary to his normal legal rights, he had no opportunity during preparation for the court martial hearings to speak for himself, and there were no responses to requests by him or his wife to other authorities. Depositions he paid a private attorney $5000 to obtain, which he felt would have destroyed the government's case, were never used. Nevertheless, he was able to resign in view of the weakness of the prosecution's case, albeit with none of the usual benefits — retirement, unemployment, the Veterans Administration loan on his home, the right to be buried in a military cemetery, and even access to the American Legion. Thirty days after agreeing to resign his commission in the Army ("for the good of the service"), the charges against him were dropped, his resignation was accepted, and an "other than honorable" discharge was bestowed upon him. No evidence had been presented on his behalf.

The senior psychiatrist who had believed Morehouse's story suffered also. She later told him that the government, via her supervisors, had ordered her to change his diagnosis to psychotic and delusional, alter his records, and give him drugs. She had refused as far as possible, giving him the smallest possible doses of antipsychotic drugs. She was forced to resign after 12 years of government service and was professionally destroyed, and she also lost all her benefits, including a pension.

Whereas even the very existence of the Stargate (formerly Sun Streak) program had been denied, the CIA, in cooperation with the Defense Intelligence Agency, started a carefully planned and executed media blitz revealing the government's psychic research and, purportedly, former psychic warfare program. It was apparently time to do so for purposes of self-interest.

Morehouse (1996, p. 249) recalled that, as a young captain, the Army's deputy Chief of Staff for intelligence (the highest ranking intelligence officer in the Army) told him and two others: "The CIA does nothing, says nothing, allows nothing unless its own interests are served. They are the biggest assembly of liars and thieves this country ever put under one roof and they are an abomination."

Efficacy Questions

How can a democratic government not only permit but support the kinds of covert and, in the last analysis, often lethal programs that have been carried out by the CIA for the past 50 years? As noted earlier, the CIA had noble parentage. Democratic nations were defending themselves in a hot war against tyrants who blatantly broke the rules not only of diplomacy but of war itself. As the old Spanish proverb says, it was necessary to "fight fire with fire". Since World War II, however, the U.S. has been directly subject to very little active fire. Yet, during the 1960s, for example, the CIA committed massive murders and tortures through the Phoenix Program, as noted in Table 15.2.

Part of the answer is that the general populace has had a positive image of the CIA even after the Church and Pike Congressional hearings in the 1970s, which disclosed extreme CIA violations. A 1979 Opinion Research Corporation opinion poll showed that 62% of U.S. citizens had a favorable opinion of the CIA; only 24% had an unfavorable opinion, while 14% had no opinion. Unfavorable opinions were highest among citizens who were college educated and had higher incomes (Kessler, 1992, p. 9). By implication, positive imagery of the CIA would be lessened if people were better educated in general and, perhaps, about the CIA in particular. For an agency such as the CIA to continue to exist within an essentially democratic society, most of the populace must support the concept of covert activity, albeit without necessarily knowing its exact nature or outcomes.

Besides its political efficacy, however, there are many important substantive questions about the CIA's actual effects. While the answers to these questions cannot be complete because much of the CIA's activities remain shrouded in secrecy, considerable knowledge is now available.

How efficacious has the CIA been in accomplishing its stated missions of predicting and controlling important events affecting national security? The CIA failed to predict both the Korean War and the end of the Cold War; it failed to accomplish its mission in the Bay of Pigs fiasco, which led to the Cuban missile crisis (the closest we have come to nuclear destruction); and its attempts to assassinate foreign leaders have been both outside of the bounds of its charter and ineffective. And, as noted earlier in this chapter, apparently most CIA veteran officers have come to believe that most of their missions were failures, sometimes because the information they gathered was ignored in favor of political expediency. On the other hand, the CIA is inclined to take credit for the end of the Cold War and for avoiding an all-out "hot war".

Has the CIA actually promoted the well-being of the U.S. and its people? While it may claim to have done so, it has also clearly violated the rights of U.S. citizens as well as the laws and rights of citizens of other countries. And it has contributed substantially to distrust and "paranoia" among the people of the U.S. Its clandestine nature has been antithetical to the democratic spirit that it is supposed to preserve and protect.

Has the CIA actually promoted freedom and well-being among the world's other nations and their citizens? The results are mixed at best. The CIA's methods may have been expedient in some cases but the methods themselves have exacted a high price in human life and well-being and conveyed the opposite of the democratic spirit. Often, through the CIA, the U.S. has equated freedom with its own capitalistic system and promoted rightist autocrats rather than allowing the citizens of other nations to determine their own leaders and governmental systems. In some cases, as exemplified by information in Table 15.2, the CIA and the U.S. have committed what can be termed second order genocide.

Overall, the CIA has probably "succeeded" at many missions, albeit at the expense of massive destruction of human lives and well-being, corrosive distrust of the U.S. and its "democratic" government, and the sacrifice of more enlightened and longer term goals in the service of what is increasingly a one-world economy and culture. For example, as the foremost seller and exporter of weapons in the world, the U.S., including through the CIA, has been helping to perpetrate lethal violence. These weapons have begun to come back into the U.S. through weapons importers and other nations that are or have been allies who received them from the U.S. originally. The U.S. Congress has even considered a measure that could place 2.5 million more rifles and pistols onto its streets ("The surplus gun invasion...", 1997). What goes around comes around.

Prospects and Recommendations

It would be naive to believe that the CIA will soon be scaled down or eliminated. CIA supporters can point to the rapidly accelerating growth in technology, including weapons systems and detection methodology that are or soon will be available to most nations. Supporters can argue that the U.S. had better be not only the most advanced nation technologically, but that it must also slow down or stop sophisticated, potentially hostile actions against the U.S. Furthermore, methodology to invade personal privacy has become so common that there are threats to personal security everywhere. For a price ranging from $75 to $450, depending on the particular personal facts the purchaser wishes to acquire, information brokers will obtain an individual's bank balance, salary, investment funds amounts, credit card number, telephone records, or 10-year medical history (Bernstein, 1997).

In view of the acceleration of information technology and what is perceived as the CIA's inadequacy to analyze and monitor world developments, Congress' House Permanent Select Committee has wanted to increase secret intelligence spending by at least 5%, which would raise the overall intelligence budget to over $30 billion, its biggest budget in 5 years (Weiner, 1997d). Thus, if anything, the CIA budget and operations may be increased in the near future.

Let us suppose that a great deal of valuable intelligence has been gathered by the CIA over its 50 years. Must the actions of the CIA be kept secret lest national security be severely compromised? Allegations of a link between the CIA and the introduction of crack cocaine into Los Angeles in the 1980s have been subjected to independent investigation within the CIA and by Congressional oversight committees. John M. Deutch (1977), the former DCI, has endorsed unclassifying the results of these investigations; he suggested that making these documents available for public scrutiny will improve the CIA's image and thus help gain the necessary public support to further its missions: fighting terrorism, countering weapons proliferation, and serving as our nation's first line of defense.

George F. Kennan (1997, p. E17) stated: "It is my conviction, based on some 70 years of experience, first as a government official and then in my 45 years as a historian, that the need by our government for *secret* intelligence about affairs elsewhere in the world has been vastly overrated." He views spying as inducing extensive counterintelligence operations by other nations and believes that most of what is needed can be acquired openly and without deadly competition.

Clearly, every effort should be made to limit harmful covert operations and to monitor those that are planned or performed. The overwhelmingly most important measures the United States can take to protect its own security and to help other nations become free is to empathize with the needs and feelings of its own citizens and those of other nations, and to respond with constructive, not clandestine, actions. The U.S. Peace Corps programs have been enormously effective in these ways. Not coincidentally, the Peace Corps is purportedly the only U.S. organization abroad which has not been infiltrated by the CIA.

The constructive spirit of the Peace Corps communicates the best message we can give other nations and ourselves. This federal government organization, established by President Kennedy in the 1960s, trains and sends U.S. volunteers abroad to work with people of developing countries on projects for technological, agricultural, and educational improvement. Its message of peace, goodwill, and good deeds is ethical, efficacious, economical, and trustworthy. Many similarly spirited organizations exist. Let us make every effort to proliferate such efforts as these and we will have far less need for the unethical, generally ineffective, expensive, clandestine and often lethal activity that so readily alienates other peoples and our own citizens.

In conclusion, our national priorities should be reset by publicizing destructive actions for what they are and promoting constructive projects at home and abroad. We must remember that the best way to counter the threat of one world technology is to cultivate one world empathy and caring for humankind.

Annotated Bibliography

1. Earley, P. (1997) *Confessions of a Spy: The Real Story of Aldrich Ames*. New York: G.P. Putnam's Sons. This is the story of a CIA spy who became and was ultimately discovered to be a mole, a spy operating as a double agent against his own government from within its own intelligence establishment. The man the media called "America's most damaging traitor" was said to be responsible for the deaths of as many as 20 Soviet informers whose own mole status he revealed. The book is also a personal portrait of the inherently duplicitous spying mentality. Even as a traitor, Ames felt that he had remained faithful, in his words, to "...what is at the core of the intelligence officer's world — betraying another person's trust in you" (p. 43).

2. Kessler, R. (1986) *The Richest Man in the World*. New York: Warner Books. This book shows that violence is golden. Its subject, the weapons broker Adnan Khashoggi, became the world's richest man as an unstinting practitioner of sociopathy accepted and aided by a myriad of governments, celebrities, industries, and even a university unable to decline his gifts. He came to the attention of the CIA partly through the Iran-Contra affair. Khashoggi's public relations skills made ready accomplices among the famous, who were willing to overlook his and their own contributions to lethal violence throughout the world, a perfect example of the effectiveness of this advice by Niccolo Macchiavelli (in *The Prince)*: "The prince must ... avoid those things which will make him hated or despised; and whenever he succeeds in this, he will have done his part, and will find no danger in other vices."

3. Kessler, R. (1992) *Inside the CIA*. New York: Pocket Books. The author, who had the CIA's cooperation, gives a guided tour of the agency and an evenhanded account of the structure and operations of the CIA since its beginnings in 1947. He found the CIA "sloppy" in its early years but basically effective as well as essential to national security into the 1990s. Kessler is critical and laudatory by turns, depending on the specific CIA project. His book is an especially good account of the complicated structure of the CIA itself, its relationships with the broader intelligence community, and its oversight by the President, Congress, and other governmental and non-governmental groups.

4. Thomas, E. (1995) *The Very Best Men*. New York: Simon & Schuster Touchstone Edition. This book relates the story of the early "glory days" of the CIA from its beginning in 1947 until its decline in the mid-1960s, through the careers of four daring officers who tried to contain the

Soviet threat. Thomas' vivid biographical accounts bring to life the personalities and the complex webs woven in the paradoxical processes of using trickery and violence to try to serve democracy.

5. Weinstein, H.M. (1990) *Psychiatry and the CIA: Victims of Mind Control.* Washington, D.C.: American Psychiatric Press. This is the excellently told story of nine Canadian citizens, out of over 100 unwitting patient-victims, who were "treated" and experimented on by world famous psychiatrist D. Ewen Cameron. Financed in part by the CIA as part of Project MKULTRA, his work was also endorsed by the Canadian government. It is told by the psychiatrist son of one of the victims. Like other unwitting patients, the author's father was subjected to ruthless experiments with drugs, electric shock, sensory isolation, enforced sleep, and auditory "driving" of messages into their brains. The "patients" all got worse to the point of irreversible, at least largely incapacitating, harm. This extreme violation of the traditional injunction of "physician, do no harm" was only faintly acknowledged and recompensed decades later after many years of heroic legal and journalistic efforts. This book is a powerful object lesson in the synergistically powerful destructiveness of authoritarianism and secrecy.

References

A&E 20th Century (1997) September 17.

American Heritage Dictionary of the English Language, 3rd ed. (1992).

Beaty, J. and Gwynne, S.C. (1991) The dirtiest bank of all. *Time,* July 29, 42–47.

Bellis, D.J. (1981) *Heroin and Politicians: The Failure of Public Policy To Control Addiction in America.* Westport, CT: Greenwood.

Bernstein, N. (1997) Online, high-tech sleuths find private facts. *The New York Times*, Sept. 15, p. A1.

Blight, J. and Lang, J. (1995) Burden of nuclear responsibility: reflections on the critical oral history of the Cuban missile crisis. *Peace and Conflict, 11*, 225–264.

Branfman, F. (1978) South Vietnam's police and prison system: the U.S. connection. In H. Frazier (Ed.), *Unlocking the CIA*, pp. 110–27. New York: Free Press.

Brody, R. (1985) *Contra Terror in Nicaragua: Report of a Fact-Finding Mission, September 1984–January 1985.* Boston: South End Press.

Burns, R. (1997) Former senator to review Gulf War investigations. *Honolulu Advertiser*, May 2, p. A6.

Castro, J. (1988) The cash cleaners. *Time*, Oct. 24, 65–66.

Chomsky, N. and Herman, E.S. (1977) The United States versus human rights in the third world. *Monthly Review, 29*, 22–45.

Chomsky, N. (1985) *Turning the Tide: U.S. Intervention in Central America and the Struggle for Peace.* Boston: South End Press.

"CIA traitor, saying he wanted cash for family, gets 23 years" (1997) *The New York Times*, June 6, p. A19.

Clarridge, D.R. (1997) *A Spy for All Seasons: My Life in the CIA*. New York: Scribner & Sons.

Corn, D. (1988) Bush's CIA: the same old dirty tricks. *The Nation*, Aug. 27–Sept. 31, 57–60.

C-Span *Washington Journal* (1997) September 16.

C-Span (1997a) September 17.

C-Span (1997b) September 9.

C-Span (1997c) September 16.

Deutch, J.M. (1997) *The New York Times*, May 18, p. E17.

Earley, P. (1997) *Confessions of a Spy: The Real Story of Aldrich Ames*. New York: G.P. Putnam's Sons.

Emerson, S. (1988) *Secret Warriors Inside the Covert Military Operations of the Reagan Era*. New York: G.P. Putnam's Sons.

Faden, R. (1996) *Final Report of the Advisory Committee on Human Radiation Experiments*. New York: Oxford Press.

"FBI agent who spied is sentenced to 27 years" (1997) *The New York Times*, June 24, p. A14.

Flanders, S.A. and Flanders, C.N. (1993) *Dictionary of American Foreign Affairs*. New York: Macmillan.

Gerth, J. (1997) New CIA chief picks veteran staff. *The New York Times,* July 22, p. A12.

Goodman, W. (1997) The tragic human toll of the early Stalin years. July 14, *The New York Times*, p. C13.

Herman, E. (1982) *The Real Terror Network*. Boston: South End Press.

Hinckle, W. and Turner, W. (1981) *The Fish Is Red — The Story of the Secret War Against Castro*. New York: Harper & Row.

Hoffman, A. and Silvers, J. (1980) An election held hostage. *Playboy, 35*(10), 73–74.

Holmes, S. (1997) Call for CIA cocaine inquiry is renewed. *The New York Times*, May 15, p. B15.

Human Rights Exploitation Manual (1983) Declassified and redacted by CIA, January, 1997.

Kaplan, J., Gen. Ed. (1992) Harry S. Truman. In J. Bartlett, *Familiar Quotations*, 16th ed., p. 655. Boston: Little, Brown & Company.

"Keeping track: empty posts at CIA" (1997) *The New York Times*, August 25, p. A 15.

Kennan, G.F. (1997) *The New York Times*, May 18, p. E17.

Kessler, R. (1986) *The Richest Man in the World*. New York: Warner Books.

Kessler, R. (1992) *Inside the CIA*. New York: Pocket Books.

Kessler, R. (1993) *The FBI*. New York: Simon & Schuster.

Kruger, H. (1980) *The Great Heroin Coup*. Boston: South End Press.

Kubark Counterintelligence Interrogation Manual (1963) Declassified and redacted by CIA, January, 1997.

Lifschultz, L. (1988) Inside the kingdom of heroin. *The Nation, 477*, 492–496.

Marshall, J., Scott, P.D., and Hunter, J. (1987) *The Iran-Contra Connection*. Boston: South End Press.

Maas, P. (1986) *Manhunt*. New York: Random House.

Macklin, W. (1997) In the name of protest. *Philadelphia Inquirer*, Aug. 4, pp. D5, D12.

McCoy, A. (1997) CIA covert actions and drug trafficking. *North Coast Express*, pp. 5, 16.

Morehouse, D. (1996) *Psychic Warrior: Inside the CIA's Stargate Program: The True Story of a Soldier's Espionage and Awakening*. New York: St. Martin's.

Morrison, D. (1995) Recollections of a nuclear war. *Scientific American, 273*, 42–46.

Moyers, B. (1988) *The Secret Government: The Constitution in Crisis*. Washington, D.C.: Seven Locks Press.

Myers, L. (1997) After CIA offered $150,000, mob said it would kill Castro for free. *West Hawaii Today*, July 2, p. A3.

"Opening up CIA history [editorial]" (1997) *The New York Times*, May 30, p. A28.

Parenti, M. (1983) *Democracy for the Few*. New York: St. Martin's.

Pearce, F. (1976) *Crimes of the Powerful*. London: Pluto Press.

Prados, J. (1986) *Presidents' Secret Wars*. New York: William Morrow.

Priest, D. (1996) U.S. instructed Latins on executions, torture. *Washington Post*, Sept. 21, pp. A1, A9.

"Prying open the spy budget [editorial]" (1997) *The New York Times*, Oct. 17, p. A34.

Richelson, J.T. (1995) *The U.S. Intelligence Community*, 3rd ed. San Francisco: Westview Press.

Scheffer, D.J. (1987) U.S. law and the Iran-contra affair. *The American Journal of International Law, 81*(3), 696–723.

Schmalz, J. (1988) Bank indicted for money laundering case. *The New York Times*, October 12, p. A56.

Sciolino, E. (1988) Fighting narcotics: U.S. urged to shift tactics. *The New York Times*, April 10, p. A56.

Sheehan, D. (1988) *Inside the Shadow Government*. Washington, D.C.: The Christie Institute.

Simon, C.P. and Eitzen, D.S. (1986) *Elite Deviance*. Boston, MA: Ally & Bacon.

Stanton, D. (1976) Drugs, Vietnam, and the Vietnam veteran: an overview. *American Journal of Drug and Alcohol Abuse, 3*, 557–570.

"The surplus gun invasion [editorial]" (1997) *The New York Time*, Sept. 9, p. A26.

Thomas, E. (1995) *The Very Best Men*. New York: Touchstone.

U.S. Army (1963) *Counterintelligence Interrogation*.

U.S. Army (1983) *Human Resource Exploitation*.

Valenstein, E.S. (1973) *Brain Control*. New York: John Wiley & Sons.

Weiner, T. (1997a) CIA's openness derided as a "snow job". *The New York Times*, May 20, p. A16.

Weiner, T. (1997b) CIA traitor severely hurt U.S. security, judge is told. *The New York Times*, June 2, p. A24.

Weiner, T. (1997c) House panel says CIA lacks expertise to carry out its duties. *The New York Times*, June 19, p. A20.

Weiner, T. (1997d) Research group is suing CIA to reveal size of spy budget. *The New York Times*, July 22, p. A16.

Weiner, T. (1997e) CIA destroyed files on 1953 Iran coup. *The New York Times*, May 29, p A19.

Weiner, T. (1997f) Veteran CIA official quits but will finish investigations. *The New York Times*, October 3, p. A 13.

Weinstein, H.M. (1990) *Psychiatry and the CIA: Victims of Mind Control*. Washington, D.C.: American Psychiatric Press.

Whitaker, L.C. (1987) Macho and morbidity: the emotional need versus fear dilemma in men. *Journal of College Student Psychotherapy, 1*(4), 33–47.

Whitaker, L.C. (1996a) Social inducements to paralethal and lethal violence. In H.V. Hall (Ed.), *Lethal Violence 2000: A Sourcebook on Fatal Domestic, Acquaintance and Stranger Aggression*, pp. 143–173. Kamuela, HI: Pacific Institute for the Study of Conflict and Aggression.

Whitaker, L.C. (1996b) The persistence of shrinking: remembrance of things not so past. *Journal of College Student Psychotherapy, 11*(3), 47–59.

Wise, D. (1997) Big lies and little green men. *The New York Times*, Aug. 8, p. A27.

Woodward, B. (1988) *Veil: The Secret Wars of the CIA 1981–1987*. New York: Pocket Books.

The Author

Leighton C. Whitaker, Ph.D., ABPP, is in private practice, is Adjunct Clinical Professor at Widener University's Institute for Graduate Clinical Psychology, and is the editor of the *Journal of College Student Psychotherapy*. His 70 professional publications address a wide variety of clinical and social subjects and include the *Whitaker Index of Schizophrenic Thinking* (Western Psychological Services, 1980) and *Schizophrenic Disorders* (Plenum Press, 1992). His previous positions include Associate Professor and Director of Adult Psychology for the University of Colorado Health Sciences Center, Professor and Director of the University of Massachusetts Mental Health Services, and Director of Swarthmore College Psychological Services. He has done forensic work for many years and has been a consultant to the U.S. Department of Labor's Job Corps. His work with youth has been featured on television and in newspapers.

Acknowledgments

The author thanks Harold V. Hall for providing Table 15.2 and the list of references indicated therein, as well as other source materials; Sandra B. McPherson for providing this author with the English-language training manuals used by the School of the Americas and for her commentary on the manuals; and Benjamin A. Whitaker for assistance with final preparation of the manuscript.

Chapter 16

CAPITAL PUNISHMENT: IMPLICATIONS FOR INSTITUTIONAL VIOLENCE VS. INDIVIDUAL RIGHTS

Sandra B. McPherson

As a boy, Fred Leuchter liked to play in the electric chair, "risking" death according to an old superstition. As an adult, Leuchter used his talent for engineering innovation to build instruments that would execute quickly and presumably painlessly (Trombley, 1992). As will be discussed, Leuchter's success and some associated exploits not only implemented questionable personal psychology, but are metaphors for the social and legal capital justice scene.

Americans only briefly relinquished the ultimate penalty. Upon reenactment of capital punishment statutes, curious trends developed. There was increasing use of the penalty, along with a search for more humane methods. Nonetheless, modernization failed to resolve or even adequately address the problems inherent in capital punishment. This chapter examines the death penalty as a form of institutionally sanctioned violence. Issues are presented in a consideration of its effectiveness and legitimacy.

Thesis

Various levels of violence in a society converge and have multiplicative effects upon each other. Violence in the family sets the stage for the emergence of violent behavior on the part of individuals. A society that is socio-economically constructed to victimize significant portions of its citizens creates a starting point for interrupted nurturing. The inadequate parenting then potentiates destructive and antisocial acts by members of affected groups. The next step in a downward spiral involves failure to provide meaningful medical and mental health care and rehabilitation.

Some acts of lethal criminal violence arise out of interactions between personal and social conditions. When such acts qualify for the imposition of the death penalty, the society reaches the end point of the spiral. Out of the foundation of individual violence and failed early remediation, there is a final response to aggression with ultimate sanction. With the help of media images which demonize perpetrators and enhance public perceptions of threat, the sequence may serve a variety of unforeseen purposes, including victimization of identifiable subgroups and legitimization of government violence.

Legal, Political, and Social Aspects

For a brief period, the U.S. joined the rest of the western democratic world and ended the use of the death penalty following the Furman v. Georgia (1972) decision. That decision, however, was anything but clear-cut. It did not find that the death penalty was unconstitutional. It allowed only that the then-current arbitrary administration of the penalty did not meet the necessary expectations of impartially applied equal justice. Furman v. Georgia rested at least in part on social science data, but it was not written as one opinion. Rather, it consisted of five differing statements from the concurring justices. The plurality basically affirmed that jury discretion was unconstitutional and that capricious application of the death penalty violated Eighth Amendment expectations of equal justice. It was analogized that just as being struck by lightning is cruel and unusual, inconsistent applications of the death penalty resulting from unconstrained jury discretion offended constitutional principles (Paternoster, 1991). After the Furman v. Georgia decision, the states were without the death penalty until such time as they fashioned acceptable statutes. The attempts which followed considered both guided discretion and mandatory penalty statutes in order to meet the Furman demands. Only discretionary approaches were supported (Gregg v. Georgia, 1976; Jurek v. Texas, 1976; Proffitt v. Florida, 1976; Roberts v. Louisiana, 1976; Woodson v. North Carolina, 1976).

Court watchers noted two trends as capital statutes were re-enacted and tested. The first phase lasted from 1976 to 1983 and focused on the protection of defendants' rights (White, 1991). A landmark case from this period was Lockett v. Ohio (1978), which invalidated the sentence of Sandra Lockett, a young black female accused of participating in a robbery. Her confederate was the gunman, there was no intention to commit the robbery, and mitigating circumstances such as youth and minor participation had not been presented. Lockett v. Ohio widened the mitigation (sentencing) stage to allow presentation of any aspect of a defendant's character or record or any of the circumstances of the offense that the defendant might proffer. Other safeguards preserved during this period included the opportunity to confront witnesses against the defendant in the penalty stage (Gardner v. Florida, 1977), the privilege against self-incrimination, protection from double jeopardy, and the potential for judicial instruction on lesser included charges (Beck v. Alabama, 1980).

The second trend, beginning about 1983, took quite a different tack and involved the promotion of more expeditious executions. As time dragged on and the appeals process moved slowly through various levels of the court system, significant effort and frustration led to decisions such as Barefoot v. Estelle (1983), in which the U.S. Supreme Court upheld the lower court's refusal to stay an execution pending an appeal that was accepted but could not be processed in the time remaining. By 1990, this trend was solidly established, with 27 of 35 capital cases that term decided in favor of the prosecution (Smith, 1990). This reasoning found its apex in Herrera v. Collins (1993), in which the Supreme Court decided that a well-founded claim of innocence was not a constitutional claim, and that executive clemency was an adequate safeguard where any new evidence surfaced. Herrera remained vulnerable to the death penalty in the face of clear evidence indicating his innocence and was duly executed in 1993.

This second trend has continued up to the present at both local and national levels. Ohio Attorney General Betty Montgomery, in the spring of 1996, campaigned for legislation to hasten the appeals process.

Ohio's death penalty law took effect in 1981, but there have been as yet no executions in that state. Montgomery's efforts in that regard illustrated not only the trend to expedite executions, but also reflected complex political factors. She was embroiled in an ongoing fight with the state public defender whose actions to restructure that office may have been at times poorly framed. Both sides were thus "posturing" and were facilitated by an appeals court's selective attention to the facts of procedural adequacy in the cases selected for grandstanding ("Politics pervades...", 1996).

A major rationale for capital punishment is the belief that it serves as a deterrent; however, historical applications and social science research have provided little support for significant crime prevention effects. In any country where procedural safeguards exist, extended time is necessary to implement the death penalty. Its administration is less certain, which may also contribute to its lack of impact. One comprehensive study of statistical data on a state-by-state basis indicated a weak deterrent effect that was initially proportionate to the number executed but was unaffected thereafter (Lester, 1987). Some studies have supported the proposition that rescinding the death penalty reduces crime, where other research has concluded that executions stimulate increased violence, or that other factors — especially war — account for homicide rate fluctuations (Archer, 1983; Fattah, 1983; Forst, 1983; Wilkes, 1987).

Other issues are also raised. One is the issue of racism. Others involve political factors as determinants in decisions, mental health concerns, and innocence. Finally, problems of inconsistency and illogic permeate all aspects of capital punishment from legislation to implementation.

It is perhaps instructive that as the final draft of this chapter was being written, the American Bar Association (ABA), by a vote of 280 to 119, called for a moratorium on executions. The ABA acted in response to its task force report detailing the injustice characteristic of administration of the death penalty throughout the country's capital jurisdictions (ABA, 1997; "Death penalty criticized", 1997).

Literature and Lore

Historical Factors

Early Christians opposed capital punishment. Believers could not hold offices where duties included authorizing capital punishment. However, when church and state joined at the end of the fourth century, this prohibition ended. Aquinas justified the use of the death penalty on the basis of the protection of society. Small sects such as Waldensions, Anabaptists, and Mennonites opposed the death penalty but were oftentimes executed for their efforts. Protestant reformers continued, rather than opposed, capital punishment. Their belief system was peculiarly structured to support the penalty, holding that people were intrinsically flawed and evil (Potter, 1993).

The first recorded execution in England occurred in 695 A.D. It was imposed to punish a thief and thus be a deterrent. In a mixed-message reform, Alfred the Great repealed many capital offenses and hanged 44 judges because they had been too quick to hang others. King Canute made it illegal to put to death Christian men "on any slight cause" (Potter, 1993, p. 2). William the Conqueror abolished the death penalty but substituted castration. The Anglican monarchs were quite active in implementing capital punishment. Thousands of people were executed under the reign of Henry VIII. His daughter, Elizabeth, continued vigorous application of the death penalty, including, among other things, using it to solve the "gypsy problem" genocidally (Potter, 1993). Capital statutes were fashioned in a way that made it inevitable that lower classes would suffer and the upper classes would be protected. For example, the Waltham Black Act of 1723 included more capital provisions than were found in the entire criminal codes of other countries of the time. It remained in effect for 100 years, though it was intended to be a temporary preventive for deer stealing and other offenses against the property and lifestyle of the landed gentry (Potter, 1993).

Similarly, Linebaugh (1992), in a study of the period from 1690 to 1800, focused on the interplay of the working and upper classes. His position was that, with the development of an ownership class and the concomitant exploitation of labor, a have-not group evolved and functioned in ways that were perceived as increasingly dangerous to the society as a whole and especially to those who owned property. With that perception, the need for repression and the use of repressive punishments increased.

Class issues were intertwined with religious precept and practice. Edmond Burke was quoted as saying (Potter, 1993, p. 6): "If a country gentleman can obtain no other favor from Government, he is sure to be accommodated with a new felony without benefit of clergy." The quote refers to the ease with which those in power could have new laws crafted to fit their particular aims which might be very specific and personal and always protected their interests. (Benefit of clergy was an interesting concept. It meant that if a person was designated a clergyman, then all power to discipline that person's behavior was removed to the Bishop, and the state ceased to have the power to punish him.)

Throughout the 1600s and 1700s, English church and state functioned more in concert than at odds; perhaps predictably, the church rather quickly came to view capital punishment as a blessing for the recipient. The notion was that a sentence of death could so adequately refocus the felon on his or her sins that it would bring a kind of contrition that allowed entrance into Heaven; therefore, the state was actually doing the person a favor by killing him or her (Potter, 1993).

As has often been noted in the study of war, people actually find it difficult to kill people (Dyer, 1985). Consistently, the presence on the English books of many capital crimes did not necessarily lead to many executions. Over time, the use of capital justice declined rather than increased. During the first half of the 19th century, reform of the so-called "bloody code" took place. The death penalty was applied only to murder. Much of the religion-based opposition to the death penalty evaporated except among Quakers and a few Anglicans. By the mid-1880s, reform included specification of first- and second-degree murder (which further proportionalized capital punishment) and ending of public executions (Potter, 1993).

Where political, social, and economic issues intersected with religion, the results were interesting. For example, the Archbishop of Canterbury, Geoffrey Fisher, took the position that while the death penalty was not a deterrent, it was a "denunciation" and was necessary to preserve the capitalistic state. Sidney Silverman, a Jewish Member of Parliament and an abolitionist, after reading Fisher's views on capitalism and capital punishment, referred to him as "the Archbishop of Cant" (Collins, 1965).

International tensions, perception of threat, and the increasing reinforcement of aggressive behavior which occur before wars break out seem to encourage the use of capital punishment. The periods before World War I and II were characterized by reduced enthusiasm for the abolition of the death penalty (Collins, 1965). Interestingly, support for capital punishment continued and increased immediately after World War II (Collins, 1965), perhaps reflecting the emergence of the largely contrived Cold War and its tensions (Swomley, 1970).

Historical foundations in the U.S. began with the early years of settlement. The Pilgrims and Puritans of New England brought with them capital punishment using a variety of methods and a tradition of selective implementation. The more vulnerable groups included women, Quakers, slaves (blacks), and indentured servants (disenfranchised whites). Throughout the colonial period, the death penalty was used to control the sexuality of women and to limit freedom of speech that confronted existing values. Imposition of the penalty was a public event, accompanied by a great deal of carousing, the liberal use of alcohol, and, not infrequently, subsequent misbehavior. Although desecration of the Sabbath was a capital crime, corporal punishments, some of which resulted in death, were forms of Sunday entertainment for an otherwise unoccupied public. Even children were a vulnerable class, with status offenses (slapping one's parent, incorrigibility, disobedience to parent or teacher) punishable by death. Methods of execution included not only hanging, but also severe whippings, along with "burning, boiling, and beheading" (Cahill, 1994).

The first execution occurred in 1608. There were 50 capital crimes in the Colonies, including witchcraft, vagrancy, and manstealing. In Virginia, there were five capital crimes for whites and 70 for blacks. Inter-state variation has been the rule. In 1794, Pennsylvania had the death penalty only for first-degree murder, with no public executions. In 1846, Michigan abolished the death penalty except for treason. Four major trends emerged over time: (1) the reduction of crimes classified as capital, (2) the reduction of cruelty through improved technology, (3) attempts through law to impose a rational framework on the process, and (4) the sanitizing of executions (Costanzo and White, 1994).

Legal Factors

Table 16.1 provides some recent legal history. The decisions clearly illustrate the initial focus on defendants' rights and the more current focus on protection of procedure and reduction of defendants' options.

Social factors impact upon and direct the administration of capital justice through both informal and formal means. For example, the wording of the Ohio statute includes among aggravating specifications fleeing the scene of a crime or killing in the course of a felonious activity — characteristics which happen to be those more likely to be present in the life of a young, black, inner-city resident than in the life of a white, middle-class citizen. In effect, the statute itself defines an arena where the probability of occurrence favors black males (Hilliard, 1982). Although more subtle, the current code is consistent with the early legislative traditions that specified more capital crimes for blacks than for whites.

It is also noteworthy that while the Furman v. Georgia (1972) decision represented a breakthrough in the use of social science research by the Supreme Court, a review of 28 capital punishment cases between 1986 and 1989 showed that during that period, the Court discredited or discounted social science research rather than relied upon it (Acker, 1993).

Cross-National Aspects

Capital punishment has been theorized to fulfill various functions. It has been present in all cultures at some point, where it has served such purposes as legitimizing political power during periods of formation and stabilization of a nation state, resolving issues between power holders in tribal situations, and ensuring the survival of the group (Otterbein, 1986). Boehm (1984) developed the thesis with regard to group survival that the death penalty can be a form of ostracism. By killing a clan member, the group distanced itself from the behavior of that member. Such an execution eliminated the need of another clan to carry out vengeance, ending the cycle of reciprocal interclan violence.

Honor-, tribal-, or feud-based issues continue to lead to executions. In Afghanistan, members of fundamentalist Islamic groups, who control in what is a state of virtual anarchy, recently executed two men for murder. The right to do so was based on family relationship to the victims (Yusufzai, 1996).

All European countries have abolished the death penalty, usually after a prolonged period of decreasing use and narrowing of enabling legislation. For example, France, in 1789, had 115 capital crimes but by 1960 had only six. Jury nullification resulted in

Table 16.1

Select Capital Cases, 1968 to Present

Case Name	Year	Content
Witherspoon v. Illinois (391 U.S. 510)	1968	State's rights limited in regard to the exclusion of jurors from capital crimes
Furman v. Georgia (408 U.S. 238)	1972	All death penalty statutes ended on the basis of arbitrary application among other things, but the constitutionality of the death penalty remained.
Gregg v. Georgia (428 U.S. 153)	1976	The issue of constitutionality of the death penalty penalty was again maintained.
Woodson v. N. Carolina (428 U.S. 280)	1976	Mandatory death penalties did not meet constitutional tests.
Coker v. Georgia (433 U.S. 584)	1977	Crimes not involving murder were eliminated.
Lockett v. Ohio (438 U.S. 586)	1978	Mitigation must be broadly construed rather than minimally specified.
Godfrey v. Georgia (446 U.S. 420)	1980	Heinousness was maintained as a capital specification, but the need for clear definitions was supported in principle.
Enmond v. Florida (458 U.S. 782)	1982	The reversal held that Enmond was not directly responsible and focused on the issue of intent.
Barefoot v. Estelle (463 U.S. 880)	1983	In spite of a pending appeal, the Supreme Court refused to stay the execution on the basis that such action would encourage the misuse of the process to defeat the death penalty.
Pulley v. Harris (465 U.S. 376)	1984	The absence of a proportionality review did not invalidate a state's law.
Ford v. Wainwright (477 U.S. 699)	1986	Execution of a legally insane defendant was not permitted. States must therefore establish procedures for determining sanity and, by extension, competency to die.
Lockhart v. McCree (476 U.S. 162)	1986	Death qualification of jurors does not invalidate the trial process.
McCleskey v. Kemp (581 U.S. 279)	1987	The presence of social science data indicating racial disparities does not invalidate the use of the penalty which must be evaluated in terms of whether racism occurred in the instant case.
Booth v. Maryland (482 U.S. 496)	1987	Victim impact statements are not to be used in the presentation of evidence to the jury.
Thompson v. Oklahoma (47 U.S. 815)	1988	Persons under the age of 16 may be executed only if there is a state statute expressly permitting same.
Penry v. Lynaugh (492 U.S. 302)	1989	Mental retardation is not in and of itself a barrier to execution but must be considered in mitigation.
Payne v. Tennessee (501 U.S. 808)	1991	Victim impact statements are permissible in the course of trial.

few actual impositions, and the penalty was subsequently abolished. Other Western countries abolished the penalty either *de jure* (by law) or *de facto* (in practice) in the 19th or early 20th century (Laurence, 1960).

The situation in Russia reflected an interesting history that clearly combined political with criminal justice concerns. Historically, capital punishment was used to deal with political dissent and constituted a form of state-supported terrorism. It was particularly in evidence during the last years of the Czarist rule and in the early years of the Bolshevik regime when white Russians and counter-revolutionaries were viewed as major threats (Brown, 1996). The "show trials" (public admissions of guilt and immediate executions) as well as the terroristic use of the penalty in Stalin's purges made capital punishment a synonym for totalitarian and illegitimate social control (Schein, 1961). Organized crime increased in importance as a factor in public consciousness in the late Brezhnev years and is a contemporary major source of concern, especially with the period of near anarchy that ensued following the ending of the Soviet system.

Within Russia, attitudes toward capital punishment among the intelligentsia, and probably also the public at large, involve much ambivalence and complexity, perhaps because the penalty has so overtly served both political and crime control purposes. In an interesting twist, the government's preference for maintaining capital punishment as a last resort (McPherson, 1994) was confronted by the European Convention (EC), which refuses admission to any nation imposing the death penalty. As a part of petitioning for membership in the EC, Yeltsin signed a decree to phase out the penalty gradually (Brown, 1996).

Japan retains the death penalty. Predictably, capital punishment became a focus when the Aum Supreme Truth cult was involved in acts of terrorism including a lethal gas attack on a Tokyo subway and a plan to mass produce nerve gas. One cultist admitted having committed murder, claiming that he was ordered to perform the act by the guru, Shoko Asahara. It was anticipated that the legal system would consider social and psychological factors, along with religious aspects, as part of evaluating the capital cases involved ("Aum's terrorist plans...", 1996; Mitsuta, 1996).

As has been generally true of westernized countries imposing the death penalty, Japanese citizens have mixed opinions as to its appropriateness. With the emergence of cult-based terrorism, that debate was enhanced by anxiety of the community on the one hand and, on the other, the commitment to end violence that emerged post-Hiroshima and World War II. While Japan renounced using aggression in acts against other nations, within its own boundaries, 550 of its citizens have been put to death. In a published debate series, the usual reasons for opposing capital punishment — morality, possibility of executing an innocent — were present along with more systemic concerns about police brutality, 60-day incommunicado detention, and judicial deference to prosecution (Matsumoto, 1996).

The use of capital punishment in China has long been a feature of its legal landscape. By 1996, social changes, the introduction of limited capitalism, and the emergence of social protest were co-occurring. An anti-crime push called "Strike Hard" resulted in the application of the death penalty to 1000 persons. Prior to the partial opening of China to involvement with the West in the late 1970s, there was little crime, and totalitarian control was relatively entrenched. "Strike Hard" confronted a return of criminal activity including gangs, murders, robberies, and rapes similar to that seen in China prior to Communism. The heavy use of the death penalty was to serve both practical and political purposes. Implementation was immediate, often within days or weeks of a finding of guilt, which was a *pro forma* approval of the findings of investigation. Nonetheless, there was no apparent impact on the crime rate (Tyler, 1996).

TABLE 16.2

DEATH PENALTY PROPORTIONALITY STATISTICS

Victim Ethnic Identification	Defendant Identification: Black	White	Latino	Native American	Other	Total
Black	38	4	0	0	0	42
White	39	74	2	1	1	117
Latino	0	0	0	1	0	1
Native American	0	0	0	0	0	0
Unknown	3	2	0	0	1	6
Other	4	0	0	0	0	4
Total	84	80	2	2	2	170[a]

[a] 169 males were on death row; however, one defendant was serving two death sentences.

Racism

Radelet and Pierce's 1985 study evaluated the processing of 1017 Florida cases from the years 1973 to 1977. The defendant-victim-race combination impacted upgrade (to capital levels) vs. downgrade (straight murder or second-degree murder) charging decisions in racist directions. Plea bargains were less likely to occur under conditions where the defendant was black and the victim was white. In 1989, Radelet examined 15,978 executions in the U.S. and identified only 30 cases in which whites were executed for crimes against blacks. Factors that played a part in this phenomenon included the fact that for a period of time, blacks could not testify against whites regardless of what information they might have had. Other constraints built into the law clearly favored death penalty outcomes for black against white crimes and held the opposite to be of less consequence. Evaluation of the 30 cases also showed the sex of the victim (female) to be a factor. The category with the highest frequency (n = 10) involved execution for crimes that harmed slaves; execution thus served the purpose of supporting the institution of slavery and protecting property. Analysis of some of these cases also showed other economic factors. Generally, the defendants were of lower socio-economic origin. Extreme heinousness of the crime was not a statistically important factor in determining whether white on black crime merited the death penalty (Radelet, 1989; Radelet and Pierce, 1985).

Patterning consistent with Radelet's work has been found elsewhere. For example, Ekland-Olsen (1988) studied types of crimes as well as the races of offenders. Results indicated that the proportionately most over-represented cases were rape-homicides with a black offender and white victim. The most under-represented cases involved robbery-homicides with a black offender and black victim.

As indicated in Table 16.2, recent statistics from the office of the Ohio Public Defender illustrate the same trends. Reviews of overall homicide statistics show that these proportions do not reflect population base rates.

Alternative interpretations of findings such as these have been presented. Rothman and Powers

(1994) suggested that these patterns did not reveal racism in society, but rather actual differences in the qualities of crimes committed. It was their thesis that black on white crime is, in general, qualitatively more heinous than black on black crime and that there is so little white on black crime that its qualitative factors cannot be identified and generalized. As support, they cited the testimony of Joseph Katz, prosecution expert in the McCleskey v. Kemp (1987) case. During the 1980s, Baldus et al. (1990) completed a massive study commissioned by the National Association for the Advancement of Colored People. Results were cited in McCleskey's defense and then rebutted by Katz, who reported that the 11% death penalty rate for Georgia blacks with white victims (as compared to the 1% for blacks with black victims) was due to the former having more aggravating specifications. (It is noteworthy that Rothman and Powers omitted any mention of the available and relevant studies by Radelet and colleagues, which showed the charging process to be impacted racially.)

Mental Health Issues

The mentally ill have always comprised an outgroup that threatens the comfort level of any society in which they exist. At the same time, the exculpatory nature of mental illness, when it comes to penalties for crimes committed where reason was impaired, is also a long-standing tradition formally stemming from M'Naghten in 1843 in English law tradition. A landmark decision in this area is Ford v. Wainwright (1986), in which the Supreme Court, in a very limited way, exempted mentally ill death row inmates from execution. It did not address whether mental illness should eliminate defendants from capital punishment, and it opened up the questions of competency and restoration. However, a flawed system is not repaired through moral and ethical error. The evaluator at this level must render a statement about the cognitive capacity of the defendant to manage legal requirements and intervene in any deficit through therapeutic/educative techniques. The role is not dissimilar to that of obtaining emergency medical intervention to arouse an overdosed defendant so that he may only a few hours later be executed in a fully aware state ("A doomed inmate...", 1995).

As an example, along with three others, Alvin Ford, a black male, attempted to rob a restaurant. Their plans did not work, and Ford's confederates fled without him. In a panic, he shot and killed a white police officer. Initially alert and able to assist his trial and appeals counsel, Ford's mental illness manifested after several years' incarceration on death row and left him unable to provide any reasonable input to his own case (Miller and Radelet, 1993).

Ford died on February 28, 1991, allegedly of acute pancreatitis. Miller and Radelet's (1993) review of the Ford case showed it to be flawed in many respects, procedurally and factually, as well as to reflect an individual who was seriously dysfunctional. However, the importance of this case did not lie in its individual characteristics, but in the issue that it raised and illustrated (Miller and Radelet, 1993).

Whereas Ford and his attorneys worked to obtain a reversal, there are many defendants who seek their own executions. It is not uncommon for persons on death row to become demoralized, depressed, and actively mentally ill while awaiting execution. Even those who maintain rationality and who, in actuality, may not have committed the crimes can reach a point of asking to be put to death ("Death penalty focus...", 1993). The death penalty as state-assisted suicide represents a combination of social, psychological, and other factors. In any case of that sort, the competency issue is never fully resolved in a fashion that eliminates serious potential error.

The case of Anthony Apanovitch of Ohio is illustrative. He has been on death row since 1984 for rape and murder. The prosecutor admitted that there was a lack of physical evidence but pursued the death penalty when Apanovitch refused a plea offer. Even though he wants to be exonerated, he states that he would rather die than continue to fight indefinitely (Rice, 1991).

A different picture presents for those who, like David Mason, have been mentally ill and chronically suicidal and have long histories of documented violent behavior. Mason killed four elderly persons. While in jail before his trial, he killed his cellmate. His personal history included massive physical and sexual abuse with serious suicidal attempts beginning at age 5 ("Execution crisis!", 1993). Execution of such persons would ensure no further violent acts on their part. Given the higher degree of certainty for aggression that pertains in such cases, some rational basis for the death penalty can be asserted. However, execution based, in part, mental illness seems inconsistent with the long-standing premise that such conditions either exculpate from criminal responsibility or at least mitigate the degree of warranted punishment.

Mumia Abu-Jamal (1994), a Pennsylvania death row inmate, citing statistics from the National Coalition to Abolish the Death Penalty, pointed out what for him was a curious racial imbalance in the death-demanding population. Of about 2600 people on death row at the time of his article, whites constituted about 51%, but of the 26 people requesting that they be put to death, 21 (80%) were white. Abu-Jamal believes imprisonment, including on death row, has become for black males a kind of society, but that the same setting for white males is an expulsion from meaningful existence. His argument is flawed in that it presumes that the only relevant factors leading to the racial imbalance come from the death row experience rather than deriving from other sources. For example, whites are significantly underrepresented on death row and blacks overrepresented. It may be that proportionately fewer highly disturbed personalities are preselected among blacks, but that such personal deviance is more frequently found among whites. Nonetheless, Abu-Jamal's more general point that life on "the row" leads to depression and enhanced suicide potential is well taken.

On the other hand, and perhaps illustrating that the death penalty admits of no good solutions to its defects, there was the French case of 1958. James French demanded death, did not receive it, and subsequently murdered his cellmate in order to return to court and argue for his own execution (White, 1991).

In the absence of empirical data, another case example may illustrate many of the common presenting factors.

Case Illustration

It is generally agreed that Wilford Berry, who killed Cleveland banker Charles Mitroff, has the best chance of being the first person to be executed in Ohio since 1963. Throughout the legal proceedings, Berry has sought his own execution. When arrested, he agreed to cooperate with the police, provided he was given the death sentence; when he went to trial, he refused to assist his own counsel and personally asked the jury to impose a death sentence. He requested that there be no appeals. Questions of his competency were confronted by his apparent rationality. He clearly understood the legal system and acted to influence it in a purposive manner, with the aim of achieving his own death. At trial, for example, he did the one thing that would almost guarantee a death sentence — he told the jury he would kill them if they did not kill him.

Berry has a history of suicidal intent since he was 11 years of age, including 10 documented attempts. At the age of 14, he was diagnosed as having a severe schizoid personality disorder, for which he had never received proper treatment. His father was admitted three times to a psychiatric hospital for the criminally insane with a diagnosis of schizophrenia, paranoid type. His mother was described as having significant psychological difficulties ("Commute Wilford Berry...", 1996; Fulmer, 1997). Berry's death wish was a step closer to becoming reality as of June 16, 1997, when a post-conviction appeal based on competency was turned down. In that hearing, he was ruled competent to waive all rights to appeal to higher authority (Ewinger, 1997).

It is perhaps an ultimate irony that a "political correctness" argument has been offered for executing the mentally retarded. Calnen and Blackmun (1992) took the position that it impairs the ability of the mentally retarded to participate fully in society unless they have the same vulnerability to execution as do all other members. Their argument ignores the fact that persons with developmental defects are subject to influence and manipulation by aggressive peers, which is not an unusual scenario with a retarded offender.

The Issue of Innocence

In 1936, Richard Hauptmann died in the New Jersey electric chair, a victim of prewar hysteria, media frenzy, German ethnic identity, and suppressed exculpatory evidence (Bryan, 1996). Bedau and Radelet (1987) investigated the factor of innocence and determined that since 1900, at least 23 people have been executed who were later found to have not committed the specified crimes. Their criteria were purposely conservative and included only cases in which there was evidence that the defendant did not commit the homicide or rape or that the act specified never occurred. To be eligible for either of those categories, crimes were selected on the basis of the following types of evidence: (1) legislated indemnification or compensation for wrongful conviction, (2) executive pardon, (3) state decisions indicating significant error, (4) judicial indemnity, (5) reversals and appeals with either no re-trial attempted by the prosecution or an acquittal upon re-trial, (6) confession by another individual or another individual implicated, (7) public statements made by state officials, and (8) subsequent scholarly judgment. In 88% of the cases selected, there was official recognition of error in the processing of the case. The above categories were not mutually exclusive and most cases fulfilled several of them. Using these criteria, Bedau and Radelet found over 400 people who were convicted of capital crimes (though not necessarily given the ultimate penalty) in the context of overzealous prosecution, false testimony of witnesses, and police coercion. Their original study caused enough of a stir that two officials rebutted it — Markman (Assistant Attorney General, Office of Legal Policy, U.S. Department of Justice) and Cassell (Special Assistant, U.S. Attorney).

In their article, the best Markman and Cassell (1988) could do was acknowledge that there may, in fact, have been 23 people executed without cause and argue that this was such a small error that it validated the death penalty. It was their opinion that dangerous people who would have committed further crimes were eliminated, thus saving many more innocent lives than the 23 that were lost in the process (Markman and Cassell, 1988). This effort to silence or otherwise reduce the impact of the work of Bedau and Radelet clearly did not work. Not only did Bedau and Radelet (1988) have the opportunity to reply to the criticisms, but they subsequently published a book in which the case histories of many of these people were grouped by category and made available to the general public (Bedau et al., 1992).

As with most aspects of capital punishment, there is an interaction of individual case-related factors with racial, social, and environmental issues that raises the likelihood of injustice. Thus, Huff et al. (1996), in their review of wrongful convictions, noted that prosecutors' need to process cases efficiently, the inherent fallibility of eyewitness testimony which is measurably increased in cross-racial situations, media exposure, and aroused public opinion all combine to raise the vulnerability of innocent defendants from socially disapproved groups to receive the severest penalties, including death.

Characteristics of the Application of the Death Penalty

As of this writing, the oldest man on death row in the U.S. is Ray Copeland, born in 1914. He is hard of hearing, disorganized, and barely competent. Unkind and macabre jokes are made about him by the guards. On the same death row is Keith Wilkins, one of the youngest offenders. His background is the typical one of major abuse, suicide attempts prior to the age of 10, and improper legal procedures.

Copeland claims to be innocent of the murders for which he was given the death penalty and carries around a batch of papers to support his position. The fact picture from the crime involved Copeland and his wife killing several persons over a period of time and appropriating the victims' property. Mention of his wife, now deceased, reduces him to tears (Trombley, 1992). At the other end of the age spectrum is Keith Wilkins, the subject of the Supreme Court's 1989 Wilkins v. Missouri decision. Wilkins' background includes his being beaten by his mother and father and then his mother's boyfriend during the first 8 years of his life. He began committing minor delinquencies in early childhood. At the age of 10, he attempted to murder his mother and her boyfriend and was sent to a mental institution. He made the first of three suicide attempts at that point. He was diagnosed as a schizotypal personality. He was treated with psychotropic medication and wound up in institutions for most of his life. He was living on the streets at the time he committed the murder for which he received a death sentence. His purpose was to obtain money to buy a motorbike. Now on death row, he professes conversion to Christianity and maintains that the murder was a fourth suicidally motivated act in which he had decided to let the state kill him. At the time of his trial, he was allowed to dismiss his appointed attorney and argue his own case. He chose not to have a jury and asked for the death penalty. The Wilkins v. Missouri decision denied an appeal which argued that the youthful age of the offender met the criteria for cruel and unusual punishment (Trombley, 1992).

Content of United States Death Penalty Statutes

The author reviewed all U.S. death penalty statutes for content in several areas, including mitigating and aggravating specifications. Results are shown in Tables 16.3 and 16.4. With respect to the mitigating factors, the most popular ones are no prior criminal history, extreme emotion or a lesser *mens rea*, youthfulness of the defendant, duress, participation/facilitation by the victim, and the defendant's minor role in the crime. Review of the content for aggravating factors indicated the most popular of these specifications to be that the victim was a law enforcement official, the murder was heinous, the murder was for hire, the defendant had a history of violence or homicide, and the defendant was viewed as a risk to others. The most common aggravating specification (victim was a law enforcement official), did not reflect any aspect of the crime, but rested entirely upon a victim characteristic.

Among the "popular" aggravating characteristics was risk of reoffending. That factor is also unrelated to the crime and is something that neither juries nor highly trained mental health specialists can specify at high levels of confidence. Nonetheless, some statutes and many courts and juries focus on recidivism in sentencing decisions. As a result, an individual may be charged with a capital crime on the basis of a factor which cannot be strongly supported, and then at the end point that same potentially flawed judgment may again play a part, including being mandated as part of a decision-tree scheme for sentencing recommendations. Finally, by virtue of the legislated aggravating specifications, the usually prohibited presentation of prior acts is introduced into the case at bar.

In the meantime, the more common mitigators are qualities that often define non-death penalty cases as opposed to capital crime, and thus may be in short supply in the capital case population. It is features such as these which facilitate arbitrary or prejudicial applications of the penalty.

The Heinousness Concept

Since the Furman decision (1972), the concept of heinousness has been held out as a justification for

Table 16.3

Categories of Aggravating Factors in All State Death Penalty Statutes

Characteristic		Number of Statutes Represented
1.	Victim characteristics	
a.	Nonpersonal identification as in law enforcement, government or other official, inmate status	25
b.	Crime related: victim was witness	9
c.	Personal quality, including status as child, elder, infirm, or pregnant	7
2.	Crime characteristics	
a.	Murder for hire or by agreement	26
b	Felony murder or murder to escape	25
c.	Heinous murder	23
d.	Specifications generally definitive for heinousness as in torture, poisoning, sexual murder, gratuitous violence	17
e.	Mass murder (2 or more victims)	12
f.	Murder with kidnaping	11
g.	Murder with arson or explosives	10
h.	Other (gang related, racial, ambush, drug related)	10
i.	Terroristic acts, including hijacking, hostage-related, train wrecking	9
j.	Treason	2
3.	Defendant characteristics	
a.	History of murder	22
b.	Dangerousness	21
c.	History of violence or felony	21
d.	Prison status	14
e.	Depravity of mind	2
f.	Presence of plan to kill more than one	2

the use of the death penalty, even where its lack of deterrence value was considered. Heinousness implies a proportionality concept with the ultimate penalty reserved for the ultimate crimes. However, attempts at definition found in various statutes and case law decisions across the country do not provide clarity. Heinous murder has been defined as murder which takes place in a house of worship prior, during, or immediately after services (Illinois); causing the victim to go through a period of time where he or she is uncertain of the outcome (Walton v. Arizona, 1990); and killing by methods showing serious mutilation, dismemberment, or the presence of physical and mental pain before death occurs (Mississippi). The inadequacy of a legal definition itself has been treated inconsistently. Thus, on one hand, it was ruled that in a case where the defendant shot a woman in the legs, stabbed her, slit her throat, and killed her husband,

TABLE 16.4

CATEGORIES OF MITIGATING FACTORS IN ALL STATE DEATH PENALTY STATUTES

Category		Number of Statutes Represented
1.	Extreme emotion	25
2.	Age of defendant	25
3.	No significant prior history	24
4.	Duress, coercion, or domination of another	24
5.	Participation of the defendant was minor	24
6.	Lesser degree of *mens rea*	22
7.	Participation or facilitation by the victim; victim provoked defendant	19
8.	Any factors defendant believes mitigating	12
9.	Influence of drugs/alcohol	8
10.	Defendant is mentally retarded	8
11.	Character of defendant	7
12.	Circumstance of crime	6
13.	Defendant's cooperation with authority	4
14.	Defendant could not foresee grave risk potential	3
15.	Defendant believed the act was justified	3
16.	Likelihood of future dangerousness	2
17.	Other defendants equally culpable but not given the death penalty	1
18.	Defendant has rehabilitation potential	1

the sentence should be revised to life imprisonment because the definition of heinousness was too vague for the jury to find its presence (Maynard v. Cartwright, 1988). Nonetheless, in John v. Florida (1992), the Court held that the trial judge was able to apply the concept of heinousness even though decisions were inconsistent and the statute vague.

This author conducted a preliminary investigation into how people think about heinousness and how they may use the concept in capital cases. Results based on a sample of 54 capital indictments showed some potential for highly heinous ratings to be associated with death outcomes. However, raters' definitions of the concept and their applications reflected the same kinds of inconsistency seen in the legal literature (McPherson, 1997).

Penal authorities are no different. For example, when David Doughton, an Ohio appeals attorney, asked a state parole board official what type of murder would not be heinous and therefore not merit the death penalty, the only example given was an instance in which a man comes home, finds his wife in bed with another man, and shoots the man (Doughton, personal communication, 1996). Doughton (1996) pointed out that such a crime does not qualify as a capital offense.

Conflicts of Interest

Not surprisingly, the use of the death penalty may take place in a context of competing and sometimes questionable motives or goals. There is now confirmation that China's pattern of 4000 executions per year continues and that healthy condemned criminals are selected for special care, assuring a source of organ donations. Aiming guns at the cerebellum and administering anticoagulant drugs are among the procedures which assure the usefulness of harvested kidneys. The organs are preordered on the international market, including the U.S., and are available to high officials in China. The medical equipment used and the facility where the operations are conducted were part of a joint venture between a U.S. company and China (Schwartz, 1997).

The specter of personal gain is raised in the case of Larry Lonchar. In Georgia, it was planned to file a federal lawsuit which would support the desire to emulate China's organ farming. If successful, ailing Detective Melvin Cobb could receive a kidney from Lonchar, one of his own death row cases (Rose, 1996).

The same source provided a further illustration of how Georgia deals with conflicts of interest. While vigorously supporting and implementing the death penalty, Georgia officials deferred to international sensitivities and chose to place a moratorium on executions so as to look good during the Olympic games (Rose, 1996).

Overall Statistical Trends

Since 1930, the U.S. government has provided statistical information on the application of the death penalty. Recent data from the U.S. Department of Justice are presented in Figures 16.1 and 16.2, and Tables 16.5 and 16.6. Figure 16.1 illustrates the reduction in absolute numbers of executions carried out in the U.S. since 1930. Figure 16.2 shows that although the current and increasing number of executions has not reached the 1955 level, the population on death row is rising rapidly, probably a result of increased appeals activity. Tables 16.5 and 16.6 provide information regarding demographic characteristics of defendants.

Additional analyses were made of geographic factors by race, sentencing outcomes, and other relevant social and historical dimensions. The data showed that the use of the death penalty was increasing in the U.S., that there was a disproportionate application of the penalty to minority groups and those of lower socio-economic status, and that significant numbers of reversals occurred of convictions and sentences. Reversals were on both procedural/technical and substantive grounds.

Elapsed time from the point of sentencing to execution has increased from 1977 to 1994. The death rate on death row other than by execution was approximately 4%, representing nearly 30% of those who died, the others having been executed. Significant numbers of younger people are found on the nation's death rows, which is a violation of United Nations resolutions regarding capital punishment (General Assembly Resolution 2857, 1971; Council Resolution, 1984/50, 1984).

A review of statutory changes occurring during 1995 indicated that 19 (50%) of the capital punishment laws were altered as follows. Ten of those changes involved the addition of new crimes, including, in two cases, the purposeful discharge of a firearm from a vehicle resulting in someone's death. Such a crime would not necessarily involve premeditation. Two changes involved the addition of the young age of the victims, 16 and 13, respectively, as an aggravating specification. Murder to interfere with First Amendment rights, murder with "object sexual penetration", and murder involving mutilation of a corpse or during child abuse were added aggravating factors. In only one case was there an increase in the difficulty of meeting capital criteria rather than a reduction — namely, a move from felony involvement to

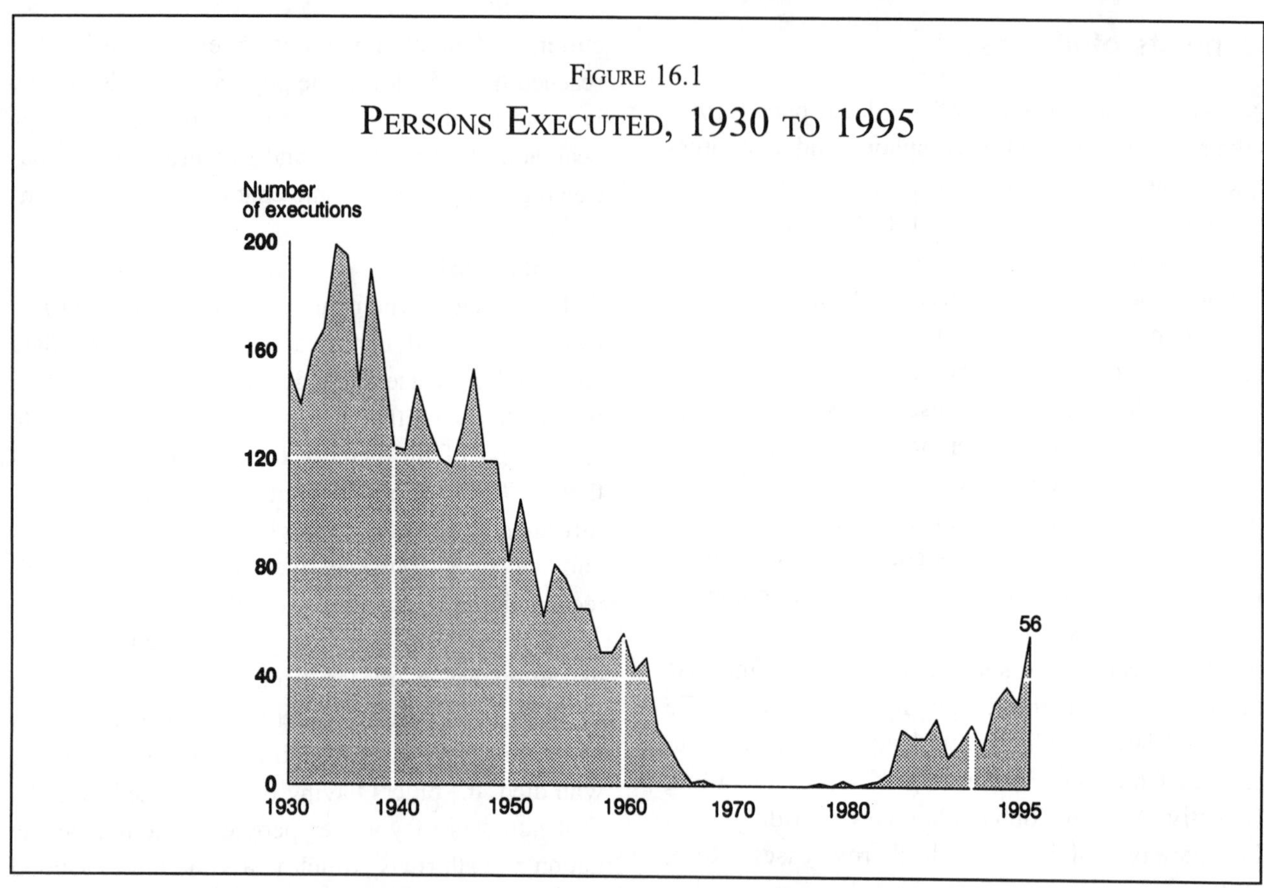

Source: Snell, T.L. (1996) Capital punishment 1995. In *Bureau of Justice Statistics Bulletin* (NCJ-162043), U.S. Department of Justice, Office of Justice Programs, December, p. 2.

knowing involvement as an aggravating factor. Procedures were changes in 13 statutes. Most of the procedural changes facilitated the imposition of the death penalty, such as reducing time limits and, in one case, allowing a defendant to waive the statutory stay of execution that allows the filing of appeals. Three of the changes favored presentation of victim impact testimony. There was one instance (Ohio) where the already mandated state Supreme Court review of cases was specified to include a weighing of aggravating vs. mitigating factors and a proportionality consideration. Finally, there were five changes in the method of execution, all reflecting a preference for lethal injection.

Consistent with minority over-representation, Native Americans constituted almost 2% of the death row inmates, but actually represent less than 1% of the U.S. population. An analysis of this over-representation revealed that in the 14 states where Native Americans were on death row, Florida was the only state in which their numbers approximated the population statistics. One state, Arizona, had a slightly lesser proportion (3% on death row vs. 4.4% of the population), which likely reflected the fact that most of the Native Americans in Arizona live on reservations, where the death penalty does not apply. Analyses of these cases showed that over 70% involved an individual who was a substance abuser and under the influence of alcohol, drugs, or both, at the time of the crime. The usual histories of neglect, loss, and poverty pertained, and there was a tendency to be from tribes not represented in the locale; thus, the cultural

FIGURE 16.2

PERSONS UNDER SENTENCE OF DEATH, 1955 TO 1995

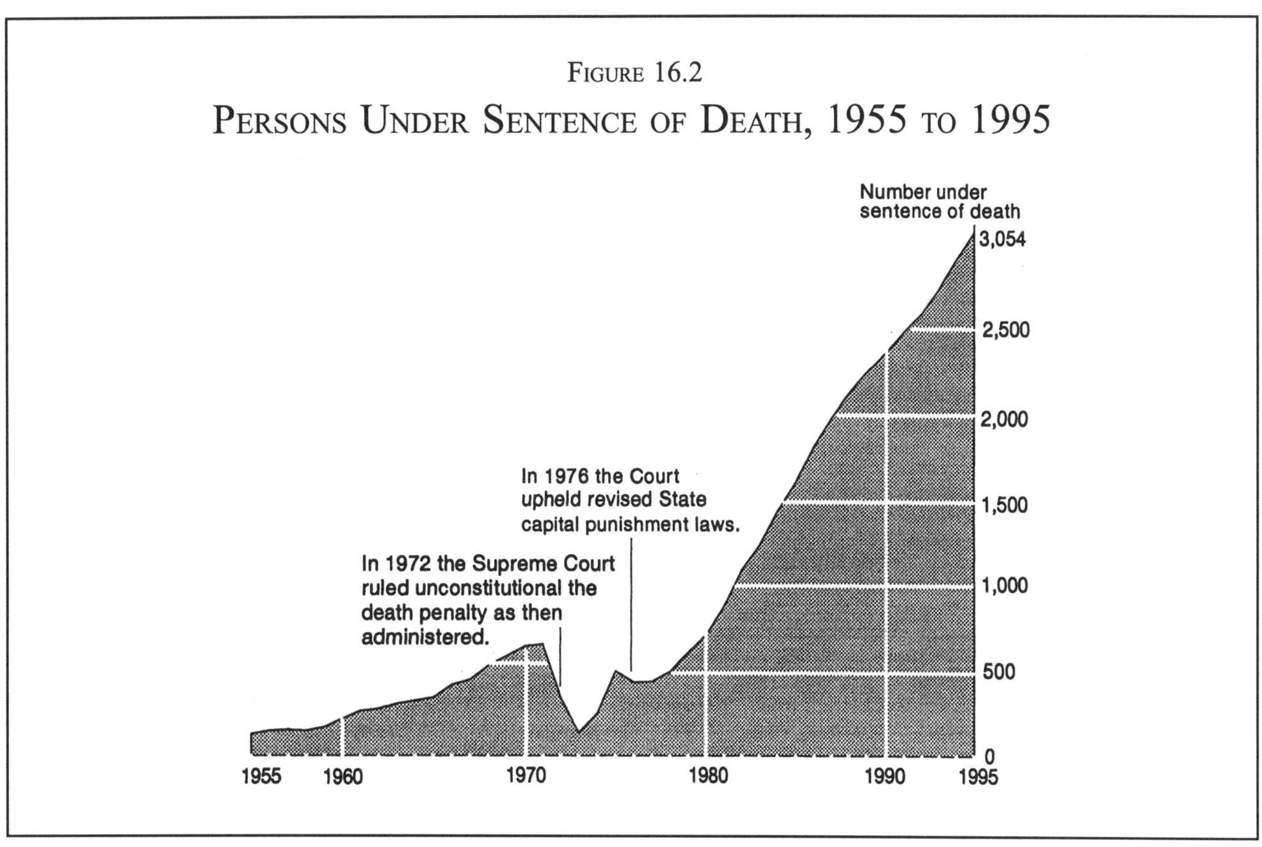

Source: Snell, T.L. (1996) Capital punishment 1995. In *Bureau of Justice Statistics Bulletin* (NCJ-162043), U.S. Department of Justice, Office of Justice Programs, December p. 12.

support of the group was not available to the individual (Hart, 1996).

One of the more serious inequities in the capital punishment scene occurred as a function of the interaction of federal and state law. In 1991, there was an attempt to extend the federal death penalty to Indian reservations. Had that bill passed, a murder committed on an Indian reservation by a Native American and a non-Native American would have involved differential liabilities. The Native American would have been vulnerable to the death penalty; the non-Native American would have been processed by the state, which, in some cases, would mean a jurisdiction with no death penalty. The exclusionary clause to that legislation, however, created the opposite inequity. In a state which has the death penalty, the two hypothetical defendants referenced above would be treated differently, with the non-Native American being vulnerable to the death penalty, and the Native American exempt unless the tribal authority elects the federal death penalty (Hart, 1996).

Ohio Death Penalty Cases

Some investigations into relevant characteristics of Ohio (the author's home state) death penalty cases were conducted, including reviews of newspaper clipping files and the post-conviction relief petitions archived by the State Public Defender. Newspaper clipping files were available for 187 cases, most involving persons currently on death row. In a few instances, the inmates had died or their status had

TABLE 16.5

DEMOGRAPHIC CHARACTERISTICS OF PRISONERS UNDER SENTENCE OF DEATH, 1995[a,b]

Characteristic	Year-End	Admissions	Removals
Number of prisoners	3054	310	161
Sex (%)			
Male	98.4	98.1	99.4
Female	1.6	1.9	.6
Race (%)			
White	56.6	54.2	56.5
Black	41.7	44.5	41.0
Other[c]	1.6	1.3	2.5
Hispanic origin (%)			
Hispanic	8.5	9.3	8.6
Non-Hispanic	91.5	90.7	91.4
Education (%)			
8th grade or less	14.7	12.1	21.8
9th–11th	37.2	41.5	42.3
High school graduate/GED	37.8	35.5	26.8
Any college	10.3	10.9	9.2
Median	11th grade	11th grade	11th grade
Marital status (%)			
Married	25.6	20.4	31.5
Divorced/separated	21.6	22.6	19.2
Widowed	2.5	2.6	2.1
Never married	50.3	54.4	47.3

[a] From Snell, T.L. (1996) Capital punishment 1995. In *Bureau of Justice Statistics Bulletin* (NCJ-162043), U.S. Department of Justice, Office of Justice Programs, December, p. 8.

[b] Calculations are based on those cases for which data were reported. Missing data by category were as follows:

	Year-end	Admissions	Removals
Hispanic origina	257	29	10
Education	422	62	19
Marital status	247	36	15

[c] At year-end 1994, "other" consisted of 24 Native Americans, 17 Asians, and 8 self-identified Hispanics. During 1995, 4 Asians were admitted; 2 Native Americans and 2 Asians were removed.

changed as a function of appeals. However, in all cases examined, there was an original charge, a subsequent conviction for a capital crime, and a recommendation of death.

Crime Characteristics

Out of the 187 cases examined, 34% (63) involved murder secondary to associated crimes, primarily burglary and robbery. An additional 16% involved

Table 16.6

Age at Time of Arrest for Capital Offense and Age of Prisoners Under Sentence of Death at Year-end 1995[a,b]

	Prisoners Under Sentence of Death			
	At Time of Arrest		On December 31, 1995	
Age	**Number[c]**	**Percent**	**Number[a]**	**Percent**
Number of prisoners	2661	100.0	2661	100.0
17 or younger	51	1.9	0	0
18–19	262	9.8	20	.8
20–24	741	27.8	257	9.7
25–29	626	23.5	428	16.1
30–34	441	16.6	556	20.9
35–39	272	10.2	575	21.6
40–44	137	5.1	343	12.9
45–49	77	2.9	261	9.8
50–54	34	1.3	125	4.7
55–59	13	.5	56	2.1
60 or older	7	.3	40	1.5
Mean age	28 yrs		36 yrs	
Median age	27 yrs		35 yrs	

[a] From Snell, T.L. (1996) Capital punishment 1995. In *Bureau of Justice Statistics Bulletin* (NCJ-162043), U.S. Department of Justice, Office of Justice Programs, December, p. 8.

[b] The youngest person under sentence of death was a white male in Nevada, born in January 1977 and sentenced to death in November 1994. The oldest person under sentence of death was a white male in Arizona, born in September 1915 and sentenced to death in June 1983.

[c] Excludes 393 inmates for whom the date of arrest for the capital offenses were not available.

murders, usually in association with such other crimes, but also with additional significant degrees of gratuitous violence, including mutilation of corpses and extensive beatings. Of the crimes, 15% involved sexual acts, including rape, mutilation, and torture; 13% were relationally based crimes. The remaining 22% of the murders involved drug transactions gone bad, attempts to avoid detection or to escape, murder of law enforcement officials, and murder with obsessional behavior. There were two serial killings and one murder for hire in which both the assassin and his "employer" who contracted the killing were placed on death row. One murder was a product of mental illness in which a man with a long-term psychiatric history opened fire in a library. Such characteristics as sexual rape, indiscriminate or non-rational violence (one defendant indicated he wanted to practice Special Forces techniques he had learned to see how effectively he could kill and chose his victims for no particular reason other than their availability), serial killing, murder for hire, and murders with gratuitous violence may well meet some subjective or intuitive notions of heinousness.

However, nearly 50% of the crimes did not include characteristics usually associated with the concept of heinousness as a special case of murders.

Victim Characteristics

Of the victims, 12%were biological relatives of the defendant or persons in current or former close relationships with the defendant, and 66% of the victims were killed during robberies, burglaries, or similar crimes. Eight of these were elderly females, three were older men, and six were elderly couples. Twenty-three victims were in family groups and were killed in what would be mass murder specifications as a function of some other crime. Eighteen of the victims were prison or law enforcement related personnel, including some prisoners as well as guards and police officers. Random violence where the victim was not selected for any characteristic occurred in 11 cases.

Offender Characteristics

Reviews of the background of death row inmates in Ohio showed the following to be common descriptors:

1. History of child abuse
2. History of alcoholism and drug abuse by parents
3. History of alcoholism and drug abuse by defendant beginning at or before adolescence
4. History of domestic violence, especially abuse of mother by father
5. History of early criminal and antisocial activity prior to the onset of adolescence, which then continued into adulthood
6. Lower socio-economic status
7. Minority group status

Post-Conviction Relief Petition Content

Post-conviction relief petitions (PCRPs) are filed as one of the rights of appeal in death penalty cases. A successful PCRP results in the case being returned to the trial court for a new hearing or, if denied, allows another door into the federal appeals process.

Forty-five recent PCRPs filed in the state of Ohio were available for review. These petitions addressed a variety of aspects and encompassed the entire trial process. The reviewers examined whether or not (1) evidence met the beyond a reasonable doubt standard of proof, (2) there was prosecutorial misconduct including withholding of exculpatory evidence, (3) the defendant was offered an opportunity to present all of the evidence in the defendant's favor, (4) the defendant had adequate resources and access to experts to evaluate evidence in the case in chief and to provide evidence and assistance at the mitigation stage, (5) undue publicity impeded a fair trial, (6) there was presentation of visual evidence (gruesome pictures) by the prosecution such that probative value was outweighed by prejudicial impact, and (7) the *voir dire* of jurors was adequate. The reviewers also looked at constitutional issues, especially referencing the cruel and unusual punishment factor with substantial information about the execution process often accompanying a presentation. (Commonly included, for example, were the 18 "botched" executions in the U.S. since 1985; three men had to be electrocuted three times each before they stopped reviving spontaneously.)

Analysis of these petitions indicated that some cases, but only a few, involved convictions on circumstantial evidence alone at a level that was highly questionable, with defendants continuing to maintain their innocence. It was frequently difficult to obtain records, with law enforcement agencies and other resources in the criminal justice system reluctant to provide information to defense counsel at both mitigation and post-conviction appeals levels. There were frequent indications of violations of defendants' rights. In what may have been technically adequate ways in some cases, the prosecution was allowed to enter evidence of prior acts unrelated to the charges involved, which potentially could have prejudiced the jury. There were several cases in which significant minority subculture issues were ignored that would have had a direct bearing on understanding not only the criminal, but the crime. For example, sudden violence on the part of Native Americans has been shown to be a frequent concomitant of alcohol-related problems. There were several instances of significant inadequacy of representation. In one case, defense counsel met with the defendant a total of three times. In that case, the court-appointed mitigation psychologist recommended to counsel that there be more lawyer-client involvement. The defendant had shown some inability to deal with legal concepts unless there was careful explanation. The advice to increase contact time was ignored.

In one case, the presiding judge systematically refused to allow defense objections to be registered for the record, threatened defense counsel with jail if protests continued, and insisted that the entire two-stage trial, including selection of jury, take place in a period of three days. According to a sworn affidavit, the judge stated in chambers during the course of the trial that he wanted to see the defendant's "nigger ass in the chair for messing with white women." In that case, the identification of the suspect depended upon the victim's death having occurred at a certain point; evidence that she was still alive and well a day later was suppressed. The mitigatory phase encompassed a period of 30 minutes (the defendant's appeals continue; he has been on death row since 1988).

In another case, the coroner was able to conclude that the victim was dead, but not that she had died from any identifiable foul play. However, upon later learning that the victim had been found in the nude in her bathroom, the coroner decided that the death was due to foul play. The defendant was alleged to have known Ted Bundy and therefore to have known how to kill people without foul play being obvious.

Some criticisms of the PCRPs can be made. They are advocacy products. Where the mitigatory facts were not adequate to convince the jury that aggravating factors were outweighed, petitions at times alleged that insufficient weight had been given to some factor, or presented a new factor belatedly discovered. Thus, in one case, the mitigation team was faulted for not having the subcultural knowledge that would have allowed a proper presentation of the impact of the defendant being a dark-skinned black rather than a light-skinned black. The notion was that this detail would have added to the weight of mitigating factors in a substantial fashion. Some of the petitions contained a great deal of essentially theoretical material about the sociology or social psychology of membership in certain groups. Equally powerful arguments can be made on either side of such issues where there is no direct connection to the crime at hand. There are no subcultures that condone the acts involved in these cases. On the other hand, subcultural factors need to be elicited and reported as part of mitigation data.

Political Applications

Perhaps the most serious nonstatutory determiners of decision-making in death penalty legislation and applications are political considerations. As already noted, capital punishment has frequently served political purposes. There is, for example, the contemporary expansion of death penalty legislation in the face of the current social enemy — terrorism.

Terrorism is generally considered to involve acts of individuals, groups, or national governments, the purposes of which are to make a statement to and to raise apprehension in a target population. The media plays an important if ambiguous and complex role in terroristic sequences, being used by both perpetrators to deliver their message and by victims to respond, often with enemy image projections that distract from the government's failure to protect or even its complicity in or contribution to the problems that led to the act (Picard, 1993).

The randomness of the violence and difficulty of prevention make terrorism a potent stimulus for defensive aggression by the public. Thus, in the early 1970s, as there was increasing awareness of regional terrorism, debates surfaced about the reintroduction of capital punishment in Israel (which has the death penalty only for persons convicted of certain Holocaust crimes) and Britain ("Or such less penalty", 1974; Sheleff, 1974; Weiler, 1974; "Must night fall?", 1975; "Reinstatement of capital punishment", 1975).

Terroristic acts often become a rationale for governments to assume power and reduce individual rights. In Israel, there is indefinite detention. The U.S., during World War II, set up the now infamous internment camps for Japanese Americans. More recently, there has been an expansion of capital legislation to meet political agendas. In 1970, the death penalty for fatal bombings went into effect in California ("Law that provides death penalty", 1970). By the 1980s, President Reagan was instructing Secretary of State Schultz to utilize "retribution and retaliation" to deal with terrorism (Wardlaw, 1982; Stohl, 1988).

Most recently, federal legislation has included the Violent Crime Control and Law Enforcement Act of 1994 and the Antiterrorism and Effective Death Penalty Act of 1996. The latter legislation targets immigrants and sets a precedent for suspension of legal rights to any person belonging to government-specified subversive groups. It also reduces *habeas corpus* rights for all state death row inmates, regardless of whether there was any terroristic connection.

From the standpoint of international comparisons, U.S. death penalty statutes include no political crimes, while in certain other notably totalitarian countries, the opposite has been true. Thus, the case of Mumia Abu-Jamal (detailed below), who is considered by many throughout the world to be a political prisoner of the U.S., did not involve charges or specifications of illegal political activism. Rather, Abu-Jamal was charged with the conventional criminal act of murder of a police officer, but his arrest, treatment, trial, and subsequent incarceration all involved significant references to his politics.

By contrast, Amnesty International (1984), in its evaluation of China's use of the death penalty, indicated significant statutory political applications. In 1983, the official count was 90,000 criminal cases processed, of which only 450 (.5%) were "counter-revolutionary" (e.g., political) crimes. Unofficial estimates were far higher, in some periods being upwards of 70%. In 1984, the categories of political prisoners included young people involved in the democratic movement, human rights violations protesters, Roman Catholic priests, Tibetan nationals in favor of religious or regional independence, alleged spies, and officials "holding wrong opinions". (There was also a variety of conventional crimes such as murder, rape, robbery leading to death or serious injury, drug trafficking, pimping, and "passing on methods of committing crime".)

Event Characteristics

It is in the implementation of the death penalty that the most bizarre and institutionally pathological characteristics can be found, along with some equally strange role players. Fred Leuchter, mentioned earlier, was a minor inventor, uncertified engineer, and death-obsessed personality. In and of himself, he is a major study. He designed the first electronic sextant and the helicopter mapping system used in Vietnam and then devised major improvements on electrocution, gassing, and lethal injection. Death penalty states have been his customers and his enemies. He served as an expert witness against the use of inadequate death technologies, perhaps as a marketing technique which backfired in that several Attorneys General became quite unhappy with his appearances and communicated the same.

His business at one point included a partner appropriately named Lynch. In one of the more colorful moments of his career, Leuchter agreed to be an expert witness in the Toronto trial of Ernst Zundel, a Holocaust revisionist and neo-Nazi. Leuchter's role was to evaluate the Nazi gas chambers in Poland and testify that they could not have been efficient enough to do the job. Leuchter claimed long after the trial that he was not a Nazi, but to little avail. The so-called Leuchter Report was carried worldwide and translated into 10 languages. Among his collection of macabre memorabilia is a picture of his son sitting in an electric chair (Trombley, 1992).

Leuchter's aberrations do not make him exceptional in a world where death is purposefully inflicted. The street slang of young criminals who commit random killings often involves their stating that they "did someone". The same phrase was used by two corrections personnel interviewed about their roles in execution. It was hard, they said, to "do someone" (Johnson, 1990).

In fact, any exposure to the violence of unnecessary death creates massive, significant psychological reactivity which reflects the unacceptability of such an event. Koopman et al. (1994) evaluated 15 journalists who observed an execution by gassing and 36 employees who observed a gunman shooting and fatally injuring eight persons. Both groups developed post-traumatic psychological symptomology, including dissociation, anxiety symptoms, and other stress markers.

In preparing armies, there is a great deal of propagandizing that dehumanizes the enemy in order to make it possible for the troops to engage in combat and for civilians to support the war effort (Keen, 1986; Silverstein, 1989). In the case of the administration of the death penalty, there is a "death protocol". The person in charge may be referred to as an "event coordinator". Code terminology that does not reflect the actual event is used for communication purposes. For example, in one setting, the physician who pronounces death simply says "number eight". The anomalous presence of a chaplain whose job is to prepare the inmate for death creates a role conflict that harkens back to years when early Christians were not allowed to participate in capital punishment. One death row chaplain stated that the presence of the ritual is what makes it possible for the procedure to be carried out (Trombley, 1992).

The ritual is essentially make believe. It incorporates a pretense of not assigning blame; thus, members of firing squads do not all have live ammunition in their guns. However, experienced marksmen know the difference between the firing of a gun with live bullets and with blanks and thus have to pretend not to know whether they fired a possibly lethal shot. Coping techniques are legion. Philip Hamma, a hangman, would take no pay for his work, but would accept a fifth of whiskey (Dicks, 1990).

An execution procedure is a fully documented template that details in semi-military fashion the time, place, and activity that will occur in the necessary sequence. In model form, one such protocol referred to the inmate as "Cain" which was another way of dehumanizing and distancing the inmate from the staff. Violations of the protocol cause immense anxiety and are avoided at all costs. It is particularly distressing if the inmate does not cooperate and go peacefully to his or her appointment (Trombley, 1992).

Any procedural problems cause consternation in "event management". Utah allows execution by firing squad, but has not done so since Gary Gilmore requested it in 1976. A current death penalty convict in Utah has fired his lawyer, dropped his appeals, and said that he will accept execution but only by firing squad. The building where Gilmore was shot has been razed, and authorities express considerable conflict regarding finding an appropriate setting (Carter, 1995).

Case Illustration

Perhaps the best case example of the politicization of the death penalty in the U.S. is that of Mumia Abu-Jamal. In 1981, after Pennsylvania had reenacted its death penalty statute, Abu-Jamal, a cab driver, came across a police officer beating Abu-Jamal's brother. Various accounts then diverged. At the end point, Abu-Jamal was shot, his brother was lying bleeding, and the police officer was dead. Abu-Jamal was subsequently beaten by the police when they arrived and again at the hospital. It was reported that a police officer standing guard in the hospital forced urine back into Abu-Jamal's body from the collection bag attached to the catheter, creating pain that woke him from unconsciousness. Abu-Jamal was known to be anti-establishment, and his trial involved a very different kind of justice than usual. He was not allowed to defend himself; he was often not allowed in the courtroom during his own trial. His assigned attorney was subsequently disbarred. The prosecutor's summation focused on Abu-Jamal's history of activism with the Black Panthers and quoted his writings. The prosecution's contention was that he should receive the death penalty because of his group membership and advocacy of unpopular positions. In the meantime, the evidence that led to his conviction included a confession which the police had not recorded, but later "remembered". If Abu-Jamal had, in fact, confessed, it was during the course of being beaten. Other witnesses recalled another man being responsible, though the adequacy of their reports would also be questionable.

Abu-Jamal continues to live on death row and to be at the center of controversy and the object of widespread international support for a re-trial ("Will the United States...", 1995; Henderson and Calahan, 1996). Political factors continue to impact on his case, with Abu-Jamal as well as his supporters now censored by National Public Radio in response to pressure from the Fraternal Order of Police and ex-Senator Robert Dole (Espada, 1997).

Is Abu-Jamal guilty? Entirely possible. Was his trial fair? Clearly, not. Can there be any real security in a society where politics and racism determine procedural aspects of justice? Certainly not.

Intervention

The death penalty is no different from many human institutions in that it is flawed and vulnerable to multiple uses and purposes. It is different, however, in its finality and specificity. Because it has served so many masters and sometimes multiple masters simultaneously, the vicissitudes of use and misuse have created a theater of the absurd.

As noted, the evidence for deterrence is mixed at best. Lester (1987) documented a slight reduction in homicides following executions but found it to be a "diminished return". In fact, studies have shown that violence indicators increase when the state functions as a model for killing. Western countries ended public executions because of the negative impact on behavior which was clearly perceived even at the time of Charles Dickens and reflected in satirical literature of that era (Collins, 1965).

Despite the efforts to define the death penalty as a specific remedy for specified problems, the ambiguity of language, along with complex psychological and social factors, provide a foundation for arbitrary and nonlegitimate applications. Thus, the interventions which seem indicated must look at all levels of social violence, from the factors that contribute to increased crime to the punishments imposed in consequence of the proscribed acts. The death penalty offers a threatened social group false confidence that there is control over the forces that apparently lurk nearby. Reducing perceptions of threat as well as addressing real social problems are part of the solution. The current trend to exclude media from the penal system (Hinckle, 1996) while not holding the media accountable for its inflammatory functions needs to be reversed in both aspects.

Irresponsible journalism may detail sordid individual behavior and demonize perpetrators. Such sensationalistic presentations and reportage may ultimately backfire and could conceivably increase violence in the society.

Silverstein's (1989) article on enemy images explored the influence of the media — both news and entertainment — on attitudes that support violence toward identified groups. The same mechanisms, including selective attention, skewed attributions, predictions of hostility, lowered empathy, objectification, and demonization, are found with respect to criminals viewed as deserving of the death penalty.

Serial killers are given significant focus in straight news stories and are also found in television movies, becoming larger than life. The greater the exposure, the more the public experiences an apparent threat to safety, in spite of no actual increases in this relatively rare phenomenon. Similarly, publicity is given to terrorist acts.

However, just as distorted images can support bad public policy, increased knowledge by the public may allow rejection of those policies and the installation of more positive and prosocial programming. For example, in the case of "Gangsta Rap", C. DeLores Tucker, a leader of the National Political Congress of Black Women, has engaged in an ongoing battle with the music world where she took action in some fairly creative ways (see also Schwartz and Matzkin, 1996). She bought stock in Time Warner and attended a meeting where she challenged its executives to read the lyrics from a number of popular groups. The lyrics in question glorified violent criminality and specifically interwove sexuality, aggression, and hatred of women into the lyrics. The executives stopped verbally supporting their product, but the contest is far from decided, with the music industry suing Tucker for attempting to subvert their business. Perhaps fittingly, one of the organizations filing those lawsuits was Death Row Records ("Battling the lyrics...", 1996).

Haines (1992) tracked reports of "flawed" executions. He surveyed eight major daily newspapers for the period 1979 through 1991. He categorized news items as to types of errors reported. Based on a theory that a suddenly apparent social inequity mobilizes reform movements, it was his thesis that execution mistakes or incongruities would lead the public to revise support for the death penalty. In effect, he hypothesized that by exercising the death penalty in a less than perfect fashion, the potential for reorganizing public perception and obtaining a revocation of the penalty would be raised. Haines identified four types of flawed executions, including the following: technical failure, prisoner role failure (departure from that of compliant victim), behavior in the death chamber inconsistent with solemnity, and execution of an innocent individual, especially where justice has been administered inconsistently. Events with these characteristics were judged to affront public sensibilities in such a way that support for the institution itself would be eroded.

Doughton's (personal communication, 1996) theory was that in any state where the death penalty is vigorously implemented, there will be negative reactions by decision-makers such that the number of capital cases will start to reduce spontaneously. This theory is perhaps augmented by economics in that in some states where many executions have occurred, there has been a move to reduce the use of, if not eliminate, the death penalty because managing costs has become unfeasible.

Ethical dilemmas, actual and potential, clearly exist for mental health professionals. There is the spectacle of Dr. Grigson's "100% accurate" testimony — "Dr. Death," as Grigson was dubbed, testified in Barefoot v. Estelle (1983) that his ability to forecast potential dangerousness was 100% accurate even when he had not directly examined the defendant. Given victim impact legislation, there is the possibility that a therapist for a grieving mother could be called to testify to the mother's state of mind as evidence against the defendant. In addition to potentially violating a given therapist's own scruples regarding participating in a capital proceeding, victim impact evidence of any kind refocuses the process from the defendant to the victim, thus canceling the Supreme Court's ruling in Furman (1972) and its later insistences on a process that reduces arbitrariness through a consideration of defendant characteristics (Leong et al., 1993).

In the meantime, as evidence that biological factors contribute to aggression has grown (see, for example, Patrick et al., 1993), the economic support for specialized evaluations has diminished. It is difficult, if not impossible, to obtain for indigent clients court authorized investigations into neurological status or other special medical or health related problems which may have relevance for the mitigatory phase.

Another aspect to consider from an intervention perspective is the plight of juries. Jurors clearly suffer as a result of participation in capital cases, with provisions sometimes recommended for therapeutic debriefing (DeAngelis, 1995; Hafemeister and Ventis, 1992). Sources of stress include not only the impact of making a death decision, but also the sequestration and impact of the evidence itself.

Capital juries are comprised of a nonrepresentative sample of the population in that they are "purged" of death penalty opponents — potential jurors who verbalize opposition to the death penalty are systematically excluded. The resulting pool is overweighed with authoritarian, conservative, and conviction-prone individuals, potentially measurably impacting both guilt and mitigatory phases (Bray and Noble, 1987; Kadane and Powers, 1987; Luginbuhl and Powers, 1987; Costanzo and Costanzo, 1992). However, the only remedy would be to open the panels to a true random sample of the population and thereby run the risk of increasing the potential for hung jury or jury nullified outcomes.

The issue of intervention turns upon whether the problems solved by the use of capital punishment are best addressed by reforming but retaining the penalty or through abolition. While the death penalty may serve no reasonable deterrence goals, it does effectively end any further antisocial acts by the executed individuals. In the case of early societies, it may have served another function — that of ending a cycle of reciprocal violence. Capital punishment allows for the satisfaction of revenge, especially where it is imposed by aggrieved parties, as is the case in Afghanistan.

The psychological benefits of revenge, however, have yet to be demonstrated, whereas the contrary strategy of forgiveness has both psychological and religious foundation. Most major religions make explicit reference to the power of forgiveness. The Moslem faith has its process of Salkha; Judaism has Selichot, the holiday preceding Yom Kippur reserved for prayers of forgiveness. Various Christian denominations have rituals, and believers recite the well-known "Lord's Prayer", which commits to forgiveness. From a psychological perspective in psychodynamically oriented therapy, the goal is often one of overcoming resentments and hostilities that have occurred because of real or imagined injury in earlier years. The Fourth Step in Alcoholics Anonymous requires acts of forgiveness. Relatively recently, therapy specifically focused on victimization and post traumatic stress has emphasized not only the expression of anger, but also the importance of eliminating revenge fantasies. One approach incorporates the Twelve Step Program, tailoring it to victimization (Black et al., 1993; Brende, 1993; Pynoos and Nader, 1993; Pynoos et al., 1993).

The implications for society of maintaining the death penalty appear to be generally negative. Public executions historically have increased violence (Collins, 1965); private and delayed executions do not clearly impact upon crime levels but have created systems that are irrational and involve extraordinary exercises in distorted roles and reasoning. If, however, it is maintained that for a few crimes and criminals, it is necessary to have an ultimate penalty, then the negative impact may be reduced by narrowing the scope of application.

Specific changes in death penalty statutes would allow less arbitrary and inequitable applications. The following are recommended:

1. Maintenance of appeal options as opposed to the current trend toward reduction. For example, as Ohio continues to increase the number of people on death row without any executions actually occurring, the state attorney general has increasingly mounted a public campaign to end access to the appeals process (Lane, 1996; McCarthy, 1997). To the extent that such efforts are successful, however, the chances of applying the death penalty to the less culpable or the truly innocent will increase.
2. All references to future dangerousness as a basis for execution should be eliminated. In the rare cases of severe sociopaths with a history of repetitive homicide, it is possible to predict the high likelihood under specified conditions of future violence. However, it is not possible with the general population of capital murderers to reach the levels of confidence in such predictions that justify a conclusion of death vs. life for individuals. In addition, mental health

professionals' participation in this decision-making process violates the ethical directive to do no harm.

3. Competency-to-die examinations should be eliminated. The American Medical Association and the American Psychiatric Association have both banned physician participation in executions. Both of those organizations, as well as the American Psychological Association, have ethical prohibitions to participation in acts of harm to other human beings. Certifying an individual for death readiness or providing treatment to restore competency is participation in the death protocol. Further, the task of a competency-to-die evaluation is logically flawed in that any scientific and clinical attempts contain an embedded error — that an individual is competent to die if he or she appreciates the appropriateness of the proposed execution.
4. There should be a constitutionally based elimination of the death penalty for persons under the age of 18 on the basis of cruel and unusual punishment, and in conformance with world standards.
5. Similarly, death penalty vulnerability for the chronically mentally ill and the mentally retarded, regardless of the relationship of the condition to the crime, should be eliminated from all statutes. Such a prohibition should not rest on assessment of competency, but on diagnostic status alone.
6. Death row procedures and management should be reformed to reach reasonable and humane conditions including involvement of inmates with the general population if behavior warrants, access to other human beings including physical contact, conjugal visitation contacts, and access to all necessary legal assistance.
7. Legal procedures should be reformed, especially those which potentially arbitrarily reduce access to appeals, such as requirements for early filing which cannot be completed by virtue of bureaucratic barriers (e.g., the obtaining of required transcripts within an unrealistic period of time).
8. Felony murder should be eliminated from the lists of capital specifications. The concept of felony murder allows broad, rather than narrow, discretion to charging authorities. It encourages the use of the death penalty in a macabre plea bargaining process and facilitates the procedural inadequacies that underlie the racial imbalances that have been characteristic of the application of the death penalty.

In mitigation work, the current thinking is that even testimony regarding psychopathy as an explanation, with the presentation of data as to biological and social formative agents beyond the control of the individual, provides some basis for a legal finding of life over death (Mehler, 1990). The nonpresentation of psychological data, which has been the only other option, may result in a situation in which only or mainly aggravating factors are presented, and the weighing process is thereby reduced to an automatic outcome (Doughton, personal communication, 1996).

Interventions common to the presence or absence of the death penalty would deal with the social inequities that feed criminality, including the following:

1. Increased support for prenatal care
2. Increased support for child welfare
3. Increased support for the study and early identification of personality disorders in young children and the institution of interventions including especially empathy training and opportunities for socially responsible roles that are reinforced by recognition and status
4. Effective intervention programs at early stages to address drug- and alcohol-related problems and especially the creation of work-study programs that will compete with the immediate gains that the drug and alcohol trade offers to inner city youths
5. Increased employment opportunities and the potential for stable, psychologically healthy work environments
6. Immediate negative sanctions for violence against women, which weds sexuality to aggression, coupled with treatment requirements
7. Intervention into the exploitation of young people by the media and entertainment industries, where combinations of sexuality, violence, and lack of consequences for aggression are presented as models for behavior

Abolishing capital punishment would end its overt or covert misdirection against society's current outgroups. Abolition would require effective corrections systems, including alternatives to long-term imprisonment for nonviolent crimes. With lower populations and shorter sentences, the overcrowding of prisons would be reduced, thus allowing the necessary space for those who must be restrained for long periods. Barzun (1962) raised concerns regarding long-term imprisonment as dehumanizing and resulting in insanity. He considered life terms more punitive than death; however, those views are not necessarily supported by empirical data. A review of data by Wormith (1984) showed that long-term incarceration may result in positive adjustment features under certain complex conditions.

Barzun (1962) spoke from his experience in England; however, over time, significant changes occurred in western European penology. Prison environments were humanized, and the basic philosophy became one of rehabilitation. As Europe now moves to more and more political unity, several current trends exist. Drug-related crime has led to more concern for control and prevention of recidivism, but the policies of decarceration and rehabilitation continue to be supported. Currently, emphasis is placed on identification of those persons for whom rehabilitation is possible and the development of broad alternatives for judicial response. In the meantime, those persons identified on behavioral bases as not reformable are placed in higher levels of managed environments necessary for secure control (Ruggiero et al., 1995).

Summary

An argument in favor of the death penalty which is admitted by anti-death penalty advocates is that it forecloses the possibility that the individual so eliminated will ever again commit murder. The argument against the death penalty which is generally acknowledged by pro-death advocates is that the death penalty, if applied to an innocent person, can never be rescinded. Both positions represent valid departure points. Merciless killers who clearly show every potential to kill again have been removed from forever doing so by their deaths at the hands of the state. It is also a matter of record that innocent persons have been victims of the capital penalty.

The ultimate argument between these two positions is one of protection of society vs. protection of the rights of the individual. This is an old tension in the history of law predating the U.S. system of jurisprudence and its evolution. Administration of the capital penalty is formal, institutionalized, legal violence against an individual. It is promulgated in the service of protecting the larger society, but, if it is the treatment for violent crimes, its side effects may be worse than the disease. Capital punishment has always served many nonlegitimate political and social goals. Accompaniments and sequelae cause harm to society in ways that are both subtle and obvious and need to be considered in the ultimate weighing of the appropriateness and usefulness of this penalty, which has been eliminated from all other Western democracies to include countries in the Eastern bloc.

Annotated Bibliography

1. Otterbein, K. (1986) *The Ultimate Coercive Sanction*. New Haven, CT: HIF Press. Intriguingly, in his acknowledgments regarding this broad-based inquiry into capital punishment across various cultures — notably, more primitive ones — Otterbein indicated that he was viewed as suspect in the U.S. as to "politics, my motivations, and even my personality structure." He concludes that all states use capital punishment if they feel the individuals threaten the society and that a "stable, mature state — one that is not at war" is one where the sense of threat is reduced. Thus, he suggests that those who oppose capital punishment need to enhance the stability and integrity of their societies. He notes that any other punishment alternatives will be potentially, at some

level, ineffective in protecting society from a given individual since even true life imprisonment leaves open the possibility of escape.

2. Radelet, M., Bedau, H., and Putnam, C. (1992) *In Spite of Innocence: Erroneous Convictions in Capital Cases.* Boston: Northeastern University Press. This case-focused volume provides extended discussions of examples reflecting different error categories. The chapter headings include Bearing False Witness, Pride and Prejudice, Corrupt Practices, and Rush to Judgment. In addition to detailing 13 cases, there is an inventory of all of the data on which the authors base their conclusion that significant numbers of people have either been vulnerable to the death penalty or actually suffered same but, in fact, were innocent. Clear evidence of the misapplication of the death penalty is provided. The book illustrates that the capital justice system carries within it such variability and unpredictability that the constitutional concerns for arbitrary justice are well merited.

3. Trombley, S. (1992) *The Execution Protocol.* New York: Crown Publications. Trombley entered the world of the death penalty in a very personal way, spending time on death row and in prison. His purpose was to develop a television documentary. In the course of doing so, he came to know those whose working lives were intimately connected to the death penalty. Out of the project, he wrote *The Execution Protocol.* In keeping with the usual distortions that accompany capital punishment, there was actually a request made by the network that an execution be scheduled to coincide with the airing of the program. The request was not granted.

4. Young, T. and French, L. (1992) Myths about aggression and attitudes about the death penalty. *Psychological Reports, 71,* 1337–1338. This brief article lists 10 myths which have relevance for attitudes toward the death penalty and one's ability to accept and include factors such as evidence regarding deterrence and the obvious racial bias: (a) humans are instinctively aggressive; (b) aggression can be controlled by substitute activity; (c) children have to play aggressively to get it out of their system; (d) failure to express anger leads to heart disease, stress, and hypertension; (e) child and spousal abuse are inflicted by the mentally ill; (f) violent crimes are proof of the aggressive instinct; (g) men are more aggressive than women; (h) emotions are uncontrollable; (i) expressing anger makes a person feel better; and (j) war is unavoidable because humans have inborn needs to express aggression.

References

Abu-Jamal, M. (1994) Demanding death. *Prison Legal News, 5*(9).

Acker, J. (1993) A different agenda: the Supreme Court, empirical research evidence, and capital punishment decisions 1986–1989. *Law and Society Review, 27*(1), 65–88.

American Bar Association (1997) *Resolution on Capital Punishment.*

Amnesty International (1984) *China, Violations of Human Rights: Prisoners of Conscience and the Death Penalty in The People's Republic of China.* London: Amnesty International.

Archer, D. (1983) Homicide and the death penalty: a cross-national test of a deterrent hypothesis. *Journal of Criminal Law and Criminology, 74*(3), 991–1013.

"Aum's terrorist plans described" (1996) *Daily Yomiuri,* April 27, p. A2.

Baldus, D., Woodworth, G., and Pulaski, C. (1990) *Equal Justice and the Death Penalty: A Legal and Empirical Analysis.* Boston: Northeastern University Press.

Barefoot v. Estelle (1983) 463 U.S. 880.

Barzun, J. (1962) In favor of capital punishment. *The American Scholar, 31*(2), 181–181.

"Battling the lyrics of gansta rap" (1996) *The Plain Dealer,* Nov. 23, p. B1.

Beck v. Alabama (1980) 442 U.S. 625.

Bedau, H. and Radelet, M. (1987) Miscarriages of justice in potentially capital cases. *Stanford Law Review, 40,* 21–179.

Bedau, H. and Radelet, M. (1988) The myth of infallibility: a reply to Markman and Cassell. *Stanford Law Review, 41,* 161–170.

Bedau, H., Radelet, M., and Putnam, C. (1992) *In Spite of Innocence: Erroneous Convictions in Capital Cases.* Boston: Northeastern University Press.

Black, D., Kaplan, T., and Hendricks, J. (1993) Father kills mother: effects on the children in the United Kingdom. In J. Wilson and B. Raphael (Eds.), *International Handbook of Traumatic Stress Syndromes.* New York: Plenum Press.

Boehm, C. (1984) Execution within the clan as an extreme form of social ostracism. *Science Information, 24*(2), 309–321.

Booth v. Maryland (1987) 482 U.S. 496.

Bray, R. and Noble, A. (1987) Authoritarianism and decisions of mock juries. In S. Wrightsman, E. Kassin, and C. Willis (Eds.), *In the Jury Box.* Beverly Hills, CA: Sage.

Brende, J. (1993) A 12-step recovery program for victims of traumatic events. In J. Wilson and B. Raphael (Eds.), *International Handbook of Traumatic Stress Syndromes.* New York: Plenum Press.

Brown, E. (1996) Translation of detail from O. Schischov, *Capital Punishment: For and Against.* Moscow: Legal Literature, 1989.

Bryan, R. (1996) The Lindbergh mystery. *The Plain Dealer,* April 2, p. B9.

Cahill, R. (1994) *New England's Cruel and Unusual Punishments.* Salem, MA: Old Salt Box Publishing House.

Calnen, T. and Blackmun, L. (1992) Capital punishment and offenders with mental retardation: response to the Penry brief. *American Journal on Mental Retardation, 96*(6), 557–564.

Carter, M. (1995) Firing squad execution poses problem in Utah. *The Plain Dealer,* Dec. 25, p. A5.

Coker v. Georgia (1977). 433 U.S. 584.

Collins, P. (1965) *Dickens and Crime.* New York: Macmillan.

Commute Wilford Berry from Ohio's Death Row (1996) Flier from Catholic Conference of Ohio.

Costanzo, M. and Costanzo, S. (1992) Jury decision making in the capital penalty phase: legal assumptions, empirical findings, and a research agenda. *Law and Human Behavior, 16*(2), 185–202.

Costanzo, M. and White, L. (1994) An overview of the death penalty and capital trials: history, current status, legal procedures, and cost. *Journal of Social Issues, 50*(2), 1–18.

Council Resolution 1984/50 (1984, May 25).

DeAngelis, T. (1995) Juror stress can influence final verdict. *The Monitor,* June, pp. 5–6.

"Death penalty criticized" (1997) *The Plain Dealer,* Feb. 4, p. A5.

"Death penalty focus policy on voluntary executions" (1993) *The Sentry,* Summer, p. 1.

Dicks, S. (1990) *Death Row: Interviews with Inmates, Their Families, and Opponents of Capital Punishment.* Jefferson, ND: McFarlandaa and Co.

"A doomed inmate drugs himself, is revived, and then executed" (1995) *The New York Times,* August 12, p. A1.

Dyer, G. (1985) *War.* New York: Crown Publications.

Ekland-Olsen, S. (1988) Structured discretion, racial bias, and the death penalty: the first decade after Furman v. Texas. *Social Science Quarterly, 69,* 853–873.

Enmond v. Florida (1982) 458 U.S. 782.

Espada, M. (1997) All things censored. *The Progressive,* July, pp. 20–22.

Ewinger, J. (1997) Judge says killer can be executed. *The Plain Dealer,* Feb. 27, pp. A1, A8.

"Execution crisis" (1993) *The Sentry,* Summer, p. 1–2.

Fattah, E. (1983) Canada's successful experience with the abolition of the death penalty. *Canadian Journal of Criminology, 25*(4), 421–431.

Ford v. Wainwright (1986) 477 U.S. 699.

Forst, B. (1983) Capital punishment and deterrence: conflicting evidence? *Journal of Criminal Law and Criminology, 74*(3), 927–942.

Fulmer, D. (1997) Warming up the hot seat. *The Cleveland Free Times,* Jan. 29, p. 8.

Furman v. Georgia (1972) 408 U.S. 238.

Gardner v. Florida (1977) 430 U.S. 349.

General Assembly Resolution 2857 (XXVI) (1971, December 20).

Godfrey v. Georgia (1980) 446 U.S. 420.

Gregg v. Georgia (1976) 428 U.S. 15.

Hafemeister, T. and Ventis, W. (1992) Juror stress: what burden have we placed on our juries? *The State Court Journal,* Fall, pp. 35–46.

Haines, H. (1992) Florida executions, the anti-death penalty movement, and the politics of capital punishment. *Social Problems, 39*(2), 125–137.

Hall, N. and Brace, P. (1994) The vicissitudes of death by decree: forces influencing capital punishment decision making in state supreme courts. *Social Science Quarterly, 75*(1), 137–151.

Hart, S. (1996) *Native Americans on Death Row in the United States*. Philadelphia, PA: American Friends Service Committee publication.

Henderson, S. and Calahan, W. (1996) *Letter of Appeal for Mumia*. Hyattesville, MD: Quxiote Center.

Herrera v. Collins (1993) 506 U.S. 390.

Hilliard, E. (1982) Capital punishment in Ohio: aggravating circumstances. *Cleveland State Law Review, 31,* 485–58.

Hinckle, P. (1996) Prisons to journalists: drop dead. *Extra!* July/August, pp. 13–15.

Huff, C., Rattner, A., and Sagarin, E. (1996) *Convicted But Innocent: Wrongful Conviction and Public Policy.* Thousand Oaks: Sage.

John v. Florida (1992) 112 S.Ct. 2114.

Johnson, R. (1990) *Death Work: A Study of The Modern Execution Process.* Belmont: Brooks Cole Publishers.

Jurek v. Texas (1976) 428 U.S. 262.

Kadane, J. and Powers, T. (1987) *Penalty Supports and Conviction Proneness.* Paper presented at the annual meeting of the American Psychological Association, New York.

Keen, S. (1986) *Faces of the Enemy: Reflections of the Hostile Imagination.* San Francisco: Harper & Row.

Koopman, C., Classen, C., Freinkel, A., and Spiegel, D. (1994) *Psychological Reactions to Two Kinds of Violence: Legal Execution Versus Mass Shooting.* Paper presented at the annual meeting of the American Psychological Association, Los Angeles.

Lane, M. (1996) Attorney general stumps to curb execution appeals. *The Plain Dealer,* April 5, p. B1.

Laurence, J. (1960) *The History of Capital Punishment.* Secaucus, NJ: Citadel Press.

"Law that provides death penalty" (1970) *The New York Times,* August 23, p. 6.

Leong, G., Weinstock, R., Silva, J., and Feth, S. (1993) Psychiatry and the death penalty: the past decade. *Psychiatric Annals, 23*(1), 41–47.

Lester, D. (1987) *The Death Penalty: Issues and Answers.* Springfield: Charles C Thomas.

Linebaugh, P. (1992) *The London-Hanged: Crime and Civil Society in the 18th Century.* London: Cambridge University Press.

Lockett v. Ohio (1978) 438 U.S. 586.

Lockhart v. McCree (1986) 476 U.S. 162.

Luginbuhl, J. and Powers, T. (1987) *Jurors' Death Penalty Support and Conviction Proneness.* Paper presented at the annual meeting of the American Psychological Association, New York.

Markman, S. and Cassell, P. (1988) Protecting the innocent: a response to the Bedau-Radelet study. *Stanford Law Review, 41,* 121–160.

Matsumoto, S. (1996) Soapbox: debate forum. *Daily Yomiuri,* April 8.

Maynard v. Cartwright (1988) 486 U.S. 356.

McCarthy, J. (1997) Execution appeals limits OK. *The Plain Dealer,* October 16, p. B5.

McCleskey v. Kemp (1987) 481 U.S. 279.

McPherson, S. (1994) *Mental Health and Russian Law: Notes From Volgograd.* Paper presented at the annual meeting of the American Psychological Association, Los Angeles.

McPherson, S. (1997) *Heinousness in Capital Crimes: The Myth of Proportionality.* Paper presented at the XXII International Congress on Law and Mental Health, Montreal, Canada.

Mehler, B. (1990) Antisocial personality disorder as mitigating evidence. *The Champion,* June, pp. 20–26.

Miller, K. and Radelet, M. (1993) *Executing the Mentally Ill.* Newbury Park: Sage.

Mitsuta, Y. (1996) Trial must determine cult's motivation. *Daily Yomiuri*, April 27, p. A2.

M'Naghten's Case, 10 Cl. F. 200, 8 Eng. Rep. 718 (H.L. 1843).

"Must night fall?" (1975) *Economist,* December, pp. 69–18.

"Or such less penalty" (1974) *Economist,* Dec. 7, pp. 17–18.

Otterbein, K. (1986) *The Ultimate Coercive Sanction: A Cross-Cultural Study of Capital Punishment.* New Haven, CT: HIF Press.

Paternoster, R. (1983) Race of victim and location of crime: the decision to seek the death penalty in South Carolina. *Journal of Criminal Law and Criminology, 74*(3), 754–785.

Paternoster, R. (1991) *Capital Punishment in America.* New York: Lexington Books.

Patrick, C., Bradley, M., and Long, P. (1993) Emotion in the criminal psychopath: startle reflex modulation. *Journal of Abnormal Psychology, 102*(1), 82–92.

Payne v. Tennessee (1991) 501 U.S. 808.

Penry v. Lynaugh (1989) 492 U.S. 302.

Picard, R. (1993) *Media Portrayals of Terrorism.* Ames: Iowa State Press.

"Politics pervades death penalty" (1996) *The Ohio Observer,* April, pp. 3–5.

Potter, H. (1993) *Hanging in Judgment.* New York: Continuum Publications.

Proffitt v. Florida (1976) 428 U.S. 242.

Pulley v. Harris (1984) 465 U.S. 376.

Pynoos R. and Nader, K. (1993) Issues in the treatment of posttraumatic stress in children and adolescents. In J. Wilson and D. Raphael (Eds.), *International Handbook of Traumatic Stress Syndromes*. New York: Plenum Press.

Pynoos, R., Sorenson, S., and Steinberg, A. (1993) Interpersonal violence and traumatic stress reactions. In L. Goldberger and Breznitz (Eds.), *Handbook of Stress*, 2nd ed. New York: The Free Press.

Radelet, M. (1989) Executions of whites for crimes against blacks: exception to the rules? *The Sociological Quarterly, 30*(4), 529–544.

Radelet, M., Bedau, H., and Putnam, C. (1992) *In Spite of Innocence: Erroneous Convictions in Capital Cases.* Boston: Northeastern University Press.

Radelet, M. and Pierce, G. (1985) Race and prosecutorial discretion in the homicide cases. *Law and Society Review, 19*(4), 487–619.

Reinstatement of capital punishment (1975) *The New York Times,* Nov. 11, p. 7.

Rice, J. (1991) Life term lacks allure. *The Plain Dealer,* April 29, p. C1.

Roberts v. Louisiana (1976) 428 U.S. 325.

Rose, D. (1996) The empty seat in Atlanta. *The Observer Review,* July 14, pp. 3–4.

Rothman, S. and Powers, S. (1994) Execution by quota? *The Public Interest,* Summer, pp. 5–17.

Ruggiero, V., Ryan, N., and Sim, J. (1995) *Western European Penal Systems: A Critical Anatomy.* Thousand Oaks, CA: Sage.

Schein, E. (1961) *Coercive Persuasion.* New York: W.W. Norton and Co.

Schwartz, L. and Matzkin, R. (1996) Violence, viewing, and development: does violence in the media cause violence in youth? In H.V. Hall (Ed.), *Lethal Violence 2000: A Source Book on Fatal Domestic, Acquaintance and Stranger Aggression*, pp. 113–142. Kamuela, HI: Pacific Institute for the Study of Conflict and Aggression.

Schwartz, R. (1997) *ABC News Good Morning America*, Oct. 15.

Sheleff, L. (1974) A case against capital punishment. *New Outlook, 17,* 51–55.

Silverstein, B. (1989) Enemy images. *American Psychologist, 44*(6), 903–913.

Smith, S. (1990) 1990 Supreme Court Review. *Bulletin of the American Academy of Forensic Psychology, 11*(1), p. 4.

Snell, T.L. (1996, December) Capital punishment 1995. In U.S. Department of Justice, Office of Justice Programs, *Bureau of Justice Statistics Bulletin* (NCJ-162043), pp. 2, 8, 12.

Stohl, M. (1988) *The Politics of Terrorism.* New York: Marcel Dekker.

Swomley, J. (1970) *American Empire.* New York: Macmillan.

Thompson v. Oklahoma (1988) 47 U.S. 815.

Trombley, S. (1992) *The Execution Protocol.* New York: Crown Publications.

Tyler, P. (1996) Crime (and punishment) rages anew in China. *The New York Times*, July 11, pp. A1, A6.

Walton v. Arizona (1990) 497 U.S. 639.

Wardlaw, G. (1982) *Political Terrorism.* Cambridge: Cambridge University Press.

Weiler, G. (1974) A case for capital punishment. *New Outlook,* (17), 46–50.

White, W. (1991) *The Death Penalty in the 90s.* Ann Arbor: University of Michigan Press.

Wilkes, J. (1987) Murder in mind. *Psychology Today, 21*(6), 26–32.

Wilkins v. Missouri (1989) 492 U.S. 937.

Will the United States Resume Executing Political Prisoners? (1995) Pamphlet of Philadelphia Refuse and Resist.

Witherspoon v. Illinois (1968) 391 U.S. 510.

Woodson v. North Carolina (1976) 428 U.S. 280.

Wormith, S. (1984) The controversy over the effects of long-term incarceration. *Canadian Journal of Criminology, 26*(4), 423–437

Young, T. and French L. (1992) Myths about aggression and attitudes about the death penalty. *Psychological Reports, 71*, 1337–1338.

Yusufzai, R. (1996) Victim's kin execute killers in Afghanistan. *The Plain Dealer,* February 11, p. A15.

About the Author

Sandra B. McPherson, Ph.D., received her Ph.D. from Case Western Reserve University in Cleveland, OH. She has diplomate status in both clinical and forensic psychology from the American Board of Professional Psychology. She divides her time between a largely forensic practice in Cleveland and teaching for the Fielding Institute based in Santa Barbara, CA. She has developed special expertise in death penalty mitigation, having worked with many defendants currently on Ohio's death row. Her work in this area began with the first case to be brought under the state's revised capital punishment statute. In addition to the other areas of criminal responsibility work, she is particularly active in domestic relations cases, with special emphasis on problems of sexual abuse allegations and the development of courtworthy psychological evaluations. She is a member of the American Psychological Association and the Ohio Psychological Association, of which she has served as president. She is a former president of the State Board of Psychology. Any correspondence concerning this article should be addressed to Sandra B. McPherson, 12434 Cedar Road, Suite 15, Cleveland, Ohio 44106.

Chapter 17

OPPRESSION BY SCIENCE: THE INTELLECTUAL JUSTIFICATION OF COLLECTIVE VIOLENCE

William H. Tucker

Some of the worst instances of collective violence have occurred when evil takes to itself the fiat of intellectual obligation; cruelty, motivated neither by anger nor terror, but carried out by the clean white hand of scientific necessity, is less likely to be encumbered by pangs of conscience.

The Political Expression of Our Biological Knowledge

The most well known, and certainly the most well studied, example of collective violence in the 20th century has been the massive slaughter committed as the official policy of the Third Reich; perhaps more books have been written about the Holocaust than about any other event in human history. It is only in the last decade, however, that scholars have begun to appreciate the significant role played by geneticists and anthropologists in providing the Nazi atrocities with biological justification (see, for example, Müller-Hill, 1988; Proctor, 1988). Indeed, the deadly mechanisms designed and implemented by the Nazis were intended to attain goals that the scientists had proclaimed necessary for the health and welfare of German society when Hitler was still an obscure corporal recovering from his wounds in World War I.

Examining Germany's post-war difficulties during the Weimar period, many of the country's eminent scientists concluded that the problems of reconstruction were primarily biological and that they needed solutions to match. They saw the process of natural selection being vitiated by medical advances and welfare institutions, resulting in a proliferation of the biologically unfit.

One solution to the presence of so many human liabilities was offered by two distinguished professors, Karl Binding and Alfred Hoche (1920), who argued, in a widely read book entitled *Die Freigabe der Vernichtung lebensunwerten Lebens* ("Permission for the Extermination of Life Unworthy of Life"), for the official, therapeutic killing of "worthless" individuals, especially the feebleminded, mentally ill, and deformed. Binding, a psychiatrist, explained that the value of a life was properly determined not only by its worth to the individual but also by its worth to society (see Friedlander, 1995). Thus, the elimination of those who were already "mentally completely dead" (quoted in Lifton, 1986, p. 46) was a scientifically defensible and useful act that relieved society of the difficult burden of caring for them. Hoche, a jurist, argued that any diagnostic errors would be insignificant in comparison with the social benefit of therapeutic killing, not only from the reduction in national resources expended on these "empty human shells" (quoted in Friedlander, 1995, p. 15), but from the expanded opportunities to conduct brain research.

The major scientific proposal for eliminating the impact of biological undesirables on German society, however, was involuntary sterilization. In 1921, three internationally recognized German scientists — Erwin Baur, Eugen Fischer, and Fritz Lenz — published a massive two-volume textbook on genetics, the first volume of which, *Human Heredity and Racial Hygiene*, was eventually translated into English (Baur et al., 1931) and hailed by reviewers as "a masterpiece" (Strong, 1931, p. 482), "the best existing general book on human inheritance" (*Menschliche Erblichkeitslehre*..., 1928, p. 136). Baur, who died just as the Nazis were taking power, had been the head of a major institute on genetic research, Lenz was a geneticist and Professor of Racial Hygiene (*Rassenhygiene*) at the University of Munich, and Fischer was the doyen of German anthropologists, a Professor at the University of Berlin as well as Director of the Kaiser Wilhelm Institute for Anthropology. The second volume, authored solely by Lenz, recommended that the "least competent third of the population ... have no descendants" (Lenz, 1932, p. 273). In fact, as an important influence on his own thought, Lenz acknowledged the work of American biologist Harry H. Laughlin, who had written the model sterilization statute adopted in some 30 states (Laughlin, 1922); the sterilization law eventually enacted by the Third Reich was patterned after this model, and in recognition of his contribution, Laughlin was awarded an honorary doctorate by the University of Heidelberg.

In addition to the presence of so many infirm and disabled, the scientists warned that racial impurity constituted another major threat to the health of German society. Though they were absolutely certain that the Nordic race was far superior, not only to people of color but also to other Europeans, the scientists' concern over racial purity was informed by more Darwinian theoretical considerations. As Lenz explained (1932, p. 503), "The hereditary traits of every race have been uniquely adapted to them through thousands of years of natural selection, and this harmony would be destroyed by racial mixture." In particular, Lenz focused on the Jews as a group with distinctive characteristics produced by the evolutionary process. Even though outsiders, their "instinctive desire not to look singular" had resulted in sexual selection for similarity to their "hosts". And having been generally excluded from a society's productive opportunities, they had developed racial traits of "shrewdness and ... an amazing capacity for putting themselves in others' places and for inducing others to accept their guidance" (Baur et al., 1931, pp. 667–668). As a result of their persuasiveness, Lenz explained, the Jews had been particularly successful in those professions requiring an ability to exert influence over others — like trader, moneylender, lawyer, or doctor — and, for the same reason, were equally effective as merchants or revolutionaries, thus providing a nicely Darwinian account for the apparently contradictory claims that Jews were both avaricious capitalists and dedicated Marxists. Though he did not judge the Jews to be unintelligent, Lenz concluded that, unlike the straightforward Nordics, they were inclined to attain their goals through "cunning" and that any intermixture between the two groups would be genetically unfavorable.

Actually, Lenz's analysis of the *Judenfrage* — the Jewish question — was fairly sophisticated in comparison to the claims offered by cruder race scientists in Germany at the time. A less nuanced view, for example, was offered in 1927 by Hans F.K. Günther, a social anthropologist at the University of Jena, whose work provided much of the theoretical foundation for Nazi racial theory. A student of Eugen Fischer — the prominent anthropologist and one of the co-authors of *Human Heredity and Racial Hygiene* — Günther was particularly concerned with the need to protect "Nordic blood", which, he claimed, had characterized the ruling class of every great past civilization. Yet, he now saw the biological integrity of these superiors threatened by intermixture with alien elements, chiefly the Jews, whom Günther (1927/1970, pp. 78–79) termed a wedge of "ferment and disturbance" that posed "the very greatest danger for the life of the European peoples and of the North American people alike." To safeguard its heritage from such deleterious intrusion, Germany needed the "courage … to make ready for future generations a world cleansing itself racially and eugenically" (Günther, 1927/1970, p. 267).

Thus, as the Nazi movement began to gather steam, it could, without exaggeration, declare that its policies enjoyed the imprimatur of science. The first volume of the party's journal, *Nationalsozialistische Monatshefte* (National Socialist Monthly), featured a cover article entitled "Der Nationalsozialismus als politischer Ausdruck unserer biologischen Kenntnis" ("National Socialism as the Political Expression of our Biological Knowledge"), which announced that the party's program had been derived from the latest research in anthropology, genetics, and other scientific disciplines. In the National Socialist state, the article emphasized, scientific results would be "directly and continuously applied to national reconstruction" (Lang, 1930, p. 397).

Clearly flattered at the prospect of their own conclusions being translated into national policy, the scientists became enthusiastic supporters of the Nazi movement and its charismatic leader, who understood the practical importance of scientific concepts. Indeed, portions of *Mein Kampf* sounded like a reprise of the ideas in the Baur-Fischer-Lenz genetics text, which Hitler had read while in prison — a fact noted by Lenz, who was impressed with the future Führer's sophisticated grasp of the principles of *Rassenhygiene* despite his limited education. Shortly before the Nazi takeover, Lenz (1931, p. 300) termed National Socialism merely "applied biology" and hailed the Nazis as "the first political party, not only in Germany but anywhere, that makes racial hygiene a central priority of its program." The leader of this "great movement," Lenz (1931, p. 308) concluded, "is the first politician of really significant influence who has recognized racial hygiene as a crucial political issue and is ready to fight for it energetically."

National Socialism in action gave Lenz no reason to regret his support. When Hitler actually seized power early in 1933, the new regime proclaimed its policies nothing more than "applied biology" and insisted that all Nazi officials become familiar with basic genetic principles; the Third Reich was to usher in the reign of science. The first major piece of legislation enacted under National Socialism was the Law for the Prevention of Genetically Defective Progeny (see Müller-Hill, 1988; Proctor, 1988). Based on scientific advice from the newly appointed Expert Advisory Council for Population and Race Politics, a group that included Lenz, Günther, and a number of other prominent scientists and physicians, the law called for the involuntary sterilization of individuals judged to suffer from any of a number of putatively hereditary conditions, including feeblemindedness, insanity, schizophrenia, epilepsy, blindness, deafness, bodily deformity, and alcoholism. In addition to providing the scientific expertise that informed the law, Fischer and Lenz would eventually participate in its implementation, evaluating the "genetic health" of individuals being considered for sterilization. Two years later, the Marriage Health Law was passed, prohibiting marriage if either individual suffered from one of the conditions specified in the involuntary sterilization statute or from a number of other illnesses.

To implement further the "national biologic measures", within the first 2 years, the Third Reich also enacted a series of restrictions on "non-Aryans" culminating in the so-called Nuremberg Laws (see Müller-Hill, 1988; Proctor, 1988). Again based on a consensus of the most prestigious scientists in the country, who agreed that Jews were a genetically unassimilable group posing a biological danger to the German people, the new legislation prohibited marriage or "extramarital congress" between Jews and Aryans and excluded non-Aryans and anyone married to a non-Aryan from government office, civil service, university professorship, and the practice of medicine. Other laws at various levels of government would follow, all designed to exclude Jews from the social and cultural life of the nation.

Elated by the wisdom of these policies and extremely proud of their own contributions to realizing them, the scientists lavished praise on the new government and its Führer for providing this opportunity to demonstrate the value of their research to the state and the life of the people. Professor of Psychiatry Ernst Rüdin, for example, who had labored fruitlessly for years to alert the public to the danger of hereditary defectives and racial impurity, acclaimed the man whose efforts had produced such a change. "The significance of *Rassenhygiene*," observed Rüdin, "did not become evident to all aware Germans until the political activity of Adolf Hitler and only through his work has our 30 year long dream of translating *Rassenhygiene* into action finally become a reality"; it was a "duty of honor" to aid in implementing Hitler's program (Rüdin, 1934, p. 228). An editorial comment in one of the leading German scientific journals praised Hitler for ushering in "an age of revolution in racial biology" ("Ansprache des Herrn Reichministers", 1933, p. 419). And Fischer (quoted in Müller-Hill, 1988, p. 10) also hailed the "new leadership" for ...

"... deliberately and forcefully intervening in the course of history and in the life of the nation, precisely where this intervention is most urgently, most decisively, and most immediately needed. To be sure, this need can only be perceived by those who are able to see and think within a biological framework, but it is understood by those people to be a matter of the gravest and most weighty concern. This intervention can be characterized as a biological population policy, biological in this context signifying the safeguarding by the state of our hereditary endowment and our race, as opposed to the unharnessed processes of heredity, selection, and elimination."

Underlying all these sincere expressions of gratitude by the scientists was their professional and personal satisfaction — not in some petty, egotistical sense, but in the more high-minded sense of having long ago enunciated the principles now, finally, recognized as essential to the biological salvation of the state. *They* had not joined the National Socialist movement; *it* had joined *them*.

Nor was it only in Germany that scientists expressed such enthusiasm over the reign of science; many biologists in the U.S. were equally ecstatic at National Socialism's commitment to genetic progress. When the sterilization law was enacted by the Reich, Paul Popenoe, the editor of the *Journal of Heredity*, cited a number of passages from *Mein Kampf* to demonstrate Hitler's clear grasp of science and concluded that the Führer's program was based "solidly on the application of biological principles to human society" (Popenoe, 1934, p. 257). An unsigned editorial in the *Eugenical News* ("Eugenical sterilization in Germany," 1933, p. 90) praised Germany for leading "the great nations of the world in the recognition of the biological foundations of national character" and termed the sterilization statute "a milestone ..., comparable in importance only with the states [sic] legal control of marriage." And in celebration of Germany's progress, the *News* also reprinted an address by Reichminister for the Interior Dr. Wilhelm Frick (1934, pp. 35, 38), who was later hanged as a war criminal, deploring the costs of a health system that provided "exaggerated care for the single individual" and calling for "the courage to rate our population according to its hereditary value."

Even after the racial purity laws were passed, some American scientists continued to cheer wildly for Germany's decision to follow "Adolf Hitler ... towards a biological salvation of humanity" (see "Eugenical propaganda in Germany", 1934, p. 45).

When criticisms of the Nuremberg Laws arose, the President of the Eugenics Research Association, whose membership at the time included some of the most prominent American psychologists, denounced the "irresponsible and hysterical charges" that had obscured "the correct understanding and the great importance of the German racial policy," which was merely "the integration of the well-considered conclusions of … anthropologists, … biologists, … and sociologists, … [who] take full cognizance of the biological basis of collective life" (Campbell, 1936, pp. 27, 25). Almost until the outbreak of war, some scientists continued to support German racial policy, promoting a Nazi propaganda film in the U.S. and (successfully) opposing the admission of German Jewish immigrants seeking to escape from the Reich on the grounds that they were not assimilable here either (see Tucker, 1994, pp. 126–127).

As is well known, between 1935 and 1941, the Third Reich escalated its efforts to eliminate from German society the deleterious influence of those groups identified by the scientists as genetically inimical. Sterilization for those suffering from various disorders and physical separation for Jews — and then for gypsies, as science demonstrated that they, too, were hereditary degenerates (see Friedlander, 1995, pp. 246–262) — eventually gave way to wholesale slaughter. Such extreme measures represented the logical extension of the scientists' determination to cleanse the German gene pool of defective and alien elements, and the scientists continued, not only to support them wholeheartedly, but also to provide intellectual justification. Over a year after the T-4 Program for killing the unfit had begun, for example, a number of professors attempted to draft a law sanctioning the practice. The decisive article, crafted by Lenz (quoted in Müller-Hill, 1988, pp. 39–40), stated, "The life of a patient, who would otherwise need lifelong care, may be ended by medical measures of which he remains unaware."

Even as the Final Solution was implemented, the scientists never wavered in their commitment to racial purity. In 1943, Rüdin (quoted in Müller-Hill, 1988, p. 61) celebrated National Socialism's first decade by congratulating Hitler and the Nazis for "such brilliant race-hygienic achievement … the fight against parasitic alien races such as the Jews and the Gypsies … and preventing the breeding of those with hereditary diseases and those of inferior stock." In 1939, 2 years before the onset of systematic extermination, Fischer (quoted in Müller-Hill, 1988, pp. 36–37) declared that "the Jew is an alien and … must be warded off" as a matter of biological "self-defense," and in 1944, with the Holocaust in full swing, he called for the creation of a "scientific front line" against Jewry (quoted in Müller-Hill, 1988, p. 80; see also Weinrich, 1946). Though pleased that National Socialism had eliminated the biological danger posed by Jews and gypsies, in 1944, Otmar Freiherr von Verschuer, another prominent researcher in genetics and Director of the Frankfurt Institute for *Rassenhygiene*, maintained that an even larger effort was required throughout Europe to protect Germany from other "foreign racial elements" (quoted in Proctor, 1988, p. 211). Had the Nazis not been defeated, science might have decreed the necessity to eliminate yet other ethnic groups.

Although it would be far too simplistic to blame the Holocaust on the German scientists, they certainly played an instrumental role in the creation, acceptance, and implementation of Nazi doctrine. Indeed, it is the participation of academics and intellectuals that makes the Holocaust unique in the annals of genocide; mass extermination, unfortunately, has occurred more than once in human history. Only in the Third Reich were the victims designated, in both theory and practice, by science. First, by defining specific groups — Jews, gypsies, and those with certain disorders — as biologically threatening, the scientists cast them in the role of "other", thus facilitating their exclusion from German society, initially through physical separation but eventually through extermination, the latter being merely the ultimate extension of the former. The scientists maintained that biology *should* be destiny, and the Nazis ensured that, one way or another, it *would* be.

In addition, the scientists conducted the research and provided the precise definitions necessary to determine who qualified for membership in the groups to be excluded. By studying, for example, everything from facial features to posture, the scientists sought to determine who was *really* — that is, biologically — Jewish, thus making Jews a danger to German society, neither by belief nor behavior, but by birth. Similar studies produced objective methods for the classification of gypsies and hereditary defectives. While the scientists may not have participated in the killing themselves, they provided an intellectual justification, transmuting evil into normative behavior essential to the genetic health of German society.

Rooted in Man's Nature

"The past," observed Faulkner, "is not yet dead; it's not even past." Though the Third Reich is gone, its intellectual underpinnings linger on in the work of a number of contemporary social scientists, not in exactly the same form, but still obsessed with racial purity, still suggesting that the physical separation of certain groups is a scientific necessity, and still containing the potential for justification of violence against them.

The major academic gathering point for scholars with this perspective has been the *Mankind Quarterly*, a journal founded in 1960 and devoted, according to its introductory editorial, to the "racial aspects of man's inheritance" which had been particularly neglected "during the last two decades," i.e., since the Nazi emphasis on racial hygiene ("Editorial", 1960, p. 4). Behind this rhetoric lies a coalition of two groups united by their desire for a social policy informed by racial differences: American scientists opposed to the civil rights movement and European scientists seeking to resurrect many of National Socialism's racial concepts.

The *Quarterly*'s editorial leadership left little doubt about its orientation. Editor-in-Chief Robert Gayre, a Scottish physical anthropologist, boasted of his acquaintance with Hans F.K. Günther, Hitler's leading social anthropologist, and had written a book during the war based on "Günther's authoritative work on German racial science," recommending a revision of the boundary between Germany and Poland in order to make Germany "considerably more Nordic" (Gayre, 1944, p. 11–12).

The two "honorary associate editors" symbolized the two groups united by the journal. Henry E. Garrett, one of the most prestigious names in American psychology at the time — formerly chair of the department at Columbia University, once President of the American Psychological Association and the Psychometric Society, a fellow of the American Association for the Advancement of Science, member of the National Research Council, and for 10 years editor of the American Psychology Series — led the "scientific" defense of legal segregation in the 1960s, maintaining that (Garrett, 1962, p. 984): "No matter how low an American white may be, his ancestors built the civilizations of Europe, and no matter how high … a Negro may be, his ancestors were (and his kinsmen still are) savages in an African jungle." Earlier, Garrett (1961a, p. 320) had declared that, "The Negro has nothing to offer the White man." Besides, he wrote (1961b, p. 256), the real goal of the civil rights movement, led by "Jewish organizations … [with a] preoccupation with racial matters" was "widespread amalgamation" which would cause "our country … [to] inevitably deteriorate intellectually, morally, and materially" (1961a, p. 320). The appropriate response to such a serious threat, he observed, was for white parents to "teach their children to hate Negroes" ("Racial mixing could be catastrophic," 1963, p. 93).

Prominent British geneticist, R. Ruggles Gates, the other honorary associate editor, had been a contributor to the Reich's literature on racial hygiene and had long argued that the different human races were actually separate species. He had also warned of biological danger from race crossing in general and from intermarriage between Jews and Germans in particular (Gates, 1929; 1948; see also Thompson, 1936). When Gates died only a year after the *Mankind Quarterly*'s appearance, he was replaced by Italian sociologist, Corrado Gini, another contributor to the Nazi racial literature and former scientific advisor to Mussolini, who explained after the war that National Socialism had been an understandable attempt "to eliminate heterogeneous socio-cultural as well as anthropological elements" in Germany, a consequence of the natural tendency toward biological homogeneity in nations (Gini, 1967, pp. 270–271).

Also involved with the *Mankind Quarterly* — as an assistant editor and frequent book reviewer — was Robert E. Kuttner, a biochemical researcher and, in addition, a leading member of the Liberty Lobby, a neo-Nazi organization founded by the Far Right activist Willis A. Carto, who had termed "Hitler's defeat … the defeat of Europe and America" and had written that behind the "niggerfication of America" was "Public Enemy No. 1:" the Jews (quoted in Simonds, 1971, p. 979).

As a spokesman for the Lobby, Kuttner testified before the House Committee on the Judiciary in 1963 during its deliberations over proposed civil rights legislation, ominously reminding the committee members of the last time a society had been forced to accept a minority in its midst: prewar Germany. Hostility was always the natural reaction to such "compulsory tolerance," insisted Kuttner (1963, p. 1971), and "perhaps we should consider," he concluded, that the Nazis "had justice on their side." In an address to the New Orleans Leadership Conference some time after passage of the civil rights laws, Kuttner (1972, p. 24) explained the true purpose of the integration movement for black males:

"If you have a drug habit costing $60 or $80 a day, you can survive only if you catch a white girl. And if you want to keep her, you better put her on a habit too, because when she wakes up, she'll run back to mother with her brown baby, if mother will take her. ...Believe me, no Black male can steal enough color TV's out of hotels to support a drug habit. You can't rob pension checks off senior citizens except one day a month, when the mail brings the check. ...You can't rob liquor stores and grocery stores forever. ...The only answer is to catch a white girl, and integration makes that much easier today."

The first volume of the *Mankind Quarterly* established the themes which have informed the journal up to the present. A reprinted article (Hall, 1960, pp. 118–119), which had originally been published 14 years earlier, at the end of the second World War, declared that "permitting the immigration of Orientals, and … granting citizenship … to Orientals … violates every biological law … that relates to harmonious existence" and recommended the "deportation of 'invaders'" as well as restriction of "citizenship rights to one species only."

Another article (Purves, 1960, pp. 51, 54) proposed that existing multi-racial communities in the U.S. be "resolv[ed] … into separate societies on a racial basis" because hostility to other races is an "instinctive" response "rooted in man's nature" and serving an essential "biological function …, namely, the prevention of interbreeding." As proof of this effect, Purves (1960, p. 54) offered "the behavior of Whites in the Southern States …, who are often kindly disposed to negroes [sic] but tend to go berserk against those suspected of physical relations with Caucasoid women." According to the *Mankind Quarterly*, science could provide a compelling biological rationale for a lynch mob.

Any residual doubt concerning the *Quarterly*'s true nature was eliminated shortly after the appearance of its initial issue when a Yugoslavian anthropologist, who had been named to the "honorary advisory board", submitted his resignation, explaining that the journal's racism was "incompatible with my conscience as a scientist" and also "an affront to [my] bitter memories … while a prisoner in Dachau"

(Skerlj, 1960, p. 172). In his response on behalf of the journal, Gates stated frankly that the anthropologist would never have been considered for the board had the editors been aware of his imprisonment in a concentration camp, which "naturally had such an effect on [his] mental outlook" (quoted in Skerlj, 1960, p. 172).

Especially during its first two decades, the *Mankind Quarterly* found little value in subtlety or euphemism; though written by scientists, many of the journal's articles were little more than hate literature with footnotes. A typical article (Arnold, 1969, pp. 86, 94) labeled blacks not only inferior, but "misfit[s] in white society," though in the long run they would be of little consequence, because the "major conflict," predicted the author with certainty, "is that between the Yellow and White races," in which "the other races and mixtures will be used by one side or the other when to do so brings benefits; and they will be annihilated by one side or the other when they become an obstruction." Another contribution, entitled "The Black Brainwash in America" (Nevin, 1967, pp. 233–234), warned of "the perversion of history and the social sciences to magnify the role of putatively under-privileged groups," as falsified textbooks "palm off colored mediocrities as statesmen and geniuses."

In addition to its own articles, the *Quarterly* glorified the most repulsive works by racial extremists. It reviewed, for example, *White America* (written in 1923 by the White supremacist and Klansman Ernest Sevier Cox and reissued by Noontide Press, the publishing arm of Carto's Liberty Lobby) praising it as "a classic book by this truly great man" (Ford, 1966, p. 118). Observing that "the White man's contact with the colored races" continued to be "the most difficult [problem] confronting civilization," the *Quarterly* concluded that *White America*'s "greatest contribution" was its "proposal of a practical solution for the United States" — to "preserve racial integrity," Cox had recommended that all blacks be sent back to Africa (Ford, 1966, p. 118).

Another work highly praised by the *Mankind Quarterly* was *The Dispossessed Majority* by Wilmot Robertson (in all likelihood, a pseudonym), a book contending that almost all contemporary problems in the U.S. stemmed from the presence of "unassimilable minorities," not just blacks but also Asians, Hispanics, Greeks, Southern Italians, Arabs, American Indians, and Jews. These groups, estimated by Robertson at 30% of the population, were not entitled to the Bill of Rights and other constitutional protections because "rights *earned* by one [racial] group" cannot be "*donated* to another" (Robertson, 1972, p. 405; emphasis in original). Robertson's neo-*Mein Kampf* obsessed, in particular, over "Jewish hegemony" in the U.S. As a result of "their fear and loathing of Western civility" and their "vendetta … against all things non-Jewish," Robertson (1972, pp. 198, 200) wrote, Jews "have been in the forefront of every divisive force of the modern era, from class agitation to minority racism, from the worst capitalist exploitation to the most brutal collectivism." A good indication of "the Jewish contribution to society," observed Robertson (1972, pp. 194-195), is the condition of New York, the city "where Jews are most heavily concentrated" and which "can only be described as the greatest municipal catastrophe of the day — a scabrous pile of ugliness, tastelessness, and lawlessness." Noting that Jews have infected Western Europe with the same social diseases, Robertson (1972) pointed out that, despite its severe defeat in World War II, Germany emerged from the conflict as "the one large Western nation free of Jewish domination" (p. 194) and, as a consequence, had become "the most affluent and stable nation in Europe" (Robertson, 1972, p. 365). "To put a stop to the Jewish envelopment of America," he concluded (Robertson, 1972, pp. 200–201), "history should not be repeated;" *this time* "the operation should be accomplished with finesse." Although the major conservative journals found *The Dispossessed Majority* too distasteful to review, Kuttner applauded this hateful screed in the *Quarterly*, agreeing with its author that the Anglo-Saxon majority was threatened by "the presence of indigestible ethnic and racial elements" and "highly recommend[ing]" the book for its "original and penetrating" insights (Kuttner, 1973, pp. 118–119).

Despite its academic facade and its impressive list of degreed editors and advisors, the *Mankind Quarterly* has provided a scholarly appearing platform for ideas more commonly associated with Klansmen and Nazis.

Temperamentally Unsuited for Citizenship

Because of the longevity and the importance of their contributions to the scientific justification of collective violence, two social scientists — Roger Pearson and Raymond B. Cattell, both associated with the *Mankind Quarterly* and both coincidentally born and educated in Britain before spending the bulk of their professional lives in the U.S. — merit more detailed consideration.

Roger Pearson, an anthropologist in the tradition of Hans F.K. Günther, established the Northern League in Europe a decade after the war as a gathering point for former Nazi intellectuals and S.S. officers, with Günther himself as one of the founding members (see Billig, 1979). The League's first conference, held in Detmold, Germany, was termed "national socialism revived" by German officials (quoted in Anderson and Anderson, 1986, p. 94). At about the same time, Pearson began publication of the journal *Northern World*, dedicated to Nordic racial solidarity, in which he bemoaned the fact that nationality was no longer determined "by the common blood ties of a shared biological heritage, but by the accident of geographical location" (Pearson, 1959, p. 4). The resulting "racial chaos" could be remedied and — of particular importance — the superior Nordic preserved, wrote Pearson (1959, p. 6), only by realizing "the falsity of modern political 'nationality' laws which are playing havoc with our natural loyalties and result too often in mongrelisation at home and fratricidal warfare abroad." This was a clarion call for resurrection of the Nuremberg Laws, not just in Germany but also in Britain, the U.S., and other racially Nordic countries where, in Pearson's view, the policy on citizenship should be: only Nordics need apply.

In *Race and Civilization* (Pearson, 1966) — which acknowledged Günther as its inspiration and, in emulation of his work, is filled with photos of beady-eyed, hook-nosed "Hither Asiatics" (i.e., Jews) and aristocratic-appearing "Distinguished Nordics" — Pearson provided further detail on the threat to Nordic purity. That "symbol ... of human dignity," he wrote, the "world-conquering ... Nordic or Aryan species," in the attempt to hold onto their ancestral estates in the face of rising taxes against the aristocracy, was being "persuaded ... to intermarry with Jewish and other non-Nordic elements," thereby "sacrific[ing] their biological heritage ... and ... their real claim to nobility" (Pearson, 1966, pp. 26, 122). The Nordic countries, Pearson (1966, p. 126) concluded — the U.S., Britain, Germany, and several others — had embarked on a policy of "racial self-destruction through State-aided immigration and even State-aided miscegenation."

Although Pearson's postwar efforts to create a Fourth Reich were largely unrewarded, they did catch the attention of the American neo-Nazi activist Willis A. Carto, who persuaded Pearson to emigrate to the U.S., where he took over editorship of *Northern World*'s successor *Western Destiny*, founded by Carto and based on his view of Jews as "Culture Distorters" conspiring to destroy the racial basis of Western civilization, and "aliens ... inherently unable to be in tune with ... Western Culture and Spirituality" ("Challenge to the liberals," 1964, p. 5). (As Carto proudly acknowledged ["Word from the publisher," 1964, p. 3], his own thought was largely influenced by Francis Parker Yockey's [1962] *Imperium*, a book dedicated to "the Hero of the Second World War" — Adolf Hitler — and published by Carto's own press with an introduction by Carto himself.) Pearson's first editorial in *Western Destiny* offered South Africa under apartheid and Rhodesia (renamed Zimbabwe at the end of white minority rule) as "the only countries in which there exists any general understanding of the true racial and historical foundation of Western Culture" and pledged to prevent the "Culture Distorters," who sought to "pervert morality" through their insistence on freedom in place of race consciousness, "from capturing the minds, morals and souls of our own children" ("New look", 1965, p. 3). Under Pearson's editorship, the journal attacked the New York bankers, those "masters of international finance" who had insisted on the "Second Fratricidal War" in order to reimpose the usurious payments on Germany that the Nazis had so heroically resisted (Paul, 1966, pp. 8, 9).

As the country in general grew less tolerant of overt racism in the 1960s, the rhetoric of *Western Destiny* was unlikely to win any new adherents, and it was necessary to adopt a more subtle approach to peddling hatred. Pearson soon parted company with Carto and spent the better part of the next decade in a series of academic positions, teaching anthropology and writing an introductory text in the field. In the mid-1970s, he moved to Washington, D.C., where he founded the Council on American Affairs and the Institute for the Study of Man, not only creating for himself a new, more respectable image as a mainstream conservative, but quickly gaining a position on the editorial boards of such think tanks as the Heritage Foundation, the Foreign Policy Research Institute, and the American Security Council. Pearson also brought publication of a now more sophisticated appearing *Mankind Quarterly* to his own Institute, replaced Gayre as its editor, and began publication of two new journals — one for technical studies in linguistics, the other a political journal featuring contributions by such well known conservatives as Jack Kemp and Jesse Helms — as well as a series of books and monographs; a few years later, he initiated yet another political journal, *Conservative Review*. (Many of the monographs, as well as the *Quarterly*, were issued by Cliveden Press, an allusion to the Cliveden Set, the group of British aristocrats sympathetic to Hitler; see Kuhn, 1938, p. E4.) Pearson had become a recognized intellectual in New Right circles and could even exhibit a letter from Ronald Reagan, congratulating him for "performing a valuable service in bringing to a wide audience the work of leading scholars" (quoted in Anderson and Anderson, 1986, p. 92).

Behind Pearson's newly minted facade, however, lurked the same neo-Nazi beliefs. When his Council on American Affairs became the American affiliate of the World Anti-Communist League (WACL), Pearson used the opportunity to turn the WACL into a new version of the Northern League, filling it with former S.S. officers and Nazi officials, Nazi collaborators from other European countries, and new recruits to the cause (see Anderson and Anderson, 1986). In 1978, the new organization gathered in Washington, D.C., for its annual conference with Pearson as its chair, aided by the assistant from his own Council, a former American Nazi Party stormtrooper. According to the *Washington Post*, conference workers distributed literature from the Liberty Lobby, containing, along with its political analyses, advertisements for Klan T-shirts, swastika-marked coins from the Third Reich, and cassette tapes of Nazi marching songs. One official delegation to the conference circulated materials calling a recent television show on the Holocaust "another gigantic campaign of Jewish propaganda to conceal their objectives of world domination" (quoted in Valentine, 1978, p. C1). During the conference, the French representatives met with William Pierce, a former American Nazi Party functionary and now head of a Virginia group promoting white superiority on the basis of scientific evidence, because, said Pierce, the two groups were "working along lines very close" to each other (quoted in Valentine, 1978, p. C1). Pierce (writing under the pseudonym Andrew MacDonald) is also the author of *The Turner Diaries*

(1978/1980), the blueprint for race war that was of particular interest to Timothy McVeigh, who was convicted of the terrorist bombing of a federal office building in Oklahoma City.

Yet even at such a notorious gathering, Pearson was anxious not to tarnish his new image of moderation. When members of the virulently racist National States Rights Party — a group whose by-laws state that "Jew-devils have no place in a White Christian nation" (quoted in George and Wilcox, 1992, p. 384) — showed up at the entrance to the conference distributing reprints from their newspaper, Pearson asked them to leave. "Not that I'm not sympathetic with what you're doing," he was reported as saying, "but don't embarrass me and cut my throat" (quoted in Valentine, 1978, p. C2). Clearly, Pearson had previously worked with the organization's leadership — he asked them to "give my regards" to Edward Fields, their national secretary; Fields has written that "every Jew who holds a position of power or authority must be removed from that position. If this does not work, then we must establish (the) Final Solution!!" (quoted in George and Wilcox, 1992, p. 383).

Under Pearson's editorship, the *Mankind Quarterly* too moved toward greater respectability, eschewing the worst rhetorical excesses of its earlier years, eliminating from its editorial staff unreconstructed right-wingers like Robert Kuttner, and no longer featuring enthusiastic praise for the work of Klansmen and Nazis. Nevertheless, Pearson remained faithful to the journal's founding principles, even if in a more subtle manner necessary to the post-civil rights era when overt calls for apartheid in the U.S. were no longer politically acceptable. The *Quarterly* continued, for example, to publish articles regularly insisting that integration had inevitably failed because of genetic differences between races and that interracial hostility was an automatic, hence inevitable, biological response serving an essential evolutionary purpose.

Many of these articles were written by Pearson, but typically under one of a host of aliases. In a civil proceeding in 1994, Pearson was forced to admit under oath what had long been suspected — that many articles purportedly written by others in the journals he has edited were actually his own work. In a deposition, he claimed to be able to recall only two such pseudonyms until prompted with some specific names, leading him to acknowledge at least two more, one of which — J.W. Jamieson — had authored 14 articles in the *Mankind Quarterly* alone as well as other works; there is little doubt that he has used many other aliases in print but was reluctant to acknowledge them. As his own explanation for this apparently deceptive behavior, Pearson declared it "not uncustomary for an editor of a journal to refrain from publishing too frequently under his own name in his own journal" and insisted that other "distinguished scholars" engaged in the same practice but could provide no examples (quoted in Institute for the Study of Academic Racism, 1997). While it is true that, without his use of pseudonyms, Pearson would have occasionally appeared as author of a number of articles in the same issue, sometimes but a single contribution on his part would nevertheless appear under one of his aliases.

In addition, his various identities appeared not only in the *Mankind Quarterly* but also as author or editor of other monographs published by Cliveden; in one instance, he even edited a book as "J.W. Jamieson" and then reviewed it as "Alan McGregor" (McGregor, 1987).

It is more likely that Pearson employed pseudonyms as a device primarily to avoid any responsibility for the opinions offered by his alter egos; the articles appearing under his own name emphasized racial differences but did not provide the scientific justification for hatred and violence presented under the aliases. But as editor, he could claim an intellectual responsibility to offer students of ethnology the opinions of other scholars.

In contrast to "real" scholarly journals, in which no article would be accepted for publication that merely repeated an idea that had already appeared in print, Pearson's pseudonymous contributions hammered away at the same themes time and again, often reprinting large sections verbatim. "Alan McGregor," alone, authored three articles (1981, 1986, 1993) declaring that racial prejudice was a biological necessity, "an honored quality" essential to evolutionary development, leading "healthy-minded people ... to maintain a healthy reproductive distance" from other races in order to "maintain the integrity of the gene pool" (McGregor, 1993, pp. 426, 431). The tendency to "distrust and repel" members of other races "as well as to love and to assist" one's own kind was not only normal and "a natural part of the human personality" but "one of the main pillars on which civilization was built, and one without which civilization might well collapse" (McGregor, 1993, pp. 431, 423).

Unfortunately, according to McGregor (1993, p. 428), the natural human tendency toward racial prejudice was "weakening under the pressure of human ideologies which are antithetical to biological realities." And the result of this breakdown, he observed, was "heavily urbanized and intellectually distorted human beings," who, just like caged animals attempting "to mate with animals of other breeds," exhibited numerous "perversions" of their natural instincts — "abnormal patterns of behavior ranging from homosexuality to a quest for abnormal erotic experiences including interracial sexual experimentation" (McGregor, 1993, pp. 430-431). Indeed, McGregor complained, our appreciation of biological imperatives had so deteriorated that acts of racial prejudice had come to be considered as "immoral" or — worse yet — as "hate crimes" (1993, p. 423). According to science, loving someone of another race was a violation of nature's law; to react violently to such a transgression was normal and natural. In the 1990s, it was still possible for a scientific journal to provide a biological rationalization for a lynch mob.

Perhaps the most revealing examples of Pearson's attempt to encode his original ideology somewhat more euphemistically are the two articles written 30 years apart by "William A. Massey", almost certainly another of his many aliases. In 1962, "The New Fanatics" appeared in the *Mankind Quarterly*, a lengthy and hateful diatribe against "intellectuals" who were using their influence as writers and teachers to manipulate an unsuspecting public into supporting integration and equal rights for blacks. It is an "uncomfortable fact," declared Massey (1962, p. 81), "that the Negro may never make a good American citizen. Even if he is of adequate intelligence he may be temperamentally unsuited for citizenship in a democracy, ... a form of government restricted to a few places and few races."

Although Massey (1964) also contributed to *Western Destiny* during Pearson's editorship, none of the standard abstracts or databases lists him as an author again until 1992 when "The New Fanatics" reappeared — an almost verbatim reprint of the original article — in two installments in *Conservative Review*, another of Pearson's publishing ventures (Massey, 1992a,b). In the updated version, however, it was now "crime-ridden minority welfare-receivers" who "may never make productive citizens" and "even if ... of adequate intelligence" were "by inheritance temperamentally unsuited for citizenship in a democracy" (Massey, 1992a, p. 33). Though the new language suggested a slightly more selective definition of those individuals unworthy of their constitutional entitlements, there could be little doubt that this was the same exclusionary ideology Pearson had offered 34 years earlier in *Northern World*. Nationality should be based on race; non-whites — indeed, in his opinion "non-Nordics" — did not belong in the U.S. or in other Nordic countries.

Eliminating "Moribund Races"

The other scientist associated with the *Mankind Quarterly* who played a particularly noteworthy role in the justification of group hatred and collective violence is the well-known late psychologist Raymond B.

Cattell, a frequent contributor to the journal and a member of its Editorial Advisory Board. The author of 56 books and hundreds of articles during a remarkable career lasting through seven decades, Cattell (who died in 1998), made significant contributions to psychometric methodology and to the fields of personality, motivation, and abilities. In 1997, the American Psychological Foundation named him the recipient of its Gold Medal Award for Lifetime Achievement in Psychology and the accompanying statement termed him, without exaggeration, "among a very small handful of people in this century who have most influenced the shape of psychology as a science" ("Gold medal award…", 1997, p. 798). (After the Foundation was informed of Cattell's ideological work, actual presentation of the award was postponed pending the report of a Blue Ribbon Panel, but shortly before the Panel was scheduled to submit its conclusions, Cattell withdrew his name from consideration.)

Hand in hand with his undeniable contributions to psychology, however, Cattell had also developed an elaborate scientific rationale, not merely justifying, but *requiring*, rigid racial separation so that "moribund" races could be segregated and eventually subjected to "genthanasia" — prevented from reproducing any of their kind — to keep the Earth from being converted into a "living museum … choked with … primitive forerunners" (Cattell, 1972, pp. 220, 221). For many of the other scientists associated with the *Mankind Quarterly*, science provided a convenient justification — a pseudo-scholarly patina — for opinions and policies that had doubtlessly been informed by other, less respectable motivations; despite the rash of articles written by "Alan McGregor", a deep appreciation of evolutionary biology was hardly what had led Roger Pearson to pronounce Jews a threat to Nordic purity in 1966. In contrast, Cattell developed not just a sociopolitical ideology but also an elaborate belief system termed "Beyondism" as an organic outgrowth of the evolutionary dynamic. Indeed, the titles of his two books on the subject (Cattell, 1972, 1987) refer to Beyondism, respectively, as "A New Morality from Science" and "Religion from Science."

Rooted in Herbert Spencer's Social Darwinism, the central tenet of Cattell's system is the claim that both morality and religion must be branches of natural science. Standards for moral behavior — our fundamental beliefs about the way human beings should treat each other — should not be derived from "mystical" religious teachings or from abstract humanitarian principles such as "social justice and equality", "basic freedom", and "human dignity" — all of which Cattell (1972, p. 411) called "whore phrases" — but must be "discovered by an examination of nature" (Cattell, 1933, p. 175). And what nature reveals, according to Cattell (1933, p. 140), is that progress toward higher levels of evolution is the "true aim of life;" hence, in order to produce a system of morality "compatible with the real nature of ourselves and the universe," evolutionary progress also must be the "end and aim of all moral laws" (Cattell, 1938, p. 88).

In Cattell's Social Darwinist view, however, evolutionary progress could be assured "only by our co-operating with Nature in its vigilant and ruthless elimination of the less fit," but such a *bellum omnium contra omnes*, he recognized, would lead to moral laws that "are apparently the exact opposite of those which religion and humanity have bred into our bones" (Cattell, 1938, p. 89). He resolved this paradox by declaring that, neither the species nor the individual, but *race*, was the basic unit of evolution; some races were biologically superior to others and thus deserved to survive and expand at the expense of the less fit. As a consequence, "altruistic modes of behavior which are at first sight biologically perverse" (Cattell, 1933, p. 69) — qualities such as "sympathy, unselfishness, self-sacrifice, and the capacity for enthusiastic co-operation" (Cattell, 1938, p. 91) — were morally acceptable only when employed to benefit one's own race; their extension to members of an "alien" race, Cattell maintained (1933, p. 69), was "abominable".

Because race was the unit of evolutionary progress, societies had to be "composed entirely of their own types" (Cattell, 1933, p. 47) — i.e., be racially homogeneous — because in a racially mixed society, Cattell warned, an inferior group would unfairly enjoy the advantages produced by its betters. Besides, temperament, natural preferences in music and art, ways of thinking, choice of amusement, and other cultural traits were all a consequence of race, and the presence of more than one race in the same society would only produce conflict and confusion. "To treat alien individuals as if they belonged to the same race, simply because their intelligence is on the same ... level," wrote Cattell (1933, pp. 65–66), "is a mistake;" an intelligent Englishman was naturally "more at one" with a less capable member of his own race than with a Jew who was his intellectual equal, and in no way "could a less gifted Scot be replaced by an advanced member of the negro [sic] race."

Yet another reason for the strict separation of races, according to Cattell (1933, pp. 155, 151) was to avoid the deleterious effects created by the "mixture of bloods between racial groups." Evolutionary morality decreed that "there shall be no miscegenation." In a "pure race," he explained (Cattell, 1933, p. 63):

"The inheritance of impulses in each individual is bound to be well balanced. The innate forces which are the innate material of character-building must have reached a certain compatibility and potential power of good integration. If two such races inter-breed, the resulting re-shuffling of impulses and psychic forces throws together in each individual a number of items which may or may not be compatible and capable of being organized into a stable unit."

Thus, "hybrids," he continued, were not only inferior to either parent race and suffered from various anatomical and glandular abnormalities, but were "frequently positively vicious," displaying "seriously defective ... intellectual and moral development" and "an abnormal liability to moral conflict and disorder" (Cattell, 1933, pp. 61–62). As an example of the problems caused by such mismatched genes, Cattell pointed out the "unstable governments" among Celtic and Eastern European people, a consequence of their mixture of Alpine and Mediterranean strains (Cattell, 1933, p. 63). Although some of the apparent silliness in these observations may be attributed to the essentialist notions of an earlier scientific zeitgeist, even in 1987 Cattell was still insisting that the "Melting Pot" in the U.S. has been largely a disaster because "90% of the hybrids" it produced were "unsuccessful" (Cattell, 1987, p. 202). Indeed, he added, the "unfortunate combinations" of various ethnic groups resulting from the Melting Pot were "responsible for the higher crime and insanity rates in the U.S.A. than in the parent countries."

In the pre-war period, however, when Cattell first developed his scientifically based morality, he saw that most nations were a "crazy pattern" of different races, and he worried that there would be no "true human progress" until some sort of racial order was established (Cattell, 1933, p. 81); in order to be of any evolutionary value, national competition had to be racial competition. And everywhere he looked in Europe, the major threat to racial order was the Jews, a group of introverted outsiders characterized by "a crafty spirit of calculation" and frequently accused of "cowardice, treason and avarice" (Cattell, 1933, pp. 48, 47). As an example of the social chaos produced by differing races living in the same nation, wrote Cattell (1933, p. 300), "think of the Jews anywhere." But quite apart from the Jews' personal traits, he explained, Europeans could not help but experience a "feeling of strangeness" in response to these racial "intruders" (Cattell, 1933, p. 47). "Hatred and abhorrence ... for the Jewish practice of living in other nations instead of forming an independent, self-sustained group of their own" was, according to Cattell (1933, p. 70), the normal and appropriate response to a group that refused "to play the game correctly," and only "would-be intellectuals" suffering from biological ignorance foolishly regarded such a natural reaction as "prejudice".

Although Cattell was disappointed with the shortsightedness of so many of his contemporaries, he was gratified to see that one European country displayed a deep appreciation of evolutionary morality. Only in the Third Reich, where the Nuremberg Laws had been passed, systematically removing the intruders and eliminating their influence from Aryan culture, did Cattell find a society based on biological wisdom. In 1937, he praised the Nazi regime for its "positive emphasis on racial improvement" (Cattell, 1937, p. 141) and, a year later (1938, p. 149), observed that Germany and its fascist allies were scientifically enlightened countries ...

"... in which individuals have disciplined their indulgences as to a religious purpose ... in comparison with the vast numbers in our democracies lacking any super-personal aim. Their rise should be welcomed by the religious man as reassuring evidence that in spite of modern wealth and ease, we shall not be allowed to sink into stagnation or adapt foolish social practices in fatal detachment from the stream of evolution."

Cattell was pleased to see that the Nazis were forcing the Jews "to play the game correctly" whether the Jews wanted to or not.

Of course, the major purpose of racially homogeneous societies in Cattell's moral system was to allow for a scientific assessment of their respective "validities," a determination of which races were destined to be "hammer" and which to be "anvil" in the shaping of the future (Cattell, 1979, p. 308). To ensure the accuracy of this judgment, it was essential, he emphasized, that advances developed by one group not be available to another because "culture borrowing" would separate the rewards of progress from their racial origin (Cattell, 1972, p. 187). It was similarly "immoral" for one race to provide "external 'charitable' support" to another, even if the result seemed "ruthless", because such assistance would merely reinforce genetically defective groups that did not deserve to survive. Indeed, Cattell insisted (1972, p. 178), the failure of a superior race to "expand" at the cost of a "defective group" was also an "immoral act militating against evolution." He further stated (1972, p. 95) that, "Failing groups" should "go to the wall" while "successful groups" deserved to "increase their power, influence, and size." The implication was unmistakable: If Third World peoples were slaughtered by famine, disease, or intertribal conflicts, it was not the role of the "advanced" nations to offer assistance, but rather, to confiscate the remains.

In the 1930s, Cattell did not hesitate to name names. While he was certain that Nordics were the most "highly evolved", a bold, intelligent race naturally fit to rule others, he was more concerned with pointing out the losers in the evolutionary competition, the races that should be pruned from the tree of humanity, so that their elimination might be both speedy and unmourned. In particular, he noted (1938, p. 145) that "the negro [sic]" was obviously an inferior race, whose lower "mental capacity ... arises from a smaller skull capacity ... as racially characteristic as the greater projection of his heel at the other end of the skeleton." Although blacks were "constitutionally good-natured and lovable," for all "their endearing qualities of humour and religiosity," wrote Cattell (1938, p. 94), they had contributed "practically nothing to social progress and culture," and all the attempts to "graft" more sophisticated cultural notions onto blacks had only resulted in further "crudity" (Cattell, 1937, p. 56). In "such clearly established cases," he declared (1933, p. 360), "interference is called for ... it is time to call a halt to a certain line of evolution."

Because the elimination of such an inferior group was imperative for evolutionary progress, the only question for Cattell was how the process should be accomplished. In the past, he noted, the "surgical operation of lopping off the backward branches of the tree of mankind was done violently," as losers in the evolutionary competition were "driven with bloodshed from their lands, ... blindly unconscious of the biological rationality of that destiny"; in the present, the same end was typically attained "by machine guns and the diseminating [sic] of disease and alcohol" (Cattell, 1933, p. 360). In place of such inhumane methods, Cattell (1938, p. 94) urged that the elimination of backward peoples be carried out with "kindness and consideration. ...By gradual restriction of births, and by life in adapted reserves and asylums, must the races which have served their turn be brought to euthanasia." That is, to escape the outright butchery that had characterized previous evolutionary progress, groups deemed inferior by the "advanced" races would be forced onto reservations where they would be prevented from reproducing. Should they resist this "humane" approach, however, the more traditional methods would be inevitable.

When other social scientists in the U.S. turned to the study of racial "prejudice" against blacks in the post-war period, Cattell called it a "sad blot on the escutcheon of the social sciences" (1948, p. 195). He found nothing prejudicial — that is, nothing "which cannot be rationally defended" — in the desire to segregate an inferior group and prevent its contact with the majority (Cattell, 1948, p. 195). According to Cattell, such an attitude was not only rational but scientifically imperative, and anyone who thought otherwise should be "automatically disqualif[ied] as a social scientist" (Cattell, 1948, p. 195). Even in the 1990s, he was still insisting that racism was a "natural innate" tendency with evolutionary "virtue" (Cattell, 1992, p. 284).

After the civil rights movement, however, it was no longer acceptable to recommend bluntly that blacks be systematically eliminated in the U.S., even if the process were carried out with "kindness and consideration" and, just as Pearson changed his tone, Cattell too then offered a slightly more subtle formulation of the same underlying message. Without mentioning blacks by name, he warned that "the musical beat from the jungle" was incompatible with "Anglo-Saxon culture" (Cattell, 1972, p. 211) and complained of the social "parasitism" created by a "genetic sub-group" with genes for resistance to malaria but low intelligence (Cattell, 1972, p. 153); because blacks carry the sickle cell gene, which also provides malarial immunity, there was little doubt about the identity of the "sub-group". A society faced with such a problem, he predicted, would eventually crash "like a great ceiling beam ... eaten from within by death watch beetles" (Cattell, 1972, p. 154) unless appropriate measures were taken. Clearly, blacks were still first on Cattell's list of "moribund" races that had already "served their turn." And though he himself may still have believed that such a "primitive" group should be "phas[ed] out" (Cattell, 1972, p.221) with kindness, others were likely to find more violent methods justified by such a severe threat to society, especially if individual members of the "failing" race proved reluctant to accept their scientifically decreed fate. In the Third Reich, in order to ensure racial homogeneity, the scientists had called only for the separation of the Jews — the central tenet of Beyondism — but other forces eventually used the professionals' own argument to justify more extreme measures.

To promote "Beyondism", in 1993, the then 88-year-old Cattell organized the Beyondist Foundation, which publishes an eponymous quarterly. The first issue of *The Beyondist* featured Cattell's review of *The Ethnostate*, the latest work by one of Beyondism's most enthusiastic adherents, Wilmot Robertson, whose hateful fulmination against "unassimilable" minorities, *The Dispossessed Majority*, had been so highly recommended by Robert Kuttner in the *Mankind Quarterly* after the major conservative journals found it too racist to review. Robertson is also the publisher of the neo-Nazi journal *Instauration*, which argues for "rational anti-Semitism" on the grounds that Jews are "arrogant obnoxious, and hypocritical ... aliens," who "distort our culture" and "promote race-mixing" ("Rational anti-Semitism," 1978, p. 14). In another book, Robertson wrote that Hitler's failure "to establish German racial hegemony in Europe ... was shattering" to Nordics in the U.S. and called the war "an unforgettable warning of the danger of placing nation or nationality above race" (Robertson, 1974, pp. 54, 76). As the solution to the country's social problems, for some time Robertson (1974, p. 55) had been promoting a racial balkanization of the U.S. that would deliver "whites of Northern European extraction" from their racial enemies — "an agglomeration of minorities consisting of Jews, dark-skinned Mediterranean whites, Chicanos, Indians, Puerto Ricans and Negroes." Based directly on Beyondism, this plan would relocate each "unassimilable" minority to its own enclave, thus producing a biologically correct "order whose geographical frontiers matched its racial frontiers" (Robertson, 1972, p. 556) as well as "accomplish[ing] the most urgent item … to sever Jews politically, economically and culturally from their host populations" (Robertson, 1974, pp. 102–103).

The Ethnostate (Robertson, 1992) presented the ultimate example of Beyondism in action. Offering science as the basis for morality and claiming that altruism is a "drag" on evolution, Robertson concluded that the highest race was "the one that has a patent on white genes" and that only Nordics were genetically fit for democracy and the Bill of Rights (Robertson, 1992, pp. 163, 224). Because this superior group was now surrounded by parasitic and incompatible racial elements, however, Robertson saw no chance for it to recapture the country it once ruled, and as the only hope for Nordic preservation, he proposed the partitioning of the U.S. into a large number of independent, racially homogeneous "ethnostates". Because citizenship in such states would be racially defined, laws against intermarriage would be unnecessary, though abortion would be "mandatory in the rare cases where mixed-race pregnancies occur" (Robertson, 1992, p. 120).

Cattell was quite pleased by this practical application of his own thinking, calling *The Ethnostate* "a timely supplement to the argument of the *Beyondist*" (quoted in Mehler, 1997, p. 158). Moreover, Cattell (1987, p. 2) acknowledged being personally "indebted" to Robertson for "improvements and clarifications" in Beyondism; apparently, Cattell was not only familiar with the work of this leading neo-Nazi theorist and found it compatible with his own scientifically derived system of morality, but he also knew the pseudonymous Robertson personally and solicited his opinion on Cattell's own thinking. And they both agreed: Nordic societies must be, not only *Judenrein*, but also free of any taint from blacks, Latinos, and other ethnic interlopers. Half a century after the unthinkable, one of the most influential psychologists of the century still found it scientifically necessary to achieve racial purity by excluding "incompatible" groups.

Evading and Fulfilling Professional Responsibility

It is possible, of course, to argue that scientists, who only propose ideas and theories, have no responsibility for violent acts committed by others. Fritz Lenz, for example, the German geneticist who offered a scientific explanation for Jewish "parasitism" and praised Hitler for soundly basing social policy on science, later disavowed any responsibility for the Reich's crimes because he "did not participate in the drafting" of the laws (Lenz, 1962, p. 309). It is true that scientists do not pull triggers, wield clubs, or give orders to those who do, whether they be Nazis in the 1930s or skinheads in the 1990s. But through their designation of some groups as biological burdens or dangers and their rationalization of racial hatred as natural, normal, and even mandatory for evolutionary progress, scientists give "permission" for acts of violence, becoming, in essence, intellectual accomplices to the crime. As one institutional official who participated in the gassing of mental patients in the Third Reich explained, despite being "torn" by his victims' agonies, he continued his ghoulish activities, reassured that "eminent scientists" had supported the policy (quoted in Wertham, 1966, p. 160).

Although nothing as horrible as the Nazi policies has occurred in the U.S., the often violent resistance to the civil rights movement in the 1950s and 1960s was regularly predicated on the authority of science. The literature list of the Citizens' Council, the center of organized, and often violent, resistance to the extension of full citizenship to blacks, was filled with articles by scientists, many of them reprinted directly from the *Mankind Quarterly* ("Timely articles on race…", 1966). Hundreds of thousands of copies of Henry Garrett's repulsive pamphlet, "How Classroom Desegregation Will Work", were distributed to suburban school districts undergoing integration (see Folsom, 1965; "Lesson in bias," 1966), informing parents and teachers that "demoralization, … disorganization, and eventually … ruin" were the inevitable result of allowing blacks and whites to attend the same school and that "intermarriage [is] a primary goal of the integrationist"; an accompanying photograph of a smiling white schoolgirl surrounded by happy black playmates was entitled "Will YOUR Child Be Exposed to THIS?" (Garrett, 1965, pp. 13, 14).

More recent racist organizations also claim the imprimatur of science and provide mail order lists of recommended reading, including many works by scientists. David Duke's National Association for the Advancement of White People, for example, offers its followers a list of "Suppressed Books" which includes a number of reprints from the *Mankind Quarterly*. Articles by Henry Garrett and lesser known psychologists appear on the list along side books "exposing … the intense hatred and duplicity of Jews" and providing the details of "Jew-Marxist domination" of Aryans ("Suppressed books", n.d.). Duke himself claimed to have espoused a "liberal, humanist viewpoint on race" until he discovered "the hard scientific facts" (quoted in Zatarain, 1990, p. 80). William Pierce, once a high-ranking official in the American Nazi Party and now head of the Nazi National Alliance also operates a mail order bookselling operation, providing the works of Roger Pearson and other scientists as justification for racism and anti-Semitism, along with books that glorify the Third Reich and expose the "enemy", that "extraordinarily dangerous parasite" — Jews. As an inducement to subscribe to his group's periodical *National Vanguard*, Pierce offers a free copy of Pearson's *Eugenics and Race* (National Vanguard Books, 1988). Pierce's catalog also offers the technical manuals on small arms, munitions, incendiaries, explosives, and demolitions that have been of particular interest to the militia movement. His own book, *The Turner Diaries* (1978/1980), provided the model for the underground group, The Order, which assassinated Denver talk show host Alan Berg because he was Jewish (see Coates, 1987). In the 1990s, National Alliance and other white supremacist groups also have web sites that offer numerous scientific references as justification for their policies.

Quite apart from their responsibility as citizens, social scientists who find this use of their discipline reprehensible have a *professional* responsibility to oppose it. At a time of overreaction to the excesses of political correctness, however, it is particularly important to distinguish criticism from the desire for proscription. Opposition to the misuse of science should never attempt to deprive the Pearsons and Cattells of the world of their own rights; the solution to bad speech, as Jefferson observed, is not restriction but effective response. Nor is the issue in this case "politically incorrect" science that judges one race less capable than another; rather, it is the attempt, on the basis of science, to deprive people of their rights or to justify hating and excluding them from full participation in society.

Social scientists are often unaware of the oppressive claims made in the name of their discipline; the *Mankind Quarterly* and other venues for this seamy side of science are not exactly mainstream journals. The average psychologist is more likely to learn of the existence of hate science from a news report on David Duke or some other extremist than from running across the actual literature.

However it may come to attention, though, with awareness comes obligation. There are a number of actions that psychologists and other social scientists can and should take to oppose the misuse of science. Naturally, when supremacist groups cite scientific authority for their own claims, other professionals should be quick to speak out, ensuring the lay public that there is no evidence in support of innate interracial hostility, and that, in any case, moral behavior is properly shaped, not by science, but by such traditional sources of values as religion, constitution, and conscience. Evolutionary psychology, for example, argues — and with substantially more evidence than is offered in support of racial conflict — that men are genetically programmed to attempt to impregnate as many women as possible, but our notions of moral behavior nevertheless demand restraint of such "innate" urges (see, for example, Wright, 1994).

More important, scientists and clinicians should encourage their professional associations at various levels to take an official stand on hate science. The American Psychological Association (APA), for example, has already frequently announced its opposition to racism, most recently through its "Psychology and Racism Project," which included a year-long series of conferences and lectures as well as a miniconvention, all designed "to educate psychologists and the public about the prevalence of racism and explore what can be done to change it" (APA, 1997a). The APA has also issued a statement of opposition to hate crimes, "condemn[ing] harassment, violence, and crime motivated by ... prejudice" (APA, 1991), and, in testimony before a congressional committee, has called for "education programs ... [to] reduce the prejudice and hostility that lead to hate crimes and violence against social groups" (APA, 1997b, p. 2). Given these official positions, it would seem only logical to also deplore the use of science to justify racism, especially in a context that rationalizes violence against members of other races as "innate" behavior. State associations as well should be encouraged to take similar stands. And because there is still considerable nonsense being peddled by scientists about the "abnormality" of both interracial marriages and their offspring, professional associations should go on record denouncing these assertions, also, as scientifically baseless.

Yet another matter of professional concern — not substantive but ethical — is the use of pseudonyms. While scientists are, of course, free to express their opinions, even when conducive to hatred and violence, they must then assume responsibility for their words. It is certainly ethically suspect and may be a violation of professional standards to publish, under a fictitious name, a highly provocative article arguing that violent behavior directed against members of other races is a biological imperative.

Finally, it is also essential that psychologists and other social scientists who are aware of the misuse of their disciplines raise the issue with their colleagues in as specific a fashion as possible. This can be done in many different contexts — in informal groups, as well as at more formal gatherings such as state, regional, and national conferences. Organizing symposia at such conferences is a particularly useful method for sensitizing colleagues to the ways in which social science has been exploited to justify hatred and violence. Specific groups within the APA, such as the Society for the Psychological Study of Social Issues (Division 9) and the Society for the Psychological Study of Ethnic Minority Issues (Division 45), would be likely candidates for sponsorship of such symposia.

In discussing this issue within the discipline, accuracy is essential, especially because other professionals may react with disbelief to the information that esteemed scientists have provided support for hate groups; the initial response to unpalatable news is often a rejection of the messenger. The revelations of Cattell's moral system, for example, produced outraged denials from some social scientists who refused to believe that one of the most influential psychologists of the century had created such a hateful ideology as an organic outgrowth of his scientific work, and when the American Psychological Foundation decided to postpone presentation of the Gold Medal Award, some of Cattell's defenders resigned from the APA in protest. (In an open letter to the APA, Cattell himself claimed that his writings had been "twisted" and "misinterpreted" by critics but provided no specific example [Cattell, 1997]. Although the letter disavowed any belief in "racism and discrimination based on race" and insisted on only "voluntary eugenics as a means to contribute to the evolution of the human race," it also, revealingly, announced Cattell's desire "to publicly retract those [past] statements" that conflicted with his present position [Cattell, 1997].)

Only accurate information will eventually overcome initial, understandably emotional reactions. For those interested in pursuing the topic further, at the end of this chapter are some carefully researched works, providing greater detail on scientific support for the justification of hatred and violence. Well-documented exposure of the true nature of this misuse of science is the best way to make it unacceptable, and making it unacceptable is necessary if we are to have better social sciences and a better society.

Summary

For almost a century, there has been a scientific school of thought that can justify violence against specific groups. This tradition maintains that certain groups are biologically harmful to society and must be excluded from it. In addition, it insists that interracial hostility is innate and hence inevitable.

Long before Hitler's rise to prominence, a group of distinguished German scientists working in the above-described tradition provided the rationale for some of the most inhumane policies of the Third Reich. In the post-war era, a number of scientists in the U.S. similarly attempted to oppose the civil rights movement in the 1960s and continued to argue for some system of rigid racial segregation. One member of this group, the well-known psychologist Raymond B. Cattell, believed that races should be separated from each other so that a judgment of their respective evolutionary fitness can be made and the "less successful" groups "phased out."

Social scientists and clinicians have a responsibility to oppose such hateful ideologies proposed in the name of their disciplines. Specific actions that they can take include informing the public, encouraging their professional associations to take an official stand, and raising the issue with their colleagues.

Annotated Bibliography

1. Proctor, R. (1988) *Racial Hygiene*. Cambridge, MA: Harvard University Press; Müller-Hill, B. (1988) *Murderous Science*. Oxford: Oxford University Press. These two works offer thorough treatments of the roles of scientists and physicians in crafting and implementing policy in the Third Reich.

2. Billig, M. (1979) *Psychology, Racism and Fascism*. Birmingham, England: A.F.&R. Publications. Billig provides an excellent description of the relationships between contemporary scholars in the U.S. and Europe and fascist movements.

3. Tucker, William H. (1994) *The Science and Politics of Racial Research*. Urbana, IL: University of Illinois Press. This book provides an overview of science in the service of oppressive political policies from the mid 19th century to the present.

References

APA (1991) *Resolution on Hate Crimes*. Washington, D.C.: American Psychological Association.

APA (1997a) Miniconvention to explore race and psychology (article from the *APA Monitor* posted on the World Wide Web). Washington, D.C.: American Psychological Association.

APA (1997b) *Testimony of the American Psychological Association on Juvenile Justice and Delinquency Prevention Act submitted to the Education and Workforce Committee Early Childhood, Youth and Families Subcommittee U.S. House of Representatives*. Washington, D.C.: American Psychological Association.

Anderson, S. and Anderson, J.L. (1986) *Inside the League*. New York: Dodd, Mead & Co.

"Ansprache des Herrn Reichministers des Innern Dr. Wilhelm Frick auf der ersten Sitzung des Sachverständigenbeirats für Bevölkerungs-und Rassenpolitik" (1933) *Archiv für Rassen-und Gesellschaftsbiologie*, *27*, 412–419.

Arnold, W. (1969) The evolution of man in relation to that of the Earth. *Mankind Quarterly*, *10*, 78–99.

Baur, E., Fischer, E., and Lenz, F. (1931) *Human Heredity*. New York: Macmillan.

Billig, M. (1979) *Psychology, Racism and Fascism*. Birmingham, England: A.F. and R. Publications.

Binding, K. and Hoche, A. (1920) *Die freigabe der vernichtung lebensunwerten lebens*. Leipzig: Felix Meiner.

Burnette, E. (1997) Retrieved Dec. 20 from the World Wide Web: http://www.apa.org/monitor/may97/race.html.

Campbell, C.G. (1936) The German racial policy, *Eugenical News*, *21*, 25–29.

Cattell, R.B. (1933) *Psychology and Social Progress*. London: C.W. Daniel.

Cattell, R.B. (1937) *The Fight for Our National Intelligence*. London: P.S. King.

Cattell, R.B. (1938) *Psychology and the Religious Quest*. London: Thomas Nelson & Sons.

Cattell, R.B. (1948) Ethics and the social sciences. *American Psychologist*, *91*, 193–198.

Cattell, R.B. (1972) *A New Morality from Science: Beyondism*. New York: Pergamon Press.

Cattell, R.B. (1979) Ethics and the social sciences: the "Beyondist" solution. *Mankind Quarterly*, *19*, 298–310.

Cattell, R.B. (1987) *Beyondism: Religion from Science*. New York: Praeger.

Cattell, R.B. (1992) Virtue in "racism"? *Mankind Quarterly*, *32*, 281–284.

Cattell, R.B. (1997) *An Open Letter to the APA*. Letter posted on the World Wide Web by E.D. Cattell, Stanford, CA. Retrieved Feb. 26, 1998, from http://www-leland.stanford.edu/~cattell/rbcachie.htm.

"Challenge to the liberals" (1964) *Western Destiny*, *9*, 5.

Coates, J. (1987) *Armed and Dangerous*. New York: Hill & Wang.

"Editorial" (1960) *Mankind Quarterly*, *1*, 4.

"Eugenical propaganda in Germany" (1934) *Eugenical News*, *19*, 45.

"Eugenical sterilization in Germany" (1933) *Eugenical News*, *18*, 89–93.

Folsom, M. (1965) Anti-Negro, anti-Semitic booklets flood suburbs. *The New York Times*, Dec. 19, p. 48.

Ford, R. (1966) Review of white America. *Mankind Quarterly*, *7*, 117–119.

Frick, W. (1934) German population and race politics, *Eugenical News*, *19*, 33–38.

Friedlander, H. (1995) *The Origins of Nazi Genocide*. Chapel Hill, N.C.: University of North Carolina Press.

Garrett, H.E. (1961a) Comment. *Current Anthropology, 2*, 319–320.

Garrett, H.E. (1961b) The equalitarian dogma. *Mankind Quarterly, 1*, 253–257.

Garrett, H.E. (1962) Letter to the editor. *Science, 135*, 982–984.

Garrett, H.E. (1965) How classroom desegregation will work, *Citizen*, October, pp. 5–17.

Gates, R.R. (1929) *Heredity in Man*. London: Constable & Co.

Gates, R.R. (1948) *Human Ancestry from a Genetical Point of View*. Cambridge, MA: Harvard University Press.

Gayre, R.G. (1944) *Teuton and Slav on the Polish Frontier*. London: Eyre & Spottiswoode.

George, J. and Wilcox, L. (1992) *Nazis, Communists, Klansmen and Others on the Fringe*. Buffalo, NY: Prometheus.

Gini, C. (1967) Race and sociology. In R.E. Kuttner (Ed.), *Race and Modern Science*, pp. 261–277. New York: Social Science Press.

"Gold medal award for lifetime achievement in psychological science" (1997) *American Psychologist, 52*, 797–799.

Günther, H.F.K. (1927/1970) *The Racial Elements of European History*. Port Washington, NY: Kennikat.

Hall, E.R. (1960) Zoological subspecies of man. *Mankind Quarterly, 1*, 113–119.

Institute for the Study of Academic Racism. (1997) In the circuit court. Announcement posted on the World Wide Web by B. Mehler, Lansing, MI. Retrieved Nov. 10, 1997, from http://www.ferris.edu/htmls/othersrv/isar/court.html

Kuhn, F. (1938) Friends of Hitler strong in Britain. *The New York Times*, April 17, p. E4.

Kuttner, R. (1963) Statement. In *Hearings before Subcommittee No. 5 of the Committee on the Judiciary on Miscellaneous Proposals Regarding the Civil Rights of Persons Within the Jurisdiction of the United States*, HR 88-1, July 19, pp. 1963–1980.

Kuttner, R.E. (1972) Northern light on southern scene. *Citizen*. December, pp. 22–29.

Kuttner, R.E. (1973) Review of the dispossessed majority. *Mankind Quarterly, 14*, 118–119.

Lang, T. (1930) Der Nationalsozialismus als politischer Ausdruck unserer biologischen Kenntnis. *Nationalsozialistische Monatshefte, 1*, 393–397.

Laughlin, H.H. (1922) Full text for a model state law. In H.H. Laughlin, *Eugenical Sterilization in the United States*, pp.441–447. Chicago, IL: Psychopathic Laboratory of the Municipal Court of Chicago.

Lenz, F. (1931) Die Stellung des Nationalsozialismus zur Rassenhygiene. *Archiv für Rassen- und Gesellschaftsbiologie, 25*, 300–308.

Lenz, F. (1932) *Menschliche Auslese und Rassenhygiene (Eugenik)* Munich: J.F. Lehmans.

Lenz, F. (1962) Letter to the editor. *Journal of Human Genetics, 14*, 309.

"Lesson in bias" (1966) *Time*, May 30, p. 63.

Lifton, R.J. (1986) *The Nazi Doctors*. New York: Basic Books.

MacDonald, A. (W. Pierce) (1978/1980) *The Turner Diaries*. Hillsboro, WV: National Vanguard Books.

Massey, W.A. (1962) The new fanatics. *Mankind Quarterly, 2*, 70–104.

Massey, W.A. (1964) Are all races equal? *Western Destiny, 9 (July)*, 10.

Massey, W.A. (1992a) The new fanatics: part one. *Conservative Review, 3* (Oct.), 28–35.

Massey, W.A. (1992b) The new fanatics: part two. *Conservative Review, 3* (Dec.), 34–41.

McGregor, A. (1981) Group conflict: an evolutionary residual? *Mankind Quarterly, 22*, 43–48.

McGregor, A. (1986) The evolutionary function of prejudice. *Mankind Quarterly, 26*, 277–284.

McGregor, A. (1987) Altruism, war and cultural selection. *Mankind Quarterly, 28*, 171–188.

McGregor, A. (1993) The double nature of prejudice. *Mankind Quarterly, 33*, 423–432.

Mehler, B. (1997) Beyondism: Raymond B. Cattell and the new eugenics. *Genetica, 99*, 153–163.

Menschliche Erblichkeitslehre und Rassenhygiene. (1928) *Quarterly Review of Biology, 3*, 136.

Müller-Hill, B. (1988) *Murderous Science.* Oxford: Oxford University Press.

National Vanguard Books (1988) *Catalog No. 11.* Hillsboro, WV.

Nevin, E. (1967) The black brainwash in America. *Mankind Quarterly, 7*, 233–235.

"New look" (1965) *Western Destiny, 10*, 3.

Paul, A. (1966) Hitler's economic policies 1933–39. *Western Destiny, 11*, 7–9.

Pearson, R. (1959) Pan-Nordicism as a modern policy. *Northern World, 3*, 4–7.

Pearson, R. (1966) *Race and Civilization.* Jackson, MS: New Patriot.

Popenoe, P. (1934) The German sterilization law. *Journal of Heredity, 25*, 257–260.

Proctor, R. (1988) *Racial Hygiene.* Cambridge, MA: Harvard University Press.

Purves, D. (1960) The evolutionary basis of race consciousness. *Mankind Quarterly, 1*, 51–54.

"Racial mixing could be catastrophic" (1963) Interview with Dr. Henry E. Garrett. *Time*, Nov. 18, pp. 92–93.

"Rational anti-Semitism" (1978) In W. Robertson (Ed.), *Best of Instauration 1978*, pp. 14, 78–79. Cape Canaveral, FL: Howard Allen.

Robertson, W. (1972) *The Dispossessed Majority.* Cape Canaveral, FL: Howard Allen.

Robertson, W. (1974) *Ventilations.* Cape Canaveral, FL: Howard Allen.

Robertson, W. (1992) *The Ethnostate.* Cape Canaveral, FL: Howard Allen.

Rüdin, E. (1934) Aufgaben und Ziele der deutschen Gesellschaft für Rassenhygiene. *Archiv für Rassen- und Gesellschaftsbiologie, 28*, 228–233.

Simonds, C.H. (1971) The strange story of Willis Carto. *National Review*, Sept. 10, pp. 978-989.

Skerlj, B. (1960) Correspondence. *Man, 60*, 172–173.

Strong, L.A.G. (1931) Full circle. *New Statesman and Nation*, 482–483.

"Suppressed books" (n.d.) *NAAWP News, 37,* 15.

Thompson, N.A. (1936) Letter to the editor. *Eugenics Review, 28*, 164–165.

"Timely articles on race relations and science" (1966) *The Citizen*, January, pp. 24–26.

Tucker, W.H. (1994) *The Science and Politics of Racial Research.* Urbana, IL: University of Illinois Press.

Valentine, P.W. (1978) The Fascist specter behind the world anti-red league. *Washington Post*, May 28, pp. C1–C2.

Weinrich, M. (1946) *Hitler's Professors.* New York: Yiddish Scientific Institute.

Wertham, F. (1966) *A Sign for Cain.* New York: Macmillan.

"Word from the publisher" (1964) *Western Destiny, 9* (June), 3.

Wright, R. (1994) *The Moral Animal*. New York: Pantheon.

Yockey, F.P. (1962) *Imperium*. New York: Truth Seeker.

Zatarain, M. (1990) *David Duke: Evolution of a Klansman*. Gretna, LA: Pelican.

About the Author

William H. Tucker, Ph.D., is a graduate of Bates College in Lewiston, ME, and received his M.A. and Ph.D. in Psychology from Princeton University. His book, *The Science and Politics of Racial Research*, was named winner of the Cleveland Foundation's Anisfield-Wolf Award and the American Political Science Association's Ralph J. Bunche Award. He is presently Professor of Psychology at Rutgers University in Camden, NJ, where he received the Rutgers College Public Service Award for his work in the Camden community.

Chapter 18

A STRATEGY FOR INSTITUTIONAL VIOLENCE: *SATYAGRAHA* AND GANDHIAN SYNTHESIS

Lucien A. Buck

Institutional violence is characteristic of Western civilization from its earliest stages. Fine (1985), for example, described modern Western civilization as a hate culture. These cultures foster antagonism, harshness, and competitiveness. The primary atmosphere is one of discord and an ever-present fear of death. A desire for vengeance is omnipresent, dependence on magic and sorcery is widespread, sex is oriented toward conquest, and women and children are devalued. As with all typologies, such distinctions do not adequately characterize every person, and no culture can be satisfactorily classified in a simplistic fashion. Nevertheless, as Fine (1985) demonstrated, Greece and Rome glorified violence and conquest, subjugated women, and supported slavery. The idealized hero was defined by achievements in killing. Jewish tradition is similarly derived from a warlike people whose angry god supported violent conquest. Absolute obedience by and the inferiority of women were central. Christianity, originally based upon principles of love and nonviolence, was converted to violence by arguments that rationalized the "justified war" and the "holy war". Given these tools, the aggressive traditions of Greece and Rome became the primary business of Christianity. The conquests that followed were paralleled by a physical assault on heretics through the inquisition and psychological tyranny through sexual repression. These traditions were built upon a fundamental belief in the innate aggressiveness of human beings.

Eventually, the justification of violence within Western civilization was converted into admiration. Craig (1989), for example, pointed out that war was used as an acceptable means of regulating human affairs and as a desirable instrument for eliminating objectionable and inferior members of society. This veneration of violence was apparent in the Victorian period in terms of the culture of honor (Gay, 1993) and clearly exists, in this form, today particularly in the American South (Nisbett et al., 1995). Weigley (1991) labeled the modern period the "age of battles" in view of the preoccupation with war as a means of solving international relations, and a variety of authors continue to discuss the contemporary employment of weapons in the service of deterrence or conflict (e.g., Kull, 1989; Zuckerman, 1989; Lifton and Markusen, 1990; Draper, 1991, 1992; Hall, 1996).

The pinnacle of institutional violence, however, is found in nuclear war (Lifton, 1967), which grew out of 20th century technological advances in warmaking and the psychological methods of converting ordinary people into agents of terror and killing. Lifton (1986), for example, demonstrated the effectiveness of Nazi ideology to convert physicians, sworn to preserve life, into the primary instruments for killing in the death camps, and Muller (1991) described how this system turned judges and lawyers, dedicated to the administration of justice, into servants of extermination. Goldhagen (1996) extended the lethal consequences of German anti-Semitism to all professions, religions, and economic groups. Similarly, Fromm's (1973) analysis of Nazi leaders led to the conclusion that there are a multitude of people ready to serve the government as its agents for torture and killing, and Todorov (1996) substantiated this warning by his analysis of Hitler's extermination camps and Stalin's gulags. The generalizability of these conclusions was verified by Gibson's (1991) evidence regarding the ease with which ordinary people can be trained to become torturers for the state, by Kelman and Hamilton's (1989) analysis of crimes of obedience, and by Lifton's (1973) work with Vietnam veterans.

War, however, is not the only form of official violence promoted by Western society. Straus, Gelles, and Steinmetz (1980) and Gelles and Cornell (1990) described the long history of cruelty displayed toward women and children within this culture. It is only during relatively recent times that physical punishment of one's wife has become undesirable and illegal in the U.S., and the physical punishment of children remains a valued, if controversial, means of discipline (Gelles and Cornell, 1990). Wife abuse is now clearly defined, but the borderline between physical punishment and child abuse remains murky. In fact, Tedeschi and Felson (1994) concluded that most severe punishment grows out of a disciplinary situation. Violence in the family, nevertheless, continues to be a primary source of homicide (Bixenstine, 1996; Poirier, 1996). In addition, Toch (1992) and Wertham (1969) discussed the organization of violent games and sports as part of the preparation of young men for war, and Ember and Ember (1995) demonstrated that societies which encourage warlike sports and severe punishment have more wars. The institutionalization of violence has taken many other forms within American society, such as what Farrell (1993) called the death professions, Rappaport and Holden (1981) described as corporate violence, Whitaker (1996) proposed as social inducements to homicide, Jordan (1968) probed as the roots of slavery, and Brown (1970) analyzed as the subjugation and extermination of Native Americans. Consistent with this evidence, Buck (1996b) tied criminal violence to the socialization of normal people in the West.

American culture, therefore, provides fertile ground for the cultivation of hate groups and terrorist activity. In fact, Stock (1996, pp. 4–5) proposed that the roots of radicalism and vigilantism predate the colonization of the U.S. She distinguished between "producer radicalism" and the culture of vigilantism in America, but illustrated the difficulty of interpreting either form as only progressive or regressive or as liberal or conservative. What is clear is that as early as 1676, settlers protested "unfair land laws, unresponsive provincial assemblies, and the imposition of new taxes." Radicalism in America has continued up to the present day with a period of "relative calm" during the time of Jefferson and Jackson. Stock (1996, p. 7) proposed that the origins of radicalism are derived from conditions of frontier life, class differences, racism, sexism, and evangelism. All forms of radicalism resorted to violence, at times, but the culture of vigilantism is the more extreme root of current hate groups. Bacon's Rebellion in 1676 was one of the earliest terrorist actions resulting in violence toward Native Americans (Stock, 1996, p. 113). However, between 1767 and 1902, more than 326 vigilante organizations were identified (Stock, 1996, p. 97), and during the 1930s and 1940s, more than 120 fascist groups were categorized (Stock, 1996, p.

140). While these groups exploited racism, sexism, and other hate ideologies, the origins of their protests were, paradoxically, related to individual rights and the antiauthoritarian roots of American democracy.

Satyagraha

The origins of human violence remain controversial (Buck, 1995a; 1996a,b), but its pervasive presence within Western civilization, within many cultures, is evident. Gandhi's (1940) view was that good and evil are inseparable in life. Comparable with Freud (1949) and May (1972), Gandhi believed that *himsa* (violence) cannot be entirely eliminated from life (Gandhi, 1940, pp. 257, 258). The necessities of living — eating, working, and building — lead to some destruction. *Himsa* is rooted even in the conditions of social existence. The primary goal is to minimize violence. *Ahimsa* (nonviolence) cannot be achieved with perfection, and Gandhi (1969) readily acknowledged his own failures. The essence of Gandhi's contribution lies in his demonstration of the extent to which people can rise above destructiveness (Buck, 1984, 1994, 1995b). This applies to both parties involved in a disagreement even if the other party is, initially, predisposed to aggressive or violent solutions. It offers a means, then, of responding to the terrorist or person driven by hatred. The process of moving toward nonviolence, however, is a complex undertaking. Nonviolence must go beyond outward appearances; it grows out of the basic attitudes and values of the person; further, the nonviolence of different people will not always take the same form, and the determinants of *himsa* are multiple and often outside of conscious awareness (Gandhi, 1970, pp. 48, 81–82).

Satyagraha is the term Gandhi (1950) chose to represent a variety of nonviolent strategies for solving problems when the other party is unwilling or unable to work cooperatively. Its primary purpose is to return the efforts toward resolution to a cooperative framework. The meaning of *Satyagraha* is derived from *Satya*, which is translated as truth, and *Agraha*, usually interpreted as love and firmness; it represents a force which grows out of truth and love (Gandhi, 1950, p. 109). Force here refers to the inner strength of the autonomous person; it does not imply the manipulation or exploitation of others. Parekh (1995, p. 143) proposed that *Agraha* is better translated as an invitation to join in a cooperative search. While called noncooperation, *Satyagraha* reflects the temporary withdrawal of cooperation, but it never seeks to take advantage of others or direct violence toward the other group. *Satyagraha* must be clearly understood in order to apply any of its varieties within a Gandhian context. Such forms of direct action can be easily abused when limited to superficial imitations (Gandhi, 1964, p. 11). *Satyagraha* is based upon openness and honesty. The other party is told what the exact demands are, which are kept to an essential minimum, and all the details of the planned action are stated in advance. This allows for a cooperative response but also permits exploitation or violence by the other party. Gandhi (1940, p. 259) recognized this and proposed that, "A Satyagrahi is born to be deceived." A Satyagrahi requires extensive training in order to learn to handle such burdens.

Gandhi's (1940) search for truth was an endless process both conceptually and personally. He titled his autobiography *The Story of My Experiments With Truth*, and proposed that "... my life consists of nothing but those experiments" (p. 8, introduction). Truth can be ascertained only by means of a search, and there can be no certainty regarding one's conclusions (Gandhi, 1962a, 1969). Because the search for truth is experimental, one's choices will vary over time and be incorrect occasionally. As a result, Gandhi has frequently been accused of inconsistency. However, an unfolding process cannot be circumscribed in advance. As Gandhi (1966a, p. 313) put it, "I have never made a fetish of consistency." As one attempts to adapt action to ideals, some segments of the path will appear inconsistent. The implementation of a

Gandhian search for truth focuses upon means rather than ends. If the means are applied appropriately, the goal is assured (Gandhi, 1954, p. 6).

Gandhi's "experiments" do not reflect the efforts of an Eastern mystic or a manipulative politician in the Western tradition. Rather, he blended an orientation toward action with a set of values that is an alternative to the use of power over people. Gandhi (1940, 1950) sought truth through the practical lessons learned on the streets and in the jails of South Africa and India, but he did not believe that he had described all of the possible applications of *Satyagraha*. For Gandhi (1961a, p. 385), "The experiment is still in the making."

Himsa is a powerful influence on life which cannot be entirely eliminated, but love is a comparable, or stronger, force. Loving includes the intention to enhance the other party's potential while simultaneously enlarging one's own (Erikson, 1969, p. 437). Loving, for Gandhi (1962a, p. 187), is concerned with giving, not receiving. It does not focus upon resentments or retaliation for disappointments. Gandhi (1970, p. 2) captured the essence of loving in the statement, "Love is reckless in giving away, oblivious as to what it gets in return." Love provides the strength to master other feelings and the world. This interpretation is essentially identical with Fromm's (1963) definition of the art of loving. For Gandhi, loving is a means of diminishing the distance between people and of maximizing their commonality (Parekh, 1995, p. 96).

Ahimsa (nonviolence) is equivalent to love. Gandhi (1970, pp. 13–14) defined *Ahimsa* first as the fullest expression of love and second as a rejection of violence toward any living being. Because *Himsa* cannot be entirely eliminated from life, *Ahimsa* needs to be understood as a principle of least violence rather than an idealistic goal of complete absence of destructiveness. Nonviolent noncooperation is often responded to violently, but it is likely to result in less violence than other options. Nonviolence, however, needs to go beyond outward appearances; it grows out of the basic attitudes and values of the person (Gandhi, 1970, p. 1). *Ahimsa* requires a respect for all forms of life (p. 12).

Satyagraha is oriented toward a loving, nonviolent search for truth but must be distinguished from pacifism. The term *Satyagraha* was intentionally chosen to reflect a direct, active response to tyranny and violence. It includes acceptance of the other party parallel to pacifism, but requires action. *Satyagraha* refuses to tolerate (in fact, demonstrates an overt, nonviolent reaction to) the demeaning or destructive behavior of the other person or group. Gandhi (1950, p. 114) proposed that passive resistance is a position of weakness which includes hatred. The Satyagrahi is not passive or weak, but a person does not seek concessions or to overcome or destroy others. Bondurant (1965) described these as the goals of Duragraha (violent coercion). *Satyagraha* attempts to redress the opponent's grievances without giving up one's own conscience. If coercive consequences cannot be entirely eliminated, they can be transformed by an orientation that is based upon trust, a concern with the problems of the other, and an attempt to solve all issues. Gandhi (1950) emphasized that the Satyagrahi cannot be afraid of trusting those originally viewed as the enemy. Duragraha intends to cause suffering in others while the nonviolent force of the Satyagrahi attempts to submit oneself to suffering as a means of getting in touch with the humanity of the "enemy".

Satyagraha can be applied effectively only within a unique value framework. It requires extensive modification of one's attitudes and values, or the acceptance of working with the leadership of an individual who has learned the necessary self-discipline. Courage is the foundation for all other values. Gandhi (1967, p. 170) proposed that, "A Satyagrahi bids good-bye to fear." Courage, as defined by May (1975, p. 13), is the value which underlies all other characteristics (Buck, 1986; Parekh, 1995). Nonviolent action, in Gandhi's (1967, pp. 174–175) view, can begin with one person and is dependent upon individual action. It takes only one person to launch a *Satyagraha* campaign. Nonviolent action does not depend upon masses of people, although it is anticipated that the Satyagrahi's responses will attract supporters. Gandhi began as a single individual (Buck, 1984) and progressed to become the leader of one of the most successful programs of political action in the course of history (Dalton, 1982, pp. 186-187).

The process of becoming a Satyagrahi requires courage, but also serves to foster further growth of fearlessness (Gandhi, 1962a, p. 153). Courage requires an inner guide, the "voice within", that may require disagreement with the whole world (Gandhi, 1967, p. 20). Courage results from the attitudes and actions of a relatively autonomous human being, not from externally imposed duties. Independence, however, must be distinguished from the rugged individualism or macho posturing of American society (Gandhi, 1939, p. 4). Inner directed capacity for self-choice as a foundation for courage needs to be balanced by humility (Gandhi, 1967, p. 19). Further, the autonomy of the Satyagrahi avoids the isolation and dehumanization of individualism. People are inherently social (Gandhi, 1967, p. 47). Courage includes the strength to offer service to the community without being coerced by conformist pressures. However, service for a Satyagrahi cannot be based on egotism; it reflects an altruistic act directed to the welfare of others (Gandhi, 1961a, p. 47). Service by the individualist is derived from arrogance and pity, therefore, from inner weakness. Arrogance and aggressiveness are indications of fear, rather than courage (Gandhi, 1967, p. 60). Gandhi called for "the bravery of the meek, the gentle and the nonviolent" (p. 61). This concept of courage is consistent with May's (1975, pp. 15-17) call for a new form which blends an abhorrence of violence with a sensitivity to the suffering of others.

Swaraj is the term Gandhi (1967) chose to reflect the personal independence necessary for *Satyagraha*. Typically, he converted this Vedic word to convey his own meaning. *Swaraj* is applicable to national and personal independence. It emphasizes self-rule, but not freedom from all limits (Gandhi, 1967, p. 317). Independence grows out of the necessity of living within limits. Because all things cannot be chosen simultaneously, boundaries provide the opportunity for the direction chosen even as they restrict access to others. Opportunities often contradict one another, and choices need to be made (Gandhi, 1949, p. 64). *Swaraj*, as with all Gandhian concepts, is best viewed as a process (Buck, 1993). It allows for the internal strength to resist external authority when that authority has become dictatorial (Gandhi, 1960, p. 180). As a process, *Swaraj* has to be worked out uniquely by each person (Gandhi, 1939, p. 65). It provides the psychological competence to choose; however, external authorities are not the only source of compulsion. It is necessary to seek autonomy from all sources: "fear of disease, bodily injury or death, of dispossession, of losing one's nearest and dearest, of losing one's reputation or giving offense, and so on" (Gandhi, 1967, p. 59).

If *Swaraj* is a process that requires continuous striving, it needs to be strengthened through self-discipline. Gandhi (1940, p. 153) interpreted the term *Brahmacharya* to mean self-control which is implemented in "thought, word and deed." Attention is usually focused upon Gandhi's efforts toward celibacy, but self-discipline applies to all aspects of living including diet and aggression. While celibacy may carry self-control too far, indulgence obstructs the self-mastery required for freedom of action. It is necessary to free oneself from the "bondage of the body" (Gandhi, 1962b, p. 70). *Brahmacharya*, however, is not a process of hard penance; it is intended to be a matter of consolation and joy (Gandhi, 1940, p. 152). Self-control is necessary for the autonomy fundamental to *Satyagraha*, but it is not martyrdom or self-punishment that is sought. Acting in ways consistent with one's conscience may end with imprisonment or death, but the purpose is to enhance life. Self-restraint cannot be coerced; it is derived from action consistent with one's conscience (Gandhi,

1966a, p. 44). *Brahmacharya*, as with *Swaraj*, is a process which is not capable of complete achievement. For example, Gandhi (1962b, p. 318) acknowledged his incessant struggle with sexuality long after his vow of celibacy.

Freedom and self-restraint can be undermined by excessive attachment to possessions. This is a particular problem for implementing *Satyagraha* within Western societies in general and the U.S. in particular. Gandhi was a critic of materialist societies, which he believed were built upon an assumption of inherent selfishness and the multiplication of human wants (Buck, 1993, 1996d; Parekh, 1995). Freedom from the constraints of ownership and from the belief that security and happiness come from possessions is essential for growth of the courage of independence. Gandhi (1967, p. 60), therefore, added the concept of *Aparagraha* or nonpossession as a facilitator of the freedom to choose that is essential to the Satyagrahi and included the need to reduce attachments to the body and family as well as to money. Efforts to own people restrict one's capacity to act independently as much as they control the other individual's freedom of action.

Aparagraha, however, must go beyond circumventing the hoarding of excessive wealth. It rejects the effort wasted in accumulating and protecting possessions, and accepts what is realistically sufficient for human needs (Gandhi, 1954, p. 29). Attachments leave people vulnerable to coercion by dictatorial threats or actions directed toward the loss of possessions. The Satyagrahi who gives up attachments frees himself or herself from a variety of punitive actions by the government or other groups. Gandhi (1962b, p. 101) also warned that one can become too attached to the goals of a *Satyagraha* campaign. This could convert the process into a willingness to do anything to succeed, but success can only come from a nonviolent search for truth. Extending the principle of *Aparagraha* to his focus upon inner strength, Gandhi (1954, p. 32) emphasized that "there is no wealth but life."

The life-oriented perspective of the Satyagrahi means a focus on serving the community without desiring any return. Gandhi (1961a, p. 47) defined this service directed toward the welfare of others as *Yayna*. This prosocial responsiveness is interrelated with *Samabhara*, or equality. Equality pervaded Gandhi's orientation toward all people. Raised in a sexist society, similar to the U.S., he fought for equality between daughters and sons (Gandhi, 1940, p. 7), and husbands and wives (p. 18). Gandhi went beyond equality between the sexes and transformed traits traditionally associated with femininity and, therefore, weakness, into strengths of the Satyagrahi (Buck and Nimbark, 1982; Erikson, 1969). The pervasiveness of the value of *Samabhara* is indicated by its application to social, economic, religious, and international spheres underlining Gandhi's (1955, p. 8) belief in the commonality among all human beings. Striving for *Samabhara*, however, is not equivalent to sameness. It is more compatible with equality of opportunity and a sufficiency of goods to provide for basic needs (Gandhi, 1954, p. 34); social justice provides for the good of all (p. 33). A Satyagrahi cannot accept the superiority or inferiority of other people (Gandhi, 1962a, p. 143).

The focus upon commonality is extended by *Advaita* which reflects a unity with all human beings and all that lives. *Advaita* indicates that *Satyagraha* needs to be implemented within a framework that recognizes the brotherhood of people (Gandhi, 1967, p. 28). Ashe (1969, p. 243) made clear, however, that this is unity in diversity rather than conformist in nature. Further, this value extends to a bond with all life. Gandhi (1967) proposed that *Advaita* requires unity not only with attractive animals such as horses or the noble lion, but also the snake and scorpion (Gandhi, 1967, p. 424). *Advaita* involves living in harmony with the universe. This is a reflection of the interconnectedness of life and goes beyond nonviolence. *Advaita* includes working for the enhancement of life. The context for unity is a cooperative relationship with life and the environment rather than the competitiveness and exploitation promoted by Western ideology. Gandhi (1954, p. 33) spoke of "oppressive competition" which "poisons all human intercourse." The *charkha* (spinning wheel) utilized by Gandhi (1967, p. 405) as part of the *Satyagraha* campaign to break British economic control over India symbolized the circle of life, nonviolent unity with life.

Concepts of nonviolence, equality, and unity were developed from practical experience and applied to *Satyagraha* campaigns, but the implications go beyond these immediate goals. Gandhi attempted to revolutionize society by implementing the Constructive Program (Bondurant, 1965, pp. 180–181), which was a promotion of community and a rejection of materialist society (Parekh, 1995, pp. 21–22). At the local level, the Ashram was established to implement a harmonious community (Gandhi, 1955), and at the national level Gandhi (1954) advocated a society concerned with the welfare of all people which he called *Sarvodaya*. *Sarvodaya* goes beyond the utilitarian principle of the greatest good for the greatest number to insist upon seeking the greatest good for all. Sarvodaya is consistent with a democratic system concerned with the welfare of minorities rather than simplistic rule by the majority (Gandhi, 1961b, p. 45). A cooperative, nonviolent society has to be worked from the bottom up beginning with the Ashram (p. 7). In the final analysis, *Satyagraha* is the means for establishing *Sarvodaya* (Gandhi, 1954, p. 3). Gandhi concluded that the reduction of violence in society could not be accomplished by a limited focus upon technique. Violence has to be understood as a function of the total social context and can be significantly reduced only by dealing with the complexities of its origins. *Sarvodaya* would make *Satyagraha* unnecessary.

Gandhi balanced the total renovation of society with change at the personal level. The goal is *Sarvodaya*, but the practice of *Satyagraha* requires the humanizing growth of the individual. The consolidation of the values of the Satyagrahi is reflected in Gandhi's (1940, p. 14) interpretation of the concept *Moksha*. He considered his life efforts to be a struggle for self-realization or *Moksha*. As Parekh (1995, p. 93) pointed out, *Moksha* requires shedding the separateness characteristic of selfhood. This process of self-actualization incorporates forgiveness, trust, faith in the universality of a potential for growth, humility, ceaseless striving, a focus upon means rather than ends, fearlessness, respect, infinite patience, gentleness, nonviolence, and a striving for unity. Any discussion of self-actualization is open to a charge of idealization, but Gandhi was not a theoretician. He applied his tactics, and never anticipated perfection. In the end, *Satyagraha* is the means of overcoming violence both through personal actualization and social reconstruction. It becomes a total philosophy of life (Gandhi, 1967, p. 394).

Gandhian Synthesis

Any discussion of Gandhi's attempts to solve the problem of violence or to conceptualize personal growth and the construction of a just society is obstructed by the fact that he provided a new analysis which stands outside of the usual categories framing Western thought. Because he proposed that he was a capitalist, a socialist, a communist, and a democrat in various writings, or that he was a Hindu, Muslim, Christian, and Jew, confusion is inevitable. As a result, Gandhi was accused of inconsistency or even deceit. Of course, there is some inconsistency in his thinking, as in all human beings, but this must be distinguished from the fact that his approach is oriented toward reconciling what appears to be in opposition (Buck, 1996c, 1996d). This is what Bondurant (1965) proposed as Gandhi's talent for creative solutions and is the basis for Parekh's (1995) contention that Gandhi's approach sometimes leads to entirely new concepts.

Gandhi's creative synthesis provides an approach to violence that revised the traditional Western perspective which includes a conception of human beings whose pursuit of self-interest leads inevitably to conflict, competition, and violence (Buck, 1995a, 1996a,b,d). Gandhi, however, refused to think in terms of opposing interests (conflict), or of solutions that required conceding essential positions (compromise; Buck, 1996c). Gandhian synthesis translates conflict into difference where all parties are respected as having legitimate views.

With Gandhian synthesis, no victory over the other person is sought (no competition); there is a readiness to allow oneself to be persuaded by the evidence and even to embrace part or all of an alternative position. Such change is neither concession nor thought of as concession but is a reassessment based upon new information. The best information available is presented in order to maximize the options available to both parties, and no solution is accepted until a fair hearing takes place. This permits creative solutions where there is no victory or defeat. It is an effort to seek the best synthesis of the total situation. This provides the possibility of mutual enhancement similar to May's (1972, p. 109) conception of integrative power. Successful resolution begins with a cooperative effort by either person or group, but eventually requires mutual cooperation. When cooperation cannot be obtained, noncooperation is used to return the situation to a joint effort to search for a satisfactory outcome. Force or violence must be avoided in thought, word, or action.

The process of moving toward creative solutions involves a sequence of steps (Bondurant, 1965). The first effort is the persistent search for avenues of cooperation. Gandhi (1972, p. 71) stated that, "Not killing competition, but life-giving-cooperation, is the law of the human being." A search for cooperation requires an effort to work *with* the other party; however, the central issue is the attitude and intent to work *with* rather than having a unified purpose. In this way, cooperation can serve as a means for moving toward a single goal, or for developing creative solutions for diverse goals. In either case, Gandhian synthesis is an orientation directed toward the enhancement of the desires of the other party even as one advances one's own position. This remains true whether the other is interpreted as an ally or an enemy. Success is determined by utilizing the proper approach rather than the achievement of a particular goal. Therefore, as long as one maintains a cooperative stance, success is guaranteed. Failure can only result from an unwillingness or an inability to try.

Cooperative efforts are independent of the behavior of others; therefore, it is possible to cooperate with a competitor, a nonresponder, a person filled with hatred. As cooperation is used and tested and self-confidence in its application is enhanced, faith in its strength is experienced. The respect central to this framework allows for the legitimacy of positions not previously considered. Creativity flourishes more openly in an environment that minimizes a fear of failure and enhances a willingness to risk. Because cooperation begins by granting legitimacy to the other parties' point of view, it transcends conflict. That is, it removes the quality of opposition inherent in conflict, and translates it into a difference of opinion where both parties can work toward creative solutions (Buck, 1995a, 1996a,c,d).

If cooperative efforts do not reach a mutually acceptable solution, an attempt is made to reason with the other party (Bondurant, 1965). Compromise is not adequate, because it requires both sides to accept solutions that include some dissatisfaction. This will be a foundation for future grievances. The deceptiveness of compromise can be replaced by problem solving which is based upon the premise that answers can be reached without giving up or giving in. Where the interaction is based upon respect and acceptance between equals, the legitimate goals of all participants can be satisfied. Mutual gain can be achieved by cooperative reasoning that seeks to solve the legitimate needs of both parties. Reasoning within a Gandhian framework simplifies the task by reducing demands to an essential minimum and by its refusal to add new issues during the negotiations.

Additional questions that arise, if legitimate, are postponed. New requirements presented after the original issues are solved reflect an attempt to take unfair advantage.

Rational discussion is likely to be successful only if it moves toward a cooperative interaction; however, a solution cannot come through reason alone (Gandhi, 1967, p. 63). It is necessary to go beyond the intellect and "move the heart also" (Gandhi, 1966a, p. 171). Gandhi believed that traditional rationalism resulted in making violence respectable. For example, the pervasive effort to justify war in the West is rationalized as an effective solution for international conflicts. *Satyagraha* is ultimately a means of realizing the integration of the moral and the rational (Parekh, 1995, pp. 165–166). When the total situation is taken into account, the inadequacy of aggressive systems becomes evident (p. 198), but it was typical of Gandhi to leave ambiguity in a settlement as a way of testing the trustworthiness of the other party (p. 159).

When cooperation and reason fail, self-suffering can be initiated in order to get through to the humane potential that Gandhi believed exists in all people. If there are some individuals, such as Hitler, who cannot be reached, self-suffering can still serve the self-questioning of the Satyagrahi (Gandhi, 1942, p. 163). Fasting is oriented, then, primarily toward the growth of the Satyagrahi, but is intended to affect the other party. Fasting, however, can be abused in both directions. Gandhi (1940, p. 236) recognized that it can become a form of indulgence. It can also be used for masochistic pleasure, but "true sacrifice" is not based on the promotion of pain (Gandhi, 1962a, p. 74). Self-sacrifice is consistent with the necessity of avoiding violence while refusing to submit to coercion. It is based upon love (Gandhi, 1962a, pp. 88–89). Self-suffering serves as a brake on violence as well as an alternative where only the person using it can suffer (Gandhi, 1962b, p. 6). An alternative to the fast, which is compatible with self-sacrifice, is evident in the acceptance of dictatorial justice. If one breaks the law, even unjust laws, one must accept the sentence of the court, but acceptance of the state's laws does not imply passivity. The court appearance is used to defend one's position, and to question the law. In addition, imprisonment can be used as a time for self-reflection as well as an attempt to promote the humanity of the other party. Gandhi (1962a, p. 177) proposed that, "The cell door is the door to freedom." Influence, Gandhi (1971, p. 42) understood, can be used manipulatively, and he warned against such practice.

When cooperation, reason, and self-suffering have not led to a creative synthesis, direct action is required. Direct action refers to a variety of nonviolent methods including *Satyagraha*, civil disobedience, parallel government, mass meetings, economic boycott, public education, sitting dharna (sitdown strike), general strikes, nonpayment of taxes, boycott of schools, etc. Gandhi (1961a, p. 385) made it clear that no list of direct action techniques can be complete: "The experiment is still in the making." The purpose of direct action is to return the situation to a cooperative framework. Therefore, all forms of direct action are nonviolent, noncompetitive, nonconforming, nonsubmissive, and nonavoiding. The objective is to restructure the differences between the parties in order to create an entirely new set of circumstances (Bondurant, 1965, p. 195). Direct action is never initiated without a set of tactics and a strategy that is made clear to those viewed as opponents as well as to one's supporters, but it is necessary to be ready to depart from this plan if persuaded by the other party. Creative synthesis seeks to turn an opponent into a collaborator where both parties seek the best solution to the "total human needs" in the situation (Bondurant, 1965, p. 196).

The Application of *Satyagraha*

Satyagraha provides an alternative to the Western self-interest/conflict/competition/violence approach to problem solving. It requires revision of the Western bias that views human beings as inherently selfish. Human infants are not born selfish; self-interest requires the time necessary to develop a sense of self. Considerable evidence (Buck, 1995a, 1996d) is available which indicates that prosocial ability can appear as early as egocentric behavior. It is observed by 12 months and is dependent upon parental socialization. Ideally, altruistic and empathic skills need to be taught early in life, but it is clear that these options can be learned after competition/violence values have been incorporated. The primary obstacle for the acceptance of cooperation and of *Satyagraha* is the pervasive belief that one is inherently driven by self-interest, and that conflict and competition are the primary, and best, means of dealing with others. A valuable starting point is to observe the extent of being cooperative that characterizes each of us. A simple exercise, carefully carried out, can demonstrate that the vast majority of most people's behavior is cooperative. A journal that records all behavior for a day, or better a week, will indicate that our responses are overwhelmingly cooperative, but that we may have paid excessive attention to the few conflicts or competitive situations that occur. If this is true, everyone, even the terrorist, has a large reservoir of cooperative experience to utilize for creative solutions.

Cooperative, nonviolent, empathetic skills are valuable but are secondary to basic attitudes. No list of techniques can be considered complete, because a Gandhian framework seeks creative solutions. Creativity requires originality that fits the unique conditions of each situation. A set of rules has a tendency to become a prescription for success that limits the imagination, but each problem requires a novel synthesis.

Satyagraha reflects an effort to move the interaction to a cooperative framework, but it must operate within a prosocial, empathic context even though cooperation is temporarily withdrawn by one of the parties. Noncooperation must be ready to return to cooperativeness, and it continues to grant legitimacy to the other individual's position. This requires growth in empathic ability in order to collect appropriate information. One must develop competence in learning to take the other person's perspective. The first step comes from the awareness that it is the Satyagrahi's responsibility to become a more effective listener and observer even when the other person's message is incompatible with one's own values or is filled with hatred. Whatever the communication difficulties of the other side, the Satyagrahi needs to take the initiative. There is little power to change other people, but unlimited capacity to change oneself in order to become more empathic and a more effective communicator.

The unwillingness or inability of the other individual to clarify his or her perspective can be overcome by the Gandhian requirement of honesty and openness regarding one's goals and actions. This is consistent with the concept of self-disclosure. As with interpersonal relationships, honesty provides an atmosphere that makes it safer for the other person to achieve the openness necessary for full disclosure and creative settlements. Honesty encourages a spiral of honesty which allows an understanding of the other party's needs so that they can be incorporated in potential solutions. However, a Gandhian approach requires training which prepares for deception. Honesty does not automatically or immediately lead to honesty. The Satyagrahi must be able to accept deception or violence without being manipulated or derailed from the pursuit of understanding. The refusal to respond violently to violence will unsettle the competitor or exploiter, and provide an opportunity for new directions.

Satyagraha requires training in converting conflict into difference. A difference does not have to be opposed. The tendency, learned in America, to view others as antagonists focuses attention on attack or defense rather than understanding. A good example of this proclivity is described by Thompson and Hrebec (1996) as the "lose-lose" effect. This reflects a failure to recognize and utilize compatible interests.

They provide evidence that lose-lose agreements are pervasive, and difficult to avoid. They estimated that more than 20% of negotiations in which there are compatible issues end in lose-lose solutions (Thompson and Hrebec, 1996, p. 406). Practice can be provided that requires tolerance for disagreement. Respect for different ideas, however incompatible with one's own, opens people to a continuing effort to grasp the other's point-of-view. Understanding, however, does not require agreement. If it is effective, empathy clarifies difference as well as similarity. It is easy to understand people with compatible positions; the difficult task is to empathize with those initially viewed as enemies or terrorists. A grasp of the total human situation is necessary because Gandhian synthesis requires maximum information.

Empathic understanding requires tolerance for feelings and attitudes that reveal criticism, complaints, and other unpleasant communications. It is difficult to examine differences without blaming, offending, or ridiculing, but a Satyagrahi requires the skill to state grievances without resorting to these tactics. Honesty is dependent upon maximum disclosure but does not include any intention to hurt or offend. Nonviolence, least violence, aims to minimize hostile words or thoughts in addition to actions. The Satyagrahi must learn to take responsibility for establishing a nonblaming, nonviolent interaction while accepting imperfection in the process. People, at times, will be offended or respond violently to honesty in spite of one's best efforts to avoid provocation. Nonviolent means can be guaranteed, but ideal ends can never be achieved with perfection.

The empathic understanding of the Satyagrahi promotes cooperation. The ability to work *with* another individual or group is built upon an accurate grasp of the others' perspective, but cooperation requires additional skill. One of the defining characteristics of cooperation is that it is a process which can be initiated regardless of the behavior of the other person. The Satyagrahi needs to offer cooperation in response to aggressive, competitive, avoidant, or cooperative responses. As with empathy, the responsibility for cooperation begins with one's own choices. This is also inherent in the Graduated and Reciprocated Initiatives in Tension Reduction (GRIT) strategy (Tetlock et al., 1991). In this approach, unilateral cooperation is announced, specific steps are taken, and cooperative responses continue regardless of the other party's actions. GRIT is consistent with Gandhian synthesis and is more effective than responding in kind to the other person's last move (Tetlock et al., 1991, p. 262). GRIT is particularly effective when cooperation is pursued persistently (p. 263). The training of the Satyagrahi, therefore, needs to promote the patience to persist in spite of a lack of reciprocal cooperation. Persistence needs to be creative by repeating, rephrasing, and reassessing without weakening one's own position.

Neither victory nor concession is sought; therefore, it is possible to restructure the problem in order to reconcile antagonistic positions. This requires practice in viewing differences as legitimate rather than as opposition. The goal of cooperation is to seek a new synthesis that satisfies the essential interests of both parties. While submissiveness or conformity is not compatible with cooperation, one must be prepared to rethink one's position and accept a reformulated goal. Gandhian synthesis seeks to solve the vital needs of all people involved. The power of a cooperative approach is derived from independence of action. A competitive strategy requires two people willing to compete, but cooperation can be initiated by the action of either individual or group. The effectiveness of cooperative learning has been clearly established by a number of investigators (e.g., Deutsch, 1993; Johnson and Johnson, 1995).

The ability to work *with* others is best implemented in a context that aims for equality. This includes changing one's attitudes toward taking advantage of or having the upper hand over another. Cooperation focuses on what one gives to the interaction rather than what one gains. Cooperation does not seek an unfair return. This can be taught by practice with developing solutions that enhance the other person's goals even as they further one's own purposes. Cooperation includes promoting an awareness that it can be to each individual's advantage if others do well. It involves solutions derived from efforts to expand the assets available rather than thinking in terms of scarcity or the concept that gain can come only from someone's loss. A shift from an achievement to a process orientation is necessary. A process perspective allows people to place any solution within a context of long-term relationships; it views any agreements as temporary and as open to new solutions in response to changing circumstances. An achievement perspective relates to goals which are expected to provide final arrangements. Cooperation includes a willingness to give up a preoccupation with achieving success. It recognizes that success comes from a continuing process of working *with* the other party.

Learning to cooperate requires rethinking the value of compromise. The traditional advice that one must give in on important issues in order to gain some advantage frames the best solution within a win-lose perspective, but limits creative alternatives. Compromise is better than continuing an antagonistic interaction but reflects the continuation of a competitive orientation. Gandhian synthesis must be formulated outside of an adversary relationship. It must be distinguished from conformity or agreement. Cooperation can include working toward a common goal, but it can be consistent with disagreement and controversy. A Satyagrahi requires training that seeks a diversity of solutions, looks for multiple options, and permits different goals for the two parties. The essential attitude is a willingness to agree to disagree and to respect the legitimacy of different points of view. Win-win solutions (e.g., Carnevale and Pruitt, 1992) to diverse goals include a reduction of needs to the minimum that obtains what is most important for both parties, an expansion of the options available, or new choices that represent better satisfaction of the essential requirements for both parties than the original proposals. None of these options includes giving up or giving in for either individual or group.

Gandhian synthesis requires an effort to respect the unique conditions specified by the other party, to demonstrate an active concern for those issues, and a voluntary responsiveness to the needs represented. This orientation is comparable to Fromm's (1963) definition of loving. A relationship between adversaries needs to be converted into one that is complementary. This requires a solution that changes irreconcilable issues into pieces that fit together in a fashion that adds to both positions. The Satyagrahi needs to develop what Erikson (1987) called a "wider identity". This involves the transcendence of we-they boundaries that can permit shared decision-making. The Satyagrahi works to restructure a competitive interaction into a cooperative exchange.

A Satyagrahi must go beyond the conversion of self-interest, conflict, and competition in order to overcome violence. This begins with an awareness of one's education in violence, and a struggle with the admiration for hitting, aggressiveness, and killing that has been encouraged by physical punishment, athletics, the death penalty, and war. Learning nonviolent options is not enough. The Satyagrahi needs to be educated in self-reliance, courage, and the strength necessary for a nonviolent campaign. Passivity is derived from a position of weakness, but so is most violence. The disciplined violence of the soldier includes courage and power, but the nonviolent, noncooperator maximizes bravery. The Satyagrahi requires the courage to keep the initiative in his or her own hands whatever the threat or violence from the opponent. The noncooperator needs the discipline to respond in terms of the sequence of steps that is consistent with the tactics and strategy of the *Satyagraha* campaign. As this plan is pursued, the discipline and morale of the noncooperators need to be reviewed and enhanced. Throughout the action, there is a persistent search for a return to cooperation that permits honorable terms for both parties. *Satyagraha* is an active means of achieving specific goals while simultaneously striving to help the other person or group reach an equitable solution.

The Satyagrahi does not resist arrest or the confiscation of property, but does not submit to any order given in anger or intended to abuse. Cooperation with all laws or rules is required except the one or few that are viewed as unjust. Noncooperation cannot be applied to everything at once. All of the other party's positions cannot be unjust if that perspective is understood properly. The right of the other group to seek particular goals must be accepted. That group must be protected from being insulted or attacked. These requirements are particularly difficult for people indoctrinated with the values of violence and retaliation. The goal is to seek victory over the situation and reconciliation of the differences, not victory over an opponent.

Gandhian Synthesis: The Spinning Wheel

Extensive applications of Gandhian synthesis demonstrate its effectiveness in a variety of contexts. Gandhi's (1967) genius for political action is clearly confirmed by his use of the *charkha* (spinning wheel) as part of the strategy to achieve Indian independence. The spinning wheel combined a symbolic message with the practical advantage of undermining the British economic stranglehold on India. Gandhi promoted the idea that every Indian (man, woman, and child) spend time each day spinning on a hand wheel. The *charkha* provided homespun cloth which could be used to break the economic control exercised by the British monopoly on manufactured cloth. It also served to decentralize industry and enhance local control and thereby encouraged democracy from the bottom up. The *charkha* fostered handicrafts, a central requirement of his educational philosophy. In addition, spinning each day served to provide the self-discipline essential to *Satyagraha*. Finally, its geometric form symbolized unity, the circle of life. Gandhi (1967) grasped its meaning for promoting Indian independence while simultaneously enhancing a culture of democracy and self-reliance. He proposed (Ghandi, 1967, p. 405) that, "The *charkha* is the symbol of nonviolence on which all life, if it is to be real life, must be based." Because the spinning wheel provided cloth for others as well as oneself, Gandhi (1954, p. 136) added the meaning of service to its practice. If all Indians participated, rich and poor, the *charkha* increased the equality necessary for a *Satyagraha* campaign.

Gandhi's Salt Satyagraha

One of Gandhi's most famous campaigns was the Salt *Satyagraha*. This action continued for about a year (Bondurant, 1965) and was a national movement of civil disobedience with the immediate goal of removing the Salt Acts (laws that provided a British monopoly on salt). These taxes were a particular financial burden for the poor. The long-term purpose was to challenge British control of India (Bondurant, 1965, pp. 89–90). Gandhi was the primary leader along with other prominent figures of the Indian National Congress, but the opening phase was carried out by trained Satyagrahis. Gandhi initiated the action by marching 200 hundred miles to the sea in order to collect salt directly and, therefore, illegally. Participation spread throughout the country and large numbers of women participated. This illustrated the enhancement of the power provided by *Satyagraha* for women who often lived under the domination of men. In some ways, women were viewed as more effective campaigners than men. Erikson (1969, p. 402) proposed that Gandhi transformed traits traditionally associated with femininity and weakness into the strength of the Satyagrahi. However, as Lifton (1973) demonstrated with anti-war Vietnam veterans, men trained as killers also can be transformed from a war to a peace orientation.

The Salt *Satyagraha* was planned as an action of the Indian National Congress, and a succession of replacement leaders was established in anticipation of the imprisonment of the initial leaders. Self-sufficiency was stressed in preparation for jail, civil disobedience, or constructive work such as the spinning wheel. Planning took place through open discussion, and volunteers took training courses to help maintain the values of *Satyagraha*. All Satyagrahis were instructed to wear Khadi (homespun) clothing. This served as a unifying symbol and as a boycott of British manufactured cloth. All trained Satyagrahis took a pledge to work for independence by peaceful means, to accept jail or other punishments, and to obey orders. The wide discussions of the Congress provided advance warning to the British, but Gandhi also sent Lord Irwin (the Viceroy) a letter reviewing the issues and advising him of the nonviolent action. In his letter, Gandhi appealed for a cooperative settlement before initiating the *Satyagraha* (Bondurant, 1965, pp. 91–93).

The march was considered a form of "penance and discipline" and was intended to attract national attention (Bondurant, 1965, pp. 93–96). After breaking the Salt Act himself, Gandhi invited everyone to participate, and masses of people began to collect salt. As the leaders of the action were arrested, shops closed, village officers resigned, and demonstrations were conducted. After the leaders were arrested, others came forward, and they continued the nonviolent campaign. Following Gandhi's arrest, volunteers marched to take over salt depots. As the police beat the marchers, others stepped forward. British violence was extensive. The first reaction of a powerful government is to suppress dissent. The continuation of the campaign led the British, eventually, to seek other solutions. Consistent with Gandhian synthesis, the British were allowed a face-saving solution. The salt laws were not officially repealed but were modified to make them irrelevant. In addition, amnesty was provided, restraining orders were withdrawn, and confiscated property was returned. Finally, future discussions on constitutional reform were announced (Bondurant, 1965, pp. 98–99). The specific goal was essentially accomplished, but the process of working toward independence needed to continue.

The Versatility of Satyagraha

The Salt *Satyagraha* represented an action toward unjust government laws, but noncooperation can be applied toward any group. The Vykom Temple Road *Satyagraha*, for example, was primarily directed toward the practice of discrimination against untouchables advocated by orthodox Hindus (Bondurant, 1965, p. 46–52). The Ahmedabad Labor *Satyagraha* was an action directed toward the mill owners of Ahmedabad in support of the textile workers (Bondurant, 1965, p. 65–73). One of the unique characteristics of this action was Gandhi's acceptance of the justice of the workers' need for a pay increase even though he had close relationships with the mill owners (Bondurant, 1965, p. 71). Not only was the *Satyagraha* able to achieve significant pay increases, but Gandhi was also able to continue to maintain good relationships with the owners. The essence of Gandhian synthesis is reflected in the potential for positive relationships and respect between individuals who begin as potential opponents or enemies. Diwakar (1969, pp. 142-143) described a variety of *Satyagraha*s including the Borsad action in the province of Gujarat. This represented a successful campaign in response to a local criminal group. Similarly, Malik (1986, pp. 87–112) reported the success of Jayaprakash Narayan's campaign in response to the Nexalite violent movement in West Bengal. Finally, in Dharmaj, a village in Gujarat, a group of students and young children initiated an effective *Satyagraha* toward local, caste-oriented social customs (Diwakar, 1969, p. 146).

Satyagraha can be applied to empires, government institutions, social customs, industry, violent uprisings, and criminal groups. It can be initiated by large organizations such as the Congress Party, village groups, workers, outcastes, women, children, and single individuals. Noncooperation can be carried out toward friends and enemies. *Satyagraha*, however, is not limited to India. Gandhi (1950) first developed these techniques in South Africa. In addition, nonviolent noncooperation was central to Martin Luther King, Jr.'s civil rights movement in the U.S. Gandhi's connection to the American Civil rights movement predated King's work, and involved meetings with earlier leaders (Malik, 1986, p. 58–82). Malik pointed out Gandhi's influence on the Congress of Racial Equality and the Student Nonviolent Coordinating Committee in their early stages, but the principles of *Satyagraha* are most clearly evident in King's writings. The connection of Gandhi's thinking to the civil rights movement and many of its leaders, including King, James Farmer, Bayard Rustin, and James Lawson, was also pointed out by Muste (1967) and Branch (1988).

The Montgomery Bus Boycott Satyagraha

Gandhian techniques developed slowly and erratically within the American Civil rights movement. The Montgomery Bus Boycott was not a systematic campaign with tactics organized and announced in advance. It began as a result of chance circumstances and was organized as issues progressed (Branch, 1988, pp. 105–142). However, as the boycott unfolded, pressure from Southern opposition increased, and King became the acknowledged leader of the resistance. He intuitively developed a nonviolent orientation (Branch, 1988, pp. 143–166). One of the first Gandhians to join the movement was Bayard Rustin (p. 168). Rustin had already brought the wisdom of organization, training, and nonviolence to the Congress of Racial Equality, but now served as a Gandhian consultant to King (pp. 174–179). Later, King recruited James Lawson, another Gandhian, to lead the organization and training of blacks in the South in preparation for the continuation of a mass, nonviolent campaign (p. 205). By this time, the necessity of careful preparation of tactics and strategy was clear. A *Satyagraha* campaign takes the initiative rather than reacting to the actions of the other party. Utilizing Gandhi's well-tested techniques, King chose to stay in jail instead of paying an unjust fine. His explanation to the judge clearly resembled Gandhi's statement to Justice Broomfield in Ahmedabad on March 18, 1922 (Branch, 1988, p. 241). King's visit to India resulted in a decision to organize an American Salt March (p. 259), and solidified an understanding of the need for meticulous planning, training, execution of a *Satyagraha* campaign (p. 260).

The Birmingham Satyagraha

The most effective Gandhian campaign of the civil rights movement was carried out in Birmingham, AL. Andrew Young (1996) provided extensive detail regarding his involvement. He was attracted to Gandhi's nonviolent tactics long before this period and played a central role in the organization and implementation of this *Satyagraha*. King was the primary leader of this campaign which was carefully planned in advance. Consistent with the first step of Gandhian synthesis, cooperation was sought with the community leaders of Birmingham (Young, 1996, pp. 189–190). In addition, citizenship schools were organized where Gandhian techniques were "meticulously taught." From the beginning, Young sought to grant legitimacy to the point of view of the "opponents" by trying to understand the threat and painful change confronting the white community. In an effort to solve the problems of the situation rather than win a conflict, Young proposed that the protesters "had to help white people embrace" the changes. The campaign proceeded within the context that "people were people." That is, the black and white communities were simply human beings with a common problem to solve.

The Birmingham *Satyagraha* began with a specific set of goals (Young, 1996, pp. 203–204). This included the desegregation of lunch counters, restrooms, drinking fountains, and fitting rooms. Second, there was a request to hire blacks in local businesses as clerks and cashiers. Finally, charges were to be dropped against nonviolent demonstrators and a biracial committee established to plan for school desegregation and to provide continuing dialogue on racial concerns. Violence in response to the proposed demonstrations was anticipated in view of Birmingham's turbulent history. The campaign's strategy and tactics were discussed openly with Birmingham's community leaders, in advance, in order to seek cooperative solutions. It was made clear that demonstrations would continue, and, if necessary increase, until desegregation was ended. Satyagrahis were ready for jail, or even death (their own) in the service of this campaign.

Understanding and trust were established with community leaders in advance, but no progress was made in changing discrimination (Young, 1996, p. 205). The earliest volunteers were the elderly (p. 207), which demonstrated the Gandhian principal of converting apparent weakness into strength. Sit-ins were coordinated with boycotts, and effectiveness was continuously monitored in order to assure that people were provided adequate information. When the city obtained a state court injunction, King announced that he would not obey court orders that did not apply equal justice (p. 212). King stated, in advance, that he would demonstrate, and, if necessary, go to jail, on Good Friday of 1963 (p. 215). The boycott was planned in order to put pressure on Birmingham stores during the busy Easter shopping period. King's arrest and the use of night sticks and dogs by the police brought considerable national attention and sympathy to the movement (pp. 215–219). The nonviolence of the demonstrators maintained "the moral high ground," but included an attempt to help the opponents raise themselves. King's Easter "Letter from a Birmingham Jail" attracted national and international attention and provided a turning point in the campaign.

The final stage, however, was set in motion by enlisting volunteers from local high schools. The students had to sign a pledge of nonviolence before they could participate (Young, 1996, p. 236). This included a pledge of discipline and "reconciliation" rather than victory. Following the example of the high school students, young children insisted on demonstrating and going to jail (pp. 238–239). When police chief Bull Connor, ordered the use of fire hoses and police dogs against the children on May 3, 1963 (p. 239), the success of the campaign was assured. As predicted, nonviolence was stronger than violence. Local businessmen now sought an end in order to solve their moral and economic losses. National attention finally prodded action by the Justice Department, and President Kennedy pressured national business leaders to intervene in their local stores (pp. 242–243). Police violence brought masses of new volunteer demonstrators (p. 240).

Birmingham's business leaders assigned the power for a settlement to two local attorneys. Consistent with the Gandhian goal of seeking a creative solution to the total situation rather than victory, the civil rights leaders sought a face-saving approach (1996, p. 245). A "stair-step" strategy was used. On the day of the settlement, all "whites only" signs were to be removed, and private interviewing for hiring blacks was to begin. A 10-day period was allowed before the changes were tested. On the tenth day, small, disciplined groups would visit the lunch counters of one store each day for 10 days, and then visits would be expanded. The stores chosen for a visit would be notified in advance. After 30 days, everything would be desegregated. After 45 days, each business would begin hiring blacks, school desegregation would be planned, and harassment of blacks attempting to vote would be ended. Face-saving for Alabama courts was arranged by temporary bail payments made by national unions. This successful campaign did not end all violence in the South nor did it provide full equality. It did solve some of the overt forms of racism. While a fine example of *Satyagraha*, this campaign adapted strategy to local creativity.

Contemporary Nonviolent Action

The continuing importance of *Satyagraha* and programs consistent with Gandhian synthesis are described in recent volumes by Oza (1991) and Shepard (1987). The activities discussed include noncooperation movements to solve government and industrial tyrannies. However, some are more consistent with community-oriented, cooperative programs that utilized Gandhian synthesis but did not require *Satyagraha* campaigns. Shepard (1987) also described a variety of contemporary Gandhian actions around the world including Cesar Chavez's leadership of the United Farm Workers of America. His discussion is consistent with Buck's (1991) analysis of the parallels between Gandhi's approach and the nonviolent, noncooperative resistance of Andrei Sakharov, Anatol Scharansky, Nelson Mandela, Vaclav Havel, and many others. Finally, the direct-action, nonviolent approaches of the environmental group, Greenpeace, and the human rights organization, Amnesty International, demonstrate continuing worldwide relevance. While the proponents of violence are widespread, there are many demonstrations of the effectiveness of nonviolence.

Peace Brigades

One of Gandhi's (1961a, pp. 88–90) most notable proposals was the concept of peace brigades and its national parallel, the peace army. Gandhi (1966b, p. 230) stated that there was no way out of violence by means of violence. Peace could come only from nonviolent means. He considered deterrence (1962b, pp. 125–126) and military strength (1966a, p. 173) to be provocative forms of violence rather than nonviolent alternatives. The attempt to establish peace by means of superior weapons inevitably led to the creation of nuclear weapons (Gandhi, 1967, p. 146). Gandhi (1966b, pp. 23–24) suggested that it is brave to die fighting the enemy, but it is more courageous to die working nonviolently toward humane goals.

Gandhi proposed peace brigades (1961a, pp. 89–90) as a substitute for the violent techniques of the police or the army. Such groups (although individuals can serve the same functions) should be composed of local people who are dedicated to nonviolence and tolerance of diversity. Peace brigades need to work continuously in the community rather than wait for problems to develop, and they need to establish a reputation for impartiality. Generally, the participants should be volunteers, but some full-time workers may be necessary. Members of a peace brigade, according to Gandhi (1954, p. 105), "must have a faith in non-violence." In addition, members "must have equal regard for all the principle religions of the Earth." This requirement applied particularly to the Hindu-Muslim problem, but, more generally, it is a call for respect toward all points of view that divide a community. The work of the peace brigade is best accomplished by people who cultivate through "personal service" relationships to the community.

Violent police activities require strong physiques, but the peace brigade emphasizes nonviolent individuals for whom "soul force must mean everything and physique must take a second place" (Gandhi, 1954, pp. 106–107). No weapons are to be carried, but considerable preparation, such as medical training is valuable. Nonviolent units, because they require special people, are likely to be small. Small forces are more easily mobilized than large groups (Gandhi, 1966b, p. 19): "I will say that a minority can do much more in the way of non-violence than a majority."

Consistent with his conception of the peace brigade, Gandhi (1961a) applied the techniques of *Satyagraha* to criminals. Instead of punishment, the cause of the criminal behavior should be understood, and an attempt should be made to correct the situation.

The Satyagrahi needs to realize that the criminal is not very different from himself or herself and should teach the criminal a vocation and provide work (Ghandi, 1961a, pp. 350–351). The rich who accumulate money by exploitation are as guilty as the robber. As with all *Satyagraha* campaigns, the Satyagrahi does not retaliate or submit to the criminal, but cures the criminal by curing himself or herself. Consistent with this, a prison "should be a house of correction and not punishment" (Gandhi, 1962a, p. 276). Gandhi perceived a strange contradiction between Western attitudes toward crime and disease. We sympathize with the ill and provide treatment, although much sickness relates to poor diets, smoking, alcohol, and other unhealthy lifestyles that people have chosen. Crime, however, is punished with great severity even though it is often rooted in society's ills. Both disease and crime are often a result of poor self-discipline, lack of responsibility, and inadequate social concern (Parekh, 1995, pp. 130–132).

Although no direct connection with Gandhian methods was stated, Twemlow and Sacco (1996) reported successful applications of the peace brigade concept in Jamaica and in cities in the U.S. They emphasized the use of carefully selected and trained community leaders whom they labeled peacemakers/peacekeepers. The primary task of the peacemaker is to defuse crisis situations before they escalate into violence (Twemlow and Sacco, 1996, pp. 628–630). "Altruistic" projects were developed in relation to potential trouble spots such as assisting the homeless and mentally ill. The peacemakers, operating in teams, worked as nonpartisan advocates for all elements of the community. This required, from a Gandhian perspective, a capacity to understand the legitimacy of alternative points of view. The "essential qualities" established for peacemakers are equivalent to the Satyagrahi: prosocial, service to the community, courage, cooperation, independence, dedication, self-discipline, advocates of equality and justice, nonviolence, and commitment. While there are people who exhibit such characteristics, Gandhian training emphasizes the need for continuing personal growth. The reduction of violent crime produced by the peacemakers was interpreted as being due to a focus on treating the causes of violence in community attitudes and conditions rather than resorting to punishment and prisons. There are also Gandhian parallels to the recommendations of Call (1996) for hostage negotiation. The recognition that hostage taking is a problem-solving effort leads to the necessity of empathic understanding (p. 578). With this understanding and the establishment of a trusting relationship, new, creative solutions to the hostage situation become possible. Utilizing this approach, Call reported that most incidents are solved by negotiated surrender with no one injured or killed (pp. 570–574).

The Republic of Texas Militia

The evaluation of a current militia group is necessarily speculative due to incomplete and uncertain information. The reconstruction of historical events never achieves complete agreement, but time provides the opportunity for careful analysis. The present analysis of the Republic of Texas group, therefore, is intended to illustrate Gandhian synthesis, but does not claim complete accuracy regarding the data available at this time. All of the information used in this analysis is taken from the reports of Verhovek (1997) as printed in the New York Times.

Richard L. McLaren is the primary initiator of a loose-knit group of individuals claiming to represent Texas as a separate nation independent of the U.S. This interpretation is based upon the conception that the U.S. illegally annexed Texas in 1845.

On April 27, 1997, Joseph Rowe and his wife were taken hostage by the Republic of Texas group. This precipitated a confrontation with the Fort Davis County Sheriff's Department, the State of Texas, and federal authorities. Information regarding the goals and size of the group was initially unclear. Estimates suggested one or two dozen well-armed, hard-core followers and hundreds of potential sympathizers. The goals of this group included a long-term legal effort to clog the state courts by a series of liens and other legal documents. Lawsuits were initiated against local landowners, and a number of out-of-court settlements achieved success in obtaining land and cash. In addition, liens were filed against Governor Bush, the state's chief judge, and hundreds of other state officials. Finally, approximately $3 million in bogus checks were passed. This long-term legal battle was escalated on April 27, 1997, not only by the taking of the hostages (Joseph Rowe was shot during this confrontation), but also by an announcement that paramilitary groups were prepared to take Texas officials hostage. This set the stage for a situation that could lead to considerable violence in Fort Davis County, and possibly throughout the State. McLaren heightened the tension by his announcement of a declaration of war against U.S. federal agencies and the United Nations. Rowe and his wife were called prisoners of war. These statements were made from the compound which was called the embassy of the Republic of Texas.

Two groups had attempted to deal with McLaren and his followers prior to the April 27, 1997, incident. Rowe, as head of the local property owner's association, had fought McLaren's legal tactics for several years without much success. The property owners' association settled out of court rather than continuing to pursue the issues legally. The agreement conceded 20 lots, $87,000, and two buildings. Some other local people also gave in to McLaren's demands, but those who continued to pursue issues legally were generally successful in court. However, legal fees were substantial. The expense of litigation was the basis for out-of-court settlements with McLaren.

The approach of the homeowners' association and other local individuals failed to implement a Gandhian approach (see Table 18.1). They were involved in a long-term effort to defend themselves against the Republic of Texas Group, but they either gave in to unjust local threats or limited their response to the courts. From a Gandhian perspective, one never accepts injustice or a violation of one's essential values. In addition, the Satyagrahi always takes the initiative rather than respond to the actions of others. A legal response is limited rather than flexible and accepts an antagonistic or conflict context for seeking a solution.

If one or more local people were informed of, or even better trained in, Gandhian techniques, an unlimited number of creative options would have become available. As Table 18.1 indicates, a Satyagrahi would begin with a process perspective that looked toward new solutions consistent with the unique conditions of this situation, emphasized flexibility, and attempted to avoid escalation. Functioning as a peace brigade, these individuals would initiate a public search for truth which made information available to the total community in order to solve the problem existing between two groups (local neighbors and the Republic of Texas militia). They would begin with the belief that there were legitimate concerns held by both groups. Efforts to understand the legitimate beliefs held by both parties would take place within a context that accepted differences between the groups but not conflict, and unilaterally sought cooperation. Cooperation would be pursued until each group had been given extensive opportunity to accept a cooperative framework. Only when either group, or both, continued to reject cooperation would direct action be implemented. At this point, specific strategic and tactical objectives would be established, and all parties would be informed in advance, of these objectives and of any actions to be taken. This *Satyagraha* would be limited to nonviolent alternatives such as public education, mass meetings, picketing the militia compound, and so forth.

The ingenuity of a peace brigade might not have succeeded in preventing the incident of April 27, 1997, but it would have obtained more detailed information regarding the Republic of Texas group. It would also have established a prior relationship with

Table 18.1

Gandhian Synthesis

1. *Process Perspective*

Issues are part of a continuing series of events.
Focus on the minimum number of essential questions at the present time.
Postpone additional issues for future negotiations.
Accept imperfection in order to allow flexibility.
Success is guaranteed by efforts not by achievements.
Each situation is unique, and this provides a readiness for new solutions.
Continuous engagement allows for solutions prior to escalation.

2. *Preparation by the Satyagrahi*

Training begins with a willingness to change, to grow (*Moksha*)
Synthesis reflects a search for truth not personal advantage.
The values of altruism, diversity, cooperation, and peaceful action guide all efforts.
Firmness, perseverance, and patience continue regardless of the response of others.
Openness and honesty are pursued in spite of deception by others.
Least violence in word, thought, and action (*Ahimsa*) is sought even in the face of violence by others.
An orientation of service to the community (*Yayna*) is developed.
Equality (*Samabhara*) is the framework for all interactions.
Unity is sought with all that lives (*Advaita*), but this is unity within diversity not conformity.
A concern with the welfare of all (*Sarvodaya*) is developed.
Direct action must be initiated in order to solve injustice in spite of coercion or violence.
Independence (*Swaraj*) must be developed as a basis for action, but this reflects power over self not over others.
Courage is essential for the necessity of taking action, but this is a courage that blends humility and sensitivity.
Discipline (*Brahmacharya*) is necessary to control competitiveness and aggression and to be prepared for assault, imprisonment, or death.
Nonpossession (*Aparagraha*) is sought in order to promote freedom from fear of loss, and from excessive attachment to goals.
An oath of nonviolence and acceptance of the *Satyagraha* strategy is pledged.
Skills such as listening, empathy, understanding, communication, and full disclosure must be learned.
Defensive, medical, and other training is desirable.

McLaren and provided a continuing foundation for a cooperative solution that solved the needs of all groups. It is possible that the violent action of the Republic of Texas group could have been prevented by facilitating an open and public discussion of McLaren's position regarding the illegal annexation of Texas by the U.S. Recognition and respect for this position may have been the primary purpose of the

Table 18.1 (continued)

Gandhian Synthesis

3. *Negotiations*

Strategy: Specific objectives are provided to the other party in advance, and these minimal, essential issues are not changed unless one is persuaded by the evidence.
Tactics: Specific, detailed, flexible actions are planned, and they are provided to the other party in advance.
Negotiations are open to the total community, never secret.
The Satyagrahi is responsible for taking the initiative.
Negotiations begin with efforts to cooperate within an atmosphere of respect between equals.
- Cooperation seeks to work with others, but includes agreeing to disagree.
- Cooperative efforts persist in response to competition, avoidance, or violence by the other party.
- Cooperation does not seek self-interest, competition, victory, or concession.
- A willingness to rethink one's position is maintained.
- An initial lack of reciprocated cooperation is accepted as part of the process.
- Failure to achieve mutual cooperation requires a search for new means for reaching the other party.

Reasoning is attempted when unilateral cooperation does not succeed.
- Work to solve the total problem solving the essential needs of all.
- Grant legitimacy to the other party's position.
- Reconcile opposite views by transcending conflict, by converting opposition to legitimate difference.
- Do not concede essential positions.
- Do not seek a new advantage if the other party changes its position.
- Do not add new issues when the original problems are solved, postpone for future negotiations.
- Maintain a readiness to be persuaded by the evidence, and an openness to seek new information.
- Actively seek new alternatives for the most effective solution thereby maximizing options.
- No solutions are accepted until a fair hearing is provided.

Self-suffering
- Seek penance to assess one's imperfections.
- Fasting can be used as a time for self-questioning, re-evaluation, self-growth.
- Accept punishment and imprisonment according to current law.
- Self-suffering limits violence to oneself.
- Self-suffering is an attempt to touch the humanity of the other party.

Direct Action: *Satyagraha*, parallel government, mass meetings, economic boycott, public education, strikes, nonpayment of taxes, parallel schools, etc.
- An attempt to create new circumstances as a basis for new solutions.
- Noncooperation seeks a return to cooperation, and is never violent.

Acceptable solutions seek mutual gain.
- Face saving respectful alternatives are created in order to avoid any implications of victory or defeat.

group or at least of McLaren. Many of his actions were oriented toward seeking public attention rather than violence. The solution achieved following a 7-day siege was, in fact, based upon just such recognition. The agreement allowed McLaren to surrender following a military-style ceremony and the signing of an agreement that he would be given an opportunity to publicly state his case. This simple recognition prevented further violence by McLaren, but under the U.S. Constitution, the group already had the right to this freedom of speech.

In addition to the local community, the State of Texas had dealt with McLaren before April 27, 1997; however, state officials were constrained by regulations that limit the flexibility which a peace brigade is able to implement. In spite of this, state and federal authorities appear to have proceeded patiently and cautiously in serving warrants that had been issued. The State Legislature established a law making the filing of false liens a criminal act in response to McLaren's activities (a confrontational response to the other group's initiative). The restraint in forcing a confrontation by serving warrants was a result of caution in response to the violence which erupted at Waco, TX, with the Branch Davidians and in Idaho at Ruby Ridge. In those cases, excessive force resulted in unnecessary killing. Instead, there was an effort to pursue the type of patient negotiations used with the Freemen in Montana. While that standoff lasted 81 days, no one was hurt and no shots were fired. Further, the Freemen were not made into martyrs whose deaths could be avenged by other militia. The patience exhibited was remarkable in view of McLaren's provocations. In addition to the liens and phony checks, McLaren refused to pay taxes and ignored judgments against him in the court cases he lost. The legal system, however, forced state and federal officials to proceed in an adversary fashion that sought victory over the Republic of Texas group. This made it difficult to solve the total situation, grant any legitimacy to the opponents, or maximize creative synthesis. The legal perspective also appeared to have diverted attention from seeking full information regarding the group that could have facilitated negotiations, and the possibility of seeking cooperation.

On April 27, 1997, state and federal officials and members of the local community were confronted by a crisis that might have been averted by a process approach (see Table 18.1). The taking of hostages was responded to by the application of force. The Republic of Texas compound was surrounded by the entire Jeff Davis County Sheriff's Department, 13 state troopers, two Texas Rangers, and members of the FBI. The crisis began with the arrest of two Republic of Texas members. The militia group escalated the action by taking hostages and, in the process, wounding Rowe. State and federal officials responded by a further escalation of force, armed police surrounding and cutting off McLaren and his supporters. This set the stage for a violent confrontation. The local community was eliminated from the situation, thus perhaps losing valuable information and potential intermediaries.

The negotiators, however, appear to have sought a peaceful solution from the beginning. While restricting the actions of the Republic of Texas members, a reasonably cooperative approach was used. It was believed that the two hostages would be killed if the militia members were not released from jail. Consistent with seeking least violence, the two prisoners were released in exchange for Rowe and his wife. This appears to be the result of patient communication in the service of a unilateral cooperative effort. This action also represented some degree of granting legitimacy to McLaren's position. In addition, respect for the group's views was illustrated by agreeing to a referendum on independence. This led to a quick release of the hostages on April 28, 1997. The position of the negotiators was remarkable considering the widespread opinion of no concessions to terrorists. In fact, the negotiators were criticized heavily for these actions. Nevertheless, this first stage of negotiations released the hostages without further injury and deprived McLaren of his most valuable asset in the situation. The lack of hostages defused the confrontation rather than further escalating it and reduced media coverage that might have increased tension. The ambivalence or disagreement among the negotiators, however, was illustrated by a continuing build up of military force. A 15-member special assault force was flown to the area. Violent intervention was held in reserve as an alternative or a negotiating chip. In either case, force was mixed with peaceful efforts.

The initial success of negotiations slowed on April 29 although officials continued to emphasize that they were seeking a peaceful solution. McLaren offered further negotiation, but sought full diplomatic immunity for the group. This would grant full recognition to his position on the status of Texas rather than an open discussion of the issue. While negotiations may have been proceeding within a cooperative framework at this time, other pressures were obstructing this context. Isolation of the militia compound led to 80 people being removed from their homes, and they pressed for the immediate use of force. At the same time, Attorney General Morales insisted that the group members were terrorists and should be treated as such. Finally, even the negotiators allowed, or were coerced into, further military build up when two armored personnel carriers were added in possible preparation for armed intervention. A potential ally for cooperative negotiation appeared when Terence O'Rourke sought to provide legal representation for McLaren. O'Rourke was a long-term associate of McLaren who appeared to be a trusted intermediary for further negotiations. It is not clear that this resource for cooperation was used effectively.

On the surface, the events of April 30, 1997, seemed to be a return to an escalation of force, and a rejection of cooperation by McLaren when he broke off negotiations. This was probably an effort to gain a competitive advantage rather than seek cooperation. Further pressure was added when police in Pecos, about 80 miles to the north, arrested seven men carrying Republic of Texas membership cards. These men were armed with weapons and explosives and could have represented an advance guard of a massive effort to reinforce the group in Fort Davis. The law enforcement group was expanded to approximately 100 state agents, and this force was supplied with horses and bloodhounds. This escalation was combined with the announcement that the state was determined to seek a peaceful settlement and had no intention of a military assault. On May 1, 1997, McLaren responded to the offer of cooperation rather than the invitation to violence and began to negotiate again.

Patient negotiation began to pay off on May 2, 1997, when one of the Republic of Texas members previously arrested and then released in the hostage exchange left the compound and surrendered to police. Robert Scheidt was called the captain of the embassy guard, and his defection indicated internal disagreement that might provide an asset for peaceful negotiation. On the same day, McLaren again appeared to escalate by dismissing his lawyer, O'Rourke, and by broadcasting Mayday appeals for armed assistance. At this time, comparisons to the Alamo were made, suggesting a readiness for a violent conclusion. It also indicated that martyrdom was an important goal, perhaps the most important issue. The spokesman for the Department of Public Safety, however, announced that no military operation was imminent. This countered rumors that continued to indicate the use of force by the state. In addition, there was a public denial of any ultimatum. This continued the state's position emphasizing a flexible, cooperative approach rather than a no negotiation confrontation.

Further desertions from the militia group began on May 3 with the surrender of McLaren's wife, Evelyn. This was followed by a negotiated surrender of most of the remaining group. McLaren and three others laid down their weapons following a military style ceremony. O'Rourke announced that there was a signed agreement by McLaren for a statewide cease fire and a commitment that he would be able to state his case regarding the Republic of Texas. State officials stated that there was no agreement other than a cease fire, with the group members surrendering peacefully. Of course, McLaren had a right to state his case, but this was true without any need for official approval. At this point, most of the group had surrendered without any violence after the wounding of Rowe by the militia. The State negotiators had succeeded in this case without a single shot fired. In order to maintain this cooperative stance, they allowed two members, who refused to surrender, to escape. After McLaren, and those who followed him, gave up and the firearms and explosives in the compound were secured, the other two were pursued by agents on horseback aided by bloodhounds and other agents in a helicopter. At this point, a win-win solution had been established. McLaren received considerable media attention regarding his cause, even painting himself as a heroic martyr in the style of the Alamo disaster. The state had most of the group in prison where legal measures could proceed in a nonviolent fashion, and people in the local community could return to their homes without further intimidation by McLaren. It is evident that the negotiators had to resist calls for violent intervention from some state officials (obvious in the dual approach of force and peaceful negotiation), from many in the media, and from people in the local community who were disappointed that McLaren was not killed in a violent assault.

The negotiators, for the most part and consistent with an informed, peaceful approach, appear to have pursued a unilateral cooperative stance while granting legitimacy to some aspects of McLaren's position. It was stated that the seeds of an agreement were always there, even when McLaren broke off negotiations or threatened the use of force. The State agreed not to interfere with any petition to a federal judge regarding diplomatic immunity or a referendum on nationhood for Texas, but McLaren already had those rights. In addition, it was agreed that he had the right to make an appeal to the United Nations, but this was also a right that was already available. Officials also allowed McLaren and his wife to spend the first night in jail together — a small concession that enhanced nonviolence. Perhaps McLaren's threats of violence were all bluff, but other members appeared to be ready to die fighting, using the image of the Alamo as a basis for a glorious death. Unfortunately, the peaceful actions of the negotiators were undercut on May 5, 1997, when one of the two escaped militia members was killed after firing on the police helicopter and the pursuing dogs. This is a frequent consequence of what appears to have been a confrontational pursuit inviting a violent response. Perhaps these two could have been followed with less urgency for capture and greater patience for peaceful surrender. This aggressive pursuit endangered the lives of police officials and, in spite of the use of force, one member remained at large as of May 6, 1997.

Direct information from the state negotiators, McLaren, and his lawyer is not available at this time. A more adequate analysis requires additional information. It is clear that official negotiating style has moved in the direction of Gandhian synthesis (Table 18.1) without being able to give up, entirely, the use of confrontation and force. Given the general success of these negotiations compared with Waco, it is possible that a more systematic Gandhian approach initiated before the hostage crisis could have avoided all violence. Further, an early intervention in the style of a peace brigade could have avoided some of the early psychological abuse by McLaren toward his neighbors. Finally, a nonviolent solution can avoid attempts to seek the type of vengeance characteristic of the Oklahoma bombing in response to Waco. Gandhian synthesis breaks the cycle of violence.

Peace Armies

Gandhi's (1961a, p. 86) concept of a peace army parallels that of the brigade but refers to larger numbers of people capable of dealing with larger potential conflicts. Shanti Sena, as Gandhi referred to the peace army, became a reality in India and, according to Shepard (1987, pp. 44–62), was used successfully on many occasions. In addition, it was implemented in a number of other countries. The recent activities of the United Nations in working to solve differences rather than fight wars is consistent with the Peace Army. These activities have not always been sufficiently nonviolent or completely successful, but the operations in Haiti and Bosnia certainly illustrate the Gandhian principle of working to reduce violence.

Unfortunately, peace is usually criticized as impractical and unaffordable; however, while there was a cumulative reduction in the world's military spending of $935 billion between 1987 and 1994 (Renner, 1995, p. 150), only about $16 billion, 2% of military expenditures, was used for peace building in 1994 (p. 166). Most of the peace dividend was diverted to purposes other than the elimination of war as a means of international problem solving. Rather than focus on the cost of peace, Renner (1995, pp. 151–153) pointed out that the price of militarism since World War II added up to $30–35 trillion. The costs of military solutions and deterrence include decontamination and rehabilitation of land, the devastations of war, ecological damage, loss of harvests and industrial production, uprooting populations, resettlement and humanitarian assistance, and the elimination of arsenals. The price of military solutions is hundreds of billions of dollars each year. Renner optimistically proposed that there is a growing recognition of the need for disarmament and cooperation in an interdependent world, and of the greater importance of economic vitality and environmental quality as a basis for a country's success. This prospect will be better served by peace armies than by military might.

Conclusions

Gandhi is often misunderstood within Western society because people are constrained by a set of values that considers human beings to be inherently driven by self-interest. The consequence of this perspective is the conclusion that conflict is inevitable, competition is an effective means of solving disagreements, and violence is a typical and acceptable aspect of human affairs. Even worse, many in the West, including professionals, advocate the desirability of self-interest and power as foundations for effective living and war as a valuable means of solving international affairs. These values promote the suspiciousness and divisiveness that are foundations for hate groups.

Gandhian problem solving requires an openness to the conception that community interest is as fundamental as self-interest, that differences do not have to be interpreted as conflict, that cooperation is more effective and powerful than competition, and that prosocial, nonviolent alternatives are superior to violence for personal and international affairs (Buck, 1995a,b, 1996a,c). Institutional violence can be dealt with most adequately by assuming that people have considerable capacity for cooperativeness. Cooperation should be sought regardless of the behavior of others. Cooperative approaches, however, are not enough; it is necessary to communicate honestly and to seek solutions through rational discussion. It is also necessary to attempt to reach the humaneness that is part of all human beings. This is a difficult task in view of the extent to which humanity has been suppressed in some people. As a result, one must persist in spite of resistance, work to understand and grant legitimacy to the other party's position, and keep the initiative in one's own hands by avoiding the traps of conflict and competition. This indicates that there is likely to be some core legitimacy to the grievances of terrorists, however extreme their general perspective. Recognition of this sense of injustice or persecution provides a foundation for rational discussion and win-win negotiation.

It is necessary to be prepared for the failure of reasoning and the initial offers of cooperation. Even more difficult, it is necessary to anticipate deception and violence. These responses cannot be allowed to deter the search for cooperation. At times, *Satyagraha* needs to be utilized to avoid deadlock or the temptation to resort to violent methods. *Satyagraha* is a means of returning the interaction to a cooperative exchange, and is always open to the other person's offers of cooperation. *Satyagraha*, as with all forms of Gandhian synthesis, attempts to solve the situation rather than win out over an opponent. It seeks a solution that satisfies the essential and legitimate needs of all parties. It avoids victory or defeat. When one side comes to believe that it is right to change some position, a solution is offered that avoids a loss of dignity. *Satyagraha*, as with all Gandhian synthesis, is a process. This means that only the most important issues are negotiated at the present time. Secondary concerns are left to future consideration. The end result of this approach is often the opportunity to reconcile positions that appear to be contradictory.

The reconciliation of opposite positions and the striving for creative solutions requires freedom of thought. As a result, concrete rules for *Satyagraha* and Gandhian synthesis cannot be prescribed in advance. Past experience and previous methods are valuable, but Gandhi always considered his approach to be an open-ended experiment. Each situation is unique. Gandhi (1969, pp. 42–43), however, rejected the term "Gandhism" and discouraged followers from using that word. He preferred to think of others as collaborators and constantly encouraged people to think for themselves.

The heart of a Gandhian perspective is based upon a search for alternatives to violence. Cooperation, community interest, and *Satyagraha* are oriented toward the minimization of violence. Gandhi never anticipated the complete elimination of violence, but he demonstrated a series of practical means for reducing violence. This position begins with the proposition that violence cannot be reduced by violent means. One can avoid violence only by nonviolent methods, but this requires extensive patience and a rejection of simplistic solutions. Gandhi (1966b, p. 30) concluded that competition for armaments, even in the name of defense, would lead inevitably to mass destruction. "If there is a victor left, the very victory will be a living death for the nation that emerges victorious." This conclusion applies equally to the suppression of crime within society by violent means such as police action or the death penalty.

Annotated Bibliography

1. Branch, T. (1988) *Parting the Waters: America in the King Years 1954–63*. New York: Simon & Schuster. Branch describes the extensive use of Gandhian techniques by Martin Luther King, Jr., and many of his associates during the civil rights campaigns in the American South. *Satyagraha* is evident during the Montgomery Bus Boycott and King's use of prison as a means of touching the humanity of the general American population. The Birmingham Campaign illustrates the ability of children, using nonviolent resistance, to overcome the power of police dogs, high-pressure hoses and jail.

2. Gandhi, M.K. (1940) *An Autobiography: The Story of My Experiments With Truth, 2nd ed.* Ahmedabad: Navajivan. This volume represents Gandhi's description of his personal search for "truth". It focuses upon his efforts toward self-realization as a basis for nonviolent resistance and service to the community. Gandhi's analysis demonstrates how *Satyagraha* grew out of the practical realities of developing creative solutions to oppression in South Africa and India.

3. Gandhi, M.K. (1961) In B. Kumarappa (Ed.), *Nonviolent Resistance*. New York: Schocken. Kumarappa presents a selection of Gandhi's writings that define *Satyagraha* and describe the value context necessary for its practice. This volume also evaluates a number of *Satyagraha* campaigns.

4. Gandhi, M.K. (1967) In R.K. Prabhu and U.R. Rao (Eds.), *The Mind of Mahatma Gandhi*. Ahmedabad: Navajivan. This volume provides representative selections of Gandhi's writing that give a good overview of his thinking. The discussion of basic values, *Sarvodaya,* and democracy are an essential context for the application of *Satyagraha*.

5. Young, A. (1996) *An Easy Burden*. New York: Harper Collins. Young's memoirs provide an excellent account of the application of *Satyagraha* to the American Civil rights movement. This volume provides a fine contrast between the well planned, successful Birmingham campaign and other demonstrations that were less effective due to inadequate preparation.

References

Ashe, G. (1969) *Gandhi*. New York: Stein & Day.

Bixenstine, V.E. (1996) Spousal homicide. In H.V. Hall (Ed.), *Lethal Violence 2000: A Sourcebook on Fatal Domestic, Acquaintance and Stranger Aggression*, pp. 231–257. Kamuela, HI: Pacific Institute for the Study of Conflict and Aggression.

Bondurant, J.V. (1965) *Conquest of Violence*, Rev. ed. Berkeley: University of California.

Branch, T. (1988) *Parting the Waters: America in the King Years 1954–63*. New York: Simon & Schuster.

Brown, D. (1970) *Bury My Heart at Wounded Knee*. New York: Holt, Rinehart & Winston.

Buck, L.A. (1984) Nonviolence and Satyagraha in Attenborough's Gandhi. *Journal of Humanistic Psychology, 24*, 130–141.

Buck, L.A. (1986) *Courage: A Gandhian Perspective*. Paper presented at International Conference on Eastern Approaches to Self and Mind, University College, Cardiff and Welsh Branch of the British Psychological Society, Cardiff, U.K.

Buck, L.A. (1991) *Courage, Autism and Schizophrenia*. Paper presented at 49th Annual Convention International Council of Psychologists, San Francisco, CA.

Buck, L.A. (1993) *Gandhi and Secular Democracy*. Paper presented at 22nd Annual Conference on South Asia, University of Wisconsin Center for South Asia, Madison, WI.

Buck, L.A. (1994) Gandhian synthesis. *Journal of Developing Societies, 11*, 112–119.

Buck, L.A. (1995a) *Empathy, Altruism and Gandhian Synthesis*. Paper presented at 53rd Annual Convention, International Council of Psychologists, Taipei, Taiwan.

Buck, L.A. (1995b) Gandhi and Jefferson: democracy and humanism. *Gandhi Marg, 17*, 175–192.

Buck, L.A. (1996a) Beyond conflict and competition: diversity, cooperation and life affirmation as alternatives to violence. In H.V. Hall (Ed.), *Lethal Violence 2000: A Sourcebook on Fatal Domestic, Acquaintance and Stranger Aggression*, pp. 589–611. Kamuela, HI: Pacific Institute for the Study of Conflict and Aggression.

Buck, L.A. (1996b) *Normal Violence*. Paper presented at 54th Annual Convention, International Council of Psychologists, Banff, Alberta, Canada.

Buck, L.A. (1996c) *Gandhian Reconciliation of Opposites Beyond Conflict, Competition and Compromise*. Paper presented at New York Conference on Asian Studies, Dowling College, Oakdale, NY.

Buck, L.A. (1996d) *Cooperation and Altruism as Alternatives for Violence*. Paper presented at Lethal Violence 2000, The Pacific Institute for the Study of Conflict and Aggression, Honolulu, HI.

Buck, L.A. and Nimbark, A. (1982) *India in Year 2000 — A Gandhian Alternative: Psychosexual Alternatives*. Paper presented at 11th Annual Conference on South Asia, University of Wisconsin, Madison, WI.

Call, J.A. (1996) The hostage triad: takers, victims and negotiators. In H.V. Hall (Ed.), *Lethal Violence 2000: A Sourcebook on Fatal Domestic, Acquaintance and Stranger Aggression*, pp. 561–587. Kamuela, HI: Pacific Institute for the Study of Conflict and Aggression.

Carnevale, P.J. and Pruitt, D.G. (1992) Negotiation and mediation. In M.R. Rosenzweig and L.W. Porter (Eds.), *Annual Review of Psychology*, pp. 537–582. Palo Alto, CA: Annual Reviews.

Craig, G.A. (1989) The grand decider. *New York Review of Books, 36*, 31–36.

Dalton, D. (1982) *Indian Idea of Freedom*. Gurgaon, India: Academic Press.

Deutsch, M. (1993) Educating for a peaceful world. *American Psychologist, 48*, 510–517.

Diwakar, R.R. (1969) *Saga of Satyagraha*. Bombay: Bharatiya Vidya Bhavan.

Draper, T. (1991) Presidential wars. *New York Review of Books, 38*, pp. 64–74.

Draper, T. (1992) The true history of the Gulf War. *New York Review of Books, 39*, 38–45.

Ember, C.R. and Ember, M. (1995) Issues in cross-cultural studies of interpersonal violence. In R.B. Ruback and N.A. Weiner (Eds.), *Interpersonal Violent Behaviors*, pp. 25–42. New York: Springer.

Erikson, E.H. (1969) *Gandhi's Truth*. New York: Norton.

Erikson, E.H. (1987) Remarks on the "wider identity". In E.H. Erikson (Ed.,), *A Way of Looking at Things*. New York: Norton.

Farrell, W. (1993) *The Myth of Male Power*. New York: Simon & Schuster.

Fine, R. (1985) *The Meaning of Love in Human Experience*. New York: Wiley.

Freud, S. (1949) *An Outline of Psychoanalysis*. New York: Norton.

Fromm, E. (1963) *The Art of Loving*. New York: Bantam.

Fromm, E. (1973) *The Anatomy of Human Destructiveness*. New York: Holt, Rinehart & Winston.

Gandhi, M.K. (1939) *Hind Swaraj*, Rev. ed. Ahmedabad: Navajivan.

Gandhi, M.K. (1940) *An Autobiography: The Story of My Experiments With Truth*, 2nd ed. Ahmedabad: Navajivan.

Gandhi, M.K. (1942) *Nonviolence in Peace and War*, Vol. 1. Ahmedabad: Navajivan.

Gandhi, M.K. (1949) *For Pacifists*. Ahmedabad: Navajivan.

Gandhi, M.K. (1950) *Satyagraha in South Africa*, 2nd ed. Ahmedabad: Navajivan.

Gandhi, M.K. (1954) *Sarvodaya*. Ahmedabad: Navajivan.

Gandhi, M.K. (1955) *Ashram Observances in Action*. Ahmedabad: Navajivan.

Gandhi, M.K. (1960) In K. Kripalani (Ed.), *All Men Are Brothers*. Ahmedabad: Navajivan.

Gandhi, M.K. (1961a) In B. Kumarappa (Ed.), *Nonviolent Resistance*. New York: Schocken.

Gandhi, M.K. (1961b) In R.K. Prabhu (Ed.), *Democracy: Real and Deceptive*. Ahmedabad: Navajivan.

Gandhi, M.K. (1962a) In L. Fischer (Ed.), *The Essential Gandhi*. New York: Vintage.

Gandhi, M.K. (1962b) In A.T. Hingorani (Ed.), *The Science of Satyagraha*. Bombay: Bharatiya Vidya Bhavan.

Gandhi, M.K. (1964) In V.B. Kher (Ed.), *Stone Walls Do Not a Prison Make*. Ahmedabad: Navajivan.

Gandhi, M.K. (1966a) In A.T. Hingorani (Ed.), *To the Perplexed*. Bombay: Bharatiya Vidya Bhavan.

Gandhi, M.K. (1966b) In A.T. Hingorani (Ed.), *Towards Lasting Peace*, Bombay: Bharatiya Vidya Bhavan.

Gandhi, M.K. (1967) In R.K. Prabhu and U.R. Rao (Eds.), *The Mind of Mahatma Gandhi*. Ahmedabad: Navajivan.

Gandhi, M.K. (1969) *Towards Non-Violent Politics*. Thanjavur, Tamilnad: Sarvodaya Prachuralaya.

Gandhi, M.K. (1970) In A.T. Hingorani (Ed.), *The Law of Love*. Bombay: Bharatiya Vidya Bhavan.

Gandhi, M.K. (1971) In A.T. Hingorani (Ed.), *Service Before Self*. New Delhi: Bharatiya Vidya Bhavan.

Gandhi, M.K. (1972) *On Myself.* Bombay: Bharatiya Vidya Bhavan.

Gay, P. (1993) *The Cultivation of Hatred.* New York: Norton.

Gelles, R.J. and Cornell, C.P. (1990) *Intimate Violence in Families*, 2nd ed. Newbury Park: Sage.

Gibson, J.T. (1991) Training people to inflict pain: state terror and social learning. *Journal of Humanistic Psychology, 31*, 72–87.

Goldhagen, D.J. (1996) *Hitler's Willing Executioners.* New York: Knopf.

Hall, H.V. (1996) Death by institutions: Fatal collective violence. In H.V. Hall (Ed.), *Lethal Violence 2000: A Sourcebook on Fatal Domestic, Acquaintance and Stranger Aggression*, pp. 1–51. Kamuela, HI: Pacific Institute for the Study of Conflict and Aggression.

Johnson, D.W. and Johnson, R.T. (1995) Social interdependence: cooperative learning in education. In B.B. Bunker and J.Z. Rubin (Eds.), *Conflict, Cooperation and Justice*, pp. 205–251. San Francisco: Jossey-Bass.

Jordan, W.D. (1968) *White Over Black.* Chapel Hill: University of North Carolina.

Kelman, H.C. and Hamilton, V.L. (1989) *Crimes of Obedience.* New Haven: Yale.

Kull, S. (1989) *Minds at War: Nuclear Reality and the Inner Conflicts of Defense Policymakers.* New York: Basic Books.

Lifton, R.J. (1967) *Death in Life.* New York: Basic Books.

Lifton, R.J. (1973) *Home From the War.* New York: Simon & Schuster.

Lifton, R.J. (1986) *The Nazi Doctors.* New York: Basic Books.

Lifton, R.J. and Markusen, E. (1990) *The Genocidal Mentality.* New York: Basic Books.

Malik, S. (1986) *Gandhian Satyagraha and Contemporary World.* Rohtak, India: Manthan.

May, R. (1972) *Power and Innocence.* New York: Norton.

May, R. (1975) *The Courage To Create.* New York: Norton.

Muller, I. (1991) *Hitler's Justice: The Courts of the Third Reich.* Cambridge: Harvard.

Muste, A.J. (1967) Nonviolence and Mississippi. In G. Ramachandran and T.K. Mahadevan (Eds.), *Gandhi: His Relevance for Our Times*, pp. 209–221. Bombay: Bharatiya Vidya Bhavan.

Nisbett, R.E., Polly, G., and Lang, S. (1995) Homicide and U.S. regional culture. In R.B. Ruback and N.A. Weiner (Eds.), *Interpersonal Violent Behaviors*, pp. 135–151. New York: Springer.

Oza, D.K. (1991) *Voluntary Action and Gandhian Approach.* New Delhi: National Book Trust.

Parekh, B. (1995) *Gandhi's Political Philosophy.* Delhi: Ajanta.

Poirier, J.G. (1996) Violence in the family. In H.V. Hall (Ed.), *Lethal Violence 2000: A Sourcebook on Fatal Domestic, Acquaintance and Stranger Aggression*, pp. 259–292. Kamuela, HI: Pacific Institute for the Study of Conflict and Aggression.

Rappaport, J. and Holden, K. (1981) Prevention of violence. In J.R. Hays, T.K. Roberts, and K.S. Soloway (Eds.), *Violence and the Violent Individual*, pp. 409–440. New York: Spectrum.

Renner, M. (1995) Budgeting for disarmament. In L.R. Brown (Ed.), *State of the World* 1995, pp. 150–169. New York: Norton.

Shepard, M. (1987) *Gandhi Today.* Arcata, CA: Simple Productions.

Stock, C.M. (1996) *Rural Radicals.* Ithaca: Cornell University.

Straus, M.A., Gelles, R.J., and Steinmetz, S.K. (1980) *Behind Closed Doors*. Garden City, NY: Anchor.

Tedeschi, J.T. and Felson, R.B. (1994) *Violence, Aggression and Coercive Actions*. Washington, D.C.: American Psychological Association.

Tetlock, P.E., McGuire, C.B., and Mitchell, G. (1991) Psychological perspectives on nuclear deterrence. In M.R. Rosenzweig and L.W. Porter (Eds.), *Annual Review of Psychology*, pp. 239–276. Palo Alto, CA: Annual Reviews.

Thompson, L. and Hrebec, D. (1996) Lose-lose agreements in interdependent decision making. *Psychological Bulletin, 120*, 396–409.

Toch, H. (1992) *Violent Men*. Washington, D.C.: American Psychological Association.

Todorov, T. (1996) *Facing the Extreme*. New York: Holt.

Twemlow, S.W. and Sacco, F.C. (1996) The violent community: a view from an evolving nation. In H.V. Hall (Ed.), *Lethal Violence 2000: A Sourcebook on Fatal Domestic, Acquaintance and Stranger Aggression*, pp. 613–634. Kamuela, HI: Pacific Institute for the Study of Conflict and Aggression.

Verhovek, S.H. (1997) Reports to *The New York Times* April 27, 1997, to May 6, 1997, *The New York Times, CXLVI*(50), 776–50,785.

Weigley, R.F. (1991) *The Age of Battles*. Bloomington: Indiana University Press.

Wertham, F. (1969) *A Sign for Cain*. New York: Warner.

Whitaker, L. (1996) Social inducements to paralethal and lethal violence. In H.V. Hall (Ed.), *Lethal Violence 2000: A Sourcebook on Fatal Domestic, Acquaintance and Stranger Aggression*, pp. 143–174. Kamuela, HI: Pacific Institute for the Study of Conflict and Aggression.

Young, A. (1996) *An Easy Burden*. New York: Harper Collins.

Zuckerman, L. (1989) Converging on peace? *New York Review of Books, 36*, 26–32.

About the Author

Lucien A. Buck, Ph.D., is a Professor of Psychology at Dowling College in Oakdale, NY. He is a Diplomate in Clinical Psychology from the American Board of Professional Psychology and a Fellow of The Academy of Clinical Psychology. He has numerous publications and presentations in the areas of conflict, competitiveness and violence, perception, altered consciousness, and psychotherapy. He has presented at a variety of international conferences on Gandhian concepts as they apply to the definition of normality, democracy, humanism, and life affirmation.

Chapter 19

A MULTI-LEVEL CONCEPTUAL FRAMEWORK FOR UNDERSTANDING THE VIOLENT COMMUNITY

Stuart W. Twemlow and Frank C. Sacco

Lethal violence does not occur in a vacuum. Most traditional psychological approaches to violence focus on family violence, battering, and child abuse. These approaches see violence as an event that stems principally from individual causes such as genetic predisposition, addiction, past abuse, and other family dynamics. The role of the violent community often serves only as a backdrop or an after-the-fact tally sheet for these individual events. In this chapter, the authors argue that diagnosis of the violent community is a necessary first step before interventions to deal with the lethal violence can be successful. While acknowledging the importance of individual and family factors, the authors have found that such factors are significantly affected by the mores of the large group — the community and the socio-economic conditions which reflect those mores. The authors' findings derive mainly from projects in Jamaica, but also from work in progress in east coast and midwestern cities in the U.S. (Twemlow, 1995a,b; Twemlow and Sacco, 1996; Sacco and Twemlow, 1997).

Studies have shown varying and often contradictory trends in lethal violence rates. Browne and Williams (1993) studied homicide reports and discovered little variance in victim rates for men but found that unmarried women experienced a dramatic increase in homicide victimization by their partners. Brownstein et al. (1994), in a detailed study of female murderers, discovered that women involved in the drug trade resorted to violence to resolve their conflicts. Thus, domestic violence alone does not explain women's lethal violence.

Bachman (1993) studied patterns of lethal victimization in older persons. Results suggested that they are more at risk in their own homes. The highest levels of violence toward older persons were nonlethal attacks by strangers during the commission of another felony. Thus, it seems the elderly are more passive targets for criminals, while younger, predominantly female victims die at the hands of more familiar males.

In a Canadian study, Silverman and Kennedy (1993) found that males chose to shoot their victims more often than did females, but that shooting overall has declined for most males. Surprisingly, males have more often beaten or stabbed their victims, according to crime/stranger homicide rates. These findings may point to an evolving cultural influence driving the shifts in how lethal violence is perpetrated.

Block (1993) and Block and Block (1992) studied Hispanic Americans in Chicago. Again, there was a clear link to community and cultural factors in how lethal violence unfolded. This study found a comparatively high risk overall for homicide in Hispanic Americans vs. whites. Further, there was a clear age factor within the Hispanic American community, with teenage males ages 15 to 19 being at high risk to be the victims of lethal violence, but this effect decreased dramatically with age. The two main causes of lethal violence were gang-related homicides and male-on-male expressive confrontations. These patterns suggest how culture and community shape the violence response. Baron (1993) studied the differences in child murder from state to state in the U.S. The findings support the hypothesis that as the level of gender inequality increases, child homicide increases. Thus, gender inequality, a culturally transmitted attitude, contributes to the social climate conducive to lethal violence toward children. These findings point to specific mechanisms within violent communities that lead to the acceptance of a domination and submission dialectic between the sexes which transfers directly to children. If it is culturally acceptable to hurt women, then it is likewise acceptable to hurt children. These studies also pointed to the impact of single-parent families and alcoholism as causal factors in explaining variances in the child homicide cases.

In an Australian study, Polk and Ransom (1991) found that 51% of homicides involved victims and offenders linked by some form of sexual intimacy. Possessiveness was the dominant characteristic of male violence toward their female partners. The younger the female, the more likely jealousy was the causal factor in the lethal violence. Older females were most often the victims of desperate males in the *folie a deux* of murder-suicide. Men were most often killed by women partners in self-defense. The culture, the authors argued, shapes the lethal violence response according to the values and attitudes of the community, male/female relationships, and the care of the young and the old.

Rose and McClain (1990) studied black homicide rates in large urban environments. Citing Federal Bureau of Investigation (FBI) statistics over a 25-year span, they found that the transition from the industrial to the post-industrial state generated trends for increased black male involvement in lethal violence both as victims and perpetrators. The age of involvement also slowly decreased. Thus, as job opportunities faded, black males often entered the illegal economy, which clearly increases the risk of involvement in lethal violence. In contrast with this more usual statistic is a highly creative study by Greenberg and Schneider (1994), who found that in three marginalized communities (high incidence of ghettos, unwanted land use, and unwanted people), the homicide rate traditionally seen as highest in young black males, ages 15 to 24, is *no* higher in this group than in whites, Hispanic Americans, females, middle-aged, and older people.

As American families shift away from traditional relationships, there is a decrease in the affiliation and association of blood kin. Daly and Wilson (1988) posited that increased lethality is related to a lowering of blood-kin immunity to violence. Children are abused more frequently and severely by nonblood relatives within a family. Their study further found that the rate of lethal violence between blood relatives in Miami in 1980 was 1.8%, while the rate of homicide between marital relatives (nonblood) was 10%. Similarly, in Detroit in 1972, 19% of homicide victims were related by marriage, and 6% were related by blood.

Zimring et al. (1983) studied 151 homicide victims in Chicago and discovered that white males killed females with whom they were intimate twice as frequently as white males were killed; whereas, black males were twice as likely to be killed by their female intimates as to kill them. This cultural pattern suggests a different code of ethics among black males that leads them to kill their intimates less frequently than white males. Smith and Parker (1980) confirmed the importance of social variables in predicting homicide rates. Poverty was shown to be a causal factor in motivating higher rates of homicide for economically disadvantaged individuals.

Living in violent communities increases the probability of violent behavior, according to Liddell et al. (1994), who studied South African children from four different communities. It was shown that children from violent communities were significantly more likely to be involved in aggressive acts, particularly when the children had more contact with older boys and men. Paddock (1975) studied communities in Oaxaca, Mexico, where there was an opportunity to compare several towns, some of which were nonviolent without heavy police activity, and others more violent. Low violence in communities seemed to result from (1) the near absence of "machismo", (2) contrasting practices of child rearing, (3) very few close friendships linking adults of the same sex, and (4) a strong social role for women.

Cicchetti and Lynch (1993) outlined a model for understanding the causes and consequences of community violence, emphasizing that violence within cultures impacts on children's development. Fitzpatrick and Boldizar (1993) described how young black children suffer symptoms of post-traumatic stress disorder (PTSD) due to living in violent communities. Friedlander (1993) argued that living in a violent community, not violent media programs, accounts for increased violence. In fact, he reported that prosocial messages on television have a greater effect on behavior than do violent messages. Richters and Martinez (1993) brought to light the complex interaction between environmental context and family. They investigated the early predictors of adaptational success and failure of 72 children living in a violent community. It was not the mere accumulation of environmental adversities, but the erosion of the home life that explained success or failure in adaptive behavior. Thus, if the family is strong, the impact of the violent community is lessened, and if the family is weak, adaptability is greatly at risk.

Responding to violence in the community demands a balanced approach. Clarke (1994) found that increasing per capita incarceration from 1975 to 1992 did not significantly reduce the per capita violent crime index or motor vehicle theft. Cahn and Cahn (1993) suggested collaborative efforts based on Project Alliance, an approach developed by the Massachusetts Attorney General, stressing coordination of law enforcement and treatment. DeJong (1994) offered school-based intervention called the Resolving Conflict Creatively Program (RCCP), based on work in the New York city schools. In this model, peaceful schools were the beginning of the evolution of a peaceful neighborhood.

Jaros (1992) saw community violence as a public health problem requiring the promotion of community education and the development of problem-solving work groups. Munoz and Tan (1994) described a program that brought youth, police, and community leaders together for a 2-day retreat to solve problems and develop projects to reduce community violence. Cordner (1993), Mastrofski (1993), and Walker (1993) suggested ways police could work with citizen groups to reduce violence in the community.

The National Crime Prevention Council, through the U.S. Department of Justice Assistance, has developed kits to help create safer communities — Working Together To Stop the Violence: A Blueprint for Safer Communities (1994). The U.S. Department of Child and Maternal Health also offers a model program titled Building Safer Communities (1994). DeBryn et al. (1988) describe community efforts that address reducing violence in Native American and Alaskan Inuit communities.

There have been many studies linking violence and poverty. Hanson (1997) took an interesting historical viewpoint; in his article, "Why Don't We Care About the Poor Anymore?", he noted that today poverty has lost its meaning; the modern view of the poor is that they are responsible for their own plight, with little attempt by communities to understand or make a place for the poor. Hanson (1997) pointed out that during the middle ages, poverty was "no social pathology but, rather, an intrinsic part of the established social order. Rich and poor alike were said to owe their positions to the grace of God rather than to anything they themselves had done, and all were expected to accept their lot with humility." In those days, there was no stigma attached to poverty; in fact, there was significant social status, because the poor were considered to have certain mystical powers and to be available to the rich as a means to atone for their sins like the Sadhu — the holy man — who begs in India. By the 19th century, however, the poor were despised instead of honored. Poverty became a social cancer to be eradicated. The mystical poor had been replaced by poor people who were enraged and criminal. In the 20th century, there was a brief respite through socialism when the poor were considered to be helpless victims of a corrupt political system dominated by the wealthy. Now, instead, modern contemporary individualism blames the poor for their lot. This hard-nosed approach to poverty led to the abolition of welfare programs in parts of many countries, including the U.S. The failure to deal with the psychological underpinnings of poverty will and has led to conditions that approach anarchy in countries where politicians legislate or demand that the poor care for themselves. Poverty wreaks havoc with the logically functioning, anxiety-free mind; the rage of the poor can auger poorly for the safety and health of the wealthy.

A violent community is particularly harsh with regard to the place of the poor. At best, the poor are seen as freeloaders with a possibility of rehabilitation if sufficient incentives, punishments, or both, are given for laziness. At worst, the poor are seen as a danger to the stability of the affluent middle class and are considered to be a sub-human group that needs to be eliminated. This all-or-nothing, oversimplified approach to human psychology is characteristic of violent communities. The literature reflects some of these findings: Hsieh and Pugh (1993) concluded that poverty and income inequality are both associated with violent crime. Sampson and Laub (1994) pointed to social class and poverty as inhibitors of normal family functioning and thus as facilitators of violence. Hagan (1994) noted that, in Norway, inequality breeds violence, especially when inequality involves segregation by race and residence.

Huff-Corzine et al. (1991) reviewed crime statistics in the U.S. and concluded that severe poverty is related to increased lethal violence rates for both blacks and whites. Kruttschnitt et al. (1994) found that poverty increased the likelihood of child abuse. White (1994), in an Australian study, pointed to the power of poverty to create a permanent "underclass" blocked from advancement through limited access to employment. Anderson (1990) conducted field work in two urban communities and concluded that poverty contributed to loss of leadership in a community, ultimately resulting in increased violence. Osman (1992) studied street gangs in the U.S. and concurred that reducing violence requires targeting the community, not alienated or aggressive individuals. Warner and Price (1993) clearly outlined the link between violent crime and neighborhood characteristics, including poverty, social disorganization, and isolation of racial groups.

The great "War on Poverty" declared by President Lyndon Johnson in the 1960s illustrates how global targeting of poverty failed to eradicate the negative impact of poverty on communities. Despite entitlement programs, community mental health centers, and anti-poverty programs, the problems of poverty and violence persist, and the federal dollars to fund such initiatives have become scarce. According to a study by the Children's Defense Fund (1993), black children are poorer today than in 1968; the gap between infant mortality of black and white infants was greater in 1993 than at any other time since 1940. The Children's Defense Fund and the Annie E. Casey Fund (1993) advocate courses of action that target the enrichment of community life for poor black children.

This chapter reports first on direct observation of the community of Montego Bay, Jamaica, by a group of psychodynamically oriented professionals who worked within that community to reduce violence and improve the residents' quality of life. The community was viewed as an organism with structures, roles, and dysfunctions, much like a patient; the diagnosis of "violent community" was based on criteria summarized by Twemlow and Sacco (1996a). They were derived from questionnaire data administered to Jamaican police officers, direct observation of the city, analysis of crime information, content analysis of media reports, and talks with local and central government officials. These criteria will be elaborated upon in much more detail to form the substance of this chapter.

A smaller scale project in two elementary schools in midwestern U.S. is then briefly described to show how schools function as a barometer of community health. Violent communities always have violent and dysfunctional schools. The project's approach enabled the school to stabilize and its surrounding community support structure became participant-observers in the school, rather than mere critics and skeptics.

If community intervention is to be successful, the diagnosis must be accurate. There is a critical mass or optimal anxiety level within the group which, when attained, can lead to widespread change with relatively small input of catalyzing resources (Yalom, 1985; Twemlow and Sacco, 1996).

Montego Bay, Jamaica

The intervention team included mental health professionals, police, and martial artists who visited Montego Bay, Jamaica, for 2 years, delivering approximately 100 hours of specialized leadership training to the police and school teachers. Programs were developed with the police and teachers as partners within the community. This project is described in detail in other works by the authors (Sacco and Twemlow, 1997; Twemlow and Sacco, 1994, 1996). Table 19.1 summarizes the training procedures and theory of community growth used in the project.

A core group of visionary private sector individuals observed that the emerging violent nature of Montego Bay directly threatened its commerce, tourism, and quality of life for citizens, and approached the team for help. The community of Montego Bay is a mid-sized community in St. James parish with a population of approximately 125,000. Although it did not have the devastating inner-city problems of Kingston, Montego Bay's homicide rate was climbing. The police had search-and-seizure powers similar to those existing during emergency conditions, and corruption of police and other officials was pervasive.

Cross-Cultural Comparison

The team's interventions and observational analysis would likely be more difficult in a more evolved nation such as the U.S. The complex nature of the politics and bureaucracy even in the most destitute communities of the U.S. would likely prohibit as much involvement, dialogue, and freedom to initiate experimental programs as was possible in Jamaica. Working in an evolving nation often allows for more innovation in both the study and the application of community development principles.

There were striking differences between the roles of men and women in Jamaica and in the U.S.; for example, in the percentage of female police officers — some 20% or more in Jamaica, compared to single-digit figures in the U.S. At the same time, although women appeared to be generally assertive, male chauvinistic roles seemed entrenched in the day-to-day husband/wife relationships, with men often being violent and conjugal rape common. Jamaica had no formal entitlement programs for financial aid, other

Table 19.1

A Seven-Step Flow Chart for Community Violence Prevention

	Theory	Features
Step 1		
Data gathering	Anti-intellectual, action-oriented leadership	1. Counter attack approach to law and order 2. Community fragmentation 3. Increased crime and corruption of community leaders 4. Altruism seen as weak and naive 5. Lack of positive male role models 6. High stress, few healthy outlets
Step II		
Community diagnosis	Violent community	1. Diagnosis established
Step III		
Identification of community stabilizing systems	1. Law and Order 2. Education 3. Health 4. Spirituality	1. Police and military 2. School teachers 3. Medical personnel 4. Church leaders
	Guiding Principles	**Source**
Step IV. Peacekeeper/peacemaker training		
Training of community change agents	Leaders catalyze large group change by role modeling	Psychoanalytic group theory
	Common goals increase cohesiveness and reduce community violence	Sociology and psychoanalytic theory
	Leaders should be strong and gentle	Martial arts training and theory
	Mental clarity, self-awareness, present centeredness and personal responsibility	Zen theory and practice
	Sublimations reduce impulsivity	Psychoanalytic ego psychology
	Reflective self is enhanced by self-awareness and role modeling	Psychoanalytic object relations theory
	Altruistic impulses can motivate change in individuals and community	Literature on altruism

than child care for children up to age 15 months. There was no formal Aid to Families With Dependent Children (AFDC) equivalent. There was a Women, Infant, and Children (WIC) program which provided minimal foodstuffs for younger mothers until their babies reached 15 months of age. Jamaica was similar to the U.S. approximately 40 years ago in its attitude toward teenage pregnancy. Young women who became pregnant while in junior high or high school were not welcomed at school and experienced significant rejection by their families and home communities.

Table 19.1 (continued)

A Seven-Step Flow Chart for Community Violence Prevention

	Guiding Principles	Source
Step V. Community leaders will catalyze change in the quality of life in the community		
Factors motivating community to change	Community groups which fight each other unproductively	"Engineered conflict" community forums resolve differences
	Aggression in schools	Antiviolence and school programs
	Homeless and indigent	Care and service programs
	Children and domestic violence	Protection and care programs for orphans and abused women
	Tourism	Protection and community clean-up with beautification
	Crime	Training in effective nonviolent alternatives
Step VI		
Maintenance of the effectiveness of the intervention	Improve conditions of employment and status of peacemaker/peacekeeper	
	Continue regular supervision and training over several years	
	Transfer training of personnel to local authorities as quickly as possible	
	Faculty function as low-profile advocates.	
	Credit goes to local community activists where possible	
Step VII		
Ongoing evaluation	Development of measures of community violence and growth	
	Ongoing review of the "Violent Community" diagnosis	

Source: Adapted from Twemlow, S.W. and Sacco, F.W. (1996) Peacekeeping and peacemaking: the conceptual foundations of a plan to reduce violence and improve the quality of life in a mid-sized community in Jamaica. *Psychiatry, 59*, 156–174.

During 10 years of visiting and working with Jamaica's school children, the authors have observed, through hundreds of conversations, that Jamaican children have a much different attitude toward education than do American youth. In almost every case, a Jamaican child is highly motivated to pursue an education. Actually, education is seen as the sole road to economic security. Even in homes for delinquent youth, the children still value education and welcome the opportunity to absorb available information. This attitude remains fixed throughout the Jamaican citizen's life cycle. When the intervention team provided workshops for the Jamaican Constabulary Force (JCF), all of the faculty marveled at how intensely focused, energetic, and absorbed these very undereducated, poorly paid Jamaican police officers were.

In the U.S., there is often a built-in adversarial relationship between school and home because of the "them vs. us" approach of required meetings between parents and school personnel. In Jamaica, authority was questioned far less. Parents usually did not engage in ongoing conflict with the school concerning strong disciplinary action with their children. They more often cooperated with the school and police around disciplinary issues. It was virtually unheard for parents to take legal action against a school concerning harsh disciplinary action against their children. It was clear that Jamaicans value education, devalue entitlement of financial aid, and prefer simple social systems over more complex ones. Whatever the etiology of these cultural differences, Jamaicans tended to accede to international authority and to value educational intervention more highly than we do in the U.S. Although there were remnants of a form of racism derived from strong British colonial rule until 1963, racism of the kind seen in the U.S. was not prominent. Splits within communities were more usually along political, religious, or socio-economic issues rather than on racial grounds.

Psychological Attributes of a Violent Community

The community can be viewed as having certain beliefs that drive cultural attitudes and, ultimately, the actions of its members. Freud (1920) studied large groups, more particularly, the functioning of the church and the military. He observed that such large groups exert a contagious effect on other groups and on their members, who become suggestible. Often, there is a submersion of the critical facility of individuals to a group agenda, resulting in impulsivity, a loss of the search for the truth, and an increase in affective pitch. He also observed that group members often subjugate their own personal goals to the ideals of their leader. The psychiatric literature abounds with research studies on how groups remain cohesive, work-oriented, and rational (e.g., Yalom, 1985). Some, McDougall (1920) for example, concluded that to be cohesive, groups must have continuity, a tradition, and a definite structure. The individual must understand how the group works, and the group must recognize that other groups are equally valid. In spite of these and other complex factors which maintain the peaceful structure of a community, identification of the central role of leadership in cohesiveness and work function of a group is the unique contribution of psychoanalytic authors in the field; leadership training was the main focus of this multi-level community intervention. Bion (1959) concluded that small groups search for three types of leaders: (1) a caring and reliable leader (dependency assumption); (2) a frightening, ruthless leader (fight/flight assumption); and (3) a messianic, omnipotent leader who will solve problems in his or her own unique way and in a way that does not need to be understood by the members of the group, as in cults, (pairing assumption). From the authors' observations, at different times, large groups, including violent communities, also react in these various ways toward their leaders.

Another valuable conceptualization of how a community obtains and constructively uses knowledge is relevant to the functioning of healthy as compared to violent communities. Bion (1970) stated that the knowledge a group develops is always in a context. It does not arise *a priori* and is not fixed or permanent. Thus, knowledge is not a possession but a process and not individual property but a function of a relationship and a cultural context. Knowledge changes constantly, or, as Bion stated, the individual learns from experience in a process of continuous reflection and transformation. Knowledge, according to Bion, can be employed for discovery and exploration and can also be employed to avoid painful and frustrating experiences (Grinberg, 1985). Knowing something exists within the context of a container — the community. Without that containing function, knowledge does not become useful, according to Bion. Bion referred to useful knowledge as *plus K-linked.* The opposite of knowledge — *minus K* — is an envious and greedy spoiling of the cultural context or the container for the knowledge. Parker (1996) called it "the celebration of deliberate and studied stupidity, the pushing away and ruin of knowledge." In violent communities, as the leadership structure collapses, minus K dominates groups and solutions that involve working together break down. The individualist solution to problems dominates in an attempt to avoid catastrophe or chaos, i.e., minus K is substituted for plus K and thus for conscious collective cooperation. Thus, the rules that hold communities together become tangled and meaningless; for example, organized crime flourishes and sick and destructively tyrannical leaders emerge. Sick leadership cannot be indicted as the cause of the violent community, because the violent community and the leadership structure are in an intimate dialectical relationship with each other. Thus, each is interdependent on the other for its destructive functioning in a way similar to Bion's (1970) "container and contained" concept.

In the team's model (summarized in Table 19.1), the community peacemakers/peacekeepers function to return the violent community to a collaborative work group mode, modeling qualities of self-reflection, and caring and compassion for others and the environment.

The intervention team in Jamaica observed the following psychological trends within Montego Bay that were considered to contribute to the violent climate there.

Anti-Intellectualism. A trend of anti-intellectualism was clearly observed during many dialogues with various individuals in the Montego Bay community. The concepts of abstract thinking and intellectual discussion were seen as luxuries beyond most citizens' grasp. Despite the value Jamaicans place on education, the idea of reflection, intellectual dialogue and debate, and other methods of reflective regulation of aggression in dealing with community problems were minimized under the regressive drag of the violent community group dynamics.

Thinking and intellectual pursuits were seen as gentle arts that were antithetical to the everyday struggle for survival. Thus, the community placed much greater emphasis on action and shorter term, stop-gap solutions than on reflection, abstraction, and the use of thought-through intellectual solutions to a wide spectrum of community problems. Intellectual discussion was reduced to a form of street debate. The average Jamaican was quite readily able to debate most world topics; however, this type of debate and dialogue was not used when it came to dealing with local community problems.

This nonthoughtful, action-oriented dynamic was evidenced in two police initiatives observed during the project period of 1992 to 1994. The first was titled Operation ARDENT, a response to increased citizen violence involving the use of police and military personnel in joint patrols of the Montego Bay tourist areas. Military personnel dressed in fatigues and carrying automatic weapons were visible along the main tourist strip (Gloucester Avenue). This approach quickly failed because it frightened off tourists and did not reduce violence.

After ARDENT came Operation ACID. This approach used police and military personnel in cooperative raids and roadblocks designed to strike at the heart of Jamaica's criminal gangs or posses. This operation, again, failed to reduce community violence and certainly did not improve the community's or the tourists' sense of safety.

Personal Power Comes From Violence; Altruism Is Weakness. Community forums were organized by the intervention team using an engineered conflict model (Twemlow and Sacco, 1996). Members of the community were challenged to debate their views of violence in the community with a large group of JCF police officers. The moderator, a clinical psychologist, engineered the debate to elicit the deep feelings of mistrust and disgust felt by both the community and the police for each other, while moving the group to a realization of convergent concerns and goals.

Both the community and the police shared the belief that action or violence was the most desirable response toward ensuring the public's safety. Through seminars and supervision, the intervention team addressed the false basis of this approach to lasting peace.

Anyone who offered goods or services *gratis* was viewed as weak and their motives as suspicious. There was very little trust that good could come from being altruistic, and being anything other than strongly self-interested was viewed as not only weak, but ridiculous. The concept that powerful individuals can be altruistic seemed quite contradictory to most Jamaicans. The notion that criminals would respect strong, yet minimally violent interventions was viewed as ludicrous. Thus, the pretest primary vision of power revolved around domination, coercion, and ultimately, violence, to induce submission, exemplified within organized crime.

There was also clear evidence of a high rate of lethal violence used by the JCF in fighting crime. The JCF was reported to be responsible for upwards of 20% of deaths by weapons in Jamaica. There were a host of causes advanced for this phenomenon, including (1) very strict gun laws which forced gun fights during arrests, (2) unbelievably poor working conditions and pay for the police, and (3) an almost total lack of community support and respect for the police.

There was little emphasis on police training of any sort. Police were neither oriented to a community police model nor trained to see themselves as involved, stable, police officers who helped prevent crime as interactive members of the community. Some older JCF officers communicated to team members that this punitive social control attitude of the police began during the colonial period. The police were expected to be the tools of oppression against the field hands working the sugar plantations. When the JCF was first commissioned in 1867, its primary role was to maintain law and order among oppressed workers for the plantation industry. Thus, rank and status within the community were obtained by exerting unquestioning control over the oppressed workers in the plantations. The roots of an oppressive law enforcement approach ran deep in this evolving nation, despite the fact that Jamaica has been valiantly struggling to evolve into an independent nation since 1963.

Immediate vs. Delayed Gratification. It appeared that much of the everyday activities of the citizens of Montego Bay did not reflect a concern for the future development and security of their community, but was more self-centered and focused on short-term gains. In fact, the primary driving force from most levels of the community, including government, involved satisfying immediate needs with short-term solutions. This was in great part the result of being an extremely poor community where the increasing population had decreasing resources.

This phenomenon was most clearly evident by observing the Montego Bay community's view of tourism. Jamaica has traditionally enjoyed approximately 30,000 new visitors a week to the island. From the mid-1980s to the mid-1990s, Jamaica had a steadily increasing $1 billion a year travel industry. Tourism grew to be the third largest industry supporting the nation's economy as reported by the Jamaican Tourist Board in 1994.

Within Montego Bay, it could be clearly observed that less and less energy was being focused on creating a friendly and safe environment for visitors. Eventually, the community became hostile toward tourists and developed an impulsive frenzy to take as much as they could from passing visitors. The concept of respecting a growing industry was over-shadowed by immediate need.

Beyond slogans on billboards, there was little organized community effort to protect tourism as a valuable economic entity. Many citizens of the community argued that there were fewer opportunities for them to survive and provide for their families, justifying whatever rude and intrusive behavior was required to profit from the dwindling stock of visitors. There was little organized community effort to address the core issues involved in this process. Again, the community's response was to dispatch its already overwhelmed and demoralized police force to use outdated tactics toward crime. Near the end of the project, the JCF began to respond to the increasing tourist conflict by appointing an intellectually oriented leader (Assistant Superintendent L.B. Rose) from within its own ranks to develop solutions for the tourist/police/community interface. Assistant Superintendent Rose later trained a team of hand-picked community police officers for the entire island.

Driving from the airport in Montego Bay to most of the tourist hotels, it was abundantly clear that the larger private sector community was not concerned about the upsetting perceptions tourists may have developed while traveling through the downtown section. There was little effort to protect visitors from the hard realities of daily life of the citizenry of Montego Bay. Tourists became upset and scared when confronting poverty and violence directly after leaving the airport. In Montego Bay, it is common to see homeless and mentally ill people and cardboard shanty towns. There seemed to be a prevailing attitude within the tourism industry that it was sufficient to transport tourists to the nice beach areas, with little organized efforts being directed toward improving the quality of life in downtown Montego Bay. Simple fences, local art, and planting shrubs could have done much to protect tourists from the harsh visions of life on the downtown streets. All-inclusive Club Med-style hotels were built outside the cities with the idea that visitors could be protected from these realities and the daily struggles of the citizens of Montego Bay and others at various tourist locations in Jamaica. But, of course, tourists want to explore local color and are usually not at all happy being confined in American-style vacation complexes.

The unfortunate result of this lack of forethought was a decreasing number of visitors and an increasing perception in the U.S. travel industry that Jamaica was a violent place and should be avoided. This was simply no longer true. Most visitors were safer in Montego Bay than they were taking a downtown shopping trip in their home community in the U.S. Thus, a cycle of violence within the Montego Bay community was accelerated by a lack of forethought and preoccupation with immediate gratification and greed rather than strategic, nonviolent planning for an improved longer term stable future. The intervention team was able to help turn around this attitude by presenting workshops and meetings with the Chamber of Commerce, government officials, and private citizens in the area.

Lack of Stable Political and Family Systems. When a community becomes self-absorbed and feels impotent, there is often a perceived lack of respect for the leader. This was very obvious in Jamaica. The team members initially observed that the community was not cohesive; a lack of confidence in the national government was evident. There was a prevailing belief that politicians and police were corrupt, resulting in a lack of faith that the leadership could provide safety.

Since the mid-1960s, there was a reported decrease in the integrity of the nuclear family within Jamaica, with a concomitant increase in single parent households with absent or marginally involved fathers, according to the team members' communications with citizens during community forums from 1992 to 1994. The male population within Jamaica was generally a highly mobile and unattached group, with many sub-family units. There was a movement away from the nuclear family, monogamy, and traditional Christian values, in spite of the many churches in St. James parish.

This observation parallels post-1960s development in the U.S. For example, in Springfield, MA, the percentage of children in the public school system who were on AFDC was nearly 80% as reflected in the 1994 Springfield Public School Records. This suggested that 8 out of 10 children were psychologically and economically fatherless within the Springfield system. This was almost a replica of the Montego Bay Secondary School, which, according to the staff of the school, also had an estimated 80% fatherless student population, with most children living in households headed by single mothers with only intermittent contact with biological fathers. This highly mobile and unattached family system was mirrored by the JCF. The JCF was designed to be a centrally trained national security force in which all officers were expected to be ready to change station with little notice. There was little opportunity for any of the officers to develop stable family relationships within any one community because they were often transferred suddenly at unpredictable intervals.

The team members considered this instability to be a causal factor in the high levels of police stress which contributed to the violence of the police. Some JCF officers reported that they often had four or five "families" in different towns because of this requirement to leave one community and live in another. The net result was that the police families became destabilized by a lack of consistent positive male role models because the strong male models were highly mobile and unattached to any one community. This destabilized the basic structure within the community and created a nonattached and highly narcissistic male population which believed that self-indulgence was their right. Responsibility and involvement within the community were subjugated by narcissism, sexual entitlement, and hedonism.

Powerlessness, Despair, and Anomie. Violent communities seem to lose a sense of purpose in the expression of their emotions and actions. As a community becomes more violent, there is an increased feeling of powerlessness and a perceived lack of purpose, with a clear lack of motivation to be harmonious and peaceful. Individuals do not feel connected to others or do not share common goals. Groups become dispersed individuals propelled by self-interest.

In Jamaica, there was a high incidence of volatile domestic disputes, including conjugal rape, with random acts of violence stemming from senseless jealousy, envy, and petty rivalries. This was immediately observable while walking around communities, where it was not uncommon to see amputated body parts due to the preference for machetes for self-defense. This absence of skill and compassion in practical problem-solving seemed to stem from a lack of perceived alternative response options, motivated by a sense of despair, fear, and powerlessness.

Escapism as a Response to Helplessness. It is no surprise that a violent community would want to create as many quick escapes as possible. The increase in alcohol and drug addiction within any one community is inversely proportional to the amount of hope and stability of a community. The more helpless and powerless individuals in a community feel, the greater the temptation to seize readily available escapes, such as chemicals.

The intervention team quickly observed that alcoholism within the police force was rampant. Within the community, alcohol was an accepted part of the overall culture, with rudimentary drinking laws and no minimum drinking age. Police stations had bars attached to them, and driving under the influence of alcohol was not expressly prohibited in Jamaica.

There was a clear increase in the use of "crack" cocaine by males, with a noticeable difference between the sexes with regard to drug abuse in Jamaica. Within the U.S., crack cocaine has seen a widely expanded use by females, especially among single-parent heads of household. This has resulted in staggering increases in addicted babies. This phenomenon was rarely observed or reported in Jamaica, where crack addiction appeared to be primarily a male phenomenon. Although less true with alcohol, there appeared to be a strong preference by males rather than females to use escapism as a primary way of coping with helplessness.

Montego Bay had very few escapes and sublimations available to its citizenry. The local government did not sponsor camps or many recreational activities.

Although the JCF, local churches, and other groups made struggling efforts to develop athletic programs, these leagues were woefully underfunded, underequipped, overpopulated, and struggled with a lack of facilities, transportation, and basic equipment.

Thus, the dwindling resources and growing anomie blended tragically with a lack of healthy sublimatory outlets, resulting in an increase of pathological escapism at all socio-economic levels of the community. These psychological factors provide the dynamic forces driving dysfunctional community behaviors by individual community members. The intervention team members hypothesized that change would stem from impacting these psychological variables within the community. Education and community program development were the techniques employed.

The Bully/Victim/Bystander Relationship and Its Destructive Effects. According to Edmond Burke, "The only thing necessary for the triumph of evil is for good men to do nothing." In a violent community, one sure way to assess the level of violence is to measure the frequency of bullying, sexual harassment, and weapon violence in schools. Middle and high schools are especially prone to eruptions of violence based on a pervading community sense of disconnection and anomie. A Montego Bay Secondary School was observed closely over a 2-year period (Sacco and Twemlow, 1997). There was noticeable violence at this school of approximately 2400 students. Reports of five to six serious physical attacks per day, with at least three sexual assaults per week, were not unusual; countless incidents of sexual harassment were reported by young females. Everyone at the school, including the administration, teachers, and especially the students, became acculturated to the high level of violence. They were numb to its impact on them as individuals.

Although the schoolyard bully is the stereotypical model for bullying, the authors have found that similar complex coercive power struggles occur between adults, between adults and children, and vice versa between children and adults in communities whose cohesiveness is collapsing. A harassing bully/victim/bystander interaction is frequently seen in workplace harassment, not only sexual but also other combinations of coercive power struggles that involve a stronger bully and a weaker victim with a facilitating bystanding audience (Twemlow 1998). Most of us met our first bullies at school, and most research into bullying has been done in school settings (Twemlow et al., 1996a). In violent communities, the complex interaction of the structural and psychological factors described in this chapter creates a context favoring bullying coercive power relationships. The authors define community harassment in a way very similar to how bullying in schools is described. It is the exposure of an individual over and over again to negative interactions on the part of one or more dominate persons or community groups, who gain in some way from the discomfort of the victim. These negative actions are intentional inflictions of injury or discomfort and may involve physical contact, words, or insulting gestures, forms, or sexual bribery and coercion, including *quid pro quo* manipulation. Essential to this definition is that there is an imbalance of power — an asymmetrical power relationship — and that the victims have problems defending themselves.

Although the main actors in this drama are the bullies and victims, a great deal of pain comes from the passive and facilitating role of the bystanders. This bystanding audience gives the supportive context or foundation for the bully/victim interaction. There are two types of bystanders. The *bully bystander* typically enjoys seeing the victimization but does not want to participate directly. Essentially, these individuals function as the bullies' helpers and are vicariously involved in the bullying. The *bystander victim* is often a frozen and frightened individual who is too afraid to deviate from the social norm and from the strong charismatic leadership of the bully and the bully bystander. Frequently, in communities, there may be lack of support for activists for social change, especially if it involves a dangerous confrontation with arbitrary and punishing authority represented by the leadership. Those who might be quite supportive in private, including friends and families, may be too afraid of job loss or other recrimination and may unconsciously socially isolate the complaining victim. In the authors' experience, it is quite common for the victims of community harassment to find that they do not have the support of friends which they previously had or thought they had under these conditions. Unsupportive friends and family may even apologize to the harassed individual for being so lacking in courage. The important point here is that this interactionist perspective defines the bully/victim/bystander relationship dialectically.

The relationship between the victim and the victimizer has been defined as a classical dialectic (Twemlow, 1995a,b). It is role-dependent relationships, with each having no meaning without the existence of the other. From this practical point of view, a dialectic coercive power relationship in the community usually involves everyone in that community who become involved in some way, usually in a bystanding role based on gossip and rumor, creating a complete milieu of pathological interpersonal relationships dominated by coercive power struggles. These conditions can result in violent and damaging consequences, for example, outbursts of homicide or gang violence.

The Denial of Violence. The single most powerful ingredient in contributing to a violent community is community-wide denial of violence. To close one's eyes to violence is a very easy and natural thing to do for most people. When an entire community closes its eyes to how violent it has become, real solutions become difficult to identify and almost impossible to accomplish through creative action plans. This was quite noticeable in Montego Bay and is also very evident in the U.S. When a public meeting is held about violence, usually few people attend. On the other hand, if there is a meeting about how much money a school should spend, the meeting is usually overwhelmed with parents who want their children to have a little bit more in school. The idea of violence is related to death, and people have a universal aversion to thinking about death.

The government and community of Montego Bay were aware of the impact that the perception of violence would have on the tourism industry. During the period of the intervention, the external perception of violence was so high that it was highlighted in the travel literature. At one point, when a large German tour boat docked in Montego Bay, not one of the 700 passengers disembarked. Travel companies issued warnings to avoid Jamaica because of the violence. Foreign visitors avoided Montego Bay. It was experiences like these that shocked the community into facing the economic disaster that would likely result from a drop in tourist revenues.

There are four fundamental varieties of community denial of violence:

1. *Direct denial.* The effect of this model is to encourage typical citizens to say to themselves that they are not, in fact, criminals, nor are they part of the problem, although it is known that, under certain circumstances (for example, the extreme stress of warfare), that the ordinary law-abiding citizen is quite capable of violent responses (Bradshaw et al., 1991, 1993). Denial allows an individual to distance himself or herself from any responsibility for the problem.
2. *Over-simplification.* As we have already observed, a common over-simplification in this model is to reduce the solution to the problem of violence to the elimination of violent individuals using severe legal penalties. For example, it is commonly accepted that the death penalty does not deter violent crime. Jamaica had severe automatic penalties for crimes involving weapons. Paradoxically, according to JCF personnel, a crime involving a gun usually led to a shootout with a fatality because the felon did not want mandatory life imprisonment. Such shootouts were common in Jamaica, even for minor crimes.
3. *Over-generalization.* Sometimes, the successful use of force to quell a riot in one circumstance is

generalized to the complicated problems of the community. In the U.S., this has led to extraordinary situations in which small towns have spent enormous amounts of money on sophisticated weaponry without saving enough of the town's budget to train personnel in the use of this weaponry. If one can arm oneself with weaponry surpassing or equal to that of the sophisticated aggressor, then one feels safe.

4. *Stereotyped response patterns*. In the martial arts, there is a truism that admonishes the fighter never to underestimate the enemy. Military training often emphasizes the skill and strength of the individual and the incompetence and ineptness of the enemy, and has often led to an underestimation of the enemy. Continuing the use of force when it does not work often results in the failure to observe how stereotyped response patterns are not useful, sometimes due to an underlying contempt of the enemy. In Jamaica, there was also the possible artifact of the racial bias of the colonial lawmakers.

Basic Structures of the Violent Community

A violent community will have a number of *a priori* structural deficits that can be observed and influenced in larger scale community interventions. Because Jamaica offered the intervention team an opportunity to observe the inner workings of a community unencumbered by complex bureaucracies and tangled social helping networks, the team's observations of these elements of a violent community were greatly enhanced. Violent communities, in the team's view, consist of the following basic structural elements:

Disconnection of the Police. It was dramatically clear that the JCF was viewed by the community as a corrupt, untrustworthy, violent group, often called "animals" by the populace. The police maintained that the community was ignorant, selfish, and unresponsive. Both the community and the police shared a lack of understanding for one anothers' perceptions, and each group struggled with gross misperceptions and a lack of accurate information about what the other thought or did.

The perception of the police as uninvolved, roving, somewhat mad watch dogs was readily observable by simply reading the daily newspaper. Any one of the three national newspapers ran several articles each day detailing how violent and out-of-control or corrupt the JCF was. There was an unlimited community appetite for information through all of the media outlets concerning the lack of discipline or corrupt and violent nature of the police. Little rapprochement was attempted between the police and the community.

Several of the community forums, outlined and described in more detail by the authors (Twemlow and Sacco, 1996) revealed that the JCF often had few vehicles, no radios, and no method by which to respond to reported crimes. The community participants were alarmed to discover that most police officers were required to take local taxis to the scene of crimes, seldom with a buddy back-up system for police work. There was virtually no understanding of the altruistic work performed by the police, such as picking up orphans and coping with the homeless and mentally ill. These forums introduced awareness and mutual understanding and concern for each other, which are fundamental to peaceful communities.

Population Increase and Redistribution. There was a dramatic increase in the St. James parish population over the 20 years prior to the study. Jamaica had evolved from an agricultural nation to one with a more expanded base of manufacturing, mining, and eventually, tourism. This drew people into communities such as Montego Bay, Ocho Rios, and Kingston. The increased pressure from the population explosion was easily observable in Jamaica through what is known as the "captured land" phenomenon. People with no housing began to migrate into areas where there was secondary access to resources generated from tourism and manufacturing. Without housing, these refugees were forced into "capturing" land. During the team's intervention period, team members was made aware of several "rebellions" in which the police were forced to break up unplanned communities made up of poor squatters who had seized open land for personal housing.

Lack of Social Welfare Programs. There were no nationally subsidized social welfare programs in Jamaica. Many conservative politicians involved in the U.S. welfare reform have turned to the idea that entitlement in the U.S. is the primary reason for the growth of poverty and single-parent families. Although very limited welfare programs existed in Jamaica, the same phenomenon of increased single-parent families existed there.

Overwhelmed Schools Dominated by Bullies. Violent communities have violent schools. As populations shift, inner-city schools become increasingly populated with children from dysfunctional homes. One clear signal of a violent community is a school run by bullies, often with extensive protection rackets. Montego Bay Secondary School was the targeted school in the team's intervention. When the team first began to make observations at the school, there was a startling amount of physical, emotional, and sexual bullying occurring on a daily basis (Sacco and Twemlow, 1997).

Beginning in elementary school, aggression becomes a primary tool of expression of dominance to counter feelings of worthlessness. Children become bullies, teachers become bullies, and the school becomes dominated by aggression and intimidation. Teachers soon become demoralized; children become distant, uninvolved participants in the educational process, with a high degree of absenteeism; and poor relationships develop between students and teachers, teachers and teachers, and students and students. Dysfunctional and aggressive adults are at home writing the scripts for angry children who later become bullies and disrupt schools at an ever-increasing rate.

Evolution of Criminal Enterprises. Violent communities often become more violent because of the presence of structured and semi-structured criminal enterprises or gangs. In Jamaica, the posse controlled vice and drug activity. In the U.S., a wide spectrum of gangs control street-level crime. The lower level gangs within both countries typically consist of young men under the direction of an older generation. These criminal enterprises vary in the sophistication of organization, rules, and methods of operation, but they often provide money, status, protection, and a sense of purpose to the destitute and lonely. Both Jamaica and the U.S. have a significant proportion of young men becoming randomly violent. In more sophisticated criminal operations, violence is a tool to enforce the rules of the criminal enterprise, whether it is drugs, gambling, or prostitution. Violence is not tolerated unless there is a "business" purpose; also, each act of violence must be allowed or ordered by a clearly defined criminal boss or leader. Young street gangs or posses do not have this "code" and thus, are more likely to experience random, nonstrategic acts of lethal violence.

Often, criminal organizations form the backbone of the violent community. The community's fear slowly begins to increase and hope for anything positive decreases because of the presence of these groups. Police are often asked to track down and invade these groups. The net result of these pure vigilante activities has been observed, in both the U.S. and Jamaica, to be, at best, a short-term solution. Gang members are driven underground by such tactics, only to spring up as soon as the intensity of the crack-down diminishes.

Abuse and Rejection of the Vulnerable. Violent communities usually do not take the time to care for the old and the young or those who are disabled or hurt. The more violent a community, the less tolerance there is for the underprivileged, neglected, mentally ill, homeless, aged, and abandoned children. In Jamaica, there were a number of examples of how children were warehoused in woefully understaffed and minimally supported orphanages, such as Blossom Garden. These programs housed 50 to 75 abandoned children who were often picked up off the street by the police and placed in these orphanages. Many of these children suffered from severe medical and psychological disorders resulting directly from neglect.

In the U.S., violent communities ignore the vulnerable despite the presence of government and private resources. Responsibility for the weak is subcontracted, and the citizens brush off daily concern for the vulnerable, believing that it is someone else's job. Injustice to the weak is rationalized away because someone else is supposed to do something to help. This is the modern, evolved community's way of turning its back on the needy. Helping the weak strengthens, and not helping weakens, the moral fabric of individuals within the community. In a previous work (Twemlow and Sacco, 1996), the authors outlined ways of appealing to altruistic traits, especially to angry and demoralized people, which can evoke a remarkable turn around in individual and community attitudes and self-esteem.

Gender Myths and Their Impact on Violence

The violent community can be seen from a perspective where cultural myth dictates attitude, with individuals within the community acting in accordance with their understanding of the dominant cultural myth. One such myth that the authors considered as fueling domestic and community violence was that Jamaican men often believe it is important, and in fact, necessary to "thump" (physically abuse) "their" women. This myth allows for a wide spectrum of highly dysfunctional male behavior that cumulatively weakens the very fabric of the community. If violence toward women is acceptable, then the very essence of good mothering and nurturance of the community's young is at risk. The cycle of violence is thus fueled.

Similar attitudes were observed concerning sexual entitlement of males. The JCF officers reported that marital rape was not an issue in Jamaica. This belief involved the idea that marriage and rape could not co-exist: If you are married, then rape is not possible. This attitude flowed from a general lack of respect for women and the acceptance of male dominance and violence.

Table 19.2 summarizes the results of an opinion survey concerning sexual attitudes administered to 33 male and 19 female members of the JCF participating in the seminar in 1992. No attempt was made to attach statistical significance in this small survey, but examination of opinion trends suggested that male police officers saw rapists as choosing victims on the basis of physical attractiveness and that female police officers suggested a need for women to be submissive as the motive. Paradoxically, female officers recommended submission to a rapist and felt unable to control the likelihood of rape when compared to male police officers. When asked if a husband has the right to engage in sexual intercourse regardless of his wife's consent, 11% of female police officers and 39% of male officers answered in the affirmative. These results suggested a strict dominance submission attitude based on gender roles even in the police force which administered the domestic law.

Intervention in Violent Communities

There are few alternatives to trying to rebuild a violent community using any systematic approach which can be applied with minimal resources yet gain maximal impact. In Jamaica, there were very sparse resources and expertise with which to initiate and maintain a sophisticated intervention to reduce violence. In the U.S., there are often so many resources that competing interests over-complicate potentially simple solutions.

The Montego Bay project provided an interesting opportunity to demonstrate how minimal resources directed toward key structures within a community could catalyze an improved quality of life. Although this 2-year project was not studied using a rigorous

TABLE 19.2

JAMAICAN CONSTABULARY FORCE SEXUAL ATTITUDE SURVEY[a]

	Female		Male	
	Yes	**No**	**Yes**	**No**
1. Men choose their rape victims because:				
a. Women are physically attractive	10 (53%)	—	26 (79%)	—
b. They threaten the men	—	—	1 (3%)	1 (3%)
c. They are abusive	6 (32%)	—	4 (12%)	—
d. They appear self-confident	3 (16%)	2 (6%)	1 (3%)	—
2. Should a woman submit to a potentially violent rapist?	12 (63%)	7 (37%)	15 (45%)	17 (52%)
3. Can a woman control the likelihood of being raped?	14 (74%)	5 (26%)	29 (88%)	4 (12%)
4. Is there a likelihood of rape being preventable?	16 (84%)	2 (11%)	26 (79%)	7 (21%)
5. Does a husband have the right to have sex regardless of the wife's consent?	2 (11%)	17 (89%)	13 (39%)	20 (61%)
6. If a man with a knife or gun orders you into a car, should you go, hoping you will be released or get a chance to break away later?	10 (53%)	8 (42%)	23 (70%)	10 (30%)
7. Does submission to a rapist increase or decrease the likelihood of the rapist continuing with the act?	Increase 9 (47%)	Decrease 7 (31%)	Increase 13 (39%)	Decrease 19 (58%)

[a] N = 52 (33 males/19 females).

hypothetical-deductive model, it showed clearly observable results and the team was able to demonstrate how to develop projects that could target interventions to create peaceful communities (Twemlow and Sacco, 1996).

The key to rebuilding a violent community is to identify peacemakers/peacekeepers (Table 19.1). These special individuals are active citizen leaders willing to stand tall against violence. These people work in the police force, schools, health and community agencies, churches, and the health professions. They represent a special kind of person with strength, honor, and a dedication to peaceful solutions to community problems. Peacemakers have to be identified and then trained. It is not possible to create them from scratch, as the team found that certain personality and behavioral characteristics need to be present first. The peacemaker functions to defuse crises and deal with emergency situations necessary to prevent the physical sequelae of violence. These individuals then become peacekeepers, whose role is to create the conditions necessary for a lasting nonviolent and creative community atmosphere. These peacemakers/peacekeepers were selected from groups that the team defined as critical to peacefulness and the quality of life in the communities. Rather than treating the symptoms of community disorganization, such as disease, child abuse, etc., the team attempted to get to the fundamental cause of the disorganization. This had to do, in the team members' minds, with the failure to provide an effective mechanism for preserving community cohesion and to develop a feeling of safety within the community and a communal concern for economic growth from tourism.

Team members felt that the stability of a community is largely dependent on four major community systems — law and order, education, health, and spirituality domains. These four community roles embody the heart and soul of a functioning community. When any of these four domains become "infected" with violence, there is a weakening of the overall community's ability to decrease impulsivity and increase positive community action.

Law and order are maintained through the traditional social control element of the police and military. In most successful nonviolent communities, the police and military serve only as a last resort measure to control crime and violence in the community.

The internal control of the community is enhanced through the spiritual rootedness of the members of the community in various altruistic organizations, such as the church. In choosing peacekeepers, it was clear that there was a strong relationship between the JCF and the ministry, with a need for the police and the various community organizations to work collaboratively on altruistic projects. This began to occur when JCF officers developed projects that were purely altruistic. The most notable of these was the evolution of the role of JCF officers as outreach street workers assisting the homeless and mentally ill.

Education is the lifeblood of any community. When violence begins to reduce a community's fundamental structures to anarchy, the most dramatic signs can often be seen in the schools. In Montego Bay, violence was a daily occurrence at the test school — Montego Bay Secondary School — and other schools. This shroud of violence created a sense of despair and a lack of interest in or opportunity for effective learning and teaching. Teachers and students felt unsafe and bullies ran the school. It was imperative for the JCF to work collaboratively with the intervention team and for school teachers and local community sponsors to develop programs that would reduce the violence at the school. When the schools are violent, the community is fed more and more bullies, and the overall long-term evolution of the community is directed toward increased violence.

The last element of a nonviolent community is proper health and nutrition of its citizens. With few exceptions, the Jamaican citizenry relied mostly on private medical care. The social welfare system was essentially developed and implemented informally by the JCF officers who were solely responsible for picking up abandoned children. Entitlement programs were virtually nonexistent. The Family Court was responsible for most probate decisions relating to child abuse, neglect, and abandonment. Unfortunately, public health and recreation also are primary targets for reduction when financial resources become slim. This reduction in the focus on health further adds fuel to the violent community evolution.

The team selected the JCF as the first target for training because JCF officers were under the greatest pressure to change. Ministers were already participating in the daily work of police officers as their spiritual guides and counselors. Later, school teachers and students participated, and finally, the medical community became involved through the team's workers in child care and mental health programs. To achieve these objectives, clearly a comprehensive leadership training program was needed.

In Jamaica, the intervention team members were nonpartisan and nonpolitical, and acted as advocates for all of the agencies in the community. From a distance, the intervention team was able to provide the necessary information, intervention, and back-up to allow the natural healing forces within the community to gel and be guided from a point outside of the community, with these peacemakers/peacekeepers taking most of the credit and criticism for any changes in the community atmosphere. Thus, no one element of the community worked alone, and the goals of the peaceful community could be set and monitored as long as necessary by a more objective, professional team with a clear, nonviolent philosophical orientation

Table 19.3

The Peacekeeper/Peacemaker Code of Conduct[a]

The peacekeeper/peacemaker:

1. "Enforces" peace nonviolently with courage and self-confidence, and if force is necessary, uses the least injurious strategy possible.
2. Values relationships with others and is more altruistic than self-centered.
3. Is committed to peace, kindness, and protecting others from harm.
4. Shows humility, accepts difference in others, and is not judgmental.
5. Is a leader and role model who takes the initiative to better the community.
6. Is mentally alert and mindful, and acts swiftly and effectively when appropriate.
7. Is physically and mentally healthy and flexible.
8. Is able to overcome fear by self-awareness and self-control.
9. Is quiet and self-restrained.
10. Has a commitment to seek new knowledge, and to maintain the knowledge necessary to keep this code.

[a] This code epitomizes the GOALS of the leadership training.

toward raising consciousness and improving the quality of life. The team followed up on the interventions with frequent telephone reports and site visits.

Successful interventions in the violent community demand both the identification and organization of peacemakers and their direction by a professional entity outside of the community. It is important for the professional force to represent a cross-section of disciplines and races sufficient to be able to develop individualized creative responses to the emerging problems that a community may have. The professional team should be able to respond to the wide spectrum of community needs including in the medical, recreational, educational, spiritual, and law enforcement domains.

In Jamaica, the team identified several peacemakers. One such individual worked in the Montego Bay Secondary School. Team members worked cooperatively for 2 years with a JCF police officer who was single-handedly able to turn around a violent school of 2400 children (Sacco and Twemlow, 1997). It was clear that this intervention at the Montego Bay Secondary School was due mainly to the efforts and characteristics of this one individual peacemaker who provided the intervention. The team also identified other JCF officers who began to take on altruistic roles within their law enforcement duties by responding to the needs of the homeless, mentally ill, and orphaned children (Twemlow and Sacco, 1996).

It is essential to be able to choose peacemakers who have the necessary attitude and personality characteristics, as it is very easy for peacemakers to become caught up in their own importance. Without the proper leadership, they can stray from the stated goals. Although these individuals must be highly motivated, they require clear boundaries and very firm guidance. A code of conduct for Peacemakers was provided to each JCF trainee (Table 19.3).

The qualities that were identified as being essential for peacemakers include the following:

1. More altruistic than egoistic
2. Aware of and takes responsibility for community problems
3. Willing to take risks for peace, not easily frightened
4. Relationship-oriented and humanistic

5. Self-motivated and motivator of others
6. Alert, strong, and positive
7. Self-rewarding with low need for praise
8. Personally well-organized
9. Advocate for the vulnerable and disempowered
10. Optimist who sees the best in people
11. Low in sadism
12. Highly enthusiastic advocate of the project with a personal understanding and commitment to it

These key characteristics need to be identified in peacemakers, and, once identified, the selected leaders should be strategically located in key organizations within the community. The outside professional agency needs to more objectively supervise and fully apply limited resources to motivate change within the various organizations. Teams of peacemakers could be developed; police can work in schools, teachers can work with police, churches can work with child protective agencies and police, etc. All peacemakers/peacekeepers should keep in touch with each other with the cooperation of the primary agency with which they are affiliated.

The observable fruits of this intervention were discussed in more detail by the authors in an earlier work (Twemlow and Sacco, 1996). In summary, the project was credited with promoting a significant increase in tourism (which continues) and a reduction in violent crime. Although complex factors make the crime-reduction figures suspect, there was no doubt about the enthusiasm of the community for what was seen by all as a highly successful collaborative venture.

Lasting and successful projects established by the team included:

1. Rape and domestic crime prevention liaison services
2. School violence prevention services
3. Program for the homeless mentally ill
4. Rape prevention teacher training
5. Community youth rap and recreation groups
6. Shifts in the training of police to a community policing model with significant improvements in salaries and conditions of employment for police officers

The authors believe that this type of intervention worked because of its focus on treating causes of violence (community attitudes and demoralization) rather than treating symptoms (increased building of prisons, tougher sentences, etc.). Training those who have an assigned leadership role in the community was also felt to be of major import for the widespread change seen, inspite of relatively minimal expenditure of resources.

Creating a Peaceful School Learning Environment (C.A.P.S.L.E. Program)

The principles for a successful intervention within the primary school grades can be drawn from an active program, currently working in two elementary schools in the midwestern U.S. (Twemlow et al., 1996b). This program has several components — it uses an outside martial arts school as a resource for special classes targeting kindergarten through the fifth grades as a whole. These classes, known as the "Gentle Warrior" programs, develop a psycho-educational approach to bullying. The roles of bully, bystander, and victim are clearly explained and enacted through role playing. The specially trained martial artists provides alternative defensive physical and psychological response patterns for all the children in a fun and active program. The classes are conducted during regular school time as part of the physical education and health curriculum.

The schools provide additional internal motivations by creating a variety of "zero tolerance for bullying" programs such as the "peace flag programs". Each classroom has a peace flag flying outside when there was no conflict; but if a student causes a disruption, that student is responsible for taking the flag down for the day.

The schools also adopted a poster campaign reinforcing the message, "Bullying is not tolerated here." The school walls are covered with posters defining the terms bully, victim, and bystander and illustrating ways to recognize them and to recognize anger and how to respond to it, including personal relaxation techniques and positive, empathic, and courteous communications. Additional aspects of the intervention include involvement of peer mentors from a nearby high school to assist the children in conflict resolution, and adult mentors (often senior citizens) to provide role models for children and to assist them in developing manners and other social skills.

This program has been operational since 1992 and has seen out-of-school suspensions cut in half within the first year, with subsequent significant continued reductions. Additional beneficial effects of the program compared to a control school included a decrease in referrals of problem students for special treatment, an increase in standardized academic achievement test scores, and a decrease in disciplinary referrals to the principal. The feeling of being able to play safely and learn without interruption in the classroom improved dramatically, together with significant improvement in classroom behaviors characteristic of the bully/victim/bystander interaction. Projective tests revealed that bullies changed in the direction of being able to inhibit aggressive behaviors and that victims increased their assertiveness. Details of these findings were reported by Twemlow et al. (1996b).

In the model schools, there was a common language concerning the bully/victim/bystander relationship. It was not uncommon to hear teachers communicating with students and students communicating with students using the learned vocabulary of bully, victim, and bystander. The saying for the day often invoked that theme. The message was kept simple, reinforcing the idea that everyone communicated better in the absence of power struggles. After the initial dramatic effect on school climate in the 1996–1997 year, only one parent in the entire school withheld consent for his or her child to participate in the program.

Comparison of the Standardized Academic Achievement tests (Metropolitan Achievement test) math percentile ranks revealed that the lowest ranking was for victims at 30.5%, with bully-bystanders at 33.8%, bullies at 42%, victim-bystanders at 48.0%, and children with no problems at 56.9% (Twemlow et al., 1996b). It was such findings that highlight the very low academic achievement of victims, whose quietness compared to bullies often leads to less attention from teachers. Programs that over-focus on bullies run the risk of inadvertently promoting similar errors.

Conclusion and Summary

This chapter develops a psychodynamic approach to violent communities as functioning entities interdependent with the individual dynamics of its members. Two successful, inexpensive interventions are described which focus on the development of leadership skills of altruism, fearlessness, and strength with compassion and diplomatic skills in the case of the Jamaica Project and a focus on the importance of group solutions identifying power struggles and sharing responsibility for the working of the group as a whole as in the case of the C.A.P.S.L.E. project. The effectiveness of interventions of these types depends on the urgency of the need as perceived by private citizens and their willingness to get involved, together with an accurate diagnosis of the characteristics of a "violent community", the expertise of its leadership, and the cohesiveness of all member components to meet a common goal.

References

Annie E. Casey Foundation (1993) *Annual Report*, Document #B1777. Available from Annie E. Casey Foundation, 701 St. Paul Street, Baltimore, MD 21202.

Bachman, R. (1993) Double edged sword of violent victimization against the elderly: patterns of family and stranger perpetration. *Journal of Elder Abuse and Neglect, 5*, 59–76.

Baron, L. (1993) Gender inequality and child homicide: a state-level analysis. In A.V. Wilson (Ed.), *Homicide: The Victim/Offender Connection*, pp. 207–226. Anderson, OH: Anderson Publishing.

Bion, W.R. (1959) *Experiences in Groups and Other Papers*. New York: Basic Books.

Bion, W.R. (1970) *Attention and Interpretation*. London: Heinemann.

Block, C.R. (1993) Lethal violence in the Chicago Latino community. In A.V. Wilson (Ed.), *Homicide: The Victim/Offender Connection*, pp. 267–342. Anderson, OH: Anderson Publishing.

Block, R. and Block, C. (1992) Homicide syndromes and vulnerability: violence in Chicago community areas over 25 years. *Studies in Crime and Crime Prevention, 1*, 61–87.

Bradshaw, S.L., Ohlde, C.D., and Horne, J.B. (1991) The love of war: Vietnam and traumatized veterans. *Bulletin of the Menninger Clinic, 55*, 96–103.

Bradshaw, S.L., Ohlde, C.D., and Horne, J.B. (1993) Combat and personality change. *Bulletin of the Menninger Clinic, 57*(Fall), 466–478.

Browne, A. and Williams, K.R. (1993) Gender, intimacy and lethal violence: trends from 1976 through 1987. *Gender and Society, 7*, 78–98.

Brownstein, H.H., Spunt, B.J., Crimmins, S., Goldstein, P.J., and Langley, S. (1994) Changing patterns of lethal violence by women: a research note. *Women and Criminal Justice, 5*, 99–118.

Cahn, M.E. and Cahn, A.L. (1993) *Project Alliance Handbook: Guidelines for the Development of a Collaborative Relationship Between Leaders in Law Enforcement and Education*. Massachusetts Atty. General Office.

Children's Defense Fund (1993) *Progress and Peril: Black Children in America*, Doc. #A4227. Washington, D.C.

Children's Safety Network National Center for Education in Maternal and Child Health (1994) *Building Safe Communities: State and Local Strategies for Preventing Injury and Violence*.

Cicchetti, D. and Lynch, M. (1993) Toward an ecological/transactional model of community violence and child maltreatment: consequences for children's development. *Psychiatry: Interpersonal and Biological Processes, 56*(Feb.), 96–118.

Clarke, S.H. (1994) Increasing imprisonment to prevent violent crime: is it working? *Popular Government*, Summer, pp. 16–24.

Cordner, G.W. (1993) Getting serious about community involvement. *American Journal of Police, 12*, 79–88.

Daly, M. and Wilson, M. (1988) Evolutionary social psychology and family homicide. *Science, 242*, 519–524.

Debryn, L.M., Hymbaugh, K., and Valdez, N. (1988) Helping communities address suicide and violence: the special initiatives team of the Indian Health Service. *American Indian and Alaskan Native Mental Health Research, 1*, 56–65.

DeJong, W. (1994) School-based violence prevention: from the peaceable school to the peaceable neighborhood. *Forum, 25*, 8–14.

Fitzpatrick, K. and Boldizar, J.P. (1993) The prevalence and consequences of exposure to violence among African-American youth. *Journal of the American Academy of Child and Adolescent Psychiatry, 32*, 424–430.

Freud, S. (1920) *Group Psychology and the Analysis of the Ego, 18*. London, Standard Edition: Hogarth Press.

Friedlander, B.Z. (1993) Community violence, children's development and mass media: In pursuit of new insights, new goals, and new strategies. Special issue: children and violence. *Psychiatry: Interpersonal and Biological Processes, 56*, 66–81.

Greenberg, M. and Schneider, D. (1994) Violence in American cities: young black males is the answer, but what was the question? *Social Science and Medicine, 39*, 179–187.

Grinberg, L. (1985) Bion's contribution to the understanding of the individual and the group. In M. Pines (Ed.), *Bion and Group Psychotherapy*, pp. 176–191. London: Routledge.

Hagan, J. (1994) New sociology of crime and inequality in America. *Studies in Crime and Crime Prevention, 3*, 7–23.

Hanson, F.A. (1997) Why don't we care about the poor anymore?. *The Humanist*, 11–14.

Hsieh, C.C. and Pugh, M.D. (1993) Poverty, income inequality, and violent crime: a meta-analysis of recent aggregate data studies. *Criminal Justice Review, 18*, 182–202.

Huff-Corzine, L., Corzine, J., and Moor, D.C. (1991) Deadly connections: culture, poverty, and the direction of lethal violence. *Social Forces, 69*, 715–732.

Jaros, K.J. (1992) *Violence as a Public Health Problem: Developing Culturally Appropriate Prevention Strategies for Adolescents and Children*. Washington, D.C.: U.S. Department of Health and Human Services, Bureau of Maternal and Child Health Resources Development.

Kruttschnitt, C., McLeod, J.D., and Dornfield, M. (1994) The economic environment of child abuse. *Social Problems, 41*, 299–313.

Liddell, C., Kvalsvig, J., Qotyana, P., and Shabalala, A. (1994) Community violence and young South African children's involvement in aggression. *International Journal of Behavioral Development, 17*, 613–628.

Mastrofski, S.D. (1993) Varieties of community policing. *American Journal of Police, 12*, 65–77.

McDougall, W. (1920) *The Group Mind*. New York: G.P. Putnam's Sons.

Munoz, S. and Tan, N. (1994) Organizing police-youth-community dialogues to prevent violence. *Forum, 25*, 20–24.

Osman, K. (1992) *Gangs*. Lucent Overview Series.

Paddock, J. (1975) Studies on antiviolent and "normal" communities. *Aggressive Behavior, 1*, 217–233.

Parker, I. (1996) Staff-student relationships in universities: boundary disasters and "minus-K". *Group Analysis, 29*, 99–111.

Polk, K. and Ransom, D. (1991) Role of gender in intimate homicide. *Australian and New Zealand Journal of Criminology, 24*, 15–24.

Richters, J.E. and Martinez, P.E. (1993) Violent communities, family choices, and children's chances: an algorithm for improving the odds. *Development and Psychopathology, 5*, 609–627.

Rose, H.M. and McClain, P.D. (1990) *Race, Place and Risk: Black Homicide in America*. New York: State University of New York Press.

Sacco, F.C. and Twemlow, S.W. (1997) School violence reduction: a model Jamaican secondary school program. *Community Mental Health, 33*, 229–234.

Sampson, R.J. and Laub, J.H. (1994) Urban poverty and the family context of delinquency: A new look at structure and process in a classic study. *Child Development, 65*, 523–540.

Silverman, R.A. and Kennedy, L.W. (1993) Interpersonal relationships and means of lethal violence in Canada. In A.V. Wilson (Ed.), *Homicide: The Victim/Offender Connection*, pp. 383–392, Anderson, OH: Anderson Publishing.

Smith, M.D. and Parker, R.N. (1980) Type of homicide and variation in regional rate. *Social Forces, 59*, 136–147.

Twemlow, S.W. (1995a) The psychoanalytic foundations of a dialectical approach to the victim/victimizer relationship. *Journal of the American Academy of Psychoanalysis, 23*, 545–561

Twemlow, S.W. (1995b) Traumatic object relations configurations seen in victim/victimizer relationships. *Journal of the American Academy of Psychoanalysis, 23*, 563–580.

Twemlow, S.W. (1998, in press) A dialectical model for sexual and other forms of workplace harassment.

Twemlow, S.W. and Sacco, F. (1994) A successful psychodynamic approach to community violence. *Psychiatric Times, IX, 2*, 36.

Twemlow, S.W. and Sacco, F. (1996) The violent community: a view from an evolving nation. In H.V. Hall (Ed.), *Lethal Violence 2000: A Sourcebook on Fatal Domestic, Acquaintances and Stranger Aggression*, pp. 613–634. Kamuela, HI: Pacific Institute for the Study of Conflict and Aggression.

Twemlow, S.W. and Sacco, F.C. (1996) Peacekeeping and peacemaking: the conceptual foundations of a plan to reduce violence and improve the quality of life in a mid-sized community in Jamaica. *Psychiatry, 59*, 156–174.

Twemlow, S.W., Sacco, F.C., and Williams, P. (1996a) A clinical and interactionist perspective on the bully-victim-bystander relationship. *Bulletin of the Menninger Clinic, 60*, 296–313.

Twemlow, S.W., Sacco, F.C., Gies, M.L., Hess. D., and Osbourn, J. (1996b) Creating a peaceful school learning environment: findings from a controlled study of an elementary school prevention focused, antiviolence intervention. Presented at a seminar entitled Adolescent Violence at The Menninger Clinic, December 13–14.

U.S. Department of Child and Maternal Health (1994) *Building Safer Communities*. Washington, D.C.: (author).

U.S. Department of Justice Bureau of Justice Assistance (1994) *Working Together To Stop the Violence: Blueprint for Safer Communities*. Washington, D.C.: National Crime Prevention Council.

Walker, S. (1993) Involving citizens in violence prevention: a reply to Rosenfeld, Decker, and Givens. *American Journal of Police, 12*, 59–64.

Warner, B.D. and Pierce, G.L. (1993) Reexamining social disorganization theory using calls to the police as measure of crime. *Child Development, 65*, 523–540.

Yalom, I.D. (1985) *The Theory and Practice of Group Psychotherapy*, 3rd ed. New York: Basic Books.

Zimring, F.E., Mukherjee, S.K., and Winkle, B.V. (1983) Intimate violence: a study of intersexual homicide in Chicago. *University of Chicago Law Journal, 50*, 910–930.

About the Authors

Stuart W. Twemlow, M.D., is in private practice of psychiatry and psychoanalysis in Topeka, KS. He is also a faculty member of the Topeka Institute for Psychoanalysis at the Menninger Foundation, Topeka, KS, and Clinical Professor of Psychiatry at the University of Kansas School of Medicine, Wichita, KS. He is an advanced black belt and master teacher in Kempo Karate and Kobudo. **Frank C. Sacco, Ph.D.,** is a Clinical Psychologist; President of Community Services Institute in Agawam, MA; and a member of the adjunct faculty at the American International College, Springfield, MA

Acknowledgments

A large team of people helped with this project — too numerous to name individuals; however, Ms. Vanessa and Mr. Kirky Taylor were the heart of the project in Montego Bay. It was their initiative.

Chapter 20

THE URGENT TASK AHEAD: PREDICTIONS AND RECOMMENDATIONS FOR PREVENTING COLLECTIVE VIOLENCE

Harold V. Hall and Leighton C. Whitaker

As we approach the end of this volume, the reader may still wonder if there is really ample cause for concern about the future of lethal violence, particularly for the beginning of the 21st century. Aren't we failing to see the bright side and, in so doing, aren't we excessively concerned with prevention?

After all, the Cold War is over. The Union of Soviet Socialist Republics (U.S.S.R.), that "evil empire", is no more. What remains of the empire is Russia, whose economy and military forces are now weak by U.S. standards. Meanwhile, U.S. military strengths and preparedness dwarf that of other nations. And, as of this writing, the U.S. economy is strong and getting stronger still. Criminal violence in the U.S. has been falling overall. So, why worry?

Our society is the most technologically advanced in the world and potentially able to solve a myriad of problems domestically and internationally. Why try to reform a society that is clearly already on top? These are serious questions that should be answered.

Isn't the Cold War over? Supposedly, yes. But the U.S. government and its military industrial complex are behaving as if it is not. The militaristic momentum established during the Cold War has carried us into even more dangerous territory. As Brian Hall (1998) documented, not only can the U.S. and Russia still fire off thousands of nuclear warheads in just a few minutes, the destructive power of these weapons is growing rapidly. For example, some U.S. warheads are being increased in destructive impact from 170 kilotons to 300 kilotons, making the 13-kiloton Hiroshima bomb seem very limited by comparison. As stated by Hall (1998, p. 45):

> *"At any given time, the United States has on alert more than 2300 warheads, delivering a combined explosive power of about 550 megatons (550 million tons of TNT) — the equivalent, to use a popular measure, of 44,000 Hiroshimas."*

So our destructive capability is greater than ever, but does that really make it more dangerous? Don't we now have superior safeguards that make an "accidental strike" virtually impossible? Probably not. We have had close calls even in the past two decades (B. Hall, 1998, p. 49):

> *"In 1980, a computer-chip failure at Norad — the United States command post in Colorado for assessing nuclear*

attacks — generated a false alarm of an all-out Soviet missile attack. The officer in charge, who fretted for eight minutes about whether the attack was real, was subsequently fired. Regulations called for him to decide in three minutes."

In 1995, a U.S. research rocket meant to study the aurora borealis was sent up off the coast of Norway. It alarmed the Russians to the point that they were just a couple of minutes from deciding to launch their nuclear missiles, before they determined that the U.S. rocket was not headed toward Russia. Thus, even if the U.S. develops adequate safeguards of its own, the Russian safeguards are increasingly inadequate, in part due to reliance on obsolete, unworkable systems. For example, a recurrent Russian computer malfunction has lately been switching part of its nuclear force to combat mode automatically. The U.S. Central Intelligence Agency (CIA) appears correct in regarding Russian Strategic Rocket forces as unsafe.

Nor have the U.S. and Russia developed what would be a rather simple and inexpensive communication safeguard: a direct link between the U.S. Norad station and its counterpart near Moscow. But, even if both the U.S. and Russia develop further safeguards, we will still have attendant extreme economic, political, and emotional costs. And all it will take to begin massive devastation is a misperception or technical or political miscommunication, or perhaps even an instance of ill will. Meanwhile, many other nations have or are developing massive nuclear destruction potential in what amounts to a continuing and escalating nuclear arms race.

Won't U.S. military strength protect us? By becoming vastly "superior" to any other nation in military strength and preparedness, the U.S. is creating a dangerous instability. Just as a nation needs within itself a system of checks and balances to maintain equilibrium, so the world's nations need to check and balance one another. Otherwise, the old adage applies: absolute power corrupts absolutely. Thus, our "overkill" orientation, manifest in our ever-greater readiness for armed conflict, threatens the already inadequate sense of proportion between other countries and our own. Most clearly, our armament "superiority" inspires other nations to emulate us in this regard. Thus, we have a very dangerous violence interlock in the form of the current arms race. The resulting struggle for power and prestige definitely emphasizes who has the biggest and best weapons. (One does not have to be a psychoanalyst to understand the macho symbolism behind this mania.) And, because other nations can no longer compete in terms of our particular weapons systems, they are inspired to develop alternative, equally destructive systems, such as biological and chemical weaponry, as has already happened in Iraq. It would be far better for us and the world at large for the U.S. to be emulated for something else, as will be discussed later.

Can't we depend on the growing U.S. economy to deter civil unrest? Ordinarily, an economically prosperous nation tends to be peaceful. But the U.S. has been on a trend toward still greater income disparity between our poorest and richest (Holmes, 1996). If the trend is allowed to continue, we will have even more homeless people as well as millions of others who have housing of some sort but exist below the poverty level, including children, who represent our future. Children suffer increasingly from these economic hardships. Frequently, children lack parental care, even in ostensibly two-parent homes, because both parents work outside of the home and no adequate child care is provided. In these cases, we are facilitating already high levels of youth illiteracy, delinquency, and mental and emotional problems. As discussed in previous chapters, such internal disparities are major determinants for civil unrest.

Won't our increasing technological advances solve our problems? Ironically, because our tremendous national economic and technical resources are being invested more and more disproportionately in weapons research, we are becoming less able to focus on technological advances that would alleviate pain, suffering, and civil unrest, and would contribute to solving global problems.

In at least one crucial technological development area, the disproportion is accelerating so rapidly as to suggest that dedication to nuclear weapons development will soon dwarf civilian science funding. According to Markoff (1998, p. D7), "Since the cold war, the Government has given civilian and military scientists rough parity in parceling out time on supercomputers. But the parity became a 2-to-1 ratio in favor of the military in 1996, and it will tilt to a 5-to-1 ratio in 1999." One consequence is that, according to the National Center for Atmospheric Research, the U.S. has dropped to sixth place globally, behind Germany, Canada, Britain, France, and Australia, in climate research capability (Markoff, 1998). The National Science Foundation, which finances the supercomputers used in civilian research, will have $74 million to allocate in 1999, while the U.S. Energy Department's Accelerated Strategic Computing Initiative, which is devoted to nuclear weapons research, will have $518 million to spend (Markoff, 1998). To put these expenditures in further perspective, however, consider that merely maintaining and operating the present U.S. nuclear arsenal will cost $25 billion in 1998 (B. Hall, 1998).

Predictions and Recommendations

Predicting is always hazardous, even if based on valid principles of behavior. No matter how expert the forecasters, we may be wrong far more than we are right. One danger is that we may rely too much on highly credentialed, powerful people who "should" be able to predict future events. The CIA, with its vast resources and multi-layered global intelligence, failed, among other notable mispredictions, to predict the breakup of the U.S.S.R. in 1991 (Morrison, 1995), one of the major events of this century. Edmund Ruffin, in his 1860 book *Anticipations of the Future*, as reported by Strauss and Howe (1997), forecast a bloody civil war in the U.S. beginning with an attack on Fort Sumter but predicted that it would not start until Christmas Eve, 1867, 6 years after it actually began. The first author of this chapter remembers his own mispredictions concerning potentially violent individuals and would much rather speak of the true positives and true negatives for which, of course, he tends to have better recall.

The unfortunate truth about predictions of any sort is that there are only five possible outcomes — and at least three of these are unhappy. We can be (1) too early, (2) too late, (3) just plain wrong about the event in question, (4) right on target or, (5) depending on how many implied predictions we have embedded within an overall prediction, both right and wrong in a combination of the above. Let's consider these outcomes in relation to the interventions recommended in this book to prevent collective violence until the middle of the next decade (to about 2005).

Too Early

Current U.S. policies and strategies for controlling collective lethal violence may prevail for most or all of the decade, including, but not limited to, increasing use of the death penalty, containment strategies resulting in the world's highest incarceration rate, continuing lack of real accountability or punishment for lethal behaviors by various government agencies and departments, and a discriminatory and senseless drug policy that appears to create even more substance abuse and related hazards. Unless there is a widespread, catastrophic disaster, the power elite may simply do more of the same. Why modify policies and strategies that seem to be working for them?

Key interventions suggested in this book, summarized in Table 20.1, may be delayed or never carried out because they represent threats to the power elite. These include more investigations into covert matters such as the chemical and biological experiments

TABLE 20.1

RECOMMENDED INTERVENTIONS FOR LESS COLLECTIVE VIOLENCE

Goal	Possible Strategy	Rationale
Increase cooperative and altruistic behavior in youth.	Proactive training in nonviolent approaches from pre-school to college.	The key to a nonviolent future lies in youth preventive programs.
Eliminate death penalty.	Legislative action based on findings that death penalty has no deterrent value.	Capital punishment models the acceptability of killing.
Reduce media violence.	Impose mandatory rating systems and sanctions.	Media violence increases violence in vulnerable youth.
Reduce sexism, racism, counter-racism.	Class action suits, legislative action. Training in shared decision-making.	Parity in relationships and opportunities reduces violence.
Greatly increase funding for social sciences.	Reduce unnecessary military spending, increase support on human relationship research.	Most talents and skills of scientists currently used for warfare.
Psychologically screen government leaders and political candidates.	Build in mandatory psychometric testing in civil service regulations and electoral process.	Much collective violence can be prevented by screening for high-risk persons.
Increase right-to-carry privileges for persons with no violent history; ban firearms for those with violent history.	Legislative action balanced against increased number of some types of violence to others.	Violent entities typically avoid armed individuals who refuse to be a victim. Inordinate violence caused by repeat, armed offenders.
Ban international sales of weapons without Congressional action on a case-by-case basis.	Congressional action and legislation. Allow United Nations to impose sanctions on weapons-selling enterprises.	Many wars and revolutions are made possible by U.S. weapons sales.
Punish government wrongdoing (e.g., Ruby Ridge, Waco, CIA murders).	Appoint special prosecutors and impose criminal sanctions on perpetrators.	Government transgressions breed contempt for the law and beget reactive violence.
Hold medical practitioners accountable for results of human radiological/biological/ chemical research.	Civil suits against individual practitioners; contact ethical board of relevant profession.	Violation of trust in doctor-patient relationships (and wrongful death) should be punished.
Fundamentally reorganize violent government agencies with greater accountability for violent deeds.	Congressional mandate, Executive branch reorganization, Supreme Court action.	Expected results would be decrease in anti-government sentiment and violence.

performed on human subjects by our government with the threat of prosecution of the individuals responsible. This threat would act as a disincentive to design systems for monitoring and control to prevent further such experiments.

A further, probably threatening recommendation is the appointment of a special prosecutor and initiation of a Congressional investigation, disclosure, apology, and compensation for the hundreds of thousands of non-U.S. allies who, outside of war, were tortured, detained, mutilated, or killed by the CIA or parties supported by that agency, as discussed in Chapter 2 by Leighton Whitaker, noted in Appendix A on the CIA's interrogation manuals provided by Sandra McPherson, and discussed at various other points in this book. This publicly available information suggests possible wrongdoing by our government which has not been sufficiently brought to light. The CIA itself should be increasingly limited in its operations, with some of its functions being taken over by other intelligence agencies. Recognizing that many of the atrocities committed by the CIA were encouraged or even directed by the then-Presidents of the U.S. (with built-in plausible deniability if the mission should be uncovered, thus giving the President a covert violent option to all problems), the President should be required by law to obtain written approval from Congress before authorizing violent actions by the CIA or its subsidiary agencies. Most of the covert operations, from the Bay of Pigs to the failure to support the Kurds in their uprising against Saddam Hussein, have not worked and have involved terrible suffering on the part of the victims. The present system involving the Inspector General of the CIA and Congressional oversight has not prevented a continuing pattern of violence and aggression. Our recommendations on this matter are not likely to meet with enthusiastic support from those currently in power.

We need to learn the art of apology, even though apology is seen as a reflection of weakness in the West, just as we expect apologies from other nations (e.g., Japan) for misdeeds. We need to inform the Peoples Republic of China, for example, that a CIA officer, operating out of a supersecret task force in Indochina in 1966, parachuted into Southern China and that this operative, by his own account, shot a Chinese soldier or North Vietnamese conscript in China in a successful quest to gather information on SAM missiles transported to Hanoi (see autobiography of Warner Smith, 1996). If the roles were reversed and a Chinese spy parachuted into southern California for the purpose of stealing U.S. military secrets, killing an American soldier in the process, we would be outraged and see this assassination as an act of war.

Apology as an intervention harkens back to the ancient wisdom that the path to atonement starts with confession. A few glimmers of hope have emerged. President Clinton, for example, recently apologized to the victims in the Tuskegee Syphilis Study, which involved 399 black males who were duped and denied treatment during the period from 1932 to 1974 (Faden, 1996). The U.S. Public Health Service physicians promised the subjects free medical care in return for participating in the study at local white churches, thus creating a supposedly benign setting. Subjects were never told that they had syphilis and were denied penicillin even after it became available in 1947. When the story broke in 1972, 28 of the men had died of syphilis and another 100 of complications. In 1997, only eight survivors remained. While apologies do not reverse events, they do acknowledge misdeeds and thus undo deception, a critical initial step for real reform. Apology should not be perceived as weakness by the power elite but as a sign of strength and compassion for the people.

Another recommendation not likely to win the endorsement of the power elite concerns psychological testing of all presidential candidates, department/agency heads, and military commanders in critical stations and missions. If one individual, such as the President or a captain of a strategic submarine, has the power to end all life on this planet as well as to effect lesser destruction, don't we have the right to know if he or she is sociopathic, mentally deranged, deteriorating from massive stress, or suffering from dementia? The public's right to this information about high officeholders outweighs the latter's right to privacy. In response to those who assert that psychological test screening of candidates for positions of power is dangerous in itself, we recommend the current methods for police screening, in which multiple objective tests with built-in scales to detect deception and distortion, in addition to an interview and a background investigation, are utilized. If only conservative conclusions are rendered, identifying disturbed leaders who are likely to aggress against others rather than seek mediation or compromise, there would be some protection of the public interest.

Too Late

Even advocates of the espoused principles and recommendations may not appreciate the proliferation of deadly collective entities with planned violence in the works. Discussions throughout this book note the increase of membership in groups and institutions such as the Patriot movement, hate groups, organized crime, and youth gangs. And, because most government entities have strong financial support, their violent-related activities are not expected to diminish.

Even given the immediate and full implementation of the recommendations, the condition of our current government may simply be terminal. Aside from resentment toward the government on the parts of various collective entities and a large portion of the American population, we have the problem of economics. How can the U.S. possibly pay its debts, given our massive national debt and the increasing interest on that debt, without a financial catastrophe of unprecedented magnitude taking place? As the U.S.S.R. collapsed because it could not pay its debts, so our country may follow suit. Even with downsizing, the U.S. military and related agencies spend more than we could possibly raise in taxes.

More broadly, are we too late to prevent the end of Western civilization? Other perspectives and predictions are instructive in this regard. Richardson (1969) was interested in the length of time humans wait before engaging in a war of a given magnitude with a proportionate number of victims. Although wars seem, with intervals of peace in between, to occur in cycles, the world's population could be destroyed in one vast Armageddon (shown by the projected intersection of the curves) toward the end of the next millennium (see Figure 20.1). In *Cosmos*, Carl Sagan (1980) reformulated the now famous Richardson Curve to take into account nuclear realities and the rapid proliferation of nuclear capabilities since World War II (i.e., the shaded area in Figure 20.1). Although Sagan suggested that the shape of the curve is partially within our control, he predicted that the destruction of civilization through global nuclear war may occur in the next several decades. The essential point of this illustration, whether Richardson or Sagan is believed, is that the chances of large scale warfare increase as a function of time. According to both men, history shows an increased willingness of humankind to engage in wars of larger magnitude.

Robert Toplin (1975, p. 291), a renowned historian, predicted a future for the U.S. that has largely been realized in the 23 years since his prediction:

"Violent crime will become even more serious. In turn, police departments, courts, and prisons will enlarge and the law will jettison more civil liberties in order to capitalize on opportunities to catch criminals. Guns will become even more commonplace, approved appurtenances of modern living as citizens load up to protect themselves. Over the years there will be more presidential assassinations as angry and deranged men blast more holes in the fabric of democracy as well as in the bodies of leaders. Bomb explosions will rock public buildings as confused individuals plan indiscriminate attacks to call attention to their personal grievances. There will be more wars over petty, emotional matters, and generations following these wars will again look back wondering how the hostilities could have been justified. In short, many Americans will suffer serious

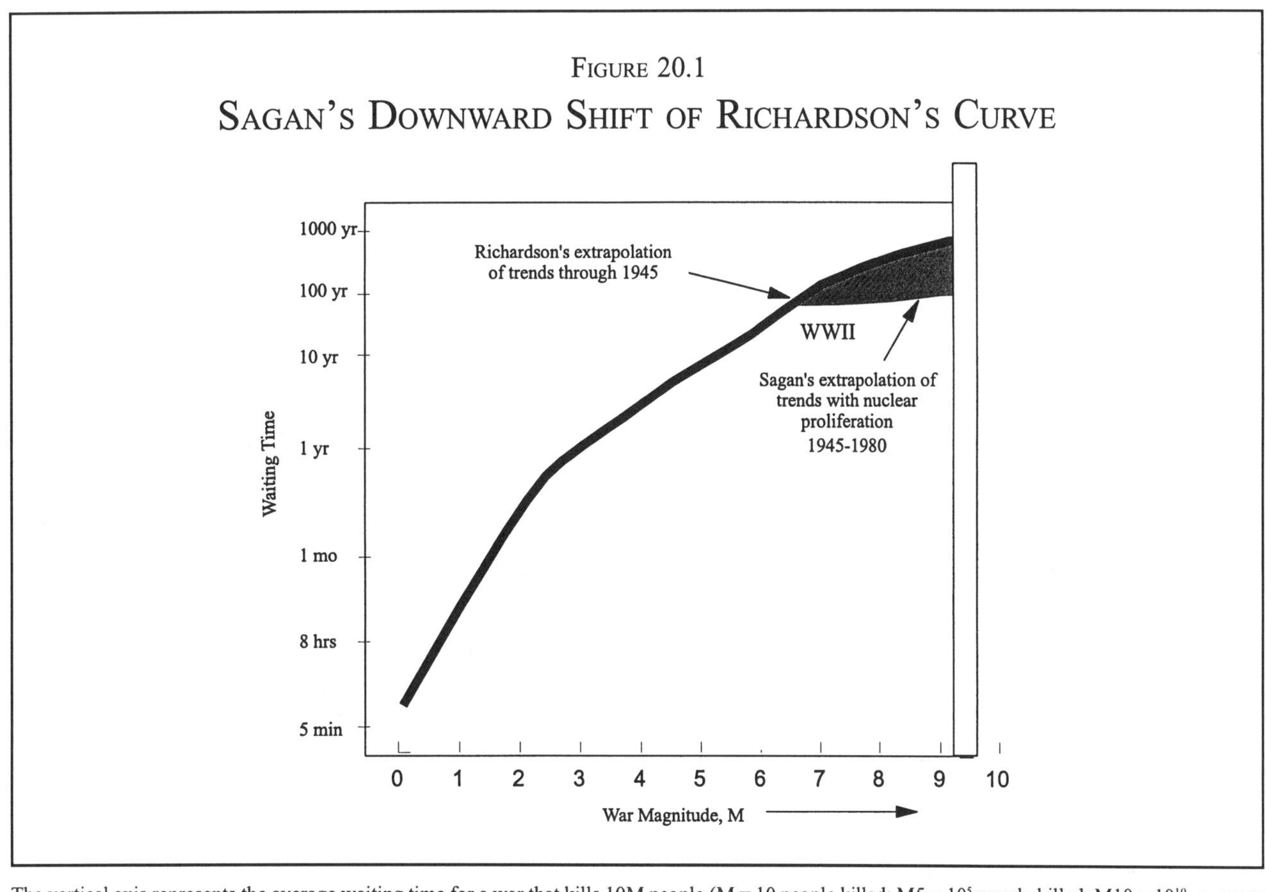

FIGURE 20.1
SAGAN'S DOWNWARD SHIFT OF RICHARDSON'S CURVE

The vertical axis represents the average waiting time for a war that kills 10M people (M = 10 people killed; M5 = 10^5 people killed; M10 = 10^{10}, or every human on the planet). the horizontal axis represents war dead magnitude, which Richardson's data showed has been increasing since 1820. Extrapolations of data through 1945 (Richardson) and 1980 (Sagan) are presented. No convincing data as of 1995 have substantially changed Sagan's extrapolation. (Adapted from Sagan, 1980, 1995.)

injury or die unnecessarily. And, many others will suffer seriously from the fear of violence." [emphasis added]

Massive intervention for even a portion of the victims in catastrophes may be beyond the capacities of the helping professions. A glimpse into the future is provided by Joseph Davis in Appendix E, which focuses on the 1995 bombing in Oklahoma City. In this true account, Davis notes that, despite timely and comprehensive critical stress debriefing to members of the community, an enormous toll was taken on both victims and professional staff. A country-wide event would quickly overwhelm our ability to respond.

Observing the cyclic nature of violence, Toplin (1975, p. 292) predicted accurately that, during lulls in the overall decline, violence will not appear likely. He ended with a prophetic note:

"At times these predictions will appear inordinately bleak. Trends do not usually move in a linear direction. There are ups and downs, periods of optimism and periods of despair. We should expect halcyon years of plenty when many will enjoy a temporary sense of relief. It is likely there will be stretches of time notable for the lack of civil, collective violence and fairly long intervals where there will not be a single attempt on the life of a President or a presidential candidate. Violent crime rates may even dip significantly. But the roots of

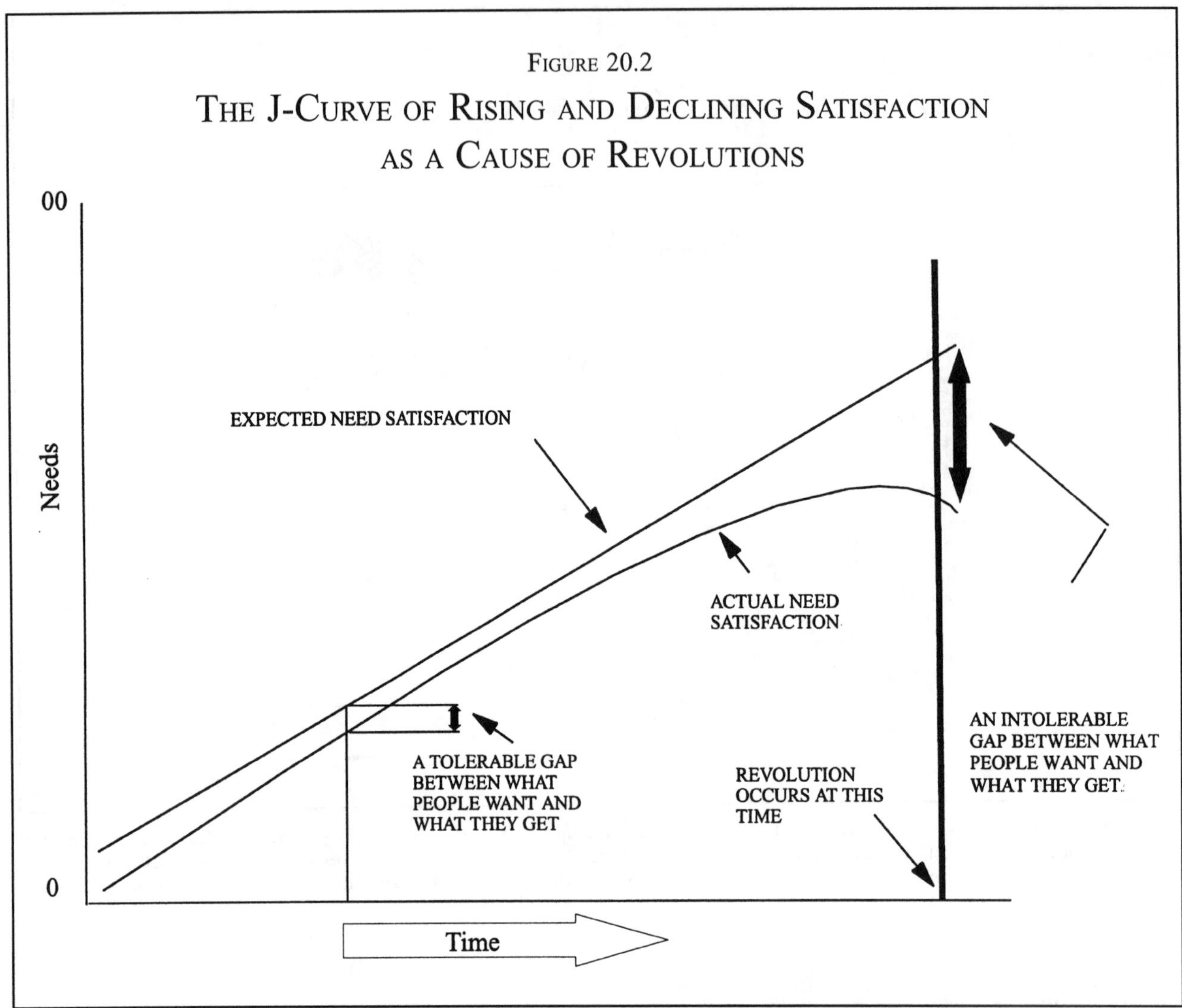

The J-curve is an assertion that the mood of citizens is one of hostility and anxiety stemming from an ever-widening gap between expected and actual need fulfillment. What constitutes an "intolerable" gap triggering revolution is unknown. (Adapted from Davies, 1969.)

trouble are too deep for the hopeful signs to prevail over the tendency towards violence, fear and cultural deterioration. Over the long haul this condition will seriously undermine the quality of American life. In a more dramatic sense, it will bring a veritable decline in American civilization."

When will it be too late for America? The J-curve, presented in Figure 20.2, has been used to explain retrospectively violent change in government (Davies, 1969). Basically, the concept suggests that revolution is more likely when a prolonged period of rising expectations and gratifications is followed by a brief period of sharp reversal (the "U" portion of the "J"), during which time the gap between expectations and gratifications becomes intolerable. Davies (1969) argued that the French Revolution of 1789, the American Civil War of 1861, and the Nazi Revolution of 1933, among other events, are explainable by the J-curve.

The J-curve is a psychological explanation — sudden deprivation of needs and gratifications creates tension and anger and increases the likelihood of willingness to break conventions, by violence if necessary, in order to satisfy those wants again. If the ever-increasing expectations of the people are gratified (an impossible task), then revolution and rebellion are unlikely. The model holds that people of all walks of life will react the same way if deprived of the goods and dignity they have previously enjoyed. When heretofore disparate elements in a fragmented society feel they have the same foe — the federal government, for example — they can unite long enough to overthrow it. Such a movement may be occurring presently to some degree. Colvard (1997, p. 3) noted:

"The conservative militants who envision a last bastion of white patriarchal America in the far Northwest find a strange agreement with disenfranchised black communities in the U.S. inner cities who believe in 'The Plan' — elite America's reputed program of genocide via drugs, demoralization, poverty, and AIDS. Both groups, and many in the middle, fear the power of a government with which they feel completely out of touch."

So which revolutions will be successful? Generally, after years of attitude formation, violence occurs when a few peoples — and the number of revolutionaries can be small — despite awareness of the illegality of their acts consider them morally acceptable given the failure of government to act in a moral fashion. They form small, cohesive bands (i.e., cells) and have an agenda of destruction. The insurgents' actions simply have to demonstrate that the government cannot provide public safety. Because states are constituted to provide security from violence (Turpin and Kurtz, 1997), destruction of their ability to provide protection leads to a perception that the government cannot do its job. Widespread natural disaster, economic upheaval, or war with other countries can trigger a concerted attack by the otherwise largely independent cells.

A second function of revolutionary violence is to induce the government to *overrespond* against uncommitted citizens, thus perpetrating repressive acts that citizens consider illegitimate and garnering more support for the revolutionary movement. As shown in Figure 20.3, excessive police and military action then leads to a temporary reduction of revolutionaries but at a cost of alienating greater numbers of heretofore uncommitted citizens. Hence, fighting revolutionaries often leads paradoxically to the downfall of the extant government by alienating third parties and producing a groundswell of protest until a power shift takes place.

Gude (1969) discussed how Fidel Castro overcame Batista with only several thousand guerillas. By terrorizing the Batista government, counter-terrorism by the government became the weapon of response resulting in the arrest, torture, and execution of tens of thousands of innocent Cubans. The urban underground then expanded to include students and the political and professional elite. Again, the crucial factor was the perception of legitimacy (not legality) of the violence. Overresponding by counterviolence and repressive means upsets a delicate political process which depends on public perception of legitimacy.

Some needs and expectations relevant to revolution take priority over others. Abraham Maslow (1970) constructed what is now a well-accepted model showing a hierarchy of needs. Although criticized (e.g., people have starved themselves in order to make a political statement), several reviews of the literature generally support Maslow's model (Corsini, 1997), which appears true both on a nomothetic (group) basis and on an idiographic (individual) basis, the latter in accord with the individual's personal history. Although individual differences emerge, thirst and hunger quickly become preoccupying when one is deprived of sustenance, and focus on higher needs is diminished. Thus, threatening people's lives by accusing them of crimes quickly suppresses any altruistic thoughts and feelings they might have otherwise.

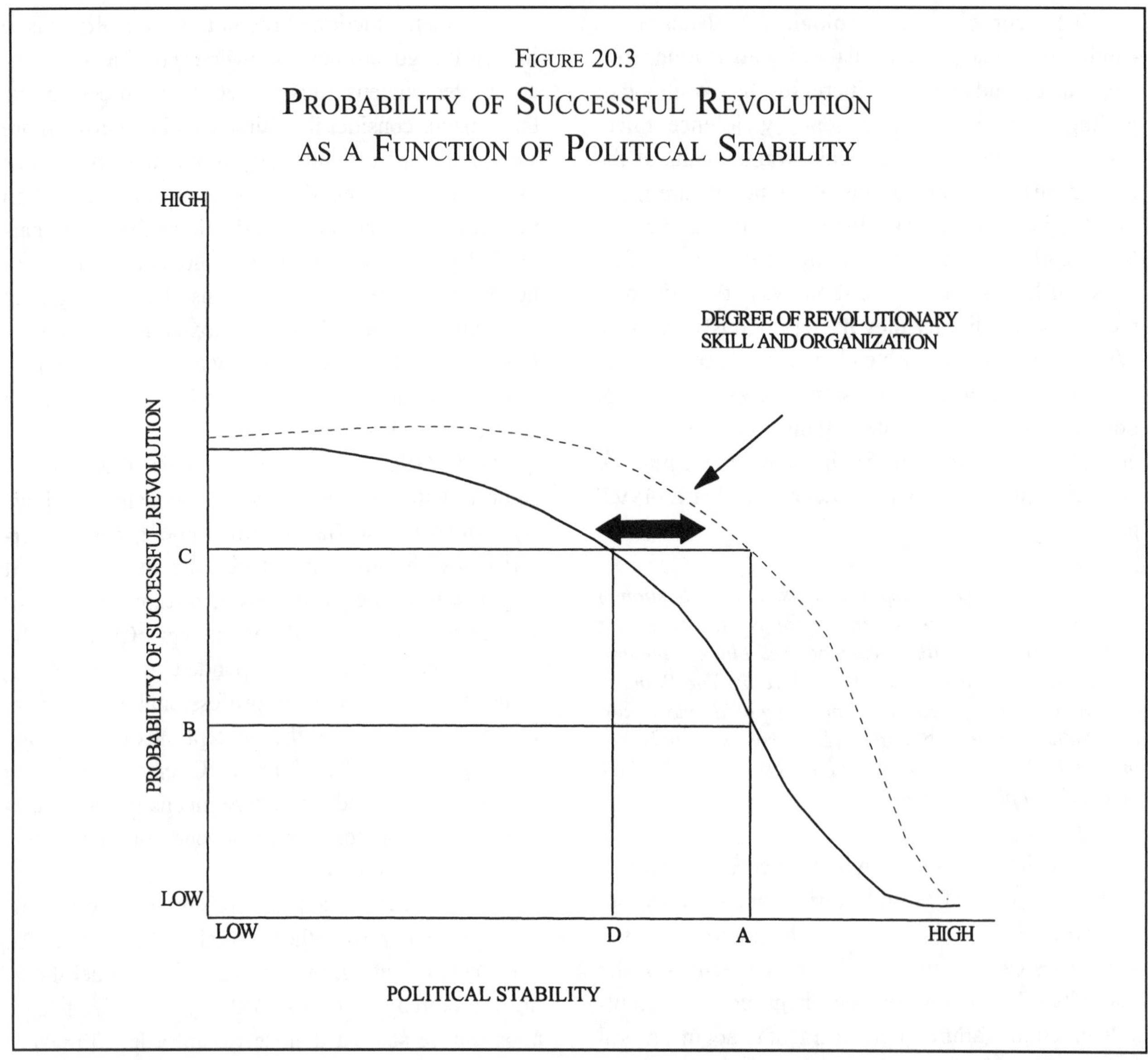

Effective police and military tactics reduce the strength of revolutionaries, but they may be accompanied by a shift toward perceived illegitimacy, which then reduces the stability of the government. more revolutionary activity may result. (Adapted from Gude, 1969.)

Maslow's hierarchy may have relevance to understanding revolution, as Figure 20.4 shows. Deprive citizens of an effective means to protect themselves and their safety needs emerge as a priority. Ban assembly of groups of like-minded individuals, such as militia groups, and needs for belongingness are thwarted, so people will strive hard to meet anyway and will tend to bind closer together in their now common cause. Deprive workers of jobs and a vocation, and their esteem needs surge to the fore. If the federal government is *perceived* as the proximate cause of these deprivations, it will be exceedingly difficult to continue to maintain government power and control.

FIGURE 20.4
MASLOW'S HIERARCHY OF NEEDS
APPLIED TO REVOLUTION ISSUES

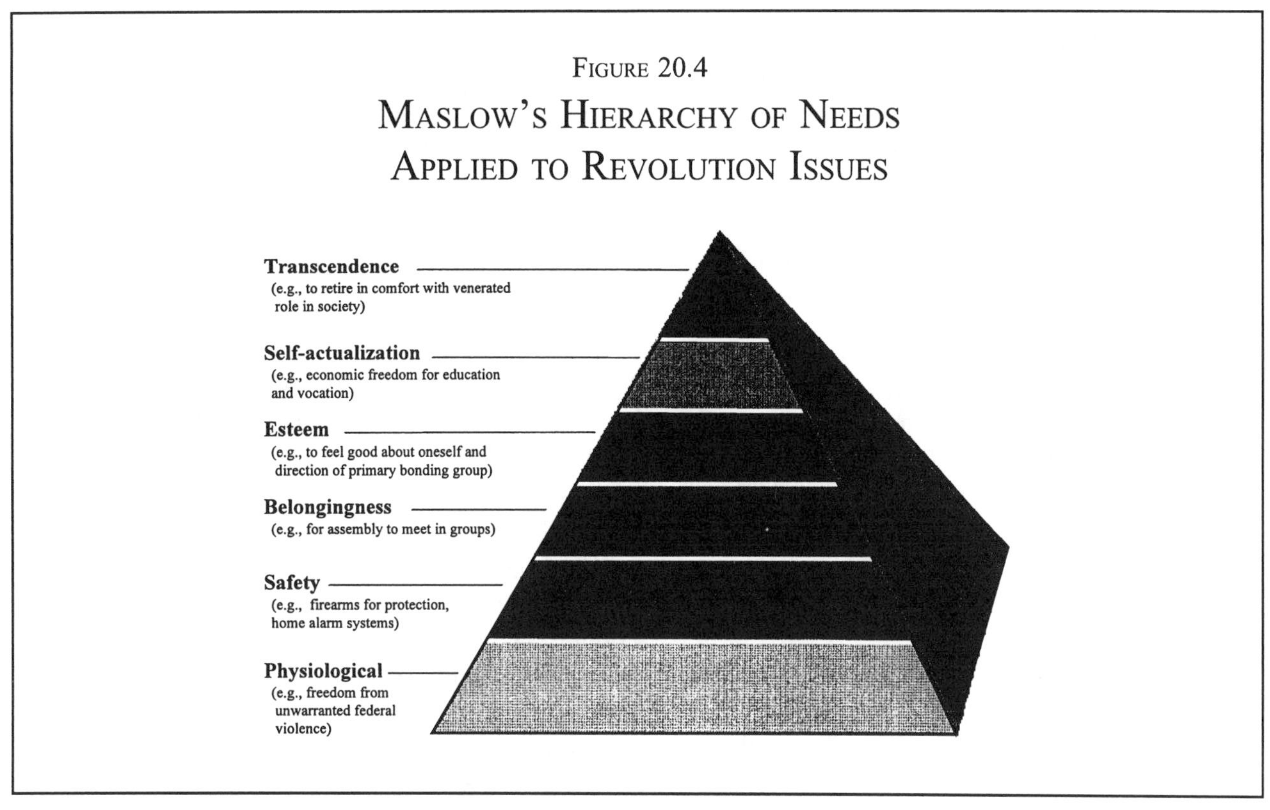

Short of killing all the revolutionaries, or otherwise "neutralizing" them, at the risk of inspiring others to become revolutionaries, the dynamics suggested by this model give an inordinate advantage to even a few dedicated and persistent insurgents. The skill, perseverance, organization, and timing of the terrorist groups, combined with a natural advantage in surprise and the ease with which it can be demonstrated that the people cannot be protected by the incumbent government, appear to be the main factors in determining the success of a revolution.

Being Wrong

However unlikely, our recommendations for intervention may become irrelevant if the U.S. shifts to a full democracy and virtually eliminates human rights abuses. Nongovernment collective entities (e.g., Patriot groups) may then disband of their own volition. The government would succeed by practicing full disclosure and restraint in dealing with its citizens.

Our recommendations may be effectively countered or bypassed. Much as the Nuremberg recommendations were simply ignored by those who conducted human radiation experiments, these recommendations are vulnerable to manipulation. They may be proclaimed as a standard for ethical behavior but, hypocritically, violated by those who make or enforce the rules.

Being Right

If implemented, the recommendations in this book may provide the U.S. with ultimately more domestic and global security and a radically enhanced capacity to promote self-actualization of its citizens. If implemented, these recommendations would mean that the U.S. would provide a model for the world and nurture a cooperative global environment in which war is rendered functionally obsolete. We have the tools. As Sagan explained (1980, p. 318):

"In our tenure on the planet, we have accumulated dangerous evolutionary baggage, hereditary propensities for aggression and ritual, submission to leaders and hostility to outsiders, which place our survival in some question. But we have also acquired compassion for others, love for our children and our children's children, a desire to learn about history, and a great soaring passionate intelligence — the clear tools for our continued survival and prosperity."

A Combination

Some recommendations may be selected for implementation by the government (e.g., development of more accurate systems of analysis for predicting violence and deception), some may be partially and begrudgingly implemented (e.g., shifting to primary prevention strategies with children or providing more opportunities for women and minorities in leadership positions), while others may be ignored completely (e.g., disclosure of government wrongdoing with appropriate changes). A combination is seen as the most likely scenario by the authors of this volume.

Conclusion

Lethal violence has continued unabated in this country since its founding. Since the end of World War II, there have been breakthrough medical advances, an increase in longevity and reduction of infant mortality, increased power for women and minorities, an expanded database on human behavior and successful treatment strategies, and a revolution in military methodology. Yet, Americans believe and feel that things are getting worse. Respect for human life is eroding. For example, at any one time, between 35 and 55 serial murderers stalk the streets of the U.S., gunfire is heard nightly in most large cities in the U.S., and unwanted babies are dumped into trash bins (Hall, 1996). Despite a much-heralded recent overall reduction in violence (which took criminologists and law enforcement agencies by total surprise), our homicide rate is still the highest of all Western nations for which records are accurately kept. The U.S. is still the world's largest supplier of weapons. From 1991 to 1996, over 75% of U.S. arms sales to developing countries went to nations where the citizens had no right to choose their own government (Barnaby, 1997). The vast majority of states now have the death penalty. We employ the majority of our scientists in war-oriented activities, while having more people in prison than any other country in the Western world. In sum, there continue to be both emerging trends for the resolution of violence and powerful forces for its continuation.

As our analyses from many contributors to this volume have revealed, U.S. government agencies and departments are directly or indirectly responsible for far more deaths and misery than all nongovernment collective entities combined. In a shameful display of failure to see the long-term likely consequences of their violent acts, they have brought us to the brink of thermonuclear destruction, threatened our environment, and diminished the well-being of our citizens. It is ironic that the decision to create an electronic environment and a nuclear capability, which has dominated U.S. science policy since 1940, has created a more violent, unsafe world in spite of the opposite intent. There is something bizarre about a nation that can produce attack submarines, each capable of destroying 160 cities with their multiple head nuclear missiles, as we developed in the 1980s, or to have equipment with visual resolution so fine you can see person-size images from our planetary orbit, and yet have hunger and violent deaths of innocent people on its streets and perform harmful radiological and biochemical research on its people. At the very least, vastly more support for the social sciences in the service of humane causes is needed to right the skewed balance created by a science of domination and command control.

Non-government violent entities are no better, and, though the victims of these groups are fewer than government groups, it may be only because of lack of opportunity. Groups and institutions range from gangs to hate groups to syndicated crime excuse and extoll their own lethal violence and condemn violence to their own members. Some collective entities such as groups in the Patriot movement have been caught with and have indicated a desire to use biological weapons (e.g., bubonic plague) and poison (e.g., Ricin), and they possess the information needed to construct atomic weapons, which they may do if they are able to buy component parts and assemble them. This willingness costs them the moral high ground with which they would differentiate themselves from the government which they claim represses them unfairly.

The means to resolve violence are tentative, fragile, and poorly supported. We in the U.S., particularly, have a difficult time letting go of violence as a problem-solving option. Nonviolent approaches such as those espoused and used by Gandhi and Martin Luther King, Jr., are increasingly popular but not yet widespread. (What do a few peace psychologists and other do-gooders know about violence and war anyway?) Yet, for all the fragility, we currently have the knowledge and technology to reverse violent trends in one or two generations. We have the broad outlines of how to foster win-win conditions, nurture positive children who abhor violence, and teach people how to share control with no loss of dignity.

By the end of the decade of our predictions, we will know which of the outcomes discussed becomes dominant overall and which of the five possibilities are fulfilled. Movement toward peaceful prosperity may occur. On the other hand, conditions within and between the U.S. and other countries may seriously deteriorate. It is quite possible that our country could be thrown into violent revolution, especially if those groups which distrust and hate the government join forces. Given our history, most likely, a combination of the possibilities will occur.

Whatever the outcome, suppression of dissidents or even suspension of common liberties is a highly probable outcome. Counterterrorist methods are not democratic. The U.S. government would be forced to suspend rights in order to fight terrorism effectively, should a revolution commence. The terrorist groups themselves, should they win, would hardly share governing with the group they despise and fear, namely minorities and all opposition groups which comprise a majority of citizens.

On a global scale, U.S.-Russian and U.S.-Chinese relations may deteriorate completely. With China, the conflict may start with aggressive Chinese action toward Taiwan, whose independence has been resented for almost half a century. Representatives of U.S. military and think tanks consider the threat of cyberspace wars to represent possible destruction of our economy and society via possible attacks on key national strategic infrastructures, especially the global financial system. Cyberspace construction and exploitation are themselves a threat because of their uncertainty while increasing by rapid and unpredictable transformations of societies and economies throughout the world.

Strauss and Howe (1997), in their well-researched *The Fourth Turning: An American Prophecy*, predicted differential outcomes in the short vs. long term. Analyzing the last 500 years, these historians discovered a distinct pattern of cycles lasting about 80 years each. First, a "high" takes place after a new regime takes power, characterized by confidence, expansion, feelings of security and euphoria (e.g., in the U.S., the period from 1946 to 1964). Second, "awakening" takes place, where values of the new order are questioned and there is a search within (1964 to 1984), followed by an "unraveling" where individualism becomes primary as institutions crumble in an increasingly fragmented society (1984 to about 2005). The model explains what is happening now in the U.S., including the temporary reduction of overall violence that we are now experiencing. In the third, unraveling period, characterized by what Strauss and Howe call the "Culture Wars", the mood of the people will be more anxious as they perceive that fundamental change will occur within their lifetimes. Around 2005, a startling crisis or triggering event (e.g., devaluation of the dollar, the spread of a deadly virus) will take place and galvanize attention and eventually lead to the death of the old order through global war, violent revolution in the U.S., or mass genocide (2005 to the 2020 decade). A new order is then established and the cycle moves once more in inexorable progression. The entire cycle represents history's recapitulation of the birth and death of seasonal variations — growth, maturation, entropy, and death or rebirth.

Based on a survey of authors contributing chapters to this book and similar to predictions by Strauss and Howe (1997), our prediction for the next several years until the middle of the next decade (2005, plus or minus 2 years) is as follows: No global wars, no violent revolution in the U.S., no elimination of federal agencies, and no economic catastrophes will occur. No external or domestic collective organization, from China or Russia alone or in combination, or any Patriot group or collection of groups will be sufficiently strong to challenge the U.S. military successfully or incite the people to revolt. The economy, though it may bounce high and low, will sustain the population and hence not act as a trigger to widespread revolution. Instead, both positive and negative trends will occur as the underlying foundations of American society continue to unravel and fragment as the nation as a whole swings to the right. An increase in the use of the death penalty, government intrusion in response to collective lawlessness, and continuation of covert activities and undeclared warfare by federal agencies (e.g., Department of Defense, CIA, Federal Bureau of Investigation [FBI], National Security Council) can be anticipated. Suspension or at least erosion of human rights and liberties follows naturally and is a safe bet. As a response, more assassinations and assassination attempts of American leaders are predicted, primarily by solo perpetrators, but they will be less successful due to improved methods for providing security for protected persons as developed by the U.S. Secret Service and other agencies. Collective efforts will move to unite currently disparate anti-government groups in a common cause, at least on the Internet, if not in cohesively organized groups. Hate groups and hate crimes by the various ethnic and racial groups will increase as differences in cultural and economic status become less tolerated. A white backlash to disproportionate black violence in particular is likely. Efforts to ban firearms will continue as part of an overall governmental response to a deteriorating society and loss of control, but will be vigorously resisted by the white middle class and reflected in more "right to carry" laws and formation of opposition groups such as the National Rifle Association and Patriot groups. To a large extent, the above predictions describe what is already occurring in this country.

For the two decades following the triggering stimulus, to about the middle of the 2020 decade, at the latest, similar to the explicit and implied predictions of Toplin (1975), Strauss and Howe (1997), Sagan (1980, 1993, personal communication), and others, the contributors to this volume believe that the chances are exceedingly high that cataclysmic events on the order of the American Civil War, World War II, the Holocaust, or worse, will occur.

Why does the long-term prediction differ from the short-term prediction until the middle of the next decade? Recognizing that human events are cyclic, as Strauss and Howe (1997) have convincingly demonstrated, we are subject to the enduring patterns of our violent history here on Earth. A total war occurs on the average of every 80 years, they found, and, more importantly, *every* Fourth Turning (i.e., the crisis period when the triggering event galvanizes the population) since the 15th century has culminated in wars of large magnitude. Wars reflect the mood of the period and are usually fought to unambiguous outcomes. It is important to remember that war can mean domestic revolution against the incumbent government (as in the Glorious Revolution of 1675 to 1704), characterized by civil upheavals and deadly Indian Wars, American Revolution, and American Civil War). Trends discussed previously reveal that the U.S. is more vulnerable to domestic than external violence. This likelihood suggests that had the FBI; the Bureau of Alcohol, Tobacco, and Firearms; and other government agencies not bungled the attacks by overkill at Ruby Ridge and Waco, militia groups would have seized on some other provocation to declare war against the federal government and that if the militia groups join forces, especially with non-militia dissident groups, and start a widespread revolution, that revolution will be to the death. No quarter would be given or expected. Under the umbrella of the revolutionary war, both winners and losers would probably commit genocide.

Even if we knew for certain that many of the more negative predictions will come to pass, the recommendations in this book should be followed for the eventual rebirth of the country. The principles of violence discussed throughout this book, upon which the recommendations are based, should be built into intervention efforts. Basic to the principles and postulates we have espoused is a spirit of compassion, understanding, peace, solicitude, love, and respect for our fellow human beings. Vaclav Havel (1997), the great president-playwright of Czechoslovakia, noted that the foundation for all constructive intervention is a moral stance. While none of us alone can save the world, each individual must act as though it were in his or her power to do so. Positive intervention implies a search for the unvarnished truth, the application of nonviolent interventions, and respect for the adversary in order to break violence interlocks. We should prepare now for what may come for our loved ones, living and not yet born, and the greater community on this planet.

What is needed to reduce institutional violence, in addition to specific predictions and recommendations, is firm resolve based on realistic awareness of the dangers and consequences of complacency and the courage to take a moral stance. We need to cultivate faith in one another and to do what is simultaneously right for ourselves and for others. Our moral stance, supported by actions, can lift our own moral well-being and convey an example that is provocative, contagious in its influence, and deserving of emulation.

The U.S. is in an ideal position to take this moral stance. By doing so, we can make our own and others' lives far more meaningful and less subject to despair. Whatever one's religious or spiritual convictions or doubts, we need to practice respect for life for ourselves and others. The basic commandment, "Thou shalt not kill", is already fundamental to Judaism, Christianity, and Islam. It is a good place to start. When we and the people of other nations learn, not just through our statements but through our actions, that we respect life, the message sent will be one of love and security instead of violence and fear. It is a case of being moral to improve morale in the very deepest sense.

To take this position, we must be willing to be kind and generous unilaterally rather than waiting for others to initiate or match our efforts. That is the spirit needed. In fact, it is to our own advantage to take the first steps. Only then do we show ourselves and others that we are truly spirited. Clearly, unilateral giving makes us vulnerable, and letting oneself be vulnerable interpersonally is at odds with the macho mentality that fuels our fanatical development of weaponry. But love inherently requires making ourselves vulnerable to others. Loving means having the courage to be vulnerable, rather than the "courage" (if such courage is needed) to practice domination. Often, of course, no real courage is needed to dominate, especially when the aggressor already possesses greater destructive power.

All of this means that we need to change from a predominantly dominator culture to a partnership culture. Instead of trying to subdue others, the partnership culture emphasizes respect for others, including their differences. In many ways, it has been respect for and cultivation of diversity that has been responsible for whatever greatness we have as a nation. Just as inbreeding eventually destroys the breed genetically, so a society that insists on cultural conformity — so emphasized in all autocratic and dominator societies — eventually and inevitably is destroyed from within as well as by outside forces.

We have the choice in our hands. Do we attempt to dominate other peoples and in the process degrade them and ourselves, or do we cultivate a national identity that really conveys what the Statue of Liberty is about? It is about welcoming, not dominating. The reforms we are suggesting are offered in this spirit that our nation cultivated so successfully in welcoming the world's rich variety of people. Let us reaffirm our traditional spiritual foundation by doing what is morally right and empowering to the people.

Annotated Bibliography

1. Archer, D. and Gartner, R. (1984) *Violence and Crime in Cross-National Perspective*. New Haven, CT: Yale University Press. This book provides a cross-national, quantitative comparison of violence and relates the findings to critical questions such as (a) Does the level of domestic violence in a society increase after that nation has participated in a war? (For most nations, the answer is a strong "yes".) (b) Does the death penalty deter violence and crime? (Almost universally, the answer is "no"; in fact, the death penalty may even indirectly increase violence.) (c) Do large cities have unusually high homicide rates? (The answer depends on the size of the city relative to the overall homicide rate of the country.)

2. Baron, R.A. and Richardson, D.R. (1994) *Human Aggression*, 2nd ed. New York: Plenum Press. This second edition of a comprehensive popular book covers virtually all aspects of human aggression. Updated discussions are presented on the development of aggressive behavior, biological bases of human violence, and aggression in natural settings. A very strong point is the continued examination of theoretical frameworks and lines of empirical investigation from the 1977 edition.

3. Gerzon, M. (1992) *A Choice of Heroes: The Changing Faces of American Manhood*. Boston: Houghton Mifflin. Gerzon provides an insightful perspective on the quick-to-violence hero images that have most influenced young men over the last few decades. He combines his own investigative travels with recent cultural history to explain how our youth adopt are constructed by ill-fitting stereotypes. The frontiersman, soldier, and even the expert and the breadwinner are too often obsolete, so the author suggests new kinds of masculinity.

3. Graham H.D. and Gurr, T.R., Eds. (1969) *The History of Violence in America. Historical and Comparative Perspectives*. New York: Frederick A. Praeger. This edited work stems from a report submitted to the National Commission on the Causes and Prevention of Violence. Presented at a time when this country was in the midst of both Vietnam and domestic turmoil, this book outlines the history of violence in America in splendid detail. Findings suggest that the conflict in the 1960s was not unique, but represented a shift in attitude on the part of Americans toward each other and their society. The value of the book lies is the historical treatment of both individual and collective violence.

4. Tedeschi, J. and Felson, R. (1994) *Violence, Aggression and Coercive Actions*. Washington,

D.C.: American Psychological Association. In this well-documented book, a theory of coercive action (the preferred term for violence and aggression), focuses on social identity, power, influence, retributive justice, and other social psychological concepts. A social interactionist approach emerges that explores face-to-face confrontations and the intent of the violent perpetrator.

References

Barnaby, F. (1997) Can we redefine national security in time? *Peace and Conflict: Journal of Peace Psychology, 3*, 217–219.

Corsini, R. (1997) *Concise Encyclopedia of Psychology*, 2nd ed. New York: John Wiley & Sons.

Colvard, K. (1997) What we already know about terrorism: violent challenges to the state and state response. *HFG Review, 1*(1).

Davies, J. (1969) The J-curve of rising and declining satisfaction as a cause of some great revolutions and a contained rebellion. In H. Graham and T. Gurr (Eds.), *The History of Violence in America. Historical and Comparative Perspectives*, pp. 690–730. New York: Frederick A. Praeger.

Faden, R. (1996) *Final Report of the Advisory Committee on Human Radiation Experiments* (Chairperson). New York: Oxford University Press.

Gude, E. (1969) Batista and Betancourt: alternative responses to violence. In H. Graham and T. Gurr (Eds.), *The History of Violence in America: Historical and Comparative Perspectives*, pp. 731–748. New York: Frederick A. Praeger.

Hall, B. (1998) Overkill is not dead. *The New York Times Magazine*, March 15, pp. 42–47, 49, 64, 76, 77, 84, 85.

Hall, H.V. (1996) Overview of lethal violence. In H.V. Hall (Ed.), *Lethal Violence 2000: A Sourcebook of Fatal Domestic, Acquaintance and Stranger Violence*, pp. 1–52. Kamuela, HI: Pacific Institute for the Study of Conflict and Aggression.

Havel, V. (1997) *The Art of the Impossible: Politics as Morality and Practice*. New York: Alfred A. Knopf.

Holmes, S.A. (1996) Income disparity between poorest and richest rises. *The New York Times*, June 20, pp. A1, A18.

Markoff, J. (1998) Military gets main use of big computers. *The New York Times*, March 23, pp. D1, D7.

Maslow, A. (1954/1970) *Motivation and Personality*. New York: Harper & Row.

Morrison, D. (1995) The intelligence community: time for reform. In R. Ullman (Ed.), *Great Decisions*, pp. 13–23. New York: Foreign Policy Associates.

Richardson, L. (1969) *Statistics of Deadly Quarrels*, Pacific Grove, CA: Boxwood Press.

Sagan, C. (1980) *Cosmos*. New York: Random House.

Smith, W. (1996) *Covert Warriors: Fighting the CIA's Secret War in Southeast Asia and China 1965–1967*. U.S.: Presidio.

Strauss W. and Howe, N. (1997) *The Fourth Turning: An American Prophecy*. New York: Broadway Books.

Toplin, R.B. (1975) *Unchallenged Violence: An American Ordeal*. Westport, CT: Greenwood Press.

Turpin, J. and Katz, L. (1997) *The Web of Violence: From Interpersonal to Global*. Chicago: University of Illinois Press.

About the Authors

Harold V. Hall, Ph.D., a forensic neuropsychologist, is the Director of the Pacific Institute for the Study of Conflict and Aggression. He has served as a consultant for a wide variety of criminal and civil justice system agencies, including the Federal Bureau of Investigation, the National Bureau of Prisons, the U.S. Secret Service, and district, family, and circuit courts at state and federal levels. Dr. Hall is a Diplomate in both Forensic Psychology and Clinical Psychology from the American Board of Professional Psychology and is a Fellow of the American Psychological Association. He is board certified in Forensic Neuropsychology from the American Board of Psychological Specialties. Most recently, he was inducted into the National Academy of Practice in Psychology, which, as with other National Academy disciplines such as medicine and dentistry, limits its membership to 100 living professionals from that discipline in the U.S. and Canada. He has investigated and trained others in individual and collective violence since the late 1960s in the Pacific Basin, on the continental U.S., and in Europe. **Leighton Whitaker, Ph.D.,** is in private practice and is Adjunct Clinical Professor at Widener University's Institute for Graduate Clinical Psychology and Editor of the *Journal of College Student Psychotherapy*. His 70 professional publications address a wide variety of clinical and social subjects and include the *Whitaker Index of Schizophrenic Thinking* (Western Psychological Services, 1980) and *Schizophrenic Disorders*, (Plenum Press, 1992) His previous positions include Associate Professor and Director of Adult Psychology for the University of Colorado Health Sciences Center, Professor and Director of the University of Massachusetts Mental Health Services, and Director of Swarthmore College Psychological Services. He has done forensic work for many years and has been consultant to the U.S. Department of Labor's Job Corps. His work with youth has been featured on television and in newspapers.

APPENDICES

Appendix A

THE MISUSE OF PSYCHOLOGICAL TECHNIQUES UNDER U.S. GOVERNMENT AUSPICES: INTERROGATION AND TERRORISM MANUALS

Sandra B. McPherson

In 1947, the School of the Americas (SOA) was established in Panama by the U.S. Army. Its purpose was to train central and southern hemisphere nationals in the art of war. Currently based at Ft. Benning, GA, the SOA has graduated over 57,000 students, many of whom have engaged in significant human rights violations throughout Latin America. The United Nations Truth Commission Report of El Salvador (1993) indicated that over 60 Salvadoran officers were responsible for the major atrocities during the Civil War. Over two thirds of those named had trained at the SOA.

Exposés and disclosures of the materials used and activities involved in instruction at the SOA clearly document a variety of serious human rights abuses. There have been reports of the use of the homeless from Panama as torture subjects and of a medical doctor from the U.S. who instructed on methods to keep subjects alive through prolonged torture projects (Fischer, 1997).

In 1982, Captain George Dollard (a fictitious name), at the time 27 years old, was given only a few months to create a training manual, copies of which, along with an earlier 1963 product, were obtained through the efforts of various researchers and study groups in the U.S. and Canada. The manuals contained explicit descriptions of many activities, including assassination, subversion of foreign governments, and the use of torture, which are inconsistent with specific U.S. policies as well as general U.S. values. Even given the pressure to perform, it is hard to believe that Dollard and others involved were unaware that their program so egregiously violated accepted limits (Fischer, 1997; Walters, 1997).

Scientists value knowledge for its own sake and explicitly or implicitly accept that increases in human knowledge benefit the human condition. Psychology as a science and as a profession rests on traditions of research, objectivity, and "the welfare and protection of the individuals and groups with whom psychologists work" (APA, 1992, p. 1598). However, as discussed below, psychologists, along with other mental health colleagues, have been willing participants in government-supported human rights violations.

Knowledge is a resource that can be used for any purpose, and the myths of Pandora's Box or Eve and the Apple are warnings that the possession of information is a power that can corrupt. In recent history, the poster children for the misuse of scientific knowledge were the medical experimenters who worked under the Nazi regime (Lifton, 1986). Contemporary moralists have expressed ambivalence about using the results from those medical records because to profit from the activities might in some way condone them.

The myth as to the U.S., however, has been that it is somehow different. It is "the democracy" and the leader of the free world with a commitment to human rights. Consistent with that notion, Milgram's (1974) research was based on the presumption that the German mind would be different from the American mind, only to find that some of the cream of the U.S. crop (e.g., university students) would, under the right conditions of authority and control, engage in the torture of other human beings. His work may have been instructive to him and to the psychological community, but it was itself a basis for ethical consternation and ultimately reform in academia (Korn, 1997). However, while the social science community worked to purge itself of exploitation (APA, 1982, 1992), there was little impact on the government and the military.

Legitimate Scientific Work Relevant to Mind Control

Following revelations of the "brainwashing" that occurred in North Korea, studies subsequently conducted by Lifton (1954, 1957, 1961), Ofshe and Singer (1986), Schein (1961), and others shed light on the psychological variables that play a part in obtaining compliance from resistant subjects. The studies of the returned prisoners of war (POWs) showed that the so-called brainwashing did not hold and that people could be repatriated psychologically as well as physically; on the other hand, methods for thought control were clearly delineated and shown to be temporarily effective.

Subsequent work in the area of destructive cults showed the same kind of techniques at work and the same outcomes. Definite stages mark the progress of people in a controlled situation where the purposes are to obtain their endorsement and compliance to an ideology and behavioral changes consistent with such agreement (Conway and Siegelman, 1978; West and Singer, 1980; Singer, 1987; Hassan, 1988;).

Whether one looks at the POW experience, the destructive cult sequence, or the manuals of interrogation that have been used by police forces (Inbau et al., 1986; Raskin, 1989; Gudjonsson, 1992), the same principles appear. These principles, to greater or lesser degrees, involve the control of the environment, differentiation of power, inducement of some anxiety or insecurity, and the use of trickery (in legitimate police interviewing, lying to subjects is explicitly condoned in the U.S., and explicitly illegal in Great Britain).

There is substantial material available on interrogation of legitimate as well as nonlegitimate types which reference a significant amount of psychological theory and scientific investigation. Gudjonsson's (1992) work alone has over 700 references, ranging from material gained in the study of psychological testing to the conformity studies in social psychology, as well as including direct investigations into witness behavior. Generally, this psychological work has been undertaken for appropriate scientific purposes and has been ethical, at least at the time it was conducted. The research increased knowledge about the functioning of humans under certain kinds of circumstances and allowed better understanding of the workings of human cognition and other aspects of behavior. The use to which the results of this research would be put were presumed to be prosocial. Thus, understanding the mechanisms of persuasion allowed some potential to reduce destructive cultic control over individuals or at least enhanced understanding of how to deal with victims; understanding the factors that went into social conformity to national aberrations such as Nazism raised the hope of avoiding repetitions on the world scene. Investigations such as Gudjonsson's focused on the dangers of inducing false confessions under conditions of psychological pressure, with the hope of increasing the soundness of enforcement while reducing victimization of innocents.

Examples of Government-Sponsored Misuse of Psychological Science

The KUBARK Counterintelligence Interrogation Manual, 1963

This manual, which became available to the public in January 1997, was redacted substantially but it is still possible to surmise the general content of many of the sections in which attempts to redact were made. Most of the acronyms used are not defined and therefore have to be understood in light of the context in which they are used. KUBARK refers to some branch of the intelligence community which was involved in foreign settings and was notably during this era an anti-Communist operation. Most likely, it was a Central Intelligence Agency (CIA) entity.

KUBARK was governed by regulations that came out of enabling legislation involving intelligence-gathering operations. The manual notes that KUBARK was not given any law enforcement rights; therefore, to the extent that it operated to restrict the freedom of people and to coerce individuals into acting against their wishes and their rights, potential illegality was involved. There are several cautions throughout the manual suggesting the importance of obtaining prior approval and of judicious use of techniques that are likely to be illegal.

The purpose of the manual was to obtain information from unwilling sources using scientifically based means and by violating the subject's rights to freedom of movement for some period of time as necessary. Classes of potential interrogatees included "defectors, escapees, or repatriates" (p. 7), and PBPRIME (apparently referring to the U.S.) citizens. In that context, it is noted that the extraterritoriality clause to the Espionage Act, passed by Congress on October 4, 1961, extended enforcement to include acts of U.S. citizens occurring outside the country.

The manual emphasizes the importance of using interrogation techniques that are not likely to backfire in the case of interrogatees who may ultimately be arrested and tried in accordance with due process. It acknowledged that what must be done is to decide when, how, and to what degree to violate human and legal rights in view of the fact that the information developed, on the basis of which one may wish to pursue a conviction, would then be tainted by the methods which are used.

An annotated bibliography at the end of the manual contains the work of Lifton, Singer, Schein, and others, who conducted research on brainwashing and descriptions of North Korean, Chinese, and Russian methodologies. Also included is work by Orne (1961), an authority on hypnosis and interrogation. Orne was involved in CIA experimentation to develop techniques of brainwashing. (In 1984, Orne testified in Commonwealth of Pennsylvania v. DiNicola that he was not allowed to discuss the kind of work that he had done.)

There is an attempt to delineate ideal interrogator qualities, but those identified would lead to success in almost any occupation, including: intelligence, experience, psychological knowledge, integrity, patience, and flexibility. The manual does, however, suggest that the following characteristics are essential (p. 10):

1. Enough operational training and experience to permit quick recognition of leads
2. Real familiarity with the language to be used
3. Extensive background knowledge about the interrogatee's native country (and Intelligence Service, if employed by one)
4. A genuine understanding of the source as a person

The manual provides a discussion of different types of personalities and their likely manipulation points, although a large portion has been redacted. It also details the importance of establishing rapport and combining a personal approach with some distance and objectivity in order to manage the setting from both a psychological and an environmental standpoint. Many of the specific techniques as well as the general approaches which are referenced are found in interrogation/investigative interviewing texts (see Inbau et al., 1986).

There is a very interesting excursion into research done at the University of Minnesota which combined studies of anxiety, affiliative needs, and ordinal position in the family. Although this research has never been developed fully, perhaps due to the logistics involved, results were cited as providing tentative guidance for varying approaches to different subjects. The manual cautions that all applications must be individualized on a case-by-case basis in order to overcome subject resistance to cooperation.

Screening techniques which are psychologically based and which emphasize getting at the themes of the person's childhood and relationships to original authorities are detailed. Singer and Schein's (1958) studies of collaborators vs. active and passive resisters to POW indoctrination yielded criteria for identifying types on the basis of which coercive strategies would be tailored. Eight pages which encompassed further information of that sort have been redacted, at which point the manual discusses the impact of an accusation and how it puts the person at a psychological disadvantage, placing the accuser in a position of authority and automatically reducing the power and adequacy experienced by the interrogatee. Suggestions are then made for ways to increase the psychological weakness in the interrogatee, including decreasing the interrogatee's ability to understand what is going on, decreasing emotional support, increasing the belief that the interrogator's power is immense, and finding ways to increase the sense of personal guilt.

The manual (p. 39) notes that "if the person does not feel guilt, he is not in his own mind guilty and will not confess to an act which others may regard as evil ... and he ... considers correct. Confession in such a case can come only with duress... ." Recommended steps paralleled the procedures in the interrogation and cult literature.

Clinical lore is also explicitly present. For example, the manual states:

"Meerlo, for example says that every verbal relationship repeats to some degree the pattern of early verbal relationships between child and parent. An interrogatee, in particular, is likely to see the interrogator as a parent or parent symbol, an object of suspicion and resistance, or of submissive acceptance. If the interrogator is unaware of this unconscious process, the result can be a confused battle of submerged attitudes, in which the spoken words are often merely a cover for the unrelated struggle being waged at lower levels of both personalities. On the other hand, the interrogator who does understand these facts and who knows how to turn them to his advantage may not need to resort to any pressures greater than those that flow directly from the interrogation setting and function." (see Meerlo, 1956, p. 48)

The manual goes on to acknowledge that with resistant subjects, other more manipulative methods for inducing regression are necessary. The techniques may range from "simple isolation to hypnosis and narcosis," the purpose of which is to bring the interrogatee to a "more infantile state" (p. 48).

There is considerable concern for environmental control for psychological effect. For example, it is recommended that there be no telephone and no interruptions so as to enhance the feeling of being "cut off" from the outside world. Research into sensory deprivation and resulting decompensation is cited.

The following clinically sophisticated discussion about the psychology of the interrogator is included (p. 38):

"Once questioning starts, the interrogator is called upon to function at two levels ... achieve rapport ... remain an essentially detached observer. Poor interrogators often confuse this bi-level functioning with role-playing, but there is a vital difference ... to be persuasive, the sympathy or

anger must be genuine; but to be useful, it must not interfere with the deeper level of precise, unaffected observation. Bi-level functioning is not difficult or even unusual; most people act at times as both performer and observer unless their emotions are so deeply involved in the situation that the critical faculty disintegrates."

Providing there is time available, there is a recommendation that sessions with resistant sources be held at varying hours to increase disorientation (pp. 49–50): "The subject may be left alone for days; and he may be returned to his cell, allowed to sleep for five minutes, and brought back ... the principle is that the session should be so planned as to disrupt the source's sense of chronological order."

In the manual, the term "coercive" is reserved for physical methods and threats of violence; however, there is some acknowledgment that the so-called non-coercive approaches represent significant pressure. A number of specific techniques are detailed which involve psychological trickery. The best known, of course, is the "good guy, bad guy" technique, but others involve playing on the potential for anxiety, guilt, and fear, often by setting up scenarios that convey false information to the interrogatee. Many of the mechanisms used within these scenarios are found in the hypnosis literature, especially referencing (Ericksonian) techniques that involve embedded messages and confusional communications.

In the section on coercive interrogations, moral issues are recognized but are quickly brushed aside as not within the province of the manual. As a practical matter, it is noted that psychological research supports that physical coercion may not produce accurate information. However, where the objective is to obtain generally low-level data, such as whether or not an individual is an agent, considerations of technical accuracy may not pertain.

There is a definite procedure for coercive interrogation. The sequence of events includes (p. 85): "arrest, detention, deprivation of sensory stimuli through solitary confinement or similar methods, threats and fear, debility, pain, heightened suggestibility and hypnosis, narcosis, and induced regression." This sequence and the techniques used to induce the various states are taken directly from psychological studies of brainwashing techniques used by the North Koreans as well as the work on sensory deprivation. Procedures also derived from experimentation that was at its midpoint by 1963 involving the use of drugs, alcohol, and hypnotic techniques were carried out by the CIA in clandestine ways (see Table A1). This work included as unwitting subjects such sources as military personnel, patients at a federal drug rehabilitation facility in Tennessee, and government employees. Included were both U.S. and non-U.S. citizens (Scheflin, 1978).

After pointing out some methods to reduce an individual's sense of integrity, such as not allowing clothing or providing clothing that does not fit, the focus is on sensory deprivation. There is a reference to experiments conducted at McGill University, where the now infamous Cameron work was completed. Among his other respected credentials, Cameron was president of the Canadian Psychiatric Association. He conducted drug regression experiments on civilians as part of CIA and U.S.-Canada sponsored research. His experimental subjects included a Member of Parliament's wife who was seriously deteriorated at the end of her so-called treatment for which she, of course, had not given informed consent. Ultimately, the knowledge of his malpractice was brought to the attention of authorities, and he was subjected to civil suit remedies. However, these steps did not succeed until 1988, 21 years after Cameron's death (Thomas, 1989).

With respect to hypnosis, after referencing Orne's work the manual proceeds to discuss its use to obtain admissions on the basis of false presumptions. Additionally, on the rare occasion when hypnosis is used, the importance of confusional techniques is emphasized as a means to obtain admissions in the face of internal resistance. This discussion is consistent with the experiments the CIA conducted which combined

TABLE A1

SELECTED EXAMPLES OF THE MISUSE OF PSYCHOLOGICAL AND RELATED SCIENCES

Date	Description	Source
11/16/51	Side-tone delay. Instrument which creates confusion by delayed feedback of speech during interrogation. Believed to increase changes of admission to guilt (Project Artichoke).	Office memorandum, U.S. Government, OSI
01/31/52	ESP Project. Presented as potentially beneficial. Related to the ongoing Project Bluebird. Noted the work of the Rhine Group at Duke University, where potentials of sensitive individuals were studied for capacity to predict future events or accurately represent distant current data.	Office memorandum, U.S. Government, OSI
02/12/52	Report of meeting where it was proposed to have stateside and overseas labs staffed by scientists, physicians (especially psychiatrists), and psychologists work on projects as described above.	Office memorandum, U.S. Government
07/14/52	Successful application of narco-hypnotic interrogation (Project Artichoke). Interrogated Soviet agents using CIA and medical personnel with drugs and hypnosis and obtained regression and amnesia for the interrogation.	Memorandum to the Director of the CIA
1954	Proposed experiment on a foreign national in which the subject was to be drugged and then attempts made to hypnotically implant an assassination act. Apparently rejected due to lack of control over the subject. Use of LSD and marijuana, and other drugs in experiments were noted. Possibilities of using electric shock, drugs, electromagnetic field, and ultrasonics, with lobotomy. The use of nonvoluntary subjects was contemplated with surreptitious hypnosis and narcosis to implement. The results obtained suggested the best subjects would be those already in medical treatment. Deprivation of food to reduce resistance was recommended per results of a study of POWs in Korea. Reactions noted to "deep hypnosis" included illness, negative psychological actions, and fatigue. Specific induction techniques were recommended (referencing the work of Adler and Secunder, Indirect techniques to induce hypnosis, *Journal of Nervous and Mental Disorders, 106*, 190–193, 1947).	Memorandum titled "Artichoke"
07/14/54	Results of experiments with increasing dosages of LSD and derivatives of marijuana.	Department of Health, Education, and Welfare; Public Health Service; National Institute of Mental Health; letter from Addiction Center of Lexington

Table A1 (continued)

Selected Examples of the Misuse of Psychological and Related Sciences

Date	Description	Source
03/21/55	Funding of Subproject 43 in the MKULTRA series for drugs and hypnosis; $20,000 granted to a "Dr. _____" at a university. Materials indicate there is a "true nature" of the project which required top-secret clearance.	Memo and letter; Source Handbook
11/15/55	Prediction of hypnotic susceptibility from knowledge of subject's attitudes, referencing the work of Morgan and Murray (1935) using the Thematic Apperception Test. Use of drugs and increased hypnotic susceptibility were discussed, referencing four sources (Baernsteain, 1928, 1929; Gorton, 1949; Wilson, 1927; Wolburg, 1948).	
1959+	Dr. Ewen Cameron, Allen Memorial Institute, Montreal, Canada. MKULTRA involved. Developed "psychic driving", which used drugs, prolonged sleep, regression, and tape recordings to impact selected psychiatric patients.	Memorandum MKULTRA, Subproject 68; see also Scheflin (1978), Thomas (1989); U.S. document
Undated	Proposal for research on aspects of mass conversion, study of cultic experiences. Purpose is to learn how to impact/control large groups of unwitting subjects.	U.S. document
11/20/59	Study of children's conceptions of occupational roles and status with the notion that it would serve government purposes.	Letter from government files stamped "Psycho"
12/17/63	Memo stamped "Eyes Only" that asserted the importance of using unwitting subjects.	Memo to Deputy Director of CIA on testing psycho-chemical and related material
1975	MKNAOMI projects. "Insofar as affecting human behavior was concerned, interests ranged from very temporary, minor displacement (such as inability to deliver a speech well) to more serious and longer incapacitation to death." Guidelines for the project included in records to be kept; assassination was included as an activity.	Memo on MKNAOMI
10/11/77	Unknown to Dr. Doris Twitchel Allen, the CIA was studying the children in her International Summer Village Program for possible future recruits. Research being done by Dr. Carolyn Scharoff on this project was funded by the CIA (unknown to Dr. Scharoff) One of the communications mentioned that an APA meeting was the setting for a contact for operatives who knew what was really occurring.	*NBC Nightly News* (John Chancellor); Department of Defense and CIA memoranda

Table A1 (continued)

Selected Examples of the Misuse of Psychological and Related Sciences

Date	Description	Source
1950–1980	Details for implementation of experiments, complete with the original and reputable scientific sources for some of the work, as well as commentary by the compiler. Emphasis was on experimentation with unwitting persons and children. This resource contains considerable speculative material, but the theories presented are not implausible. Examples of both experiments and individual victims of procedures are presented in detail, with sources which can be checked.	*Mind Control PWR-832* (1994; Prevailing Winds Research, P.O. Box 23511, Santa Barbara, CA)
1960–present	Gittinger's work began with the WAIS and use of subtest scores to identify personality types. Gittinger was recruited early on to work with the CIA in the experimentation programs including MKULTRA, Project Artichoke, and the like. Gittinger continues to occasionally present at CIA training sessions. His work was formalized as the Personality Assessment System Foundation (PASF) and was detailed by DuVivier (1992) There are ongoing seminars and CIA-sponsored organizations involved. The content of his manual (*An Introduction to the Personality Assessment System,* by John F. Winne and John W. Gittinger), as well as DuVivier's handbook, involve theory and applications consistent with CIA manuals. These seminars also feature Myers-Briggs typology approaches and information from that literature.	Scheflin (1978); Gorton (1989). Gittinger's publications can be found in the psychological literature for the 1950s and 1960s. Other sources are protected.

trickery and hypnotic states in order to get people to do things that they would not ordinarily do (Scheflin, 1978; Thomas, 1989).

Because of the importance in hypnosis of subject compliance with the procedure, the use of hypnotic drugs is recommended. An example of a sequence is as follows (p. 98):

"... administer a silent drug to a resistant source, persuade him as the drug takes effect and he is slipping into a hypnotic trance, place him under actual hypnosis as conscious[ness] is returning, shift his frame of reference so that his reasons for resistance become reasons for cooperating, interrogate him, and conclude the session by implanting the suggestion that when he emerges from trance, he will not remember anything about what has happened."

Human Resource Exploitation Training Manual, 1983

This manual was used in a number of Latin American countries from November 1982 through March 1987. An addendum, apparently dated 1984, states that torture is not authorized or condoned. Nonetheless, the manual goes into some detail regarding the arrest and detainment of persons. A process of psychological victimization is initiated, including blindfolding, showering with the blindfold on and others present, and a medical examination including body cavity searches. Questioning takes place after there is evidence of disorientation and regression.

The manual also discusses the use of interpreters and makes the point that psychological research suggests that "men and women both respond better to questioning by a male" (section C-4). It also references the fact that in societies where women are viewed as of inferior status, it is problematic to use them as interpreters. There are some fairly explicit discussions of the different ways of using interpreters — for example, alternate vs. simultaneous — which rest on findings from the study of language and the interpretation process.

As with the 1963 version of the KUBARK manual, the 1983 Human Resources Exploitation Training Manual contains a description of personality types. This typology is much more specifically developed in the 1983 manual with suggested approaches for specific personality types. Thus, the interrogation of a so-called orderly-obstinate subject whose childhood features often included acts of rebellion calls for a friendly, non-controlling interrogator. By contrast, the optimistic subject, often the youngest (and overindulged) member of a large family, is best handled by the "friend and foe" technique. The manual opines that a guilt-ridden subject often succumbs to punishment. It makes the point that these are guidelines and that specific individuals will have some combination of the various qualities. The typologies rest upon a psychological evaluation of the subject from both records, where possible, and initial screening that yields biographical data. Some of the screening techniques emphasize obtaining incidental information that is not viewed as important by the subject. Those data reflect associations, attitudes, and childhood events which may be useful in specifying the subject's type.

In the section on coercive techniques (which are officially disavowed), there are a number of handwritten changes, many of which accompany redacted sections. This "reform" was sloppily accomplished in a way that insured that all of the unacceptable instructions remain present. For example, the following handwritten note appears in the discussion about the use of force and coercion: "The use of most coercive techniques is improper and violated laws" (page number indecipherable). The manual then details ways to induce regression through prolonged exertion, heat, cold, moisture, and deprivation of food or sleep, etc. A section is crossed out about the importance of having a psychologist available because the subject may "sink into a defensive apathy from which it is hard to arouse him," and there is added: "this illustrates why this coercive technique may produce torture" (page number undecipherable). A series of specific psychological pressures are then detailed, including the randomization of events, which will lead to disorientation and lack of control.

The CIA's Nicaragua Manual

The main purpose of this manual was to train guerrilla forces to overthrow the then-existing government in Nicaragua. In the preface, it defines guerrilla warfare as "essentially a political war" (Omang and Neier, 1985, p. 33). The preface also states that the "human being should be considered the priority objective in a political war." The manual then proceeds to detail propaganda techniques and group dynamics methods. There is significant emphasis on group discussions, joining with the peasantry, and redefining in the tradition of double-speak the conditions under which they lived and understood their situation (p. 41): "The group discussion method and self-criticism are a general guerrilla training and operations technique." The description of these activities is similar to what Schein (1961) identified as POW brainwashing techniques. There is a discussion of devices which define an "us vs. them" re-education. The manual notes that while there must be a joining with the people, the fact that the guerrillas are armed allows a perception of them as potentially dangerous. Maintaining that implicit terror, while ostensibly being protective, is an appropriate part of controlling the populace. With regard to political oratory, there is a section that specifically instructs in the use of rhetoric and speech-making to persuade; these techniques are consistent with psychological research on primacy and recency. In addition to psychological techniques, there are very specific military techniques for infiltration, subversion of local autonomy, and overthrow of the government.

Other Examples

Table A1 provides a partial list of additional research and activities that reflect some government-sponsored misuses of psychological knowledge and techniques.

Conclusion

The recently released KUBARK and Human Exploitation manuals, as well as the Nicaraguan manual originally made public by *Soldier of Fortune* magazine ("Guerrilla war manual", 1995), contain considerable references to psychological research and techniques. The 1963 KUBARK manual includes an annotated bibliography. Much of the work was done in the pursuit of legitimate knowledge — understanding factors of social conformity, identifying variables that affect relationships and communications for purposes of psychotherapy enhancement, and understanding the scope and limitations of brainwashing techniques utilized in the 1930s and 1940s in the USSR and Communist China.

The manuals also reference materials on the study and training of police interrogation methods and the study of transference phenomena; however, a close reading of these manuals shows that they have also benefited from experiments that never involved legitimate aims and which were conducted under morally bankrupt auspices and procedures. This is particularly the case with hypnosis, where data from both therapeutic and scientific inquiries and from attempts to develop assassins have been included (Inbau and Reid, 1953; Meerlo, 1956; Biderman, 1959; Biderman and Zimmer, 1961; Scheflin, 1978; Thomas, 1989; Prevailing Winds Research, 1994, undated).

In the face of the overwhelming evidence that government agencies of the U.S. have supported, or continue to support, activities which violate the values of society, there has been denial, cover up, or minimization. No less an authority than the U.S. Supreme Court supported the CIA in maintaining secret the names of investigators and institutions involved in conducting the experiments (Central Intelligence Agency et al. v. Simms et al., 1986). The use of the manuals continued at least until 1992. In the Department of Defense's Inspector General's Report of February 21, 1997, there was reference to a March 1992 memorandum as to proper supervision of experiments. However, "little corrective action has been taken to insure that such abhorrent training materials are no longer used" (National Council of Churches, 1997, p. 1).

Finally, this author has obtained documentation of current use of psychological techniques, funded by the U.S. government and continuing under CIA auspices (see Table A1), involving the Gittinger Personality System and its accompaniment, the Myers-Briggs typology. Ostensibly new discoveries are often found to have historical referents. Certainly, torture techniques and the government-sponsored terrorism which now are dignified by psychological/scientific terminology are in many cases very old knowledge parading as new. The ability to extend torture and to use it for terroristic purposes is not a modern phenomenon. Nonetheless, the modern refinements of those primitive strategies serve to underscore the lack of moral development that characterizes a now highly technically competent society. The scientific and academic communities have clearly been not only sources of, but complicit partners in, U.S. versions of these activities. The changes which are needed depend upon trained professionals refusing to assist in, or ceasing to studiously ignore, the misuses which victimize and destroy instead of heal and actualize.

References

APA (1982) *Ethical Principles in the Conduct of Research with Human Participants*. Washington, D.C.: American Psychological Association.

APA (1992) *Ethical Principles in the Conduct of Research with Human Participants*. Washington, D.C.: American Psychological Association.

Biderman, A. (1959, March) *A Study of Development of Improved Interrogation Techniques*: Stud. SR (77-DW), Secret. Final report of contract AF 18 (600) 1797. Washington, D.C.: Bureau of Social Science Research.

Biderman, A. and Zimmer, H., Eds. (1961) *The Manipulation of Human Behavior*. New York: John Wiley & Sons.

Central Intelligence Agency et al. v Sims et al. (1986)

Commonwealth of Pennsylvania v. Nicola (1984) Suppression Hearing, Court of Common Pleas, Criminal Division, Erie County, 1980. Case Nos. 631–634.

Conway, F. and Siegelman, J. (1978) *Snapping*. New York: J.P. Lippincott & Co.

DuVivier, J. (1992) *Diagnosis and Treatment in Education*. New York: University Press of America.

Fischer, M. (1997) Teaching torture. *GQ*, June, pp. 182–189, 237–240.

Gudjonsson, G. (1992) *The Psychology of Interrogations, Confessions and Testimony*. New York: John Wiley & Sons.

Guerrilla war manual (1995) *Soldier of Fortune*. February, pull-out section: FM 95-1A.

Hassan, S. (1988) *Combating Cult Mind Control*. Gloucester, VT: Park Street Press.

Human Resource Exploitation Training Manual (1983).

Inbau, F. and Reid, J. (1953) *Lie Detection and Criminal Investigation*. New York: Williams & Wilkins.

Inbau, F., Reid, J., and Buckley, J. (1986) *Criminal Interrogation and Confessions*, 3rd ed. Baltimore: Wilkens & Wilkins.

Korn, J. (1997) *Illusions of Reality: A History of Deception in Social Psychology*. Albany: State University of New York Press.

KUBARK Counterintelligence Interrogation Manual (1963) July.

Lifton, R. (1954) Home by ship: reaction patterns of American prisoners of war repatriated from North Korea. *American Journal of Psychiatry, 110*, 732–739.

Lifton, R. (1957) Chinese communist "thought reform": confession and re-education of western civilians. *Bulletin of the New York Academy of Medicine*, September, p. 33.

Lifton, R. (1961) *Thought Reform and the Psychology of Totalism*. New York: W.W. Norton.

Lifton, R. (1986) *The Nazi Doctors: Medical Killing and the Psychology of Genocide*. New York: Basic Books.

Meerlo, J. (1956) *The Rape of the Mind*. Cleveland: World Publishing.

Milgram, S. (1974) *Obedience to Authority: An Experimental View*. New York: Harper & Row.

National Council of Churches (1997) *Inspector General's Report on Army Manuals: A Feeble Response; What the Recently Declassified Manuals Contain*. February 24.

Ofshe, R. and Singer, M. (1986) Attacks on peripheral versus central elements of self and the impact of thought reforming techniques. *The Cultic Studies Journal, 3*(1), 3–24.

Omang, J. and Neier, A. (1985) *Psychological Operations in Guerrilla Warfare*. New York: Random House.

Orne, M. (1961) The potential uses of hypnosis in interrogation. In A. Biderman and H. Zimmer (Eds.), *The Manipulation of Human Behavior*. New York: John Wiley & Sons.

Prevailing Winds Research (1994) *Project MKULTRA: Secret Documents From the CIA's Infamous Program To Control the Human Mind.* PWR-831.

Prevailing Winds Research (undated) *Mind Control*. PWR-832.

Raskin, D. (1989) *Psychological Methods in Criminal Investigation and Evidence*. New York: Springer Publishing.

Scheflin, A. (1978) *The Mind Manipulators: Techniques of Coercive Mind Control*. New York: Grosse & Dunlap, Paddington Press.

Schein, E. (1961) *Coercive Persuasion*. New York: W.W. Norton.

Singer, M. (1987) Group psychodynamics. In R. Berkow (Ed.), *The Merck Manual of Diagnosis and Therapy*, 15th ed., pp. 1461–1471. NJ: Merck, Sharp and Cohme Research Laboratories.

Singer, M. and Schein, E. (1958) Projective test responses of prisoners of war following repatriation. *Psychiatry*, (21).

Sullivan, H. (1954) *The Psychiatric Interview*. New York: W.W. Norton.

Thomas, G. (1989) *Journey Into Madness*. New York: Bantam Books.

United Nations Truth Commission Report on El Salvador (1993) March 15.

Walters, N. (1997) The secret of SOA's "torture manuals". *Columbus Ledger Enquirer*, April 20.

West, L. and Singer, M. (1980) Cults, quacks and nonprofessional psychotherapies. In H. Kaplan, A. Freedman, and B. Sadoch (Eds.), *Comprehensive Textbook of Psychiatry*, III, pp. 3245–3258. Baltimore: Williams & Wilkins.

About the Author

Sandra B. McPherson, Ph.D., received her Ph.D. from Case Western Reserve University in Cleveland, OH. She has diplomate status in both clinical and forensic psychology from the American Board of Professional Psychology. She divides her time between a largely forensic practice in Cleveland and teaching for the Fielding Institute based in Santa Barbara, CA. She has developed special expertise in death penalty mitigation, having worked with many defendants currently on Ohio's death row. Her work in this area began with the first case to be brought under the state's revised capital punishment statute. In addition to the other areas of criminal responsibility work, she is particularly active in domestic relations cases, with special emphasis on problems of sexual abuse allegations and the development of court-worthy psychological evaluations. She is a member of the American Psychological Association and the Ohio Psychological Association, of which she has served as president. She is a former president of the State Board of Psychology. Any correspondence concerning this article should be addressed to Sandra B. McPherson, 12434 Cedar Road, Suite 15, Cleveland, Ohio 44106.

Appendix B

PHOENIX PROGRAM

John Doe

As I crouch in the underbrush at the southern edge of the jungle clearing, the early morning sounds are soothing, reminiscent of the farm in rural Tennessee. Chickens are strutting in front of the house, clucking to be fed and watered, scrambling and scuffling with each other, creating a subdued din of chatter. A peaceful scene.

Out of the corner of my eye, I see the old man come out of the hooch. He bends over, picks up the bag of rough, brown cornfeed and starts feeding the chickens. I've spent a long time studying this scenario, playing the options over and again, until I'm certain that I can get the job done without being seen. Certain, too, that what I am about to do is necessary.

I have been told that the old man is a traitor to the South Vietnamese cause, a Communist sympathizer, and a clear danger to achieving pacification and political stability in this area of South Vietnam. His dossier is fat, full of information collected about him since before the French were overthrown in 1952. He's been around for a long time, had a lot to do with how the war has not progressed in this area. The dossier says he fought with the Viet Minh against the Japanese, and later the French, and was a leader in the overthrow of the Bao Dai. He is considered a patriarch of freedom, and nationalism in his sphere of influence. The reports describe him as a quiet, unassuming man, a rice farmer, family man, and as wise politically as he is influential. Too bad he is on the wrong side.

Overall, we have not been particularly successful in convincing these particular villagers that the South's political future is assured as soon as the fighting ends and that the politicians can hammer out a democratic form of government that will bring about the desperately needed changes in the government, the economy, and the society as a whole. This man stands in the way of all that.

His looks are deceiving, actually, disarming. He doesn't resemble any of my pictures of a political big wig, or even a soldier, although I can imagine him 30 years younger, lean and mean after spending so much time in the jungle commanding Nationalist forces against the Japanese and French. He looks like everyman, everyone, and no one.

The old man is making a dance of the feeding ritual. From here, it looks like the Tai Chi movements I learned early on in my career as part of my martial arts training. Very smooth, easy movements, precisely placing his feet and gracefully tossing the corn pellets to the birds.

The bullet hits him in the head as he turns to answer someone talking to him from inside the building. He never knows what hit him. The silencer effectively muffles the sound of the shot. There is a cry from inside the hut. People are gathering around the body, and the alarm sounds. Younger men are scurrying about, some with weapons.

I quickly disassemble the sniper rifle and pack it away. Picking up my gear in a large briefcase, I hurry back to the old jeep parked a couple of hundred meters away, hidden among the brush along the side of the road. The drive back to Hue is pleasant.

I send a brief radio message to my headquarters states, "The bird is nested." And I'm done for the day.

Breakfast at the Circle Sportif is leisurely and satisfying, as is the conversation with the waiters and some of the well-to-do locals; they inquire about my latest news story. I tell them I am writing a story about the pacification efforts and the civic action programs being introduced to them by the Vietnamese government. To them, I am one of hundreds of civilian newspaper people who wander about the country these days. They don't know I am a soldier.

As I reflect on the mission, I wonder about this very special kind of warfare. Counter-insurgency. The teachings of Sun Tsu, Mao Tse Tsung, and Che Gueverra provide the blueprints for what we are doing now.

Not so surprisingly, the other side has been using these same tactics and strategies since the 1930s; they're more practiced and effective, their intelligence is better and more timely, but we have the technological advantage in this war. We can win this war at will by applying that technology. It is a sacred duty we have taken upon ourselves, to help the Vietnamese people win their freedom. That is the party line.

So, why are we losing?

The Phoenix Program is supposed to be secret. The oath and the warnings that came with accepting this assignment made it clear. A $10,000 fine, 10 years in prison — the minimum punishment for divulging anything about this operation to unauthorized personnel. Not a warning to be taken lightly. And, that may be why there are so few of us involved. Or, maybe it's just that I don't know all the people involved.

I know only three other soldiers who have been brought into the operation, one of whom is my boss, Lieutenant Colonel John Ballard, who wears Infantry brass and no nametapes on his camouflage fatigues. It did not take long in our first meeting to figure out that that was likely a cover. He did not come across as a soldier's soldier the way most Infantry officers do. No. There was something about him. His jeep was unmarked. The chopper that brought him to the base camp was also unmarked. CIA trappings, non-standard weaponry and tactics.

He has been in this part of the world for a long time, speaks the language like a native, knows the history, cultural traditions, the economic and political landscapes with precision and certainty. He has all the answers to the questions that came up for me when we were planning this particular sortie. I admired his skill and his extensive knowledge. He was a little on the scary side.

For all intents and purposes, he could pass for a university professor, on sabbatical, doing economic and cultural research for the U.S. Agency for International Development. I think that's how some people knew him. Maybe the uniform was a gimmick to help him deal with any potential problems with the few of us who actually were soldiers.

A few weeks later, I off-load the chopper in a distant base camp. This place looks more like a military post. A lot of other Green Berets. I feel at home instantly.

Ballard tells me that we're going to interdict a medium-size border crossing from Cambodia into the delta region of the country. The North Vietnamese Army (NVA) has a couple of infantry divisions camped out just across the border, guarding the routes into Vietnam along the rivers and trails that lace the area like spider webs. We are set to jump off at first light, following a Rolling Thunder blast over the area earlier in the morning. The fighter support from the Marine base at Danang is due in just before we hit the silk, so we'll very likely be moving into a hot Landing Zone.

At 0400, we are alerted that there is a village along the way that has to be taken out before we cross the border. This area has been in Communist hands for years, in spite of the fact that we run search and destroy operations almost daily in some part of the Corps zone. Ballard tells me that I will move in ahead of the main force, along with two other snipers. Our job is to get into close proximity to the village, on the Cambodian side, and set up Claymore mines along one of the main trails out of the village, then position ourselves so that we can snipe at anything moving along the trail, once the fireworks start. We are told that we are not to take prisoners, that all of these people are Communist sympathizers. There are no civilian friendlies in the area.

As the dawn breaks, we're in position, well-hidden in the tall trees that form the canopy over the narrow jungle trail, and far enough away from the village proper to be relatively safe from any stray ordinance from the bombers and fighters. The sound of the heavy bombs from the B-52s is deafening for a few minutes. I think, had I not been aware of it happening, the sudden breaking of the silence of the jungle with all of the explosives would have rattled me to the bone. As it was, it was an awesome experience.

As soon as the first bomb exploded, people in the village began moving. In the village itself, there must have been panic and chaos. Here in the jungle, we waited for the stream of villagers to approach. Looking down the trail toward the village, people were scrambling for cover, many of them opening spider holes, escaping into a network of underground tunnels that offered the only possible escape from the death and destruction of the bombing raid.

The fighters were now overhead, making strafing runs along the riverbanks and right down through the middle of the village. Bodies were everywhere, mutilated dead and wounded, men, women, and children. There was no mercy in this little campaign.

Then the first group of people moved along the trail. Flanking the trail like dutiful soldiers, they stepped into the line of fire of the Claymores. Another brief holocaust from the blast of the mines, then silence. No survivors.

The second group came on, more slowly and cautiously than the first. And, they were armed. This looks more like the conventional ground battle. The odds are more even. They, too, step into the kill zone of the Claymores. Several big blasts, then silence.

We climb out of the safety of the trees, moving slowly along the trail. Half a dozen dead in various states of dismemberment. Two villagers are alive, a man and a woman, both seriously wounded. This is mercy killing. They expected it. I think they were almost thankful.

I didn't see the kids at first. Three boys. They must be about 14 or 15 years old. One of them has a rifle; the other two are unarmed. A short burst from the Swedish K and it's over. They knew, too. They didn't run when they saw us. They didn't cry, or offer any resistance. They knew.

The debriefing for this mission was short. We reported the success of the mission. There were no prisoners, no survivors. And, we lost no one on this outing.

The Phoenix Program was built around the notion that in order to establish a viable pro-American, pro-democratic form of government, it is necessary to rid the current government of corruption and adversarial political influences. This philosophy has afforded conquering military forces disposition of the vanquished for as long as humankind has waged war. The means for accomplishing this goal, for many of the oppositional elements, is simple: kill them, and by doing so, weaken the resistance and create terror and confusion among the enemy. In this effort, there are no rules, beyond individual survival of each of us as operatives, and total secrecy with regard to who we are, where we come from, and for whom we work.

My bases of operations are Saigon, Danang, and Hue City. In all three areas, the cover is that of being civilian technicians, journalists, and advisors to the civilian communities, under the auspices of the Agency for International Development.

Overtly, the Agency provides technical assistance to local governments, down to and including villages, along with equipment, supplies, and monies. Everyone knows, or likely suspects, that the Agency is also doubling as a collection resource for information on the political, economic, and diplomatic status of all government agencies and personnel working for the South Vietnamese.

The Vietnamese who work for the Agency are all bilingual, at least, and many of them speak French as well as English, in addition to their native tongue. Very few Americans speak Vietnamese with any kind of fluency; fewer still have any appreciation of the historical struggle of the Vietnamese people against the Chinese for over 300 years, then the French and Dutch Colonialists, and now, the Americans.

These people are enured to hardships occasioned by their continuous fight to preserve the autonomy and integrity of their culture and lands. They are a proud people, and, like the Chinese, have a grasp of history that allows them to see their future over the long term. Their commitment to sovereignty is unshakable. This alone accounts for our losing the war.

In the military establishment, the Phoenix Program included another aspect of counter-insurgency that got a lot more attention — the Chieu Hoi Program. The Chieu Hoi were those South Vietnamese Communists and North Vietnamese soldiers captured alive, recruited as double agents, and sent back to the field with combat units to lead them to Viet Cong (VC) and NVA hideouts, supply depots, and enemy controlled areas of the countryside, with the idea of ferreting out other Communist sympathizers and destroying them. Similar to other aspects of the Phoenix Program, Chieu Hoi were killed outright at the first sign of defection back to the other side. The defection rates were high, in the 70 to 80% range. Even so, they were often lower than the desertion rates in some of the active military units conscripted by the South Vietnamese government.

Both sides conscripted in similar ways. Objections were often met with brutal violence against individuals or families, or even whole villages. At a place called Phu Loc, deep in the rice country of the Delta region, I witnessed the vicious retaliation exacted on its residents by a South Vietnamese officer, Dai Oui Ai, who burned the entire village because a handful of young conscripts escaped into the marshland and successfully evaded being drafted into military service.

More than 30 people died as the village was razed. Dai Oui Ai called it his version of the "scorched Earth" philosophy taught to him by his American advisor, U.S. Army Captain George K. Hodges. Hodges was proud of his accomplishment, and took credit for a body count of enemy soldiers and insurrectionists. He was a former Green Beret officer who struck me as having "lost it" on his second tour of duty in Vietnam, when his base camp was overrun and most of his troops were either killed or captured. He hated "gooks" and, being an Arkansas redneck, he also hated "niggers", Poles, Jews, and Russians. Rumor had it, he also likes to rape young girls captured and believed to be VC soldiers or sympathizers. Rape was a part of his routine interrogation techniques.

Some weeks later, much farther north, a group of us moved into a hut in the MACV compound in Hue City. Spartan accommodations, down to the French latrine that accommodated both sexes, sometimes simultaneously — a hole in the floor over which one squatted to defecate into a drainage pipe that emptied into the gutter like a waterway leading to the Perfume River. Raw sewage. No processing plant. And, a smell that would, on particularly hot days, sicken the stomach.

The occasion for this trip was taking out a source of resistance in the civilian community — a Lutheran missionary and his family, who ran a small chapel and a medical clinic that provided assistance to refugees and the homeless. The dossier indicated that he was also very active politically, encouraging villagers not to become involved in supporting either the Viet Cong or the South Vietnamese government. The area was a no man's land, not particularly hostile and very little enemy activity that we could find. It did, however, flank a known North Vietnamese supply route that began some 45 klicks north of the DMZ and wound its way south along the coastal sand dunes and marshes, making it considerably easier to transport weapons and ammunition than via the alternate route along the densely jungled Laotian border route to the west.

This operation would be about "discouraging" the missionary from his activities, sort of a warning to him to disengage from the political arena. The mission was to simply stage an "attack" on him and make it look like the Viet Cong were responsible. The actual plan was to rocket his home and mission at a time when he and his family were away from the facility. We were to recruit a few local Regional Popular Forces (RF/PF) troops whom we would dress in black pajamas and who would supervise the attack. The RF/PF troops would put up a smoke screen, fire a lot of ordinance in the general direction of the facility, then fade away into the night.

What actually happened was the attack went as planned, only the good Reverend and his family members were in the house when the attack began. The missionary himself was not wounded, but his two children were critically injured, and his wife was killed outright.

After the attack, we put on our "good guys" hat and "rescued" the missionary and his family and medivaced them to Danang. We then mounted a "chase" for the alleged attackers with a Mike Force contingent from Phu Bai, American regular troops who were not involved in the "attack". Plausible denial, in the face of an operational fuckup that cost the life of one innocent civilian and untold injury to others. Routine stuff that.

The Agency's command centers looked like any business office, except for the unusual communications gear visible throughout the installation — high frequency microwave antennas and relay stations, steel-lined communications bunkers, and a range of weapons, explosive devices, and equipment that were far more sophisticated and advanced than the equipment routinely issued to American soldiers assigned to ground combat units or support facilities.

High-ranking military officers were frequent visitors, but beyond that, there were no uniforms in sight. The "technicians" were, on the whole, academic types, bright, articulate, solidly indoctrinated into the party line. It was in this complex arena that the targets were identified and the information organized and provided to the specific operatives whose mission was to eliminate them.

Somewhere, higher in the chain of command, there was someone who approved each mission on an individual basis. The country team, whose chief was the U.S. Ambassador, issued the orders; dossiers were assembled and disseminated via courier to each of the smaller teams, whose job it was to complete the missions. Highly compartmentalized, few knew who did what, particularly among the actual shooters. I came to believe that the whole program was the brainchild of the Central Intelligence Agency, sold to the President based on an analysis of the history of colonial involvement in this part of the world.

The Chinese and Japanese provided the structural architecture for the general operations, based on their operations in Indochina, Cambodia, Thailand, and Burma during World War II, and, later in Korea, where it was necessary to disrupt the political will and structure of any organized resistance to being taken over by force.

The State Department denies the purpose and intention of the program and, specifically, its methods. I often wondered why they didn't just hire mercenaries, the Mafia, or someone like that. The conclusion I came to is that it was about security, plausible denial, closely held control, and political cover your ass. There was always a question of trust and loyalty with outsiders; a home-grown hit team was more reliable and secure.

Ballard was a stickler for detail. Every individual mission usually called for at least several weeks of intense study of the area of operation (AO), escape routes, and access routes, schedules, routines, and the specific information regarding each target. There was no margin for error. Rehearsals — skills drills, he called them — made for perfection in planning and execution. As far as I know, there was never an unsuccessful mission on our team (in spite of the occasional errors, as noted above with the Missionary), and we never lost an operative on a mission during my three tours of duty in-country.

I don't think I was alone in questioning a lot of what we were doing in Vietnam. At the time, however, I was as "gung ho" a young soldier as any Army could want. I was already a committed career soldier, and had, from the moment of entry into active duty, been selected from a small group of volunteers for special assignments. All of my training, from Basic Infantry throughout my "Advanced Individual Training" and the subsequent specialized training, groomed me for the kinds of assignments described above.

Politically, I was unsophisticated, though not quite naive, and my values were to "God and Country" followed by the Agency and anything else, including family. I was exactly the kind of soldier the Agency wanted for the "dirty tricks" details that became so popular during the earlier stages of the war. The earlier stages included most of what went on prior to our committing ground combat units to the effort. During the early and mid-1960s, few Americans knew anything about Vietnam, much less where in the world it is, and what we were doing there. If anything, most people were only aware of a place called "French Indochina", where the French colonialists had been unseated from power during the 1950s, an area being contested by the democratic "free world" and the awesome specter of communist domination. This was a recurring political theme that provided most of us with the emotional commitment to do things we ordinarily might not. I learned early on that what we were doing was preventing the "domino effect" from occurring in Southeast Asia, a favorite political theory of the time, in a world scared silly of being overrun by the "Red Hordes", whether Russian or Chinese.

It was also during this time that I began to be aware of the degree to which our own propaganda might be just that and based on a faulty set of political precepts. What I experienced on the ground in Vietnam didn't fit the pictures painted for me by my tutors at Langley, Fort Holabird, and the Defense Intelligence Agency.

The more I got into the history of the region, the more I began to realize that the Vietnamese were (and are) a proud and very nationalistic group of people. One whose culture and traditions extend much further into the past than our own. They boast a history of successfully defeating a wide range of threats to their sovereignty — from the Chinese, the Dutch, and the French — during the previous 300 years.

I began to question the wisdom of our intervention in their political and domestic affairs. Gnawing questions that I didn't have the answers to and, as I soon discovered, would not be encouraged to explore any further. Such is the nature of the internal politics of the military. Questioning the command's wisdom wasn't part of the job description.

So much of the confusion for me, personally, that came as I had to eventually deal with being a Vietnam veteran, came about by virtue of the way in which we were being treated, and especially so after the conclusion of the fighting and we were running in defeat for our own shores. Being met at the airports and railways at home by people hostile to the war and dealing with the derision and public ridicule offered to us by "protesters" and others whom we collectively referred to as the "long-haired hippy freaks" caused a lot of heartache for most of us who participated in the war, and particularly those of us who were wounded in the fights. The feeling of being unsupported by our government, and even our friends and families, was as traumatic as any of the events that occurred to us individually or collectively, and made healing virtually impossible for many of us.

Years after these experiences, my analysis of the events, including the political considerations, was much different from what I came to during the immediacy of the experiences. Of particular concern were those issues which define the parameters of the struggle with my own PTSD issues, and recovery from those experiences.

So, what did I learn? Actually, quite a bit, particularly about the things needed for recovery from the devastation that the war was for me. I speak of the devastation not from a victim perspective, but in acknowledgment of the impact that those events had, and continue to have, on my life, even today. The personal costs for me included losing a family, three failed marriages altogether, being unable to commit to or work with external authority figures, hence a record of employment problems that most folks likely don't face in the normal course of their socialization. Talk to any Vietnam veteran. The themes are so consistent and similar it's scary.

What was damaged the most, from one point of view, were the values to which I subscribed during most of my military career. I bought into the American dream of the 1950s — hard work pays, loyalty to God and Flag, and "our way of life." All of that. The war destroyed any illusions I have had, and absolutely killed any hope of regaining that trust in the government which for me was so important for so many years.

I don't know if there's any way to prevent the institutionalized violence that these stories depict, given the nature of governments in the modern world. The arts of diplomacy fail us on a regular enough basis that we can count on there being wars and conflicts for the foreseeable future. Short of disarming the whole planet, peace will likely continue to elude us. The "cause", if you will, of this kind of problem solving, from one perspective appears to lie in our basic predatory nature.

Civilization has not developed to a level where all men can breathe freely without fear, and prosper in harmony with Great Nature. We are still savages, so close to our barbaric natures that the veneer of civilization quickly falls away as we decompensate into defensive strategies based on the fear of losing political or economic advantage in a world that still prizes competition in the extreme. Sane men, in a world that is essentially insane, often have a difficult time being heard, much less heeded. Yet, sanity exists, and eventually Great Nature brings us to our knees when we tread too far afield from the natural order of things. Ultimately, I believe that we will evolve as a species; I just don't expect to be on board when it happens. Not in my lifetime.

The practical matters that emerge for those of us caught up in the institutional violence depicted above, are not without some hope, or help. If we are capable of learning from our experiences, then there are some lessons free for the taking. From my perspective, some of them are as follows:

In the *political arena*, attending to the influence and directions that governments take in administering the public good, we would be better served by a government in which the people are more active participants. Many Americans don't vote, their voices are never heard, and an overwhelming sense of powerlessness encroaches on our historical values around freedom, democracy, human dignity and rights, and good social order which are debilitated by a professional governmental bureaucracy that has long since abandoned its highest ideals.

Our current political process more closely resembles the forms we have for such a long time rebelled against (e.g., the dictatorial fascist, Communist, or autocratic forms that we so vehemently decry) but, in practice, embrace by virtue of our laziness and lack of understanding of history. We are, therefore, doomed to repeat it until we get it right.

For as long as individuals and governments devalue human life, atrocities will persist, the biggest of which is war. From my personal perspective, I recognized just how uncivilized I can be under certain circumstances. Years of reflecting on this question lead me to understand that, as a species, we are not far removed from our Neanderthal cousins; our brains are those of the earliest members of our tribes, psychologically and emotionally hard-wired for survival in the wild. The physiological responses we carry around are poorly organized for the current conditions in the world, and even more poorly mediated by our current social agendas and conditioning responses. I don't know what the answer to this one is; perhaps, only time and conscious effort in the direction of becoming more socially responsive will elicit the changes in our basic natures in the direction of civilization, peace, and harmony with Nature, not the current stance of challenging Nature and blatant disruption of the inherent dynamic balance that Nature is.

Our current political attitudes and behaviors are shaped by philosophies of one sort or another, the foci of which are primarily on the issues of the distribution of wealth; power over and control of physical and personal space; and economic growth or advantage, or both. These philosophies embody the concepts of individualism and competition rather than community and cooperation. In short, our social institutions are ill-equipped to consider alternatives; they are too busy with the business of perpetuating themselves, much like the professional politician seeking term after term.

In the area of *prevention of institutional violence*, for as long as humanity persists in its current struggle for dominance, wars will persist, and all the things that go with the savagery and barbarisms of war. Individually and collectively, our attitudes do not support peace and balance. On the contrary, we steep ourselves in vicarious violence, even while we attempt to deny our use of it as a political tool. The schism thus created by a government in denial and distortion affects us all and creates and perpetuates a sense of distrust, fear, and avoidance from the masses. Practically, our government is not one of, for, and by the people, but is only one more form of tyranny, exacted in both subtle and not-so-subtle disinformation, duplicity, and corruption from the top to the bottom. We are approaching a time of revolution rather than evolution. A populace overburdened by unfair taxation, unreasonable laws, selective enforcement of laws, and non-representation of the public in governmental decision-making is currently experiencing the same conditions that led to our rebellion as a group over 200 years ago and to the founding of the Republic. One has to wonder how this revolution will come about. Perhaps, another civil war, as well as other wars based on economic issues. The future does not look rosy.

So, how do we deal with these issues? I would begin by impeaching the current political structures, replacing all of the professional politicians with ordinary people; reducing the size of government and its influence over the states in shaping social policies and standards, avoiding the tendency to legislate morality and civic sameness. Our hopes really lie in promoting and negotiating our creative diversity, achieving accommodation and inclusion, rather than the current push toward social conformity and compliance.

With respect to the question of how to prevent future young Americans from participating in these kinds of operations, I doubt that there is a preventative so long as the Government continues to indoctrinate its young soldiers into the political and social beliefs that inform government operations (e.g., as long as we believe that other nations are engaging in similar activities, then we effectively have no choice but to counter with similar strategies and tactics). The appeal, of course, is to our sense of what it takes not only to survive in a hostile environment, but what it may take to prevail in such local conflicts.

Another just as important question has to do with the matter of treating soldiers who are suffering from

PTSD as a result of their involvement in these kinds of operations. I can't speak to the issues from having treated other Phoenix-type exposure clients; however, I have treated PTSD in a range of combat-related exposure scenarios with considerable success. And, I have my own experiences of the war upon which to reflect and consider these questions as they relate to my own PTSD symptoms. The truth is, the symptoms persist; however, they have abated somewhat in terms of frequency and intensity over the years, and my judgment with regard to what helped and what didn't may be useful to some.

First, I think that my status as a career soldier did, in some sense, mitigate some of the symptoms insomuch as I was embedded in a support system in which the experiences of war are a part of the normal set of expectation for soldiers. In that system, I was fortunate enough to have been associated with a psychiatrist who was, himself, a World War II and Korean combat veteran and who knew all that was known about how to treat "battle fatigue", as it was then still being called.

Secondly, I think my general understanding of the political and historical issues surrounding the war itself was helpful to me in coming to terms with the more pervasive, secondary traumata associated with having our own political structure operating in a system of denial, avoidance of responsibility and disinformation regarding our involvement in the war, and the manner in which veterans, in general, were treated by the system. I speak now of things like the denial of our use of such chemicals as Agent Orange and other biological weaponry, and the impact such things had on our own troops as well as the Vietnamese.

Having been married to a Vietnamese woman (who was killed by the Viet Cong) was another assist, in some very important ways. That relationship and the learning that it offered me with regard to the history, language, and culture of the Vietnamese people were critical supports for me in dealing with the lack of integrity and deceptiveness of my own government regarding most aspects of the war. My Vietnamese wife gave me a much clearer sense of the historical and cultural values that dominate the daily lives of the Vietnamese people. Understanding that allowed me to sort through the propaganda promulgated by our own system, and come to a valuing of their civilization, and my role in the war effort. A very sobering and difficult body of knowledge to reconcile.

Over the years, I have come to believe that the U.S. Government was the aggressor in that war and that we allied ourselves with our political clones in the Vietnamese government, most of whom were of a dictatorial bent, and all of whom were corrupted by our influence and political persuasion, not to mention the millions of dollars we spent to buy political influence and economic advantage.

I think sometimes of General Nguyen Kao Ki, whom we bought while he was head of the Vietnamese air forces and who later became one of a string of Vietnamese political puppets. He now lives someplace in California and owns a string of franchise food establishments. He lives high on the hog with monies stolen from the Vietnamese people and the U.S. Government. His payoff continues to this day, and there are literally hundreds of other such people whom we bought and paid for, now living in the U.S., part of their reward for betraying their country, and politically selling out to our "promises" of wealth in the land of the big PX.

My personal bitterness and resentments are very troublesome at times, particularly when, in the course of my routine work, I have to deal with government bureaucrats. They are the same in all times and places — inept, corrupt, small-minded, and lacking both vision and integrity with respect to the business of the public.

What I have seen evolving during the past 30 years with respect to the federal and state governments frightens me to no end. The corruption, disinformation, denial, and malfeasance on the part of government workers at all levels appear to have created a level of distrust and dissatisfaction with the way things are, such that the citizenry is quickly becoming fed up with the lies, the corruption, the lack of focus, and callous disregard for the public trust, such that I fear an insurrection on our own soil: a revolution against what may be the most viable form of government the world has ever known.

Sadly, the events of recent years, e.g., the Oklahoma City bombing, the Waco, Texas, stand-off, and other terroristic and socially disruptive acts by a variety of individuals and groups, speak to the level of frustration ordinary people experience in dealing with a government that has become unfair, inept to the extreme, and disabusing of the ordinary rights of citizens. One doesn't have to be a genius to figure out that something is seriously wrong with how things are going. One does have to be circumspect and have a perspective on the events within the context of our history, in order to understand the meaning of such social tragedies. As a nation, Vietnam tore us apart; the aftermath of that hasn't abated in the 30 years since it became apparent that the federal government was both imprudent and wrong in engaging in the War. The series of lies and betrayals foisted upon the citizenry since then have only exacerbated the levels of distrust and the lack of confidence in the political process.

At some level, I can't help but believe that all of that is a part of a much larger plan by the bureaucrats in power, to further extend the powers of the State into the lives of all of us as individuals, and a denial and erosion of the fundamental principles of human freedom and dignity upon which our Republic was founded.

APPENDIX C

TOWARD A GENOCIDE EARLY WARNING SYSTEM*

Israel W. Charny and Chanan Rapaport

"I came home a little afraid for my country, afraid of what it might want and get, and like, under pressure of combined reality and illusion. I felt — and feel — that it was not Germany Man that I had met, but Man. He happened to be in Germany under certain conditions. He might, under certain conditions, be me." —Milton Mayer

"Ideas, even simple ones, have remarkable vitality, even propagate themselves and spread to new areas. History is full of examples of ideas which seemed at first too naive to be taken seriously, developing finally into movements of great power. Any voice raised against evil is better than no voice." —Anna W.M. Wolf

Frequently we read in *The New York Times* or its counterparts around the world that in such and such a place on our planet, groups of people of such and such color, nationality, or religion have been murdered. Those of us who care sigh and worry a moment but soon return to our immediate concerns. Were we to track the process of our inner experience during such moments, we would probably find that we feel a deep sense of impotence mingled with sadness and concern. However, since it is painful to continue to feel a deep sense of helplessness, with rare exceptions we turn the experience off, and it is all over in a flash of a few minutes. Once we feel that there is really nothing we can do about what is happening, it is maddening to continue feeling so deeply. We turn off our emotions and return to the small and large events of our lives about which we feel we can do something. We turn our energies to areas of our living in which we can continue to feel alive, and we turn away from a problem of death about which we feel so helpless that it might draw us further toward our own death.

Now and then, journalists pick up news of genocidal events and provide some degree of continuity of coverage in their reports to their newspapers or broadcast stations. These are not "big stories", generally speaking. Sometimes a story is covered in an in-depth feature in a Sunday newspaper section or magazine, but reports of genocide are not treated with the electricity that is accorded to news reports of other types of societal upheaval or disaster. Nor are reports of genocide treated with a sense of immediacy or

* Reprinted in its original form with permission of the senior author, Israel W. Charny. Originally published in 1982 in *How Can We Commit the Unthinkable? Genocide: The Human Cancer*, Boulder, Co: Westview Press, pp. 283–331. A paperback edition was published in 1983 under the title *Genocide, the Human Cancer: How Can We Commit the Unthinkable?* New York: Hearst Professional Books. A Portuguese translation of the book, retitled *Thinking the Unthinkable*, with an updated introduction and bibliography, was published in 1997 by Editora Rosa dos Tempos in Rio de Janeiro, Brazil.

urgency. For the most part, the tacit understanding is that the peoples and nations of our world do not react to news of genocidal events with any great emotion, and certainly they are not going to take any collective action to stop a slaughter.[1]

There are some public groups, sometimes organized as quasi-governmental or quasi-international agencies, that do take a professional responsibility for following and reporting the facts of genocides that erupt in our strange world. However, these groups do not represent a major force in the shaping of world public opinion or of the responses of international agencies. To our knowledge, no such agency is significant by way of its reputation for accuracy and comprehensiveness of information or by way of its actual or symbolic status in the spectrum of agencies that represent man's efforts at international organizations, although the fact that the Nobel Peace Prize was awarded to Amnesty International in 1977 for its reporting and efforts on behalf of the imprisoned and tortured is an indication that some significant progress has been made.[2]

In the years after the Holocaust of the Jewish people in Europe and the explosion of the atomic bomb on Hiroshima and Nagasaki began to be assimilated, there have been some indications of a growing concern about genocide. However, if such a concern is to build a meaningful momentum, new organizations and institutions will be needed to translate the concern about genocide into effective international law, communication, and action.[3] In December 1948, the United Nations drafted a Convention on the Prevention and Punishment of the Crime of Genocide. This extension of international law gained sufficient signatures to go into effect on January 12, 1951, but it has never been tested as a legal reality.[4]

At this point in its evolution, mankind is deeply limited in its readiness to experience and take action in response to genocidal disasters. Most events of genocide are marked by massive indifference, silence, and inactivity. Some isolated events are followed by a measure of concern, outcry, and protest; but even those genocidal events that do trigger some degree of awareness and protest are rarely followed by any significant efforts to correct or limit the genocidal process by people who are not connected to the events by reason of kinship or geographical closeness.

The Symbolic and Practical Significance of a Genocide Early Warning System

In the treatment or correction of many human problems, there are fairly long stages in which the most that can be done is to observe systematically how and when a problem begins, the way in which it unfolds, under what conditions it is naturally arrested, and under what conditions it gathers momentum. Even this process of carefully monitoring the problem can begin to bring a certain amount of relief to the suffering. Even though real treatment of some diseases does not yet exist, the caring and involvement of a physician can bring the patient some relief from terror. Over and above the humanitarian meaning of such relief, the patient is also assisted in this way to gather new strength for however much of a fight for life he or she may be able to make. We also know that there are rare instances in which people survive even killer diseases, although no one seems to know exactly why. Some cancers, for example, even severe ones, have been known to recede by themselves. It is interesnting for our concept of a Genocide Early Warning System that some cancer researchers suggest that these recoveries signify that the organism has recovered its natural ability to recognize the cancer cells as its enemy and so is able to successfully redirect its powerful immunologic "troops" against the enemy.[5] The efforts of organized medicine also try to provide for the comfort of the patient and the protection of the community from contagious diseases. Thus, although there may be no treatment for a specific disease, these side measures can help reduce the toll of a disease even as man awaits the breakthrough of new knowledge and the development of directly effective therapies.

There is little question that mankind as a whole would enjoy at least some sense of relief if there were a designated institution to monitor and report the terrible events that destroy so many human lives. As an official activity of such a responsible institution, an established Genocide Early Warning System would represent a new statement of concern about human life.

An early warning system would mean that some effort was being made to combat the primitive madness that has killed millions of people in every period of human history. Even if at the outset the tools and procedures of an early warning system were inevitably to suffer the weaknesses and limitations of most beginning programs and technologies and even if an early warning system initially were to result in very little practical aid to the victims, there would be a profound evolutionary meaning to the development of such an agency.

Such an agency would speak not only to the immediate present, but to the long flow of human history as well. A Genocide Early Warning System would announce to all of us that mankind was gaining a new awareness of the widespread tragedy of mass murder and was seeking to develop new processes to control and remove this terrible cancer.

Admittedly, there is always some danger that the spotlight of world public opinion would impel some genociders to do their work with even greater haste and ruthlessness. But it seems far more conceivable that the major impact of the spotlight of world public opinion would be to reduce the number of fatalities. Ultimately, in a long evolutionary process, it should be entirely possible to turn the concept of mass extermination into an odious, unacceptable relic of man's onetime primitiveness, much as cannibalism is almost universally inconceivable today. The possibility that an insistent world public opinion would turn humans away from genocide is, after all, also based on our built-in wishes to respect and advance life. Our natural life-seeking side would be strengthened by the pressure of information from a worldwide early warning system and its representation of human caring.

The basic principle of an early warning system is to create an information feedback system. Just as biofeedback has shown us that a person can exert control over his body — rate of heartbeat, blood circulation, muscle tension, and so on — when informed of the current levels and told what level to strive for, social and cultural systems may have untapped adaptive capacities as well. Ervin Laszlo (1974)

A Human Environment Ombudsman

Statement of the Union of International Associations of the Preparatory Committee for the United Nations Conference on the Human Environment, Stockholm, 1972:

Specific recognition ... needs to be given to the function of national and international ... "lookout" institutions which, through their specialized interest and sensitivity:

- Identify *new* threats to the human environment at an early stage.
- Mobilize support to draw public attention to the nature of each new threat.
- Encourage governments to take legislative action to counteract the threats to the environment.
- Help to generate the political will without which governments cannot act.
- Support government agencies by providing a pool of experts to monitor the problems and steps towards its solutions, and to advise on legislation.
- Supply a non-political forum in which the problem can be discussed before it is handled between governments in a political setting.

has proposed an "ecofeedback system". "Ecofeedback is the principle that the existing states of the world system can be measured, evaluated in terms of preferred states, and the pertinent information fed back to the population directly concerned in maintaining or changing the given states."[6]

Levels of Information in a Genocide Early Warning System

Our concept of a Genocide Early Warning System involves at least three different levels of data collection, which are to be put into operation at different stages of the system's development.

1. A genocide warning data system begins by assembling the facts of ongoing genocide around the world in a comprehensive and systematic way. Incredible as it may seem, there is no such integrated data source anywhere in the world today — neither for current reports of genocide nor for past genocides. Moreover, a genocide warning system not only treats the data of genocide as facts in themselves, but it organizes the information into meaningful patterns and sequences that add to our understanding of how these events unfold and gather momentum.
2. A second level of information in an early warning system concerns the wide range of human rights violations that fall short of genocide, such as murder on a smaller scale, concentration camps, torture, imprisonment without due process, and a denial of rights to emigrate. In recent years, there has been an increasing amount of information about such human rights violations and suggestions for global information systems, but the need for such systems has not yet been met.[7] This level of human rights data in the genocide warning system not only treats information about violations in their own right, but also connects those violations to predictions of the likelihood of a buildup of momentum toward mass murder.
3. The third level of information in the early warning system branches out to track a broad spectrum of social indicators. First, some social indicators cover a variety of societal and cultural processes that are not immediately related to overt violent behavior or to the ideology of genocide, but they are nonetheless considered potentially relevant to the unfolding of possible tendencies toward genocide. These indicators include the valuing of life in a society, the valuing of the quality of life, a culture's orientation to the distribution of power, and so on. Second, other indicators are specifically connected to the subsequent emergence of genocide. These indicators include the development of an ideology of genocide, patterns of dehumanization, legitimation of violence in a society, and so on. Unlike the first two levels, which could be put into operation at once, this level of information gathering and analysis would require longitudinal studies to develop and test the relevant indicators.

Level 1: Monitoring Ongoing Genocides

The major function of a Genocide Early Warning System is to report ongoing events of genocide anywhere on the globe. Such an early warning system means developing a worldwide, computerized data bank to collate, according to nations and other groups such as tribes or religions, all allegations, reports, and investigations of genocidal events. The basic charge of the early warning system is to develop the best possible means for gathering and verifying information about mass exterminations. Of course, a true megalomaniac won't simply open the doors of his extermination camps to visiting investigators or otherwise stop his determined plans to remove a victim group just because an international agency makes inquiries, but it is not inconceivable that dedicated, relentlessly effective investigative reporting would at least hamper the course of an ongoing genocidal process.

The potential impact of authoritative, insistent reports on world public opinion is becoming greater and greater in our day and age as the penetration of an already incredibly powerful mass media continues to grow apace all over the world. An international Genocide Early Warning System could be expected to change considerably the continuity of coverage and the impact of information about mass murders when they are revealed to the world. It is no longer a matter of haphazard, short-lived journalistic reports that are dropped when a story is no longer "news", but instead is a process of systematic reports, rendered at regular time intervals in addition to emergency alerts, followed up by careful investigations and verifications by an institution that represents a significant public or collective authority that news reports alone do not. Many outlets are used: the mass media, reports to national governments and international bodies, reports to scholarly organizations and publications, the development of learning and information resources for university and high school curricula, and so on.

Under a world spotlight, the momentum of at least some genocidal processes could conceivably be slowed. Many genocidal campaigns do not reach their zenith for some time and usually not until it has become clear that it is possible "to get away with it" in an unknowing and uncaring world.[8] Within the ranks of the genociding people, more dissidents might be emboldened to fight the genocidal policy. The role of "ignorant" bystandards to the genocide would be made far more uncomfortable by the glare of the international spotlight. In addition, the insistent reality of reports in the international news media might help a potential victim people recognize the danger to their lives so that they could flee in time. Under certain circumstances, such publicity might also lead to the organization of more effective campaigns of self-defense and counterattack.

Incredible as it may seem, not only have there been (and are) genocides that were ignored by an indifferent world, but there also have been genocides that were not "at all known" until many years later. Robert Conquest[9] describes how it was not until 1966 that it became known that during World War II, 200,000 Meskaji, a Turkish people of Islamic faith in the Georgian Soviet Socialist Republic, were deported by the Soviets from the geographic area of Mesketia and sustained heavy casualties during that deportation.

A genocide data warning system will report events of mass murder as quickly as possible and carefully follow up all reports of genocide. The immediate life-serving purpose of such an information system is apparent. At the same time, the information bank should also be developed to include systematic data of past events of genocide and to organize past and current data in meaningful categories so that researchers can study how genocides have unfolded in different cultures and eras.

Level 2: Monitoring Violations of Basic Human Rights

The Genocide Early Warning System also gathers, evaluates, and reports information on human rights violations that fall short of actual genocide, as well as on trends toward possible new genocides. Such data constitute a critical information mass as to present human suffering and also provide indications of possible momentum toward genocidal events in the future. Even in the current stage of mankind's "humanistic consciousness", it is possible to specify a large variety of actions that constitute clear-cut violations of basic human rights. The United Nations Universal Declaration of Human Rights lists certain violations of basic human rights, such as slavery, torture, and imprisonment without due process. Although there are always problems of interpretation, such rights and their violations are, relatively speaking, objectively definable.[10]

When combined with the data on actual genocide, this second level of information in the early warning system data bank provides a comprehensive picture of actual, overt events that deny human beings their fundamental rights — first to stay alive and second to be secure from torture, abuse, and denial of basic liberties. When analyzed and categorized in meaningful ways, these data provide a basis for seeing the pattern and sequential development of abuses of human rights, up to and including the occurrence of actual genocide. The following are categories for information assembly:

1. *Events: reports of genocide and other major human rights violations.* Information is collected on current reports of mass murder around the world as well as on other major human rights violations that fall short of genocide: murder, detention in concentration camps, torture, imprisonment without due process, slavery, denial of the right to emigrate freely, denial of free speech, and so on, according to categories selected from the United Nations Universal Declaration of Human Rights.
2. *Peoples.* The above events are recorded as to the nations or peoples involved, both as initiators and as targets. The classification also includes power blocs such as NATO, Warsaw Pact countries, and the Arab League and religious groups such as Jews, Protestants, Catholics, Hindus, and Moslems.
3. *Stages.* Events are analyzed according to a sequential classification of stages.
   - 00 Historical events and transitions
   - 01 Psychological events and transitions
   - 02 Economic and cultural events and transitions
   - 03 Political and geographic events and transitions
   - 04 Legal events and transitions
   - 05 Social events and transitions
   - 06 Communication events and transitions
   - 07 Ideological events and transitions
   - 08 Religious events and transitions
   - 09 Nationalistic and racial events and transitions
   - 10 Formulation of genocidal fantasy
   - 20 Precipitating factors or context
   - 30 Mobilization of means to genocide
   - 40 Legalization and institutionalization of genocide
   - 50 Execution of genocide
   - 51 Denial of commission of genocide
4. *Reported causes.* The overt causes, precipitating events, and background causes that are reported to have led to the events are classified. The data and explanations of these causes are provided by the same data sources that provide the information concerning genoicidal events and human rights violations.
5. *Data sources.* Initially, the data sources are news items gathered by those news agencies around the world that are judged as achieving relatively high levels of objectivity and accuracy in their reports. Data are also received from specialized agencies that investigate and report serious cases of genocide and human rights violations when they are brought to the agencies' attention. At a much later stage in the development of the early warning system, there are direct investigative procedures to supplement these data, especially for purposes of systematic follow-up reports.

Level 3: Predicting Buildups of Possible Genocidal Violence

The further development of an early warning system concerns information about social indicators within a national group or culture that are known to be linked to the possibility of future genocide. These social indicators include attitudes such as defining other peoples as inferior or not deserving equal rights, defining people or minitory groups as dangerous, and taking a ruthless attitude toward national warfare rather than accepting humanitarian principles of combat under international law. There are, of course, many complex problems to be solved before such a prediction system can be developed. First of all, there is no existing social science methodology for forecasting future events of genocide, and social indicator researchers, in general, are in a very beginning stage of development.

Nonetheless, until such research is done and actual predictions can be attempted, the collection of data about societal processes is useful in its own right. Thus, weather information that "heavy cloud cover is seen over Kansas today" is useful even when no effort is made to predict the probability of precipitation in the next two 24-hour periods. Similarly, it is useful to have observations such as "a certain head of state is demanding a variety of tributes from citizens on pain of punishment, including the requirement that shopkeepers wear clothing made of fabric on which the president's picture has been printed" or "the government in a certain country has announced the suspension of civil liberties for all members of a certain tribe or subspopulation."

Social psychologist Herman Kelman emphasizes the importance of studying the conditions under which genocide occurs. Kelman discusses what he calls sanctioned massacres, or violent events in the context of a genocidal policy, that are directed at groups that have not themselves threatened or engaged in hostile actions against those who do violence to them. In contrast to other violent events, Kelman suggests that, "The psychological environment in which such massacres occur lacks the conditions normally perceived as providing some degree of moral justification for violence. ... [The] question for the social psychologist is: what are the conditions under which normal people become capable of planning, ordering, committing, or condoning acts of mass violence?"[11]

The observations collected will increasingly be based on research showing which indicators are historically relevant to the buildup of genocidal acts of violence. However, it is important that this level of data collection not be turned prematurely into prediction statements. Any concrete information that a responsible early warning institution would choose to make public would carry considerable weight, and a public reporting of social indicators by an international agency committed to the monitoring of potential genocide would in itself constitute a kind of prediction. An early warning agency carries a heavy responsibility for evaluating the kind of information it is proper to report publicly. Premature reporting could easily destroy the potential of such an agency. However, in principle, it seems both entirely proper and feasible for an international agency to identify a wide range of events that are linked to actual and potential violations of basic human rights and to release this information to the public.[12]

There is also a danger that one or more ideological blocs will seek to politicize the early warning system so that it will attack other ideological groups. In recent years, terrorist groups have justified their murderous actions against innocent citizens as self-defense against alleged genocide — a justification that has been aptly called the rhetoric of genocide. Historically, there have always been groups that subvert man's finest concepts to serve the purposes of the satanic; thus, once-profound religious ideals have sometimes been involved to justify killing some "heretics", and the concept of democracy is regularly appropriated by dictatorial states, which then condemn free nations as fascist. No doubt efforts would be made to use the authority and prestige of an early warning system for the very purpose of dehumanizing other people. In fact, the machinery of the early warning system could be taken as a basis for rationalizing repressive measures against one population group or another. The data of a system that purports to identify the potential mass murderers might even be taken to justify the murder of some people as potential killers.[13]

It is therefore essential that a Genocide Early Warning System be established as an independent scientific agency that is safeguarded, as much as possible, from political entry. One way of doing this, which also suits the requirements of scientific development, is to encourage the development of multiple, independent early warning systems around the world. This procedure will make possible a healthy cross-checking of information and stimulate a variety of creative efforts toward the development, testing, and refinement of a "genocide meteorology". Strictly from the point of view of effective data gathering, it seems wisest to develop a variety of regional centers that will focus on the regional "climate" of their more immediate geographical or cultural zones. Today, for example, Westerners hardly know about the extermination of peoples in remote areas, such as Indians in

TABLE C1

LEVELS OF INFORMATION TO BE MONITORED IN A GENOCIDE EARLY WARNING SYSTEM

	Current Operational Feasibility	**Appropriateness of Reports to World Public**
1. Monitoring ongoing genocides		
Multi-source information-gathering and investigative system (e.g., collation of available news-service reports; reports from international health, environmental, and legal agencies; mobile teams for interviewing international travelers and refugees; and official field investigation teams dispatched to scenes of reported mass murders).	Requires development of reliable data-gathering system; does not pose major conceptual or technical problems given adequate resources.	Appropriate on completion of reliable system of gathering, verifying, assembling, and retrieving information; calls for creative development of effective ways to deliver information.
2. Monitoring violations of basic human rights		
Expansion of information-gathering and investigative system to include a wide range of human rights violations such as torture, imprisonment without due process, denial of right to emigrate, and denial of free speech, according to rights defined in United Nations Universal Declaration of Human Rights.	*Yes*, as above.	*Yes*, as above.
3. Monitoring and predicting buildups of possible genocidal violence		
Further expansion of information-gathering and investigative system to track a broad spectrum of social indicators that are seen in the build-up of potential genocide violence (e.g., cultural attitudes toward human life as expendable, prejudices and dehumanization of a minority, societal allowance of violence, acceptance of a fantasy or folk theme of genocide).	*No*; requires long-range research program to develop and test relevant social indicators and to formulate a valid approach to prediction of possible future violence.	*Yes* as to description of ongoing, objectively defined social processes that are public knowledge, following research demonstration of linkage to buildup of genocide; *no* as to statements of predictions of possible buildups of genocidal violence until research confirms reliability and validity of such predictions.

Brazil, the Kurds in Iraq, or Christians and other non-Moslem Africans in southern Sudan. Regionally based centers can be staffed with knowledgeable, local behavioral scientists who are close to the pulse of the local people, can observe events at first hand, and are more sensitive to local symbolism and cultural indicators.

The same principle applies to the professional setting of the agencies. No doubt it would be good to see an early warning system within the framework of a legal international agency such as the United Nations. However, a strong argument can be made for the simultaneous development of early warning systems in a variety of settings, such as major universities and research institutes. University campuses today include a great many innovative centers that seek to apply traditional knowledge to the frontier problems that face human beings. All over the world, there are centers for the study of international relations, world law, social planning, peace, conflict resolution, world health, environment, and strategic matters. Any one of these settings could appropriately take on the project of monitoring and recording genocide and other violations of human rights.

For many years, the fantasy of one of the authors (Charny) has been the establishment of a center for the study of genocide, human rights, and the potential for peace. About 1966, I came to a deeply felt decision that I wanted to study what was known about the psychology of man's ability to engage in mass murder. I wrote to Yad Vashem, The Heroes and Martyrs Remembrance Authority, in Jerusalem, to inquire about what information they had assembled in their archives on the subject. The brief and courteous reply I received stunned me: "There is very little material." In many ways, I owe to that reply a good deal of my resolution to work harder at the possible contribution of the psychological sciences to our understanding of how human beings can be so incredibly destructive — a crucial question in my opinion.

In such a center, people would link the study of all that takes place in the terrible holocausts with the study of the human potential to be peaceful and nonviolent. The center would invite groups of scholars from a variety of disciplines — psychology, sociology, political science, international relations and law, anthropology, economics, communications, and other fields — to work together in a collaborative search for a study of the causes and treatment of cancers of human destructiveness. An effort would be made to seek to understand scientifically the causes, processes, and sequences that lead to genocidal destructiveness, and, at the same time, the tools of science and ingenuity would be used to create new designs for human evolution toward the potential for peace.

Understandably, the Nazi Holocaust has generated a good number of memorial agencies and traditions — the most significant being Yad Vashem. But these memorials — like the memorials to other peoples who have suffered genocide — generally fail to project a particular tragedy as a universal tragedy of the many peoples who have suffered, and will yet suffer, extermination. Moreover, the intent of the memorial basically does not go beyond a pious hope that the simple act of memoralizing or remembering events that took place will make people more aware of the past and thereby reduce the possibility of genocidal brutalities in the future. Although it is essential that we be aware of the past, there is nothing that says that historical awareness and heartfelt memorializing alone will correct man's ways. There is little hope of ending genocide until we truly learn to understand the sequences and processes that lead to genocide.[14]

Reservations About the Proposal for an Early Warning System

There are many problems involved in setting up a Genocide Early Warning System. A system that in no way showed promise of development into a meaningful, practical instrument would not only fail to lead to a new sense of symbolic hope and aliveness, but conceivably could set us back. The fact that even when we tried, we were nothing more than naive fools railing against the prevailing realities of life would be another demonstration of man's utter impotence. Inaccuracies of reporting and prediction would be a serious problem and, in some instances, would touch off painful national and cultural sensitivities. The actual operational beginnings of all levels of a working early warning system would need to be very carefully planned, tested, and developed to a point of significant technical success.

Finally, it has to be clear that such a system in itself cannot be expected to bring about any immediate major changes on this mad globe. Only people who are naive and innocent about power and human life could subscribe to the illusion that just having the "weather reports" and "weather forecasts" of a Genocide Early Warning System will change the reality of life on earth in any immediate way. One might also say wryly that a world that has seen millions die for so many centuries will not be in much of a rush for early warning information. Nonetheless, even a beginning effort to build a genocide early warning system as a tool of future international process could arouse hope and other positive actions by various people. Although no "messianic" changes can be expected because of a genocide data system, mankind's taking responsibility for new levels of knowing and reporting how people treat human life could represent a step toward a better future.

The Early Warning Processes: Life Experience Processes as a Frame of Reference for an Early Warning System

In the long-range development of a Genocide Early Warning System, beyond reporting information about present genocides and other major violations of human rights, we want to look at those social forces and processes in a culture that predictably generate genocidal momentums and bring them to a head.

We have chosen very specifically to begin with a series of statements about basic life experience processes of individuals, families and groups, and society. These experience processes are, to our minds, universal attributes of the human condition, and all people must encounter them, constructively or otherwise. They are the basic conditions of being alive, staying alive, and feeling alive. However, these same conditions can be turned toward destructiveness, and then these processes can combine to build increasing momentums toward violence and can culminate in genocide. These processes are detailed in Appendix A [not available in this text], which shows how the basic life experience processes are sources of life satisfaction but can also be turned toward destructiveness. The negative restatements of these basic processes as destructive processes constitute the early warning indicators on the societal level.

Note that these concepts of the life experience processes generate terms that refer at one and the same time to specific behavior and to underlying human values.[15] Another advantage of this approach is that behavior on the larger societal level is linked to processes on the other levels of individual, family, and smaller group experiences.[16]

Other researchers of early warning systems may choose to define their categories strictly in terms of the behavior of large groups *vis-a-vis* human rights and life, and it may well be that the "weather predictions" that someday issue from those other early warning systems will, in fact, prove more effective. However, our own preference is to try for concepts that will be useful to us both along the roads to Auschwitz and Hiroshima and in relation to many everyday events. We are fascinated by pedestrian, everyday power plays, such as in an academic community when an entire department is eliminated or a department chairman is squeezed out, or in a family that scapegoats one member of the family into the role of a victim-patient to suffer a condition that represents a larger family problem. Other early warning studies may focus exclusively on concrete behavioral acts, without reference to their intrinsic value or experiential meanings, and not use concepts that can be applied to levels of human organization that are smaller than large groups. But, the whole thrust of the book, *How Can We Commit the Unthinkable? Genocide: The Human Cancer*, is to attempt to link genocidal events to the underlying sources of such behavior, because we believe that, ultimately, genocide takes form through a series of processes that extend across the whole continuum of human experience.

We believe not only that eventually there must be legal and institutional processes to outlaw discriminatory and life-destructive behavior, but that it is also crucial that people's underlying value processes evolve toward a basic commitment to life. We therefore prefer to work from concepts that encompass the psychophilosophical principles (*weltanschauung*) of a culture or people and descriptions of actual behavior toward other human beings. An analogy in psychotherapy is that psychotherapists attempt to correct both the behavior and the underlying psychophilosophical processes. For example, they not only teach a family member the specific behavior of not being abusive to another family member, but they also attempt to teach the larger principle of not trying to gain emotional security by putting down someone else.

This simultaneous approach to human values and behavior provides us with more linkages between the issues of a society's madness and the day-to-day problems of individuals, families, and small groups. Much the same dynamics are at work when people defend themselves against the terrors of life within a family that unwittingly "murders" one of its members emotionally, as when a nation of people chooses to murder a "lesser" race. If we were to build our warning system more exclusively in behavioral terms that referred only to the political and power forces at work in large groups, the concept would not be so readily translatable into a framework for looking at individuals, families, and small groups as well as larger societies.

Nothing in what we are saying is intended to equate one level of human experience with another. The same mechanism of defense — say, projection of one's fears of inadequacy onto another — is not exactly the same in individual psychology, between members of a family group, between persons in a mob, or between persons in mobs heading en masse to kill their victims. However, there is a continuity of the human experiencing process, or what has been called transactional connections, from one level to the next, and we can learn a great deal by understanding the continuities of behavior from one level of human experiencing to the next.

This frame of reference also makes it possible to focus on positive, life-respective values and behavior of a people, not just on destructiveness and violations of human rights. Such a frame of reference also makes it possible to record a society's positive values and attitudes toward the right of human beings to experience their life without harassment as well as to record a society's infringements of human rights.

Defining Early Warning Processes

Early warning processes represent a society's methods for managing certain basic life experiences or basic value processes that all societies have to contend with, e.g., the people's orientation to the value of human life, the importance placed on the quality of life experience, or the people's orientation to power. These societal processes are extensions of universal life issues that we must grapple with on all levels of individual and collective experience.

The early warning processes are grouped under four headings:

1. *Devaluing humanness*: how people devalue human life; also how people devalue the experience of

aliveness, seek power over others, and resort to overt violence and destructiveness

2. *The illusion of self-defense*: the absence of control machinery for monitoring and managing escalations of threats and the application of excessive force in self-defense
3. *The ideology of victimization*: how human beings utilize natural defense mechanisms in response to the inevitable anxieties of life — especially the universal tendency to project onto others qualities of nonhumanness and dangerousness and then to legitimize their victimization; also the corresponding degree of availability of a group to be victimized
4. *The cancer of genocidal destructiveness*: tracking the sequences of the actual buildup of genocidal destructiveness as it moves from stage to stage in a society

Devaluing Humanness

Early Warning Process 01: The Devaluing of Human Life

Although we have assumed that from the beginning of life all people experience a basic desire to live and have a reverence for life, many events and influences are capable of leading people away from valuing life. Moreover, there is also a natural side of human experiencing that moves in the direction of death. As a result, people develop vastly different attitudes toward the value of human life.

In gathering data about a culture, we ask, "Does the culture speak to the sanctity and dignity of human life, or does the culture teach capriciousness of a callousness toward life?" Some cultures insist on the value of life even under highly problematic conditions such as war. Other cultures are indifferent to or depreciate the value of life or readily define many conditions under which life may be taken without regret.

How does the value assigned to life compare with the value assigned to achieving power over others? Which does a culture value more? Is power always so important that it justifies eliminating lives? To what extent does the pursuit of power become the dominant value of life?

A people's perception of the relationship between life and death also enters into their valuing of life. Some cultures link preparation for death with accepting life's challenge to honor life until the time to die comes. Other cultures separate the reality of death from any linkage with the challenge of life, and death awareness is denied in every possible way. We know from clinical studies of suicide that very frequently the suicide's unconscious conception of his death is that death will not *really* occur, that he will really continue to live after he "dies", and that he will be able to reap the pleasure of his vengeance against certain intimates whom he is seeking to punish through his death. This individual psychological experience is quite similar to the larger ideological teaching of some cultures or religions that death, in effect, is not real so long as one gives up one's life on behalf of one's people or ideology. Such cultures or religions may teach and encourage a cult of suicidal missions against one's enemies on the grounds of the enormous rewards that will follow to the true believers. One psychologist has found a crucial link between suicide and murder and argues that the suicide-homicide linkage is the central dynamic of mass murders and genocide.[17]

In the cruel course of life, peoples and cultures are likely to have to choose between their values of life and other values more than once. The question then becomes, "How does the valuing of human life stand up under the competition?" For example, in certain religions or cultures, death may be so highly valued that it can even win out over life. Or at various times, the value of life must compete against money — how deeply will a people value life when billions of dollars are at stake, say for new agents of chemical warfare?

Early Warning Process 02: The Irrelevance of Human Experience

How does a society relate to the quality of the human experience? Which is ultimately more important — production standards and efficiency (no matter what the human cost) or a combination of efficient production and decent work conditions and satisfaction? How a culture values the natural environment and ecology as a whole has a good deal to do with that people's approach to the quality of life. Respect for the environment means concern with how an environment will support human experiencing. It also includes concern with the public health of not only the present generation but future generations as well. A people that is oblivious to present and future human suffering caused by illness, blight, or pollution is not likely to care much about any loss of human life because of violence. On the other hand, a stated concern about the quality of the ecology and environment can also be taken, and has been taken, as a basis for the extermination of a people who are said to be a blight on the environment or to the genetic purity of the race. This fact illustrates what is emphasized elsewhere: Any ideology that is considered to be more important than human life necessarily becomes a possible basis for rationalizing the destruction of human life.

Another aspect of the quality of human life involves the way pleasure and responsibility are viewed. Are both joy in living and responsibility seen as necessary to human integrity? Is responsibility presumed to be the one overriding source of meaning in life? Are pleasures treated as entirely separate from responsibility, thereby inviting orgies and sadism?

In collecting data about the quality of human experiencing, we are often far from the actualities and tragedies of violence. However, by examining a group's attitude toward the quality of human experiencing, we seek to identify those group processes that, in time, may conspire to permit the emergence of violence. We would like to believe that, overall, those people who truly succeed in loving the opportunity that is life would not countenance genocidal violence.[18]

Early Warning Process 03: The Pursuit of Power Over Others

All human beings need to attain a reasonable degree of objective control over their own destiny and a sense of their power over the flow of life's events. We are forever living with an awareness of our mortality. Without a sense of present and potential power over our environment, we would be doomed to total terror. It is not a matter of whether or not to have power; it is a matter of how to go about having power, how to exercise one's power, how to safeguard one's power, and how to express one's power in relation to the equally legitimate needs of others. Both excesses of power and insufficiencies of power are to be seen as dangerously supporting possible sequences toward destructiveness.

The early warning indicators that have to do with the development of power essentially probe the question, "For what purpose is power sought?" When power is intended as energy for people to experience their own aliveness more fully, power is a tool for fulfilling human potential. The focus of life is one's own experiencing and not control over another person or people. On the other hand, when power is seen as being vested in controlling another people, the focus of life is not the richness of one's own experiencing, but taking over, possessing, and dominating others. We are interested in gauging the extent to which a given culture seeks the further development of its own power potential and the extent to which a people turns its cultural and governmental destiny toward the fulfillment of power ambitions at the expense of others.

TABLE C2

ILLUSTRATIONS OF EARLY WARNING PROCESS 03: THE PURSUIT OF POWER OVER OTHERS

	Supporting Human Life	Moving Toward Destruction
Use of power in conflict resolution	1. Society maintains pride in its power to face and resolve problems. 2. Serious chronic problems are acknowledged and processes toward solutions are initiated.	1. Weaknesses and problems of society are handled by compensatory effort at power over others, such as by scapegoating. 2. Major weakness in society is likely to stimulate compensatory efforts to power; tangible loss of power. a. Political instability b. Loss of significance in international affairs c. Loss of national purpose, confidence, or pride

In any society, no matter how much a people tries, there inevitably arise enormous inequalities of power. How does a society relate to its inequalities? Are the inequalities taken as a challenge to social change, or does society tolerate and exploit the emergence of inadequate, excluded, or fringe groups? What kinds of checks and balances exist to prevent an excessive use of power?

It is also important to note any situations of national weakness that may lead a people to compensate by attacking a scapegoat victim. We look to see whether a people has recently suffered any tangible loss of power to which it is still reacting, whether there is any significant threat to the internal stability of the nation, or whether the society has experienced a sense of loss of significance about itself and its purpose.

Finally, the ways in which a society defines its intentions to other peoples are crucial. Although some societies are drawn, despite sincere and good intentions, into destructiveness, others define their power as strength at the expense of others and see the legitimacy of their power as justifying any means, regardless of the cost to human life. The latter societies will very probably become great destroyers, whereas a people that makes a commitment to equality and cooperation with other people at least has a fighting chance of containing the carnage.

Early Warning Process 04: Overt Violence and Destructiveness

In the psychology of the individual personality, we have known for a long time that the greatest potential for violence is in those who are too removed from their natural rage and potential for violence and those who are too readily given to an impulsive expression of violent impulses.[19] The same seems to be true of societies in general. Whereas a society's momentum toward genocide is often marked by increasing violence, a society that fails to make provisions for a

TABLE C3

ILLUSTRATION OF EARLY WARNING PROCESS 04: OVERT VIOLENCE AND DESTRUCTIVENESS

	Supporting Human Life	Moving Toward Destruction
Availability of tools of violence	1. Sale of weapons carefully regulated and minimized.	1. Weapons are easily, even promiscuously, available with little or token regulation.
	2. Official use of weapons is discouraged and subject to careful regulation following of weapons as tools to preserve life.	2. Official use of weapons automatically justified by position of authority; weapons are intended to impose and protect reign of authority.
	3. Arms development limited according to existing international conventions, and active effort made to extend scope or disarmament and weapons-control conventions.	3. Arms development is maximized, and efforts are made to subvert existing international conventions.
	4. Culture educates against use of weapons except in self-defense.	4. Culture glorifies use of weaponry.

sufficient discharge of violent impulses is also a prime candidate for a sudden eruption of genocidal violence (see news report of a mass murder in erstwhile peaceful Indonesia). In developing an early warning system, therefore, we look at the extent to which violent impulses are accepted as natural and universal on various levels of human experience or, conversely, the extent to which they are denied and suppressed. By the same token, societies that condone, officially sanction, and encourage the spread of armaments and localized warfare are societies in which fuller onslaughts of mass murder are likely to take form.

What happens when a society must resort to violence in response to a realistic threat? To what extent does a culture seek to limit its official violence, even at the risk of some degree of error? Is violence in the name of self-defense sanctioned largely unquestioningly and even relished? Is the destruction of an enemy or oppressor gleefully sought? Are retaliation killings sanctioned and celebrated? Is the destruction of enemy civilians considered justifiable? Is a systematic large-scale destruction of the enemy people allowed to become the goal of the war response?

The Illusion of Self-Defense

Early Warning Process 05: Absence of Control Machinery for Managing Escalatory Spirals

It is certainly a natural requirement of life that there must be a machinery for the management of threat, for we live in constant threat as to our immediate

TABLE C4

ILLUSTRATION OF EARLY WARNING PROCESS 05: ABSENCE OF CONTROL MACHINERY FOR MANAGING ESCALATORY SPIRALS

	Supporting Human Life	Moving Toward Destruction
Societal responses to threat	1. Group conscience and individual conscience within group is encouraged; negative group passions are discouraged and limited by leadership.	1. Contagion of negative group passions encouraged. a. Loss of individual identity and conscience is encouraged and accepted. b. Projection of natural weakness onto outsiders is encouraged. c. Controlled media used to indoctrinate for hatred and rehearsals of violence. d. Crowd experiences stated to inflame passions.
	2. Decision-making mediated by process of checks and balances.	2. Decision-making is authority-dominated. a. Machinery of government does not readily allow for differences of opinion. b. Centers of influence on government in society are lacking. c. Major power is in hands of military. d. Dictator or dictatorial elite is in power.

future and the unknowns of the powerful natural forces around us and within us. However, the basic problem in all threat-management machinery is that of graduation of response.

The early warning data begin with the extent to which provision is made for some way to respond to threat. An absence of machinery to deal with threat is no more to be valued than are excessive responses to threat; both characteristically stimulate the escalation of a crisis. The important question is whether a people and their leadership accept the necessity and responsibility for monitoring and checking their management of threat, which also includes the necessity of evaluating the impact of any steps taken in response to threat. Monitoring is required at any and every step of managing the escalating of a threat, not just at the beginning and not just when critical action-decision points are approached, but at every step along the intricate system of communication and response to another frightened people.

There is the great danger at every step of a sequence of responses to threat that an uncontrollable process of escalation and counterescalation will be unleashed. It is proper to meet serious threat courageously and directly with appropriate strength, but just how is that strength posed and to what extent is the show of strength linked to creative offers and invitations to find a way to remove the threat?

In the early warning indicators of the handling of threat, we include such information as whether or not there are monitors and ombusmen within a government whose job it is to check undisciplined counterthreat behavior and to develop peace-encouraging initiatives as well as alternative, nonviolent responses to conflict. Similarly, we want to observe whether and to what extent societal institutions influence government policy through their monitoring and criticism (e.g., watchdog foundations, labor and business interests, the communications media, and public opinion).

We also ask if the already existing channels of communication, such as diplomacy and mediation, are being utilized fully to try to ascertain the other party's intentions. Perhaps most important, to what extent is a people prepared to reach out directly to potential enemies to seek common purposes and interests that might be served by cooperative activity?

When it is felt that the time has come for overt power, what alternatives to out-and-out military or even quasi-military actions are sought? If and when actual military means are applied, what further decisions as to control and limiting of the military means are made? Are there efforts to negotiate? Are the military means withdrawn as rapidly as possible?

As the escalation of threat builds, the basic orientation of a people toward peoples other than themselves is subject to the most critical tests and pressures. At this time, a society that had previously maintained a climate of relative respect for other people may begin dehumanizing and scapegoating another people. One of the trends that we look at most carefully in a serious threat situation is whether natural passions of hate and vengeance seeking are fanned and encouraged, or whether the fighting back and natural rage of war are contained and focused on the immediate threat. Throughout history, an almost surefire solution of a present threat seems to have been to turn the flaming excitement of prejudice and hate onto an outsider. How many people are prepared to forego this cheap solution?[20]

Early Warning Process 06: Applying Excessive Force in Self-Defense and in Solution of Conflicts

In the course of history, a few societies have managed to maintain a noncombatant role, almost no matter what the circumstances around them. Just how this is best done or how this status can be developed is not entirely clear. One way seems to be for a nation to be useful to all the combatant parties, say, as a financial repository for the combatant countries (and for their leaders). Some peoples seem to take on a noncombatant status after they have lost a great deal at war and subsequently choose to withdraw from further "games" of conflict, perhaps by decisively reducing military expenditures or by withdrawing from an active striving for leadership or a visible role in international affairs. Another way to develop this status is for a people to choose purposefully to stand for peace and to build a noncombatant tradition. Of course, such peoples' lack of military strength can be exploited by a stronger and violent nation, but there have been instances in which the essential dignity and principle of standing for life in this mad world have survived even invasion and occupation.[21]

The issue is how a people can strive for peace when all peoples face enormous forces of destruction is extremely complex. The immediate purpose in the data system is to collect information about a culture's orientation toward force and violence. We begin with the prevailing motif of a people. Is peace or force valued? Is the major ideal to live cooperatively with neighboring peoples, or is there pleasure associated with the use of force and violence? Cultures that idealize force are often characterized as cultivating "hypermasculinity". There are many societies with military elites; there are others in which the military is valued but kept in check lest the values it can represent become too dominant.

If and when a society does find itself at war, what choices are made in the execution of that war? Is the nation's philosophy of war to take the least possible action consistent with self-defense? Are all possible efforts made to protect human life even in wartime? When the war is won, are the occupation policies humane or harsh and exploitative?

Within each society, there are many choices to be made concerning the use of force in solving ethnic and religious differences, economic rivalry, and political competitions. How does a culture instruct people to solve conflicts? Are conflicts to be worked out essentially through some version of the doctrine of survival of the fittest or in a more orderly fashion within the framework of the law? Does the legal tradition allow and encourage the triumph of raw power, or is the law developed more as a tool to help people solve problems equitably?

One of the crucial tests of a culture's stand on violence is how its members relate to force and acts of violence against those people within the culture who represent the least desirable elements, hence potential scapegoats of that society. There have always been societies that enforce laws against wanton crime, excessive force, and murder except when those acts are directed against the Jews, blacks, heathens, sexual deviants, or who have you of their time.

To our knowledge, no people to date has successfully achieved an ideal balance between a commitment to peace and the ability to stand up to the evils of the world. It may be one thing for the Swiss to use their skills as world financiers as a hedge against being involved in international conflicts, but some still question the rightness of that country's serving as a financial prostitute for a killer nation such as Nazi Germany. So, too, if for many generations the Jewish people cultivated a commitment for peace by leaving themselves weak and available to pogroms and forced marches to gas chambers, that was not a satisfactory solution to the quest for peace. These collective processes raise profound philosophical and political questions we do not presume to be able to answer. However, within the framework of an early warning system, data about a culture's orientation to force and violence may indicate whether that culture is or is not likely to produce genociders.

The Ideology of Victimization

Early Warning Process 07: Dehumanization of Potential Victim Group

The underlying machinery for the dehumanization of a potential victim group is housed in the attitudes of a culture toward differences between people. Even cultures that do seek to emphasize some sense of man's equality or godliness — that all people are God's creatures — still have to deal with the powerful realities of differences between people and the natural processes those differences set off in human beings. Some of the provocative realities surrounding man's differences are these:

1. People are remarkably different from one another — in color, build, and appearance, let alone in tradition and culture.
2. Human beings naturally tend to react very strongly to differences — with fear, distaste, and repugnance.
3. People who are different become likely objects of projection.

No matter how humanistically oriented a particular culture is toward the brotherhood of all human beings, the fact remains that each culture must also provide ways for dealing with natural experiences caused by differences. Only in a relatively few instances are people educated toward accepting and enjoying differences. The exciting philosophy of such a positive approach to experiencing people who differ from us is that differences are the other side of the sameness and universality of man — both should be taught simultaneously. However, the prevailing

TABLE C5

ILLUSTRATION OF EARLY WARNING PROCESS 07: DEHUMANIZATION OF POTENTIAL VICTIM GROUP

	Supporting Human Life	Moving Toward Destruction
Definition of potential victim	All people are like us, one of us, equal to us, deserving of life like us.	Other people are defined as being not of our kind, not one of us. a. Alien, different b. Unattractive, distasteful, not valuable c. Repulsive, repugnant d. Less than us e. As if not human, as if not of our species

situation in most cultures has been and is to make people feel that the differences are disturbing and problematic, so people who are different are assigned one degree or another of "not-being-the-same-as-us-ness" and, progressively, "less-than-us-ness".

In the data of the early warning system, we seek to define the attribution of less-than-us-ness along a continuum from arousing distaste and/or disapproval to virtually lacking humanness, being as if not of our species.

Early Warning Process 08: Perception of Potential Victim Group as Dangerous

One of the important elements that spark the eruption of violence against a potential target group is a perception of the victim group as a source of serious danger to one's actual survival. This is a paradoxical situation. On the one hand, the victim group has been defined as so seriously lacking in quality and value that they are less than us. They are not human as we are. Yet these same people are also endowed with characteristics of such great power that they are literally seen as threatening our annihilation.

Annihilation is defined in many different ways, from the simple threat of conquest and death to a more symbolic threat to a people's racial, religious, and/or cultural survival. What is so striking is that people treat threats of the destruction of their symbolic continuity as virtually the same as, if not more dangerous than, threats of actual physical annihilation. Historically, we have been all too ready to kill those other people who threaten to wipe out our names, our God's name, our flag, our economic system, and so on.

It is, of course, possible to believe that another people is threatening us with massive annihilation without the enemy also being regarded as less than us or not of our species. When fear is not linked with dehumanizing another people, genocidal campaigns are not as likely. However, human weakness being what it is, projections of nonhuman status are likely to form with relentless suddenness if and when war erupts. Once such projections of "not-us-ness" and being nonhuman take hold, the door is open to cruelties, atrocities, and genocides.

TABLE C6

ILLUSTRATION OF EARLY WARNING PROCESS 08: PERCEPTION OF POTENTIAL VICTIM GROUP AS DANGEROUS

	Supporting Human Life	Moving Toward Destruction
Perception of victim group	Potential victim group is not perceived as threat.	Potential victim group is perceived as threatening actual annihilation. 1. Physical annihilation a. Military b. Other territorial expansionism c. Population invasion 2. Racial annihilation 3. Economic annihilation 4. Religious annihilation (heresy) 5. Other spiritual or psychological annihilation a. Weakens our culture b. Destroys our customs and way of life c. Infects our culture with evil d. Destroys our continuing identity (symbolic immortality)

Early Warning Process 09: Legitimation of Victimization by Leadership Individuals and Institutions

The sequence of the early warning processes, which defines the buildup of a momentum of genocidal violence, is now nearing its tragic climax of manifest events of killing. Yet even now, the likelihood of genocide depends to a large extent on the basic cultural and legal definitions set by the leaders and societal institutions as to whether or not killing the victims is legitimate. When the idea of genocide begins to take form in a culture, the issue of whether or not violence and genocide will be legitimate, approved, and legal becomes supreme.[22]

Many levels of social organization are involved in the decision as to whether or not to legitimize victimization of a target people. In addition to the leaders, whom most people will follow, we look in our early warning system for individuals, groups, and institutions that might challenge the legitimacy of deliberate, officially sanctioned violence and perhaps check the government's excesses.

It is true that even major trends toward violence can be initiated and established by relatively small groups of "brown shirts" before a society wakes up to the danger. William A. Westley (1966) sees the legitimization of violence as a three-stage process: initial support by the public for mild violence by a special group, support for extreme forms of violence by that group, and support for systematic extreme violence — which often is executed by the same small group of people. Given the permission of society, the perpetrators become their own supporting

Table C7

Illustration of Early Warning Process 09: Legitimation of Victimization by Leadership Individuals and Institutions

	Supporting Human Life	Moving Toward Destruction
Social approval and legal definition of victimization	1. Victimization is socially unacceptable and is prosecuted under the law.	1. Victimization is socially acceptable (even when there are laws against it).
	2. Leaders and institutions stand personally and through the law against victimization.	2. Leaders and institutions sanction and progressively legalize destruction of victims.
	3. Persecution of a group, overt or covert, direct or indirect, is to be exposed and stopped, and the persecutors and their accomplices are to be prosecuted.	3. Persecution of a group is overt or covert, pursued as a legitimate and major goal of the society.

audience and allow deeper and more fanatic kinds of violence on the part of their sick members. At the same time, the public can dissociate itself from responsibility for the violence done by that small group; in fact, the small group can even initiate a sequence of violence despite the official disapproval of the society's leaders.[23]

If and when a tragic, full-scale policy of genocide is launched by a society, there is still a final choice for each person and each institution in the society. Even when an order comes from on high, each army commander has to decide whether to send his troops to commit genocide, and even then the troops must decide whether or not to execute the order. Even when a policy of genocide is well under way, each person and group within the society must elect whether or not to fight, directly or indirectly, against the policy. The legitimation of genocidal violence is a function of all segments of a society — the leaders, institutions, and people.

Early Warning Process 10: Availability of Victim Group

In order for the definitions of a given people as being less than human and highly dangerous to take hold, a certain compliance, acceptance, or tacit support of the definitions on the part of the victim group itself seems to be required. In our early warning data, we look to see if definitions of availability to be a victim are rooted in the culture. To what extent do the folklore and traditions of a people identify them as historic victims? Does the culture place tangible values on the status of being victims? "We shall remain valuable despite their attacking us. We shall become the more valuable because they persecute us." Granted, there can be in such a spirit a beautiful and courageous stand in the face of real danger, but there often are also a kind of self-righteousness and a sense of martyrdom, which are unconsciously enjoyed for their "secondary gains". Although there may be great

Table C8

Illustration of Early Warning Process 10: Availability of Victim Group

	Supporting Human Life	**Moving Toward Destruction**
Expectation of potential victim	Expectation of not being victim	Expectation of being victim 1. Value in being victims a. We shall remain valuable despite their attacking us b. We shall become the more valuable because they persecute us 2. Honor extended to victims as serving group's destiny of martyrdom 3. Tradition of preparing to be victims

heroism on the part of the certain victim peoples, the idealization of survival as the persecuted ones can become a way of life, through which people unconsciously find meaning for their existence and/or for their spiritual eternity after death. There is, we know, a deep magnetic pull to the apocalyptic-messianic images in the folklores of peoples.

How does a people honor its members who are the victims? Over and above the caring for those who have fallen, are the victims regarded as heroes and martyrs who, in effect, represent the group's desire for martyrdom? To what extent does a people's tradition prepare its children to be victims — even to intimating that the punishment is deserved because of their sins — instead of concentrating on teaching new generations how to avoid being victims?

Training to be victims often includes a tradition of denying the reality of a mounting threat. It is true that human beings can exaggerate the extent of a threat, but it is also a fact that human beings are capable of denying a threat of death that is staring them in the eyes. *When Jews who escaped the early Nazi death marches returned to the ghetto to tell their fellow Jews that the Nazis were machine-gunning men, women, and children and intended to exterminate every one of them, they were angrily hooted at and yelled down by the majority who didn't want to hear the truth.*

Suppose they held a genocide and nobody came? It becomes much harder and perhaps impossible to commit genocide when a victim people is not prepared to be wiped out. In assembling early warning systems data, we seek to identify the extent to which a people makes itself available, even if unknowingly, to play the role of victim if and when such a "request" is made.

The Cancer of Genocidal Destructiveness

Early Warning Process 11: Development of Manifest Genocidal Process

We are now at the end of the road. Now the warning system can only record the tragic finale of genocide.

However, even at this stage, there still are bitterly significant processes to be determined, even as a genocidal campaign is achieving maximum momentum toward whatever measure of destruction it will achieve. Even now it need not be too late to stop a mounting campaign of genocide if one pays attention to the signals and mobilizes resources to stop the genocidal activity.

In effect, every society, every group within that society, and every individual on all levels of that society are faced with a series of critical decisions whether or not to be unknowing bystanders, knowing bystanders or accomplices, or actual executioners in the unfolding momentum of mass murder. These decisions are necessarily repeated at several stages in the sequence.

As the momentum of oppression mounts, a critical aspect of decision making in every society is what happens to the legal machinery of the society. Is the legal machinery indifferent to the victims? Does it support and legitimize the violences? In the history of many genocides, there have often been early "field experiments" to see how far one can go, and how much one can get away with. What other public and institutional forces besides the judiciary speak up against the victimization? Are there popular protests? Do legislators speak out? Do opposition political parties attack the emerging violence? Do religious leaders stand up against the increasing oppression and violence? What role does the press play?[24]

The terrible end usually approaches step by step. There first may be unofficial executions of groups of the victim people. If these first executions are not stopped, there then follow more-open campaigns of genocidal executions, though these, too, may still be kept "unofficial" so as not to arouse too much concentrated attention. Special squads of killers often are employed at first. Then civilians are encouraged to commit violence against the victims, and regular police and military forces are employed more openly. The process quickens with each wave of executions.

Robert Payne[25] studied genocide in Bangladesh, using it as a basis to examine mass slaughter throughout history. He found that mass murder "obeys predictable laws and assumes predictable stages, despite outward differences." Payne suggests that the universal scheme of a massacre follows a consistent pattern:

1. The future victims are lulled into a sense of security.
2. The death blow is delivered.
3. The victims recover from their paralysis.
4. The military mounts another massacre.
5. The victims begin to organize.
6. The military mounts a third massacre.
7. The victim "bites off the enemy's hands and feet" (the tide begins to turn against the killers).
8. The final massacre (the killers continue, relentlessly, up to their last breath).

Should there develop inquiries or investigations by various international sources attempting to track down "rumors" and "unconfirmed reports" of genocide, there are generally efforts at evasion, concealment, and denial. A common phenomenon that attends the gathering momentum of executions and killings is the capacity of the killers, and the host society at large, to deny the experience of killing their victims.[26]

Eventually, there is frankly militant, large-scale genocide. Now we hear openly of the genociders' policy. At this stage, the cancer cannot be stopped, of course, except by destroying the host. Certainly, by now it is too late for the many who have already died while the world ignored, denied, or evaded all the earlier warnings and indications, and it is also too late for the many who will now die during the terminal ravages of the cancer. The last of the many earlier warning opportunities has passed.

Tracking the Sequence of Events

The values and behavior of a society are, of course, subject to considerable change and progression. The long-range goal of an early warning system is to track and predict the sequences of events through which societies characteristically move, often unknowingly, to genocide. In order to understand the characteristic progression toward genocide in different cultures and eras, we studied a great many societies in which genocide had taken place. We found that the sequences through which genocides build were in many ways very similar, despite vast differences in historical and social contexts. On the basis of these similarities, we mapped a "time line" to use in following the progression of a group or society. We discovered that the pattern we observed in studies of genocide were remarkably similar to the pattern described by sociologist Neil Smelser (1963) in his study of collective groups.[27]

Smelser defines a series of determinants of collective behavior according to the "logic of a value-added process", which means that each stage in the process adds its value, but only as the earlier stages combine according to a certain pattern can the next stage contribute its particular value. Collective behavior is the combination of all the necessary conditions. Thus, for example: "A racist incident between a Negro and a white may spark a race riot. But unless this incident occurs in the context of a structurally conducive atmosphere, an atmosphere of strain (an atmosphere in which people perceive the incident as symbolic of a troubled state of affairs), the incident will pass without becoming a determinant in a racial outburst."[28] Smelser's stages are:

1. Structural conduciveness: What structures in the societal system promote the collective behavior?
2. Structural strain: What specific strains are operative in the group, within the context of the previously described conducive elements, that will elicit the collective behavior?
3. Growth and spread of generalized belief: The crystallization of value-oriented beliefs that impel and define the legitimacy and necessity of the collective behavior
4. Precipitating factors
5. Mobilization of participants for action
6. Operation of social control

In our proposed data system, the time line essentially follows Smelser's concept of the collective process, but our time line is elaborated and adapted to the specific phenomenon we are tracking, genocide. We use the following categories:

1. Societal forces supporting human life vs. societal forces moving toward destruction of human life
    a. Cultural values and tradition
    b. Structural processes and institutions
    c. Human rights status
2. Key historical, economic, political, legal, and social events and transitions
3. Formation of genocidal fantasy and ideology
4. Precipitating factors or context
5. Mobilization of means to genocide
6. Legitimation and institutionalization of genocide
7. Execution of genocide and experience-denying mechanisms

Societal Forces Supporting Human Life vs. Societal Forces Moving Toward Destruction of Human Life

Supporting human life: The ways in which the psychocultural processes are turned toward the support of human life by peoples and cultures who guard against destructiveness and seek the common welfare of all people. Moving toward destruction of human life: The ways in which psychocultural processes are turned toward inviting and implementing destructiveness.

The concept of an early warning system requires that we describe a baseline or starting point for any given people or group some time before there are any forces building to the point of programs of genocidal extermination. Our proposed framework begins with entries of societal case history data, recorded first as objective descriptions of processes and events and then classified, to the best of our judgment, as to whether the values and behavior processes of the society are turned toward supporting human life or the destruction of human life, or both.

Everything that we have been saying about the human condition argues that from the outset, we are all involved in experiences of creating life and destroying life. Indeed, we speculated that so long as the constructive and destructive processes balance each other and are integrated with one another in the inner individual human experience, one achieves the most vivid experiences of aliveness. Although we are far from proposing an extension of this theory to the behavior of collective groups, we do say that all societies in our world do all manner of things on behalf of life and all manner of things against human life. In our picture of each society, we want to get a picture of the flow of the forces on both sides of the ledger. Note that in all cases the value is assigned to behavior, as much as possible, without regard to the particular cultural and historical "clothing" in which the behavior is "dressed". For example, violence in the name of a group's ideology is treated as assault and destruction of a target people, regardless of what it is called in the ideology of those doing the violence.

The information we seek as to how a given society is organized both in the direction of supporting life and in the direction of potential destructiveness is organized along three major tracks of cultural values and tradition, structural processes and institutions, and human rights status.

That classification partly derives from the work of A. Paul Hare[29] on the basic needs that all groups must meet if they are to survive: Members of a group must share a common identity, members of a group must be able to generate the skills and resources necessary to reach a goal, members of a group must have rules to allow them to coordinate their activities and enough feeling of solidarity to stay together, and the group must be able to exercise control over its membership if it is to be effective in reaching the common goal. But, the classification we use also relates to the "functional autonomy" of behavior, or how certain behaviors continue long after the original reasons for them have ceased to exist.

Cultural Values and Traditions

The prevailing collective orientation and tradition of a society, what has been called in sociology at times "national character", in history the "historical tradition", or in folklore the "folkmyth"; the ideological values of a people (e.g., the traditional value placed on warring and violence or the emphasis traditionally placed on family relationships); also the goals articulated by a society (e.g., an emphasis on scientific progress, an emphasis on rescuing one's people from being victimized, a goal of military domination, a desire for peace, the pursuit of industrial supremacy).

A society's cultural values and tradition determines, to a large extent, the structures and processes that it creates, how it responds to the dilemmas that develop from structural and institutional processes, and how it responds to the inevitable tensions and pressures that can easily invite and seemingly justify the destruction of human life. Although a society that places a high value on life to begin with should have fewer threats of violence, it is inevitable that, sooner or later, tense and explosive situations will arise in all societies, and the prevailing values of a culture are then of enormous importance in determining how far the buildup toward destructiveness will go. *A military commander gives the order to imprison a group of aliens at a time when war with their homeland threatens; the press protests vehemently against the imprisonment of the alien population. A head of state threatens nuclear warfare against another nation;*

the legislature calls for impeachment of the executive. Discriminatory legislation is passed calling for the expropriation of land belonging to members of a minority group; the courts issue an order against the expropriation on the grounds that it is unconstitutional.

New events and theories are colored by the accumulated historical memories of a people, that is, the national consciousness of the society's readiness for violence and genocide, how the society responds with emergency measures at times of great distress, the tradition of freedom or suppression of expression and artistic diversity, the extent to which the people accept their polarization into more and less privileged classes. Also important are the society's prevailing beliefs about the "goodness" or "badness" of basic human nature and whether strong authority and power are required in order to contain bad elements or whether one can trust the free play of the democratic process to contain threats against the fabric of society.

In general, the prevailing atmosphere of a society is a critical index of the value system. There is no mistaking the difference between a societal atmosphere that is permeated with fear and terrror and a societal atmosphere that encourages freedom of expression, initiative, and risk.

Structural Processes and Institutions

The means a group chooses in pursuit of its goals and the structures and institutions created by the group, which develop in the course of the momentum of the societal system (e.g., a policy of military conquest and extermination by a political system that assigns unchecked power to a single leader or a system of justice that checks and balances the executive power of the state; a free press, a controlled press, or a demagogic press).

The structures and institutions of a society are, first of all, expressions of the value system of the group, but these structures and institutions themselves produce various dilemmas that grow out of the "laws of structure," not just because people "want" what is happening. *The brilliant ideas of a pioneering scientist are celebrated and adopted by students; however, as the years pass, these disciples may create an idolatrous cult around the "master's" ideas that interferes with new learning. A mental hospital permits ward personnel to make decisions about the patients' therapies, such as medication or electric shock "treatment", and the result is that many decisions are based on considerations of keeping a patient quiet and tractable rather than on the patient's real needs.*

There are "politics" or system dynamics in each of the subsystems of economic, political, legal, and social services of a society, and these service systems influence one another. It is important to see whether or not check-and-balance controls are instituted to correct the inequalities that arise in any system so that the rights of the weaker members of the population are guaranteed. A similar set of considerations obtain as to the relationship of each society to other societies. To what extent does it attempt to impose its interests on peoples in other countries or on minorities within its boundaries whose culture and ideological identities are different?

Human Rights Status

The actual status of human rights in a society, including the society's relationship to minorities and to members of other societies and the actual actions undertaken by the collective group as to human life and dignity.

Human rights data are powerful in their own right and also from the point of view of their place in a larger system of social indicators as critical indications of whether a society is likely to move in the direction of more severe infringements of life and possibly genocide. We look at the human rights status of people in connection with each of the early warning processes. Thus, the valuing of human life as a basic process to which all societies must relate finds expression in a society's attitude toward the death penalty, the nature of the military training, the presence of legal and internal professional review machinery for monitoring life-terminating events, and so on.

The quality of human rights in a society is indicated by such factors as freedom of the press, freedom of education, the right to work, decent conditions of work, the right to marry a consenting person of one's choice, and freedom of association. How does a society define human rights under conditions of stress and crisis? *Can a citizen sue a court against being inducted into the army on grounds of a moral commitment to nonviolence? Do government officials or university lecturers lose their positions if they oppose a policy of military intervention?*

The ultimate test of human rights comes when a societal process moves tragically closer to a policy of genocide toward a target group. The acid test of a society is whether some combination of the courts, legislature, press, or public opinion struggles to stop a policy of extermination, whether by the police, military, secret service, or government leaders.

Key Historical Economic, Political, Legal, and Social Events and Transitions

Life is marked by never-ending problems and changes that demand major readjustments: from without, by way of natural forces of climate, ecology, biology, and so on; from within, by way of momentous historical events and definitive transitions in maneuvering for power. These major forces and events, interpreted within the prevailing value system of the group, generate powerful dynamics, which greatly influence the subsequent collective process.

The data of major historical, economic, political, legal, and social events that have a huge impact on a people's collective experience are the data that students traditionally have gathered in their efforts to account for genocidal violence. *In Germany, a major economic depression unleashed great bitterness and stimulated a powerful, compensatory nationalism. These processes fed the emergence of Nazi fascism and the megalomaniac persecution of Jews and other "inferior" peoples, from which the Nazis drew so much of their power.* Traditional historical analyses that relate only to these powerful historical forces fall far short of explaining genocidal violence, because they ignore the critical dynamics of human experiencing that are at play both in the determination of historical events and in the response to historical forces. But it would be no less absurd to account for the unfolding of collective behavior only on the basis of psychological dynamics and without reference to these major events in human beings' lives.[30]

To a considerable extent, the major historical events that so influence us are outcomes of the issues all people and societies must deal with (e.g., how a society organizes the distribution of its power resources and whether a society scapegoats others for its difficulties as opposed to concentrating its resources on efforts to rebuilt itself). And all major historical events, in turn, shape how people define their basic values and attitudes. The ways in which individuals, groups, and larger communities experience and perceive events and the impact these events have on the values people then define for their lives interact constantly.

Vahkn Dadrian's analysis of the genocide of the Armenians by the Turks during World War I is a good illustration of the interplay between psychocultural dynamics and socio-historical processes, which, together, forge a momentum toward genocide. Dadrian[31] traces the history of the stigmatization of the Armenians to the stigma the Moslems attached to subject races and to the scorn the Turks attached to the fields of commerce and industry, which had been ceded to the Armenians. The Armenians grew powerful in those pursuits but never developed accompanying legal and political strengths.

Dadrian then places the genocide in the larger sociohistorical context of a world war — a time of disequilibrium of cataclysmic proportions — and in the context of the crumbling Ottoman Empire and its need for antidotes to internal discord to recapture lost Pan-Turkic glory. The stigmatization of the Armenians was a necessary condition of the genocide, but it was not sufficient in itself to set off the deadly process.

Also included in the data of major events and transitions are eruptions of violence in societies — how they are authorized and planned and how the society responds to them by way of containing and controlling the violence or by approving and legitimizing it. We need to see the sequences that unfold as societies turn toward increasing violence. As violence climbs and previous unheard-of brutality occurs with increasing frequency, do the society's basic institutions stand by and tacitly allow what is happening? Do the political and legal institutions openly assist, legitimize, and authorize the violence?

Note, of course, that even highly violent societies do not necessarily go on to commit genocide. The wild and woolly American West with its six-shooting cowboys had its limts — although, in truth, it is an entirely fitting subject of study to examine the relationship between the classic cowboy culture and the genocidal campaigns that did take place against the American Indians. Fiery black people's riots in any number of communities around the world need not go on to become a full-scale genocidal campaign against whites, but in some cases these riots could very well have a larger genocidal momentum in the future.

Formation of Genocidal Fantasy and Ideology

The progressive unfolding of a fantasy or goal of genocide articulated either by the leadership of a group or through the prevailing motifs of the group as a whole and progressing to the point of being codified and ritualized in the basic ideology of the group, but not the expression of extremist personalities or fringe groups.

In this category, we identify the first major transitions from societal strains and violence toward the specific direction of possible genocide as a culminating collective expression of the society. We seek to identify first what we call the formation of the genocidal fantasy and then the elaboration of an accepted genocidal ideology. Genocide is too serious and vast a matter to spring up in a vacuum of nondefinition or nonideology. There is generally a guiding ideology, and before that there generally is a fantasy of power or redemption or salvation through ridding society of a given target people. We are interested in identifying in any given society the original emergence of such a fantasy and the emergence of the ideological goal of genocide as they are articulated by a leader or an elite and/or through the motif of the group as a whole. We specifically seek to exclude expressions of genocidal fantasies by extremist personalities or groups within a culture, which, as far as can be seen at the time, do not have a significant influence on the total process of a people.[32]

The emergence of full-scale genocide is made possible by the promulgation of an accepted ideology that justifies the killing as self-defense. "They are out to destroy our people/nation/faith/right to exist/way of life; therefore, in self-defense, we must destroy them first." Typically, the victim people is redefined in this ideology as some manner of lesser or subhuman species and therefore not deserving of the protection or dignity that is naturally due other members of the society.

Precipitating Factors or Context

The dramatic events, whether realistically significant or symbolically charged, that constitute powerful threats and thereby trigger the next latent stages of threat response.

The turning point in the collective process often is marked by some dramatic precipitating event(s). Sometimes, these precipitating events have very powerful objective meanings. Famine and drought, for example, or a full-scale war are clear-cut emergencies that trigger all kinds of collective behavior. However, many times the precipitating events are powerful largely by virtue of their electrifying symbolic meanings for the collective group. Given a society whose basic value system favors superiority over other peoples and in which fantasies and a potential ideology of genocide of another people are operative, the occurrence of a major threat, whether real or symbolic, will trigger the subsequent stages of this society's latent style of response to threat. The precipitating crisis may come in the form of major competition for a society's major industry, it may be in the movement of troops to the border by a neighboring country, or it may be the "trivial" matter of another country's humiliating a nation's ambassador.

One way of testing the objective reality of a precipitating event is to judge whether the same event would be handled differently by peoples and cultures that are prepared to interpret such events as problems that need to be solved more than as threats to survival. It is in this sense that many of us question intuitively the traditional historical explanations of various wars as growing out of this or that affront, insult or challenge, border incident, or dramatic clash between ideological interests and leaders — as if any of these events really could explain and justify the unbearable hells that were unleashed. We have sensed that so much of history is more like a recurring fairy tale, in which the mad forces of war and destruction are ready to erupt and require only some essentially trivial symbol to justify triggering the forces that are lying in wait.

And yet, symbolic precipitating factors and contexts do wield tremendous power as triggers that impel and justify the next stages of a behavior process. It is therefore essential that we learn how these triggers operate and that we prepare alternative strategies to head off the destructive spiral. In collective life, the art of diplomacy concerns avoiding provoking another people, e.g., knowing the "dos and don'ts" of cultural customs and honoring a people's points of cultural pride. A high point of collective maturity has been reached when one nation does not need to send troops into action when another country threatens border incidents and yet the first nation stands firm and has the appropriate military strength should it be required.

The psychology of brinksmanship or emergency responses to precipitating events is an enormous challenge for statesmen and societies. In the early warning system, we seek to analyze these highly charged precipitating events and the roles they play in the transition from the earlier stages of the sequence toward genocide in the later, more deadly stages.

Mobilization of Means to Genocide

The mobilization of tools and the organization of the participants for action to effect the fantasy or goal of genocide.

Following identification of the fantasy of and ideological plan for genocide, we look for indications within a culture that an operative capacity is being mobilized to implement the fantasy and the ideological goal. A genociding group or society obviously must mobilize a great many tools and resources to carry out its intentions. There is a need for managers in the government who administer the genocide, or, in the case of an insurgent or a revolutionary force, in the semi-governmental leadership forces of the group.

Legitimate and Institutionalization of Genocide

The progressively formal codifications of the law and the authorization of the formal institutions of a society to allow and implement destruction of the target group.

Whether or not a society moves all the way to genocide is very much a function of the extent to which the people and the institutions agree to the legitimation and institutionalization of the unfolding genocide. Sociologist Irving Louis Horowitz[33] argues that genocide is not a random event but grows out of the structure of the state, which must give its approval. Using genocide as the focal point, he has derived a typology of social systems: genocidal societies, deportation or incarceration societies, torture societies, harassment societies, traditional shame societies, guilt societies, tolerant societies, and permissive societies.

Even when a culture is already at the stage of manifest genocide, there is a great deal of information that we seek not only for the long-range purpose of learning more, but also on the realistic grounds that even early stages of genocide still present choices to people and that some genocidal momentums can be stopped even at a late stage. We want to know, for example, what positions the heads of the major churches in a culture take before, during, and after mass executions that are committed by their religionists. We want to know the position taken by medical administrators and practitioners (e.g., whether medical people make themselves available for cruel experiments that become another chapter in the tapestry of the genocide and what kind of medical treatment is given to the survivors and escapees). What are the reactions of the judiciary — do attorneys and judges fulfill the law's historic role as guardian against killing? Does the fourth estate risk exposing, criticizing, and protesting the horrors of the genocidal events? There are also situations in which local political and other leaders are able to arrest an already ongoing genocidal process — for example, the newly installed Kallay government rejection of German demands to deport Jews. Sociologist Helen Fein[34] argues forcefully in her well-documented "accounting" of the Holocaust that genocide is a rational result of choices made by the ruling elites, given the circumstances or potential profits and costs and shows that "where state authorities had resisted discrimination and/or church leaders vocally opposed any attempts to justify anti-Semitism or discrimination against Jews, resistance movements also identified with the Jews. ...If the threat of deportation would not be deterred by the state, leadership usually arose among Gentiles and Jews to avoid the isolation of the Jews, and finally countered the mobilization of the death machine."

Execution of Genocide and Experience-Denying Mechanisms

The actual extermination of a target victim people and the various ways in which the group or people block out experiencing the human meanings of the now-increasing momentum of violence and destruction.

The final, tragic data-entry column refers to the actual leap of mankind into a hell in which all that is precious and decent in the human experience is abandoned and the actual extermination of a target people is pursued. Even at this stage, there are important data to be entered as to the facts, figures, locations, methods, and agents of death. There are, moreover, different types of process structures to genocide that need to be analyzed.[35] We also need to follow the various societal processes we have been examining as they strangely continue to play out some semblance of themselves even when the black night of noncivilization has fallen. *The churches offer communion. The courts remain open. The press functions.* Grotesquely, the civilization seems to continue at a time when the society otherwise has become an agency of the deathhead. But there are also, or could be, signs of remaining life. Just as we study terminal medical conditions and seek every possible way to battle anew for life, so it is in the study of genociding societies. Sometimes we wonder: What if the conductor of the Berlin Symphony had turned to his audience and denounced the death camps? What if the pope had railed unambiguously against the death rites of the pagan Nazi crucifiers? Are not the continuing institutions of society potentially the remarkable heart and kidney machines through which we would hope to reassert life in a dying social order that has turned to meting out death?

We also seek to identify what we all experience — denying mechanisms, or the various ways in which people in groups block out experiencing the human meanings of their overt mass exterminations. The mass murderer pyramids onto his already existing definition of the target group as not human a belief that he is doing no more than putting society "in order". For human beings to be able to bear the ultimately inescapable inner experience of what they are doing to living people, they must use powerful psychological defenses to block out the experience. We want to understand the structure of these defenses and how they are picked and supported by the group culture. Even at this terrifying stage of the genocidal momentum, there is still much that might be done to disrupt the unchallenged progression of the typical genocidal sequence.[36]

Defining Levels of Process

All of the above steps in the development of genocide take place on several different levels. For example, some events come about as dramatic critical incidents, which at one fell swoop forever change human history. There are other, no less dramatic changes that come about as the result of a longer-term process of social change.[37]

Critical Incidents and Ongoing Process

Critical incidents: Key events that are seen as shaping the historical process of people (e.g., a major declaration by the constituted leader of a people, a celebrated legal case, economic depression, defeat in war, ecological tragedy). Ongoing process: The less dramatic, steady emergence of processes that are accepted as standard for a people or culture, such as a social tradition of segregation or the legal codification of a segregation policy.

In the case of the Holocaust, there were infamous moments when the signal was given to advance violence to new heights: *Krystallnacht*, the night the Nazis burned the synagogues and pulled Jews into the streets, beat them, and in subsequent days removed thousands to concentration camps; the failure of the Conference of Allied Nations at Evian, Switzerland, in 1938 to intervene on behalf of the Jewish victims; the first orders for mass extermination of Jews during the German push eastward in the early 1940s; the later decision by the Nazis to proceed to a systematic "final solution"; and so on.[38]

Along with such critical incidents, there are also the day-by-day events, which we call the ongoing process. These are often less dramatic, yet critically significant processes in the pace of a people or a culture toward genocide via policies of segregation, discrimination, humiliation, police brutality, imprisonment, and internment in concentration camps. There must be an ongoing climate in a culture that will permit, invite, and support what becomes orders to napalm-burn villages, to separate husbands and wives, and parents and children, or to execute prisoners. Events like these grow out of the ongoing processes within a people's history and way of life that precede the climactic events. In the case of Nazi Germany, there was the emergence of a fabric of unchallenged social humiliation, discriminatory legislation against the Jews, suspension of civil liberties and elementary civil rights, police actions such as midnight arrests and removal to an unknown fate, and an increasing brutalization until the brutality escalated to a full-blown program of genocide.

Note that the same sets of events in a society may be recorded in different ways both as critical incidents and as ongoing processes. We attempt in the organization of our early warning system to line these data up alongside each other, while providing for a degree of separation between the two kinds of events so that we can study them independently.

Leadership and Societal Dynamics

Leadership: Policy designs, decisions, announcements, and implementations that are seen as issuing from the leader or leadership of a society — such as the president, prime minister, dictator, or head of the church — or by the legislature or courts (e.g., the U.S. Supreme Court decision to desegregate public facilities or the decision of a military leadership to overthrow a government). Societal dynamics: The behavior flow of a given society that is attributable to the collective social-evolutionary process (e.g., the tradition of a free press, the sanctity of the law, a growing momentum of violence in the streets, and an accepted historical tradition of prejudice against black people).

How much the major processes of a society are determined by the acts of its leaders and how much by the larger flows of societal dynamics is a never-ending, fascinating question. It is important, and enormously interesting, to track the buildup of a society toward genocidal violences on the two tracks: the events that are initiated and led by the visible leaders and the events that unfold within the larger, more anonymous process of the collective societal dynamics.[39]

What Do Intelligent People Do When They Know in Advance?

Among the great advances of modern science is the ability to forecast various possible killers, such as hurricanes and tidal waves, or sources of poison and contamination. People in danger zones often are given advance warning and leave their homes. Yet, in many instances, a considerable number of residents do not leave for safer spots, even when advised to do so by the authorities. One U.S. government study of people who refused to leave their homes in the area of an oncoming tidal wave sought to identify the characteristics of people who refused to accept warning information. A surprising finding was that a fair number of well-educated people were among those who refused to leave.[40] Similarly, in the world of personal health, people frequently ignore early warning symptoms, early professional advice, and all manner of promptings of common sense until it is too late for them to save their life. In the psychoanalytic treatment of individuals, we learn that human beings tend to repeat the same acts over and over again, even though they are deeply self-punishing. In the history of mankind, people also repeat the same mistakes again and again.[41]

Human beings are dangerously unknowing or unable to shift many of their ways, even when they are on their way to death. One of the functions of a Genocide Early Warning System, therefore, is to educate people as to the possibility and desirability of change when they are faced with the knowledge of an impending state of danger. The very existence of an early warning system is a powerful symbol of the importance of knowing and being aware.

As we pointed out earlier, knowledge, in itself, does not bring real change, nor is it impossible that knowledge can also bring about an acceleration of evil. Lewis Coser[42] points out that undercutting human being's time-honored denial of the evils about them could, paradoxically, increase their denial of people's common humanity, but he also sees the positive potential of a knowledge of evil:

"If the increased visibility brought about by the communication revolution decreases the effectiveness of the denial of knowledge by 'good people' and forces reliance upon a second line of defense, the denial of common humanity, then an increasing brutalization of public life is much to be feared. If this comes to pass, we might enter a new brutalizing age in

which the 'good people', far from trying to protect themselves from the impact of dirty work, would condone it with a good conscience. And when the conscience of 'good people' rather than being protected by more or less hypocritical maneuvers, atrophies for good, then God help us all.

"But then again, an alternative and more hopeful outcome might also be envisaged: the new visibility that certain forms of evil have attained in our days may induce intellectuals, those 'antennae of the race', and in their wake educated strata, the young and others who have relatively marginal stakes in the society, to question some of the value premises on which the society is based. ...In this case the revulsion against manifest horrors may set into operation a process of reexamination of societal values which could, in the long run, lead to a transvaluation of basic values and to a restructuring of the fundamental assumptions upon which the society rests."

In the final analysis, if a Genocide Early Warning System someday serves "only" to save several thousand potential victims by enabling them to flee the clutches of a genocider headed toward their homes, the effort and cost of building such an early warning system will have been justified.

Notes

1. Marc Pilisuk and Lyn Ober (1976) "Torture and Genocide as Public Health Problems," *American Journal Orthopsychiatry, 46*(3), 388–392.

2. For a time, Amnesty International, which was established in 1961, was viewed in some quarters as somewhat leftist, or at least as an unduly naive, liberal group that failed to distinguish between torture and the legitimate and realistic necessities of military and police functions against revolutionaries, terrorists, and other groups who clothed themselves in "liberation" semantics to disguise their own vicious assaults on human life, while charging the established governments with cruelties. More recently, however, Amnesty is emerging as a responsible organization whose annual report of torture around the world is looked to by citizens rights groups and governments with increasing respect. At the center of Amnesty's activities is a Prisoner of Conscience Library. Amnesty seeks to maintain information about people who are held as political prisoners (defined as "those physically restrained from expressing an honestly held opinion that does not advocate violence"). Information is collected from friends and relatives of prisoners, a systematic scanning of newspapers, and inquiries, including sending authorized representatives to investigate the situation of a prisoner. The group then works by methods such as approaching embassies and writing letters to newspapers to secure prisoners' releases, at the same time it provides some assistance for prisoners and their families. At this point, at least, Amnesty is concerned primarily with individual cases, and, in fact, it carefully represents itself as an advocate of individual rights rather than as an observer of the larger status of human rights in a given nation, although there is a trend in Amnesty reports toward more overviewing of torture and the legal practices of countries (see *Amnesty International Annual Reports,* Luard, 1967). Other agencies, too, concern themselves with monitoring various aspects of civil rights around the world. One important source of information about major world events is Keesing's *Contemporary Archives*. The International Commission of Jurists, based in Geneva, issues very important advice on human rights violations. The International League for the Rights of Man, a nongovernmental organization accredited to the United Nations, follows and reports on offenses against human rights. Freedom House in New York issues meaningful surveys of the status of freedom in different countries. However, to the best of our knowledge, none of these reporting agencies attempts to maintain a systematic information system as to ongoing genocides, or the broader picture of the status of human rights in different countries, and for the

most part each agency is committed to its traditional mode for distributing information, not to the development of multimedia means for arousing and alerting an informed world public.

3. In a special issue of the magazine published by the United Nations Association of the U.S., which was devoted to the thirtieth anniversary of the United Nations, William Korey, a past chairman of the observer programs of the World Assembly on Human Rights and the conference of UN representatives of the association, writes about human rights in general: "Violations of human rights appear as widespread today, if not more so, as at any time in the past. The thousands of petitions — 'communications' — reaching the U.N. annually, relating violations of human rights, constitute only the tip of the iceberg. Gross violations of human rights often go unreported. An Amnesty International report last year documented the practice of physical and psychological torture in some 60 countries of the globe. Even terrifying instances of genocide reappeared, beginning in the sixties." (William Korey [1975] "U.N. Human Rights, Illusion and Reality: Violations of Human Rights Appear as Widespread Today, If Not More So, As at Any Time in the Past," *U.N. 30, Interdependent, 2*(7), 117.)

4. For many years, the U.S. has stood out as conspicuously absent from the list of signatories to the genocide convention. In a release dated August 7, 1974, the Bureau of Public Affairs of the Department of State noted: "The U.S., although participating in the development of the Convention text, and voting for and signing it, has never ratified or acceded to it. President Nixon noted this in a message to the Senate on February 19, 1970, and urged the Senate to consider anew this Convention. He stated that its ratification would reaffirm the stringent U.S. opposition to the crime of genocide, and he added that the Attorney General and the Secretary of State believe that there are no constitutional obstacles to US ratification. The Genocide Convention outlaws action that is repugnant to the American people and contrary to the principles on which our country was founded. Our failure to adhere to this Convention is an unnecessary diplomatic embarrassment and leaves us open to criticism despite our condemnation of genocide. Conversely, by ratifying the Convention, we would be publicly reaffirming our faith in the concepts of human dignity and human rights, and we would be helping to strengthen the structure of international law."

5. A noteworthy number of cancer research projects are designed around marking cancer cells in such a way that the body will be able to recognize them as enemies. These studies follow from the conception of cancer as a process wherein the pathological cells have lost contact with the rest of the body because the normal interactive genetic message is not being communicated; hence, the cancerous cells are not triggering natural immunologic reactions that normally fight off the cancer process. (Personal communication, Alberto Podorgny, Weizmann Institute of Science.)

6. Ervin Laszlo (1974) "World System Research and Information Bureau," *International Associations, 16*(1), 36.

7. David Weisbrodt, a professor of international law, testified at a U.S. congressional hearing in 1978: "Perhaps the greatest problem facing non-governmental organizations and researchers concerned about international human rights is the need for human rights documentation." (David Weisbrodt [1978] "Testimony Before U.S. House Committee on International Relations," *Human Rights Internet, 3*(7-8), 5.)

8. Pinchas Lapid has argued that the Turks' massacre of the Armenians was significant not only in its own tragic right, but also as a "dress rehearsal" for the Holocaust that was to follow. Lapid argues that the dress rehearsal took place in several levels: not only the actual systematization of mass destruction, but also the attention given to covering up news of the massacre, the actual participation of Germans in the killings executed by the Turks, and the fact that the world was largely silent about the tragedy of the Armenians and did not punish the killers, thereby tacitly encouraging the Holocaust and other genocides in years to come. (Pinchas Lapid [1974] "The 'Dress Rehearsal' for the Holocaust," *Bulletin of Bar-Ilan University*, Summer, pp. 14–20; in Hebrew.)

9. Robert Conquest (1970) *The Nation Killers: The Soviet Deportation of Nationalities*, London: Macmillan.

10. In discussing the concept of the Universal Declaration of Human Rights, Jorge Dominguez argues that in order to bridge between the different definitions of human rights data that various governments put forth and the real human rights situations one is seeking to evaluate, a data system should be built around concepts of values as well as of facts. He reviews various available frameworks, including the framework provided by the eight basic values of social life identified by Harold Lasswell and Abraham Kaplan: power, respect, rectitude, wealth, well-being, enlightenment, skill, and affection. Dominguez then adds four "modes of enjoyment" which are to cut across those values: security, growth, equality, and liberty. He concludes, "Assessments can be made about human rights conditions by using empirical data. ...But 'What then' is a question that will continue to face us all" (Jorge I. Dominguez, Nigel S. Rodley, Bryce Wood, and Richard Falk [1979] *Enhancing Global Human Rights,* New York: McGraw-Hill. See also Harold Lasswell and Abraham Kaplan, *Power and Society*, New Haven: Yale University Press, 1965; and note 12 below). William Korey writes about the Universal Declaration of Human Rights: "If the manifesto acts as a powerful beacon that provides light and inspiration for those suffering oppression or struggling for basic rights, it nonetheless lacks the kind of machinery that can bring about compliance with its various provisions. It may constitute international law, but it is devoid of enforcement powers that could give it genuine effectiveness. Implementing machinery, with certain notable exceptions, is missing. ...*Human rights is a dangerous Pandora's box to many officials. If it were opened no government would be safe from attack."* (William Korey, *U.N. Human Rights, Illusion and Reality,* p. 118.)

11. Herbert C. Kelman (1973) "Violence Without Moral Restraint," *Journal Social Issues*, *29,* 25, 31.

12. One of the most ambitious proposals for worldwide monitoring of a wide variety of social indicators was put forth by the team of Richard Snyder, Charles Hermann, and Harold Lasswell. Their central focus is that governments can be evaluated for their effects on human dignity. Although the academic world has reacted with many of the usual, if necessary, reservations and criticisms of feasibility, this proposal has generated considerable support overall and, in many quarters, even excitement. (Richard C. Snyder, Charles Hermann, and Harold D. Lasswell [1976] "A Global Monitoring System: Appraising the Effects of Government on Human Dignity," *International Studies Quarterly, 20*(2), 221–260.)

13. In certain areas of psychiatry, we have had frighteningly real examples of how behavioral science concepts and professionals can be subverted to tasks of destruction. In Nazi Germany, psychiatrists were among the leaders of the first mass

extermination programs, which were rationalized as the legitimate treatment of the mentally ill, retarded, and incompetent. (Fredric Wertham [1966] "The Geranium in the Window: The Euthanasia Murders," in Wertham, F., Ed., *A Sign for Cain*, New York: Macmillan.)

14. President Carter's Commission on the Holocaust, under the chairmanship of Elie Wiesel, followed a commendable path toward proposing a Holocaust center that would be both a memorial to peoples who have suffered genocide and an active research center (*Report of the President's Commission on The Holocaust,* Washington, D.C.: Government Printing Office, 1974). About relating the Holocaust to the plight of the peoples, Wiesel writes: "How to reconcile the specifically Jewish victims with the universality of all victims haunted us throughout the pilgrimage. ...As if, by speaking of Jews, we were somehow turning our backs on the millions of non-Jews the Nazis slaughtered. Which, of course, is not the case. Quite the contrary: As we evoke the Jewish martyrdom, we also recall the suffering and deaths of the non-Jewish victims. The universality of the Holocaust must be realized in its uniqueness." (Elie Wiesel, reporting on the trip of President Carter's Commission on the Holocaust to Auschwitz and other death camps in the *New York Times Magazine.*)

15. See the same emphasis on values and seeing events as parts of larger patterns in the following comparison between traditional approaches to individual human problems and a world order approach which appeared in the newsletter of the Institute for World Order in New York, *Macroscope* No. 2 (Winter-Spring 1977), p. 6. A fuller development is in Burns H. Weston (1975) "Contending with a Planet in Peril and Change: An Optimum Educational Response," *Alternatives: A Journal of World Policy, 5*(1), 59–95:

Traditional Approaches	*World Order Approach*
1. Analysis presumed value free	1. Analysis is value oriented and aimed at value clarification and realization
2. Ultimate analytical goal is description	2. Ultimate analytical goal is prescription
3. Time dimension is past and present	3. Time dimension is past, present, and especially future
4. Problems seen as separate issues	4. Problems seen as interrelated issues
5. Focuses on nation-states and governmental elites	5. Focuses on range of actors from individual to supranational institutions
6. Policy goals defined in terms of national interest (designed to maximize national wealth)	6. Policy goals defined in terms of global interest (designed to meet human needs)
7. Power seen as basically basically military and economic	7. Power seen as not only the ability to coerce
8. Large-scale violence considered as an acceptable means to implement policy	8. Large-scale violence ordinarily considered unacceptable goals
9. Human survival is assumed	9. Human survival is deemed problematical

16. In a series of "commandments" to students of collective behavior, sociologists Marx and Wood (1975) comment: "Thou shalt walk an intellectual tight rope that permits collective and conventional behavior to be viewed in light of common theoretical and conceptual frameworks, but that does not claim no differences exist between them." (Gary T. Marx and James L. Wood [1975] "Strands of Theory and Research in Collective Behavior," *Annual Review Sociology, 1,* 416.)

17. Samuel Warner (1957) *The Urge to Mass Destruction,* New York: Grune and Stratton.

18. Kurt Wolff (1969) calls for a "sociology of evil," that is, a study of the etymology and semantics of evil in various languages, the place of evil in the history of philosophy, the relationships between evil and technology, evil and the law, and so on. (Kurt H. Wolff [1969] "For a Sociology of Evil," *Journal Social Issues, 25*(1), 111–125).

19. Edwin I. Megargie (1967) "Matricide, Patricide, and the Dynamics of Aggression," paper delivered at a symposium, Murder Within the Family, at the annual meeting of the American Psychological Association, Washington, D.C.; and Edwin I. Megargie (1971) "The Role of Inhibition in the Assessment and Understanding of Violence," in Jerome I. Singer (Ed.), *The Control of Aggression and Violence*, New York: Academic Press, pp. 125–147. It is intriguing, and important, that even when there is a bona fide organic basis for an individual's eruption into violence, personal psychological processes and the societal processes that affect the individual's orientation to violence still determine to a great extent whether or not the pressure of the organic process will find its expression in destructive ways. A panel of 32 specialists reporting to Texas Governor John Connally about the Whitman case, a man who went berserk on a university campus, called the tumor Whitman suffered "extremely malignant" but they were not convinced that it was responsible for his bloody acts. "The report points out that the murderer had been accustomed since childhood to handle guns. Later, during his military training for sharpshooting, he became an expert in the use of firearms." The same commission suggested that soldiers who have been trained for killing in such a way that their whole thinking process will have been shaped by their training should be reconditioned or reeducated prior to their return to civilian life (*Fellowship, 33*(3), [March], 1967; see also Mortimer D. Gross [1971] "Violence Associated with Organic Brain Disease," in Jan Fawcett, Ed., *Dynamics of Violence*, Chicago: American Medical Association, pp. 85–91.)

20. A powerful study of witch-hunting by an outstanding student of genocide, Norman Cohn of the Columbus Center at Sussex University, England (a research center that is concerned with the dynamics of persecution and extermination), describes the devastating "collective fantasy"and collective persecution of hapless men and women, especially the latter, who were accused of being witches and then destroyed by the community in its "self-defense." (Norman Cohn [1975] *Europe's Inner Demons: An Enquiry Inspired by the Great Witch-Hunt*, New York: Basic Books.) Reviewer John Demos wrote in the *New York Times* about the book, "Few previous works have demonstrated so convincingly the power of 'inner' constructs to share historical events" (John Demos, review of Norman Cohn, *Europe's Inner Demons* in *New York Times Book Review*, August 10, 1975). See also Norman Cohn (1969) *Warrant for Genocide: The Myth of the Jewish Conspiracy and the Protocols of the Elders of Zion*, New York: Harper. Here we might also take note of a book by the brilliant "prophet" Elie Wiesel, who describes, in the story form, a twentieth-century blood-libel and pogrom in a small town — using this plot as a metaphor for the Holocaust. The story centers around a missing Christian child. There are rumors in the marketplace that the Jews killed him. An air of pogrom is all about when one Jew, Moshe, steps in to offer himself as the murderer of the child, though he is not, but the moral process has already reached the point that one sacrifice will no longer satisfy the mob. The pogrom must proceed in all its raw passion. (Elie Wiesel [1973] *The Oath*, New York: Random House.)

21. Gene Sharp (1973) *The Politics of Nonviolent Action*, Boston: Porter Sargent.

22. The pressure for legitimizing violence that previously was not sanctioned becomes greater when a society undergoes major upheavals, such as during wartime or during economic or other disasters, and when the basic ideological definitions in a society change radically. Allen Grimshaw (1970) emphasizes two conditions that charactertize the emergence of collective violence: (1) when previously stable superior/subordinate relationships between peoples lose theor hold and (2) when there is a belief that societal control agencies are either weak or partisan or both. (Allen D. Grimshaw [1970] "Interpreting Collective Violence: An Argument for the Importance of Social Structure," in James F. Short, Jr., and Marvin E. Wolfgang (Eds.), *Collective Violence, Annals of the American Academy of Political and Social Science,* 391, pp. 9–20.)

23. William A. Westley (1966) "The Escalation of Violence Through Legitimation," in Marvin E. Wolfgang (Ed.), *Patterns of Violence, Annals of the American Academy of Political and Social Science,* 364, pp. 120–126.

24. When *The Holocaust* was shown on West German television, the editor in chief of the mass-circulation *Stern* magazine acknowledged: "I knew that defenceless people were being exterminated like vermin in the name of Germany. Yes, I knew about it and I was too cowardly to offer any opposition." (Reuters, *Jerusalen Post*, February 2, 1979.)

25. Robert Payne (1973) *Massacre: The Tragedy at Bangla Desh and the Phenomenon of Mass Slaughter Throughout History*, New York: Macmillan, chapter 6 ("A Schema of Massacre"), pp. 76–87. An excellent summary of the stages of the unfolding of the Holocaust will be found in a pamphlet published by Yad Vashem, *The Holcaust* (Jerusalem, 1975).

26. The story of Erich Dorf in the book and television film, *The Holocaust*, is a powerful illustration of such denial of experiencing. (Gerald Green [1978] *The Holocaust*, New York: Bantam.)

27. For a critique of Smelser's book and a response by him, see Elliott Currie and Jerome H. Skolnick, "A Critical Note on Conceptions of Collective Behavior," in Short and Wolfgang (Eds.), *Collective Violence*, pp. 34–45, and Neil J. Smelser, "Two Critics in Search of a Bias: A Response to Currie and Skolnick," ibid., pp. 46–55.

28. Smelser, *Collective Behavior*, p. 262.

29. A. Paul Hare (1974) "Cyprus — Conflict and its Resolution," pamphlet at inaugural lecture at the University of Cape Town, South Africa, May; A. Paul Hare (1973) "Theories of Group Development and Categories for Interaction Analysis," *Small Group Behavior*, *4*(3), 259–304. See also A. Paul Hare (1976) *Handbook of Small Group Research*, Glencoe, IL.: Free Press; and A. Paul Hare and Herbert H. Blumberg, Eds. (1968) *Nonviolent Direction Action: American Cases, Social-Psychological Analyses*, Washington, D.C.: Corpus.

30. A frightening example of the nonsense of one-sided explanations of human experience is the remark of a well-known family therapist who commented that there should have been relatively little suffering during the Holocaust in Jewish families whose basic family structure was psychologically sound!

31. Vahakn N. Dadrian (1974) "The Structural-Functional Components of Genocide: A Victimological Approach to the Armenian Case," in Israel Drapkin and Emilio Viano (Eds.), *Victimology*. Lexington, MA: D.C. Heath, pp. 123–136.

32. For example, when a Nazi party in Minneapolis succeeded in a municipal election, the event meant the party was no longer a fringe party but a

meaningful indicator, though in the larger perspective still a low-level indicator (see Jack Porter [1977] "A Nazi Runs for Mayor," *Present Time, 4*(4), 27–31).

33. Irving Louis Horowitz (1976) *Genocide: State Power and Mass Murder*, New Brunswick, NJ: Transaction.

34. Helen Fein (1979) *Accounting for Genocide: National Responses and Jewish Victimization During the Holocaust*, New York: Free Press, p. 325.

35. Dadrian has made an effort to classify different types of genocide as cultural; latent, e.g., via deportation; retributive or localized atrocities, as a meting out of punishment; utilitarian or regional massacres; and optimal or full-scale holocausts. (Vahakn N. Dadrian [1975] "A Typology of Genocide," *International Review Modern Sociology, 5*(2), 201–212.) Sociologist Jack Nusam Porter argues that genocide presupposes a clear intent to wipe out the target people; all other killing is more like "oppression" or "massacres," not genocide. Porter's argument has the advantage of defining genocide more clearly but the disadvantage of excluding too many situations of mass murder. (Jack Nusan Porter, "What Is Genocide?," unpublished paper. See also Lucy S. Davidowicz [1976] *The War Against the Jews 1933–1945*, New York: Bantam.)

36. Fishel Schneorson was a psychologist in Tel Aviv who called out in 1943: "We must alert the peoples of the entire world that the destruction of millions in Europe is not the tragedy of those millions alone, nor of the Jewish People mourning its sons, but this is a worldwide epidemic, in the fullest tragic sense, that threatens death and destruction to the existence of humanity itself. Although everyone knows that the Jewish People are indeed the first victims of the Nazi destruction, they are neither the only ones nor the last. It is enough to recall the slaughter of the Gypsies that the Nazis are conducting in Europe according to their plan for eliminating inferior races, as well as the mass destruction of Soviet prisoners. This is the way of epidemics, the surest victims are the weak, but in the course of time none are spared and more and more victims are added." See Fishel Schneorson (1968) *Psychohistory of the Holocaust and Rebirth: Essays and Researches*, Tel Aviv: Israel, p. 12 (in Hebrew).

37. See John C. Flanagan (1954) "The Critical Incident Technique," *Psychological Bulletin, 51,* 327–358.

38. Davidowicz, *War Against the Jews 1933–1945.*

39. "A system flow chart covering many social events ... would reveal a confluence of multiple causes of violence, where several factors come together at approximately the same time and exceed the threshhold of suppression through mutual reinforcement" (Roy Grinker, Sr. [1971] "What Is the Cause of Violence?" in Jan Fawcett (Ed.), *Dynamics of Violence*, Chicago: American Medical Association, p. 59.)

40. A bibliography of researches of such disasters is in Anita Cochran, "A Selected Annotated Bibliography on Natural Hazards," Institute of Behavioral Science, University of Colorado, September 1972. Increasingly, disaster research centers have been established at various universities, such as Ohio State, which publishes a newsletter about disaster studies, *Unscheduled Events.*

41. Years ago, the brilliant social novelist Sinclair Lewis wrote what has become a byword for the denial of potential destruction to ourselves: *It Can't Happen Here* (1935, Doubleday).

42. Lewis A. Coser (1969) "The Visibility of Evil," *Journal Social Issues, 25*(1), pp. 108–109.

Appendix D

ASSESSMENT OF DANGEROUSNESS USING HANDWRITING CHARACTERISTICS

Kimon Iannetta[1]

A Brief Historical Synopsis

Since ancient times, writing has been used to provide information regarding the potential dangerousness of people. The Roman historian Suetonius declared that he could see the meanness in Augustus Caesar's script. The Chinese philosopher and painter, Jo-Hau, stated, "Handwriting infallibly shows whether it comes from a vulgar or noble minded person."

Beginning in 1609 with the work of the Frenchman Francois Demelle, character as revealed by writing became an established field of study. Early pioneers applied scientific principles beginning in 1878, with the work of Jules Crepieux-Jamin. The Germans in the 19th century, beginning with Wilhelm Preyer, originated the idea that handwriting is "brainwriting". Later, George Meyer related handwriting to emotions. Ludwig Klages applied Gestalt theory to handwriting, Later, Max Pulver studied the unconscious through writing, applying the principles of Sigmund Freud. Others reviewed physiological principles applied to handwriting, with Robert Saudek being one of the serious researchers and writers in this area. In the 1940s, Thea Stein Lewinson studied handwriting along with psychosomatic medicine. In his *Diagrams of the Unconscious*, Werner Wolff observed that man expresses his unconscious thought in his writing. The well-known psychologists Allport and Vernon further studied handwriting and declared its importance in the study of human behavior. Alfred Binet was interested in handwriting as a means of determining intellectual traits. Early research by Binet and Crepieux-Jamin indicated that handwriting could be used as a differential diagnostic tool in establishing intelligence.

In Europe, handwriting analysis was often taught within the confines of psychology. In the U.S., Milton Bunker, who pioneered the graphoanalysis movement, evaluated specific letter traits through longitudinal studies. In 1980, the U.S. Library of Congress reclassified handwriting analysis from its previous category — the occult — to the field of psychology.

[1] The editors are indebted to Kimon Iannetta for her permission to reprint portions of her 1993 research-oriented work, *Danger Between the Lines: Facilitating Assessment of Dangerousness Using Handwriting Characteristics*, written by Kimon Iannetta, with James F. Craine and Dennis G. McLaughlin. Ms. Iannetta conducts a wide variety of nationally recognized training and consults and publishes in the area of the forensic aspects of handwriting analysis. She can be reached at Trial Run, P.O. Box 1486, Kailua, HI, 96734, telephone: (808) 262-4593, e-mail: trialrun@aloha.net.

Writing is an appropriate field for scientific study in that it has been found, like other behaviors, to be stable and consistent over time. In a research study conducted by Harvey in 1934, writings of 50 women were evaluated, with samples taken 2 months apart. Correlations between the writings were found to be significant.

In addition to utilizing handwriting as an evaluation tool in determining components of behavior, it has long been established as an instrument in rendering identification of suspected forgers, writers of anonymous notes, and perpetrators of violent crimes. This field of forensic writing or document examination includes evaluation of papers, inks, and other related characteristics. For the most part, the fields of handwriting analysis in behavioral evaluations and document examination have remained separate, although there has been some discussion regarding the overlapping techniques and characteristics of both. The skills of the document examiner and the behavioral profiler can assist in the identification of the writer and the establishment of the personality characteristics of dangerous people. It is useful to have at least a fundamental knowledge of both disciplines in order to appreciate how they can be helpful and reinforce the findings of each other. Both observe that no two persons write alike and that writing is an established behavior that can be used to identify an individual. They share some common history and principles, despite the modern divisions within the professional communities.

Review of the Literature on Psychopathology in Handwriting: Three Major Authorities

Background studies in handwriting analysis provide a foundation for our interest in the scientific study of handwriting and its use in determining dangerousness. We know that handwriting emanates from the brain. It responds and relates to physiological changes, to physical structures, and to emotional responses. Writing provides an avenue for the assessment of individual characteristics and behaviors. It is a way to describe these behaviors as they would predict violence against individuals and institutions. The need to classify and categorize these specific features as they relate to specific types of dangerous persons remains an ongoing challenge. We will briefly survey the work of three principal authors whom most professional handwriting analysts recognize as experts in the field.

Klara Roman (1952) declared that writing reflects one's inner states. Most of her research was done in the 1950s. She noted that one's script can indicate personality features and moods. Anger, depression, and anxiety can be observed by the changes in pressure, speed, and spacing. Illegible, heedless writing is indicative of depressed individuals or those for whom life has no meaning. Slow, constricted writing can depict inner sadness. Inadequate inner spaces may show a craving for contact. Every handwriting is unique and cannot be duplicated. It is always changing, yet consistently reflecting individual expression. One or two traits alone do not indicate dangerousness. The entirety, the combination of various traits and features, must be taken as a whole to be examined.

Alfred Mendel (republished 1990) observed that the most important criterion for establishing mental disturbance comes from noting parts of letters that have been left out, one or several letters that are replaced by letters that don't belong, or one letter left out and a threaded formation substituted. He differentiated among various personality types, noting that paranoids frequently have blurred spots in their writing. Schizophrenics, who have problems making lasting contacts, show their personality disorganization through the dissolution of their writing, with distorted and grotesque letters. A tendency for middle zone letters to abruptly move into the upper or lower case shows social-emotional disharmony.

Saudek noted ten graphic features to indicate psychopathological attributes. He included slow writing, unnatural pressure of the writing, general instability in the writing, touching up of letter formations, letters written as other letters, blobbed or punctuated handwriting, frequent pen lifts, important parts of letters that are omitted, marked initial emphases, and letters "o", "a", "d", "g", and "q" open at the base. Persona writing — carefully executed writing that appears almost artificial in its perfection, is a particular clue to the potentially deceptive and dangerous person.

Danger Between the Lines: A Project Study

Research at the Hawaii State Hospital, undertaken by this author, with James Craine, Ph.D., and Dennis G. McLaughlin, Ph.D., expanded our knowledge of the identifying traits of dangerousness in writing. Initially, the study was conducted to analyze the writings of potentially violent psychiatric patients as a diagnostic tool. The project was initiated in 1984; 24 subjects were studied. Two handwriting analysts, with no prior knowledge of the subjects or their histories, studied their writings. Their results in identifying potential danger were superior to the standard methods currently in use. Their evaluations were correct to a highly significant degree statistically, and the study outcome noted the predictive capability of handwriting as a diagnostic tool.

Handwriting characteristics were organized and categorized into three main classifications, including (1) a sign of dangerousness, (2) a facilitator of action, and (3) an inhibitor of violent action. The handwriting was further rated on a scale from 0 to 5, with 0 indicating no danger signs and 5 indicating extreme likelihood for exhibiting dangerous behavior. The pilot study provided evidence that the technique of handwriting analysis has considerable validity in the prediction of violence. Thus, dangerousness can be evaluated with a high degree of certainty using the classifications and identifying characteristics indicated in the study.

Handwriting as a Visual Blueprint

Handwriting can be defined as a visual blueprint in that it can efficiently register one's propensity toward violent behavior. It can provide a map to pertinent data about potentially dangerous persons. To an expert in the discipline of behavioral profiling, the study and analysis of written communication reveals a broad understanding of the inner workings of the writer's mind. Mind prints, expressed as handwriting, are used as a method of identification, just like fingerprints. No two writings are identical. The patterns of movement are established from one's specific physiological and psychological characteristics and behaviors. The patterns of writing movements are locked in time for scrutiny and observation. One is able to evaluate an individual's specific timing, cadence, rhythm, consistencies, and peculiar features.

An individual's patterns of energy are revealed through his or her symbolic movements. The individual's stream of consciousness can show subtle layers and dimensions of the person's multi-dimensional self. A person's energy patterns can be revealed through his or her writings. With this visual product, one can observe mental, emotional, physical, and biological changes. Writing is a register of an individual's state, traits, and conscious and unconscious impulse reactions. An individual's sudden or slow change in behavior can be monitored through evaluating the writing over a period of time. It can be used to predict violence in the workplace by comparing characteristics of writing done at various times. Writing, like fingerprints, leaves a written trail with patterns that expose the guilt, the anxiety, and the looming explosion or decompression of the would-be threat.

Handwriting analysis is recommended as just one factor of the total process. Criminal records, personality tests, background data, environment factors, and medical information combine with handwriting characteristics to form the basis of the evaluation.

Interpreting handwriting requires a review of traits and their relationship as they combine to form an impression. Margins, word spacing, line slopes, rhythm, and the overall organization of the writing are reviewed. An evaluation is made of the overall appearance of the writing, whether it is refined or crude, rhythmic or lacking in rhythm and balance. Pressure characteristics, orientation to the page, and special letter traits, including size, shape, and zonal distributions, are examined. The strong traits that most clearly represent the individual will stand out. Very unusual structures or styles will indicate potential emotional or thought disturbances.

Assassins and Bombers

In Chapter 1 of this book, Harold Hall discusses assassins. Iannetta (1993, pp. 20–21) cited Clarke (1988), who listed characteristics common to assassins, which he placed into the following four categories:

1. Type I assassins view their acts as probable sacrifices of self for political ideals. These assassins are fully aware of the meaning and consequences of their acts, and emotional distortion is present only to the extent that political ideals supersede survival instincts. This group includes John Wilkes Booth, who assassinated Lincoln, and Leon Czolgosz, McKinley's assassin.
2. Type II assassins have an overwhelming need for acceptance, recognition, and status. They are without delusion and are cognizant of the personal consequences of their acts. They are characterized by moderately high levels of reality-based anxiety that has a strong influence on their behavior. These assassins seek power in order to compensate for low self-worth that is frequently the result of a deprivation of love and affection in their personal lives. The exercise of power in a public manner generates attention that has been denied in the past. The Type II assassin is anxious, emotional, and depressed and is primarily concerned with personal problems and only secondarily concerned with causes or ideals. Lee Harvey Oswald, assassin of John F. Kennedy; John Hinckley, attempted assassin of Ronald Reagan; and Lynette "Squeaky" Fromme, attempted assassin of Gerald Ford, all fall into this category.
3. Type III assassins are psychopaths who feel that their lives are intolerably meaningless. These assassins have no positive political values and are highly contemptuous of morality and social convention. The rage and perversity of these people may tend toward suicide, mass murder, or assassinations, but in the case of assassination there is no political motive. Except for their intense anger, they are emotionally flat; they feel neither joy nor sadness, they are indifferent to death, and they are unable to relate to others. Type III assassins include Arthur Bremer, who shot George Wallace.
4. Type IV assassins are characterized by severe emotional and cognitive distortion that is expressed in delusions of persecution and/or grandeur and in hallucinations. Contact with reality is tenuous and they are therefore unable to grasp the significance of their actions. Their acts are typically "divinely inspired." Charles Guiteau, who assassinated President James Garfield, was a Type IV assassin.

Killers such as the Unabomber, who used explosive devices are discussed in Chapter 1, and trait descriptions such as repressed rage and dysfunctional social relationships are provided.

The following analysis of Timothy McVeigh's handwriting shows how his development and adult history, including the masterminding of the bombing of the Murrah Federal Building in Oklahoma City, are translated into a distinct writing style (see Figure D1).

Timothy McVeigh: A Case Study in Terrorism by Bombing

Background. On April 19, 1995, 168 people, 19 of them children, were killed in a bombing that destroyed the Murrah Federal Building in Oklahoma City. What kind of person would commit such an unbelievably horrendous crime? We will investigate

FIGURE D1

HANDWRITING SAMPLE OF TIMOTHY McVEIGH

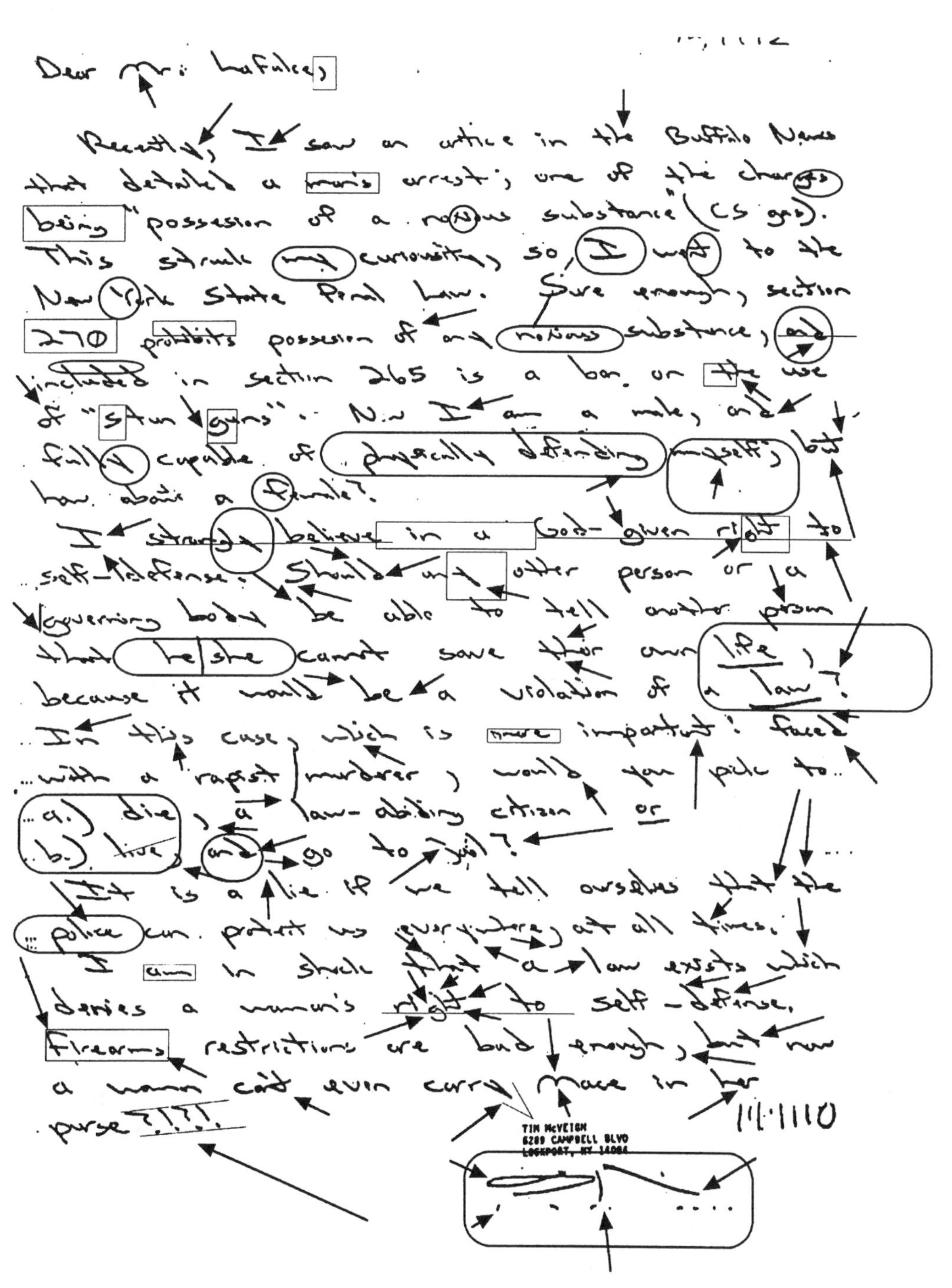

Dear Mr. LaFalce,

Recently, I saw an article in the Buffalo News that detailed a man's arrest; one of the charges being "possession of a noxious substance" (CS gas). This struck my curiosity, so I went to the New York State Penal Law. Sure enough, section 270 prohibits possession of any noxious substance, and included in section 265 is a ban on the use of "stun guns". Now I am a male, and fully capable of physically defending myself, but how about a female?

I strongly believe in a God-given right to self-defense. Should any other person or a governing body be able to tell another person that he/she cannot save their own life, because it would be a violation of a law?

In this case, which is more important: faced with a rapist/murderer, would you pick to..

a.) die, a law-abiding citizen or

b.) live and go to jail?

It is a lie if we tell ourselves that the police can protect us everywhere at all times.

I am in shock that a law exists which denies a woman's right to self-defense. Firearms restrictions are bad enough, but now a woman can't even carry Mace in her purse?!?!

TIM McVEIGH
6289 CAMPBELL BLVD
LOCKPORT, NY 14094

briefly the background of Timothy McVeigh, who was convicted of perpetrating this tragedy and then review those personality aspects in his writing that provide a glimpse of the motivating factors.

McVeigh came from a small town in upstate New York. His father was a blue collar worker who was employed making radiators. His mother worked as a travel agent. His parents were reportedly often absent during his growing up years. His father worked nights, and his mother was very active socially in addition to maintaining a regular work schedule. In school, he was considered outgoing, bright, and talkative. According to biographical accounts, his friends say that McVeigh loved guns at an early age and took them to school. He spent hours by himself shooting at targets.

Following high school, McVeigh joined the Army, serving as an artilleryman. He was a loner but made a few friends, such as Terry Nichols and Michael Fortier. Those who recall McVeigh's time in the military remember that he talked incessantly. He had paranoid descriptions about the threat of the federal government, especially with regard to individuals losing their right to have guns. During the Gulf War, he killed two enemy soldiers and bragged about it. Frustrated over his failure to complete the Green Berets training, McVeigh eventually left the Army.

He became a drifter, living in motels, frequenting gun shows, and becoming increasingly bitter about the federal government. He became outraged when the Federal Bureau of Investigation (FBI) raided the Branch Davidian compound on April 19, 1993, which happened exactly 2 years before the bombing in Oklahoma City. He visited the site to demonstrate his anger over the FBI raid. This background laid the framework for the violence in McVeigh's life. He had been described by those who knew him as someone who loved guns, had a deep philosophical hatred of government control over guns, and was a loner. He learned to kill in the military. He used the raid on the Branch Davidians as a precipitating issue of his rage. His handwriting indicated aspects of this potential for violence.

A Behavioral Profile Through Written Communication. When the author (Iannetta, 1993) first began to examine McVeigh's writing, dated 1992, she was struck by the apparent discrepancies between the signature and the body of the text. This revealed immediately an individual in great conflict with himself. Later, similarities between the two writings were found which were not so obvious at first glance, but nevertheless showed the consistent pattern of thought and behavior.

Taken alone, his signature fairly screams for attention, while hiding the writer's identity. It reveals the major precipitating factors that resulted in the destruction McVeigh later perpetrated. He has an organized design in his signature, beginning with the first stroke, the "T" for Tim, which symbolically curls into a fetal position, indicating his looking to the past and reaching for it hungrily. The central stroke of the signature divides the past from the future. The final and third stroke, which is made with powerful and forceful energy, indicates a dominant and tremendous power which culminates in an explosion of superfluous dots that grind in his unconscious. This represents the explosion that occurred 5 years later.

McVeigh's entire signature is symbolic of his inner need, his drama and myth, which are acted out in total in the body of his writing where his text portrays how he proceeds in his daily activities and habits. Overall, McVeigh's writing depicts his intelligence, his consistent patterns, his ability to be shrewdly manipulative and controlled, and his ability to control his behavior and carry out his missions within his own defined parameters. He sees himself as sane and behaves and talks normally. His inner conflict is hidden from others as he goes about his everyday life, but in fact that turmoil is reflected in his handwriting.

McVeigh further shows arrogance, a need for recognition and status. This attitude, coupled with feelings of omnipotence, could catapult him to the point where he could be convinced that he could kill and escape detection by being more clever than government officials or law enforcement personnel.

The writing also shows that this is a man who feels deprived of intimacy. Of course, there are reports that McVeigh may have experienced psychological damage from environmental deprivation caused by parental absences. In his writing, as the authors observed in the specific characteristics, he has not developed the ability to establish and maintain deep and significant interpersonal relations, proper bonding, and attachment. He may not have developed bonding at an early age, as he certainly has not learned the elements of trust. In fact, he expects and anticipates the worst and guards against the perceived threats by authority/parental/governmental figures. He therefore becomes suspicious and doubting of the motives of others, another characteristic exhibited in the writing. Other feelings of withdrawal, fears, and loneliness are exhibited

Certain patterns predominate and repeat in the body of the writing. For example, certain structures reveal McVeigh's obsessions with his dependent needs for a nurturing figure. The authors note the particular strokes in the "g"s that curl into a fetal position, as the capital "T" does in the signature, which represent this need. The "g"s reflect the emotions, the feelings of sexual intimacy, and, again, that fetal position bending into the past, indicating that McVeigh is looking for the mother figure that was missing. Specifically, the circular part of these "g"s reside in the lower zone, representing the unconscious need for that nurturance and the significant void that is felt at that level.

McVeigh has experienced deprivation of sensory imagery which is shown clearly in his "y" structures that also represent his tangible and physical acting out of his concerns, his memory, and his actions. The "y"s are retraced and angled, formed in such a way as to reveal his violent and aggressive mood as well as his hidden agenda. Again, like the "g", this unusual letter structure stands out in the body of the writing. Both the "y" and "g" structures, in their unusual formations, reveal McVeigh's improper bonding and his overwhelming need for intimacy and his inability to create it.

Much of the body of the writing visually appears to slant to the left, but certain letter structures do so in an unusual and dramatic pattern. Patterns of writing that slant unnaturally to the left further reveal the writer's emotional withdrawal, a feeling which is compounded by his need for space and his feelings of alienation and desire for distance from others. While his unconscious concerns are for intimacy, at the same time, he needs to separate himself from others. There is therefore a conflict between the conscious and unconscious drives.

McVeigh chooses to print. This reflects his desire to communicate clearly without revealing his emotional content.

There is a tension exhibited in the writing indicating a writer who has difficulty releasing feelings appropriately. The pressure of the writing shows greater intensity than the average writer would demonstrate. It shows McVeigh's energy and lasting feelings. The energy is propelled by his will power (demonstrated by the firmness and strengths of his "t" bars) which pushes and drives forward, and yet control is revealed by the downward directional focus of the crossbars.

The authors observed the grinding dots that accompany McVeigh's signature. That similar pattern is interspersed throughout his writing.

Lack of trust, resistance, and suspicion are reflected in the very unusual angles of letter strokes that dramatically turn left. Note for example, the "y" strokes that represent his personal standard, which is that lack of trust. McVeigh projects blame onto others; therefore, he has a need for self-defense. This paramount need is demonstrated in the fact that certain structures, as his "y" formations, are aggressive and weaponlike. They thrust right, revealing his hidden aggression.

The location of certain letters, or portions of letters, as well as the formation of letters reflect the personality characteristics of the writer. In McVeigh's case, his "d"s are separated by an unusually large space from the rest of the letters in his words and sometimes hide behind the baseline. This characterizes his distancing of his personal ideas and behaviors, the fact that he was able to keep these hidden from others. He has a need to hide, protect, and go about his plans in a covert and oppositional manner.

We must look closely to see certain subtle characteristics that reflect the special concerns and behaviors of this writer. He reverses the direction of his writing at certain critical junctures in a habitual manner. These occur with unique endings such as the "ht" at the end of words. Rather than end at the usual juncture, as we are taught to form the letter "h" prior to the "t" formation, McVeigh performs an upward stroke to make the "t," which has no terminal structure. (McVeigh can therefore carry out his activities in a creative, albeit bizarre, manner.)

As noted previously, McVeigh has aggressive impulses. Where is this seen in his writing? There are certain club strokes at the beginning of down structures, as well as angular strokes where they should not be in the writing. These strokes, as they often bend left, recognize the writer's clinging to his past and the pressure that it brings to his present thoughts and behavior. His "i"s and "t"s are made in a backward formation and show his need for a protective shield against the world. He is ready for battle. Capital letters, that are out of place at certain sections of the writing, again show where his feelings are particularly defiant.

The author (Iannetta, 1993) observed that McVeigh has great self-involvement and arrogance. The tallness of certain letters, such as the stems of the "d"s and "l"s and similar letters, is a symbol of that particular obsession with his own belief system.

McVeigh connects certain words in a manner that is consistent and subconsciously demonstrates how he thinks and what ideas are linked in his thought patterns. For example, the words "murder" and "law abiding" are attached. The vertical slash that occurs between the words "rapist" and "murderer" connect below with the word "law-abiding". "Die" and "live" are also connected as are "life" and "law" which are both underlined. It appears that McVeigh connects the words that have symbolic meaning for him.

The writer is attentive to detail. Almost every "i" is dotted and "t" crossed. These consistent patterns provide us with important information about this man in that he will organize carefully and ensure that every detail is considered. At the same time, the exceptions present another message. The "i" dot on the word "police" is missing, an ominous sign. The dot on the "i" in the word "jail" has a sharp, left slant, a sign of meticulous detail found on a word of some significance to McVeigh.

From McVeigh's writing, the author (Iannetta, 1993) would recognize in advance, without knowing him or his violent crime, that he is an introverted person and an organized planner. He conceives ideas based on his personal belief system. He carefully and accurately puts things together with precision and perfection. His thinking style is obsessive and driven by strong, powerful feelings and a desire to act on them. He needs to communicate and do so clearly. McVeigh wants to be important, yet feels rejected, and his final rejection brings the retaliation. His writing shows a type of superficial thinking that may not have really considered the women and children prior to the bombing as he focused on his own personal and safety concerns.

The readers are invited to explore the three tables adapted from the author's material (Iannetta, 1993) as follows: Primary indicators of dangerousness are listed in Table D1, facilitators of dangerousness are found in Table D2, and inhibitions to dangerousness are provided in Table D3. Factors on each table are numbered, labeled, given a condensed description, and interpreted psychologically. Presented for research purposes only and not for direct clinical application in predicting dangerousness in specific cases, the tables may be used to better understand written communications involving possible dangerousness.

References

Clark, James W. (1984) *American Assassins*. Princeton, NJ: Princeton University Press.

Fromm, E. (1973) *The Anatomy of Human Destructiveness*. Greenwich, CT: Fawcett Publications.

Iannetta, K., with Craine, J.F. and McLaughlin, D.G. (1993) *Danger Between the Lines: Facilitating Assessment of Dangerousness Using Handwriting Characteristics*. Kailua, HI: K. Iannetta.

Mendel, A.O. (republished 1990) *Personality in Handwriting*. Hollywood, CA: Newcastle Publishers.

Roman, K. (1952) *Handwriting: A Key to Personality*. New York: Pantheon Books.

TABLE D1

PRIMARY INDICATORS OF DANGEROUSNESS

Indicator of Dangerousness	Stroke Description	Psychological Implications
D-1 distorted personal pronoun "I"	Personal pronoun "I" written in a distorted, twisted, exaggerated, or unusual way	Direct connection to individual's self-image; distortions suggest distortion of one's self-concept
D-2 split personal pronoun "I"/signature	Personal pronoun "I" or signature broken into two or more parts	Disturbed self-concept; suggests weak boundaries between conscious thought processes and unconscious drives and urges
D-3 "rocking" printer personal pronoun "I"	Block print "I" with dish-shaped bottom cross bar	May indicate shallowness of purpose and unreliability which ties in with emotional instability
D-4 broken or segmented letters	Breaks within letters where continuous lines are the norm	Suggests weak boundaries between conscious thought processes and unconscious drives and urges
D-5 disintegrated writing	Writing strongly lacks rhythm, stability, legibility	May indicate impending or recent physical or mental breakdown; thoughts and/or emotions have become separated
D-6 club-like strokes	Stokes with club-like appearance, thick at either beginning or end	Indicates extreme decisiveness and/or forcefulness
D-7 slashes	Right-tending knife-like slashes that come to sharp points	Inner frustration at inability to follow through with one's desires; frequently found in handwriting of people who like to use weapons, especially sharp instruments
D-8 "X" formation	"X" structures where they are not normally expected	Shows that writer likes conflict and competition; may indicate thoughts, worries, or fantasies about death
D-9 tics	Straight, unnecessary strokes connected by sharp angles, either initial or final	Suggests anger, hostility, irritability, frustration, tendency to easily lose one's temper; writer has short fuse and can fly off the handle at least provocation
D-10 gouged dots	Extra-heavy ground-in dots; heavily jabbed dots	Reveals inner tension, irritability, and temper; implies ruminating or obsessional thinking

Table D1 (continued)

Primary Indicators of Dangerousness

Indicator of Dangerousness	Stroke Description	Psychological Implications
D-11 weapon-shaped letters	Structures resembling knives, guns, clubs, whips, etc.	Implies dangerous imagery; may be unconscious representation of hostile impulses
D-12 intense pressure	Writing pressure is exceptionally heavy	May indicate state of high tension and internal pressure; extreme need for sex, food, or substances
D-13 displaced pressure	Upstrokes are heavy; downstrokes light	Indicates inappropriate release and utilization of mental, emotional, and/or physical energies
D-14 erratic pressure	Erratic, changeable, arrhythmic pressure	Suggests erratic impulses and uncontrolled emotional responses and urges
D-15 blotches, puddles of ink	Excessive deposits of ink, especially in circles	Illustrates compulsive and uncontrollable indulgences in sensual and libidinal urges and possibility of impending inner or outer explosion
D-16 corrugated strokes	Writing strokes are shaky or feathery, does not flow smoothly	Indicates behavioral excesses, drug or alcohol abuse, and/or sexual excesses; may also imply increasing internal pressure and impending mental or physical breakdown
D-17 repaired strokes	Repaired, re-worked, or fixed letters	Indicates an attempt to cover up or to correct what's already been done; suggests that the writer is a fixer or perfectionist
D-18 disguised letters	Letters which look like other letters or which cannot be distinguished	Indicates fraudulent intentions; often seen in the writing of persons who are contrary, tricky, amoral, or who demonstrate active resistance to accepted and legal norms of behavior
D-19 repetitive overwriting	Repeatedly retraced structures	Suggests a loss of or lapse of consciousness, sometimes due to strong internal tension; writer may be excessively compulsive in behavior

TABLE D1 (CONTINUED)

PRIMARY INDICATORS OF DANGEROUSNESS

Indicator of Dangerousness	Stroke Description	Psychological Implications
D-20 slow or carefully drawn writing	Writing is stylized, slow, and lacking on spontaneity	Shows pretense of being conventional and conforming; acts as a cover and symbolizes lack of spontaneity or initiative
D-21 initial braced strokes	Initial strokes are rigid, angular, and braced	Illustrates feelings of deep anger or resentment; writer is inclined to focus on past hurts and injustices and is ready to retaliate
D-22 angled circle letters	Letters normally rounded have an angular appearance (especially "a" and "o")	Suggests lack of sensitivity to others' feelings and may indicate a harsh, crude, and/or brutal individual, when found in combination with other indications of dangerousness
D-23 open-bottom circles	Circle letters left open on the bottom (especially "a" and "o")	Portrays hypocrisy, lack of moral judgment
D-24 retraced letters	Downstrokes of midzone letters retraced by the following upstroke; retraced letters appear tight	Suggests that writer represses needs, desires, and emotions; implies that writer does not have coping skills or sense of logic needed to analyze his internal forces
D-25 strokes jut below line	Final strokes extend below the line and move forward	May indicate hidden aggression or sneaky, behind-the-scenes activities
D-26 letters dropped below baseline	Individual letters dip below baseline	May be an indication of unpleasant unconscious urges and desires affecting the individual's value or belief system and behavior
D-27 "felon's claw" formations	Lower zone structures are counterclockwise, reach leftward, and end in hooks	Suggests sneaky, underhanded, devious, and irresponsible behavior; implies that writer feels starved for love; may seek emotional fulfillment in deviant ways
D-28 angular lower zone	Lower zone structures are sharply angled	Signifies feelings of sexual guilt, tension, or hostility which sometimes translates into violence

Table D1 (continued)

Primary Indicators of Dangerousness

Indicator of Dangerousness	Stroke Description	Psychological Implications
D-29 distorted lower zone structures	Lower zone structures are twisted, distorted, or reversed	Points to unusual or disturbed physical or sexual desires; implies sexual confusion and/or emotional blocks
D-30 blotched upper zone	Upper zone structures are muddied by excess ink	Suggests unclean, indistinct morals and thinking; points toward immorality and morbid fantasies
D-31 distorted upper zone	Upper zone structures are twisted, distorted, reversed, or excessively retraced	Thinking and morals may be distorted or strange; writer may twist ideas or morals to fit his behavior or to justify his actions
D-32 distorted midzone letters	Midzone letters deviate from standard form; may be hard to distinguish when out of context (especially "m" and "n")	Suggests poor thinking patterns; may indicate confusion or evasiveness regarding everyday situations
D-33 distorted "d"s	Lower case "d"s that deviate from standard structure; may be hard to distinguish when out of context	Portrays distortions of one's personal value system, including ideas, morals, beliefs, appearance, or general life-style; expresses non-conformist or defiant individuality

Table D2

Facilitators of Dangerousness[a]

Facilitators of Dangerousness	Stroke Description	Psychological Implications
F-1 angular writing	Midzone formations are sharp-cornered and angular (especially "m" and "n")	Indicates that writer is militant, opinionated, resistant, and strongly principled; writer lacks softness, warmth, and flexibility and may be insensitive, rigid, inflexible, or unyielding
F-2 extreme size	Very tiny or extremely large writing	Prone to view the world and others in extremes rather than in normal proportions; extremely large writing indicates that writer sees himself as very important; extremely small writing shows introspection and very narrow vision
F-3 horizontal expansion	Loose, formless writing	Indicates very broad, expansive thinking and suggests poor boundaries, inner discipline or firm moral codes; with signs of dangerousness, writer can be impulsively violent
F-4 horizontal compression	Tight, constricted style	Indicates repressed, inhibited feelings; writer does not acknowledge inner responses or desires and may not know himself well
F-5 narrow word spacing	Midzone structures are proportionately larger than upper or lower zone structures	Writer desires close proximity to others, and may even require it, depending on amount of space between words; when combined with dangerous signs, person amy violate other people's rights
F-6 predominant midzone	Midzone structures are proportionately larger than upper or lower zone structures	Indicates that writer is oriented to the present rather than the past or future; indicates strong need for immediate gratification, immaturity, and subjective view of the world

Table D2 (continued)

Facilitators of Dangerousness[a]

Facilitators of Dangerousness	Stroke Description	Psychological Implications
F-7 erratic midzone size	Midzone structures vary in size and shape	Suggests a proneness to hypersensitivity which relates to fluctuating self-image; implies unstable responses and inner conflict
F-8 increasing size	Letters or groups of letters grow larger as they progress (especially "m" and "n")	Suggests a verbally blunt person — someone who lacks tact; points toward lack of refined social skills and implies that writer attempts to overcompensate for basic feeling of inferiority
F-9 monotonous writing	Writing follows a rigid-repetitious, or non-variable pattern	Indicates inflexibility and overly mechanical thinking; person wants to create a special image and has learned to cover the true self behind a facade
F-10 printing or disconnected writing	Lack of connections between letters	Indicates that writer has cut himself off from inner feelings and that there is an avoidance of emotion or attachment to people; naturalness is replaced by precision
F-11 overly connected writing	All letters of words connected; words may be connected to each other	Indicates compulsive tendencies; writer tends to recognize information only, relying heavily on orderly and systematic thinking and not trusting one's intuition
F-12 formless writing	Letters are formless and threadlike	Implies lack of structured thought processes and points toward uncertainty, indecision, and lack of commitment
F-13 far rightward slant	Writing slants far to right, almost leaning on the line	Indicates immediate and intense emotional responses to outer stimuli; connotes strong emotional biases; person is inclined to act impulsively and volcanically

Table D2 (continued)

Facilitators of Dangerousness[a]

Facilitators of Dangerousness	Stroke Description	Psychological Implications
F-14 increasing slant	Slant increases radically within a word or entire line	Indicates tendency to become increasingly emotional and less objective as the writer becomes involved with a person, project, or activity
F-15 variable slant	Slant is variable and inconsistent	Implies a person with an erratic emotional nature, one who is subject to the mood of the moment; writer is easily excitable and unpredictable; behavior may be erratic
F-16 erratic spacing	Word and/or letter spacing is inconsistent	Indicates erratic responses to environmental influences; suggests that writer is ambivalent about interpersonal contact, is inconsistent, unorganized, and lacks logic
F-17 irregular baseline	Line of writing is inconsistent; may appear wavy	Indicates moodiness; suggests immaturity and labile, unpredictable reactions and behavior
F-18 arched baseline	Writing line forms an arch	Indicates variable moods; projects or endeavors are started with energy or enthusiasm which wanes; writer may be bipolar manic depressive if arched baselines are consistent and seen throughout the writing
F-19 downhill baseline	Writing line goes downhill	Shows pessimism, despondency, or lack of energy; if line falls sharply, depression or tiredness is indicated
F-20 uphill baseline	Writing line goes uphill	Indicates positive mood and optimistic outlook; if lines rise steeply on the page, writer may be restless, manic, or unrealistically optimistic

Table D2 (continued)

Facilitators of Dangerousness[a]

Facilitators of Dangerousness	Stroke Description	Psychological Implications
F-21 out-of-place capitals	Capital letters in place of lower case letters (especially "k")	Indicates resistance toward authority; writer is alert to possible injustices by authority figures; may indicate rebelliousness and fear of losing one's autonomy
F-22 missing letters	Writing is illegible due to missing letters	Indicates tendency to evade the truth or to skim over part of the story; writer tends to be careless and rushed
F-23 superfluous strokes	Extra, connected, and unnecessary additions to letters	Indicates embellishment of basic truth with idiosyncratic perceptions or outright deception
F-24 simplified or omitted lead-ins	Absence of lead-ins at beginning of letters or words	Shows simplified, direct approach in speech, action, manners, dress, or taste; writer may disregard formalities and come right to the point
F-25 "m", "n" loops	Loops appear between humps of "m" and "n"	Indicates strong repression stemming from fear of unconscious thoughts and desires; indicative of anxiety, excessive worry, or obsessive ruminating over unimportant matters
F-26 initial hooks	Letters or words begin with hooks	Writer is prone to acquisitiveness — a desire to possess
F-27 "shark's teeth"	Midzone structures look like shark's teeth (especially "m", "n")	Suggests unmet emotional hunger often resulting in covert "using" of other people; connotes devious behavior, manipulation, and indirect communication
F-28 angles mixed with arches	Midzone formations are both angular and rounded (especially "m" and "n")	Illustrates tendency toward social immaturity; person may be torn between being soft (arches) or harsh (angles); when added to signs of dangerousness, brutality is a possibility

Table D2 (continued)

Facilitators of Dangerousness[a]

Facilitators of Dangerousness	Stroke Description	Psychological Implications
F-29 small initial loops	Small, reversed initial loop	Indicates jealousy, fear of rejection or loss of love; afraid of losing relationships or things; indicative of suspiciousness, insecurity, and competitiveness
F-30 forward thrust	Strokes	Rightward-thrusting strokes; end strokes thrust forward at an angle Implies aggressiveness and/or initiative (forward movement); writer employs considerable energy in their activities, whether positive or negative
F-31 finals curve up and back	Final strokes move up and to the left over midzone in upper zone (especially "m" and "n")	Indicates a need for attention, notice, and recognition; writer may use attention-getting behaviors such as flirtation, strong show of emotion, or extravagant gestures
F-32 final hooks	Words or letters end with hook-like structure	Shows tenacity; writers holds on to possessions, ideas, attitudes, or intentions; finds security in the familiar
F-33 leftward-ending strokes	Strokes with a leftward direction which normally end to the right	Implies self-castigation or self-blame. Writer may place himself in situations that result in some form of punishment; relates to unconscious guilt or self-condemnation
F-34 braced structures	Final midzone strokes are braced, tent-like structures (especially "t" and "d")	Indicative of stubborn, unreasonable, oppositional attitude
F-35 signature crossed out	Line through signature; obscured or crossed-out signature	Indicates self-negative thoughts; writer does not wish to associate with the name which is crossed out; may be dangerous to self of the first name is crossed out or obliterated

Table D2 (continued)

Facilitators of Dangerousness[a]

Facilitators of Dangerousness	Stroke Description	Psychological Implications
F-36 narrow right margin	Writing lines go all the way to right edge of paper	Indicates a proneness to rush ahead due to difficulty controlling one's impulses; writer's mental or emotional brakes are not working properly
F-37 exaggerated capitals	Capital letters are proportionately very large	Indicates incongruence between a desire to be important and the actual self-image; need to be important is not in keeping with abilities or reality, sometimes creating frustration, irritability, or anxiety
F-38 closed circle letters	Circle letters closed on tip (especially "a" and "o")	Shows reticence; writer may not be willing or able to verbally express thoughts and feelings; generally prefers to keep personal matters concealed
F-39 looped circle letters	Circle letters with initial loops (especially "a" and "o")	Indicates self-deception or self-denial; writer can be manipulative and lacking in clear communication
F-40 variable personal pronoun "I"	Varying styles of personal pronoun "I" in the same writing	Indicates vacillating self-image, someone unsure of who is the real "I"; may have different selves according to the situation
F-41 reversed personal	Pronoun "I"	"I"s written in reverse direction, opposite of standard style Implies covert defiance and/or a tendency to follow one's own rules; writer is oppositional, usually pretending to follow rules but actually doing things independent of the norm; very common sign with "bad boys"
F-42 signature different from text	Text and signature are appreciably different in style	Writer's outer expression (persona) and behavior are different from the way he really thinks and feels; may want to create an impression or to be seen as different than he really is

Table D2 (continued)

Facilitators of Dangerousness[a]

Facilitators of Dangerousness	Stroke Description	Psychological Implications
F-43 enlarged "d" circle	Circle part of lower case "d" is extra large in proportion to other letters	Suggests strong indifference to other people's opinions; writer sets his own standards and may also be defiant or live a life-style which opposes authority
F-44 "d" stem leaning far rightward	Lower case "d" stem leans far to right	Suggests a fragile self-esteem which requires a defensive posture; indicates possibility of sudden emotional outbursts or other strong reactions to perceived threats to self-esteem
F-45 very short "t," "d" stems	Lower case "t" and "d" stems are very short in proportion to midzone letters	Writer wants to make independent decisions about his own lifestyle; disregards social rules and norms and likes to "do his own thing"
F-46 very tall "t" and "d" stems	Lower case "t" and "d" are excessively tall in proportion to midzone letters	Suggests vanity, an overestimation of one's own worth and abilities; writer expects praise and recognition, whether it has been earned or not, tends to think that rules do not apply to him; may exhibit pomposity, grandiosity, or arrogance
F-47 wide "t" and "d" loops	Lower case "t" and "d" stems with extra-wide loops	Indicates fear of criticism regarding lifestyle, dress, family, customary behavior, etc.; suggests tendency to be "thin-skinned" — to imagine disapproval and to magnify criticism, which comes from guilt feelings
F-48 down-slanted cross bars	T-bars and horizontal cross strokes that slant downward and are sharp at the end	Indicates a dominating nature; writer wants things done his way; indicates a demanding, controlling personality, resulting from feelings of futility and powerlessness

Table D2 (continued)

Facilitators of Dangerousness[a]

Facilitators of Dangerousness	Stroke Description	Psychological Implications
F-49 rightward-placed t-bars	t-bars fly off to the right of t-stems	Shows habit of exploding or reacting with temper when plans or goals are thwarted; writer is irritable, impatient, apt to "fly off the handle" at slightest provocation
F-50 heavy t-bars	t-bars and horizontal strokes are thick in comparison to other strokes	Indicates a person of strong will, someone who is purposeful and self-directed
F-51 high t-bars	t-bars placed on top of or above t-stems	Suggests very high goals; writer is prone to have a rich fantasy life, especially concerning future; looks far ahead and may want to do something important or be someone special
F-52 dish-shaped t-bars	t-bars are bent upward at each end	Prone to be irresponsible and fearful of commitment; suggestive of shallow purpose and unreliability
F-53 extended t-bars	t-bars and horizontal strokes are proportionately long	Indicates enthusiasm and enjoyment of ideas and interests; writer is likely to follow through with plans and intentions
F-54 strong downstrokes	Heavy, long downstrokes in lower zone structures	Writer is determined and self-directed, has strong follow-through and does not wish to admit defeat; energy is expressed in physical or practical accomplishments
F-55 exaggerated lower zone	Lower zone structures are exaggerated in length and width	Suggests unusually strong physical and/or material drives; heavy focus on physical satisfaction (i.e., food, sex, and physical activity), or writer may be concerned with financial security
F-56 entangled lower zone	Lower zone structures are over-extended, running into lines below	Indicates subjective thinking; writer scatters his energy by being involved in many interest and activities, is prone to restlessness, and has an urge for frequent change

TABLE D2 (CONTINUED)

FACILITATORS OF DANGEROUSNESS[a]

Facilitators of Dangerousness	Stroke Description	Psychological Implications
F-57 stunted upper zone	Upper zone structures are absent, very small, or squelched	Writer thinks along practical and/or materialistic rather than spiritual or philosophical lines
F-58 exaggerated upper zone	Upper zone structures are exaggerated in height and width	Indicates a tendency to exaggerate, distort ideas, or daydream; suggestive of strong imagery, active imagination, and rich fantasy life
F-59 entangled upper zone	Upper zone structures invade the lines above	Writer's thoughts are confused and/or distorted; when exaggerated, there are possible hallucinations and loss of contact with reality
F-60 drooping finals	Final strokes of letters or words droop downward	Shows discouragement and resignation; may show chronic depression or pessimism
F-61 tall initial "p" strokes	Initial stroke for "p"s rise above main part of letter	Indicates that writer uses argumentativeness as a defense against intrusion
F-62 distorted "p"s	"p"s deviate from standard form; may be twisted, exaggerated, distorted, or squeezed	Points toward unusual attitudes regarding one's physical desires and activities; can be associated with emotional acting-out, or trouble accepting one's physical drives
F-63 tied structures	Tied letters (especially "t" and "f")	Indicates persistence and an unwillingness to admit defeat; writer is in the habit of trying over and over again, even if that means going back to the beginning
F-64 unique structures	Any letter repeatedly written in an odd, unique, or unusual way	Indicates an unusual thinking style; may indicate talents and uniquely creating abilities or pathological obsessions, especially when found consistently
F-65 phallus-shaped structures	Phallus-shaped strokes	Indicates repetitive thoughts and fantasies about sex

Table D2 (continued)

Facilitators of Dangerousness[a]

Facilitators of Dangerousness	Stroke Description	Psychological Implications
F-66 flat-topped structures	Letters are flat across the top (especially "r")	Indicates manual dexterity and an ability to work with tools and implements; sometimes found in the handwritings of killers who are deft at carrying out their murderous deeds

[a] Facilitators of dangerousness are those characteristics which, when added to the dangerous signs in Table D1, increase the possibility of violent behavior according to their relative strength and how they combine with other traits. In general, facilitators increase activity, whether positive or negative.

TABLE D3

INHIBITORS TO DANGEROUSNESS

Inhibitors to Dangerousness	Stroke Description	Psychological Implications
I-1 uniformity	Overall uniformity of the writing: good rhythm, consistency, evenness of letter size, spacing, slant, etc.	Implies clarity of thinking and organization; indicates objectivity, harmony, coordination and timing; suggests one who is self-disciplined and self-controlled
I-2 vital pressure	Writing pressure is natural and of high quality (natural alternation between thick and thin strokes)	Shows vitality, energy, and liveliness; suggests full participation in life and depth of emotional experiences; indicates integration, vitality, and emotional balance
I-3 light pressure	Writing is light, lacks pressure	Indicates lack of intensity; emotional experiences are not absorbed and are usually quickly forgotten; feelings are usually expressed immediately rather than harbored; reactions tend to be more intellectual or spiritual than physical or emotional
I-4 consistent baseline	Writing stays on an even line	Suggests internal regulation, self-discipline, emotional stability, and goal-orientation; suggests "feet on the ground" approach; writer is inclined to use thought before action
I-5 vertical writing	Writing is vertical, does not slant to left or right	Indicates objectivity and considered actions; writer exercises conscious control over desires and feelings, has less need for interpersonal relationships than more emotional people; may work better with facts and objects than with people
I-6 wide line spacing	Spacing between lines is extra wide	Lack of contact with inner feelings; writer does not allow self to be influenced by inner feelings and can therefore be quite objective; tends to feel isolated from others

TABLE D3 (CONTINUED)

INHIBITORS TO DANGEROUSNESS

Inhibitors to Dangerousness	Stroke Description	Psychological Implications
I-7 extra wide word spacing	Spacing between words is wider than normal	Indicates that self-control dominates and that writer may be isolated from his emotions and from other people; implies lack of spontaneity; thinking and objectivity predominate over feeling; suggests loneliness and need for space
I-8 soft baseline	Letter formations are rounded at the baseline	Implies a relaxed approach, little or no aggressive forces, and a gentle nature; enhances such traits as helpfulness, receptiveness, nurturing qualities
I-9 arcade formations	Midzone formations are rounded on top (especially "m" and "n")	Writer is gentle by nature and generally lacking in aggressive tendencies, tends to be soft, considerate, patient, and careful; concerned with appearances and self-protection; often secretive and guarded about personal matters
I-10 precise letter formations	Letters are clearly written, well formed, and legible (especially "m" and "n")	Suggests clearly defined, concise thinking and communication; writer thinks things through carefully, is inclined to be practical and systematic
I-11 consistent midzone size	Midzone structures are consistent in size and shape	Indicative of self-control, inner discipline, regularity, and predictability; writer is "on an even keel" socially and emotionally
I-12 diminishing size	Letters or groups of letters diminish in size as they progress (especially "m" and "n")	Suggests innate psychological insight, an ability to understand and (usually) influence others on a subtle level; writer uses tact and discretion and works toward peaceful solutions

Table D3 (continued)

Inhibitors to Dangerousness

Inhibitors to Dangerousness	Stroke Description	Psychological Implications
I-13 wavy lead-ins	Initial strokes above midzone are soft, curved, or wavy (especially "m" and "n")	Suggests an individual with humor and a generally positive attitude; adult coping mechanism which implies that writer makes use of humor to keep his attitude and surroundings light and positive
I-14 long, curved lead-ins	Initial strokes of words are long and curved	Often found in handwriting of individuals who are deliberate and who tend to carefully consider possible consequences before making a move
I-15 large initial loops	Large, initial leftward-moving loops in upper zone	Reveals a desire to take on responsibility, to do something important, or to be an integral part of a team; connotes caretaking approach often seen in writing of teachers, parents, doctors, nurses
I-16 cupped finals	End strokes cup out and upward	Indicates generosity, willingness to give or to share that which the writer feels is valuable; suggests that writer may be service oriented and wants to be fair; shows consideration for others
I-17 straight, extended finals	Finals extend straight out to fill space	Tendency to be cautious, to rethink one's decision before taking action; writer is "putting on the brakes"
I-18 consistent upper zone	Uppers zone structures are consistent in height, width, and style	Suggests consistent philosophy or code of ethics; points toward intellectual control and suggests a person whose actions and responses are consistent with his code of ethics
I-19 stunted lower zone	Lower zone structures are noticeably short	Writer is prone to sedentary preferences and may lack physical follow-through; may have weak energy or low sex drive

Table D3 (continued)

Inhibitors to Dangerousness

Inhibitors to Dangerousness	Stroke Description	Psychological Implications
I-20 clear circle letters	Circle letters are well-defined and free of loops, extra strokes, or marks (especially "a" and "o")	Indicates clarity of thought and ease of communication; writer wants to be open with his ideas and feelings
I-21 figure-8 structures	Letters made like figure 8s (especially "f" and "g")	Indicates adaptability, flexibility, and fluid thinking; suggests strong coping mechanisms; under stress, writer can change his viewpoint and adapt accordingly
I-22 Greek "e"s	"e"s made in the Greek style	Point toward aesthetic, cultural, or artistic interests; writer appreciates that which is beautiful and wants to be refined
I-23 rounded "e"s	Lowercase "e"s are round and open	Shows a tolerant attitude toward other people and their ideas, willingness to see through other's eyes, empathy, readiness to listen to and accept new approaches
I-24 arched t-bars	t-bars are bent downward at each end	Writer is making a conscious effort to change or to control something he sees as negative or undesirable; he bends his will to accomplish self-control
I-25 Accurate "i" dots and t-bars	Carefully placed i-dots and t-bars	Shows attentiveness to details and care in planning; suggests patience as a strong asset; adds to writer's stability and consistency in thought and action

APPENDIX E

CRITICAL INCIDENT STRESS DEBRIEFING, OKLAHOMA CITY, 1995

Joseph A. Davis[1]

Shortly after 9:00 a.m. on April 19, 1995, the Alfred P. Murrah Federal Building, located in downtown Oklahoma City, was devastated by a bomb blast of such gigantic proportions that it was reportedly heard over a 25- to 35-mile radius and as far away as Norman, OK. Oklahomans commuting to work on that sunny Wednesday morning had been going about their business as usual while a crude bomb made from various organic compounds, chemical fertilizer, sodium nitrate, and diesel fuel, weighing an estimated 4800 pounds or more, was transported in a rented van that blasted out a crater approximately 15 to 30 feet wide and 12 to 15 feet deep in the ground floor of the Murrah Federal Building on North West 5th Street. The building was immediately impacted; floors and windows collapsed. As far as ten blocks away, hundreds of innocent victims lay hurt, seriously injured, or dead from shards of glass that flew from office windows hundreds of feet above the street floor. Without warning, the initial impact of the bomb immediately devastated the entire city.

Psychologically in a state of shock, disbelief, and denial, acute symptoms of post-traumatic stress disorder were commonplace. Oklahomans, "numb" from the impact of the critical incident and ill-equipped to handle the chaos of such catastrophic proportions, struggled to regain control of their lives as friends, family, and loved ones went unaccounted for or were found critically injured, dying, or already dead.

The critical incident on April 19, 1995, demanded the immediate attention of our nation to come to the aid of all Oklahomans who were reaching out in a time of desperate need. One hundred sixty eight people were found dead, including 19 children and a trauma nurse who was working as an emergency services rescue worker. Still others are missing and may never be found. Over 500 other victims were injured from the blast and received emergency medical attention.

---

[1] Joseph Davis, Ph.D., is currently a Crisis Response Team member, southern California Team Leader, and Professional Trainer for the National Organization for Victim Assistance (NOVA) located in Washington, D.C. In addition to providing crisis response public services to NOVA, he is a Senior Stress Management Specialist providing disaster mental health services in times of crisis for FEMA, also located in Washington, D.C. In California, Dr. Davis is a Professional Trainer for the Governor's Office of Emergency Services and the California Specialized Training Institute, located at California Polytechnical University (Cal-Poly) in San Luis Obispo, CA. Dr. Davis specializes in disaster preparedness, disaster mental health trauma recovery services, critical incident stress debriefing, and disaster management operations planning.

Additionally, countless others were traumatized by the critical event and needed professional mental health attention or medical care for weeks, months, and quite possibly, years to come. On June 1, 1995, an exhaustive investigation revealed that as many as 30 office buildings in Oklahoma City proper had been condemned and as many as 300 others had been damaged. Overall, the full extent of the physical and psychological impact of the blast on the state and city of Oklahoma as well as our nation is yet unknown and may never realistically be estimated in terms of trauma, loss, and grief.

National Organization for Victim Assistance

Since the late 1970s and early 1980s, the victim assistance movement has received more positive attention than ever and has gained tremendous momentum with the passage of state and federal legislation designed to provide resources and services to those who are physically or emotionally traumatized or victimized (Davis, 1993). As members of the National Organization for Victim Assistance (NOVA), the Crisis Response Teams (CRT) of emergency trauma specialists are on "stand-by" for any national or international emergency considered to be a critical incident that requires on-site debriefing services to any state, city, town or community in crisis (as a standard operating procedure, NOVA becomes involved only when an invitation is made by any federal, state, or local authority).

Founded by Marlene A. Young in 1975, NOVA is a highly respected, non-profit organization that has responded to many "high profile" tragedies, such as the crisis in Washington state after the Mount St. Helen's eruption in 1980; the Air Florida airline crash of 1982; the South Korean airline flight 007 disaster of 1983; the Mexico earthquake of 1985; the Edmond, OK, post office mass murders involving postal clerk Patrick Sherrill in 1986; the Milwaukee Jeffrey Dahmer serial murder series; and the Kobe, Japan, earthquake tragedy in 1997, to name only a few (NOVA, 1994). Most of the information in this appendix, unless otherwise referenced, is attributed to NOVA.

On April 19, 1995, the author received an emergency call from NOVA's national Office in Washington, D.C., with instructions to go to Oklahoma City. NOVA had already deployed an initial CRT, sometimes called a Critical Incident Stress Debriefing Team, to the scene and surrounding community while this author was in transit. Prior to the flight, the author was briefed by telephone regarding what to expect upon arrival in Oklahoma City.

Deployment of a Community Crisis Response Team

NOVA's invitation to deploy a CRT was initiated by Oklahoma Attorney General Drew Edmundsen, former Attorney General of Oklahoma Michael C. Turpen, the Oklahoma City Board of Education, and the U.S. Department of Justice directed by Attorney General Janet Reno, to provide critical incident stress debriefing (CISD), education, and crisis intervention, as well as one-on-one services as needed for first responders (i.e., firefighters, police officers, emergency medical personnel) and the citizens, children, and families in the surrounding communities of Oklahoma City.

NOVA's CRT personnel are all highly trained specialists in disaster management, emergency disaster mental health acute care, debriefing, victim assistance, victimology, and intervention in times of community crisis (man-made, natural, or industrial). When putting together a NOVA team, each member is carefully selected and typically represents a cross-section of the community to which it is to be deployed. Most NOVA teams members represent various disciplines, including clergy, emergency service, media relations, public safety, education, nursing, psychology, psychiatry, victim advocacy, law enforcement, and medicine.

When specifically requested, NOVA's main objective is to provide intense and immediate emergency consultation and crisis intervention services, with additional follow-up during a limited period of time to individuals, families, public safety and emergency personnel, and communities impacted by a major disaster involving a critical incident. Usually, a team of ten specialists will be deployed and work for 3 to 4 days; they will then be relieved by additional teams as needed, depending upon the magnitude of the catastrophe.

Traumatic Stress, Critical Incident, and Intervention

A critical incident may involve sudden death in the line of duty, serious injury from a shooting, or a physical or psychological threat to the safety or well-being of an individual or community regardless of the type of incident. It may also be any situation or event faced by an individual, including emergency or public safety personnel, which causes a distressing, dramatic, or profound change or disruption in the person's physical or psychological functioning which has the potential to interfere with that person's ability to function (Davis, 1992a). Traumatic events and their impact upon a person, at least psychologically, are fairly predictable in a clinical sense. When a person has been "exposed" to a critical incident briefly or long term, this exposure can have a dramatic impact on their functioning. Emergency workers, public safety personnel and responders to crisis situations, rape victims, abused spouses and children, stalking victims, media personnel, and individuals who are exposed to a variety of critical incidents (fire, earthquake, floods, industrial disaster, workplace violence) can all develop short-term crisis reactions.

The Nature of Catastrophic Events

Individual trauma must be differentiated from collective trauma, which affects an entire community that is exposed to a critical incident. Individual trauma is generally a devastating blow to the psyche that triggers individual defense mechanisms so suddenly that one cannot respond effectively. The temporal stages of catastrophic events are considered next.

Objective Time Stages of Crisis

1. *Pre-disaster baseline.* A community's pre-disaster baseline includes its history of disasters and political, economic, or historical tensions.
2. *Anticipation.* This period is characterized by anxiety, wariness, and wonder. There may be excitement tempered by high vigilance.
3. *Threat of imminent danger.* Reactions at this stage are usually manifested in one of three ways: fear, fatalism or acceptance, or defiance. Threat itself can cause trauma. It triggers the physical reactions of crisis, including the rush of adrenaline and momentary paralysis. A disaster subculture develops where there are repetitive disaster impacts, periodic warnings of disaster, and the existence of consequential damage that is apparent to the community.
4. *Impact.* At the initial moment of impact, victims often feel that time stops. When the sense of time resumes, it is usually experienced as if life either is progressing in slow motion or at an extremely fast pace. The less control a person has during the crisis, the more likely that the crisis will be perceived as lasting a long time. Duration issues (the longer any of the following periods last, the greater the intensity of the experience of disaster and crisis) include: (a) duration of immediate life-threatening event, (b) duration of ongoing survival concerns, (c) duration of sensorial involvement, and (d) duration of community preoccupation. The low point is the juncture in time in most disasters when one can assess the total casualties or damage. That may be referred to as the low point of the disaster. However, certain types of disasters, such as health

epidemics, environmental spills, and chemical or nuclear attacks, continue to impact their victims over their entire lifetime. Such disaster are referred to as "no low point disasters."

5. *Personal inventory of the event and crisis.* The inventory stage of a disaster takes place immediately after the initial impact. Survivors often experience a period of time in which there is silence. The silence is usually deceptive. Observers of a disaster scene may witness the noise of ambulances or natural forces, but the survivors of the disaster hear nothing. The inventory stage is the time when the survivor make a first assessment of the amount of damage that has occurred. In addition to the experience of silence, they often feel isolated, alone in the midst of tragedy. For that reason, it is important to establish or restore the individuals' and the community's connection with others as soon as possible.
6. *Rescue.* The rescue period may last for a few minutes or days while rescuers work to assist victims. While rescue is usually thought of in physical terms, there is also a need for emotional or psychological rescue. There is some argument about when rescue efforts should be attempted. One position is that outreach addressing the trauma of disasters should be performed as soon as possible after the impact of the disaster. Interventions may be necessary if the duration of the disaster is for an extended period of time.
7. *Remedy and mitigation.* The remedy and mitigation phase is the period when an individual or a community attempts to regain control of life and face the short- and long-range consequences of the tragedy. Initially, there may be a euphoric reaction among survivors.

Subjective Dimensions of Crisis

1. *Individuals exist in normal state of equilibrium.* This equilibrium is bounded by joys and sorrows and is marked by everyday crises and developmental or life-event stressors. When a disaster strikes, it moves individuals out of their normal state of equilibrium into a new dimension. The more severe the disaster, the less likely that the individual will ever again establish a similar level of equilibrium.
2. *The crisis-reaction.*
   a. *Physical shock, disorientation, and numbness.* Adrenaline begins to pumps through the body, which may relieve itself of excess material through regurgitation, defecation, or urination. Heart rate increases. and hyperventilation, sweating, and similar reactions may take place.
   b. *Heightened sensory perception reaction.* There is a focus on one sense, but all senses are involved. Sight and sounds may leave indelible memories of things touched, smelled, or tasted.
   c. *Heightened physiological arousal and associated states* (prolonged fight or flight response). Eventually, physical and psychological exhaustion takes place. After the body rests, either as a result of sleep or faintness, an individual will feel depressed and disturbed. Sleep has served to pass the individual from the time when the disaster happened to a future time. The person has gone on with his or her life.
3. *The crisis reaction.* The emotional response parallels the physical response; there is an initial reaction of shock, disbelief, and denial. Emotions include anger or rage, fear or terror, frustration, confusion, guilt or self-blame, shame or humiliation, and grief or sorrow. As far as reconstruction of the individual's equilibrium, with good support systems and effective interventions the emotional rollercoaster may become balanced and a new equilibrium established.

Spatial Dimensions of Crisis

Spatial Convergence of the Crisis and Disaster Situation

The concept of convergence refers to the phenomenon of the gathering of people, information, and attention around a disaster site. There is positive and negative convergence. *Positive* convergence occurs when people go to the scene as trained and wanted helpers. *Negative* convergence occurs when people assemble for their own purposes. They may be looters, voyeurs, ambulance-chasing attorneys, mental health professionals, media representatives, and others.

Proximity of the Crisis Situation

The closer one is to the center of the disaster, the more likely one is to be at risk for post-disaster crisis and long-term stress reactions. The center of the disaster is defined as the point of impact. Eye witnesses and survivors of loved ones who died in the disaster are at high risk, in addition to victims who suffered major bodily injuries or certain types of property damage.

Geographic Spread of the Crisis Event and Situation

The greater the area affected by the disaster, the greater the chance that it will become a community-wide tragedy. As people identify with an affected geographic area, they extend the range of community members who feel touched by the catastrophe.

A System for Classifying Disaster

There are three major categories of disasters. *Natural disasters* are defined as those that have been part of the physical environment. *Industrial disasters* are those that arise from a serious disruption of the ecosystem as a result of the products, by-products, and waste from the manufacturing system. *Human disasters* are those that arise from efforts of judgment, deliberate action, or incompetence.

When natural disasters occur, victims often turn to mythological explanations, omens, and symbols to try to understand what happened. The catastrophe may raise issues of faith or sin. Survivors often have a greater acceptance of the consequences of acts of God or Mother Nature than they do of consequences of human-caused disasters. Many natural disasters have a clear period of warning prior to impact.

With industrial or technological disasters, political issues may have affected the installation or operation of a plant or industrial site. Economic issues relating to the reasons for the operation of the installation and the potential for community revival may be operative. Lack of personal accountability for the event and institutional depersonalization of victims may have a long-term impact.

Human disasters raise issues of justice and fairness. If the disaster was caused by purposeful human cruelty, there may be issues related to evil or the impossibility of understanding the criminal mind. For accidents caused by human conduct, there are often issues related to the preventability of the disaster. Accidents tend to cause more intense anger than crime.

Crisis Reactions in the Aftermath of a Trauma Event

The normal human response to trauma follows a similar pattern called the crisis reaction. The physical response to trauma is based on our animal instincts. It includes:

1. Frozen fright — physical shock or disorientation is experienced.
2. Fight-or-flight reaction — adrenaline begins to pump through the body; the body may relieve itself of excess materials, such as ingested food. One or more body functions may become more acute while others seem to shut down. Heart rate increases, and hyperventilation and sweating are commonly experienced.
3. Physical arousal associated with fight-or-flight cannot be prolonged indefinitely and will eventually result in exhaustion and negative emotional reaction
4. Physical reactions are heightened.

Trauma is accompanied or followed by a multitude of losses, including: (1) loss of control over one's life, (2) loss of faith in God or other people, (3) loss of a sense of fairness or justice, (4) loss of personally significant property or loved ones, (5) loss of a sense of immortality and invulnerability, and (6) loss of a sense of future. Because of the losses, trauma response involves grief and bereavement. One can grieve over the loss of loved people as well as loved things.

Trauma is often accompanied by regressive behaviors to childhood-like mental and physical states, such as doing things that appear childish. Examples include singing nursery rhymes, assuming a fetal position, crawling instead of walking, and calling a law enforcement officer or other authority for assistance. In addition, individuals may feel very childish. Examples include feeling insignificant, unimportant, or small; wanting to be taken care of by "mommy" or "daddy"; feeling weak and frail; or feeling helpless to deal with the trauma.

Recovery from an Immediate Traumatic Event

Most people live through a disaster event and are able to reconstruct their lives without outside intervention or help; however, many find that some type of outside intervention can be useful in dealing with trauma. Individual recovery from immediate trauma is often affected by (1) understanding the severity of the crisis reaction and establishing appropriate coping responses to the event, (2) understanding what happened by putting the event into perspective, (3) achieving stability and balance after the event, (4) being in a supportive environment, and (5) receiving validation of the experience.

Recovery issues for survivors generally include (1) gaining control of event in one's mind; (2) working out an understanding of the event and, as needed, redefining life and clarifying values; (3) learning to establish a new balance for one's existence; (4) learning to re-establish trust; (5) learning to establish a new future; and (6) learning to re-establish life meaning.

Not all victims or survivors suffer from long-term stress reactions; however, many victims may continue to re-experience crisis reactions over long periods of time. Such crisis reactions are normal in response to "bigger events" that remind the victim of the event itself.

Everyday events can bring back intense emotion and acute experiences that occurred during the original trauma. Events, often called "situational triggers", will vary with different victims or survivors, but may include (1) identification of a perpetrator in a police lineup; (2) sensorial experiences (seeing, hearing, touching, smelling, tasting) something that reminds the victim or survivor of the original event; (3) anniversaries of the disaster or traumatic event; (4) the proximity of holidays or significant "life events"; (5) hearings, trials, appeals or other critical phases of the criminal justice process; and (6) media and news reports about a similar event.

Long-term stress reactions may be made better or worse by the actions of others. When such reactions are perceived by others to be negative (whether they are malicious or not), the actions of others are often referred to as "secondary assaults" and the feelings are often described as a secondary injury. Sources of the secondary assaults may include (1) law enforcement personnel and the criminal justice system; (2) the news print media, radio, and television; (3) family, friends, co-workers, acquaintances, patrons, others; (4) hospital and emergency-room personnel and health and mental-health professionals; (5) social service workers, victim service workers, school teachers, and educators; (6) the victim compensation system; and (7) the religious system.

The intensity of long-term stress reactions usually decreases over time, as does the frequency of the re-experienced crisis; however, the effects of a catastrophic trauma cannot be "cured". Even survivors of trauma who reconstructed new lives, achieved a degree of normalcy and happiness in their lives and can honestly say that they prefer the new, "sadder-but-wiser" person they have become often find that new life events trigger the memories and reactions to the

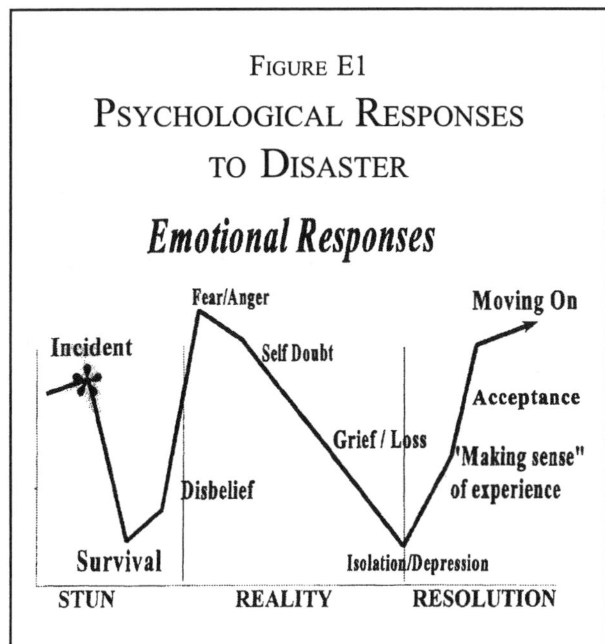

FIGURE E1
PSYCHOLOGICAL RESPONSES TO DISASTER

trauma. When someone survives a catastrophe, they often experience stress reactions for years. Long-term stress reactions are natural responses of people who have survived a traumatic event. Figure E1 presents the trauma and recovery states.

Timing, Disaster Situations, and the Media

Although each crisis is unique, there is often a common pattern to the media's response to the aftermath of any tragedy that affects entire communities. The type of information sought by the media as the trauma unfolds often follows a particular pattern. The following is a temporal unfolding of a crisis situation that follows a pattern from the initial moments of a crisis through the next several days and weeks. The pattern is broken down incrementally from 0 to 12 hours, 12 to 24 hours, 24 to 36 hours, 36 to 72 hours, and 72 hours and beyond.

0 to 12 Hours

In the immediate aftermath of a crisis, the media rapidly attempt to obtain information to answer the question, "What happened here?" They attempt to piece together a story board based on eye-witness accounts. Monitoring police radios bands and, in many cases, finding almost anyone to talk about what happened provide additional information for that story line. The results are frequently incomplete, conflicting, and inaccurate in terms of what actually happened and often provide a source of secondary injury for victims and the community.

12 to 24 Hours

As a crisis situation unfolds, the next question the media seeks to answer is, "Who are the victims of this tragedy?" There is often a struggle over the timing of the release of the names of those injured and killed as local authorities try to notify the surviving next-of-kin. Typically, no one is immune from the media's search for identifying information about the victim. The media will often seek out this information from a variety of sources including hospitals, police, fire services, emergency rescue workers, hospital emergency room personnel, families, friends, neighbors, schools, and co-workers or through encampment at the scene of the tragedy, all in an concentrated effort to identify who has information about the situation and its victims.

24 to 36 Hours

The next question the media try to answer is, "Why did this tragic event happen?" It is a normal reaction on the part of many people, including victims, survivors, and local community members to attempt to understand what happened by finding someone or something to blame and hold responsibility for the event. Typically, everyone has their story or version of who is to blame. Unfortunately for the community, the media often uses such information to speculate about who or what may have caused the tragic crisis well before the actual facts of the situation emerge from those in charge of the situation, such as police, fire, or rescue personnel.

In situations where there is an obvious person to blame or at fault, the media will often run a story line on the alleged offender and frequently blame the situation on a variety of sources such as negligent security, questioning whether the victims contributed to the event in some way, or about those who could have foreseen or prevented the tragic crime. In crisis situations involving natural disasters or faulty construction, the issues of inadequate disaster preparedness capability and insurance coverage often arise.

36 to 72 Hours

At this point during a crisis, the media continues to speculate over what happened and why, and begins to evaluate the effectiveness and timeliness of emergency rescue efforts. This occurs even as the rescue or cleanup operations continue in the aftermath. Ensuring privacy for victims is paramount as they are released from the hospital, return to work, or begin to make arrangements for funerals or memorial services.

72 Hours and Beyond

The fact-specific details of what happened during the tragedy is now old news and the media turn to focusing on the funeral services for the deceased. In order to continue media coverage, the media will often try to sensationalize the crisis by scrutinizing the lifestyles and social and religious pursuits of the victims. The media might also run stories about victims who have suffered through similar misfortunes and raise doubts about the employer, business, government agency, or whichever entity is currently being blamed for contributing to the crisis.

The aforementioned time periods are encountered during what is called an immediate crisis. When an immediate crisis occurs over extended periods such as in hostage-taking situations, wars, tornadoes, floods, or hurricanes, the media have greater opportunities to become more involved in crisis stories. As a source of secondary injury, the media often forget about protecting the innocent victim and may include the names and faces of the victims in their stories without realizing the impact of their actions in the aftermath of the tragedy. Each story potentially retraumatizes victims, survivors, and the community.

Critical Incident Stress Debriefing

Debriefing is a specific technique or method designed to assist others in dealing with the "critical incident stress response syndrome" and the typical physical or psychological symptoms generally associated with it. Typically, debriefings should be conducted as soon as possible after exposure to a stressful event. Debriefings can be conducted on-site, off-site, on-scene, or near-scene (Davis, 1992b).

Another type of critical incident stress debriefing — referred to as "defusings" — can be conducted within a few hours after the critical incident (Davis, 1992a). Most importantly, debriefings or defusings should be provided as soon as possible but typically no later than the first 24 to 72 hours after the initial impact of the critical event. As the time between exposure and debriefing or defusing lengthens and the actual impact of the critical incident diminishes, such intervention becomes less effective. Therefore, a close temporal relationship between the critical incident and the actual debriefing is imperative for it to become fully beneficial and effective (Davis, 1993).

Individuals who receive critical incident stress debriefing within a 24- to 72-hour period after the initial critical incident show fewer short-term and long-term crisis reactions or psychological trauma. Conversely, emergency service workers, rescue workers, police and fire personnel, and trauma victims who do not receive such debriefing typically respond by experiencing many of the aforementioned symptoms. When applying debriefing techniques, an appropriate and effective protocol must be followed when assisting responders and crisis victims with any critical incident.

Debriefing techniques can be quite involved and labor intensive (Davis, 1993). Initially, the emergency crisis intervention response provider must lay the constructive groundwork or framework for an initial assessment of the impact of the critical incidents on the responder or victim by carefully reviewing that person's level of involvement before, during, and after the critical incident. Most approaches incorporate the following key points into the debriefing process when providing assistance to victims and emergency rescue workers:

1. Lay the framework and groundwork for an initial audit and assessment regarding the impact of the critical incident on the responder, the rescuer, emergency worker, public safety officer, or victim.
2. Identify immediate issues surrounding problems involving safety and security.
3. Allow for ventilation of thoughts, emotions, and experiences, and validate possible reactions.
4. Predict future events and reactions, and provide assistance in preparing for those events and reactions.
5. Develop a plan for outreach and recovery back into the community and to the workplace setting.
6. Conduct a systematic review of the critical incident and its emotional, physical, and sensory impact on the responder or victim; be alert for maladaptive behaviors or responses to the crisis or trauma.
7. Bring closure to the incident or matter by anchoring or grounding responders or victims to community resources to initiate or start the rebuilding process; also, help identify possible positive experiences from the event.

Debriefing assists in the re-entry process in an adaptive manner during the initial critical stages of the aftermath. Debriefing can be done individually or in small or large groups, depending on the situation. Debriefing is not a critique or psychotherapy per se, but rather a systematic review of the events preceding, during, and after the traumatic impact.

Critical Incident Stress Debriefing Process

First, the debriefer or facilitator briefly evaluates each individual's situational involvement, the person's age, level of development, and degree of exposure to the critical incident or event (i.e., direct impact or indirect impact), whether the individual is a child, adolescent, teenager, or adult. Issues of safety and security generally arise as major themes during this time. Each person is affected differently, depending on their understanding of the event (Davis, 1992, 1993).

Second, issues surrounding safety and security surface, particularly with children. Feeling safe and secure is of major importance when, without warning, their lives are shattered by tragedy and loss.

Third, ventilation and validation are important to individuals, as each, in their own way, needs to discuss their exposure, sensory experiences, and thoughts, and feelings that are tied to the event. Ventilation and validation are necessary to give individuals an opportunity to express their feelings and emotions. This not only helps the responder or victim but also helps the debriefer place reactions or emotions in context and give them a better perspective. This also helps people prepare for events with which they will inevitably be faced in the future, such as funerals, ceremonies, anniversary dates of the event, birthdates of those who may have died as a result of the tragedy, and so on.

Fourth, the debriefer assists the victim or crisis responder in predicting the future, including the possible full-range of emotions, reactions, and problems associated with this type of exposure. By predicting, preparing, and planning for the range of emotions, thoughts, and potential psychological and physical reactions stemming from the stressful critical incident, the debriefer can also help the responder or victim prepare and plan for the near and long-term future. This also typically helps avert any long-term crisis reaction and extensive trauma resulting from the initial critical incident.

Fifth, the debriefer should conduct a thorough and systematic review of the physical, emotional/psychological, and sensorial impact of the critical incident on the individual. The debriefer should carefully listen and evaluate the responders' or victims' thoughts, mood, affect, choice of words, and perceptions of the critical incident, looking for potential clues suggesting problems in terms of managing or coping with the tragic event.

Sixth, a sense of closure is needed. Closure is an important feature of any debriefing. Information and education are provided to the victims and responders regarding ongoing support or resources. Additionally, closure can bring assistance where a plan for future action is needed to develop a basis for grounding or anchoring the person during times of high critical incident stress and for purposes of reassurance during the aftermath.

Seventh, closure assists in short-term and long-term recovery through the re-entry process. During the aftermath, victims and responders need significant assurance that each new day will bring new challenges and that resources are available to assist in making the physical and psychological adaptive changes necessary to meet these challenges appropriately.

Re-entry and Recovery from Crisis in the Community

After the Oklahoma City bombing, children in kindergarten through sixth grade, principals, school psychologists, nurses, guidance counselors, teachers, school staff members, community leaders, and public officials were debriefed. The citizens of Oklahoma City and the community-at-large were all suffering, many clearly in the midst of short-term crisis reactions. Dozens of others needed attention for acute PTSD, sleep disturbance, anxiety, acute reactive depression, and phobic disorder. Some could not be alone.

Almost everyone in this close, tight-knit community knew someone who had been hurt, seriously injured, or had died. Regardless of whether or not someone knew one of the victims, all Oklahomans suffered from the tragedy. Oklahoma was and is a community and state in crisis. One elementary school had 35 individuals wounded or killed by the bombing. During the initial aftermath, many high school students were suicidal and required an immediate mental health response during the debriefing phase.

Debriefing Can Lessen the Impact of Trauma

Debriefing can avert major long-term psychological injury; however, if symptoms persist for at least 1 month after the impact of the critical incident, a referral to a mental health professional is suggested.

In Oklahoma City, the emotions of children and their families were generally kept in check while they optimistically praying for a successful search for a loved one. Still, countless others, realizing the worst, awaited confirmation of deaths of loved ones.

For the surviving victims, grief will be difficult to resolve because many of their questions remain forever unanswered. Some remains cannot be identified, even with conventional and contemporary forensic science methods.

Working With Trauma Victims

During the 4 days the author spent in Oklahoma City, he personally debriefed over 1100 individuals in groups of 25 to 50 and provided one-on-one crisis intervention and outreach to dozens of others at various times. During the debriefings, individuals who approached the author had difficulty coping or needed one-on-one intervention and were at risk for what the author assessed to be acute psychological reaction. Many others, observed during the debriefings in groups, were so traumatized that the author could act only as a referral agent to the local public service agencies, school counselors, school psychologists, school nurses, mental health community service providers, and hospitals for assessment and further care.

Debriefing the Debriefing Team

As with all CRT members, the author had the opportunity to be debriefed by NOVA staff. As a necessary and integral part of the CRT's work during any critical incident, no debriefer can possibly be emotionally above or psychologically removed from any event of this magnitude. The Oklahoma NOVA Team's group debriefings were at times intense, particularly on the last day before departure as we prepared to turn over our responsibilities to a third CRT arriving from around the country. Individual "one-on-ones" were available when requested. Each team member was affected in his or her own way. Our CRT bonded quickly and responded admirably under tremendous pressure and long hours.

On a personal note, the author was emotionally and physically exhausted after working 12- to 15-hour days on three of the four days he was at the scene. On the third day, the author had a chance to grieve and mourn and to realize that Oklahoma City and Oklahomans represented realistically, Anytown, USA. As communities and as a nation, the Oklahoma bombing tragedy brings a sense vulnerability to us all.

References

Davis, J.A. (1992a) *Seminar on Mass Disaster Preparation and Psychological Trauma*, May, San Diego, CA.

Davis, J.A. (1992b) *Identifying Acute Post-Traumatic Stress Disorder (PTSD) in Disaster Victims and Emergency Responders*, January, San Diego, CA.

Davis, J.A. (1993) *On-Site Critical Incident Stress Debriefing Field Interviewing Techniques Utilized in the Aftermath of Mass Disaster*, training seminar for emergency responders and police personnel, March, San Diego, CA.

NOVA (1994) *Responding to Communities in Crisis*. Washington, D.C.: National Organization for Victim Assistance.

INDEX

Index

K

L

M

N

O

P

Q

R

U

V

W

Y

Z